D0382149

Cooking Light

ANNUAL RECIPES 2011

Oxmoor House®

A Year at *Cooking Light*

2010 was one of the most exciting years yet at *Cooking Light*, in part because so much change is happening on the American food front: the return of farmers' markets in so many cities and towns, the terrific national curiosity about innovative chefs, the fascination with global flavors and recipes, the boom in delicious artisanal foods, and the interest in eating sustainable seafood and humanely raised meats. In the area of nutrition, Americans are becoming more conscious of the spike in obesity and the challenge of getting better food into our schools. In turn, people are personally more interested in consuming whole foods as well as healthy fats from olives, nuts, and grains and in trying new varieties of fruits and vegetables.

◀ **Lamb Burgers with Sun-Dried Tomato Aioli**
(page 163)
These tasty burgers are ready in just 30 minutes.

This year at *Cooking Light,* we experimented with and published some our best recipes yet. Here are some of the highlights:

- As nutrition science gets more complicated, the "rules" for healthy eating actually are getting simpler. In "The *Cooking Light* Way to Eat," we summarized what we've learned about nutrition and healthy cooking in the past 23 years. Find out about it on page 31. These are rules you really can live by—and enjoy your food while you do it.

- In "Oops! 25 Common Cooking Mistakes and How to Avoid Them" (page 52), we've compiled a list of common culinary boo-boos and mishaps—and we've shown how they can be avoided. Every cook makes a blunder sooner or later, and many mistakes become habits that lead to repeated disappointment. Some of these mistakes are peculiar or even more noticeable in healthy cooking.

- In May, Mark Bittman (author of multiple cookbooks and writer of *The New York Times* "Minimalist" column) began sharing his tips and recipes for consuming more vegetables and less meat—an almost meatless approach that has myriad health benefits. Check some of them out on pages 129, 152, and 312.

- Our annual Summer Cookbook (page 143) is a glorious celebration of seasonable bounty. Fresh sweet fruits and delicious crunchy vegetables—pure heaven from earth—are the basis for this entire section.

- In September, as busy cooks jumped back into the back-to-school-and-work pace, we offered 67 tips, 10 quick side dishes, 11 superfast entrées, and a bunch of quick-cooking techniques (page 236) to help the healthy cook who's in a real hurry.

At *Cooking Light,* we hear every month from enlightened cooks who have responded to our recipes and want to share great ideas that inform our future issues. To all of you, thanks. We hope this compilation inspires all our readers in your pursuit of light, great eating.

Scott Mowbray
Editor

◀ **Pan-Seared Striped Bass All'amatriciana**
(page 199)
Don't be intimidated by the name. This quick dish makes an ideal weeknight meal.

▼ **Mississippi Mud Pie**
(page 282)
Serve this dessert with a scoop of vanilla ice cream.

Our Favorite Recipes

Not all recipes are created equal.

At *Cooking Light*, only those that have passed muster with our Test Kitchens staff and food editors—not an easy crowd to please—make it onto the pages of our magazine. We rigorously test each recipe, often two or three times, to ensure that it's healthy, reliable, and tastes as good as it possibly can. So which of our recipes are our favorites? They're the dishes that are the most memorable. They're the ones readers keep calling and writing about, the ones our staff whip up for their own families and friends.

◀ **Upside-Down Fudge-Almond Tart** *(page 35)*
Chopped almonds add crunch to this decadent chocolate dessert. A touch of golden cane syrup adds a can't-quite-place-it richness to the bittersweet chocolate base.

▼ **Pear and Prosciutto Pizza** *(page 62)*
Peppery arugula is pitted against creamy, sweet caramelized onions and salty prosciutto and cheese. The premade crust makes preparation quick and easy.

◀ **Rösti Casserole with Baked Eggs** *(page 26)*
Crisp shredded potatoes make a perfect bed for runny golden egg yolks. Gruyère and grated turnip add elegance to this simple casserole, perfect for any meal.

▼ **Poutine** *(page 27)*
Oven-frying the potatoes in duck fat adds a rich, meaty flavor and gives these potato strips a gorgeously crisp texture. With a topping of salty cheese, this meal is a divine combination of flavors.

Our Favorite Recipes

▶ Fried Catfish with Hush Puppies and Tartar Sauce

(page 92)

A tangy tartar sauce with the bite of horseradish accompanies this classic fried catfish with hush puppies. Catfish is traditional in this dish.

▼ Bacon and Wild Mushroom Risotto with Baby Spinach

(page 121)

This creamy risotto is filled with three different types of mushrooms and six slices of crisp bacon, which brings crunchy texture and smoky flavor to this dish.

Fresh Coconut Cake *(page 110)*
Shaved ribbons of toasted coconut make this cake a showstopper rather than an ordinary oversized snowball. A silky Italian meringue frosting will make you second-guess more sugary varieties.

Farmers' Market Potato Salad *(page 154)*
This vibrant potato salad is not your typical picnic fair. Multicolored finger-ling potatoes, tomatoes, fresh corn, and zucchini are tossed with a bright Dijon dressing. It's even better a day after it's made.

Our Favorite Recipes

◄ **Blueberry-Peach Cobbler** *(page 177)* Stirring the blueberries into the biscuit-like topping of this cobbler, rather than the filling, allows fresh sliced peaches to release their juices without masking a single blueberry bite.

▼ **Sheep's-Milk Yogurt Cheesecakes with Grilled Figs and Pistachios** *(page 182)* The mild flavor and silky texture of these individual cheesecakes is delicately perfumed with rose water. Grilled figs add a honey-sweetness to this beautiful dessert.

Our Favorite Recipes

▶ **Hot and Hot Tomato Salad** *(page 205)*
This salad is a mosaic of summer's best offerings: heirloom tomatoes, fresh peas, and okra—lightly fried in the Southern tradition. A tangy buttermilk dressing and smoky bacon make this first course worthy of seconds.

▼ **Two Potato and Beet Hash with Poached Eggs and Greens** *(page 318)*
Root vegetables make this hash something special. This hearty dish would make a fantastic weeknight dinner.

Braised Short Ribs with Egg Noodles *(page 70)*
The tasty browned bits at the bottom of the pan add deep, complex notes to an already hearty dish. Slow-cooked short ribs fall off the bone, and egg noodles sop up a rich, meaty broth.

Mushroom Bolognese *(page 313)*
This dish smells incredible as it cooks, with a deep, earthy, mushroomy fragrance. And the flavor lives up to the promise of the amazing aroma.

Our Favorite Recipes

◄ **Bananas Foster Bread**
(page 312)
Bananas are caramelized in brown sugar and cognac before being folded into a cinnamon-spiced batter and baked. A slightly boozy glaze makes this adult-friendly dessert anything but ordinary.

▼ **Sautéed Arctic Char and Arugula Salad with Tomato Vinaigrette** *(page 197)*
A quick balsamic vinaigrette dresses both the tender Arctic char and the peppery arugula salad in this recipe. The main and the side mingle with each other here to create one perfect plate.

Creamy Garlic-Seafood Soup *(page 20)*
A full-bodied broth captures the flavor of the sea in this soup while still letting fresh shrimp and snapper shine. A squeeze of lime cuts through the buttery finish of cream and chopped avocado.

Our Favorite Recipes

◀ **Watermelon Margaritas** *(page 194)*
A refreshing watermelon-lime margarita, served in a tall glass with a sugared rim, begs for a lawn chair and a hot summer afternoon. Tequila and Triple Sec make this drink an adult favorite.

▼ **Sausage and Sourdough Bread Stuffing** *(page 339)*
Fresh sage, thyme, and parsley add beautiful color and flavor to this lightened holiday stuffing. Tossed with chicken broth and baked, this dish stays warm and moist.

Our Favorite Recipes

▶ **Vanilla Cake with Italian Meringue Frosting** *(page 357)*
A simple, moist vanilla cake gets star treatment when iced with a glossy Italian meringue. This dessert looks so stunning your guests will think you bribed the baker.

Sour Cream Coffee Cake *(page 80)*
Toasted oats add a nutty flavor and welcome texture to both the cake and the crumb topping in this recipe. Sour cream keeps the cake moist and light.

Eggplant Parmesan *(page 301)*
Baking panko-crusted eggplant separately ensures a crispy coating without any frying. Topped with tomato sauce, mozzarella, and ricotta spiked with crushed red pepper, this entrée is so delicious you won't miss the heavy restaurant alternative.

Pink Grapefruit Sorbet *(page 86)*
This two-ingredient sorbet does double duty: It refreshes your palette while delivering nearly a full day's worth of calcium. Just another reason to truly enjoy dessert.

Crab Cakes with Spicy Rémoulade *(page 142)*
Panko (Japanese breadcrumbs) act as a unique binder for lump crabmeat, keeping the cakes light and the crab front and center. A zesty rémoulade with capers and Creole mustard serves as a dip for every bite.

Apricot-Thyme Galette *(page 146)*
Fresh, juicy apricots signal the beginning of summer in this rustic tart. Honey and apricot jam provide sweetness, while a sprinkle of fresh thyme adds a lemony fragrance.

Golden Peach Soup with Shrimp and Crab Seviche *(page 145)*
Presentation alone makes this soup a star. A centerpiece of fresh shrimp and crab, tossed with lime and cilantro floats above a golden peach puree accented with jalapeño for an extra burst of heat.

Baba Ghanoush *(page 186)*
A classic Middle-Eastern snack reinvented. This roasted eggplant dip pops with garlic, tahini, and fresh parsley. Toasted pine nuts offer a contrast in texture, and a little low-fat mayonnaise lightens the dish.

Salty Chihuahua *(page 384)*
This blushing grapefruit cocktail looks even better in a salt-rimmed glass, as the name implies. Cointreau adds a unique orange flavor to the tequila in this margarita-style drink.

Avocado-Buttermilk Soup with Crab Salad *(page 208)*
Cool and creamy, this avocado soup also gets its color from fresh tomatillos. A crab topping gets a bright boost from red bell peppers, chives, and fresh orange zest.

Key Lime Pie *(page 283)*
Tart, sweet, and crowned in a cloud of fluffy meringue, this Key lime pie will transport you to the coast of Florida and beyond.

Beef Filets with Pomegranate-Pinot Sauce *(page 327)*
Instead of drinking a glass of red wine with dinner, why not flavor your steak with it? Pomegranate juice adds a fruity complexity to a pinot noir pan sauce, and pomegranate seeds garnish each steak.

Toasted Guajillo and Pork Posole *(page 363)*
Pork shoulder simmered with cloves and cumin becomes incredibly tender in this soup—a deep red from dried guajillo chiles and smoky adobo. White hominy completes this posole, brightened with fresh cilantro, radishes, and lime.

Beef Filets with Mushroom Sauce and Parmesan Popovers *(page 336)*
Pepper-crusted tenderloin filets are paired with a rich, earthy mushroom sauce. Parmesan popovers catch all the meaty juices.

Halibut à la Provençal over Mixed Greens *(page 370)*
Herbes de Provence provides a French flair to halibut dressed in fresh lemon juice and olive oil. Serve on a bed of mixed greens tossed with a quick Dijon vinaigrette.

Brioche Rolls *(page 400)*
Buttery brioche rolls make a spectacular side for soup or a breakfast treat topped with jam. A seam on the side of each roll makes it easy to split with a friend, though you probably won't want to.

CONTENTS

©2010 by Time Home Entertainment, Inc.
135 West 50th Street, New York, NY 10020

All rights reserved. No part of this book may be reproduced in any form or by any means without the prior written permission of the publisher, excepting brief quotations in connection with reviews written specifically for inclusion in magazines or newspapers, or limited excerpts strictly for personal use.

ISBN-13: 978-0-8487-3341-4
ISBN-10: 0-8487-3341-X
ISSN: 1091-3645
Printed in the United States of America
First Printing 2010

Be sure to check with your health-care provider before making any changes in your diet.

Oxmoor House
VP, Publishing Director: Jim Childs
Editorial Director: Susan Payne Dobbs
Brand Manager: Michelle Turner Aycock
Senior Editor: Heather Averett
Managing Editor: Laurie S. Herr

Cooking Light® Annual Recipes 2011
Editor: Rachel Quinlivan, R.D.
Buying Guide Editor: Georgia Dodge
Senior Production Manager: Greg A. Amason

Contributors:
Designer: Carol Damsky
Copy Editor: Jacqueline B. Giovanelli
Proofreader: Norma Butterworth-McKittrick
Indexer: Mary Ann Laurens
Interns: Christine T. Boatwright, Perri K. Hubbard, Caitlin Watzke

To order additional publications, call 1-800-765-6400.

For more books to enrich your life, visit **oxmoorhouse.com**

To search, savor, and share thousands of recipes, visit **myrecipes.com**

Cover: *Maple-Glazed Salmon (page 238)*
Page 1: *Apple-Poblano Whole Roast Turkey (page 335), Framboise Cranberry Sauce (page 345), Sausage and Sourdough Bread Stuffing (page 339), Rosemary Mashed Sweet Potatoes with Shallots (page 340), Citrus Green Beans with Pine Nuts (page 341)*

Cooking Light®
Editor: Scott Mowbray
Creative Director: Carla Frank
Deputy Editor: Phillip Rhodes
Food Editor: Ann Taylor Pittman
Special Publications Editor: Mary Simpson Creel, M.S., R.D.
Nutrition Editor: Kathy Kitchens Downie, R.D.
Associate Food Editors: Timothy Q. Cebula, Julianna Grimes
Associate Editors: Cindy Hatcher, Brandy Rushing
Test Kitchen Director: Vanessa T. Pruett
Assistant Test Kitchen Director: Tiffany Vickers Davis
Chief Food Stylist: Charlotte Fekete
Senior Food Stylist: Kellie Gerber Kelley
Recipe Testers and Developers: Robin Bashinsky, Adam Hickman, Deb Wise
Art Director: Fernande Bondarenko
Junior Deputy Art Director: Alexander Spacher
Designer: Chase Turberville
Photo Director: Kristen Schaefer
Senior Photographer: Randy Mayor
Senior Photo Stylist: Cindy Barr
Photo Stylist: Leigh Ann Ross
Copy Chief: Maria Parker Hopkins
Assistant Copy Chief: Susan Roberts
Research Editor: Michelle Gibson Daniels
Editorial Production Director: Liz Rhoades
Production Editor: Hazel R. Eddins
Art/Production Assistant: Josh Rutledge
Administrative Coordinator: Carol D. Johnson
CookingLight.com Editor: Allison Long Lowery
CookingLight.com Nutrition Editor: Holley Johnson Grainger, M.S., R.D.
Production Assistant: Mallory Daugherty

BRIGHT FLAVORS FROM WARM PLACES

The sweetness of tropical fruits, the heat of tropical chiles, the fragrance of tropical spices: These recipes will transport you...

For us, new flavors often make the best souvenirs, the sweetest memories, of vacations. We return from interesting places with a hundred ideas and a refreshed inclination to get cooking. And there's little need to haul anything messy home in a suitcase anymore: The explosion of imported spices, condiments, oils, and staples in American markets means that playing with the flavors that seduced us in the Caribbean, Asia, Europe, or South America is easy.

Here we focus on chile peppers, lime, avocado, mango, cilantro: the foods and flavors that transport us to the warm, watery, beachy places that recharge our batteries.

Quick & Easy • Kid Friendly
Baja Fish Tacos with Mango Salsa

Be sure to heat the oil to the proper temperature, and maintain the heat. Otherwise, the fish will absorb unnecessary fat and calories as it cooks. If you can't find fresh, never-frozen halibut, substitute another firm white-fleshed fish, such as turbot or striped bass.

1 cup diced peeled ripe mango
1/4 cup finely chopped red onion
1 tablespoon fresh lime juice
1 tablespoon chopped fresh cilantro
1/8 teaspoon salt
1 jalapeño pepper, seeded and minced
5 cups canola oil
3.38 ounces all-purpose flour (about 3/4 cup)
1 cup beer
1 1/2 teaspoons freshly ground black pepper
1 teaspoon salt
1 teaspoon garlic powder
1 1/2 pounds skinless halibut fillet, cut into 16 (3 x 1-inch) strips
8 (6-inch) corn tortillas

1. Combine first 6 ingredients; set aside.
2. Clip a fry thermometer to the side of a large, heavy saucepan. Add oil to pan; heat over medium-high heat until thermometer registers 375°. Reduce heat to medium, maintaining oil temperature.
3. Weigh or lightly spoon flour into dry measuring cups; level with a knife. Combine flour and next 4 ingredients, stirring with a whisk. Add fish to batter, tossing gently to coat. Remove fish from batter. Carefully add 4 or 5 fish pieces to hot oil; cook 4 to 5 minutes or until golden brown and done, turning occasionally (maintain oil temperature at 375° throughout cooking process). Drain fish on paper towels. Repeat procedure in batches with remaining fish.
4. Heat tortillas according to package directions. Divide fish evenly among tortillas; spoon about 2 tablespoons salsa into each tortilla. Yield: 4 servings (serving size: 2 tacos).

CALORIES 356; FAT 17g (sat 1.4g, mono 9.3g, poly 4.9g); PROTEIN 6.8g; CARB 47.3g; FIBER 3.9g; CHOL 5mg; IRON 1.5mg; SODIUM 690mg; CALC 38mg

Mahimahi with Pineapple Chutney

Gold rum has a pronounced flavor and adds a decidedly Caribbean influence to this spicy-sweet dish. The rum is aged in barrels, and through this process it takes on an amber hue and develops subtle flavors of caramel and vanilla. If you can't find gold, use white rum.

2 teaspoons canola oil
1 1/2 cups finely chopped red onion
1 cup finely chopped red bell pepper
1 tablespoon minced peeled fresh ginger
1 teaspoon minced seeded habanero pepper
1 garlic clove, minced
1 teaspoon kosher salt, divided
1/4 cup gold rum
3 cups fresh pineapple, cut into 1/2-inch pieces
1/2 cup packed brown sugar
3 tablespoons fresh lime juice
1 tablespoon chopped fresh cilantro
Cooking spray
6 (6-ounce) mahimahi fillets
1/4 teaspoon freshly ground black pepper

1. Heat oil in a medium saucepan over medium-high heat. Add onion and next 4 ingredients; stir in 1/2 teaspoon salt. Cook 4 minutes, stirring constantly. Add rum to pan; cook 20 seconds or until liquid evaporates. Stir in pineapple, sugar, and juice; bring to a boil. Cook 15 minutes or until liquid thickens. Remove from heat; cool slightly. Stir in cilantro.
2. Heat a grill pan over medium-high heat. Coat pan with cooking spray. Sprinkle both sides of fish evenly with remaining 1/2 teaspoon salt and black pepper. Add fish to pan; cook 6 minutes on each side or until desired degree of doneness. Serve with chutney. Yield: 6 servings (serving size: 1 fillet and about 1/3 cup chutney).

CALORIES 337; FAT 3g (sat 0.5g, mono 1.2g, poly 0.8g); PROTEIN 32.6g; CARB 44g; FIBER 4.2g; CHOL 120mg; IRON 2.9mg; SODIUM 473mg; CALC 88mg

continued

WINE NOTE: Even if you usually drink only bone-dry wines, make an exception here. This sweet-hot chutney calls for a wine with a touch of sugar. Slightly off-dry Stanza 2008 Gewürztraminer ($13) from California's Monterey County (a wine region that's taking off) is full of lively white peach, spicy green apple, sweet jasmine, green herbs, and orange zest that match this tropical dish for fruit, spice, and exotic spirit.

Cheese and Shrimp–Stuffed Poblanos

Chihuahua cheese, a Mexican melting cheese, enriches and slightly thickens this creamy sauce. Substitute shredded cheddar cheese if you can't find Chihuahua.

1 red bell pepper
8 poblano peppers
2 tablespoons olive oil
1 pound peeled and deveined medium shrimp, chopped
½ teaspoon salt, divided
5 garlic cloves, minced
1½ tablespoons all-purpose flour
¼ teaspoon ground red pepper
½ cup half-and-half
¾ cup fat-free milk, divided
¾ cup (3 ounces) shredded Chihuahua cheese
2 tablespoons chopped fresh cilantro
2 tablespoons fresh lime juice

1. Preheat broiler.
2. Cut bell pepper in half lengthwise; discard seeds and membranes. Place bell pepper halves, skin sides up, and whole poblanos on a foil-lined baking sheet. Broil 10 minutes or until blackened, turning poblanos to blacken all sides. Place peppers in a zip-top plastic bag; seal. Let stand 10 minutes. Peel. Finely chop bell peppers. Cut tops crosswise from poblanos; remove seeds.
3. Heat a large skillet over medium-high heat. Add oil to pan; swirl to coat. Sprinkle shrimp with ¼ teaspoon salt. Add shrimp to pan; cook 3 minutes or until done. Remove from pan.
4. Add garlic to pan; sauté 30 seconds, stirring constantly. Sprinkle with flour

and ground red pepper; cook 1 minute. Slowly add half-and-half, stirring with a whisk. Stir in ½ cup milk; cook 1 minute, stirring constantly. Remove from heat; let stand 2 minutes. Add cheese and remaining ¼ teaspoon salt, stirring until smooth. Place ⅓ cup cheese mixture in a large bowl; reserve remaining cheese mixture. Add bell pepper, shrimp mixture, cilantro, and juice to ⅓ cup cheese mixture in bowl; toss to coat. Stir remaining ¼ cup milk into reserved cheese mixture. Spoon 3 tablespoons cheese sauce onto each of 4 plates. Spoon 6 tablespoons shrimp mixture into each poblano. Place 2 stuffed poblanos and two tops on each plate. Yield: 4 servings.

CALORIES 376; FAT 18.7g (sat 7.5g, mono 8g, poly 1.9g); PROTEIN 32.9g; CARB 20.2g; FIBER 2.1g; CHOL 206mg; IRON 4.4mg; SODIUM 649mg; CALC 306mg

Creamy Garlic–Seafood Soup

If served as an entrée, this is a special-occasion splurge, nutritionally. But you can serve a smaller portion as an appetizer, guilt-free.

8 ounces medium shrimp, shells and tails intact
Cooking spray
2 cups chopped onion
12 garlic cloves, crushed
2 jalapeño peppers, halved
¼ cup dry white wine
6 cups water
1 tablespoon butter
2 tablespoons all-purpose flour
¾ cup heavy whipping cream
1 teaspoon salt, divided
⅛ teaspoon saffron threads, crushed
1 pound black snapper fillets, cut into bite-sized pieces
3 tablespoons small fresh cilantro leaves
1 avocado, peeled, seeded, and chopped
6 lime wedges

1. Peel and devein shrimp, reserving shells.
2. Heat a Dutch oven over medium-high heat. Coat pan with cooking spray. Add shrimp shells, onion, garlic, and peppers; sauté 3 minutes, stirring

frequently. Add wine to pan, and cook 3 minutes or until liquid almost evaporates, stirring occasionally. Add 6 cups water, and bring to a boil. Reduce heat, and simmer 40 minutes or until liquid is reduced to 3 cups; strain over a bowl. Discard solids. Wipe pan clean.
3. Melt butter in pan over medium-high heat. Stir in flour; cook 1 minute, stirring constantly. Gradually add 1 cup shrimp broth, stirring constantly with a whisk. Stir in remaining 2 cups broth, cream, ½ teaspoon salt, and saffron, and bring to a boil. Cook 5 minutes or until slightly thick, stirring occasionally. Sprinkle shrimp and fish evenly with remaining ½ teaspoon salt; add to pan. Reduce heat, and simmer 3 minutes or until shrimp are pink and fish flakes easily. Remove from heat. Ladle about ⅔ cup soup into each of 6 bowls; top each serving with 1½ teaspoons cilantro and about 1½ tablespoons avocado. Serve with lime wedges. Yield: 6 servings.

CALORIES 305; FAT 19.8g (sat 9.2g, mono 7.2g, poly 1.8g); PROTEIN 25g; CARB 7.1g; FIBER 2g; CHOL 131mg; IRON 1.6mg; SODIUM 528mg; CALC 73mg

WINE NOTE: The ever-popular Santa Margherita Pinot Grigio from Italy, 2008 ($20), is a zesty, crisp white with notes of grapefruit and lime. With a kick of heat in your bowl, you want refreshment in your glass. This wine delivers with vibrant fruit and a clean finish.

Coconut Shrimp with Fiery Mango Sauce

(pictured on page 244)

Sweet coconut tames the heat of the sauce.

Sauce:
1 teaspoon canola oil
²/₃ cup finely chopped onion
½ teaspoon grated peeled fresh ginger
1 garlic clove, minced
1 (12-ounce) can mango nectar
¼ Scotch bonnet pepper, unseeded
1½ tablespoons fresh lime juice
⅛ teaspoon salt
Shrimp:
28 jumbo shrimp (about 1½ pounds)
½ cup flaked sweetened coconut
½ cup panko (Japanese breadcrumbs)
⅓ cup cornstarch
3 large egg whites, lightly beaten
½ teaspoon salt
8 teaspoons canola oil, divided
Cooking spray

1. To prepare sauce, heat a small saucepan over medium-high heat. Add 1 teaspoon oil to pan; swirl to coat. Add onion, ginger, and garlic; sauté 3 minutes, stirring frequently. Add nectar and pepper; bring to a boil. Cook 10 minutes or until reduced to ¾ cup. Remove from heat; let stand 10 minutes. Place mixture in a blender; process until smooth. Stir in juice and ⅛ teaspoon salt. Cool.
2. To prepare shrimp, peel and devein shrimp, leaving tails intact; discard shells.
3. Place coconut in a food processor; pulse 6 times or until finely chopped. Add panko; pulse to combine. Place coconut mixture in a shallow dish. Place cornstarch in a shallow dish. Place egg whites in a shallow dish. Sprinkle shrimp evenly with ½ teaspoon salt. Working with 1 shrimp at a time, dredge shrimp in cornstarch, shaking off excess. Dip in egg whites; dredge in coconut mixture.
4. Heat a large nonstick skillet over medium-high heat. Add 2 teaspoons oil to pan; swirl to coat. Add 7 shrimp to pan; coat tops of shrimp with cooking spray. Cook shrimp 2½ minutes on each side or until done. Repeat procedure 3 times with remaining oil and shrimp. Yield: 4 servings (serving size: 7 shrimp and about 2½ tablespoons sauce).

CALORIES 367; **FAT** 13.5g (sat 2.4g, mono 6.5g, poly 3.7g); **PROTEIN** 31g; **CARB** 29.5g; **FIBER** 1g; **CHOL** 252mg; **IRON** 5.6mg; **SODIUM** 731mg; **CALC** 76mg

Jerk Mackerel with Papaya Salad

Mackerel's assertive flavor stands up to the bold taste of jerk seasonings. Plus it's a great sustainable seafood choice. Save remaining Jamaican Jerk Paste to toss with vegetables or hot cooked rice, or stretch it with a little olive oil and use the mixture to marinate chicken.

Salad:
1 cup (2-inch) julienne-cut peeled papaya
1 cup (2-inch) julienne-cut peeled jicama
1 cup (2-inch) julienne-cut red bell pepper
1 tablespoon small cilantro leaves
2 tablespoons fresh lime juice
⅛ teaspoon salt
Fish:
¼ cup Jamaican Jerk Paste
4 (6-ounce) mackerel fillets
Cooking spray

1. Preheat broiler.
2. To prepare salad, combine first 4 ingredients; toss. Sprinkle mixture with lime juice and salt; toss gently to coat.
3. To prepare fish, rub 1 tablespoon Jamaican Jerk Paste over each fillet. Place fillets on a broiler pan coated with cooking spray. Broil 10 minutes or until desired degree of doneness. Serve with salad. Yield: 4 servings (serving size: 1 fillet and ¾ cup salad).

CALORIES 439; **FAT** 26.3g (sat 6.2g, mono 10.3g, poly 6.4g); **PROTEIN** 36g; **CARB** 13.6g; **FIBER** 3.4g; **CHOL** 110mg; **IRON** 3mg; **SODIUM** 600mg; **CALC** 52mg

Jamaican Jerk Paste:
1 Scotch bonnet pepper
½ cup chopped green onion tops
¼ cup finely chopped red onion
1 tablespoon brown sugar
1½ tablespoons fresh lime juice
1 tablespoon water
1 teaspoon salt
1 teaspoon fresh thyme leaves
1 teaspoon minced peeled fresh ginger
¼ teaspoon ground allspice
2 garlic cloves, chopped

1. Cut Scotch bonnet pepper into quarters. Remove and discard seeds and membranes from 3 pepper quarters; leave seeds and membrane intact in remaining pepper quarter. Place pepper and remaining ingredients in a mini chopper, and process until a fine paste forms. Yield: ⅓ cup (serving size: about 1 tablespoon).

CALORIES 19; **FAT** 0.1g (sat 0g, mono 0g, poly 0.1g); **PROTEIN** 0.5g; **CARB** 4.8g; **FIBER** 0.6g; **CHOL** 0mg; **IRON** 0.3mg; **SODIUM** 396mg; **CALC** 13mg

CHILE PEPPERS, LIME, AVOCADO, MANGO, AND CILANTRO ARE A FEW OF THE FOODS AND FLAVORS THAT TRANSPORT US TO THE TROPICS.

Quick & Easy • Kid Friendly

Corn and Crab Fritters with Guacamole

Fritters:
4.5 ounces all-purpose flour (about 1 cup)
¼ cup cornmeal
3 tablespoons finely chopped fresh
    chives
1½ teaspoons baking powder
½ teaspoon salt
⅛ teaspoon ground red pepper
½ cup buttermilk
2 large eggs
¾ cup frozen corn kernels, thawed
1 (8-ounce) container lump crabmeat,
    shell pieces removed
¼ cup canola oil, divided

Guacamole:
2 tablespoons finely chopped seeded plum
    tomato
1 tablespoon organic canola mayonnaise
2 teaspoons minced red onion
2 teaspoons fresh lemon juice
⅛ teaspoon salt
1 avocado, peeled and seeded

1. To prepare fritters, weigh or lightly spoon flour into a dry measuring cup; level with a knife. Combine flour and next 5 ingredients in a large bowl, stirring well with a whisk. Combine buttermilk and eggs, stirring well. Add egg mixture, corn, and crab to flour mixture, stirring gently until moist.
2. Heat a large nonstick skillet over medium-high heat. Add 2 tablespoons oil to pan; swirl to coat. Add 5 (¼-cup) batter mounds to pan, pressing each with back of a spatula to slightly flatten. Cook 4 minutes on each side or until golden and thoroughly cooked. Repeat procedure with remaining 2 tablespoons oil and batter.
3. To prepare guacamole, combine tomato and remaining ingredients in a bowl. Mash avocado with fork to desired consistency. Serve with fritters. Yield: 5 servings (serving size: 2 fritters and 2 tablespoons guacamole).

CALORIES 408; **FAT** 23.8g (sat 3.1g, mono 12g, poly 6g); **PROTEIN** 14.7g; **CARB** 36.4g; **FIBER** 3.7g; **CHOL** 130mg; **IRON** 2.9mg; **SODIUM** 710mg; **CALC** 140mg

COOKING CLASS

CHILI BASICS

Learn the secrets to making a great bowl of chili. Meat-based, bean-based, or completely vegetarian: We offer three delicious variations.

The origins of chili are uncertain, but it's natural to think of it as an American classic. Chili has many regional interpretations, and within each region almost as many recipes as there are cooks. Take chili con carne, a specialty of the Lone Star State: just beef with chiles and onions, maybe some tomatoes, garlic, and definitely seasonings, all cooked until meltingly tender. No self-respecting Texan would consider adding beans. In other regions, chili simply isn't chili unless it has beans. Here we embrace several styles and offer three different healthy bowls.

Make Ahead

Beef and Pinto Bean Chili
(pictured on page 242)

For a three-alarm chili, leave the seeds and membranes in the jalapeños. The sour cream has a cooling effect, but you can seed the peppers or use less for a milder result.

Cooking spray
1 pound boneless chuck roast, trimmed and
    cut into 1-inch pieces
¾ teaspoon salt, divided
2 tablespoons canola oil
4 cups chopped onion (about 2 medium)
¼ cup minced jalapeño peppers (about
    2 large)
10 garlic cloves, minced
1 (12-ounce) bottle beer
1 tablespoon paprika
1 tablespoon ground cumin
2 tablespoons tomato paste
3 cups fat-free, less-sodium beef broth
1 (28-ounce) can whole peeled tomatoes,
    drained and chopped
1 (15-ounce) can pinto beans, rinsed and
    drained
½ cup thinly sliced radish
1 avocado, peeled, seeded, and chopped
6 tablespoons small fresh cilantro leaves
6 tablespoons sour cream
6 lime wedges

1. Heat a Dutch oven over high heat. Coat pan with cooking spray. Sprinkle beef evenly with ¼ teaspoon salt. Add beef to pan; sauté 5 minutes, turning to brown on all sides. Remove from pan. Add oil to pan; swirl to coat. Add onion and jalapeño; sauté 8 minutes or until lightly browned, stirring occasionally. Add garlic; sauté 1 minute, stirring constantly. Stir in beer, scraping pan to loosen browned bits; bring to a boil. Cook until liquid almost evaporates (about 10 minutes), stirring occasionally. Stir in paprika, cumin, and tomato paste; cook 1 minute, stirring frequently. Return beef to pan. Add broth, tomatoes, and beans; bring to a boil. Reduce heat, and simmer 1½ hours or until mixture is thick and beef is very tender, stirring occasionally. Stir in remaining ½ teaspoon salt.
2. Ladle 1 cup chili into each of 6 bowls. Divide radish and avocado evenly among bowls. Top each serving with 1 tablespoon cilantro and 1 tablespoon sour cream. Serve with lime wedges. Yield: 6 servings.

CALORIES 421; **FAT** 23g (sat 6.8g, mono 10.9g, poly 2.6g); **PROTEIN** 21.6g; **CARB** 30.4g; **FIBER** 8.5g; **CHOL** 53mg; **IRON** 4.1mg; **SODIUM** 787mg; **CALC** 123mg

3 STEPS TO TASTY CHILI

1 BROWN TO BUILD A BASE. If making a meat-based chili, the first step is to brown the meat. This enhances the appearance of the meat and creates little bits of flavor in the bottom of the pan. For a vegetarian chili, roast peppers or vegetables to create a similar effect.

2 SAUTÉ AROMATICS TO ADD LAYERS OF FLAVOR. Cook flavorful ingredients like onions and garlic in a small amount of oil to add depth to your chili.

3 ADD LIQUID, AND REDUCE TO CONCENTRATE. Beer, wine, broth, and canned tomatoes (with their juices) are all common ingredients in chili recipes. And when you add the liquid, be sure to scrape the bottom of the pan to loosen all of the yummy browned bits.

Make Ahead
Chili con Carne

A traditional Texas-style chili, this stew packs a smoky punch from mildly spicy poblanos and a hot chipotle chile. .

8 poblano chiles
3 pounds boneless chuck roast, trimmed and cut into ½-inch cubes
1½ teaspoons salt
½ teaspoon black pepper
3 tablespoons all-purpose flour
2 tablespoons olive oil, divided
3 cups chopped onion
4 garlic cloves, minced
3 cups peeled seeded chopped plum tomato (about 10 medium)
1 tablespoon dried oregano
1 tablespoon ground cumin
1 chipotle chile, canned in adobo sauce
3 tablespoons chopped fresh cilantro
6 tablespoons shredded reduced-fat cheddar cheese

1. Preheat broiler.
2. Place poblanos on a foil-lined baking sheet; broil 8 minutes or until charred, turning after 6 minutes. Place poblanos in a zip-top plastic bag; seal. Let stand 15 minutes. Peel and cut chiles into 1-inch pieces.
3. Sprinkle beef with salt and black pepper; dredge in flour. Heat 1 tablespoon oil in a Dutch oven over medium-high heat. Add half of beef to pan; sauté for 5 minutes, turning to brown on all sides. Remove from pan. Repeat procedure with remaining oil and beef.
4. Reduce heat to medium. Add onion to pan; cook 12 minutes, stirring occasionally. Add garlic; cook 3 minutes, stirring frequently. Return beef to pan. Stir in tomato, oregano, and cumin; bring to a simmer. Cover and cook 1 hour, stirring occasionally. Stir in poblanos; simmer for 45 minutes or until beef is tender, stirring occasionally. Rinse, seed, and chop chipotle. Stir in chipotle and cilantro. Sprinkle with cheese. Yield: 10 servings (serving size: about 1 cup chili and about 2 teaspoons cheese).

CALORIES 360; **FAT** 20.9g (sat 7.6g, mono 9.3g, poly 1.1g); **PROTEIN** 29.2g; **CARB** 13.8g; **FIBER** 2.6g; **CHOL** 84mg; **IRON** 3.6mg; **SODIUM** 442mg; **CALC** 83mg

THE BASICS OF GREAT CHILI

ADD FLAVOR AND HEAT WITH CHILES. There are hundreds of different options. Each chile contributes a slightly different flavor, from fruity to bitter, with varying heat levels. For example, poblanos offer mild heat and a fruity taste. Jalapeños have a sharp, acidic flavor and a medium heat level—if you want to tame that heat, remove the seeds and membranes on the inside walls. Or use serrano peppers to crank up the heat even more. Fresh peppers are best in quick-cooking chili, but for those that simmer more than two hours, try dried or use a combination for more nuanced flavor.

CHOOSE THE RIGHT CUTS.
For beef chili, chuck is the best choice because it performs beautifully when cooked slowly. Another tough cut with connective tissue (which melts away when braised or stewed) is pork shoulder.

TAKE IT SLOW.
Let chili simmer slowly—the flavors will meld as the liquid thickens, intensifying the overall taste.

NUTRITION NOTES

▪ Add beans to boost fiber. One (15-ounce) can adds 2 or more grams of fiber per serving.
▪ Add your favorite seasonal veggies, which provide texture, color, and nutrients.

Make Ahead

Three-Bean Vegetarian Chili

Cumin and paprika add earthy flavor to this meatless chili.

2 red bell peppers
3 tablespoons extra-virgin olive oil
1 cup chopped onion
2 teaspoons ground cumin
1 teaspoon crushed red pepper
1 teaspoon paprika
½ teaspoon salt
4 garlic cloves, thinly sliced
2 cups organic vegetable broth
1½ cups (½-inch) cubed peeled butternut
   squash
1 (28-ounce) can no-salt-added tomatoes,
   undrained and chopped
1 (15-ounce) can pinto beans, rinsed and
   drained
1 (15-ounce) can cannellini beans, rinsed and
   drained
1 (15-ounce) can red kidney beans, rinsed and
   drained
½ cup thinly sliced green onions

1. Preheat broiler.
2. Cut bell peppers in half lengthwise. Remove and discard seeds and membranes. Place pepper halves, skin sides up, on a foil-lined baking sheet. Broil 15 minutes or until blackened. Place pepper halves in a zip-top plastic bag; seal. Let stand 15 minutes. Peel and chop peppers.
3. Heat a Dutch oven over medium-low heat. Add oil to pan; swirl to coat. Add onion; cook 15 minutes, stirring occasionally. Stir in cumin and next 4 ingredients; cook 2 minutes, stirring frequently. Add bell peppers, broth, squash, and tomatoes; bring to a simmer. Cook 20 minutes, stirring occasionally. Add beans; simmer 25 minutes or until slightly thick, stirring occasionally. Sprinkle with green onions. Yield: 6 servings (serving size: about 1½ cups).

CALORIES 264; **FAT** 8.3g (sat 1.2g, mono 5.2g, poly 1.3g); **PROTEIN** 9.5g; **CARB** 40.9g; **FIBER** 10.7g; **CHOL** 0mg; **IRON** 4.4mg; **SODIUM** 787mg; **CALC** 145mg

EVERYDAY VEGETARIAN

HEARTY CASSEROLES

Hot from the oven, these robust dishes are inspired by global flavors. Each is soul-warming and deeply satisfying on the coldest winter nights.

Potato, Turnip, and Spinach Baeckeoffe

Translated from the Germanic Alsatian dialect, baeckeoffe means "baker's oven," as it was traditionally a dish that was brought to the local baker to cook in his oven. Classic versions are loaded with meat, but our vegetarian riff is equally hearty and rich.

1 tablespoon butter
1 pound sliced mushroom caps
1 teaspoon minced garlic
1 cup white wine
2 tablespoons chopped fresh flat-leaf parsley
1 large fresh thyme sprig
¾ teaspoon freshly ground black pepper,
   divided
2 tablespoons ⅓-less-fat cream cheese
Cooking spray
4 cups vertically sliced onion (about 2 medium
   onions)
1 (8-ounce) Yukon gold potato, peeled and
   cut into ¼-inch-thick slices
2 cups packed baby spinach leaves
½ teaspoon salt, divided
1 (6-ounce) turnip, peeled and cut into
   ⅛-inch-thick slices
1½ teaspoons chopped fresh tarragon
¼ cup heavy whipping cream
½ cup (2 ounces) shredded Gruyère cheese

1. Preheat oven to 350°.
2. Melt butter in a large nonstick skillet over medium-high heat. Add mushrooms to pan, and sauté 2 minutes or until lightly browned. Stir in garlic; sauté 30 seconds. Add wine; cook 2 minutes. Add parsley, thyme, and ¼ teaspoon black pepper. Cover, reduce heat, and simmer 10 minutes. Uncover and cook 6 minutes or until liquid almost evaporates. Remove from heat; discard thyme. Add cream cheese, stirring until cheese melts. Remove mushroom mixture from pan. Wipe pan clean with paper towels.
3. Heat pan over medium-high heat. Coat pan with cooking spray. Add onion; sauté for 5 minutes, stirring frequently. Reduce heat to medium; continue cooking for 15 minutes or until deep golden brown, stirring frequently. Set aside.
4. Coat a 6-cup baking dish with cooking spray. Arrange potato slices in dish, and top with spinach. Sprinkle ¼ teaspoon salt and ¼ teaspoon black pepper evenly over spinach. Spoon mushroom mixture over black pepper, and arrange turnip slices over mushroom mixture. Top with caramelized onion; sprinkle with remaining ¼ teaspoon salt, remaining ¼ teaspoon black pepper, and tarragon. Pour whipping cream over tarragon, and sprinkle evenly with Gruyère cheese. Cover and bake at 350° for 40 minutes. Uncover and bake an additional 20 minutes or until vegetables are tender and cheese begins to brown. Yield: 4 servings (serving size: about 1¼ cups).

CALORIES 310; **FAT** 14.5g (sat 8.9g, mono 3.7g, poly 0.6g); **PROTEIN** 11.2g; **CARB** 29.8g; **FIBER** 4.3g; **CHOL** 48mg; **IRON** 1.9mg; **SODIUM** 445mg; **CALC** 221mg

Mexican Casserole

Look for veggie protein crumbles in the produce section, near the tofu. Zesty Mexican spices and flavorings sass up plain- (or original-) flavored crumbles. Serve with fruit salad.

4 teaspoons olive oil, divided
1 cup chopped onion
2 garlic cloves, minced
1 jalapeño pepper, minced
1 teaspoon chili powder
½ teaspoon ground cumin
¼ teaspoon freshly ground black pepper
1 (12-ounce) package meatless fat-free
    crumbles (such as Lightlife Smart Ground)
48 baked tortilla chips
Cooking spray
1 (15-ounce) can pinto beans, rinsed and
    drained
1 tablespoon fresh lime juice
2 cups chopped seeded plum tomato
2 tablespoons minced fresh cilantro
¼ teaspoon salt
1 cup (4 ounces) shredded Monterey Jack
    cheese
2 tablespoons fat-free sour cream
2 tablespoons chopped green onions
¼ cup sliced ripe olives

1. Preheat oven to 375°.
2. Heat 2 teaspoons oil in a large nonstick skillet over medium heat. Add onion to pan; cook 4 minutes or until tender. Add garlic and jalapeño; cook 1 minute. Stir in chili powder and next 3 ingredients; cook 3 minutes or until thoroughly heated. Arrange half of tortilla chips in an 11 x 7–inch baking dish coated with cooking spray; top evenly with crumbles mixture.
3. Heat remaining 2 teaspoons oil in skillet over medium heat. Add beans, mashing with back of a wooden spoon until chunky and thick; cook 2 minutes or until heated, stirring constantly. Stir in lime juice.
4. Combine tomato, cilantro, and salt. Layer beans and tomato mixture over crumbles mixture in dish. Top with remaining tortilla chips, pressing to slightly crush. Sprinkle evenly with cheese. Bake at 375° for 13 minutes or until cheese is bubbly. Cut casserole

into 6 equal pieces; top each serving with 1 teaspoon sour cream, 1 teaspoon onions, and 2 teaspoons olives. Yield: 6 servings.

CALORIES 313; FAT 12.9g (sat 4.6g, mono 5.2g, poly 2.4g); PROTEIN 20.6g; CARB 30.2g; FIBER 7.4g; CHOL 18mg; IRON 3mg; SODIUM 816mg; CALC 295mg

Baked Vegetable Lasagna

Don't press out water from the tofu; that way, the cheesy layer will remain moist and creamy. Serve with breadsticks and a green salad.

3 tablespoons olive oil, divided
½ cup chopped white onion
2 garlic cloves, minced
1 teaspoon kosher salt, divided
1 teaspoon sugar
¼ teaspoon freshly ground black pepper,
    divided
¼ teaspoon crushed red pepper
1 (28-ounce) can crushed tomatoes
½ cup chopped fresh basil
1 tablespoon chopped fresh oregano
1 cup ricotta cheese
½ cup (2 ounces) grated fresh Parmigiano-
    Reggiano cheese
1 (14-ounce) package water-packed firm tofu,
    drained
1 large egg, lightly beaten
½ cup thinly sliced green onions
3 cups finely chopped red bell pepper (about
    2 medium)
2 medium zucchini, quartered lengthwise and
    thinly sliced (about 3 cups)
⅓ cup finely chopped fresh parsley
Cooking spray
12 cooked lasagna noodles
¾ cup (3 ounces) shredded part-skim
    mozzarella cheese

1. Preheat oven to 375°.
2. Heat 2 tablespoons oil in a medium saucepan over medium-high heat. Add white onion; sauté 5 minutes or until tender. Add garlic; sauté 1 minute or until golden. Add ½ teaspoon salt, sugar, ⅛ teaspoon black pepper, crushed red pepper, and tomatoes. Cover, reduce heat to low, and simmer 15 minutes or until thoroughly heated. Remove from heat; stir in basil and oregano. Cool.

3. Place ricotta, Parmigiano-Reggiano, tofu, egg, and ¼ teaspoon salt in a food processor; process for 10 seconds or until blended. Stir in green onions. Set aside.
4. Heat remaining 1 tablespoon oil in a large nonstick skillet over medium-high heat. Add bell pepper, zucchini, and remaining ¼ teaspoon salt to pan; sauté 10 minutes or until vegetables are tender and liquid evaporates. Remove from heat; stir in parsley and remaining ⅛ teaspoon black pepper.
5. Spread ½ cup tomato mixture in the bottom of a 13 x 9–inch baking dish coated with cooking spray; top with 3 noodles. Spread ¾ cup tomato mixture over noodles; top with 1 cup tofu mixture and 1 cup zucchini mixture. Repeat layers twice, ending with noodles. Spread remaining ¾ cup tomato mixture over top. Bake at 375° for 35 minutes or until bubbly; top with mozzarella cheese. Bake an additional 5 minutes or until cheese melts. Let stand 10 minutes. Yield: 8 servings (serving size: 1 piece).

CALORIES 347; FAT 18g (sat 6.2g, mono 7g, poly 3.6g); PROTEIN 21.6g; CARB 28.8g; FIBER 5.3g; CHOL 53mg; IRON 8.1mg; SODIUM 543mg; CALC 595mg

Staff Favorite

Rösti Casserole with Baked Eggs

This dish embodies the alluring qualities you'd expect from rösti—shredded potatoes that are cooked until browned and crisp on the edges. Serve with a colorful mixed greens salad.

1¼ cups fat-free Greek-style yogurt
2 tablespoons all-purpose flour
1½ cups grated peeled turnip (about 8 ounces, 2 small)
1¼ cups (5 ounces) shredded Gruyère cheese
⅓ cup butter, melted
¼ cup chopped fresh chives
1¼ teaspoons salt
½ teaspoon freshly ground black pepper
¼ teaspoon grated whole nutmeg
1 (30-ounce) package frozen shredded hash brown potatoes, thawed (such as Ore-Ida)
Cooking spray
8 large eggs
Chopped fresh chives (optional)
Freshly ground black pepper (optional)

1. Preheat oven to 400°.
2. Combine yogurt and flour in a large bowl, stirring well. Add turnip and next 7 ingredients to yogurt mixture. Spread potato mixture evenly into a 13 x 9–inch baking dish coated with cooking spray. Bake at 400° for 30 minutes or until bubbly. Remove from oven. With back of a spoon, make 8 indentations in top of potato mixture. Crack 1 egg into each of 8 indentations. Return dish to oven. Bake at 400° for 8 minutes or until egg whites are firm and yolks barely move when pan is touched. Cut into 8 pieces. Garnish with additional chives and black pepper, if desired. Serve immediately. Yield: 8 servings (serving size: 1 piece).

CALORIES 347; **FAT** 17.4g (sat 9.3g, mono 5.7g, poly 1.4g); **PROTEIN** 18.1g; **CARB** 27.3g; **FIBER** 2.1g; **CHOL** 220mg; **IRON** 1.2mg; **SODIUM** 605mg; **CALC** 242mg

FRESH, LOCAL & FRENCH: QUÉBEC COOKING HEATS UP

A visit to Québec City shows that the revolution that is transforming U.S. food has come, finally, to the French-Canadian province.

For the longest time, the best Québécois food you could find in many parts of the province was *poutine*, which translates from French, fittingly, as "a mess." Poutine involves crisp, rough-cut fries covered in peppery chicken gravy and salty, gooey, melted cheese curds that arrive as hot as napalm and squeak against your teeth when they are fresh. The dish was, and is, fuel for keeping warm through the frigid winters. Served with steamed, cabbage-topped hot dogs, poutine is a satisfying, if decidedly low-rent and by no conceivable means healthy, meal. But in a place with as much pride in its history and identity as Québec, you couldn't help wondering if a mess was really the best they could do.

No, it wasn't—not by a long shot: Québec is experiencing a culinary revival whose most exciting dimension, for those who don't know much north-of-the-border history, is how long and rich the culinary tradition is in these parts.

The foodie soul of the region begins with the fact that Québec is not just another part of Canada. From the time the city was established in 1608, it was the seat of France's sprawling North American empire, and most Québecers insist, with good reason, that their society is profoundly distinct from any other on the continent.

Québec's culinary roots run deep indeed. For example, settlers discovered Jerusalem artichokes and introduced them to Europe. The inhabitants ate oysters, lobster, and mackerel from up the seaway, and wild game like caribou (not to be confused with the beverage known by the same name) and ducks. They made cheese, too—honest, artisanal farmhouse cheeses. Québec City in its early days probably produced more cheeses in a few square miles than you could find on the rest of the continent combined.

But the rise of factory foodmaking and the relative poverty of the province were not kind to Québec's cuisine. After the second world war, small, local producers sold out to bigger, more centralized, less regionally distinct ones. As happened all across North America, there was a flight from the kitchen, and recipes were lost.

In the last 10 years Québec has turned back to its artisanal, pastoral, food-loving roots. Where there were just a handful of distinctive cheeses here in the 1980s, the province produces hundreds today.

Québec's chefs are rediscovering long-forgotten local products like that cheese and Jerusalem artichokes (they're called *topinambours* in French, which even if you don't speak the language is one of the most beautiful words imaginable), wild game, and even the tender plants and succulents that grow wild along the St. Lawrence's shores.

Poutine might not be the city's only reliable food any longer, but for better or worse, it is tradition, too.

Staff Favorite • Kid Friendly

Poutine

The fresher the cheese curds, the better they'll be. If you can't find local, fresh curds, order them from Ellsworth Co-op Creamery at ellsworthcheesecurds.com, or substitute kasseri cheese cubes. Kasseri, a salty Greek cheese, comes close to imitating the texture of curds. (Cheddar will work but won't add texture like the curds.) Oven-frying the potatoes in duck fat adds a rich, meaty flavor and gives them a gorgeously crisp texture. Look for duck fat in specialty markets or order online.

2 tablespoons duck fat
2 pounds baking potatoes, cut into
 4 x ¼–inch strips (about 3 medium)
½ teaspoon kosher salt, divided
Cooking spray
6 ounces 50% less-fat pork sausage
1½ tablespoons butter, melted
2 tablespoons all-purpose flour
2 cups fat-free, less-sodium beef broth
2 ounces fresh cheddar cheese curds
Chopped fresh parsley (optional)

1. Place a small roasting pan in oven. Preheat oven to 450°.
2. Carefully remove hot pan from oven. Melt fat in pan; add potatoes. Sprinkle potatoes with ¼ teaspoon salt; toss. Bake at 450° for 45 minutes or until golden, turning once after 30 minutes.
3. Heat a large skillet over medium-high heat. Coat pan with cooking spray. Add sausage; cook 5 minutes or until browned, stirring to crumble. Combine butter and flour, stirring until smooth. Add butter mixture to sausage; cook 1 minute, stirring constantly. Slowly add broth to pan, stirring constantly; bring to a boil. Reduce heat; add remaining ¼ teaspoon salt, and simmer 3 minutes or until slightly thick, stirring occasionally. Spoon gravy over fries; top with cheese curds. Sprinkle with parsley, if desired. Yield: 8 servings (serving size: about ½ cup fries, 3 tablespoons gravy, and 1 tablespoon cheese curds).

CALORIES 220; FAT 11.5g (sat 5g, mono 4.1g, poly 1g); PROTEIN 8.4g; CARB 21.7g; FIBER 1.6g; CHOL 31mg; IRON 1.2mg; SODIUM 453mg; CALC 67mg

Make Ahead

Braised Beef Short Ribs

Serve this hearty winter dish over mashed potatoes. You can prepare the entire dish ahead and reheat just before serving. Reheat the beef on the grill to give a hint of smoky flavor, if you like. Veal demi-glace—veal stock reduced to a concentrated gelatin—adds depth and richness to the sauce.

1.1 ounces all-purpose flour (about ¼ cup)
8 (2½-ounce) beef short ribs, trimmed
1 teaspoon kosher salt
½ teaspoon freshly ground black pepper
2 tablespoons olive oil
¾ cup diced onion
⅓ cup diced celery
⅓ cup diced carrot
¼ cup chopped leek
1 garlic clove, minced
10 whole black peppercorns
5 juniper berries
3 fresh thyme sprigs
2 bay leaves
¼ cup veal demi-glace
¾ cup hot water
½ cup dry red wine
Thyme sprigs (optional)

1. Preheat oven to 350°.
2. Weigh or lightly spoon flour into dry measuring cup; level with a knife. Place flour in a shallow dish. Sprinkle beef evenly on all sides with salt and pepper; dredge in flour. Heat a large Dutch oven over medium-high heat. Add oil to pan, and swirl to coat. Add beef to pan; sauté for 8 minutes, turning to brown on all sides. Remove beef from pan.
3. Add onion and next 3 ingredients to pan; sauté 5 minutes, stirring occasionally. Add garlic; sauté 1 minute, stirring frequently. Place peppercorns and next 3 ingredients on a double layer of cheesecloth. Gather edges of cheesecloth together; tie securely. Place herb and spice bundle in pan; return beef to pan. Dissolve demi-glace in ¾ cup hot water, stirring well. Add demi-glace mixture and wine to pan; bring to a boil. Cover and bake at 350° for 2½ hours or until beef is fork tender. Remove beef from pan; strain cooking liquid through a fine-mesh sieve over a bowl. Discard solids. Serve cooking liquid with beef. Garnish with thyme sprigs, if desired. Yield: 4 servings (serving size: 2 ribs and 2 tablespoons cooking liquid).

CALORIES 224; FAT 13.7g (sat 3.9g, mono 7.9g, poly 1g); PROTEIN 13.4g; CARB 11.5g; FIBER 1.3g; CHOL 34mg; IRON 2.1mg; SODIUM 718mg; CALC 31mg

WINE NOTE: With the richness of short ribs, you need to pull out a cabernet as an accompaniment. (Well-marbled beef loves to tame this grape's tannins.) Slingshot 2006 Cabernet Sauvignon is a Napa bottle that, at $23, won't break the bank. But it offers beautiful nuances of cedar, spice (juniper's a big player), and aromatic dried cherries, with bright acidity.

Quick & Easy

Chocolate Cappuccino

1 cup chocolate liqueur
2 tablespoons maple syrup
2 cups hot brewed espresso
1½ cups scalded whole milk
¼ teaspoon ground cinnamon
Chocolate shavings (optional)

1. Combine liqueur and syrup in a microwave-safe dish; heat at HIGH for 30 seconds. Divide liqueur mixture among 8 mugs; add ¼ cup espresso to each. Froth milk; pour about ¼ cup milk into each mug. Top evenly with ground cinnamon; garnish with chocolate shavings, if desired. Yield: 8 servings.

CALORIES 146; FAT 1.7g (sat 0.9g, mono 0.4g, poly 0.2g); PROTEIN 1.5g; CARB 18.9g; FIBER 0g; CHOL 5mg; IRON 0.2mg; SODIUM 29mg; CALC 57mg

Kid Friendly

Tourtière

Spiced meat pie dating back to the Middle Ages is a holiday tradition in Québec. The dish is often made in a pie plate with top and bottom crusts. Our version calls to bake individual pies in ramekins with just a top crust—a simple way to shave both fat and calories from each serving. If you don't have ramekins, simply spoon the pork mixture into a (9-inch) pie plate and top with the entire store-bought pastry.

Cooking spray
1 pound ground pork
1 teaspoon salt, divided
½ teaspoon ground cinnamon
⅛ teaspoon ground red pepper
⅛ teaspoon ground cloves
1 tablespoon olive oil
1 cup finely chopped onion
½ cup finely chopped carrot
⅓ cup finely chopped celery
1 (1-pound) russet potato, peeled and cut into
    ¼-inch cubes
3 garlic cloves, minced
2 tablespoons all-purpose flour
1½ cups fat-free, less-sodium chicken broth
3 tablespoons finely chopped chives
½ (15-ounce) package refrigerated pie
    dough (such as Pillsbury)

1. Preheat oven to 400°.
2. Heat a large skillet over medium-high heat, and coat pan with cooking spray. Add pork to pan. Sprinkle pork with ½ teaspoon salt, cinnamon, red pepper, and cloves; sauté for 5 minutes or until browned, stirring to crumble. Using a slotted spoon, remove pork from pan. Add oil to pan, and swirl to coat. Add onion and next 3 ingredients; sauté for 5 minutes, stirring frequently. Add garlic, and sauté for 1 minute, stirring constantly. Return pork to pan. Stir in flour, and cook for 1 minute, stirring constantly. Add broth, scraping pan to loosen browned bits; bring to a boil. Cook 2 minutes or until slightly thick. Remove from heat; stir in chives.
3. Place 1 cup pork mixture into each of 6 (8-ounce) ramekins. Roll pie dough to an 11-inch circle. Cut 4 (5-inch) dough circles. Combine and reroll dough scraps. Cut 2 (5-inch)

circles. Place 1 dough circle on each ramekin, tucking edges inside. Cut an X in top of each circle; coat lightly with cooking spray. Place ramekins on a baking sheet. Bake at 400° for 40 minutes or until golden and bubbly. Yield: 6 servings (serving size: 1 ramekin).

CALORIES 420; FAT 22.2g (sat 7.6g, mono 9.8g, poly 2g); PROTEIN 17.5g; CARB 36.5g; FIBER 2.4g; CHOL 54mg; IRON 1.8mg; SODIUM 683mg; CALC 45mg

BEER NOTE: With traditional Canadian Tourtière, reach for the strong and spicy Québécois beer Maudite ($8.99/750 ml). Made in a Belgian style, Maudite has a peppery, spicy signature that echoes this dish's layers of cinnamon and clove. The beer is strong and full-flavored, with bold fruit, caramel, bready, and figgy flavors that work with the complex flavors of these meat pies, while remaining refreshingly drinkable.

Make Ahead

Caribou-Poached Pears and Ice Cream

Pears are poached in a Québécois beverage called caribou, which is often served during the winter carnival. Double the amount of hot spiced wine you make, reserve half, and enjoy it as a beverage.

1¼ cups fruity red wine
4 juniper berries
3 star anise
4 (1-inch) cinnamon sticks, divided
2 whole cloves
1 whole nutmeg
⅓ cup white rum
½ cup sugar, divided
4 firm Bartlett or Anjou pears, peeled and
    cored
1¼ cups whole milk
¼ cup heavy whipping cream
2 large egg yolks
3 tablespoons chopped pistachios

1. Combine wine, juniper berries, anise, 2 cinnamon sticks, cloves, and nutmeg in a saucepan, and bring to a boil. Reduce heat, and simmer for 5 minutes; remove from heat. Let stand for 30 minutes.

Strain mixture over a bowl, reserving liquid; discard solids. Stir in ⅓ cup white rum.
2. Combine rum mixture and ¼ cup sugar in a large saucepan. Cook over medium heat 2 minutes or until sugar dissolves. Place pears in pan; cook 1 hour or until pears are tender, turning occasionally. Remove pears; cool. Bring cooking liquid to a boil; cook 15 minutes or until mixture reduces to ¼ cup.
3. Combine milk, whipping cream, and remaining 2 cinnamon sticks in a heavy saucepan; bring to a boil. Remove from heat; discard cinnamon sticks. Combine remaining ¼ cup sugar and egg yolks in a large bowl. Gradually add half of hot milk mixture to yolk mixture, stirring constantly. Return mixture to pan; cook over low heat until mixture reaches 160°, stirring constantly. Place pan in an ice-filled bowl; cool completely. Pour mixture into freezer can of an ice-cream freezer, and freeze according to manufacturer's instructions. Carefully drain liquid from bucket; repack bucket with ice and salt. Cover with kitchen towels; ripen for at least 1 hour.
4. Cut pears in half lengthwise. Slice each pear half, lengthwise, cutting to but not through stem end. Fan one pear half on each of 8 small plates, and drizzle pear halves evenly with reduced syrup. Serve with ¼ cup ice cream. Sprinkle about 1 teaspoon pistachios over each serving. Yield: 8 servings.

CALORIES 237; FAT 9.4g (sat 4.7g, mono 3.1g, poly 0.9g); PROTEIN 3.3g; CARB 32.3g; FIBER 3.6g; CHOL 75mg; IRON 0.6mg; SODIUM 39mg; CALC 74mg

Habitant Pea Soup

Habitant refers to people who live in rural Québec, where this hearty soup is a popular staple.

2 tablespoons olive oil
2 cups finely chopped onion
1 cup finely chopped carrot
½ cup finely chopped celery
2 cups yellow split peas
6 cups fat-free, less-sodium beef broth
2 cups water
6 ounces salt pork
2 bay leaves
1 (12-ounce) ham hock
2 tablespoons chopped fresh flat-leaf parsley
2 tablespoons chopped fresh thyme
¾ teaspoon kosher salt
½ teaspoon freshly ground black pepper
¼ cup crème fraîche
Thyme leaves (optional)

1. Heat oil in a large Dutch oven over medium-high heat. Add onion, carrot, and celery to pan; sauté for 6 minutes, stirring occasionally. Stir in peas; sauté for 1 minute. Add broth and next 4 ingredients; bring to a boil. Reduce heat, and simmer 1½ hours or until peas are tender, skimming surface occasionally, as necessary.
2. Remove ham hock and bay leaves; discard. Remove salt pork; cool. Remove 1½ cups pea mixture; let stand 5 minutes. Puree 1½ cups pea mixture, and return to pan, stirring to thicken slightly. Stir in parsley and next 3 ingredients.
3. Dice salt pork. Heat a nonstick skillet over medium-high heat. Add pork to pan; cover and cook 5 minutes or until crisp and browned, stirring frequently. Ladle 1 cup soup into each of 8 bowls; top each serving with 1 tablespoon pork and 1½ teaspoons crème fraîche. Sprinkle with fresh thyme leaves, if desired. Yield: 8 servings.

CALORIES 426; FAT 25.2g (sat 8.7g, mono 11g, poly 2.5g); PROTEIN 14.7g; CARB 34.8g; FIBER 15.4g; CHOL 30mg; IRON 1.6mg; SODIUM 839mg; CALC 34mg

NUTRITION MADE EASY
THE POWER OF OATS

No more excuses for skipping breakfast: Our oatmeal ideas make quick work of the day's most important meal.

Oatmeal has been in the nutritional spotlight for decades. The oat bran craze of the 80s begat the Wilford Brimley "It's the right thing to do" TV ads of which, believe it or not, there is now a remix on YouTube. Today we know it's not just the bran: Two-thirds of oaty goodness is in the rest of the grain. The welcome news is that basic rolling and cutting, used to make instant and quick varieties, does not damage the nutrition. So, whether you want convenience or a slow-cooked nutty bowl of groats, it's all good.

Quick & Easy
Banana, Wheat Germ, and Oats

Wheat germ and oats make a perfect pair: You get the goodness of whole grains from the oats and a host of nutrients, such as vitamin E, iron, potassium, and folic acid, from the wheat germ.

3¾ cups water
1 cup old-fashioned rolled oats
⅔ cup toasted wheat germ
¼ teaspoon salt
1½ cups sliced banana (about 2)
3 tablespoons brown sugar
1 tablespoon butter

1. Combine first 4 ingredients in a medium saucepan, and bring to a boil over high heat, stirring occasionally. Reduce heat to medium-low, and cook for 6 minutes or until thick and thoroughly heated, stirring occasionally. Remove from heat. Divide cereal evenly among 3 bowls. Top each serving with ½ cup banana, 1 tablespoon brown sugar, and 1 teaspoon butter. Yield: 3 servings.

CALORIES 336; FAT 8.4g (sat 3.2g, mono 2g, poly 2.3g); PROTEIN 12.1g; CARB 59.1g; FIBER 8.3g; CHOL 10mg; IRON 3.9mg; SODIUM 226mg; CALC 35mg

KNOW YOUR OAT OPTIONS

Whole oats are a tough, chewy grain, as slow-cooking as brown rice, and various amounts of cutting, rolling, steaming, and precooking are used to speed the home-preparation time. Unlike with white-flour processing, however, significant amounts of nutrients are not lost.

OAT GROATS
Oats as nature intended (they're similar to wheat berries). They'll need about 45 minutes of stove-top simmering before they're tender.

STEEL-CUT (IRISH)
These are whole oat groats that have been halved or cut into three pieces, so they cook faster (about 20 minutes) and the finished dish is chewier.

REGULAR (ROLLED)
What most of us know as oatmeal is made of whole groats that have been steamed and then flattened by large rollers. They're ready in about 5 minutes.

INSTANT
Regular rolled oats are flattened even more, then cooked and dried. (Not to be confused with sugary pulverized instant oat packets.)

OATMEAL IS RICH IN SOLUBLE FIBER, WHICH CAN IMPROVE HEART HEALTH BY REDUCING LDL CHOLESTEROL LEVELS AND HELP KEEP YOU FEELING FULL LONGER.

Overnight Honey-Almond Multigrain Cereal

Steel-cut oats and barley soak up water overnight so they're ready to go in the morning. Use a big bowl because the grains will expand.

⅓ cup steel-cut oats (such as McCann's)
2 tablespoons uncooked pearl barley
1¼ cups water
⅛ teaspoon salt
¼ teaspoon ground cinnamon
⅛ teaspoon ground nutmeg
1 tablespoon sliced almonds, toasted
1 tablespoon honey

1. Combine oats, barley, and 1¼ cups water in a microwave-safe 4-cup bowl. Cover and refrigerate 4 hours or overnight.

2. Uncover bowl, and stir in salt. Microwave, uncovered, at HIGH for 6 minutes or until most of liquid is absorbed, stirring well after 3 minutes. Stir in cinnamon and nutmeg. Top with almonds and honey. Yield: 1 serving (serving size: 1 bowl).

CALORIES 388; **FAT** 7.1g (sat 0.9g, mono 3g, poly 2g); **PROTEIN** 11.2g; **CARB** 75g; **FIBER** 10g; **CHOL** 0mg; **IRON** 3.7mg; **SODIUM** 300mg; **CALC** 56mg

SUPER STIR-INS

Think beyond brown sugar to kick up the flavor and texture of your bowl. Swirl, sprinkle, or top with any one of these 18 options for less than 100 calories. (Even bacon! It's surprisingly good.)

SWEET
Molasses, 1 teaspoon
Maple syrup, 2 teaspoons
Strawberry jam, 1 tablespoon

CRUNCHY
Walnuts, 1 tablespoon chopped
Almonds, 1 tablespoon sliced
Cashews, 1 tablespoon chopped

CHEWY
Cherries, 1 tablespoon dried
Apricots, 1 tablespoon diced and dried
Figs, 1 tablespoon diced and dried

FRUITY
Blueberries, ¼ cup
Strawberries, ¼ cup sliced
Apple, 2 tablespoons diced

ADVENTUROUS
Creamy peanut butter, 1 tablespoon
Toasted coconut, 1 tablespoon
Chocolate syrup, 1 tablespoon

SAVORY
Bacon, ½ slice, crumbled
Cheddar cheese, 1½ tablespoons shredded
Nonfat Greek yogurt, ¼ cup

THE *COOKING LIGHT* WAY TO EAT

10 Rules for Healthy Eating in 2010 plus 50 Small Changes That Can Make a Big Difference

Cooking Light started 23 years ago, when the idea that healthier cooking would appeal beyond the granola and Birkenstock crowd was a radical proposition. But the timing was brilliant: Heart disease had been on the rise since the 1950s, and science was pursuing the leading suspect—saturated fat—like a posse of PhDs hunting down Bonnie and Clyde. The Dietary Guidelines for Americans had been published in 1980, nutrition labels would be standardized in 1990, and the first food pyramid appeared in 1992. Foods were indeed being villainized—the poor little egg was shown on the cover of *Time* magazine in 1984 (along with its sidekick, bacon) as the sad-faced poster child in the war on cholesterol. If you had an officially "healthy" food to sell—like oatmeal—you had a big new field to plow, and the government would allow you to make unprecedented claims.

We know where this led—to silly ideas about "superfoods" and the hero-worshiping of fiber, antioxidants, etc. "Nutritionism," as Michael Pollan, award-winning journalist and author of *In Defense of Food*, calls the excessive belief in the power of individual nutrients, led to ever more fortification of "empty" foods without really making them whole. It led to enshrined wisdom (no more than 30 percent of calories from fat) until new research began to tear the shrine down.

Some, like Pollan, see a near-collapse of the idea that nutrition knowledge per se can lead to better health. They have a point, but we're more optimistic. We think this is not a period of muddle (though, terribly, it's a period of rising obesity and diabetes), but instead it's a period when the real, deep wisdom about healthy eating is coming into new focus for those who will see. This wisdom blends science, tradition, care for the environment, love of cooking, the human need for pleasure and indulgence, and the ideal of balance into a minestrone seasoned by the good old common sense of the American cook. The power to do good—to nurture our families, to enjoy our food, to celebrate culinary traditions while being mindful of the health of the earth—is in our hands.

"The *Cooking Light* Way to Eat" sums up our thinking in 2010. Our rules are not narrow dogma; they're broad gestures designed to incorporate what we know about nutrition into the cook's life well lived. We know that when it comes to cooking and eating, it is the small choices that yield the biggest results over time. So at the end of each of the 10 rules, you'll find five fairly small ideas that support the bigger idea.

1. *Try* SOMETHING NEW

Because life is short, the menu is long, and the odds favor the adventurous appetite: Variety ensures a nutrient-rich diet and, in our view, a much happier eater. By adventurous we don't refer to the insect-munching stunt eaters of cable television. When we think about adventurous eaters, we think of Naomi Duguid, coauthor of six award-winning, intrepidly reported cookbooks, including *Mangoes and Curry Leaves; Beyond the Great Wall;* and *Hot, Sour, Salty, Sweet.* Facing a new food such as Chinese snails, yak meat, or tree ear fungus, the question for Duguid has never been "Why?" but "Why not?" She doesn't travel 10,000 miles to say no to Kazakh goat broth. New foods in (or from) foreign places help you "understand where you are, learn how people work with what they have, and engage with and be interested in the world," says Duguid. When in Rome, in other words.

New foods are not always instantly enjoyed, Duguid admits. She had to hold her breath to swallow fresh, warm camel's milk and struggled a bit with grilled guinea pig (but it was "rich-tasting and tender") and chicken sashimi ("beautifully sliced ... a favorite in Japan served with special dipping sauces"). But it's usually worth the effort to open a new culinary horizon, she finds.

You may not be able to travel, of course, and may have less expansive views about chicken sashimi (as do we). But Rome's larder has come to America, along with that of almost every other cuisine on the planet. Cookbooks by culinary adventurers like Duguid are our field reports and universal translation tools.

SMALL IDEAS FOR TRYING NEW FOODS

• Set a family new-food goal to try a new recipe or new ingredient each week.

• Grow your own winter greens or exotic Thai herbs. You'll be more likely to try them and experiment with them if they're right outside the door (or on the windowsill).

• Start a supper club with neighbors, friends, or curious and adventurous eaters. Use e-mail or Internet invitation sites to help coordinate and plan the event, which can be based on an ingredient, country, holiday, or time period.

• Try a field trip to an ethnic market for inspiration. A little mushroom soy sauce packs plenty of umami flavor that's a perfect addition to a vegetarian stir-fry. Another good find: schichmi, a somewhat spicy Japanese seasoning that's good on rice or potatoes or sprinkled over soups.

• For inspiration, read Jonathan Gold's adventurous food reviews at laweekly.com.

Duguid's Everyday Dal

1½ cups split hulled mung dal or masoor (red)
  dal, rinsed and drained
6 cups water
½ teaspoon ground turmeric
2 bay leaves
1 (3-inch) cinnamon stick
1½ teaspoons salt, divided
3 tablespoons olive oil
1 teaspoon black or brown mustard seeds
1 tablespoon minced peeled fresh ginger
1 tablespoon minced garlic
½ teaspoon nigella seeds
½ teaspoon cumin seeds
2 dried small hot red chiles, stemmed
½ cup finely chopped shallots
1 cup diced carrot
1 cup cauliflower florets
¾ cup fresh cilantro leaves
6 lime wedges (optional)

1. Combine dal and 6 cups water in a large saucepan; bring to a boil. Stir in turmeric, bay leaves, and cinnamon stick; partially cover, reduce heat, and simmer 25 minutes or until tender, stirring occasionally. Discard bay leaves and cinnamon stick. Stir in ½ teaspoon salt. Keep warm.

2. Heat oil in a large nonstick skillet over medium-high heat. Add mustard seeds; cook 1 minute or until seeds pop, stirring constantly. Add ginger and next 4 ingredients; cook 2 minutes, stirring constantly. Add shallots; cook 3 minutes or until shallots are tender, stirring frequently. Add carrot and cauliflower; cook 5 minutes or until vegetables are crisp-tender, stirring frequently. Add 1 cup dal mixture and remaining 1 teaspoon salt to carrot mixture; cook 2 minutes, stirring frequently.

3. Add carrot mixture to remaining dal mixture; bring to a boil. Cook 40 minutes or until mixture thickens. Sprinkle each serving with 2 tablespoons cilantro leaves. Garnish with lime wedges, if desired. Yield: 6 servings (serving size: about ¾ cup).

CALORIES 266; **FAT** 8.2g (sat 1g, mono 5g, poly 0.8g); **PROTEIN** 14.6g; **CARB** 35.7g; **FIBER** 8.8g; **CHOL** 0mg; **IRON** 3.7mg; **SODIUM** 619mg; **CALC** 50mg

2. Choose
HEALTHY FATS

Because the old "less fat means a healthier diet" paradigm has been shifted by research suggesting that certain fats from vegetables, nuts, and fish actually promote good health. In 2010, the fats you favor are just as important as how much fat you eat.

This wisdom is native to some food cultures. "My father and grandfather would eat a spoonful of extra-virgin olive oil every morning," says Efisio Farris, a native of Sardinia who is chef-owner of a couple of restaurants in Texas. "My father is 89, and my grandfather lived to 107."

Anecdotes aren't proof, and oil isn't medicine. But the good news about healthful, flavorful oils is getting through. Olive oil is the fat of choice for starting many cooked dishes now, although American cooks are only beginning to understand that the delicious potential of healthy fats can carry through the cooking to the "finishing" of a dish, as well.

In his restaurants in Houston and Dallas, Farris drizzles intense fruttato ("fruity") olive oil over finished dishes like pasta or roasted fish as a potent flavoring flourish.

Olive oil is only one of many healthy fats. Hazelnut oil, walnut oil, almond oil, sesame oil, avocado oil, and even pine nut oil can add beautiful nuance to salads, grains, fish, or vegetables. Something as simple and old-fashioned as excellent tinned sardines, packed in olive oil and eaten with crisp whole-grain crackers, is a gold mine of healthy fish and plant fats.

SMALL IDEAS FOR CHOOSING FATS

• Add foods high in healthy fat—like avocados, nuts, and canola-based mayo—to your salads and sandwiches.

• Splurge on top-quality extra-virgin olive oil, like Ravida ($30 for a 16.9-ounce bottle at zabars.com), which packs intense flavor: A little of this herbal-grassy oil, one of our favorites, goes a long way.

• Get to know which low-fat and fat-free products really deliver. It's important to cut saturated fat intake, but the low-fat food must taste good. We love Fage Total 2% yogurt for its thick, creamy texture, and Kerrygold Reduced-Fat Aged Cheddar, which boasts rich flavor without the plastic-like mouthfeel of some low-fat cheeses.

• Choose fish loaded with omega-3 fatty acids, such as sardines, mackerel, sablefish, and rainbow trout.

• To avoid dangerous trans fats, ignore the Nutrition Facts label and check the ingredient list: Partially hydrogenated oil of any kind means trans fats lurk within.

3. Cook
MORE OFTEN

Because if super-chef Grant Achatz can find the time to cook at home, so can you. Achatz puts in 100 hours a week at his superb Chicago restaurant, Alinea. "I get here at 10:30 in the morning, and I don't leave until 3 in the morning," says the 35-year-old father of two young boys. "But when the restaurant is closed, often I transform into what I call my Martha Stewart phase, where I'm romantically walking to the market and grilling beautiful organic foods at home." In Achatz's home kitchen, his boys grab their stools and plastic knives, and his girlfriend, Heather, rolls up her sleeves. "Everybody helps. We really enjoy that time when we get to interact and cook, and feel a sense of accomplishment and connection."

For home cooks simplicity is better. You can make an amazing omelet for dinner in very little time. What can take a little time, of course, is mastering the technique of an "amazing" omelet, but that comes from plain old book learning or a local cooking class, and a bit of practice. Better cooking is its own reward—and tends to lead to more cooking. And here's the health payoff: Cooking at home means you are the nutritional gatekeeper of the kitchen; you control what your family eats. If you want to use less salt in a marinara to cut sodium, or serve a whole-grain barley risotto, or put a double layer of nutritious, leafy green spinach in a lasagna—that's your charge.

SMALL IDEAS FOR COOKING MORE OFTEN

• Stock your pantry abundantly. You can easily pull a nutritious dinner together from well-stocked shelves and skip a trip to the store—or a call for pizza delivery.

• Use your slow cooker to do most of the cooking. Put ingredients in the pot, turn on, and return later to the heady aroma of a healthy, hearty stew or braise.

• Share the cooking duties for a casual dinner party with friends.

• Cook double-duty ingredients— grill lots of veggies for sandwiches today and pasta tomorrow, or spicy steak that can add flavor to a next-day salad.

• Learn a new technique. Nothing fancy—it could be rolling that perfect omelet, whisking together a vinaigrette, or making a custard for ice cream. Improved kitchen skills always make us want to cook more.

4. *Eat less red*
& PROCESSED MEAT

It's not good to eat like a king just because you can afford to eat like a king.

Our sea-to-shining-sea success as food producers democratized eating and made meat a dietary birthright for Americans. But as Michael Pollan says, that isn't necessarily progress: "Meat has always been a very special thing ... giant joints of meat were for banquets. We've taken banquet food and made it everyday food."

Many processed meats contain nitrites, implicated in cancer. What's more, the compounds formed when meat, fish, or poultry are browned or charred also have been associated with disease. Large servings of red meat yield a diet high in saturated fat. And meat-centric eating pushes other healthy foods from the center of the plate to the side—or right off it.

Eating less meat can be a challenge, though. Solutions include using meat for flavor rather than filler; being creative or even sneaky with alternatives like tofu and beans; using small amounts of processed meats, such as prosciutto or bacon, as a flavoring or garnish; and concentrating satisfying meat flavors in stocks and reductions for soups and sauces.

Pollan also advises paying more for meat from small producers. Industrial meat production has a big carbon footprint, and few would claim boxed-in animals are happy. The free-range message is undeniably appealing, but such meat is expensive. Pollan suggests that spending more is not bad economics, though, because you can make a delicious meal plus a flavorful stock from the chicken, which amortizes the cost over several meals, and the leftovers are delicious.

SMALL IDEAS FOR EATING LESS MEAT

• Set a goal to go meatless every Monday (or any day of the week), and try a cheese pizza, tofu stir-fry, or a casserole for dinner.

• Choose the finest bacon you can find—then use much less to flavor vegetables or other dishes. You get by with less when each bite brims with porky flavor.

• Exploit umami, the savory, meaty "fifth taste." Make a risotto with plenty of meaty mushrooms, and finish with top-grade Parmigiano–Reggiano for a double dose of umami.

• Buy grass-fed beef for its pleasing grassy, mineral-like qualities. Buying online involves a carbon cost from the shipping, but grass-fed ranching is greener, and feedlot beef in your supermarkets may not be local anyway.

• Eat more fish. Some choice sustainable and delicious options include albacore tuna, Arctic char, and U.S.-farmed tilapia.

5. *Eat more*
WHOLE FOODS

Because we don't yet know all the good things food processors are removing from what we eat. Although the list of nutrients on a nutrition label is short (fats, fibers, sugars, cholesterol, sodium, vitamins, etc.), the list of food components suspected of helping prevent disease is huge.

Why is this important? Populations whose diets are based on whole foods tend to be less afflicted by diabetes, heart disease, and cancer. A diet rich in whole foods also tends to increase your consumption of fiber and complex carbohydrates and cuts your intake of simple sugars, refined carbs, and salt.

We're not saying there is no place in the diet for processed foods. Cooking is processing. Chocolate, wine, and many of the good things in life are processed foods, far from the whole state of the bean or grape. We recommend lower-fat dairy products. And don't even think of taking away our semolina pastas! But the story of the American diet reflects a persistent, naive (and ultimately misplaced) trust that we know enough about nutrition to eat vast amounts of foods that have been reduced to pale shadows of their former selves.

SMALL IDEAS FOR EATING MORE WHOLE FOODS

• Get to know local production. Check out localharvest.org for information on u-picks, Community Shared Agriculture groups (CSAs), and discussion forums on topics from beekeeping to organic produce.

• Make your own nut butters. You can grind just what's needed at many health-food and gourmet markets. Then you can control the amount of salt or sugar added.

• Don't fear the freezer. Frozen whole-kernel corn, green peas, and lima beans are good, nutritious, and tasty. Use what you need; minimal prep is required. Add pan-toasted corn to chili or soup; toss peas into rice and stir-fries.

• Learn to break down and use a whole chicken. Buy a "pastured" bird; use the meat in stews, roasts, or chili, and then make stock with the leftover bones.

• Experiment with whole grains. In place of refined couscous, serve whole-grain quinoa with a lamb or chickpea tagine.

6. *Start the day*
OFF WELL

Because the path to weight control and weight loss probably starts with a good breakfast. An impressive 78 percent of the 5,000 participants in the National Weight Control Registry (which tracks people's weight loss and maintenance success) report eating a regular breakfast—and they have lost an average of 66 pounds, maintaining that for more than five years.

Why this is so isn't exactly clear. But consider a day without breakfast: By midmorning you have fasted for 12 hours or longer. This sets the stage for brain droop, maybe followed by some impulsive snacking. Lunch arrives and, overhungry, you may eat too much, too fast. Or, if you have been "good," you may reach the dinner hour feeling you've earned a food "credit" after a stressful day—and then binge.

Breakfast is about pacing. Modern life is about racing, of course, but good breakfast choices are not complicated or time-consuming. Indeed, morning offers the day's best opportunity to make whole grains, whole fruits, low-fat dairy, and other nutritious foods into a habit because breakfast tends to be a meal of habitual choices.

SMALL IDEAS TO START THE DAY

• Make your own breakfast cereal with rolled oats or kasha (buckwheat groats), dried fruits, and nuts. You'll gain all the nutrition benefits of a whole-grain, fruited cereal—free of crazy additives, sugary faux fruit bits, or refined grains.

• Healthy savory leftovers can be a good option, too. A piece of that veggie-rich pizza from the night before, or a slice of roast pork tenderloin tucked into 100 percent whole-grain bread, is a good savory option.

• Sprinkle on nutrition with nutrient-rich wheat germ. An old trick, but we love a little over yogurt or cold cereal. Mix into waffle and pancake batters, too.

• Think outside the oat box. Oats corner the market for hot, good-for-you cereals. But barley grits, rye flakes, or brown rice cereals are interesting whole-grain updates on the old stand-by. Check health-food stores or supermarket cereal or baking aisles.

• If drive-through is the only option, an Egg McMuffin from McDonald's, oatmeal from Starbucks, or Au Bon Pain's fruit cups and muesli are sensible selections.

7. *Indulge* ADVENTUROUSLY

Because a healthy approach to eating includes permission to satisfy that part of the soul that craves truffles, butter, chocolate, or cheese—in modest portions.

We have people like Heath Putnam to thank for the ever-growing list of indulgent treats in the American food supply. Putnam, living in Europe at the time, turned from techno-geek to pork producer after encountering the portly Mangalitsa pig, a "lard-based" breed whose woolly heads and sagging bellies produce the richest, most indulgent pork he had ever tasted.

Some pig: "It's addictive. The meat is kind of sweet and it's salty, and fatty ... but the fat on this pig is particularly light and clean," he says. The precise opposite is true of U.S. factory pork, which has been bred to often be superlean (healthy) but sometimes superbland (why bother?).

Leaving Europe, Putnam decided in 2006 to become America's only importer of the Mangalitsa. There were logistical challenges to deal with, but he's now chief Mangalitsa expert and evangelist in America. Yes, it's caloric and expensive: $13 to $19 per pound. But, as with all of the best foods, "It doesn't take much to feel satisfied." We agree: A small, pan-seared Mangalitsa chop, finished in the oven and bathed in a tart red wine–blueberry reduction, was gamy and silky—and simply the best chop ever. Permission to indulge granted.

SMALL IDEAS FOR INDULGING ADVENTUROUSLY

• Seek out the real thing. Piquant, creamy Roquefort beats a generic blue cheese, and a little goes a long way in a green salad or with walnuts and port for dessert. Try a smoky Spanish chorizo, artisanal chocolates and coffees, or real farm butters.

• Drizzle rich browned butter over humble vegetables for a nutty flavor boost; try on steamed green beans or broccoli.

• Have dessert at the ready for any number of sweet tooths by making your own slice-and-bake cookies. Freeze leftover dough; slice and bake for the next batch.

• Host a tasting party for delicious, costly foods or drinks—think sparkling wines, Spanish hams, or French cheeses. Each guest brings a favorite and a recipe (if appropriate). The variety of foods tasted in tidbit portions, and for a reasonable cost, is terrific.

• Buy a superb chef's knife. A great tool, often expensive, is an indulgence that pays off for years. Having a razor-sharp, pristine blade in a perfectly balanced knife inspires us to cook.

8. *Eat out* CREATIVELY

We're lucky to live in the golden age of restaurant eating in America. Many chefs are reviving almost-lost traditions, encouraging local provenance, and blending the multitude of ideas and ingredients that different food cultures have brought to this country. And although it is true that chefs are wanton with butterfat, salt, and portion size, a careful eater can incorporate regular restaurant meals into a healthy diet.

Eating well in restaurants is not automatic, however. Sam Sifton, who recently became *The New York Times'* new chief restaurant critic, observes a gulf between people who "invariably" order poorly and those who order well.

Sifton's first rule: Order what you don't cook. "I find that the people who invariably order poorly ... gravitate to the plain chicken breast dish, to the pasta that seems like something they might be able to make at home. And then they're disappointed because it is something they might have been able to make at home!"

Second rule: Order difficult dishes. Difficult doesn't always mean complex—simple stir-frying is rarely done as well at home as in the commercial kitchen, with its super-hot burners.

Third: Favor the labor intensive. "To order duck confit is to order a really delicious dish that is immensely time-consuming to make at home."

For those living in smaller cities and towns, Sifton's advice: Avoid chains at all cost, and have the chutzpah to interrogate the locals. According to Sifton, it almost invariably yields good results."

Interrogate the waiter, too. Waiters are there to sell. Maybe the monkfish really is superb; maybe it's about to be thrown out because it didn't sell last week. Ask them in a good-humored way what they'd really recommend, Sifton says.

SMALL IDEAS FOR EATING OUT CREATIVELY

• Bypass entrées and order several appetizers to share—you'll get to taste more of what's to offer, and portions will be smaller.

• Explore strip malls. Yes, strip malls, because some of the best restaurants (often ethnic) set up shop at these unassuming locations. Lower rents make for more affordable prices, too.

• Book the chef's table every once in a while. It'll give you a cook's-eye view of a professional kitchen.

• Go off your usual grid. It's comforting to eat in familiar favorites, but new chefs deserve support, and unfamiliar neighborhoods turn up surprises.

• Participate in the discussion: Check out deep sites like chowhound.com and egullet.org, where passionate, informed foodies post advice on what to eat and where to eat it nationwide. You'll soon be able to tell the experts from the cranky ranters.

9. *Be* PORTION-AWARE

Because the great secret of healthy eating is this: Once you know what constitutes the components of a good diet, you still need to be conscious of how much of those components to eat. Not obsessed, but aware. Consider the story of Japanese-born Makiko Itoh:

"I moved with my family from Tokyo to New York in the 1980s. In Japan my school lunch was usually a homemade bento—a compact meal in a box—lovingly prepared by my mother. In New York, though, I adapted to local eating habits: huge platters of food at the local diner; two-fisted bagels; $1.99 pancake breakfasts. I gained 70-plus pounds by the time I reached my 20s. I was busting out against the stereotype of the slim Asian chick, but that didn't make my college and young adult years very fun.

"A few years ago, I decided to get a grip on my health and eating habits. I threw out my stack of take-out menus and fad diet books, started cooking more Japanese food, and incorporated bento lunches into my daily routine.

"At first my bento boxes seemed way too small. But I discovered that the right portion sizes for me were smaller than I thought. Single portions of proteins and carbs packed neatly and attractively into a bento box—the gaps filled in with vegetables—left me comfortably satisfied instead of in an overstuffed stupor."

In 2007, Itoh started JustBento.com to share her enthusiasm for healthy bento meals. "I'm better able to judge portion sizes now, even when they're not in a bento box. I do slip up sometimes (and I'm still rounder than your average Japanese woman!), but with my 'bento brain' I know when and how to pull it back. My interest in bento took me home to my cultural and culinary roots, to find out what works for me. It did work. I'm happier and healthier."

Not everyone needs to bento, but a bento brain—deliberately and persistently conscious of portion sizes until right-sizing becomes automatic—is a necessary step toward healthier eating.

SMALL IDEAS FOR BEING PORTION-AWARE

• Use smaller plates, cups, and serving utensils—you'll dole out smaller portions.

- Serve veggie dishes and salads on the dinner table in big bowls, family-style, making it easy for folks to have extra. Then portion the meats and starches for each plate, and keep those foods in the kitchen so you won't be as tempted to reload.

- Set aside leftovers before you eat.

- Haul out, or buy, a kitchen scale. With practice, you may be able to gauge a 4-ounce portion of beef or a 2-ounce portion of pasta by sight; till then, let the scale take the guess-work out of it.

- Purchase small containers of items like yogurt and 100 percent fruit juices. With packaged foods, be label-aware: One container, even a small one, doesn't necessarily mean one serving.

10. *Drink*
WELL

Because the same awakening to the joys of variety and authenticity that is shaping American food is fermenting the wine, beer, and spirits world.

There are flavors and complexities in wine found nowhere else, and the pleasures and ritual of a well-made cocktail are deliciously grown-up. If you need another reason, here it is: One drink a day for women (two for men) is associated with heart health—and not just wine, any alcohol. Research also suggests that those who drink regularly as an integrated part of a food-centered, social lifestyle—think of the French, Spanish, and Italians—are more likely to enjoy the heart-healthy payoff. If you can't or don't want to drink, don't. But for the rest, it's fine to drink moderately and better to drink well.

SMALL IDEAS FOR DRINKING WELL

- Up the nutrition ante of cocktails by adding 100 percent fruit juice or purees.

- Flavor your own gin, fruit liqueur, or infused vodka.

- Choose better mixers. Try Stirrings ginger ale, zingy Fee Brothers bitters, or Fever-Tree or Q Tonic waters in a cocktail.

- Buy a good stopper to preserve the freshness of a good wine for the next day.

- Fall in love with fortified wines, such as a Bual Madeira or an Oloroso sherry. One dessert favorite: caramel-y Prager Tomás Port.

The Whoopsy Daisy

To make simple syrup, combine equal amounts of sugar and water in a saucepan; bring to a boil. Cook 1 minute or until sugar dissolves, stirring occasionally. Simple syrup keeps for up to two weeks in an airtight container in the fridge.

½ cup El Tesoro tequila blanco
¼ cup Del Maguey San Luis Del Rio mezcal
6 tablespoons fresh lime juice
6 tablespoons simple syrup
2 teaspoons pomegranate molasses

1. Combine all ingredients; stir with a whisk. Strain through a cheesecloth-lined colander into a bowl. Yield: 4 servings (serving size: about ⅓ cup).

CALORIES 158; FAT 0g; PROTEIN 0.1g; CARB 15.8g; FIBER 0.1g; CHOL 0mg; IRON 0.4mg; SODIUM 1mg; CALC 13mg

SPECIAL OCCASION RECIPE

Decadent, rich, and intensely chocolaty, this recipe garnered our highest rating for flavor. It's a bit of a splurge. Leftovers keep well in the fridge for up to five days.

Staff Favorite • Make Ahead
Kid Friendly

Upside-Down Fudge-Almond Tart
(pictured on page 241)

Cooking spray
1 cup coarsely chopped almonds, toasted
4 ounces bittersweet chocolate, coarsely chopped
6 tablespoons unsalted butter
2.25 ounces all-purpose flour (about ½ cup)
3 tablespoons sifted Dutch process cocoa
¼ teaspoon salt
2 large eggs
6 tablespoons sugar
2 tablespoons golden cane syrup
¾ teaspoon vanilla extract

1. Preheat oven to 350°. Set oven rack to lowest third of oven.
2. Coat a 9-inch round removable-bottom tart pan with cooking spray. Sprinkle almonds in pan.
3. Combine chocolate and butter in top of a double boiler. Cook over simmering water until chocolate melts, stirring occasionally. Remove from heat; set aside.
4. Weigh or lightly spoon flour into a dry measuring cup; level with a knife. Combine flour, cocoa, and salt in a medium bowl, stirring with a whisk.
5. Place eggs in a large bowl; beat with a mixer at medium speed 2 minutes or until thick and pale. Gradually add sugar, 1 tablespoon at a time, beating at medium speed 2 minutes or until sugar dissolves. Add golden cane syrup and vanilla; beat on low speed 1 minute or until blended. Add chocolate mixture; beat 1 minute or until blended. Add flour mixture, and beat on low speed just until combined.
6. Pour batter over nuts into prepared pan, spreading evenly. Bake in lower third of oven at 350° for 20 minutes or until a wooden pick inserted into center comes out with a few moist crumbs. Cool tart in pan 20 minutes on a wire rack. Invert tart onto a serving platter. Yield: 10 servings (serving size: 1 wedge).

CALORIES 281; FAT 19.8g (sat 7.7g, mono 8.1g, poly 2.1g); PROTEIN 5.9g; CARB 24.6g; FIBER 2.7g; CHOL 60mg; IRON 1.6mg; SODIUM 80mg; CALC 45mg

CAN THIS COCKY, YOUNG, BRITISH CHEF REALLY MAKE AMERICANS EAT HEALTHIER?

Jamie Oliver believes that by teaching ordinary Americans new cooking skills, and getting them to share those skills with others, he can improve our national diet. His idea caused a big fuss in the U.K. How will it fare here?

The first time most Americans met British Chef Jamie Oliver was in 1999, when he was host of the Food Network's *Naked Chef*. Trailing in the motorcycle exhaust fumes of the brilliant *Two Fat Ladies*, Oliver's charmingly affable presence satisfied our taste for Anglophilia but showcased a different side of British food; instead of the notoriously sludgy and greasy standards, he adopted a casual, Mediterranean-influenced approach in line with evolving U.S. tastes—baked herb-stuffed salmon or pappardelle with mixed wild mushrooms. After 2001, he practically disappeared, leaving a void that was eventually filled by the foul-mouthed macho posturings of superstar restaurant chef Gordon Ramsay.

While Oliver was away from American airwaves, he was ferociously busy in his native Britain. He dropped the silly "naked chef" moniker to become just Jamie, a still-boyish but very serious advocate for a variety of food-related causes. First, he founded Fifteen, a successful restaurant concept built around teaching culinary skills to disadvantaged kids. Next, he launched a campaign to revamp the country's school lunch program; it resulted in a £280 million government-funded overhaul. A spate of Channel 4 television specials tackled tough topics, like the sad state of mass pork and poultry production. Along the way, Oliver authored 15 books, launched a beautiful magazine and the obligatory line of kitchen products, expanded Fifteen to four locations, and opened another chain, Jamie's Italian.

Now, 10 years after his first foray, Oliver is coming back to U.S. television with a reality series on ABC. *Jamie Oliver's Food Revolution* will find him replicating his hit cooking-and-preaching U.K. show, *Jamie's Ministry of Food,* in Huntington, West Virginia. (Huntington is among the least healthy towns in the United States, statistically.) His premise: Teach a person how to cook one basic, healthy dish, and he or she can "pass it on," sharing new culinary skills and confidence with friends and family. This is reality television, but with an Oliver twist: This Brit believes that by simply telling people what "proper" food is—and teaching them how to cook it—you can change the way they eat, and then change a whole community.

Make Ahead
Leek and Potato Soup

"What a classic soup! Usually eaten hot, it's also surprisingly delicious eaten refrigerator-cold on a summer's day with a squeeze of lemon juice and a dollop of natural yogurt." —J.O. (Adapted from Jamie's Food Revolution *by Jamie Oliver. Copyright 2009. Published by Hyperion. All rights reserved.)*

2 leeks (about 1 pound)
6 cups fat-free, less-sodium chicken broth
2 tablespoons olive oil
3 cups coarsely chopped onion (about 1 pound)
1 cup chopped carrot
1 cup chopped celery
2 garlic cloves, minced
2 cups cubed peeled Yukon gold potato (about 1 pound)
½ teaspoon freshly ground black pepper
¼ teaspoon fine sea salt

1. Remove roots, outer leaves, and tops from leeks. Cut each leek in half lengthwise. Cut each half crosswise into ½-inch-thick slices. Immerse in cold water; swirl. Drain.
2. Bring broth to a boil in a large saucepan over medium-high heat.
3. Heat oil in a large Dutch oven over medium-high heat. Add leek, onion, and next 3 ingredients. Partially cover, and cook 20 minutes or until vegetables are tender, stirring occasionally. Add hot broth and potato; return to a boil. Cover, reduce heat, and simmer 10 minutes or until potato is tender. Stir in pepper and salt. Serve chunky, or puree with an immersion blender or in a blender. Yield: 8 servings (serving size: about 1¼ cups).

CALORIES 130; **FAT** 3.6g (sat 0.5g, mono 2.5g, poly 0.4g); **PROTEIN** 3.4g; **CARB** 21.5g; **FIBER** 2.9g; **CHOL** 0mg; **IRON** 1.3mg; **SODIUM** 443mg; **CALC** 42mg

MARK BITTMAN TALKS WITH JAMIE OLIVER

Mark Bittman writes the Minimalist column for *The New York Times* and is the author of *How to Cook Everything*.

DO YOU FEEL LIKE YOU'RE ON A MISSION?

I am massively driven to do what I'm doing. Part of it, in a soppy kind of way, feels right and very natural. I mean, I never wanted to be on telly! I was really happy as a sous chef. But I've learned that when I open my gob, people trust me, which then causes them to buy different chicken or pork or seek out semolina flour.

AND IT HAS COME NATURALLY?

I grew up in food. My dad ran a pub. So in 2004, when I went into Greenwich and took on feeding 24,000 schoolkids every day, yes, it was big and overwhelming and scary, but I just treated it like it was Dad's pub. It's a bit of wanting to do it, and enjoying doing it, and needing to do it.

IS IT PART OF A BIGGER "FOOD MOVEMENT"? IS THERE A FOOD MOVEMENT?

Cooking is not taught at school, they're eating crap at school, and there's largely processed food being sold to the home market. We've almost dissolved the natural skill of being able to look after ourselves. We need to create a movement so people can understand it really quickly and simply. I've done that in England and called it "pass it on." I think America has become a different place in the last 18 months, so the timing of this is amazing.

WHEN YOU SAY THINGS ARE DIFFERENT, YOU'RE TALKING ABOUT ...

Americans are looking at where they want things to go. And I think that if I'm really clever, in the next nine months we can tell a story that inspires people, upsets them enough, and makes them understand that change is easy and it doesn't necessarily involve spending more money. America could get it and change way quicker than England. When Americans go with something, they go quicker than anyone else.

WHAT KIND OF CHANGE ARE YOU HOPING FOR?

Look: I'm not a nutritionist—I love food, including burgers, and pizza, and stuff like that. I'm not yelling, "Hey you, lose weight!" That's not what it's about. It's about empowering people with the skills they need to nourish themselves and their families, to feel that sense of pride, which is really as basic as making a panini or poached egg, and getting people reconnected with the simplicity of knocking a few ingredients together and making proper food.

YOU USE THAT TERM A LOT, "PROPER FOOD." HOW DO YOU DEFINE IT?

Food from scratch, really. We know most of the problems with the health in both of our countries is largely due to huge amounts of soda, sugar, fat, deep-frying, and a load of additives. If you could at least half of the time buy, or do yourself, something that was remotely scratch-based, you probably could fix 98 percent of the [nutrition] problems in America. It's so much more than just "eat less." We need to arm the public with basic cooking skills! They don't need equations or graphs or nutritional science. Just arm them with the ability to turn a bunch of seasonal ingredients, whether they're fresh or frozen—because frozen stuff can be great—into meals.

YOU SAY STUFF LIKE THAT—FROZEN FOOD CAN BE GREAT—AND THEN YOU GET INTO COMBAT WITH FOODIES.

Well, don't get me wrong, I am a proper geek about food. I love the extreme, hard, rare stuff. But my day job involves me trying to speak a bit of common sense and be realistic. I can be talking to middle class people one minute and a family on [welfare] the next, and to be honest, I say the same thing to both.

HOW ARE YOU GOING TO ARM PEOPLE WITH BASIC COOKING SKILLS?

If people like us—of whom there are not enough—could have 18 hours with a person, we could sort them out for life. In that 18 hours, we could teach basic stewing, roasting, stir-frying, how to enjoy veggies, salads, how to batch cook and freeze, to shop in an efficient way ... it's not rocket science. That's where the "pass it on" movement came from. My idea was a pyramid model: I would teach one person how to make spaghetti Bolognese. They always bought the idea and were like, "Wow, I can do this!" Then I say, "Right, will you teach it to four of your mates?" Because if I teach one person who teaches four who teach four who teach four—if that chain repeats itself 14 times, that's the entire population of Great Britain.

WHAT ABOUT THE BIG FOOD COMPANIES?

If we're clever enough, I really do believe there will be a swell of public emotion that will ultimately take businesses to a better place. The key with the public is to remind them how important their effort is. Every single parent thinks her or his opinion doesn't matter [with schools], but get four parents together to go in and see a head teacher—that's radical.

WHAT'S THE ROLE OF TELEVISION IN ALL OF THIS?

Television can be a force. Magic can be created, and quickly. We have loads of great journalists writing great stuff, but when you take it all and roll it up into TV, then bang! Everyone is talking about it. My shows have injected money into a system, and we had regulations about nutrition in schools not only promised but delivered. TV did that.

HOW MUCH TIME WILL YOU BE SPENDING HERE FOR *FOOD REVOLUTION*?

Months.

WILL YOU BE GOING HOME?

I'm going to try. I've got three beautiful young kids who need a dad.

AND WHY HUNTINGTON? WHY WEST VIRGINIA?

Huntington, statistically, is the most unhealthy town in America—meaning it has the highest rates of lifestyle diseases, obesity, diabetes, dental problems. My goal is to get them out of the top 10—or bottom 10—within the year.

SO YOU HOPE ... ?

I want to tell a story with real people that [shows] we can move mountains. It really does come down to a few community members, a few families, a few kids, a few schools in Huntington. I'm either going to get it right, and it's going to be sweet, or if it isn't compelling and doesn't hit the spot, it will get boring.

WHAT DO YOU THINK WILL HAPPEN IF YOU GET PEOPLE TO COOK PROPER FOOD HALF THE TIME, AS YOU SAY?

Well, this sounds a bit romantic, but if once, twice, or even three times a week people cooked, and sat around the table with their family, that would have a dramatic impact on the whole country. I think kids would be happier, marriages would fail less. I suppose my belief is that by just creating an element of care in the mainstream you have a much nicer environment all 'round.

Spicy Moroccan Stewed Fish with Couscous

"You can make this recipe using any white fish or salmon fillets. It's incredibly quick to cook and a really good thing to give the kids for dinner. I like to use a mixture of beans and peas, but if you find it easier to use just one of those, that's fine—it will still be beautiful." —J.O. (Adapted from Jamie's Food Revolution by Jamie Oliver. Copyright 2009. Published by Hyperion. All rights reserved.)

1 cup uncooked couscous
3 tablespoons olive oil, divided
3 tablespoons fresh lemon juice, divided
³⁄₄ teaspoon fine sea salt, divided
¼ teaspoon freshly ground black pepper, divided
1 cup boiling water
2 (6-ounce) skinless halibut fillets, each cut in half
³⁄₄ pound peeled and deveined large shrimp
1 teaspoon cumin seeds
³⁄₄ teaspoon ground cinnamon
2 garlic cloves, thinly sliced
1 fresh hot red chile, thinly sliced
½ cup clam juice
1 (14.5-ounce) can diced tomatoes, drained
½ cup frozen green peas, thawed
Fresh basil leaves (optional)

1. Place couscous in a medium bowl. Add 1 tablespoon oil, 2 tablespoons lemon juice, ¼ teaspoon salt, and ⅛ teaspoon pepper. Pour 1 cup boiling water over couscous. Cover and let stand 10 minutes. Fluff with a fork.
2. Sprinkle ¼ teaspoon salt and remaining ⅛ teaspoon pepper evenly over fish. Toss shrimp with remaining ¼ teaspoon salt.
3. Heat a large nonstick skillet over medium-high heat. Add remaining 2 tablespoons oil, swirling to coat. Add cumin seeds and next 3 ingredients; stir to coat. Top with fish; scatter shrimp over fish. Add clam juice, tomatoes, and remaining 1 tablespoon lemon juice; bring to a boil. Cover, reduce heat, and simmer 8 minutes. Add peas; cover and simmer 2 minutes or until fish and shrimp are done. Serve with couscous; garnish with basil, if desired. Yield: 4 servings (serving size: ½ halibut fillet, about 4 shrimp, ½ cup tomato mixture, and ¾ cup couscous).

CALORIES 475; **FAT** 14.6g (sat 2.4g, mono 8.7g, poly 2.6g); **PROTEIN** 42.2g; **CARB** 43.2g; **FIBER** 4.6g; **CHOL** 191mg; **IRON** 4mg; **SODIUM** 809mg; **CALC** 107mg

SIMPLE ADDITIONS

Sautéed Snapper with Orange-Fennel Salad

The salad brings bright, fresh, Mediterranean flavors to this simple fish dish. A mandoline slices fennel evenly.

2 oranges
1 medium fennel bulb with stalks
2 tablespoons olive oil, divided
4 (6-ounce) yellowtail snapper fillets
½ teaspoon fresh thyme leaves

Peel and section oranges over a bowl, reserving 2 tablespoons juice. Thinly slice fennel bulb; chop 1 teaspoon fronds. Discard stalks. Place orange sections and sliced fennel in a medium bowl. Combine reserved juice, fronds, 1 tablespoon oil, ¼ teaspoon salt, and ¼ teaspoon freshly ground black pepper in a small bowl, stirring with a whisk. Drizzle juice mixture over fennel mixture; toss well to coat. Heat remaining 1 tablespoon oil in a large nonstick skillet over medium-high heat. Sprinkle fish evenly with ½ teaspoon salt, ¼ teaspoon freshly ground black pepper, and thyme. Add fish to pan; cook 4 minutes on each side or until desired degree of doneness. Serve with fennel salad. Yield: 4 servings (serving size: 1 fillet and about ½ cup salad).

CALORIES 283; **FAT** 9.5g (sat 1.5g, mono 5.8g, poly 1.4g); **PROTEIN** 36.3g; **CARB** 12.2g; **FIBER** 3.4g; **CHOL** 63mg; **IRON** 0.8mg; **SODIUM** 575mg; **CALC** 112mg

THE FIVE INGREDIENTS

2 oranges

+

1 medium fennel bulb with stalks

+

2 tablespoons olive oil, divided

+

4 (6-ounce) yellowtail snapper fillets

+

½ teaspoon fresh thyme leaves

READER RECIPES
CONTEST WINNERS

This year's contest winners brought a wealth of flavor to the *Cooking Light* judging table.

Of the more than 2,800 entries that flooded our mailbox for the fifth annual *Cooking Light* Ultimate Reader Recipe Contest, about 80 were tested in our kitchens to select the 12 finalists who came to Birmingham to prepare their recipes. Three category winners each took home $5,000, and the grand prize winner was awarded $20,000, plus a $5,000 prize to donate to her charity of choice. Three of our recipe developers—David Bonom, Maureen Callahan, and Jeanne Kelley—tasted, conferred, and picked the winners.

English professor Suzanne Rumsey was astounded when told she was a finalist. "I'd never participated in a recipe contest and entered on a whim," she says.

Well, Rumsey must have a natural knack. She made her dish only once before submitting the recipe. The judges loved its simplicity, its use of whole-grain barley, and the vibrant flavors of feta, citrus, cucumber, and herbs.

Angela Spengler and her husband both love spicy foods, and she especially loves breakfast recipes. So her dish was a natural, combining comforting breakfast ingredients with the heat of jalapeños in a breakfast calzone that works hot or at room temperature.

Graphic designer Michele Zanta comes from "a long line of good cooks," she says. Her mother and grandmother passed on Italian family recipes, some of which are quite labor-intensive. But her prize-winning recipe takes less than 15 minutes to prepare.

For Christmas, Marcie Dixon bakes several thousand—yes, thousand—cookies to give as gifts. "I start baking in October and freezing them in coffee cans," she says. "I'm a big baker, so cookies are a natural thing for me."

Make Ahead • Kid Friendly
Greek Chicken and Barley Salad

Grand Prize Winner—Family Dinners
"I designated Heifer International to receive my cash award. They help communities fight hunger through self-reliance and sustainability."
—Suzanne Rumsey, Fort Wayne, Indiana

Salad:
2 (6-ounce) skinless, boneless chicken breast halves
⅛ teaspoon kosher salt
1 teaspoon olive oil
4 cups fat-free, less-sodium chicken broth, divided
1 cup uncooked pearl barley
2 cups cubed seeded cucumber
1 cup grape tomatoes, halved
½ cup cubed yellow bell pepper
⅓ cup reduced-fat feta cheese
¼ cup chopped pitted kalamata olives

Dressing:
3 tablespoons extra-virgin olive oil
1 teaspoon grated lemon rind
2 tablespoons fresh lemon juice
1 tablespoon minced fresh basil
1 teaspoon minced fresh thyme
1 teaspoon red wine vinegar
½ teaspoon kosher salt
3 garlic cloves, minced

1. To prepare salad, sprinkle chicken with ⅛ teaspoon salt. Heat 1 teaspoon oil in a nonstick skillet over medium-high heat. Add chicken; cook 2 minutes on each side or until browned. Add 1 cup broth; cover, reduce heat, and simmer 10 minutes or until done. Cool; shred chicken. Discard broth.
2. Bring 3 cups broth to a boil in a large saucepan; add barley. Cover, reduce heat, and simmer 35 minutes or until liquid is absorbed. Fluff with a fork. Cool. Combine chicken, barley, cucumber, and next 4 ingredients in a large bowl.
3. To prepare dressing, combine 3 tablespoons oil and remaining ingredients; stir well. Add to barley mixture; toss well. Cover and chill. Yield: 8 servings (serving size: 1 cup).

CALORIES 230; FAT 9.8g (sat 2g, mono 5.7g, poly 1.1g); PROTEIN 18g; CARB 18.3g; FIBER 3.2g; CHOL 38mg; IRON 1.2mg; SODIUM 611mg; CALC 38mg

---

Quick & Easy • Kid Friendly
Jalapeño, Sausage, Jack, and Egg Breakfast Braid

Category Winner—Starters & Drinks
"Sweet and savory make a good flavor combination for breakfast in general, so I like to serve this with a fruit garnish like grapes or melon."
—Angela Spengler, Clovis, New Mexico

1 (13.8-ounce) can refrigerated pizza crust dough
Cooking spray
1 tablespoon olive oil
¼ cup chopped onion
4 ounces chicken sausage with jalapeño peppers, chopped
2 large eggs, lightly beaten
½ cup (2 ounces) shredded Monterey Jack cheese
¼ cup shredded cheddar cheese
¼ cup chopped seeded jalapeño peppers
1 large egg white, lightly beaten

1. Preheat oven to 425°.
2. Unroll dough onto a baking sheet coated with cooking spray; pat into a 15 x 10–inch rectangle.
3. Heat oil in a large skillet over medium heat. Add onion and sausage; cook 9 minutes or until lightly browned. Stir in eggs; cook 1½ minutes or until set. Remove from heat.
4. Sprinkle Monterey Jack lengthwise down center of dough, leaving about a 2½-inch border on each side. Spoon egg mixture evenly over cheese. Sprinkle cheddar over egg mixture; top with jalapeño peppers.
5. Make 2-inch-long diagonal cuts about 1 inch apart on both sides of dough to within ½ inch of filling using a sharp knife or kitchen shears. Arrange strips over filling, alternating strips diagonally over filling. Press ends under to seal. Brush with egg white. Bake at 425° for 15 minutes or until golden brown. Let stand 5 minutes. Cut crosswise into slices. Yield: 6 servings (serving size: 1 slice).

CALORIES 164; FAT 10.4g (sat 4.2g, mono 4.4 g, poly 1g); PROTEIN 10.6g; CARB 7.3g; FIBER 0.1g; CHOL 98mg; IRON 0.8mg; SODIUM 344mg; CALC 115mg

Fresh Mediterranean Salad

Category Winner—Sides & Salads

"The key to enjoying food is to slow down, take a sip of wine, linger. As an artist, I think presentation is just as important as taste. I like to take the time to plate things nicely—if the salad looks beautiful, it just tastes better."

—Michele Zanta, Plantation, Florida

Vinaigrette:

3 tablespoons red wine vinegar

2 tablespoons water

1 teaspoon dried oregano

1 teaspoon freshly ground black pepper

1 teaspoon Dijon mustard

1/2 teaspoon kosher salt

2 garlic cloves, chopped

3 tablespoons extra-virgin olive oil

Salad:

2 cups sliced fennel bulb (about 1 medium)

11/2 cups thinly sliced red onion

1 cup pitted ripe olives, halved

3/4 cup chopped fresh flat-leaf parsley

1/2 cup (2 ounces) crumbled feta cheese

1 (15.5-ounce) can cannellini beans, rinsed and drained

6 plum tomatoes, quartered

2 tablespoons sunflower seeds

1. To prepare vinaigrette, combine first 7 ingredients in a small bowl. Gradually add oil, stirring with a whisk until blended.

2. To prepare salad, combine fennel and next 6 ingredients in a large bowl. Drizzle vinaigrette over salad, tossing until well combined. Sprinkle with sunflower seeds. Cover and chill at least 1 hour. Yield: 10 servings (serving size: 1 cup).

CALORIES 119; **FAT** 8.1g (sat 1.8g, mono 4.5g, poly 1.5g); **PROTEIN** 3.2g; **CARB** 10g; **FIBER** 3.1g; **CHOL** 5mg; **IRON** 1.7mg; **SODIUM** 346mg; **CALC** 74mg

Chocolate-Cherry Heart Smart Cookies

(pictured on page 245)

Category Winner—Desserts

"I love chocolate and cherry flavors together, and I found great dried cherries from Maine for this recipe. I also used bittersweet instead of milk chocolate: Not only does it have less sugar, but it has a deeper flavor, too."

—Marcie Dixon, Arlington Heights, Illinois

1.5 ounces all-purpose flour (about 1/3 cup)

1.5 ounces whole-wheat flour (about 1/3 cup)

11/2 cups old-fashioned rolled oats

1 teaspoon baking soda

1/2 teaspoon salt

6 tablespoons unsalted butter

3/4 cup packed light brown sugar

1 cup dried cherries

1 teaspoon vanilla extract

1 large egg, lightly beaten

3 ounces bittersweet chocolate, coarsely chopped

Cooking spray

1. Preheat oven to 350°.

2. Weigh or lightly spoon flours into dry measuring cups; level with a knife. Combine flours and next 3 ingredients in a large bowl; stir with a whisk.

3. Melt butter in a small saucepan over low heat. Remove from heat; add brown sugar, stirring until smooth. Add sugar mixture to flour mixture; beat with a mixer at medium speed until well blended. Add cherries, vanilla, and egg; beat until combined. Fold in chocolate. Drop dough by tablespoonfuls 2 inches apart onto baking sheets coated with cooking spray. Bake at 350° for 12 minutes. Cool on pans 3 minutes or until almost firm. Remove cookies from pans; cool on wire racks. Yield: 30 cookies (serving size: 1 cookie).

CALORIES 94; **FAT** 3.2g (sat 1.6g, mono 0.6g, poly 0.2g); **PROTEIN** 1.5g; **CARB** 15.7g; **FIBER** 1.3g; **CHOL** 10mg; **IRON** 0.6mg; **SODIUM** 88mg; **CALC** 15mg

RECIPE MAKEOVER
SOUTHEAST ASIAN FRIED RICE

We added some whole-grain goodness to a less greasy, less salty version of a comforting staple.

A wok-tossed mix of rice and savory tidbits ought to be a prescription for light eating. But too often an order of fried rice turns up a greasy, salty, clumpy rice-pile low on vegetables and too rich in oily, starchy calories. This sort of fried rice can easily exceed your day's allotment for sodium. But it need not be this way! Inspired by Thai flavor profiles, our unconventional but utterly delicious fried rice keeps calories, saturated fat, and sodium in check.

Traditionally, the caramel tint of fried rice comes from cooking foods in a slick of very hot oil and then adding a soy-heavy seasoning sauce. We use a splash of lower-sodium soy sauce plus savory, oceany fish sauce that saturates the chicken and rice without overdoing the sodium. We ration oil to curb calories. For meaty flavor, we use just two slices of bacon. For chewy texture, we substitute nutty, whole-grain brown rice. And to boost the veggies, we pack in broccoli, bell pepper, and plenty of green onions. You can try green beans, carrots, bean sprouts, or tomato.

Southeast Asian Fried Rice

Save leftover brown rice to prepare this take on a Thai-style stir-fried one-dish meal. A little bacon replaces the ham or pork that can sometimes appear in this preparation.

1 tablespoon brown sugar
1 tablespoon fish sauce
1 tablespoon less-sodium soy sauce
1 tablespoon fresh lime juice
1 teaspoon sambal oelek (ground fresh chile paste), divided
1/4 teaspoon salt, divided
2 large eggs, lightly beaten
1 bunch green onions
2 tablespoons peanut oil, divided
2 1/2 cups cooked and cooled brown rice
1/4 cup vertically sliced shallots
2 (4-ounce) skinless, boneless chicken thighs, cut into 1/2-inch pieces
1 (6-ounce) skinless, boneless chicken breast, cut into 1/2-inch pieces
2 cups broccoli florets
1 cup julienne-cut red bell pepper
1 1/2 teaspoons minced garlic
Cooking spray
2 bacon slices, cooked and crumbled
4 lime wedges

OLD WAY	OUR WAY
898 calories per serving	438 calories per serving
43.8 grams total fat	16.3 grams total fat
5.7 grams saturated fat	3.7 grams saturated fat
3,401 milligrams sodium	786 milligrams sodium
Lots of vegetable oil	Just enough peanut oil
2 cups white rice per serving	2/3 cup brown rice per serving
3 tablespoons high-sodium condiments	1 1/2 teaspoons savory condiments

1. Combine first 4 ingredients, 1/2 teaspoon sambal oelek, and 1/8 teaspoon salt in a small bowl, stirring with a whisk. Combine eggs and remaining 1/2 teaspoon sambal oelek in a bowl. Separate green tops from green onions, and diagonally chop; set aside. Cut green onion bottoms into 1-inch pieces; set aside.

2. Heat a large nonstick skillet over medium-high heat. Add 2 teaspoons oil to pan, swirling pan to coat evenly. Add rice; stir-fry 1 1/2 minutes, stirring constantly. Transfer rice mixture to a large bowl. Heat 2 teaspoons oil in pan. Add shallots to pan; stir-fry 30 seconds or until tender. Add chicken; stir-fry 1 1/2 minutes or until lightly browned. Add brown sugar mixture to pan; bring to a boil. Reduce heat, and simmer 1 minute or until liquid thickens slightly, stirring occasionally. Add chicken mixture to rice mixture.

3. Wipe pan clean with a paper towel; return pan to medium-high heat. Add remaining 2 teaspoons oil to pan, swirling to coat. Add broccoli and bell pepper; stir-fry 3 minutes or until vegetables are tender. Add remaining 1/8 teaspoon salt, green onion bottoms, and garlic; stir-fry 1 minute or until fragrant. Add chicken mixture to pan, cook 2 minutes or until thoroughly heated; return chicken mixture to large bowl.

4. Return pan to medium-high heat. Coat pan with cooking spray. Add egg mixture to pan, swirling to coat pan; cook 30 seconds or just until egg is set. Transfer egg to a cutting board; chop. Stir egg and bacon into rice mixture. Top with green onion tops; garnish with lime wedges. Yield: 4 servings (serving size: 1 1/2 cups rice mixture and 1 lime wedge).

CALORIES 438; **FAT** 16.3g (sat 3.7g, mono 6.7g, poly 4.3g); **PROTEIN** 31.6g; **CARB** 41.3g; **FIBER** 5.6g; **CHOL** 167mg; **IRON** 3.3mg; **SODIUM** 786mg; **CALC** 98mg

We let bacon stand in for the ham or barbecued pork often added to Thai stir-fries.

A go-to stir-fry staple, lower-sodium soy sauce is crucial for underscoring meaty flavor. Just a touch keeps tabs on sodium.

A spritz of zingy lime juice checks the salty edge of a robust stir-fry sauce and boosts flavor without sabotaging the nutrition.

Even though many Thai dishes rely on plenty of fish sauce, we used just 1 tablespoon to add depth to the poultry and rice.

BREAKFAST, LUNCH, AND DINNER IN... DENVER

Denverites aren't afraid to play with their food. Troy Guard of TAG and Lisa Bailey of D Bar Desserts are among the city's most creative chefs.

Once left off the culinary map for its admittedly tired take on cowboy cuisine, Denver is catching up to food trends fast.

Sourcing local and ecofriendly foods is de rigueur, even in winter. Chefs preserve Colorado's warm-season foods, such as Olathe sweet corn and Western slope peaches, to use during the cold season and zealously cultivate friendships with nearby farmers for winter-ready hoophouse-grown greens and cellar vegetables.

Breakfast
Carrot Cake Pancakes

Creative versions of pancakes are Denver's top carb-loading choice for a day on the slopes or trails. Weekend lines snake out the door and around the block at Snooze (snoozeeatery.com) for flapjacks with alluring comfort-food treatments; one favorite stack uses Reese's Peanut Butter Cups. Try pineapple upside-down pancakes with vanilla crème anglaise or carrot cake pancakes with a gooey cream cheese drizzle; both are served with cinnamon-spiked butter. These cakey flapjacks feature warm spices and bright carrot flavor. Our lightened version uses low-fat buttermilk and a small dab of honey butter to top the pancakes.

5.6 ounces all-purpose flour (about 1¼ cups)
¼ cup chopped walnuts, toasted
2 teaspoons baking powder
1 teaspoon ground cinnamon
¼ teaspoon salt
⅛ teaspoon freshly ground nutmeg
Dash of ground cloves
Dash of ground ginger
¼ cup brown sugar
¾ cup low-fat buttermilk
1 tablespoon canola oil
1½ teaspoons vanilla extract
2 large eggs, lightly beaten
2 cups finely grated carrot (about 1 pound)
Cooking spray
3 tablespoons butter, softened
2 tablespoons honey

1. Weigh or lightly spoon flour into dry measuring cups, and level with a knife. Combine flour and next 7 ingredients in a large bowl, stirring with a whisk. Combine ¼ cup brown sugar and next 4 ingredients; add sugar mixture to flour mixture, stirring just until moist. Fold in 2 cups carrot.
2. Heat a large nonstick skillet over medium heat. Coat pan with cooking spray. Spoon 4 (¼-cup) batter mounds onto pan, spreading with a spatula. Cook for 2 minutes or until tops are covered with bubbles and edges look cooked. Carefully turn pancakes over; cook 1 minute or until bottoms are lightly browned. Repeat procedure twice with remaining batter. Combine butter and honey in a small bowl; serve with pancakes. Yield: 6 servings (serving size: 2 pancakes and about 2 teaspoons honey butter).

CALORIES 315; FAT 13.3g (sat 4.8g, mono 4.4g, poly 3.3g); PROTEIN 7.8g; CARB 41.6g; FIBER 2.2g; CHOL 78mg; IRON 2.3mg; SODIUM 381mg; CALC 177mg

Lunch
Lamb Sliders with Blue Cheese

Denver diners seek warm and filling food in deep winter. They find it in the juicy burger made with succulent local lamb at Jonesy's Eat Bar (jeatbar.com). Add arugula to these burgers, if desired.

2 teaspoons olive oil
2½ cups thinly sliced onion (about 1 large)
1 teaspoon brown sugar
½ teaspoon salt, divided
¼ teaspoon freshly ground black pepper
1¼ pounds lean ground lamb
Cooking spray
12 (1.3-ounce) mini sandwich buns (such as Pepperidge Farm)
3 tablespoons crumbled blue cheese

1. Heat oil in a large nonstick skillet over medium heat. Add onion and sugar to pan; cook 10 minutes, stirring frequently. Stir in ¼ teaspoon salt. Reduce heat; cook 8 minutes or until tender and browned, stirring occasionally. Keep warm.
2. Preheat broiler.
3. Combine remaining ¼ teaspoon salt, pepper, and lamb in a large bowl. Divide lamb mixture into 12 equal portions; shape each into a ½-inch-thick patty. Place patties on rack of a broiler pan coated with cooking spray; place rack in pan. Broil 6 minutes, turning once after 3 minutes. Remove from oven; let stand 3 minutes.
4. Broil buns, cut sides up, 2 minutes or until lightly toasted. Place patties on bottom halves of buns; top each patty with about 1½ tablespoons caramelized onion and about 1 teaspoon blue cheese. Cover with top halves of buns. Yield: 6 servings (serving size: 2 sliders).

CALORIES 452; FAT 20.8g (sat 7.5g, mono 9.5g, poly 2g); PROTEIN 23.5g; CARB 42.3g; FIBER 3.1g; CHOL 66mg; IRON 3.6mg; SODIUM 694mg; CALC 136mg

Dinner

Bison Steak with Poblano Mole

At Opus Restaurant (opusdine.com), Chef Michael Long updates classic Colorado bison with spicy poblano polenta and chipotle-avocado brûlée. Look for bison at gourmet grocers, or substitute beef flank steak.

1 tablespoon olive oil
⅓ cup finely chopped onion
¾ cup uncooked long-grain rice
1 tablespoon tomato paste
½ teaspoon ground cumin
¼ teaspoon salt
1 cup fat-free, less-sodium beef broth
½ cup water
¼ cup finely chopped fresh cilantro
2 tomatillos
½ teaspoon olive oil
¼ cup chopped seeded poblano chile
¼ cup chopped onion
½ teaspoon ancho chile powder
¼ teaspoon ground cumin
⅛ teaspoon salt
1 garlic clove, crushed
⅓ cup fire-roasted diced tomatoes with green chiles (such as Muir Glen)
¼ cup fat-free, less-sodium beef broth
½ teaspoon chopped chipotle chile, canned in adobo sauce
½ (6-inch) corn tortilla, torn into pieces
¼ ounce dark chocolate, chopped
1 tablespoon sliced almonds, toasted and finely chopped
1 tablespoon unsalted pumpkinseed kernels, toasted
Cooking spray
1 (1-pound) bison flank steak
¼ teaspoon salt
¼ teaspoon freshly ground black pepper

1. Heat 1 tablespoon oil in a small saucepan over medium heat. Add ⅓ cup onion to pan; cook 3 minutes or until tender. Stir in rice; cook 4 minutes, stirring frequently. Add tomato paste, cumin, and ¼ teaspoon salt; cook 1 minute, stirring constantly. Stir in 1 cup broth and ½ cup water; bring to a boil. Cover, reduce heat, and simmer 20 minutes or until rice is tender. Remove from heat; stir in cilantro. Keep warm.

2. Discard husks and stems from tomatillos; chop. Heat ½ teaspoon oil in a large saucepan over medium heat. Add poblano, ¼ cup onion, and tomatillos; cook 10 minutes, stirring occasionally. Stir in chile powder, ¼ teaspoon cumin, salt, and garlic; cook 1 minute. Stir in tomatoes, ¼ cup broth, chipotle, and tortilla; cook 5 minutes. Reduce heat; simmer 6 minutes or until vegetables are tender. Add chocolate, stirring until melted; remove from heat. Stir in almonds and pumpkinseeds. Place mixture in a blender. Remove center piece of blender lid; secure lid on blender. Place a towel over opening in lid. Blend until smooth. Keep warm.

3. Heat a grill pan over medium-high heat. Coat pan with cooking spray. Sprinkle steak with ¼ teaspoon salt and black pepper. Add steak to pan; cook 5 minutes on each side or until desired degree of doneness. Let stand 5 minutes. Cut crosswise into thin slices. Yield: 4 servings (serving size: ½ cup rice, 3 ounces meat, and ¼ cup mole).

CALORIES 354; FAT 8.9g (sat 2.1g, mono 4.7g, poly 1.1g); PROTEIN 30g; CARB 36.7g; FIBER 2.5g; CHOL 70mg; IRON 5.5mg; SODIUM 669mg; CALC 41mg

DENVER CHEFS ARE MINDFUL OF THEIR OUTDOOR-ADDICTED, CALORIE-BURNING CLIENTELE.

EASY COOKING

START WITH A...CAN OF TUNA

This convenience staple lends itself to a Spanish salad, a delicious panino, and a creamy sauce for chicken.

Quick & Easy • Make Ahead

Spanish-Style Tuna and Potato Salad

1 pound small red potatoes, quartered
1 pound haricots verts, trimmed and cut into 2-inch pieces
2 cups cherry tomatoes, halved
¼ cup thinly sliced shallots
¾ teaspoon salt
½ teaspoon smoked paprika
¼ teaspoon ground red pepper
1 (5-ounce) can albacore tuna in water, drained
¼ cup extra-virgin olive oil
3 tablespoons sherry vinegar
5 cups torn romaine lettuce

1. Place potatoes in a large saucepan; cover with water to 2 inches above potatoes. Bring to a boil; cook potatoes 6 minutes or until almost tender. Add beans; cook 4 minutes or until beans are crisp-tender and potatoes are tender. Drain; rinse with cold water. Drain.

2. Place potato mixture in a large bowl. Add tomatoes and next 5 ingredients; toss. Drizzle potato mixture with oil and vinegar; toss to coat. Arrange 1 cup lettuce on each of 5 plates; divided potato mixture evenly among plates. Yield: 5 servings.

CALORIES 239; FAT 11.7g (sat 1.6g, mono 7.9g, poly 1.3g); PROTEIN 10.3g; CARB 25.6g; FIBER 6.7g; CHOL 10mg; IRON 2mg; SODIUM 470mg; CALC 81mg

WINE NOTE: A Spanish rosé, or rosado, complements this meal. Bodegas Borsao Rosado 2008 ($8) is crisp and dry, with herbal notes to match the tart dressing.

Sautéed Chicken with Tonnato Sauce

2 tablespoons fresh lemon juice, divided
1 teaspoon dried oregano
3 garlic cloves, minced and divided
4 (6-ounce) skinless, boneless chicken breast halves
1 tablespoon olive oil
1/4 teaspoon salt
1/4 teaspoon freshly ground black pepper
1/3 cup organic canola mayonnaise
2 teaspoons capers
1 anchovy fillet
1 (5-ounce) can albacore tuna in water, drained and flaked
4 cups arugula

1. Combine 1 tablespoon juice, oregano, and 2 garlic cloves in a large zip-top bag. Add chicken to bag; seal. Let stand 10 minutes, turning once. Heat oil in a large skillet over medium-high heat. Remove chicken from bag; discard marinade. Sprinkle both sides of chicken evenly with salt and pepper. Add chicken to pan. Cook 5 minutes on each side or until done. Let stand 5 minutes; cut chicken crosswise into 1/4-inch-thick slices.
2. Place remaining 1 tablespoon juice, remaining 1 garlic clove, mayonnaise, and next 3 ingredients in a food processor; process until smooth, scraping sides. Place 1 cup arugula on each of 4 plates. Arrange 1 chicken breast half on each plate; serve each with about 3 tablespoons sauce. Yield: 4 servings.

CALORIES 364; FAT 20.9g (sat 1.9g, mono 7.8g, poly 10.5g); PROTEIN 39.1g; CARB 2.9g; FIBER 0.8g; CHOL 96mg; IRON 2mg; SODIUM 451mg; CALC 79mg

LET'S TALK TUNA

All of these recipes call for albacore tuna packed in water, as it's our favorite for everyday use. It's readily available and reasonably priced. You'll also get more healthy omega-3 fatty acids from drained tuna packed in water instead of oil.

Several types of tuna are available at a variety of price points. When shopping, read the labels carefully so you'll know exactly what's inside. Some products may have higher sodium levels due to added broth or salt, while premium products often contain nothing more than raw fish that cooks in its juices during the canning process. If you're concerned about sustainability or mercury, look for fish caught with pole and line.

Below is a quick-reference guide to inform your choices.

LIGHT MEAT
The most economical choice, light (also called chunk light) tuna is made from common varieties, such as skipjack, Yellowfin, or Bluefin tuna. And skipjack populations are healthy.

WHITE MEAT
Albacore tuna is the only variety that's allowed to be called white meat, but despite the name, not all albacore is purely white. In fact, the lighter meat likely comes from old fish caught in deep waters, while darker, pinkish flesh comes from vibrant young fish, most likely from shallow waters. In short, the darker-meat young fish probably contain fewer chemicals, like mercury, often found in large, old fish.

PREMIUM TUNA
Premium brands are available at specialty markets or online. For example, Dave's Gourmet Albacore packs their prized catch in its own juices, and they fish with sustainable practices. Ortiz Bonito del Norte is good albacore packed in olive oil.

VENTRESCA
The Champagne of tunas, buttery-tasting ventresca comes from the fish's belly. Expect to pay extra and savor this delicacy.

Tuna Noodle Casserole

Although the recipe calls for egg noodles, you can use any short pasta to make this dish.

8 ounces wide egg noodles
2 tablespoons olive oil
1/2 cup chopped yellow onion
1/3 cup chopped carrot
2 tablespoons all-purpose flour
2 3/4 cups fat-free milk
1/2 cup (4 ounces) 1/3-less-fat cream cheese, softened
2 tablespoons Dijon mustard
1/2 teaspoon salt
1/2 teaspoon freshly ground black pepper
1 cup frozen peas, thawed
1/2 cup (2 ounces) grated Parmigiano-Reggiano cheese, divided
2 (5-ounce) cans albacore tuna in water, drained and flaked
Cooking spray

1. Preheat broiler.
2. Cook noodles according to package directions, omitting salt and fat. Drain. Heat a large skillet over medium heat. Add oil to pan; swirl to coat. Add onion and carrot; cook 6 minutes or until carrot is almost tender, stirring occasionally. Sprinkle with flour; cook 1 minute, stirring constantly. Gradually stir in milk; cook 5 minutes, stirring constantly with a whisk until slightly thick. Stir in cream cheese and next 3 ingredients; cook 2 minutes, stirring constantly.
3. Remove pan from heat. Stir in noodles, peas, 1/4 cup Parmigiano-Reggiano cheese, and tuna. Spoon mixture into a shallow broiler-safe 2-quart baking dish coated with cooking spray; top with remaining 1/4 cup Parmigiano-Reggiano cheese. Broil 3 minutes or until golden and bubbly. Let stand 5 minutes before serving. Yield: 6 servings (serving size: 1 1/3 cups).

CALORIES 422; FAT 16.5g (sat 7.1g, mono 6.3g, poly 1.8g); PROTEIN 27.4g; CARB 40.6g; FIBER 3g; CHOL 88mg; IRON 2.4mg; SODIUM 756mg; CALC 293mg

Quick & Easy
Tuna Panini

Serve these hearty sandwiches with fresh apple slices or a tossed green salad.

3 tablespoons finely chopped red onion
3 tablespoons organic canola mayonnaise
1 teaspoon grated lemon rind
1/4 teaspoon fennel seeds, crushed
1/4 teaspoon freshly ground black pepper
3 slices center-cut bacon, cooked and crumbled
2 (5-ounce) cans albacore tuna in water, drained and flaked
8 slices sourdough bread
4 (1/2-ounce) slices provolone cheese
Cooking spray

1. Combine first 7 ingredients in a medium bowl, stirring well to coat. Place 4 bread slices on a flat surface; top each bread slice with 1 cheese slice. Divide tuna mixture evenly among bread slices; top each serving with 1 remaining bread slice.
2. Heat a large skillet over medium heat. Lightly coat sandwiches with cooking spray. Place sandwiches in pan; top with another heavy skillet. Cook 3 minutes on each side or until lightly browned (leave skillet on sandwiches as they cook). Yield: 4 servings (serving size: 1 sandwich).

CALORIES 405; **FAT** 17.7g (sat 4g, mono 5.1g, poly 6.9g); **PROTEIN** 28.3g; **CARB** 33.3g; **FIBER** 2.3g; **CHOL** 49mg; **IRON** 3.6mg; **SODIUM** 872mg; **CALC** 182mg

BUDGET COOKING
FEED 4 FOR LESS THAN $10

We riff off the classic BLT, roast chicken with squash, and serve shrimp with pasta.

Quick & Easy
Grown-Up Grilled Cheese Sandwiches

$2.14 per serving, $8.54 total
A new take on a familiar favorite pairs grilled cheese with a BLT for a luscious veggie-packed sandwich that feels like an indulgence. Serve with zesty dill pickle spears.

Cooking spray
1 cup vertically sliced red onion
1 large garlic clove, minced
1 cup (4 ounces) shredded reduced-fat sharp white cheddar cheese (such as Cracker Barrel)
8 (1 1/2-ounce) slices hearty white bread (such as Pepperidge Farm)
2 cups fresh spinach leaves
8 (1/4-inch-thick) slices tomato
6 slices center-cut bacon, cooked

1. Heat a large nonstick skillet over medium-low heat. Coat pan with cooking spray. Add onion and garlic, and cook 10 minutes or until tender and golden brown, stirring occasionally.
2. Sprinkle 2 tablespoons cheese over each of 4 bread slices. Top each slice with 1/2 cup spinach, 2 tomato slices, 2 tablespoons onion mixture, and 1 1/2 bacon slices. Sprinkle each with 2 tablespoons cheese; top with the remaining 4 bread slices.
3. Heat skillet over medium heat. Coat pan with cooking spray. Place sandwiches in pan, and cook for 3 minutes on each side or until golden brown and cheese melts. Yield: 4 servings (serving size: 1 sandwich).

CALORIES 376; **FAT** 11g (sat 5.3g, mono 4.8g, poly 0.6g); **PROTEIN** 20.2g; **CARB** 50.3g; **FIBER** 3.3g; **CHOL** 24mg; **IRON** 2.9mg; **SODIUM** 876mg; **CALC** 308mg

┌──────────────────────────────┐
WHAT IS BUDGET COOKING?

Prices derived from midsized-city supermarkets. For specialty or highly perishable ingredients, like some Asian sauces or fresh herbs, we account for the entire cost of the ingredient. For other ingredients, we include the cost for only the amount used. Salt, pepper, and cooking spray are freebies.
└──────────────────────────────┘

Kid Friendly
Roast Chicken with Potatoes and Butternut Squash

$1.62 per serving, $6.47 total

2 tablespoons minced garlic, divided
1 teaspoon salt, divided
3/4 teaspoon freshly ground black pepper, divided
1/2 teaspoon dried rubbed sage
1 (3 1/2-pound) roasting chicken
Cooking spray
12 ounces red potatoes, cut into wedges
1 1/2 cups cubed peeled butternut squash (about 8 ounces)
2 tablespoons butter, melted

1. Preheat oven to 400°.
2. Combine 1 1/2 tablespoons garlic, 1/2 teaspoon salt, 1/2 teaspoon pepper, and sage in a small bowl. Remove and discard giblets and neck from chicken. Starting at neck cavity, loosen skin from breast and drumsticks by inserting fingers, gently pushing between skin and meat. Lift wing tips up and over back; tuck under chicken. Rub garlic mixture under loosened skin. Place chicken, breast side up, on rack of a broiler pan coated with cooking spray. Place rack in broiler pan.
3. Combine potatoes, squash, butter, remaining 1 1/2 teaspoons garlic, remaining 1/2 teaspoon salt, and remaining 1/4 teaspoon pepper. Arrange vegetable mixture around chicken. Bake at 400° for 1 hour or until a thermometer inserted into meaty part of thigh registers 165°. Let stand 10 minutes. Discard skin. Yield: 4 servings (serving size: about 3 ounces chicken and about 3/4 cup vegetables).

CALORIES 399; **FAT** 12.1g (sat 5g, mono 3.2g, poly 1.7g); **PROTEIN** 43.8g; **CARB** 25.9g; **FIBER** 3.4g; **CHOL** 147mg; **IRON** 3.5mg; **SODIUM** 791mg; **CALC** 77mg

WINE NOTE: For an affordable wine to pair with this dish, pick a dry riesling from Washington state, like Chateau Ste. Michelle's 2007 (Columbia Valley; $9). It has peach and orange flavors that create a tempting aromatic package with the sweet flavors of this dish.

Quick & Easy

Shrimp Fra Diavolo

$2.47 per serving, $9.87 total

Be sure to use inexpensive medium-sized shrimp in this garlicky, spicy classic.

8 ounces uncooked linguine
2 tablespoons extra-virgin olive oil, divided
1½ tablespoons minced garlic, divided
1 pound medium shrimp, peeled and deveined
¾ cup diced onion
1 teaspoon crushed red pepper
½ teaspoon dried basil
½ teaspoon dried oregano
2 tablespoons tomato paste
1 tablespoon fresh lemon juice
1¾ cups canned crushed tomatoes
¼ teaspoon salt
1 (14.5-ounce) can diced tomatoes, drained

1. Cook pasta according to package directions, omitting salt and fat. Drain; keep warm.
2. While pasta cooks, heat 1 tablespoon oil in a large nonstick skillet over medium-high heat. Add 1½ teaspoons garlic and shrimp; sauté for 3 minutes or until shrimp are done. Remove from pan; keep warm.
3. Add remaining 1 tablespoon oil and onion to pan; sauté 5 minutes or until softened. Stir in remaining 1 tablespoon garlic, pepper, basil, and oregano; cook 1 minute, stirring constantly. Stir in tomato paste and lemon juice; cook 1 minute or until slightly darkened. Stir in crushed tomatoes, salt, and diced tomatoes; cook 5 minutes or until thickened. Return shrimp to pan; cook for 2 minutes or until thoroughly heated. Serve over pasta. Yield: 4 servings (serving size: 1 cup pasta and about 1¼ cups sauce).

CALORIES 477; **FAT** 10.7g (sat 1.4g, mono 5.3g, poly 1.7g); **PROTEIN** 33g; **CARB** 59.4g; **FIBER** 5.4g; **CHOL** 172mg; **IRON** 5.4mg; **SODIUM** 552mg; **CALC** 121mg

DINNER TONIGHT

Stopwatch-tested menus from the *Cooking Light* kitchen.

40 minutes

SHOPPING LIST

Roast Chicken with Balsamic Bell Peppers

2 red bell peppers
1 yellow bell pepper
1 large shallot
fresh rosemary
fennel seeds
garlic powder
dried oregano
olive oil
balsamic vinegar
fat-free, less-sodium chicken broth
4 (6-ounce) skinless, boneless chicken breast halves

Mascarpone Mashed Potatoes

1½ pounds Yukon gold potatoes
2% milk
mascarpone cheese

GAME PLAN

While oven preheats:
- Prep potatoes.
- Bring potatoes to a boil.
- Prepare spice rub.

While chicken browns:
- Slice bell peppers and shallots.

While chicken roasts:
- Finish cooking bell pepper mixture.
- Mash potatoes.

Quick & Easy

Roast Chicken with Balsamic Bell Peppers

with Mascarpone Mashed Potatoes
(pictured on page 243)

Prep Pointer: Use a stainless steel or cast-iron skillet for more tasty browned bits and a more flavorful sauce.
Simple Sub: Use red wine vinegar or sherry vinegar for a sauce with a sharper edge.
Flavor Hit: Aromatic fennel seeds lend Mediterranean flair and mild anise notes.

¾ teaspoon salt, divided
¾ teaspoon fennel seeds, crushed
½ teaspoon black pepper, divided
¼ teaspoon garlic powder
¼ teaspoon dried oregano
4 (6-ounce) skinless, boneless chicken breasts
2 tablespoons olive oil, divided
Cooking spray
2 cups thinly sliced red bell pepper
1 cup thinly sliced yellow bell pepper
½ cup thinly sliced shallots (about 1 large)
1½ teaspoons chopped fresh rosemary
1 cup fat-free, less-sodium chicken broth
1 tablespoon balsamic vinegar

1. Preheat oven to 450°.
2. Heat a large skillet over medium-high heat. Combine ½ teaspoon salt, fennel seeds, ¼ teaspoon black pepper, garlic powder, and oregano. Brush chicken with 1½ teaspoons oil; sprinkle spice rub over chicken. Add 1½ teaspoons oil to pan. Add chicken; cook 3 minutes or until browned. Turn chicken over; cook 1 minute. Arrange chicken in an 11 x 7–inch baking dish coated with cooking spray. Bake at 450° for 10 minutes or until done.
3. Heat remaining 1 tablespoon oil over medium-high heat. Add bell peppers, shallots, and rosemary; sauté 3 minutes. Stir in broth, scraping pan to loosen browned bits. Reduce heat; simmer 5 minutes. Increase heat to medium-high. Stir in vinegar, remaining ¼ teaspoon salt, and remaining ¼ teaspoon pepper; cook 3 minutes, stirring frequently. Serve bell pepper mixture

over chicken. Yield: 4 servings (serving size: 1 breast half and about ½ cup bell pepper mixture).

CALORIES 282; FAT 11g (sat 2.1g, mono 6.4g, poly 1.7g); PROTEIN 35.9g; CARB 8.8g; FIBER 19g; CHOL 94mg; IRON 2mg; SODIUM 644mg; CALC 38mg

For the Mascarpone Mashed Potatoes:
Place 1½ pounds cubed peeled Yukon gold potatoes in a large saucepan; cover with water. Bring to a boil; reduce heat, and simmer 15 minutes or until tender. Drain; return to pan. Add ⅓ cup 2% milk, 3 tablespoons mascarpone cheese, and ½ teaspoon salt. Mash to desired consistency.

SHOPPING LIST

Pan-Grilled Halibut with Chimichurri
cilantro
basil
1 shallot
1 lemon
olive oil
4 (6-ounce) halibut fillets

Charred Vegetable Rice
1 small zucchini
grape tomatoes
green onions
long-grain white rice
olive oil
frozen whole-kernel corn

GAME PLAN

While rice cooks:
■ Prepare chimichurri.
■ Cook fish.
■ Char vegetable mixture for rice.
Fluff rice, and add vegetables.

Quick & Easy
Pan-Grilled Halibut with Chimichurri
with Charred Vegetable Rice

Flavor Hit: Charring in a cast-iron skillet coaxes caramelized flavor from frozen corn.
Simple Sub: For a woodsier taste in the sauce, use 1 teaspoon chopped oregano in place of basil.
Prep Pointer: You'll get more juice from a room-temperature lemon.

1½ tablespoons chopped fresh cilantro
1 tablespoon chopped fresh basil
1 tablespoon finely chopped shallots
1½ tablespoons olive oil
1½ tablespoons fresh lemon juice
½ teaspoon salt, divided
¼ teaspoon freshly ground black pepper, divided
Cooking spray
4 (6-ounce) halibut fillets

1. Combine first 5 ingredients in a medium bowl; stir in ¼ teaspoon salt and ⅛ teaspoon pepper.
2. Heat a grill pan over medium-high heat. Coat pan with cooking spray. Sprinkle remaining ¼ teaspoon salt and remaining ⅛ teaspoon pepper over fish. Add fish to pan; cook 4 minutes on each side or until desired degree of doneness. Serve with sauce. Yield: 4 servings (serving size: 1 fillet and about 2 teaspoons sauce).

CALORIES 227; FAT 8.8g (sat 1.2g, mono 4.9g, poly 1.7g); PROTEIN 34.2g; CARB 1.1g; FIBER 0.1g; CHOL 52mg; IRON 1.5mg; SODIUM 384mg; CALC 80mg

For the Charred Vegetable Rice:
Cook 1 cup long-grain white rice according to package directions, omitting salt and fat. Heat 1½ tablespoons olive oil in a large cast-iron skillet over medium-high heat. Add ½ cup thawed frozen whole-kernel corn and ½ cup chopped zucchini to pan; sauté 3 minutes or until vegetables are charred. Stir in ½ cup halved grape tomatoes and ⅓ cup chopped green onions; sauté 1 minute or until tomatoes almost wilt. Combine vegetable mixture, rice, and ¾ teaspoon salt.

WINE NOTE: The green herbs and tangy citrus in the chimichurri here need a bright, herbal white: sauvignon blanc. Discover the Clayhouse label out of California's powerhouse Central Coast. Their 2008 Sauv Blanc ($15) is racy with lime, green apple, crisp stone fruit, and green herbs, with enough body to stand up to the meaty fish.

SHOPPING LIST

Dijon Croque Monsieur
Italian bread
6 ounces thinly sliced ham
whole-grain Dijon mustard
fat-free mayonnaise
4 ounces Gruyère cheese
egg substitute
fat-free milk

Haricots Verts Salad
¾ pound haricots verts
1 small red bell pepper
chives
1 medium shallot
white wine vinegar
extra-virgin olive oil
Dijon mustard

GAME PLAN

While water for haricots verts comes to a boil:
■ Prepare vinaigrette for salad.
■ Assemble sandwiches.
While sandwiches cook:
■ Slice bell pepper.
■ Toss salad.

continued

Quick & Easy

Dijon Croque Monsieur

with Haricots Verts Salad

Instead of your usual grilled ham and cheese, try this French-style sandwich that's enhanced by the zip of whole-grain mustard.
Kid Tweak: Ditch the spicy Dijon, and go with mayo only.
Simple Sub: Regular greens beans will work great in the salad, but you'll need to cook them a few minutes longer.
Flavor Hit: Gruyère cheese is nutty, earthy, and complex.

1 tablespoon whole-grain Dijon mustard
1 tablespoon fat-free mayonnaise
8 (1-ounce) slices Italian bread
6 ounces thinly sliced ham
1 cup (4 ounces) shredded Gruyère cheese
¼ teaspoon freshly ground black pepper
½ cup egg substitute
¼ cup fat-free milk
Cooking spray

1. Combine mustard and mayonnaise in a small bowl. Spread ¾ teaspoon mustard mixture over each of 4 bread slices; layer each slice with 1½ ounces ham and ¼ cup cheese. Sprinkle evenly with pepper. Spread ¾ teaspoon mayonnaise mixture over each remaining bread slice; place, mustard side down, on top of sandwiches.
2. Combine egg substitute and fat-free milk in a shallow dish. Dip both sides of each sandwich into egg mixture.
3. Heat a large nonstick griddle or skillet over medium heat. Coat pan with cooking spray. Add sandwiches to pan; cook 3 minutes on each side or until lightly browned and cheese melts. Yield: 4 servings (serving size: 1 sandwich).

CALORIES 350; **FAT** 11.7g (sat 6.1g, mono 3.1g, poly 0.9g); **PROTEIN** 25.1g; **CARB** 34.6g; **FIBER** 1.7g; **CHOL** 51mg; **IRON** 2.8mg; **SODIUM** 935mg; **CALC** 344mg

For the Haricots Verts Salad:
Cook ¾ pound trimmed haricots verts in boiling water 3 minutes or until crisp-tender. Drain and plunge beans into ice water; drain. Place beans in a medium bowl; add ½ cup slivered red bell pepper. Combine 2 tablespoons chopped fresh chives, 2 tablespoons minced shallots, 2 tablespoons white wine vinegar, 2 tablespoons extra-virgin olive oil, 1 teaspoon Dijon mustard, ½ teaspoon salt, and ¼ teaspoon black pepper, stirring with a whisk. Drizzle vinaigrette over bean mixture; toss to coat.

40 minutes

SHOPPING LIST

Seared Lamb with Balsamic Sauce
1 small red onion
garlic
olive oil
balsamic vinegar
1 (14-ounce) can fat-free, less-sodium beef broth
dry red wine
8 (4-ounce) lamb loin chops

Cracked Wheat–Currant Pilaf
flat-leaf parsley
quick-cooking bulgur
dried currants
butter

Spicy Chard
garlic
1 large bunch Swiss chard
olive oil
crushed red pepper
1 (14-ounce) can fat-free, less-sodium chicken broth

GAME PLAN

Sauté bulgur and bring to a boil with water. While bulgur stands:
- Cook lamb.
- Prepare balsamic sauce.
- Prepare chard. Stir currants and parsley into bulgur.

Quick & Easy

Seared Lamb with Balsamic Sauce

with Cracked Wheat-Currant Pilaf and Spicy Chard

Lamb's assertive flavor is tempered by the sweet-savory sauce and fruit-studded pilaf.
Time-Saver: Use prechopped red onion from the produce section.
Flavor Hit: Balsamic vinegar gives the sauce a sweet, rich taste.
Simple Sub: Use golden or regular raisins instead of currants.

2 teaspoons olive oil
8 (4-ounce) lamb loin chops, trimmed
½ teaspoon kosher salt
¼ teaspoon freshly ground black pepper
1 cup finely chopped red onion
2 garlic cloves, chopped
¼ cup dry red wine
⅓ cup fat-free, less-sodium beef broth
2 tablespoons balsamic vinegar

1. Heat oil in a large nonstick skillet over medium-high heat. Sprinkle lamb with salt and pepper. Add lamb to pan, and cook 3 minutes or until browned. Turn lamb over, and cook 4 minutes or until desired degree of doneness. Remove lamb from pan; keep warm. Add onion and garlic to pan; cook 3 minutes or until onion is tender. Add wine; bring to a boil. Cook 3 minutes or until liquid evaporates. Stir in broth and vinegar; bring to a boil. Cook 2 minutes or until reduced to about ⅔ cup. Serve sauce with lamb. Yield: 4 servings (serving size: 2 chops and about 2½ tablespoons sauce).

CALORIES 253; **FAT** 11.6g (sat 3.7g, mono 5.7g, poly 0.9g); **PROTEIN** 29.4g; **CARB** 5.9g; **FIBER** 0.8g; **CHOL** 90mg; **IRON** 2.2mg; **SODIUM** 357mg; **CALC** 34mg

For the Cracked Wheat-Currant Pilaf:
Sauté 1½ cups quick-cooking bulgur in 2 teaspoons butter over medium-high heat for 1 minute. Add 1½ cups water and ½ teaspoon kosher salt. Bring to a boil; cook 2 minutes. Cover, remove from heat, and let stand 25 minutes. Fluff with a fork. Stir in 3 tablespoons dried currants and 2 tablespoons chopped fresh flat-leaf parsley.

Quick & Easy • Kid Friendly

Fettuccine Alfredo with Bacon

When you're short on time and the ingredient list is short, make every ingredient the freshest and best you can find. A real wood-smoked bacon imparts lots of flavor: Applewood is mild and slightly sweet, while hardwood, such as hickory, is more assertive.

1 (9-ounce) package refrigerated fresh
  fettuccine
2 slices applewood-smoked bacon, chopped
1 teaspoon minced garlic
1 tablespoon all-purpose flour
1 cup 1% low-fat milk
$^2/_3$ cup (about 2$^1/_2$ ounces) grated
  Parmigiano-Reggiano cheese
$^1/_2$ teaspoon salt
2 tablespoons chopped fresh parsley
$^1/_2$ teaspoon freshly ground black pepper

1. Cook pasta according to package directions, omitting salt and fat. Drain in a colander over a bowl, reserving ¼ cup cooking liquid.
2. While pasta cooks, cook bacon in a large nonstick skillet over medium-high heat 4 minutes or until crisp, stirring occasionally. Remove bacon from pan, reserving drippings. Add garlic to drippings in pan; sauté 1 minute, stirring constantly. Sprinkle flour over garlic; cook 30 seconds, stirring constantly. Gradually add milk, stirring constantly; cook 2 minutes or until bubbly and slightly thick, stirring constantly. Reduce heat to low. Gradually add cheese, stirring until cheese melts. Stir in salt and reserved ¼ cup cooking liquid. Add hot pasta to pan; toss well to combine. Sprinkle with bacon, parsley, and pepper. Yield: 4 servings (serving size: about 1 cup).

CALORIES 339; FAT 11.7g (sat 5g, mono 3.8g, poly 0.7g); PROTEIN 17.3g; CARB 38.4g; FIBER 2g; CHOL 22mg; IRON 0.5mg; SODIUM 833mg; CALC 291mg

OUR FAVORITE RISOTTO WITH PORCINI MUSHROOMS AND MASCARPONE

Meaty, woodsy mushrooms and a dollop of buttery Italian cream cheese make this rich dish a risotto to remember.

Risotto with Porcini Mushrooms and Mascarpone

2 cups boiling water
1 cup dried porcini mushrooms (about 1
  ounce)
1 (14-ounce) can less-sodium beef broth
Cooking spray
1 cup uncooked Arborio rice
$^3/_4$ cup chopped shallots
2 garlic cloves, minced
$^1/_2$ cup dry white wine
¼ cup (1 ounce) grated Parmigiano-Reggiano
  cheese
1 tablespoon chopped fresh thyme
$^1/_2$ teaspoon salt
$^1/_2$ teaspoon black pepper
¼ cup (1 ounce) mascarpone cheese
Thyme leaves (optional)

1. Combine 2 cups boiling water and mushrooms; let stand 30 minutes or until soft. Drain through a colander over a bowl. Reserve 1½ cups soaking liquid; chop mushrooms.
2. Bring soaking liquid and broth to a simmer in a small saucepan (do not boil). Keep broth mixture warm.
3. Heat a large saucepan over medium-high heat. Coat pan with cooking spray. Add rice, shallots, and garlic; sauté 5 minutes. Add wine, and cook until liquid evaporates (about 2 minutes).

4. Add 1 cup broth mixture to rice mixture; cook over medium heat 5 minutes or until liquid is nearly absorbed, stirring constantly. Add remaining broth mixture, ½ cup at a time, stirring constantly until each portion of broth mixture is absorbed before adding the next (about 25 minutes total). Add mushrooms, Parmigiano-Reggiano, and next 3 ingredients; stir gently until cheese melts. Spoon 1 cup risotto into each of 4 bowls. Top each serving with 1 tablespoon mascarpone and thyme leaves, if desired. Yield: 4 servings.

CALORIES 369; FAT 15g (sat 7.9g, mono 4.1g, poly 0.6g); PROTEIN 11.5g; CARB 48g; FIBER 4.2g; CHOL 39mg; IRON 2.1mg; SODIUM 570mg; CALC 115mg

DRIED MUSHROOMS LEND A RICH MUSHROOMY ESSENSE TO THIS DISH. TO REHYDRATE, SOAK THEM IN HOT WATER UNTIL TENDER. THEY'LL BE MORE DENSE AND CHEWY THAN FRESH MUSHROOMS.

THE 25 MOST COMMON COOKING MISTAKES

And how to avoid them for success every time.

Every cook, being human, errs, bungles, botches, flubs, and screws up in the kitchen once in a while. If you have not "caramelized" fruit in salt rather than sugar (hey, it looked like sugar!), you have not suffered the most embarrassing mistake made by one of our editors. But you have probably done something like it. Indeed, we did not have to look much further than our staff—and their encounters with readers, friends, and relatives—to compile a list of 25 common, avoidable culinary boo-boos. This is by no means a complete account of kitchen snafus—it does not address the complicated error in judgment that led the mother of one of our editors to put chives in her cheesecake—but it's a very good start. The creative cook can often cook her way out of a kitchen error, but the smart cook aims to prevent such creativity from being necessary. Here are 25 ways to be smarter every time.

1. YOU DON'T TASTE AS YOU GO.

RESULT: The flavors or textures of an otherwise excellent dish are out of balance or unappealing.

For most cooks, tasting is automatic, but when it's not, the price can be high. Recipes don't always call for the "right" amount of seasoning, cooking times are estimates, and results vary depending on your ingredients, your stove, altitude … and a million other factors. Your palate is the control factor: You are directing this show. Knowing that the strawberries you bought are more tangy than sweet tells you to boost sugar a bit. Tasting, not time in the pot, tells you when dried beans have become tender, or haricots verts have reached the point of perfection. (If the beans are tough, simply cook longer. For haricots verts, taste early and often until they become crisp-tender, or you'll ruin an expensive ingredient.) Think that experienced cooks don't forget this most basic rule? *Cooking Light* Associate Food Editor Tim Cebula was

sous chef in a notable restaurant when he served up, for his boss, "caramelized" pineapple that somehow refused to brown. The chef quickly returned the dish. Turns out Tim had coated the fruit in salt, not sugar. "That's why it wouldn't caramelize."

2. YOU DON'T READ THE ENTIRE RECIPE BEFORE YOU START COOKING.

RESULT: Should-be-tender meat turns out tough, flavors are dull, entire steps or ingredients get left out.

Even the best-written recipes may not include all the headline information at the top. Three-fourths of the way down a recipe for Lemon-Garlic Roast Chicken, there may be a note to brine the bird for 24 hours. A wise cook approaches each recipe with a critical eye—studying, not skimming, looking for unfamiliar ingredients, specialty equipment, problematic steps—and reads the recipe well before it's time to cook. Review as you would any complicated, multistep plan (because that's what a recipe is).

"Trust me," says former *Cooking Light* Test Kitchens tester Mary Drennen Ankar, "you don't want to be an hour away from dinner guests arriving when you get to the part of the recipe that says to marinate the brisket overnight or simmer for two hours." Follow the pros' habit of gathering your *mise en place*—that is, having all the ingredients gathered, prepped, and ready to go before you turn on the heat. If you don't, you may leave out an ingredient or compromise the recipe by shortchanging a crucial step, and that's a tragic thing.

3. YOU MAKE UNWISE SUBSTITUTIONS IN BAKING.

RESULT: You wreck the underlying chemistry of the dish.

Substitutions are a particular temptation, and challenge, with healthy cooking. At *Cooking Light* it's our job to substitute lower-fat ingredients—to change the cooking chemistry a bit while capturing the soul of a dish. When it comes to baking, this is as much science as art, and it requires a lot of trial and error.

We learn a lot from reader disappointments. "I'll get calls about cakes turning out too dense or too gummy," says Test Kitchens Director Vanessa Pruett. "After a little interrogation, I'll get to the truth—that the reader used ALL applesauce instead of a mix of applesauce and oil or butter, subbed whole-wheat flour for all-purpose where that just wouldn't do, or went with sugar substitute in place of sugar." Applesauce makes baked goods gummy, too much whole-wheat flour can make them dense, and sugar substitutes don't react the same way as sugar. All three of those mistakes in one cupcake recipe make clay, not cake. Best practice:

Follow the recipe, period. And if you want to experiment (as we do all the time), regard it as an experiment and expect a few failures along the way.

4. YOU BOIL WHEN YOU SHOULD SIMMER.

RESULT: A hurried-up dish that's cloudy, tough, or dry.

This is one of the most common (and perhaps least recognized) kitchen errors. First, let's clarify what we mean by simmering: A bubble breaks the surface of the liquid every second or two. More vigorous bubbling than that means you've got a boil going. And the difference between the two can ruin a dish. When you boil chicken stock, you churn fat and impurities all throughout the liquid; when you simmer, though, those undesirable elements float to the surface where they're easily skimmed off so the stock turns out clean-tasting and clear. Boil a chuck roast, and it becomes tough; simmer, and the connective tissue gently melts to produce fork-tender meat. "I had a friend serve me a beef stew once that gave me a real jaw work-out," says Nutrition Editor Kathy Kitchens Downie. "She boiled the meat for 45 minutes instead of simmering it for a couple of hours. She says she just wanted it to get done more quickly. Well, it was 'done,' but meat cooked too quickly in liquid ironically turns out very dry. And tough, really tough."

BOILING WHEN YOU SHOULD BE SIMMERING IS ONE OF THE MOST COMMON AND PERHAPS LEAST RECOGNIZED KITCHEN ERRORS.

Beef Rendang

This rich Malay curry is redolent with lemongrass, garlic, ginger, and cinnamon. Cook the beef mixture at a low simmer so the sauce doesn't scorch and the meat slowly becomes tender. If you can't find unsweetened coconut, use sweetened flaked coconut and omit the added sugar.

½ cup chopped shallots
⅓ cup thinly sliced peeled ginger
1½ tablespoons minced garlic (about 5 cloves)
2 tablespoons chili garlic sauce (such as Lee Kum Kee)
1½ teaspoons ground turmeric
1¼ teaspoons salt
¼ teaspoon ground cinnamon
6 whole cloves
1 to 2 serrano chiles, chopped
1 (14-ounce) can light coconut milk, divided
⅔ cup flaked unsweetened coconut, toasted
1 teaspoon grated lime rind
2 tablespoons fresh lime juice
2 teaspoons sugar
2 (3-inch) fresh lemongrass stalks, crushed
2 pounds boneless chuck roast, trimmed and cut into 1-inch cubes
1 (14-ounce) can fat-free, less-sodium chicken broth
4 cups hot cooked basmati rice

1. Place first 9 ingredients in a food processor or mini chopper. Add ¼ cup coconut milk; process until smooth. Spoon mixture into a bowl; set aside.
2. Place 3 tablespoons coconut milk and flaked coconut in food processor; process until a smooth paste forms.
3. Heat a large saucepan over medium-high heat. Add shallot mixture; cook 1 minute or until fragrant, stirring constantly. Stir in remaining coconut milk, rind, and next 5 ingredients; bring to a boil. Cover, reduce heat to medium-low, and simmer 1½ hours or until beef is tender, stirring occasionally. Discard lemongrass. Stir in flaked coconut mixture; simmer 10 minutes or until liquid almost evaporates. Serve over rice. Yield: 6 servings (serving size: ½ cup beef mixture and ¾ cup rice).

CALORIES 449; **FAT** 14.6g (sat 10.3g, mono 2.5g, poly 0.4g); **PROTEIN** 27.4g; **CARB** 51.5g; FIBER 3.1g; **CHOL** 49mg; **IRON** 3.3mg; **SODIUM** 784mg; **CALC** 30mg

5. YOU OVERHEAT CHOCOLATE.

RESULT: Instead of having a smooth, creamy, luxurious consistency, your chocolate is grainy, separated, or scorched.

The best way to melt chocolate is to go slowly, heat gently, remove from the heat before it's fully melted, and stir until smooth. If using the microwave, proceed cautiously, stopping every 20 to 30 seconds to stir. If using a double boiler, make sure the water is simmering, not boiling. It's very easy to ruin chocolate, and there is no road back. Associate Food Editor Julianna Grimes recently made a cake with her young son but didn't pay close enough attention while microwaving the chocolate. It curdled. "It was all the chocolate I had on hand so I had to dump it and change my plans." No chocolate fix for Grimes, though her son was content to lick the vanilla-frosted beaters.

6. YOU OVERSOFTEN BUTTER.

RESULT: Cookies spread too much or cakes are too dense.

We've done it: forgotten to soften the butter and zapped it in the microwave to do the job quickly. But it's a baking error to excessively soften, let alone melt, the butter. Better to let it stand at room temperature for 30 to 45 minutes to get the right consistency. You can speed the process significantly by cutting butter into tablespoon-sized portions and letting it stand at room temperature.

Properly softened butter should yield slightly to gentle pressure, but you don't want to be able to sink your finger way down into it. Too-soft butter means your cookie dough will be more like batter, and it will spread too much as it bakes and lose shape. Butter that's too soft also won't cream properly with sugar, and creaming is essential to creating fluffy, tender cakes with a delicate crumb.

7. YOU OVERHEAT LOW-FAT MILK PRODUCTS.

RESULT: The milk curdles or "breaks," yielding grainy mac and cheese, ice cream, or pudding.

If you're new to lighter cooking, you may not know that even though you can boil cream just fine, the same is not true for other milk products, which will curdle. A cook distracted by kids or the phone can quickly produce a grainy, broken mess. The solution is to cook lower-fat dairy products to a temperature of only 180° or less. Use a clip-on thermometer, hover over the pan, and heat over medium-low or low heat to prevent curdling. And if it curdles, toss and start again: Ice cream or pudding made with curdled milk won't ever be smooth or velvety. One alternative: Stabilize milk with starch, like cornstarch or flour, if you want to bring it to a boil; the starch will prevent curdling (and it'll thicken the milk, too).

Kid Friendly

Bacon, Ranch, and Chicken Mac and Cheese
(*pictured on page 249*)

The combination of onion and garlic powders plus fresh dill creates a flavor similar to ranch dressing.

8 ounces uncooked elbow macaroni
1 applewood-smoked bacon slice
8 ounces skinless, boneless chicken breast, cut into 1/2-inch pieces
1 tablespoon butter
1 tablespoon all-purpose flour
1 1/2 cups fat-free milk
1/3 cup condensed 45% reduced-sodium 98% fat-free cream of mushroom soup, undiluted
3/4 cup (3 ounces) shredded six-cheese Italian blend (such as Sargento)
1/2 teaspoon onion powder
1/2 teaspoon garlic powder
1/2 teaspoon chopped fresh dill
1/2 teaspoon salt
Cooking spray
1/2 cup (2 ounces) shredded colby-Jack cheese

1. Cook pasta according to package directions, omitting salt and fat; drain.
2. Cook bacon in a large nonstick skillet over medium heat until crisp. Remove bacon from pan, reserving drippings in pan. Finely chop bacon; set aside. Increase heat to medium-high. Add chicken to drippings in pan; sauté 6 minutes or until done.
3. Melt butter in a large saucepan over medium heat; sprinkle flour evenly into pan. Cook 2 minutes, stirring constantly with a whisk. Combine milk and soup, stirring with a whisk; gradually add milk mixture to saucepan, stirring with a whisk. Bring to a boil; cook 2 minutes or until thick. Remove from heat; let stand 4 minutes or until sauce cools to 155°. Add Italian cheese blend and next 4 ingredients, stirring until cheese melts. Stir in pasta and chicken.
4. Preheat broiler.
5. Spoon mixture into an 8-inch square baking dish coated with cooking spray. Sprinkle evenly with reserved bacon and colby-Jack cheese. Broil 3 minutes or until cheese melts. Yield: 4 servings (serving size: about 2 cups).

CALORIES 497; FAT 17g (sat 9.2g, mono 4.7g, poly 1.4g); PROTEIN 33.3g; CARB 51.7g; FIBER 2g; CHOL 74mg; IRON 2.4mg; SODIUM 767mg; CALC 368mg

8. YOU DON'T KNOW YOUR OVEN'S QUIRKS AND IDIOSYNCRASIES.

RESULT: Food cooks too fast, too slow, or unevenly.

Ideally, every oven set to 350° would heat to 350°. But many ovens don't, including expensive ones, and some change their behavior as they age. Always use an oven thermometer. Next, be aware of hot spots. If you've produced cake layers with wavy rather than flat tops, hot spots are the problem. SaBrina Bone, who tests in our kitchen, advises the "bread test": Arrange bread slices to cover the middle oven rack. Bake at 350° for a few minutes, and see which slices get singed—their location marks your oven's hot spot(s). If you know you have a hot spot in, say, the back left corner, avoid putting pans in that location, or rotate accordingly.

9. YOU'RE TOO CASUAL ABOUT MEASURING INGREDIENTS.

RESULT: Dry, tough cakes; rubbery brownies; and a host of other textural mishaps.

In lighter baking, you're using less of the butter and oil that can hide a host of measurement sins. If you add as little as 2 extra tablespoons of flour to a cake recipe, for example, you may end up with a dry, tough texture. And adding too much flour is easy: One cook's "cup of flour" may be another cook's 1 1/4 cups.

Why the discrepancy? Some people scoop their flour out of the canister, essentially packing it down into the measuring cup, or tap the cup on the counter and then top off with more flour. Both practices yield too much flour.

"Lightly spoon flour into dry measuring cups, then level with a knife," advises Test Kitchens Director Vanessa Pruett. A dry measuring cup is one without a spout—a spout makes it difficult to level off the excess flour with the flat side of a knife. "Lightly spoon" means don't pack it in.

If you're measuring flour by weight, however, it's not important how you get the flour out of the canister. That's why we changed our recipe style in 2008 to call for flour in ounces by weight (though we still offer approximate cup amounts for those who don't have kitchen scales). Weighing is simply more accurate.

And try not to be thrown off by volume measurements. Many liquid measuring cups (those with spouts) show that 1 cup equals 8 ounces—but that means *8 fluid ounces*, and fluid ounces are volume measurements, not weight measurements.

Make Ahead • Kid Friendly

Tuscan Cake with Citrus Compote

Cake:

½ cup sugar

6 tablespoons extra-virgin olive oil

2 large eggs

1 tablespoon grated grapefruit rind

1½ teaspoons grated lime rind

½ teaspoon vanilla extract

1 (6-ounce) container plain low-fat yogurt

5.6 ounces all-purpose flour (about 1¼ cups)

1.5 ounces fine yellow cornmeal (about ¼ cup)

¾ teaspoon baking soda

¼ teaspoon baking powder

¼ teaspoon salt

Cooking spray

Compote:

2 large red grapefruit

4 large oranges

2 tablespoons fresh lime juice

3 tablespoons honey

⅛ teaspoon ground allspice

1. Preheat oven to 325°.

2. To prepare cake, place sugar and oil in a large bowl; beat with a mixer at high speed 2 minutes or until well blended. Add eggs, 1 at a time, beating well after each addition. Add rinds, vanilla, and yogurt; beat until combined.

3. Weigh or lightly spoon flour and cornmeal into dry measuring cups; level with a knife. Combine flour, cornmeal, baking soda, baking powder, and salt, stirring with a whisk. Add flour mixture to oil mixture; stir with a whisk just until combined. Pour batter into a 9-inch springform pan coated with cooking spray. Bake at 325° for 30 minutes or until golden brown and a wooden pick inserted in center comes out clean. Cool 10 minutes on a wire rack; remove sides from pan. Cool cake completely on rack.

4. To prepare compote, peel and section grapefruit and oranges over a medium bowl, reserving juices; place sections in another bowl. Combine reserved juices and lime juice in a small saucepan; bring to a boil. Stir in honey and allspice; reduce heat, and simmer 4 minutes or until syrupy. Cover and chill 30 minutes. Pour over fruit sections; toss gently.

Chill. Serve compote over cake. Yield: 9 servings (serving size: 1 cake wedge and about ¼ cup compote).

CALORIES 305; **FAT** 10.7g (sat 1.8g, mono 7.1g, poly 1.2g); **PROTEIN** 5.4g; **CARB** 48.9g; **FIBER** 2.8g; **CHOL** 48mg; **IRON** 1.4mg; **SODIUM** 211mg; **CALC** 88mg

10. YOU OVER-CROWD THE PAN.

RESULT: Soggy food that doesn't brown.

All food will release moisture as it cooks so you need to leave room for the steam to escape. Trapped moisture turns a browning exercise into a steam bath. Most cooks know this, but it's easy to overcrowd a pan when you're in a hurry, particularly if you have to brown a large amount of meat for a beef stew. But the brown, crusty bits are critical for flavor, particularly with lower-fat cooking. A soggy batch of beef going into a Dutch oven will not be a beautiful, rich, deeply flavored stew when it comes out, even if it does get properly tender. This browning principle applies equally to quick-cook foods like crab cakes, chicken breasts, and so on. Leave breathing room in the pan, and you'll get much better results. If you need to speed things up, use two pans at once.

11. YOU MISHANDLE EGG WHITES.

RESULT: The whites won't whip up. Or, over-beaten or roughly handled, they produce flat cake layers or soufflés with no lift.

Properly beaten egg whites are voluminous, creamy, and glossy, but they require care. First, separate whites from yolks carefully; a speck of yolk can prevent the whites from whipping up fully.

Our favorite tool for separating eggs: our hands. When you try to shuffle the egg from one half of a broken shell to the other, there are too many jagged edges that may puncture the yolk. Crack an egg into your hand, however, and the whites slip through your fingers, leaving the yolk intact.

We also encourage the three-bowl method, which limits the risk of any yolk contaminating the batch of whites. Here's how: Separate the egg over bowl #1, letting the white fall into the bowl. Place the yolk into bowl #2. If the white cleanly separates from the yolk, transfer it to bowl #3. If you accidentally get some yolk into bowl #1, it won't ruin the whole bowl of whites. Simply discard or cook that egg, wipe bowl #1 clean, and start over. (Use leftover yolks for custards, homemade mayonnaise, or lemon curd.)

Let the whites stand for a few minutes—at room temperature they whip up better than when cold. Whip with clean, dry beaters at high speed just until stiff peaks form—that is, until the peak created when you lift the beater out of the bowl stands upright. If you overbeat, the whites will turn grainy or dry or may separate. When the whites are perfectly beaten, gently fold them into the cake batter or soufflé base. Otherwise, you'll deflate them. We've seen roughly handled batter yield cake layers only a half-inch high.

12. YOU TURN THE FOOD TOO OFTEN.

RESULT: You interfere with the sear, food sticks, or you lose the breading.

Learning to leave food alone is one of the hardest lessons in cooking; it's so tempting to turn, poke, flip. But your breaded chicken or steak won't develop a nice crust unless you allow it to cook, undisturbed, for the specified time. One sign that it's too early to turn: You can't slide a spatula cleanly under the crust. "It'll release from the pan when it's ready," says Assistant Test Kitchens Director Tiffany Vickers Davis. "Don't try to pry it up—the crust will stick to the pan, not the chicken."

Blue Cheese–Stuffed Chicken with Buffalo Sauce

(pictured on page 248)

Resist the urge to turn the chicken before it's time; otherwise you risk having the breading stick to the pan (mistake #12).

½ cup (2 ounces) crumbled blue cheese
1 tablespoon reduced-fat sour cream
1 teaspoon fresh lemon juice
⅛ teaspoon freshly ground black pepper
4 (6-ounce) skinless, boneless chicken breast halves
¼ cup all-purpose flour
2 tablespoons 2% reduced-fat milk
1 large egg, lightly beaten
1 cup panko (Japanese breadcrumbs)
1½ tablespoons butter, divided
6 tablespoons finely chopped drained bottled roasted red bell peppers
2 teaspoons water
1 teaspoon Worcestershire sauce
1 teaspoon minced fresh garlic
½ teaspoon hot sauce

1. Preheat oven to 350°.
2. Combine first 4 ingredients in a small bowl. Cut a horizontal slit through thickest portion of each chicken breast half to form a pocket. Stuff cheese mixture evenly into pockets.
3. Place flour in a shallow dish. Combine milk and egg in a shallow dish, stirring well with a whisk. Place panko in a shallow dish. Working with 1 chicken breast half at a time, dredge chicken in flour, then dip in egg mixture; dredge in panko. Repeat procedure with remaining chicken, flour, egg mixture, and panko.
4. Heat a large ovenproof skillet over medium-high heat. Add 1 tablespoon butter to pan; swirl until butter melts. Arrange chicken in pan; cook 4 minutes or until browned. Turn chicken over; place skillet in oven. Bake at 350° for 20 minutes or until done.
5. While chicken bakes, combine remaining 1½ teaspoons butter, bell peppers, and next 3 ingredients in a small saucepan over medium heat.

Bring to a simmer; cook until butter melts. Remove from heat, and stir in hot sauce. Serve sauce with chicken. Yield: 4 servings (serving size: 1 breast half and about 4 teaspoons sauce).

CALORIES 392; FAT 12.9g (sat 6.7g, mono 3.4g, poly 1g); PROTEIN 47.4g; CARB 18.5g; FIBER 1.1g; CHOL 175mg; IRON 2.3mg; SODIUM 421mg; CALC 120mg

13. YOU DON'T GET THE PAN HOT ENOUGH BEFORE YOU ADD THE FOOD.

RESULT: Food that sticks, scallops with no sear, pale meats.

The inexperienced or hurried cook will barely heat the pan before adding oil and tossing in onions for a sauté. Next comes ... nothing. Silence. No sizzle. A hot pan is essential for sautéing veggies or creating a great crust on meat, fish, and poultry. It also helps prevent food from sticking. Associate Food Editor Tim Cebula was once advised by a restaurant chef thusly: "If you think your pan is hot enough, step back and heat it a couple more minutes. When you're about ready to call the fire department, then add oil and proceed to cook the food." This is typical pro-chef hyperbole (though they do tend to cook at higher temperatures than the home cook), but it drives home the point. Oh—and only add the oil when the pan is hot, just before adding the ingredients. Otherwise, it will smoke, and that's bad for the oil.

14. YOU SLICE MEAT WITH—INSTEAD OF AGAINST—THE GRAIN.

RESULT: Chewy meat that could have been tender.

For tender slices, look at the meat to determine the direction of the grain (the muscle fibers), and cut across the grain, not with it. This is particularly important with tougher cuts

such as flank steak or skirt steak, in which the grain is also quite obvious. But it's also a good practice with more tender cuts like standing rib roast or even poultry.

15. YOU UNDER-BAKE CAKES AND BREADS.

RESULT: Cakes, brownies, and breads turn out pallid and gummy.

Overcooked baked goods disappoint, but we've found that less experienced bakers are more likely to undercook them—and that's a travesty. Think about the joy of breaking into a crusty baguette, relishing the sugar crust that tops brownies or pound cake, savoring the hearty crunch of cast-iron–crisped corn bread. "You won't get that irresistible browning unless you have the confidence to fully cook the food," says Associate Food Editor Julianna Grimes. "Really look at the food. Even if the wooden pick comes out clean, if the cake is pale, it's not finished. Let it go another couple of minutes until it has an even, golden brownness." It's better to err on the side of slightly overcooking than producing gummy, wet, unappealing food. Once you've done this a few times and know exactly what you're looking for, it'll become second nature.

16. YOU DON'T USE A MEAT THERMOMETER.

RESULT: Your roast chicken, leg of lamb, or beef tenderloin turns out over- or undercooked.

Small, inexpensive, thoroughly unglamorous, the meat thermometer is one of the most valuable kitchen tools you can own. Using one is the surefire way to achieve a perfect roast chicken or beautiful medium-rare lamb roast because temperatures don't lie and appearances can deceive. "I had a friend," remembers Associate Food Editor Julie Grimes, "who made Thanksgiving dinner for her mother-in-law. The turkey looked beautiful, but when she cut into it she was horrified to find it still frozen in the middle." No thermometer could be fooled by that if the probe went to the proper depth.

We love digital probe thermometers, which allow you to set the device to the desired temperature. A heat-proof wire leads to an external digital unit that sits outside the oven and beeps when the meat is ready. This eliminates the frequent opening and closing of the oven door to check the temp—during which you lose valuable heat—and that speeds the cooking.

17. MEAT GETS NO CHANCE TO REST AFTER COOKING.

RESULT: Delicious juices vacate the meat and run all over the cutting board, leaving steak or roast dry.

Plan your meals so that meat you roast, grill, sear, or sauté has time to rest at room temperature after it's pulled from the heat. That cooling-off time helps the juices, which migrate to the center of the meat, to be distributed more evenly throughout. Associate Food Editor Tim Cebula is our chief evangelist in this regard; he has had nightmares (Hitchcock meets *Iron Chef*) about people cutting into a beef tenderloin too soon, his slow-motion dive to prevent the crime always futile. The resting rule, by the way, applies equally to an inexpensive skirt steak or a premium dry-aged, grass-fed steak, as well as poultry. With small cuts like a steak or boneless, skinless chicken breast, five minutes is adequate. A whole bird or standing rib roast requires 20 to 30 minutes. Tent the meat loosely with foil to keep it warm.

18. YOU TRY TO RUSH COOKING CARAMELIZED ONIONS.

RESULT: You end up with sautéed onions, which are nice but a far cry from the melt-in-your-mouth caramelized ideal.

If you want real, true, sweet, creamy caramelized onions to top your burger or pizza or for the divine tart called *pissaladière*, you need to cook them over medium-low to low heat for a long time, maybe up to an hour. If you crank the heat and try to speed up the process, you'll get a different product—onions that may be crisp-tender and nicely browned but lacking that characteristic translucence and meltingly tender quality you want. Bottom line: Know that caramelized onions take time, and plan to cook them when you can give them the time they need. The good news is that onions are not like garlic, and they will not burn in a heartbeat and ruin a dish; just stir occasionally, over low heat.

19. YOU OVER-WORK LOWER-FAT DOUGH.

RESULT: Cookies, scones, piecrusts, and biscuits turn out tough.

Recipes with lots of butter are more likely to stay moist and tender because of the fat, even if the dough is overmixed or overkneaded. But without all that fat, you absolutely must use a light hand. That's why many of our biscuit and scone recipes instruct the cook to knead the dough gently or pat it out (instead of rolling), and our cookie or piecrust recipes say to mix just until flour is incorporated. To be safe, stop machine mixing early and finish by hand. "Whenever I make any of our cookies, I stop the mixer before the flour is completely incorporated," says the Test Kitchens' Deb Wise. "I do that last bit of mixing by hand, and it makes a difference." That's because vigorous mixing encourages gluten development, which creates a chewy or tough texture—great in a baguette but not in a biscuit.

20. YOU NEGLECT THE NUTS YOU'RE TOASTING.

RESULT: Burned nuts, with a sharp, bitter flavor.

Our recipes often call for toasted nuts because toasting intensifies flavor, allowing us to use less (and thus lower the calories in a recipe). But the nut is a mighty delicate thing—in an oven it can go from perfectly toasty to charred in seconds. This has happened to every one of our Test Kitchens' cooks. Our preferred method: Arrange nuts in a single layer on a heavy baking sheet, and bake at 350° for as little as two minutes for flaked coconut to five or more minutes (for dense nuts like almonds); shake the pan or stir frequently so the nuts toast evenly—they tend to brown on the bottom more quickly. They're done when they've darkened slightly (or turned golden brown for pale nuts like pine nuts or slivered almonds) and smell fragrant and toasty. Do not start another project or walk away while they're in the oven. One final word: If you burn the nuts, toss them and start over—you don't want that acrid quality in your food. Oh, and another final word: We don't recommend toasting nuts in a pan on top of the stove: It's almost impossible not to burn them that way.

21. YOU DON'T SHOCK VEGETABLES WHEN THEY'VE REACHED THE DESIRED TEXTURE.

RESULT: Mush.

Toss green beans (or haricots verts), broccoli, or asparagus into boiling water for three to seven minutes, and they'll turn vibrant green with a crisp-tender texture—pure veggie perfection. But if you don't "shock" those vegetables at that point by spooning them out of the boiling water and plunging them into ice water (or at least rinsing under cold running water) to stop the cooking process, the carryover heat will continue to cook them to the point that they turn army-green and flabby. This is not a concern if you intend to serve the vegetables immediately. But often a recipe will call for vegetables to be finished in, say, a quick sauté with butter and mushrooms. In such a case, when the veggies will sit before their final act, they need to be shocked. This is also a convenient method for precooking vegetables for a complex meal: They can be quickly reheated when, for example, the roast is resting. You can refrigerate them overnight and warm them quickly the next day—they'll still have a toothsome crunch and bright color that even a short, warm wait will rob them of.

22. YOU PUT ALL THE SALT IN THE MARINADE OR BREADING.

RESULT: Fish, poultry, or meat that's underseasoned.

Healthy cooks try to keep sodium levels in check and only allocate a small amount of salt to a recipe—so they need to maximize the salt's impact. But a chicken that is marinating in, say, citrus juice and a teaspoon of salt will actually absorb only a tiny amount of the marinade. When you toss out the marinade, you also toss out most of the salt and its seasoning effect. It's better to use a little salt in the marinade, then directly sprinkle the majority of the salt on the chicken after it comes out of the marinade. The same goes for breaded items: If all the salt is in the panko coating for your fish fillet and you discard half of that panko after dredging, half of the flavor goes with it. Instead, sprinkle salt directly on the fish fillet, and then coat it with the breading.

23. YOU POP MEAT STRAIGHT FROM THE FRIDGE INTO THE OVEN OR ONTO THE GRILL.

RESULT: Food cooks unevenly: The outside is overdone, and the inside rare or raw.

Meats will cook much more evenly if you allow them to stand at room temperature for 15 to 30 minutes (depending on the size of the cut) to take the chill off. A large roast that goes into the oven refrigerator-cold will likely yield a piece of meat in which the outside is over-cooked while the core struggles to get to a safe eating temperature. As you slice the roast, you'll see a bull's-eye effect: The middle is rare (or even raw) while the outside is well done.

This is less of a problem with smaller cuts like chicken breasts—though even those benefit from resting at room temperature for five or 10 minutes before cooking. "If you're spending money on a good piece of meat," says Associate Food Editor Tim Cebula, "it would be a shame to end up with an easily preventable bull's-eye." This is the sort of practice that, while easily overlooked, can produce the admirable food that signals a great cook at work.

Cajun Steak Frites with Kale

Frites:

1 pound baking potatoes, cut lengthwise into ¼-inch-thick strips
1 tablespoon olive oil
1 teaspoon hot sauce
¾ teaspoon dried thyme
¼ teaspoon garlic salt
Cooking spray

Steak:

1 (1-pound) flank steak, trimmed
¼ teaspoon salt
¼ teaspoon garlic powder
¼ teaspoon dried thyme
¼ teaspoon dried oregano
⅛ teaspoon ground cumin
⅛ teaspoon paprika
⅛ teaspoon chili powder
⅛ teaspoon ground red pepper
⅛ teaspoon freshly ground black pepper

Kale:

1 tablespoon olive oil
1 garlic clove, minced
1 pound kale, stemmed and shredded
¼ cup water
1 teaspoon red wine vinegar
¼ teaspoon salt
¼ teaspoon freshly ground black pepper

1. Preheat oven to 500°.
2. To prepare frites, heat a large baking sheet in oven for 5 minutes. Combine potatoes, 1 tablespoon oil, and hot sauce in a large bowl. Add ¾ teaspoon thyme and garlic salt; toss to combine. Remove preheated pan from oven. Coat pan with cooking spray. Arrange potatoes in a single layer on prepared pan. Bake at 500° for 40 minutes or until crisp, turn-ing once after 20 minutes. Remove from oven; cover and keep warm.
3. Preheat broiler.
4. To prepare steak, let steak stand at room temperature 15 minutes. Combine ¼ teaspoon salt and next 8 ingredients; sprinkle both sides of steak with spice blend. Place steak on a broiler pan coated with cooking spray; broil 6 minutes on each side or until desired degree of doneness. Cover and let rest 5 minutes. Cut steak diagonally across grain into thin slices.
5. To prepare kale, heat a large skillet over medium heat. Add 1 tablespoon oil and minced garlic; cook 1 minute, stirring constantly. Add kale and ¼ cup water; cover and cook 5 minutes or until tender. Remove from heat; stir in vinegar and remaining ingredients. Arrange 1 cup kale and 3 ounces steak on each of 4 plates; divide frites evenly among servings. Yield: 4 servings.

CALORIES 369; FAT 14.3g (sat 3.9g, mono 7.6g, poly 1.3g); PROTEIN 28.1g; CARB 32.7g; FIBER 4.6g; CHOL 45mg; IRON 4.2mg; SODIUM 459mg; CALC 149mg

24. YOU DON'T KNOW WHEN TO ABANDON SHIP AND START OVER.

RESULT: You serve a disappointing meal. And you know it's disappointing!

If you badly burn the garlic you're sautéing for marinara sauce, you could dump it and start again fresh without losing too much time. It's human nature to try to cover up this sort of seemingly minor error and proceed, hoping against evidence (and that nagging voice in the back of your mind) that the dish will turn out OK. But after investing an hour in that slowly simmered sauce, the whole pot tastes of bitter, burned garlic.

There's no shame in making a mistake; we all do. And while it may feel a bit wasteful to throw food in the trash, tossing out burned garlic, charred nuts, or smoking oil is the right thing to do. Start again fresh (if you have extras of the ingredients). Of course, there is a no-turning-back point, too. If you've overcooked a chicken because you didn't use a meat thermometer, you're bound to serve an overcooked chicken. At that point, the best practice is to 'fess up, apologize, pass the wine, and move on.

25. YOU USE INFERIOR INGREDIENTS.

RESULT: Sigh.

We save this point for last because it's the linchpin of great cooking: Good food begins and ends with the ingredients. The dishes you cook will only be as mediocre, good, or superb as the ingredients you put in them. That's why, as a rule, we recommend using high-quality olive oil, heritage meats, imported prosciutto, real Parmigiano-Reggiano cheese, and great butter, whenever available and affordable. Lower-quality substitutes simply don't taste as good and, as with so much healthy cooking, you don't have as much fat to compensate (fat provides desirable mouthfeel and carries a lot of flavor).

Out-of-season produce (tomatoes, apples, and many other supermarket fruits and vegetables) also disappoints, even when it looks good. Winter eggplant is likely to be bitter and spongy, so it's best to wait until summer to make that grilled eggplant stack. Canned tomatoes may be a better option for pasta sauces out of season. And you can even go wrong with in-season produce if you choose a substandard product. A hard, unripe mango or avocado will ruin your fruit salsa.

Always shop for the best ingredients. They're the foundation of good cooking and why we strive not to make the mistakes described here. Choose top-notch produce, meats, and cheeses, and protect them as you would anything else precious—handle with love, respect, and care so you can be a steward of the joys of great food. Your cooking will invariably turn out better.

RUSH-HOUR RESCUE 1-2-3

Registered dietitian, mother, and culinary star Ellie Krieger shares healthy recipes that are ready in a hurry.

When it comes to the weeknight meal crunch, TV Food Network star Ellie Krieger is time deprived, tired, and not keen to work any harder than necessary in the kitchen. But she doesn't stress about what's for dinner anymore. Her secret: a simple 1-2-3 system for stocking the fridge and larder with easy-to-fix foods. "I want to come home and have the right ingredients for a delicious, healthy meal at my fingertips," says Krieger. "Then I don't have to worry about it."

Quick & Easy

Spicy Chicken Fried Rice with Peanuts

Stir-fried rice is ideal for using up leftover brown rice, veggies, and chicken. (Prepare with boil-in-bag brown rice, if you don't have leftover rice.) This flavorful entrée isn't overly fiery, despite the generous amount of crushed red pepper; you can always use less of the spice if you prefer. Serve with steamed baby bok choy.
28-Minute Stir-Fry: A savory, spicy sauce coats the whole-grain rice, chicken, and veggies in this dish.
22-Minute Bok Choy: Mild-flavored bok choy is the perfect fresh side to this hearty entrée.

¼ cup less-sodium soy sauce
1 tablespoon dark brown sugar
1 teaspoon dark sesame oil
¾ teaspoon crushed red pepper
2 tablespoons canola oil
2 cups diced red bell pepper (about 2)
1 cup diced onion
¼ cup thinly sliced green onions, divided
2 tablespoons minced peeled fresh ginger
2 large garlic cloves, minced
5 cups cold cooked brown rice
2 cups diced cooked chicken (about 1 pound)
1 (8-ounce) can sliced water chestnuts, drained and chopped
⅓ cup chopped unsalted, dry-roasted peanuts

1. Combine first 4 ingredients in a small bowl; stir well with a whisk.
2. Heat canola oil in a wok or large nonstick skillet over medium-high heat. Add bell pepper, diced onion, and 2 tablespoons green onions to pan; stir-fry 3 minutes or until tender. Add ginger and garlic; stir-fry 1 minute. Add rice, chicken, and water chestnuts; stir-fry 5 minutes or until thoroughly heated, stirring gently. Add soy sauce mixture; cook 2 minutes, tossing gently to coat. Sprinkle with remaining 2 tablespoons green onions and peanuts. Yield: 5 servings (serving size: about 1¾ cups rice mixture, about 1¼ teaspoons green onions, and 1 tablespoon peanuts).

CALORIES 482; FAT 14.8g (sat 2.1g, mono 7.2g, poly 4.6g); PROTEIN 26.3g; CARB 61.8g; FIBER 6.9g; CHOL 48mg; IRON 2.8mg; SODIUM 479mg; CALC 59mg

Maple-Mustard Pork Chops with Winter Squash Puree

(pictured on page 247)

15-Minute Pork Chops: An easy, tasty pan sauce turns plain ole pork into a guest-worthy entrée.
19-Minute Squash Puree: Frozen butternut squash offers all the nutrition of fresh. It's just easier to prep.
10-Minute Green Beans: Crisp-tender steamed green beans add fiber, flavor, and color to the plate.

4 (6-ounce) bone-in center-cut pork chops
1/2 teaspoon salt, divided
1/4 teaspoon freshly ground black pepper
Cooking spray
1 tablespoon butter
2 tablespoons finely chopped shallots
1/4 cup fat-free, less-sodium chicken broth
2 tablespoons Dijon mustard
2 tablespoons maple syrup
2 tablespoons chopped fresh flat-leaf parsley

1. Sprinkle both sides of pork with 1/4 teaspoon salt and pepper.
2. Heat a large skillet over medium-high heat. Coat pan with cooking spray. Add pork to pan; cook 3 minutes on each side or until cooked through, but with a slight blush in center. Remove from pan; keep warm.
3. Return pan to medium-high heat. Add butter to pan, swirling pan to coat. Add shallots; sauté 3 minutes or until tender and translucent. Add broth; bring to a boil, and cook 1 minute. Stir in mustard, syrup, and remaining 1/4 teaspoon salt; cook 1 minute or until slightly thick. Return pork to pan. Cook pork 1 minute on each side or until thoroughly heated (be careful not to overcook pork). Serve pork with sauce. Garnish each serving with 1 1/2 teaspoons parsley. Yield: 4 servings (serving size: 1 pork chop and 1 tablespoon sauce).

CALORIES 283; **FAT** 15.1g (sat 6.3g, mono 6.2g, poly 1g); **PROTEIN** 27.1g; **CARB** 8.2g; **FIBER** 0.3g; **CHOL** 84mg; **IRON** 1.1mg; **SODIUM** 456mg; **CALC** 44mg

Quick Winter Squash Puree:

This easy side comes together quickly with convenient frozen winter squash. Pair with Maple-Mustard Pork Chops or roast chicken for a simple, colorful, nutrient-rich dish.

1/3 cup fat-free, less-sodium chicken broth
2 (12-ounce) packages frozen cooked butternut squash
1 tablespoon butter
1/2 teaspoon grated orange rind
1 1/2 teaspoons maple syrup
1/4 teaspoon salt
1/4 teaspoon freshly ground black pepper

1. Place broth and squash in a large saucepan over medium heat. Cover and cook 15 minutes or until thoroughly heated, stirring occasionally. Add butter and remaining ingredients; stir until combined. Yield: 4 servings (serving size: 3/4 cup).

CALORIES 100; **FAT** 3g (sat 1.8g, mono 0.8g, poly 0.2g); **PROTEIN** 2.4g; **CARB** 19g; **FIBER** 4.9g; **CHOL** 8mg; **IRON** 1mg; **SODIUM** 204mg; **CALC** 37mg

Vegetable and Spicy Sausage Soup with Cheese "Crackers"

A little bit of sausage adds big flavor to this veggie-rich soup. Look for 50%-less-fat or light pork sausage near the other breakfast sausage in the refrigerated section of your supermarket. The cheese crackers can be assembled and baked while the soup simmers. Serve with a green salad and breadsticks.
8-Minute Cheese Crackers: These cheese crisps boost calcium and protein, plus they add a welcome salty note.
50-Minute Soup: This chock-full-of-veggies soup makes it easy to eat a variety of produce.

4 ounces 50%-less-fat pork sausage (such as Jimmy Dean)
1 1/2 cups finely chopped onion
1 1/4 cups finely chopped zucchini
1/2 cup finely chopped carrot
1/3 cup finely chopped celery
1/2 teaspoon kosher salt, divided
2 garlic cloves, minced
2 tablespoons tomato paste
1/8 teaspoon ground red pepper
3 cups fat-free, less-sodium chicken broth, divided
2 (15.5-ounce) cans organic cannellini beans, rinsed, drained, and divided
1/3 cup half-and-half
1 teaspoon chopped fresh rosemary
1/2 teaspoon freshly ground black pepper
5 tablespoons grated fresh Parmigiano-Reggiano cheese
1/8 teaspoon freshly ground black pepper

1. Heat a large Dutch oven over medium-high heat. Add sausage to pan, and cook 4 minutes or until browned, stirring to crumble. Remove from pan; keep warm.
2. Return pan to medium heat. Add onion, zucchini, carrot, celery, 1/4 teaspoon salt, and garlic; cook 5 minutes or until vegetables are tender, stirring frequently. Stir in tomato paste and red pepper; cook 1 minute, stirring constantly. Place 1 cup vegetable mixture, 1/2 cup broth, and 1 can of beans in a food processor, and process until smooth. Return pureed bean mixture to pan. Add remaining 2 1/2 cups broth and 1 can beans; bring to a boil. Reduce heat, and simmer 20 minutes or until vegetables are thoroughly cooked. Remove from heat, and stir in remaining 1/4 teaspoon salt, half-and-half, rosemary, and 1/2 teaspoon black pepper. Cover and keep warm.
3. Preheat oven to 500°.
4. While soup simmers, combine cheese and 1/8 teaspoon black pepper in a small bowl. Drop cheese mixture by tablespoonfuls to make 5 mounds, 4 inches apart, on a baking sheet covered with parchment paper. Pat mounds into 3-inch circles. Bake at 500° for 3 minutes or until golden and bubbling. Cool on pan 3 minutes.
5. Ladle about 1 cup soup into each of 5 bowls; top each serving with about 2 1/2 tablespoons sausage and 1 cheese "cracker." Yield: 5 servings.

CALORIES 230; **FAT** 8.6g (sat 3.5g, mono 2.4g, poly 0.8g); **PROTEIN** 13.2g; **CARB** 25.1g; **FIBER** 9g; **CHOL** 26mg; **IRON** 2.3mg; **SODIUM** 711mg; **CALC** 175mg

THE RUSH-HOUR METHOD

1 STICK WITH 10-MINUTE MEATS & SEAFOOD. During the week, rely on meat, poultry, and fish selections that cook quickly, preferably in less than 10 minutes. "I love frozen shrimp because you can thaw them in 5 minutes," says Krieger, and then fix any number of ways. "If unexpected company drops by, you can make shrimp cocktail. Or you can cook the shrimp in a little white wine or broth and toss with vegetables or pasta." Also on her easy list: boneless chicken breast and pork tenderloin. Slice them, cut them into strips or medallions, and they cook in 4 or 5 minutes.

2 SHOP FOR LOW-FUSS VEGGIES. "It can be daunting to think about peeling and chopping on a weeknight," admits Krieger. Precut veggies or varieties that take little prep are staples. Bags of prewashed greens can make a salad or add the final flourish to pasta tosses or soups. Fresh or flash-roasted grape tomatoes can dress up salads. And Krieger says she wouldn't be without her freezer stash of favorite veggies. Frozen mashed winter squash, for instance, can be cooked quickly and drizzled with maple syrup for an easy side.

3 ADD A SIDE OF FAST-COOKING WHOLE GRAINS. To round out the meal, Krieger suggests keeping fast-fix whole-grain sides in the pantry. Whole-wheat couscous, quinoa, and precooked brown rice in a pouch are all tasty and speedy options. She thinks people might feel guilty about using precooked items, but they are huge time-savers. "We all take shortcuts," says Krieger. "I think it's OK to use packaged convenience foods as long as they don't come with a lot of additives or seasonings." Unadorned varieties are not only healthier, but they also allow you to season to your family's taste.

Quick & Easy
Ravioli Toss

This recipe barely counts as cooking, yet you can take full credit as everyone devours it. Vary the veggies you toss with the ravioli. Try a combo of bell peppers and sliced red onion, or tomatoes, garlic, and plenty of fresh herbs. A simple side of blanched broccoli rabe (rapini) or broccoli rounds out the meal.
35-Minute Ravioli Toss: Your family won't know this is 100% whole-wheat pasta, it's so cheesy-good.
12-Minute Broccoli Rabe: Seasoned with salt and lemon juice, blanched broccoli rabe is a pretty side.
5-Minute Green Beans (in Ravioli Toss): Krieger saves time by cooking the green beans with the pasta.

2 (9-ounce) packages refrigerated whole-wheat four-cheese ravioli
2 cups (2-inch) cut green beans (about ½ pound)
½ cup thinly sliced sun-dried tomatoes, packed without oil (about 6)
2 tablespoons olive oil
2 tablespoons red wine vinegar
4 plum tomatoes, chopped (about 1 pound)
1 garlic clove, minced
½ teaspoon kosher salt
¼ teaspoon freshly ground black pepper
¼ cup (1 ounce) shaved fresh Parmigiano-Reggiano cheese

1. Prepare pasta according to package directions, omitting salt and fat. Add beans to pasta during last 5 minutes of cooking. Drain.
2. Combine sun-dried tomatoes and next 4 ingredients in a large bowl. Add pasta mixture, salt, and pepper; toss gently to combine. Top with cheese. Yield: 6 servings (serving size: 1½ cups pasta mixture and about 2 teaspoons cheese).

CALORIES 347; **FAT** 14.5g (sat 6.1g, mono 3.6g, poly 0.6g); **PROTEIN** 15.2g; **CARB** 40g; **FIBER** 6.5g; **CHOL** 60mg; **IRON** 2.4mg; **SODIUM** 785mg; **CALC** 178mg

---

NUTRITION MADE EASY
PIZZA, PRONTO

A healthy, nutritious pie, ready in about 20 minutes.

At the rate Americans eat pizza, you'd think it was an official Food Guide Pyramid category. The amount of pizza we consume in a day is best measured in acres—100, to be exact. (That's about the size of 100 football fields.) Factor that against the ease with which pizza can turn into a nutritional nightmare, and a window into the obesity crisis opens. Two slices of a certain purveyor's large Italian Sausage and Red Onion pizza tally up to 700 calories and 1,720 milligrams sodium. Our twist on the same pizza? A slim 420 calories and 715mg sodium. And you can have our healthy version ready in the time it would take to have one of those weighed-down pies delivered to your door.

Manchego and Chorizo Pizza

½ pound broccoli rabe (rapini), trimmed
⅛ teaspoon salt
1 (12-ounce) prebaked pizza crust (such as Mama Mary's)
½ cup (2 ounces) shredded Manchego cheese
1 link Spanish chorizo sausage (about 2 ounces), thinly sliced
⅔ cup chopped plum tomato
¼ cup vertically sliced red onion

1. Preheat oven to 450°.
2. Cook broccoli rabe in boiling water 4 minutes or until tender. Drain and rinse with cold water. Drain; squeeze excess moisture from broccoli rabe, and pat dry with paper towels. Coarsely chop, and sprinkle with salt.
3. Place crust on a baking sheet. Sprinkle evenly with cheese. Top with broccoli rabe, chorizo, tomato, and onion. Bake at 450° for 12 minutes or until crust browns. Cut into 8 wedges. Yield: 4 servings (serving size: 2 wedges).

CALORIES 382; **FAT** 15.4g (sat 4.7g, mono 3.7g, poly 5.6g); **PROTEIN** 15.1g; **CARB** 46.1g; **FIBER** 5.1g; **CHOL** 23mg; **IRON** 3.6mg; **SODIUM** 624mg; **CALC** 175mg

FIVE SMART TOPPING TRADE-OFFS

We did the nutritional math to calculate simple switches that add up to big calorie, fat, and sodium savings. Have your pie and eat it, too, with our picks.

TOMATO-BASED SAUCE
It has about half the sodium of a white sauce counterpart (made of eggs, cream, and sometimes cheese), plus going red helps you avoid 8 grams of saturated fat.

BACON
It has all the savory, porky notes of pancetta (and a comparable amount of saturated fat) but contains half the sodium of the Italian version.

SPANISH CHORIZO
For cured meat, super-seasoned chorizo beats pepperoni with 20 fewer calories and 80 fewer milligrams of sodium in similar serving sizes.

KALAMATA OLIVES
They deliver the same briny, salty notes of anchovies, but olives make a better choice because a comparable portion undercuts anchovies' sodium level by half.

CHICKEN APPLE SAUSAGE
While it's not surprising that poultry is a healthier choice than Italian pork sausage, it is shocking that the poultry version has half the calories, fat, and saturated fat, compared to the same portion of pork.

Chicken Sausage, Sweet Onion, and Fennel Pizza

Making pizza nutritious is all about proportion. The amounts of sausage and cheese are just right to keep calories, sodium, and saturated fat in check.

3 ounces chicken apple sausage, chopped (such as Gerhard's)
2 teaspoons olive oil
1½ cups vertically sliced Oso Sweet or other sweet onion
1 cup thinly sliced fennel bulb (about 1 small bulb)
¼ teaspoon salt
1 (12-ounce) prebaked pizza crust (such as Mama Mary's)
¾ cup (3 ounces) shredded Gouda cheese
1 tablespoon chopped fresh chives

1. Preheat oven to 450°.
2. Heat a large nonstick skillet over medium-high heat. Add sausage to pan; sauté 4 minutes or until browned, stirring occasionally. Remove from pan.
3. Add oil to pan; swirl to coat. Add onion, fennel, and salt; cover and cook 10 minutes or until tender and lightly browned, stirring occasionally.
4. Place pizza crust on a baking sheet. Top evenly with onion mixture; sprinkle with cheese, and top evenly with sausage. Bake at 450° for 12 minutes or until cheese melts. Sprinkle evenly with chives. Cut pizza into 8 wedges. Yield: 4 servings (serving size: 2 wedges).

CALORIES 420; FAT 18.9g (sat 6.1g, mono 5.4g, poly 5.6g); PROTEIN 16g; CARB 48.4g; FIBER 3.4g; CHOL 40mg; IRON 3.4mg; SODIUM 715mg; CALC 248mg

Staff Favorite
Pear and Prosciutto Pizza

Pit peppery arugula against a base of creamy, sweet caramelized onions. Also appearing: prudent amounts of salty prosciutto, cheese, and walnuts.

2 teaspoons olive oil
2 cups vertically sliced Oso Sweet or other sweet onion
1 (12-ounce) prebaked pizza crust (such as Mama Mary's)
½ cup (2 ounces) shredded provolone cheese
1 medium pear, thinly sliced
2 ounces prosciutto, cut into thin strips
Dash of freshly ground black pepper
2 tablespoons chopped walnuts, toasted
1½ cups baby arugula leaves
1 teaspoon sherry vinegar

1. Preheat oven to 450°.
2. Heat oil in a large nonstick skillet over medium-high heat. Add onion to pan; cover and cook 3 minutes. Uncover and cook 10 minutes or until golden brown, stirring frequently.
3. Place pizza crust on a baking sheet. Top evenly with onion; sprinkle with cheese. Top evenly with pear and prosciutto. Sprinkle with pepper. Bake at 450° for 12 minutes or until cheese melts. Sprinkle with nuts. Place arugula in a medium bowl. Drizzle vinegar over greens; toss gently to coat. Top pizza evenly with arugula mixture. Cut pizza into 8 wedges. Yield: 4 servings (serving size: 2 wedges).

CALORIES 446; FAT 18.8g (sat 4.9g, mono 5.1g, poly 7.3g); PROTEIN 16.6g; CARB 55.5g; FIBER 3.8g; CHOL 17mg; IRON 3.6mg; SODIUM 664mg; CALC 221mg

A BIT OF IRISH WARMTH

Family, tradition, hearty food, a patron saint: Share the luck of these celebrating Irish-Americans.

Long before the first band marched in Southie's (South Boston's) now-famous parade, and long before Chicago colored its river green, Irish Catholics quietly honored St. Patrick on March 17th. In Ireland it was a national holiday, the anniversary of the death of a patron saint who converted pagans to Christianity. Until the 1970s, Irish bars weren't even allowed to open.

This idea of a more reverent, religious holiday was carried to America. Margaret Johnson, a second-generation Irish-American and Irish food expert who now lives on Long Island in New York, recalls St. Patrick's Day from her childhood as a time for family, community, and food. "I grew up in Newburyport, Massachusetts," says Johnson of the small, mostly Catholic community where she lived. "Almost all my friends had last names like McLaughlin, Sullivan, or O'Keefe. My maiden name was McGlew. So we were all alike."

At home, her extended family celebrated by gathering for corned beef and cabbage prepared by her mother. Though not traditionally Irish, this dish was the closest thing they could find to approximate the bacon and cabbage Margaret's Irish-born grandmother knew in the old country, where butchers cured pork in a manner similar to Jewish-American corned beef.

Johnson, the author of seven Irish cookbooks (two published in Ireland), knows a thing or two about authentic cuisine. Asked if she cooks Irish food year-round or only for St. Patrick's Day, she responds, "People eat Italian food 365 days a year, so why not Irish?" Root veggies like parsnips, turnips, rutabagas, and of course potatoes are popular in Irish cooking. "It's not uncommon to serve potatoes three or four different ways," Johnson says. "Boiled, mashed, and fried—all in the same meal."

Although we tend to think of lamb, beef, and pork, Ireland is also known for its seafood, like smoked salmon. "And considering that the country is an island surrounded by some of the cleanest water on the planet, the fish there is wonderful," Johnson says.

A meal is typically served with hearty Irish soda bread, be it brown or white. The real deal is quite different from the American version, which is usually sweet and more cake-like, with raisins and caraway seeds.

Make Ahead • Freezable
Brown Soda Bread

Whole-wheat flour, wheat germ, and steel-cut oats (also called Irish oatmeal) make this a super-healthy interpretation of the classic Irish bread.

Cooking spray
11.25 ounces whole-wheat flour (about 2½ cups)
2.25 ounces all-purpose flour (about ½ cup)
½ cup steel-cut oats (such as McCann's)
2 tablespoons brown sugar
1 tablespoon wheat germ
1 teaspoon baking soda
1 teaspoon baking powder
½ teaspoon salt
2 cups low-fat buttermilk
1 large egg, lightly beaten

1. Preheat oven to 325°.
2. Coat a 9 x 5–inch loaf pan with cooking spray. Line pan with parchment paper, and coat with cooking spray.
3. Weigh or lightly spoon flours into dry measuring cups, and level with a knife. Combine flours and next 6 ingredients. Combine buttermilk and egg; add to flour mixture. Stir just until combined.
4. Spoon mixture into prepared pan. Bake at 325° for 1 hour and 5 minutes or until a wooden pick inserted in center comes out clean. Invert bread onto a wire rack; cool completely. Remove parchment; slice bread into 12 slices. Yield: 12 servings (serving size: 1 slice).

CALORIES 160; FAT 1.8g (sat 0.5g, mono 0.2g, poly 0.3g); PROTEIN 7.2g; CARB 30.8g; FIBER 4g; CHOL 18mg; IRON 1.7mg; SODIUM 286mg; CALC 86mg

Ploughman's Lunch Platter

A traditional pub salad made with sausages or sliced meats, cheese, and any combination of mixed lettuce, tomatoes, cucumbers, coleslaw, or chutney, this dish is always served with soda bread.

2 tablespoons white balsamic vinegar
1 tablespoon whole-grain Dijon mustard
1 tablespoon Dijon mustard
1 teaspoon honey
½ teaspoon fresh lemon juice
¼ teaspoon freshly ground black pepper
½ cup extra-virgin olive oil
8 cups chopped romaine lettuce
3 (3-ounce) links chicken apple sausage, cooked and sliced diagonally
4 ounces reduced-fat cheddar cheese (such as Kerrygold), sliced
3 slices Brown Soda Bread (page 63), each cut into quarters
2 ounces cornichons
¾ cup Tomato Chutney

1. Combine first 6 ingredients in a large bowl, stirring well. Slowly drizzle oil into vinegar mixture, stirring constantly with a whisk. Add lettuce; toss to coat. Arrange salad on a platter with sausage, cheese, Brown Soda Bread, and cornichons. Place Tomato Chutney in a bowl; add to platter. Yield: 6 servings (serving size: 1¼ cups salad, 1½ ounces sausage, ¾ ounce cheese, ½ bread slice, about 2 cornichons, and about 2 tablespoons chutney).

CALORIES 440; **FAT** 27.3g (sat 6.1g, mono 14g, poly 2.4g); **PROTEIN** 15.5g; **CARB** 36.9g; **FIBER** 5.4g; **CHOL** 50mg; **IRON** 2.5mg; **SODIUM** 968mg; **CALC** 212mg

Tomato Chutney:

1¼ cups cider vinegar
½ cup sugar
2 teaspoons sea salt
1 teaspoon ground ginger
½ teaspoon cardamom seeds, crushed
½ teaspoon mustard seeds
¼ teaspoon ground cloves
1 cup chopped onion
½ cup golden raisins
2 tablespoons minced fresh garlic
1 tablespoon olive oil
¼ teaspoon black pepper
7 plum tomatoes, peeled and quartered

1. Place first 7 ingredients in a large saucepan over medium-low heat; bring to a boil. Add onion and remaining ingredients; stir to combine. Reduce heat, and simmer 1½ hours or until thick, stirring occasionally. Yield: 2 cups (serving size: 2 tablespoons).

CALORIES 68; **FAT** 1.2g (sat 0.2g, mono 0.7g, poly 0.2g); **PROTEIN** 0.6g; **CARB** 13.3g; **FIBER** 0.7g; **CHOL** 0mg; **IRON** 0.3mg; **SODIUM** 292mg; **CALC** 9mg

---

REVIVING A TRADITION

Legend has it that St. Patrick taught the Irish to distill wine. Grapes being scant, they moved on to grains. A vast industry eventually arose and then crashed after Prohibition cut exports. A revival is now under way, and more choices are available. Irish whiskey is light and smooth, a middle ground between intense bourbon and peaty Scotch. Here are three favorites from a staff tasting.

BUSHMILLS BLACK BUSH ($36)
From the oldest licensed distillery in the world, this whiskey has a slightly sweet caramel flavor, but you'll also taste floral notes and vanilla.

REDBREAST 12 YEAR ($40)
Just as you might expect from this deep amber-colored gem, the flavor is nutty and spicy with a faint sweetness, and the finish goes on and on.

JAMESON 18 YEAR LIMITED RESERVE ($85)
Lightly smoky with a hint of leather, this outstanding whiskey has a complex buttery flavor with hints of citrus and spice.

Irish Bacon and Cabbage with Mustard Sauce

This dish is more authentic than the ubiquitous corned beef and cabbage, though it is quite similar in that Irish boiling bacon is a cured meat, too. The boiling bacon is also leaner than traditional American bacon (which does not make an appropriate substitute). Order the Irish bacon from tommymoloneys.com.

2 pounds Irish boiling bacon (such as Tommy Moloney's)
14 cups water, divided
12 ounces small red potatoes
4 medium carrots, cut into 1-inch pieces
1 (3-pound) cabbage, trimmed, cored, and quartered
2 tablespoons unsalted butter
1 small onion, finely chopped
1 garlic clove, minced
⅔ cup dry white wine
2 teaspoons whole-grain Dijon mustard
1¼ cups 2% reduced-fat milk
¼ teaspoon freshly ground black pepper
⅛ teaspoon salt

1. Place bacon in a large Dutch oven; cover with 8 cups water. Bring to a boil; cover, reduce heat, and simmer 2 hours, skimming foam from liquid as necessary.
2. Remove bacon from pan; cover and keep warm. Remove 1¼ cups cooking liquid from pan; reserve cooking liquid for mustard sauce. Discard remaining cooking liquid.
3. Add potatoes, carrots, and cabbage to pan; cover with remaining 6 cups water. Bring to a boil. Cover and simmer 20 minutes or until vegetables are tender; drain. Cut each cabbage quarter in half lengthwise.
4. Melt butter in a medium saucepan over medium heat. Add onion and garlic; cook 3 minutes or until tender, stirring occasionally. Stir in wine and mustard; cook 2 minutes. Add reserved 1¼ cups bacon cooking liquid and milk. Bring to a boil; cook 20 minutes or until reduced to 2 cups, stirring frequently. Stir in black pepper and salt. Cut bacon into 8 slices; serve with sauce and vegetables. Yield: 8 servings (serving size:

3 ounces bacon, 1 cabbage wedge, ½ cup carrot, about 1½ ounces potato, and ¼ cup sauce).

CALORIES 305; **FAT** 13g (sat 5.3g, mono 5.5g, poly 1g); **PROTEIN** 25.2g; **CARB** 24.9g; **FIBER** 5.5g; **CHOL** 76mg; **IRON** 1.6mg; **SODIUM** 909mg; **CALC** 175mg

Staff Favorite • Make Ahead
Freezable

Beef and Guinness Stew

2 tablespoons canola oil, divided
1 tablespoon butter, divided
¼ cup all-purpose flour
2 pounds boneless chuck roast, trimmed and cut into 1-inch cubes
1 teaspoon salt, divided
5 cups chopped onion (about 3 onions)
1 tablespoon tomato paste
4 cups fat-free, less-sodium beef broth
1 (11.2-ounce) bottle Guinness Draught
1 tablespoon raisins
1 teaspoon caraway seeds
½ teaspoon black pepper
1½ cups (½-inch-thick) diagonal slices carrot (about 8 ounces)
1½ cups (½-inch-thick) diagonal slices parsnip (about 8 ounces)
1 cup (½-inch) cubed peeled turnip (about 8 ounces)
2 tablespoons finely chopped fresh flat-leaf parsley

1. Heat 1 tablespoon oil in a Dutch oven over medium-high heat. Add 1½ teaspoons butter to pan. Place flour in a shallow dish. Sprinkle beef with ½ teaspoon salt; dredge beef in flour. Add half of beef to pan; cook 5 minutes, turning to brown on all sides. Remove beef from pan with a slotted spoon. Repeat procedure with remaining 1 tablespoon oil, 1½ teaspoons butter, and beef.
2. Add onion to pan; cook 5 minutes or until tender, stirring occasionally. Stir in tomato paste; cook 1 minute, stirring frequently. Stir in broth and beer, scraping pan to loosen browned bits. Return meat to pan. Stir in remaining ½ teaspoon salt, raisins, caraway seeds, and pepper; bring to a boil. Cover, reduce heat, and simmer 1 hour, stirring occasionally. Uncover and bring to a boil. Cook 50 minutes, stirring occasionally. Add carrot, parsnip, and turnip. Cover, reduce heat to low, and simmer 30 minutes, stirring occasionally. Uncover and bring to a boil; cook 10 minutes or until vegetables are tender. Sprinkle with parsley. Yield: 8 servings (serving size: about 1 cup).

CALORIES 365; **FAT** 19.4g (sat 6.8g, mono 8.6g, poly 1.7g); **PROTEIN** 25.3g; **CARB** 18.8g; **FIBER** 3.6g; **CHOL** 62mg; **IRON** 2.6mg; **SODIUM** 454mg; **CALC** 52mg

Make Ahead

Black and Tan Brownies

Historically, the phrase "black and tan" referred to the much-reviled auxiliary force of English soldiers sent to Ireland to suppress the Irish rebels after the 1916 Easter Rising. Eventually, a much-loved drink made with half Guinness Stout and half Harp Lager assumed the name, and now this two-toned brownie (with the addition of Guinness) shares it.

Tan Brownies:
6 tablespoons butter, softened
1½ cups packed brown sugar
2 large eggs
1 teaspoon vanilla extract
4.5 ounces all-purpose flour (about 1 cup)
1 teaspoon baking powder
¼ teaspoon salt
½ cup chopped pecans
Cooking spray
Black Brownies:
3 ounces unsweetened chocolate, finely chopped
4 tablespoons butter
1 cup granulated sugar
2 large eggs
1 teaspoon vanilla extract
1 cup Guinness Stout
4.5 ounces all-purpose flour (about 1 cup)
¼ teaspoon salt

1. Place one rack in lower third of oven; place another rack in center of oven. Preheat oven to 350°.
2. To prepare Tan Brownies, place 6 tablespoons butter and brown sugar in a medium bowl; beat with a mixer at medium speed until light and fluffy. Beat in 2 eggs and 1 teaspoon vanilla. Weigh or lightly spoon 4.5 ounces (about 1 cup) flour into a dry measuring cup; level with a knife. Combine 4.5 ounces flour, baking powder, and ¼ teaspoon salt, stirring well. Add flour mixture and pecans to sugar mixture, beating just until combined. Spoon into a 13 x 9–inch baking pan coated with cooking spray, spreading evenly with a knife or rubber spatula. Bake at 350° in lower third of oven for 15 minutes.
3. To prepare Black Brownies, melt chocolate and 4 tablespoons butter in a large microwave-safe bowl at HIGH 1 minute or until melted, stirring after every 20 seconds until smooth. Add granulated sugar, stirring until well combined. Add 2 eggs, 1 teaspoon vanilla, and Guinness, stirring with a whisk until well combined. Weigh or lightly spoon 4.5 ounces (about 1 cup) flour into a dry measuring cup; level with a knife. Combine 4.5 ounces flour and ¼ teaspoon salt, stirring well. Add flour mixture to chocolate mixture, stirring to combine. Pour mixture evenly over Tan Brownies.
4. Bake on center rack at 350° for 25 minutes or until a wooden pick inserted into center comes out almost clean. Cool in pan on a wire rack; cut into squares. Yield: 32 servings.

CALORIES 162; **FAT** 7g (sat 3.4g, mono 2.4g, poly 0.7g); **PROTEIN** 2.2g; **CARB** 23.7g; **FIBER** 0.8g; **CHOL** 36mg; **IRON** 1.2mg; **SODIUM** 87mg; **CALC** 29mg

Smoked Salmon with Tangy Horseradish Sauce

Although smoked Irish salmon is traditional, any smoked salmon will work in this dish—just make sure to purchase smoked wild salmon.

1/3 cup organic canola mayonnaise (such as Spectrum)
1 tablespoon chopped fresh flat-leaf parsley
1 tablespoon prepared horseradish
1 tablespoon whole-grain Dijon mustard
1/4 teaspoon freshly ground black pepper
12 slices Brown Soda Bread (page 63)
12 thin slices smoked salmon (about 8 ounces)
Dill sprigs (optional)

1. Combine first 5 ingredients in a small bowl, stirring well.
2. Place 2 slices Brown Soda Bread on each of 6 plates; top each slice with 1 salmon slice and about 1 teaspoon sauce. Garnish with dill, if desired. Yield: 6 servings.

CALORIES 460; **FAT** 15g (sat 1.8g, mono 4.6g, poly 7.5g); **PROTEIN** 21.1g; **CARB** 62.5g; **FIBER** 8g; **CHOL** 48mg; **IRON** 3.8mg; **SODIUM** 938mg; **CALC** 178mg

Irish Coffee

Irish whiskey has a smooth flavor, as opposed to the smoky quality of Scotch whisky. If you don't have Irish whiskey, substitute bourbon.

1/4 cup whipping cream
1/2 cup Irish whiskey
1/4 cup sugar
4 cups strong coffee

1. Place whipping cream in a medium bowl. Beat with a mixer at high speed until stiff peaks form.
2. Heat 6 mugs by running under very hot water; dry with paper towels.
3. Pour about 4 teaspoons whiskey into each glass. Add 2 teaspoons sugar to each serving; add 2/3 cup coffee, stirring until sugar dissolves. Top each serving with about 1½ tablespoons whipped cream (do not stir). Yield: 6 servings.

CALORIES 111; **FAT** 3.7g (sat 2.3g, mono 1.1g, poly 0.1g); **PROTEIN** 0.4g; **CARB** 8.6g; **FIBER** 0g; **CHOL** 14mg; **IRON** 0mg; **SODIUM** 7mg; **CALC** 10mgs

---

MORE CONTEST FINALISTS

In this second batch of the finalist recipes from the fifth annual *Cooking Light* Ultimate Reader Recipe Contest, we particularly loved the creativity of the contestants, manifested in recipes like oatmeal cookies with dried apple and caramel bits, a fizzy cocktail made with pureed canned fruit, a versatile and adaptable side salad, and fajitas reinvented as soup.

Chili-Spiced Chicken Soup with Stoplight Peppers and Avocado Relish

Category Finalist—Family Dinners
"My husband likes Mexican food—tacos, fajitas, burritos. This recipe is everything you'd find in a fajita in a healthy, tasty soup instead."
—Jamie Miller,
Maple Grove, Minnesota

Spice Blend:
2½ teaspoons chili powder
2 teaspoons ground cumin
1½ teaspoons ground coriander
1 teaspoon dried oregano
1 teaspoon cracked black pepper
½ teaspoon kosher salt
Soup:
1 tablespoon canola oil, divided
1¼ pounds skinless, boneless chicken breast, cut into ½-inch-wide strips
2 cups chopped sweet onion
1 cup chopped red bell pepper
1 cup chopped green bell pepper
1 cup chopped yellow bell pepper
1 tablespoon minced garlic
½ teaspoon salt
2 cups fresh corn kernels
1 (32-ounce) carton fat-free, less-sodium chicken broth
1 (28-ounce) can fire-roasted crushed tomatoes, undrained
2 tablespoons fresh lime juice

Relish:
½ cup chopped fresh cilantro
1/3 cup chopped green onions
1 teaspoon grated lime rind
3 ounces queso fresco, crumbled
1 diced peeled avocado
Cilantro sprigs (optional)

1. To prepare spice blend, combine first 6 ingredients in a small bowl.
2. To prepare soup, heat 2 teaspoons oil in a large nonstick saucepan over medium-high heat. Add chicken; sprinkle 1½ tablespoons spice blend over chicken. Sauté 8 minutes or until done; cool. Chop chicken; set aside.
3. Heat remaining 1 teaspoon oil in pan over medium-high heat; add onion and next 5 ingredients. Sprinkle vegetable mixture with remaining spice blend; sauté 8 minutes or until vegetables are tender. Stir in chicken, corn, broth, and tomatoes; bring to a boil. Reduce heat; simmer 15 minutes. Add lime juice.
4. To prepare relish, combine chopped cilantro and next 4 ingredients.
5. Ladle 1¼ cups soup into bowls; top with ¼ cup relish. Garnish with cilantro sprigs, if desired. Yield: 8 servings.

CALORIES 285; **FAT** 9.6g (sat 2.1g, mono 4.7g, poly 1.8g); **PROTEIN** 27.2g; **CARB** 23.1g; **FIBER** 5.5g; **CHOL** 65mg; **IRON** 3.1mg; **SODIUM** 773mg; **CALC** 99mg

---

GET THE MOST FROM YOUR LIME

Before juicing, roll a room-temperature lime under your palm to break down the cells inside the fruit that hold liquid. If a fruit is especially firm (and sometimes it's hard to find a good one in an entire supermarket bin), microwave the fruit for 20 seconds. You should get 2 to 3 tablespoons of juice per fruit.

Mixed Citrus Green Salad

Category Finalist—Sides & Salads

"I love to experiment, so I'm always creating recipes. The dressing in this salad is one I've been making a long time for fruit salad, but it also works well on leafy greens. Bagged salad mixes are a great time-saver, and you can throw a meal together in no time by adding a protein such as grilled chicken or shrimp."

—Debra Keil,
Owasso, Oklahoma

1 cup red seedless grapes, halved
2 (5-ounce) bags mixed salad greens
1 (11-ounce) can mandarin oranges, drained
1 (8-ounce) container pineapple chunks, drained
1 (8-ounce) container red grapefruit, drained
7 tablespoons Orange–Poppy Seed Dressing
21 walnut halves, toasted

1. Combine first 5 ingredients in a large bowl. Arrange 2 cups salad on each of 7 plates; drizzle with 1 tablespoon Orange–Poppy Seed Dressing; reserve remaining dressing for another use. Top each serving with 3 walnut halves. Yield: 7 servings.

CALORIES 173; FAT 8.6g (sat 1.4g, mono 2.3g, poly 3.8g); PROTEIN 3.3g; CARB 23.5g; FIBER 2.3g; CHOL 4mg; IRON 0.8mg; SODIUM 53mg; CALC 60mg

Orange–Poppy Seed Dressing:
½ cup fresh orange juice
¼ cup honey
¼ cup canola oil
2 tablespoons champagne vinegar
⅛ teaspoon salt
1 teaspoon poppy seeds

1. Place first 5 ingredients in a blender; process until blended. Add poppy seeds; pulse once. Cover and refrigerate. Yield: 1 cup plus 2 tablespoons (serving size: 1 tablespoon).

CALORIES 46; FAT 3.2 (sat 0.2g, mono 1.8g, poly 1g); PROTEIN 0.1g; CARB 4.6g; FIBER 0g; CHOL 0mg; IRON 0mg; SODIUM 17mg; CALC 3mg

Caramel Apple Oatmeal Cookies

Category Finalist—Desserts

"I bake a lot of cookies, but I'd never made many oatmeal cookies because I don't like raisins. I found that dried apples and caramel bits make a good replacement for the raisins."

—Helen Worthington,
Meridian, Mississippi

6.75 ounces all-purpose flour (about 1½ cups)
1½ cups old-fashioned rolled oats
1 teaspoon baking powder
½ teaspoon baking soda
½ teaspoon salt
¾ cup granulated sugar
¾ cup packed brown sugar
6 tablespoons unsalted butter, softened
2 teaspoons vanilla extract
1 large egg
¾ cup finely chopped dried apple slices
¾ cup caramel bits or 16 small soft caramel candies, chopped

1. Preheat oven to 350°.
2. Weigh or lightly spoon flour into dry measuring cups; level with a knife. Combine flour and next 4 ingredients in a bowl; stir well.
3. Place sugars and butter in a large bowl; beat with a mixer at medium speed until light and fluffy. Add vanilla and egg; beat well. Gradually add flour mixture; beat at low speed until just combined. Fold in apple and caramel bits.
4. Drop dough by 2 teaspoonfuls 2 inches apart onto baking sheets lined with parchment paper. Flatten balls slightly with hand. Bake at 350° for 9 minutes. Cool on pans 3 minutes. Remove cookies from pans; cool completely on wire racks. Yield: 4 dozen (serving size: 1 cookie).

CALORIES 83; FAT 2g (sat 1.1g, mono 0.5g, poly 0.3); PROTEIN 1.1g; CARB 15.5g; FIBER 0.5g; CHOL 8mg; IRON 0.4mg; SODIUM 74mg; CALC 17mg

Apricot-Ginger Bellinis

(pictured on page 246)

Category Finalist—Starters & Drinks

"I created this recipe for my sister-in-law's baby shower (we used ginger ale instead of prosecco for the mom-to-be). For a pretty touch, dip the edges of the Champagne flutes in a mixture of sugar and grated lime rind."

—Karen Coyne,
Hagerstown, Maryland

Sugar Syrup:
¾ cup water
¾ cup sugar
1 (2-inch) piece peeled fresh ginger, halved

Remaining Ingredients:
1 teaspoon grated lime rind
1 teaspoon fresh lime juice
1 (15-ounce) can apricot halves in light syrup, drained
1 (750-milliliter) bottle prosecco or other sparkling white wine

1. To prepare sugar syrup, combine ¾ cup water and sugar in a small saucepan. Bring to a boil; cook 2 minutes or until sugar dissolves. Add ginger. Remove from heat; cool. Chill 4 hours.
2. Strain sugar syrup through a colander into a bowl; discard ginger. Place ⅓ cup sugar syrup in a blender; reserve remaining syrup for another use. Add rind, juice, and apricots to blender; process until smooth. Spoon 2 tablespoons apricot puree into each of 8 glasses. Top each with ⅓ cup prosecco; stir gently. Yield: 8 servings.

CALORIES 111; FAT 0g; PROTEIN 0.2g; CARB 13g; FIBER 0.4g; CHOL 0mg; IRON 0.1mg; SODIUM 1mg; CALC 4mg

THE BEST OF BARLEY

This ancient grain is perfect in modern cooking: granola, risotto, burgers, or salads. Barley flakes and pearl barley also offer fiber plus a bevy of nutrients.

Make Ahead
Mediterranean Barley Salad

2¼ cups water
¾ cup uncooked pearl barley
1½ teaspoons grated lemon rind
3 tablespoons fresh lemon juice
2 tablespoons extra-virgin olive oil
½ teaspoon Dijon mustard
1 cup thinly sliced fennel bulb (about 1 small bulb)
⅓ cup chopped fresh parsley
¼ cup finely chopped red onion
¾ teaspoon kosher salt
½ teaspoon coarsely ground black pepper
8 pitted kalamata olives, halved
1 (15-ounce) can cannellini beans, rinsed and drained
⅓ cup chopped walnuts, toasted

1. Bring 2¼ cups water and barley to a boil in a saucepan. Cover, reduce heat, and simmer 25 minutes or until tender and liquid is almost absorbed. Cool to room temperature.
2. Combine rind and next 3 ingredients in a bowl; stir well with a whisk. Add barley, fennel, and next 6 ingredients; toss gently. Cover and refrigerate 30 minutes. Garnish with walnuts just before serving. Yield: 4 servings (serving size: 1¼ cups salad and about 4 teaspoons nuts).

CALORIES 313; **FAT** 16.1g (sat 1.9g, mono 7.5g, poly 6.2g); **PROTEIN** 6.6g; **CARB** 38.9g; **FIBER** 8.2g; **CHOL** 0mg; **IRON** 2.9mg; **SODIUM** 643mg; **CALC** 79mg

Lentil-Barley Burgers with Fiery Fruit Salsa

Use leftover cooked pearl barley with lentils, veggies, and seasonings for a hearty main-dish burger sans the bun. Fruit salsa adds bright flavors. Serve with lime wedges for added zest.

Salsa:
¼ cup finely chopped pineapple
¼ cup finely chopped mango
¼ cup finely chopped tomatillo
¼ cup halved grape tomatoes
1 tablespoon fresh lime juice
1 serrano chile, minced
Burgers:
1½ cups water
½ cup dried lentils
Cooking spray
1 cup chopped onion
¼ cup grated carrot
2 teaspoons minced garlic
2 tablespoons tomato paste
1½ teaspoons ground cumin
¾ teaspoon dried oregano
½ teaspoon chili powder
¾ teaspoon salt, divided
¾ cup cooked pearl barley
½ cup panko (Japanese breadcrumbs)
¼ cup finely chopped fresh parsley
½ teaspoon coarsely ground black pepper
2 large egg whites
1 large egg
3 tablespoons canola oil, divided

1. To prepare salsa, combine first 6 ingredients; cover and refrigerate.
2. To prepare burgers, combine 1½ cups water and lentils in a saucepan; bring to a boil. Cover, reduce heat, and simmer 25 minutes or until lentils are tender. Drain. Place half of lentils in a large bowl. Place remaining lentils in a food processor; process until smooth. Add processed lentils to whole lentils in bowl.
3. Heat a large nonstick skillet over medium-high heat. Coat pan with cooking spray. Add onion and carrot; sauté 6 minutes or until tender, stirring occasionally. Add garlic; cook 1 minute, stirring constantly. Add tomato paste, cumin, oregano, chili powder, and ¼ teaspoon salt; cook 1 minute, stirring constantly. Add onion mixture to lentils. Add remaining ½ teaspoon salt, barley,

and next 5 ingredients; stir well. Cover and refrigerate 1 hour or until firm.
4. Divide mixture into 8 portions, shaping each into a ½-inch-thick patty. Heat 1½ tablespoons oil in a large nonstick skillet over medium-high heat. Add 4 patties; cook 3 minutes on each side or until browned. Repeat procedure with remaining 1½ tablespoons oil and 4 patties. Serve with salsa. Yield: 4 servings (serving size: 2 patties and ¼ cup salsa).

CALORIES 315; **FAT** 12.8g (sat 1.2g, mono 6.8g, poly 3.5g); **PROTEIN** 12.8g; **CARB** 39.2g; **FIBER** 9.5g; **CHOL** 53mg; **IRON** 3.9mg; **SODIUM** 539mg; **CALC** 60mg

Barley, Butternut Squash, and Shiitake Risotto

Like risotto in texture but not in cooking method, this one-dish meal's creaminess is underscored with the addition of Taleggio, a soft Italian cheese. You can substitute Brie, if you like.

3 cups (½-inch) cubed peeled butternut squash (about 1½ pounds)
3 tablespoons olive oil, divided
¾ teaspoon kosher salt, divided
2 cups thinly sliced shiitake mushroom caps (about ½ pound)
⅓ cup finely chopped red onion
1 cup uncooked pearl barley
2 garlic cloves, chopped
⅔ cup white wine
3½ cups organic vegetable broth
¼ teaspoon black pepper
4 ounces Taleggio cheese, diced
2 tablespoons fresh thyme leaves

1. Preheat oven to 450°.
2. Combine squash, 1 tablespoon oil, and ¼ teaspoon salt; toss well to coat. Arrange squash mixture in a single layer on a baking sheet. Bake at 450° for 25 minutes, stirring once.
3. Heat 1 tablespoon oil in a large Dutch oven over medium-high heat. Add mushrooms; sauté 5 minutes or until browned, stirring occasionally. Transfer mushroom mixture to a bowl; keep warm.

4. Heat remaining 1 tablespoon oil in pan. Add onion; sauté 4 minutes or until tender, stirring occasionally. Add barley and garlic; cook 1 minute, stirring constantly. Add wine; bring to a boil. Cook 3 minutes or until liquid is nearly absorbed. Add broth, remaining ½ teaspoon salt, and pepper; bring to a boil. Cover, reduce heat, and simmer 30 minutes or until barley is tender and liquid is nearly absorbed. Remove from heat; add cheese, stirring until cheese melts. Stir in squash, mushrooms, and thyme. Serve immediately. Yield: 6 servings (serving size: about 1 cup).

CALORIES 339; FAT 11.9g (sat 3.9g, mono 6.3g, poly 1.1g); PROTEIN 9.3g; CARB 46g; FIBER 8.3g; CHOL 14mg; IRON 2.6mg; SODIUM 745mg; CALC 150mg

Make Ahead • Kid Friendly
Toasted Barley and Berry Granola

While rolled barley flakes look nearly identical to rolled oats, they pack more fiber. Look for them in whole-food shops or supermarket bulk food bins. Try this granola over plain low-fat yogurt.

¼ cup unsalted pumpkinseed kernels
¼ cup unsalted sunflower seed kernels
⅓ cup maple syrup
2 tablespoons brown sugar
2 tablespoons canola oil
1 teaspoon ground cinnamon
1½ teaspoons vanilla extract
¼ teaspoon salt
⅛ teaspoon ground cardamom
2 cups rolled barley flakes
¼ cup toasted wheat germ
⅓ cup dried blueberries
⅓ cup sweetened dried cranberries

1. Preheat oven to 325°.
2. Place pumpkinseed kernels and sunflower seed kernels on a baking sheet lined with parchment paper. Bake at 325° for 5 minutes. Cool seeds in pan on a wire rack.
3. Combine syrup and next 6 ingredients in a medium bowl. Stir in toasted kernels, barley, and wheat germ.

4. Spread barley mixture in a single layer on a baking sheet lined with parchment paper. Bake at 325° for 25 minutes or until lightly browned, stirring every 10 minutes.
5. Remove from oven; cool granola in pan on a wire rack. Stir in dried blueberries and dried cranberries. Store in an airtight container. Yield: 4 cups (serving size: ⅓ cup).

CALORIES 181; FAT 6.5g (sat 0.7g, mono 2.3g, poly 2.8g); PROTEIN 4.5g; CARB 27.4g; FIBER 3.7g; CHOL 1mg; IRON 1.4mg; SODIUM 59mg; CALC 13mg

BUDGET COOKING
FEED 4 FOR LESS THAN $10

Indulge your cravings for late-winter fare with hearty and economical menus.

Quick & Easy
Chicken Curry

$2.39 per serving, $9.56 total

1 tablespoon canola oil
3 (6-ounce) skinless, boneless chicken breast halves, cut into 1-inch pieces
½ teaspoon salt
2 cups green bell pepper strips (about 1 large)
2 tablespoons fresh lime juice
2 tablespoons less-sodium soy sauce
2 tablespoons red curry paste
1 teaspoon sugar
1 (14-ounce) can light coconut milk
3 cups hot cooked long-grain rice
Lime wedges (optional)

1. Heat a large nonstick skillet over medium-high heat. Add oil to pan; swirl to coat. Sprinkle chicken evenly with salt. Add chicken to pan; cook 6 minutes or until browned, turning once. Add bell pepper to pan; sauté 4 minutes, stirring occasionally. Remove chicken mixture from pan. Combine juice and next 3 ingredients in a small bowl, stirring with a whisk. Add juice mixture and coconut milk to pan; bring to a boil. Cook 12 minutes or until

slightly thick. Return chicken mixture to pan; cook 2 minutes or until thoroughly heated. Serve over rice. Garnish with lime wedges, if desired. Yield: 4 servings (serving size: ¾ cup chicken mixture and ¾ cup rice).

CALORIES 402; FAT 10.2g (sat 5.2g, mono 2.6g, poly 1.5g); PROTEIN 34.7g; CARB 42.4g; FIBER 1.4g; CHOL 74mg; IRON 3.1mg; SODIUM 806mg; CALC 33mg

Quick & Easy
Bacon and Butternut Pasta

$2.07 per serving, $8.26 total

3¼ teaspoons salt, divided
8 ounces uncooked fettuccine
2 bacon slices
2 tablespoons butter
3 cups (½-inch) cubed peeled butternut squash
2 garlic cloves, minced
½ cup (2 ounces) crumbled blue cheese
½ cup sliced green onions

1. Bring 3 quarts water and 1 tablespoon salt to a boil in a large saucepan. Add pasta; cook 8 minutes. Drain in a colander over a bowl, and reserve ⅓ cup cooking liquid.
2. Cook bacon in a large skillet over medium heat until crisp. Remove bacon from pan, reserving 2 teaspoons drippings in pan. Crumble bacon; set aside. Add butter to drippings in pan; cook 30 seconds or until butter melts. Increase heat to medium-high. Add squash; sauté 7 minutes or until almost tender. Add garlic; cook 1 minute, stirring constantly. Stir in remaining ¼ teaspoon salt, pasta, reserved cooking liquid, and cheese; cook 2 minutes or until pasta is al dente, stirring frequently. Sprinkle with bacon and onions. Yield: 4 servings (serving size: 1 cup).

CALORIES 385; FAT 14.1g (sat 7.8g, mono 4.1g, poly 0.8g); PROTEIN 13.1g; CARB 53.4g; FIBER 4.7g; CHOL 31mg; IRON 2.7mg; SODIUM 701mg; CALC 135mg

continued

For the spinach salad:
Combine 1½ tablespoons lemon juice, 1 tablespoon olive oil, 1½ teaspoons honey, 1 teaspoon Dijon mustard, ¼ teaspoon salt, and ¼ teaspoon pepper in a bowl, stirring with a whisk. Toss with 5 cups fresh spinach. Top with 1 cored and thinly sliced Braeburn apple.

Quick & Easy
Roast Leg of Lamb with Chile-Garlic Sauce

$2.49 per serving, $9.97 total
The base of the sauce is sambal oelek—a fiery Asian condiment you'll find on the ethnic aisle at major supermarkets or at Asian markets.

Lamb:
1 (1-pound) boneless leg of lamb, trimmed
¾ teaspoon salt
½ teaspoon freshly ground black pepper
Cooking spray
Sauce:
1 tablespoon sambal oelek (ground fresh chile paste)
½ teaspoon ground cumin
¼ teaspoon ground coriander
⅛ teaspoon salt
3 garlic cloves, minced
2 tablespoons olive oil

1. Preheat oven to 425°.
2. To prepare lamb, sprinkle lamb evenly with ¾ teaspoon salt and pepper. Place lamb on a broiler pan coated with cooking spray. Bake at 425° for 21 minutes or until a thermometer inserted in thickest part of roast registers 120°. Place lamb on a cutting board; let stand at room temperature 10 minutes before slicing.
3. To prepare sauce, combine sambal oelek and next 4 ingredients with a mortar and pestle; grind into a fine paste. Slowly drizzle oil into sambal mixture, stirring until thoroughly combined. Serve sauce with lamb. Yield: 4 servings (serving size: 3 ounces lamb and about 1 tablespoon sauce).

CALORIES 265; FAT 18.5g (sat 6.3g, mono 9.7g, poly 1.2g); PROTEIN 21.7g; CARB 1.8g; FIBER 0.2g; CHOL 71mg; IRON 2mg; SODIUM 574mg; CALC 17mg

For the green beans:
Steam ⅔ pound trimmed green beans 6 minutes or until crisp-tender. Drain beans; toss with ¼ teaspoon salt and ¼ teaspoon black pepper.

For the roasted potatoes:
Preheat oven to 425°. Cut 1 pound red-skinned potatoes into thin wedges. Combine potato wedges, 1 tablespoon olive oil, ½ teaspoon salt, and ¼ teaspoon freshly ground black pepper; toss well to coat. Arrange potato mixture in a single layer on a jelly-roll pan coated with cooking spray. Bake at 425° for 30 minutes or until potato wedges are browned and tender, stirring after 15 minutes.

Make Ahead • Freezable • Kid Friendly
Braised Short Ribs with Egg Noodles

$2.47 per serving, $9.87 total
The key to getting incredibly rich flavor in this sauce is to create tasty browned bits on the bottom of the pan. To ensure you create those bits, use a stainless steel skillet—not a nonstick pan.

1½ pounds beef short ribs, trimmed (4 ribs)
3¾ teaspoons salt, divided
½ teaspoon freshly ground black pepper
½ cup all-purpose flour
2 tablespoons olive oil, divided
2½ cups water
¾ cup chopped carrot (about 1 large)
½ cup chopped onion
1 (8-ounce) package cremini mushrooms, sliced
3 garlic cloves, minced
1 tablespoon tomato paste
3 quarts water
8 ounces uncooked medium egg noodles

1. Sprinkle beef evenly with ¼ teaspoon salt and pepper; dredge in flour. Heat a large skillet over medium-high heat. Add 1 tablespoon oil to pan; swirl to coat. Add beef to pan; cook 4 minutes or until browned, turning occasionally. Add 2½ cups water, scraping pan to loosen browned bits; bring to a boil. Cover, reduce heat, and simmer 1 hour and 45 minutes or until fork-tender. Remove beef from pan; cover and keep warm. Remove cooking liquid from pan; reserve cooking liquid.
2. Heat skillet over medium heat. Add remaining 1 tablespoon oil to pan; swirl to coat. Add carrot and onion; cook 4 minutes, stirring occasionally. Add mushrooms and ½ teaspoon salt; cook 5 minutes, stirring occasionally. Add garlic; cook 30 seconds, stirring constantly. Add tomato paste, and cook 30 seconds, stirring frequently. Stir in reserved cooking liquid; bring to a boil. Reduce heat, and simmer 6 minutes or until slightly thickened.
3. Bring 3 quarts water and remaining 1 tablespoon salt to a boil in a large saucepan. Add noodles; cook 5 minutes or until al dente. Drain; serve noodles with ribs and sauce. Yield: 4 servings (serving size: 1¼ cups noodles, 1 rib, and ¾ cup sauce).

CALORIES 488; FAT 18.2g (sat 5.4g, mono 8.5g, poly 1.1g); PROTEIN 25.2g; CARB 56.3g; FIBER 4.3g; CHOL 107mg; IRON 4.4mg; SODIUM 684mg; CALC 46mg

EASY COOKING
START WITH A...CAN OF CHICKPEAS

The versatile legume finds a home in many cuisines, from Spanish tapas to Moroccan tagines, and many dishes in between.

Quick & Easy
Roasted Cauliflower, Chickpeas, and Olives

Enjoy this tangy dish as a side with sautéed fish or roast chicken.

5½ cups cauliflower florets (about 1 pound)
24 green Spanish olives, pitted and halved
8 garlic cloves, coarsely chopped
1 (15-ounce) can chickpeas (garbanzo beans), rinsed and drained
3 tablespoons olive oil
½ teaspoon crushed red pepper
¼ teaspoon salt
3 tablespoons fresh flat-leaf parsley leaves

1. Preheat oven to 450°.
2. Combine first 4 ingredients in a small roasting pan. Drizzle with oil, and sprinkle with pepper and salt. Toss well to coat. Bake at 450° for 22 minutes or until cauliflower is browned and crisp-tender, stirring after 10 minutes. Sprinkle with parsley. Yield: 6 servings (serving size: about ⅔ cup).

CALORIES 176; FAT 10.1g (sat 1g, mono 6.4g, poly 2.4g); PROTEIN 4.2g; CARB 17.6g; FIBER 4.2g; CHOL 0mg; IRON 1.2mg; SODIUM 585mg; CALC 42mg

Quick & Easy • Kid Friendly

Chickpeas with Broccoli Rabe and Bacon

1 pound broccoli rabe, trimmed and cut into 2-inch pieces
1 tablespoon olive oil
6 center-cut bacon slices, chopped
1 cup chopped onion
½ teaspoon dried oregano
⅛ teaspoon crushed red pepper
6 garlic cloves, thinly sliced
1 (15-ounce) can chickpeas (garbanzo beans), rinsed and drained
¼ teaspoon salt
¼ teaspoon freshly ground black pepper
2 ounces Parmigiano-Reggiano cheese

1. Cook broccoli rabe in a large pot of boiling water 2 minutes or until crisp-tender; drain.
2. Heat a large skillet over medium-high heat. Add oil to pan; swirl to coat. Add bacon; sauté 3 minutes, stirring frequently. Stir in onion, oregano, and red pepper; sauté 4 minutes or until onion begins to soften, stirring occasionally. Add garlic; sauté 30 seconds, stirring constantly. Add chickpeas; sauté 1 minute. Stir in broccoli rabe, salt, and black pepper; cook 2 minutes or until thoroughly heated, tossing to combine. Place about 1½ cups chickpea mixture on each of 4 plates; shave ½ ounce cheese evenly over each serving. Yield: 4 servings.

CALORIES 263; FAT 10.3g (sat 3.8g, mono 3.8g, poly 0.9g); PROTEIN 16.8g; CARB 27.5g; FIBER 4g; CHOL 20mg; IRON 2.3mg; SODIUM 743mg; CALC 254mg

Make Ahead

Lamb and Chickpea Tagine

Serve this hearty Moroccan-inspired stew over hot cooked couscous.

1 tablespoon olive oil
1 pound lamb stew meat
1 cup chopped onion
½ teaspoon salt
¼ teaspoon ground red pepper
¼ teaspoon ground cumin
5 garlic cloves, minced
1 tablespoon tomato paste
2 teaspoons honey
2½ cups fat-free, less-sodium chicken broth
½ cup golden raisins
1 (15-ounce) can chickpeas (garbanzo beans), rinsed and drained
⅓ cup chopped pistachios
2 tablespoons small fresh cilantro leaves

1. Heat a large saucepan over medium-high heat. Add oil to pan; swirl to coat. Add lamb; sauté 4 minutes, turning to brown on all sides. Remove lamb with a slotted spoon. Add onion, and next 3 ingredients to pan; sauté 4 minutes, stirring occasionally. Add garlic; sauté 1 minute, stirring constantly. Return lamb to pan; stir in tomato paste and honey. Cook 30 seconds, stirring constantly. Add broth, raisins, and chickpeas; bring to a boil. Reduce heat to medium, and cook 50 minutes or until lamb is tender, stirring occasionally. Sprinkle with pistachios and cilantro. Yield: 5 servings (serving size: about ⅔ cup lamb mixture, 4 teaspoons pistachios, and 1½ teaspoons cilantro).

CALORIES 432; FAT 15.6g (sat 3.9g, mono 7.5g, poly 2.6g); PROTEIN 37.9g; CARB 36.2g; FIBER 5.4g; CHOL 98mg; IRON 4.8mg; SODIUM 729mg; CALC 81mg

WINE NOTE: You don't want your food to be sweeter than your wine. What to do, then, with a honeyed tagine? Go for a wine with deep fruit that seems sweet even if it isn't—a zinfandel full of jammy, spicy blackberries, plums, pepper, chocolate, and even raisins: Rodney Strong 2007 "Knotty Vines" Zin (Sonoma County, $22).

Quick & Easy • Kid Friendly

Penne with Chickpeas, Feta, and Tomatoes

Salty feta, sweet cherry tomatoes, and nutty chickpeas combine for a hearty Greek-inspired pasta dish. Use oregano instead of basil, if you prefer.

8 ounces uncooked penne (tube-shaped pasta)
2 tablespoons olive oil
½ cup chopped shallots
3 garlic cloves, minced
½ cup chopped red bell pepper
1 (15-ounce) can chickpeas (garbanzo beans), rinsed and drained
3 cups halved cherry tomatoes
¾ cup (3 ounces) crumbled feta cheese
⅓ cup small fresh basil leaves
½ teaspoon salt
½ teaspoon grated lemon rind
¼ teaspoon freshly ground black pepper

1. Cook pasta according to package directions, omitting salt and fat; drain in a colander over a bowl, reserving ¼ cup cooking liquid.
2. Heat a large skillet over medium-high heat. Add oil to pan; swirl to coat. Add shallots and garlic; sauté 45 seconds, stirring constantly. Stir in bell pepper and chickpeas; sauté 2 minutes, stirring occasionally. Add tomatoes; sauté 2 minutes. Stir in pasta and reserved cooking liquid; cook 1 minute or until thoroughly heated. Remove from heat. Add feta and remaining ingredients; toss to combine. Yield: 4 servings (serving size: 1½ cups).

CALORIES 458; FAT 13.3g (sat 4.5g, mono 6.2g, poly 1.4g); PROTEIN 16.5g; CARB 70.5g; FIBER 7.5g; CHOL 19mg; IRON 3.8mg; SODIUM 759mg; CALC 172mg

BREAKFAST, LUNCH, AND DINNER IN... AUSTIN

For Austin, geography is destiny. The Texas town's famous South by Southwest music festival takes its name from its location: To the east lies the rich farmland and green cotton fields that make the state part of the Old South. To the west, the rocky Hill Country and ranching culture of the Southwest begins. This is where catfish and corn bread meet steak and tacos—all given a creative, modern spin in a city whose unofficial motto is "Keep Austin Weird."

Breakfast

Eggs Blindfolded over Garlic Cheddar Grits

The place to go for a nostalgic Southern breakfast is Hoover's Cooking (hooverscooking. com). Hoover will make you "Eggs Blindfolded," a Southern short-order cook's version of poached eggs. The eggs are dropped on a hot griddle and then covered with a couple of pieces of ice and a lid. The sizzling ice makes for a delightful half-fried, half-poached egg. Try one on a scoop of hearty garlic cheddar grits.

Grits:
2 1/2 cups hot cooked grits
3 tablespoons grated cheddar cheese
1/2 teaspoon garlic powder
1/2 teaspoon salt
1/2 teaspoon freshly ground black pepper

Eggs:
Cooking spray
4 large eggs, divided
1/2 cup ice cubes, divided
Freshly ground black pepper (optional)
Chopped fresh chives (optional)

1. To prepare grits, combine first 5 ingredients in a large bowl; keep warm.
2. To prepare eggs, heat a small skillet over medium heat. Coat pan with cooking spray. Break 2 eggs in pan; cook 1 minute or until whites are set. Add 1/4 cup ice cubes to pan; cover and cook 2 minutes or until eggs are done. Remove from pan. Repeat procedure with remaining 2 eggs and 1/4 cup ice.

Serve eggs over grits. Garnish with black pepper and chives, if desired. Yield: 4 servings (serving size: 1 egg and about 2/3 cup grits).

CALORIES 184; FAT 7g (sat 2.7g, mono 2.5g, poly 0.9g); PROTEIN 9.8g; CARB 20.3g; FIBER 0.6g; CHOL 217mg; IRON 1.9mg; SODIUM 474mg; CALC 71mg

Lunch

Mahimahi BLT

"People in Austin love tacos, but they want them to be healthy," says David Garrido of Garrido's. His top seller is a taco with grilled fish on a bed of lettuce and tomatoes with a topping of aioli or salsa and bacon.

Salsa:
1 tablespoon olive oil
1/2 cup chopped onion
1 garlic clove, minced
2 cups coarsely chopped tomato
1/4 cup finely chopped red bell pepper
1 1/2 teaspoons minced seeded habanero pepper
1/4 teaspoon salt

Tacos:
1 pound mahimahi or other firm white fish fillets
1 onion, cut into 1/4-inch-thick slices
2 tablespoons olive oil
2 teaspoons guajillo chile powder
1/2 teaspoon salt
2 cups shredded Boston lettuce
8 corn tortillas
2 cups chopped seeded tomato
2 bacon slices, cooked and crumbled

1. Preheat broiler.
2. To prepare salsa, heat 1 tablespoon oil in a small skillet over medium heat. Add chopped onion to pan; cook 3 minutes or until slightly softened. Add garlic; sauté 30 seconds. Stir in tomato; bring to a boil and cook 2 minutes. Place tomato mixture in a blender; pulse 10 times or until almost smooth. Combine tomato mixture, bell pepper, habanero, and 1/4 teaspoon salt in a small bowl; cover and keep warm.
3. To prepare tacos, place fish and onion slices on a broiler pan. Brush both sides of fish and onion evenly with 2 tablespoons olive oil. Sprinkle fish and onion evenly with chile powder and 1/2 teaspoon salt. Broil 4 minutes; carefully turn fish. Broil 4 minutes. Remove from oven; flake fish with a fork.
4. Place 1/4 cup shredded lettuce on each tortilla. Top each tortilla evenly with fish, onion slices, 1/4 cup chopped tomato, and crumbled bacon. Spoon about 2 1/2 tablespoons salsa on top of each taco. Yield: 4 servings (serving size: 2 tacos).

CALORIES 337; FAT 14.6g (sat 2.6g, mono 7.6g, poly 2g); PROTEIN 26.7g; CARB 27.8g; FIBER 4.4g; CHOL 88mg; IRON 2.2mg; SODIUM 718mg; CALC 74mg

Dinner

Grilled Flatiron Steaks with Kale and Beet Risotto

The locavore trend meets the "nose to tail" movement (the idea of using as much of the animal as possible) at Olivia (olivia-austin. com). Chef James Holmes is receiving acclaim for a menu that includes Southern and Southwestern offal dishes like lamb hearts with green chile salsa and foie gras grits. In late winter, look for a hearty dish of risotto made with organic beets topped with a Texas grass-fed flatiron steak sprinkled with crumbled local "Pure Luck" blue cheese. Flatiron steaks are cuts from the top blade with the shoulder tendon removed. Olivia restaurant uses local grass-fed beef, but grain-fed beef will also work in this dish.

1 pound beets
¼ cup red wine vinegar
1 tablespoon tarragon
3 tablespoons olive oil, divided
Cooking spray
1 teaspoon minced garlic
6 cups chopped kale (about 1 bunch)
2 cups fat-free, less-sodium chicken broth
2 cups water
½ cup chopped onion
1 cup Arborio rice or other medium-grain rice
¼ cup white wine
¾ teaspoon salt, divided
2 (8-ounce) flatiron steaks
¼ teaspoon freshly ground black pepper
¼ cup (1 ounce) crumbled blue cheese

1. Preheat oven to 350°.
2. Leave root and 1-inch stem on beets; scrub with a brush. Wrap beets in heavy-duty aluminum foil. Bake at 350° for 1 hour and 15 minutes or until tender. Remove from oven; cool. Trim off beet roots and stems; rub off skins. Cut beets into quarters. Place beets, vinegar, tarragon, and 1 tablespoon oil in a blender. Process until smooth; set aside.
3. Heat a large skillet over medium heat. Coat pan with cooking spray. Add garlic to pan; cook 30 seconds, stirring constantly. Add kale to pan; cook 5 minutes or until kale wilts, stirring frequently. Remove kale mixture from pan; wipe pan clean.
4. Bring broth and 2 cups water to a simmer in a small saucepan (do not boil). Keep warm over low heat.
5. Heat remaining 2 tablespoons oil in skillet over medium heat. Add onion; cook 5 minutes or until tender, stirring occasionally. Add rice; cook 1 minute, stirring constantly. Stir in wine; cook 2 minutes or until liquid is absorbed, stirring constantly. Add broth mixture, ½ cup at a time, stirring constantly until each portion of broth is absorbed before adding next (about 20 minutes total). Stir in pureed beet mixture, kale, and ½ teaspoon salt. Remove from pan; keep warm. Wipe pan clean.
6. Heat skillet over medium-high heat. Coat pan with cooking spray. Sprinkle beef evenly with remaining ¼ teaspoon salt and pepper. Add beef to pan; cook

3 minutes on each side or until desired degree of doneness. Remove from pan; let stand at room temperature 5 minutes before cutting across grain into thin slices. Serve beef with risotto; sprinkle with blue cheese. Yield: 4 servings (serving size: 1¼ cups risotto, 3 ounces beef, and 1 tablespoon cheese).

CALORIES 524; FAT 19.9g (sat 6.8g, mono 9.4g, poly 1.3g); PROTEIN 30.9g; CARB 55.3g; FIBER 6.2g; CHOL 77mg; IRON 4.4mg; SODIUM 952mg; CALC 127mg

SIMPLE ADDITIONS

Quick & Easy

Pan-Grilled Pork Chops with Grilled Pineapple Salsa

Seed the jalapeño if you prefer a milder salsa.

4 (4-ounce) boneless center-cut loin pork chops (about ½ inch thick)
1 tablespoon plus 2 teaspoons fresh lime juice, divided
4 (½-inch-thick) slices pineapple
1 medium red onion, cut into ½-inch-thick slices
1 tablespoon minced jalapeño pepper

Combine pork and 1 tablespoon juice; let stand 10 minutes. Heat a grill pan over medium-high heat. Coat pan with cooking spray. Add pineapple and onion; cook 4 minutes on each side or until onion is tender. Coarsely chop pineapple and onion; combine in a medium bowl with remaining 2 teaspoons lime juice, jalapeño, and ⅛ teaspoon salt. Sprinkle pork with ½ teaspoon salt and ¼ teaspoon freshly ground black pepper. Heat grill pan over medium-high heat. Coat pan with cooking spray. Add pork; cook 4 minutes on each side or until done. Yield: 4 servings (serving size: 1 chop and about ½ cup salsa).

CALORIES 215; FAT 7g (sat 2.5g, mono 3.1g, poly 0.5g); PROTEIN 26.4g; CARB 10.9g; FIBER 1.4g; CHOL 70mg; IRON 1mg; SODIUM 416mg; CALC 42mg

THE FIVE INGREDIENTS

4 (4-ounce) boneless center-cut loin pork chops (about ½ inch thick)

+

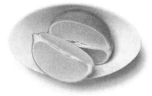

1 tablespoon plus 2 teaspoons fresh lime juice, divided

+

4 (½-inch-thick) slices pineapple

+

1 medium red onion, cut into ½-inch-thick slices

+

1 tablespoon minced jalapeño pepper

DINNER TONIGHT

Here are a handful of wonderful stopwatch-tested menus from the *Cooking Light* Test Kitchens.

SHOPPING LIST

Maple and Soy–Glazed Flank Steak

less-sodium soy sauce
dark sesame oil
Sriracha
maple syrup
1-pound flank steak
sake or dry sherry

Silky Sesame Cucumbers

1 English cucumber
seasoned rice vinegar
dark sesame oil
toasted sesame seeds

Scallion Noodles

carrots
green onions
8 ounces wide rice noodles
seasoned rice vinegar
dark sesame oil
crushed red pepper

GAME PLAN

While steak marinates:
- Preheat broiler.
- Salt cucumbers.
- Bring water to a boil.

While steak cooks:
- Finish cucumber side dish.
- Cook noodles.

While steak rests:
- Complete noodle side dish.

Quick & Easy • Kid Friendly

Maple and Soy–Glazed Flank Steak

with Silky Sesame Cucumbers and Scallion Noodles

Flavor Hit: Readily available Sriracha (in the Asian foods section) offers sweet heat.
Buy The Best: Maple syrup has a vanilla-caramel flavor; do not substitute pancake syrup.
Make-Ahead Tip: You can make and chill the cucumbers up to one day ahead.

1 (1-pound) flank steak, trimmed
¼ cup less-sodium soy sauce
3 tablespoons maple syrup
2 tablespoons sake or dry sherry
2 teaspoons dark sesame oil
1 teaspoon Sriracha (Asian hot chile sauce)
⅛ teaspoon freshly ground black pepper
Cooking spray

1. Pierce steak gently on both sides. Combine steak and next 6 ingredients in a shallow dish; turn to coat. Marinate at room temperature 20 minutes, turning occasionally.
2. Preheat broiler.
3. Remove steak from marinade, reserving marinade. Place steak on a broiler pan coated with cooking spray. Pour marinade into a small skillet; bring to a boil, stirring well. Cook over medium-high heat 3 minutes or until thick and syrupy.
4. Brush steak with half of glaze; broil 5 minutes. Turn steak over, and brush with remaining glaze; broil 5 minutes or until desired degree of doneness. Place steak on a cutting board; let stand 5 minutes. Cut steak diagonally across grain into thin slices. Yield: 4 servings (serving size: 3 ounces).

CALORIES 232; FAT 9.1g (sat 3.2g, mono 3.6g, poly 1.2g); PROTEIN 23.4g; CARB 11.9g; FIBER 0.2g; CHOL 45mg; IRON 2mg; SODIUM 580mg; CALC 25mg

For the Silky Sesame Cucumbers:
Cut 1 English cucumber into very thin slices. Toss cucumber with 1 teaspoon kosher salt; let stand 15 minutes. Drain; firmly squeeze dry, and place in a bowl. Drizzle with 2 tablespoons seasoned rice vinegar and ¾ teaspoon dark sesame oil; toss well. Stir in 2 teaspoons toasted sesame seeds.

For the Scallion Noodles:
Cook 8 ounces wide rice noodles according to package directions; drain and rinse with cold water. Combine noodles, ½ cup shaved carrots, ¼ cup green onion strips, 2 tablespoons seasoned rice vinegar, 1 tablespoon dark sesame oil, ¼ teaspoon crushed red pepper, and ¼ teaspoon salt.

SHOPPING LIST

Pasta with Asparagus, Pancetta, and Pine Nuts

1 pound asparagus
1 large lemon
garlic
8 ounces cavatappi pasta
extra-virgin olive oil
pine nuts
2 ounces pancetta
1 ounce Parmigiano-Reggiano cheese

White Bean and Thyme Crostini

garlic
1 lemon
fresh thyme
1 small baguette
extra-virgin olive oil
1 can cannellini beans

GAME PLAN

While oven heats and water comes to a boil:
- Slice asparagus.
- Mince garlic.
- Dice pancetta.

While pasta cooks:
- Toast nuts.
- Cook pancetta and crostini together.
- Make bean spread.
- Crumble cheese.

Pasta with Asparagus, Pancetta, and Pine Nuts
with White Bean and Thyme Crostini

Simple Sub: Pine nuts are particularly delicious in this dish, but walnuts would also be tasty.
Buy The Best: Look for asparagus that's firm and brightly colored with tightly packed tips.
Time-Saver: If your supermarket deli carries it, pre-diced pancetta saves time.

8 ounces uncooked cavatappi pasta
1 pound asparagus, trimmed and cut diagonally into 1½-inch pieces
1 teaspoon minced garlic
3 tablespoons pine nuts
2 ounces diced pancetta
2 tablespoons fresh lemon juice
2 teaspoons extra-virgin olive oil
½ teaspoon kosher salt
¼ teaspoon freshly ground black pepper
¼ cup (1 ounce) crumbled Parmigiano-Reggiano cheese

1. Preheat oven to 400°.
2. Cook pasta according to package directions, omitting salt and fat; add asparagus to pan during last 3 minutes of cooking. Drain. Sprinkle pasta mixture with garlic; return to pan, and toss well.
3. Arrange pine nuts in a single layer on a jelly-roll pan. Bake at 400° for 3 minutes or until golden and fragrant, stirring occasionally. Place in a small bowl.
4. Increase oven temperature to 475°.
5. Arrange pancetta on jelly-roll pan. Bake at 475° for 6 minutes or until crisp.
6. Combine lemon juice and next 3 ingredients, stirring with a whisk. Drizzle over pasta mixture; toss well to coat. Sprinkle with pine nuts, pancetta, and cheese. Yield: 4 servings (serving size: about 2 cups).

CALORIES 385; FAT 14.3g (sat 3.9g, mono 5.2g, poly 2.8g); PROTEIN 14.9g; CARB 47.2g; FIBER 3.6g; CHOL 15mg; IRON 3.6mg; SODIUM 584mg; CALC 113mg

For the White Bean and Thyme Crostini:
Arrange 8 (¼-inch-thick) baguette slices on a baking sheet; brush with 2 teaspoons extra-virgin olive oil. Bake at 475° for 4 minutes or until golden.

Sauté ½ teaspoon minced garlic in 2 teaspoons extra-virgin olive oil for 30 seconds or until fragrant. Stir in ⅓ cup rinsed and drained cannellini beans, ⅛ teaspoon kosher salt, and ⅛ teaspoon black pepper; mash with a fork. Add 1 tablespoon warm water and ½ teaspoon fresh lemon juice. Spread 1 teaspoon on each baguette slice; sprinkle evenly with 1 teaspoon fresh thyme leaves.

30 minutes

SHOPPING LIST

Halibut with Caper Salsa Verde
fresh flat-leaf parsley
fresh basil
1 small shallot
1 lemon
extra-virgin olive oil
capers
Dijon mustard
anchovy paste
2 (6-ounce) halibut fillets

Asiago Roasted Fennel
1 large fennel bulb
extra-virgin olive oil
Asiago cheese

GAME PLAN

While oven preheats:
- Trim and slice fennel.
- Prepare salsa verde.
While fennel roasts:
- Cook fish.

Halibut with Caper Salsa Verde
with Asiago Roasted Fennel

The robust salsa (more of a leafy, less saucy sauce) is a dominant presence on the plate. Sweet and mellow roasted fennel makes a particularly fitting side.
Simple Sub: The salsa would be delicious with just about any other fish—tuna in particular.
Prep Pointer: Use a sharp knife to chop the herbs; a dull one will crush them rather than cut them cleanly.
Flavor Hit: A tiny bit of anchovy paste adds depth and complexity to the salsa.

4 teaspoons extra-virgin olive oil, divided
¼ teaspoon freshly ground black pepper, divided
2 tablespoons chopped fresh flat-leaf parsley
2 tablespoons chopped fresh basil
1½ teaspoons capers, drained and minced
1 teaspoon minced shallots
¼ teaspoon Dijon mustard
¼ teaspoon grated lemon rind
⅛ teaspoon anchovy paste
2 (6-ounce) skinless halibut fillets
¼ teaspoon kosher salt

1. Combine 1 tablespoon oil, ⅛ teaspoon pepper, parsley, and next 6 ingredients in a small bowl, tossing well; set aside.
2. Heat a large nonstick skillet over medium-high heat. Add remaining 1 teaspoon oil to pan; swirl to coat. Sprinkle fish fillets evenly with salt and remaining ⅛ teaspoon pepper. Add fish fillets to pan; cook 4 minutes on each side or until desired degree of doneness. Serve fish with salsa verde. Yield: 2 servings (serving size: 1 fillet and about 2 tablespoons salsa verde).

CALORIES 325; FAT 14.5g (sat 2.1g, mono 8.3g, poly 3g); PROTEIN 45.7g; CARB 1.1g; FIBER 0.4g; CHOL 71mg; IRON 2.2mg; SODIUM 454mg; CALC 113mg

continued

For the Asiago Roasted Fennel:
Preheat oven to 400°. Remove outer leaves from 1 large fennel bulb; cut into ¼-inch-thick slices. Place fennel on a jelly-roll pan; drizzle with 1 tablespoon extra-virgin olive oil. Sprinkle with ⅛ tea-spoon kosher salt and ⅛ teaspoon freshly ground black pepper. Bake at 400° for 12 minutes. Toss with 2 tablespoons grated fresh Asiago cheese. Bake an additional 12 minutes or until lightly browned and tender.

SHOPPING LIST

Shiitake and Sweet Pea Risotto
1 small onion
garlic
8 ounces shiitake mushroom caps
fresh thyme
1 (32-ounce) package fat-free, less-sodium chicken broth
Arborio rice
extra-virgin olive oil
dry white wine
butter
Parmigiano-Reggiano cheese
frozen green peas

Romaine-Tomato Salad
1 shallot
1 lemon
fresh thyme
romaine lettuce
1 pint grape tomatoes
extra-virgin olive oil

GAME PLAN

While broth comes to a simmer:
■ Chop onion, garlic, and thyme.
■ Slice mushroom caps.
While risotto cooks:
■ Sauté mushrooms.
■ Prepare salad.
■ Grate cheese.

Quick & Easy • Kid Friendly
Shiitake and Sweet Pea Risotto
with Romaine-Tomato Salad

Prep Pointer: Look for ingredients used multiple times in a menu, and chop all at once.
Simple Sub: Fresh mint, a classic springtime partner for peas, is a fine substitute for thyme.

4 cups fat-free, less-sodium chicken broth
1 tablespoon butter
½ cup finely chopped onion
1½ teaspoons minced garlic, divided
1 cup uncooked Arborio rice
½ cup dry white wine
1 tablespoon extra-virgin olive oil
4 cups thinly sliced shiitake mushroom caps
2 teaspoons chopped fresh thyme, divided
¾ cup frozen green peas
6 tablespoons grated fresh Parmigiano-Reggiano cheese, divided
¼ teaspoon freshly ground black pepper

1. Bring broth to a simmer in a medium saucepan; keep warm over low heat.
2. Melt butter in a large skillet over medium heat. Add onion; cook 2 minutes. Add 1 teaspoon garlic; cook 30 seconds, stirring constantly. Add rice; cook 1 minute, stirring constantly. Add wine; cook 2 minutes or until liquid is absorbed, stirring frequently. Stir in ½ cup broth; cook 2 minutes or until liquid is absorbed, stirring constantly. Add remaining broth, ½ cup at a time, stirring constantly until each portion of broth is absorbed before adding the next (about 20 minutes).
3. Heat oil in a large nonstick skillet over medium-high heat. Add mushrooms to pan; sauté 5 minutes or until tender. Add remaining ½ teaspoon garlic and 1 teaspoon thyme; sauté 1 minute. Set aside.
4. Stir mushrooms, remaining 1 teaspoon thyme, peas, ¼ cup cheese, and pepper into risotto; cook 3 minutes. Spoon about 1¼ cups risotto into each of 4 bowls; sprinkle each with 1½ teaspoons cheese. Yield: 4 servings.

CALORIES 324; FAT 10g (sat 3.7g, mono 3.9g, poly 0.8g); PROTEIN 11.7g; CARB 48g; FIBER 4.5g; CHOL 14mg; IRON 1.3mg; SODIUM 710mg; CALC 101mg

---

For the Romaine-Tomato Salad:
Combine 2 tablespoons minced shallots, 1 tablespoon lemon juice, 1 tablespoon extra-virgin olive oil, ½ teaspoon minced fresh thyme, ¼ teaspoon salt, and ¼ teaspoon pepper, stirring with a whisk. Combine 5 cups torn romaine lettuce and 2 cups halved grape tomatoes. Drizzle with dressing; toss.

SHOPPING LIST

Farfalle with Lamb Ragù, Ricotta, and Mint
1 small onion
carrots
fresh rosemary
fresh mint
garlic
extra-virgin olive oil
large can crushed tomatoes
fat-free, less-sodium chicken broth
8 ounces farfalle
8 ounces lean ground lamb
part-skim ricotta cheese
dry white wine

Baby Greens Salad
1 lemon
5-ounce package baby greens
Dijon mustard
honey
extra-virgin olive oil

GAME PLAN

While lamb browns:
■ Bring water to a boil.
■ Chop onion and carrot.
■ Mince rosemary and garlic.
While sauce simmers:
■ Cook pasta.
■ Prepare dressing.
■ Toss salad just before serving.

Quick & Easy
Farfalle with Lamb Ragù, Ricotta, and Mint
with Baby Greens Salad

Lemon juice prevents apple slices from discoloring, but it also dulls the hue of some green vegetables (or even turns them brown). To avoid this, dress the greens with citrus just before serving.
Time-Saver: Use packaged shredded carrots instead of chopping whole ones.
Leaner Lamb: Prepackaged supermarket ground lamb can have a high fat content; ask your butcher to grind a lean cut for you.
Kid Pleaser: The whimsical bow-tie shape will entice less adventurous eaters to try this dish.

4 teaspoons extra-virgin olive oil, divided
8 ounces lean ground lamb
3/4 teaspoon kosher salt, divided
1/2 cup finely chopped onion
1/4 cup finely chopped carrot
1 teaspoon minced fresh rosemary
2 garlic cloves, minced
1/2 cup dry white wine
1/8 teaspoon freshly ground black pepper
11/2 cups canned crushed tomatoes, undrained
1/2 cup fat-free, less-sodium chicken broth
8 ounces uncooked farfalle (bow-tie pasta)
1/2 cup part-skim ricotta cheese
1/4 cup small fresh mint leaves

1. Heat 1 teaspoon oil in a large skillet over medium-high heat. Add lamb; cook 5 minutes, stirring to crumble. Remove lamb from pan with a slotted spoon; sprinkle with 1/4 teaspoon salt. Discard drippings from pan. Reduce heat to medium-low. Add 2 teaspoons oil, onion, and carrot; cook 5 minutes or until tender, stirring occasionally. Add rosemary and garlic; cook 1 minute, stirring constantly.
2. Return lamb to pan; add wine. Increase heat to medium-high; cook 3 minutes or until liquid almost evaporates. Add remaining 1/2 teaspoon salt and pepper. Stir in tomatoes and broth; bring to a simmer. Partially cover and simmer 10 minutes, stirring occasionally.
3. While sauce simmers, cook pasta according to package directions. Drain; return pasta to pan. Stir in 1 cup sauce and remaining 1 teaspoon oil. Spoon 1 cup pasta mixture onto each of 4 plates; top each serving with 3/4 cup remaining sauce, 2 tablespoons ricotta, and 1 tablespoon mint. Yield: 4 servings.

CALORIES 464; **FAT** 16.9g (sat 5.9g, mono 7.6g, poly 1.5g); **PROTEIN** 23.9g; **CARB** 54.7g; **FIBER** 4.5g; **CHOL** 51mg; **IRON** 4.8mg; **SODIUM** 629mg; **CALC** 157mg

For the Baby Greens Salad:
Combine 2 teaspoons fresh lemon juice, 1/2 teaspoon Dijon mustard, 1/2 teaspoon honey, 1/4 teaspoon kosher salt, and 1/8 teaspoon black pepper in a large bowl, stirring well with a whisk. Whisk in 11/2 tablespoons extra-virgin olive oil. Add 1 (5-ounce) package baby greens; toss gently to coat.

SUPERFAST

We're not talking wimpy, two-alarm dishes. Adjust the heat to really warm up your weeknights with these easy and spicy 20-minute entrées.

Quick & Easy
Jerk-Rubbed Catfish with Spicy Cilantro Slaw

For maximum heat, leave the seeds and membranes in the pepper; habanero will be much hotter than serrano. Ever touched your lips or eyes after chopping hot peppers? Avoid those burns by wearing gloves to prevent the pepper's heat from penetrating your skin.

3 cups cabbage-and-carrot coleslaw mix
2 tablespoons chopped fresh cilantro
3 tablespoons canola mayonnaise
2 tablespoons fresh lime juice
11/2 teaspoons sugar
1 to 11/2 teaspoons finely chopped habanero or serrano pepper
Cooking spray
4 (6-ounce) catfish fillets
4 teaspoons Jamaican jerk seasoning

1. Combine first 6 ingredients in a medium bowl; toss well to coat.
2. Heat a grill pan over medium-high heat. Coat pan with cooking spray. Sprinkle fish evenly with jerk seasoning. Add fish to pan; cook 3 minutes on each side or until desired degree of doneness. Remove from heat; serve fish with slaw. Yield: 4 servings (serving size: 1 fillet and about 1/2 cup slaw).

CALORIES 256; **FAT** 12.6g (sat 3.1g, mono 6.5g, poly 2.8g); **PROTEIN** 26.6g; **CARB** 6.2g; **FIBER** 1.5g; **CHOL** 76mg; **IRON** 0.3mg; **SODIUM** 426mg; **CALC** 24mg

Quick & Easy • Make Ahead
Fiery Beef and Rice Noodle Salad

2 ounces uncooked rice stick noodles
12 ounces flank steak, trimmed
1/4 teaspoon salt
1/4 teaspoon black pepper
Cooking spray
2 cups shredded iceberg lettuce
1/3 cup thinly vertically sliced red onion
1 cucumber, peeled, halved lengthwise, and thinly sliced
1/2 habanero pepper, minced
1/4 cup fresh lime juice
1 tablespoon sugar
1 tablespoon fish sauce
12 fresh basil leaves, torn

1. Cook noodles according to package directions. Drain and rinse with cold water; drain. Coarsely chop noodles.
2. While noodles cook, freeze steak 5 minutes. Remove from freezer; cut across grain into 1/8-inch-thick slices. Sprinkle with salt and black pepper.
3. Heat a large cast-iron skillet over medium-high heat. Coat with cooking spray. Add beef; sauté 4 minutes.
4. Combine steak, noodles, lettuce, and next 3 ingredients. Combine juice, sugar, and fish sauce; pour over noodle mixture, tossing gently. Sprinkle with basil. Yield: 4 servings (serving size: 11/2 cups salad and about 1 tablespoon basil).

CALORIES 197; **FAT** 4.3g (sat 1.7g, mono 1.6g, poly 0.2g); **PROTEIN** 20g; **CARB** 20.2g; **FIBER** 1.3g; **CHOL** 27mg; **IRON** 1.8mg; **SODIUM** 545mg; **CALC** 35mg

Spicy Shrimp and Grits

3 cups 1% low-fat milk
1 cup water
1 tablespoon butter
½ teaspoon salt, divided
¼ teaspoon black pepper, divided
1 cup uncooked quick-cooking grits
½ cup (2 ounces) grated fresh Parmesan
   cheese
4 applewood-smoked bacon slices
1 pound peeled, deveined large shrimp
1 cup thinly vertically sliced white onion
2 cups grape tomatoes, halved
1 teaspoon hot pepper sauce or chopped
   chipotle chile, canned in adobo sauce
⅛ teaspoon ground or crushed red pepper
¼ cup green onion strips

1. Combine milk, water, butter, ¼ teaspoon salt, and ⅛ teaspoon black pepper in a saucepan over medium-high heat. Bring to a simmer; gradually add grits, stirring constantly with a whisk. Reduce heat to medium; cook 4 minutes or until thick, stirring occasionally. Remove from heat; stir in cheese.
2. While grits cook, cook bacon in a large nonstick skillet over medium heat until crisp. Remove bacon from pan, reserving 2 teaspoons drippings; crumble bacon. Add shrimp to drippings in pan; cook 2 minutes on each side or until done. Remove shrimp from pan. Add white onion to pan; sauté 1 minute. Stir in bacon, tomatoes, remaining ¼ teaspoon salt, and remaining ⅛ teaspoon black pepper; sauté 2 minutes, stirring occasionally. Add shrimp, pepper sauce, and red pepper; cook 1 minute or until shrimp are heated. Serve over grits; sprinkle with green onions. Yield: 4 servings (serving size: 1 cup grits, about 1½ cups shrimp mixture, and 1 tablespoon green onions).

CALORIES 510; **FAT** 15.9g (sat 7.5g, mono 4.9g, poly 1.8g); **PROTEIN** 41.1g; **CARB** 49.5g; **FIBER** 2.4g; **CHOL** 206mg; **IRON** 5mg; **SODIUM** 972mg; **CALC** 481mg

Szechuan-Style Tofu with Peanuts

2 (3½-ounce) bags boil-in-bag jasmine rice
1 (14-ounce) package water-packed firm tofu,
   drained and cut into 1-inch pieces
Cooking spray
½ cup fat-free, less-sodium chicken broth
1 tablespoon sambal oelek (ground fresh chile
   paste)
1 tablespoon less-sodium soy sauce
1 teaspoon cornstarch
2 teaspoons black bean garlic sauce
1 tablespoon canola oil
¼ teaspoon salt
1 (8-ounce) package presliced mushrooms
½ cup matchstick-cut carrots
1 tablespoon bottled ground fresh ginger
   (such as Spice World)
½ cup chopped green onions
¼ cup unsalted dry-roasted peanuts,
   chopped

1. Preheat broiler.
2. Cook rice according to package directions, omitting salt and fat.
3. Arrange tofu in a single layer on a foil-lined jelly-roll pan coated with cooking spray; broil 14 minutes or until golden.
4. While tofu cooks, combine broth and next 4 ingredients, stirring with a whisk; set aside.
5. Heat oil in a large nonstick skillet over medium-high heat. Add salt and mushrooms; sauté 4 minutes or until mushrooms begin to release liquid, stirring occasionally. Stir in carrots and ginger; cook 1 minute. Add broth mixture; cook 30 seconds or until sauce begins to thicken. Remove from heat; stir in tofu and onions. Serve over rice; sprinkle with peanuts. Yield: 4 servings (serving size: ¾ cup rice, about ¾ cup tofu mixture, and 1 tablespoon peanuts).

CALORIES 389; **FAT** 14.3g (sat 2.1g, mono 5.5g, poly 6.2g); **PROTEIN** 17.2g; **CARB** 51.6g; **FIBER** 2.4g; **CHOL** 0mg; **IRON** 4mg; **SODIUM** 619mg; **CALC** 92mg

3 WAYS TO CRANK UP THE HEAT

HOT SAUCES
Chiles mixed with vinegar add tang and spice.

FRESH CHILE PEPPERS
Fresh fire, hot to superhot

RED PEPPER
Ground or crushed red pepper adds piquant taste.

RECIPE HALL OF FAME

OUR FAVORITE WHOLE-WHEAT BUTTERMILK PANCAKES

Light, fluffy flapjacks, topped with butter and drizzled with sweet syrup, guarantee you'll start the day off right.

Quick & Easy • Freezeable
Kid Friendly

Whole-Wheat Buttermilk Pancakes

3.4 ounces all-purpose flour (about ¾ cup)
3.6 ounces whole-wheat flour (about ¾ cup)
3 tablespoons sugar
1½ teaspoons baking powder
½ teaspoon baking soda
½ teaspoon salt
1½ cups low-fat buttermilk
1 tablespoon canola oil
1 large egg
1 large egg white
Cooking spray
¾ cup maple syrup
3 tablespoons butter

1. Weigh or lightly spoon flours into dry measuring cups; level with a knife. Combine flours, sugar, and next 3 ingredients in a large bowl, stirring with a whisk. Combine buttermilk and next 3 ingredients, stirring with a whisk. Add buttermilk mixture to flour mixture, stirring just until moist.

2. Heat a nonstick griddle or nonstick skillet over medium heat. Coat pan with cooking spray. Spoon about ¼ cup batter per pancake onto griddle. Turn pancakes over when tops are covered with bubbles and edges look cooked. Serve with syrup and butter. Yield: 6 servings (serving size: 2 pancakes, 2 tablespoons syrup, and 1½ teaspoons butter).

CALORIES 347; **FAT** 9.9g (sat 4.4g, mono 3.4g, poly 1.3g); **PROTEIN** 7.4g; **CARB** 59.2g; **FIBER** 2.3g; **CHOL** 53mg; **IRON** 2.1mg; **SODIUM** 520mg; **CALC** 197mg

SPECIAL OCCASION RECIPE

PAVLOVAS FOR PASSOVER

Nests of fluffy egg whites become crisp meringues to fill with berries and lemon curd.

Make Ahead • Kid Friendly

Pistachio Pavlovas with Lemon Curd and Berries
(pictured on page 248)

You can make the components ahead, and assemble at the last minute. If serving on an occasion other than Passover, try adding one teaspoon vanilla extract to the meringues.

Meringues:
¼ teaspoon kosher-for-Passover cream of tartar
4 large egg whites
¾ cup granulated sugar
¼ cup dry-roasted pistachios, chopped

Lemon Curd:
2 large eggs
1 large egg white
½ cup granulated sugar
2 teaspoons grated lemon rind
½ cup fresh lemon juice (about 3 lemons)
1 teaspoon potato starch
Dash of salt
2 (6-ounce) packages fresh raspberries
1 tablespoon kosher-for-Passover powdered sugar (optional)

1. Preheat oven to 250°.

2. To prepare meringues, cover 2 baking sheets with parchment paper. Draw 4 (4-inch) circles on each piece of paper. Turn paper over; secure with masking tape.

3. Place cream of tartar and 4 egg whites in a large bowl; beat with a mixer at high speed until foamy. Gradually add ¾ cup granulated sugar, 1 tablespoon at a time, beating until stiff peaks form.

4. Divide egg white mixture among 8 circles on baking sheets. Shape meringues into nests with 1-inch sides using back of a spoon. Sprinkle with nuts.

5. Bake at 250° for 1 hour, rotating baking sheets after 30 minutes. Turn oven off; cool meringue nests in closed oven 2 hours. Remove from oven, and carefully remove nests from paper.

6. To prepare lemon curd, combine whole eggs and 1 egg white in a medium bowl; stir well with a whisk. Heat ½ cup granulated sugar and next 4 ingredients over medium-high heat in a small, heavy saucepan to 180° or until tiny bubbles form around edge. Gradually add hot juice mixture to egg mixture, stirring constantly with a whisk. Return juice mixture to pan. Cook over medium heat for 2 minutes or until thick, stirring constantly. Spoon curd into a bowl; cool to room temperature. Cover and chill.

7. Arrange about ¼ cup raspberries in each meringue nest; top with about 2 tablespoons lemon curd. Sprinkle nests evenly with powdered sugar, if desired. Serve immediately. Yield: 8 servings (serving size: 1 pavlova).

CALORIES 199; **FAT** 3.3g (sat 0.6g, mono 1.4g, poly 0.9g); **PROTEIN** 5.3g; **CARB** 39.4g; **FIBER** 3.3g; **CHOL** 53mg; **IRON** 0.7mg; **SODIUM** 71mg; **CALC** 25mg

HOW TO MAKE PERFECT MERINGUE NESTS

1 CHOP PISTACHIOS. Chop the pistachios—but not too finely. You want them to provide a burst of nutty flavor and firm crunch to every bite.

2 MAKE A TEMPLATE. Trace circles onto parchment paper as a guide for shaping the nests; a standard oatmeal can is the perfect size. Turn the paper (and pencil markings) over before securing to the pans.

3 SHAPE THE NESTS. Shape the egg white mixture into nest shapes with the back of a spoon—smooth the inside of the nests to create a bowl-like shape.

SOUR CREAM COFFEE CAKE

Whole grains. Toasty oats and nuts. Mmm....

Some coffee cakes might as well be called fatty cakes: They're so heavy with butter, sugar, and nuts that a slice is no good way to begin your day. We slimmed down this classic and used whole grains in the batter. The result: a moist and satisfying breakfast cake. Here's how we did it.

Light baking is always tricky, and adding the whole-grain goal upped the ante again. A combination of all-purpose, whole-wheat, and homemade whole-grain rolled oat flour anchored the batter. With a little butter, light sour cream, and a mix of granulated and brown sugars, we achieved the best texture and flavor for the fewest calories and saturated fat. Instead of an overly sweet, heavy, and caloric breakfast, our trimmed-down version is so good, you won't believe half the grains are whole. A slice, with a hot cuppa, is a great way to start incorporating more whole grains into your diet.

LIGHT, WHOLE-GRAIN BAKING 101

• Toasting rolled oats removes some of the raw flavor from the whole grain and enhances its natural nuttiness. Toast oats ahead; store in an airtight container.

• Because we grind some of the oats in a food processor, the batter remains a tad lumpy. For a tender, moist cake, do not overmix.

• Because we use only 1 tablespoon butter, you won't see big clumps of sugar and oats as in traditional streusel-like toppings. Ours yields a sweet, crunchy top.

Staff Favorite • Make Ahead
Freezable • Kid Friendly

Sour Cream Coffee Cake

Mix the dry ingredients with the wet until just combined (don't overstir) for the best result. This is tastiest warm from the oven, but leftovers are also delicious.

¾ cup old-fashioned rolled oats (about 2.5 ounces), divided
Cooking spray
4.5 ounces all-purpose flour (about 1 cup)
1 ounce whole-wheat flour (about ¼ cup)
1 teaspoon baking powder
½ teaspoon baking soda
¼ teaspoon salt
½ cup granulated sugar
½ cup packed brown sugar, divided
⅓ cup butter, softened
2 large eggs
1 teaspoon vanilla extract
1 (8-ounce) carton light sour cream (such as Daisy)
2 tablespoons finely chopped walnuts, toasted
½ teaspoon ground cinnamon
1 tablespoon chilled butter, cut into small pieces

1. Preheat oven to 350°.
2. Spread oats in a single layer on a baking sheet. Bake at 350° for 6 minutes or until oats are barely fragrant and light brown.
3. Coat a 9-inch springform pan with cooking spray; set aside.
4. Reserve ¼ cup oats; set aside. Place remaining ½ cup oats in a food processor; process 4 seconds or until finely ground. Weigh or lightly spoon flours into dry measuring cups; level with a knife. Combine processed oats, flours, baking powder, baking soda, and salt; stir with a whisk.
5. Place granulated sugar, ¼ cup brown sugar, and ⅓ cup butter in a large bowl. Beat with a mixer at medium speed 3 minutes or until light and fluffy. Add eggs, 1 at a time, beating well after each addition. Beat in vanilla. Add flour mixture to sugar mixture alternately with sour cream, beginning and ending with flour mixture. (Batter will be slightly lumpy because of oats.) Spoon batter into prepared pan; spread evenly.
6. Combine remaining ¼ cup oats, remaining ¼ cup brown sugar, nuts, and cinnamon in a bowl. Cut in 1 table-spoon butter with a pastry blender or 2 knives until well blended. Sprinkle top of batter evenly with nut mixture. Bake at 350° for 38 minutes or until a wooden pick inserted in center comes out clean, top is golden, and cake begins to pull away from sides of pan. Cool cake in pan for 10 minutes; remove from pan. Yield: 10 servings (serving size: 1 piece).

CALORIES 276; FAT 11.5g (sat 6.5g, mono 2.5g, poly 1.2g); PROTEIN 5.5g; CARB 38.5g; FIBER 1.4g; CHOL 61mg; IRON 1.5mg; SODIUM 247mg; CALC 59mg

OLD WAY	OUR WAY
501 calories per serving	276 calories per serving
32.2 grams total fat	11.5 grams total fat
14.7 grams saturated fat	6.5 grams saturated fat
3 sticks of butter	¾ stick of butter
Refined all-purpose and cake flours	All-purpose and whole-wheat flours
1 pound full-fat sour cream	½ pound light sour cream

A FEAST OF SPRING

What fresh, savory surprises this updated menu for Easter brings! Best of all, it's really doable: Just follow our plan.

Baked ham, glazed with aromatic vermouth ... a brisk and effervescent Champagne Limoncello Cocktail ... dill and smoked salmon–stuffed eggs (a delightful variation on the old deviled standard) ... the glorious spring blessings of peak-season asparagus, sweet carrots, fingerling potatoes, baby artichokes, and strawberries ... Do we have your appetite's attention yet? We had great fun putting fresh twists on this classic ham dinner for Easter. It's a feast to take proudly to the table. Promise: With our tips and make-ahead timeline, you can pull off the whole menu with ease.

EASTER DINNER

serves 8

Champagne Limoncello Cocktails

Deviled Eggs with Smoked Salmon and Herbs

Carrot Soup with Yogurt

Asparagus and Spring Greens Salad with Gorgonzola Vinaigrette

Baked Ham with Rosemary and Sweet Vermouth

Roasted Fingerling Potatoes and Baby Artichokes

No-Knead Overnight Parmesan and Thyme Rolls

Lavender-Scented Strawberries with Honey Cream

Make Ahead • Kid Friendly

Deviled Eggs with Smoked Salmon and Herbs

Use any combination of herbs you like for this easy and tasty starter.

8 large eggs
1/4 cup fat-free sour cream
1 tablespoon chopped fresh chives
2 tablespoons reduced-fat mayonnaise
1 tablespoon Dijon mustard
2 teaspoons minced fresh tarragon
2 teaspoons minced fresh dill
1/4 teaspoon freshly ground black pepper
2 ounces cold-smoked salmon, finely chopped
16 small fresh dill sprigs (optional)
16 small fresh tarragon sprigs (optional)

1. Place eggs in a large saucepan. Cover with cool water to 1 inch above eggs; bring just to a rolling boil. Remove from heat; cover and let stand 15 minutes. Drain and rinse with cold running water until cool.
2. Peel eggs; cut in half lengthwise. Place yolks in a medium bowl; mash with a fork until smooth. Add sour cream and next 7 ingredients; stir well. Spoon mixture into egg white halves (about 1 tablespoon in each half). Garnish with dill and tarragon sprigs, if desired. Yield: 8 servings (serving size: 2 stuffed egg halves).

CALORIES 95; FAT 5.8g (sat 1.6g, mono 2.1g, poly 1g); PROTEIN 8.1g; CARB 2.6g; FIBER 0g; CHOL 214mg; IRON 1mg; SODIUM 295mg; CALC 44mg

---

COUNTDOWN TO DINNER

Follow this timeline to get a lot of the work done in advance.

5 DAYS AHEAD:
- Hard-cook eggs; refrigerate in shells.

2 DAYS AHEAD:
- Make Gorgonzola Vinaigrette.
- Blanch asparagus for salad.
- Make vermouth glaze for ham.
- Make lavender syrup for dessert.

1 DAY AHEAD:
- Fill eggs (leave off herb garnish).
- Make soup.
- Rub ham with seasonings.
- Make roll dough.
- Make Honey Cream.

3 HOURS AHEAD:
- Start cooking ham.

1 TO 2 HOURS AHEAD:
- Shape dough and allow to rise.
- Prep artichokes.
- Quarter strawberries.

WHILE HAM RESTS:
- Cook potatoes and artichokes.
- Reheat soup (add water or chicken broth if soup is too thick).
- Top eggs with herb garnish.

LAST-MINUTE:
- Bake rolls.
- Make cocktails.
- Toss salad just before serving.
- Assemble dessert.

Asparagus and Spring Greens Salad with Gorgonzola Vinaigrette

1 pound green and white asparagus, trimmed and cut into (2-inch) pieces
2¼ teaspoons salt, divided
2 tablespoons minced shallots
2 tablespoons white balsamic vinegar
2 tablespoons extra-virgin olive oil
½ teaspoon grated lemon rind
¼ teaspoon freshly ground black pepper
½ cup (2 ounces) crumbled Gorgonzola cheese, divided
1 (5-ounce) package mixed salad greens

1. Cook asparagus and 2 teaspoons salt in boiling water 2 minutes or until crisp-tender. Drain and rinse asparagus under cold water; drain.
2. Combine remaining ¼ teaspoon salt, shallots, and next 4 ingredients in a small bowl, stirring with a whisk. Stir in ¼ cup cheese.
3. Combine asparagus and greens in a large bowl. Drizzle with dressing; toss gently to coat. Sprinkle with remaining ¼ cup cheese. Yield: 8 servings (serving size: about 1 cup).

CALORIES 77; **FAT** 5.5g (sat 1.8g, mono 3g, poly 0.5g); **PROTEIN** 3.1g; **CARB** 4g; **FIBER** 1.6g; **CHOL** 5mg; **IRON** 1.6mg; **SODIUM** 239mg; **CALC** 63mg

Carrot Soup with Yogurt

A hint of toasted sesame oil lends depth to this velvety soup. Garnish with sautéed carrot strips.

2 teaspoons dark sesame oil
⅓ cup sliced shallots (about 1 large)
1 pound baby carrots, peeled and cut into 2-inch pieces
2 cups fat-free, less-sodium chicken broth
1 teaspoon grated peeled fresh ginger
½ cup 2% Greek-style plain yogurt
8 fresh mint sprigs

1. Heat oil in a medium saucepan over medium heat. Add shallots to pan; cook 2 minutes or until almost tender, stirring occasionally. Add carrots; cook 4 minutes. Add broth; bring to a boil. Cover, reduce heat, and simmer 22 minutes or until tender. Add ginger; cook 8 minutes or until carrots are very tender. Cover and let stand 5 minutes at room temperature.
2. Pour half of carrot mixture into a blender. Remove center piece of blender lid (to allow steam to escape); secure blender lid on blender. Place a clean towel over opening in blender lid (to avoid splatters). Blend until smooth. Pour into a large bowl. Repeat procedure with remaining carrot mixture. Return pureed soup to pan; heat over medium heat 2 minutes or until heated.
3. Spoon soup into small bowls, and top with plain yogurt and fresh mint sprigs. Yield: 8 servings (serving size: ½ cup soup, 1 tablespoon yogurt, and 1 mint sprig).

CALORIES 47; **FAT** 1.6g (sat 0.4g, mono 0.5g, poly 0.5g); **PROTEIN** 2.2g; **CARB** 6.5g; **FIBER** 1.7g; **CHOL** 1mg; **IRON** 0.6mg; **SODIUM** 163mg; **CALC** 36mg

Champagne Limoncello Cocktails

For a pretty touch, rub a cut lemon wedge on the rim of the glass, and roll in sugar.

8 (3 x ½-inch) strips lemon rind
8 tablespoons Limoncello (lemon-flavored liqueur)
4 teaspoons fresh lemon juice
1 (750-milliliter) bottle brut Champagne, chilled

1. Roll up each strip of lemon rind; place 1 into each of 8 Champagne flutes. Add 1 tablespoon liqueur and ½ teaspoon juice to each glass. Divide Champagne evenly among glasses. Serve immediately. Yield: 8 servings (serving size: about ½ cup).

CALORIES 105; **FAT** 0g; **PROTEIN** 0g; **CARB** 1.8g; **FIBER** 0g; **CHOL** 0mg; **IRON** 0mg; **SODIUM** 0mg; **CALC** 0mg

Lavender-Scented Strawberries with Honey Cream

⅓ cup water
⅓ cup sugar
½ teaspoon dried lavender (such as McCormick)
½ teaspoon unflavored gelatin
1 tablespoon water
¼ cup honey
2 tablespoons cornstarch
⅛ teaspoon salt
3 large egg yolks
1 cup 2% reduced-fat milk
1 (6-ounce) container 2% Greek-style plain yogurt
2 cups quartered strawberries

1. Bring first 3 ingredients to a boil in a small saucepan; cook 1 minute or until sugar dissolves, stirring occasionally. Remove from heat; let stand 10 minutes. Strain syrup through a sieve into a small bowl; discard solids. Chill.
2. Sprinkle gelatin over 1 tablespoon water in a small bowl. Let stand 1 minute or until gelatin dissolves.
3. Combine honey and next 3 ingredients in a medium bowl; stir well with a whisk.
4. Heat milk over medium-high heat in a small heavy saucepan to 180° or until tiny bubbles form around edge (do not boil). Gradually add hot milk to egg mixture, stirring constantly with a whisk. Return milk mixture to pan. Cook over medium heat until thick and bubbly (about 2 minutes), stirring constantly. Remove from heat; add gelatin mixture, stirring well. Pour milk mixture into a bowl; stir occasionally until cool but not set (about 20 minutes). Stir in yogurt. Spoon ¼ cup yogurt mixture into each of 8 dessert glasses or bowls. Cover and chill at least 2 hours.
5. Top each serving with ¼ cup strawberries, and drizzle with 2 teaspoons syrup. Yield: 8 servings.

CALORIES 135; **FAT** 2.8g (sat 1.3g, mono 0.9g, poly 0.4g); **PROTEIN** 4.3g; **CARB** 24.6g; **FIBER** 0.9g; **CHOL** 80mg; **IRON** 0.4mg; **SODIUM** 63mg; **CALC** 72mg

Make Ahead • Kid Friendly

No-Knead Overnight Parmesan and Thyme Rolls

(pictured on page 252)

Stir the dough together quickly the day before shaping and baking—no kneading necessary. The dough is more like a thick batter; don't add additional flour or the rolls will turn out dry.

½ teaspoon dry yeast
2 tablespoons warm water (100° to 110°)
2 tablespoons extra-virgin olive oil, divided
1 teaspoon dried thyme
⅓ cup 2% reduced-fat milk
½ cup (2 ounces) grated Parmigiano-
   Reggiano cheese, divided
1 tablespoon sugar
½ teaspoon kosher salt
1 large egg, lightly beaten
1.1 ounces whole-wheat white flour (about
   ¼ cup)
5.6 ounces all-purpose flour (about 1¼ cups),
   divided
Cooking spray
½ teaspoon cracked black pepper

1. Dissolve yeast in 2 tablespoons warm water in a large bowl; let stand 5 minutes or until bubbly.
2. Heat 1 tablespoon oil in a small saucepan over medium heat. Add thyme to pan; cook 1 minute or until bubbly and fragrant. Add thyme mixture and milk to yeast mixture, stirring with a whisk; add ¼ cup cheese, sugar, salt, and egg, stirring well.
3. Weigh or lightly spoon whole-wheat white flour into a dry measuring cup; level with a knife. Using a wooden spoon, stir whole-wheat white flour into yeast mixture. Weigh or lightly spoon 4.5 ounces (about 1 cup) all-purpose flour into a dry measuring cup; level with a knife. Add all-purpose flour to yeast mixture, stirring well. Add enough of remaining 1.1 ounces (about ¼ cup) all-purpose flour, 1 tablespoon at a time, to form a smooth but very sticky dough. Place dough in a large bowl coated with cooking spray, turning to coat top. Cover and refrigerate overnight. (Dough will not double in size.)

4. Remove dough from refrigerator. Do not punch dough down. Turn dough out onto a floured surface; sprinkle dough lightly with flour. Roll dough into a 12 x 7–inch rectangle. Brush dough with remaining 1 tablespoon oil. Sprinkle remaining ¼ cup cheese evenly over dough; sprinkle with pepper. Beginning with a long side, roll up dough jelly-roll fashion. Pinch seam to seal (do not seal ends of roll). Cut roll into 8 (1½-inch) slices. Place slices, cut sides up, on a baking sheet covered with parchment paper. Cover and let rise in a warm place (85°), free from drafts, 1 hour or until rolls have risen slightly.
5. Preheat oven to 400°.
6. Place pan in oven, and immediately reduce heat to 375°. Bake rolls at 375° for 12 minutes or until golden brown. Serve warm. Yield: 8 servings (serving size: 1 roll).

CALORIES 161; FAT 6.3g (sat 2g, mono 3.3g, poly 0.6g); PROTEIN 6.3g; CARB 19.7g; FIBER 1.3g; CHOL 32mg; IRON 1.4mg; SODIUM 246mg; CALC 112mg

Roasted Fingerling Potatoes and Baby Artichokes

6 cups water
2 tablespoons fresh lemon juice
2 pounds baby artichokes
2 tablespoons extra-virgin olive oil
1¼ pounds small red fingerling potatoes,
   halved lengthwise
Cooking spray
1 tablespoon butter
2 teaspoons chopped fresh parsley
1 teaspoon grated lemon rind
1 teaspoon kosher salt
½ teaspoon black pepper

1. Preheat oven to 425°.
2. Combine 6 cups water and lemon juice in a large bowl. Cut off stem of each artichoke to within 1 inch of base; peel stem. Remove bottom leaves and tough outer leaves, leaving tender heart and bottom. Cut each artichoke in half lengthwise. Remove fuzzy thistle from bottom with a spoon. Place artichokes in lemon water.

3. Combine oil and potatoes; toss well. Arrange potatoes in a single layer on a jelly-roll pan coated with cooking spray. Bake at 425° for 15 minutes. Drain artichokes; add artichokes to potatoes, tossing to combine. Bake an additional 15 minutes or until tender. Place vegetables in a large bowl. Toss with butter and remaining ingredients. Serve immediately. Yield: 8 servings.

CALORIES 123; FAT 4.9g (sat 1.4g, mono 2.8g, poly 0.4g); PROTEIN 3.2g; CARB 17.4g; FIBER 3.4g; CHOL 4mg; IRON 1.3mg; SODIUM 292mg; CALC 22mg

Kid Friendly

Baked Ham with Rosemary and Sweet Vermouth

This ham takes cues from the Mediterranean with piney rosemary and sweet vermouth.

2 cups sweet vermouth
2 tablespoons honey
1 (6-pound) 33%-less-sodium smoked, fully
   cooked ham half
Cooking spray
2 tablespoons chopped fresh rosemary
1 teaspoon freshly ground black pepper
3 garlic cloves, minced

1. Preheat oven to 350°.
2. Bring vermouth and honey to a boil in a small heavy saucepan; cook 16 minutes or until reduced to about ¾ cup. Remove pan from heat.
3. Trim fat and rind from ham. Score outside of ham in a diamond pattern. Place ham on a broiler pan coated with cooking spray. Rub ham evenly with rosemary, pepper, and garlic. Bake at 350° for 1½ hours. Brush ham with ¼ cup vermouth mixture; cover loosely with foil. Bake an additional 45 minutes or until a thermometer inserted in center of ham registers 135°, basting with vermouth mixture every 15 minutes. Place ham on a serving platter; let stand 30 minutes before slicing. Yield: 16 servings (serving size: about 3 ounces meat).

CALORIES 147; FAT 6.1g (sat 2g, mono 2.9g, poly 0.7g); PROTEIN 14.2g; CARB 4.5g; FIBER 0.1g; CHOL 51mg; IRON 0.8mg; SODIUM 872mg; CALC 3mg

HERBED RACK OF LAMB WITH LINGONBERRY SAUCE

Juicy rib meat with a sweet-tangy sauce is sure to wow your guests.

Herbed Rack of Lamb with Lingonberry Sauce

Lingonberry preserves are available at many supermarkets and gourmet shops; substitute whole-berry cranberry sauce.

2 tablespoons finely chopped fresh thyme
2 tablespoons finely chopped fresh parsley
1 teaspoon minced fresh rosemary
2 teaspoons Dijon mustard
1 large garlic clove, minced
5 tablespoons raspberry vinegar, divided
2 (1½-pound) French-cut racks of lamb
   (8 ribs each), trimmed
½ teaspoon salt, divided
½ teaspoon freshly ground black pepper,
   divided
Cooking spray
¼ cup tawny port
3 tablespoons finely chopped shallots
½ cup fat-free, less-sodium beef broth
⅓ cup lingonberry preserves
1½ teaspoons butter

1. Preheat oven to 400°.
2. Combine first 5 ingredients in a bowl; stir in 1 tablespoon vinegar.
3. Sprinkle lamb with ¼ teaspoon salt and ¼ teaspoon pepper. Heat a large ovenproof skillet over medium-high heat. Coat pan with cooking spray. Add lamb to pan; cook 2 minutes on each side or until browned. Remove lamb from pan; pat thyme mixture over lamb. Return lamb to pan; place pan in oven. Bake at 400° for 15 minutes or until a thermometer registers

138°. Remove lamb from pan, and let stand for 10 minutes. Cut into chops.
4. Return pan to medium-high heat; add remaining ¼ cup vinegar, port, and shallots. Bring to a boil. Boil 1 minute or until mixture is reduced by half; stir in broth. Bring to a boil; cook 3 minutes or until liquid measures about ½ cup. Stir in remaining ¼ teaspoon salt, remaining ¼ teaspoon pepper, and preserves. Cook 1 minute; remove from heat. Add butter, stirring until butter melts. Serve sauce with lamb. Yield: 4 servings (serving size: 4 chops and about 3 tablespoons sauce).

CALORIES 408; **FAT** 16.6g (sat 7.5g, mono 6.3g, poly 1g); **PROTEIN** 37g; **CARB** 26.1g; **FIBER** 0.4g; **CHOL** 144mg; **IRON** 3.3mg; **SODIUM** 451mg; **CALC** 36mg

LAMB—STATESIDE VS. DOWN UNDER

Although sheep are raised all over the world, the most readily available racks of lamb originate in the United States, Australia, and New Zealand. New Zealand lamb, which makes up about 20 percent of the U.S. market, elicits the most robust, gamey flavor. It's also grass-fed, leaner, and smaller—a rack usually weighs a pound or less. Because of their size, these lamb chops are often favored for appetizers.

Domestic and Australian lamb are similar in taste and texture. Much heavier than New Zealand racks, these two options often feed on grass, though American lamb is usually finished on grain. Both also have a lighter, milder flavor. The racks range from 1¼ to 2 pounds and have slightly more marbling. The cooked meat from our Frenched racks is comparable in calories and fat to an equal weight of cooked beef skirt steak.

American lamb, which makes up about 50 percent of the U.S. market, is sometimes called Colorado lamb. This moniker is often misleading: Although much of the meat is processed in the state, the lambs often arrive from Texas, California, or any Rocky Mountain states. Domestic racks are also the most expensive at $18 to $20 per pound. Australian costs $15 to $18, and New Zealand lamb ranges from $14 to $17.

Imported lamb usually arrives vacuum-sealed and frozen to maintain its quality, while American varieties are often sold fresh. Ask your butcher to French the rack.

DUMPLINGS: FUN, EASY, FULL OF FLAVOR

Hearty yet delicately textured, these little pasta packages are favorites from Italy to India to Japan.

Gyoza with Soy-Citrus Sauce

1 tablespoon minced peeled fresh ginger
1 tablespoon less-sodium soy sauce
½ teaspoon grated orange rind
1 teaspoon fresh orange juice
¼ teaspoon kosher salt
⅛ teaspoon crushed red pepper
8 ounces shiitake mushrooms, stemmed
   and chopped
8 ounces button mushrooms, chopped
2 green onions, cut into 2-inch pieces
2 garlic cloves
Cooking spray
6 ounces chopped fresh spinach
28 gyoza skins
2 teaspoons peanut oil, divided
½ cup organic vegetable broth, divided
⅓ cup fresh orange juice
1 tablespoon less-sodium soy sauce
2 teaspoons rice vinegar
Fresh chives (optional)

1. Place first 10 ingredients in a food processor, and process until finely chopped.
2. Heat a large nonstick skillet over medium heat. Coat pan with cooking spray. Add mushroom mixture and spinach to pan; cook 10 minutes or until liquid evaporates, stirring frequently. Cool slightly.
3. Working with 1 gyoza skin at a time (cover remaining skins to prevent drying), moisten edges of skin with water. Spoon about 1 tablespoon spinach mixture into center of circle. Fold in

half, pinching edges together to seal. Place dumpling, seam side up, on a baking sheet (cover loosely with a towel to prevent drying). Repeat procedure with remaining skins and filling.

4. Heat 1 teaspoon oil in a large non-stick skillet over medium-high heat. Add half of dumplings to pan; cook 2 minutes on each side or until lightly browned. Remove from pan; keep warm. Repeat procedure with remaining 1 teaspoon oil and remaining dumplings. Add ¼ cup broth, ⅓ cup juice, 1 tablespoon soy sauce, and vinegar to pan; bring to a boil. Place dipping sauce in a small bowl.

5. Add remaining ¼ cup broth to pan; bring to a boil. Add dumplings; cover and cook 2 minutes or until tender. Remove from pan. Serve with dipping sauce; top with chives, if desired. Yield: 4 servings (serving size: 7 dumplings and 2 tablespoons sauce).

CALORIES 200; FAT 3.1g (sat 0.5g, mono 1.2g, poly 1g); PROTEIN 9.4g; CARB 33.3g; FIBER 3.4g; CHOL 7mg; IRON 4mg; SODIUM 748mg; CALC 74mg

Potato Gnocchi with Lemon-Thyme Sauce

2 (10-ounce) baking potatoes
2.5 ounces all-purpose flour (about ½ cup plus 1 tablespoon)
1¾ teaspoons kosher salt, divided
Cooking spray
1 gallon water
4 teaspoons butter
4 teaspoons extra-virgin olive oil
½ cup finely chopped shallots
1 tablespoon grated lemon rind
2 teaspoons chopped fresh thyme
2 teaspoons fresh lemon juice
Dash of kosher salt
2 tablespoons shaved fresh Parmigiano-Reggiano cheese
¼ teaspoon freshly ground black pepper

1. Preheat oven to 400°.
2. Pierce potatoes with a fork; bake at 400° for 1 hour or until tender. Cool slightly. Peel potatoes; discard peels. Press cooked potatoes through a potato ricer into a large bowl. Weigh or lightly spoon flour into a dry measuring cup and spoon; level with a knife. Combine potatoes, flour, and ¾ teaspoon salt. Stir well to form a dough.

3. Turn dough out onto a lightly floured surface. Knead until smooth. Divide dough into 4 equal portions, shaping each portion into a 20-inch-long rope. Cut each rope into 20 (1-inch) pieces; roll each piece into a ball. Working with 1 dough piece at a time (cover remaining dough to prevent drying), using your thumb, roll dough piece down the tines of a lightly floured fork (gnocchi will have ridges on 1 side and an indentation on the other). Place gnocchi on a baking sheet coated with cooking spray. Cover and set aside.

4. Bring 1 gallon water and remaining 1 teaspoon salt to boil in a large Dutch oven. Add half of gnocchi to boiling water; cook gnocchi for 1½ minutes or until done (gnocchi will rise to surface). Remove gnocchi with a slotted spoon, and place in a colander to drain. Repeat procedure with remaining gnocchi.

5. Heat butter and olive oil in a medium skillet over medium heat. Add shallots to pan; cook 10 minutes or until tender, stirring occasionally (do not brown). Stir in rind and next 3 ingredients. Combine butter mixture, gnocchi, cheese, and pepper in a large bowl; toss gently to coat. Yield: 6 servings (serving size: ⅔ cup).

CALORIES 182; FAT 6.3g (sat 2.4g, mono 3g, poly 0.7g); PROTEIN 3.8g; CARB 28.5g; FIBER 1.7g; CHOL 8.2mg; IRON 1.1mg; SODIUM 337mg; CALC 32mg

Curried Vegetable Samosas with Cilantro-Mint Chutney

Chutney:
½ cup fresh cilantro leaves
½ cup fresh mint leaves
¼ cup chopped red onion
2 tablespoons fresh lemon juice
1 tablespoon water
¼ teaspoon kosher salt
⅛ teaspoon sugar
1 serrano chile, coarsely chopped
1 (½-inch) piece peeled fresh ginger

Samosas:
1¼ cups mashed cooked peeled baking potatoes
¼ cup cooked yellow lentils
1 tablespoon minced fresh mint
1 teaspoon Madras curry powder
1 teaspoon butter, softened
¼ teaspoon kosher salt
¼ teaspoon ground cumin
½ cup frozen petite green peas, thawed
10 egg roll wrappers
1 large egg, lightly beaten
Cooking spray

1. To prepare chutney, place first 9 ingredients in a blender; process until smooth. Set aside.
2. To prepare samosas, combine potatoes and next 6 ingredients. Gently fold in peas.
3. Working with 1 egg roll wrapper at a time (cover remaining wrappers to prevent drying), cut down middle to form 2 long rectangles. Moisten edges of wrapper with egg. Spoon 1 tablespoon potato mixture near bottom edge of wrapper. Fold up from 1 corner to opposite outer edge of wrapper, making a triangle. Fold over to opposite side again as if folding up a flag. Repeat fold to opposite side to form a triangle. Repeat with remaining wrappers and filling.
4. Heat a large cast-iron skillet over medium-high heat. Coat pan with cooking spray. Lightly coat samosas with cooking spray. Add samosas to pan, and cook 1 minute on each side. Drain on paper towels. Serve with chutney. Yield: 4 servings (servings size: 5 samosas and about 1 tablespoon chutney).

CALORIES 288; FAT 2.6g (sat 0.9g, mono 0.5g, poly 0.2g); PROTEIN 11g; CARB 58.3g; FIBER 5.4g; CHOL 29mg; IRON 4.6mg; SODIUM 574mg; CALC 43mg

Steamed Vegetable Sui-Mai Dumplings with Chili-Sesame Oil

2 tablespoons chopped fresh cilantro

2 green onions, cut into 2-inch pieces

1 garlic clove

1 (½-inch) piece peeled fresh ginger

1 cup sliced napa (Chinese) cabbage

½ cup chopped peeled Granny Smith apple

1 tablespoon less-sodium soy sauce

2 teaspoons mirin (sweet rice wine)

¼ teaspoon Sriracha (hot chile sauce, such as Huy Fong)

¼ teaspoon kosher salt

1 large egg white

6 ounces firm water-packed tofu, drained and finely chopped

20 gyoza skins

2 teaspoons sesame oil

½ teaspoon Asian chili sesame oil or other chili oil

1. Place first 4 ingredients in a food processor; process until finely chopped. Add cabbage and next 5 ingredients; pulse 10 times or until finely chopped. Add egg white; pulse until combined. Place cabbage mixture in a medium bowl, and stir in tofu.

2. Moisten edge of gyoza skin with water, working with 1 skin at a time (cover remaining skins to keep them from drying). Spoon about 1 tablespoon tofu mixture into center of circle. Gather up edges of skin around filling; lightly squeeze skin to adhere to filling, leaving top of dumpling open. (If skins do not open enough to see tofu mixture, use the tip of a knife to separate dough and form pockets.) Repeat procedure with remaining skins and filling.

3. Place dumplings in a large bamboo steamer lined with parchment paper or cabbage leaves. Working in batches, steam 9 minutes or until filling and wrappers are lightly firm. Combine oils, and drizzle over tops of dumplings. Yield: 4 servings (serving size: 5 dumplings).

CALORIES 185; FAT 6.4g (sat 1g, mono 1.6g, poly 1.6g); PROTEIN 9.3g; CARB 21.7g; FIBER 1.6g; CHOL 50mg; IRON 2mg; SODIUM 460mg; CALC 125mg

10 NUTRITION MYTHS THAT SHOULDN'T KEEP YOU FROM THE FOODS YOU LOVE!

Some nutrition myths bounce around on crazy e-mail chain letters and pop up on goofy evening news reports. Others fuel the sale of rip-off diet books. Some are so accepted they seem hardwired into our brains. Take deep-fried foods, for example. They're universally bad for you, right? Well, no. When we challenged ourselves to explore whether fried foods could be made healthy (see Cooking Class on page 92), we discovered that, when done properly under conditions any home cook can mimic, fried foods don't have to be forever banished from a healthy diet.

The exercise inspired us to take on some other ingrained nutrition misconceptions. We talked with leading nutrition researchers, chefs, and food scientists and did some sleuthing of our own to debunk 10 myths so you can enjoy many once-forbidden foods without that old familiar twinge of guilt. Ready to dig in?

1. ADDED SUGAR IS ALWAYS BAD FOR YOU.

TRUTH: You can use the sweet stuff to ensure that sugar calories are far from "empty" calories.

Sugar is essential in the kitchen. Consider all that it does for baking, creating a tender cake crumb and ensuring crisp cookies. Then there's its role in creating airy meringue or soft-textured ice cream. Keep in mind that other sweeteners like "natural" honey are basically refined sugar anyway—and they are all metabolized by your body the same way, as 4 calories per gram. Sugar also balances the flavors in healthy foods that might not taste so great on their own. "Add a little bit of sugar to help boost your intake of nutrient-rich foods by making them tastier," says Jackie Newgent, RD, author of the *All-Natural Diabetes Cookbook*. A wee bit of sugar to balance a too-tart tomato sauce is a good thing; so is a teaspoon of honey on a tart grapefruit half or in plain yogurt. Don't go overboard, of course. Most health experts suggest that added sugar supply no more than 10 percent of your total calories—about 200 in a 2,000-calorie diet.

Make Ahead • Freezable

Pink Grapefruit Sorbet

In this refreshing palate cleanser, the sugar tames the tartness of grapefruit juice.

3 cups fresh pink grapefruit juice (about 4 grapefruits), divided

¾ cup sugar

1. Combine ½ cup juice and sugar in a small saucepan over medium heat. Cook until sugar dissolves, stirring frequently.

2. Combine sugar mixture and remaining 2½ cups juice in a medium bowl; cover and refrigerate until chilled.

3. Pour mixture into freezer can of an ice-cream freezer, and freeze according to manufacturer's instructions. Spoon sorbet into a freezer-safe container; cover and freeze 1 hour or until sorbet is firm. Yield: 6 servings (serving size: ⅔ cup).

CALORIES 145; FAT 0.1g (sat 0g, mono 0g, poly 0g); PROTEIN 0.6g; CARB 36.4g; FIBER 0.1g; CHOL 0mg; IRON 0.3mg; SODIUM 1mg; CALC 11mg

2. EATING EGGS RAISES YOUR CHOLESTEROL LEVELS.

TRUTH: Dietary cholesterol found in eggs has little to do with the amount of cholesterol in your body.

The confusion can be boiled down to semantics: The same word, "cholesterol," is used to describe two different things. Dietary cholesterol—the fat-like molecules in animal-based foods like eggs—doesn't greatly affect the amount of cholesterol circulating in your bloodstream. Your body makes its own cholesterol, so it doesn't need much of the kind you eat. Instead, what fuels your body's cholesterol-making machine is certain saturated and trans fats. Eggs contain relatively small amounts of saturated fat. One large egg contains about 1.5 grams saturated fat, a fraction of the amount in the tablespoon of butter many cooks use to cook that egg in. In healthy people, "the research with eggs has never shown any link of egg consumption with blood lipids or with risk of heart disease," says Don Layman, PhD, professor emeritus in the Department of Food Science and Human Nutrition at the University of Illinois at Urbana-Champaign. Cutting eggs out of your diet is a bad idea; they're a rich source of 13 vitamins and minerals.

Quick & Easy

Huevos Revueltos

2 teaspoons canola oil
1 jalapeño pepper
3/4 cup thinly sliced green onions
2 garlic cloves, minced
1 3/4 cups chopped plum tomatoes
1/2 teaspoon salt
6 large eggs, lightly beaten
1/2 cup (2 ounces) shredded Monterey Jack cheese with jalapeño peppers
1/4 cup chopped fresh cilantro
8 (6-inch) corn tortillas, warmed
4 lime wedges (optional)
Hot pepper sauce (such as Tabasco, optional)

1. Heat oil in a large nonstick skillet over medium-high heat. Cut jalapeño in half lengthwise; discard seeds from one half and leave seeds in remaining half. Mince both jalapeño halves. Add jalapeño, green onions, and garlic to pan; sauté 3 minutes or until tender. Add tomatoes and salt; cook 2 minutes or until thoroughly heated, stirring frequently.
2. Add eggs; cook 3 minutes or until soft-scrambled, stirring constantly. Sprinkle evenly with cheese and cilantro. Serve with tortillas and, if desired, lime wedges and hot sauce. Yield: 4 servings (serving size: 2/3 cup egg mixture and 2 tortillas).

CALORIES 289; FAT 14.1g (sat 4.5g, mono 4.3g, poly 2.4g); PROTEIN 15.6g; CARB 25.3g; FIBER 3.4g; CHOL 285mg; IRON 1.9mg; SODIUM 503mg; CALC 156mg

3. ALL SATURATED FATS RAISE BLOOD CHOLESTEROL.

TRUTH: New research shows that some saturated fats don't.

Just when we'd all gotten comfortable with the idea that there are good-for-you mono- and polyunsaturated fats (like those found in olive oil and walnuts), along comes new research calling into question the one principle most health professionals thought was sacrosanct: All saturated fat is bad. Researchers have long known that there are many kinds of saturated fats; the main ones are lauric, myristic, palmitic, and stearic acid. What's interesting is that they are handled differently by the body when consumed. Stearic acid, a type of saturated fat found naturally in cocoa, dairy products, meats, and poultry, as well as palm and coconut oils, has attracted the most scientific interest because it appears to act similarly to monounsaturated fat in that it does not raise harmful LDL cholesterol but boosts beneficial HDL cholesterol levels. This is not a license to eat freely of anything containing stearic acid, of course: rib-eye steak, for example, has some, but also has a high proportion of the other saturated fats that raise LDL—one of many contributors to heart disease risk. But there are foods, like coconut and chocolate, that contain what may eventually be called the "good" saturated fat—and so the moderate consumption of these is healthier than once thought. We say moderate, though, because foods rich in any type of fat tend to be dense in calories, as well.

Make Ahead • Freezable
Kid Friendly

Toasted Coconut Chocolate Chunk Cookies

Given that both chocolate and coconut are not as "bad" as once thought, and given that they taste mighty good together, we baked up a batch of these toasty, chocolaty treats to celebrate. Like all sweets with few other nutrients, though, they are treats—perfectly healthy every once in a while.

1 cup flaked sweetened coconut
4.5 ounces all-purpose flour (about 1 cup)
1/2 teaspoon baking powder
1/4 teaspoon baking soda
1/8 teaspoon salt
3/4 cup packed brown sugar
1/4 cup unsalted butter, softened
1 teaspoon vanilla extract
1 large egg
2 ounces dark chocolate (70% cacao), chopped
Cooking spray

1. Preheat oven to 350°.
2. Arrange coconut in a single layer in a small baking pan. Bake at 350° for 7 minutes or until lightly toasted, stirring once. Set aside to cool.
3. Weigh or lightly spoon flour into a dry measuring cup; level with a knife. Combine flour, baking powder, baking soda, and salt in a medium bowl; stir with a whisk until blended. Place sugar and butter in a large bowl; beat with a mixer at medium speed until well blended. Beat in vanilla and egg. Add flour mixture, beating at low speed just until combined. Stir in toasted coconut and chocolate.
4. Drop by level tablespoons 2 inches apart onto baking sheets coated with cooking spray. Bake at 350° for 10 minutes or until bottoms of cookies just begin to brown. Remove from pan, and cool completely on wire racks. Yield: 25 servings (serving size: 1 cookie).

CALORIES 88; FAT 3.8g (sat 2.5g, mono 0.6g, poly 0.1g); PROTEIN 1g; CARB 13g; FIBER 0.4g; CHOL 12mg; IRON 0.6mg; SODIUM 38mg; CALC 15mg

4. THE ONLY HEART-FRIENDLY ALCOHOL IS RED WINE.

TRUTH: Beer, wine, and liquors all confer the same health benefits.

The so-called French Paradox elevated red wine to health-food status when researchers thought it was the antioxidants in the drink that protected the foie gras- and cheese-loving French from heart disease.

More recent research, however, has shown that antioxidants aren't the answer after all. Alcohol—the ethanol itself—raises levels of protective high-density lipoproteins (HDL, or good cholesterol), which help protect against plaque buildup in the arteries and reduce clotting factors that contribute to heart attack and stroke, according to Eric Rimm, ScD, associate professor of nutrition at the School of Public Health at Harvard University. Any kind of beverage that contains alcohol, when consumed in moderation (and that means one to two drinks a day), helps reduce heart disease risk.

5. ADDING SALT TO THE POT ADDS SODIUM TO THE FOOD.

TRUTH: Salt added to boiling water may actually make vegetables more nutritious.

New York City launched the National Salt Reduction Initiative early this year to reduce salt levels in packaged and restaurant foods. This is the city that limited trans fats in restaurants and banned smoking, so if history is any indication, the country will follow with public health messages encouraging us to shake our salt-in-everything habits. In general it's a good initiative; sodium is a potential problem even for non-hypertensive people. But it's easy to overlook how sodium can actually help in recipes.

"Salt in the cooking water reduces the leaching of nutrients from vegetables into the water," says Harold McGee, author of *On Food & Cooking*. That means your blanched broccoli, green beans, or asparagus likely retains more nutrients—although there aren't studies to prove it. McGee recommends using about 1 teaspoon of salt per cup of water. The amount of sodium absorbed by the food is minuscule. Remember, the vast majority of sodium in our diets (about 75 percent) comes from processed foods, not fresh vegetables taking a brief dip in salted cooking water.

Quick & Easy • Kid Friendly

Green Beans with Orange and Hazelnuts

Salted boiling water helps blanched veggies retain their structure and nutrients and doesn't add much sodium. Substitute olive oil for hazelnut oil, if it's easier.

¼ cup hazelnuts
2 quarts water
¼ cup salt
1 pound green beans, trimmed
1 tablespoon thin orange rind strips
2 teaspoons roasted hazelnut oil
⅛ teaspoon salt

1. Preheat oven to 350°.
2. Place hazelnuts on a baking sheet. Bake at 350° for 8 minutes; stir once. Turn nuts out onto a towel. Roll up towel; rub off skins. Chop nuts.
3. Combine 2 quarts water and ¼ cup salt in a large saucepan; bring to a boil. Add beans; cook 5 minutes or until crisp-tender. Drain. Place in a serving bowl. Add nuts, rind, oil, and ⅛ teaspoon salt; toss well to coat. Yield: 6 servings (serving size: about ⅔ cup).

CALORIES 110; **FAT** 7.5g (sat 0.6g, mono 5.6g, poly 1g); **PROTEIN** 3.4g; **CARB** 9.9g; **FIBER** 4.8g; **CHOL** 0mg; **IRON** 1.6mg; **SODIUM** 81mg; **CALC** 54mg

6. FRIED FOODS ARE ALWAYS TOO FATTY.

TRUTH: Healthy deep-fried food is not an oxymoron.

We did a lot of research in our Test Kitchens to prove that, done right, fried foods are nutritionally fine (we already knew they were delicious, of course; see page 92).

Here's how frying works: When food is exposed to hot oil, the moisture inside boils and pushes from the interior to the surface and then out into the oil. As moisture leaves, it creates a barrier, minimizing oil absorption into the food—when the frying is done right. Meanwhile, the little oil that does penetrate the food's surface forms a crisp, tasty crust. To keep foods from soaking up oil (and calories), fry according to recipe instructions. For most foods, 375°F is

optimal. Oil temperatures that are too low will increase fat absorption. When we added tempura-coated veggies (see recipe on page 94) to cooler-than-optimal oil, the result was greasy and inedible—they absorbed more than 1 cup of oil instead of ⅓ cup. Also, overcooked food will soak up oil.

Keep in mind that we're not giving fast-food fried chicken dinners with French fries a passing grade. Such a meal contains an entire day's worth of calories and sodium, thanks to large portion sizes, excessive breading, and globs of sauces. But in the hands of a careful home cook, a delicately breaded and fried catfish fillet with a few hush puppies can be a perfectly reasonable—and delicious—dinner.

7. THE MORE FIBER YOU EAT, THE BETTER.

TRUTH: Not all fibers are equally beneficial. Consider the source.

Yogurt is a dairy food that's a great source of calcium. But it doesn't naturally come with fiber. Yet the grocery aisles now boast fiber-supplemented yogurt, along with cereals, energy bars, even water. What's the deal?

Fiber is a fad-food component right now, and food manufacturers are isolating specific types of fiber and adding them to packaged foods to take advantage. But the science isn't entirely clear yet: Just as we're learning more about different types of fat and their functions (see Myth #3), research is helping us understand how complex fiber is as well. Gone are the days of just two types of fiber: water-soluble (the kind found in oats, fruits, and legumes) and insoluble (the kind found in whole grains, nuts, and seeds). We now know that different fibers have different functions (wheat bran helps move foods along; oat bran lowers cholesterol; inulin supports healthy gut bacteria, etc.).

Some experts are skeptical that the so-called faux-fiber foods offer the same beneficial effect as naturally fiber-rich ones. "Foods fortified with fiber will not provide all the inherent goodness of whole foods like whole grains, legumes, vegetables, and fruits," says Joanne Slavin, PhD, RD, professor in the Department of Food Science and Nutrition at the University of Minnesota. Fact is, most processed foods lack a bevy of vitamins, minerals, and phytonutrients. So while it's true that only half of us eat the fiber we need for good health, added fiber doesn't get us off the hook.

Meanwhile, nutritional watchdog organizations are campaigning to prohibit the inclusion of added fibers in the total fiber count that's listed on the Nutrition Facts Panel on packaged foods.

Wheat Berry Salad with Raisins and Pistachios

Eating fiber-rich whole foods is the best way to gain this essential component of your diet. Whole-grain wheat berries are chewy, mild, and packed with fiber. Prep all the ingredients while the grain cooks.

1 cup uncooked wheat berries (hard winter wheat)
¾ teaspoon salt, divided
3 tablespoons shelled pistachios
2 tablespoons olive oil
2 tablespoons fresh lemon juice
2 teaspoons honey
½ teaspoon ground coriander
½ teaspoon grated peeled fresh ginger
½ cup golden raisins
¼ cup thinly sliced green onions
2 tablespoons chopped fresh cilantro
½ cup (2 ounces) crumbled goat cheese

1. Preheat oven to 350°.
2. Place wheat berries and ½ teaspoon salt in a medium saucepan. Cover with water to 2 inches above wheat berries, and bring to a boil. Cover, reduce heat to medium-low, and simmer 1 hour or until tender. Drain.
3. Place pistachios on a baking sheet. Bake at 350° for 8 minutes, stirring once. Cool slightly, and chop.
4. Combine oil, juice, honey, coriander, ginger, and remaining ¼ teaspoon salt in a large bowl, stirring with a whisk. Add hot wheat berries and raisins; stir well to combine. Let stand 20 minutes or until cooled to room temperature.
5. Add nuts, green onions, and cilantro to wheat berry mixture. Transfer to a serving bowl, and sprinkle with goat cheese. Yield: 6 servings (serving size: about ½ cup).

CALORIES 240; **FAT** 8.9g (sat 2.3g, mono 4.8g, poly 1.3g); **PROTEIN** 7.2g; **CARB** 36.8g; **FIBER** 5g; **CHOL** 4mg; **IRON** 0.7mg; **SODIUM** 284mg; **CALC** 28mg

8. YOU SHOULD ALWAYS REMOVE CHICKEN SKIN BEFORE EATING.

TRUTH: You can enjoy a skin-on chicken breast without blowing your sat-fat budget.

Half the pleasure of eating roast chicken comes from the gloriously crisp, brown skin that seems to melt in your mouth. Yet the skinless, boneless chicken breast—one of the more boring protein sources on Earth—became the health-conscious cook's gold standard somewhere along the way. Fortunately, the long-standing command to strip poultry of its skin before eating doesn't hold up under a nutritional microscope. A 12-ounce bone-in, skin-on chicken breast half contains just 2.5 grams of saturated fat and 50 calories more than its similarly portioned skinless counterpart. What's more, 55 percent of the fat in the chicken skin is monounsaturated—the heart-healthy kind you want more of, says Amy Myrdal Miller, MS, RD, Program Director for Strategic Initiatives at The Culinary Institute of America at Greystone. Tuesday night's chicken dinner just got a lot more interesting—and appetizing.

Oregano and Lime Roasted Chicken Breasts

A chicken breast will always be lean—skinned or not. If you're tired of plain skinless, boneless chicken breasts, splurge on the skin-on option from time to time.

Chicken:
1 tablespoon chopped fresh oregano
2 teaspoons grated lime rind
1 teaspoon ground cumin
2 teaspoons minced garlic
¼ teaspoon freshly ground black pepper
4 bone-in, skin-on chicken breast halves (about 3 pounds)
2 teaspoons olive oil
½ teaspoon salt
Sauce:
1 tablespoon all-purpose flour
¼ teaspoon ground cumin
1 cup fat-free, less-sodium chicken broth
1 tablespoon tequila
½ teaspoon lime juice

1. To prepare chicken, combine first 5 ingredients in a small bowl. Loosen skin from breast halves by inserting fingers, gently pushing between skin and meat. Rub oregano mixture evenly under loosened skin of each breast half. Arrange chicken breasts in a shallow dish; cover and refrigerate at least 4 hours.
2. Preheat oven to 375°.
3. Heat oil in a large ovenproof skillet over medium-high heat. Sprinkle chicken with salt. Add chicken to pan, skin sides down; cook 5 minutes or until browned. Turn chicken over, and transfer to oven. Bake at 375° for 25 minutes or until chicken is done. Remove chicken from pan, reserving 1½ tablespoons drippings; set chicken aside, and keep warm.
4. To prepare sauce, heat reserved drippings in pan over medium-high heat. Add flour and ¼ teaspoon cumin to pan, and cook 30 seconds, stirring constantly with a whisk. Add broth, tequila, and juice, scraping pan to loosen browned bits. Bring to a boil, and cook until reduced to about ⅔ cup (about 2 minutes), stirring occasionally. Serve with chicken. Yield: 4 servings (serving size: 1 breast half and about 2½ tablespoons sauce).

CALORIES 446; **FAT** 18.8g (sat 4.9g, mono 8.1g, poly 3.8g); **PROTEIN** 60.2g; **CARB** 2.9g; **FIBER** 0.7g; **CHOL** 167mg; **IRON** 2.6mg; **SODIUM** 534mg; **CALC** 46mg

9. ORGANIC FOODS ARE MORE NUTRITIOUS THAN CONVENTIONAL.

TRUTH: There are many good reasons to choose organic, but nutrition isn't one of them.

If you buy organic because you believe that sustainable farming supports the health of the soil, the work of small farmers, or the well-being of livestock, that's all good. And you may find it more tasty. However, it's not accurate to also promote organic as inherently more nutritious. Researchers at the London School of Hygiene & Tropical Medicine provided the most comprehensive review of organic foods to date, including some 50 years of organic research. Their conclusion: No significant nutritional difference exists between conventional and organic crops and livestock. A good radish by any other name is still a radish. There is, of course, still the issue of trace amounts of pesticides or herbicides—wash conventional produce carefully.

10. COOKING OLIVE OIL DESTROYS ITS HEALTH BENEFITS.

TRUTH: Even delicate extra-virgin oils can take the heat without sacrificing nutrition.

This one has been kicking around ever since olive oil became a "good" fat: Cook with premium versions and you heat away the healthful properties. It simply isn't true.

First of all, heart-healthy monounsaturated fats aren't unfavorably altered by heat. They survive a sauté intact. Now, research from Italy and Spain is showing that other plant-based compounds—the elements that likely give olive oils their complex flavor profiles as well as other healthful properties—can also stand up to standard cooking procedures. They're surprisingly stable, as long as the oil isn't heated past its smoking point, which for extra-virgin olive oil is pretty high—about 405°F. (Canola oil's smoke point is 400°F.)

How you store the oil is more important. Fats and phytonutrients stay stable for up to two years in unopened opaque bottles stored at room temperature and away from light. Heat, light, and air drastically affect stability. Store in a room-temp cupboard, and use within six months.

Quick Skillet Asparagus

Extra-virgin olive oil adds great flavor to this simple dish, and sautéing with it doesn't burn away the oil's healthful antioxidants.

4 teaspoons extra-virgin olive oil
1 pound medium asparagus spears, trimmed
½ teaspoon grated lemon rind
1 teaspoon fresh lemon juice
¼ teaspoon salt

1. Heat a large cast-iron or nonstick skillet over medium-high heat. Add oil to pan; swirl to coat. Add asparagus to pan; cook 3 minutes or until asparagus is crisp-tender and browned, stirring frequently. Transfer to a serving platter. Add rind, juice, and salt, tossing to coat. Yield: 4 servings (serving size: about 3 ounces).

CALORIES 71; FAT 4.7g (sat 0.7g, mono 3.3g, poly 0.7g); PROTEIN 2.5g; CARB 5g; FIBER 2.5g; CHOL 0mg; IRON 0.4mg; SODIUM 148mg; CALC 25mg

NUTRITION MADE EASY
THE SPIN ON HEALTHY SALADS

Made fresh at home, or even using convenience foods like rotisserie chicken, salads are nutrition powerhouses. But beware the overloaded versions.

Nine cups of fruits and vegetables per day—the amount recommended for most of us—sounds like a Mount Everest of produce. Many Americans get just three. Eating the *Cooking Light* way (more plants, less meat, "good" fats in the right proportion, lots of variety) increases fruit and vegetable consumption. But reaching the nine-cup mark requires a healthy dedication.

Enter the salad: easy to make, infinitely variable, seasonally adjustable, and the best way to sample the many fresh gifts provided by the garden and the farmers' market. Variety is the key: You want to benefit from the huge number of potentially healthful compounds in different plants. Variety also helps prevent salad fatigue. The recipes we offer here illustrate the supple balance of bitter, sweet, crunch, acid, and creaminess possible in a nutrition-packed salad.

Watch for "loaded" salads, though—greens buried under piles of bacon, shredded cheese, and gloppy dressings. As you'll see, some restaurant salad choices are higher in fat than burgers or burritos.

Spring Salad with Grapes and Pistachio-Crusted Goat Cheese

You could simplify this by just topping the salad with goat cheese and chopped pistachios. But our method ensures that each grassy, creamy bite of cheese contrasts with the salty, crunchy nuts.

¼ cup shelled dry-roasted pistachios, finely chopped
½ cup (4 ounces) goat cheese
¼ cup Easy Herb Vinaigrette (page 91)
1 (5-ounce) package gourmet salad greens or spring lettuce mix
1 cup seedless red grapes, halved
¼ teaspoon freshly ground black pepper

1. Place pistachios in a shallow dish. Divide cheese into 12 equal portions, rolling to form 12 balls. Roll each ball in pistachios until well coated. Set aside.
2. Combine Easy Herb Vinaigrette and greens in a large mixing bowl, and toss gently to coat evenly. Divide greens mixture evenly among 4 salad plates. Top each serving with ¼ cup grapes and 3 cheese balls. Sprinkle salads evenly with pepper, and serve immediately. Yield: 4 servings.

CALORIES 235; FAT 18.4g (sat 5.2g, mono 8.4g, poly 3.9g); PROTEIN 7.8g; CARB 11.8g; FIBER 1.7g; CHOL 13mg; IRON 1.4mg; SODIUM 192mg; CALC 67mg

NEWS FROM THE SALAD-SCIENCE DESK

CHOOSE FAT-FREE DRESSING, AND YOU'LL MISS OUT ON MANY NUTRIENTS.

Researchers have long known that fat aids in the absorption of certain vitamins and antioxidants. But does that mean low-fat dressings are ineffective in helping your body get its needed share, too? No: A small Iowa State study revealed that people who ate salads with low-fat dressing absorbed more nutrients than people who opted for fat-free. No fat, no nutrients.

SALAD BARS ARE A GOOD INFLUENCE ON KIDS—EVEN AFTER LUNCH.

When UCLA researchers stuck salad bars in three elementary schools, they found that fruit and veggie consumption rose roughly 25 percent—a sign that poor eating habits at school may in part be the fault of poor selection, not resistance to fresh food. Strikingly, the healthy eating benefit persisted: 16 percent of total fruit and veggie consumption took place outside the lunch hour.

SALAD NUTRIENTS MAY HELP PREVENT BREAST CANCER.

A 10-year study of more than 8,900 Italian women found that a regular salad habit might be a factor in a 35 percent reduction in breast cancer risk, compared to women who ate fewer raw vegetables. In a follow-up study, researchers found that salad consumption significantly correlated with reduced risk for a specific HER-2-positive type of breast cancer. More studies are needed to confirm the effect, but plants are rich sources of a variety of antioxidants, which may help protect cells from cancer-causing damage.

SALAD MAKES YOU UPBEAT—OR DO UPBEAT PEOPLE FAVOR SALADS?

It's a chicken-and-egg sort of phenomenon, but Finns who described themselves as optimistic were more likely to eat fresh vegetables and salads, according to a study of nearly 9,000 men and women. Pessimists tended to go for junk food, smoking, or other unhealthy activities.

Quick & Easy • Make Ahead

Easy Herb Vinaigrette

This recipe makes plenty of dressing to keep on hand, so having a salad with dinner is effortless any night of the week.

9 tablespoons white wine vinegar
1½ tablespoons wildflower honey
½ teaspoon fine sea salt
1 cup canola oil
3 tablespoons chopped fresh basil
3 tablespoons minced fresh chives

1. Combine first 3 ingredients in a medium bowl; slowly whisk in oil until combined. Stir in basil and chives. Store, covered, in refrigerator for up to 5 days. Yield: about 1⅔ cups (serving size: 2 tablespoons).

CALORIES 160; FAT 17.2g (sat 1.2g, mono 10.2g, poly 5.1g); PROTEIN 0.1g; CARB 2.1g; FIBER 0.1g; CHOL 0mg; IRON 0mg; SODIUM 89mg; CALC 2mg

---

Quick & Easy

Superfast Chef Salad

Start with a bag of prechopped romaine lettuce and a rotisserie chicken from the grocery store for an easy, healthy dinner any night of the week. Serve with a crusty multigrain baguette and a glass of wine.

10 cups torn or chopped romaine lettuce
1 cup shredded skinless, boneless rotisserie chicken breast
½ cup thinly sliced Texas 1015 or other sweet onion
⅓ cup shaved carrot
1 avocado, seeded, peeled, and sliced
3 tablespoons crumbled blue cheese
½ cup Easy Herb Vinaigrette (above)

1. Arrange 2½ cups lettuce on each of 4 plates. Top lettuce evenly with chicken, onion, carrot, avocado, and blue cheese. Drizzle each serving with 2 tablespoons Easy Herb Vinaigrette; serve immediately. Yield: 4 servings.

CALORIES 367; FAT 28.2g (sat 3.4g, mono 15g, poly 6.2g); PROTEIN 18.5g; CARB 12.6g; FIBER 4.6g; CHOL 43mg; IRON 2.0mg; SODIUM 451mg; CALC 66mg

---

Quick & Easy

Spinach Strawberry Salad

This simple starter salad is an ideal accompaniment to grilled or roast chicken or pork.

1½ cups quartered strawberries
¼ cup Easy Herb Vinaigrette (recipe at left)
1 tablespoon finely chopped fresh mint
1 (6-ounce) package fresh baby spinach
2 tablespoons sliced almonds, toasted
¼ teaspoon freshly ground black pepper

1. Combine first 4 ingredients in a large bowl; toss gently to coat. Sprinkle with almonds and pepper; serve immediately. Yield: 4 servings (serving size: 2 cups).

CALORIES 136; FAT 10.3g (sat 0.7g, mono 6g, poly 3g); PROTEIN 2.1g; CARB 11g; FIBER 3.6g; CHOL 0mg; IRON 1.7mg; SODIUM 113mg; CALC 50mg

---

RESTAURANT SALAD SHOCKERS

When you find yourself in restaurants that offer things like No Rules Parmesan Pasta (70 grams fat) or Big Mouth Burgers (62 grams fat, undressed), it's tempting to default to a salad. Beware.

OUTBACK
Queensland Salad with Blue Cheese Dressing
Radically improve nutrition by trading this for a 6-ounce sirloin, green beans, and small house salad.

1,097 calories
82g fat (30g saturated)
3,100mg sodium

QDOBA
Build-Your-Own Taco Salad
For half the sodium and a fraction of the saturated fat and calories, try a naked burrito with pulled pork (yes!), beans, guac, fajita vegetables, and mango salsa.

1,090 calories
62g fat (20g saturated)
1,900mg sodium

FRYING BASICS

We were surprised—and delighted—to perfect some frying techniques that fill the bill for healthy eating.

Upon tasting a perfectly fried food, people often swoon and exclaim, "It's not greasy at all!" As if that were a miracle. And we've said it, too. Yet even with the ungreasy evidence in our hands, we instinctively regard a perfect beer-battered shrimp or French fry as a fat bomb. But here's the happy truth: If you fry in the right oil and follow our guidelines carefully, fried foods can have a place in a healthy diet. Science shows how proper frying minimizes oil absorption while creating that sublime, toasty crust. In our Test Kitchens, six breaded, fried catfish fillets and a basket of hush puppies absorbed only ¼ cup oil! It's all in the technique. Read on for the secrets of healthy frying.

Staff Favorite • Kid Friendly

Fried Catfish with Hush Puppies and Tartar Sauce

Coat the fillets and prepare the batter for hush puppies while you wait for the oil to come up to temperature. You can also make the tartar sauce up to two days ahead and keep it refrigerated. If you don't like catfish, use halibut, tilapia, or another flaky white fish.

Tartar Sauce:
¼ cup organic canola mayonnaise (such as Spectrum)
1 tablespoon dill pickle relish
1 tablespoon chopped fresh flat-leaf parsley
1 teaspoon prepared horseradish
¾ teaspoon fresh lemon juice
⅛ teaspoon salt

Catfish:
8 cups peanut oil
6 (6-ounce) catfish fillets
½ teaspoon salt
9 ounces all-purpose flour (about 2 cups), divided
1¼ cups cornmeal
1 teaspoon freshly ground black pepper
2 cups buttermilk
2 large eggs

Hush Puppies:
3.4 ounces all-purpose flour (about ¾ cup)
⅓ cup cornmeal
⅓ cup buttermilk
3 tablespoons grated onion
1 teaspoon baking powder
¼ teaspoon salt
¼ teaspoon ground red pepper
1 large egg, lightly beaten

1. To prepare tartar sauce, combine first 6 ingredients. Cover and chill.
2. To prepare catfish, clip a candy/fry thermometer to a Dutch oven; add oil to pan. Heat oil to 385°.
3. Sprinkle fillets evenly with ½ teaspoon salt. Place 4.5 ounces (1 cup) flour in a shallow dish. Combine remaining 4.5 ounces flour, cornmeal, and black pepper in a shallow dish. Combine 2 cups buttermilk and 2 eggs in a shallow dish. Dredge fillets in flour; dip in buttermilk mixture. Dredge in cornmeal mixture; shake off excess breading. Place 2 fillets in hot oil; cook 5 minutes or until done, turning occasionally. Make sure oil temperature does not drop below 375°. Remove fillets from pan using a slotted spoon; drain on paper towels. Return oil temperature to 385°. Repeat procedure twice with remaining fillets.
4. To prepare hush puppies, weigh or lightly spoon 3.4 ounces (¾ cup) flour in dry measuring cups; level with a knife. Combine 3.4 ounces flour and remaining ingredients. Drop batter 1 tablespoonful at a time into pan; fry at 375° for 5 minutes or until browned, turning frequently. Remove hush puppies from pan using a slotted spoon; drain on paper towels. Yield: 6 servings (serving size: 1 fillet, 2 hush puppies, and 4 teaspoons tartar sauce).

CALORIES 507; FAT 23.8g (sat 4.1g, mono 8.4g, poly 9.4g); PROTEIN 29.4g; CARB 43g; FIBER 2.6g; CHOL 153mg; IRON 3.6mg; SODIUM 846mg; CALC 171mg

THE BASICS OF HEALTHY FRYING

KEEP OIL CLEAN.
If debris builds up in the pan, it will burn after a few minutes. This is especially a problem when frying breaded and battered ingredients. Burned particles in the oil will cause it to discolor and infuse it with an off flavor that will taint the food. So use a slotted spoon to remove crumbs as you go.

MAKE BETTER BATTER OR BREADING.
Coating foods yields a tasty crust, but breadings and batters done wrong can inflate calories and promote oil absorption. All-purpose flour adheres well because it contains gluten, but too much flour causes the food to absorb more oil. Adding gluten-free ingredients like cornmeal or rice flour reduces absorption. And batters that use leaveners or carbonated beverages produce gas bubbles that discourage oil absorption as well.

NUTRITION NOTES

■ Choose a healthy oil that's low in saturated fat. We use peanut oil. Soybean and canola oils are also good.
■ Watch oil temperature like a hawk: If it's not hot enough, the food will soak up extra oil.

4 STEPS TO HEALTHY FRYING

1 HEAT THE OIL. Once you've selected a heart-healthy oil with a high smoke point, place the oil in a large pan like a deep skillet or Dutch oven. The pan you should choose depends on the foods you'll cook—you don't want to overcrowd the pan. Clip a fry thermometer to the side of the pan.

2 COAT YOUR INGREDIENTS. Some foods, like our doughnut holes, don't require an exterior coating before they're fried; the batter forms its own coating. Others, like fish, chicken, or veggies, benefit from breading or a batter. If battered, simply dip and fry. If breaded, use a three-step process (see fried catfish recipe, page 92).

3 MAINTAIN THE TEMPERATURE AS YOU COOK. As you add foods, temperature can drop. Watch the thermometer, and slow the pace or adjust the heat. Too-hot oil will burn the exterior before the interior is fully cooked. Oil that's not hot enough will slow the cooking process and result in greasy, soggy food.

4 DRAIN. Always use a slotted spoon to transfer foods into hot oil so the batter doesn't clump. Then use that spoon to remove foods from the pan so they don't sit in pools of oil. Drain fried foods on paper towels for a minute or two; the towels will absorb any exterior oil that may still be clinging to them.

Maple-Glazed Sour Cream Doughnut Holes

Sour cream enriches these yeasted dough-nut holes. Omit the maple glaze and dip the doughnut holes in a mixture of granulated sugar and ground cinnamon for more texture. Enjoy them for breakfast or dessert.

6 tablespoons warm water (100° to 110°)

¼ cup granulated sugar

1⅛ teaspoons dry yeast

6.75 ounces all-purpose flour (about 1½ cups), divided

⅛ teaspoon salt

3 tablespoons sour cream

1 large egg, lightly beaten

Cooking spray

6 cups peanut oil

1½ cups powdered sugar

2 tablespoons maple syrup

2 tablespoons water

1. Combine first 3 ingredients in a large bowl. Let stand 5 minutes or until bubbly. Weigh or lightly spoon 5.63 ounces (about 1¼ cups) flour into dry measuring cups; level with a knife. Combine 5.63 ounces flour and salt. Add sour cream and egg to yeast mixture; stir until smooth. Add flour mixture, and stir until a moist dough forms.

2. Turn dough out onto a lightly floured surface. Knead until smooth and elastic (about 3 minutes); add enough of remaining 1.13 ounces flour (about ¼ cup), 1 tablespoon at a time, to prevent dough from sticking to hands (dough will feel slightly sticky). Place dough in a clean bowl coated with cooking spray. Cover dough with plastic wrap. Let rise in a warm place (85°), free from drafts, 1 hour or until almost doubled in size.

3. Punch dough down. Divide dough into 36 equal portions; roll each portion into a ball. Cover dough with plastic wrap coated with cooking spray; let stand 30 minutes.

4. Clip a candy/fry thermometer onto side of a Dutch oven; add oil to pan. Heat oil to 375°. Combine powdered sugar, syrup, and 2 tablespoons water; stir until smooth. Place 9 dough balls in hot oil; fry 2 minutes or until golden and done, turning as necessary. Make sure oil temperature remains at 375°. Remove doughnut holes from pan; drain. Dip doughnut holes into syrup mixture; remove with a slotted spoon. Drain on a cooling rack over a baking sheet. Repeat procedure 4 times with remaining dough balls and syrup mixture. Yield: 12 servings (serving size: 3 doughnut holes).

CALORIES 178; FAT 5.9g (sat 1.4g, mono 2.5g, poly 1.6g); PROTEIN 2.4g; CARB 29.3g; FIBER 0.5g; CHOL 19mg; IRON 0.9mg; SODIUM 33mg; CALC 11mg

Tempura Tofu and Spring Vegetables

Tempura is a versatile batter. Substitute peeled shrimp for the tofu. Or use asparagus and fresh green beans for veggies.

1 (14-ounce) package water-packed extra-firm tofu, drained
12 cups peanut oil
6 tablespoons rice vinegar
1½ tablespoons sugar
3 tablespoons reduced-sodium tamari
1½ teaspoons grated peeled fresh ginger
1 pound baby carrots with green tops
4.5 ounces all-purpose flour (about 1 cup)
6.75 ounces rice flour (about 1 cup)
1 teaspoon baking soda
½ teaspoon salt
2 cups club soda, chilled
12 ounces sugar snap peas, trimmed

1. Place tofu on several layers of paper towels; cover with paper towels. Top with a heavy skillet; let stand 30 minutes. Discard paper towels. Cut tofu in half horizontally; cut blocks into 16 (½-inch-thick) slices. Cut slices in half, crosswise, to form 32 (1 x ½–inch) rectangles.
2. Clip a candy/fry thermometer onto side of a large skillet; add oil to pan. Heat oil to 385°. Combine vinegar and next 3 ingredients. Trim carrot tops to 1 inch; peel carrots.
3. Weigh or lightly spoon flours into dry measuring cups; level with a knife. Combine flours, baking soda, and salt, stirring well with a whisk. Gradually add club soda, stirring until smooth. Using a slotted spoon, dip tofu in batter. Place tofu in hot oil, and fry 1 minute or until golden, turning once. Make sure oil temperature remains at 375°. Remove tofu, and drain.
4. Return oil temperature to 385°. Using a slotted spoon, dip carrots in batter. Place carrots in oil; fry 2 minutes or until golden, turning once. Make sure oil temperature remains at 375°. Remove carrots; drain. Return oil temperature to 385°.
5. Using a slotted spoon, dip peas in batter. Place peas in oil; fry 1 minute or until golden, turning once. Make

sure oil temperature remains at 375°. Remove peas, and drain. Serve tofu and vegetables with tamari mixture. Yield: 5 servings (serving size: about 6 tofu pieces, 5 carrots, 7 peas, and 2½ tablespoons dipping sauce).

CALORIES 428; FAT 19.4g (sat 3g, mono 10.2g, poly 5.2g); PROTEIN 12.9g; CARB 46.2g; FIBER 4.9g; CHOL 0mg; IRON 3.5mg; SODIUM 826mg; CALC 201mg

AND NOW TO REVIEW...

Although it's true that properly fried foods aren't as bad as we once thought, frying should be an occasional treat. A few critical factors to keeping fat and calories in check bear repeating; keep these in mind every time you fry.

■ Use moderation. Pair fried entrées with a healthy side or salad.

■ Choose a heart-healthy oil with a high smoke point (see Nutrition Notes, page 92).

■ Heat oil to the proper temperature, and use a candy/fry thermometer to monitor it.

■ Maintain the proper oil temperature during cooking; otherwise, the food begins absorbing excess oil, not only adding fat and calories but also rendering it soggy. Greasy fried food is badly fried food.

■ When breading foods before frying, use a mixture of glutinous all-purpose flour and nonglutinous ingredients, like rice flour or cornmeal, to minimize oil absorption.

■ When battering foods before frying, be sure to use carbonated liquids, a small amount of leavening (baking soda), or both in the batter. These release gas bubbles as the food cooks, further reducing oil absorption.

■ Drain cooked foods on paper towels for a minute or two after cooking, so any excess oil doesn't cling and soak into the food.

START WITH A...BLOCK OF TOFU

Tofu—a healthy vehicle for bold flavors.

Ma Po Tofu with Steamed Broccolini

1 (14-ounce) package firm water-packed tofu, drained
1 to 2 tablespoons Sriracha (hot chile sauce, such a Huy Fong)
1½ tablespoons mirin (sweet rice wine)
1 tablespoon black bean garlic sauce
2 teaspoons sugar
1 cup fat-free, less-sodium chicken broth
1 tablespoon cornstarch
2 tablespoons less-sodium soy sauce
1 teaspoon chili oil
1 tablespoon canola oil
4 ounces ground sirloin
1 tablespoon finely chopped garlic
2 teaspoons grated peeled fresh ginger
2 cups hot cooked long-grain white rice
8 ounces steamed Broccolini
¼ cup fresh cilantro leaves

1. Place tofu on paper towels; cover with paper towels. Top with a heavy skillet; let stand 30 minutes. Discard towels. Cut tofu into 1-inch cubes.
2. Combine Sriracha and next 3 ingredients. Combine broth and next 3 ingredients, stirring until smooth.
3. Heat canola oil in a large skillet over medium-high heat. Add beef; stir-fry 3 minutes. Add garlic and ginger; stir-fry 30 seconds. Add Sriracha mixture; cook 1 minute, stirring occasionally. Add broth mixture; bring to a boil. Cook 1 minute. Stir in tofu. Serve with rice and Broccolini; sprinkle with cilantro. Yield: 4 servings (serving size: ½ cup rice, ¾ cup tofu mixture, and 2 ounces Broccolini).

CALORIES 335; FAT 11.5g (sat 1.7g, mono 7.2g, poly 2.1g); PROTEIN 19.7g; CARB 37.1g; FIBER 1.7g; CHOL 15mg; IRON 3.8mg; SODIUM 661mg; CALC 243mg

Indian-Style Tofu and Cauliflower with Chutney

This is a riff on the Indian dish aloo gobi, *with tofu standing in for traditional potatoes.*

1 (14-ounce) package firm water-packed tofu, drained
1 medium onion, cut into 6 wedges
2 tablespoons canola oil
1 teaspoon brown mustard seeds
3/4 teaspoon cumin seeds
2 teaspoons curry powder
4 garlic cloves
1 (1/2-inch) piece fresh ginger, peeled and coarsely chopped
4 cups cauliflower florets (about 1 1/4 pounds)
1/4 cup water
1 teaspoon salt
1 (14.5-ounce) can diced tomatoes, undrained
4 1/2 cups hot cooked basmati rice
1/4 cup plain fat-free yogurt
1/4 cup chopped fresh cilantro

1. Place tofu on several layers of paper towels. Cover tofu with several more layers of paper towels; top with a cast-iron or other heavy skillet. Let stand 30 minutes. Discard paper towels. Cut tofu into 1/2-inch cubes.
2. Place onion in a food processor; pulse until finely chopped. Heat a large skillet over medium heat. Add oil to pan; swirl to coat. Add mustard seeds and cumin; cook 10 seconds or until mustard seeds begin to pop. Add onion and curry powder; cook 10 minutes, stirring frequently. Increase heat to medium-high; cook 2 minutes or until onion is golden, stirring constantly.
3. Place garlic and ginger in food processor; process until a smooth paste forms. Stir garlic mixture into onion mixture; sauté 1 minute, stirring constantly. Stir in tofu, cauliflower, and next 3 ingredients; bring to a simmer. Cover, reduce heat to medium-low, and cook 15 minutes. Uncover, increase heat to medium, and simmer 10 minutes or until cauliflower is tender.
4. Spoon 3/4 cup rice onto each of 6 plates; top each serving with 1 cup tofu mixture. Spoon 2 teaspoons yogurt over each serving; sprinkle with cilantro. Yield: 6 servings.

CALORIES 312; **FAT** 8.8g (sat 0.8g, mono 5.5g, poly 1.5g); **PROTEIN** 12.5g; **CARB** 47.6g; **FIBER** 5g; **CHOL** 0mg; **IRON** 3.5mg; **SODIUM** 517mg; **CALC** 187mg

Lo Mein with Tofu

Although lo mein is traditionally made with Chinese egg noodles, here we substitute whole-wheat linguine. Pan-frying the tofu gives it a crisp exterior.

1 (14-ounce) package firm water-packed tofu, drained and cut crosswise into 4 (1-inch-thick) pieces
8 ounces whole-wheat linguine
1 teaspoon dark sesame oil
1/2 teaspoon salt, divided
1/4 teaspoon freshly ground black pepper, divided
2 tablespoons canola oil, divided
3 tablespoons oyster sauce
1 1/2 tablespoons mirin (sweet rice wine)
1 1/2 tablespoons less-sodium soy sauce
1 teaspoon rice vinegar
3/4 cup vertically sliced onion
2 cups shredded cabbage
2 cups peeled, thinly diagonally sliced carrot
2 large garlic cloves, thinly sliced
1 1/2 cups fresh bean sprouts
1/4 cup chopped green onions

1. Place tofu in a single layer on several layers of paper towels. Cover tofu with several more layers of paper towels, and top with a cast-iron skillet or other heavy pan. Let stand 30 minutes. Discard paper towels.
2. Cook pasta in boiling water until al dente; drain. Combine pasta, sesame oil, 1/4 teaspoon salt, and 1/8 teaspoon pepper; toss. Set aside.
3. Sprinkle remaining 1/4 teaspoon salt and remaining 1/8 teaspoon pepper evenly over tofu. Heat a large cast-iron skillet over medium-high heat. Add 1 tablespoon canola oil to pan; swirl to coat. Add tofu to pan; cook 4 minutes on each side or until golden. Remove from pan; cut into bite-sized pieces. Combine oyster sauce and next 3 ingredients in a small bowl, stirring well.
4. Heat a wok or cast-iron skillet over medium-high heat. Add remaining 1 tablespoon canola oil to pan; swirl to coat. Add onion; stir-fry 2 minutes or until lightly browned. Add cabbage, carrot, and garlic; stir-fry 2 minutes or until cabbage wilts. Reduce heat to medium; stir in tofu and vinegar mixture, tossing to coat. Add pasta and bean sprouts; toss. Cook 2 minutes or until thoroughly heated. Sprinkle with green onions. Yield: 4 servings (serving size: 1 3/4 cups).

CALORIES 397; **FAT** 15.4g (sat 1.3g, mono 8.8g, poly 4.1g); **PROTEIN** 18.2g; **CARB** 55.1g; **FIBER** 9g; **CHOL** 0mg; **IRON** 4mg; **SODIUM** 736mg; **CALC** 248mg

KNOW YOUR TOFUS

If you've never worked with tofu, the main consideration is matching type to recipe. Tofu is made in two different ways, and each process yields different results.

SILKEN TOFU: As the name implies, this type of tofu has a smooth texture, similar to that of crème fraîche or yogurt. It's soy milk that's simply thickened with a coagulant, and although packages are often labeled soft, firm, and extra-firm, you shouldn't rely on this tofu to hold its shape in a vigorously cooked dish like a stir-fry. Silken is your best bet for making dips and sauces, smoothies, or dessert recipes.

WATER-PACKED TOFU: In a process similar to that of making cheese, soy milk is heated, and salts are added to separate the milk into curds and whey. Then the curds are scooped out, pressed into molds, drained, and blocks of tofu are the result. Water-packed is the type to use in stir-fries and other savory applications where you want the tofu to hold its shape after it's cooked.

Hot and Sour Soup with Tofu

Since this appetizer soup is a good source of protein, it works as a main dish if you double the portion size. White pepper gives the soup mild heat; for more spice, stir in sambal oelek.

1 (14-ounce) package firm water-packed tofu, drained
1¾ cups water, divided
1 (½-ounce) package dried sliced shiitake mushroom caps
4 cups fat-free, less-sodium chicken broth
¼ cup white vinegar
2 tablespoons less-sodium soy sauce
1 tablespoon finely chopped peeled fresh ginger
2 teaspoons sugar
¾ teaspoon white pepper
1 garlic clove, minced
2½ tablespoons cornstarch
½ cup canned sliced bamboo shoots, drained and cut into julienne strips
1 large egg, lightly beaten
½ cup thinly diagonally sliced green onion tops

1. Place tofu on several layers of paper towels. Cover tofu with several more layers of paper towels; top with a cast-iron skillet or other heavy pan. Let stand 30 minutes. Discard paper towels. Cut tofu into 1-inch cubes.
2. Bring 1½ cups water to a boil in a small saucepan; remove from heat. Stir in mushrooms; let stand 30 minutes. Stir in broth and next 6 ingredients; bring to a boil. Reduce heat, and simmer 10 minutes, stirring occasionally. Combine remaining ¼ cup water and cornstarch in a small bowl, stirring with a whisk until smooth. Stir cornstarch mixture, tofu, and bamboo shoots into broth mixture; bring to a boil. Cook 1 minute, stirring occasionally; remove from heat. Slowly drizzle egg into broth mixture (do not stir). Place pan over low heat; cook 1 minute. Stir soup gently to combine. Sprinkle with green onions. Yield: 6 servings (serving size: about 1¼ cups).

CALORIES 110; **FAT** 4.1g (sat 0.6g, mono 3g, poly 0.2g); **PROTEIN** 8.6g; **CARB** 10.1g; **FIBER** 0.8g; **CHOL** 30mg; **IRON** 1.4mg; **SODIUM** 445mg; **CALC** 141mg

THE YOUNG MAN AND THE SEA

All this sustainability talk makes Barton Seaver hungry. How one chef wants to raise your consciousness, deliciously.

Barton Seaver is only half kidding when he throws up his hands and says the way to save the oceans is to eat more broccoli.

The seafood chef and save-the-fish advocate drops the broccoli provocation on a conservation-minded crowd that has come, in part, to hear Seaver's green-blue message, but also most emphatically to chow down on his wood-grilled barramundi. He passionately and actively campaigns to save the fish, but at the same time, he's quickly becoming one of America's best-known seafood chefs. (He was anointed Chef of the Year last fall by *Esquire.*) It's not always easy wearing both hats.

"Sometimes I don't know what I'm doing here. I see myself as mainly a cook, but I was given a megaphone and am willing to use it," he says of his crusader persona. "It's intellectually engaging and a way to connect with a surprising number of people." Surprising because more and more diners are beginning to care what fish they're eating and where it came from. They sense that the seas, boundless on their surface but hidden below, are in peril—that broccoli may be the only choice if decisions to conserve aren't urgently made.

Seaver wants consumers to expand their fish horizons: Choose barramundi, which has the same sweet, clean flavor as endangered red snapper; experiment with lower-profile varieties of sustainable wild Alaskan salmon, like chum, along with the more familiar king, coho, and sockeye; and give bluefish, mackerel, and sardines a chance. He insists that sustainable varieties can save money. Tilapia is cheaper than endangered species it resembles, like orange roughy.

SEAFOOD SAVVY

GET EDUCATED. Conservation organizations, such as Blue Ocean Institute (blueocean.org) and Monterey Bay Aquarium (montereybayaquarium.org/cr/seafoodwatch.aspx), offer easy-to-use information with pocket guides and downloadable lists on their Web sites.

ASK QUESTIONS. How was the fish caught? Where did it come from? How was it raised? If farmed, what kind of farm? The answers will determine whether the seafood is a sustainable choice. For instance, wild-caught Alaskan salmon is one of Monterey Bay's Super Green picks; other types of salmon and most farmed-at-sea salmon aren't. If you can't get satisfactory answers, take your business elsewhere.

SUPPORT LEGISLATION AND LOBBY LAWMAKERS. Safeguarding the oceans requires legal action to stop dangerous and unethical fishing practices. Make your legislators aware of your convictions.

CONSIDER FROZEN SEAFOOD. New technology allows fishermen greater profitability and more time to transport the fish from the water to the table. And for the consumer: Markets are able to buy the seafood in bulk and sell inventory slowly, which can drive prices down. Unlike fresh fish, frozen fish can be transported via slower, less expensive, more ecofriendly means, like trains or trucks.

Mackerel with Herb Salad

Brining the fish in water with salt and sugar heightens its natural flavor, but it also provides a little added insurance that the fish will remain moist, even if it's slightly overcooked. Mackerel has a firm texture and full-bodied flavor, making it a perfect candidate for the grill.

1 cup cold water
3½ teaspoons salt, divided
1 teaspoon sugar
4 (6-ounce) mackerel fillets
Cooking spray
2 cups fresh flat-leaf parsley leaves
1 cup thinly sliced Vidalia or other sweet onion
1 teaspoon grated orange rind
1 cup orange sections (about 2 medium)
¾ cup fresh tarragon leaves
⅔ cup walnuts, toasted and coarsely chopped
2 tablespoons extra-virgin olive oil
1 tablespoon balsamic vinegar
½ teaspoon grated garlic

1. Preheat grill to medium-high heat.
2. Combine 1 cup water, 1 tablespoon salt, and sugar in a shallow dish. Add fillets; let stand 15 minutes. Remove fillets; pat dry. Discard brine. Place fillets, skin side down, on a grill rack coated with cooking spray. Grill 10 minutes or until desired degree of doneness. (Do not turn fillets.) Keep warm.
3. Combine parsley and next 4 ingredients in a bowl. Sprinkle herb mixture with ¼ teaspoon salt; toss. Combine walnuts and remaining ingredients, stirring with a whisk until blended. Stir in remaining ¼ teaspoon salt. Place 1 fillet on each of 4 plates; top each serving with 1 cup herb mixture. Drizzle 2 tablespoons walnut mixture over each serving. Yield: 4 servings.

CALORIES 459; **FAT** 22g (sat 2.7g, mono 8g, poly 9.5g); **PROTEIN** 43.7g; **CARB** 23.3g; **FIBER** 5.1g; **CHOL** 99mg; **IRON** 6.1mg; **SODIUM** 795mg; **CALC** 202mg

Pasta with Mussels, Pine Nuts, and Orange

(pictured on page 250)

This dish combines two economical ingredients, mussels and pasta, to create an elegant dish.

1 pound uncooked linguine
3¾ teaspoons salt, divided
4 pounds mussels, scrubbed and debearded
1 cup white wine
1 tablespoon olive oil
¾ cup pine nuts, toasted
1 garlic clove, sliced
½ teaspoon grated orange rind
½ cup fresh orange juice
½ cup chopped fresh flat-leaf parsley

1. Cook pasta in boiling water with 1 tablespoon salt 9 minutes; drain.
2. Combine mussels and wine in a Dutch oven over medium-high heat. Cover and cook 7 minutes or until shells open; discard any unopened shells. Line a fine sieve with 2 layers of cheesecloth; place over a bowl. Strain cooking liquid through prepared sieve; reserve 2 cups cooking liquid. Remove mussels from shells; keep warm. Discard cheesecloth and shells.
3. Heat a large saucepan over medium heat. Add oil to pan; swirl to coat. Add pine nuts and garlic; cook 1 minute, stirring constantly. Add reserved cooking liquid, remaining ¾ teaspoon salt, rind, and juice, stirring well; bring to a simmer. Add pasta to pan; cook 5 minutes or until liquid thickens and coats pasta. Remove from heat; stir in parsley and mussels. Serve immediately. Yield: 8 servings (serving size: 1 cup).

CALORIES 490; **FAT** 15.7g (sat 2g, mono 4.7g, poly 5.8g); **PROTEIN** 33.6g; **CARB** 53.7g; **FIBER** 2.4g; **CHOL** 56mg; **IRON** 10.8mg; **SODIUM** 889mg; **CALC** 74mg

Quick & Easy

Crispy Broiled Sablefish

Also known as black cod, sablefish is a fantastic substitution for its endangered cousin, Chilean sea bass, because it has similar rich flesh. However, it can be difficult to find and sometimes expensive. If you can't find it, substitute halibut.

1 cup cold water
3¼ teaspoons salt, divided
1 teaspoon sugar
4 (6-ounce) sablefish fillets
1 teaspoon Dijon mustard
1 large egg white
½ cup panko (Japanese breadcrumbs)
1 tablespoon orange rind
Cooking spray

1. Preheat oven to 400°.
2. Combine 1 cup water, 1 tablespoon salt, and sugar in a shallow dish. Add sablefish fillets; let stand 15 minutes. Remove fillets from brine; pat dry. Discard brine. Sprinkle fillets with remaining ¼ teaspoon salt. Combine mustard and egg white, stirring with a whisk until blended. Brush mustard mixture over fillets.
3. Combine panko and rind. Press panko mixture evenly over top of fillets. Place fillets on a broiler pan coated with cooking spray. Bake at 400° for 10 minutes. Remove pan from oven.
4. Preheat broiler.
5. Broil fillets 3 minutes or until brown. Yield: 4 servings (serving size: 1 fillet).

CALORIES 353; **FAT** 25.3g (sat 5.2g, mono 13.2g, poly 3.3g); **PROTEIN** 23.9g; **CARB** 5.6g; **FIBER** 0.4g; **CHOL** 80mg; **IRON** 2.1mg; **SODIUM** 462mg; **CALC** 60mg

Bloody Mary Oyster Shooters

This recipe calls for a small amount of alcohol, so it's really more of a fun canapé than a beverage. If you want to make a nonalcoholic version, omit the vodka and add an extra 1/4 cup veggie juice and a bit more lemon juice.

10 live oysters in shell
1 cup vegetable juice (such as V-8)
3 tablespoons vodka
1 tablespoon prepared horseradish
1 tablespoon Worcestershire sauce
2 teaspoons fresh lemon juice
1/8 teaspoon salt
1/2 teaspoon hot sauce (optional)

1. Scrub oysters thoroughly, and rinse under cold running water until all grit is removed. Shuck oysters (leaving meat on the half shells); carefully cut the foot of each oyster with shucking knife.
2. Combine vegetable juice and next 5 ingredients in a liquid measuring cup. Stir in hot sauce, if desired. Fill each of 10 shot glasses with 2½ tablespoons juice mixture. Place meat from one oyster in each glass. Discard shells. Yield: 10 servings (servings size: 1 shooter).

CALORIES 28; **FAT** 0.2g (sat 0.1g, mono 0g, poly 0.1g); **PROTEIN** 1g; **CARB** 2.4g; **FIBER** 0.3g; **CHOL** 4mg; **IRON** 1mg; **SODIUM** 139mg; **CALC** 13mg

IT'S IMPORTANT TO SEAVER THAT FISH BE AFFORDABLE, LIKE TILAPIA, AND FUN, LIKE OYSTER SHOOTERS.

Broiled Tilapia with Frisée-Apple Salad and Mustard-Parsley Sauce

Because it's sustainably farm-raised and widely available, tilapia is a great option. And since it doesn't have an assertive flavor, it pairs well with a variety of ingredients.

1 cup cold water
4 teaspoons salt, divided
1 teaspoon sugar
6 (6-ounce) tilapia fillets
3 tablespoons olive oil, divided
1/4 teaspoon freshly ground black pepper
Cooking spray
8 cups arugula
6 cups trimmed frisée
1/2 cup fresh mint leaves
2 Gala apples, cored and thinly sliced
1 tablespoon chopped fresh flat-leaf parsley
2 tablespoons sour cream
1 tablespoon whole-grain Dijon mustard
1 tablespoon fresh lemon juice
1 tablespoon water

1. Combine 1 cup water, 1 tablespoon salt, and sugar in a shallow dish. Add fillets, and let stand 15 minutes. Remove fillets from brine; pat dry. Discard brine. Brush fillets with 1 tablespoon olive oil. Sprinkle with ½ teaspoon salt and pepper.
2. Preheat broiler.
3. Place fillets on a broiler pan coated with cooking spray; broil 7 minutes or until desired degree of doneness.
4. Combine arugula, frisée, and mint in a large bowl. Combine apple and 1 tablespoon oil; toss well. Add apple mixture and 1/4 teaspoon salt to arugula mixture, and toss gently.
5. Combine remaining 1 tablespoon oil, remaining 1/4 teaspoon salt, parsley, and remaining ingredients, stirring with a whisk until blended. Divide arugula mixture evenly among 6 plates; top each serving with 1 fillet. Drizzle about 1 tablespoon sour cream mixture over each serving. Yield: 6 servings.

CALORIES 294; **FAT** 11.5g (sat 2.8g, mono 6.5g, poly 1.7g); **PROTEIN** 35.4g; **CARB** 15.2g; **FIBER** 4.1g; **CHOL** 75mg; **IRON** 2.9mg; **SODIUM** 676mg; **CALC** 90mg

EASY GUIDE TO BETTER CHOICES

Sites like blueocean.org list sustainable seafood choices. When in doubt, go with one of Seaver's top 10.

TOP 5 FISH FOR THE HOME COOK

1 FARM-RAISED MUSSELS, CLAMS, AND OYSTERS These bivalves are easy to prepare, and they're one of the most super-green foods we can eat. They help restore the quality of the waters where they live and provide great economic opportunities for struggling coastal communities.
2 AMERICAN FARMED CATFISH Produced in a clean and sustainable way, this humble yet familiar fish has a long shelf life, but it also freezes well, making it a convenient option on a busy day.
3 ARCTIC CHAR A great substitution for the less sustainable farmed Atlantic salmon, arctic char has the same luxurious flavor and deep, rich color with a slightly milder flavor. Although it's farmed in many places, the majority comes from the pristine waters off Iceland.
4 RAINBOW TROUT Available in a variety of forms, ranging from whole fish to smoked fillets, trout are versatile and easy to prepare.
5 ALASKAN SALMON Experiment with the five different species to find your favorite: King salmon is meaty, oily, and rich. Sockeye is gamey. Coho is well-balanced, and pink is the lightest. Chum is the most similar to farmed Atlantic salmon in flavor.

TOP 5 TO TRY IN RESTAURANTS

1 BARRAMUNDI Sustainably farmed in western Massachusetts, this fish has a clean, light flavor similar to snapper.
2 KONA KAMPACHI Another farmed species, this one from the cold waters near Hawaii. It is great as a raw preparation, and many chefs use it for appetizers. It has an unparalleled richness and a clean flavor.
3 ALASKAN SABLEFISH Very similar to the endangered Chilean sea bass, sablefish has a delicate buttery flavor and supple, meaty texture.
4 FRESH SARDINES Vastly different from canned, these fish have a sweet, fresh, clean flavor. Ordering them in a restaurant is a good way to get someone else to do the filleting.
5 MACKEREL Spanish mackerel has an assertive flavor that works with robust flavors. In restaurants, mackerel dishes tend to be playful and highlight the chef's talent.

MORE WINNING RECIPES

This month we complete our series featuring the remaining finalist entries from the 2009 *Cooking Light* Ultimate Reader Recipe Contest. These dishes rose to the top of the four contest categories: starters and drinks, family dinners, side salads and side dishes, and desserts.

Quick & Easy • Kid Friendly

Black Bean Burgers with Mango Salsa
(pictured on page 251)

Category Finalist—Family Dinners

"I try to cook vegetarian as much as possible. My then-16-month-old daughter loved black beans, so I decided to make black bean burgers. My now-2-year-old loves them! I like a sweet bite with savory dishes, so I added mango to an avocado salsa to top the burgers."

— Marina Delio,
Santa Barbara, California

2 (15-ounce) cans black beans, rinsed and drained
¾ cup finely chopped fresh cilantro, divided
¾ cup (3 ounces) shredded Monterey Jack cheese
¼ cup panko (Japanese breadcrumbs)
2 teaspoons ground cumin
1 teaspoon dried oregano
½ teaspoon sea salt
½ medium jalapeño pepper, finely chopped
2 large egg whites
Cooking spray
1¼ cups chopped peeled mango (about 1 medium)
3 tablespoons chopped shallots
1½ tablespoons fresh lime juice
1 avocado, peeled and chopped
1 garlic clove, minced
6 (2-ounce) whole-wheat hamburger buns, lightly toasted
6 green leaf lettuce leaves

1. Preheat oven to 350°.
2. Place black beans in a medium bowl; mash with a fork. Stir in ½ cup finely chopped cilantro and next 7 ingredients. Shape bean mixture into 6 (½-inch-thick) patties. Arrange patties on a baking sheet coated with cooking spray. Bake at 350° for 20 minutes, carefully turning once.
3. Combine remaining ¼ cup cilantro, mango, and next 4 ingredients in a medium bowl. Place a patty on bottom half of each hamburger bun; top each with 1 lettuce leaf, ⅓ cup salsa, and top half of bun. Yield: 6 servings (serving size: 1 burger).

CALORIES 320; FAT 11.9g (sat 3.9g, mono 5g, poly 1.7g); PROTEIN 13.4g; CARB 46.2g; FIBER 10.1g; CHOL 13mg; IRON 3.3mg; SODIUM 777mg; CALC 201mg

Make Ahead • Kid Friendly

Tart and Tangy Bulgur Salad

Category Finalist—Sides & Salads

1 cup uncooked bulgur
1 cup boiling water
2 tablespoons olive oil
2 tablespoons lime juice
½ teaspoon salt
8 large fresh basil leaves, finely chopped
1 garlic clove, minced
¼ cup chopped red onion
12 large olives, sliced (about ¾ cup)
1 large tomato, chopped
Lime wedges (optional)

1. Combine bulgur and boiling water in a large bowl. Cover and let stand 45 minutes.
2. Combine oil and next 4 ingredients in a small bowl, stirring with a whisk until combined. Add oil mixture, onion, olives, and tomato to bulgur; toss well. Garnish with lime wedges, if desired. Yield: 4 servings (serving size: about 1 cup).

CALORIES 210; FAT 8.7g (sat 1.2g, mono 6g, poly 1.1g); PROTEIN 5g; CARB 31g; FIBER 7.6g; CHOL 0mg; IRON 1.5mg; SODIUM 420mg; CALC 35mg

Quick & Easy

Steamed Clams Fagioli

Category Finalist—Starters & Drinks

"I use a small amount of high-quality olive oil for flavor. This first course soup is mostly vegetables, but the clams make it more substantial."

— Christine Losurdo,
Campbell Hall, New York

1 tablespoon olive oil
2 garlic cloves, minced
½ cup finely chopped onion
¼ cup finely chopped celery
⅛ to ¼ teaspoon crushed red pepper
¼ cup dry white wine
1 (14.5-ounce) can diced tomatoes, undrained
¾ cup fat-free, less-sodium chicken broth
¼ cup clam juice
1 tablespoon chopped fresh parsley
½ teaspoon dried oregano
⅛ teaspoon salt
⅛ teaspoon black pepper
1 (15.5-ounce) can cannellini beans, rinsed and drained
24 littleneck clams
8 (½-inch-thick) slices whole-wheat French bread baguette (about 8 ounces), toasted

1. Heat oil in a Dutch oven over medium-high heat. Add garlic; sauté 1 minute, stirring frequently. Add onion and celery; sauté for 1 minute, stirring frequently. Add red pepper; cook 1 minute. Stir in wine; cook 1 minute. Stir in tomatoes; bring to a simmer. Cook 5 minutes, stirring frequently. Add broth and next 6 ingredients; bring to a boil. Cover and reduce heat; simmer 2 minutes. Add clams to pan. Cover and cook over medium-high heat 5 minutes or until clams open; discard unopened shells. Ladle ⅔ cup soup into 8 bowls; top each with 3 clams. Serve with toast. Yield: 8 servings.

CALORIES 170; FAT 3.4g (sat 0.5g, mono 1.8g, poly 0.6g); PROTEIN 10.8g; CARB 24g; FIBER 4.9g; CHOL 20mg; IRON 3mg; SODIUM 406mg; CALC 84mg

Make Ahead • Freezable
Kid Friendly

Mexican Spiced Shortbread Cookies

Category Finalist—Desserts

"The inspiration for these sinfully rich-tasting cookies combines my obsession with short-bread, dulce de leche, and a restaurant cream cheese dessert."

—Jennifer Brumfield,
Bellingham, Washington

Cookies:
6.75 ounces all-purpose flour (about 1½ cups)
⅓ cup unsweetened cocoa
¼ teaspoon ground cinnamon
¼ teaspoon salt
⅛ teaspoon chipotle chile powder
⅛ teaspoon ancho chile powder
½ cup unsalted butter, softened
½ cup canola oil
¾ cup powdered sugar

Icing:
2 tablespoons unsalted butter
½ cup packed light brown sugar
½ cup 1% low-fat milk
1¼ cups powdered sugar
1 teaspoon vanilla extract

Nuts:
1 teaspoon light brown sugar
1 teaspoon sea salt
1 teaspoon unsalted butter, softened
36 small pecan halves

1. To prepare cookies, weigh or lightly spoon flour into dry measuring cups; level with a knife. Combine flour, cocoa, and next 4 ingredients in a bowl; stir with a whisk.
2. Place ½ cup butter in a large bowl; beat with a mixer at medium speed until light and fluffy. Gradually add oil; beat 3 minutes or until well blended. Gradually add ¾ cup powdered sugar; beat well. Add flour mixture; beat at low speed until well blended. Cover and chill 30 minutes.
3. Preheat oven to 325°.
4. Shape dough into 36 balls. Place 2 inches apart on an ungreased baking sheet. Flatten cookies to ¼ inch thickness. Bake at 325° for 20 minutes. Cool 1 minute on baking sheet. Remove

from baking sheet to a wire rack; cool completely.
5. To prepare icing, melt 2 tablespoons butter in a large saucepan over medium heat. Add ½ cup brown sugar and milk; cook 1 minute or until sugar dissolves, stirring constantly. Bring to a boil; reduce heat, and simmer 3 minutes or until slightly thickened, stirring occasionally. Remove from heat; cool to room temperature. Add powdered sugar and vanilla, stirring with a whisk until smooth.
6. To prepare nuts, combine 1 teaspoon brown sugar, sea salt, and 1 teaspoon butter in a medium bowl. Arrange pecans on a baking sheet. Bake at 325° for 10 minutes or until toasted. Add hot pecans to butter mixture, tossing well to coat. Cool.
7. Spread 1 teaspoon icing over each cookie; top each with 1 pecan half. Yield: 3 dozen cookies (serving size: 1 cookie).

CALORIES 125; FAT 7.5g (sat 2.4g, mono 3.3g, poly 1.4g); PROTEIN 1g; CARB 14.5g; FIBER 0.6g; CHOL 9mg; IRON 0.5mg; SODIUM 85mg; CALC 11mg

BUDGET COOKING
FEED 4 FOR LESS THAN $10

Fresh, inspired springtime meals can be surprisingly economical.

Pork Tenderloin, Pear, and Cranberry Salad

$2.38 per serving, $9.53 total

1 tablespoon cider vinegar
1 teaspoon Dijon mustard
¾ teaspoon brown sugar
1½ teaspoons minced fresh garlic, divided
1¼ teaspoons dried thyme, divided
1 pound pork tenderloin, trimmed and cut crosswise into ¼-inch-thick slices
¾ teaspoon salt, divided
¾ teaspoon freshly ground black pepper, divided

2 tablespoons all-purpose flour
¼ cup olive oil, divided
¼ cup sliced shallots
¼ cup dried cranberries
¼ cup cranberry juice cocktail
6 cups baby spinach leaves
1 ripe red Anjou pear, thinly sliced

1. Combine vinegar, mustard, sugar, ½ teaspoon garlic, and ¼ teaspoon thyme; set aside.
2. Combine pork and remaining 1 teaspoon garlic, remaining 1 teaspoon thyme, ½ teaspoon salt, and ½ teaspoon pepper; toss well to coat. Sprinkle pork mixture with flour; toss well. Let stand 5 minutes.
3. Heat 1 tablespoon oil in a medium saucepan over medium heat. Add shallots to saucepan; cook 3 minutes or until shallots are tender and lightly browned, stirring occasionally. Add cranberries and juice; cook until liquid is reduced to 2 tablespoons (about 2 minutes). Reduce heat to medium-low. Add vinegar mixture; cook 1 minute. Gradually add 1 tablespoon oil, remaining ¼ teaspoon salt, and remaining ¼ teaspoon pepper, stirring well with a whisk. Cover and keep warm.
4. Heat 1 tablespoon oil in a large nonstick skillet over medium-high heat. Add half of pork to skillet; cook 3 minutes or until browned, turning once. Remove pork from skillet. Repeat procedure with remaining 1 tablespoon oil and remaining pork. Toss pork with 1 tablespoon warm cranberry mixture.
5. Combine spinach and pear in a large bowl. Drizzle with remaining cranberry mixture; toss well to coat. Arrange about 2 cups spinach mixture on each of 4 plates; top evenly with pork. Yield: 4 servings.

CALORIES 360; FAT 17.7g (sat 3.3g, mono 11.6g, poly 1.9g); PROTEIN 25.8g; CARB 25.6g; FIBER 4.4g; CHOL 74mg; IRON 3.3mg; SODIUM 593mg; CALC 71mg

Quick & Easy

Peppery Pasta with Arugula and Shrimp

$2.15 per serving, $8.61 total

Splitting the shrimp in half helps a small amount stretch further. You can sub baby spinach for arugula, if you prefer.

1 tablespoon minced fresh garlic, divided
1¼ teaspoons black pepper, divided
½ teaspoon salt, divided
1 (5-ounce) package fresh baby arugula
4 quarts water
8 ounces uncooked linguine
1 tablespoon olive oil
½ pound peeled and deveined medium
   shrimp, cut in half horizontally
2 tablespoons minced shallots
¾ cup fat-free, less-sodium chicken broth
2 tablespoons fresh lemon juice
1 tablespoon butter
½ cup (2 ounces) shaved fresh Romano
   cheese

1. Combine 2 teaspoons garlic, 1 teaspoon pepper, ¼ teaspoon salt, and arugula in a large bowl; toss well.
2. Bring 4 quarts water to a boil in a large Dutch oven. Add pasta; cook 10 minutes or until al dente; drain. Add hot pasta to arugula mixture, and toss well until arugula wilts.
3. Heat oil in a large skillet over medium-high heat. Add shrimp, remaining ¼ teaspoon salt, and remaining ¼ teaspoon pepper; sauté 1 minute. Add remaining 1 teaspoon garlic and shallots; sauté 1 minute or until shrimp are done. Remove shrimp from pan. Add broth and juice to pan, scraping pan to loosen browned bits; cook 5 minutes or until liquid is reduced by half. Return shrimp to pan. Remove from heat; stir in butter.
4. Arrange 1½ cups pasta on each of 4 plates. Spoon ⅓ cup shrimp mixture over each serving. Top each serving with 2 tablespoons cheese. Yield: 4 servings.

CALORIES 409; **FAT** 12.5g (sat 5g, mono 4.5g, poly 1.1g); **PROTEIN** 26.1g; **CARB** 46g; **FIBER** 2.1g; **CHOL** 107mg; **IRON** 3.3mg; **SODIUM** 671mg; **CALC** 231mg

Kid Friendly

Mushroom-Stuffed Chicken

$2.49 per serving, $9.95 total

Serve with 3 cups cooked egg noodles tossed with 2 tablespoons butter and green onions.

2 (1-ounce) slices white bread, torn
Cooking spray
¼ cup chopped green onions
8 ounces presliced mushrooms
½ teaspoon dried thyme
1 garlic clove, minced
½ cup (2 ounces) shredded part-skim
   mozzarella cheese
¾ teaspoon salt, divided
½ teaspoon black pepper, divided
4 (6-ounce) skinless, boneless chicken
   breast halves
¼ cup all-purpose flour
2 large eggs, lightly beaten
1 tablespoon olive oil

1. Preheat oven to 350°.
2. Pulse bread in a food processor to form fine crumbs. Place in a dish.
3. Heat a large ovenproof skillet over medium-high heat. Coat pan with cooking spray. Add onions and mushrooms; sauté 10 minutes. Stir in thyme and garlic. Cool mixture 10 minutes; stir in cheese, ¼ teaspoon salt, and ¼ teaspoon pepper.
4. Cut a slit through thickest portion of each breast half to form a pocket. Stuff each with ¼ cup mushroom mixture. Sprinkle chicken with remaining ½ teaspoon salt and remaining ¼ teaspoon pepper. Place flour in a shallow dish. Place eggs in a shallow dish. Dredge chicken in flour. Dip in eggs; dredge in breadcrumbs.
5. Heat oil in skillet over medium-high heat. Add chicken; cook 2 minutes on each side or until browned. Place pan in oven. Bake at 350° for 15 minutes or until a thermometer registers 165°. Yield: 4 servings (serving size: 1 stuffed breast half).

CALORIES 376; **FAT** 13.4g (sat 4.3g, mono 5.7g, poly 1.9g); **PROTEIN** 44.9g; **CARB** 17.4g; **FIBER** 1.4g; **CHOL** 207mg; **IRON** 3mg; **SODIUM** 717mg; **CALC** 170mg

Chicken with Lemon and Olives

$2.39 per serving, $9.56 total

¼ cup fresh orange juice
¼ cup fresh lemon juice
3 tablespoons olive oil
2 tablespoons honey
¾ teaspoon ground cumin
6 garlic cloves, coarsely chopped
4 chicken leg quarters, skinned
½ teaspoon salt
½ teaspoon black pepper
16 pimiento-stuffed green olives, halved
1 lemon, thinly sliced
¼ cup fresh flat-leaf parsley leaves

1. Preheat oven to 400°.
2. Combine first 7 ingredients; marinate at room temperature 30 minutes.
3. Pour marinade into a 13 x 9–inch baking dish. Heat a large skillet over medium-high heat. Add chicken; cook 3 minutes on each side or until browned. Arrange chicken in dish; sprinkle with salt and pepper. Top with olives and lemon slices. Bake at 400° for 40 minutes or until a thermometer registers 165°.
4. Remove chicken from dish; keep warm. Strain sauce over a saucepan, reserving solids. Bring sauce to a boil; cook 3 minutes or until slightly thick. Stir in olives and garlic; serve with chicken and lemons. Top with parsley. Yield: 4 servings (serving size: 1 leg quarter and 2 tablespoons sauce).

CALORIES 343; **FAT** 19.2g (sat 2.7g, mono 11.9g, poly 3.3g); **PROTEIN** 27.2g; **CARB** 18.4g; **FIBER** 1.7g; **CHOL** 105mg; **IRON** 2mg; **SODIUM** 852mg; **CALC** 46mg

For the green pea rice:
Heat 2 teaspoons olive oil in a small saucepan over medium-high heat. Add 1 teaspoon minced garlic; sauté 1 minute. Add 1 (14-ounce) can fat-free, less-sodium chicken broth; bring to a boil. Stir in 1 cup long-grain white rice. Cover, reduce heat, and simmer 20 minutes. Stir in ½ cup thawed frozen green peas.

BREAKFAST, LUNCH, AND DINNER IN... PORTLAND

Portland, Oregon, is quickly stealing Berkeley's mantle as the city that fresh, local, seasonal food built. Little wonder; Portland is surrounded by bounty—a mild climate allows a year-round growing season for farmers dedicated to sustainable agriculture; forested hills nearby yield wild mushrooms; small independent vineyards produce world-class wines; and the Pacific Ocean, which is just an hour away, provides succulent seafood.

Quick & Easy
Breakfast

Frittata with Morels, Fava Beans, and Pecorino Romano Cheese

At Simpatica Dining Hall (simpaticacatering.com), shared tables and stiff coffee promote bonhomie over familiar breakfast fare with seasonal twists, like savory crepes stuffed with squash and house-cured bacon, or a frittata brimming with freshly foraged morels. Chef Scott Ketterman of Simpatica Dining Hall uses crème fraîche to add richness to this spring vegetable frittata. We've cut fat and calories by using light sour cream and replacing two of the whole eggs with egg whites. If you can't find fresh morel mushrooms or fava beans, try the recipe with shiitake mushrooms and shelled edamame.

1/3 cup shelled fava beans
1/2 cup fresh morel mushrooms (about 2 ounces)
1 tablespoon olive oil
2 tablespoons grated fresh pecorino Romano cheese, divided
1 tablespoon finely chopped fresh parsley
2 tablespoons light sour cream
1 teaspoon chopped fresh tarragon
1/4 teaspoon salt
1/8 teaspoon freshly ground black pepper
4 large eggs
2 large egg whites
Tarragon leaves (optional)

1. Preheat oven to 350°.
2. Cook fava beans in boiling water 30 seconds. Remove with a slotted spoon, and plunge beans into ice water; drain well. Peel tough skins from beans.
3. Place mushrooms in a small bowl of cold water; swirl mushrooms gently to remove any grit. Drain; rinse well. Drain on paper towels, patting mushrooms dry.
4. Heat oil in an 8-inch ovenproof skillet over medium-high heat. Add mushrooms to pan; sauté 5 minutes or until browned. Combine 1 tablespoon cheese, parsley, and next 6 ingredients in a medium bowl; stir with a whisk. Stir in mushrooms and beans. Add egg mixture to pan; cook 1 minute, stirring gently. Place pan in oven; bake at 350° for 8 minutes or until edges are puffed and center is almost set. Remove from oven.
5. Preheat broiler.
6. Sprinkle top of frittata with remaining 1 tablespoon cheese. Broil 1 minute or until cheese melts. Garnish with fresh tarragon leaves, if desired. Yield: 2 servings (serving size: ½ frittata).

CALORIES 356; FAT 20.3g (sat 6g, mono 9.4g, poly 2.6g); PROTEIN 26.2g; CARB 19g; FIBER 6.6g; CHOL 435mg; IRON 3.9mg; SODIUM 586mg; CALC 153mg

Make Ahead
Lunch

Chickpea, Bread, and Leek Soup with Harissa and Yogurt

One of Portland's healthiest choices is Garden State Cart (gardenstatecart.com), where ingredients like locally raised free-range chicken and vegetables direct from a partnering farm are done up Mediterranean-style. This hearty Middle Eastern–inspired soup is based on a favorite at Garden State Cart. Look for harissa—a fiery North African condiment incorporating chile peppers, tomatoes, and paprika—in tubes and cans at ethnic grocery stores and specialty shops.

4 large leeks (about 2½ pounds)
2 tablespoons olive oil
4 teaspoons ground cumin
4 garlic cloves, minced
6 cups fat-free, less-sodium chicken broth
1 (19-ounce) can chickpeas (garbanzo beans), rinsed and drained
2 tablespoons chopped fresh flat-leaf parsley
4½ cups cubed day-old bread (about 6 ounces)
3/4 cup plain low-fat yogurt
6 teaspoons harissa

1. Remove roots, outer leaves, and tops from leeks, leaving white and light green parts of each leek. Cut each leek in half lengthwise. Cut each half crosswise into thin slices. Rinse with cold water; drain.
2. Heat olive oil in a large Dutch oven over medium heat. Add leeks to pan; cook 10 minutes or until tender, stirring frequently. Add cumin and garlic; cook 1 minute.
3. Add chicken broth and chickpeas; bring to a boil. Reduce heat to medium-low, and simmer 15 minutes. Stir in parsley. Place about ⅔ cup bread in each of 6 bowls; ladle about 1⅓ cups soup over each serving. Combine yogurt and harissa in a small bowl. Top each serving with 2 tablespoons yogurt mixture. Yield: 6 servings.

CALORIES 334; FAT 7.6g (sat 1.1g, mono 3.5g, poly 1.1g); PROTEIN 11.8g; CARB 57g; FIBER 6.7g; CHOL 2.5mg; IRON 6mg; SODIUM 805mg; CALC 226mg

Dinner

Flank Steak with Roasted Endive, Spring Onion Agrodolce, and Arugula

Spring onions stewed in vinegar and honey make a delightful sweet-sour garnish for this beef dish, inspired by Chef Ben Bettinger of Beaker and Flask (beakerandflask.com), who often uses inexpensive shoulder steak, sometimes labeled "shoulder tender." If you can't find spring onions, substitute cipollini onions or shallots.

½ cup honey

12 ounces spring onions, trimmed and quartered

½ cup sherry vinegar

2 tablespoons olive oil, divided

6 heads Belgian endive (about 1 pound), halved lengthwise

¾ teaspoon salt, divided

¾ teaspoon freshly ground black pepper, divided

2 tablespoons chopped fresh oregano, divided

1½ teaspoons Hungarian sweet paprika

1 (1-pound) flank steak, halved crosswise

6 cups arugula leaves (about 4 ounces)

2 tablespoons extra-virgin olive oil

1 tablespoon fresh lemon juice

1. Place honey in a medium saucepan over medium heat; cook 2 minutes or until heated. Add onions to pan; stir to combine. Stir in vinegar; bring to a boil. Cover, reduce heat, and simmer 30 minutes or until onions are tender. Cook, uncovered, 20 minutes or until syrupy.
2. Preheat oven to 375°.
3. Heat an ovenproof grill pan over medium-high heat. Add 1 tablespoon olive oil to pan, swirling to coat. Sprinkle endive evenly with ¼ teaspoon salt and ¼ teaspoon black pepper. Add endive, cut sides down, to pan. Cook 1 minute or until lightly browned. Turn endive; place pan in oven. Bake at 375° for 15 minutes or until endive is tender. Remove endive from oven; cover and keep warm. Wipe pan clean.
4. Combine remaining ½ teaspoon salt, remaining ½ teaspoon pepper, 1 tablespoon oregano, and paprika in a small

bowl. Sprinkle beef evenly with oregano mixture. Heat grill pan over medium-high heat. Add remaining 1 tablespoon olive oil to pan, swirling to coat. Add beef to pan; cook 4 minutes on each side or until desired degree of doneness. Let stand 10 minutes before cutting across grain into thin slices.
5. Combine remaining 1 tablespoon oregano, arugula, 2 tablespoons extra-virgin olive oil, and juice in a medium bowl; toss gently. Serve steak with endive and arugula salad; top steak with onion mixture. Yield: 4 servings (serving size: about 3 ounces steak, about 1 cup salad, 3 endive halves, and about 5 tablespoons onion mixture).

CALORIES 484; **FAT** 19.9g (sat 4.3g, mono 12.5g, poly 1.7g); **PROTEIN** 27.4g; **CARB** 49.5g; **FIBER** 5.3g; **CHOL** 37mg; **IRON** 3mg; **SODIUM** 505mg; **CALC** 120mg

RECIPE HALL OF FAME
OUR FAVORITE FLATBREAD

Salty Italian bacon and fresh asparagus make this crisp-chewy flatbread unforgettable. Use a mandoline to slice the asparagus, or just cut it into 2-inch pieces.

Flatbread with Pancetta, Mozzarella, and Asparagus

½ cup warm water (100° to 110°)

1 teaspoon dry yeast

6.7 ounces all-purpose flour (about 1½ cups), divided

½ teaspoon sea salt

Cooking spray

1 teaspoon dried thyme

2 ounces pancetta, finely chopped

1 garlic clove, minced

⅛ teaspoon freshly ground black pepper

1 tablespoon cornmeal

1 cup very thinly vertically sliced asparagus

¼ cup (1 ounce) shredded part-skim mozzarella cheese

¼ cup (1 ounce) grated Parmigiano-Reggiano cheese

1. Combine warm water and yeast in a large bowl; let stand 5 minutes. Weigh or lightly spoon flour into dry measuring cups; level with a knife. Add 5.6 ounces (about 1¼ cups) flour and salt to yeast mixture; stir until blended. Turn dough out onto a floured surface. Knead dough until smooth and elastic (about 8 minutes); add enough of remaining 1.1 ounces (about ¼ cup) flour, 1 tablespoon at a time, to prevent dough from sticking to hands (dough will feel sticky).
2. Place dough in a large bowl coated with cooking spray, turning to coat top. Cover and let rise in a warm place (85°), free from drafts, 45 minutes or until doubled in size. (Gently press two fingers into dough. If an indentation remains, dough has risen enough.)
3. Heat a small skillet over medium heat. Add thyme, pancetta, and garlic to pan; sauté 5 minutes or until pancetta is crisp. Stir in pepper.
4. Preheat oven to 475°.
5. Place a baking sheet in oven 15 minutes to preheat. Punch dough down; cover and let rest for 5 minutes. Stretch dough into a 10-inch circle on a floured surface. Sprinkle cornmeal on preheated baking sheet, and place dough on sheet. Spread pancetta mixture evenly over dough. Arrange asparagus over pancetta mixture; sprinkle evenly with cheese. Bake flatbread at 475° for 10 minutes or until crust is golden. Remove from oven. Sprinkle with Parmigiano-Reggiano cheese. Cut flatbread into 8 wedges. Yield: 8 servings (serving size: 1 wedge).

CALORIES 147; **FAT** 4.1g (sat 2.1g, mono 0.5g, poly 0.2g); **PROTEIN** 6.3g; **CARB** 20.4g; **FIBER** 1.3g; **CHOL** 10mg; **IRON** 1.6mg; **SODIUM** 339mg; **CALC** 84mg

SIMPLE ADDITIONS

Quick & Easy

Mango Shrimp Kebabs

These fresh-flavored skewers are a great option for entertaining.

1½ pounds large peeled and deveined shrimp
2 large red bell peppers, cut into 1-inch
  pieces
2 mangoes, peeled and cut into 1-inch cubes
1 small red onion, cut into 1-inch pieces
2 limes, cut into wedges

Prepare grill to medium-high heat. Sprinkle shrimp evenly with ½ teaspoon salt and ⅛ teaspoon freshly ground black pepper. Thread shrimp, bell pepper, mango, and onion alternately onto each of 8 (12-inch) skewers. Place skewers on a grill rack coated with cooking spray; grill 2 minutes on each side or until shrimp are done. Squeeze juice from lime wedges over kebabs. Yield: 4 servings (serving size: 2 skewers).

CALORIES 277; **FAT** 3.3g (sat 0.7g, mono 0.5g, poly 1.2g); **PROTEIN** 35.8g; **CARB** 27.1g; **FIBER** 4.2g; **CHOL** 259mg; **IRON** 4.5mg; **SODIUM** 551mg; **CALC** 109mg

THE FIVE INGREDIENTS

1½ pounds large peeled and deveined shrimp

+

2 large red bell peppers, cut into 1-inch pieces

+

2 mangoes, peeled and cut into 1-inch cubes

+

1 small red onion, cut into 1-inch pieces

+

2 limes, cut into wedges

Quick & Easy

Turkey Reuben Panini

Here's authentic deli-style flavor in a lower-fat package.

8 (½-ounce) slices thin-slice rye bread
¼ cup fat-free Thousand Island dressing
8 (½-ounce) thin slices reduced-fat Swiss
  cheese
¼ cup refrigerated sauerkraut, rinsed and
  drained
8 ounces deli, low-sodium turkey breast (such
  as Boar's Head)

Spread one side of each bread slice evenly with 1½ teaspoons dressing. Place one cheese slice on dressed side of each of four bread slices; top each with 1 tablespoon sauerkraut and 2 ounces turkey. Top each sandwich with 1 cheese slice and 1 bread slice, dressed side down. Coat outside of sandwich (top and bottom) with cooking spray. Heat a large skillet over medium-high heat. Add sandwiches to pan. Place a cast-iron or other heavy skillet on top of sandwiches; press gently to flatten sandwiches (leave cast-iron skillet on sandwiches while they cook). Cook 2 minutes on each side or until browned and cheese melts. Yield: 4 servings (serving size: 1 sandwich).

CALORIES 268; **FAT** 7.5g (sat 3g, mono 0.6g, poly 0.4g); **PROTEIN** 25.2g; **CARB** 25.7g; **FIBER** 3.1g; **CHOL** 35mg; **IRON** 1.7mg; **SODIUM** 819mg; **CALC** 304mg

THE FIVE INGREDIENTS

8 (½-ounce) slices
thin-slice rye bread

¼ cup fat-free
Thousand Island dressing

8 (½-ounce) thin slices
reduced-fat Swiss cheese

¼ cup refrigerated sauerkraut,
rinsed and drained

8 ounces deli, low-sodium
turkey breast (such as Boar's Head)

DINNER TONIGHT

Here are a handful of stopwatch-tested menus from the *Cooking Light* Test Kitchens.

30 minutes

SHOPPING LIST

Spaghetti with Sausage and Simple Tomato Sauce

garlic
fresh basil
spaghetti
28-ounce can no-salt-added whole
   tomatoes
olive oil
crushed red pepper
sugar
8 ounces hot Italian turkey sausage
Parmigiano-Reggiano cheese

Mixed Greens Salad

1 lemon
4 cups mixed microgreens
1 bunch watercress
Dijon mustard
sugar
extra-virgin olive oil

GAME PLAN

While broiler heats:
  ■ Bring water to boil.
  ■ Puree tomatoes.
  ■ Mince garlic.
While sausage cooks:
  ■ Cook pasta.
  ■ Cook tomato sauce.
  ■ Shave cheese.
  ■ Tear basil.
  ■ Prepare salad.

Quick & Easy • Make Ahead

Spaghetti with Sausage and Simple Tomato Sauce
with Mixed Greens Salad

Make-Ahead Tip: Prepare the sauce up to three days ahead.
Flavor Hit: A good amount of crushed red pepper infuses the sauce with heat.
Simple Sub: In place of sausage, try sautéed shrimp.

8 ounces hot Italian turkey sausage links
8 ounces uncooked spaghetti
1 (28-ounce) can no-salt-added whole
   tomatoes, undrained
2 tablespoons olive oil
½ teaspoon crushed red pepper
5 garlic cloves, minced
1 teaspoon sugar
½ teaspoon kosher salt
¼ cup torn fresh basil
½ cup (2 ounces) shaved Parmigiano-
   Reggiano cheese

1. Preheat broiler.
2. Arrange sausage on a small baking sheet. Broil sausage 5 minutes on each side or until done. Remove pan from oven (do not turn broiler off). Cut sausage into ¼-inch-thick slices. Arrange slices in a single layer on baking sheet. Broil sausage slices 2 minutes or until browned.
3. Cook pasta according to package directions, omitting salt and fat; drain.
4. Place tomatoes in a food processor; process until almost smooth. Heat oil in a large nonstick skillet over medium-high heat. Add pepper and garlic; sauté 1 minute. Stir in tomatoes, sugar, and salt; cook 4 minutes or until slightly thick. Add sausage and cooked pasta to pan; toss well. Top with basil and cheese. Yield: 4 servings (serving size: 1¼ cups pasta, 2 tablespoons cheese, and 1 tablespoon basil).

CALORIES 460; **FAT** 16.9g (sat 5.1g, mono 8.1g, poly 2.8g); **PROTEIN** 24.4g; **CARB** 53.3g; **FIBER** 4g; **CHOL** 57mg; **IRON** 4.7mg; **SODIUM** 895mg; **CALC** 253mg

continued

For the Mixed Greens Salad:
Combine 1 tablespoon fresh lemon juice, ½ teaspoon Dijon mustard, ¼ teaspoon salt, ¼ teaspoon sugar, and ¼ teaspoon black pepper in a medium bowl. Gradually add 2 tablespoons extra-virgin olive oil, stirring constantly with a whisk. Drizzle dressing over 4 cups mixed microgreens and 2 cups trimmed watercress; toss to coat.

40 minutes

SHOPPING LIST

Shrimp and Okra Gumbo
1 small onion
1 medium bell pepper
celery
garlic
½ pound fresh okra pods
fresh flat-leaf parsley
canola oil
all-purpose flour
dried thyme
ground red pepper
paprika
ground allspice
fat-free, less-sodium chicken broth
1 (28-ounce) can diced tomatoes
4 ounces smoked ham
¾ pound peeled and deveined large shrimp

Creamy Yogurt Grits
quick-cooking grits
fat-free Greek-style yogurt

GAME PLAN

Prepare roux mixture; remove from pan.
While onion and ham cook:
- Bring water to a boil for grits.
- Prep bell pepper, celery, and okra.
While broth mixture simmers:
- Cook grits.
- Chop parsley.

Quick & Easy • Make Ahead
Shrimp and Okra Gumbo
with Creamy Yogurt Grits

Simple Sub: Use cubed skinless, boneless chicken breast in lieu of shrimp.
Buy The Best: Look for firm, bright-green okra.

2 tablespoons canola oil, divided
3 tablespoons all-purpose flour
10 tablespoons fat-free, less-sodium chicken broth
1 cup chopped onion
4 ounces smoked ham, chopped
1 cup chopped green bell pepper
⅔ cup diced celery
½ teaspoon dried thyme
3 garlic cloves, minced
½ pound fresh okra pods, sliced
¼ cup water
½ teaspoon ground red pepper
½ teaspoon paprika
½ teaspoon freshly ground black pepper
¼ teaspoon salt
¼ teaspoon ground allspice
1 (28-ounce) can diced tomatoes, drained
¾ pound peeled and deveined large shrimp
2 tablespoons chopped fresh flat-leaf parsley

1. Heat 1 tablespoon oil in a large saucepan over medium-high heat. Add flour; cook 1 minute or until lightly browned, stirring constantly with a whisk. Add broth; stir with a whisk until thick. Pour into a bowl; set aside. Wipe pan clean with paper towels.
2. Heat remaining 1 tablespoon oil in pan over medium heat. Add onion and ham; cook 10 minutes, stirring occasionally. Add bell pepper and next 4 ingredients; cook 5 minutes or until vegetables are almost tender, stirring occasionally. Add broth mixture, ¼ cup water, and next 6 ingredients. Bring to a boil; reduce heat, and simmer 10 minutes or until vegetables are tender. Stir in shrimp; cook 4 minutes or until shrimp are done. Sprinkle with parsley. Yield: 4 servings (serving size: 1½ cups gumbo and 1½ teaspoons parsley).

CALORIES 300; FAT 10.5g (sat 1.4g, mono 4.4g, poly 2.8g); PROTEIN 26.6g; CARB 26.5g; FIBER 7.3g; CHOL 143mg; IRON 4mg; SODIUM 918mg; CALC 162mg

---

For the Creamy Yogurt Grits:
Bring 2½ cups water to a boil in a medium saucepan. Gradually whisk in ¾ cup uncooked quick-cooking grits; cover, reduce heat, and simmer 8 minutes or until thick. Stir in 1 cup fat-free Greek-style yogurt, ½ teaspoon salt, and ½ teaspoon black pepper.

30 minutes

SHOPPING LIST

Vietnamese Beef-Noodle Soup with Asian Greens
1 large yellow onion
garlic
3-inch piece fresh ginger
4 heads baby bok choy
5 ounces snow peas
1 small Thai chile
5 ounces fresh bean sprouts
fresh basil
fresh mint
1 lime
4 ounces wide rice stick noodles
less-sodium soy sauce
fish sauce
32-ounce container fat-free, less-sodium beef broth
whole cloves
cardamom pods
star anise
brown sugar
1 (8-ounce) sirloin steak

Sesame Wontons
wonton wrappers
dark sesame oil

GAME PLAN

While oven heats for wontons:
- Chill beef in freezer.
- Bring water to a boil for noodles.
- Heat aromatics in broth.
While vegetables simmer in broth:
- Slice beef.
- Bake wontons.

Vietnamese Beef-Noodle Soup with Asian Greens

with Sesame Wontons

Prep Pointer: Take care not to overcook the noodles as they'll turn soggy in the soup.
Simple Sub: Use a serrano or habanero pepper in place of the Thai chile; seed for less heat.

1 (8-ounce) sirloin steak
4 ounces uncooked wide rice stick noodles
1½ cups thinly sliced yellow onion
3 whole cloves
2 cardamom pods
2 garlic cloves, halved
1 (3-inch) piece peeled fresh ginger, thinly sliced
1 star anise
4 cups fat-free, less-sodium beef broth
2 cups water
1 tablespoon less-sodium soy sauce
1 teaspoon brown sugar
2 teaspoons fish sauce
4 cups baby bok choy leaves
1 cup snow peas, trimmed
1 small fresh Thai chile, thinly sliced into rings
1 cup fresh bean sprouts
¼ cup fresh basil leaves
¼ cup fresh mint leaves
4 lime wedges

1. Freeze beef for 10 minutes; cut across grain into ⅛-inch-thick slices.
2. Cook noodles according to package directions. Drain and rinse with cold water; drain.
3. Place onion and next 5 ingredients in a large saucepan; cook over medium-high heat 5 minutes, stirring frequently. Add broth and 2 cups water; bring to a boil. Strain broth mixture though a fine sieve over a bowl; discard solids. Return broth to pan. Add soy sauce, sugar, and fish sauce; bring to a boil. Add bok choy and snow peas; simmer 4 minutes or until peas are crisp-tender and bok choy wilts.
4. Arrange ½ cup noodles into each of 4 large bowls. Divide raw beef and chile slices evenly among bowls. Ladle about 1⅔ cups hot soup over each serving (broth will cook beef). Top each serving

with ¼ cup bean sprouts, 1 tablespoon basil, and 1 tablespoon mint. Serve with lime wedges. Yield: 4 servings.

CALORIES 303; FAT 8.3g (sat 3.2g, mono 3.5g, poly 0.4g); PROTEIN 24.2g; CARB 31.1g; FIBER 2.8g; CHOL 51mg; IRON 4.2mg; SODIUM 900mg; CALC 120mg

For the Sesame Wontons:
Cut 16 wonton wrappers in half diagonally; arrange on 2 baking sheets coated with cooking spray. Brush 2 teaspoons dark sesame oil over wrappers. Sprinkle evenly with ¼ teaspoon salt. Bake at 375° for 7 minutes or until crisp and edges are browned.

30 minutes

| SHOPPING LIST |

Chicken Carne Asada Tacos with Pickled Onions
1 large orange
2 limes
1 (10-ounce) red onion
1 avocado
1 lime (optional)
sugar
cumin seeds
dried oregano
ground cumin
corn tortillas
1½ pounds skinless, boneless chicken thighs
Cotija cheese

Spicy Black Beans
fresh cilantro
1 (7-ounce) can chipotle chiles in adobo sauce
fat-free, less-sodium chicken broth
1 (15-ounce) can black beans

| GAME PLAN |

While water and onions come to a boil:
 ■ Prepare citrus marinade for onions.
While onions marinate:
 ■ Brown chicken.
 ■ Heat tortillas.
 ■ Prepare beans.
 ■ Chop avocado, and crumble cheese.

Chicken Carne Asada Tacos with Pickled Onions

with Spicy Black Beans

Prep Pointer: You'll get more juice from room-temperature citrus.
Buy The Best: Choose authentic corn tortillas made with masa harina.
Flavor Hit: Adobo sauce (from canned chipotle chiles) imparts nuanced smokiness to the beans.

½ cup fresh orange juice (about 1 orange)
⅓ cup fresh lime juice (about 2 limes)
1 teaspoon sugar
1 teaspoon cumin seeds
1 medium red onion, thinly vertically sliced
1½ pounds skinless, boneless chicken thighs, trimmed and cut into thin strips
1 teaspoon dried oregano
1 teaspoon ground cumin
¾ teaspoon salt
¾ teaspoon freshly ground black pepper
Cooking spray
8 (6-inch) corn tortillas
1 cup diced peeled avocado (about 1 avocado)
½ cup (2 ounces) crumbled Cotija cheese
Lime wedges (optional)

1. Combine first 4 ingredients in a bowl, stirring until sugar dissolves. Place onion in a small saucepan; cover with water. Bring to a boil; drain and plunge onion in ice water. Drain onion; add to juice mixture. Chill until ready to serve.
2. Heat a large cast-iron skillet over high heat. Sprinkle chicken with oregano and next 3 ingredients; toss to coat. Coat pan with cooking spray. Add chicken to pan; cook 4 minutes or until browned and done, stirring occasionally.
3. Heat tortillas according to package directions. Divide chicken evenly among tortillas. Drain onion; divide evenly among tortillas. Top each tortilla with 2 tablespoons avocado and 1 tablespoon cheese; fold over. Serve with lime wedges, if desired. Yield: 4 servings (serving size: 2 tacos).

CALORIES 413; FAT 17.1g (sat 5.2g, mono 7.1g, poly 2.7g); PROTEIN 33.4g; CARB 33.6g; FIBER 4.9g; CHOL 123mg; IRON 3.2mg; SODIUM 825mg; CALC 237mg

continued

For the Spicy Black Beans:
Remove 1 teaspoon adobo sauce from 1 (7-ounce) can chipotle chiles in adobo sauce; reserve remaining chiles and sauce for another use. Combine 1 teaspoon adobo sauce; ¼ cup fat-free, less-sodium chicken broth; and 1 (15-ounce) can rinsed and drained black beans in a saucepan; bring to a boil. Mash bean mixture. Sprinkle with 1 tablespoon chopped fresh cilantro.

30 minutes

SHOPPING LIST

Crispy Fish with Lemon-Dill Sauce
2 lemons
fresh dill
panko (Japanese breadcrumbs)
paprika
onion powder
garlic powder
canola mayonnaise
dill pickles
eggs
4 (6-ounce) skinless Alaskan cod fillets

Sautéed Zucchini
2 large zucchini
olive oil

GAME PLAN

While broiler heats:
- Arrange breading ingredients in separate dishes.
- Prepare and chill sauce.
- Bread fish.

While fish cooks:
- Prepare zucchini.

Quick & Easy • Kid Friendly
Crispy Fish with Lemon-Dill Sauce
with Sautéed Zucchini

For sustainability reasons, be sure to choose Alaskan cod or substitute halibut or tilapia. Simple Sub: Though not as crispy, regular dry breadcrumbs will work fine in place of panko. Prep Pointer: A broiler pan allows air to circulate under the fish, preventing sogginess.

2 large egg whites, lightly beaten
1 cup panko (Japanese breadcrumbs)
½ teaspoon paprika
¾ teaspoon onion powder
¾ teaspoon garlic powder
4 (6-ounce) skinless cod fillets
1 teaspoon black pepper
½ teaspoon salt
Cooking spray
¼ cup canola mayonnaise
2 tablespoons finely chopped dill pickle
1 teaspoon fresh lemon juice
1 teaspoon chopped fresh dill
4 lemon wedges

1. Preheat broiler.
2. Place egg whites in a shallow dish. Combine panko and next 3 ingredients in a shallow dish. Sprinkle fish evenly with pepper and salt. Dip each fillet in egg white, then dredge in panko mixture; place on a broiler pan coated with cooking spray. Broil 4 minutes on each side or until desired degree of doneness.
3. Combine mayonnaise and next 3 ingredients. Serve with fish and lemon wedges. Yield: 4 servings (serving size: 1 fillet, about 2 tablespoons sauce, and 1 lemon wedge).

CALORIES 245; **FAT** 5.2g (sat 0.2g, mono 2.7g, poly 1.4g); **PROTEIN** 34.5g; **CARB** 11.5g; **FIBER** 0.8g; **CHOL** 63mg; **IRON** 0.7mg; **SODIUM** 654mg; **CALC** 18mg

For the Sautéed Zucchini:
Heat a large nonstick skillet over medium-high heat. Cut 2 large zucchini diagonally into ½-inch-thick slices. Add 1 tablespoon olive oil to pan; swirl to coat. Add zucchini, ¼ teaspoon salt, and ¼ teaspoon black pepper; sauté 5 minutes or until browned.

SUPERFAST

Fragrant spices imbue poultry, fish, and lamb with rich, authentic flavors in these easy Middle Eastern recipes that take just 20 minutes to prepare..

Quick & Easy
Spicy Chicken Shawarma

2 tablespoons finely chopped fresh parsley
½ teaspoon salt
½ teaspoon crushed red pepper
¼ teaspoon ground ginger
¼ teaspoon ground cumin
⅛ teaspoon ground coriander
5 tablespoons plain low-fat Greek-style yogurt, divided
2 tablespoons fresh lemon juice, divided
3 garlic cloves, minced and divided
1 pound skinless, boneless chicken breast halves, thinly sliced
2 tablespoons extra-virgin olive oil
1 tablespoon tahini
4 (6-inch) pitas, halved
½ cup chopped cucumber
½ cup chopped plum tomato
¼ cup prechopped red onion

1. Combine first 6 ingredients in a large bowl; stir in 1 tablespoon yogurt, 1 tablespoon juice, and 2 garlic cloves. Add chicken; toss to coat. Heat oil in a large nonstick skillet over medium-high heat. Add chicken mixture to pan; sauté 6 minutes or until browned and done, stirring frequently.
2. While chicken cooks, combine remaining ¼ cup yogurt, remaining 1 tablespoon lemon juice, remaining 1 garlic clove, and tahini, stirring well. Spread 1½ teaspoons tahini mixture inside each pita half; divide chicken evenly among pita halves. Fill each pita half with 1 tablespoon cucumber, 1 tablespoon tomato, and 1½ teaspoons onion. Yield: 4 servings (serving size: 2 stuffed pita halves).

CALORIES 402; **FAT** 10.7g (sat 1.9g, mono 6g, poly 2g); **PROTEIN** 36.4g; **CARB** 40g; **FIBER** 2.1g; **CHOL** 67mg; **IRON** 4.1mg; **SODIUM** 541mg; **CALC** 93mg

Quick Lamb Kofta with Harissa Yogurt Sauce

Rice:
1 (3½-ounce) bag boil-in-bag jasmine rice
1 teaspoon saffron threads
2 tablespoons thinly sliced green onions
Kofta:
2 tablespoons minced fresh cilantro
2 tablespoons grated fresh onion
2 tablespoons 2% Greek-style plain yogurt
1 teaspoon ground cumin
1 teaspoon ground coriander
1 teaspoon turmeric
2 teaspoons bottled minced garlic
½ teaspoon salt
¼ teaspoon black pepper
1 pound lean ground lamb
Cooking spray
Sauce:
½ cup 2% Greek-style plain yogurt
¼ cup chopped bottled roasted red bell
    pepper
1 teaspoon ground cumin
1 teaspoon ground coriander
2 teaspoons bottled minced garlic
½ teaspoon crushed red pepper
¼ teaspoon salt

1. To prepare rice, cook boil-in-bag jasmine rice and saffron in boiling water according to package directions. Drain; fluff rice with a fork. Sprinkle with green onions.
2. While rice cooks, prepare kofta. Combine cilantro and next 9 ingredients; shape into 12 oblong patties.
3. Heat a large nonstick skillet over medium-high heat. Coat pan with cooking spray. Add patties to pan; cook 10 minutes or until done, turning occasionally to brown on all sides.
4. While kofta cooks, prepare sauce. Combine ½ cup yogurt and remaining ingredients. Serve sauce with kofta and rice. Yield: 4 servings (serving size: 3 patties, about ¼ cup sauce, and about ⅓ cup rice).

CALORIES 344; **FAT** 16.3g (sat 6.9g, mono 6.4g, poly 1.1g); **PROTEIN** 24.8g; **CARB** 24.4g; **FIBER** 0.8g; **CHOL** 77mg; **IRON** 2.9mg; **SODIUM** 563mg; **CALC** 72mg

Saffron Fish Stew with White Beans

Be sure to choose a sustainable fish, like wild-caught Pacific flounder or wild-caught Alaskan halibut.

1 tablespoon extra-virgin olive oil
1 cup prechopped onion
1 teaspoon ground fennel
½ teaspoon ground coriander
2 garlic cloves, crushed
1 fresh thyme sprig
½ teaspoon grated fresh orange rind
¼ teaspoon saffron threads, crushed
1½ cups water
1½ cups clam juice
1 (14.5-ounce) can diced tomatoes, undrained
¼ teaspoon salt
1 pound flounder fillet, cut into (2-inch) pieces
1 (14-ounce) can great Northern beans,
    rinsed and drained
Thyme leaves

1. Heat oil in a large Dutch oven over medium-high heat. Add onion and next 4 ingredients; sauté 5 minutes. Stir in rind and saffron; add water, clam juice, and tomatoes. Bring to a boil; reduce heat, and simmer 5 minutes. Stir in salt, fish, and beans; cook 5 minutes. Top with thyme leaves. Yield: 4 servings (serving size: 2 cups).

CALORIES 249; **FAT** 5.1g (sat 0.9g, mono 2.8g, poly 0.9g); **PROTEIN** 27.9g; **CARB** 23g; **FIBER** 5.7g; **CHOL** 57mg; **IRON** 2.2mg; **SODIUM** 569mg; **CALC** 101mg

Lamb Chops with Pistachio Gremolata

(pictured on page 251)

Serve with a side of Israeli couscous tossed with golden raisins and diced red bell pepper.

½ teaspoon salt
½ teaspoon ground cumin
¼ teaspoon ground coriander
¼ teaspoon black pepper
⅛ teaspoon ground cinnamon
8 (4-ounce) lamb loin chops, trimmed
Cooking spray
2 tablespoons finely chopped pistachios
2 tablespoons chopped fresh flat-leaf parsley
1 tablespoon chopped fresh cilantro
2 teaspoons grated lemon rind
⅛ teaspoon salt
1 garlic clove, minced

1. Heat a large nonstick skillet over medium-high heat. Combine first 5 ingredients; sprinkle evenly over both sides of lamb. Coat pan with cooking spray. Add lamb to pan; cook 4 minutes on each side or until desired degree of doneness.
2. While lamb cooks, combine pistachios and remaining ingredients; sprinkle over lamb. Yield: 4 servings (serving size: 2 lamb chops and about 1 tablespoon gremolata).

CALORIES 233; **FAT** 11.2g (sat 3.5g, mono 5g, poly 1.2g); **PROTEIN** 29.6g; **CARB** 1.9g; **FIBER** 0.8g; **CHOL** 90mg; **IRON** 2.4mg; **SODIUM** 467mg; **CALC** 32mg

Halibut with Lemon-Fennel Salad

1 teaspoon ground coriander
½ teaspoon salt
½ teaspoon ground cumin
¼ teaspoon freshly ground black pepper
5 teaspoons extra-virgin olive oil, divided
2 garlic cloves, minced
4 (6-ounce) halibut fillets
2 cups thinly sliced fennel bulb (about 1 medium)
¼ cup thinly vertically sliced red onion
2 tablespoons fresh lemon juice
1 tablespoon chopped flat-leaf parsley
1 teaspoon fresh thyme leaves

1. Combine first 4 ingredients in a small bowl. Combine 1½ teaspoons spice mixture, 2 teaspoons oil, and garlic in a small bowl; rub garlic mixture evenly over fish. Heat 1 teaspoon oil in a large nonstick skillet over medium-high heat. Add fish to pan; cook 5 minutes on each side or until desired degree of doneness.
2. Combine remaining ¾ teaspoon spice mixture, remaining 2 teaspoons oil, fennel bulb, and remaining ingredients in a medium bowl, tossing well to coat. Serve salad with fish. Yield: 4 servings (serving size: 1 fillet and about ½ cup salad).

CALORIES 259; **FAT** 9.7g (sat 1.3g, mono 5.4g, poly 1.8g); **PROTEIN** 36.3g; **CARB** 5.3g; **FIBER** 1.7g; **CHOL** 54mg; **IRON** 2.1mg; **SODIUM** 411mg; **CALC** 111mg

Pita Salad with Cucumber, Fennel, and Chicken

2 (6-inch) pitas
2 cups thinly sliced fennel bulb
1 cup shredded skinless, boneless rotisserie chicken breast
½ cup chopped fresh flat-leaf parsley
¼ cup vertically sliced red onion
½ English cucumber, halved lengthwise and thinly sliced
½ teaspoon salt, divided
¼ teaspoon black pepper, divided
¼ cup fresh lemon juice
1 tablespoon white wine vinegar
½ teaspoon chopped fresh oregano
3 tablespoons extra-virgin olive oil

1. Preheat oven to 350°.
2. Arrange pitas on a baking sheet. Bake at 350° for 12 minutes or until toasted; cool 1 minute. Tear into bite-sized pieces. Combine pita pieces, fennel, and next 4 ingredients. Sprinkle with ¼ teaspoon salt and ⅛ teaspoon pepper.
3. Combine juice, vinegar, oregano, remaining ¼ teaspoon salt, and remaining ⅛ teaspoon pepper. Gradually add oil, stirring with a whisk. Drizzle dressing over pita mixture; toss to coat. Serve immediately. Yield: 4 servings (serving size: 1½ cups).

CALORIES 257; **FAT** 11.6g (sat 1.8g, mono 7.9g, poly 1.4g); **PROTEIN** 15.6g; **CARB** 23.3g; **FIBER** 2.7g; **CHOL** 30mg; **IRON** 2.7mg; **SODIUM** 429mg; **CALC** 68mg

RECIPE MAKEOVER
DIVINE FRESH COCONUT CAKE

A towering, tender cake covered with fluffy frosting—with plenty of real coconut—makes a showstopping dessert that isn't a nutritional splurge.

This recipe received our Test Kitchen's highest rating. To trim calories, we swapped butter for shortening and used less. We kept the sugar the same and added a few whipped egg whites for structure. The trade-off for saturated fat in the butter is balanced by the frosting: We ditched whipped heavy cream and used an Italian meringue to give a fluffy texture. And instead of putting coconut meat in the cake and frosting, we used a prudent amount of the caloric shavings—toasted to deepen flavor—and pressed them onto the outside of the cake. Rather than knocking you out with fake coconut extract overtones, this cake offers balanced flavor.

Staff Favorite • Make Ahead
Kid Friendly

Fresh Coconut Cake

If your coconut water does not measure 1 cup (8 fluid ounces), add enough tap water so the liquid measures 1 cup. Even though fresh coconut is sublime, you can use Goya brand coconut water in place of fresh coconut water and buy coconut flakes in the baking aisle.

Cake:
Cooking spray
1 tablespoon cake flour
12 ounces sifted cake flour (about 3 cups)
2 teaspoons baking powder
¼ teaspoon salt
1¾ cups sugar, divided
⅔ cup butter, softened
1 cup warm coconut water (from 1 small brown coconut)
1 teaspoon vanilla extract
6 large egg whites

Frosting:
4 large egg whites
¼ teaspoon cream of tartar
⅛ teaspoon salt
2 tablespoons sugar
1¼ cups sugar
¼ cup water
1 teaspoon vanilla extract
2 cups shaved fresh coconut, toasted

1. To prepare cake, preheat oven to 350°.
2. Lightly coat 3 (9-inch) round cake pans with cooking spray; line bottom of pans with wax paper. Lightly coat wax paper with cooking spray; dust pans with 1 tablespoon flour.
3. Combine 12 ounces (about 3 cups) flour, baking powder, and salt; stir with a whisk. Place 1½ cups plus 2 tablespoons sugar and butter in a large bowl; beat with a mixer at medium speed for 2½ minutes or until well blended. Add flour mixture and coconut water alternately to sugar mixture, beginning and ending with flour mixture. Beat in 1 teaspoon vanilla. In a separate bowl, beat 6 egg whites on high speed until foamy using clean, dry beaters. Add remaining 2 tablespoons sugar, 1 tablespoon at a time, beating until stiff peaks form (do not overbeat). Carefully fold egg whites into batter; pour batter into prepared

pans. Bake at 350° for 18 minutes or until a wooden pick inserted in center comes out clean. Cool in pans 10 minutes on wire racks; remove from pans. Discard wax paper. Cool completely on wire racks.
4. To prepare frosting, combine 4 egg whites, cream of tartar, and ⅛ teaspoon salt in a large bowl; beat with a mixer at high speed until foamy. Add 2 tablespoons sugar, 1 tablespoon at a time, beating until stiff peaks form. Combine 1¼ cups sugar and ¼ cup water in a saucepan; bring to a boil. Cook, without stirring, until candy thermometer registers 250°. With mixer on low speed, pour hot sugar syrup in a thin stream over egg whites. Gradually increase speed to high; beat 8 minutes or until thick and cool. Stir in 1 teaspoon vanilla.
5. Place 1 cake layer on a serving plate, and spread with 1 cup frosting. Top with another cake layer. Repeat procedure with 1 cup frosting and remaining cake layer, ending with cake layer on top. Spread remaining frosting over top and sides of cake. Gently press shaved coconut onto top and sides of cake. Store cake loosely covered in refrigerator. Yield: 16 servings (serving size: 1 slice).

CALORIES 332; FAT 10.8g (sat 7.5g, mono 2.1g, poly 0.4g); PROTEIN 4.3g; CARB 55.8g; FIBER 1.3g; CHOL 20mg; IRON 1.7mg; SODIUM 207mg; CALC 54mg

OLD WAY	OUR WAY
622 calories per slice	332 calories per slice
38.5 grams total fat	10.8 grams total fat
19.5 grams saturated fat	7.5 grams saturated fat
1 cup shortening	⅔ cup butter
Frosting made with heavy cream	Frosting made with Italian meringue
Icing filled with shredded coconut	Coconut shavings pressed onto icing

FRESH COCONUT 101

1 HANDY (KITCHEN) TOOLS
Use a clean nail and small hammer to make 3 holes in the eyes of the coconut; pour coconut water into a clean measuring cup.

2 CRACK THE SHELL WITH EASE
Warm the coconut in a preheated 350° oven for 25 to 30 minutes. Wrap the whole coconut in a kitchen towel. On a steady, hard surface, give the coconut several good raps all over to crack open. (Cooking the coconut helps separate the coconut meat from the shell.)

3 CUT WITH CARE With a small, sharp knife, cut the creamy white flesh from the shell and tough inner brown layer. Shave into large, thin pieces.

THE DELICIOUS ART OF KEEPING IT SIMPLE

How to use the less-is-more principle for easier, better cooking

All of us who cook are subject to the temptation to add just one more ingredient to a dish that doesn't quite measure up. Feeling adventurous, we add a cardamom pod and coriander seeds to sautéed mushrooms, say, and then find we've taken the flavor profile from interesting to strange—when just a knob of butter would have rounded out the veggie's earthy flavors. Often, with this "just one more ingredient" approach, the more you add, the further you wander from the original idea, and there's no way back.

Confidence building starts with excellent ingredients. These may require you to reach a bit deeper into your wallet, but the results are worth it. For example, a gorgeous grass-fed steak, which can cost a lot more than its feedlot counterpart, can be seasoned thoughtfully with a minimalist spice rub that's nuanced enough to stand up to the meat's pleasantly mineral-like beefiness: You'll be eating smaller, healthier portions anyway, so the value is doubly there.

Cooking in season is unquestionably the key to cooking simple. Ingredients are at their best and, if abundant, at their cheapest. A little salt, pepper, butter, herbs, or cheese is enough to bring out incredible flavor. Oily, meaty, sumptuous Alaskan salmon is just coming into season and will need little more than a simple sauce when cooked just right. The recipes here exemplify the less-is-more principle for kitchen confidence.

Quick & Easy • Kid Friendly
Spring Linguine with Basil

Pasta should be easy and delicious, like this entrée. Prep the peas, cheese, and basil while the pasta water heats. Serve with a green salad.

9 ounces uncooked fresh linguine
1 cup shelled fresh green peas
4 teaspoons extra-virgin olive oil
1 tablespoon unsalted butter
2 tablespoons fresh lemon juice
1/2 teaspoon salt
1/4 teaspoon freshly ground black pepper
1/4 cup thinly sliced fresh basil
2 ounces shaved fresh Parmigiano-Reggiano cheese

1. Cook pasta according to package directions, omitting salt and fat. Add peas to pasta during last 2 minutes of cooking time. Drain pasta mixture in a colander over a bowl, reserving 1/4 cup pasta liquid.
2. Heat oil and butter in pan over medium heat 1 minute or until butter melts. Remove from heat; stir in pasta mixture, reserved pasta water, juice, salt, and pepper; toss well.
3. Divide pasta mixture evenly among 4 bowls; top each serving with 1 tablespoon basil and about 2 tablespoons cheese. Serve immediately. Yield: 4 servings (serving size: about 1 cup).

CALORIES 324; FAT 12g (sat 4.4g, mono 5.1g, poly 1.6g); PROTEIN 13.2g; CARB 41.4g; FIBER 4.5g; CHOL 63mg; IRON 2.9mg; SODIUM 467mg; CALC 135mg

WINE NOTE: Spring Linguine with Basil is filled with the fresh, green flavors of spring peas and basil. While sauvignon blanc will work well, wines from Austria's grüner veltliner grape make a fun and adventurous choice. Look for Fred Loimer "Lois" 2008 ($15), with its bright green apple and herbal flavors, and a peppery quality that works well with this dish.

Quick & Easy • Kid Friendly
Spring Vegetable Skillet

Enjoying vegetables—and their simple crunchy, woodsy, or creamy textures—is part of the beauty of produce. When you have gorgeous seasonal offerings, they barely need any seasoning. No need to get fancy—it just confuses the clear, clean flavors of spring.

16 baby carrots with tops (about 10 ounces)
3/4 teaspoon kosher salt, divided
12 ounces sugar snap peas, trimmed
1 1/2 tablespoons butter
1 tablespoon chopped fresh tarragon
1/4 teaspoon freshly ground black pepper
1 teaspoon grated lemon rind
1 teaspoon fresh lemon juice

1. Peel carrots, and cut off tops to within 1 inch of carrot; cut in half lengthwise.
2. Place 1/4 teaspoon salt in a large saucepan of water; bring to a boil. Add carrots and peas; cook 3 minutes or until crisp-tender. Drain.
3. Melt butter in a large nonstick skillet over medium-high heat. Add vegetables, and cook 1 minute, stirring to coat. Stir in remaining 1/2 teaspoon salt, tarragon, and pepper; cook 1 minute. Remove from heat; stir in rind and juice. Yield: 6 servings (serving size: 2/3 cup).

CALORIES 69; FAT 2.9g (sat 1.8g, mono 0.7g, poly 0.1g); PROTEIN 1.7g; CARB 8.8g; FIBER 2.8g; CHOL 8mg; IRON 1.2mg; SODIUM 221mg; CALC 58mg

Quick & Easy

Pan-Seared Scallops with Bacon and Spinach

Scallops in the pan are always in danger of steaming rather than searing, so the first lesson in simplicity is this: big pan, plenty of heat. Our approach keeps delicate seafood bare-bones simple with a hot skillet, salt, pepper, and bacon. Spinach rounds out the flavors. Serve with a multigrain baguette and a glass of wine.

3 center-cut bacon slices
1½ pounds jumbo sea scallops (about 12)
3/8 teaspoon kosher salt, divided
¼ teaspoon freshly ground black pepper, divided
1 cup chopped onion
6 garlic cloves, sliced
12 ounces fresh baby spinach
4 lemon wedges (optional)

1. Cook bacon in a large cast-iron skillet over medium-high heat until crisp. Remove bacon from pan, reserving 1 tablespoon drippings in pan; coarsely chop bacon, and set aside. Increase heat to high.
2. Pat scallops dry with paper towels. Sprinkle scallops evenly with ¼ teaspoon salt and ⅛ teaspoon pepper. Add scallops to drippings in pan; cook 2½ minutes on each side or until done. Transfer to a plate; keep warm. Reduce heat to medium-high. Add onion and garlic to pan; sauté 3 minutes, stirring frequently. Add half of spinach; cook 1 minute, stirring frequently. Add remaining half of spinach; cook 2 minutes or just until wilted, stirring frequently. Remove from heat; stir in remaining ⅛ teaspoon salt and remaining ⅛ teaspoon pepper. Divide spinach mixture among 4 plates; top each serving evenly with crumbled bacon and 3 scallops. Serve immediately with lemon wedges, if desired. Yield: 4 servings (serving size: 3 scallops and ¾ cup spinach mixture).

CALORIES 323; **FAT** 6.5g (sat 1.9g, mono 2.3g, poly 0.6g); **PROTEIN** 45.3g; **CARB** 22.7g; **FIBER** 5g; **CHOL** 106mg; **IRON** 6.8mg; **SODIUM** 885mg; **CALC** 141mg

Quick & Easy

Easy Penne and Tuna Salad

Pasta and tuna can sound boring, so the temptation is to jazz it up a bit too much. But great tuna married to al dente pasta is sublime. We start with premium fish packed in oil. A simple vinaigrette, crispy shallots, and peppery arugula bring it all together. Serve with a torn baguette.

1 large red bell pepper
4 quarts water
2¼ teaspoons salt, divided
6 ounces uncooked penne pasta
2 cups coarsely chopped arugula
¼ cup thinly sliced shallots
2 tablespoons red wine vinegar
1 tablespoon capers, drained
1 tablespoon extra-virgin olive oil
1 (7.8-ounce) jar premium tuna packed in oil (such as Ortiz), drained and flaked

1. Preheat broiler.
2. Cut bell pepper in half lengthwise; discard seeds and membranes. Place pepper halves, skin sides up, on a foil-lined baking sheet; flatten with hand. Broil 15 minutes or until blackened. Place in a zip-top plastic bag; seal. Let stand 15 minutes. Peel and chop.
3. Bring 4 quarts water and 2 teaspoons salt to a boil in a large saucepan. Cook pasta according to package directions, omitting additional salt and fat. Drain and rinse with cold water; drain well.
4. Combine bell pepper, pasta, remaining ¼ teaspoon salt, arugula, and remaining ingredients in a large bowl; toss well. Yield: 4 servings (serving size: 2 cups).

CALORIES 310; **FAT** 8.8g (sat 1.4g, mono 4.3g, poly 2.3g); **PROTEIN** 21.4g; **CARB** 36.3g; **FIBER** 2.5g; **CHOL** 17mg; **IRON** 2.2mg; **SODIUM** 556mg; **CALC** 34mg

Quick & Easy

Seared Salmon with Jalapeño Ponzu

The "fusion" idea has been an excuse for many a restaurant chef to jumble up a lot of flavors and ingredients that just don't work together. Here we simply take a Japanese soy-citrus sauce and spice up the dish with fiery jalapeño pepper slices. The tang/heat blend is the perfect counterpoint for rich fish, and beautifully easy. You'll be amazed at how quickly this stellar entrée comes together. Serve with a side of long-grain rice to sop up the extra sauce.

¼ cup less-sodium soy sauce
2 tablespoons fresh orange juice
2 tablespoons mirin (sweet rice wine)
1 tablespoon fresh lemon juice
1 tablespoon dark sesame oil
4 (6-ounce) salmon fillets
1 large jalapeño pepper, cut crosswise into thin slices

1. Combine first 4 ingredients in a small bowl; mix well.
2. Heat oil in a large nonstick skillet over medium-high heat. Add salmon, skin sides down; cook 4 minutes on each side or until fish flakes easily with a fork or until desired degree of doneness. Arrange 1 fillet on each of 4 plates. Top fillets evenly with jalapeño slices. Spoon about 2 tablespoons soy sauce mixture over each serving; let stand 10 minutes before serving. Yield: 4 servings.

CALORIES 333; **FAT** 16.6g (sat 3.6g, mono 7.2g, poly 4.7g); **PROTEIN** 37.2g; **CARB** 5g; **FIBER** 0.3g; **CHOL** 87mg; **IRON** 0.9mg; **SODIUM** 621mg; **CALC** 24mg

Chile-Rubbed Flat-Iron Steak

This cut of meat is actually from the top blade steak and is named for its triangular shape that's similar to an iron. A simple smoky, hot spice rub and a quick run on the grill cooks this cut into a flavorful, tender entrée. We take care to cook the meat until pink in the center; then rest it to ensure that it's juicy when sliced. To maintain the simple theme, serve with a salad of cilantro leaves and thinly sliced radishes.

2 tablespoons brown sugar
2 teaspoons canola oil
1 teaspoon chipotle chile powder
1 teaspoon ground cumin
3/4 teaspoon kosher salt
1 (1-pound) flat-iron steak, trimmed
Cooking spray
4 lime wedges
4 (6-inch) corn tortillas, warmed
Cilantro leaves (optional)

1. Preheat grill to medium-high heat.
2. Combine first 5 ingredients in a small bowl. Rub sugar mixture evenly over steak; let stand 10 minutes. Place steak on a grill rack coated with cooking spray; cook 4 minutes on each side or until desired degree of doneness. Let stand 10 minutes; cut diagonally across grain into thin slices. Serve with lime wedges and tortillas. Garnish each serving with cilantro leaves, if desired. Yield: 4 servings (serving size: 3 ounces steak, 1 lime wedge, and 1 tortilla).

CALORIES 268; FAT 11.7g (sat 2.9g, mono 5.4g, poly 1.3g); PROTEIN 23.4g; CARB 17.9g; FIBER 1.9g; CHOL 51mg; IRON 2.8mg; SODIUM 420mg; CALC 27mg

THE PEERLESS PLEASURES OF MAKING GREAT PIZZA

There is nothing more satisfying. Here, four pizza styles. Plenty of healthy toppings. And weeknight shortcuts for when you're in a hurry to get home-made pie to table.

America's ultimate convenience food, which built home-delivery empires and frozen-pie fortunes, is one of the most satisfying and easy dishes to cook at home. The work is pure sensory pleasure: handling the silky dough, simmering the tangy-sweet sauce, topping the pizza with a Jackson Pollock flourish, then enjoying the bakery aromas of the crust as it browns and blisters in the oven. Rolling the pizza cutter across the pie should be done with gusto. And, as you tuck into that irresistible second slice, there's more comfort in the fact that your pizza is not only impeccably fresh and delicious, but it's also a lot healthier than most pies you could order in.

Pizza has come a long way in the past 25 years. California-style pie, with its sometimes kooky toppings, ascended and, to a degree, receded. Breathless reports came back from Italy as American food writers sought the holy grail, the Naples überpizza. Lately the pizza fanatics have been debating the merits of coal-fired versus wood-fired artisanal pizzas, while the Web set up tents for the pizza geeks to parse "nominal thickness factor" and "bowl residue compensation."

Yes, fine, OK, but pizza is a simple combination of delectable crust (whether thick, medium, or cracker-thin) and fresh, well-chosen ingredients. Nor is there one perfect style; here we offer four—Neapolitan, grilled, thin-crust, and Chicago deep-dish—along with easy tips for making professional-grade pizzas at home.

Wait—doesn't homemade crust slow this process down for a weeknight cook? Dough is slow food, yes; that's what makes it so delicious. But ours is made the night before so actual cooking time is quite quick. And you can make dough on a weekend and freeze it—see notes for defrosting on page 118.

Pizza Margherita

Because this classic Neapolitan-style pizza is so simple, it depends on quality ingredients: Use the best fresh mozzarella and basil you can find.

1 cup warm water (100° to 110°), divided
10 ounces bread flour (about 2 cups plus
  2 tablespoons)
1 package dry yeast (about 2¼ teaspoons)
4 teaspoons olive oil
¾ teaspoon kosher salt, divided
Cooking spray
1 tablespoon yellow cornmeal
¾ cup Basic Pizza Sauce (page 116)
1¼ cups (5 ounces) thinly sliced fresh
  mozzarella cheese
⅓ cup small fresh basil leaves

1. Pour ¾ cup warm water in the bowl of a stand mixer with dough hook attached. Weigh or lightly spoon flour into dry measuring cups and spoons; level with a knife. Add flour to ¾ cup water; mix until combined. Cover and let stand 20 minutes. Combine remaining ¼ cup water and yeast in a small bowl; let stand 5 minutes or until bubbly. Add yeast mixture, oil, and ½ teaspoon salt to flour mixture; mix 5 minutes or until a soft dough forms. Place dough in a large bowl coated with cooking spray; cover surface of dough with plastic wrap lightly coated with cooking spray. Refrigerate 24 hours.
2. Remove dough from refrigerator. Let stand, covered, 1 hour or until dough comes to room temperature. Punch dough down. Press dough out to a 12-inch circle on a lightly floured baking sheet, without raised sides, sprinkled with cornmeal. Crimp edges to form a ½-inch border. Cover dough loosely with plastic wrap.
3. Position an oven rack in the lowest setting. Place a pizza stone on lowest rack. Preheat oven to 550°. Preheat pizza stone for 30 minutes before baking dough.
4. Remove plastic wrap from dough. Sprinkle dough with remaining ¼ teaspoon salt. Spread Basic Pizza Sauce evenly over dough, leaving a ½-inch border. Arrange cheese slices evenly over pizza. Slide pizza onto preheated pizza stone, using a spatula as a guide. Bake at 550° for 11 minutes or until the crust is golden. Cut pizza into 10 wedges, and sprinkle evenly with basil. Yield: 5 servings (serving size: 2 wedges).

CALORIES 421; FAT 10.9g (sat 4.7g, mono 4.7g, poly 1g); PROTEIN 16.9g; CARB 62.8g; FIBER 6.5g; CHOL 22mg; IRON 4.4mg; SODIUM 754mg; CALC 267mg

Kid Friendly

Four-Cheese Pizza

1 cup warm water (100° to 110°), divided
10 ounces bread flour (about 2 cups plus
  2 tablespoons)
1 package dry yeast (about 2¼ teaspoons)
7 teaspoons olive oil, divided
½ teaspoon kosher salt
Cooking spray
1 tablespoon yellow cornmeal
2 tablespoons chopped garlic
⅓ cup (about 3 ounces) part-skim ricotta
  cheese (such as Calabro)
1¼ ounces taleggio cheese, thinly sliced
¼ cup (1 ounce) crumbled Gorgonzola
  cheese
¼ cup (1 ounce) finely grated Parmigiano-
  Reggiano cheese
2 tablespoons chopped fresh chives

1. Pour ¾ cup warm water in the bowl of a stand mixer with dough hook attached. Weigh or lightly spoon flour into dry measuring cups and spoons; level with a knife. Add flour to ¾ cup water; mix until combined. Cover and let stand 20 minutes. Combine remaining ¼ cup water and yeast in a small bowl; let stand 5 minutes or until bubbly. Add yeast mixture, 4 teaspoons oil, and salt to flour mixture; mix 5 minutes or until a soft dough forms. Place dough in a large bowl coated with cooking spray; cover surface of dough with plastic wrap lightly coated with cooking spray. Refrigerate 24 hours.
2. Remove dough from refrigerator. Let stand, covered, 1 hour or until dough comes to room temperature. Punch dough down. Press dough out to a 12-inch circle on a lightly floured baking sheet, without raised sides, sprinkled with cornmeal. Crimp edges to form a ½-inch border. Cover dough loosely with plastic wrap.
3. Position an oven rack in the lowest setting. Place a pizza stone on lowest rack. Preheat oven to 550°. Preheat stone 30 minutes before baking dough.
4. Remove plastic wrap from dough. Combine remaining 1 tablespoon oil and garlic; gently brush garlic mixture evenly over dough, leaving a ½-inch border. Spread ricotta evenly over dough; arrange taleggio and Gorgonzola evenly over ricotta. Top with Parmigiano-Reggiano. Slide pizza onto preheated pizza stone, using a spatula as a guide. Bake at 550° for 10 minutes or until crust is golden. Cut pizza into 10 wedges; sprinkle with chives. Yield: 5 servings (serving size: 2 wedges).

CALORIES 370; FAT 14.1g (sat 5.2g, mono 6.7g, poly 1.4g); PROTEIN 14.6g; CARB 45.7g; FIBER 1.9g; CHOL 22mg; IRON 1.2mg; SODIUM 344mg; CALC 174mg

NEAPOLITAN-STYLE PIZZA

The style defined: The thin, lightly crisp yet chewy crust is blistered and bubbly. Toppings feature bold Mediterranean flavors: Bright, peppery basil; creamy, fresh mozzarella; and robust San Marzano tomatoes are Neapolitan-style staples. This brand of pie originated in Naples, Italy, widely considered the birthplace of pizza in general.
How it's made: Neapolitan-style pizzerias use incendiary ovens ratcheted up to 800° or higher to achieve a lightly charred crust on pizzas that cook in a few minutes. Your home oven tops out at 550° (or maybe 500°), so charring won't happen. But you can still get a wonderful crust with contrasting textures—crisp bottom, chewy inside—that makes an impressive base for quickly cooked toppings.

Start with an autolyse—mixing the flour and water together and letting it rest for 20 minutes—which helps flour absorb the water, making the dough softer and the crust crumb more open.

Rest the dough overnight, which makes the crust's flavor more complex. Finally, gently press the dough into a 12-inch circle by hand; a rolling pin presses out air pockets that keep the crust's texture light.

Basic Pizza Sauce

San Marzano tomatoes are traditionally used in Neapolitan pizza sauce. We like their balanced sweet-acidic quality.

2 tablespoons extra-virgin olive oil
5 garlic cloves, minced
1 (28-ounce) can San Marzano tomatoes
1/2 teaspoon kosher salt
1/2 teaspoon dried oregano

1. Heat oil in a medium saucepan over medium heat. Add garlic to pan; cook 1 minute, stirring frequently. Remove tomatoes from can using a slotted spoon, reserving juices. Crush tomatoes. Stir tomatoes, juices, salt, and oregano into garlic mixture; bring to a boil. Reduce heat, and simmer 30 minutes, stirring occasionally. Yield: 6 servings (serving size: about 1/3 cup).

CALORIES 66; **FAT** 4.7g (sat 0.7g, mono 3.3g, poly 0.6g); **PROTEIN** 1.2g; **CARB** 6.2g; **FIBER** 1.4g; **CHOL** 0mg; **IRON** 1.4mg; **SODIUM** 175mg; **CALC** 48mg

DEEP-DISH, CHICAGO-STYLE PIZZA

The style defined: Thick, bready, chewy crust; meaty toppings; and loads of tomato sauce—it's a knife, fork, and two napkins kind of pie, invented at Pizzeria Uno in Chicago more than 60 years ago.
How it's made: You need more dough, so use more flour. Roll it into shape with a rolling pin, creating a denser crust texture. The architecture of a Chicago-style pizza is defined by a layer of cheese on top of the dough, then meat and veggie toppings, then tomato sauce. This has a practical advantage: Because the dough cooks longer and at a lower temperature than other styles of pizza, separating the dough from the sauce with a layer of cheese helps keep the crust from becoming soggy. (We layer our dough with some cheese, but for eye appeal, we put the pepperoni and some extra cheese on top.) Cook it in a baking pan set atop a preheated baking sheet, which helps the bottom of the crust crisp.

Pepperoni Deep-Dish Pizza

This Chicago-style classic features pepperoni, America's favorite pizza topping.

1 cup warm water (100° to 110°), divided
12 ounces bread flour (about 2 1/2 cups)
1 package dry yeast (about 2 1/4 teaspoons)
4 teaspoons olive oil
1/2 teaspoon kosher salt
Cooking spray
1 1/4 cups (5 ounces) shredded part-skim mozzarella cheese, divided
1 1/2 cups Basic Pizza Sauce (at left)
2 ounces pepperoni slices
2 tablespoons grated Parmigiano-Reggiano cheese

1. Pour 3/4 cup warm water in the bowl of a stand mixer with dough hook attached. Weigh or lightly spoon flour into dry measuring cups; level with a knife. Add flour to 3/4 cup water, and mix until combined. Cover and let stand 20 minutes. Combine remaining 1/4 cup water and yeast in a small bowl; let stand 5 minutes or until bubbly. Add yeast mixture, oil, and salt to flour mixture, and mix 5 minutes or until a soft dough forms. Place dough in a large bowl coated with cooking spray, and cover surface of dough with plastic wrap lightly coated with cooking spray. Refrigerate 24 hours.
2. Remove dough from refrigerator. Let stand, covered, 1 hour or until dough comes to room temperature. Punch dough down. Roll dough out to a 14 x 11–inch rectangle on a lightly floured surface. Press dough into bottom and partially up sides of a 13 x 9–inch metal baking pan coated with cooking spray. Cover dough loosely with plastic wrap.
3. Place a baking sheet in oven on bottom rack. Preheat oven to 450°.
4. Arrange 3/4 cup mozzarella evenly over dough; top with Basic Pizza Sauce, pepperoni, Parmigiano-Reggiano, and remaining 1/2 cup mozzarella. Place pan on baking sheet in oven; bake at 450°

for 25 minutes or until crust is golden. Cut pizza into 6 rectangles. Yield: 6 servings (serving size: 1 rectangle).

CALORIES 404; **FAT** 16.3g (sat 5.9g, mono 7.8g, poly 1.5g); **PROTEIN** 16.9g; **CARB** 47.1g; **FIBER** 2.7g; **CHOL** 26mg; **IRON** 3.9mg; **SODIUM** 607mg; **CALC** 244mg

Veggie Grilled Pizza

A sprinkling of bright, sweet mint complements the smoky grilled vegetables in this dish.

1 cup warm water (100° to 110°), divided
10 ounces bread flour (about 2 cups plus 2 tablespoons)
1 package dry yeast (about 2 1/4 teaspoons)
10 teaspoons olive oil, divided
1 teaspoon kosher salt, divided
Cooking spray
2 tablespoons yellow cornmeal
12 ounces baby eggplant, cut crosswise into 1-inch-thick slices
1 medium zucchini, cut crosswise into 1-inch-thick slices
1 large red bell pepper, quartered and seeded
3 garlic cloves, minced
2/3 cup Basic Pizza Sauce (at left)
1/4 teaspoon freshly ground black pepper
1 cup (4 ounces) shredded fontina cheese
1/4 cup small mint leaves
2 teaspoons fresh thyme leaves

1. Pour 3/4 cup warm water in the bowl of a stand mixer with dough hook attached. Weigh or lightly spoon flour into dry measuring cups and spoons; level with a knife. Add flour to 3/4 cup water; mix until combined. Cover and let stand 20 minutes. Combine remaining 1/4 cup water and yeast in a small bowl; let stand 5 minutes or until bubbly. Add yeast mixture, 4 teaspoons oil, and 1/2 teaspoon salt to flour mixture; mix 5 minutes or until a soft dough forms. Place dough in a large bowl coated with cooking spray; cover surface of dough with plastic wrap lightly coated with cooking spray. Refrigerate 24 hours.
2. Prepare grill to high.
3. Remove dough from refrigerator. Let stand, covered, 1 hour or until dough comes to room temperature. Punch

dough down. Press dough out to a 12-inch oval on a lightly floured baking sheet sprinkled with cornmeal. Crimp edges to form a ½-inch border. Cover dough loosely with plastic wrap.

4. Brush eggplant, zucchini, and bell pepper with remaining 2 tablespoons oil. Grill eggplant 4 minutes on each side or until tender; place in a bowl. Grill zucchini 3 minutes on each side or until tender; add to eggplant. Place pepper quarters, skin sides down, on grill rack; grill 6 minutes or until blistered. Place peppers in a zip-top plastic bag; seal. Let stand 10 minutes. Peel peppers; add to vegetable mixture. Coarsely chop vegetables. Add garlic to vegetables; toss to combine.

5. Place pizza dough, cornmeal side up, on grill rack coated with cooking spray, and grill 4 minutes or until blistered. Turn dough over; grill 3 minutes. Remove from grill. Spread Basic Pizza Sauce evenly over top side of crust, leaving a ½-inch border. Arrange vegetable mixture evenly over sauce; sprinkle evenly with remaining ½ teaspoon salt and black pepper. Top with cheese. Return pizza to grill rack, and grill 4 minutes or until thoroughly cooked. Cut pizza into 10 pieces; sprinkle with mint and thyme. Yield: 5 servings (serving size: 2 pieces).

CALORIES 454; FAT 19.7g (sat 6.2g, mono 10.1g, poly 2.5g); PROTEIN 15.6g; CARB 55.7g; FIBER 6g; CHOL 26mg; IRON 4.1mg; SODIUM 637mg; CALC 176mg

GRILLED PIZZA

The style defined: Cooking dough over an open flame yields crust that's crisp outside and airy inside, with a little chew and some light charring that lends pleasantly bitter notes to the flavor. Introduced to America by Al Forno restaurant in Providence, Rhode Island, some 30 years ago, this style has become a fun alternative to backyard barbecues with burgers and dogs.

How it's made: The dough is the same as for our Neapolitan-style pizzas. Cook times will vary from grill to grill (and from charcoal to gas), but the game plan stays constant: Cook the top side of the pizza first, letting it brown and lightly char in spots. It will release from the grill when it's ready to be turned. Flip to cook a few minutes on the other side, top the pizza, and finish cooking.

Garlicky Clam Grilled Pizza

We use littleneck clams in this dish. Use the cooking liquid from the clams—it can be frozen for up to three months—to make clam chowder.

1 cup warm water (100° to 110°), divided
10 ounces bread flour (about 2 cups plus 2 tablespoons)
1 package dry yeast (about 2¼ teaspoons)
10 teaspoons olive oil, divided
½ teaspoon kosher salt
Cooking spray
2 tablespoons yellow cornmeal
2 tablespoons butter
⅓ cup chopped shallots
6 garlic cloves, minced
½ cup dry white wine
5 dozen small clams in shells, scrubbed
½ cup (2 ounces) grated Parmigiano-Reggiano cheese
1 tablespoon finely chopped fresh flat-leaf parsley
1 tablespoon finely chopped fresh oregano

1. Pour ¾ cup warm water in the bowl of a stand mixer with dough hook attached. Weigh or lightly spoon flour into dry measuring cups and spoons; level with a knife. Add flour to ¾ cup water; mix until combined. Cover and let stand 20 minutes. Combine remaining ¼ cup water and yeast in a small bowl; let stand 5 minutes or until bubbly. Add yeast mixture, 4 teaspoons oil, and salt to flour mixture; mix 5 minutes or until a soft dough forms. Place dough in a large bowl coated with cooking spray; cover surface of dough with plastic wrap lightly coated with cooking spray. Refrigerate 24 hours.

2. Remove dough from refrigerator. Let stand, covered, 1 hour or until dough comes to room temperature. Punch dough down. Press dough out to a 12-inch circle on a lightly floured baking sheet, without raised sides, sprinkled with cornmeal. Crimp edges to form a ½-inch border. Cover dough loosely with plastic wrap.

3. Prepare grill to high.

4. Heat a Dutch oven over medium-high heat. Add remaining 2 tablespoons oil to pan; swirl to coat. Add butter;

swirl until butter melts. Add shallots; sauté 2 minutes. Add garlic; sauté 1 minute. Stir in wine and clams; bring to a boil. Cover and cook 8 minutes or until shells open; discard any unopened shells. Remove clams from pan using a slotted spoon. Strain cooking liquid through a fine sieve over a bowl, reserving solids. Reserve cooking liquid for another use. Remove clams from shells; discard shells. Chop clams; toss with reserved solids.

5. Place pizza dough, cornmeal side up, on grill rack coated with cooking spray; grill 4 minutes or until blistered. Turn dough over; grill 3 minutes. Remove from grill. Spread clam mixture evenly over top side of crust, leaving a ½-inch border; top with cheese. Return pizza to grill rack; grill 4 minutes or until thoroughly cooked. Remove from grill. Sprinkle with parsley and oregano. Cut pizza into 10 wedges. Yield: 5 servings (serving size: 2 wedges).

CALORIES 420; FAT 11.5g (sat 3.6g, mono 5.1g, poly 1.5g); PROTEIN 26.3g; CARB 51.2g; FIBER 2g; CHOL 50mg; IRON 18.4mg; SODIUM 435mg; CALC 201mg

STORE-BOUGHT SHORTCUTS

If you can't make homemade dough the night before, here are some ways to get a jump on the pizza process.

Store-bought crusts, prebaked items from makers such as Boboli and Mama Mary's, will cut significant time from your prep work. Our toppings will still taste great on these crusts. A couple of tips: They may be higher in sodium than our homemade crusts, so if sodium is a concern, use less added salt in the recipe. They will also likely require a different baking time and temperature, so heed the package guidelines.

Refrigerated canned dough from makers like Pillsbury is also an option, and fresh pizza dough is available at many supermarkets (ask for it in the bakery section). You can also sometimes buy pizza dough from pizzerias. Check out the smaller neighborhood pizzerias rather than nationwide chains. Many will sell you dough balls for about $3 to $5 that will make 14- to 16-inch pizzas. Since that's bigger than our pizzas, you can freeze leftover raw dough to make smaller pizzas another time.

THIN-CRUST, CALIFORNIA-STYLE PIZZA

The style defined: The crust—sometimes cracker-crisp, sometimes light, airy, and tender—is a vehicle for delightfully nontraditional toppings: Pepperoni and sausage make way for smoked salmon, apricots, and arugula. This style was popularized by chefs like Wolfgang Puck and chains such as the California Pizza Kitchen.

How it's made: Roll the dough as thin as possible with a rolling pin. (For our cracker crust Smoked Salmon Thin-Crust Pizza (below), we roll the dough to 14 inches instead of 12, making it even thinner.) Pierce the rolled surface several times with a fork to keep bubbling to a minimum and help it retain its shape as it bakes. Blind bake the dough before adding the toppings, which keeps the crust crisp.

Smoked Salmon Thin-Crust Pizza

The crisp cracker crust of this pizza makes a pleasing contrast to the velvety soft salmon.

½ cup warm water (100° to 110°)
½ teaspoon dry yeast
2 tablespoons olive oil
¼ teaspoon kosher salt
6 ounces bread flour (about 1¼ cups)
Cooking spray
2 tablespoons yellow cornmeal
⅓ cup (3 ounces) ⅓-less-fat cream cheese, softened
1½ tablespoons capers, drained
4 (⅛-inch-thick) slices red onion, separated into rings
4 ounces cold-smoked salmon, thinly sliced
1 tablespoon chopped fresh dill

1. Combine ½ cup warm water and yeast in the bowl of a stand mixer with dough hook attached; let stand 5 minutes or until bubbly. Add oil and salt to yeast mixture. Weigh or lightly spoon flour into dry measuring cups; level with a knife. Sprinkle flour over yeast mixture; mix 2 minutes or until a soft dough forms. Place dough in a large bowl coated with cooking spray; cover surface of dough with plastic wrap lightly coated with cooking spray. Refrigerate 24 hours.

2. Position an oven rack in lowest setting. Place a pizza stone on lowest rack. Preheat oven to 550°. Preheat pizza stone 30 minutes before baking dough.

3. Remove dough from refrigerator. Let stand, covered, 1 hour or until dough comes to room temperature. Punch dough down. Roll dough out to a very thin 14-inch circle on a lightly floured baking sheet, without raised edges, sprinkled with cornmeal. Crimp edges to form a ½-inch border. Pierce dough several times with a fork.

4. Slide dough onto preheated pizza stone, using a spatula as a guide. Bake at 550° for 4 minutes. Remove from oven; spread cheese evenly over dough. Arrange capers and onion over cheese. Bake an additional 5 minutes or until crust is golden brown. Top evenly with salmon; sprinkle with dill. Cut pizza into 8 wedges. Yield: 4 servings (serving size: 2 wedges).

CALORIES 326; FAT 13.8g (sat 4.5g, mono 7g, poly 1.5g); PROTEIN 13.1g; CARB 36.6g; FIBER 1.6g; CHOL 23mg; IRON 2.6mg; SODIUM 867mg; CALC 30mg

Apricot and Prosciutto Thin-Crust Pizza

Look for apricots that are slightly underripe so they'll stand up to the heat, or you can substitute two medium peaches.

½ cup warm water (100° to 110°)
½ teaspoon dry yeast
8½ teaspoons olive oil, divided
½ teaspoon kosher salt, divided
6 ounces bread flour (about 1¼ cups)
Cooking spray
2 tablespoons yellow cornmeal
1 teaspoon chopped fresh thyme
¼ teaspoon freshly ground black pepper
3 apricots, each pitted and cut into 8 wedges
2 shallots, peeled and thinly sliced
¾ cup (3 ounces) crumbled goat cheese
1½ tablespoons finely chopped fresh flat-leaf parsley
1 tablespoon minced fresh chives
1 cup arugula
1 ounce thinly sliced prosciutto
1 ounce shaved fresh Parmigiano-Reggiano cheese

1. Combine ½ cup warm water and yeast in the bowl of a stand mixer with dough hook attached; let stand 5 minutes or until bubbly. Add 4 teaspoons oil and ¼ teaspoon salt to yeast mixture. Weigh or lightly spoon flour into dry measuring cups; level with a knife. Sprinkle flour over yeast mixture; mix 2 minutes or until a soft dough forms. Place dough in a large bowl coated with cooking spray; cover surface of dough with plastic wrap lightly coated with cooking spray. Refrigerate 24 hours.

2. Remove dough from refrigerator. Let stand, covered, 1 hour or until dough comes to room temperature. Punch dough down. Roll dough out to a thin 12-inch circle on a lightly floured baking sheet, without raised edges, sprinkled with cornmeal. Crimp edges to form a ½-inch border. Pierce dough several times with a fork. Cover dough loosely with plastic wrap.

3. Position an oven rack in lowest setting. Place a pizza stone on lowest rack. Preheat oven to 550°. Preheat pizza stone 30 minutes before baking dough.

4. Combine 1 tablespoon oil, thyme, pepper, apricots, shallots, and remaining ¼ teaspoon salt; toss gently. Remove plastic wrap from dough; slide dough onto preheated pizza stone, using a spatula as a guide. Bake at 550° for 4 minutes. Top dough with goat cheese and apricot mixture. Bake an additional 5 minutes or until crust is golden brown. Sprinkle with parsley and chives. Toss arugula with remaining 1½ teaspoons oil; arrange arugula over apricot mixture. Top with prosciutto and Parmigiano-Reggiano cheese. Cut into 10 wedges. Yield: 5 servings (serving size: 2 wedges).

CALORIES 307; FAT 14.3g (sat 4.8g, mono 6.9g, poly 1.2g); PROTEIN 12.1g; CARB 32.7g; FIBER 2g; CHOL 17mg; IRON 2.9mg; SODIUM 459mg; CALC 120mg

FREEZING AHEAD

You can make your pizza dough ahead of time, and freeze it after its 24-hour rest. To defrost, put the dough back in the refrigerator overnight. Once the dough is thawed, proceed with the recipe from the step that calls for removing the dough from the refrigerator to bring it to room temperature.

A HAITIAN-AMERICAN TRADITION

Maud Cadet serves three generations of Haitian-Americans the hearty island dishes of her youth. In the year of an earthquake tragedy, hers is a heartwarming story of a cook, a kitchen, and a clan.

As a girl in Port-au-Prince in the 1950s, Maud Cadet wasn't even allowed into the kitchen of her prosperous family's home. Now, she's a mother of five and grandmother of nine, and her San Jose, California, kitchen is at the center of family life: Maud welcomes her close-knit clan every other Sunday for a lively family feast. It's a ritual that keeps the family strong, she says, nourishing relationships, and it forms the highlight of Maud's week: "I'm not myself when they don't come," says Maud. "I don't like to be in the house by myself on Sundays."

Maud and her husband, Raymond, met in Haiti but did not marry until Maud followed him to the United States in 1963 after studying fashion design; he was an electrical engineer who eventually ended up at Intel. When children came, she left a clothing business behind to raise them (though once they started elementary school, she put her energy into 17 years of running a day care). Four sons—Ron, Rudy, Rick, and Marc—and their wives and children, who range in age from just under a year to 13, live nearby. Daughter Marjorie Cadet-Martinez lives in Maryland and visits annually. The group has happily outgrown the dining room and eats in the heart of the home: the comfortable, aroma-filled kitchen.

Their communal Sunday meals tap into the Cadets' Haitian roots: Raised by her godmother—her own mother died when Maud was 5—Maud grew up with a dozen relatives. But she didn't cook.

"In Haiti, the food is usually prepared by the household cook, and the kids are not allowed in the kitchen," says Maud in her lilting tones, which retain a French-Caribbean note. "But I used to sneak in. I sometimes got in trouble because I loved cooking!"

Maud did take home-economics classes after high school, but Haitian home cooking was the real influence: dishes like *soupe au giraumon* (a squash soup traditional for the New Year, thanks to its lucky golden color), braised seafood, and pâtés, which in Haitian cuisine consist of spiced chicken in flaky pastry, reminiscent of a Jamaican patty—a beloved family favorite. "I can have all kinds of appetizers, and they say, 'Where are the pâtés?'" says Maud.

And so the food traditions of a land left almost five decades before are passed to a second and third generation—the story of so much American cooking. Maud's Sunday dinners feed a family's spirit, fostering deep connections among the siblings, nieces, and nephews. "The way the tradition started had a lot to do with Haitian culture," says Rudy. "In our youth, we had rules: We had to get cleaned up for dinner, and we didn't excuse ourselves until everyone was done. We had dinner together, and it bred the habit."

Snapper in Haitian Court-Bouillon

Part French technique, part personalized spin, this main-course fish dish is the essence of good family classics. In the Cadet family, it's always served over rice. For the prettiest results, slice the red bell pepper and onion with a mandoline, making paper-thin strips. Choose a sustainable snapper species, like black snapper, or go with black bass or striped bass.

1½ teaspoons chopped fresh thyme
1 teaspoon dry mustard
½ teaspoon salt
½ teaspoon freshly ground black pepper
4 (6-ounce) skinless black snapper fillets
1 cup fat-free, less-sodium chicken broth
½ cup clam juice
2 garlic cloves, crushed
1 small yellow onion, quartered
½ to 1 whole habanero pepper, seeded
1½ cups thinly sliced red bell pepper
¾ cup thinly sliced red onion
1 tablespoon tomato paste
1 tablespoon honey

1. Combine first 4 ingredients in a small bowl. Sprinkle fish evenly with thyme mixture.
2. Place broth and next 4 ingredients in a large sauté pan over medium-high heat; bring to a boil. Cover, reduce heat, and simmer 10 minutes. Discard onion and habanero. Add fish; cover and simmer 10 minutes or until fish flakes easily with a fork. Carefully remove fish from pan; keep warm.
3. Add bell pepper and remaining ingredients to cooking liquid in pan; cover and cook 5 minutes or until vegetables are tender. Top fish with sauce. Yield: 4 servings (serving size: 1 fillet and about ⅓ cup sauce and vegetables).

CALORIES 214; FAT 2.7g (sat 0.5g, mono 0.4g, poly 0.8g); PROTEIN 36.3g; CARB 9.8g; FIBER 1.5g; CHOL 64mg; IRON 0.9mg; SODIUM 587mg; CALC 70mg

Griot with Sauce Ti-Malice

This dish involves braising chunks of pork, sautéing them until crisp, and then cooking with some braising liquid as the pork slowly caramelizes. Ti-Malice, a Haitian condiment, is named for a trickster in voodoo mythology. It's a piquant, sour sauce, a foil to the sweeter pork. For the most authentic taste, serve with rice and pan-fried plantains. Garnish with cilantro leaves, and serve with lime wedges, if desired.

1 habanero pepper
³/₄ cup fresh orange juice (about 3 large oranges)
6 tablespoons fresh lime juice, divided
3 tablespoons minced shallots
2 tablespoons minced garlic
1 tablespoon Dijon mustard
1 tablespoon honey
2 teaspoons salt
4 fresh thyme sprigs
3 pounds boneless pork shoulder, trimmed and cut into 1¹/₂-inch pieces
2 cups fat-free, less-sodium chicken broth
¹/₂ cup thinly sliced shallots
1 teaspoon cider vinegar
1 teaspoon freshly ground black pepper
1 tablespoon canola oil

1. Cut habanero in half. Seed one half of pepper, and leave seeds in other half. Mince both pepper halves. Combine habanero, orange juice, ¼ cup lime juice, minced shallots, and next 5 ingredients in a large bowl; stir with a whisk. Add pork; toss to coat. Cover and chill 12 to 24 hours.
2. Place pork and marinade in a Dutch oven over medium-high heat. Add broth; bring to a boil. Cover, reduce heat, and simmer 1½ hours or until meat is tender. Remove pork from pan with a slotted spoon, reserving cooking liquid. Strain cooking liquid through a sieve into a bowl; discard solids. Place a large zip-top plastic bag in a bowl. Pour reserved cooking liquid into bag; let stand 5 minutes. Snip off 1 bottom corner of bag; drain liquid into a medium saucepan, stopping before the fat layer reaches opening. Discard fat. Set ½ cup cooking liquid aside.

3. Place saucepan with cooking liquid over medium-high heat; bring to a boil. Cook 20 minutes or until reduced to about 1 cup. Add sliced shallots, vinegar, black pepper, and 1 tablespoon lime juice. Cover and keep warm.
4. Heat oil in a large nonstick skillet over medium heat. Add pork; cook 10 minutes, turning to brown well on all sides. Add reserved ½ cup cooking liquid and remaining 1 tablespoon lime juice. Increase heat to medium-high; cook 4 minutes or until liquid nearly evaporates, stirring occasionally. Place pork in a bowl; pour sauce over pork. Yield: 10 servings (serving size: about 3 ounces pork and 2 tablespoons sauce).

CALORIES 223; **FAT** 8.8g (sat 2.6g, mono 4.2g, poly 1.2g); **PROTEIN** 27.3g; **CARB** 7.3g; **FIBER** 0.3g; **CHOL** 75mg; **IRON** 1.4mg; **SODIUM** 668mg; **CALC** 33mg

Chicken and Okra Stew

This hearty stew is something like Brunswick stew, that old-fashioned Southern favorite—only the Haitian version is certainly fierier, thanks to the habanero. If you don't like it quite so spicy, use a seeded, minced jalapeño.

4 teaspoons canola oil, divided
2 pounds skinless, boneless chicken thighs, quartered
1 habanero pepper
1¹/₂ cups chopped green bell pepper
1 cup finely chopped onion
²/₃ cup finely chopped celery
2¹/₂ cups chopped plum tomato
2 tablespoons chopped fresh parsley
1 tablespoon chopped fresh oregano
1 teaspoon salt
1 teaspoon freshly ground black pepper
¹/₈ teaspoon ground cloves
1 (14-ounce) can fat-free, less-sodium chicken broth
1 pound fresh okra pods, cut into 1-inch pieces

1. Heat 2 teaspoons oil in a Dutch oven over medium-high heat. Add half of chicken to pan; cook 6 minutes, browning on all sides. Remove chicken from pan. Add remaining chicken to pan; cook 6 minutes, browning on all sides. Remove chicken from pan.

2. Cut habanero in half. Seed one half of pepper, and leave seeds in other half. Mince both pepper halves. Add remaining 2 teaspoons oil to pan; swirl to coat. Add minced habanero, bell pepper, onion, and celery; sauté 5 minutes or until tender, stirring occasionally. Add tomato; cook 3 minutes or until tomato softens. Add parsley and next 5 ingredients; bring to a boil. Return chicken to pan; cover, reduce heat, and simmer 10 minutes. Add okra; cover and simmer 15 minutes or until okra is just tender. Yield: 6 servings (serving size: 1¹/₃ cups).

CALORIES 269; **FAT** 9.4g (sat 1.8g, mono 3.7g, poly 2.5g); **PROTEIN** 33g; **CARB** 13.4g; **FIBER** 4.8g; **CHOL** 126mg; **IRON** 2.8mg; **SODIUM** 692mg; **CALC** 106mg

Haitian Chicken Pâté Puffs

Rather than a more traditional pâté, a chicken picadillo is first made and then whirred up for a filling in these little first-course puff-pastry packets. The filling is then sealed in the dough and baked.

1 habanero pepper
Cooking spray
¹/₄ cup chopped yellow onion
2 teaspoons minced garlic
¹/₂ pound ground chicken breast
¹/₄ cup shredded carrot
2 teaspoons no-salt-added tomato paste
2 teaspoons fresh lime juice
1 teaspoon cider vinegar
1 tablespoon chopped green onions
1 tablespoon chopped fresh parsley
1 teaspoon chopped fresh thyme
¹/₂ teaspoon freshly ground black pepper
¹/₄ teaspoon salt
¹/₈ teaspoon ground cloves
¹/₈ teaspoon grated whole nutmeg
1 (14-ounce) package frozen puff pastry, thawed (such as Dufour)
1 large egg
1 tablespoon water

1. Cut habanero in half. Seed one half of pepper, and leave seeds in other half. Mince both pepper halves. Heat a large nonstick skillet over medium-high heat. Coat pan with cooking spray.

Add minced habanero, yellow onion, and garlic to pan; sauté 3 minutes or until tender, stirring frequently. Add chicken; cook 5 minutes or until browned, stirring to crumble. Add carrot; cook 2 minutes. Add tomato paste; cook 1 minute, stirring constantly. Add lime juice and vinegar, scraping pan to loosen browned bits. Add green onions and next 6 ingredients; stir well. Remove from heat; cool mixture to room temperature.

2. Place cooled chicken mixture in a food processor; process until almost smooth (mixture will begin to clump).

3. Preheat oven to 400°.

4. Roll puff pastry into a 15 x 12–inch rectangle on a lightly floured surface. Cut puff pastry into 20 (3-inch) squares. Combine egg and 1 tablespoon water, stirring with a whisk. Brush egg mixture along edges of pastry squares; spoon about 1 scant tablespoon filling in center of each pastry square. Fold each pastry square in half; press edges closed with tines of a fork. Brush top with egg wash; arrange 1 inch apart on a baking sheet. Bake at 400° for 20 minutes or until puffed and golden brown. Yield: 20 servings (serving size: 1 pâté puff).

CALORIES 102; **FAT** 5.7g (sat 1.6g, mono 3.2g, poly 0.3g); **PROTEIN** 4.5g; **CARB** 7.7g; **FIBER** 0.6g; **CHOL** 17mg; **IRON** 0.7mg; **SODIUM** 139mg; **CALC** 6mg

THE FILLING IN HAITIAN CHICKEN PÂTÉ PUFFS IS HIGHLY SPICED FOR SURE, BUT IT'S ALSO VERY AROMATIC, A NICE START TO ANY MEAL

THE FIRST RISOTTO OF SPRING

As an entrée, side, or even dessert, this dish is a versatile partner for fresh spring produce. Our easy tips will help you turn out perfect risottos every time.

If you think of risotto as a cold-weather comfort food, think again. Some of spring's best ingredients make themselves at home in a pot of creamy, cheese-laced risotto. Asparagus, fava beans, and green peas serve as bright-flavored counterpoints to the starchiness of the dish, while fresh morel mushrooms lend an earthy touch. Likewise, the richness of the risotto softens the puckery tartness of rhubarb and balances arugula's peppery bite.

Cooking risotto is, admittedly, a bit of a process, but it's really a fairly simple one, even if you are a beginner: Toast the rice, then continue to stir as it slowly absorbs liquid and releases starch, softening to the point where it offers just the slightest resistance to the bite—the state of risotto perfection known as al dente. Just follow our simple tips for preparing risotto (see page 123), and you're sure to turn out a perfect batch every time.

Staff Favorite
Bacon and Wild Mushroom Risotto with Baby Spinach

4 cups Homemade Chicken Stock (page 122)
6 bacon slices, chopped
1 cup chopped shallots
1 tablespoon extra-virgin olive oil
1 teaspoon chopped fresh thyme
4 garlic cloves, minced
4 ounces cremini mushrooms, sliced
4 ounces shiitake mushrooms, stemmed and sliced
4 ounces oyster mushrooms, sliced
1 cup uncooked Carnaroli or Arborio rice or other medium-grain rice
1/3 cup Madeira wine or dry sherry
4 cups baby spinach
1/2 cup (2 ounces) grated fresh Asiago cheese
1/2 teaspoon salt
1/4 teaspoon freshly ground black pepper

1. Bring Homemade Chicken Stock to a simmer in a small saucepan (do not boil); keep warm over low heat.

2. Heat a large Dutch oven over medium heat. Add bacon to pan; cook 8 minutes or until crisp, stirring occasionally. Remove bacon from pan with a slotted spoon. Add shallots and next 3 ingredients to drippings in pan; cook 6 minutes or until shallots are tender, stirring occasionally. Stir in mushrooms; cook 8 minutes, stirring occasionally. Add rice, and cook 1 minute, stirring constantly. Stir in Madeira; cook 1 minute or until liquid is nearly absorbed, stirring constantly. Stir in 1 cup stock; cook 4 minutes or until liquid is nearly absorbed, stirring constantly. Add remaining stock, 1/2 cup at a time, stirring constantly until each portion of stock is absorbed before adding the next (about 25 minutes total). Stir in spinach; cook 1 minute. Remove from heat; stir in cheese, salt, and pepper. Sprinkle with bacon. Yield: 5 servings (serving size: about 1 1/4 cups risotto and about 1 tablespoon bacon).

CALORIES 405; **FAT** 19.1g (sat 6.6g, mono 8.4g, poly 2g); **PROTEIN** 16.5g; **CARB** 42.6g; **FIBER** 3.5g; **CHOL** 38mg; **IRON** 2.4mg; **SODIUM** 555mg; **CALC** 145mg

USE RISOTTO LIKE A BLANK CANVAS: ALLOW IT TO SPOTLIGHT THE SEASON'S BEST FRESH PRODUCE.

Make Ahead • Freezable

Homemade Chicken Stock

This rich, brown stock adds deep flavor to risotto. Skim foam from the top of the stock as it cooks. Freeze any leftover stock, and use it for soups, stews, and sauces.

8 pounds chicken wings
Cooking spray
5 quarts water, divided
4 celery stalks, cut into 3-inch pieces
2 onions, quartered
2 carrots, cut into 3-inch pieces
15 fresh parsley sprigs
10 fresh thyme sprigs
3 bay leaves

1. Preheat oven to 425°.
2. Place chicken wings on 2 jelly-roll pans coated with cooking spray. Bake wings for 1 hour or until browned. Place wings in a stockpot. Pour ½ quart water into each jelly-roll pan, scraping to loosen browned bits. Pour water mixture into stockpot.
3. Add remaining 4 quarts water, celery, and remaining ingredients to stockpot. Bring to a boil. Reduce heat to low, and simmer 4 hours, skimming off and discarding foam as needed. Strain stock through a fine sieve into a large bowl; discard solids. Cool stock to room temperature. Cover and refrigerate 8 hours. Skim solidified fat from surface of stock; discard fat. Yield: 18 cups (serving size: 1 cup).

CALORIES 26; **FAT** 0.7g (sat 0.2g, mono 0.2g, poly 0.2g); **PROTEIN** 4.5g; **CARB** 0.2g; **FIBER** 0.1g; **CHOL** 11mg; **IRON** 0.2mg; **SODIUM** 18mg; **CALC** 4mg

Pan-Seared Shrimp and Arugula Risotto

Serve with steamed or roasted asparagus.

4 cups Homemade Chicken Stock (at left)
2 tablespoons extra-virgin olive oil, divided
1 pound large shrimp, peeled and deveined
½ teaspoon salt, divided
¼ teaspoon freshly ground black pepper, divided
½ cup chopped shallots
6 garlic cloves, minced
1 cup uncooked Carnaroli or Arborio rice or other medium-grain rice
½ cup dry white wine
½ cup (2 ounces) grated fresh Parmigiano-Reggiano cheese
2 tablespoons butter
3 cups baby arugula
½ cup thinly sliced fresh basil

1. Bring Homemade Chicken Stock to a simmer in a small saucepan (do not boil). Keep warm over low heat.
2. Heat 1 tablespoon oil in a large nonstick skillet over medium-high heat. Sprinkle shrimp with ¼ teaspoon salt and ⅛ teaspoon pepper. Add shrimp to pan; cook 1 minute. Remove pan from heat; set aside.
3. Heat remaining 1 tablespoon oil in a large saucepan over medium heat. Add shallots and garlic to pan; cook 5 minutes or until tender, stirring frequently. Add rice; cook 1 minute, stirring constantly. Stir in wine; cook 1 minute or until liquid is nearly absorbed, stirring constantly. Add 1 cup stock; cook 4 minutes or until liquid is nearly absorbed, stirring constantly. Stir in remaining stock, ½ cup at a time, stirring frequently until each portion of stock is absorbed before adding the next (about 25 minutes total). Stir in shrimp; cook 1 minute or until done. Stir in cheese, butter, remaining ¼ teaspoon salt, and remaining ⅛ teaspoon pepper. Remove from heat; stir in arugula and basil. Yield: 6 servings (serving size: 1 cup).

CALORIES 344; **FAT** 13.4g (sat 4.8g, mono 5.8g, poly 1.5g); **PROTEIN** 26g; **CARB** 30.3g; **FIBER** 1.9g; **CHOL** 139mg; **IRON** 2.6mg; **SODIUM** 521mg; **CALC** 210mg

Lemon Risotto with Peas, Tarragon, and Leeks

Pair this pleasantly tart side-dish risotto with roasted salmon or halibut. Garnish with long strips of lemon rind and fresh tarragon sprigs, if desired.

1 cup fresh green peas
4 cups Homemade Chicken Stock (at left)
2 tablespoons extra-virgin olive oil
1½ cups finely chopped leek (about 2)
½ cup chopped shallots
1 cup uncooked Carnaroli or Arborio rice or other medium-grain rice
3 tablespoons dry white wine
½ cup (2 ounces) grated fresh Parmigiano-Reggiano cheese
1 teaspoon grated lemon rind
2 tablespoons fresh lemon juice
½ teaspoon salt
⅛ teaspoon freshly ground black pepper
2 tablespoons chopped fresh tarragon
1 tablespoon butter

1. Bring a small saucepan of water to a boil. Add peas; boil 1 minute. Drain and rinse with cold water; drain well. Bring Homemade Chicken Stock to a simmer in a small saucepan (do not boil). Keep warm over low heat.
2. Heat oil in a large saucepan over medium heat. Add leek and shallots to pan; cook 7 minutes or until tender, stirring frequently. Add rice; cook 1 minute, stirring constantly. Add wine; cook 30 seconds or until liquid is nearly absorbed, stirring constantly. Stir in 1 cup stock; cook 4 minutes or until liquid is nearly absorbed, stirring constantly. Add remaining stock, ½ cup at a time, stirring constantly until each portion of stock is absorbed before adding the next (about 25 minutes total). Stir in peas; cook 1 minute. Stir in cheese and next 4 ingredients. Remove from heat; stir in tarragon and butter. Yield: 8 servings (serving size: about ½ cup).

CALORIES 205; **FAT** 7.7g (sat 2.5g, mono 3g, poly 0.7g); **PROTEIN** 8.8g; **CARB** 26.4g; **FIBER** 2.4g; **CHOL** 15mg; **IRON** 1mg; **SODIUM** 298mg; **CALC** 124mg

Morel Risotto

Serve with roast chicken or pan-seared pork chops. If you can't find fresh morels, substitute 1 ounce dried ones. Soak in 1 cup hot water for 30 minutes; drain and halve lengthwise.

4 cups Homemade Chicken Stock (page 122)
2 tablespoons extra-virgin olive oil
1/4 cup chopped shallots
1/4 cup finely chopped onion
1 teaspoon fresh thyme leaves
1/2 pound morel mushrooms, halved
  lengthwise
1 cup uncooked Carnaroli or Arborio rice or
  other medium-grain rice
1/4 cup dry vermouth
1/2 cup (2 ounces) grated fresh pecorino
  Romano cheese
1/4 cup heavy whipping cream
1/2 teaspoon salt
1/4 teaspoon freshly ground black pepper
2 tablespoons chopped fresh chives

1. Bring Homemade Chicken Stock to a simmer in a small saucepan (do not boil). Keep warm over low heat.
2. Heat oil in a large saucepan over medium heat. Add shallots, onion, and thyme to pan; cook 5 minutes or until tender, stirring frequently. Add mushrooms; cook 1 minute. Add rice; cook 1 minute, stirring frequently. Stir in vermouth; cook 30 seconds or until liquid is nearly absorbed, stirring constantly. Stir in 1 cup stock; cook 4 minutes or until liquid is nearly absorbed, stirring frequently. Add remaining stock, 1/2 cup at a time, stirring constantly until each portion of stock is absorbed before adding the next (about 25 minutes total). Add cheese and next 3 ingredients; cook 2 minutes. Remove from heat; top with chives. Yield: 8 servings (serving size: about 1/2 cup).

CALORIES 198; **FAT** 8.7g (sat 3.4g, mono 3.9g, poly 0.8g); **PROTEIN** 7.5g; **CARB** 21.9g; **FIBER** 1.5g; **CHOL** 22mg; **IRON** 0.5mg; **SODIUM** 237mg; **CALC** 78mg

5 TIPS FOR GREAT RISOTTO

Yes, you can even cook it for a dinner party—and use leftovers the next day.

1. CHOOSE THE RIGHT RICE
To make risotto, you need to use medium-grain rice, which absorbs more liquid than long-grain rice but won't become sticky like short-grain (think sushi) rice. The most common varieties are Arborio, Carnaroli, and Vialone Nano. Each will produce satisfying results. Of the three, Arborio is typically cheapest and most widely available. But our staff prefers Carnaroli to the others.

In a side-by-side taste test, we found that Carnaroli yielded the creamiest results. Moreover, it stays perfectly al dente longer than the other varieties, making it less likely to become mushy, which is a huge plus for less-experienced risotto cooks. By contrast, Vialone and particularly Arborio can turn from undercooked to overcooked relatively quickly. Carnaroli is more expensive than Arborio, but in our opinion, it's worth every penny. Search it out in specialty stores and gourmet grocers.

2. USE THE BEST INGREDIENTS
As with most simple dishes, good ingredients make all the difference. We find that rich, homemade stocks (see Homemade Chicken Stock, page 122) make risotto considerably more flavorful than canned broths, although commercial broths will work just fine in a pinch—just be sure to use less-sodium versions. Full-sodium broths will make the risotto too salty as they reduce.

Likewise, use the freshest produce you can find. Search out pristine asparagus stalks and newly dug morels at your local farmers' market, for instance. And use fresh, fragrant herbs to finish the risotto. Adding them at the end preserves their color and keeps their flavor intense.

3. ENSURE CREAMINESS
There's some debate over whether risotto needs to be stirred constantly. We've certainly found that the more it's stirred, the creamier it becomes. The stirring also helps the rice grains cook evenly. But food scientists will tell you risotto becomes creamy from the gradual addition of warm liquid. So even if you have to step away for a moment, make sure your cooking liquid is hot, and incorporate it 1/2 cup or so at a time, waiting until it's nearly absorbed before adding more.

Creaminess is a matter of taste, however: Some people like their risotto to flow like porridge, while others prefer it tighter. If you prefer a looser, more flowing risotto, stir in a little extra stock toward the end of the cooking process. Either way, serve immediately once you've reached the desired consistency and the rice is al dente: tender on the outside, slightly firm (but not crunchy) in the middle. It doesn't take long before perfectly cooked risotto will turn gummy or dry.

4. PREP AHEAD
Conventional wisdom says risotto isn't a good dish for dinner parties because it pretty much chains you to the stove for close to half an hour. But if you prep in advance, you can pull it together in about 10 minutes on the night of the event.

The plan: Make your risotto the day before, cooking it until the rice is only about 5 minutes away from being perfectly al dente. Stir in cheese and seasonings, but hold off on any add-ins like asparagus, peas, parsley, shrimp, or anything else that might lose color or overcook upon reheating. Pour the risotto onto a jelly-roll pan, and spread it into an even layer (this gives the rice more surface area to help it cool faster). Put the jelly-roll pan in the refrigerator. Once the rice has cooled thoroughly, wrap the pan in plastic wrap. Chill your remaining stock.

To complete the risotto, blanch, cook, or chop any items you plan to add to the rice, and have them at the ready. Heat the remaining stock in a saucepan. Add the risotto to the pan, and stir until it reaches the desired texture and consistency. Stir in your prepped extra items and herbs, and then serve it up to your grateful—and likely quite impressed—guests.

5. MAKE GREAT USE OF LEFTOVERS
True, leftover risotto just won't be the same the next day; reheat it in more stock and it'll likely turn mushy. But risotto cakes are every bit as delicious as the original risotto and a snap to make. Just take a handful of the leftover rice and form it into a 1/2-inch patty. Dredge it in flour or panko, if you like, but it's not necessary. Then cook the patties for about 3 minutes on each side in hot olive oil over medium-high heat, or until the cakes have turned golden brown and are thoroughly heated. Presto—a quick and satisfying side dish that complements all manner of meat, fish, or poultry dishes.

Ruby Port and Rhubarb Risotto with Sugared Strawberries

Risotto becomes a kind of rice pudding in this dish and is drizzled with a sweet-tart syrup.

2 cups sliced strawberries
3/4 cup plus 1 tablespoon sugar, divided
2/3 cup ruby port
1 1/2 cups chopped rhubarb
3 1/2 cups water
2 cups whole milk
1/4 teaspoon salt
1/8 teaspoon freshly ground nutmeg
2 tablespoons butter
1 cup uncooked Carnaroli or Arborio rice or other medium-grain rice
1/2 teaspoon vanilla extract
1/4 cup (2 ounces) mascarpone cheese

1. Combine strawberries and 1 tablespoon sugar in a small bowl. Set aside.
2. Combine port and 1/4 cup sugar in a small saucepan over medium-high heat. Bring to a boil; cook 7 minutes or until slightly thickened. Stir in rhubarb; cook 7 minutes.
3. Bring 3 1/2 cups water to a simmer in a small saucepan (do not boil). Keep warm over low heat. Combine milk, remaining 1/2 cup sugar, salt, and nutmeg in a separate saucepan; bring to a simmer (do not boil). Keep warm over low heat. Melt butter in a large Dutch oven. Add rice to pan; cook 1 minute, stirring constantly. Stir in 1 cup hot water; cook 3 minutes or until liquid is nearly absorbed, stirring constantly. Add remaining water, 1/2 cup at a time, stirring constantly until each portion of water is absorbed before adding the next. Add milk mixture, 1/2 cup at a time, stirring constantly until each portion of milk is absorbed before adding the next (about 30 minutes total). Stir in vanilla; cook 1 minute. Remove from heat; stir in mascarpone until cheese melts. Place about 1/2 cup risotto in each of 8 bowls. Top each serving with 2 tablespoons port mixture and 1/4 cup strawberry mixture. Yield: 8 servings.

CALORIES 306; FAT 11.8g (sat 6.5g, mono 3.1g, poly 0.6g); PROTEIN 5.5g; CARB 46.6g; FIBER 2.3g; CHOL 31mg; IRON 0.4mg; SODIUM 129mg; CALC 118mg

---

Kid Friendly
Risotto with Spring Vegetables

Saffron adds a hint of color and exotic flavor.

2 cups shelled fava beans (about 1 1/2 pounds unshelled)
1/2 cup fresh green peas
4 cups Homemade Chicken Stock (page 122)
2 tablespoons extra-virgin olive oil
1 cup chopped shallots
1/2 cup chopped carrot
1 cup uncooked Carnaroli or Arborio rice or other medium-grain rice
1/8 teaspoon saffron threads, crushed
1/2 cup white wine
8 ounces thin asparagus, cut into 2-inch pieces
1 cup (4 ounces) grated fresh Parmigiano-Reggiano cheese
1/4 cup chopped fresh parsley
1/4 teaspoon salt
1/4 teaspoon freshly ground black pepper

1. Cook beans in boiling water 2 minutes. Drain and rinse with cold water; drain. Remove tough outer skins from beans; discard skins. Cook peas in boiling water 2 minutes. Drain and rinse with cold water; drain well.
2. Bring Homemade Chicken Stock to a simmer in a small saucepan (do not boil). Keep warm over low heat.
3. Heat oil in a large Dutch oven over medium heat. Add shallots and carrot to pan; cook 4 minutes or until tender, stirring occasionally. Add rice and saffron; cook 1 minute, stirring constantly. Stir in wine; cook 30 seconds or until liquid is nearly absorbed, stirring constantly. Add 1 cup stock; cook 4 minutes or until liquid is nearly absorbed, stirring constantly. Add remaining stock, 1/2 cup at a time, stirring constantly until each portion of stock is absorbed before adding the next (about 25 minutes total). Stir in fava beans, peas, and asparagus with last addition of stock. Remove from heat; stir in cheese and remaining ingredients. Yield: 6 servings (serving size: 1 cup).

CALORIES 371; FAT 10.2g (sat 3.3g, mono 4.7g, poly 1.4g); PROTEIN 21.8g; CARB 54.8g; FIBER 3.4g; CHOL 19mg; IRON 3mg; SODIUM 354mg; CALC 221mg

---

EVERYDAY VEGETARIAN
BRING ON THE BRINE

Brined ingredients such as capers, olives, and preserved citrus get their bright flavor from being cured in salted liquid. Used judiciously, they deliver major flavor while keeping sodium levels in check.

Stuffed Grape Leaves

This classic Mediterranean dish makes a great party hors d'oeuvre. Brined flavor comes from both the grape leaves and the salty feta cheese. For convenience, assemble and cook the stuffed grape leaves the day before. Refrigerate overnight, then set out for a couple of hours to come to room temperature.

42 bottled large grape leaves (about 6 ounces)
2 tablespoons extra-virgin olive oil, divided
1 1/2 cups minced yellow onion (about 1 medium)
1 cup thinly sliced green onions (about 1 bunch)
1/3 cup sliced almonds, chopped
3 cups water, divided
3/4 cup uncooked long-grain rice
1/2 teaspoon salt
1/4 teaspoon freshly ground black pepper
1/4 teaspoon ground cinnamon
1 cup (4 ounces) crumbled feta cheese
3 tablespoons chopped fresh flat-leaf parsley
3 tablespoons chopped fresh mint
2 tablespoons chopped fresh dill
3 tablespoons fresh lemon juice, divided
Lemon wedges (optional)
Fat-free Greek-style plain yogurt (optional)

1. Rinse grape leaves with cold water; drain well. Pat dry with paper towels. Remove stems; discard.
2. Heat 1 tablespoon oil in a saucepan over medium heat. Add yellow onion to pan; cook 10 minutes or until tender, stirring occasionally. Add green onions and almonds; cook 3 minutes, stirring occasionally. Stir in 2 cups water; bring

to a boil. Add rice and next 3 ingredients; cover, reduce heat, and simmer 22 minutes or until rice is tender. Remove from heat; cool. Stir in cheese and next 3 ingredients.

3. Spoon 1½ heaping tablespoons rice mixture onto center of 1 grape leaf. Bring 2 opposite points of leaf to center; fold over filling. Beginning at 1 short side, roll up leaf tightly, jelly-roll fashion. Repeat procedure with remaining rice mixture and 35 grape leaves. Place 12 stuffed grape leaves, seam sides down, in large saucepan lined with 3 grape leaves. Drizzle with 1 teaspoon oil and 1 tablespoon juice. Top with 12 stuffed grape leaves; drizzle with 1 teaspoon oil and 1 tablespoon juice. Repeat procedure with remaining 12 stuffed grape leaves, 1 teaspoon oil, and 1 tablespoon juice. Cover with remaining 3 grape leaves; pour remaining 1 cup water over leaves. Invert a small heatproof plate on top of leaves. Bring to a boil. Cover, reduce heat, and simmer 1½ hours. Remove from heat, and let stand in saucepan 2 hours. Serve at room temperature with lemon wedges and yogurt, if desired. Yield: 12 servings (serving size: 3 stuffed grape leaves).

CALORIES 128; FAT 6.5g (sat 1.9g, mono 3.4g, poly 0.8g); PROTEIN 4g; CARB 14.4g; FIBER 1.2g; CHOL 8.4mg; IRON 2.1mg; SODIUM 210mg; CALC 175mg

Olive Piadine with Arugula Salad and Caper Vinaigrette

If you don't have a pizza stone, use a preheated jelly-roll pan or baking sheet.

Dough:
5.1 ounces all-purpose flour (about 1 cup plus 2 tablespoons), divided
7 tablespoons warm water (100° to 110°), divided
1 teaspoon dry yeast
6 tablespoons coarsely chopped pitted picholine olives
1 teaspoon extra-virgin olive oil
¼ teaspoon salt
Cooking spray
1 teaspoon cornmeal

Salad:
1½ cups arugula
1½ cups frisée
¼ cup pine nuts, toasted
1½ tablespoons capers, coarsely chopped
2 tablespoons extra-virgin olive oil
½ teaspoon grated lemon rind
1 tablespoon fresh lemon juice
1½ teaspoons white wine vinegar
½ teaspoon caper brine
¼ teaspoon freshly ground black pepper
⅛ teaspoon kosher salt
½ shallot, thinly sliced
1 small garlic clove, minced

1. To prepare dough, weigh or lightly spoon flour into a dry measuring cup and spoons, and level with a knife. Combine 2 tablespoons flour, 3 tablespoons warm water, and yeast in a large bowl; let stand 20 minutes. Add remaining 4.5 ounces flour (about 1 cup), remaining ¼ cup warm water, olives, oil, and ¼ teaspoon salt; stir until smooth. Turn dough out onto a lightly floured surface. Knead until smooth and elastic (about 8 minutes); add enough flour, 1 tablespoon at a time, to prevent dough from sticking to hands (dough will feel sticky).

2. Place dough in a large bowl coated with cooking spray, turning to coat top. Cover and let rise in a warm place (85°), free from drafts, 2 hours or until doubled in size. (Gently press two fingers into dough. If indentation remains, dough has risen enough.) Punch dough down; cover and let rest 5 minutes. Divide in half. Working with one portion at a time (cover remaining dough to prevent drying), roll each portion into an 8-inch circle on a floured surface. Place dough on a baking sheet coated with cooking spray and sprinkled with cornmeal.

3. Position an oven rack in the lowest setting. Place a pizza stone on lowest rack. Preheat oven to 500°. Preheat pizza stone for 30 minutes before baking dough.

4. Slide rolled dough onto preheated pizza stone, using a spatula as a guide. Bake on lowest oven rack at 500° for 7 minutes. Remove flatbread to cutting board.

5. To prepare salad, combine arugula and remaining ingredients in a bowl; toss to coat. Place 1½ cups salad on each flatbread. Fold flatbread over salad; cut piadines in half. Yield: 4 servings (serving size: ½ piadine).

CALORIES 300; FAT 16.9g (sat 1.6g, mono 9.3g, poly 4.8g); PROTEIN 6.4g; CARB 33.5g; FIBER 1.8g; CHOL 0mg; IRON 2.7mg; SODIUM 610mg; CALC 41mg

Make Ahead
Preserved Lime Tabbouleh Salad

Preserved citrus is a key to many Moroccan and Middle Eastern dishes. Traditional recipes take weeks. Our version is ready in a few hours.

1 cup uncooked bulgur
1½ cups hot water
1 cup chopped English cucumber
¾ cup chopped seeded plum tomato
¾ cup chopped fresh flat-leaf parsley
¼ cup finely chopped shallots
3 tablespoons coarsely chopped pitted kalamata olives
1 (14-ounce) can chickpeas (garbanzo beans), rinsed and drained
3 tablespoons extra-virgin olive oil
3 tablespoons fresh lime juice
3 tablespoons water
1 teaspoon minced garlic
½ teaspoon kosher salt
½ teaspoon freshly ground black pepper
Dash of sugar
2 quarters Quick Preserved Limes (page 126), finely chopped

1. Combine bulgur and 1½ cups hot water in a medium bowl; let stand 1 hour. Drain. Combine bulgur, cucumber, and next 5 ingredients in a large bowl.

2. Place oil and remaining ingredients in a blender; process until smooth. Pour dressing over bulgur mixture; toss well to coat. Yield: 6 servings (serving size: about 1 cup).

CALORIES 226; FAT 9.4g (sat 1.1g, mono 6.3g, poly 1.4g); PROTEIN 5.7g; CARB 31.5g; FIBER 7.2g; CHOL 0mg; IRON 1.6mg; SODIUM 440mg; CALC 42mg

continued

LIGHT ICE CREAM

Forget the endless wait for summer: Infinite flavor variations make this a year-round homemade treat. Learn the basics, then riff.

The sweetest evidence of the progress made in American food can be seen in what's happened with ice cream over the last few decades. We're just not that nostalgic about the basic Neapolitan blocks of our youth—not against the deliciously dizzying array of Ben and Jerry's or other premium ice creams now available. And light ice cream has evolved even further from its watery ice-milk days. In the Test Kitchens, we like to get creative with ingredients and flavors, but we hold fast to this basic rule: We settle for no less than smooth, creamy, rich results. Read on to learn how to churn out lighter versions of your favorite flavors.

Make Ahead

Quick Preserved Limes:

This recipe works equally well with lemons—use 3 quartered. Use in grain salads or pasta dishes.

2 cups water
¼ cup kosher salt
4 limes, quartered
10 black peppercorns
1 cinnamon stick
1 bay leaf

1. Combine all ingredients in a saucepan; bring to a boil. Reduce heat, and simmer 1 hour. Cool to room temperature; cover and refrigerate. Discard peppercorns, cinnamon, and bay leaf before using. Yield: 16 servings (serving size: 1 drained lime quarter).

CALORIES 5; FAT 0g; PROTEIN 0g; CARB 1.8g; FIBER 0.5g; CHOL 0mg; IRON 0mg; SODIUM 289mg; CALC 1mg

---

Curried Cauliflower with Capers

Look for olive-size caperberries at gourmet grocers or specialty stores.

6 cups cauliflower florets (about 1 large head)
¼ cup extra-virgin olive oil, divided
2 teaspoons grated lemon rind
2 tablespoons lemon juice
½ teaspoon salt
½ teaspoon curry powder
¼ teaspoon freshly ground black pepper
⅓ cup caperberries, thinly sliced
¼ cup chopped fresh flat-leaf parsley
¼ cup capers, drained

1. Preheat oven to 450°.
2. Combine cauliflower and 1 tablespoon oil on a jelly-roll pan, tossing to coat. Bake at 450° for 30 minutes or until browned, turning once.
3. Combine remaining 3 tablespoons oil, rind, and next 4 ingredients in a large bowl; stir with a whisk. Add cauliflower, caperberries, parsley, and capers; toss mixture well to combine. Yield: 6 servings (servings size: about 1 cup).

CALORIES 107; FAT 9.5g (sat 1.3g, mono 6.6g, poly 1.2g); PROTEIN 2.1g; CARB 5.3g; FIBER 2.6g; CHOL 0mg; IRON 0.7mg; SODIUM 445mg; CALC 24mg

---

Make Ahead • Freezable

Strawberry-Rhubarb Ice Cream

Make a nonalcoholic version of this grown-up ice cream by substituting cranberry juice cocktail for the wine.

2½ cups whole milk
¾ cup half-and-half
1 cup sugar, divided
3 large egg yolks
2 cups chopped fresh rhubarb
⅓ cup fruity red wine (such as merlot)
3 cups chopped fresh strawberries (about 1 pound)

1. Combine milk and half-and-half in a heavy saucepan over medium-high heat. Heat milk mixture to 180° or until tiny bubbles form around edge (do not boil). Combine ½ cup sugar and egg yolks in a large bowl, stirring with a whisk until pale yellow. Gradually add half of hot milk mixture to egg yolk mixture, stirring constantly with a whisk. Pour egg yolk mixture into pan with remaining milk mixture; cook over medium-low heat until a thermometer registers 160° (about 2 minutes), stirring constantly. Place pan in a large ice-filled bowl for 20 minutes or until custard cools completely, stirring occasionally.
2. Combine remaining ½ cup sugar, rhubarb, and wine in a saucepan over medium-high heat; bring to a boil. Reduce heat, and simmer 8 minutes or until rhubarb is tender and liquid is syrupy. Remove from heat; let stand 10 minutes. Place rhubarb mixture and strawberries in a blender; process until smooth. Strain mixture through a sieve over a bowl, pressing with a wooden spoon; discard solids. Stir rhubarb mixture into custard mixture.
3. Pour custard into the freezer can of an ice-cream freezer; freeze according to manufacturer's instructions. Drain ice water from freezer bucket; repack with salt and ice. Cover with kitchen towels, and let stand 1 hour or until firm. Yield: 10 servings (serving size: about ¾ cup).

CALORIES 173; FAT 5.6g (sat 2.9g, mono 1.7g, poly 0.5g); PROTEIN 3.8g; CARB 28.2g; FIBER 1.3g; CHOL 74mg; IRON 0.4mg; SODIUM 36mg; CALC 123mg

---

NUTRITION NOTES

- Get at least 10% of your daily calcium needs with just one serving of any of our ice cream recipes.
- Because we use mostly reduced-fat milk with a little cream, our recipes keep saturated fat in check.

Fresh Mint Ice Cream

This make-ahead creamy treat is an ideal dessert for summertime entertaining. The basic custard lends itself to tons of flavors. Instead of mint, try ginger, cinnamon sticks, or toasted coconut flakes.

2 cups 2% reduced-fat milk
1 cup half-and-half
1 (1-ounce) package fresh mint sprigs
³⁄₄ cup sugar
Dash of salt
2 large egg yolks
Small fresh mint leaves (optional)

1. Combine first 3 ingredients in a medium heavy saucepan over medium-high heat. Heat milk mixture to 180° or until tiny bubbles form around edge (do not boil). Remove from heat; cover and let stand 10 minutes.

2. Pour milk mixture through a fine sieve over a bowl, pressing slightly with a wooden spoon; discard solids. Return liquid to pan.

3. Place sugar, salt, and egg yolks in a bowl; stir with a whisk until pale yellow. Gradually add half of hot milk mixture to egg mixture, stirring constantly with a whisk. Pour egg yolk mixture into pan with remaining milk mixture; cook over medium-low heat until a thermometer registers 160° (about 2 minutes), stirring constantly. Place pan in a large ice-filled bowl until custard cools completely, stirring occasionally. Pour mixture into the freezer can of an ice-cream freezer; freeze according to manufacturer's instructions. Drain ice water from freezer bucket; repack with salt and ice. Cover with kitchen towels, and let stand 1 hour or until firm. Garnish with mint leaves, if desired. Yield: 6 servings (serving size: about ½ cup).

CALORIES 207; **FAT** 7.6g (sat 4.4g, mono 2.4g, poly 0.5g); **PROTEIN** 4.8g; **CARB** 30.8g; **FIBER** 0g; **CHOL** 89mg; **IRON** 0.2mg; **SODIUM** 84mg; **CALC** 148mg

4 STEPS TO A SMOOTH, LIGHT ICE CREAM

1 HEAT THE MILK. The first step is to scald the milk or heat it to about 180°. If you want to infuse the custard with any herbs or spices, let those ingredients steep in the hot milk mixture, as we do for Fresh Mint Ice Cream (at left).

2 TEMPER THE EGG YOLKS. Combine sugar and yolks. Then slowly add the hot milk mixture to the yolk mixture, stirring constantly. This is a process known as tempering: slowly heating the yolks without "scrambling" them.

3 CHILL THE CUSTARD. Chilling the custard ensures it will freeze quickly and more smoothly. In fact, if you make the custard up to a day ahead and refrigerate it overnight or until it's thoroughly chilled, you'll get the best results.

4 FREEZE. Although tabletop freezers are handy and certainly work in a pinch, we like the old-fashioned churns because they typically whip more air into the custard, yielding light and fluffy results. They also have a lower freezing point.

THE BASICS OF ICE CREAM

IF YOU CHURN
If using an old-fashioned churn, pour about ½ cup salt over every 4 cups ice. Any salt will do the trick, but the smaller the grains, the faster the custard will freeze.

TIME TO FIRM UP
Ice cream from a traditional churn can be eaten right after it's frozen. A tabletop freezer yields softer results, so you need to transfer it to a container and freeze until firm.

HEAT THE MILK
It's important to scald the milk, especially if you plan to infuse it with flavors. You can steep fresh herbs, fresh ginger, a vanilla bean, or other ingredients in the hot milk. Be sure, though, not to add sugar to the milk before heating as sugar can cause the milk to curdle when hot.

Make Ahead • Freezable • Kid Friendly

Salted Caramel Ice Cream
(pictured on page 253)

If you prefer a more straightforward caramel ice cream, reduce the sea salt to ⅛ teaspoon, and omit the flake salt garnish.

3½ cups 2% reduced-fat milk
3 large egg yolks
1¼ cups packed brown sugar
¼ cup heavy cream
1 tablespoon butter
½ teaspoon sea salt
½ teaspoon flake salt

1. Place milk in a medium saucepan over medium-high heat. Heat to 180° or until tiny bubbles form around edge of pan (do not boil). Place egg yolks in a large bowl; stir with a whisk. Gradually add half of hot milk to yolks, stirring constantly. Return yolk mixture to pan.
2. Combine sugar, cream, and butter in a large saucepan over medium heat; bring to a boil, stirring until sugar melts. Cook 3 minutes without stirring. Remove from heat; stir in sea salt. Gradually add caramel mixture to yolk mixture, stirring constantly. Return pan to low heat; cook until a thermometer registers 160°.

Place pan in a large ice-filled bowl until completely cooled, stirring occasionally. Pour mixture into the freezer can of an ice-cream freezer; freeze according to manufacturer's instructions. Drain ice water from freezer bucket; repack with salt and ice. Cover with kitchen towels, and let stand 1 hour or until firm. Scoop about ½ cup ice cream into each of 10 dishes; sprinkle with flake salt. Yield: 10 servings.

CALORIES 241; FAT 7.9g (sat 4.5g, mono 2.5g, poly 0.5g); PROTEIN 4.7g; CARB 39g; FIBER 0g; CHOL 99mg; IRON 0.9mg; SODIUM 370mg; CALC 173mg

SIMPLE ADDITIONS

Quick & Easy

Mussels in Fennel Broth

Serve with a crusty baguette to soak up the flavorful broth.

1 large fennel bulb with stalks
2 garlic cloves, thinly sliced
½ cup dry vermouth
4 pounds mussels, scrubbed and debearded
2 tablespoons butter

Chop fennel to measure 2 cups. Chop fennel fronds to measure 1 tablespoon. Heat a large Dutch oven over medium-high heat. Add chopped fennel bulb and garlic; sauté 3 minutes. Add 1 cup water and vermouth to pan; bring to a boil. Cover, reduce heat, and simmer 3 minutes or until fennel is tender. Add mussels to pan; cover and cook 5 minutes or until shells open. Remove mussels from pan and keep warm; discard any unopened shells. Remove pan from heat, and add 2 tablespoons butter, stirring until butter melts. Serve fennel broth over mussels, and sprinkle with fennel fronds. Yield: 4 servings (serving size: about 1 pound mussels and ½ cup broth).

CALORIES 288; FAT 11.4g (sat 4.7g, mono 2.7g, poly 1.7g); PROTEIN 30.7g; CARB 14.4g; FIBER 1.9g; CHOL 85mg; IRON 10.5mg; SODIUM 788mg; CALC 100mg

THE FIVE INGREDIENTS

1 large fennel bulb with stalks

+

2 garlic cloves, thinly sliced

+

½ cup dry vermouth

+

4 pounds mussels, scrubbed and debearded

+

2 tablespoons butter

LESS MEAT, MORE FLAVOR

JUST AS SLOPPILY GOOD

By Mark Bittman

The *How to Cook Everything* author tackles an American handful, with satisfying results.

I am not a vegetarian. But I now eat way more vegetables than meat.

About three years ago—after some scary news about my cholesterol and blood sugar—I flipped my diet so that plant foods provide at least 70 percent of my daily calories and the rest come from animal protein and everything else. (You can do this informally, like I did, or keep a log and count.)

Swapping in a lot more plants delivers more disease-fighting nutrients and can also help you lose weight and reduce the risk of obesity-related diseases. In my case, I lost more than 30 pounds in the first few months without paying attention to much of anything aside from the proportion of plants I was eating. And there's a second benefit: Eating this way is good for the planet because raising animals puts more stress on the environment than growing plants.

Meat is undeniably delicious, and that's why my approach to cooking will always be almost meatless. The idea is to augment small quantities of meat (generally no more than a couple of ounces per person at a sitting—even less than in many *Cooking Light* recipes) with satisfying and nutritious foods that fit the "mostly plants" bill. I now eat whole grains whenever possible, after drastically reducing my intake of refined carbohydrates. No denial or guilt, and nothing strange. Just a shift in mind-set. Easy, successful, and sane.

My goal is simple: I'll remake traditional dishes so they contain more vegetables, learning new techniques that maximize the flavor and impact of meat and other animal products, and

introducing new ways of thinking about meals, snacks, and holiday fare. I'll also tackle some "convenience food" make-ahead dishes that, for me, form the backbone of everyday sane cooking.

Quick & Easy

Almost Meatless Sloppy Joes

2 tablespoons olive oil
1/2 cup finely chopped white onion
1 tablespoon minced garlic
1/2 teaspoon salt
1/4 teaspoon freshly ground black pepper
6 ounces ground sirloin
1/2 cup grated carrot
2 teaspoons chili powder
1 teaspoon brown sugar
1/2 teaspoon dried oregano
1/4 teaspoon ground red pepper
2 cups canned crushed tomatoes
1 (15.5-ounce) can low-sodium red beans, rinsed, drained, and divided
4 (2-ounce) whole-wheat sandwich rolls, split and toasted
4 (1/4-inch-thick) red onion slices, separated into rings

1. Heat olive oil in a large skillet over medium-high heat. Add onion and next 4 ingredients to pan; cook 5 minutes or until meat is browned and vegetables are tender, stirring occasionally to crumble beef.
2. Add carrot and next 4 ingredients; cook 2 minutes, stirring occasionally. Stir in tomatoes; bring to a boil. Reduce heat to medium; cook 10 minutes or until thickened and carrot is tender, stirring occasionally.
3. Partially mash 1 cup beans with a fork or potato masher. Add mashed beans and remaining whole beans to pan; cook 1 minute or until thoroughly heated. Spoon 1 cup bean mixture onto bottom half of each roll; top each serving with 1 red onion slice and top half of roll. Yield: 4 servings (serving size: 1 sandwich).

CALORIES 405; FAT 14.4g (sat 3.2g, mono 7.5g, poly 2.3g); PROTEIN 19.4g; CARB 53.3g; FIBER 10.4g; CHOL 28mg; IRON 5.1mg; SODIUM 781mg; CALC 148mg

Quick & Easy

Sloppy Lentils in Pita

1 tablespoon olive oil
3/4 cup finely chopped onion
1 tablespoon minced garlic
1/2 teaspoon salt
1/4 teaspoon freshly ground black pepper
8 ounces lean ground lamb
3/4 cup dried brown lentils
1 teaspoon ground cumin
1 teaspoon dried thyme
1 cup water, divided
2 cups diced plum tomatoes or boxed diced tomatoes, undrained
1 bay leaf
4 (6-inch) whole-wheat pitas, cut in half
1/2 cup plain 2% Greek-style yogurt
1 cup thinly sliced cucumber
Chopped fresh mint (optional)

1. Heat olive oil in a large skillet over medium-high heat. Add onion and next 4 ingredients; cook 5 minutes or until lamb is browned and vegetables are tender, stirring occasionally to crumble lamb.
2. Add lentils, cumin, and thyme; stir until seasonings become fragrant. Add 1/2 cup water, tomatoes, and bay leaf; bring to a boil. Cover, reduce heat to medium, and cook 15 minutes. Stir lentil mixture; add remaining 1/2 cup water. Cover and cook 15 minutes or until lentils are tender and mixture is thick (add additional water as needed). Discard bay leaf. Fill each pita half with 1/2 cup lentil mixture. Spoon 1 tablespoon yogurt into each pita half, and top with 2 tablespoons cucumber. Sprinkle with mint, if desired. Yield: 4 servings (serving size: 2 filled pita halves).

CALORIES 454; FAT 13.8g (sat 4.4g, mono 5.8g, poly 1.4g); PROTEIN 28.2g; CARB 57.4g; FIBER 11.6g; CHOL 39mg; IRON 4.9mg; SODIUM 716mg; CALC 115mg

A READER'S TACO SALAD

Margee Berry enjoys grilling year-round, even during the rainy winters in Washington state. She created her own version of a taco salad. Chipotle hot sauce and cumin bring a smoky Southwestern flavor, and the shrimp, black beans, and fresh vegetables add color and texture.

Quick & Easy • Kid Friendly

Southwestern-Style Shrimp Taco Salad

"Taco salads in restaurants are tasty but loaded with calories, fat, and sodium. That's why I make my own with the same Mexican smokiness and spices."

—Margee Berry, Trout Lake, Washington

1/4 cup fresh lime juice
2 tablespoons olive oil
1 teaspoon ground cumin
2 teaspoons minced garlic
2 teaspoons maple syrup
2 teaspoons chipotle hot sauce
3/4 pound medium shrimp, peeled and deveined
2 ears shucked corn
Cooking spray
1 cup chopped romaine lettuce
1/2 cup chopped green onions
1/4 cup chopped fresh cilantro
1 (15-ounce) can black beans, rinsed and drained
3 plum tomatoes, chopped
2 ounces baked blue corn tortilla chips (about 1 1/2 cups)
1/3 cup light sour cream
1/4 cup diced peeled avocado
Lime wedges (optional)

1. Prepare grill to medium-high heat.
2. Combine first 6 ingredients in a small bowl, stirring with a whisk. Place shrimp in a shallow bowl. Drizzle 1 tablespoon lime juice mixture over shrimp, tossing gently to coat. Reserve remaining lime juice mixture; set aside. Thread shrimp onto metal skewers. Lightly coat corn with cooking spray. Place shrimp kebabs and corn on a grill rack coated with cooking spray. Grill 8 minutes, turning kebabs once and turning corn frequently until browned. Remove from grill; cool slightly.
3. Remove shrimp from skewers, and place in a large bowl. Cut kernels from ears of corn. Add corn, lettuce, and next 4 ingredients to shrimp. Drizzle reserved lime juice mixture over shrimp mixture, and toss gently to combine.
4. Divide tortilla chips evenly among 6 shallow bowls; top each serving with 1 cup shrimp mixture. Combine sour cream and avocado in a small bowl; mash with a fork until well blended. Top each serving with about 1 tablespoon sour cream mixture. Serve with a lime wedge, if desired. Yield: 6 servings.

CALORIES 228; FAT 8.5g (sat 1.8g, mono 4.4g, poly 1.4g); PROTEIN 16.2g; CARB 25.5g; FIBER 4.5g; CHOL 91mg; IRON 2.7mg; SODIUM 327mg; CALC 79mg

Kid Friendly

Lemon-Rosemary Chicken Breasts

A former personal chef, Wendy Collett uses fresh asparagus and creamy polenta to make an easy and elegant dinner for company.

1 1/2 tablespoons olive oil
1/2 teaspoon salt, divided
1/2 teaspoon black pepper, divided
4 (8-ounce) bone-in chicken breast halves, skinned
1 1/2 cups fat-free, less-sodium chicken broth
1/3 cup fresh lemon juice
1 fresh rosemary sprig

1. Preheat oven to 375°.
2. Heat a large skillet over medium-high heat; add oil. Sprinkle 1/4 teaspoon salt and 1/4 teaspoon pepper over chicken. Add chicken; cook 3 minutes on each side. Arrange chicken in a 13 x 9–inch baking dish. Bake at 375° for 25 minutes or until a thermometer registers 165°. Remove from oven; cover and let stand 15 minutes.
3. Heat skillet over medium-high heat. Add broth, juice, and rosemary sprig. Bring to a boil, scraping pan to loosen browned bits; reduce heat, and simmer 20 minutes or until broth mixture measures 1/3 cup. Discard rosemary sprig; stir in remaining 1/4 teaspoon salt and 1/4 teaspoon pepper. Serve sauce with chicken. Yield: 4 servings (serving size: 1 breast half and about 1 tablespoon sauce).

CALORIES 230; FAT 8.9g (sat 1.8g, mono 5g, poly 1.4g); PROTEIN 33.4g; CARB 2.3g; FIBER 0.5g; CHOL 89mg; IRON 1.3mg; SODIUM 518mg; CALC 24mg

Make Ahead • Kid Friendly

Almond Butter Snickerdoodles

"Other nut butters, such as cashew or peanut, work equally well in these cookies."

—Michaela Rosenthal
Woodland Hills, California

1 cup packed brown sugar
1/3 cup (about 3 ounces) 1/3-less-fat cream cheese, softened
1/4 cup unsalted butter, softened
2 tablespoons smooth almond butter
1 teaspoon grated lemon rind
1 teaspoon vanilla extract
2 large egg yolks, lightly beaten
4.75 ounces white whole-wheat flour (about 1 cup)
1.5 ounces whole-wheat flour (about 1/3 cup)
1 teaspoon baking soda
1 1/2 teaspoons ground cinnamon, divided
1/2 teaspoon salt
2 tablespoons granulated sugar

1. Preheat oven to 350°.
2. Line a large baking sheet with parchment paper.
3. Place first 4 ingredients in a medium bowl, and beat with a mixer at high speed until well combined (about 2 minutes). Add rind, vanilla, and egg yolks; beat until well blended.
4. Weigh or lightly spoon flours into dry measuring cups; level with a knife. Combine flours, baking soda, 1/2 teaspoon cinnamon, and salt; stir with a whisk. Add flour mixture to butter mixture; beat at low speed until well combined. Drop half of dough by rounded tablespoons onto prepared baking sheet. Combine remaining 1 teaspoon

cinnamon and granulated sugar in a small bowl; sprinkle half of cinnamon-sugar mixture evenly over cookies. Bake at 350° for 6 minutes; flatten cookies with back of a spatula. Bake an additional 6 minutes. Cool on pans 1 minute. Remove from pans, and cool on wire racks. Repeat procedure with remaining dough and sugar mixture. Yield: 2 dozen (serving size: 1 cookie).

CALORIES 104; FAT 3.8g (sat 1.9g, mono 1.2g, poly 0.3g); PROTEIN 1.6g; CARB 16.2g; FIBER 0.5g; CHOL 25mg; IRON 0.7mg; SODIUM 127mg; CALC 19mg

Quick & Easy

Roasted Corn and Radish Salad with Avocado-Herb Dressing

"Make the dressing first, and refrigerate the remaining half in plastic wrap. Serve the extra dressing with crudités or baked tortilla chips."
—Riki Senn, Milford, Delaware

1/2 ripe peeled avocado, sliced
1 teaspoon fresh lime juice
2 ears yellow corn with husks
2 heads Boston or Bibb lettuce
1/2 cup thinly sliced radishes
1/2 cup Avocado-Herb Dressing

1. Preheat oven to 450°.
2. Combine avocado and juice in a small bowl; cover and refrigerate. Trim both ends of corn cobs, leaving husks intact. Place corn on a baking sheet. Bake at 450° for 20 minutes or until tender. Cool. Remove husks from corn; scrub silks from corn. Cut kernels from ears of corn; discard cobs.
3. Reserve 4 whole lettuce leaves. Chop remaining lettuce to measure 4 cups. Combine chopped lettuce, avocado mixture, corn, and radishes. Spoon lettuce mixture into lettuce leaves. Serve with Avocado-Herb Dressing. Yield: 4 servings (serving size: 1 lettuce leaf, 1 cup salad, and 2 tablespoons dressing).

CALORIES 151; FAT 7.7g (sat 1.3g, mono 3.6g, poly 1.6g); PROTEIN 4.4g; CARB 209g; FIBER 4.8g; CHOL 4mg; IRON 1.8mg; SODIUM 192mg; CALC 38mg

Quick & Easy
Avocado-Herb Dressing:
1/2 cup light mayonnaise
1/4 cup finely chopped green onions
1/4 cup reduced-fat sour cream
1 tablespoon chopped fresh flat-leaf parsley
1 tablespoon chopped fresh chives
1 teaspoon chopped fresh tarragon
1 teaspoon anchovy paste
1/8 teaspoon salt
1/2 ripe peeled avocado
1 garlic clove, minced
2 tablespoons water
1 tablespoon white wine vinegar
3 drops hot sauce

1. Place first 10 ingredients in a food processor; process until smooth. With processor running, pour 2 tablespoons water, vinegar, and hot sauce through food chute, processing until blended. Store dressing in an airtight container in refrigerator. Yield: 1¼ cups (serving size: 1 tablespoon).

CALORIES 19; FAT 1.4g (sat 0.3g, mono 0.5g, poly 0.3g); PROTEIN 0.3g; CARB 1.8g; FIBER 0.3g; CHOL 2mg; IRON 0.1mg; SODIUM 87mg; CALC 2mg

RECIPE HALL OF FAME
OUR FAVORITE STRAWBERRY-ALMOND CREAM TART

Nestled in a creamy filling and crumbly graham cracker crust, strawberries shine in this delectable tart.

Make Ahead • Kid Friendly
Strawberry-Almond Cream Tart
Crust:
36 honey graham crackers (9 sheets)
2 tablespoons sugar
2 tablespoons butter, melted
4 teaspoons water
Cooking spray

Filling:
2/3 cup (about 5 ounces) 1/3-less-fat cream cheese
1/4 cup sugar
1/2 teaspoon vanilla extract
1/4 teaspoon almond extract
Topping:
6 cups small fresh strawberries, hulled and divided
2/3 cup sugar
1 tablespoon cornstarch
1 tablespoon fresh lemon juice
2 tablespoons sliced almonds, toasted

1. Preheat oven to 350°.
2. To prepare crust, place crackers in a food processor; process until crumbly. Add 2 tablespoons sugar, butter, and 4 teaspoons water; pulse just until moist. Place cracker mixture in a 9-inch round removable-bottom tart pan lightly coated with cooking spray, pressing into bottom and up sides of pan to ¾ inch. Bake at 350° for 10 minutes or until lightly browned. Cool completely on a wire rack.
3. To prepare filling, combine cream cheese and next 3 ingredients in a medium bowl; stir until smooth. Spread cream cheese mixture evenly over bottom of tart shell.
4. To prepare topping, place 2 cups strawberries in food processor, and process until smooth. Combine strawberry puree, 2/3 cup sugar, and cornstarch in a small saucepan over medium heat; stir with a whisk. Bring to a boil, stirring constantly. Reduce heat to low; cook 1 minute. Remove glaze from heat. Cool to room temperature, stirring occasionally.
5. Combine remaining 4 cups strawberries and juice, and toss to coat. Arrange berries, bottoms up, in a circular pattern over filling. Spoon half of glaze evenly over berries (reserve remaining glaze for another use). Sprinkle nuts around edge. Cover and chill 3 hours. Yield: 10 servings (serving size: 1 wedge).

CALORIES 235; FAT 7.8g (sat 2.9g, mono 1.2g, poly 0.4g); PROTEIN 4.1g; CARB 38.6g; FIBER 2.4g; CHOL 14mg; IRON 0.6mg; SODIUM 176mg; CALC 33mg

NUTRITION MADE EASY
GOOD TO GO

Smoothies make a refreshing snack. Keeping them simple and sanely sized also keeps them healthy.

Silly is the kindest word to describe the national habit of finding something good for us and then supersizing it. Start with a nutritious-if-humble blend of fresh fruit and low-fat dairy, then bloat it into a calorie monster, courtesy of a 40-ounce smoothie-shop cup. Locate some "fat-blasting, energy-boosting" stuff, and throw that in, as well. Voilà—as much as a thousand calories in a cup.

More of a good thing isn't always better. We're here to reclaim the healthy essence of the smoothie: fruits, vegetables, and lower-fat dairy, lightly sweetened, and whirred into a refreshing drink. Sized sensibly, it's ideal as a snack or healthy on-the-go breakfast. Start your blenders!

Quick & Easy • Kid Friendly

Peach-Mango Smoothie

⅔ cup frozen sliced peaches
⅔ cup frozen mango pieces (such as Dole)
⅔ cup peach nectar
1 tablespoon honey
1 (6-ounce) container organic peach fat-free
    yogurt

1. Place all ingredients in a blender; process 2 minutes or until smooth. Serve immediately. Yield: 2 servings (serving size: 1 cup).

CALORIES 184; FAT 0.3g (sat 0.1g, mono 0.1g, poly 0.1g);
PROTEIN 4.1g; CARB 44g; FIBER 2.4g; CHOL 2mg;
IRON 0.4mg; SODIUM 50mg; CALC 107mg

Quick & Easy • Kid Friendly

Strawberry-Guava Smoothie

1 cup quartered strawberries (about
    5 ounces)
½ cup guava nectar
1 (6-ounce) container organic strawberry
    fat-free yogurt
1 frozen sliced ripe small banana
5 ice cubes (about 2 ounces)

1. Place all ingredients in a blender; process 2 minutes or until smooth. Serve immediately. Yield: 2 servings (serving size: about 1¼ cups).

CALORIES 156; FAT 0.5g (sat 0.1g, mono 0.1g, poly 0.2g);
PROTEIN 4.2g; CARB 36.2g; FIBER 3.6g; CHOL 2mg;
IRON 0.5mg; SODIUM 49mg; CALC 116mg

Quick & Easy • Kid Friendly

Banana Breakfast Smoothie

Prepare this and take along a handful of granola for a quick breakfast on the go. Adding the yogurt at the very end imparts a creamy texture to the smoothie.

½ cup 1% low-fat milk
½ cup crushed ice
1 tablespoon honey
⅛ teaspoon ground nutmeg
1 frozen sliced ripe large banana
1 cup plain Greek 2% yogurt

1. Place first 5 ingredients in a blender; process 2 minutes or until smooth. Add yogurt; process just until blended. Serve immediately. Yield: 2 servings (serving size: 1 cup).

CALORIES 212; FAT 3.6g (sat 2.5g, mono 0.2g, poly 0.1g);
PROTEIN 14.2g; CARB 34.2g; FIBER 2g; CHOL 9mg;
IRON 0.3mg; SODIUM 75mg; CALC 200mg

Quick & Easy • Kid Friendly

Cucumber, Apple, and Mint Cooler

Each serving of this smoothie offers a half-cup of vegetables, plus a little fruit.

1 cup chopped seeded peeled cucumber
    (about ½ pound)
⅓ cup unsweetened frozen 100% apple juice
    concentrate, undiluted
¼ cup cold water
¼ cup chopped fresh mint
10 ice cubes (about 4 ounces)

1. Place all ingredients in a blender; process 2 minutes or until smooth. Serve immediately. Yield: 2 servings (serving size: 1 cup).

CALORIES 91; FAT 0.4g (sat 0.1g, mono 0g, poly 0.1g);
PROTEIN 1g; CARB 21.6g; FIBER 1.4g; CHOL 0mg;
IRON 2mg; SODIUM 16mg; CALC 41mg

Quick & Easy • Kid Friendly

Carrot, Apple, and Ginger Refresher

½ cup 100% carrot juice, chilled
½ cup unsweetened applesauce
½ cup organic vanilla fat-free yogurt
1 teaspoon fresh lemon juice
½ teaspoon grated peeled fresh ginger
1 frozen sliced ripe banana
5 ice cubes (about 2 ounces)

1. Place all ingredients in a blender; process 2 minutes or until smooth. Serve immediately. Yield: 2 servings (serving size: about 1¼ cups).

CALORIES 138; FAT 0.1g (sat 0g, mono 0g, poly 0.1g);
PROTEIN 4.3g; CARB 32.7g; FIBER 2.3g; CHOL 2mg;
IRON 0.3mg; SODIUM 79mg; CALC 126mg

BREAKFAST, LUNCH, AND DINNER IN... WASHINGTON, D.C.

Conservative politics were not all that dominated the nation's capital for most of the past quarter-century. Washington, D.C., was culinarily conservative, too, to a degree that no recent tourist or transplant can perhaps appreciate. Most downtown dining rooms were formal places, and if you weren't wealthy, then you probably weren't going to dine all that well. No more. The city has witnessed an unprecedented boom of activity over the past seven years as a slew of cooking styles has transformed where and how Washingtonians eat.

"We now have some of the best restaurants in the world, an enormous variety of ethnic restaurants, and a good crop of high-quality casual restaurants," says Phyllis Richman, former food critic for the *Washington Post*, adding that while the city belongs, for the first time, in the culinary company of New York and L.A., it's also blessedly free of "the high-powered tension that comes with their dining scenes."

Breakfast
Savory Buckwheat Crepes with Ham and Mornay Sauce

No place in the city is more evocative of European elegance than Café du Parc (cafeduparc.com). The restaurant is part of the famous Willard Hotel, a block away from the White House, and its menus are overseen by Antoine Westermann, a 3-star Michelin chef with restaurants in Paris and Strasbourg. Tradition trumps innovation; classic French dishes evince a reverence for technical mastery that results in precise, cleanly cooked dishes. At breakfast, look to the buckwheat crepes, light and nutty, filled with ham and Gruyère. In this recipe, inspired by Café du Parc, use a younger Gruyère rather than well-aged cheese to help prevent the sauce from breaking.

Crepes:
3 ounces all-purpose flour (about ²/₃ cup)
1 cup fat-free milk
2 tablespoons buckwheat flour
¼ teaspoon salt
1 large egg, lightly beaten
Cooking spray

Filling:
1 cup chopped 33%-less-sodium smoked ham
1 garlic clove, thinly sliced
4 cups sliced shiitake mushroom caps (about 10 ounces)
½ cup fat-free, less-sodium chicken broth
1 tablespoon minced fresh flat-leaf parsley
¼ teaspoon freshly ground black pepper
6 tablespoons (1½ ounces) shredded Gruyère cheese

Sauce:
2 tablespoons butter
3 tablespoons minced shallots
1 tablespoon all-purpose flour
1½ cups fat-free milk
½ cup (2 ounces) shredded Gruyère cheese
¼ teaspoon salt
¼ teaspoon freshly ground black pepper
Dash of freshly grated nutmeg

1. To prepare crepes, weigh or lightly spoon 3 ounces (about ²/₃ cup) all-purpose flour into dry measuring cups; level with a knife. Combine all-purpose flour and next 4 ingredients in a medium bowl, stirring with a whisk until smooth. Cover and let stand at room temperature 30 minutes.
2. Heat a 9-inch crepe pan or nonstick skillet over medium heat. Coat pan with cooking spray. Pour about ¼ cup batter into center of pan; quickly tilt pan in all directions so batter covers pan with a thin film. Cook about 1 minute. Carefully lift edge of crepe with a spatula to test for doneness. Turn crepe over when it can be shaken loose from pan and underside is lightly browned; cook 30 seconds. Place crepe on a towel; cool. Repeat procedure five times with remaining batter. Stack crepes between single layers of wax paper or paper towels to prevent sticking.
3. Preheat oven to 300°.
4. To prepare filling, heat a large nonstick skillet over medium heat. Coat pan with cooking spray. Add ham and garlic to pan; cook 3 minutes or until garlic is tender and ham is lightly browned, stirring frequently. Add mushrooms; reduce heat to medium-low. Cover and cook 10 minutes or until mushrooms start to soften, stirring occasionally. Add broth, parsley, and pepper; cook, uncovered, 10 minutes or until liquid evaporates and mushrooms are tender. Remove from heat.
5. Spoon ⅓ cup ham mixture into center of each crepe. Top each with 1 tablespoon cheese; fold sides over. Place filled crepes in an 11 x 7–inch baking dish. Cover with foil; bake at 300° for 20 minutes or until thoroughly heated.
6. To prepare sauce, melt butter in a medium saucepan over medium-low heat. Add shallots; cook 5 minutes or until tender, stirring frequently. Sprinkle 1 tablespoon all-purpose flour into pan; cook 2 minutes, stirring constantly. Slowly add 1½ cups milk, stirring constantly with a whisk until smooth; bring to a simmer over medium heat. Reduce heat, and simmer 10 minutes or until sauce thickens, stirring frequently. Remove from heat. Strain sauce through a fine mesh sieve into a bowl; discard solids. Rinse and dry pan; place over low heat, and return strained sauce to pan. Stir in ½ cup cheese and remaining ingredients; stir until cheese melts. Serve sauce with crepes. Yield: 6 servings (serving size: 1 filled crepe and about 2½ tablespoons sauce).

CALORIES 249; **FAT** 11.3g (sat 6.2g, mono 3.5g, poly 0.7g); **PROTEIN** 15.1g; **CARB** 22g; **FIBER** 1.5g; **CHOL** 74mg; **IRON** 1.8mg; **SODIUM** 515mg; **CALC** 308mg

Lunch

Spicy Ethiopian Red Lentil Stew

The large population of Ethiopian immigrants in the D.C. metro area has a considerable influence on the city's cultural life. It's not a stretch to say that feasting on the various wats, or slow-simmered stews, of the city's Ethiopian restaurants when visiting D.C. is akin to chowing down on pizza in New York or cheesesteaks in Philadelphia. Etete (eteterestaurant.com), which translates as "mama" in Amharic, is one of the city's best. It resides in the heart of Little Ethiopia. "Mama" is Tiwaltenigus Shenegelegn, and if you're lucky, she may swing by your table. For this dish, inspired by Etete, you'll need Ethiopian Berbere spice, a mixture of dried chiles, cloves, ginger, coriander, and allspice. Look for it at gourmet markets and specialty stores, or order it from americanspice.com.

2 teaspoons canola oil
2 cups chopped red onion
1 tablespoon minced peeled fresh ginger
3 garlic cloves, minced
3 tablespoons tomato paste
1½ tablespoons Berbere spice
3 cups organic vegetable broth
1 cup dried small red lentils
¼ teaspoon salt
¼ cup finely chopped fresh cilantro
4 cups hot cooked basmati rice

1. Heat oil in a large Dutch oven over medium heat. Add onion to pan; cook 15 minutes or until tender, stirring occasionally. Add ginger and garlic; cook 5 minutes, stirring frequently. Stir in tomato paste and Berbere spice; cook 1 minute, stirring to combine. Gradually add broth, stirring with a whisk until blended. Increase heat to medium-high; bring to a simmer.
2. Rinse lentils under cold water; drain. Add lentils to broth mixture; simmer, partially covered, 35 minutes or until lentils are tender, stirring occasionally. Stir in salt. Sprinkle with cilantro; serve over rice. Yield: 4 servings (serving size: 1 cup lentils and 1 cup rice).

CALORIES 454; FAT 3.9g (sat 0.3g, mono 1g, poly 1g); PROTEIN 19g; CARB 85.5g; FIBER 9.5g; CHOL 0mg; IRON 5.1mg; SODIUM 867mg; CALC 43mg

Dinner

Grilled Sardines with Beluga Lentils

Komi (komirestaurant.com) is a Mediterranean restaurant that speaks with a pronounced Greek accent (Chef Johnny Monis's parents grew up along the Aegean). This is no place for rushed power dining—each meal is a long, leisurely affair, from a multicourse procession of meze that shows off Monis's willingness to splurge (the seafood, in particular, tastes as if it has just been pulled from the deep) to a communal-style platter of roasted baby goat or pig.

2 tablespoons cardamom pods, crushed
1½ teaspoons cumin seeds
3 cups water
2 cups organic vegetable broth
1 bay leaf
1½ cups uncooked dried beluga lentils
1 tablespoon olive oil
¼ cup finely chopped shallots
4 garlic cloves, minced
½ teaspoon salt, divided
½ teaspoon ground black pepper
12 (3-ounce) cleaned whole fresh sardines
Cooking spray
2 tablespoons fresh lemon juice
4 cups gourmet salad greens
3 tablespoons sherry vinegar

1. Place cardamom and cumin in a large saucepan over medium heat; cook 5 minutes or until toasted, stirring occasionally. Add 3 cups water, broth, and bay leaf; bring to a boil. Reduce heat to low; simmer 40 minutes. Strain mixture through a sieve over a bowl, reserving liquid. Discard solids.
2. Combine cooking liquid and lentils in pan; bring to a boil. Remove from heat; cover. Let stand 18 minutes or until lentils are just tender; drain.
3. Heat olive oil in a large skillet over medium-high heat. Add shallots; sauté 2 minutes or until tender. Add garlic; cook 1 minute, stirring constantly. Add lentils, ¼ teaspoon salt, and pepper. Remove from heat; set aside.
4. Prepare grill to medium-high heat.
5. Arrange fish on grill rack coated with cooking spray; grill 4 minutes or until skin is crisp. Turn; grill 3 minutes or until desired degree of doneness. Remove from grill. Sprinkle with remaining ¼ teaspoon salt; drizzle with juice.
6. Combine greens and vinegar. Arrange 1 cup greens on each of 4 plates; top each with 1 cup lentils. Arrange 3 sardines on each plate. Yield: 4 servings.

CALORIES 521; FAT 7.3g (sat 1.2g, mono 3.9g, poly 1.4g); PROTEIN 57.9g; CARB 57.1g; FIBER 12.1g; CHOL 90mg; IRON 11.9mg; SODIUM 866mg; CALC 106mg

BUDGET COOKING
FEED 4 FOR LESS THAN $10

Enjoy inspired, international flavors without breaking the bank.

Kid Friendly
Zucchini, Cherry Tomato, and Fresh Ricotta Pasta

$1.62 per serving, $6.48 total
Our quick ricotta method is inexpensive and easy, and it truly makes this weeknight pasta dish shine.

3 cups whole milk
½ cup buttermilk
3½ teaspoons salt, divided
6 quarts water
8 ounces uncooked fettuccine
1 tablespoon olive oil
2 medium zucchini, halved lengthwise and sliced crosswise
¼ teaspoon freshly ground black pepper
1 teaspoon minced garlic
1½ cups cherry tomatoes, halved
2 tablespoons small fresh mint leaves

1. Combine milk and buttermilk in a small heavy saucepan over medium heat; bring to a boil, stirring occasionally. Remove from heat; drain. Place milk solids in a small bowl; sprinkle with ⅛ teaspoon salt. Toss gently to combine.

2. Bring 6 quarts water to a boil in a large Dutch oven. Stir in 1 tablespoon salt and pasta; cook 7 minutes or until al dente. Drain.

3. Heat a large nonstick skillet over medium-high heat. Add oil to pan; swirl to coat. Add zucchini; sauté 2 minutes, stirring occasionally. Stir in ¼ teaspoon salt, pepper, and garlic; sauté 2 minutes, stirring frequently; stir in tomatoes. Combine remaining ⅛ teaspoon salt, pasta, and tomato mixture in a large bowl; toss. Top with ricotta and mint. Yield: 4 servings (serving size: 1½ cups).

CALORIES 380; **FAT** 11.4g (sat 4.8g, mono 4g, poly 0.8g); **PROTEIN** 14.5g; **CARB** 56.5g; **FIBER** 3.2g; **CHOL** 23mg; **IRON** 2.3mg; **SODIUM** 593mg; **CALC** 235mg

Kid Friendly

Chicken Enchiladas

$2.46 per serving, $9.85 total

This dish offers make-ahead options: You can assemble the enchiladas up to two days ahead, cover, refrigerate, and bake them before serving. And if your family eats in shifts, just make individual servings.

2 tablespoons olive oil, divided
4 (8-ounce) bone-in chicken thighs, skinned
¼ cup (2 ounces) ⅓-less-fat cream cheese, softened
2 tablespoons chopped fresh cilantro
¼ teaspoon salt
¼ teaspoon black pepper
2 cups chopped onion
3 garlic cloves, minced
1 teaspoon chili powder
½ teaspoon ground red pepper
¼ teaspoon ground cumin
1 cup fat-free, less-sodium chicken broth
¾ cup water
1 (14.5-ounce) can diced tomatoes
9 (6-inch) corn tortillas, divided
Cooking spray
¼ cup (1 ounce) shredded cheddar cheese
2 green onions, thinly sliced

1. Preheat oven to 375°.

2. Heat 1 tablespoon oil in a large oven-proof skillet over medium-high heat. Add chicken to pan; sauté 6 minutes on each side. Place skillet in oven; bake

at 375° for 10 minutes or until done. Remove chicken from pan; let stand 15 minutes. Remove meat from bones; shred. Discard bones. Place chicken in a medium bowl; stir in cream cheese and next 3 ingredients.

3. Heat a medium saucepan over medium-high heat. Add remaining 1 tablespoon oil to pan, and swirl to coat. Add onion, and sauté 5 minutes or until tender, stirring occasionally. Add garlic; sauté 30 seconds, stirring constantly. Remove 3 tablespoons onion mixture; add to chicken. Add chili powder, red pepper, and cumin to remaining onion mixture in pan; sauté 30 seconds, stirring constantly. Stir in chicken broth, ¾ cup water, and tomatoes; bring to a boil. Tear 1 tortilla into small pieces; add to tomato mixture. Reduce heat to medium, and simmer 30 minutes, stirring occasionally. Remove from heat; let stand 10 minutes. Carefully pour tomato mixture into a blender, and process until smooth.

4. Spread ½ cup tomato mixture in the bottom of an 11 x 7–inch glass or ceramic baking dish lightly coated with cooking spray. Warm remaining 8 tortillas according to package directions. Spoon about ¼ cup chicken mixture down center of each tortilla; roll up. Place seam-side down in prepared dish. Pour remaining tomato mixture over filled tortillas. Sprinkle filled tortillas with cheddar cheese. Bake at 375° for 25 minutes or until bubbly and lightly browned. Sprinkle with green onions. Yield: 4 servings (serving size: 2 enchiladas).

CALORIES 496; **FAT** 23.4g (sat 7.3g, mono 10.5g, poly 3.7g); **PROTEIN** 30.9g; **CARB** 42g; **FIBER** 6.4g; **CHOL** 99mg; **IRON** 2.8mg; **SODIUM** 711mg; **CALC** 221mg

Quick & Easy • Kid Friendly

Spring Vegetable Carbonara

$1.93 per serving, $7.71 total

Cavatappi, spiral-shaped pasta, adds an element of whimsy to this budget-friendly dish. If you can't find it, substitute fusilli.

½ cup frozen green peas, thawed
12 ounces asparagus, trimmed and cut into 1-inch pieces
8 ounces uncooked cavatappi pasta
½ cup (2 ounces) grated pecorino Romano cheese
½ teaspoon kosher salt
½ teaspoon freshly ground black pepper
3 large eggs, lightly beaten
4 slices center-cut bacon, chopped
1 cup chopped seeded red bell pepper

1. Cook peas and asparagus in boiling water 3 minutes or until asparagus is crisp-tender; drain. Plunge into ice water; drain. Cook pasta according to package directions, omitting salt and fat. Drain pasta in a colander over a bowl, reserving ¼ cup cooking liquid. Combine pasta and vegetables.

2. Combine cheese and next 3 ingredients in a bowl, stirring well with a whisk. Gradually add hot cooking liquid to egg mixture, stirring constantly with a whisk. Cook bacon in a large skillet over medium heat until crisp, stirring occasionally. Remove bacon from pan, reserving 1 tablespoon drippings in pan. Add bacon to pasta mixture. Cook bell pepper in drippings 3 minutes, stirring occasionally. Add pasta mixture; cook 1 minute or until thoroughly heated. Remove pan from heat, and stir in egg mixture. Return pan to low heat; cook 2 minutes or until sauce thickens slightly, stirring constantly. Yield: 4 servings (serving size: 1¾ cups).

CALORIES 425; **FAT** 14.4g (sat 5.9g, mono 5.3g, poly 1.6g); **PROTEIN** 22.2g; **CARB** 52g; **FIBER** 5.4g; **CHOL** 183mg; **IRON** 3.6mg; **SODIUM** 614mg; **CALC** 210mg

Korean-Style Beef Skewers with Rice Noodles

$2.49 per serving, $9.97 total
Find the noodles and sambal on the ethnic aisle at the supermarket or in an Asian market.

6 tablespoons less-sodium soy sauce

1/3 cup sugar

1½ tablespoons sambal oelek (chile paste, such as Huy Fong)

1 tablespoon canola oil

1 tablespoon fresh lime juice

4 garlic cloves, minced

1 (1-pound) top sirloin steak, sliced against the grain into thin strips

½ cup water

8 ounces wide rice sticks

3 tablespoons thinly sliced green onions

1. Prepare grill to medium-high heat.
2. Combine first 6 ingredients in a zip-top bag. Add beef to bag; seal. Marinate at room temperature 30 minutes, turning once. Remove steak from bag; reserve marinade. Thread steak evenly onto 8 (8-inch) skewers. Grill 2 minutes on each side or until desired degree of doneness. Combine reserved marinade and ½ cup water in a small saucepan; bring to a boil. Cook 1 minute.
3. Soak noodles in boiling water until tender; drain. Place noodles in a large bowl. Pour reserved marinade mixture over noodles. Sprinkle with onions; toss. Serve with skewers. Yield: 4 servings (serving size: 2 skewers and ½ cup noodles).

CALORIES 303; **FAT** 8g (sat 2g, mono 3.8g, poly 1.2g); **PROTEIN** 23.9g; **CARB** 33.3g; **FIBER** 0.5g; **CHOL** 42mg; **IRON** 2.3mg; **SODIUM** 850mg; **CALC** 34mg

DINNER TONIGHT

Stopwatch-tested menus from the *Cooking Light* Test Kitchens.

30 minutes

SHOPPING LIST

Asparagus and Smoked Trout Frittata

8 ounces thin asparagus

fresh dill

green onions

canola oil

4 ounces smoked trout

2% reduced-fat milk

eggs

Parmigiano-Reggiano cheese

Watercress-Radish Salad

2 bunches watercress

radishes

olive oil

cider vinegar

whole-grain Dijon mustard

sugar

GAME PLAN

While oven heats and water comes to a boil:
- Trim asparagus.
- Skin and flake trout.
- Grate cheese.

While asparagus cooks:
- Chop dill.

While frittata bakes:
- Prepare salad.

Asparagus and Smoked Trout Frittata
with Watercress-Radish Salad
(pictured on page 253)

Shopping Tip: Smoked trout is located wherever you usually find smoked salmon. Vegetarian Swap: Omit trout, add sautéed mushrooms, and increase salt to ½ teaspoon.

8 ounces thin asparagus, trimmed and cut into 1-inch pieces

1 tablespoon 2% reduced-fat milk

¼ teaspoon freshly ground black pepper

1/8 teaspoon salt

4 large eggs

4 large egg whites

¼ cup (1 ounce) grated fresh Parmigiano-Reggiano cheese, divided

1½ teaspoons chopped fresh dill

4 ounces smoked trout, skinned and flaked into large pieces

Cooking spray

1 teaspoon canola oil

½ cup minced green onions

1. Preheat oven to 450°.
2. Cook asparagus in a large saucepan of boiling water 2 minutes. Drain and plunge asparagus into ice water; drain and pat dry.
3. Combine milk and next 4 ingredients in a medium bowl, stirring with a whisk. Stir in asparagus, 2 tablespoons cheese, dill, and trout.
4. Heat a 10-inch ovenproof skillet over medium heat. Coat pan with cooking spray. Add oil and onions to pan; cook 1 minute, stirring occasionally. Pour egg mixture into pan; stir once. Cook without stirring 2 minutes or until edges begin to set. Place pan in oven. Bake at 450° for 8 minutes or until eggs are just set. Remove from oven; sprinkle evenly with remaining 2 tablespoons cheese.
5. Preheat broiler.
6. Broil frittata 2 minutes or until lightly browned. Remove from oven; let stand 5 minutes. Cut into 8 wedges. Yield: 4 servings (serving size: 2 wedges).

CALORIES 186; **FAT** 10.2g (sat 3.4g, mono 4.2g, poly 1.5g); **PROTEIN** 19.9g; **CARB** 4.3g; **FIBER** 1.6g; **CHOL** 239mg; **IRON** 1.9mg; **SODIUM** 687mg; **CALC** 140mg

For the Watercress-Radish Salad:
Combine 1 tablespoon olive oil, 1¼ teaspoons cider vinegar, 1 teaspoon whole-grain Dijon mustard, ¼ teaspoon sugar, and ⅛ teaspoon salt in a bowl, stirring with a whisk. Toss with 2 bunches trimmed watercress and ½ cup thinly sliced radishes.

SHOPPING LIST

Chicken Milanese with Spring Greens
1 lemon
1 small shallot
spring mix salad greens
white wine vinegar
olive oil
sugar
all-purpose flour
dry breadcrumbs
2 (6-ounce) skinless, boneless chicken breast halves
egg
Parmigiano-Reggiano cheese

Parmesan–Browned Butter Orzo
fresh chives
orzo pasta
fat-free, less-sodium chicken broth
dry white wine
butter
Parmesan cheese

GAME PLAN

While shallots soak:
  ▪ Start preparing orzo.
While orzo simmers:
  ▪ Pound chicken.
  ▪ Bread chicken.
  ▪ Cook chicken.
While orzo rests:
  ▪ Toss salad.

Quick & Easy • Kid Friendly

Chicken Milanese with Spring Greens
with Parmesan-Browned Butter Orzo

¾ teaspoon fresh lemon juice
¾ teaspoon white wine vinegar
½ teaspoon minced shallots
¼ teaspoon kosher salt, divided
Dash of sugar
2 (6-ounce) skinless, boneless chicken breast halves
⅓ cup dry breadcrumbs
2 tablespoons grated Parmigiano-Reggiano cheese
2 tablespoons all-purpose flour
1 large egg white, lightly beaten
¼ teaspoon black pepper, divided
5 teaspoons olive oil, divided
2 cups packed spring mix salad greens
2 lemon wedges

1. Combine juice, vinegar, shallots, ⅛ teaspoon salt, and sugar; let stand 15 minutes.
2. Place chicken between 2 sheets of heavy-duty plastic wrap; pound to ½-inch thickness using a meat mallet or small heavy skillet.
3. Combine breadcrumbs and cheese in a shallow dish. Place flour in a shallow dish. Place egg white in a shallow dish. Sprinkle chicken with remaining ⅛ teaspoon salt and ⅛ teaspoon pepper. Dredge chicken in flour; dip in egg white. Dredge in breadcrumb mixture. Place chicken on a wire rack; let stand 5 minutes.
4. Heat 1 tablespoon oil in a large nonstick skillet over medium-high heat. Add chicken; cook 3 minutes. Turn chicken over; cook 2 minutes or until browned and done.
5. Add remaining 2 teaspoons oil and remaining ⅛ teaspoon pepper to shallot mixture; stir with a whisk. Add greens; toss gently. Place 1 chicken breast half and 1 cup salad on each of 2 plates. Serve with lemon wedges. Yield: 2 servings.

CALORIES 402; FAT 15.4g (sat 3g, mono 9g, poly 1.8g); PROTEIN 45.9g; CARB 17.7g; FIBER 1.4g; CHOL 102mg; IRON 2.2mg; SODIUM 539mg; CALC 80mg

For the Parmesan-Browned Butter Orzo:
Cook 1 tablespoon butter in a small saucepan over medium-low heat 4 minutes or until browned. Add ½ cup orzo; cook 1 minute. Add 2 tablespoons white wine; cook over medium-high heat 1 minute. Add 1¼ cups fat-free, less sodium chicken broth. Bring to a boil; reduce heat, and simmer 13 minutes. Stir in 1 tablespoon grated Parmesan; cover and let stand 5 minutes. Sprinkle with 1 tablespoon chopped chives.

SHOPPING LIST

Herbed Arugula-Tomato Salad with Chicken
1 lemon
1 pint cherry tomatoes
garlic
1 (5-ounce) package baby arugula
extra-virgin olive oil
white wine vinegar
dried herbes de Provence
Dijon mustard
pitted kalamata olives
4 (4-ounce) chicken breast cutlets

Asiago–Black Pepper Bread
garlic
French bread
Asiago cheese
olive oil

GAME PLAN

While broiler heats for bread:
  ▪ Marinate chicken.
  ▪ Halve tomatoes.
  ▪ Grate cheese for bread.
While chicken cooks:
  ▪ Prepare vinaigrette.
  ▪ Broil bread.
Toss salad and top with chicken and olives just before serving.

continued

Herbed Arugula– Tomato Salad with Chicken

with Asiago–Black Pepper Bread

Time-Saver: Thin-cut chicken cutlets cook in only four minutes.
Simple Sub: In place of arugula, try baby spinach.
Flavor Hit: Herbes de Provence lend floral complexity to the salad.

3 tablespoons extra-virgin olive oil, divided
1 teaspoon grated lemon rind
1 tablespoon fresh lemon juice
4 (4-ounce) chicken breast cutlets
Cooking spray
3/4 teaspoon salt, divided
1/2 teaspoon freshly ground black pepper, divided
2 cups halved cherry tomatoes
1 (5-ounce) package baby arugula
1 1/2 tablespoons white wine vinegar
1 teaspoon dried herbes de Provence
1/2 teaspoon Dijon mustard
1 garlic clove, minced
3 tablespoons halved pitted kalamata olives

1. Combine 1 tablespoon oil, rind, juice, and chicken; let stand 5 minutes.
2. Heat a large nonstick skillet over medium-high heat. Coat pan with cooking spray. Sprinkle chicken evenly with 1/2 teaspoon salt and 1/4 teaspoon pepper. Add chicken to pan; cook 2 minutes on each side or until done. Remove from heat; keep warm.
3. Combine tomatoes and arugula in a large bowl. Combine vinegar, herbes de Provence, mustard, garlic, remaining 1/4 teaspoon salt, and remaining 1/4 teaspoon pepper; gradually add remaining 2 tablespoons oil, stirring constantly with a whisk. Drizzle vinaigrette over salad; toss gently to coat. Divide salad evenly among 4 plates. Cut chicken cutlets across grain into thin slices; arrange 1 sliced cutlet over each salad, and top each serving with about 2 teaspoons olives. Yield: 4 servings.

CALORIES 265; **FAT** 14.2g (sat 2.1g, mono 9.5g, poly 1.8g); **PROTEIN** 28g; **CARB** 6.2g; **FIBER** 1.8g; **CHOL** 66mg; **IRON** 1.8mg; **SODIUM** 683mg; **CALC** 87mg

For the Asiago–Black Pepper Bread:
Combine 1 tablespoon olive oil and 1 minced garlic clove; brush evenly over 4 (1 1/2-ounce) French bread slices. Sprinkle 1/4 cup finely grated Asiago cheese and 1/2 teaspoon cracked black pepper evenly over bread. Broil 2 minutes or until lightly browned.

40 minutes

SHOPPING LIST

Grilled Balsamic Skirt Steak
garlic
balsamic vinegar
Worcestershire sauce
dark brown sugar
1 pound skirt steak

Sautéed Baby Spinach
garlic
1 (10-ounce) package fresh baby spinach
butter

Tomato-Vidalia–Blue Cheese Salad
2 pints grape tomatoes
1 small Vidalia onion
extra-virgin olive oil
white wine vinegar
blue cheese

GAME PLAN

While steak marinates:
- Slice garlic.
- Prepare vinaigrette.
- Prep vegetables for salad.

While steak cooks and rests:
- Prepare spinach.
- Toss salad.

Grilled Balsamic Skirt Steak

with Sautéed Baby Spinach and Tomato-Vidalia-Blue Cheese Salad

Cut the steak into smaller pieces so all of it will fit in the grill pan at once.
Prep Pointer: For bagged greens, check the use-by date and rinse even if it says "prewashed."
Simple Sub: Vidalias are particularly sweet, but any onion will work fine in the salad.

1/4 cup balsamic vinegar
1 tablespoon Worcestershire sauce
2 teaspoons dark brown sugar
1 garlic clove, minced
1 pound skirt steak, trimmed and cut into 4 pieces
Cooking spray
1/2 teaspoon kosher salt, divided
1/4 teaspoon freshly ground black pepper

1. Combine first 4 ingredients in a large zip-top plastic bag. Add steak, turning to coat; seal and marinate at room temperature 25 minutes, turning once. Remove steak from bag; discard marinade.
2. Heat a large grill pan over medium-high heat. Coat pan with cooking spray. Sprinkle both sides of steak with 1/4 teaspoon salt and pepper. Add steak to pan; cook 3 minutes on each side or until desired degree of doneness. Remove steak from pan; sprinkle with remaining 1/4 teaspoon salt. Tent with foil; let stand 5 minutes. Cut steak diagonally across grain into thin slices. Yield: 4 servings (serving size: 3 ounces).

CALORIES 201; **FAT** 10.3g (sat 4g, mono 5.2g, poly 0.4g); **PROTEIN** 22.3g; **CARB** 3.1g; **FIBER** 0g; **CHOL** 51mg; **IRON** 2.6mg; **SODIUM** 323mg; **CALC** 16mg

For the Sautéed Baby Spinach:
Melt 2 teaspoons butter in a large skillet over medium heat. Add 3 thinly sliced garlic cloves; cook 1 minute. Sprinkle with 1/4 teaspoon kosher salt and 1/8 teaspoon black pepper. Gradually add 1 (10-ounce) package fresh baby spinach; cook 1 minute or until spinach just wilts, tossing frequently.

For the Tomato-Vidalia-Blue Cheese Salad:

Combine 1 tablespoon extra-virgin olive oil, 1¼ teaspoons white wine vinegar, ¼ teaspoon kosher salt, and ⅛ teaspoon black pepper. Toss with 2½ cups halved grape tomatoes and ⅓ cup diced Vidalia onion. Sprinkle with 3 tablespoons crumbled blue cheese.

30 minutes

SHOPPING LIST

Grilled Chicken with Mint and Pine Nut Gremolata

fresh mint
1 large lemon
garlic
extra-virgin olive oil
pine nuts
4 (6-ounce) skinless, boneless chicken breast halves

Sugar Snap and Feta Salad

1 small red onion
12 ounces fresh sugar snap peas
1 small lemon
extra-virgin olive oil
white wine vinegar
honey
feta cheese

GAME PLAN

While onion slices soak:
- Bring water to a boil for peas.
- Prepare gremolata.
- Heat grill pan.

While chicken cooks:
- Cook peas.
- Prepare vinaigrette.
- Toss salad.

Quick & Easy

Grilled Chicken with Mint and Pine Nut Gremolata
with Sugar Snap and Feta Salad

Flavor Hit: Toasting pine nuts takes a few minutes but greatly intensifies their flavor. Prep Pointer: Remove only the outer yellow rind from the lemon to avoid any bitterness. Simple Sub: Most any leafy herb will work nicely—basil, parsley, or cilantro in particular.

Gremolata:
1 cup loosely packed fresh mint leaves
2 tablespoons pine nuts, toasted
2 teaspoons grated lemon rind
2 garlic cloves, minced
4 teaspoons extra-virgin olive oil
¼ teaspoon kosher salt

Chicken:
2 teaspoons extra-virgin olive oil
4 (6-ounce) skinless, boneless chicken breast halves
½ teaspoon kosher salt
¼ teaspoon freshly ground black pepper

1. To prepare gremolata, place first 4 ingredients in a mini chopper; process just until combined. Add 4 teaspoons olive oil and ¼ teaspoon salt; process to combine. Set aside.

2. To prepare chicken, heat a large grill pan over medium-high heat. Brush 2 teaspoons olive oil evenly over chicken; sprinkle chicken evenly with ½ teaspoon salt and pepper. Add chicken to pan; cook 5 minutes on each side or until done. Remove chicken from pan; let stand 5 minutes. Serve gremolata with chicken. Yield: 4 servings (serving size: 1 chicken breast half and about 4 teaspoons gremolata).

CALORIES 236; FAT 11.3g (sat 1.6g, mono 6.1g, poly 2.6g); PROTEIN 30.4g; CARB 2.3g; FIBER 0.8g; CHOL 74mg; IRON 1.6mg; SODIUM 438mg; CALC 35mg

For the Sugar Snap and Feta Salad:
Place ½ cup thinly vertically sliced red onion in a bowl of ice water for 10 minutes; drain and pat dry. Cook 12 ounces trimmed sugar snap peas in boiling water 2 minutes. Drain and plunge peas in ice water; drain and pat

dry. Combine 1 tablespoon fresh lemon juice, 1 tablespoon extra-virgin olive oil, 1 teaspoon white wine vinegar, ½ teaspoon honey, ¼ teaspoon kosher salt, and ¼ teaspoon freshly ground black pepper in a medium bowl, stirring with a whisk. Add peas, onion, and ⅓ cup crumbled feta cheese; toss well.

SUPERFAST

From salad-stuffed flatbread to a knife-and-fork open-faced option—hearty sandwiches are on the menu in these easy 20-minute weeknight entrées.

Quick & Easy

Arctic Char Sandwiches with Lemon-Tarragon Slaw

1 tablespoon olive oil
½ teaspoon salt, divided
½ teaspoon black pepper, divided
4 (4-ounce) arctic char fillets
1¼ cups cabbage-and-carrot coleslaw
1 tablespoon chopped fresh tarragon
2 tablespoons organic canola mayonnaise (such as Spectrum)
1 tablespoon fresh lemon juice
1 teaspoon Dijon mustard
4 (2-ounce) Kaiser rolls, toasted

1. Heat oil in a large nonstick skillet over medium-high heat. Sprinkle ¼ teaspoon salt and ¼ teaspoon pepper evenly over both sides of fish. Add fish to pan; cook 4 minutes on each side or until desired degree of doneness.

2. Combine coleslaw, remaining ¼ teaspoon salt, remaining ¼ teaspoon black pepper, tarragon, and next 3 ingredients; toss well. Arrange 1 fillet over bottom half of each roll; top with ¼ cup slaw and top half of roll. Yield: 4 servings (serving size: 1 sandwich).

CALORIES 406; FAT 18.4g (sat 2.7g, mono 7.9g, poly 6.5g); PROTEIN 26.7g; CARB 32g; FIBER 1.9g; CHOL 56mg; IRON 2.4mg; SODIUM 727mg; CALC 77mg

Turkey Panini with Watercress and Citrus Aioli

2 tablespoons canola mayonnaise
¼ teaspoon grated lime rind
¼ teaspoon grated lemon rind
1 teaspoon fresh lemon juice
¼ teaspoon freshly ground black pepper
1 garlic clove, minced
8 (1-ounce) slices white bread
½ pound deli-sliced smoked turkey (such as Boar's Head)
2 cups trimmed watercress
4 (½-ounce) slices provolone cheese
Cooking spray

1. Heat a large grill pan over medium-high heat.
2. Combine first 6 ingredients; spread evenly over 4 bread slices. Top evenly with turkey, watercress, cheese, and remaining 4 bread slices.
3. Coat grill pan with cooking spray. Arrange 2 sandwiches in pan. Place a cast-iron or heavy skillet on top of sandwiches; press gently to flatten. Cook 2 minutes on each side (leave cast-iron skillet on sandwiches while they cook). Repeat procedure with remaining 2 sandwiches. Yield: 4 servings (serving size: 1 sandwich).

CALORIES 304; FAT 11.8g (sat 2.7g, mono 2.8g, poly 3.6g); PROTEIN 21.3g; CARB 29g; FIBER 1.2g; CHOL 38mg; IRON 2mg; SODIUM 810mg; CALC 210mg

Open-Faced Sandwiches with Ricotta, Arugula, and Fried Egg

4 (2-ounce) slices whole-wheat country bread
Cooking spray
2 cups arugula
1 tablespoon extra-virgin olive oil, divided
1½ teaspoons fresh lemon juice
½ teaspoon salt, divided
½ teaspoon freshly ground black pepper, divided
4 large eggs
¾ cup part-skim ricotta cheese
¼ cup (1 ounce) grated fresh Parmigiano-Reggiano cheese
1 teaspoon chopped fresh thyme

1. Preheat broiler.
2. Coat both sides of bread with cooking spray. Broil 2 minutes on each side or until lightly toasted.
3. Combine arugula, 2 teaspoons oil, juice, ⅛ teaspoon salt, and ¼ teaspoon pepper; toss gently.
4. Heat remaining 1 teaspoon oil in a large nonstick skillet over medium heat. Crack eggs into pan; cook 2 minutes. Cover and cook an additional 2 minutes or until whites are set. Remove from heat.
5. Combine ¼ teaspoon salt, ricotta, Parmigiano-Reggiano, and thyme; spread over bread slices. Divide salad and eggs evenly over bread. Sprinkle with remaining ⅛ teaspoon salt and remaining ¼ teaspoon pepper. Yield: 4 servings (serving size: 1 sandwich).

CALORIES 337; FAT 15.8g (sat 5.9g, mono 6.9g, poly 1.6g); PROTEIN 21.8g; CARB 27.2g; FIBER 4.1g; CHOL 231mg; IRON 2.8mg; SODIUM 807mg; CALC 316mg

CHOOSE THE RIGHT BREAD FOR THE SANDWICH

BAGUETTE
Sturdy texture stands up to hefty fillings.

FLATBREAD
Wrap and roll up smaller ingredients.

COUNTRY BREAD
Thick, dense slices for open-faced options.

SUB OR HOAGIE ROLLS
Great for saucy sandwiches.

Chipotle Chicken Cheesesteaks

1 (7-ounce) can chipotle chiles in adobo sauce
2 teaspoons olive oil, divided
12 ounces chicken cutlets, thinly sliced
1 cup vertically sliced onion
1 cup red bell pepper strips
2 teaspoons bottled minced garlic
¼ teaspoon dried thyme
¼ teaspoon salt
1 cup (4 ounces) shredded reduced-fat sharp cheddar cheese
4 (2-ounce) submarine or hoagie rolls

1. Remove 1 chile and 1 tablespoon adobo sauce from can; mince chile. Set chile and sauce aside. Reserve remaining chiles and sauce for another use.
2. Heat 1 teaspoon oil in a large cast-iron skillet over medium-high heat. Add chicken; sauté 4 minutes or until done. Remove chicken from pan. Heat remaining 1 teaspoon oil in pan over medium-high heat. Add onion and next 3 ingredients; sauté 4 minutes. Stir in chile and adobo sauce; cook 30 seconds. Add chicken and salt; cook 1 minute, stirring frequently. Remove from heat. Add cheese, stirring until cheese melts. Divide mixture evenly among rolls. Yield: 4 servings (serving size: 1 sandwich).

CALORIES 388; FAT 13g (sat 5.7g, mono 5.1g, poly 1.2g); PROTEIN 32.8g; CARB 35.2g; FIBER 3.3g; CHOL 71mg; IRON 2.8mg; SODIUM 605mg; CALC 322mg

Banh Mi–Style Roast Beef Sandwiches

⅛ teaspoon kosher salt
⅛ teaspoon freshly ground black pepper
¾ pound flank steak, trimmed
2 tablespoons rice vinegar
1 tablespoon fish sauce
1 tablespoon less-sodium soy sauce
1½ teaspoons sugar
1 jalapeño pepper, thinly sliced
1 cup matchstick-cut carrots
½ cup thinly sliced radishes
1 (8-ounce) baguette, halved lengthwise and toasted
½ cup fresh cilantro leaves

1. Heat a large cast-iron skillet over medium-high heat. Sprinkle salt and pepper evenly over steak. Add steak to pan; cook 5 minutes on each side or until desired degree of doneness. Remove steak from pan; let stand 5 minutes. Cut steak diagonally across grain into thin slices.
2. While steak cooks, combine vinegar and next 4 ingredients in a medium bowl. Combine carrots and radishes in a medium bowl; add 1 tablespoon vinegar mixture, tossing to coat. Let vegetable mixture stand 5 minutes. Add steak to remaining 5 tablespoons vinegar mixture; toss well to coat.
3. Arrange steak on bottom half of bread; top with carrot mixture and cilantro. Top with top half of bread; cut into 4 equal pieces. Yield: 4 servings (serving size: 1 sandwich).

CALORIES 302; FAT 6g (sat 2.5g, mono 2.4g, poly 0.3g); PROTEIN 23.4g; CARB 39.4g; FIBER 2.3g; CHOL 32mg; IRON 3.3mg; SODIUM 907mg; CALC 29mg

Caprese Wraps with Chicken

2 tablespoons olive oil
2 tablespoons white wine vinegar
¼ teaspoon kosher salt
¼ teaspoon black pepper
4 cups prechopped hearts of romaine lettuce
1½ cups shredded skinless, boneless rotisserie chicken breast
¾ cup (3 ounces) fresh mozzarella cheese, chopped
½ cup fresh basil leaves, torn
1 pint cherry tomatoes, quartered
Cooking spray
4 (2.8-ounce) multigrain flatbreads (such as Flatout)
1 large garlic clove, halved

1. Combine first 4 ingredients in a large bowl, stirring with a whisk. Add lettuce and next 4 ingredients, tossing to coat.
2. Heat a large nonstick skillet over medium-high heat. Coat pan with cooking spray. Working with 1 flatbread at a time, cook bread 1 minute on each side or until toasted. Rub 1 side of each flatbread with cut sides of garlic. Arrange 1½ cups chicken mixture in center of each flatbread; roll up. Yield: 4 servings (serving size: 1 wrap).

CALORIES 328; FAT 15.9g (sat 4.5g, mono 6.2g, poly 2.7g); PROTEIN 30.3g; CARB 22g; FIBER 9.5g; CHOL 61mg; IRON 2.9mg; SODIUM 573mg; CALC 180mg

Sausage-Fennel Subs

Cooking spray
1½ cups vertically sliced onion
1 cup thinly sliced fennel bulb
4 garlic cloves, thinly sliced
6 ounces chicken and sun-dried tomato sausage, thinly diagonally sliced
4 (2-ounce) submarine rolls or hoagie rolls
½ cup tomato-basil pasta sauce
8 (½-ounce) slices provolone cheese

1. Preheat broiler.
2. Heat a large nonstick skillet over medium-high heat. Coat pan with cooking spray. Add onion, fennel, and garlic; sauté 4 minutes. Add sausage, and sauté 3 minutes or until sausage is lightly browned and vegetables begin to brown.
3. Arrange rolls, cut sides up, in a single layer on a baking sheet; broil 2 minutes or until toasted. Spoon about ⅔ cup sausage mixture on bottom half of each roll, and top each with 2 tablespoons sauce. Place 2 cheese slices over sauce. Arrange sandwiches on baking sheet; broil 2 minutes or until cheese melts. Yield: 4 servings (serving size: 1 sandwich).

CALORIES 395; FAT 16.9g (sat 7.7g, mono 5.4g, poly 2.3g); PROTEIN 21.5g; CARB 39g; FIBER 3.5g; CHOL 55mg; IRON 2.8mg; SODIUM 981mg; CALC 324mg

DELICIOUSLY LIGHTER CRAB CAKES

With less filler and no deep-frying to overwhelm the crab, this iconic seafood entrée is healthier and tastier.

Instead of being light and refreshing—what we crave this time of year—many crab cakes are heavy in calories, sodium, and saturated fat. Plus they're often junked up with caloric and sodium-laden fillers and then deep-fried (a tasty technique, but the caramelizing powers of deep-frying overwhelm the delicate, sweet crab). Often there's too much sauce, too. Here's how we put this seasonal treat within nutritional reach.

We lightly season sweet, premium crab and use just enough mayonnaise, low-sodium panko (Japanese bread-crumbs), and egg to bind it all together. We don't add any salt to the mixture, to keep sodium in check. The cakes are cooked in a slick of oil instead of deep-fried. We love a good rémoulade but overhaul the condiment to add a flavor punch without as much sodium.

Our version of crab cakes is ideal for the season: a vibrant and light dish that pairs perfectly with a crisp salad and glass of wine.

OLD WAY	OUR WAY
734 calories per serving	292 calories per serving
8.6 grams saturated fat	1.6 grams saturated fat
1,285 milligrams sodium	571 milligrams sodium
High-sodium breadcrumbs	Panko (Japanese breadcrumbs)
At least ¼ cup oil absorbed in deep-frying	1 tablespoon oil for sautéing
Rémoulade overload	Just enough rémoulade

Crab Cakes with Spicy Rémoulade
(pictured on page 254)

We keep fillers to a minimum with this fresh take on crab cakes. This lower-sodium, streamlined rémoulade (there are no gherkins, anchovies, or green olives) is best made one day ahead to allow flavors to marry.

Crab Cakes:
2 tablespoons finely chopped fresh chives
1 tablespoon chopped fresh flat-leaf parsley
1½ tablespoons canola-based mayonnaise
   (such as Spectrum brand)
½ teaspoon grated lemon rind
1 tablespoon fresh lemon juice
¼ teaspoon freshly ground black pepper
⅛ teaspoon ground red pepper
1 large egg
⅓ cup panko (Japanese breadcrumbs)
1 pound lump crabmeat, drained and shell
   pieces removed
1 tablespoon olive oil, divided

Rémoulade:
¼ cup canola-based mayonnaise
1 tablespoon chopped shallots
1½ tablespoons capers, drained and chopped
2 teaspoons Creole mustard
1 teaspoon fresh lemon juice
¼ teaspoon ground red pepper
⅛ teaspoon kosher salt

1. To prepare crab cakes, combine first 8 ingredients. Add panko and crab, tossing gently to combine. Cover and refrigerate 30 minutes.
2. Fill a ⅓-cup dry measuring cup with crab mixture. Invert onto work surface; gently pat into a ¾-inch-thick patty. Repeat procedure with remaining crab mixture, forming 8 cakes.
3. Heat 1½ teaspoons oil in a large skillet over medium-high heat. Add 4 crab cakes to pan; cook 4 minutes or until bottoms are golden. Carefully turn cakes; cook 4 minutes or until bottoms are golden and crab cakes are thoroughly heated. Remove cakes from pan; keep warm. Wipe pan dry with paper towels. Heat remaining 1½ teaspoons oil in pan. Repeat procedure with remaining 4 crab cakes.
4. To prepare rémoulade, combine ¼ cup mayonnaise and remaining ingredients in a small bowl; stir with a whisk. Serve with crab cakes. Yield: 4 servings (serving size: 2 crab cakes and 1½ tablespoons rémoulade).

CALORIES 292; **FAT** 22g (sat 1.6g, mono 7.8g, poly 10.2g); **PROTEIN** 18.7g; **CARB** 5g; **FIBER** 0.5g; **CHOL** 161mg; **IRON** 1.2mg; **SODIUM** 571mg; **CALC** 53mg

SUMMER COOKBOOK

O summer...celebrate with us the sweet joys of fruit and the luscious crunch of vegetables.

FRUITS

Fruits are nature's candy: luscious, succulent, brimming with juice, divinely sweet. They're perfect with savory summer dishes, too.

AN AL FRESCO DINNER MENU

serves 6

Sparkling Rosemary-Peach Cocktails (below)

Muhammara with Crudités (page 148)

Grilled Chicken with Cucumber-Melon Salsa (page 145)

Green salad

Apricot-Thyme Galette (page 146)

Sparkling Rosemary-Peach Cocktails

A heady punch of woodsy rosemary creates an herbaceous riff on the classic Bellini.

¾ cup water
½ cup sugar
1 (3-inch) rosemary sprig
2 ripe peeled peaches, cut into 1-inch pieces
1 (750-milliliter) bottle Champagne or sparkling wine, chilled

1. Combine first 3 ingredients in a small saucepan; bring to a boil. Remove from heat; cool to room temperature. Strain rosemary syrup in a sieve over a bowl; discard solids. Cover and chill at least 1 hour.
2. Place rosemary syrup and peaches in a blender, and process until smooth. Strain mixture through a sieve over a bowl; cover and chill at least 4 hours. Spoon about 2 tablespoons peach syrup into each of 8 Champagne flutes, and top each serving with about ⅓ cup Champagne. Yield: 8 servings.

CALORIES 126; FAT 0.1g (sat 0g, mono 0.1g, poly 0g); PROTEIN 0.2g; CARB 16.5g; FIBER 0.1g; CHOL 0mg; IRON 0.1mg; SODIUM 1mg; CALC 3mg

Make Ahead
Fig and Lime Jam

We tested this recipe with not-too-sweet Brown Turkey figs; if using sweeter Black Mission figs, you may need to decrease the sugar. The mashed fig mixture can stand overnight.

2 cups sugar
¼ cup fresh lime juice (about 3 limes)
2 pounds fresh Brown Turkey figs, cut into (¼-inch) pieces (about 6 cups)

1. Combine all ingredients in a large heavy saucepan; mash fig mixture with a potato masher until combined. Let stand 2 hours. Bring mixture to a boil over medium heat. Reduce heat; simmer 35 minutes or until mixture begins to thicken slightly, stirring occasionally. Cool completely. Cover and chill overnight. Yield: 4 cups (serving size: 2 tablespoons).

CALORIES 70; FAT 0.1g (sat 0g, mono 0g, poly 0.1g); PROTEIN 0.2g; CARB 18.1g; FIBER 0.8g; CHOL 0mg; IRON 0.1mg; SODIUM 0mg; CALC 10mg

Kid Friendly
Peach, Plum, and Apricot Crisp

4½ cups sliced peaches
2 cups sliced plums
2 cups sliced apricots
¾ cup granulated sugar
3 tablespoons all-purpose flour
¼ teaspoon grated whole nutmeg
Cooking spray
1 cup old-fashioned rolled oats
½ cup packed brown sugar
3.4 ounces all-purpose flour (about ¾ cup)
½ teaspoon salt
¼ cup butter, melted
4 cups vanilla low-fat ice cream

1. Combine first 6 ingredients in a large bowl; let stand 15 minutes.
2. Preheat oven to 400°.
3. Spoon fruit mixture into a 13 x 9–inch glass or ceramic baking dish coated with cooking spray. Bake at 400° for 35 minutes or until bubbly.
4. Combine oats and next 3 ingredients in a bowl. Drizzle with butter, stirring until crumbly. Sprinkle oat mixture over fruit. Bake an additional 15 minutes or until topping is lightly browned and fruit is bubbly. Serve warm with ice cream. Yield: 12 servings (serving size: about ½ cup crisp and ⅓ cup ice cream).

CALORIES 299; FAT 6g (sat 3.2g, mono 1.6g, poly 0.4g); PROTEIN 5.1g; CARB 58.3g; FIBER 3.4g; CHOL 13mg; IRON 1.3mg; SODIUM 160mg; CALC 88mg

Lemon-Cornmeal Pound Cake with Berries and Cream

Cake:
7.9 ounces all-purpose flour (about 1¾ cups)
½ cup cornmeal
1 teaspoon baking soda
¼ teaspoon salt
1½ cups granulated sugar
10 tablespoons butter, softened
3 large eggs
2 teaspoons grated lemon rind
1 teaspoon vanilla extract
⅔ cup nonfat buttermilk
3 tablespoons fresh lemon juice
3 large egg whites
Cooking spray
2 tablespoons all-purpose flour
Topping:
1½ cups fresh blueberries
1½ cups sliced fresh strawberries
1 cup fresh blackberries
¼ cup granulated sugar
1 tablespoon fresh lemon juice
½ cup heavy whipping cream
2 tablespoons powdered sugar

1. Preheat oven to 350°.
2. To prepare cake, weigh or lightly spoon 7.9 ounces (about 1¾ cups) flour into dry measuring cups; level with a knife. Combine flour and next 3 ingredients. Combine 1½ cups granulated sugar and butter in a large bowl; beat with a mixer at high speed until fluffy. Add eggs, one at a time, beating until blended; stir in rind and vanilla. Combine buttermilk and 3 tablespoons juice. Add flour mixture to butter mixture alternately with buttermilk mixture, beginning and ending with flour mixture.
3. Place egg whites in a large, clean bowl; beat at high speed using clean, dry beaters until stiff peaks form. Gently fold half of egg whites into batter. Gently fold in remaining egg whites. Spoon batter into a 10-inch tube pan coated with cooking spray and dusted with 2 tablespoons flour. Bake at 350° for 1 hour or until a wooden pick inserted in center comes out clean. Cool in pan on wire rack 10 minutes.

Remove cake from pan; cool completely on wire rack.
4. To prepare topping, combine blueberries and next 4 ingredients. Chill 30 minutes. Beat cream with a mixer at high speed until soft peaks form. Gradually add powdered sugar, beating until stiff peaks form. Serve cake with berries and cream. Yield: 16 servings (serving size: 1 cake slice, about ¼ cup berries, and 1 tablespoon cream).

CALORIES 287; **FAT** 11.2g (sat 6.5g, mono 3g, poly 0.7g); **PROTEIN** 4.7g; **CARB** 43.4g; **FIBER** 1.7g; **CHOL** 69mg; **IRON** 1.3mg; **SODIUM** 147mg; **CALC** 55mg

Make Ahead

Cracked Wheat Salad with Nectarines, Parsley, and Pistachios

Great with grilled chicken, lamb, or salmon, this side-dish salad also packs well for a picnic. Almost any fruit would work well in place of nectarines—try apricots, peaches, or figs.

1 cup uncooked bulgur
1 cup boiling water
1½ cups thinly sliced nectarines (about 3)
½ cup thinly sliced green onions
¼ cup chopped fresh flat-leaf parsley
1 tablespoon chopped fresh dill
3 tablespoons extra-virgin olive oil
3 tablespoons white balsamic vinegar
¾ teaspoon salt
¼ teaspoon freshly ground black pepper
3 tablespoons chopped pistachios

1. Combine bulgur and 1 cup boiling water in a large bowl. Cover and let stand 1 hour. Stir in nectarines and next 7 ingredients; toss well. Sprinkle with nuts. Yield: 6 servings (serving size: about ¾ cup).

CALORIES 188; **FAT** 9g (sat 1.2g, mono 5.9g, poly 1.4g); **PROTEIN** 4.2g; **CARB** 24.7g; **FIBER** 5.7g; **CHOL** 0mg; **IRON** 1.2mg; **SODIUM** 307mg; **CALC** 29mg

Make Ahead • Freezable • Kid Friendly

Minted Watermelon and Lemon Ice Pops

Watermelon Layer:
¼ cup sugar
¼ cup water
¼ cup coarsely chopped fresh mint
2 cups packed (½-inch) cubed seeded watermelon
1 tablespoon fresh lime juice
Lemon Layer:
6 tablespoons sugar
½ cup water
⅔ cup fresh lemon juice
⅓ cup fresh orange juice
¼ teaspoon orange extract

1. To prepare watermelon layer, combine ¼ cup sugar and ¼ cup water in a small saucepan over medium-high heat. Bring to a boil; cook 30 seconds, stirring until sugar dissolves. Stir in mint; cover and let stand 30 minutes. Strain through a sieve into a bowl.
2. Place watermelon in a blender; process until smooth. Strain puree through a sieve into bowl with mint syrup; press with back of a spoon to extract juice. Discard solids. Stir in lime juice; cover and chill 1 hour.
3. Pour about 2½ tablespoons watermelon mixture into each of 8 ice pop molds. Freeze 1½ hours or until almost set. Arrange 1 wooden stick into mixture, being careful not to push through to bottom of mold. Return to freezer. Freeze 1 hour or until frozen.
4. To prepare lemon layer, combine 6 tablespoons sugar and ½ cup water in a small saucepan over medium-high heat. Bring to a boil; cook 30 seconds, stirring until sugar dissolves. Pour into a bowl; stir in lemon juice, orange juice, and extract. Cool 15 minutes; cover and chill at least 1 hour.
5. Remove molds from freezer. Pour about 3 tablespoons lemon mixture over frozen watermelon mixture in each mold. Freeze 2 hours or until completely frozen. Yield: 8 servings (serving size: 1 ice pop).

CALORIES 82; **FAT** 0g; **PROTEIN** 0.3g; **CARB** 22.1g; **FIBER** 0.4g; **CHOL** 0mg; **IRON** 0.2mg; **SODIUM** 3mg; **CALC** 8mg

Golden Peach Soup with Shrimp and Crab Seviche

As intriguing as it is beautiful, this sweet-tangy-slightly spicy soup makes a stunning first course.

Seviche:

8 ounces chopped cooked shrimp

1 cup fresh lime juice (about 6 large limes)

4 ounces lump crabmeat, shell pieces removed

3 tablespoons finely chopped red onion

3 tablespoons chopped fresh cilantro

1 tablespoon minced seeded jalapeño pepper

1 tablespoon extra-virgin olive oil

¼ teaspoon salt

Soup:

3 pounds peaches, peeled, pitted, and chopped

⅓ cup fresh lime juice (about 2 large limes)

½ teaspoon salt

¼ cup finely chopped red onion

¼ cup matchstick-cut radishes

¼ cup minced red bell pepper

3 tablespoons chopped fresh cilantro

1 tablespoon minced seeded jalapeño pepper

¼ teaspoon fine sea salt

Cilantro sprigs (optional)

1. To prepare seviche, combine shrimp and 1 cup juice in a medium bowl; chill 1 hour. Add crab; toss gently to combine. Drain thoroughly; return shrimp and crab to bowl. Stir in 3 tablespoons onion and next 4 ingredients. Chill at least 30 minutes or up to 6 hours.

2. To prepare soup, combine peaches, ⅓ cup juice, and ½ teaspoon salt. Place half of peach mixture in a blender; process until smooth. Pour pureed peach mixture into a large bowl. Repeat procedure with remaining peach mixture. Stir in ¼ cup onion and next 4 ingredients. Cover and chill 30 minutes.

3. Arrange ¼ cup seviche in each of 8 small shallow bowls; ladle about ½ cup soup around seviche. Sprinkle evenly with sea salt; garnish with cilantro sprigs, if desired. Yield: 8 servings.

CALORIES 139; **FAT** 3g (sat 0.3g, mono 1.3g, poly 0.4g); **PROTEIN** 10.2g; **CARB** 20.6g; **FIBER** 2.8g; **CHOL** 53mg; **IRON** 1.3mg; **SODIUM** 391mg; **CALC** 32mg

---

Quick & Easy

Grilled Chicken with Cucumber-Melon Salsa

A combination of green and orange melons is colorful and speaks to the beauty of summer. You can substitute ½ teaspoon granulated sugar for agave nectar, if desired. We left the seeds in the jalapeño for some heat, but you can discard them for a milder dish.

1 cup (½-inch) cubed honeydew melon

1 cup (½-inch) cubed cantaloupe

½ cup diced peeled English cucumber

½ cup diced red onion

¼ cup chopped fresh mint

1 teaspoon grated lime rind

3 tablespoons fresh lime juice

2 tablespoons extra-virgin olive oil

2 teaspoons minced jalapeño pepper

1 teaspoon light agave nectar

¾ teaspoon kosher salt, divided

½ teaspoon freshly ground black pepper, divided

6 (6-ounce) skinless, boneless chicken breast halves

Cooking spray

Mint sprigs (optional)

1. Prepare grill to medium-high heat.

2. Combine first 10 ingredients; stir in ¼ teaspoon salt and ¼ teaspoon black pepper, tossing well to combine.

3. Sprinkle chicken evenly with remaining ½ teaspoon salt and remaining ¼ teaspoon black pepper. Coat chicken with cooking spray. Place chicken on a grill rack coated with cooking spray; grill 5 minutes on each side or until done. Serve with salsa; garnish with mint sprigs, if desired. Yield: 6 servings (serving size: 1 breast half and about ½ cup salsa).

CALORIES 255; **FAT** 8.6g (sat 1.8g, mono 4.7g, poly 1.4g); **PROTEIN** 35.1g; **CARB** 8.1g; **FIBER** 0.8g; **CHOL** 94mg; **IRON** 1.4mg; **SODIUM** 327mg; **CALC** 29mg

---

Make Ahead • Freezable • Kid Friendly

Bittersweet Chocolate–Cherry Sorbet with Fresh Cherry Compote

Tart-sweet cherry and strong dark chocolate flavors meld beautifully in this surprisingly rich sorbet crowned with juicy fresh cherries. Use a high-quality jam for the sorbet, and be sure to start the process a day ahead for the best flavor and texture.

Sorbet:

¾ cup red cherry jam (such as Bonne Maman)

½ cup Dutch process cocoa

¼ cup sugar

⅛ teaspoon salt

2 cups water

Compote:

¼ cup sugar

1 pound fresh Bing or tart cherries, pitted and halved

1. To prepare sorbet, combine first 4 ingredients in a heavy saucepan, stirring with a whisk. Gradually add 2 cups water, stirring with a whisk. Bring mixture to a boil, stirring well with a whisk. Cool to room temperature; cover and chill overnight.

2. Stir sorbet mixture with a whisk. Pour mixture into freezer can of an ice-cream freezer; freeze according to manufacturer's instructions. Spoon sorbet into a freezer-safe container; cover and freeze 1 hour or until firm.

3. To prepare compote, combine ¼ cup sugar and cherries; toss well. Let stand at room temperature 1 hour. Serve compote with sorbet. Yield: 7 servings (serving size: ½ cup sorbet and about ¼ cup compote).

CALORIES 197; **FAT** 1.3g (sat 0.5g, mono 0.3g, poly 0g); **PROTEIN** 1.7g; **CARB** 50.6g; **FIBER** 3.4g; **CHOL** 0mg; **IRON** 0.9mg; **SODIUM** 45mg; **CALC** 19mg

Kid Friendly

Grilled Halibut with Peach and Pepper Salsa

A fresh fruit salsa is a lovely accompaniment to grilled fish in the summer; try it also with striped bass or arctic char. Here, the season's juiciest peaches pair with fiery habanero pepper for a sweet-spicy flavor.

Salsa:

2½ cups coarsely chopped peeled yellow peaches (about 1¼ pounds)

1⅓ cups chopped red bell pepper (about 1 large)

½ cup thinly sliced green onions

½ cup chopped fresh arugula

⅓ cup fresh lemon juice (about 2 lemons)

2 tablespoons chopped fresh oregano

¼ teaspoon salt

1 habanero pepper, seeded and minced

1 garlic clove, minced

Fish:

2 tablespoons fresh lemon juice

2 tablespoons olive oil

1 teaspoon paprika

2 garlic cloves, minced

6 (6-ounce) skinless halibut fillets

½ teaspoon salt

½ teaspoon freshly ground black pepper

Cooking spray

1. To prepare salsa, combine first 9 ingredients; toss gently. Let stand 30 minutes before serving.

2. Prepare grill to medium-high heat.

3. To prepare fish, combine 2 tablespoons juice and next 3 ingredients in a large, shallow glass baking dish, stirring with a whisk. Add fish to juice mixture; turn to coat. Cover and let stand 15 minutes.

4. Remove fish from marinade; discard marinade. Sprinkle fish evenly with ½ teaspoon salt and black pepper. Place fish on a grill rack coated with cooking spray; grill 3 minutes on each side or until desired degree of doneness. Serve fish with salsa. Yield: 6 servings (serving size: 1 fillet and about ⅔ cup salsa).

CALORIES 267; **FAT** 8.6g (sat 1.2g, mono 4.6g, poly 1.8g); **PROTEIN** 35.3g; **CARB** 11.8g; **FIBER** 2.3g; **CHOL** 52mg; **IRON** 2mg; **SODIUM** 389mg; **CALC** 104mg

Staff Favorite • Kid Friendly

Apricot-Thyme Galette

A little bit of almond flour (also labeled "almond meal") makes the dough more tender. Look for it on the baking aisle or in the gluten-free section of your supermarket.

6.2 ounces all-purpose flour (about 1¼ cups plus 2 tablespoons), divided

3 tablespoons ice water

½ teaspoon cider vinegar

⅛ teaspoon almond extract

⅓ cup turbinado sugar, divided

¼ cup almond flour

¼ teaspoon salt

¼ cup chilled butter, cut into pieces

1½ tablespoons cornstarch

2 pounds firm ripe apricots, pitted and cut into quarters

¼ cup apricot jam

1 tablespoon honey

1 teaspoon fresh thyme leaves

1. Preheat oven to 400°.

2. Weigh or lightly spoon 1.1 ounces (about ¼ cup) all-purpose flour into a dry measuring cup; level with a knife. Combine 1.1 ounces all-purpose flour, 3 tablespoons ice water, vinegar, and almond extract in a small bowl; stir with a fork until well blended to form a slurry.

3. Combine remaining 5.1 ounces (about 1 cup plus 2 tablespoons) all-purpose flour, 2 tablespoons sugar, almond flour, and salt, stirring with a whisk. Cut in butter with a pastry blender or 2 knives until mixture resembles coarse meal. Add slurry, and stir just until moist. Turn dough out onto a lightly floured surface; knead lightly 5 times. Gently press dough into a 4-inch circle on heavy-duty plastic wrap. Cover with additional plastic wrap. Carefully roll dough into a 14-inch circle; freeze 10 minutes.

4. Remove dough from freezer; remove top sheet of plastic wrap. Let stand 1 minute or until pliable. Place dough, plastic wrap side up, onto a baking sheet lined with parchment paper; remove remaining plastic wrap.

5. Combine cornstarch and 2 tablespoons sugar; sprinkle over dough, leaving a 2-inch border. Arrange apricots spokelike on top of cornstarch mixture, leaving a 2-inch border. Fold edges of dough over apricots (dough will only partially cover apricots).

6. Combine jam and honey in a small microwave-safe bowl; microwave at HIGH 45 seconds. Brush jam mixture over apricots and dough edges. Sprinkle with remaining sugar. Bake at 400° for 35 minutes or until crust browns. Remove from oven; sprinkle with thyme. Cool 10 minutes. Yield: 8 servings (serving size: 1 wedge).

CALORIES 271; **FAT** 8.1g (sat 3.8g, mono 2.8g, poly 0.4g); **PROTEIN** 4.7g; **CARB** 47.7g; **FIBER** 3.3g; **CHOL** 15mg; **IRON** 1.7mg; **SODIUM** 121mg; **CALC** 30mg

Brined Pork Tenderloin with Plum and Jicama Relish

A quick brine keeps the pork moist and juicy.

8 cups cold water

½ cup kosher salt

2 (1-pound) pork tenderloins, trimmed

1 tablespoon extra-virgin olive oil

½ teaspoon freshly ground black pepper, divided

1½ cups diced plums (¾ pound)

¾ cup finely chopped peeled jicama

½ cup finely chopped red onion

2 teaspoons grated lime rind

2 tablespoons fresh lime juice

1 tablespoon honey

⅛ teaspoon kosher salt

1 serrano chile, seeded and chopped

Parsley sprigs (optional)

1. Combine 8 cups cold water and ½ cup salt in a 13 x 9–inch glass or ceramic baking dish, stirring until salt dissolves. Add pork to brine; let stand at room temperature 1 hour.

2. Prepare grill to medium-high heat.

3. Drain pork; pat dry. Brush pork with oil; sprinkle with ¼ teaspoon pepper. Place pork on grill rack; grill 15 minutes or until a thermometer registers 155° (slightly pink), turning pork occasionally. Remove pork from grill; let stand 5 minutes. Cut across grain into ½-inch-thick slices.

4. Combine remaining ¼ teaspoon pepper, plums, and next 7 ingredients; toss gently to combine. Serve relish with pork. Garnish with parsley sprigs, if desired. Yield: 8 servings (serving size: 3 ounces pork and about ¼ cup relish).

CALORIES 221; **FAT** 8.4g (sat 2.7g, mono 4g, poly 0.8g); **PROTEIN** 25.2g; **CARB** 10g; **FIBER** 1.4g; **CHOL** 78mg; **IRON** 1.4mg; **SODIUM** 792mg; **CALC** 10mg

VEGETABLES

In which we exult in the crunch and color of the season. Raw and cooked. Spiced and diced. Pure heaven from earth.

Quick & Easy • Make Ahead

Romano Bean Salad

Also called Italian flat beans or runner beans, this snap bean variety looks like a wide, flat green bean. You can easily substitute an equal amount of regular green beans.

2 quarts water
1 pound Romano beans, trimmed and
    cut into ½-inch pieces
1 tablespoon kosher salt
1 garlic clove
¼ cup chopped fresh flat-leaf parsley
2 tablespoons capers
1 tablespoon extra-virgin olive oil
1 teaspoon grated lemon rind
¼ teaspoon kosher salt
¼ teaspoon freshly ground black pepper

1. Bring 2 quarts water to a boil in a large saucepan. Add beans, 1 tablespoon salt, and garlic; cook 8 minutes or until tender. Drain and plunge beans into ice water; drain. Place beans in a medium bowl. Finely chop garlic, and add to beans. Add parsley and remaining ingredients, tossing gently to coat. Yield: 6 servings (serving size: ½ cup).

CALORIES 46; **FAT** 2.4g (sat 0.3g, mono 1.7g, poly 0.3g); **PROTEIN** 1.5g; **CARB** 6g; **FIBER** 2.8g; **CHOL** 0mg; **IRON** 1mg; **SODIUM** 247mg; **CALC** 34mg

Agua Fresca de Pepino

Serve this refreshing cooler on a hot day—it's perfect with spicy Mexican food. Because we only include a tiny amount of seeded serrano pepper, the beverage doesn't become very spicy but picks up the "green" vegetal flavors of the pepper. Use the remaining serrano pepper in your favorite salsa recipe, or toss it into a lime-based salad dressing with cilantro.

3 cups chopped seeded peeled cucumber
    (about 2 medium)
¼ cup sugar
3 tablespoons fresh lime juice
¼ serrano pepper, seeded
3 cups water
Ice
Lime slices (optional)
Cucumber slices (optional)

1. Place first 4 ingredients in a blender; process until smooth. Add 3 cups water; cover and refrigerate overnight.
2. Strain cucumber mixture through a fine sieve over a pitcher; discard solids. Serve over ice; garnish with lime or cucumber slices, if desired. Yield: 4 servings (serving size: about 1 cup).

CALORIES 54; **FAT** 0.1g (sat 0g, mono 0g, poly 0g); **PROTEIN** 0.2g; **CARB** 14g; **FIBER** 0.2g; **CHOL** 0mg; **IRON** 0.1mg; **SODIUM** 6mg; **CALC** 11mg

---

**QUICK SUMMER MEAL
FOR A PASTA FIX MENU**

serves 6

**Quick-Roasted Cherry Tomato
Sauce with Spaghetti** (at right)

Romano Bean Salad (at left)

Garlic bread

Quick & Easy • Kid Friendly

Quick-Roasted Cherry Tomato Sauce with Spaghetti

OK, so tomatoes are fruits, not vegetables—but you use them like veggies. For the prettiest dish, use multicolored tomatoes.

4 quarts water
1 tablespoon kosher salt
12 ounces uncooked spaghetti
2 pints cherry tomatoes
3 tablespoons extra-virgin olive oil, divided
1 tablespoon red wine vinegar
½ teaspoon kosher salt
⅛ teaspoon crushed red pepper
¼ cup chopped or torn fresh basil leaves
¼ cup chopped fresh flat-leaf parsley
¾ cup (3 ounces) crumbled semisoft goat
    cheese

1. Preheat oven to 450°.
2. Bring 4 quarts water to a boil in a large Dutch oven. Add 1 tablespoon salt and spaghetti to boiling water; cook 10 minutes or until spaghetti is al dente. Drain spaghetti in a colander over a bowl, reserving ½ cup cooking water. Return spaghetti to pan; set aside, and keep warm.
3. While spaghetti cooks, combine tomatoes, 1 tablespoon olive oil, and next 3 ingredients on a jelly-roll pan, tossing well to coat. Bake tomato mixture at 450° for 10 minutes or until tomatoes are soft and lightly charred in places.
4. Add tomatoes and any tomato juice to spaghetti in Dutch oven. Add ¼ cup reserved cooking water to jelly-roll pan, scraping pan to loosen browned bits; carefully pour water mixture and remaining 2 tablespoons oil into spaghetti mixture. Place Dutch oven over medium heat. Add remaining ¼ cup reserved cooking water, 2 tablespoons at a time, until spaghetti mixture is moist, tossing frequently. Stir in basil and parsley. Sprinkle with cheese. Serve immediately. Yield: 6 servings (serving size: about 1⅓ cups).

CALORIES 328; **FAT** 10.8g (sat 3.2g, mono 5.8g, poly 1.2g); **PROTEIN** 11g; **CARB** 46.6g; **FIBER** 3.2g; **CHOL** 7mg; **IRON** 2.7mg; **SODIUM** 376mg; **CALC** 48mg

Muhammara with Crudités

Muhammara is a sweet-spicy Middle Eastern dip made from roasted bell pepper, walnuts, and, traditionally, Aleppo pepper and pomegranate molasses. We subbed in readily available crushed red pepper and honey with delicious results.

3 red bell peppers
¼ cup walnut halves, toasted and divided
¼ cup plain dry breadcrumbs
3 tablespoons extra-virgin olive oil
2 tablespoons tomato paste
1 teaspoon ground cumin
1 teaspoon honey
½ teaspoon salt
¼ teaspoon crushed red pepper
⅛ teaspoon ground cinnamon
1 garlic clove
2 tablespoons fresh lime juice
18 radishes, halved
18 baby carrots with tops, trimmed
18 baby lettuce leaves (such as baby romaine)

1. Preheat broiler.
2. Cut bell peppers in half lengthwise; discard seeds and membranes. Place pepper halves, skin sides up, on a foil-lined baking sheet; flatten with hand. Broil 20 minutes or until blackened. Place in a zip-top plastic bag; seal. Let stand 20 minutes. Peel peppers, and discard skins.
3. Place 4 bell pepper halves, 3 tablespoons walnuts, breadcrumbs, and next 8 ingredients in a food processor, and process until smooth. Add remaining 2 bell pepper halves; pulse until coarsely chopped. Spoon dip into a bowl; stir in juice. Top with remaining 1 tablespoon walnuts. Serve with radishes, carrots, and lettuce. Yield: 6 servings (serving size: about ½ cup dip, 6 radish halves, 3 carrots, and 3 lettuce leaves).

CALORIES 155; FAT 10.1g (sat 1.3g, mono 5.4g, poly 3g); PROTEIN 2.7g; CARB 14.5g; FIBER 3.6g; CHOL 0mg; IRON 1.5mg; SODIUM 317mg; CALC 42mg

Sweet Corn Relish

With our simple refrigerator relish recipe, you can preserve a bumper crop of corn for up to six weeks. Serve with any grilled meat or fish, or spoon over salad greens.

6 cups fresh corn kernels (about 8 ears)
3 cups chopped green cabbage
1 cup chopped red bell pepper
1 cup cider vinegar
½ cup sugar
½ cup chopped shallots (about 2 large)
2 teaspoons celery seeds
2 teaspoons mustard seeds
1 teaspoon salt
1 teaspoon cumin seeds
½ teaspoon ground turmeric
⅛ teaspoon crushed red pepper

1. Combine all ingredients in a Dutch oven; bring to a boil. Reduce heat; simmer, uncovered, 20 minutes or until vegetables are tender and most of liquid evaporates, stirring frequently. Cool; pour into airtight containers. Yield: 6 cups (serving size: ¼ cup).
Note: Refrigerate relish in airtight containers for up to six weeks.

CALORIES 59; FAT 0.6g (sat 0.1g, mono 0.2g, poly 0.3g); PROTEIN 1.6g; CARB 13.7g; FIBER 1.2g; CHOL 0mg; IRON 0.6mg; SODIUM 107mg; CALC 12mg

---

FARMERS' MARKET VEGGIE PLATE MENU

serves 6

Cranberry Beans with Parsley Pesto (at right)

Roasted Summer Squashes with Caper Gremolata (page 150)

Summer Peach and Tomato Salad (page 149)

Corn bread

Cranberry Beans with Parsley Pesto

Fresh-from-the-pod cranberry beans are creamy and delicious, especially when adorned with a mixture of herbs, nuts, and cheese. Serve alongside grilled lamb or pork, or enjoy a larger serving as a vegetarian entrée.

2 quarts water
4 cups shelled fresh cranberry beans (about 2¼ pounds unshelled beans)
1 teaspoon salt
1¼ cups chopped seeded plum tomato (about 2 large)
½ cup finely chopped red onion
¾ cup fresh parsley leaves
½ cup fresh basil leaves
2 tablespoons grated fresh Parmesan cheese
2 tablespoons chopped walnuts, toasted
3 tablespoons extra-virgin olive oil
2 tablespoons water
1 tablespoon fresh lemon juice
½ teaspoon salt
⅛ teaspoon freshly ground black pepper
1 garlic clove

1. Bring 2 quarts water to a boil in a large saucepan; stir in cranberry beans and 1 teaspoon salt. Reduce heat, and simmer, uncovered, 40 minutes or until beans are tender. Drain beans; place in a large bowl. Stir in tomato and onion.
2. Place parsley and remaining ingredients in a food processor; process until finely chopped, scraping sides of bowl occasionally. Add herb mixture to bean mixture, and toss to combine. Serve at room temperature. Yield: 8 servings (serving size: about ¾ cup).

CALORIES 193; FAT 7.1g (sat 1.2g, mono 4g, poly 1.6g); PROTEIN 9.5g; CARB 24.3g; FIBER 9.6g; CHOL 1mg; IRON 2.5mg; SODIUM 246mg; CALC 77mg

Eggplant, Zucchini, and Tomato Tian

Tian, a French word used throughout Provence, refers to both a shallow cooking vessel and the food cooked in it. An 11 x 7–inch glass or ceramic baking dish works well for this recipe, but if you have a 2-quart tian or gratin dish, all the better.

1 pound Japanese eggplant, cut diagonally into 1/4-inch-thick slices
1 pound zucchini, cut diagonally into 1/4-inch-thick slices
Cooking spray
1 pound large beefsteak tomatoes, peeled, seeded, and cut into 1/4-inch-thick slices
1 1/2 tablespoons extra-virgin olive oil, divided
1/4 teaspoon salt, divided
1/4 teaspoon freshly ground black pepper, divided
4 ounces French bread baguette
1 cup (4 ounces) grated fresh Parmigiano-Reggiano cheese
2 tablespoons chopped fresh flat-leaf parsley
2 teaspoons chopped fresh oregano
1 1/2 teaspoons chopped fresh thyme
2 garlic cloves, minced
1/4 cup fat-free, less-sodium chicken broth

1. Preheat oven to 375°.
2. Arrange eggplant and zucchini in a single layer on a baking sheet coated with cooking spray. Lightly coat vegetables with cooking spray. Bake at 375° for 15 minutes. Arrange half of eggplant in a single layer in an 11 x 7–inch glass or ceramic baking dish coated with cooking spray. Top with half of zucchini and half of tomato. Drizzle 2 1/4 teaspoons oil evenly over vegetables. Sprinkle vegetables evenly with 1/8 teaspoon salt and 1/8 teaspoon black pepper.
3. Place bread in a food processor; process until coarse crumbs measure 2 cups. Add cheese and next 4 ingredients to processor; process until combined. Sprinkle 1 1/2 cups breadcrumb mixture evenly over tomato. Repeat layers with remaining eggplant, zucchini, tomatoes, oil, salt, pepper, and breadcrumb mixture. Pour broth over top. Bake at 375° for 1 hour or until vegetables are tender and topping is browned. Yield: 6 servings (serving size: about 1 cup).

CALORIES 191; FAT 8.1g (sat 3g, mono 3.7g, poly 1g); PROTEIN 10g; CARB 22.3g; FIBER 4g; CHOL 12mg; IRON 1.6mg; SODIUM 459mg; CALC 178mg

---

Kid Friendly

Bell Pepper, Tomato, Cucumber, and Grilled Bread Salad

Summer's freshest veggies combine in a colorful side-dish salad. Toss in grilled shrimp or chicken for an easy one-dish dinner.

4 (1-ounce) slices day-old country-style bread
4 cups coarsely chopped tomatoes (about 1 1/2 pounds)
1 cup finely chopped red onion
3/4 cup chopped yellow bell pepper
3/4 cup chopped orange bell pepper
1/2 cup torn fresh basil leaves
1 English cucumber, peeled and coarsely chopped
1/4 cup red wine vinegar
1/2 teaspoon freshly ground black pepper
1/4 teaspoon salt
2 garlic cloves, minced
1/4 cup extra-virgin olive oil

1. Prepare grill to medium-high heat.
2. Place bread slices on grill rack; grill 1 minute on each side or until golden brown with grill marks. Remove from grill; tear bread into 1-inch pieces.
3. Combine tomatoes and next 5 ingredients in a large bowl. Add bread; toss gently.
4. Combine vinegar and next 3 ingredients in a small bowl, stirring with a whisk. Gradually add oil, stirring constantly with a whisk. Drizzle dressing over salad; toss gently to coat. Cover and chill 20 minutes before serving. Yield: 6 servings (serving size: 1 2/3 cups).

CALORIES 178; FAT 9.7g (sat 1.3g, mono 6.6g, poly 1g); PROTEIN 3.5g; CARB 19.5g; FIBER 3.1g; CHOL 0mg; IRON 1.6mg; SODIUM 237mg; CALC 43mg

---

Quick & Easy • Kid Friendly

Summer Peach and Tomato Salad

Simplicity has never looked so beautiful. A stunning combination of skin-on peaches and heirloom tomatoes of various colors, sizes, and shapes creates a sweet-savory salad that pairs well with grilled pork.

1/3 cup thinly vertically sliced red onion
3 ripe peaches, pitted and each cut into 8 wedges (about 1 pound)
1/2 pound heirloom beefsteak tomatoes, cut into thick wedges
1/2 pound heirloom cherry or pear tomatoes, halved
2 tablespoons sherry vinegar
1 tablespoon extra-virgin olive oil
2 teaspoons honey
1/2 teaspoon salt
1/8 teaspoon freshly ground black pepper
1/2 cup (2 ounces) crumbled feta cheese
1/4 cup small fresh basil leaves or torn basil

1. Combine first 4 ingredients in a large bowl.
2. Combine vinegar and next 4 ingredients in a small bowl, stirring with a whisk. Drizzle vinegar mixture over peach mixture; toss well to coat. Sprinkle with cheese and basil. Yield: 8 servings (serving size: 1 cup).

CALORIES 75; FAT 3.5g (sat 1.3g, mono 1.6g, poly 0.3g); PROTEIN 2.1g; CARB 9.9g; FIBER 1.7g; CHOL 6mg; IRON 0.4mg; SODIUM 230mg; CALC 47mg

Indian-Spiced Okra

Quick & Easy

Even folks who usually don't like okra enjoy the taste and texture of this highly seasoned dish. We left the seeds in the chile for moderate spice. Serve with grilled chicken or lamb.

¾ teaspoon brown mustard seeds
1 tablespoon canola oil
1 teaspoon ground coriander
1 teaspoon finely chopped serrano chile
½ teaspoon kosher salt
¼ teaspoon curry powder
1 pound small to medium okra pods, trimmed

1. Cook mustard seeds in a large heavy skillet over medium-high heat 30 seconds or until toasted and fragrant. Add oil and remaining ingredients; cook 1 minute, stirring occasionally. Cover, reduce heat to low, and cook 8 minutes, stirring occasionally. Uncover and increase heat to high; cook an additional 2 minutes or until okra is lightly browned. Yield: 6 servings (serving size: ⅔ cup).

CALORIES 47; FAT 2.6g (sat 0.2g, mono 1.4g, poly 0.7g); PROTEIN 1.7g; CARB 5.7g; FIBER 2.7g; CHOL 0mg; IRON 0.7mg; SODIUM 163mg; CALC 66mg

Quick & Easy • Kid Friendly

Grilled Flank Steak with Avocado and Two-Tomato Salsa

Fresh tarragon offers an unexpected but delightful flavor to the salsa. Serve as a simple entrée or as soft tacos with warmed corn tortillas.

½ cup diced avocado
½ cup diced red tomato
½ cup diced yellow tomato
1 tablespoon finely chopped red onion
1 tablespoon fresh lime juice
2 teaspoons chopped fresh tarragon
1½ teaspoons extra-virgin olive oil
¾ teaspoon salt, divided
½ teaspoon black pepper, divided
1 (1½-pound) flank steak, trimmed
Cooking spray

1. Prepare grill to medium-high heat.
2. Combine first 7 ingredients, ⅛ teaspoon salt, and ¼ teaspoon pepper.
3. Sprinkle steak evenly with ½ teaspoon salt and remaining ¼ teaspoon pepper. Place steak on a grill rack coated with cooking spray; grill 6 minutes on each side or until desired degree of doneness. Remove steak from grill; let stand 5 minutes. Cut steak across grain into thin slices; sprinkle evenly with remaining ⅛ teaspoon salt. Serve with salsa. Yield: 6 servings (serving size: about 3 ounces steak and about 2 tablespoons salsa).

CALORIES 208; FAT 11g (sat 3.7g, mono 5.2g, poly 0.7g); PROTEIN 23.8g; CARB 2.5g; FIBER 1g; CHOL 43mg; IRON 1.8mg; SODIUM 345mg; CALC 21mg

Quick & Easy • Kid Friendly

Herbed Green and Wax Beans

Adding a bundle of herbs (bouquet garni) to the steaming liquid imparts subtle flavor and aroma to the vegetables.

4 fresh thyme sprigs
4 fresh parsley sprigs
1 bay leaf
1 cup water
½ pound green beans, trimmed
½ pound fresh yellow wax beans, trimmed
1 tablespoon extra-virgin olive oil
½ teaspoon butter, softened
¼ teaspoon salt
¼ teaspoon freshly ground black pepper

1. Tie thyme, parsley, and bay leaf together with twine. Place in a large skillet with 1 cup water. Bring to a boil; cook 1 minute. Add beans; cover, reduce heat, and simmer 8 minutes or until crisp-tender. Drain well; discard herbs. Place beans in a bowl. Add oil and remaining ingredients; toss well to coat. Yield: 4 servings (serving size: about 1 cup beans).

CALORIES 49; FAT 1.7g (sat 0.5g, mono 1g, poly 0.2g); PROTEIN 1.7g; CARB 6.9g; FIBER 2g; CHOL 1mg; IRON 0.9mg; SODIUM 161mg; CALC 36mg

Quick & Easy • Kid Friendly

Roasted Summer Squashes with Caper Gremolata

A traditional gremolata (garnish) features lemon rind, garlic, and parsley. We include briny capers in the mix to add excitement to this side.

Gremolata:
¼ cup chopped fresh flat-leaf parsley
1 teaspoon grated lemon rind
2 tablespoons fresh lemon juice
1 tablespoon capers
2 teaspoons extra-virgin olive oil
1 garlic clove, minced
Squash:
4 cups multicolored pattypan squash, halved lengthwise
3 cups baby zucchini, trimmed
2 teaspoons extra-virgin olive oil
¼ teaspoon kosher salt
¼ teaspoon freshly ground black pepper

1. Preheat oven to 475°.
2. To prepare gremolata, combine first 6 ingredients in a small bowl. Set aside.
3. To prepare squash, combine squash, zucchini, and 2 teaspoons oil. Sprinkle with salt and pepper. Arrange squash, cut sides down, in a single layer on a jelly-roll pan. Bake at 475° for 15 minutes or until squash is tender and lightly browned, stirring after 7 minutes. Sprinkle gremolata over squash. Serve immediately. Yield: 8 servings (serving size: about ¾ cup).

CALORIES 43; FAT 2.4g (sat 0.3g, mono 1.7g, poly 0.3g); PROTEIN 1.5g; CARB 4.7g; FIBER 1.5g; CHOL 0mg; IRON 0.2mg; SODIUM 92mg; CALC 5mg

NUTRITION MADE EASY
HEALTHY GRILLING

Everyone's favorite summertime cooking technique has suffered from alarming research about carcinogens. Here's how to grill food that's flavorful and safe.

Meat, fire, flavor, fast: These make grilling summer's go-to cooking method. And for a long time grilling was assumed to be one of the healthier cooking methods going: It doesn't require any additional cooking fat, and in fact, a fair amount of the fat from the meat melts and drips away, producing delicious smoky flavors when it explodes on the coals below.

But you'd have to live in a cave not to know that grilling has developed a bit of a reputation. Research has shown that the high temperatures achieved on the grill (whether gas or charcoal) can cause carcinogenic compounds—heterocyclic amines (HCAs)—to form in proteins from meat, fish, and poultry. Meanwhile, the smoke from incomplete combustion of fuel—exacerbated by all that dripping fat—contains other potentially harmful compounds.

The sensible thing is not to back away from the grill, but to approach the grill with a plan to minimize the risks. What foods you choose to grill; how they are cut, handled, and marinated; how long they remain over the fire—all these matter. Use our strategies, and the recipes that embody them, for healthy grilling this summer.

Kid Friendly
Lemon and Sage Chicken

Antioxidant compounds in citrus fruits and herbs may reduce the formation of HCA compounds. Here, we leave the skin on for moisture while grilling, then discard it.

1 (4-pound) roasting chicken
1 tablespoon grated lemon rind
1/3 cup fresh lemon juice
1/3 cup Sauternes or other dessert white wine
1/4 cup minced fresh sage leaves
1 tablespoon olive oil
1 teaspoon paprika
1/4 teaspoon freshly ground black pepper
2 large garlic cloves, grated
1/2 teaspoon salt

1. Remove and discard giblets and neck from chicken. Cut chicken into drumsticks, thighs, and breasts; cut each breast in half crosswise to form 4 breast pieces total. Reserve wings and back for another use.
2. Combine rind and next 7 ingredients in a small bowl, and stir with a whisk. Place juice mixture in a large zip-top plastic bag. Add chicken to bag; seal and marinate in refrigerator 1 hour. Remove chicken from bag, and discard marinade. Sprinkle chicken evenly with salt.
3. Prepare grill to medium-high heat. After preheating, turn left burner off (leave right burner on), or arrange charcoal on one side of grill for indirect heat.
4. Place chicken on grill rack covering right burner; grill over direct heat 15 minutes, turning every 5 minutes. Move chicken to grill rack covering left burner; grill over indirect heat 10 minutes or until a thermometer registers 165°. Discard chicken skin. Yield: 4 servings (serving size: 2 breast pieces or 1 leg and 1 thigh).

CALORIES 246; **FAT** 13.7g (sat 3.9g, mono 5.7g, poly 3g); **PROTEIN** 26.3g; **CARB** 2.2g; **FIBER** 0.1g; **CHOL** 84mg; **IRON** 1.3mg; **SODIUM** 374mg; **CALC** 15mg

MARINATE, CHAR LIGHTLY, AND MIND THE BEEF

■ **MARINATE YOUR MEAT.** It may help reduce those nasty HCAs. Kansas State University researchers marinated steaks in three different mixtures of oil, vinegar, and herbs and spices. After grilling, HCAs in the marinated steaks were cut by 57 to 88 percent. Dozens of studies confirm the effect. The reason it works is not so clear: The marinade may create a protective barrier between the meat's proteins and the heat of the grill. Or antioxidants in the marinade may combat HCAs head-on.

■ **BEWARE OF BURNT.** A bit of char is unavoidable (and it tastes good), but inc inerated meat will contain more cancer-causing compounds. Don't get coals super-hot and then plop fatty meats directly over them. Work the whole grilling surface.

■ **REDUCE BACTERIA IN BURGERS.** To kill the common E. coli bacteria, the USDA recommends cooking ground beef to 160°. If you want to go for medium-rare, grind your own beef, then cook immediately. If you use store-bought meat, flip burgers frequently: A study in the *Journal of Food Protection* advised flipping every 30 seconds for optimal E. coli reduction! Another study found that even when two patties both reached 160°, the one flipped more often had one-fifth the E. coli.

Lemongrass and Garlic Shrimp

Shrimp is a great grilling option because it's lean (that means less likelihood of flare-ups that cause burning or charring) and also because it cooks so quickly. Look for fresh or frozen lemongrass in Asian markets and gourmet grocery stores. You can substitute 1 teaspoon grated lemon rind for the lemongrass in a pinch.

1/4 cup sugar
3 tablespoons canola oil
2 tablespoons fish sauce
1 fresh lemongrass stalk, trimmed and
    coarsely chopped
1 large garlic clove, grated
36 jumbo Tiger shrimp, peeled and deveined
    (about 2 pounds)

1. Place first 5 ingredients in a food processor or mini chopper; process until lemongrass is finely chopped. Transfer sugar mixture to a large zip-top plastic bag. Add shrimp; seal and marinate in refrigerator 45 minutes.
2. Prepare grill to high heat.
3. Remove shrimp from bag; discard marinade. Thread 6 shrimp onto each of 6 (12-inch) skewers. Place skewers on grill rack; grill 2 minutes on each side or until done. Yield: 4 servings (serving size: 9 shrimp).

CALORIES 314; FAT 9.2g (sat 1.1g, mono 3.7g, poly 3.1g); PROTEIN 46.4g; CARB 9g; FIBER 0g; CHOL 345mg; IRON 5.6mg; SODIUM 621mg; CALC 120mg

Lamb Kebabs

Zesty marinades make for healthier grilling.

1 cup plain whole-milk yogurt
1 1/2 teaspoons salt, divided
1/4 teaspoon plus 1/8 teaspoon freshly
    ground black pepper, divided
1 tablespoon grated peeled fresh ginger
2 teaspoons Madras curry powder
1/2 teaspoon ground cumin
1 large garlic clove, grated
2 1/2 pounds boneless leg of lamb, trimmed
    and cut into 1-inch pieces

1. Combine yogurt, 1/4 teaspoon salt, 1/8 teaspoon pepper, and next 4 ingredients; stir with a whisk. Place yogurt mixture in a large zip-top plastic bag. Add lamb; seal and marinate in refrigerator 45 minutes.
2. Prepare grill to medium heat.
3. Remove lamb from bag; discard marinade. Thread lamb evenly onto 20 (10-inch) skewers; sprinkle evenly with 1 teaspoon salt and remaining 1/4 teaspoon pepper. Place kebabs on grill rack, and grill 4 minutes for medium-rare or desired degree of doneness, turning once. Sprinkle evenly with remaining 1/4 teaspoon salt. Yield: 10 servings (serving size: 2 kebabs).

CALORIES 201; FAT 11.9g (sat 5.5g, mono 4.8g, poly 0.5g); PROTEIN 21.7g; CARB 0.4g; FIBER 0g; CHOL 71mg; IRON 1.7mg; SODIUM 361mg; CALC 16mg

---

LESS MEAT, MORE FLAVOR

A LIGHT TAKE ON PAN ROASTS

By Mark Bittman

Invert the ratios of the classic dish—more summer vegetables, accents of seafood—for the season's best one-dish meals.

Many pan roasts are cooked on top of the stove, usually in a fair amount of cream. (Why this is called a "roast," when it's clearly a stew, is beyond me.) This is nice—if you have good cream—but it's hardly a dish that's going to make it into your healthy weekly repertoire. It's rich, expensive, and practically vegetable-free.

I prefer this rule-breaking method, where you cook assorted vegetables and a little seafood (sometimes with sausage, sometimes not) in a big (ahem) roasting pan. The dry heat ensures some browning and crispness, and pushes the liquid into service for deglazing and making a little sauce, not poaching, so you use a lot less.

And, because you're not drowning the whole thing in cream, you can still taste the ocean, which is kind of what you want. Kitchen cleanup is a snap (especially if you cook it outdoors as described below). As a bonus, you get a meal that isn't a salad but still provides a variety of colors and textures.

Buying fish can be tricky: Not only are there flavor and freshness to consider, but also sustainability and contaminants. Fortunately, pan roasts are perfect for mussels, clams, and oysters. When these come from domestic or Canadian waters, they're generally raised in a way that doesn't trash the environment. (For shrimp, look for wild.) You can also make a pan roast with fin fish, but you'll be missing out on the delicious briny liquid generated by simmering mollusks and crustaceans.

---

6 MORE HEALTHY GRILLING STRATEGIES

Even if you don't have time for a quick marinade to help protect proteins, try these other smart practices for the healthiest grilling.

1 FLIP AT THE RIGHT TIME. You want to avoid burning but not rip the meat apart. Give it a gentle tug; it's ready to flip when it comes loose without pulling.
2 SIZE MATTERS. Cube or slice meats into smaller portions to speed cook time, or choose quick-cooking options like shrimp or fish.
3 THE SHORTER THE COOK TIME, THE BETTER. The faster foods are cooked, the less likely they'll develop dangerous charring. Don't cook meat past its goal temperature:

165° for ground poultry; 160° for ground red meats and fresh pork; or 145° for red meat steaks or chops.
4 MOVE MEAT AWAY FROM FLARE-UPS. Water on a grease fire...not a good idea. Move food to a cooler part of the grill or set aside while the fire dies down.
5 GRILL SOMETHING OTHER THAN MEAT. You'll reduce your exposure to carcinogenic compounds. Opt for low- or no-protein peaches, plums, tomatoes, eggplant, corn, or breads.
6 CLEAN THAT GRILLING MACHINE. Keep your grill rack spick-and-span to prevent other bits from causing flare-ups.

When it comes to vegetables, consider these recipes as guidelines. The idea is to start the longest-cooking ones in the pan first, then build in more tender vegetables before adding the seafood. A potato is always nice but hardly mandatory; cauliflower florets—though more intensely flavored—are a sound option. Or put down a layer of summer squash chunks, and cook them dry before proceeding. If you're using raw sausage or bacon, roast them along with the sturdy vegetables in this first turn in the oven.

When these begin to brown, stir in aromatic vegetables like garlic, shallots, or onion; this is also a good time for cooked or smoked meat, like prosciutto, ham, or Spanish-style chorizo—even a teeny bit adds a lot of flavor. If you're adding some vegetables that require a moderate amount of cooking—like green beans, cabbage, corn, or carrots—add them now, too, and cook until they just begin to get tender.

Wait to add the seafood until the vegetables are just about ready, since they'll return to the oven for only a few minutes more. Here's when the liquid goes in. Although it isn't much, it helps you scrape the tasty browned bits from the bottom of the pan and keeps everything moist for the last blast in the oven. I wait until this stage to add spices so they don't burn but their raw taste cooks off. Instead of the curry powder and Spanish smoked paprika in these recipes, you might try Old Bay seasoning, chili powder, a pinch of cayenne, or even five-spice powder; or use only salt and pepper, if you like.

You can move the whole pan roast operation outside, if you prefer: To cook it on a grill, build a medium-high fire (or heat a gas grill) off to one side for indirect cooking. Cover the grill, and roast as you would in the oven, adding ingredients in stages as described above.

Or cook it over a live fire. Simply place the pan just to the side over the fire. You can cover it with foil, though the results will be more like those from steaming. Or leave the pan open to the sky over a moderately high heat—which, come to think of it, sounds suspiciously like a traditional pan roast.

Kid Friendly
Smoky Spanish-Style Pan Roast

1 pound small red new potatoes, halved
2 tablespoons olive oil
3/4 teaspoon salt, divided
1/2 teaspoon freshly ground black pepper, divided
3/4 pound unpeeled large shrimp
1/4 pound Spanish chorizo, thinly sliced
1 pound green beans, trimmed
4 garlic cloves, chopped
1/2 cup pilsner beer
1/2 teaspoon Spanish smoked paprika
2 red bell peppers, cut into thin strips
1/4 cup fresh flat-leaf parsley leaves

1. Preheat oven to 400°.
2. Combine potatoes, oil, ½ teaspoon salt, and ¼ teaspoon black pepper in a large roasting pan, tossing well to coat potatoes. Arrange potatoes in a single layer, cut sides down, in pan. Bake at 400° for 15 minutes or until potatoes are lightly browned.
3. While potatoes cook, peel shrimp, leaving tails intact. Devein shrimp, if desired. Set shrimp aside.
4. Stir chorizo, green beans, garlic, remaining ¼ teaspoon salt, and remaining ¼ teaspoon black pepper into pan. Bake at 400° for 10 minutes. Add beer, paprika, and bell pepper, scraping pan to loosen browned bits. Nestle shrimp into vegetable mixture. Bake at 400° for 10 minutes or until potatoes and green beans are tender and shrimp are done. Sprinkle with parsley. Yield: 4 servings (serving size: 1½ cups).

CALORIES 392; FAT 15.5g (sat 3.8g, mono 8.5g, poly 2.4g); PROTEIN 28g; CARB 36.6g; FIBER 7.7g; CHOL 129mg; IRON 4mg; SODIUM 590mg; CALC 127mg

Curried Mussel Pan Roast

Use either regular curry powder or, for more kick, Madras curry powder.

1 pound Yukon gold potatoes, cut into 1½-inch pieces
2 tablespoons olive oil
1/2 teaspoon salt
1/2 teaspoon freshly ground black pepper
3 cups cherry tomatoes
1/2 cup light coconut milk
1 teaspoon curry powder
4 medium ears fresh corn, shucked and cut crosswise into 2-inch pieces
1 pound mussels, scrubbed
1 cup chopped green onions
3 tablespoons chopped fresh mint
Lime wedges

1. Preheat oven to 400°.
2. Combine first 4 ingredients in a large roasting pan, tossing well to coat. Arrange potatoes in a single layer in pan. Bake at 400° for 20 minutes or until lightly browned, stirring after 10 minutes. Stir in tomatoes and next 3 ingredients, scraping pan to loosen any browned bits. Nestle mussels into vegetable mixture. Bake at 400° for 15 minutes or until potatoes are tender and mussels open. Discard any unopened shells. Stir in onions and mint.
3. Spoon about 3 cups mussels mixture into each of 4 bowls; spoon cooking liquid evenly over top. Serve with lime wedges. Yield: 4 servings.

CALORIES 373; FAT 11.8g (sat 3g, mono 5.8g, poly 1.9g); PROTEIN 18.6g; CARB 51.2g; FIBER 6.2g; CHOL 28mg; IRON 6.5mg; SODIUM 625mg; CALC 65mg

LIGHT POTATO SALAD

Reinvent this popular staple by replacing saturated fat with heart-healthy options and slashing sodium without losing flavor.

Americans can definitely agree on one thing: Potatoes are our favorite veggie. Each of us eats about a whopping 130 pounds per year. During the summer months (if not year-round), you can safely bet that loads of potatoes find their way into the ubiquitous potato salad. Honestly, can you have a cookout or picnic without one? Despite regional interpretations, there's really one basic way to make this popular dish. And here, we'll show you how to master the technique and turn out a variety of unique, healthy salads.

Staff Favorite • Quick & Easy
Make Ahead • Kid Friendly

Farmers' Market Potato Salad

Look for a mix of red, purple, and brown-skinned fingerling potatoes, so named because of their oblong shapes, to prepare this stunning salad. If you can't find them, substitute small red potatoes. You can serve this dish at room temperature just after it's tossed together, or make it ahead, refrigerate, and serve chilled.

1 cup fresh corn kernels (about 2 ears)
2 pounds fingerling potatoes, cut into 1-inch pieces
2½ tablespoons olive oil, divided
2 tablespoons chopped fresh tarragon
2 tablespoons cider vinegar
2 tablespoons whole-grain Dijon mustard
½ teaspoon hot pepper sauce (such as Tabasco)
¾ teaspoon salt
½ teaspoon freshly ground black pepper
Cooking spray
¾ cup vertically sliced red onion
¾ cup diced zucchini
1 cup cherry tomatoes, halved

1. Preheat oven to 425°.
2. Place corn and potatoes on a jelly-roll pan. Drizzle vegetables with 1 tablespoon oil; toss to coat. Bake at 425° for 30 minutes or until potatoes are tender. Place mixture in a large bowl. Combine tarragon and next 5 ingredients in a small bowl, stirring with a whisk. Gradually add remaining 1½ tablespoons oil, stirring constantly with a whisk. Drizzle potato mixture with dressing; toss gently to coat.
3. Heat a large skillet over medium heat. Coat pan with cooking spray. Add onion and zucchini to pan; cook 4 minutes or until lightly browned, stirring occasionally. Add zucchini mixture and tomatoes to potato mixture; toss gently to combine. Yield: 6 servings (serving size: about 1 cup).

CALORIES 198; FAT 6.6g (sat 0.9g, mono 4.1g, poly 0.7g); PROTEIN 4.5g; CARB 32.7g; FIBER 3.8g; CHOL 0mg; IRON 1.4mg; SODIUM 438mg; CALC 28mg

---

NUTRITION NOTES

- Potatoes are a good source of complex carbohydrates, potassium, and phytonutrients.
- Spuds are low in calories. Keep potato salads healthy by adding heart-healthy oils in moderation.

Quick & Easy • Make Ahead
Kid Friendly

Lemon-Arugula Potato Salad

If you want to make this potato salad ahead, prepare the recipe through step two. Once the potato mixture is completely cooled, cover and refrigerate. Toss with fresh arugula just before serving so the greens don't wilt or get bruised. Peppery arugula contrasts the tangy lemon and creamy potatoes. Watercress would also work, or try a bitter green like frisée.

2 pounds Yukon gold potatoes, peeled and cut into 1-inch pieces
7 teaspoons extra-virgin olive oil, divided
½ cup finely chopped shallots (about 3 small)
1½ tablespoons sherry vinegar
2 teaspoons stone-ground mustard
1 teaspoon grated lemon rind
1 teaspoon fresh lemon juice
½ teaspoon salt
¼ teaspoon freshly ground black pepper
2½ cups loosely packed arugula

1. Place potato pieces in a medium saucepan; cover with cold water to 2 inches above potatoes. Bring to a boil over medium-high heat. Reduce heat to medium, and gently simmer 10 minutes or until potatoes are tender. Drain potatoes.
2. Heat a small skillet over medium-high heat. Add 1 teaspoon oil to pan; swirl to coat. Add shallots to pan; sauté 3 minutes or until lightly browned, stirring occasionally. Remove from heat. Combine shallots, vinegar, and next 5 ingredients in a small bowl, stirring well with a whisk. Gradually add remaining 2 tablespoons oil, stirring constantly with a whisk until combined. Drizzle dressing over warm potatoes; toss gently to coat. Cool completely.
3. Add arugula to potato mixture; toss gently. Serve immediately. Yield: 6 servings (serving size: about 1 cup).

CALORIES 155; FAT 5.3g (sat 0.7g, mono 3.8g, poly 0.6g); PROTEIN 3.2g; CARB 23.1g; FIBER 1.6g; CHOL 0mg; IRON 1.3mg; SODIUM 247mg; CALC 19mg

4 STEPS TO PERFECT POTATO SALAD

1 CUT TO SIZE. Cut potatoes into uniform shapes and sizes so they'll cook evenly. If they're different sizes, some will become mushy while others still have an undesirable crunch. Low-starch varieties, like red potatoes, work best in potato salads.

2 START IN COLD WATER. Be sure to start with cold water when boiling potatoes. This works to solidify the outer surfaces and helps prevent them from getting too soft as the interior cooks, so the potatoes will hold their shape nicely in a potato salad.

3 ADD DRESSING. Make the dressing while the potatoes cook, and toss them with the dressing while they're still warm so they'll absorb maximum flavor. If using dairy products, like sour cream, allow the potatoes to cool slightly before tossing to prevent curdling.

4 ADD ADDITIONAL FLAVORS AND INGREDIENTS. Customize your salad. For example, add your favorite veggies, fresh herbs, or salad greens. You can even give the salad an international flair: Lemongrass adds Thai flavor; chutney lends an Indian taste.

WAXY, LOW-STARCH VARIETIES, LIKE RED-SKINNED POTATOES, YUKON GOLDS, AND FINGERLINGS, WORK BEST IN POTATO SALADS BECAUSE WHEN COOKED PROPERLY, THEY DON'T BECOME MUSHY.

EVERYDAY VEGETARIAN

THE JOY OF EGGS

Whether they're enriching cheese-laced tarts, enveloping fresh, seasonal vegetables, or puffing savory soufflés, eggs are a versatile ingredient in meatless meals—and a good protein source.

Herbed Ricotta Tart

Serve with a mixed greens salad.

1 (11-ounce) can refrigerated pizza crust dough
Cooking spray
2 cups thinly sliced green onions
1⅓ cups part-skim ricotta cheese
½ cup thinly sliced fresh chives
2 tablespoons minced fresh dill
½ teaspoon salt
½ teaspoon freshly ground black pepper
2 large eggs, lightly beaten
1 large egg white, lightly beaten
2 tablespoons finely grated fresh Parmigiano-Reggiano cheese

1. Preheat oven to 375°.
2. Unroll dough, and press into bottom and up sides of a 9-inch round removable-bottom tart pan coated with cooking spray.
3. Heat a medium nonstick skillet over medium heat. Coat pan with cooking spray. Add onions to pan; cook 5 minutes, stirring occasionally. Combine cooked green onions, ricotta cheese, and next 6 ingredients. Pour onion mixture into prepared crust; sprinkle mixture with Parmigiano-Reggiano cheese. Bake at 375° for 35 minutes or until center is set. Let stand 5 minutes. Cut into 6 wedges. Yield: 6 servings (serving size: 1 wedge).

CALORIES 259; FAT 8.4g (sat 3.5g, mono 2.1g, poly 0.4g); PROTEIN 14.9g; CARB 30.4g; FIBER 1.7g; CHOL 89mg; IRON 2.5mg; SODIUM 673mg; CALC 206mg

Parmesan and Eggplant Soufflé

There's no need to beat egg whites for this soufflé; it rises nicely with whisked eggs and egg whites. For overnight preparation, assemble and refrigerate the night before. Pull the baking dish out of the refrigerator as the oven preheats, and bake as instructed.

Cooking spray
4 cups (1-inch) cubed eggplant (about 1 pound)
1 cup chopped red bell pepper (about 1 medium)
½ cup chopped red onion
½ teaspoon salt, divided
1.1 ounces all-purpose flour (about ¼ cup)
2 cups fat-free milk
5 tablespoons grated fresh Parmigiano-Reggiano cheese, divided
⅛ teaspoon ground red pepper
4 large eggs
3 large egg whites
1 tablespoon chopped fresh oregano
Chopped fresh parsley (optional)

1. Preheat oven to 350°.
2. Heat a large nonstick skillet over medium-high heat. Coat pan with cooking spray. Add eggplant, bell pepper, and onion; sauté 5 minutes or until tender. Stir in ¼ teaspoon salt; sauté 5 minutes. Set aside.
3. Weigh or lightly spoon flour into a dry measuring cup; level with a knife. Place flour in a medium saucepan; add milk, stirring with a whisk. Bring to a boil over medium heat, and cook milk mixture 1 minute or until thick, stirring constantly. Add 3 tablespoons cheese, stirring until cheese melts. Remove from heat; stir in remaining ¼ teaspoon salt and ground red pepper. Let stand 15 minutes.
4. Combine eggs and egg whites in a medium bowl, stirring with a whisk. Stir in oregano. Gradually add hot milk mixture to egg mixture, stirring constantly with a whisk. Fold in eggplant mixture; pour into an 11 x 7–inch glass or ceramic baking dish coated with cooking spray. Sprinkle with remaining 2 tablespoons cheese. Bake at 350° for 30 minutes or until puffy and set. Garnish with parsley, if desired. Serve immediately. Yield: 4 servings.

CALORIES 221; FAT 7.3g (sat 2.8g, mono 2.5g, poly 0.9g); PROTEIN 17.7g; CARB 21.5g; FIBER 3.9g; CHOL 219mg; IRON 1.8mg; SODIUM 557mg; CALC 270mg

Quick & Easy
Scrambled Eggs with Morel and Tarragon Cream Sauce

This dish is great served with fruit for breakfast or brunch, or paired with a salad and crisp white wine for dinner. Use fresh morel mushrooms if they're available—substitute 1 cup cleaned, fresh mushrooms for dried.

½ cup (about ½ ounce) dried morel mushrooms
2 teaspoons butter
¼ cup finely chopped shallots
½ cup organic vegetable broth
1 teaspoon fresh lemon juice
⅓ cup reduced-fat sour cream
2 teaspoons chopped fresh chives, divided
2 teaspoons chopped fresh tarragon, divided
½ teaspoon salt, divided
¼ teaspoon freshly ground black pepper, divided
Cooking spray
3 large eggs
3 large egg whites
4 English muffins, split and toasted

1. Place mushrooms in a bowl, and cover with boiling water. Cover and let stand 20 minutes or until tender. Drain well; coarsely chop.
2. Melt butter in a large nonstick skillet over medium-high heat. Add shallots; sauté 1 minute. Add mushrooms; sauté 2 minutes. Add broth and juice; cook 2 minutes. Remove from heat; stir in sour cream. Stir in 1 teaspoon chives, 1 teaspoon tarragon, ¼ teaspoon salt, and ⅛ teaspoon pepper. Place mushroom sauce in a small bowl; cover and keep warm. Wipe pan clean with a paper towel.
3. Heat pan over medium heat, and coat with cooking spray. Combine remaining 1 teaspoon chives, 1 teaspoon tarragon, ¼ teaspoon salt, ⅛ teaspoon black pepper, eggs, and egg whites, stirring with a whisk. Pour egg mixture into pan. Cook 4 minutes or until soft-scrambled, stirring frequently.
4. Place 2 muffin halves, cut sides up, on each of 4 plates. Top each serving with about 3 tablespoons sauce and ¼ cup eggs. Yield: 4 servings.

CALORIES 265; FAT 9.2g (sat 4.1g, mono 2.9g, poly 1.2g); PROTEIN 14.3g; CARB 31.6g; FIBER 1.8g; CHOL 171mg; IRON 3.4mg; SODIUM 732mg; CALC 152mg

Quick & Easy
Summer Vegetable Frittata

1½ tablespoons olive oil
1 cup diced zucchini
½ cup chopped red bell pepper
⅓ cup chopped onion
1 tablespoon chopped fresh thyme
½ teaspoon salt, divided
¼ teaspoon freshly ground black pepper, divided
2 garlic cloves, minced
½ cup chopped seeded tomato
9 large eggs

1. Heat oil in a 10-inch nonstick broiler-proof skillet over medium heat. Add zucchini, bell pepper, onion, thyme, ¼ teaspoon salt, ⅛ teaspoon black pepper, and garlic. Cover and cook 7 minutes or until vegetables are tender, stirring occasionally. Stir in tomato. Cook, uncovered, 5 minutes or until liquid evaporates.
2. Combine eggs, remaining ¼ teaspoon salt, and remaining ⅛ teaspoon black pepper in a medium bowl; stir with a whisk until frothy. Pour egg mixture into pan over vegetables, stirring gently. Cover, reduce heat, and cook 15 minutes or until almost set in center.
3. Preheat broiler.
4. Broil frittata 3 minutes or until set. Invert onto a serving platter; cut into 8 wedges. Yield: 4 servings (serving size: 2 wedges).

CALORIES 227; FAT 16.4g (sat 4.2g, mono 8g, poly 2.1g); PROTEIN 15.1g; CARB 5.5g; FIBER 1.1g; CHOL 476mg; IRON 2.4mg; SODIUM 458mg; CALC 80mg

A CHINESE-AMERICAN TRADITION

For as long as anyone can remember, Sutseng Liu's home and kitchen have been gathering places for those in want of good food and good company.

I t was January 15, 2010, and Friday night was family night at Sutseng Liu's house. Two daughters and her granddaughter headed to join Sutseng for dinner at the Burlingame, California, home she shared with her sister and her third daughter, the way they had ended most weeks for more than a decade.

The get-togethers had been a tradition Sutseng started years ago to keep everyone connected, and while the Friday-night dinners were intimate and casual, larger gatherings for holidays and other occasions regularly brought together a dozen or more relatives and friends. For decades, Sutseng spent the better part of her days planning menus and preparing meals for her loved ones. By the age of 90, she had passed along the cooking responsibilities to the younger generations, but her home remained the place where her family cooked together and caught up. This was her gift to them.

Born in Taiwan, Sutseng was an elementary school teacher when she met her husband, Jiachi Liu. After they married, the couple moved to Tokyo, where daughter Wendy Lee and son Ben Liu were born. Several years later, the young family moved back to Taiwan, where they had two more daughters, Fanny Liu and Ginger Wigby. Since their home was then located in a central area that friends and relatives frequented, it was natural for the always welcoming Sutseng to host as many as 10 guests for dinner nearly every night.

Beginning in the late '60s, Sutseng's children left Taiwan for America, spreading across the states to Alabama, Missouri, Kansas, and New York. Eventually, her daughters made their way to the San Francisco Bay Area to be near one another; today they live just a few miles apart. In the early '80s, Sutseng moved with her husband and sister Sue Chan from Taiwan to join them; son Ben lives near Las Vegas and visits regularly. As in her homeland, Sutseng's California home became the hub of family activity, with food at the heart of the action.

Yet in the tradition of immigrants, they blend culinary traditions, fusing Chinese, Japanese, and American flavors. The menu on any given night might include sticky rice, sashimi, porcini risotto, and roasted Brussels sprouts. They adapt favorite recipes using healthier techniques—as in Garlic-Ginger Shrimp Stir-Fry (page 158), which relies on flavorful seasonings, rather than excessive oil, for richness—and welcome new foods just as their mother welcomed unexpected guests to the table. "If it's good, we adopt it," says Wendy.

All are well fed in this house—friends, strangers, and family. They add helpings to each others' plates as dishes are passed. "But what's most important is getting together," says daughter Ginger. By the time plates are cleared and the conversation has wound down, everyone has been nourished—body and soul.

Note: Two months after that January dinner, Sutseng Liu passed away. Her family will continue to gather over food and nurture each other through cooking, carrying on the tradition she started so many years ago.

Shanghai-Inspired Fish Stew

Traditionally, this comfort-food stew is made with flash-fried and then long-simmered fish heads. Tilapia fillets make an excellent, quick-cooking substitute.

3 ounces uncooked bean threads (cellophane noodles)
2 cups boiling water
1 ounce dried wood ear mushrooms
4 cups fat-free, less-sodium chicken broth
2 tablespoons julienne-cut peeled fresh ginger
1 tablespoon rice vinegar
1 tablespoon less-sodium soy sauce
1 tablespoon Chinese black vinegar or Worcestershire sauce
½ teaspoon ground white pepper
½ teaspoon dark sesame oil
¼ teaspoon salt
1 pound tilapia fillets, cut into bite-sized pieces
8 ounces silken firm tofu, drained and cubed
¼ cup thinly sliced green onions

1. Prepare noodles according to package directions. Drain and rinse with cold water. Drain. Snip noodles several times with kitchen shears.
2. Combine 2 cups boiling water and mushrooms in a medium bowl; let stand 20 minutes. Drain mushrooms in a sieve over a bowl; discard mushrooms. Combine mushroom soaking liquid, broth, and next 7 ingredients in a Dutch oven. Bring to a boil. Cover, reduce heat, and simmer 20 minutes. Add tilapia; cover and simmer 10 minutes. Stir in noodles and tofu; simmer, uncovered, 5 minutes. Ladle 1 cup soup into each of 8 bowls; sprinkle each serving with 1½ teaspoons green onions. Yield: 8 servings.

CALORIES 121; **FAT** 2g (sat 0.5g, mono 0.6g, poly 0.8g); **PROTEIN** 14g; **CARB** 11.1g; **FIBER** 0.5g; **CHOL** 28mg; **IRON** 0.8mg; **SODIUM** 407mg; **CALC** 19mg

Pan-Fried Egg Rolls

Rather than the usual filling mishmash, these family-tradition egg rolls keep the ingredients more distinct, similar to spring or summer rolls. The family likes to pan-fry these so they're crisp without the fuss and mess of deep-frying.

¼ cup sweet chili sauce, divided
12 ounces fresh bean sprouts, chopped
12 (8-inch) egg roll wrappers
12 cooked jumbo shrimp, peeled, deveined, and split in half lengthwise (about 13 ounces)
6 tablespoons chopped fresh cilantro
¼ cup peanut oil
1 tablespoon rice vinegar
2 teaspoons less-sodium soy sauce
¼ teaspoon grated peeled fresh ginger
⅛ teaspoon freshly ground black pepper

1. Combine 3 tablespoons chili sauce and bean sprouts, tossing well to coat.
2. Working with 1 egg roll wrapper at a time (cover remaining wrappers to prevent drying), place wrapper onto work surface with 1 corner pointing toward you (wrapper should look like a diamond). Spoon about 2 heaping tablespoons bean sprout mixture into center of wrapper; top with 2 shrimp halves and 1½ teaspoons cilantro. Fold lower corner of wrapper over filling; fold in side corners. Moisten top corner of wrapper with water; roll up jelly-roll fashion. Place egg roll, seam sides down, on a baking sheet. Repeat procedure with remaining wrappers, bean sprout mixture, shrimp, and cilantro.
3. Heat 2 tablespoons oil in a large nonstick skillet over medium-high heat. Add 6 egg rolls, seam sides down, and cook 7 minutes or until golden, turning occasionally. Place on a wire rack. Repeat procedure with remaining 2 tablespoons oil and 6 egg rolls.
4. Combine remaining 1 tablespoon chili sauce, vinegar, and remaining ingredients. Serve sauce with egg rolls. Yield: 12 servings (serving size: 1 egg roll and 1½ teaspoons sauce).

CALORIES 103; FAT 4g (sat 0.7g, mono 1.7g, poly 1.3g); PROTEIN 7.9g; CARB 8.7g; FIBER 0.7g; CHOL 48mg; IRON 1.3mg; SODIUM 207mg; CALC 23mg

Tee Pon Pork

This aromatic, irresistible braise uses a technique similar to the one employed for Sutseng Liu's lamb stew. Look for Shaoxing at Asian markets—try to get the kind that's made for drinking, as products labeled "Shaoxing cooking wine" are loaded with salt. Serve over rice.

1 tablespoon canola oil
3½ pounds boneless pork shoulder, trimmed
½ cup less-sodium soy sauce
½ cup Shaoxing wine or dry sherry
⅓ cup packed brown sugar
2 tablespoons julienne-cut peeled fresh ginger
2 (3-inch) cinnamon sticks
1 star anise
8 teaspoons chopped fresh cilantro

1. Heat oil in a Dutch oven over high heat. Add pork to pan; cook 5 minutes or until browned, turning frequently. Remove from pan; set aside.
2. Combine soy sauce and next 5 ingredients in pan over medium heat, and stir until sugar dissolves. Return pork to pan. Cover, reduce heat, and simmer 2½ hours or until pork is fork-tender. Discard cinnamon and anise. Shred meat into large pieces using 2 forks; toss with sauce. Sprinkle with cilantro. Yield: 8 servings (serving size: about 3 ounces meat and 2 tablespoons sauce).

CALORIES 269; FAT 10.1g (sat 3g, mono 4.8g, poly 1.4g); PROTEIN 31g; CARB 10.7g; FIBER 0.2g; CHOL 85mg; IRON 1.8mg; SODIUM 615mg; CALC 36mg

WINE NOTE: The perfect wine for this spiced pork is a variety growing in spades in California, but few people know about it or have tasted it: barbera. One of the most important red grapes in Italy, barbera in this country has mostly disappeared into generic red wine blends—until recently. Now winemakers are capitalizing on the grape's beautifully high level of acidity (it makes a fantastic food wine) and spicy cherry flavors, and they are bottling it on its own. In the Sierra Foothills, for some reason, barbera often has an edge of cinnamon that makes a lovely link to this pork. You can't go wrong with the

2007 Terra d'Oro Barbera from Amador County ($18), with a rush of sweet red fruit and warm spices.

Garlic-Ginger Shrimp Stir-Fry

Family traditions often make adjustments to classic recipes. In this case, there's no soy sauce in the stir-fry—rather, the shrimp is salted first, a fantastic adaptation that causes the shrimp to become a little firmer, almost crisper over the heat.

1¼ pounds large shrimp, peeled and deveined
1 teaspoon salt
1 tablespoon dark sesame oil
1½ tablespoons minced peeled fresh ginger
5 garlic cloves, thinly sliced
1½ cups coarsely chopped red bell pepper
3 tablespoons Shaoxing (Chinese rice wine) or dry sherry
2 tablespoons rice vinegar
1 cup orange sections (about 2 large oranges)
3 cups hot cooked short-grain rice
1 cup (1-inch) cut green onions

1. Place shrimp in a bowl; sprinkle with salt, tossing well. Let stand 10 minutes.
2. Combine oil, ginger, and garlic in a wok or large nonstick skillet. Place over medium-high heat; cook 4 minutes or until ginger and garlic begin to brown. Add shrimp; stir-fry 2 minutes. Add bell pepper; stir-fry 2 minutes. Add wine and vinegar; bring to a simmer. Cook 1 minute or until wine mixture is syrupy. Gently stir in orange sections. Serve over rice; sprinkle with onions. Yield: 4 servings (serving size: 1½ cups stir-fry and ¾ cup rice).

CALORIES 417; FAT 6.5g (sat 1.1g, mono 1.9g, poly 2.6g); PROTEIN 33.4g; CARB 53.8g; FIBER 4.8g; CHOL 215mg; IRON 6.2mg; SODIUM 814mg; CALC 125mg

BREAKFAST, LUNCH, AND DINNER IN... SANTA FE

There's something to be said for knowing what you have and sticking with it. In the case of Santa Fe, New Mexico, chefs, that something is the chile pepper.

Long isolation from the rest of the Southwest and Mexico produced a distinctive style of local food featuring robust and often-fiery chiles in everything from enchiladas to eggs. Santa Fe's classic dishes might bear the same names as their Tex-Mex or Mexican cousins, but here they differ significantly in taste. Much more of their flavor is derived from local chiles; the New Mexican pepper, a crossbreed of two other varieties, was developed here in the late 1800s. You'll find other distinctive regional ingredients, too, ranging from blue cornmeal to chicos (dried corn kernels roasted in outdoor wood-fired ovens). The cuisine includes dishes that are seldom found outside the state, such as carne adovada, pork slow simmered in a fiery red chile sauce.

But change is afoot as Santa Fe celebrates its 400th anniversary in 2010. The city finds itself turning more of its culinary attention to the Spanish side of its roots. (Santa Feans used to call their New Mexican cooking "Spanish," not realizing how much it had evolved in frontier circumstances away from the mother country's food.) The Spanish renaissance here has awakened Santa Feans to other international flavors, too—from Afro-Caribbean to Vietnamese and El Salvadorean. And if you want a taste of tradition, dozens of Santa Fe restaurants continue to specialize in classic New Mexican food; skipping it altogether would be like visiting Boston without tasting its chowder.

> "WHAT EXCITES ME ABOUT CHOOSING AND PRESENTING LOCAL DISHES ALONG WITH THE EMPHATIC FLAVORS OF MEXICO AND EL SALVADOR ARE THE SHARED INGREDIENTS COMMON TO THE CUISINES."
>
> —*Katharine Kagel, chef-owner of Cafe Pasqual's*

Breakfast
Eggs Barbacoa

The long-reigning star of the Santa Fe breakfast scene is Cafe Pasqual's (pasquals.com), where Chef-Owner Katharine Kagel merges local ingredients and global ideas. Griddled polenta is topped with red chile. There are a smoked trout hash and a magnificent eggs barbacoa with chile d'arbol, which inspired our simplified home version.

1 (15-ounce) can pinto beans, rinsed and drained
6 tablespoons bottled low-sodium salsa (such as Green Mountain Gringo), divided
2 tablespoons water
8 (6-inch) corn tortillas
Cooking spray
4 large eggs
1/4 teaspoon kosher salt
1/4 teaspoon freshly ground black pepper
1 cup hot Beef Barbacoa (recipe on page 160)
1/2 cup (2 ounces) queso fresco, crumbled
1/4 cup finely chopped green onions
1/4 cup finely chopped fresh cilantro
4 lime wedges

1. Place beans in a food processor; process until smooth. Combine beans, 2 tablespoons salsa, and 2 tablespoons water in a small saucepan; heat over low heat until warm, stirring occasionally. Keep warm.
2. Heat a large nonstick skillet over medium-high heat. Lightly coat both sides of each tortilla with cooking spray. Place 1 tortilla in pan, and cook 30 seconds on each side or until toasted. Repeat procedure with remaining tortillas.
3. Add water to a large skillet, filling two-thirds full; bring to a boil. Reduce heat; simmer. Break 1 egg into each of 4 (6-ounce) custard cups coated with cooking spray. Place custard cups in simmering water in pan. Cover pan; cook 8 minutes. Remove custard cups from water. Sprinkle salt and pepper evenly over eggs.
4. Place 2 tortillas on each of 4 plates, and top each tortilla with 2 tablespoons bean mixture. Top beans with 2 tablespoons Beef Barbacoa. Place 1 poached

continued

egg on each plate so it overlaps both tortillas. Top each serving with 1 tablespoon remaining salsa. Sprinkle each serving with 2 tablespoons cheese, 1 tablespoon green onions, and 1 tablespoon cilantro. Serve with lime wedges. Yield: 4 servings.

CALORIES 362; FAT 11.9g (sat 3.9g, mono 4.1g, poly 1.6g); PROTEIN 32.2g; CARB 33g; FIBER 5.7g; CHOL 273mg; IRON 4.3mg; SODIUM 604mg; CALC 132mg

Make Ahead
Beef Barbacoa:
1 teaspoon freshly ground black pepper
1 teaspoon dried oregano
3/4 teaspoon kosher salt
3/4 teaspoon ground cumin
3/4 teaspoon ancho chile powder
1 (2 1/4-pound) boneless chuck steak, trimmed
Cooking spray
1 cup water
2 garlic cloves, thinly sliced
1 tablespoon fresh lime juice

1. Preheat oven to 300°.
2. Combine first 5 ingredients in a small bowl; rub oregano mixture evenly over beef. Heat a large Dutch oven over high heat. Coat pan with cooking spray. Add beef to pan; cook 3 minutes on each side or until browned. Add 1 cup water and garlic to pan, scraping pan to loosen browned bits. Cover and bake at 300° for 3 hours or until beef is very tender. Cool to room temperature. Cover and chill 8 hours or overnight.
3. Skim fat from surface of broth. Remove beef; shred with 2 forks. Return beef to pan; bring to a simmer over medium-high heat. Simmer mixture 3 minutes or until liquid evaporates; stir in lime juice. Reduce heat to medium, and cook beef 3 minutes or until crisp in spots. Yield: 10 servings (serving size: 2 ounces).

CALORIES 121; FAT 4.2g (sat 1.5g, mono 1.7g, poly 0.2g); PROTEIN 18.9g; CARB 0.8g; FIBER 0.2g; CHOL 57mg; IRON 2.3mg; SODIUM 179mg; CALC 11mg

Quick & Easy
Lunch
Cantaloupe, Prosciutto, and Cabrales Salad

Lunch at La Boca (labocasf.com) includes this summer-time specialty: Chef James Campbell Caruso slices cantaloupe thinly to cover a dinner plate, then tops it with olive oil, rosemary-infused honey, bits of Spanish blue cheese and ham, and a tangle of greens. You'll want to save room for dessert: Caruso's wife and pastry chef, Leslie Campbell, excels with fruity desserts, such as strawberry slices marinated in sherry vinegar syrup and topped with crème anglaise and a skinny, crunchy lengua de gato ("cat's tongue") cookie.

3 tablespoons extra-virgin olive oil, divided
2 teaspoons sherry vinegar
3 cups loosely packed arugula
1 (3 1/4-pound) cantaloupe, peeled, seeded, and cut lengthwise into 20 (1/4-inch-thick) wedges
4 (1/2-ounce) slices prosciutto, cut into thin strips
1/2 cup (2 ounces) Cabrales cheese, crumbled
2 tablespoons honey
1/4 teaspoon kosher salt
1/4 teaspoon freshly ground black pepper

1. Combine 1 1/2 tablespoons oil and vinegar, stirring with a whisk. Combine vinegar mixture and arugula in a bowl. Fan 5 cantaloupe wedges on each of 4 plates; top cantaloupe with about 3/4 cup arugula mixture. Place 1/2 ounce prosciutto on each plate; top each serving with 2 tablespoons cheese. Drizzle remaining 1 1/2 tablespoons oil and honey over salad; sprinkle with salt and pepper. Yield: 4 servings.

CALORIES 269; FAT 16.6g (sat 4.8g, mono 9.3g, poly 2.1g); PROTEIN 8.3g; CARB 25g; FIBER 0.3g; CHOL 21mg; IRON 1mg; SODIUM 621mg; CALC 137mg

Dinner
Grilled Salmon with Chorizo and Fingerlings

Executive Chef Megan Tucker of Amavi (amavirestaurant.com) focuses on regional Mediterranean cuisine—paying homage to Santa Fe when possible. The menu changes regularly but might include the Spanish-accented salmon that inspired our version.

Cooking spray
1/4 cup minced shallots
2 garlic cloves, minced
1 1/2 cups fat-free, less-sodium chicken broth, divided
3/4 pound fingerling potatoes, cut into 1/2-inch pieces
2 ounces Spanish chorizo sausage, diced
3/4 teaspoon kosher salt, divided
2 1/2 cups baby spinach leaves
1 teaspoon Spanish smoked paprika
4 (6-ounce) salmon fillets
1 tablespoon extra-virgin olive oil

1. Prepare grill to medium-high heat.
2. Heat a medium nonstick skillet over medium heat. Coat pan with cooking spray. Add shallots and garlic to pan; cook 1 minute, stirring frequently. Add 1/4 cup chicken broth. Cover, reduce heat, and cook 3 minutes or until shallots are tender. Stir in remaining 1 1/4 cups broth, potatoes, and chorizo; bring to a simmer. Simmer 20 minutes or until potatoes are tender; stir in 1/4 teaspoon salt. Add spinach to pan; cover. Remove from heat; stir to combine. Keep warm.
3. Sprinkle remaining 1/2 teaspoon salt and paprika over fillets. Lightly coat fillets with cooking spray; arrange in a single layer, skin sides up, on grill rack. Grill 2 minutes. Rotate a quarter turn on same side; grill 3 minutes or until well marked. Turn over; grill 5 minutes or until desired degree of doneness.
4. Place 1 fillet in each of 4 shallow bowls; ladle 3/4 cup potato mixture over fish. Drizzle 3/4 teaspoon oil over each serving. Yield: 4 servings.

CALORIES 462; FAT 25.5g (sat 5.5g, mono 10.8g, poly 7.7g); PROTEIN 39.3g; CARB 17.7g; FIBER 3g; CHOL 100mg; IRON 1.7mg; SODIUM 653mg; CALC 46mg

FROM YOUR KITCHEN TO OURS

Bored with traditional salmon recipes, Meagan Jensen looked to the aromatic spices found in Indian cuisine to jazz up her favorite fish. "One of my friends never liked salmon, but I definitely changed his mind," she says. Jensen, who has been cooking since she was 13, says the secret to this recipe is packing a lot of flavor with a few well-chosen ingredients.

When it comes to experimenting with recipes, Marie Meyer encourages friends and family to be fearless. "Some of the things I come up with are not that good," she says. But Meyer found a winner with her spicy Asian marinade. An avid griller, Meyer wanted to create a marinade made with accessible ingredients and versatile enough to apply to a variety of meats. She also uses it with pork tenderloin and cuts of chicken.

To create something new from leftover vegetables, Marie Rizzio's mother frequently made fritters out of eggplant, broccoli, and zucchini. Years later, Rizzio replicated her mother's vegetable patties but made them healthier and incorporated summer squash. Rizzio avoids full-fat frying by lightly browning the croquettes in a touch of canola oil.

Pasta dishes are perfect for Christin Holcomb and her husband, who try to avoid eating leftovers: She cooks only as much as she needs and can vary the ingredients and amount depending on the number of guests. Holcomb created this recipe after looking for a new and healthful way to present her favorite pasta, orecchiette. Instead of a heavy, creamy sauce, the flavors are kept light and bright with fresh summer produce and a tangy vinaigrette. She opted for colorful bell peppers, but choose your favorite in-season vegetables.

Quick & Easy
Indian-Spiced Salmon with Basmati Rice
(pictured on page 256)

"I try to cut calories wherever I can without compromising taste. If you season properly, you can compensate with flavor."
—Meagan Jensen, Reno, Nevada

Rice:
2 cups water
1 cup uncooked basmati rice
¼ teaspoon salt
3 tablespoons chopped fresh flat-leaf parsley
4 teaspoons roasted salted cashew pieces
Salmon:
½ teaspoon ground ginger
½ teaspoon garam masala
½ teaspoon ground coriander
¼ teaspoon ground turmeric
Dash of kosher salt
Dash of ground red pepper
4 (6-ounce) skinless salmon fillets
Cooking spray

1. To prepare rice, bring 2 cups water to a boil in a small saucepan. Stir in rice and ¼ teaspoon salt; cover, reduce heat, and cook 20 minutes or until rice is tender. Remove from heat; stir in parsley and cashews. Keep warm.
2. To prepare salmon, preheat broiler.
3. Combine ginger and next 5 ingredients. Rub spice mixture evenly over salmon. Place fillets on a broiler pan or baking sheet coated with cooking spray. Cover with foil; broil 7 minutes. Remove foil; broil an additional 4 minutes or until desired degree of doneness. Serve salmon with rice. Yield: 4 servings (serving size: 1 fillet and about ½ cup rice).

CALORIES 511; FAT 19.8g (sat 4g, mono 7.4g, poly 6.9g); PROTEIN 37.1g; CARB 47.1g; FIBER 1.8g; CHOL 100mg; IRON 2.5mg; SODIUM 297mg; CALC 29mg

Spicy Asian Marinated Flank Steak
(pictured on page 255)

For a quick side dish you can prepare while the steak stands, sauté fresh sugar snap peas, chopped red bell pepper, and vertically sliced red onions just until crisp-tender. "Cooking brings your family together. One of our traditions was to have sit-down meals. Although two of my boys are in college now, they both like to cook and have turned into fellow foodies. The guys like to grill, and this is easy for them to prepare."
—Marie Meyer, Greensboro, North Carolina

2 tablespoons less-sodium soy sauce
1 tablespoon fresh lime juice
1 teaspoon curry powder
1 teaspoon ground red pepper
2 teaspoons minced peeled fresh ginger
1½ teaspoons rice wine vinegar
1 teaspoon olive oil
1 teaspoon dark sesame oil
1 (8-ounce) can crushed pineapple in juice, drained
4 garlic cloves, minced
1 (1-pound) flank steak, trimmed
Cooking spray
¼ teaspoon salt

1. Combine first 10 ingredients in a large zip-top plastic bag. Add steak; seal and marinate in refrigerator 24 hours, turning occasionally.
2. Prepare grill to medium-high heat.
3. Remove steak from bag; discard marinade. Place steak on grill rack coated with cooking spray, and grill 4 minutes on each side or until desired degree of doneness. Sprinkle with salt, and let stand 5 minutes. Cut steak diagonally across grain into thin slices. Yield: 4 servings (serving size: 3 ounces).

CALORIES 236; FAT 8.6g (sat 3.2g, mono 3.6g, poly 0.7g); PROTEIN 32.2g; CARB 5.9g; FIBER 0.5g; CHOL 49mg; IRON 2.2mg; SODIUM 365mg; CALC 32mg

Summer Squash Croquettes

"I enjoy experimenting with food, and my husband is chief taster. These croquettes will please even picky eaters who need to incorporate more vegetables into their diet."

—Marie Rizzio, Interlochen, Michigan

$4^2/_3$ cups coarsely chopped yellow squash (about $1^1/_4$ pounds)

$^1/_2$ cup chopped green onions

1 cup crushed saltine crackers (about 30 crackers)

$^1/_2$ teaspoon salt

$^1/_2$ teaspoon sugar

2 large eggs

$^1/_4$ cup yellow cornmeal

Cooking spray

1 tablespoon canola oil, divided

Sliced green onions (optional)

1. Steam squash and $^1/_2$ cup onions, covered, 15 minutes or until tender. Drain well. Mash mixture with a fork. Stir in crackers and next 3 ingredients. Cover and chill 3 hours; drain well in a fine mesh strainer.

2. Place cornmeal in a shallow dish. Divide squash mixture into 12 equal portions, shaping each portion into a $^1/_2$-inch-thick patty. Lightly coat each patty with cooking spray. Sprinkle patties with cornmeal.

3. Heat 1 teaspoon oil in a large non-stick skillet coated with cooking spray over medium-high heat. Place 4 patties in pan; cook $1^1/_2$ minutes on each side or until golden. Remove patties from pan. Repeat procedure 2 times with remaining 2 teaspoons oil and 8 patties. Garnish with onions, if desired. Serve immediately. Yield: 6 servings (serving size: 2 patties).

CALORIES 151; **FAT** 6.3g (sat 1g, mono 3.1g, poly 1.4g); **PROTEIN** 6.6g; **CARB** 18.6g; **FIBER** 2.1g; **CHOL** 71mg; **IRON** 2.2mg; **SODIUM** 387mg; **CALC** 45mg

---

Orecchiette with Roasted Peppers, Arugula, and Tomatoes

"I love how the cupped shape of the orecchiette pasta holds the sauce so each bite is full of flavor. It works great with simple ingredients and lets subtle elements shine."

—Christin Holcomb
Rancho Santa Margarita, California

1 orange bell pepper

1 yellow bell pepper

8 ounces uncooked orecchiette pasta ("little ears" pasta)

1 teaspoon olive oil

1 teaspoon minced garlic, divided

8 ounces cherry tomatoes, halved

3 tablespoons champagne or white wine vinegar

2 tablespoons olive oil

$1^1/_2$ teaspoons sugar

$^3/_4$ teaspoon salt

$^1/_4$ teaspoon dried herbes de Provence

$^1/_4$ teaspoon freshly ground black pepper

3 cups loosely packed arugula

$^1/_2$ cup (about 2 ounces) shaved fresh Parmesan cheese

1. Preheat broiler.

2. Cut bell peppers in half lengthwise; discard seeds and membranes. Place pepper halves, skin sides up, on a foil-lined baking sheet; flatten with hand. Broil 15 minutes or until blackened. Place in a zip-top plastic bag; seal. Let stand 10 minutes. Peel and cut into 1-inch strips.

3. Cook pasta according to package directions, omitting salt and fat. Drain.

4. Heat 1 teaspoon oil in a large non-stick skillet over medium heat. Add $^1/_4$ teaspoon garlic; cook 30 seconds. Add bell peppers and tomatoes to pan; cook 4 minutes or until tomatoes are tender, stirring occasionally. Remove from heat.

5. Combine remaining $^3/_4$ teaspoon garlic, vinegar, and next 5 ingredients in a small bowl; stir with a whisk. Add pasta and oil mixture to bell pepper mixture in pan; toss well to coat. Cool

---

slightly. Stir in arugula. Top each serving with cheese. Yield: 4 servings (serving size: $1^3/_4$ cups pasta mixture and 2 tablespoons cheese).

CALORIES 365; **FAT** 12g (sat 3.1g, mono 6.8g, poly 1.4g); **PROTEIN** 12.8g; **CARB** 52.4g; **FIBER** 4.4g; **CHOL** 7mg; **IRON** 2.8mg; **SODIUM** 627mg; **CALC** 190mg

DINNER TONIGHT

Here are more stopwatch-tested Menus from the *Cooking Light* Test Kitchens.

SHOPPING LIST

Lamb Burgers with Sun-Dried Tomato Aioli

garlic

arugula

1 large beefsteak tomato

sun-dried tomatoes, packed without oil

canola mayonnaise

multigrain hamburger buns

1 pound lean ground lamb

pecorino Romano cheese

Sweet and Tangy Slaw

cabbage-and-carrot coleslaw

1 small red onion

fresh parsley

sugar

cider vinegar

canola oil

GAME PLAN

While tomatoes rehydrate:
- Preheat grill pan.
- Combine lamb mixture.

While burgers cook:
- Prepare aioli.
- Prepare slaw.

Lamb Burgers with Sun-Dried Tomato Aioli

with Sweet and Tangy Slaw

Simple Sub: Use ground beef in place of lamb.
Make-Ahead Tip: Prepare the aioli up to two days in advance.

10 sun-dried tomatoes, packed without oil
1 cup water
¼ cup canola mayonnaise
½ teaspoon black pepper, divided
2 garlic cloves, minced and divided
2 tablespoons grated pecorino Romano cheese
½ teaspoon kosher salt
1 pound lean ground lamb
Cooking spray
4 (2-ounce) multigrain hamburger buns
2 cups arugula
4 (½-inch-thick) slices tomato

1. Place sun-dried tomatoes and 1 cup water in a microwave-safe bowl; microwave at HIGH 2 minutes. Let stand 3 minutes. Drain. Place sun-dried tomatoes, mayonnaise, ¼ teaspoon pepper, and 1 garlic clove in a mini food processor; pulse 10 times or until tomatoes are finely chopped. Set aside.
2. Combine remaining 1 garlic clove, remaining ¼ teaspoon pepper, cheese, salt, and lamb in a large bowl. Divide mixture into 4 portions, shaping each into a ½-inch-thick patty. Heat a grill pan over medium-high heat. Coat pan with cooking spray. Add patties to pan; cook 4 minutes on each side or until done. Remove from pan; cover and keep warm.
3. Arrange 4 bun halves, cut sides down, in pan over medium-high heat; cook 1 minute or until toasted. Repeat procedure with remaining bun halves. Spread about 1 tablespoon mayonnaise mixture on bottom half of each bun; top each with ½ cup arugula, 1 patty, 1 tomato slice, and top half of bun. Yield: 4 servings (serving size: 1 burger).

CALORIES 448; **FAT** 23.8g (sat 7.3g, mono 10.7g, poly 3.2g); **PROTEIN** 27.5g; **CARB** 28.9g; **FIBER** 4.2g; **CHOL** 78mg; **IRON** 4mg; **SODIUM** 765mg; **CALC** 104mg

---

For the Sweet and Tangy Slaw:
Combine 1 tablespoon sugar, 3 tablespoons cider vinegar, 1 tablespoon canola oil, and ¼ teaspoon salt in a large bowl. Add 4 cups packaged cabbage-and-carrot coleslaw, ⅓ cup vertically sliced red onion, and 2 tablespoons fresh parsley leaves; toss to combine.

40 minutes

SHOPPING LIST

Thai Red Curry Shrimp
1 medium red bell pepper
1 lime
dark brown sugar
jasmine rice
14-ounce can light coconut milk
red curry paste
fish sauce
butter
1¼ pounds large shrimp

Ginger-Garlic Green Beans
12 ounces green beans
fresh ginger
garlic
canola oil

GAME PLAN

While rice cooks:
  ■ Sauté shrimp.
  ■ Slice bell pepper.
While curry cooks:
  ■ Cook green beans.
  ■ Juice lime.

Thai Red Curry Shrimp

with Ginger-Garlic Green Beans

Time-Saver: Red curry paste is a potent blend of herbs and aromatics that creates speedy sauces.
Prep Pointer: Sautéing curry paste in the coconut "cream" maximizes its flavor.
Time-Saver: Purchase peeled and deveined shrimp from the seafood counter.

1¾ cups water
1 cup uncooked jasmine rice
2 teaspoons butter
¼ teaspoon kosher salt
Cooking spray
1¼ pounds large shrimp, peeled and deveined
1 (14-ounce) can light coconut milk
1 tablespoon red curry paste
1½ tablespoons fish sauce
4 teaspoons dark brown sugar
1 red bell pepper, seeded and thinly sliced
2 teaspoons fresh lime juice

1. Bring first 4 ingredients to a boil in a saucepan. Cover, reduce heat, and simmer 15 minutes. Remove from heat; let stand 10 minutes. Fluff with a fork.
2. Heat a large skillet over medium-high heat. Coat pan with cooking spray. Add shrimp; sauté 3 minutes or until done. Remove shrimp from pan; keep warm. Spoon coconut cream (the thick part from top of the can) into pan using a slotted spoon. Add curry paste; cook 2 minutes or until liquid almost evaporates, stirring constantly.
3. Stir in remaining coconut milk, fish sauce, and sugar. Reduce heat to medium; simmer 10 minutes or until sauce thickens, stirring frequently. Add bell pepper; toss to coat. Increase heat to medium-high; cook 5 minutes or until crisp-tender. Add shrimp; cook 1 minute or until thoroughly heated. Remove from heat; stir in lime juice. Spoon 1 cup rice onto each of 4 plates; top each serving with 1 cup shrimp mixture. Yield: 4 servings.

CALORIES 330; **FAT** 9.8g (sat 6.7g, mono 0.9g, poly 1.1g); **PROTEIN** 32.4g; **CARB** 28.8g; **FIBER** 1g; **CHOL** 220mg; **IRON** 4.4mg; **SODIUM** 865mg; **CALC** 83mg

continued

For the Ginger-Garlic Green Beans:
Cook 12 ounces trimmed green beans in boiling water 5 minutes or until crisp-tender. Drain and plunge beans into ice water; drain. Heat 1 teaspoon canola oil in a large skillet over medium-high heat. Add 2 teaspoons minced peeled fresh ginger and 1 teaspoon minced garlic; sauté 1 minute. Add beans, ¼ teaspoon salt, and ¼ teaspoon black pepper; cook 2 minutes or until heated.

SHOPPING LIST

Arugula, Italian Tuna, and White Bean Salad

2 lemons
garlic
grape tomatoes
1 small red onion
1 (5-ounce) package fresh baby arugula
extra-virgin olive oil
Dijon mustard
2 (6-ounce) cans Italian tuna packed in olive oil
1 (15-ounce) can cannellini beans
Parmigiano-Reggiano cheese

Rosemary Focaccia

fresh rosemary
extra-virgin olive oil
coarse sea salt
1 (13.8-ounce) can refrigerated pizza crust dough

GAME PLAN

While oven heats:
- Prepare dough.
- Make salad dressing.
While bread bakes:
- Prepare salad.

Quick & Easy

Arugula, Italian Tuna, and White Bean Salad

with Rosemary Focaccia

Vegetarian Swap: Use 1½ cans of beans, and replace the tuna with a fistful of kalamata olives.
Buy The Best: Imported tuna packed in oil is moist and flavorful, adding richness to the salad.
Flavor Hit: Shaved cheese has a bigger impact than grated, adding a salty, nutty punch.

3 tablespoons fresh lemon juice
1½ tablespoons extra-virgin olive oil
½ teaspoon minced garlic
¼ teaspoon kosher salt
¼ teaspoon freshly ground black pepper
¼ teaspoon Dijon mustard
1 cup grape tomatoes, halved
1 cup thinly vertically sliced red onion
2 (6-ounce) cans Italian tuna packed in olive oil, drained and broken into chunks
1 (15-ounce) can cannellini beans, rinsed and drained
1 (5-ounce) package fresh baby arugula
2 ounces Parmigiano-Reggiano cheese, shaved

1. Combine first 6 ingredients in a large bowl, stirring with a whisk. Add tomatoes and next 4 ingredients; toss. Top with cheese. Yield: 4 servings (serving size: 2¼ cups).

CALORIES 301; FAT 14.5g (sat 4.1g, mono 6.7g, poly 2.8g); PROTEIN 27.5g; CARB 15g; FIBER 3.8g; CHOL 21mg; IRON 2.5mg; SODIUM 709mg; CALC 263mg

For the Rosemary Focaccia:
Preheat oven to 400°. Unroll dough from a 13.8-ounce can refrigerated pizza crust; pat into a 12 x 8–inch rectangle on a baking sheet coated with cooking spray. Fold dough in half to form an 8 x 6–inch rectangle; press together lightly. Using fingertips, gently dimple dough. Brush dough with 2 teaspoons extra-virgin olive oil; sprinkle with ½ teaspoon chopped fresh rosemary and ¼ teaspoon coarse sea salt. Bake at 400° for 15 minutes or until golden.

SHOPPING LIST

Grilled Lime-Soy Tuna with Noodles

2 limes
fresh ginger
garlic
matchstick-cut carrots
green onions
less-sodium soy sauce
rice vinegar
dark sesame oil
mirin
4 ounces wide rice noodles
canola oil
toasted sesame seeds
honey
ground red pepper
2 (6-ounce) tuna steaks

Miso–Mixed Vegetable Salad

sugar snap peas
radishes
1 red bell pepper
rice vinegar
canola oil
dark sesame oil
white miso

GAME PLAN

While tuna marinates:
- Prepare noodles.
- Prep vegetables for salad.
- Prepare salad dressing.
While tuna cooks:
- Toss salad.

Grilled Lime-Soy Tuna with Noodles
with Miso-Mixed Vegetable Salad

Shopping Tip: Look for mild-tasting white miso in the refrigerated section of your supermarket.
Time-Saver: Matchstick-cut carrots are a versatile staple for busy weeknights.
Flavor Hit: Dark sesame oil adds rich, nutty complexity to the noodles.

8 teaspoons fresh lime juice
8 teaspoons less-sodium soy sauce
4 teaspoons canola oil
4 teaspoons honey
2 teaspoons minced peeled fresh ginger
Dash of ground red pepper
1 garlic clove, minced
2 (6-ounce) tuna steaks (about 1 inch thick)
4 ounces wide rice noodles
¼ cup matchstick-cut carrots
4 teaspoons rice vinegar
1½ teaspoons toasted sesame seeds
1½ teaspoons dark sesame oil
1 teaspoon mirin (sweet rice wine)
Cooking spray
1 tablespoon finely minced green onions

1. Combine first 7 ingredients in a small bowl. Pour 2 tablespoons juice mixture into a zip-top plastic bag; reserve remaining juice mixture. Add tuna to bag; seal and marinate at room temperature 20 minutes, turning bag once.
2. Cook noodles according to package directions. Drain and rinse with cold water; drain. Combine noodles, carrots, and next 4 ingredients.
3. Heat a grill pan over medium-high heat. Coat pan with cooking spray. Remove tuna from bag; discard marinade. Place tuna in pan; cook 1½ minutes on each side or until desired degree of doneness. Divide noodle mixture between 2 plates; sprinkle each with 1½ teaspoons onions. Cut tuna into thin slices; arrange 1 sliced tuna steak on each plate. Drizzle each serving with 3 tablespoons reserved dressing. Yield: 2 servings.

CALORIES 541; FAT 13.5g (sat 1.6g, mono 6.4g, poly 4.6g); PROTEIN 43.9g; CARB 63.6g; FIBER 2.2g; CHOL 74mg; IRON 2.1mg; SODIUM 625mg; CALC 66mg

For the Miso-Mixed Vegetable Salad:
Steam 1 cup sugar snap peas 3 minutes or until crisp-tender; rinse with cold water, and drain. Combine peas, ¼ cup sliced radishes, and ¼ cup finely chopped red bell pepper. Combine 2 teaspoons rice vinegar, 1 teaspoon white miso, 1 teaspoon canola oil, and ¼ teaspoon dark sesame oil; toss with salad.

30 minutes

SHOPPING LIST

Walnut and Rosemary Oven-Fried Chicken
fresh rosemary
Dijon mustard
panko
chopped walnuts
low-fat buttermilk
Parmigiano-Reggiano cheese
4 (6-ounce) chicken cutlets

Toasted Garlic Escarole
1½-pound head escarole
garlic
1 lemon
olive oil

GAME PLAN

While oven heats:
• Coat chicken with buttermilk mixture.
• Toast panko.
While chicken bakes:
• Prepare escarole.

TOASTING PANKO IN A SKILLET MAKES IT CRUNCHIER AND GOLDEN BROWN.

Walnut and Rosemary Oven-Fried Chicken
with Toasted Garlic Escarole

¼ cup low-fat buttermilk
2 tablespoons Dijon mustard
4 (6-ounce) chicken cutlets
⅓ cup panko (Japanese breadcrumbs)
⅓ cup finely chopped walnuts
2 tablespoons grated fresh Parmigiano-Reggiano cheese
¾ teaspoon minced fresh rosemary
¼ teaspoon kosher salt
¼ teaspoon freshly ground black pepper
Cooking spray
Rosemary leaves (optional)

1. Preheat oven to 425°.
2. Combine buttermilk and mustard in a shallow dish, stirring with a whisk. Add chicken to buttermilk mixture, turning to coat.
3. Heat a small skillet over medium-high heat. Add panko to pan; cook 3 minutes or until golden, stirring frequently. Combine panko, nuts, and next 4 ingre-dients in a shallow dish. Remove chicken from buttermilk mixture; discard buttermilk mixture. Dredge chicken in panko mixture.
4. Arrange a wire rack on a large baking sheet; coat rack with cooking spray. Arrange chicken on rack; coat chicken with cooking spray. Bake at 425° for 13 minutes or until chicken is done. Garnish with rosemary leaves, if desired. Yield: 4 servings (serving size: 1 cutlet).

CALORIES 287; FAT 9.4g (sat 1.6g, mono 1.6g, poly 5.1g); PROTEIN 42.7g; CARB 6g; FIBER 0.9g; CHOL 101mg; IRON 1.6mg; SODIUM 379mg; CALC 66mg

For the Toasted Garlic Escarole
Cut a 1½-pound escarole head crosswise into 1-inch strips; place in a large bowl. Heat 1½ tablespoons olive oil in a small skillet over medium-high heat. Add 4 thinly sliced garlic cloves to pan; sauté 2 minutes or until golden. Remove from heat; add 1½ tablespoons fresh lemon juice, ¼ teaspoon kosher salt, and ¼ teaspoon freshly ground black pepper. Drizzle dressing over escarole, and toss to coat.

SUPERFAST

These easy 20-minute entrées utilize well-chosen cuts of beef, which offer speed, convenience, versatility, and—most importantly—great flavor.

Quick & Easy

Grilled Polenta with Spicy Steak

Look for tubes of prepared polenta in the refrigerated part of the produce section.

4 teaspoons canola oil, divided
¾ teaspoon kosher salt, divided
½ teaspoon ground cumin
½ teaspoon chipotle chile powder
¼ teaspoon freshly ground black pepper
1 (1-pound) flank steak, trimmed
1 (18-ounce) tube of polenta, cut into 8 slices
1 ripe peeled avocado, sliced
½ cup fresh cilantro leaves
½ cup (2 ounces) crumbled queso fresco
½ cup refrigerated fresh salsa
Lime wedges (optional)

1. Heat a grill pan over medium-high heat. Combine 1 teaspoon oil, ½ teaspoon salt, cumin, chile powder, and pepper; rub evenly over steak. Add steak to pan; cook 6 minutes on each side or until desired degree of doneness. Remove steak from pan; let stand 5 minutes. Cut steak diagonally across grain into thin slices.
2. While steak rests, brush remaining 1 tablespoon oil over both sides of polenta slices; sprinkle evenly with remaining ¼ teaspoon salt. Add polenta to pan; cook 3 minutes on each side or until browned. Arrange 2 polenta slices on each of 4 plates; divide avocado evenly among servings. Top each serving with about 3 ounces steak, 2 tablespoons cilantro leaves, 2 tablespoons queso fresco, and 2 tablespoons salsa. Serve with lime wedges, if desired. Yield: 4 servings.

CALORIES 397; **FAT** 19.2g (sat 4.6g, mono 10.1g, poly 2.6g); **PROTEIN** 28.9g; **CARB** 24g; **FIBER** 5.1g; **CHOL** 41mg; **IRON** 3.1mg; **SODIUM** 739mg; **CALC** 70mg

Quick & Easy

Balsamic Steak au Poivre

Crack the peppercorns with the back of a heavy skillet or in a mortar and pestle or spice grinder (don't grind too finely).

2 (8-ounce) New York strip steaks (about 1 inch thick), trimmed
¼ teaspoon kosher salt
2 tablespoons cracked mixed peppercorns
1 tablespoon olive oil
⅓ cup finely chopped shallots
½ cup fat-free, less-sodium beef broth
2 tablespoons balsamic vinegar
1 tablespoon butter

1. Heat a large cast-iron skillet over high heat. Pat steaks dry with paper towels; sprinkle steaks evenly with salt. Press peppercorns onto both sides of steaks. Add oil to pan; swirl to coat. Add steaks to pan; cook 3 minutes on each side or until desired degree of doneness. Remove steaks from pan; let stand 5 minutes. Cut each steak in half.
2. While steaks rest, add shallots to pan; cook 1 minute or until almost tender. Stir in broth and vinegar, scraping pan to loosen browned bits. Bring to a boil; cook 2 minutes or until reduced by half. Remove from heat; stir in butter. Yield: 4 servings (serving size: 3 ounces steak and 1½ tablespoons sauce).

CALORIES 236; **FAT** 12.7g (sat 4.8g, mono 5.9g, poly 0.7g); **PROTEIN** 25g; **CARB** 3.6g; **FIBER** 0.1g; **CHOL** 57mg; **IRON** 1.8mg; **SODIUM** 246mg; **CALC** 26mg

Quick & Easy • Kid Friendly

Garlic-Thyme Burgers with Grilled Tomato

1 tablespoon chopped fresh thyme
½ teaspoon kosher salt
¼ teaspoon freshly ground black pepper
2 garlic cloves, minced
1 pound ground sirloin
4 (½-inch-thick) slices beefsteak tomato
1 tablespoon Dijon mustard
4 (2-ounce) Kaiser rolls or other sandwich rolls
4 baby romaine lettuce leaves

1. Heat a grill pan over medium-high heat. Combine first 5 ingredients in a medium bowl. Divide mixture into 4 equal portions, shaping each into a ½-inch-thick patty. Add patties to pan; cook 4 minutes on each side or until desired degree of doneness. Remove patties from pan. Add tomato slices to pan; cook 1 minute on each side. Spread about ¾ teaspoon mustard over bottom half of each roll; top each with 1 lettuce leaf, 1 patty, 1 tomato slice, and top half of roll. Yield: 4 servings (serving size: 1 burger).

CALORIES 354; **FAT** 12g (sat 4.4g, mono 4.6g, poly 1.5g); **PROTEIN** 28.5g; **CARB** 30.9g; **FIBER** 1.9g; **CHOL** 73mg; **IRON** 4.7mg; **SODIUM** 651mg; **CALC** 101mg

Quick & Easy

Seared Filet with Mixed-Herb Gremolata

A great sear on the steaks depends on getting the pan very hot and not moving the meat too much while it's cooking.

4 (4-ounce) beef tenderloin steaks (1 inch thick)
½ teaspoon kosher salt, divided
¼ teaspoon freshly ground black pepper
2 tablespoons chopped fresh parsley
1 tablespoon chopped fresh rosemary
1 tablespoon chopped fresh thyme
1 tablespoon olive oil
1 tablespoon grated lemon rind
1 teaspoon fresh lemon juice
1 small garlic clove, minced

1. Heat a large cast-iron skillet over high heat. Sprinkle steaks with ¼ teaspoon salt and pepper. Add steaks to pan; cook 3 minutes on each side or until desired degree of doneness. Remove steaks from pan; let stand 5 minutes.
2. While steaks rest, combine remaining ¼ teaspoon salt, parsley, and remaining ingredients; serve over steaks. Yield: 4 servings (serving size: 1 steak and 1½ teaspoons gremolata).

CALORIES 218; **FAT** 12.8g (sat 4.1g, mono 6.3g, poly 0.7g); **PROTEIN** 23.5g; **CARB** 1.1g; **FIBER** 0.4g; **CHOL** 71mg; **IRON** 1.8mg; **SODIUM** 284mg; **CALC** 28mg

Quick & Easy
Spicy Beef and Bell Pepper Stir-Fry

1 tablespoon canola oil
12 ounces flank steak, cut diagonally across the grain into thin slices
1 red bell pepper, cut into thin strips
1 yellow bell pepper, cut into thin strips
1/4 cup less-sodium soy sauce
1 1/2 tablespoons rice wine vinegar
1 tablespoon minced peeled fresh ginger
2 teaspoons chili garlic sauce (such as Lee Kum Kee)
4 green onions, cut into 2-inch pieces
2 teaspoons toasted sesame seeds

1. Heat a large nonstick skillet over medium-high heat. Add oil to pan; swirl to coat. Add steak to pan; cook 2 minutes, searing on one side. Add bell peppers; cook 2 minutes or until beef loses its pink color, stirring constantly. Remove beef mixture from pan.
2. Add soy sauce and next 3 ingredients to pan; bring to a boil. Cook 1 minute or until slightly thickened. Add beef mixture and green onions to pan; toss well to coat. Sprinkle with sesame seeds. Yield: 4 servings (serving size: 1 cup).

CALORIES 216; FAT 11.5g (sat 3.1g, mono 5.4g, poly 1.8g); PROTEIN 20.8g; CARB 7.7g; FIBER 2.2g; CHOL 35mg; IRON 2.9mg; SODIUM 624mg; CALC 54mg

Quick & Easy
Grilled Steak with Baby Arugula and Parmesan Salad

1 teaspoon chopped fresh thyme
1/4 teaspoon kosher salt
1/2 teaspoon freshly ground black pepper, divided
4 (4-ounce) flat-iron steaks
2 lemons, halved
1 tablespoon chopped fresh chives
1 tablespoon extra-virgin olive oil
1 tablespoon fresh lemon juice
1/2 teaspoon Dijon mustard
1/8 teaspoon kosher salt
4 cups loosely packed baby arugula
1/4 cup (1 ounce) shaved fresh Parmigiano-Reggiano cheese

1. Heat a grill pan over medium-high heat. Rub thyme, 1/4 teaspoon salt, and 1/4 teaspoon pepper over steaks. Add steaks to pan; cook 4 minutes on each side or until desired degree of doneness. Remove steaks from pan. Add lemon halves, cut sides down, to pan; cook 3 minutes. Cut steaks across grain into thin slices.
2. Combine remaining 1/4 teaspoon pepper, chives, and next 4 ingredients, stirring with a whisk. Drizzle over arugula; toss to coat. Arrange 1 steak, 1 cup arugula, and 1 lemon half on each of 4 plates; top each salad with 1 tablespoon cheese. Yield: 4 servings.

CALORIES 255; FAT 16.2g (sat 6g, mono 7.5g, poly 0.9g); PROTEIN 24.4g; CARB 2g; FIBER 0.5g; CHOL 75mg; IRON 2.9mg; SODIUM 376mg; CALC 124mg

RECIPE HALL OF FAME
OUR FAVORITE BANANA SPLIT ICE-CREAM SANDWICHES

Thin, crisp vanilla cookies add a textural twist to the conventional banana split ingredients in this delightful sweet treat.

Kid Friendly
Banana Split Ice-Cream Sandwiches

Cookies:
7 tablespoons powdered sugar
6 tablespoons sifted all-purpose flour
1/4 teaspoon vanilla extract
1 large egg
Filling:
2 cups vanilla low-fat ice cream, softened
3/4 cup ripe mashed banana (about 1 1/2 medium bananas)
6 tablespoons coarsely chopped dry-roasted peanuts, divided

Remaining Ingredients:
6 tablespoons frozen fat-free whipped topping, thawed
6 tablespoons chocolate syrup
6 maraschino cherries, drained

1. To prepare cookies, combine sugar and flour, stirring with a whisk. Add vanilla and egg; beat with a mixer at medium speed 2 minutes. Cover and refrigerate 2 hours.
2. Preheat oven to 350°.
3. Cover a large baking sheet with parchment paper. Draw 6 (3-inch) circles on paper. Turn paper over; secure with masking tape. Spoon about 1 tablespoon batter into center of each drawn circle; spread batter to outside edge of each circle. Bake at 350° for 6 minutes or until edges begin to brown. Carefully remove cookies from paper, and cool completely on wire racks. Repeat procedure with remaining batter, reusing parchment paper.
4. To prepare filling, combine ice cream and banana in a chilled bowl, stirring well. Place 1/4 cup peanuts in a shallow bowl. Place 1 cookie on each of 6 plates. Carefully spread about 1/3 cup ice cream mixture over flat side of each cookie. Top with remaining cookies, flat sides down, pressing gently. Lightly roll sides of each sandwich in peanuts.
5. Top each sandwich with 1 tablespoon whipped topping, 1 tablespoon chocolate syrup, remaining 1 teaspoon peanuts, and 1 cherry. Serve immediately. Yield: 6 servings (serving size: 1 sandwich).

CALORIES 292; FAT 7.7g (sat 2.2g, mono 3.2g, poly 1.7g); PROTEIN 6.9g; CARB 49.8g; FIBER 2g; CHOL 47mg; IRON 1.1mg; SODIUM 136mg; CALC 84mg

FEED 4 FOR LESS THAN $10

Enjoy the vibrant flavors of the season with these economical meals.

Risotto Primavera

$2.48 per serving, $9.92 total
This risotto is studded with the vibrant flavor of fresh veggies. Although inexpensive, this dish is attractive and tasty enough to serve guests.

1 tablespoon olive oil, divided
½ teaspoon salt, divided
1 pint cherry tomatoes
3¼ cups water
2¼ cups fat-free, less-sodium chicken broth
1½ cups chopped onion
1½ cups Arborio rice
2 tablespoons white wine vinegar
½ cup frozen green peas
12 ounces asparagus, trimmed and cut into
   1-inch pieces
2 ounces pecorino Romano cheese, divided
1 tablespoon lemon juice
¼ teaspoon black pepper

1. Preheat oven to 400°.
2. Toss 1½ teaspoons olive oil, ⅛ teaspoon salt, and tomatoes on a parchment-lined jelly-roll pan. Bake at 400° for 15 minutes or until tomatoes burst.
3. Heat 3¼ cups water and broth in a saucepan over medium heat (do not boil).
4. Heat remaining 1½ teaspoons oil in a large Dutch oven over medium-high heat. Add onion to pan; cook 5 minutes, stirring frequently. Add rice; cook 1 minute. Stir in vinegar; cook 30 seconds or until liquid is absorbed, stirring constantly. Add broth mixture, ½ cup at a time, stirring constantly until each portion is absorbed before adding the next (about 20 minutes total). Add peas and asparagus to pan

with last ½ cup of broth mixture. Remove from heat; grate 1 ounce cheese. Stir in grated cheese, remaining ⅜ teaspoon salt, and juice. Spoon about 1¾ cups risotto into each of 4 bowls; top evenly with tomatoes. Shave remaining 1 ounce cheese evenly over each serving; sprinkle with pepper. Yield: 4 servings.

CALORIES 428; **FAT** 8.1g (sat 2.7g, mono 3.6g, poly 0.7g); **PROTEIN** 16g; **CARB** 75.3g; **FIBER** 8.3g; **CHOL** 13mg; **IRON** 3.2mg; **SODIUM** 672mg; **CALC** 192mg

Quick & Easy
Linguine with Spicy Shrimp

$2.46 per serving, $9.83 total
The combo of Cajun seasoning and ground red pepper really packs a punch of heat in this dish, but the creamy sauce takes the edge off. Serve with sliced French bread.

8 ounces uncooked linguine
2 tablespoons butter
½ cup finely chopped onion
3 garlic cloves, minced
2 plum tomatoes, chopped
1 pound peeled and deveined medium shrimp
1½ teaspoons Cajun seasoning
½ teaspoon ground red pepper
⅛ teaspoon salt
½ cup half-and-half
⅓ cup chopped fresh flat-leaf parsley

1. Cook pasta according to package directions, omitting salt and fat. Drain. Place pasta in a large bowl; keep warm.
2. Melt butter in a large skillet over medium-high heat. Add onion; sauté 3 minutes, stirring occasionally. Add garlic and tomatoes; sauté 2 minutes, stirring constantly. Sprinkle shrimp with Cajun seasoning, red pepper, and salt. Add shrimp mixture to pan; sauté 3 minutes or until shrimp are almost done; remove from heat. Stir in half-and-half. Pour shrimp mixture over pasta; toss. Sprinkle with parsley. Yield: 4 servings (serving size: 1¼ cups).

CALORIES 436; **FAT** 12.1g (sat 6.4g, mono 2.8g, poly 1.2g); **PROTEIN** 32.5g; **CARB** 49.1g; **FIBER** 2.7g; **CHOL** 199mg; **IRON** 5.1mg; **SODIUM** 694mg; **CALC** 120mg

WINE NOTE: Linguine with Spicy Shrimp combines peppery heat with a creamy sauce, making a fuller-bodied white a good partner. Little Penguin Chardonnay 2008 ($6), from Australia, has tropical and pear fruit, with just a bit of sweetness and refreshing acidity.

Quick & Easy
BLT Bread Salad

$2.32 per serving, $9.26 total
Think of this hearty tossed salad as a deconstructed BLT sandwich, where the bread appears in the form of croutons. Round out the plate with fresh cantaloupe.

6 ounces French bread baguette, cut into
   ½-inch cubes
Cooking spray
4 slices hickory-smoked bacon
1 tablespoon olive oil
¼ cup red wine vinegar
¼ teaspoon freshly ground black pepper
⅛ teaspoon salt
6 cups torn romaine lettuce
1½ pounds plum tomatoes, cut into ½-inch
   wedges
3 green onions, thinly sliced
½ cup (2 ounces) crumbled feta cheese

1. Preheat oven to 350°.
2. Layer bread on a baking sheet; coat with cooking spray. Bake at 350° for 18 minutes or until toasted.
3. Cook bacon in a large nonstick skillet over medium heat until crisp. Remove bacon from pan, reserving 1 tablespoon drippings in pan. Cut bacon into ½-inch pieces. Stir oil into bacon drippings in pan; remove from heat. Stir in vinegar, pepper, and salt.
4. Combine lettuce, tomatoes, and onions in a large bowl; drizzle with vinaigrette. Add bread; toss well to coat. Sprinkle with bacon and cheese. Serve immediately. Yield: 4 servings (serving size: about 2 cups).

CALORIES 315; **FAT** 14.4g (sat 6g, mono 6.4g, poly 1.6g); **PROTEIN** 10.5g; **CARB** 37.6g; **FIBER** 4.7g; **CHOL** 26mg; **IRON** 3.3mg; **SODIUM** 788mg; **CALC** 116mg

Kid Friendly
Root Beer–Can Chicken
$2.48 per serving, $9.92 total

1½ teaspoons Hungarian sweet paprika
1 teaspoon brown sugar
½ teaspoon garlic powder
½ teaspoon onion powder
½ teaspoon ground red pepper
½ teaspoon chili powder
¼ teaspoon ground allspice
¾ teaspoon kosher salt, divided
2 (12-ounce) cans root beer, divided
2 tablespoons chilled unsalted butter,
   cut into pieces
2 teaspoons cider vinegar
1 (3½-pound) whole chicken, skinned

1. Prepare grill for indirect grilling, heating one side to medium.
2. Combine first 7 ingredients and ½ teaspoon salt in a small bowl.
3. Open both root beer cans, and pour 18 ounces into a small saucepan. Set remaining root beer aside (in the can). Bring 18 ounces root beer to a boil. Cook until reduced to ⅓ cup (about 20 minutes). Remove from heat. Add remaining ¼ teaspoon salt, butter, and vinegar, stirring until smooth.
4. Rub paprika mixture evenly over chicken. Holding chicken upright with cavity facing down, insert reserved opened root beer can into cavity. Place chicken on unheated side of grill. Spread legs out to form a tripod to support chicken. Cover and grill 1 hour and 30 minutes or until a meat thermometer inserted into meaty portion of thigh registers 160°, basting chicken every 20 minutes with sauce.
5. Lift chicken slightly using tongs; place spatula under can. Carefully remove chicken and can from grill; place on a cutting board. Let stand 10 minutes. Gently lift chicken using tongs or insulated rubber gloves; carefully twist can and remove from cavity. Discard can. Yield: 4 servings (serving size: 1 breast half or 1 leg quarter).

CALORIES 371; **FAT** 15.1g (sat 6.2g, mono 5g, poly 2.4g); **PROTEIN** 35.6g; **CARB** 21.4g; **FIBER** 0.2g; **CHOL** 121mg; **IRON** 1.9mg; **SODIUM** 502mg; **CALC** 32mg

For the potatoes: Preheat oven to 400°. Cut 1½ pounds red potatoes into thin wedges. Toss potato wedges with 2 tablespoons olive oil and ¾ teaspoon kosher salt. Roast at 400° for 29 minutes or until browned, stirring once.

For the slaw: Combine 1 (12-ounce) bag broccoli slaw mix, ½ cup sweetened dried cranberries, ⅓ cup canola mayonnaise, 1 tablespoon fresh lemon juice, ¾ cup thinly sliced red onion, and ¼ teaspoon salt; toss.

SIMPLE ADDITIONS

Latin Baked Chicken

¼ cup fresh lime juice
3 tablespoons less-sodium soy sauce
2 tablespoons honey
2 tablespoons minced chipotle chile in adobo
   sauce
8 (4-ounce) bone-in chicken thighs, skinned

Preheat oven to 400°. Combine lime juice, soy sauce, honey, and chipotle in a large bowl. Add chicken, and toss well to coat. Let stand 10 minutes at room temperature. Arrange chicken on a broiler pan coated with cooking spray, reserving marinade. Bake at 400° for 15 minutes. Place reserved marinade in a blender, and process until smooth. Place pureed marinade in a small saucepan. Bring to a boil, and cook 3 minutes. Brush chicken with half of cooked sauce; return to oven and bake an additional 10 minutes. Brush chicken with remaining sauce; bake an additional 10 minutes or until a thermometer registers 165°. Yield: 4 servings (serving size: 2 chicken thighs).

CALORIES 316; **FAT** 9g (sat 2.3g, mono 2.8g, poly 2.2g); **PROTEIN** 45.3g; **CARB** 11.9g; **FIBER** 0.8g; **CHOL** 188mg; **IRON** 2.8mg; **SODIUM** 677mg; **CALC** 28mg

THE FIVE INGREDIENTS

¼ cup fresh lime juice

3 tablespoons less-sodium soy sauce

2 tablespoons honey

2 tablespoons minced chipotle chile in adobo sauce

8 (4-ounce) bone-in chicken thighs, skinned

Swordfish Kebabs with Orange Basil Sauce

Leave a little space between the swordfish pieces on the kebabs so they cook evenly.

1 orange
2 cups fresh basil leaves
2 tablespoons olive oil
2 garlic cloves, peeled
1½ pounds swordfish, cut into (1-inch) pieces

Prepare grill to medium-high heat. Squeeze orange to extract ¼ cup juice. Place orange juice, basil, oil, and garlic in a mini chopper; add ¼ teaspoon salt. Process basil leaf mixture until finely chopped. Sprinkle ¼ teaspoon salt and ⅛ teaspoon freshly ground black pepper evenly over fish; thread fish onto 4 (12-inch) skewers. Grill fish 10 minutes or until fish flakes easily when tested with a fork or until desired degree of doneness, turning occasionally. Drizzle fish with sauce, or serve sauce separately. Garnish sauce with orange rind, if desired. Yield: 4 servings (serving size: 1 skewer and 2 tablespoons sauce).

CALORIES 280; **FAT** 14g (sat 2.9g, mono 7.7g, poly 2.6g); **PROTEIN** 34.3g; **CARB** 2.8g; **FIBER** 0.7g; **CHOL** 66mg; **IRON** 1.9mg; **SODIUM** 449mg; **CALC** 36mg

---

THE FIVE INGREDIENTS

1 orange

+

2 cups fresh basil leaves

+

2 tablespoons olive oil

+

2 garlic cloves, peeled

+

1½ pounds swordfish, cut into (1-inch) pieces

Cheesy Margherita Pizza

This easy, kid-friendly pizza is sure to be a family favorite.

1 (16-ounce) refrigerated fresh pizza crust dough
2 plum tomatoes, each cut into 8 slices
1½ cups (6 ounces) shredded part-skim mozzarella cheese, divided
½ cup (2 ounces) grated fresh Romano cheese
12 fresh basil leaves, thinly sliced

Roll dough into a 16-inch circle on a lightly floured surface. Place dough on a 16-inch pizza pan or baking sheet coated with cooking spray. Cover loosely; let stand in a warm place (85°) for 15 minutes. Drain tomato slices on paper towels. Preheat oven to 425°. Sprinkle dough with ½ cup mozzarella; arrange tomato slices in a single layer over mozzarella. Sprinkle remaining 1 cup mozzarella and Romano cheeses evenly over tomatoes. Bake at 425° for 20 minutes or until crust and cheese are browned. Cut pizza into 8 wedges, and sprinkle evenly with basil. Yield: 4 servings (serving size: 2 wedges).

CALORIES 442; **FAT** 17.1g (sat 7.8g, mono 6.9g, poly 0.8g); **PROTEIN** 24g; **CARB** 54.2g; **FIBER** 2.7g; **CHOL** 38mg; **IRON** 3.2mg; **SODIUM** 777mg; **CALC** 503mg

1 (16-ounce) refrigerated fresh pizza crust dough

2 plum tomatoes, each cut into 8 slices

1½ cups (6 ounces) shredded part-skim mozzarella cheese, divided

½ cup (2 ounces) grated fresh Romano cheese

12 fresh basil leaves, thinly sliced

Mediterranean Stuffed Chicken Breasts

This versatile dish is easy enough for a week-night supper but elegant enough for company.

1 large red bell pepper
¼ cup (1 ounce) crumbled feta cheese
2 tablespoons finely chopped pitted kalamata olives
1 tablespoon minced fresh basil
8 (6-ounce) skinless, boneless chicken breasts

Preheat broiler. Cut bell pepper in half lengthwise; discard seeds and membranes. Place pepper halves, skin sides up, on a foil-lined baking sheet; flatten with hand. Broil 15 minutes or until blackened. Place in a zip-top plastic bag; seal. Let stand 15 minutes. Peel and finely chop. Prepare grill to medium-high heat. Combine bell pepper, cheese, olives, and basil. Cut a horizontal slit through thickest portion of each chicken breast half to form a pocket. Stuff 2 tablespoons bell pepper mixture into each pocket; close opening with a wooden pick. Sprinkle chicken with ¼ teaspoon salt and ¼ teaspoon black pepper. Place chicken on a grill rack coated with cooking spray. Grill 6 minutes on each side or until done. Remove from grill; cover loosely with foil, and let stand 10 minutes. Yield: 8 servings (serving size: 1 stuffed chicken breast half).

CALORIES 210; **FAT** 5.9g (sat 1.9g, mono 2.3g, poly 1g); **PROTEIN** 35.2g; **CARB** 1.8g; **FIBER** 0.5g; **CHOL** 98mg; **IRON** 1.3mg; **SODIUM** 266mg; **CALC** 43mg

1 large red bell pepper

+

¼ cup (1 ounce) crumbled feta cheese

+

2 tablespoons finely chopped pitted kalamata olives

+

1 tablespoon minced fresh basil

+

8 (6-ounce) skinless, boneless chicken breasts

A LIGHTER BOWL OF BAKED BEANS

We give this picnic side dish a flavor and nutrition makeover.

Baked beans are a picnic or barbecue version of comfort food, balancing starchy, creamy, and sweet notes. Even better, beans are full of fiber and good nutrients. But some recipes smother the beans with loads of fatty pork, grease, and a salt shaker's worth of sodium. We tweaked this staple to keep the yum factor without walking on the bland side.

Starting with dried beans allowed us to customize the flavor while keeping tabs on calories, saturated fat, and sodium. Instead of a half-pound of bacon, we use 3 slices and just 1½ tablespoons rendered bacon grease to infuse the beans with porky goodness without tipping the calorie and saturated fat scales. We balance high-sodium elements—salt, bacon, and mustard—with maple syrup and bourbon. Some tart-sweet cider vinegar perks up the taste. This dish has complex flavors and smooth texture, plus all the fiber and one-fourth the sodium of many recipes. Best of all, these beans maintain the legume's nutrition all-star status.

OLD WAY	OUR WAY
458 calories per serving	199 calories per serving
8.6 grams saturated fat	1.1 grams saturated fat
1,111 milligrams sodium	307 milligrams sodium
High-sodium canned pork and beans	Dried beans
½ pound bacon	3 ounces bacon
¼ cup rendered bacon grease	1½ tablespoons rendered bacon grease

Make Ahead

Bourbon Baked Beans

Check your beans 10 to 15 minutes ahead of time to make sure they're not drying out.

1 pound dried navy beans (about 2½ cups)
3 applewood-smoked bacon slices
1 cup finely chopped onion
5 cups water, divided
½ cup maple syrup, divided
¼ cup plus 2 tablespoons bourbon, divided
¼ cup Dijon mustard
1½ teaspoons Worcestershire sauce
¼ teaspoon freshly ground black pepper
1 tablespoon cider vinegar
1 teaspoon salt

1. Sort and wash beans; place in a large Dutch oven. Cover with water to 2 inches above beans; cover and let stand 8 hours or overnight. Drain beans. Wipe pan dry with a paper towel.
2. Preheat oven to 350°.
3. Heat pan over medium-high heat. Add bacon to pan, and cook 4 minutes or until crisp. Remove from pan, reserving 1½ tablespoons drippings in pan; crumble bacon. Add onion to drippings in pan; cook 5 minutes or until onion begins to brown, stirring frequently. Add beans, bacon, 4 cups water, ¼ cup maple syrup, ¼ cup bourbon, and next 3 ingredients to pan. Bring to a boil; cover and bake at 350° for 2 hours.

4. Stir in remaining 1 cup water, remaining ¼ cup maple syrup, and remaining 2 tablespoons bourbon. Cover and bake 1 hour or until beans are tender and liquid is almost absorbed. Stir in vinegar and salt. Yield: 6½ cups (serving size: ½ cup).

CALORIES 199; FAT 3.1g (sat 1.1g, mono 0.7g, poly 0.5g); PROTEIN 7.8g; CARB 31.8g; FIBER 5.6g; CHOL 4mg; IRON 2.1mg; SODIUM 307mg; CALC 66mg

FLAVOR BOOSTERS

Beans—whether canned or dried—need bold flavor builders to bring out their leguminous best. Pork is a natural flavor pal to beans, but here are a few other accents that make the humble vegetable plate-worthy:

■ Worcestershire sauce's tantalizing mix of tangy tamarind, briny anchovies, and a laundry list of ingredients adds rich savoriness. A little goes a long way.

■ Dijon also adds some sodium, but with it comes a tart, sharp note with the slightest hint of heat that pairs well with beans.

■ Sweet, mild maple syrup not only adds rich flavor but also helps create the thick, creamy texture of the cooked navy beans.

BUILDING BETTER, LIGHTER BURGERS

Juicy meats! Rich flavors! Zesty condiments!

The great American burger has been gaining weight like a cartoon sumo wrestler lately. In fast-food joints and fancy restaurants alike, it's all about superdupersizing.

It's time to reclaim America's national food for folks who want to grill a juicy, delicious, and satisfying burger that is plenty big enough but fits into a healthy diet, too. Humbly, we present five candidates. Beef, of course, in two versions, but also lamb, salmon, and turkey for good measure. Each meat is paired with spices and condiments that elevate these sandwiches to new flavor glory. (OK, maybe we're not so humble.)

The secrets to healthy burgers are now revealed. Less fat in the patty requires a few tricks to keep things juicy. If you like it simple, try the brisket cheeseburger. If you like spice, the poblano burger is very nice. If you want fish, the salmon burger is the alpha and the omega 3 of fishburgers. There are flavors for every palate. So fire up the grill this weekend and get your better, lighter burger summer going.

Kid Friendly

Turkey Burgers with Roasted Eggplant

(pictured on page 258)

1 (8-ounce) eggplant
Cooking spray
2 tablespoons finely chopped fresh parsley, divided
4 teaspoons olive oil, divided
1 teaspoon fresh lemon juice
1 garlic clove, minced
3/4 teaspoon kosher salt, divided
1/2 teaspoon freshly ground black pepper, divided
1 pound turkey tenderloins, cut into 1-inch pieces
1 teaspoon lower-sodium soy sauce
1/4 teaspoon Marmite
4 (1 1/2-ounce) hamburger buns, toasted
4 Bibb lettuce leaves
4 (1/4-inch-thick) tomato slices

1. Preheat oven to 400°.
2. Lightly coat eggplant with cooking spray; wrap eggplant in foil. Place eggplant on a jelly-roll pan; bake at 400° for 45 minutes or until very tender, turning once. Remove from foil; cool slightly. Cut eggplant in half. Carefully scoop out pulp to measure 1 1/4 cups; discard skin. Place pulp in a food processor; process until smooth. Reserve 1/4 cup pureed pulp. Combine remaining pulp, 1 tablespoon parsley, 2 teaspoons oil, juice, and garlic. Stir in 1/2 teaspoon salt and 1/4 teaspoon pepper; set aside.
3. To prepare grinder, place feed shaft, blade, and 1/4-inch die plate in freezer 30 minutes or until well chilled. Assemble grinder just before grinding.
4. Arrange turkey pieces in a single layer on jelly-roll pan, leaving space between each piece. Freeze 15 minutes or until meat is firm but not frozen. Combine meat and remaining 2 teaspoons oil in large bowl; toss to combine. Pass meat through meat grinder completely. Immediately pass meat through grinder a second time. Combine reserved 1/4 cup eggplant puree, turkey, remaining 1 tablespoon parsley, soy sauce, and Marmite in a large bowl. Divide mixture into 4 equal portions, gently shaping each into a 1/2-inch-thick patty. Press a nickel-sized indentation in center of each patty. Cover and chill until ready to grill.
5. Preheat grill to medium-high heat.
6. Lightly coat patties with cooking spray; sprinkle with remaining 1/4 teaspoon salt and remaining 1/4 teaspoon pepper. Place patties on grill rack, and grill 4 minutes until well marked. Carefully turn patties over, and grill 3 minutes or until desired degree of doneness. Place 1 patty on bottom half of each bun; top each serving with 1 tablespoon eggplant mixture, 1 lettuce leaf, 1 tomato slice, and top half of bun. (Reserve remaining eggplant mixture for another use.)
Yield: 4 servings (serving size: 1 burger).

CALORIES 311; **FAT** 12.5g (sat 3g, mono 2.8g, poly 1.5g); **PROTEIN** 26.9g; **CARB** 23.3g; **FIBER** 1.9g; **CHOL** 65mg; **IRON** 3.6mg; **SODIUM** 522mg; **CALC** 70mg

WINE NOTE: These burgers have a rich and meaty flavor, accentuated by the addition of Marmite. This savory, meaty character is often identifiable in the affordable and intriguing reds of France's Languedoc region, like Jean-Luc Colombo Syrah La Violette 2007 ($12), with chewy black fruit and notes of fresh herbs and smoked meat that pump up the flavor even more.

TURKEY BURGER

How do you get a burger made from mild, low-fat turkey to have some of the meaty richness of beef? Add some rich, meaty flavors! Here's the kitchen science: Beef and other red meats contain compounds called *glutamates*. So do soy sauce and Marmite, which is a powerfully strong yeast extract found in a lot of supermarkets (the Aussies love a version called Vegemite). We add a bit of both to our turkey mixture, lending this burger the umami flavors of real red meat.

As for juiciness, another challenge with turkey, that comes from the addition of mildly flavored eggplant. We simply roast the eggplant with olive oil, then puree it, then blend it with the ground meat.

LAMB BURGER

This burger is kept lean by using lamb shoulder, which has about two-thirds less fat than preground lamb from the supermarket. For a lighter texture, grind it yourself (see tips, page 175), or ask a butcher to do it. *Vadouvan*, an Indian spice mix, flavors the meat. The patties get tantalizingly aromatic when charred on a hot grill.

Mint and yogurt provide the perfect counterpoint to the spice mix. Finally, sweet roasted red peppers and bitter radicchio round out a deliciously tasty burger.

Lamb Burgers with Indian Spices and Yogurt-Mint Sauce

Vadouvan is an Indian condiment made by cooking onions, shallots, and garlic until deeply caramelized, then flavoring them with a combination of toasted dried spices. You can substitute 2 teaspoons of garam masala or Madras curry powder for all the ground spices here.

1 pound boneless lamb shoulder, trimmed
    and cut into 1-inch pieces
2 tablespoons olive oil, divided
3/4 cup finely chopped onion
1/4 cup finely chopped shallots
2 tablespoons minced garlic, divided
3/4 teaspoon ground cumin
3/4 teaspoon ground coriander
1/4 teaspoon ground cardamom
1/4 teaspoon ground mustard
1/4 teaspoon ground turmeric
1/8 teaspoon ground red pepper
Dash of grated whole nutmeg
2 tablespoons finely chopped fresh mint,
    divided
3/4 teaspoon kosher salt, divided
2 red bell peppers
1/2 cup plain 2% reduced-fat Greek yogurt
1 tablespoon fresh lemon juice
1/4 teaspoon freshly ground black pepper,
    divided
Cooking spray
4 (1 1/2-ounce) hamburger buns, toasted
2 cups torn radicchio

1. To prepare grinder, place feed shaft, blade, and 1/4-inch die plate in freezer 30 minutes or until well chilled. Assemble grinder just before grinding.

2. Arrange lamb pieces in a single layer on a jelly-roll pan, leaving space between each piece. Freeze 15 minutes or until meat is firm but not frozen. Combine lamb and 1 tablespoon oil in large bowl; toss to combine. Pass lamb through meat grinder completely. Immediately pass meat through grinder a second time. Cover and chill.

3. Heat remaining 1 tablespoon oil in a medium nonstick skillet over medium heat. Add onion and shallots; cook 15 minutes or until onions are golden, stirring frequently. Stir in 1 1/2 tablespoons garlic, cumin, and next 6 ingredients; cook 1 minute. Remove from heat; cool to room temperature.

4. Combine lamb mixture, onion mixture, 1 tablespoon mint, and 1/4 teaspoon salt. Divide mixture into 4 equal portions, gently shaping each into a 1/2-inch-thick patty. Press a nickel-sized indentation in center of each patty. Cover and chill until ready to grill.

5. Preheat broiler.

6. Cut bell peppers in half lengthwise; discard seeds and membranes. Place pepper halves, skin sides up, on a foil-lined baking sheet; flatten with hand. Broil 9 minutes or until blackened. Place in a zip-top plastic bag; seal. Let stand 10 minutes. Peel and cut each pepper portion in half.

7. Preheat grill to medium-high heat.

8. Combine remaining 1 1/2 teaspoons garlic, remaining 1 tablespoon mint, yogurt, juice, 1/4 teaspoon salt, and 1/8 teaspoon black pepper in a bowl. Set aside.

9. Sprinkle patties evenly with remaining 1/4 teaspoon salt and remaining 1/8 tea-spoon black pepper. Place patties on a grill rack coated with cooking spray; grill 4 minutes or until grill marks appear. Carefully turn patties; grill 3 minutes or until desired degree of doneness. Place 1 patty on bottom half of each bun; top each serving with 2 tablespoons yogurt mixture, 1/2 cup radicchio, 2 bell pepper strips, and top half of bun. Yield: 4 servings (serving size: 1 burger).

CALORIES 398; FAT 15.7g (sat 4.1g, mono 7.8g, poly 2.3g); PROTEIN 31.5g; CARB 32.9g; FIBER 3.3g; CHOL 74mg; IRON 4.5mg; SODIUM 656mg; CALC 153mg

BRISKET BURGER

This is the purist's burger and the best argument of all for using fresh-ground meat. Preground supermarket beef is often made from trim and scraps. The result can be inconsistent flavor. Not only that, but preground meat compresses the longer it sits in tight packaging, which affects texture. So it's much better to start with whole cuts of beef and grind them yourself, or get the butcher to do it at the shop or supermarket.

Grinding also lets you control fat. We use lean brisket, which is lower in saturated fat, and then add olive oil, which ensures juiciness and a rich, meaty flavor.

Kid Friendly

Simple, Perfect Fresh-Ground Brisket Burgers

We loved the flavorful patty we got from grinding inexpensive beef brisket (see page 175 for grinding tips). Ask for the flat cut of brisket for the leanest choice. Traditional condiments like ketchup and mustard are an option, but we found this burger so good on its own that all we added was cheese, lettuce, and tomato.

1 (1-pound) beef brisket, trimmed and cut into
    1-inch pieces
2 tablespoons olive oil
1/4 teaspoon kosher salt
1/8 teaspoon freshly ground black pepper
Cooking spray
4 (1/2-ounce) cheddar cheese slices
4 (1 1/2-ounce) hamburger buns, toasted
4 green leaf lettuce leaves
4 (1/4-inch-thick) slices tomato

1. To prepare grinder, place feed shaft, blade, and 1/4-inch die plate in freezer 30 minutes or until well chilled. Assemble grinder just before grinding.

2. Arrange meat in a single layer on jelly-roll pan, leaving space between each piece. Freeze 15 minutes or until meat is firm but not frozen. Combine meat and oil in large bowl, and toss to combine. Pass meat through meat grinder completely. Immediately pass meat through grinder a second time. Divide mixture into 4 equal portions, gently shaping each into a 1/2-inch-thick patty. Press a nickel-sized indentation in the center of each patty. Cover and chill until ready to grill.

3. Preheat grill to medium-high heat.
4. Sprinkle patties with salt and pepper. Place on a grill rack coated with cooking spray; grill 2 minutes or until grill marks appear. Carefully turn patties; grill 3 minutes. Top each patty with 1 cheese slice; grill 1 minute or until cheese melts and beef reaches desired degree of doneness. Place 1 patty on bottom half of each bun; top each serving with 1 lettuce leaf, 1 tomato slice, and top half of bun. Yield: 4 servings (serving size: 1 burger).

CALORIES 386; **FAT** 17.9g (sat 6.1g, mono 8.7g, poly 1.9g); **PROTEIN** 32.4g; **CARB** 22.1g; **FIBER** 1.2g; **CHOL** 64mg; **IRON** 4mg; **SODIUM** 496mg; **CALC** 181mg

THE THUMBPRINT TRICK

Overworking and compressing the meat results in dense, dry hamburgers. Form the patty gently, then make a small indentation in the center of each one with your thumb. The indentation helps the patty hold its shape—rather than swelling—as it shrinks during cooking.

SALMON BURGER

This light, tasty burger proves that salmon can be every bit as satisfying as beef. The trick is to get the texture right. Ground beef will stick together firmly to form a patty, but ground salmon alone can be soft and difficult to work with, and a binder like breadcrumbs or eggs can blur the salmon flavor. Solution: For perfect texture, we puree one quarter of the salmon into a fine paste and use it to bind the rest of the roughly chopped salmon.

The burgers are then flavored with classic fish condiments. Adding shallots offers a great oniony kick. Lemon zest and tarragon add complexity. They are finished with a deliciously tangy honey-mustard glaze.

Salmon Burgers
(pictured on page 258)

For best results, choose salmon from the meaty center of the fish and avoid portions cut from the tail section.

1 pound skinless center-cut salmon fillets, cut into 1-inch pieces, divided
2 tablespoons Dijon mustard, divided
2 teaspoons grated lemon rind
2 tablespoons minced fresh tarragon
1 tablespoon finely chopped shallots (about 1 small)
1/2 teaspoon kosher salt
1/4 teaspoon freshly ground black pepper
1 tablespoon honey
1 cup arugula leaves
1/2 cup thinly sliced red onion
1 teaspoon fresh lemon juice
1 teaspoon extra-virgin olive oil
Cooking spray
4 (1 1/2-ounce) hamburger buns, toasted

1. Place 1/4 pound salmon, 1 tablespoon mustard, and rind in a food processor; process until smooth. Spoon puree into a large bowl. Place remaining 3/4 pound salmon in food processor; pulse 6 times or until coarsely chopped. Fold chopped salmon, tarragon, and next 3 ingredients into puree. Divide mixture into 4 equal portions, gently shaping each into a 1/2-inch-thick patty. Cover and chill until ready to grill.
2. Preheat grill to medium heat.
3. Combine remaining 1 tablespoon mustard and honey in a small bowl, and set aside.
4. Combine arugula and next 3 ingredients in a medium bowl. Set aside.
5. Lightly coat both sides of burgers with cooking spray. Place patties on a grill rack; grill 2 minutes. Carefully turn patties, and grill an additional 1 minute or until desired degree of doneness. Place 1 patty on bottom half of each bun; top each serving with 1 1/2 teaspoons honey mixture, 1/4 cup arugula mixture, and top half of bun. Yield: 4 servings (serving size: 1 burger).

CALORIES 372; **FAT** 16g (sat 3.2g, mono 5.9g, poly 5.8g); **PROTEIN** 27.3g; **CARB** 28.2g; **FIBER** 1.5g; **CHOL** 67mg; **IRON** 2.1mg; **SODIUM** 569mg; **CALC** 92mg

WHY GRINDING'S GOOD

There's no question: Fresh-ground beef, lamb, or turkey yields a superior, juicier burger. That includes meat you've had ground to order in a butcher shop or at a supermarket and loosely wrapped (tight wraps compress the meat). At home, a grinder attachment for your stand mixer is ideal, or an old-fashioned hand grinder. Or you can use your food processor; in that case, be sure to work in small batches, pulsing the meat 8 to 10 times or until the meat is finely chopped but not pureed.

No matter what grinding tool you use, it's important to keep the meat and the grinding equipment as cold as possible. If the meat gets too warm, it will begin to smear rather than grind cleanly, giving the finished product a nasty mashed texture. Putting the meat and grinding equipment in the freezer for at least 15 minutes beforehand helps guarantee optimum results.

No time? In a pinch, you can of course use preground beef, lamb, or turkey for these recipes. The spices and condiments will still produce a better, lighter burger.

A MIXTURE CALLED A *PANADE*, SOMETIMES USED IN MEATBALLS, HELPS KEEP THE LEAN, SUPERMARKET GROUND SIRLOIN TENDER AND JUICY.

Spicy Poblano Burgers with Pickled Red Onions and Chipotle Cream

A poblano chile is the perfect mix of fruity flavor with a little bit of heat. Leave the seeds in your poblano if you want more fiery flavor.

2 poblano chiles
1 tablespoon 1% low-fat milk
1 (1-ounce) slice white bread, crusts removed, and torn into ½-inch pieces
3 tablespoons minced fresh cilantro, divided
1 teaspoon ground cumin
½ teaspoon ground coriander
½ teaspoon paprika
½ teaspoon kosher salt, divided
½ teaspoon freshly ground black pepper, divided
1 pound ground sirloin
½ cup light sour cream
1 tablespoon minced shallots
1 teaspoon fresh lime juice
1 (7-ounce) can chipotle chiles in adobo sauce
Cooking spray
4 (1½-ounce) hamburger buns, toasted
¼ cup Pickled Red Onions (recipe at right)

1. Preheat broiler.
2. Place poblano chiles on a foil-lined baking sheet, and broil 8 minutes or until blackened, turning after 6 minutes. Place in a zip-top plastic bag; seal. Let stand 15 minutes. Peel chiles, and discard seeds and membranes. Finely chop.
3. Place milk and bread in a large bowl; mash bread mixture with a fork until smooth. Add poblano chile, 1½ tablespoons cilantro, cumin, coriander, paprika, ¼ teaspoon salt, ¼ teaspoon black pepper, and beef to milk mixture, tossing gently to combine. Divide mixture into 4 equal portions, gently shaping each into a ½-inch-thick patty. Press a nickel-sized indentation in center of each patty. Cover and chill until ready to grill.
4. Preheat grill to medium-high heat.
5. Combine remaining 1½ tablespoons cilantro, remaining ¼ teaspoon salt, and remaining ¼ teaspoon black pepper in a medium bowl. Stir in sour cream, shallots, and juice. Remove 1 chipotle pepper and 2 teaspoons adobo sauce from can; reserve remaining chipotle peppers and adobo sauce for another use. Chop chile. Stir chopped chipotle and 2 teaspoons adobo sauce into sour cream mixture. Set aside.
6. Place patties on a grill rack coated with cooking spray; grill 3 minutes or until grill marks appear. Carefully turn patties; grill an additional 3 minutes or until desired degree of doneness. Place 1 patty on bottom half of each bun; top each serving with 3 tablespoons chipotle cream and 1 tablespoon Pickled Red Onions. Yield: 4 servings (serving size: 1 burger).

CALORIES 325; FAT 9.8g (sat 4.5g, mono 2.5g, poly 1.4g); PROTEIN 29.5g; CARB 30.2g; FIBER 2.1g; CHOL 70mg; IRON 3.9mg; SODIUM 621mg; CALC 81mg

Make Ahead
Pickled Red Onions

The tangy zip of these pickled onions cuts through the rich chipotle cream. Use leftovers in bean burritos, on a beef sandwich, or mixed with fresh cilantro and orange sections for a quick relish for grilled Alaskan salmon.

½ cup sugar
½ cup rice vinegar
½ cup water
1 jalapeño pepper, halved lengthwise
2½ cups thinly vertically sliced red onion

1. Combine first 4 ingredients in a medium saucepan; bring to a boil, stirring until sugar dissolves. Add onion to pan, and cover. Remove from heat, and cool to room temperature. Store in an airtight container in refrigerator for up to 1 month. Yield: 2 cups (serving size: 1 tablespoon drained pickled onions).

CALORIES 3; FAT 0g; PROTEIN 0.1g; CARB 0.8g; FIBER 0.1g; CHOL 0mg; IRON 0mg; SODIUM 0mg; CALC 1mg

POBLANO BEEF BURGER

The secret to this burger, which is made of lean, preground supermarket sirloin, is the addition of a mixture called a *panade*, a mash of milk and bread used to keep meatballs tender and moist. Also in the mix are warm spices often found in Mexican chorizo sausage—such as coriander, paprika, and cumin. There's a creamy, smoky poblano sauce, and the burger is finished with a quick red onion pickle that lends a wonderful tang. (The pickled onion recipe yields more than you'll need for a single batch of burgers, but it keeps for several weeks in the fridge. Use on sandwiches or salads—or the next batch of these poblano burgers.)

SUMMER FRUIT COBBLERS

Stone fruit and berries star in these stunning and deliciously healthy desserts.

Seasonal fruits find sweet-tart perfection during the summer, and what better way to highlight their flavors than a cobbler? Of course, peaches, plums, and berries work in savory applications, but they seem tailor-made for these simple, down-home desserts—so simple, in fact, that all you need is a baking dish, some fruit, and a few ingredients to make a biscuit-style topping to get cooking. We went beyond the basics with these cobblers, then got creative with toppings. For example, Blueberry-Peach Cobbler is like a blueberry muffin canoodling with fresh peaches. You can even make them ahead. We're sure you'll love the results.

Staff Favorite • Make Ahead
Kid Friendly

Blueberry-Peach Cobbler

Use peaches that aren't superripe for this recipe so they'll hold their shape when cooked. The baking dish will be brimming with fruit and topping, so it's a good idea to place it on a foil-lined baking sheet before putting it in the oven.

5 pounds peaches, peeled, pitted, and
    sliced
2 tablespoons fresh lemon juice
1 cup granulated sugar, divided
3/8 teaspoon salt, divided
6.75 ounces (about 1 1/2 cups) plus
    2 tablespoons all-purpose flour, divided
Cooking spray
1 teaspoon baking powder
1/2 cup butter, softened
2 large eggs
1 teaspoon vanilla extract
3/4 cup buttermilk
2 cups fresh blueberries
2 tablespoons turbinado sugar

1. Preheat oven to 375°.
2. Place peaches in a large bowl. Drizzle with juice; toss. Add 3/4 cup granulated sugar, 1/8 teaspoon salt, and 2 tablespoons flour to peach mixture, and toss to combine. Arrange peach mixture evenly in a 13 x 9–inch glass or ceramic baking dish coated with cooking spray.
3. Weigh or lightly spoon 6.75 ounces flour (about 1 1/2 cups) into dry measuring cups; level with a knife. Combine 6.75 ounces flour, remaining 1/4 teaspoon salt, and baking powder in a bowl, stirring well with a whisk. Place remaining 1/4 cup granulated sugar and butter in a medium bowl, and beat with a mixer at medium speed until light and fluffy (about 2 minutes). Add eggs, 1 at a time, beating well after each addition. Stir in vanilla extract. Add flour mixture and buttermilk alternately to butter mixture, beginning and ending with flour mixture, beating just until combined. Stir in blueberries.
4. Spread batter evenly over peach mixture; sprinkle with turbinado sugar. Place baking dish on a foil-lined baking sheet. Bake at 375° for 1 hour or until topping is golden and filling is bubbly. Yield: 12 servings (serving size: about 3/4 cup).

CALORIES 303; **FAT** 9.6g (sat 5.4g, mono 2.4g, poly 0.7g); **PROTEIN** 5.1g; **CARB** 52.2g; **FIBER** 3.5g; **CHOL** 58mg; **IRON** 1.5mg; **SODIUM** 189mg; **CALC** 51mg

Make Ahead

Plum Cobbler

5 pounds plums, peeled, pitted, and
    quartered
1 tablespoon fresh lemon juice
1 1/2 teaspoons grated peeled fresh ginger
3/4 cup granulated sugar, divided
1/4 teaspoon salt, divided
6.75 ounces (about 1 1/2 cups) plus
    1 1/2 tablespoons all-purpose flour,
    divided
Cooking spray
3/4 teaspoon baking powder
1/4 cup chilled butter, cut into pieces
1 teaspoon grated lemon rind
6 ounces chilled 1/3-less-fat cream cheese,
    cut into pieces
1/2 cup buttermilk
2 tablespoons turbinado sugar

1. Preheat oven to 375°.
2. Combine first 3 ingredients in a bowl. Add 1/4 cup granulated sugar, 1/8 teaspoon salt, and 1 1/2 tablespoons flour; toss. Arrange mixture in a 13 x 9–inch glass or ceramic baking dish coated with cooking spray.
3. Weigh or lightly spoon 6.75 ounces flour (about 1 1/2 cups) into dry measuring cups; level with a knife. Place flour, remaining 1/2 cup granulated sugar, remaining 1/8 teaspoon salt, and baking powder in a food processor; pulse 3 times. Add butter, rind, and cheese; pulse until mixture resembles coarse meal. Add buttermilk; pulse until blended.
4. Drop dough by spoonfuls over plum mixture; sprinkle with turbinado sugar. Bake at 375° for 55 minutes or until golden. Yield: 12 servings (serving size: about 1/2 cup).

CALORIES 293; **FAT** 8.7g (sat 4.8g, mono 2.7g, poly 0.5g); **PROTEIN** 5g; **CARB** 52g; **FIBER** 3.2g; **CHOL** 22mg; **IRON** 1.1mg; **SODIUM** 169mg; **CALC** 45mg

TASTE TEST

The level of natural sugar in most fruits is set when harvested, so sample the fruit before making your cobbler. If the fruit is underripe and tastes tart, you can add an extra couple tablespoons of sugar to the fruit filling.

4 STEPS TO MAKING CREATIVE COBBLERS

1 PICK OR BUY JUST-RIPE FRUIT. Select fruit that ripened on the vine (or tree); it shouldn't be overripe, especially in the case of stone fruit like peaches or plums. Fruit that's too soft won't hold up to the heat while the topping fully cooks.

2 MAKE THE FILLING. The fruit filling can be as simple or as creative as you like. Combine two or more fruits, and add flavors like grated fresh ginger, ground spices, or grated citrus rind. Toss it all together, and place in a ceramic or glass baking dish.

3 PREPARE THE TOPPING. There are many interpretations of toppings, ranging from tender biscuit-style to pastry dough, and you can customize them to your tastes. Then sprinkle (or pour) the topping over the top of the fruit mixture.

4 BAKE UNTIL BUBBLY AND BROWNED. The key to success is timing: Bake the fruit until it's tender but not mushy, and the topping until it's cooked fully. The best visual cues for doneness are browned topping and pockets of fruit bubbling up to the top.

Make Ahead • Kid Friendly

Lattice-Topped Blackberry Cobbler
(pictured on page 259)

Using whole almonds in the topping gives it a little color from the skins, but substituting sliced or slivered almonds will also work in this recipe. Serving Suggestion: Although the cobbler is tasty on its own, if you want to serve it with low-fat ice cream, reduce the serving size to about 1/2 cup.

1 cup granulated sugar, divided
6 tablespoons butter, softened
1 large egg yolk
1/2 teaspoon vanilla extract
3/4 cup whole almonds, toasted
6 ounces all-purpose flour (about 1 1/3 cups)
1/4 teaspoon baking powder
1/4 teaspoon salt
3 tablespoons ice water
10 cups fresh blackberries (about 5 [12-ounce] packages)
3 tablespoons cornstarch
1 tablespoon fresh lemon juice
Cooking spray
2 tablespoons turbinado sugar

1. Place 1/3 cup granulated sugar and butter in a large bowl; beat with a mixer until combined (about 1 minute). Add egg yolk, beating well. Stir in vanilla.
2. Place almonds in a food processor; pulse 10 times or until finely ground. Weigh or lightly spoon flour into dry measuring cups; level with a knife. Combine nuts, flour, baking powder, and salt, stirring well with a whisk. Gradually add nut mixture to butter mixture, beating at low speed just until a soft dough forms, adding 3 tablespoons ice water, as necessary. Turn dough out onto a lightly floured surface; knead lightly 6 times or until smooth. Divide dough into 2 equal portions; wrap each portion in plastic wrap. Chill 1 hour or until firm.
3. Preheat oven to 375°.
4. Combine remaining 2/3 cup granulated sugar, blackberries, cornstarch, and lemon juice; toss gently. Arrange berry mixture in a 13 x 9–inch glass or ceramic baking dish coated with cooking spray.

5. Unwrap dough. Roll each dough portion into a 13 x 9–inch rectangle on a lightly floured surface. Cut 1 rectangle, crosswise, into (1-inch-wide) strips. Cut remaining rectangle, lengthwise, into (1-inch-wide) strips. Arrange strips in a lattice pattern over fruit mixture; sprinkle dough with turbinado sugar. Bake at 375° for 50 minutes or until golden. Let stand 10 minutes. Yield: 12 servings (serving size: about ⅔ cup).

CALORIES 301; FAT 11.5g (sat 4.1g, mono 4.6g, poly 1.8g); PROTEIN 5.7g; CARB 47g; FIBER 8.6g; CHOL 32mg; IRON 2mg; SODIUM 103mg; CALC 75mg

TEST KITCHEN TIP

Add a dash of salt to baked goods and other sweets—it intensifies the sweetness and rounds out the dish's flavor.

SIZING THEM UP

Some folks like the homey appeal of one large cobbler baked in a glass or ceramic casserole dish. Baking in individual-sized dishes is another option that makes a statement at the table. Any of our recipes can be baked in ramekins or other earthenware, but if you opt for that route, they won't need to bake as long. For example, individual Plum Cobblers (page 177) bake for only 35 minutes.

CITRUS SENSE

Acidic ingredients like lemons or limes heighten and brighten the flavor of dishes they grace, so all of our recipes call for a little splash of fresh lemon juice.

NUTRITION NOTES

- Each serving of Blackberry Cobbler has 8.6 grams of fiber.
- Blueberries are rich in vitamin C and natural antioxidants.

A SHRIMP, A BARBIE, AND A SYDNEY BEACH

The beer-and-meat-centric clichés of Australian cooking are banished with this light, bright, down-under summer menu from Sydney's Jane and Jeremy Strode.

Australia has always offered a thrill to those immigrants who love the strangeness of its animals, plants, landscape, and even its light. No less to its immigrant chefs: Jeremy Strode arrived from London in 1992 and found himself agog over the unfamiliar things that were pulled from local waters.

"I reveled in all the species I had never encountered," Jeremy remembers. "Deliciously plump, sweet, and rather prehistoric-looking crayfish called 'bugs,' 'marron,' and 'yabbies.' Crabs unlike any I'd ever tasted. And wonderful fish such as the meaty, firm, and grill-friendly Hiramasa kingfish (also known as amberjack), or the Red Emperor and Trevalla, with their delicate flavor yet moist, large flake. Not to mention the scallops and abalone from Tasmania, which are just amazing!"

He arrived, though, with a background of culinary training that was more rigid than playful. Britain had not fully embarked on the cooking revolution that has since turned London into a world culinary capital. In Sydney and other big cities, things were looser, and cooks were experimenting. "Because this is a relatively new country," explains Jeremy's Australian wife and cooking partner, Jane, "we don't have a long history of, say, French tradition that governs the way we do things. We have fewer rules when it comes to cooking." The Aussies were making things up, in other words, and so it was a lucky chef who found his way there to play with those pristine ingredients—not only the seafood, but also produce both familiar and strange.

Jeremy began cooking in Melbourne restaurants in 1992—The George Hotel, the Adelphi, his own restaurant Pomme, and Langton's, where he met pastry chef Jane Booth. In 2002, the couple moved to Sydney, and they married in 2004. In 2005, they opened their own restaurant, Bistrode. The Bistrode menu speaks of a fusion of Jeremy's British cooking (the cooking of that country having undergone a momentous revolution) flecked with the brightness of Jane's modern Oz taste.

When they opened Bistrode, Jeremy knew he'd need a grill. Aussie eating, like Aussie life, favors the outdoors. "In the summer," Jane says, "we head outside with picnic baskets laden with fresh seafood, seviche, Greek and Thai salads, terrines, panforte, and wine." And out there, on the beaches, in the backyards, is the grill—the legendary barbie.

The Strodes' talents merge in the meal featured here. Jane's flourishes are seen in a Vietnamese noodle salad topped with grilled tiger prawns, the simplest panzanella with brilliant heirloom tomatoes and lightly charred sourdough, and a delicate dessert blending sheep's-milk yogurt and a whiff of rose water into creamy cheesecakes served with grilled figs. Jeremy's hand can be felt in the unexpected and surprisingly upscale use of coleslaw and back bacon to enhance crispy-skinned ocean trout. It's a meal, like a kitchen partnership, that's inspired.

Tiger Prawn, Noodle, and Herb Salad

A beautiful and delicious starter, this Asian-influenced noodle dish offers a different interpretation of shrimp on the barbie. Here Jane brings in some Vietnamese influences to pair with Australia's moist, sweet tiger prawns.

¼ cup fresh lime juice
1 tablespoon palm sugar or brown sugar
1 tablespoon fish sauce
2 garlic cloves, crushed
12 tiger prawns (about 20 ounces)
Cooking spray
2 ounces rice vermicelli
½ cup thinly diagonally sliced green onions
½ cup loosely packed fresh cilantro leaves
½ cup loosely packed fresh mint leaves, torn
¼ cup shredded unsweetened coconut
¼ cup chopped salted dry-roasted peanuts
2 finger hot chiles, thinly sliced

1. Combine first 4 ingredients in a medium bowl, stirring until sugar dissolves. Let stand 30 minutes; discard garlic.
2. Preheat grill to medium-high heat.
3. Peel prawns, leaving tails intact. Arrange prawns on a grill rack coated with cooking spray; grill 4 minutes or until done, turning once.
4. Cook noodles according to package directions. Combine noodles, green onions, and remaining ingredients in a large bowl. Drizzle with juice mixture, tossing to coat. Top with prawns. Yield: 6 servings (serving size: 2 prawns and ½ cup noodle mixture).

CALORIES 128; FAT 5.1g (sat 2.5g, mono 1.2g, poly 0.9g); PROTEIN 5.4g; CARB 15.8g; FIBER 1.8g; CHOL 21mg; IRON 1.2mg; SODIUM 260mg; CALC 33mg

Whole Baby Snapper and Green Sauce

An Australian grill isn't complete without the essential whole fish, and a local-waters snapper is a common choice. A bright, fresh, anchovy-flecked sauce adorns the simply seasoned fish in this first course. If you can't find baby snapper, use one or two larger fish, and adjust the cook time accordingly; a 4-pound fish will take about 25 minutes to cook.

3 whole baby snapper (about 12 ounces each), cleaned
½ teaspoon freshly ground black pepper, divided
¼ teaspoon kosher salt
1 lemon, cut into ⅛-inch-thick slices
Cooking spray
1 cup loosely packed fresh flat-leaf parsley leaves
⅔ cup loosely packed fresh mint leaves
¼ cup loosely packed fresh dill
¼ cup loosely packed fresh basil leaves
3 tablespoons extra-virgin olive oil
2 tablespoons capers
4 anchovy fillets
3 garlic cloves, peeled

1. Preheat grill to medium-high heat.
2. Score snapper by making 4 (1-inch) crosswise cuts on each side of skin with a sharp knife. Sprinkle ¼ teaspoon pepper and salt evenly inside cavities; arrange lemon slices evenly in cavities. Wrap fish tightly in foil coated with cooking spray. Place fish on grill rack; grill 15 minutes or until fish flakes easily when tested with a fork or until desired degree of doneness, turning once. Let stand 5 minutes before unwrapping.
3. Place parsley and remaining ingredients in a food processor; process until finely chopped. Stir in remaining ¼ teaspoon pepper. Serve sauce with fish. Yield: 6 servings (serving size: ½ fish and about 2 tablespoons sauce).

CALORIES 146; FAT 8.1g (sat 1.2g, mono 5.2g, poly 1.2g); PROTEIN 16.1g; CARB 1.9g; FIBER 0.8g; CHOL 29mg; IRON 1.3mg; SODIUM 300mg; CALC 57mg

Ocean Trout with Coleslaw and Crispy Smoked Bacon

Skin-on fish holds together better on the grill—plus the skin gets deliciously crisp and lightly charred. The Strodes use Australian bacon, called bacon rashers or back bacon. Because that's less available in the States, we recommend Canadian bacon.

6 (¾-ounce) pieces Canadian bacon
6 (6-ounce) skin-on ocean trout, steelhead trout, or salmon fillets
¼ teaspoon kosher salt
½ teaspoon freshly ground black pepper, divided
Cooking spray
2¼ cups thinly sliced red cabbage
2 cups thinly sliced green cabbage
¾ cup fresh flat-leaf parsley leaves
½ cup thinly sliced red onion
1½ tablespoons white wine vinegar
1 tablespoon extra-virgin olive oil
1 teaspoon Dijon mustard
2 tablespoons canola mayonnaise (such as Spectrum)
⅛ teaspoon kosher salt

1. Preheat grill to medium-high heat.
2. Place bacon on grill rack; grill 1½ minutes on each side or until browned. Remove from grill; set aside.
3. Sprinkle fish evenly with ¼ teaspoon salt and ¼ teaspoon pepper. Arrange fish on a grill rack coated with cooking spray; grill 4 minutes on each side or until desired degree of doneness.
4. Combine red cabbage and next 3 ingredients in a large bowl. Combine vinegar, oil, and mustard in a small bowl, stirring with a whisk; stir in mayonnaise. Add vinegar mixture, ⅛ teaspoon salt, and remaining ¼ teaspoon pepper to cabbage mixture, tossing to coat. Top slaw with bacon just before serving with fish. Yield: 6 servings (serving size: 1 fillet, ⅔ cup slaw, and 1 bacon piece).

CALORIES 327; **FAT** 17.7g (sat 3.4g, mono 8g, poly 5.2g); **PROTEIN** 35.3g; **CARB** 5.1g; **FIBER** 1.6g; **CHOL** 90mg; **IRON** 1.5mg; **SODIUM** 457mg; **CALC** 51mg

WINE NOTE: The rich pink meat of ocean trout (or salmon) can easily handle a lighter red wine, especially when prepared with crispy smoked bacon. Bogle Pinot Noir 2008 ($14), from California's cool Russian River Valley, is medium-bodied with light berry and cherry flavors that won't overpower the dish, while a beam of bright acidity helps to balance the fish's healthful natural fats.

Marinated Chicken Thighs with Sweet Potato

In Australia, the chefs make this dish with pumpkin; sweet potato wedges are a good stand-in.

3 tablespoons lower-sodium soy sauce
1½ tablespoons honey
1½ tablespoons grated peeled fresh ginger
1 tablespoon mirin
¼ teaspoon five-spice powder
2 garlic cloves, sliced
2 tablespoons canola oil, divided
12 skin-on, bone-in chicken thighs
3 small sweet potatoes (about 7 ounces each)
½ teaspoon kosher salt, divided
¼ teaspoon freshly ground black pepper
Cooking spray
1 medium yellow onion, vertically sliced
1 cup red bell pepper strips
1 cup yellow bell pepper strips
3 tablespoons tomato sauce
1 teaspoon white wine vinegar
3 tablespoons thinly sliced green onions

1. Combine first 6 ingredients in a large zip-top plastic bag. Add 1½ teaspoons oil and chicken; seal. Marinate in refrigerator 2 hours, turning bag occasionally.
2. Preheat grill to medium-high heat.
3. Cut potatoes in half lengthwise; cut each potato piece in half crosswise. Add potato wedges to a large pot of boiling water; reduce heat, and simmer 5 minutes. Drain. Combine potatoes, 1½ teaspoons oil, and ¼ teaspoon salt.

4. Remove chicken from marinade; discard marinade. Sprinkle chicken with remaining ¼ teaspoon salt and black pepper. Arrange on a grill rack coated with cooking spray; grill 8 minutes on each side or until done. Remove from grill; keep warm. (Discard skin before serving.) Arrange potato on grill rack; grill 4 minutes on each side or until done.
5. Heat remaining 1 tablespoon oil in a large skillet over high heat. Add yellow onion; stir-fry 1 minute. Add bell peppers; stir-fry 2 minutes. Add tomato sauce and vinegar; cook 1 minute, stirring constantly. Serve bell pepper mixture with chicken and potatoes. Top with green onions. Yield: 6 servings (serving size: 2 thighs, ½ cup bell pepper mixture, 2 potato wedges, and 1½ teaspoons green onions).

CALORIES 361; **FAT** 16.2g (sat 3.5g, mono 7.1g, poly 4.1g); **PROTEIN** 29.3g; **CARB** 23.8g; **FIBER** 3.8g; **CHOL** 99mg; **IRON** 2.4mg; **SODIUM** 508mg; **CALC** 48mg

WINE NOTE: Aussie-style Marinated Chicken Thighs with Sweet Potato includes honey and five-spice, flavors that are often apparent in viognier wines. Australia's Yalumba makes several versions of this aromatic white, including Yalumba Eden Valley 2008 ($19), with exotic spice, supple apricot, and lemon curd flavors. A substantial, almost viscous, body allows this wine to linger on the palate with even the most flavorful foods.

Heirloom Tomato, Baby Basil, and Sourdough Salad

Heirloom tomatoes are relatively new to Australia, and due to the growing influx of farmers' markets gracing Sydney's streets, Jane and Jeremy can now access them readily in summer months. This is their take on a classic panzanella salad.

3 (2-ounce) slices sourdough bread, crusts removed
1¼ pounds heirloom cherry tomatoes (larger tomatoes halved)
¼ cup olive oil
2 tablespoons balsamic vinegar
1 teaspoon superfine or granulated sugar
¼ teaspoon kosher salt
¼ teaspoon freshly ground black pepper
1 cup loosely packed fresh baby basil leaves

1. Preheat grill to medium-high heat.
2. Arrange bread on grill rack; grill 1 minute on each side or until well marked. Cool slightly; tear into chunks. Combine bread and tomatoes in a bowl.
3. Combine oil, vinegar, and sugar in a small bowl, stirring until sugar dissolves. Drizzle over bread mixture; sprinkle with salt and pepper. Toss gently to coat. Sprinkle with basil leaves. Yield: 6 servings (serving size: ⅔ cup).

CALORIES 157; **FAT** 9.6g (sat 1.4g, mono 6.7g, poly 1.2g); **PROTEIN** 3.4g; **CARB** 15.4g; **FIBER** 1.5g; **CHOL** 0mg; **IRON** 1.4mg; **SODIUM** 239mg; **CALC** 25mg

Staff Favorite • Make Ahead

Sheep's-Milk Yogurt Cheesecakes with Grilled Figs and Pistachios

Jane's skills as a pastry chef shine in this stunning dessert. Look for rose water with the extracts in gourmet stores, or in Indian or Mediterranean food markets. Although it adds a floral essence, you can omit it and substitute ½ teaspoon vanilla extract. We call for 3-inch ring molds, but for more drama, go for 1½- to 2-inch molds with high sides.

Cooking spray
¾ cup graham cracker crumbs
2 tablespoons canola oil
½ cup superfine sugar
1½ tablespoons fresh lemon juice
1 (8-ounce) block ⅓-less-fat cream cheese, softened
½ cup plain sheep's whole-milk yogurt
1 teaspoon rose water
1½ teaspoons unflavored gelatin
⅓ cup water
1 tablespoon pasteurized egg white, lightly beaten
6 figs, halved
2 tablespoons shelled pistachios, coarsely chopped

1. Arrange 6 (3-inch) ring molds on a parchment-lined baking sheet. Lightly coat molds with cooking spray. Combine crumbs and oil in a small bowl, stirring with a fork until moist. Gently press 2 tablespoons crumb mixture into bottom of each mold. Chill 30 minutes.
2. Place sugar, lemon juice, and cream cheese in a food processor, and process until smooth. Add yogurt and rose water; process until combined.
3. Sprinkle gelatin over ⅓ cup water in a small microwave-safe bowl; let stand 1 minute. Microwave at HIGH 15 seconds, stirring until gelatin dissolves. Stir gelatin mixture thoroughly into yogurt mixture. Fold in egg white. Pour ⅓ cup yogurt mixture over crust in each mold. Chill at least 2 hours or until set.
4. Preheat grill to medium-high heat.
5. Arrange figs, cut sides down, on a grill rack coated with cooking spray; grill 2 minutes or until lightly browned and tender. Run a knife around outside edge of each ring mold; remove molds from cheesecakes. Place 1 cheesecake and 2 fig halves on each of 6 dessert plates; sprinkle each serving with 1 teaspoon pistachios. Yield: 6 servings.

CALORIES 333; **FAT** 16.9g (sat 6.9g, mono 6.4g, poly 2.5g); **PROTEIN** 7.8g; **CARB** 40.1g; **FIBER** 2.4g; **CHOL** 32mg; **IRON** 0.9mg; **SODIUM** 233mg; **CALC** 90mg

LESS MEAT, MORE FLAVOR
GRILL PRIMER
By Mark Bittman

Vegetables and fruits get char-wonderful over outdoor heat. Here are my techniques for great results.

Before you throw another burger on the grill (or shrimp on the barbie, for that matter), make sure there's room for the up-and-coming grilling star: vegetables. Veggies are just as varied as meat or fish, they're equally amenable to most sauces, and—unlike animal products—the more of them you eat, the better.

Here's a quick primer for better balance on the grill, using loads of veggies along with smaller amounts of the still-beloved meat and fish.

Setting up the grill: If you have a gas grill, set the burners so that you have half on high and half on medium. You want the same deal for a charcoal grill, so light a large fire, then spread the coals so that they're heavily concentrated under one half of the grates and less so in the other half. If you plan on cooking a lot, be prepared to add a handful of coals in between batches to keep the heat steady and stoked. Right before cooking, brush the grates down well and run an oil-soaked towel over them.

Prep work: Some vegetables (like corn and asparagus) require only trimming. Cut most other vegetables lengthwise, whenever possible, into nice thick slices—think "planks"—or wedges. Skewers are good for small items like cherry tomatoes. But it's easier to control doneness if you don't mix and match different foods on the same kebabs.

Seasoning: Rub, or brush, everything with a thin film of oil, and sprinkle with salt and pepper. A brightly flavored sauce like the Asian-inspired chimichurri here will bring the vegetables and meat together on the plate, but adding it during grilling will promote burning, so add it to the vegetables right after they come off the grill. If you're going for Asian flavors, use a neutral-tasting oil like grapeseed.

(I'm not a fan of canola, but if you like it, that's another option.) For everything else, use good olive oil.

Types of vegetables and fruits to try: Eggplant, summer squash, onions, mushrooms—these are the old standbys. But go for some unusual summer produce, too: whole radishes and small carrots; sliced jicama, beets, or kohlrabi; or sweet or white potatoes cut into planks.

Maximizing the meat: Since you're eating less of it (figure 3 ounces or so, raw and boneless, per person), go for cuts with lots of flavor. I like shellfish, fatty whole fish, steaks, chicken thighs, and shoulder lamb chops. Do a rib-eye, skirt, or flank steak, and serve it sliced to share; ditto thick-cut bone-in pork chops. Sausages—cut in halves or thirds for portion management—get nice and crisp on the grill. And sliders (small burgers) are fun.

Technique and equipment: Fishing food out of the hot coals is no fun, and you can use a basket if you're really worried. But I find that simply putting food against the grain of the grill rack usually keeps things from slipping into the abyss. Long-handled tongs and spatulas are the tools of choice, and if you really want to work a roaring, jam-packed grill, you're going to need to work one in each hand.

Timing: Work in batches, starting with the foods that taste best at room temperature and ending with the fish, chicken, or meat. Just keep things moving from the hottest spot of the grill for searing, working them through the medium heat and eventually onto a platter. (Don't be afraid to peek underneath.) The idea is to color and soften the vegetables a bit without turning them to mush. Obviously the harder a vegetable is raw—think potatoes and other tubers and roots—the longer it's going to take. You can parboil to get a bit of a head start, or just let them cruise over indirect heat with the cover on for a while.

To serve: Put the meat on top of the vegetables or around the outside of the plate, almost like a garnish. Pass the sauce at the table, or serve simply with lemon or lime wedges and a final sprinkling of sea salt.

Quick & Easy

Grilled Jicama, Radishes, Scallions, and Chicken with Asian-Style "Chimichurri"

2 cups packed fresh cilantro leaves
1 cup packed fresh parsley leaves
3 tablespoons fresh lime juice (about 1 lime)
¼ teaspoon sugar
⅛ teaspoon ground red pepper
4 canned anchovy fillets
1 small garlic clove, chopped
6 tablespoons water
1 pound jicama, peeled and cut into (½-inch-thick) slices
½ pound radishes, trimmed
8 green onions, trimmed
2 tablespoons grapeseed oil
½ teaspoon salt, divided
4 skinless, boneless chicken thighs (about 12 ounces)
½ teaspoon freshly ground black pepper

1. Preheat grill to high heat using both burners. After preheating, turn left burner to medium heat (leave right burner on high heat).
2. Place first 7 ingredients in a mini food processor; process until finely chopped. With processor on, gradually add water, 1 tablespoon at a time; process until smooth.
3. Combine jicama and next 3 ingredients, tossing to coat. Arrange jicama and radishes on right side of grill rack (over high heat) and onions on left side of grill rack (over medium heat); grill 4 minutes on each side or until tender and well marked. Remove from grill; cut radishes in half. Sprinkle vegetables with ¼ teaspoon salt. Keep warm.
4. Sprinkle chicken with remaining ¼ teaspoon salt and black pepper. Arrange chicken on right side of grill rack (over high heat); grill 4 minutes on each side or until done. Place 1 chicken thigh on each of 4 plates; divide vegetables evenly among plates. Serve each with about ¼ cup sauce. Yield: 4 servings.

CALORIES 266; **FAT** 14g (sat 2.6g, mono 3.8g, poly 6.4g); **PROTEIN** 18.9g; **CARB** 17.2g; **FIBER** 8g; **CHOL** 59mg; **IRON** 3.4mg; **SODIUM** 535mg; **CALC** 95mg

Quick & Easy

Grilled Vegetables with Yogurt-Tahini Sauce

Serve with grilled flatbread or pita for a complete vegetarian meal.

1 cup plain fat-free Greek yogurt
1½ tablespoons tahini
1 tablespoon fresh lemon juice
½ teaspoon ground cumin
1 teaspoon minced garlic
½ teaspoon salt, divided
3 tablespoons olive oil
½ teaspoon hot Spanish smoked paprika
12 large button mushrooms, halved
2 tomatoes, halved horizontally
1 large eggplant (about 1½ pounds) cut lengthwise into 8 wedges
1 head radicchio, quartered
¼ teaspoon black pepper
Chopped fresh parsley (optional)

1. Preheat grill to high heat using both burners. After preheating, turn left burner to medium heat (leave right burner on high heat).
2. Combine first 5 ingredients and ¼ teaspoon salt, stirring with a whisk.
3. Combine oil and paprika in a small bowl. Brush oil mixture evenly over mushrooms, tomatoes, eggplant, and radicchio. Sprinkle evenly with remaining ¼ teaspoon salt and pepper.
4. Arrange vegetables on right side of grill rack (over high heat); grill vegetables 8 minutes or until just tender, turning once. Move any vegetables to left side of grill rack (over medium heat) if they get done more quickly. Place vegetables on a platter. Sprinkle with chopped parsley, if desired. Serve with sauce. Yield: 4 servings (serving size: ½ tomato, 2 eggplant wedges, 1 radicchio quarter, 6 mushroom halves, and about ¼ cup sauce).

CALORIES 249; **FAT** 14.2g (sat 2g, mono 8.6g, poly 2.8g); **PROTEIN** 11.7g; **CARB** 23.7g; **FIBER** 8.6g; **CHOL** 0mg; **IRON** 2mg; **SODIUM** 350mg; **CALC** 86mg

THE PLEASURES OF PROVENCE

Bold flavors from the sun-soaked South of France brighten up meatless dishes.

Penne with Zucchini Pistou

A touch of cream enriches the sauce in this hearty dish.

4 teaspoons extra-virgin olive oil, divided
2½ cups (¼-inch-thick) slices small zucchini
    (about ¾ pound)
1 cup packed fresh basil leaves
½ cup (2 ounces) shaved Parmigiano-
    Reggiano cheese, divided
2 tablespoons pine nuts, toasted
4 garlic cloves, chopped
2 cups chopped Vidalia or other sweet onion
    (about 1 large)
6 quarts water
1¾ teaspoons kosher salt, divided
8 ounces uncooked penne pasta
¼ cup heavy whipping cream
½ teaspoon freshly ground black pepper

1. Heat 2 teaspoons oil in a large skillet over medium-high heat. Add zucchini to pan; sauté 5 minutes or until tender and golden. Remove from pan; cool.
2. Place ¼ cup cooked zucchini, basil, ¼ cup cheese, pine nuts, and garlic in a food processor; process until finely chopped. (Keep mixture in processor.)
3. Heat remaining 2 teaspoons oil in a large skillet over medium-high heat. Add onion to pan; sauté 10 minutes or until golden. Return remaining cooked zucchini to pan. Remove from heat.
4. Combine 6 quarts water and 1 teaspoon salt in a large Dutch oven, and bring to a boil. Cook pasta in boiling water according to package directions, omitting salt and fat. Drain in a sieve over a bowl, reserving ⅓ cup cooking liquid. Add pasta to vegetables.

5. With processor on, add reserved liquid to basil mixture; process until smooth. Add basil mixture to pasta mixture. Add cream, remaining ¾ teaspoon salt, and pepper; stir. Top with remaining ¼ cup cheese. Yield: 4 servings (serving size: 1½ cups pasta mixture and 1 tablespoon cheese).

CALORIES 420; FAT 17.2g (sat 6.1g, mono 6.6g, poly 2.6g); PROTEIN 13.9g; CARB 52.9g; FIBER 3.4g; CHOL 29.2mg; IRON 2mg; SODIUM 575mg; CALC 173mg

WINE NOTE: This veggie pasta calls for Dry Creek Vineyard 2007 DCV3 Estate Fumé Blanc from Sonoma County's Dry Creek Valley ($25). It's minerally and herbal, but also rich with pink grapefruit, melon, and white nectarine.

Brandade of White Beans with Baby Artichokes

Brandade most often refers to a salt cod puree popular throughout France, but in this vegetarian version, it's a rich puree of beans topped with grilled artichokes.

6 baby artichokes (about 2 pounds)
Cooking spray
1 teaspoon extra-virgin olive oil
2 cups chopped onion (about 1 large)
4 garlic cloves, chopped
⅔ cup water
2 teaspoons chopped fresh rosemary
½ teaspoon grated lemon rind
2 (15-ounce) cans cannellini beans or other
    white beans, rinsed and drained
½ cup dry rosé wine
4 garlic cloves, thinly sliced
1 shallot, thinly sliced
½ cup organic vegetable broth
2 tablespoons chopped fresh flat-leaf
    parsley
2 teaspoons chopped fresh thyme

1. Preheat grill to medium-high heat.
2. Cut ¼ inch off stems of artichokes; peel stems. Remove bottom leaves and tough outer leaves from each artichoke, leaving tender heart and bottom. Trim

about 1 inch from tops of artichokes. Place artichokes in a Dutch oven filled two-thirds with water; bring to a boil. Cover, reduce heat, and simmer 20 minutes or until a leaf near center of each artichoke pulls out easily. Drain and cool. Cut in half lengthwise. Place artichoke halves, cut sides down, on grill rack coated with cooking spray; grill 4 minutes on each side or until golden.
3. Heat oil in a large skillet over medium-high heat. Add onion to pan; sauté 4 minutes or until tender. Add chopped garlic; sauté 4 minutes or until onion is golden. Add ⅔ cup water and next 3 ingredients; cook 2 minutes or until thoroughly heated. Place bean mixture in a food processor; process until smooth. Keep warm.
4. Combine wine, sliced garlic, and shallot in a small saucepan; bring to a boil. Reduce heat, and simmer 4 minutes or until liquid almost evaporates. Add broth; simmer until reduced to ½ cup (about 3 minutes).
5. Spoon about ½ cup bean mixture into each of 6 shallow bowls, and top each serving with 2 artichoke halves. Drizzle about 1½ tablespoons broth mixture over top of each serving; sprinkle each serving with 1 teaspoon parsley and about ¼ teaspoon thyme. Yield: 6 servings.

CALORIES 167; FAT 1.7g (sat 0.2g, mono 0.6g, poly 0.2g); PROTEIN 9.7g; CARB 32.3g; FIBER 12.2g; CHOL 0mg; IRON 3.4mg; SODIUM 210mg; CALC 115mg

Chickpea Bajane

Bajane is a Provençal term for the midday meal. Chickpeas are a staple in Provence, where they are often stewed and served with pasta and vegetables. In this version, chickpeas, leeks, carrots, fennel, and spinach are served atop protein-rich quinoa.

Quinoa:
2 teaspoons extra-virgin olive oil
1 garlic clove, minced
1 cup organic vegetable broth
1 cup water
1 cup uncooked quinoa
1½ teaspoons chopped fresh thyme
¼ teaspoon salt

Chickpea Mixture:

2 teaspoons extra-virgin olive oil, divided
2 cups thinly sliced leek (about 1 large)
4 garlic cloves, chopped
2½ cups sliced fennel bulb (about 1 large)
1¾ cups (¼-inch-thick) slices carrot (about
  ¾ pound)
½ teaspoon fennel seeds
½ cup white wine
1 cup organic vegetable broth
4 teaspoons chopped fresh thyme, divided
1 (14½-ounce) can no-salt-added chickpeas
  (garbanzo beans), rinsed and drained
1 tablespoon fresh lemon juice
¼ teaspoon salt
¼ teaspoon freshly ground black pepper
1 (5-ounce) package baby spinach

1. To prepare quinoa, heat 2 teaspoons oil in a large saucepan over medium-high heat. Add minced garlic to pan; sauté 1 minute. Add 1 cup broth and next 4 ingredients; cover, reduce heat, and simmer 15 minutes or until liquid is absorbed and quinoa is tender.
2. To prepare chickpea mixture, heat 1 teaspoon oil in a Dutch oven over medium-high heat. Add leek and chopped garlic to pan; sauté 5 minutes or until tender. Add remaining 1 teaspoon oil, fennel bulb, carrot, and fennel seeds; sauté 10 minutes or until vegetables are golden. Add wine; cook 3 minutes or until liquid almost evaporates. Stir in 1 cup broth, 2 teaspoons thyme, and chickpeas; cook 1 minute or until thoroughly heated. Remove from heat; stir in juice, ¼ teaspoon salt, pepper, and spinach.
3. Place about ⅔ cup quinoa in each of 4 bowls; top each serving with about 1½ cups chickpea mixture. Sprinkle each serving with ½ teaspoon thyme. Yield: 4 servings.

CALORIES 357; **FAT** 7.8g (sat 0.7g, mono 4.4g, poly 1.9g); **PROTEIN** 11.8g; **CARB** 60.4g; **FIBER** 11.3g; **CHOL** 0mg; **IRON** 5.9mg; **SODIUM** 728mg; **CALC** 168mg

Grilled Tofu with Ratatouille Vegetables

This attractive, summery barbecue dish combines the vegetables of the famous Provençal stew with meaty grilled tofu.

1 cup organic vegetable broth
½ cup fresh orange juice
½ cup dry rosé wine
2 teaspoons dried herbes de Provence
2 tablespoons olive oil
1 tablespoon olive paste
½ teaspoon kosher salt
¼ teaspoon freshly ground black pepper
4 garlic cloves, minced
1 (14-ounce) package extra-firm tofu, cut into
  8 (¾-inch-thick) slices
3 small eggplants, each cut lengthwise into
  4 slices
3 small zucchini, each cut lengthwise into
  4 slices
1 Vidalia or other sweet onion, cut into
  ½-inch-thick slices
1 large red bell pepper, cut into 8 wedges
4 small tomatoes
Cooking spray
2 tablespoons chopped fresh basil
1 tablespoon chopped fresh parsley
1 tablespoon chopped fresh thyme

1. Preheat grill to medium-high heat.
2. Place first 4 ingredients in a medium saucepan over medium-high heat; bring to a boil. Cook until slightly syrupy and reduced to ⅓ cup (about 10 minutes). Remove from heat; cool. Stir in oil and next 4 ingredients.
3. Place tofu and next 5 ingredients on grill rack coated with cooking spray. Brush half of juice mixture over tofu and vegetables; grill 4 minutes. Turn tofu and vegetables over; brush with remaining juice mixture. Cook 3 minutes or until vegetables are golden brown and tender.
4. Combine basil, parsley, and thyme. Divide vegetables and tofu equally among 4 plates. Sprinkle each serving with 1 tablespoon herb mixture. Yield: 4 servings.

CALORIES 309; **FAT** 13.6g (sat 1.9g, mono 6.2g, poly 4.3g); **PROTEIN** 13.9g; **CARB** 33.1g; **FIBER** 9.7g; **CHOL** 0mg; **IRON** 3.4mg; **SODIUM** 440mg; **CALC** 296mg

READER RECIPES
FROM YOUR KITCHEN TO OURS

As a doctoral student, Sara Best looks for quick, uncomplicated dishes for weeknight dinners. "I wanted something fast, easy, fresh, and tasty, made with ingredients that I already had in the house," she says. By using tilapia, Best kept her meal wallet-friendly and was able to stretch one fillet to make two filling tacos. Her homemade fresh fruit salsa gives bright flavor and color. Instead of mango, Best suggests using any sweet, fresh fruit you have on hand for a low-cost substitution.

Inspired by friends who adore Mexican flavors, Christine Datian decided to reinvent traditional Middle Eastern tabbouleh with Southwestern spices. After substituting cilantro for parsley and adding peppers, cumin, and chili powder, she knew she had a unique dish that was quick and easy to throw together. "If you're working, you can do a lot of prep before, when you do have time," she says. Datian recommends buying prechopped vegetables from the grocery store for a fast weeknight meal. If necessary, you can even soak the bulgur overnight.

Dissatisfied with the baba ghanoush recipes she was finding, Karen Waldman decided to create her own. By combining mayonnaise and tahini, she tinkered, found her perfect combination, and even incorporated it into a Greek-themed Thanksgiving meal. The unique dinner was an instant hit with her family. She plans to explore another cuisine by making this year's holiday menu an Indian feast. "I find this part of cooking, the creativity, very rewarding, especially when it turns out tasty," she says.

continued

Fish Tacos with Mango Salsa Verde

"Keep in mind that 'healthy' doesn't have to mean tasteless and unsatisfying. If you fill your pantry with wholesome ingredients, then it's that much easier to come up with something flavorful and new. Sometimes I add steamed rice and sautéed fresh spinach on the side."
—Sara Best, Nashville, Tennessee

Salsa:
1/2 cup chopped peeled mango
1/2 cup chopped green tomato
2 tablespoons finely chopped red onion
4 teaspoons chopped fresh cilantro
1 teaspoon fresh lemon juice
1/4 teaspoon black pepper
1/4 teaspoon chili powder
Tacos:
2 (6-ounce) tilapia fillets
Cooking spray
1/2 teaspoon Old Bay seasoning
4 (8-inch) whole-wheat flour tortillas
1 cup mixed salad greens

1. To prepare salsa, combine first 7 ingredients in a small bowl; toss well.
2. To prepare tacos, preheat broiler.
3. Place fish on a broiler pan coated with cooking spray; sprinkle fish evenly with seasoning. Broil 6 minutes or until desired degree of doneness.
4. Heat a medium nonstick skillet over medium-high heat. Lightly coat tortillas with cooking spray. Add tortillas to pan, 1 at a time; cook 1 minute on each side or until lightly toasted. Divide fish evenly among tortillas; top each taco with 1/4 cup greens and 1/4 cup salsa. Serve immediately. Yield: 2 servings (serving size: 2 filled tacos).

CALORIES 488; **FAT** 9.2g (sat 3.4g, mono 3.5g, poly 1.6g); **PROTEIN** 43.4g; **CARB** 55g; **FIBER** 6.1g; **CHOL** 85mg; **IRON** 3.7mg; **SODIUM** 609mg; **CALC** 45mg

Spicy Southwestern Tabbouleh

"You can make this salad a meal by adding some shredded rotisserie chicken."
—Christine Datian, Las Vegas, Nevada

3/4 cup uncooked bulgur
1 1/4 cups boiling water
1 1/2 teaspoons extra-virgin olive oil
1 cup chopped fresh cilantro
1 cup vertically sliced red onion
3/4 cup diced seeded tomato
1/2 cup sliced green onions
1/2 cup diced yellow bell pepper
1/2 cup chopped peeled avocado
1/4 cup diced seeded peeled cucumber
1/4 cup (1 ounce) crumbled queso fresco
1/4 cup extra-virgin olive oil
2 tablespoons fresh lemon juice
2 tablespoons fresh lime juice
2 teaspoons diced seeded jalapeño pepper
3/4 teaspoon dried oregano
1/2 teaspoon salt
1/4 teaspoon ground cumin
1/4 teaspoon ground red pepper
1/4 teaspoon paprika
1/4 teaspoon chili powder
1/4 teaspoon freshly ground black pepper
1/8 teaspoon ground allspice
1 garlic clove, minced
Dash of hot pepper sauce (such as Tabasco)

1. Combine bulgur, 1 1/4 cups boiling water, and 1 1/2 teaspoons oil in a medium bowl; cover and let stand 20 minutes. Drain bulgur through a fine sieve; place bulgur in a medium bowl. Add cilantro and remaining ingredients; toss well. Yield: 6 servings (serving size: 3/4 cup).

CALORIES 212; **FAT** 13.7g (sat 2.4g, mono 9g, poly 1.9g); **PROTEIN** 4.6g; **CARB** 21.1g; **FIBER** 5.4g; **CHOL** 3mg; **IRON** 1.1mg; **SODIUM** 224mg; **CALC** 61mg

Baba Ghanoush

"Besides serving this dip with the usual pita wedges, baba ghanoush is also good on bagels, English muffins, or with crisp raw vegetables."
—Karen Waldman, Brookfield, Connecticut

1 large eggplant (about 1 1/2 pounds)
Cooking spray
1/4 cup pine nuts, toasted
3/4 teaspoon cumin seeds, toasted and crushed
1/2 teaspoon minced garlic
3 tablespoons fresh lemon juice
2 tablespoons low-fat mayonnaise
2 tablespoons tahini (roasted sesame seed paste)
1 teaspoon kosher salt
1/4 teaspoon freshly ground black pepper
3 tablespoons chopped fresh parsley
Parsley sprigs (optional)

1. Preheat oven to 375°.
2. Pierce eggplant several times with a fork; place on a foil-lined baking sheet coated with cooking spray. Bake at 375° for 45 minutes or until tender. Cut eggplant in half. Scoop out pulp; discard skins. Drain eggplant pulp in a colander 30 minutes.
3. Place pine nuts, cumin seeds, and garlic in a food processor; pulse until finely chopped. Add eggplant, lemon juice, and next 4 ingredients to food processor. Process until smooth. Spoon eggplant mixture into a medium bowl; stir in parsley. Garnish with parsley sprigs, if desired. Yield: 2 cups (serving size: 1/4 cup).

CALORIES 75; **FAT** 5.3g (sat 0.5g, mono 1.6g, poly 2.5g); **PROTEIN** 2.1g; **CARB** 6.7g; **FIBER** 2.8g; **CHOL** 0mg; **IRON** 0.8mg; **SODIUM** 277mg; **CALC** 17mg

SINGAPORE SPICE & SMOKE

Here it is: the mecca of street foods, the outdoor global carnival of piping-hot grilled goodies and sublime spices. Can't fly around the world right now? We bring Singapore's secrets home.

Singapore's cuisine, like its population, draws from Chinese, Indonesian, Malay, and Indian influences. At its best, that combination produces dishes that are both healthy and delicious. At its worst, it's heavy—and still delicious. The best way to experience Singapore's food is to avoid the fancy restaurants and spend a lazy evening at a hawker center, one of the city's many astounding outdoor food courts. One fantastic option is in the Tiong Bahru neighborhood, where dozens of whirring fans whip up steam from a hundred flaming woks and boiling pots into a fragrant fog. There are all kinds of treats, from the standards, like *popiah* (translucent spring rolls) and *chwee kueh* (rice cakes with chile sauce and pickled radish), to the exotic, such as raw fish porridge and grilled stingray. Taking a deep breath is like inhaling a complex, flavorful meal.

Chile Crabs

This iconic dish is a favorite in Singapore, but traditionally, the crabs are fried in the chile mixture. Here we offer a healthier grilled version. Place each crab on its back, and snip off the small pointed flap at the lower part of the shell known as the apron; remove the fat beneath the apron. Rinse the entire crab well, and pat dry. Once cleaned, pop the crabs in the freezer for 30 minutes before marinating them.

10 fresh red Thai chiles, stemmed
9 large garlic cloves
1/2 medium red bell pepper, chopped
1/3 cup ketchup
1 1/2 tablespoons sugar
1 teaspoon salted bean paste or red miso
1 teaspoon fresh lime juice
8 (8-ounce) fresh blue crabs, rinsed and aprons removed (see recipe note above)
2 spring onions, trimmed and chopped
1 bunch fresh cilantro (optional)

1. Place first 3 ingredients in a food processor; process until finely ground. Stir in ketchup and next 3 ingredients.

Place crabs in a large bowl; top with 1/2 cup chile mixture. Toss to combine. Set remaining chile mixture aside. Marinate in refrigerator 1 hour.
2. Preheat grill to medium-high heat.
3. Remove crabs from marinade, and discard marinade. Arrange crabs, shell sides up, on grill rack; grill 12 minutes or until shells turn red. Serve with remaining chile sauce and onions. Garnish with cilantro, if desired. Yield: 4 servings (serving size: 2 crabs, 1/2 onion, and 1 tablespoon sauce).

CALORIES 158; **FAT** 2g (sat 0.3g, mono 0.3g, poly 0.8g); **PROTEIN** 20.9g; **CARB** 14.7g; **FIBER** 1.1g; **CHOL** 96mg; **IRON** 1.5mg; **SODIUM** 638mg; **CALC** 133mg

WINE NOTE: Always a good bet with seafood, gewürztraminer pairs perfectly with Chile Crabs. The lychee and spice flavors of Chateau Ste. Michelle Gewürztraminer Columbia Valley 2008 ($10), from Washington, complement the Asian flavors, while the wine's slight sweet apple and pear fruit counter the heat.

Sotong Bakar (Barbecue Squid)

The spice rub and dipping sauce are hot, hot, hot (but quite good). Serve with slices of cucumber and fresh cilantro leaves for a cooling effect in the mouth. Thai chiles are very spicy, so you can use fewer (and increase the mild bell pepper) to tame the heat.

1 1/2 pounds whole cleaned skinless squid tubes
1/3 cup chopped red bell pepper
13 fresh red Thai chiles, stemmed
6 large garlic cloves
3 large peeled shallots, coarsely chopped
1 (1-inch) piece peeled fresh ginger, coarsely chopped
6 tablespoons sugar
2 tablespoons lower-sodium soy sauce
1 1/2 teaspoons freshly ground black pepper
1/4 teaspoon kosher salt
Cooking spray

1. Score squid by making 4 (1/2-inch) crosswise cuts in each tube.
2. Place bell pepper and next 4 ingredients in a food processor; process until finely ground. Stir in sugar and next 3 ingredients. Combine squid and 2/3 cup chile mixture in a large zip-top plastic bag; seal. Marinate in refrigerator 3 hours, turning bag occasionally. Reserve remaining 2/3 cup chile mixture for dipping sauce.
3. Preheat grill to medium heat.
4. Remove squid from bag; discard marinade. Arrange squid in a single layer on grill rack coated with cooking spray. Grill 2 minutes on each side or until charred and squid begins to curl around edges. Serve with reserved sauce. Yield: 4 servings (serving size: 4 1/2 ounces squid and about 2 1/2 tablespoons sauce).

CALORIES 263; **FAT** 2.6g (sat 0.6g, mono 0.2g, poly 1g); **PROTEIN** 28.1g; **CARB** 30.9g; **FIBER** 1.1g; **CHOL** 396mg; **IRON** 1.8mg; **SODIUM** 466mg; **CALC** 75mg

Satay (Grilled Skewers)

This all-time favorite is part of Singapore's Malay culinary tradition. Here we use beef, but chicken, pork, and lamb are also popular. Satay is usually served with wedges of cucumber and raw onions. Substitute fresh gingerroot for galangal, if you can't find it. Order the Malaysian shrimp paste from malaysianfood.net.

3 tablespoons (about 1½ ounces) palm sugar or brown sugar
¼ cup water, divided
1 teaspoon tamarind paste
1 tablespoon coriander seeds
½ teaspoon cumin seeds
¼ teaspoon fennel seeds
2 tablespoons chopped peeled fresh galangal
4 teaspoons chopped peeled fresh lemongrass
4 shallots, coarsely chopped
3 candlenuts or macadamia nuts
1 garlic clove, chopped
1 fresh red chile, chopped
½ teaspoon ground turmeric
½ teaspoon salt
2 pounds rib-eye steak, trimmed and cut into (¼ x 1-inch) strips
1 tablespoon canola oil
Cooking spray
1 cup Peanut Dipping Sauce (recipe at right)

1. Place sugar and 2 tablespoons water in a small saucepan over low heat; cook 8 minutes or until sugar dissolves. Strain through a fine sieve over a bowl, and discard solids. Cool completely. Combine tamarind paste and remaining 2 tablespoons water, stirring until smooth. Combine sugar mixture and tamarind mixture in a large zip-top plastic bag; seal. Set aside.
2. Heat a small skillet over medium-high heat. Add coriander, cumin, and fennel seeds; cook 2 minutes, shaking pan occasionally. Cool. Place mixture in a spice or coffee grinder, and process until finely ground. Place galangal and next 5 ingredients in a food processor, and process until finely chopped.
3. Add galangal mixture, coriander mixture, turmeric, and salt to sugar mixture; seal. Knead to combine. Add beef to

bag, turning to coat; seal. Marinate in refrigerator 1 hour, turning twice. Add oil to bag, turning to coat; seal. Marinate in refrigerator overnight, turning occasionally.
4. Preheat grill to medium-high heat.
5. Remove beef from bag; discard marinade. Thread beef evenly onto each of 32 (8-inch) skewers. Place skewers on grill rack coated with cooking spray. Cook 1 minute on each side or until desired degree of doneness. Serve with Peanut Dipping Sauce. Yield: 8 servings (serving size: 4 skewers and about 2 tablepoons sauce).

CALORIES 339; FAT 22.8g (sat 6.4g, mono 9.3g, poly 3.5g); PROTEIN 25g; CARB 8.5g; FIBER 1.9g; CHOL 139mg; IRON 2.4mg; SODIUM 312mg; CALC 42mg

---

HOW TO HAVE A SINGAPORE FLING AT HOME

GAME PLAN: Think of it as an Asian-style small plates party. Have fun shopping, then fire up the grill.

1 Most midsized cities now have Southeast Asian stores or Chinese stores that sell these ingredients. Or order online from sites like importfood.com or malaysianfood.net. You can find substitution suggestions in the Ingredient Guide, page 189.

2 All the recipes can be made or marinated ahead, so simply have your grill hot when your guests arrive.

3 Include hot steamed white rice, cooling cucumber slices or cucumber salad, extra sambal, and fresh fruit (pineapple, papaya, mango) on your buffet. Shrimp crackers, available at specialty stores, are fun.

4 Serve food on recyclable plates—balsa or paper. Use fresh banana leaves if you can find them.

5 Make a pitcher of Singapore slings, and have Tiger beer on hand.

Make Ahead
Peanut Dipping Sauce

4 dried hot red chiles
½ cup unsalted, dry-roasted peanuts
2 teaspoons chopped peeled fresh galangal
1½ teaspoons chopped peeled fresh lemongrass
½ teaspoon belacan (Malaysian shrimp paste) or 1 teaspoon fish sauce
1 garlic clove, chopped
1 shallot, chopped
1 tablespoon vegetable oil
¾ cup water
5 teaspoons palm sugar
2 teaspoons tamarind paste
½ teaspoon rice vinegar
¼ teaspoon salt

1. Place chiles in a bowl, and cover with hot water. Let stand 30 minutes or until tender. Drain. Place chiles, peanuts, and next 5 ingredients in a food processor; process until finely chopped.
2. Heat a medium saucepan over medium-high heat. Add oil to pan, and swirl to coat. Add chile mixture; cook 1 minute, stirring constantly. Add ¾ cup water and remaining ingredients; bring to a boil. Reduce heat; simmer 4 minutes, stirring occasionally. Let stand 30 minutes. Yield: 8 servings (serving size: about 2 tablespoons).

CALORIES 80; FAT 6.4g (sat 0.8g, mono 3g, poly 2.2g); PROTEIN 2.6g; CARB 3.9g; FIBER 1g; CHOL 37mg; IRON 0.4mg; SODIUM 118mg; CALC 9mg

WINE NOTE: Beef satay is a tasty wine problem: All those heady Southeast Asian aromatics—tamarind, coriander, lemongrass—suggest an aromatic white match. But underneath the spice is beef, so go with pink! Look to a bone-dry, crisp, fruity rosé from California that's full of spicy red fruit flavors. Try Zaca Mesa 2009 "Z Gris" from Santa Ynez Valley ($16). Tart cherry and sweet, wild strawberry flavors are surrounded by aromatic spices, lime, and herbs.

INGREDIENT GUIDE

1. FRESH GINGERROOT: Adds slightly sweet, peppery zing to most Asian dishes.

2. GALANGAL: Galangal looks similar to fresh gingerroot and has a similar though milder peppery flavor. Best substitute: fresh ginger.

3. SOY SAUCE: We prefer lower-sodium soy sauce.

4. MIRIN: Mild, slightly sweet Japanese rice wine with a low alcohol content. Best substitute: sake or other rice wine.

5. SHAOXING: Look for this Chinese fermented rice wine (pronounced shaow-SHEEN) at Asian markets. Try to find the type made for drinking as the cooking wine is loaded with sodium. Best substitute: dry sherry.

6. LEMONGRASS: Fibrous herb that releases remarkable lemony fragrance and flavor when minced or pounded. It's increasingly available in the produce section of major supermarkets. Or look in an Asian specialty market. Best substitute: grated lemon rind (about 1/2 teaspoon for every teaspoon called for).

7. KETCHUP: Yup! The classic American condiment can lend a sweet-tart flavor to many Singaporean foods.

8. GARLIC: Aromatic staple that helps build a strong flavor base in many dishes.

9. FRESH TURMERIC: This orange-yellow root has a unique musty flavor. Best substitute: dried ground turmeric (add 1/4 teaspoon dried for every teaspoon fresh).

10. SHALLOTS: Small, mild members of the onion family—the go-to onions in Southeast Asian cooking.

11. CANDLENUTS (BUAH KERAS): Oily, macadamia-like nuts that flavor and thicken Singaporean soups, stews, and curries. Always cook before eating—they are toxic raw. Best substitute: macadamias.

12. CHILES: As in Mexican food, there is no single chile that lends heat. Experiment with a combination of dried and fresh peppers that range in pungency from fiery hot Thai chiles to mild and sweet bell peppers. Look at your local supermarket or Asian market, or order blazing hot Thai chiles and dried red chiles from ImportFood.com.

13. HOISIN SAUCE: Thick, salty-sweet Asian sauce.

14. FENNEL SEEDS: Have an aniselike flavor.

15. DRIED GROUND TURMERIC: Mild, slightly musty version of the fresh stuff.

16. PALM SUGAR: Worth seeking out— similar to maple sugar, but the darkest versions have a unique, deep, almost tart flavor: a tangy sugar. Look for it in Asian markets or online at ImportFood.com. Best substitute: maple sugar or dark brown sugar.

17. CORIANDER SEEDS: Seeds of the plant that produces cilantro leaves, with a distinctive flavor.

18. BELACAN (SHRIMP PASTE): Like a funky cheese, this Malaysian staple packs a pungent stink. A little goes a long way, adding richness, complexity, and subtle background notes to dishes it graces. Best substitute: fish sauce (use about 2 teaspoons fish sauce per teaspoon belacan).

19. COCONUT MILK: Full-fat coconut milk separates into a cream layer and a thin milky layer. It's the thick, creamy layer that adds characteristic flavor and silky texture to Southeast Asian foods.

20. CUMIN SEEDS: Deliver a unique musty, almost smoky, note.

21. TAMARIND PASTE: Tart tamarind pulp, mixed with water and without the pesky seeds. Look for it at Asian or Hispanic markets. The best substitute is fresh lime juice.

22. KAFFIR LIME LEAVES: Worth seeking out for their sublime fragrance, which suffuses a whole dish. Often sold frozen, sometimes dried, but the latter are much milder even after soaking. Best substitute: grated lime rind (about 1/4 teaspoon for every leaf called for).

23. SESAME OIL (DARK): A full, roasted-flavor sesame oil.

24. RICE VINEGAR: Mild, slightly sweet vinegar used in many Asian dishes.

25. FRESH CILANTRO: Bright, fragrant, love-it-or-hate-it herb with a uniquely pungent flavor.

26. SALTED BEAN PASTE: Fermented soybean paste is used in Chinese cooking and is usually available at Asian markets in cans or jars. Best substitute: red miso.

Cantonese-Style Grilled Pork

Hoisin sauce gives this dish its salty-sweet aromatic flavor. Serve these succulent slices of pork with steamed Chinese buns, or sandwich them in a hot dog bun.

1 pound boneless pork shoulder, trimmed
1/2 teaspoon salt
1 tablespoon sugar
2 tablespoons hoisin sauce
2 tablespoons ketchup
1 tablespoon Shaoxing (Chinese cooking wine) or dry sherry
2 teaspoons mirin (sweet rice wine)
1 teaspoon grated peeled fresh ginger
1 garlic clove, minced
Cooking spray

1. Cover and freeze pork 45 minutes. Cut pork across grain into 1/8-inch-thick slices. Sprinkle pork evenly with salt.
2. Combine sugar and next 6 ingredients in a large zip-top plastic bag; knead to blend. Add pork to bag; seal. Marinate in refrigerator 3 hours, turning bag occasionally.
3. Preheat grill to medium-high heat.
4. Remove pork from bag, and discard marinade. Place pork on a grill rack coated with cooking spray. Grill 1 minute on each side or until desired degree of doneness. Yield: 4 servings (serving size: 3 ounces).

CALORIES 221; **FAT** 8.9g (sat 2.9g, mono 3.3g, poly 0.6g); **PROTEIN** 23.4g; **CARB** 9.4g; **FIBER** 0.1g; **CHOL** 67mg; **IRON** 0.9mg; **SODIUM** 560mg; **CALC** 20mg

Otak Otak (Grilled Fish Quenelles)

Assemble and cook these parcels a day ahead. Cool and chill until you're ready to serve. Order candlenuts from importfood.com, or look for them in Southeast Asian markets. Always cook the nuts before eating as they're toxic if eaten raw. You can substitute 2 teaspoons grated lime rind for the Kaffir lime leaves. The creamy layer that forms on top of full-fat canned coconut milk adds a rich flavor to the dish. Be sure not to shake the can so the cream stays separated, and use only the thick top layer. Look for banana leaves at Asian or Latin markets (fresh or frozen), or order them from grocerythai.com.

15 dried hot red chiles, seeded
2 tablespoons chopped peeled fresh
   lemongrass (about 2 stalks)
5 candlenuts or macadamia nuts
1 (2-inch) piece fresh galangal, peeled and
   coarsely chopped
1 (2-inch) piece fresh turmeric, peeled and
   coarsely chopped
15 shallots, peeled and coarsely chopped
   (about 1 pound)
1 teaspoon belacan (Malaysian shrimp paste)
   or 2 teaspoons fish sauce
2 tablespoons coriander seeds
2 tablespoons canola oil
½ cup thick regular coconut milk
½ cup light coconut milk
1 large egg, lightly beaten
1 pound Spanish or other mackerel fillet,
   skinned
¼ cup superfine sugar (such as castor sugar)
1 teaspoon salt
8 Kaffir lime leaves, stemmed and cut into
   thin strips
18 banana leaves, cut into 6-inch squares

1. Place chiles in a medium bowl; cover with boiling water. Let stand 30 minutes or until tender, and drain. Place chiles, lemongrass, and next 3 ingredients in a food processor, and process until finely ground. Add shallots and belacan; process until ground.
2. Heat a large skillet over medium heat. Add coriander seeds to pan; cook 1 minute or until toasted, shaking pan occasionally. Add seeds to chile mixture; process until ground.

3. Increase heat to medium-high. Add oil to pan, and swirl to coat. Add chile mixture to pan. Stir-fry 5 minutes or until fragrant. Combine regular and light coconut milks, stirring with a whisk. Add coconut mixture to spice mixture, stirring to combine, and bring to a boil. Remove from heat. Cool 15 minutes; stir in egg.
4. Place fish in food processor, and process until finely ground. Combine spice mixture, fish, sugar, salt, and lime leaves in a large bowl. Divide mixture into 18 equal portions (about 3½ tablespoons each).
5. Preheat grill to medium-high heat.
6. Working with 1 banana leaf at a time, place leaf on grill. Grill 1 minute or until leaf color brightens and texture softens; remove leaf from grill. Spoon 1 portion fish mixture into center of leaf, shaping mixture into a 2 x 3–inch rectangle, and fold sides of banana leaf over fish mixture. Secure leaf with wooden picks. Repeat procedure with remaining banana leaves and fish mixture to yield 18 parcels.
7. Arrange parcels on grill rack, and grill 3 minutes on each side or until desired degree of doneness. Chill at least 1 hour before serving. Yield: 18 servings (serving size: 1 parcel).

CALORIES 108; **FAT** 6g (sat 2.4g, mono 1.7g, poly 1.2g); **PROTEIN** 6.2g; **CARB** 7.7g; **FIBER** 1.1g; **CHOL** 28mg; **IRON** 0.7mg; **SODIUM** 177mg; **CALC** 19mg

> YOU SHOULD ALWAYS COOK CANDLENUTS BEFORE EATING THEM AS THEY'RE TOXIC IF EATEN RAW.

Ikan Bakar (Barbecue Fish)

Aji (also called horse mackerel) ranges in size. Small fish about the size of fresh sardines are common in Singapore. If you can't find aji, sardines or larger mackerel will work. If using larger fish, adjust the cooking time accordingly.

Fish:
8 (4-ounce) whole dressed aji or fresh
   sardines
1 teaspoon fresh lime juice
½ teaspoon ground turmeric
¾ teaspoon salt, divided
¼ cup chopped red bell pepper
5 large garlic cloves, peeled
5 fresh Thai chiles, stemmed
1 small shallot, peeled
1 tablespoon canola oil
Cooking spray
Sauce:
⅓ cup thinly sliced shallots (about 1 small)
1 tablespoon finely chopped red bell pepper
1 tablespoon fresh lime juice
1 tablespoon lower-sodium soy sauce
1 finger hot chile pepper, thinly sliced

1. Preheat grill to medium-high heat.
2. To prepare fish, rinse fish with cold water; pat dry. Combine 1 teaspoon juice, turmeric, and ½ teaspoon salt; rub evenly over fish. Place remaining ¼ teaspoon salt, bell pepper, and next 3 ingredients in a food processor; process until finely ground. Heat a small skillet over medium heat. Add 1 tablespoon oil to pan; swirl to coat. Add garlic mixture; cook 5 minutes or until mixture begins to brown, stirring frequently. Remove from heat; cool 15 minutes. Spoon 1 tablespoon garlic mixture into cavity of each fish. Arrange fish on a grill rack coated with cooking spray; grill 2 minutes on each side or until desired degree of doneness.
3. To prepare sauce, combine ⅓ cup shallots and remaining ingredients in a small bowl. Serve with fish. Yield: 4 servings (serving size: 2 fish and 1 tablespoon sauce).

CALORIES 279; **FAT** 18.9g (sat 4g, mono 7.5g, poly 5.2g); **PROTEIN** 21.4g; **CARB** 5.7g; **FIBER** 1g; **CHOL** 64mg; **IRON** 1.9mg; **SODIUM** 650mg; **CALC** 28mg

AN ITALIAN-AMERICAN TRADITION

Gabriella Manzone cultivated a deep love of Piedmontese food traditions in her three daughters. Decades later, her dinner table remains the hub of family life.

When Italian immigrant Gabriella Manzone's three daughters were growing up in suburban California, Gabriella and her husband, Domenico, sent them to Italy every summer. That way, the Manzones figured, the girls—Ughetta, 37; Liliana (or Lilly), 34; and Yolanda, 31; all named for female ancestors—would grow up connected to their family and its distinctive, dairy-rich cuisine in northern Italy's Piemonte region. "My mom used to call it watering our roots," says Lilly affectionately. Gabriella chimes in, "I told my girls: 'You have to grow your Italian roots with Italian water!'"

Gabriella's plan worked, and today, the sisters have a tight family bond centered around the food traditions their mother fostered throughout their uniquely Italian-American childhood. That bond is best expressed in weekly dinners the sisters host for friends and family.

Today, Gabriella's and her daughters' cooking updates the rich Piedmontese tradition, which includes French influences, including cream and butter sauces, as well as Italian standbys like risottos, pastas, and vegetable dishes. Much of their favorite fare is simple, in classic Italian tradition, from a tomato and green bean salad to thin chicken cutlets, which Yolanda adapted and lightened from the original veal. A barely sweet dessert of peaches baked with crushed amaretti cookies and cocoa that puffs delectably when baked follows from Gabriella's love of fruit sweets.

The weekend dinners stem from the emphasis that Gabriella placed on family meals when the girls were growing up. "For us, dinner was the real family meal," she says. "It was very important to me that the kids learn that we eat together." Although Domenico, a busy doctor, often didn't arrive home until late, Gabriella set a place for him when the girls ate dinner, and sat the girls down again when he arrived. "Sometimes, she'd wake us up!" recalls Yolanda. "If we were in our pajamas, we'd still sit at the table while he ate so we got that time together."

Family dinners strengthened family connections, says Gabriella. "My girls learned the difference between eating and dining," she says. "The conversation is just as important as the food. What they came away with from our dinners, I hope, is that we are interested in each other's lives."

The pleasures of family dinner might seem simple, but for the Manzones its effects run deep, nurturing bonds and reinvigorating the whole family. Indeed, says Gabriella—who at 64 has a spirit as youthful as her daughters'—it might just keep them young. "In Italian, we have a saying: *A tavola, non si invecchia*," she says. "At the table, you don't get old."

Chocolate-Amaretti Peaches

Adapted from Gabriella's dessert of peaches filled with amaretti and cocoa powder, our version of this quick dessert uses shaved bittersweet chocolate for added richness. Look for amaretti cookies at specialty or gourmet markets; they have a distinct almond-amaretto flavor and crunchy texture that make this dish memorable. In a pinch, you can substitute crumbled almond biscotti.

½ cup crushed amaretti cookies (about 8 cookies)
2 tablespoons brown sugar
4 large ripe peaches, halved and pitted
Cooking spray
8 teaspoons butter
1 ounce bittersweet chocolate, shaved

1. Preheat broiler.
2. Combine cookie crumbs and sugar in a small bowl.
3. Hollow center of peach halves using a melon baller. Fill each peach half with 1 rounded tablespoon cookie crumb mixture. Arrange peaches in an 11 x 7–inch glass or ceramic baking dish coated with cooking spray. Place 1 teaspoon butter on top of each filled half. Broil 2 minutes or until butter melts. Sprinkle evenly with chocolate. Cool 5 minutes before serving. Yield: 8 servings (serving size: 1 peach half).

CALORIES 117; FAT 5.4g (sat 3.2g, mono 1.1g, poly 0.2g); PROTEIN 1.5g; CARB 17g; FIBER 1.6g; CHOL 10mg; IRON 0.3mg; SODIUM 42mg; CALC 9mg

"IN ITALIAN WE HAVE A SAYING: AT THE TABLE, YOU DON'T GET OLD."

—Gabriella Manzone

Yolanda's Famous Chicken

The family serves these crispy sautéed chicken breasts with lemon wedges only (no sauce). Because they're so flavorful, a spritz of citrus is all they need. You can easily double the recipe to accommodate a larger group—crisp two breast halves at a time in a skillet (or four at a time in two skillets), then finish cooking the whole batch in the oven.

2 (1½-ounce) bread slices
4 (6-ounce) skinless, boneless chicken
   breast halves
¼ cup all-purpose flour
¼ cup (1 ounce) finely grated Parmigiano-
   Reggiano cheese
1½ teaspoons dried rosemary, crushed
1½ teaspoons dried marjoram
½ teaspoon salt
½ teaspoon freshly ground black pepper
1 tablespoon 2% reduced-fat milk
1 large egg
Cooking spray
4 teaspoons olive oil, divided
4 lemon wedges

1. Tear bread into pieces. Place bread in a food processor, and pulse until breadcrumbs measure about 1¾ cups.
2. Place each chicken breast half between 2 sheets of heavy-duty plastic wrap, and pound chicken to ½-inch thickness using a meat mallet or small heavy skillet.
3. Place flour in a shallow dish. Combine breadcrumbs, cheese, and next 4 ingredients in a second shallow dish. Combine milk and egg in a third shallow dish, stirring with a whisk. Working with 1 breast half at a time, dredge chicken in flour, shaking off excess. Dip into egg mixture; dredge in breadcrumb mixture, pressing to coat evenly on both sides. Place chicken on a large plate. Repeat procedure with remaining breast halves, flour, egg mixture, and breadcrumb mixture; refrigerate 30 minutes.
4. Preheat oven to 375°.
5. Heat a 12-inch nonstick skillet over medium-high heat. Coat pan with cooking spray; add 2 teaspoons olive oil, swirling to coat. Add 2 breast halves to pan; cook 3 minutes on each side or until browned. Place on a broiler pan coated with cooking spray. Lightly coat chicken with cooking spray. Repeat procedure with remaining 2 teaspoons olive oil and remaining breast halves. Bake at 375° for 12 minutes or until a thermometer registers 165°. Serve with lemon wedges. Yield: 4 servings (serving size: 1 breast half and 1 lemon wedge).

CALORIES 362; FAT 10.7g (sat 3g, mono 4.7g, poly 1.2g); PROTEIN 45.7g; CARB 18.4g; FIBER 1.1g; CHOL 156mg; IRON 2.8mg; SODIUM 625mg; CALC 146mg

WINE NOTE: As the Manzones state, a shot of fruity acidity is all this chicken dish needs. You'll find it aplenty in a New Zealand sauvignon blanc, like Stoneleigh Sauvignon Blanc Marlborough 2009 ($17), with its vivacious, citrusy acidity and bright flavors of tropical fruit.

Green Bean and Tomato Salad

1 pound green beans, trimmed and cut into
   2-inch pieces
2 pounds beefsteak tomatoes, seeded and
   cut into ½-inch-thick wedges
5 tablespoons balsamic vinegar
2 teaspoons minced garlic
½ teaspoon salt
½ teaspoon freshly ground black pepper
1 anchovy fillet, minced
3 tablespoons extra-virgin olive oil

1. Bring a large pot of water to a boil over high heat. Add green beans; cook 3 minutes or until crisp-tender. Drain and rinse well with cold water. Drain thoroughly; place in a bowl. Add tomatoes.
2. Combine vinegar and next 4 ingredients in a bowl; gradually add oil, stirring constantly with a whisk. Drizzle over bean mixture; toss gently to coat. Serve at room temperature or chilled. Yield: 8 servings (serving size: about 1 cup).

CALORIES 90; FAT 5.4g (sat 0.8g, mono 3.8g, poly 0.7g); PROTEIN 2.1g; CARB 9.6g; FIBER 3g; CHOL 0mg; IRON 1mg; SODIUM 177mg; CALC 35mg

Celery, Walnut, and Parmesan Salad

Because the salt draws water out of the celery, it's best to serve this simple salad shortly after tossing the ingredients together.

5 cups thinly sliced celery (about 1 pound)
¾ cup (3 ounces) finely diced Parmigiano-
   Reggiano cheese
⅔ cup coarsely chopped walnuts, toasted
1½ tablespoons extra-virgin olive oil
1½ tablespoons fresh lemon juice
1 teaspoon freshly ground black pepper
½ teaspoon kosher salt

1. Combine all ingredients in a large bowl; toss well. Yield: 8 servings (serving size: ¾ cup).

CALORIES 131; FAT 11.1g (sat 2.3g, mono 3.4g, poly 5g); PROTEIN 4.9g; CARB 4.2g; FIBER 1.8g; CHOL 5mg; IRON 0.6mg; SODIUM 305mg; CALC 135mg

BREAKFAST, LUNCH, AND DINNER IN... BOSTON

You probably won't find Boston's typical top chef having his or her own national cooking show, peddling an expansive line of branded products, or opening flashy outposts in Vegas and Shanghai (OK, with the exception of Todd English or Ming Tsai). Instead, they stay home and cook. And when they're not cooking at their restaurants—as they are, night after night—you'll likely find them eating at each other's places. When it comes to trends, Boston may give a nod to what's current—even an occasional full-body embrace—but it often comes a year or three after trends start in New York City or the Bay Area, and not every trend makes it to town. Those that do are executed better here than anywhere else—and that's just the way Bostonians like it.

Breakfast

Greek Yogurt Parfaits

Start the day at Sofra (sofrabakery.com). Chef Ana Sortun blends little-known Turkish regional and eastern Mediterranean cuisines with fantastically fresh produce in a way unlike anything other chefs are doing. The breakfast that will redefine your idea of the meal is shakshuka, eggs poached in a thin, spicy tomato sauce with curry and pita crumbs. And the Greek yogurt parfait, made with creamy yogurt topped with grano and honey, tastes like decadent crème fraîche—yet is still light and refreshing in the heat of summer. Grano, which means "grain" in Italian, are the polished whole berries from durum semolina wheat. If you can't find grano, try wheat berries, barley, or brown rice instead.

1 cup uncooked grano
12 cups water, divided
1/4 cup orange blossom honey
1/4 teaspoon kosher salt
4 cups plain 2% reduced-fat Greek yogurt
2 cups fresh berries (such as blackberries, blueberries, or sliced strawberries)

1. Soak grano in 6 cups water overnight. Drain. Place in a medium saucepan with remaining 6 cups water over medium-high heat; bring to a boil. Reduce heat, and simmer 20 minutes or until grano is just tender. Drain well. Stir in honey and salt. Cool to room temperature.

2. Spoon 1/4 cup yogurt into each of 8 parfait glasses. Top yogurt with 3 tablespoons grano and 2 tablespoons berries; repeat layers. Yield: 8 servings (serving size: 1 parfait).

CALORIES 228; FAT 3.1g (sat 2.1g, mono 0.1g, poly 0.2g); PROTEIN 14.1g; CARB 38.9g; FIBER 4.8g; CHOL 7mg; IRON 0.8mg; SODIUM 106mg; CALC 130mg

> SLOW TO ADAPT BOSTON MAY BE, BUT ONCE THE CITY TACKLES A TREND, IT'S NOT JUST DONE MORE CALMLY (EASILY CONFUSED WITH "BORINGLY"), BUT BETTER.

Lunch

Lobster Salad Rolls with Shaved Fennel and Citrus

Although sourcing ingredients locally has become yesterday's news, Boston-area chefs were doing so before just about anybody outside the San Francisco Bay Area. Here, Boston is gloriously provincial. Jasper White, with his demand for local fish and direct buying from New England farms, was a pre-locavore locavore. New to the downtown scene, Chef Mark Goldberg is serving local fare family-style at Woodward (woodwardatames.com) in the hip Ames Hotel. He gives a New England classic—lobster salad—a modern update with crisp fennel and citrus aioli. We use New England–style hot dog buns, which are top-split and have an open crumb on the sides.

3 cups coarsely chopped cooked lobster meat (about 3 [1¼-pound] lobsters)
3 tablespoons canola mayonnaise
2 teaspoons chopped fresh tarragon
½ teaspoon kosher salt, divided
2 cups thinly sliced fennel bulb (about 1 medium)
½ teaspoon grated orange rind
1 tablespoon fresh orange juice
1 tablespoon fresh lemon juice
1 tablespoon rice wine vinegar
2 teaspoons extra-virgin olive oil
¼ teaspoon freshly ground black pepper
Cooking spray
6 (1½-ounce) hot dog buns

1. Combine lobster, mayonnaise, 2 teaspoons tarragon, and ¼ teaspoon salt; cover and refrigerate.

2. Combine fennel, remaining ¼ teaspoon salt, orange rind, and next 5 ingredients.

3. Heat a large nonstick skillet over medium heat. Coat pan with cooking spray. Add buns to pan; cook 2 minutes on each side or until lightly browned. Place ⅓ cup fennel salad in each bun. Top each serving with ½ cup lobster salad. Yield: 6 servings (serving size: 1 lobster roll).

CALORIES 238; FAT 6.2g (sat 0.8g, mono 3g, poly 1.9g); PROTEIN 19.4g; CARB 24.9g; FIBER 1.9g; CHOL 52mg; IRON 1.9mg; SODIUM 699mg; CALC 120mg

Dinner

Ricotta-Pea Ravioli with Asparagus and Mushrooms

Boston's devotion to its chefs is evident in a popular new string of casual spin-offs of fine dining spots. Ken Oringer and Jamie Bissonnette, the duo behind Toro, opened Coppa (coppaboston.com) last summer to almost-immediate acclaim. The casual trattoria offers house-made charcuterie, wood-fired pizzas, seasonal small-plate pastas, and a small sampling of snout-to-tail dishes that more than hold their own against cult New York establishments. 00 flour, or "doppio zero" (double zero), is high-protein Italian flour that's as fine as talcum powder, so it makes an especially silky dough. It's available in many Italian markets, as well as online. You can substitute all-purpose flour, but the pasta won't be as finely textured. Use a mandoline or vegetable peeler to shave the asparagus.

Filling:
²/₃ cup whole-milk ricotta cheese
½ cup frozen petite green peas, thawed and coarsely chopped
¼ cup (1 ounce) finely grated Parmigiano-Reggiano cheese
2 tablespoons chopped fresh chives
¼ teaspoon kosher salt
¼ teaspoon ground nutmeg
¼ teaspoon freshly ground black pepper
¼ teaspoon grated lemon rind

Pasta:
7½ ounces 00 flour (about 1½ cups)
¼ teaspoon kosher salt
2 tablespoons water
2 large eggs

Sauce:
2 tablespoons extra-virgin olive oil
½ cup finely chopped shallots (about 2)
5 teaspoons chopped fresh chives
½ teaspoon chopped fresh thyme
2 (8-ounce) packages presliced exotic mushroom blend (such as shiitake, cremini, and oyster)
1 cup fat-free, lower-sodium chicken broth
¼ teaspoon freshly ground black pepper

Remaining Ingredients:
½ pound asparagus, thinly shaved
½ cup (2 ounces) shaved Parmigiano-Reggiano cheese

1. To prepare filling, combine first 8 ingredients in a bowl. Cover and refrigerate 1 hour.

2. To prepare pasta, weigh or lightly spoon flour into dry measuring cups; level with a knife. Place flour and ¼ teaspoon salt in a food processor; pulse 3 times or until blended. With processor on, slowly pour 2 tablespoons water and eggs through food chute; process until dough forms a ball. Turn dough out onto a lightly floured surface; knead until smooth and elastic (about 5 minutes). Wrap dough in plastic wrap; refrigerate 30 minutes.

3. Divide dough into 8 equal portions. Working with 1 portion at a time, pass dough through smooth rollers of pasta machine on widest setting (cover remaining dough to keep from drying). Continue moving width gauge to narrower settings; pass dough through rollers once at each setting, dusting with flour if needed. Lay pasta sheet flat on a lightly floured surface; cover. Repeat procedure with remaining dough.

4. Spoon 1½ teaspoons filling mixture at about 2-inch intervals along length of 1 pasta sheet. Moisten edges and in between each filling portion with water; place 1 pasta sheet on top, pressing around filling to seal. Cut pasta sheet into 6 (3 x 3-inch) ravioli, trimming edges with a sharp knife or pastry wheel. Brush excess flour from ravioli. Place ravioli on a lightly floured baking sheet (cover to prevent drying). Repeat procedure with remaining dough portions and filling mixture to form 24 ravioli.

5. To prepare sauce, heat oil in a large skillet over medium heat. Add shallots and next 3 ingredients to pan, and cook 8 minutes or until mushrooms are browned and tender, stirring occasionally. Add broth and ¼ teaspoon pepper; cook 4 minutes or until liquid almost evaporates. Remove from heat; keep warm.

6. Bring 6 quarts water to a boil in each of 2 large Dutch ovens. Add 12 ravioli to each pan; cook 4 minutes or until ravioli float to the surface. Remove ravioli from water with a slotted spoon. Place ravioli on a tray, making sure they do not overlap; cover and keep warm.

Return water in 1 Dutch oven to a boil. Add shaved asparagus; cook 15 seconds. Drain.

7. Place 4 ravioli on each of 6 plates; top each serving with ½ cup sauce and ¼ cup asparagus. Sprinkle each serving with 4 teaspoons cheese. Yield: 6 servings.

CALORIES 363; FAT 14.6g (sat 5.5g, mono 6g, poly 1.2g); PROTEIN 19.9g; CARB 41g; FIBER 8.3g; CHOL 83mg; IRON 4.6mg; SODIUM 498mg; CALC 249mg

RECIPE HALL OF FAME
OUR FAVORITE WATERMELON MARGARITAS

A long, tall version of the great summer sipper with only 105 calories.

Quick & Easy

Watermelon Margaritas

2 teaspoons sugar
1 lime wedge
3½ cups cubed seeded watermelon
½ cup tequila
2 tablespoons sugar
3 tablespoons fresh lime juice
1 tablespoon Triple Sec (orange-flavored liqueur)
Lime wedges or watermelon balls (optional)

1. Place 2 teaspoons sugar in a saucer. Rub rims of 6 glasses with 1 lime wedge; spin rim of each glass in sugar to coat. Set prepared glasses aside.

2. Place watermelon and next 4 ingredients in a blender; process until smooth. Fill each prepared glass with ½ cup crushed ice. Add ½ cup margarita to each glass. Garnish with lime wedges or melon balls, if desired. Yield: 6 servings.

CALORIES 105; FAT 0.2g (sat 0g, mono 0g, poly 0.1g); PROTEIN 0.6g; CARB 14.1g; FIBER 0.4g; CHOL 0mg; IRON 0.2mg; SODIUM 1mg; CALC 7mg

FEED 4 FOR LESS THAN $10

Seasonal ingredients shine in these economical summer meals.

Quick & Easy

Penne with Pistachio Pesto and White Beans

$1.85 per serving, $7.38 total

Pistachios make an interesting and tasty addition to this pesto. Look for roasted pistachios that are in the shell because they're more economical than shelled nuts.

8 ounces uncooked penne pasta
1 cup packed fresh basil leaves
1/4 cup roasted shelled pistachios
6 garlic cloves
2 tablespoons olive oil
1 1/2 cups chopped seeded peeled tomato
1 teaspoon freshly ground black pepper
3/4 teaspoon kosher salt
1 (15-ounce) can cannellini beans, rinsed and drained
1 (5-ounce) package arugula
1/4 cup (1 ounce) shredded fresh pecorino Romano cheese

1. Cook pasta according to package directions, omitting salt and fat. Drain and rinse with cold water. Drain.
2. Place basil, nuts, and garlic in a food processor; process until finely chopped. Heat a large skillet over medium heat. Add oil to pan, and swirl to coat. Add basil mixture, and cook 2 minutes, stirring frequently. Stir in pasta, tomato, and next 3 ingredients; cook 2 minutes or until thoroughly heated, tossing to combine. Remove from heat. Add arugula to pan, and toss to slightly wilt. Place about 1 1/4 cups pasta mixture in each of 4 bowls, and top each serving with 1 tablespoon cheese. Yield: 4 servings.

CALORIES 423; **FAT** 13.7g (sat 2.9g, mono 7.4g, poly 2.3g); **PROTEIN** 16.4g; **CARB** 60.2g; **FIBER** 7.2g; **CHOL** 7mg; **IRON** 4.4mg; **SODIUM** 613mg; **CALC** 204mg

Braised Chicken Thighs with Plums

$2.50 per serving, $9.99 total
Serve this dish over couscous tossed with grated lemon rind.

3/4 teaspoon salt, divided
1/2 teaspoon black pepper, divided
1/8 teaspoon ground allspice
8 bone-in chicken thighs, skinned
2 tablespoons butter
1 cup chopped onion
2 garlic cloves, minced
1/4 cup brandy
3/4 cup fat-free, lower-sodium chicken broth
1 teaspoon dried rubbed sage
3 pitted plums, cut into wedges
1 tablespoon fresh lemon juice

1. Combine 1/2 teaspoon salt, 1/4 teaspoon pepper, and allspice, stirring well; sprinkle evenly over both sides of chicken.
2. Melt butter in a large nonstick skillet over medium-high heat. Add chicken to pan; cook 3 minutes on each side or until browned. Remove chicken from pan. Add onion to pan; sauté 4 minutes or until tender. Add garlic; sauté 1 minute, stirring frequently. Stir in brandy; cook 30 seconds or until liquid evaporates. Stir in remaining 1/4 teaspoon salt, remaining 1/4 teaspoon pepper, broth, and sage; bring to a boil. Return chicken to pan. Cover, reduce heat, and simmer 12 minutes. Arrange plums in pan; cook 8 minutes or until chicken is done. Drizzle with juice. Yield: 4 servings (serving size: 2 chicken thighs and about 1/2 cup plum mixture).

CALORIES 357; **FAT** 16.9g (sat 6.6g, mono 5.8g, poly 2.8g); **PROTEIN** 29g; **CARB** 11.5g; **FIBER** 1.8g; **CHOL** 114mg; **IRON** 1.8mg; **SODIUM** 640mg; **CALC** 33mg

WINE NOTE: Braised Chicken Thighs with Plums pairs well with a dry rosé. La Vieille Ferme Rosé 2009 ($9), from France's Rhône Valley, has big flavors of berry, currant, and plum. The wine's fruitiness and caramel flavors work with this dish.

Quick & Easy

Greek-Style Pork Chops

$2.46 per serving, $9.85 total
Cut two pita rounds in half, and cut each half into quarters and toast. Serve the pita wedges with the pork chops.

2 tablespoons red wine vinegar, divided
1 teaspoon dried oregano
2 teaspoons olive oil, divided
2 garlic cloves, minced
4 (4-ounce) boneless center-cut loin pork chops
3/4 cup plain fat-free Greek yogurt
1 tablespoon chopped fresh dill
1/2 teaspoon salt, divided
1 1/2 cups diced plum tomatoes (about 2 medium)
1 cup diced seeded cucumber
1/2 cup diced red onion
Cooking spray

1. Combine 1 tablespoon red wine vinegar, oregano, 1 teaspoon olive oil, and garlic in a zip-top plastic bag. Add pork to bag, and seal. Marinate 20 minutes at room temperature, turning after 10 minutes. Combine remaining 1 tablespoon vinegar, remaining 1 teaspoon oil, yogurt, dill, and 1/8 teaspoon salt, stirring well with a whisk. Cover and chill. Combine tomatoes, cucumber, and onion. Sprinkle tomato mixture with 1/8 teaspoon salt; toss to combine.
2. Heat a grill pan over medium-high heat. Coat pan with cooking spray. Remove pork from bag, and discard marinade. Sprinkle both sides of pork evenly with remaining 1/4 teaspoon salt. Add pork to pan, and cook 4 minutes on each side or until desired degree of doneness. Remove pork from pan, and let stand 2 minutes. Place 3/4 cup tomato mixture on each of 4 plates, and top each serving with 1 pork chop and about 3 tablespoons yogurt mixture. Yield: 4 servings.

CALORIES 233; **FAT** 9.3g (sat 2.8g, mono 4.8g, poly 0.8g); **PROTEIN** 30.1g; **CARB** 5.7g; **FIBER** 1g; **CHOL** 70mg; **IRON** 1.2mg; **SODIUM** 361mg; **CALC** 74mg

Grilled Pork Tacos with Summer Corn and Nectarine Salsa

$2.49 per serving, $ 9.96 total

Be sure to zest your lime before you slice and juice it. Serve this refreshing summer taco with an easy side dish of smoky-spicy rice: Toss 2 cups hot cooked white rice with ¼ teaspoon ground red pepper and 1 cooked, crumbled bacon slice.

2 tablespoons fresh lime juice, divided
1½ tablespoons extra-virgin olive oil, divided
4 (4-ounce) boneless center-cut loin pork chops
¾ teaspoon salt, divided
½ teaspoon ground cumin
¼ teaspoon freshly ground black pepper
1 garlic clove, minced
Cooking spray
1 ear shucked corn
¼ cup diced red bell pepper
½ cup diced ripe nectarine
½ teaspoon grated lime rind
1 minced seeded jalapeño pepper
8 (6-inch) corn tortillas
1 cup shredded cabbage

1. Preheat grill to medium-high heat.
2. Combine 2 teaspoons lime juice, 1 tablespoon oil, and pork in a zip-top plastic bag; seal. Marinate 10 minutes at room temperature. Remove pork from bag; discard marinade. Sprinkle both sides of pork with ½ teaspoon salt, cumin, pepper, and garlic. Place pork on a grill rack coated with cooking spray; grill 3 minutes on each side or until desired degree of doneness. Let stand 5 minutes. Slice pork into thin strips.
3. Lightly coat corn with cooking spray. Place corn on a grill rack coated with cooking spray; grill 6 minutes or until lightly charred, turning occasionally. Let corn stand 5 minutes; cut kernels from cob. Combine kernels, 2 teaspoons juice, remaining 1½ teaspoons oil, remaining ¼ teaspoon salt, bell pepper, and next 3 ingredients in a bowl; toss.
4. Place tortillas on a grill rack coated with cooking spray, and grill 1 minute on each side or until lightly browned. Toss cabbage with remaining 2 teaspoons lime juice. Place 2 tortillas on each of 4 plates, and divide pork evenly among tortillas. Top each taco with about 1 tablespoon cabbage mixture and about 2 tablespoons salsa. Yield: 4 servings (serving size: 2 tacos).

CALORIES 332; **FAT** 16.4g (sat 4.4g, mono 8.1g, poly 2g); **PROTEIN** 21.6g; **CARB** 27.1g; **FIBER** 4.1g; **CHOL** 60mg; **IRON** 1.3mg; **SODIUM** 519mg; **CALC** 57mg

PEARL BARLEY IS A VERSATILE, INEXPENSIVE INGREDIENT THAT ADDS MORE WHOLE GRAINS TO YOUR DIET, AND IT PAIRS WELL WITH SUMMER PRODUCE.

Summer Barley Salad

$1.91 per serving, $7.65 total

Serve this colorful summer salad with buttery lemon green beans.

1½ cups uncooked pearl barley
1 cup fresh corn kernels (about 2 ears)
1 cup diced seeded plum tomato (about 2 small)
½ cup chopped green onions
¼ cup chopped fresh flat-leaf parsley
20 kalamata olives, pitted and coarsely chopped
3 tablespoons fresh lemon juice
2 tablespoons olive oil
¼ teaspoon salt
¼ teaspoon freshly ground black pepper
1 garlic clove, minced
¾ cup (3 ounces) crumbled feta cheese

1. Cook barley according to package directions, omitting salt. Drain and rinse with cold water; drain. Cool completely. Combine barley, corn, and next 4 ingredients in a bowl. Combine juice and next 4 ingredients, stirring well with a whisk; drizzle over barley mixture. Toss to coat. Sprinkle with cheese. Yield: 4 servings (serving size: about 1 cup).

CALORIES 494; **FAT** 18.5g (sat 4.9g, mono 9.8g, poly 1.9g); **PROTEIN** 13.5g; **CARB** 73.8g; **FIBER** 13.7g; **CHOL** 19mg; **IRON** 2.9mg; **SODIUM** 704mg; **CALC** 152mg

Lemon green beans:
Steam 1 pound fresh green beans until crisp-tender. Toss beans with 1 tablespoon butter, 1 teaspoon grated lemon rind, and ¼ teaspoon salt.

SUPERFAST

These 20-minute main-dish salads put fresh spins on bright salad flavors. The additions of chicken, seafood, or grains make them ideal for dinnertime appetites.

Quick & Easy

Thai Seafood Salad

¼ cup water
8 ounces sea scallops
1 pound peeled and deveined medium shrimp
5 tablespoons fresh lime juice
2½ tablespoons fish sauce
1 teaspoon sugar
1 teaspoon chile paste with garlic
1 cup red bell pepper strips
½ cup prechopped red onion
¼ cup fresh mint leaves, finely chopped
8 ounces lump crabmeat, drained and shell pieces removed
2 fresh lemongrass stalks, trimmed and thinly sliced
1 cucumber, halved lengthwise and thinly sliced

1. Bring ¼ cup water to a simmer in a large skillet. Add scallops to pan; cover and cook 3 minutes or until done. Remove scallops from pan with a slotted spoon; pat scallops dry with paper towels. Place scallops in a large bowl. Add shrimp to simmering water in pan; cover and cook 3 minutes or until done. Drain well; add to scallops.
2. While scallops and shrimp cook, combine lime juice and next 3 ingredients; stir to dissolve sugar.
3. Add juice mixture, bell pepper, and remaining ingredients to scallop mixture; toss gently to combine. Yield: 6 servings (serving size: about 1⅓ cups).

CALORIES 180; **FAT** 2.4g (sat 0.4g, mono 0.3g, poly 0.9g); **PROTEIN** 30.9g; **CARB** 8.5g; **FIBER** 1g; **CHOL** 165mg; **IRON** 3mg; **SODIUM** 756mg; **CALC** 110mg

Quick & Easy

Grilled Chicken and Spinach Salad with Spicy Pineapple Dressing

(pictured on page 257)

1 pound skinless, boneless chicken breast
1 teaspoon chili powder
½ teaspoon salt
Cooking spray
1¼ cups (1-inch) cubed fresh pineapple (about 8 ounces), divided
2 tablespoons chopped fresh cilantro
2 tablespoons fresh orange juice
4 teaspoons apple cider vinegar
½ teaspoon minced habanero pepper
1 large garlic clove
¼ cup extra-virgin olive oil
¾ cup julienne-cut peeled jicama
⅔ cup thinly sliced red bell pepper
½ cup thinly sliced red onion
1 (5-ounce) package fresh baby spinach (about 8 cups)

1. Heat a grill pan over medium-high heat. Place chicken between 2 sheets of plastic wrap, and pound to an even thickness using a meat mallet or small heavy skillet. Sprinkle both sides of chicken evenly with chili powder and salt. Lightly coat chicken with cooking spray. Add chicken to pan; cook 3 minutes on each side or until done. Remove from pan; set aside.
2. Place half of pineapple, cilantro, and next 4 ingredients in a blender; process until smooth. With blender on, gradually add olive oil until blended.
3. Combine remaining pineapple, jicama, and remaining ingredients in a large bowl. Drizzle with ¾ cup dressing, and toss gently to coat. Divide salad evenly among 4 plates. Cut chicken across grain into thin slices; divide chicken evenly over salads. Drizzle salads evenly with remaining ¼ cup dressing. Yield: 4 servings.

CALORIES 313; **FAT** 15.2g (sat 2.3g, mono 10.2g, poly 1.8g); **PROTEIN** 28g; **CARB** 16.8g; **FIBER** 4.3g; **CHOL** 66mg; **IRON** 2.6mg; **SODIUM** 444mg; **CALC** 58mg

Quick & Easy

Sautéed Arctic Char and Arugula Salad with Tomato Vinaigrette

If you can't find arctic char, substitute another sustainable option like Alaskan salmon.

4 (6-ounce) arctic char fillets
¾ teaspoon salt, divided
½ teaspoon black pepper, divided
Cooking spray
4 teaspoons balsamic vinegar
2 tablespoons extra-virgin olive oil
2 teaspoons minced shallots
1 pint grape tomatoes, halved
5 cups loosely packed arugula
2 tablespoons pine nuts, toasted

1. Heat a large nonstick skillet over medium-high heat. Sprinkle fillets evenly with ½ teaspoon salt and ¼ teaspoon pepper. Coat pan with cooking spray. Add fillets to pan; cook 3 minutes or until browned. Turn fillets over; cook 4 minutes or until desired degree of doneness. Remove fish from pan; loosely cover, and keep warm. Wipe pan clean with paper towels.
2. While fish cooks, place vinegar in a medium bowl. Gradually add oil, stirring with a whisk. Stir in shallots.
3. Return pan to medium-high heat. Add tomatoes, remaining ¼ teaspoon salt, and remaining ¼ teaspoon black pepper; sauté 3 minutes or until tomatoes soften. Add tomatoes to vinaigrette; toss to combine.
4. Arrange 1¼ cups arugula on each of 4 plates; top each serving with 1 fillet. Spoon about ½ cup tomato mixture over each salad, and sprinkle with 1½ teaspoons nuts. Yield: 4 servings.

CALORIES 342; **FAT** 20.5g (sat 3.7g, mono 10.4g, poly 4.8g); **PROTEIN** 33.1g; **CARB** 5.9g; **FIBER** 1.6g; **CHOL** 80mg; **IRON** 1.5mg; **SODIUM** 522mg; **CALC** 72mg

Lemony Orzo-Veggie Salad with Chicken

¾ cup uncooked orzo
¼ teaspoon grated lemon rind
3 tablespoons fresh lemon juice
1 tablespoon extra-virgin olive oil
½ teaspoon kosher salt
½ teaspoon minced garlic
¼ teaspoon honey
⅛ teaspoon freshly ground black pepper
1 cup shredded skinless, boneless rotisserie
    chicken breast
½ cup diced English cucumber
½ cup prechopped red bell pepper
⅓ cup thinly sliced green onions
1 tablespoon chopped fresh dill
½ cup (2 ounces) crumbled goat cheese

1. Cook orzo according to package directions, omitting salt and fat. Drain and rinse with cold water; drain and place in a large bowl.
2. While orzo cooks, combine lemon rind and next 6 ingredients, stirring well with a whisk. Drizzle juice mixture over orzo; toss to coat. Add chicken and next 4 ingredients; toss gently to combine. Sprinkle with cheese. Yield: 4 servings (serving size: about 1¼ cups).

CALORIES 275; **FAT** 9.7g (sat 3.8g, mono 3.9g, poly 0.9g); **PROTEIN** 18.2g; **CARB** 28g; **FIBER** 1.8g; **CHOL** 41mg; **IRON** 0.9mg; **SODIUM** 338mg; **CALC** 60mg

Seashell Salad with Buttermilk-Chive Dressing

8 ounces uncooked seashell pasta
1 cup frozen green peas
¼ cup organic canola mayonnaise
¼ cup fat-free buttermilk
1 tablespoon minced fresh chives
1 teaspoon chopped fresh thyme
½ teaspoon salt
½ teaspoon freshly ground black pepper
2 garlic cloves, minced
2 cups loosely packed baby arugula
1 teaspoon olive oil
2 ounces finely chopped prosciutto
    (about ½ cup)

1. Cook pasta according to package directions, omitting salt and fat. Add peas to pasta during last 2 minutes of cooking. Drain and rinse with cold water; drain well.
2. While pasta cooks, combine mayonnaise and next 6 ingredients in a large bowl. Add pasta mixture and arugula; toss to coat.
3. Heat oil in a skillet over medium-high heat. Add prosciutto; sauté 2 minutes. Drain on paper towels. Sprinkle prosciutto over salad. Yield: 4 servings (serving size: about 1¼ cups salad and 1 tablespoon prosciutto).

CALORIES 373; **FAT** 14.9g (sat 1.4g, mono 4.4g, poly 7.5g); **PROTEIN** 13.6g; **CARB** 45.7g; **FIBER** 3.6g; **CHOL** 18mg; **IRON** 2.8mg; **SODIUM** 677mg; **CALC** 50mg

Couscous Salad with Chickpeas

1 cup uncooked whole-wheat couscous
½ teaspoon salt, divided
½ teaspoon black pepper, divided
⅛ teaspoon ground cinnamon
1 cup boiling water
3 tablespoons extra-virgin olive oil
3 tablespoons fresh lemon juice
1½ teaspoons minced garlic
Dash of sugar
⅓ cup chopped fresh mint
¼ cup thinly sliced green onions
⅛ teaspoon smoked paprika
1 (15-ounce) can chickpeas (garbanzo beans),
    rinsed and drained
1 large ripe tomato, chopped
¾ cup (3 ounces) crumbled feta cheese

1. Place couscous, ¼ teaspoon salt, ¼ teaspoon pepper, and cinnamon in a bowl. Stir in boiling water; cover and let stand 10 minutes. Fluff with a fork.
2. Combine oil and next 3 ingredients in a small bowl.
3. Add oil mixture, remaining ¼ teaspoon salt, remaining ¼ teaspoon pepper, mint, and next 4 ingredients. Sprinkle with cheese. Yield: 4 servings (serving size: 1⅓ cups salad and 3 tablespoons cheese).

CALORIES 351; **FAT** 16.2g (sat 4.7g, mono 8.6g, poly 1.6g); **PROTEIN** 11g; **CARB** 43.6g; **FIBER** 7.7g; **CHOL** 19mg; **IRON** 2.6mg; **SODIUM** 655mg; **CALC** 154mg

BUILD A GREAT SALAD WITH THESE CHOICE INGREDIENTS

POULTRY OR FISH
Boneless poultry, fish fillets, and shellfish cook in a flash.

QUICK-COOKING PASTA
Try small seashells, orzo, or couscous.

PACKAGED FRESH GREENS
Save time with convenient options.

CANNED OR FROZEN BEANS OR PEAS
Legumes add protein.

Southwestern Cobb Salad

Vinaigrette:

3 tablespoons white wine vinegar

1 teaspoon honey

3/4 teaspoon ground cumin

1/2 teaspoon smoked paprika

1/2 teaspoon garlic powder

1/4 teaspoon ground red pepper

2 tablespoons canola oil

Salad:

3 slices center-cut bacon

Cooking spray

8 ounces skinless, boneless turkey breast, cut into 1/2-inch pieces

1/4 teaspoon salt

8 cups torn romaine lettuce

1/2 cup refrigerated fresh pico de gallo

1/2 cup diced avocado

1/2 cup (2 ounces) crumbled queso fresco

1/4 cup chopped green onions

1 (15-ounce) can low-sodium black beans, rinsed and drained

1. To prepare vinaigrette, combine first 6 ingredients in a medium bowl, stirring with a whisk. Gradually add oil, stirring constantly with a whisk; set aside.

2. To prepare salad, cook bacon in a nonstick skillet over medium heat until crisp. Remove bacon from pan; crumble. Wipe pan clean with paper towels. Increase heat to medium-high. Coat pan with cooking spray. Sprinkle turkey with salt. Add turkey to pan; sauté 4 minutes or until done.

3. Arrange 2 cups lettuce on each of 4 plates. Top each serving with about 2 teaspoons bacon, 5 tablespoons turkey, 2 tablespoons pico de gallo, 2 tablespoons avocado, 2 tablespoons queso fresco, 1 tablespoon onions, and about 1/3 cup beans. Drizzle vinaigrette evenly over salads. Yield: 4 servings.

CALORIES 293; FAT 13.6g (sat 2.5g, mono 7.2g, poly 3g); PROTEIN 22.4g; CARB 19.9g; FIBER 6.6g; CHOL 44mg; IRON 3.1mg; SODIUM 455mg; CALC 117mg

DINNER TONIGHT

Here are a handful of fast weeknight menus from the *Cooking Light* Test Kitchens.

40 minutes

SHOPPING LIST

Pan-Seared Striped Bass All'amatriciana

1 small onion

garlic

1 pint cherry tomatoes

crushed red pepper

balsamic vinegar

extra-virgin olive oil

4 (6-ounce) striped bass fillets

2 ounces pancetta

Arugula, Fennel, and Parmesan Salad

baby arugula

1 large fennel bulb

1 lemon

extra-virgin olive oil

Parmigiano-Reggiano cheese

GAME PLAN

While fish cooks:
- Chop pancetta.
- Chop onion.
- Mince garlic.
- Quarter tomatoes.

While sauce cooks:
- Prepare salad.

Pan-Seared Striped Bass All'amatriciana
with Arugula, Fennel, and Parmesan Salad

While dishes all'amatriciana are traditionally made with guanciale (cured Italian pork jowl), we substituted pancetta, which is more readily available.

Flavor Hit: Balsamic vinegar adds a touch of sweet depth to the sauce.

Simple Sub: If you can't find pancetta, substitute prosciutto or unsmoked bacon.

Buy The Best: Purchase firm fennel bulbs with stiff stalks and fresh, bright-green fronds.

1 tablespoon extra-virgin olive oil, divided

4 (6-ounce) striped bass fillets

1/4 plus 1/8 teaspoon salt, divided

2 ounces pancetta, finely chopped

1/2 cup chopped onion

1/8 teaspoon crushed red pepper

3 garlic cloves, minced

2 cups cherry tomatoes, quartered

1 teaspoon balsamic vinegar

1. Heat 2 teaspoons oil in a large nonstick skillet over medium-high heat. Sprinkle fish evenly with 1/4 teaspoon salt. Add fish to pan, skin sides up; cook 3 minutes or until lightly browned. Turn fish over; cook 4 minutes or until desired degree of doneness. Remove fish from pan; keep warm.

2. Return pan to medium-high heat. Add remaining 1 teaspoon oil and pancetta; cook 1 minute, stirring occasionally. Add onion, pepper, and garlic; cook 5 minutes or until pancetta is browned, stirring occasionally. Add tomatoes and vinegar; cook 3 minutes or until tomatoes soften, stirring frequently. Add remaining 1/8 teaspoon salt, stirring well. Serve sauce with fish. Yield: 4 servings (serving size: 1 fillet and 1/4 cup sauce).

CALORIES 272; FAT 12.1g (sat 3.4g, mono 5.4g, poly 2.1g); PROTEIN 33.2g; CARB 5.8g; FIBER 1.3g; CHOL 146mg; IRON 1.7mg; SODIUM 577mg; CALC 42mg

continued

For the Arugula, Fennel, and Parmesan Salad:

Toss 4 cups baby arugula, 2 cups thinly sliced fennel bulb, 2 tablespoons fresh lemon juice, 4 teaspoons extra-virgin olive oil, ¼ teaspoon salt, and ⅛ teaspoon black pepper in a large bowl. Divide salad evenly among 4 bowls; top each serving with 2 tablespoons shaved Parmigiano-Reggiano cheese.

SHOPPING LIST

Grilled Miso-Marinated Filet Mignon

green onions
rice vinegar
lower-sodium soy sauce
dark sesame oil
Dijon mustard
honey
miso paste
4 (4-ounce) beef tenderloin steaks

Sugar Snap Noodle Salad

1 cup sugar snap peas
1 orange bell pepper
green onions
bottled ground fresh ginger
dark sesame oil
sambal oelek
4 ounces wide rice noodles

GAME PLAN

While steaks marinate:
- Preheat grill.
- Slice bell pepper.
- Slice green onions.

While steaks cook:
- Prepare salad.

Quick & Easy

Grilled Miso-Marinated Filet Mignon

with Sugar Snap Noodle Salad

Shopping Tip: Find miso in the refrigerated section of Asian markets and supermarkets. Flavor Hit: A touch of Dijon mustard adds sharp, pungent notes to the marinade. Simple Sub: In place of sambal oelek, use ¼ to ½ teaspoon crushed red pepper.

3 tablespoons finely chopped green onions
2 tablespoons miso paste
1 tablespoon rice vinegar
1 tablespoon honey
1 tablespoon lower-sodium soy sauce
2 teaspoons Dijon mustard
1 teaspoon dark sesame oil
4 (4-ounce) beef tenderloin steaks, trimmed
Cooking spray

1. Combine first 7 ingredients in a large zip-top plastic bag. Add steaks to bag; turn to coat. Let stand at room temperature 20 minutes, turning occasionally.
2. Preheat grill to medium-high heat.
3. Remove steaks from bag; discard marinade. Place steaks on grill rack coated with cooking spray; grill 5 minutes on each side or until desired degree of doneness. Yield: 4 servings (serving size: 1 steak).

CALORIES 207; **FAT** 10.2g (sat 3.7g, mono 4.1g, poly 0.7g); **PROTEIN** 23.9g; **CARB** 3.5g; **FIBER** 0.2g; **CHOL** 71mg; **IRON** 1.6mg; **SODIUM** 330mg; **CALC** 19mg

For the Sugar Snap Noodle Salad:

Cook 4 ounces wide rice noodles according to package directions; add 1 cup sugar snap peas during last 3 minutes of cooking time. Drain and rinse with cold water; drain. Combine noodle mixture, 1 cup orange bell pepper strips, ¼ cup sliced green onions, 1 tablespoon dark sesame oil, 1 teaspoon sambal oelek (ground fresh chile paste), ½ teaspoon bottled ground fresh ginger, and ¼ tea-spoon salt.

WINE NOTE: Big red wines don't always mean big prices, especially if you know where to look. A Spanish red like Bodegas Borsao Red 2008 ($8), from Spain's Campo de Borja region, has enough power to match this dish, with its firm tannins and smoky, dark fruit.

SHOPPING LIST

Farfalle with Tomatoes, Onions, and Spinach

1 small yellow onion
garlic
1 pint grape tomatoes
baby spinach
8 ounces farfalle
extra-virgin olive oil
dried oregano
white wine vinegar
Parmigiano-Reggiano cheese
3 ounces feta cheese

Olive Flatbread

garlic
fresh basil
olive oil
crushed red pepper
kalamata olives
11-ounce can refrigerated thin-crust pizza dough

GAME PLAN

While oven heats:
- Bring water to a boil.
- Slice onion and garlic for pasta.
- Halve tomatoes.

While pasta cooks:
- Cook flatbread.
- Prepare sauce for pasta.
- Crumble cheese.

Quick & Easy

Farfalle with Tomatoes, Onions, and Spinach

with Olive Flatbread

Prep Pointer: Vertically sliced onions (as opposed to rings) separate nicely and meld better with the pasta.
Simple Sub: Try baby arugula in place of spinach.
Time-Saver: Bagged greens require no trimming.

1 tablespoon plus ¼ teaspoon salt
8 ounces uncooked farfalle pasta
2 tablespoons extra-virgin olive oil, divided
1 cup vertically sliced yellow onion
1 teaspoon dried oregano
5 garlic cloves, sliced
2 cups grape tomatoes, halved
1 tablespoon white wine vinegar
3 cups baby spinach
3 tablespoons shaved fresh Parmigiano-
   Reggiano cheese
¼ teaspoon freshly ground black pepper
¾ cup (3 ounces) crumbled feta cheese

1. Bring a large pot of water to a boil with 1 tablespoon salt. Add pasta, and cook according to package directions; drain.
2. Heat 1 tablespoon oil in a large nonstick skillet over medium-high heat. Add onion and oregano; sauté 12 minutes or until lightly browned. Add garlic; sauté 2 minutes. Add tomatoes and vinegar; sauté 3 minutes or until tomatoes begin to soften. Add pasta and spinach; cook 1 minute. Remove from heat, and stir in Parmigiano-Reggiano, remaining 1 tablespoon oil, remaining ¼ teaspoon salt, and pepper. Sprinkle with feta. Yield: 4 servings (serving size: about 1½ cups pasta mixture and 3 tablespoons feta).

CALORIES 374; **FAT** 13.3g (sat 5g, mono 6.2g, poly 0.9g); **PROTEIN** 13.7g; **CARB** 51.1g; **FIBER** 3.8g; **CHOL** 22mg; **IRON** 2.6mg; **SODIUM** 632mg; **CALC** 212mg

For the Olive Flatbread:

Preheat oven to 450°. Unroll 1 (11-ounce) can refrigerated thin-crust pizza dough onto a baking sheet. Combine 1½ tablespoons olive oil, ½ teaspoon crushed red pepper, and 1 minced garlic clove; brush over dough. Sprinkle dough with ⅓ cup chopped kalamata olives. Bake at 450° for 11 minutes or until browned and done. Top with 2 tablespoons thinly sliced basil.

30 minutes

SHOPPING LIST

Grilled Pork Chops with Two-Melon Salsa
precut seedless watermelon
precut honeydew melon
1 small sweet onion
1 jalapeño pepper
fresh cilantro
1 lime
canola oil
chili powder
garlic powder
4 (4-ounce) boneless center-cut pork
   chops

Garlic Texas Toast
garlic
country sourdough bread
butter

GAME PLAN

While oven heats:
■ Prepare salsa.
■ Brush bread with butter mixture.
■ Prepare spice rub.
While pork cooks:
■ Cook bread.

Quick & Easy

Grilled Pork Chops with Two-Melon Salsa

with Garlic Texas Toast

Simple Sub: Use any fruit you like in place of melons—peaches, pineapple, or mango.
Kid Tweak: Seed the jalapeño for sensitive palates.
Time-Saver: Purchase precut melon from the grocery store.

Salsa:
1 cup chopped seedless watermelon
1 cup chopped honeydew melon
3 tablespoons finely chopped sweet onion
1 tablespoon finely chopped jalapeño pepper
1 tablespoon chopped fresh cilantro
1 tablespoon fresh lime juice
⅛ teaspoon salt
Pork Chops:
2 teaspoons canola oil
1½ teaspoons chili powder
½ teaspoon garlic powder
½ teaspoon salt
¼ teaspoon freshly ground black pepper
4 (4-ounce) boneless center-cut pork chops,
   trimmed
Cooking spray

1. To prepare salsa, combine first 7 ingredients; set aside.
2. To prepare pork chops, heat a grill pan over medium-high heat. Combine oil and next 4 ingredients in a small bowl. Rub oil mixture over both sides of pork chops. Coat pan with cooking spray. Add pork to pan; cook 4 minutes on each side or until desired degree of doneness. Serve with salsa. Yield: 4 servings (serving size: 1 pork chop and ½ cup salsa).

CALORIES 256; **FAT** 13.5g (sat 4.3g, mono 6.4g, poly 1.6g); **PROTEIN** 25g; **CARB** 8.7g; **FIBER** 0.9g; **CHOL** 70mg; **IRON** 0.9mg; **SODIUM** 458mg; **CALC** 37mg

For the Garlic Texas Toast:

Preheat oven to 375°. Combine 1 tablespoon melted butter and 1 minced garlic clove in a small bowl. Brush 1 side of each of 4 (1½-ounce) slices country sourdough bread with butter mixture. Place bread on a baking sheet; bake at 375° for 8 minutes or until lightly browned.

30 minutes

SHOPPING LIST

Spicy Chipotle Shrimp Salad

celery
1 small red onion
fresh cilantro
1 lime
1 head Boston lettuce
canola mayonnaise
ground cumin
1 can chipotle chiles in adobo sauce
1½ pounds peeled and deveined large shrimp

Avocado, Mango, and Pineapple Salad

pretrimmed fresh pineapple
1 large ripe mango
1 ripe avocado
1 lime
fresh cilantro
honey

GAME PLAN

While grill pan heats:
 ▪ Slice fruit.
While fruit cooks:
 ▪ Chop celery, onion, and cilantro.
While shrimp cooks:
 ▪ Prepare fruit salad.

Quick & Easy • Make Ahead

Spicy Chipotle Shrimp Salad

with Avocado, Mango, and Pineapple Salad

Simple Sub: Use ¼ to ½ teaspoon ground chipotle chile pepper for the canned chiles. Kid Tweak: Omit the chiles, and add diced red bell pepper for sweetness and crunch. Make-Ahead Tip: Prepare the shrimp salad a day ahead. Take leftovers to work for lunch.

1½ pounds peeled and deveined large shrimp
⅛ teaspoon salt
⅛ teaspoon freshly ground black pepper
Cooking spray
¼ cup finely chopped celery
2 tablespoons finely chopped red onion
2 tablespoons chopped fresh cilantro
3 tablespoons canola mayonnaise
1 tablespoon chopped chipotle chile, canned in adobo sauce
2 teaspoons fresh lime juice
½ teaspoon ground cumin
8 Boston lettuce leaves

1. Heat a grill pan over medium-high heat. Sprinkle shrimp with salt and black pepper. Coat pan with cooking spray. Add half of shrimp to pan; cook 2 minutes on each side or until done. Remove shrimp from pan; repeat procedure with remaining shrimp. Cool shrimp 5 minutes.
2. Place shrimp in a medium bowl; stir in celery and next 6 ingredients. Arrange 2 lettuce leaves on each of 4 plates; top each serving with ¾ cup shrimp mixture. Yield: 4 servings.

CALORIES 235; **FAT** 10.9g (sat 0.9g, mono 3g, poly 6.2g); **PROTEIN** 29.2g; **CARB** 3.2g; **FIBER** 0.8g; **CHOL** 219mg; **IRON** 3.8mg; **SODIUM** 400mg; **CALC** 87mg

For the Avocado, Mango, and Pineapple Salad:
Heat a grill pan over medium-high heat. Add 4 (½-inch-thick) pineapple slices and 1 cup sliced peeled mango; cook 3 minutes on each side or until browned. Divide pineapple, mango, and 1 sliced peeled avocado evenly among 4 plates. Combine 1½ tablespoons fresh lime juice, ½ teaspoon honey, and ¼ teaspoon salt; drizzle evenly over salads. Sprinkle 2 tablespoons fresh cilantro leaves evenly over salads.

RECIPE MAKEOVER
SUPER SAMOSAS

Baked phyllo wrapped around a veggie-studded filling yields a healthier version of the Indian snack.

Samosas promise the ideal appetizer, with a golden pastry enveloping a zesty spiced filling. While the flavors and textures are sublime, the promise is short-lived because many traditional recipes' appetizer portions weigh in with as many calories as an entrée, thanks to a fatty, deep-fried pastry, heavy fillings, and sauces. Inspired by the Indian street food, we devised a recipe that delivers on taste, texture, and nutrition.

We succeeded by starting with a veggie-studded filling in place of a curried lamb and potato one. Chickpeas and green peas keep calories and saturated fat in check and soak up the spicy streamlined curry mix. Instead of homemade pastry, we brush phyllo sheets with a little butter for richness. And creamy fat-free Greek yogurt is perfect in the cool raita. Our authentic-flavored appetizer offers a healthy portion size with healthy nutrition numbers.

Kid Friendly

Spicy Chickpea Samosas with Raita

Samosas:

1½ tablespoons canola oil

½ cup finely chopped carrot

½ cup thinly sliced green onions

2 tablespoons minced peeled fresh ginger

1 tablespoon minced garlic

1 tablespoon tomato paste

1½ teaspoons cumin seeds

1 teaspoon brown mustard seeds

¾ teaspoon kosher salt

¼ teaspoon ground red pepper

¼ teaspoon freshly ground black pepper

1 cup frozen green peas, thawed

1 tablespoon water

1 (15-ounce) can chickpeas (garbanzo beans), rinsed and drained

½ cup chopped fresh cilantro

1 tablespoon fresh lemon juice

24 (14 x 9-inch) sheets frozen phyllo dough, thawed

Cooking spray

2 tablespoons butter, melted

Raita:

¾ cup plain nonfat Greek yogurt

¾ cup chopped seeded peeled cucumber

2 tablespoons thinly sliced green onions

2 tablespoons chopped fresh cilantro

2 teaspoons fresh lemon juice

¼ teaspoon kosher salt

¼ teaspoon ground cumin

⅛ teaspoon freshly ground black pepper

1. To prepare samosas, heat oil in a skillet over medium heat. Add carrot; cook 3 minutes, stirring frequently. Add ½ cup onions, ginger, and garlic; cook 1 minute, stirring constantly. Add tomato paste and next 5 ingredients; cook 1 minute, stirring constantly. Add peas, 1 tablespoon water, and chickpeas; cook 1 minute. Remove from heat; stir in cilantro and juice. Cool.

2. Preheat oven to 400°.

3. Place 1 phyllo sheet on a large work surface (cover remaining dough to keep from drying); coat with cooking spray. Place another phyllo sheet on coated phyllo; coat with cooking spray. Fold layered sheets in half lengthwise. Spoon 2 tablespoons filling onto bottom end of rectangle, leaving a 1-inch border. Fold bottom corner over mixture, forming a triangle; keep folding back and forth into a triangle to end of phyllo strip. Tuck edges under; place seam side down on a baking sheet coated with cooking spray. Brush with melted butter. Repeat procedure with remaining 22 phyllo sheets, cooking spray, filling, and butter. Bake at 400° for 10 minutes or until crisp and golden.

4. To prepare raita, combine yogurt and remaining ingredients. Serve with samosas. Yield: 12 servings (serving size: 1 samosa and 1½ tablespoons raita).

CALORIES 156; FAT 5.8g (sat 1.7g, mono 2.5g, poly 1.1g); PROTEIN 5g; CARB 21.2g; FIBER 2.8g; CHOL 5mg; IRON 1.7mg; SODIUM 369mg; CALC 41mg

SAMOSAS 101

Traditionally, these pastries are folded from a round piece of dough, but we use phyllo to encase the filling. Here's how to fold with success.

1 Spoon about 2 tablespoons chickpea mixture onto bottom end of rectangle, leaving a 1-inch border.

2 Fold bottom corner over mixture, forming a triangle.

3 Keep folding back and forth to end of phyllo strip, forming a triangular packet.

OLD WAY	OUR WAY
467 calories per serving	156 calories per serving
33.1 grams fat	5.8 grams fat
7.4 grams saturated fat	1.7 grams saturated fat
Fatty ground lamb	Judiciously seasoned veggies
Deep-fried homemade pastry	Baked phyllo dough
Whole-milk plain yogurt	Fat-free Greek yogurt

AMERICA'S SUMMER BOUNTY

Take farmers' market produce, add brilliant chefs, and voilà: gorgeous summer recipes.

There's been a thrilling increase in the American appetite for farmers' markets over the last 15 years. The best example may be a thriving new market just down the road from you, but consider these encouraging numbers: There are 5,274 farmers' markets in the United States, up from just 1,755 in 1994, according to the USDA. Even during the recession, from 2008 to 2009, the number of markets jumped 13 percent.

What we have here is something nourishing to celebrate: Once again, average hungry Americans have easy access to the handiwork of local food artisans and farmers. This is very cheery news, for good health, good taste, and good land.

More and more Americans want to know where their food comes from, and it's affecting the way food is sold in supermarkets, too—not just Whole Foods but also Wal-Mart and other mainstream markets. These days people want to know not only the name of the farm where their beef and pork are raised, but also the breed of the animals and the farming practices used to raise them.

One of the spurs for this trend has been chefs, who are advocates and ambassadors for farms and markets, shopping by morning and plastering menus with the names of suppliers by night. That spirit of local appreciation has sent many home cooks to the same markets, giving them access to restaurant-quality ingredients for their own cooking.

It's a delightful relationship, the alliance of restaurants, markets, farmers, and home cooks. So we tagged along with a few market-focused chefs as they shopped and cooked. The pages here highlight their stories and offer healthy recipes that use the freshest ingredients you'll find right now.

BOSTON

MARKETS: Copley Square Market and New Deal Fish Market
CHEF: Barry Maiden, Hungry Mother

The first time Barry Maiden tasted an oyster, he was standing on the beach with his feet in the ocean, the shell just plucked out of the sand moments earlier. He and a friend were raking for clams. Maiden recalls the serendipitous oyster as one of the best things he has ever eaten. "You connect the moment and the food and your surroundings," he says.

Maiden expresses his passion for these types of connections in his soulful cooking at Hungry Mother in Cambridge, Massachusetts. To create his menus, he scours the offerings from local farmers and talks with fishermen and his fishmonger regularly.

For Maiden, bluefish signals summer, and you'll find this fish on his menus from June through September. (In October the fish migrate back south to warmer waters.) He makes a delicious smoked bluefish paté. Here he pairs the fish with sweet and spicy *maque choux*, a Cajun-inspired corn dish.

Quick & Easy

Crisp Chatham Bluefish with Maque Choux

Although bluefish are available from the southern Atlantic during cooler months, they're a summer delicacy off the coast of Massachusetts. Substitute fresh Spanish mackerel if you can't find bluefish.

3 tablespoons butter
1 cup finely chopped sweet onion
½ cup finely chopped red bell pepper
¼ cup finely chopped celery
3 tablespoons finely chopped jalapeño pepper
1½ tablespoons minced garlic
3 cups fresh corn kernels (about 6 ears)
1 teaspoon Spanish smoked paprika
1½ cups chopped seeded peeled tomato
1 tablespoon chopped fresh basil
1½ teaspoons kosher salt, divided
Dash of ground red pepper
2 tablespoons canola oil, divided
6 (6-ounce) bluefish fillets, skin-on
¼ teaspoon freshly ground black pepper

1. Melt butter in a saucepan over medium-high heat; add onion and next 4 ingredients to pan. Reduce heat to medium-low, and cook 7 minutes or until vegetables are tender. Add corn and paprika; cook 5 minutes, stirring occasionally. Add tomato; cook 10 minutes, stirring occasionally. Remove from heat. Stir in basil, ½ teaspoon salt, and red pepper.
2. Heat a 10-inch cast-iron skillet over high heat. Add 1 tablespoon oil to pan; swirl to coat. Sprinkle fillets evenly with remaining 1 teaspoon salt and black pepper. Add 3 fillets to pan, skin sides down; sauté 3 minutes or until skin is crisp. Turn fillets over; sauté 3 minutes or until desired degree of doneness. Remove from pan; keep warm. Repeat procedure with remaining 1 tablespoon oil and fillets. Spoon about ⅔ cup corn mixture onto each of 6 plates; top each serving with 1 fillet. Yield: 6 servings.

CALORIES 481; FAT 18.7g (sat 5.4g, mono 7g, poly 3.3g); PROTEIN 36.4g; CARB 40.5g; FIBER 4.6g; CHOL 107mg; IRON 2mg; SODIUM 636mg; CALC 35mg

BOULDER

MARKET: Boulder County Farmers' Market
CHEF: Lachlan Mackinnon-Patterson, Frasca Food and Wine

Armed with experience working in prestigious restaurants in Paris, Chef Lachlan Mackinnon-Patterson opened Frasca Food and Wine to considerable acclaim in Boulder. His techniques are sharp, befitting his European gigs. His tastes run to Italy right now, but his menus cite the names of his favorite farms. Local, organic Cure Farms supplied turnips for a late-spring dish this year of pickled ramps and turnips, and for a plate of wilted greens with pasta, chanterelles, and leeks. The green bean salad offered here is simple and straightforward but jazzed up by the addition of a mustard crema.

Quick & Easy

Green Bean Salad with Mustard Crema

Cooking the beans in salted water helps them retain a bright green color. Serve beans chilled or at room temperature.

3 pounds fresh green beans, trimmed
2¼ teaspoons sea salt, divided
1½ tablespoons minced fresh chives
4½ tablespoons crème fraîche
3 tablespoons whole-grain mustard
1 teaspoon chopped fresh thyme
¼ teaspoon freshly ground black pepper
3 tablespoons sliced almonds, toasted

1. Cook beans 5 minutes or until crisp-tender in boiling water with 2 teaspoons salt. Drain and plunge beans into ice water. Drain and pat dry.
2. Combine remaining ¼ teaspoon salt, chives, and next 4 ingredients in a large bowl, stirring well with a whisk. Add beans to mustard mixture; toss. Divide beans evenly among 6 plates; top each serving with 1½ teaspoons almonds. Yield: 6 servings.

CALORIES 90; **FAT** 5.4g (sat 2.5g, mono 1g, poly 0.4g); **PROTEIN** 2.3g; **CARB** 8.9g; **FIBER** 4.4g; **CHOL** 11mg; **IRON** 0.7mg; **SODIUM** 356mg; **CALC** 62mg

Staff Favorite

Hot and Hot Tomato Salad

This recipe is a lightened interpretation of Hastings' summer staple. For his original recipe, check out Hot and Hot Fish Club Cookbook. Use whatever varieties of colorful tomatoes you find at your local market. Hastings likes to use red beefsteak, yellow globe, and green zebra tomatoes. Cherokee purple tomatoes add unique flavor and color to the plate, if you can find them. Outside the South, black-eyed peas are a fine sub for lady peas. Okra is a regional delicacy that's optional in this dish. If you omit it from the recipe, the salad is a mere 207 calories with 3.6 grams saturated fat and 323 milligrams sodium.

7 large ripe heirloom tomatoes, cored and sliced crosswise into ¼-inch-thick slices
1 cup small cherry tomatoes, halved
1 teaspoon freshly ground black pepper, divided
¾ teaspoon kosher salt, divided
2 tablespoons extra-virgin olive oil, divided
2 tablespoons red wine vinegar
1 cup fresh shelled lady peas (about 6 ounces) or black-eyed peas, rinsed well and drained
1 (6-ounce) smoked ham hock
1 large onion, peeled and quartered
1 fresh thyme sprig
2 cups peanut oil
6 tablespoons buttermilk, divided
2.25 ounces all-purpose flour (about ½ cup)
¼ cup coarse-ground cornmeal
30 whole baby okra, trimmed
3 slices applewood-smoked bacon, cooked and coarsely crumbled
6 tablespoons minced fresh chives
1 small garlic clove, minced
2 tablespoons fresh lemon juice
2 tablespoons crème fraîche
6 tablespoons torn fresh basil

1. Sprinkle cut sides of tomatoes with ½ teaspoon pepper and ¼ teaspoon salt; drizzle with 1 tablespoon olive oil and vinegar. Set aside.
2. Combine peas and next 3 ingredients in a medium saucepan; cover with cold water. Bring to a simmer over medium heat; simmer 15 minutes or until peas are just tender, stirring occasionally. Remove from heat; drain and cool. Discard ham hock, onion, and thyme.

3. Clip a candy/fry thermometer onto side of a large skillet; add peanut oil to pan. Heat peanut oil to 350°. Place ¼ cup buttermilk in a shallow dish. Combine flour, cornmeal, ¼ teaspoon salt, and ¼ teaspoon pepper in a shallow dish, stirring well. Dip okra in buttermilk; dredge in flour mixture. Place okra in hot oil; fry 2 minutes or until golden, making sure oil temperature remains at 350°. Remove okra using a slotted spoon, and drain on paper towels.
4. Divide tomato slices evenly among 6 plates; top each serving evenly with cherry tomatoes. Spoon 2 heaping tablespoons peas over each tomato stack. Arrange 5 pieces fried okra on each serving; sprinkle evenly with bacon.
5. Combine remaining 2 tablespoons buttermilk, chives, and garlic in a small bowl. Add remaining ¼ teaspoon salt, remaining ¼ teaspoon pepper, and juice; stir well with a whisk. Gradually add remaining 1 tablespoon olive oil, while whisking vigorously. Stir in crème fraîche. Drizzle 2 tablespoons dressing mixture over each serving; top with 1 tablespoon basil. Yield: 6 servings.

CALORIES 357; **FAT** 20.6g (sat 5.3g, mono 7.8g, poly 3.7g); **PROTEIN** 10.7g; **CARB** 35.5g; **FIBER** 6.5g; **CHOL** 17mg; **IRON** 2.2mg; **SODIUM** 419mg; **CALC** 69mg

BIRMINGHAM

MARKET: Jones Valley Urban Farm
CHEF: Chris Hastings, Hot and Hot Fish Club

In a rural state like Alabama, sweet corn, tomatoes, okra, and a profusion of field peas thrive in the extreme summer heat. For Chris Hastings of Hot and Hot Fish Club, good cooking is a matter of bringing this bounty together simply and laying on some Southern touches. His early summer menu included fried green tomatoes with crabmeat rémoulade, Fudge Farms pork with pea salad, and smoked quail with local beans. Hastings and his wife, Idie, even use local potters to supply their restaurant's serving pieces.

Hastings' signature Hot and Hot Tomato Salad, adapted here, combines crisp fried whole baby okra and delicate lady peas served over fresh heirloom tomato slices and topped with smoky bacon and a creamy herbed dressing.

Make Ahead

Drunken Figs with Black Pepper Granola

An exotic-sounding but absolutely delicious dessert. Fernet is an herby liqueur imported from Italy. If you can't find it, substitute pastis or ouzo.

Figs:

1 cup water

1 cup honey

¼ cup Fernet Branca or anisette liqueur

2 teaspoons fresh lemon juice

¼ teaspoon salt

24 fresh figs, quartered

Granola:

2 tablespoons butter

3 tablespoons brown sugar

1¾ cups old-fashioned rolled oats

¼ cup pine nuts, toasted

½ teaspoon freshly ground black pepper

Dash of salt

Remaining Ingredient:

¼ cup mascarpone cheese

1. To prepare figs, combine first 5 ingredients in a small saucepan; bring to a boil. Place figs in a shallow dish; add hot syrup to dish. Cool fig mixture to room temperature; cover and refrigerate overnight.

2. Preheat oven to 325°.

3. To prepare granola, melt butter in a large nonstick skillet over medium heat; stir in sugar, and increase heat to medium-high. Cook 2 minutes or until sugar browns lightly. Add oats and next 3 ingredients; stir to coat. Cook 2 minutes, stirring frequently. Arrange oat mixture in a single layer on a baking sheet lined with parchment paper. Bake at 325° for 16 minutes or until toasted, stirring after 8 minutes. Cool completely.

4. Remove figs from liquid using a slotted spoon, and discard liquid. Divide fig quarters evenly among 8 bowls, and top each serving with ½ cup granola. Spoon 1½ teaspoons mascarpone on each serving. Yield: 8 servings.

CALORIES 321; FAT 13.8g (sat 5.8g, mono 3.9g, poly 2.4g); PROTEIN 5.6g; CARB 48.3g; FIBER 6.4g; CHOL 25mg; IRON 1.6mg; SODIUM 59mg; CALC 87mg

SAN FRANCISCO

MARKET: Ferry Plaza Farmers' Market
CHEF: Luis Villavelazquez, Absinthe Brasserie & Bar and Arlequin Café

For San Francisco chef Luis Villavelazquez, shopping at the Ferry Plaza Farmers' Market gets him in touch with ingredients that are absolutely of-the-moment from local farms. Although he could have ingredients delivered to his doors at Absinthe Brasserie & Bar and Arlequin Café (and sometimes he does), Villavelazquez relishes the opportunity to yak with the farmers who grow the fruits he uses in his dreamy desserts.

Last October he opened his own stall at the market. He sells some of the most popular menu items from his restaurant kitchens and test drives wacky new flavor combinations at the Arlequin booth. In early summer his offerings include strawberry and tobacco-infused scones; in the fall he has beignets filled with maple-bacon cream. And here he offers a wonderfully inventive dessert based on fresh figs, one of California's finest—but fleeting—late summer fruits.

Quick & Easy

Eggplant Crostini

Although this recipe calls for a regular globe eggplant, if you see baby eggplants or other fresh seasonal varieties, they will work just as well in this tangy appetizer.

1 (1-pound) eggplant

¼ cup extra-virgin olive oil, divided

Cooking spray

16 (½-ounce) slices multigrain baguette

½ teaspoon salt, divided

2½ tablespoons fresh lemon juice, divided

¼ cup plain whole-milk Greek yogurt

½ teaspoon freshly ground black pepper, divided

1 garlic clove, minced

1 cup arugula

1 cup red, orange, yellow, and green cherry tomatoes, quartered

2 tablespoons fresh mint leaves, torn

1 ounce Parmigiano-Reggiano cheese, shaved

1. Preheat grill to medium-high heat.

2. Slice eggplant into 1-inch-thick slices; brush both sides evenly with 1 tablespoon oil. Place eggplant in a single layer on a grill rack coated with cooking spray; grill 6 minutes on each side or until eggplant is tender. Brush both sides of bread slices evenly with 2 tablespoons oil. Place bread slices in a single layer on a grill rack coated with cooking spray; grill 1 minute on each side or until toasted.

3. Place eggplant, ¼ teaspoon salt, 1 tablespoon juice, and next 3 ingredients in a food processor; pulse until coarsely chopped. Spoon about 1 heaping tablespoon eggplant mixture on each bread slice.

4. Combine arugula, tomatoes, and mint in a bowl. Drizzle with remaining 1½ tablespoons juice and remaining 1 tablespoon oil. Sprinkle with remaining ¼ teaspoon salt; toss to coat. Divide salad mixture evenly among bread slices; top evenly with cheese. Yield: 8 servings (serving size: 2 crostini).

CALORIES 175; FAT 9.5g (sat 2.1g, mono 5.3g, poly 0.8g); PROTEIN 6.2g; CARB 17.7g; FIBER 5.9g; CHOL 4mg; IRON 1.2mg; SODIUM 330mg; CALC 195mg

WINE NOTE: Bourillon-D'orleans Vouvray Sec, Vieilles Vignes, Coulee d'Argent 2008 ($22), is a bright, crisp, medium-bodied chenin blanc from the Touraine region of the Loire Valley. Its racy backbone of lemongrass and straw has enough body and acid to stand up to the grill flavors and cut the creamy tartness of the yogurt.

CHICAGO

MARKET: Chicago Green City Market
CHEF: Koren Grieveson, Avec

The menu at the popular Chicago eatery Avec changes often, dictated by the best ingredients acclaimed chef Koren Grieveson buys from local farmers. Grieveson thinks locally, but seasons globally: She loves mixing and matching a variety of flavors on a single plate. So when she sees fresh summer tomatoes and piquant peppers at the market, she adds a dish like chorizo-stuffed Medjool dates with smoked bacon and tomato and piquillo pepper sauce to that night's menu.

Here Grieveson offers a Mediterranean-inspired appetizer that highlights fresh summer eggplant, made tangy with yogurt and fragrant with mint.

TA-DAH!

Faster, fresher no-cook entrées for the hottest days in summer.

Quick & Easy

Prosciutto, Peach, and Sweet Lettuce Salad

Serve this light main-course salad with a hunk of crusty baguette and a glass of chilled riesling. Choose ripe, juicy peaches, and leave the peel on for more texture. Ricotta salata is a milky, mild, slightly salty cheese that's easy to crumble; you can substitute feta or goat cheese.

2 tablespoons fresh lemon juice
2 teaspoons honey
¼ teaspoon freshly ground black pepper
⅛ teaspoon salt
2 tablespoons extra-virgin olive oil
1 tablespoon finely chopped fresh mint
1 (6.5-ounce) package sweet butter
   lettuce mix
2 large ripe peaches, cut into wedges
3 ounces very thin slices prosciutto, cut
   into 1-inch pieces
3 ounces ricotta salata cheese, divided
   into 4 equal pieces
2 tablespoons dry-roasted sunflower seed
   kernels
Small mint leaves (optional)

1. Combine first 4 ingredients, stirring with a whisk. Gradually drizzle in olive oil, stirring constantly with a whisk. Stir in chopped mint.
2. Combine lettuce mix and peaches in a large bowl. Drizzle lettuce mixture with dressing; toss gently to coat. Arrange about 2 cups salad in each of 4 bowls; top each serving with ¾ ounce prosciutto, 1 piece ricotta salata, and about 2 teaspoons sunflower seed kernels. Garnish with mint, if desired. Yield: 4 servings (serving size: 1 salad).

CALORIES 209; **FAT** 13.5g (sat 3.2g, mono 5.9g, poly 2.2g); **PROTEIN** 10.4g; **CARB** 14.3g; **FIBER** 2.1g; **CHOL** 26mg; **IRON** 1.4mg; **SODIUM** 530mg; **CALC** 87mg

WINE NOTE: With this salad, you need a wine that can take the sweetness of peaches and honey. Riesling's the ticket. It has a honeyed character built right in, and it adores cured pork. Apex Cellar's 2008 Riesling from Washington state's Columbia Valley (about $18) would be a great choice, with a spritz of lemon offsetting its off-dry stone fruit.

Quick & Easy

Tuna, Arugula, and Egg Salad with Pita Chips

If your budget allows, try a premium jarred tuna, like Ortiz, which is rich, firm, and meaty. Purchase precooked, peeled eggs from your supermarket.

3 tablespoons fresh lemon juice
2 tablespoons extra-virgin olive oil
1 teaspoon Dijon mustard
¼ teaspoon freshly ground black pepper
⅛ teaspoon salt
6 cups loosely packed baby arugula
1 cup halved cherry tomatoes
½ cup very thinly vertically sliced red onion
¼ cup chopped kalamata olives
1 tablespoon capers
2 hard-cooked large eggs, halved
1 (5-ounce) can light tuna in olive oil, drained
2 ounces plain pita chips

1. Combine first 5 ingredients, stirring with a whisk. Drizzle dressing over arugula; toss gently to coat. Divide arugula evenly among 4 bowls; top evenly with tomatoes and next 5 ingredients. Serve with pita chips. Yield: 4 servings (serving size: about 2 cups salad and ½ ounce pita chips).

CALORIES 269; **FAT** 17.1g (sat 2.7g, mono 10g, poly 3.2g); **PROTEIN** 13.7g; **CARB** 16.2g; **FIBER** 2.5g; **CHOL** 115mg; **IRON** 1.3mg; **SODIUM** 635mg; **CALC** 78mg

Quick & Easy • Kid Friendly

Chicken and Guacamole Tostadas

(pictured on page 259)

Smoked paprika gives the chicken rich, grill-like flavor—with no cooking. Look for tostada shells (fried, flat corn tortillas) near the flour and corn tortillas or in the Mexican food section of your grocery store. Serve with lime wedges.

1 ripe peeled avocado
1 cup plus 2 tablespoons finely chopped
   tomato, divided
3 tablespoons minced fresh onion, divided
3 tablespoons fresh lime juice, divided
½ teaspoon salt, divided
1 small garlic clove, minced
1 tablespoon chopped fresh cilantro
1 tablespoon minced seeded jalapeño pepper
2 cups shredded skinless, boneless rotisserie
   chicken breast
¼ teaspoon smoked paprika
8 (6-inch) corn tostada shells

1. Place avocado in a small bowl; mash with a fork. Stir in 2 tablespoons tomato, 1 tablespoon onion, 1 tablespoon juice, ¼ teaspoon salt, and garlic.
2. Combine remaining 1 cup tomato, remaining 2 tablespoons onion, 1 tablespoon juice, remaining ¼ teaspoon salt, cilantro, and jalapeño; toss well.
3. Combine chicken, remaining 1 tablespoon juice, and paprika; toss well to combine. Spread about 1 tablespoon guacamole over each tostada shell; top each with ¼ cup chicken mixture and about 2 tablespoons salsa. Yield: 4 servings (serving size: 2 tostadas).

CALORIES 345; **FAT** 15.4g (sat 3g, mono 6.9g, poly 4.5g); **PROTEIN** 25.4g; **CARB** 26.9g; **FIBER** 5.4g; **CHOL** 60mg; **IRON** 1.9mg; **SODIUM** 548mg; **CALC** 24mg

Avocado-Buttermilk Soup with Crab Salad

Simple orange-infused crabmeat floats atop a rich, creamy soup. If the soup seems a little too thick, add 1 to 2 tablespoons more buttermilk.

3/4 cup fat-free buttermilk
1/2 cup chopped fresh tomatillos
1/2 cup fat-free, lower-sodium chicken broth
3/8 teaspoon salt
2 ripe peeled avocados, pitted
1 serrano pepper, seeded
1 small garlic clove
2 tablespoons minced red bell pepper
1 tablespoon chopped fresh chives
1 teaspoon fresh lemon juice
1/2 teaspoon grated orange rind
8 ounces lump crabmeat, drained and shell pieces removed

1. Place first 7 ingredients in a blender; process until smooth.
2. Combine bell pepper and remaining ingredients; toss gently to combine. Spoon about 3/4 cup soup into each of 4 bowls; top each serving with about 1/3 cup crabmeat mixture. Yield: 4 servings.

CALORIES 252; FAT 16.3g (sat 2.6g, mono 9.8g, poly 2.3g); PROTEIN 16.9g; CARB 12.4g; FIBER 5.7g; CHOL 44mg; IRON 1.5mg; SODIUM 540mg; CALC 107mg

WINE NOTE: The fresh and healthful ingredients of this soup scream California—or, specifically, California chardonnay. The full body and supple texture of a well-balanced wine like Bogle Chardonnay, California 2008 ($11), permit it to partner with the creamy soup and sweet shellfish, while the wine's tart apple flavors and lively finish cleanse the palate for the next delicious bite.

Chicken and Glass Noodle Salad

To ensure the noodles get soft, soak them in the hottest water you can get from your tap. The salad is moderately spicy; reduce the chile paste by 1 teaspoon or omit it for a milder dish.

1 (3.75-ounce) package uncooked bean threads (cellophane noodles)
2 tablespoons rice vinegar
2 tablespoons fresh lime juice
1 1/2 tablespoons fish sauce
1 teaspoon sugar
2 teaspoons sambal oelek (ground fresh chile paste) or chile paste with garlic
2 cups shredded skinless, boneless rotisserie chicken breast
1/2 cup matchstick-cut or grated carrot
1/2 cup red bell pepper strips
1/3 cup thinly sliced shallots
2 tablespoons fresh cilantro leaves
1 tablespoon chopped fresh mint
1/2 cup chopped unsalted dry-roasted peanuts

1. Place noodles in a large bowl. Cover with very hot tap water, and let stand 15 minutes.
2. While noodles soak, combine vinegar and next 4 ingredients, stirring until sugar dissolves. Combine chicken and next 5 ingredients, tossing well.
3. Drain and rinse noodles with cold water; drain well, squeezing to remove excess water. Snip noodles several times with kitchen shears. Combine noodles and chicken mixture, tossing well to combine. Drizzle noodle mixture with vinegar mixture; toss well to coat. Top with peanuts. Yield: 4 servings (serving size: about 1 1/2 cups salad and 2 tablespoons peanuts).

CALORIES 346; FAT 11.7g (sat 2g, mono 5.4g, poly 3.5g); PROTEIN 27.1g; CARB 34.1g; FIBER 2.4g; CHOL 60mg; IRON 2.1mg; SODIUM 589mg; CALC 44mg

---

RECIPE HALL OF FAME
OUR FAVORITE HEIRLOOM TOMATO SALAD

This simple salad features the delightful contrast of icy, crunchy granita crowning juicy, room-temperature tomatoes.

Heirloom Tomato Salad

Granita:
1 tablespoon red wine vinegar
2 teaspoons extra-virgin olive oil
1/4 teaspoon kosher salt
8 ounces seeded peeled heirloom tomato
Salad:
4 assorted heirloom tomatoes, cut into 1/4-inch-thick slices (about 2 pounds)
1/2 teaspoon freshly ground black pepper
1/4 teaspoon kosher salt
Small basil leaves (optional)

1. To prepare granita, place first 4 ingredients in a blender or food processor; process until smooth. Place tomato mixture in an 8-inch square baking dish; cover and freeze until firm, stirring twice during first 2 hours. Remove mixture from freezer; scrape entire mixture with a fork until fluffy.
2. To prepare salad, divide tomato slices evenly among 6 plates. Sprinkle tomatoes evenly with pepper and 1/4 teaspoon salt. Top each serving with 2 tablespoons granita. Sprinkle with basil leaves, if desired. Yield: 6 servings.

CALORIES 49; FAT 1.9g (sat 0.3g, mono 1.3g, poly 0.3g); PROTEIN 1.7g; CARB 7.6g; FIBER 2.3g; CHOL 0mg; IRON 0.6mg; SODIUM 166mg; CALC 20mg

THE BRIGHT, LIGHT FLAVORS OF ASIA

The vibrant cooking of China and Southeast Asia perfectly complements the freshest produce in local markets.

Any traveler dazzled by the food markets of Thailand, Vietnam, or Hong Kong returns with a new appreciation of the value that the great Asian cuisines place on fresh produce. These are among the original plant-based diets, and cooking is oriented around the crunch, flavor, and earthy essence of greens and herbs. Sweet, salty, sour, and bitter notes are used not to mask but to highlight plant flavors. Steaming and stir-frying respect the texture of fresh food. Dishes can be bold and balanced, complex and restrained.

Which is why Asian cooking is summer cooking. Mustard greens, pea tendrils, bean sprouts, mint, Thai basil, and much more are now abundant at many farmers' markets, often grown by immigrant market-gardeners. Look for rice sticks, rice paper, lo mein, and cellophane noodles in Asian sections of big supermarkets or in specialty stores.

Quick & Easy
Cilantro Shrimp

Cilantro lends a pleasant grassy edge to a simple shrimp dish. Look for sambal oelek in the Asian section of supermarkets or specialty stores, or substitute hot sauce. Serve with steamed bok choy or sugar snap peas.

1 tablespoon dark sesame oil
3 cups (1-inch) slices green onions
2 tablespoons minced peeled fresh ginger
5 garlic cloves, minced
1 pound large shrimp, peeled and deveined
3½ tablespoons lower-sodium soy sauce
½ teaspoon sambal oelek (ground fresh chile paste) or hot sauce
2 cups chopped fresh cilantro
3 cups hot cooked brown rice

1. Heat a wok or large skillet over high heat; add oil to pan, swirling to coat. Add onions, ginger, and garlic to pan; stir-fry 1 minute. Add shrimp; stir-fry 2 minutes. Stir in soy sauce and sambal oelek; stir-fry 1 minute or until shrimp are done. Remove pan from heat, and add cilantro, stirring constantly until cilantro wilts. Serve over rice. Yield: 4 servings (serving size: 1 cup shrimp mixture and ¾ cup rice).

CALORIES 356; FAT 6.9g (sat 1.2g, mono 2.3g, poly 2.8g); PROTEIN 29g; CARB 44.3g; FIBER 5.1g; CHOL 172mg; IRON 5.1mg; SODIUM 653mg; CALC 143mg

Coconut Noodles with Scallops and Pea Tendrils
(pictured on page 262)

Pea tendrils, also called pea shoots, are the leafy, tender stem portion of young pea plants. We use small, delicate tendrils, which can be eaten raw. If the pea tendrils you choose are too firm, you might need to cook them with the cabbage mixture for up to 6 minutes. If you can't find tendrils, use mâche or spinach. Shrimp paste—made from salted, fermented ground shrimp—is a condiment common in Southeast Asian cooking. Look for it at Asian markets, or use anchovy paste instead. We use thin rice stick noodles in this dish. Use vermicelli if they are unavailable, and cook according to package directions.

1 (6.75-ounce) package uncooked rice sticks (rice-flour noodles)
½ cup chopped fresh cilantro
⅓ cup coarsely chopped peeled fresh lemongrass (about 2 stalks)
1 tablespoon grated peeled fresh ginger
2 teaspoons shrimp paste or anchovy paste
3 to 4 Thai chiles, halved and seeded
3 garlic cloves, peeled
2 shallots, peeled
1 tablespoon dark sesame oil
1 cup fat-free, lower-sodium chicken broth
2 tablespoons brown sugar
3½ tablespoons lower-sodium soy sauce
¼ teaspoon salt
1 (14-ounce) can light coconut milk
4 cups thinly sliced napa (Chinese) cabbage (1 small head)
1½ cups thinly sliced green onions, divided
1 cup fresh or frozen green peas, thawed
1 pound sea scallops, halved horizontally
4 cups pea tendrils (about ¼ pound), coarsely chopped

1. Cook noodles in boiling water 1½ minutes; drain. Rinse under cold water; drain and place in a large bowl.
2. Place cilantro and next 6 ingredients in a food processor; process until a paste forms. Heat a Dutch oven over medium-high heat; add oil to pan, swirling to coat. Add cilantro mixture to pan; sauté 5 minutes. Stir in broth, scraping pan to loosen browned bits. Stir in sugar and next 3 ingredients. Add cabbage and 1¼ cups onions to pan; cook 3 minutes, stirring occasionally. Stir in peas and scallops; cook 3 minutes or until scallops are done. Remove pan from heat; stir in noodles. Spoon 1¼ cups noodle mixture into each of 8 bowls; top each serving with 1½ teaspoons remaining onions and ½ cup pea tendrils. Yield: 8 servings.

CALORIES 250; FAT 5.1g (sat 2.8g, mono 0.8g, poly 1g); PROTEIN 15g; CARB 37.6g; FIBER 2.7g; CHOL 20mg; IRON 2.3mg; SODIUM 550mg; CALC 83mg

Honey-Wine Braised Chicken Thighs with Mustard Greens

Serve with rice or lo mein noodles.

2½ teaspoons dark sesame oil
6 skinless, boneless chicken thighs (about 2 pounds)
2 cups chopped red onion (about 1 large)
¾ cup fat-free, lower-sodium chicken broth
⅓ cup Shaoxing (Chinese rice wine) or dry sherry
2½ tablespoons minced peeled fresh ginger
3 tablespoons oyster sauce
2 tablespoons honey
4 garlic cloves, minced
1½ pounds mustard greens, stems removed and coarsely chopped
1 tablespoon sesame seeds, toasted

1. Preheat oven to 350°.
2. Heat a large Dutch oven over high heat; add oil to pan, swirling to coat. Add chicken; cook 4 minutes on each side or until browned. Add onion; stir-fry 4 minutes. Reduce heat; add broth and Shaoxing, scraping pan to loosen browned bits. Stir in ginger and next 3 ingredients. Cover and bake at 350° for 30 minutes.
3. Remove from oven. Shred chicken with 2 forks; return to pan. Place pan over medium-low heat. Add half of greens to pan; cover. Cook 5 minutes or until greens wilt; stir well. Repeat procedure with remaining greens. Cook mixture, covered, 15 minutes. Spoon 1 cup chicken mixture into each of 6 bowls; sprinkle each serving with ½ teaspoon sesame seeds. Yield: 6 servings.

CALORIES 327; **FAT** 14.4g (sat 3.4g, mono 5.3g, poly 3.7g); **PROTEIN** 33.4g; **CARB** 13.5g; **FIBER** 0.7g; **CHOL** 101mg; **IRON** 3.8mg; **SODIUM** 281mg; **CALC** 214mg

---

Quick & Easy

Lime Shrimp Salad with Bean Sprouts and Thai Basil

Salad:
2 cups fresh bean sprouts
2 cups thinly sliced napa (Chinese) cabbage
1 cup diced fresh pineapple
¾ cup shredded carrot (about 1 large)
½ cup coarsely chopped fresh mint leaves
¼ cup coarsely chopped fresh Thai basil leaves
5 cups water
¾ pound medium shrimp, peeled and deveined
Dressing:
1 tablespoon brown sugar
3 tablespoons fresh lime juice (about 1 lime)
2 tablespoons fish sauce
2 garlic cloves, minced
2 Thai chiles, seeded and minced
¾ cup chopped unsalted, dry-roasted peanuts
Lime wedges (optional)

1. To prepare salad, combine first 6 ingredients in a large bowl.
2. Bring 5 cups water to a boil in a large saucepan. Add shrimp to pan; reduce heat, and simmer 2 minutes or until done. Drain and rinse shrimp under cold water; drain well. Cut shrimp in half lengthwise; add shrimp to sprouts mixture, tossing to combine.
3. To prepare dressing, combine sugar and next 4 ingredients in a small bowl, stirring with a whisk until sugar dissolves. Pour dressing over salad, tossing to coat. Sprinkle with peanuts. Serve with lime wedges, if desired. Yield: 6 servings (serving size: 1 cup shrimp salad and 2 tablespoons peanuts).

CALORIES 221; **FAT** 10.3g (sat 1.5g, mono 4.7g, poly 3.3g); **PROTEIN** 18.3g; **CARB** 16.5g; **FIBER** 3.3g; **CHOL** 86mg; **IRON** 2.6mg; **SODIUM** 565mg; **CALC** 82mg

---

Make Ahead

Asian-Style Veggie Rolls

Mint and cilantro give the vegetable mixture bright taste. For a milder dipping sauce, seed the Thai chile pepper. Allow the sauce to stand for about 30 minutes before serving so the flavors can meld.

Rolls:
8 (8-inch) round sheets rice paper
2 cups thinly sliced Bibb lettuce leaves (about 4 large)
2 cups cooked bean threads (cellophane noodles)
1 cup fresh bean sprouts
1 cup shredded carrot (about 1 large)
½ cup coarsely chopped fresh mint
½ cup fresh cilantro leaves
¼ cup thinly sliced green onions
Sauce:
1 tablespoon sugar
3 tablespoons fresh lime juice (about 1 lime)
3 tablespoons water
2 tablespoons fish sauce
1 garlic clove, minced
1 Thai chile, thinly sliced

1. To prepare rolls, add hot water to a large, shallow dish to a depth of 1 inch. Place 1 rice paper sheet in dish, and let stand 30 seconds or just until soft. Place sheet on a flat surface. Arrange ¼ cup lettuce over half of sheet, leaving a ½-inch border. Top with ¼ cup bean threads, 2 tablespoons sprouts, 2 tablespoons carrot, 1 tablespoon mint, 1 tablespoon cilantro leaves, and 1½ teaspoons green onions. Folding sides of sheet over filling and starting with filled side, roll up jelly-roll fashion. Gently press seam to seal. Place roll, seam side down, on a serving platter (cover to keep from drying). Repeat procedure with remaining roll ingredients.
2. To prepare sauce, combine sugar and remaining ingredients in a small bowl, stirring with a whisk until sugar dissolves. Serve sauce with rolls. Yield: 8 servings (serving size: 1 roll and about 2 teaspoons sauce).

CALORIES 83; **FAT** 0.3g (sat 0g, mono 0g, poly 0.1g); **PROTEIN** 2.3g; **CARB** 18.5g; **FIBER** 1.1g; **CHOL** 0mg; **IRON** 0.7mg; **SODIUM** 371mg; **CALC** 22mg

Make Ahead
Sticky Rice Balls with Sausage and Dried Shrimp

This traditional Asian snack food would make a great party nibble. Also known as sticky or sweet rice, glutinous rice is the key to binding the elements together. Find it, along with dried baby shrimp and Chinese sausage, in Asian markets.

Rice Balls:
2 cups uncooked short-grain glutinous rice
4 cups water, divided
1/3 cup dried baby shrimp
1 (1/2-ounce) Chinese sausage link
2 1/2 teaspoons dark sesame oil, divided
3/4 cup thinly sliced green onions
4 garlic cloves, minced
1 (8-ounce) can sliced bamboo shoots, drained and coarsely chopped
1 tablespoon lower-sodium soy sauce
1 teaspoon fish sauce
1/2 teaspoon granulated sugar
1/4 teaspoon freshly ground black pepper
1 cup coarsely chopped fresh cilantro
Sauce:
1/3 cup lower-sodium soy sauce
2 tablespoons water
2 teaspoons brown sugar
1 teaspoon sesame seeds, toasted
1/2 teaspoons dark sesame oil
1/2 teaspoon chili garlic sauce (such as Lee Kum Kee)

1. To prepare rice balls, place rice in a sieve. Rinse with cold water; drain. Bring 3 cups water to a boil in a saucepan; add rice to pan. Cover, reduce heat, and simmer 20 minutes or until liquid is absorbed. Remove from heat; let stand, covered, 10 minutes. Place rice in a large bowl; cool to room temperature. **2.** Bring remaining 1 cup water to a boil in a small saucepan; add shrimp to pan. Reduce heat, and simmer 20 minutes. Drain well; finely chop shrimp. **3.** Steam sausage, covered, 15 minutes or until thoroughly heated. Cool slightly; finely chop. Heat 2 teaspoons oil in a medium nonstick skillet over medium heat. Add onions and garlic; cook 1 minute, stirring frequently. Add

shrimp, sausage, and bamboo shoots; cook 1 minute. Stir in 1 tablespoon soy sauce and next 3 ingredients. Add remaining 1/2 teaspoon oil, shrimp mixture, and cilantro to rice, stirring gently to combine. Roll rice into 36 (1-inch) balls. Arrange balls in a single layer on a baking sheet; cover and chill 2 hours. **4.** To prepare sauce, combine 1/3 cup soy sauce and remaining ingredients in a small bowl; stir with a whisk. Serve rice balls at room temperature with sauce. Yield: 12 servings (serving size: 3 balls and 2 teaspoons sauce).

CALORIES 150; **FAT** 2.3g (sat 0.5g, mono 0.8g, poly 0.8g); **PROTEIN** 3.9g; **CARB** 28g; **FIBER** 1.2g; **CHOL** 5mg; **IRON** 1mg; **SODIUM** 343mg; **CALC** 16mg

FROM OUR NEW COOKBOOK

Cooking Light First Foods: Baby Steps to a Lifetime of Healthy Eating has more than 100 simple, nutritious recipes for babies, toddlers, and their moms.

Quick & Easy • Make Ahead Kid Friendly
Pureed Apples

For 4- to 9-month-olds. *Choose Gala, Golden Delicious, Rome, or Pink Lady apples. They are sweeter and less acidic than apples such as Granny Smiths.*

4 apples (about 2 pounds), peeled, cored, and quartered

1. Place apples in a vegetable steamer. Steam, covered, 12 minutes or until very tender. **2.** Place apples in a food processor; process until smooth. Yield: 2 cups or 8 (1/4-cup) servings.

CALORIES 46; **FAT** 0.1g (sat 0g, mono 0g, poly 0.1g); **PROTEIN** 0.3g; **CARB** 12.3g; **FIBER** 1.3g; **CHOL** 0mg; **IRON** 0.1mg; **SODIUM** 0mg; **CALC** 5mg

Make Ahead • Freezable • Kid Friendly
Blueberry Oatmeal Muffins

For 12- to 18-month-olds. *Tossing frozen blueberries with flour before adding them to the batter keeps them from turning the batter purple while they bake. If you use fresh blueberries, skip that step. Serve 1/2 to 1 cooled muffin to your child.*

1 2/3 cups quick-cooking oats
3 ounces all-purpose flour (about 2/3 cup)
2.33 ounces whole-wheat flour (about 1/2 cup)
3/4 cup packed light brown sugar
2 teaspoons ground cinnamon
1 teaspoon baking powder
1 teaspoon baking soda
3/4 teaspoon salt
1 1/2 cups low-fat buttermilk
1/4 cup canola oil
2 teaspoons grated lemon rind
2 large eggs
2 cups frozen blueberries
2 tablespoons all-purpose flour
Cooking spray
2 tablespoons granulated sugar

1. Preheat oven to 400°. **2.** Place oats in a food processor; pulse 5 to 6 times or until oats resemble coarse meal. Place in a large bowl. **3.** Weigh or lightly spoon flours into dry measuring cups; level with a knife. Add flours and next 5 ingredients to oats; stir well. Make a well in center of mixture. **4.** Combine buttermilk and next 3 ingredients. Add to flour mixture; stir just until moist. **5.** Toss berries with 2 tablespoons flour, and gently fold into batter. Spoon batter into 16 muffin cups coated with cooking spray; sprinkle 2 tablespoons granulated sugar evenly over batter. Bake at 400° for 20 minutes or until muffins spring back when touched lightly in center. Remove from pans immediately; place on a wire rack. Yield: 16 adult servings (serving size: 1 muffin).

CALORIES 190; **FAT** 5g (sat 0.6g, mono 2.4g, poly 1.2g); **PROTEIN** 4.2g; **CARB** 33.3g; **FIBER** 2.4g; **CHOL** 23mg; **IRON** 1.6mg; **SODIUM** 248mg; **CALC** 74mg

BREAKFAST, LUNCH, AND DINNER IN... SAN FRANCISCO

Many cities aspire to be "the new San Francisco," foodwise, and from towns like Portland to Charleston the progress is amazing. Americans are eating more and more the way San Francisco residents eat, singing the tune of local, seasonal, and sustainable ingredients first sung more than 35 years ago by Bay Area organic farmers, ranchers, and chefs.

But when it comes to culinary innovation, the new San Francisco is ... San Francisco. Chefs here have been thinking way beyond the New American basics of grass-fed meat and organic vegetables, putting a worldly, streetwise spin on farm-to-table menus, and cooking from an ever-growing catalog of heirloom produce.

San Francisco was not immune to the financial crash despite its high-tech economy, and when the downturn dried up some dining dollars, chefs innovated: Fine dining came down to earth. Superfancy tasting menus gave way to simpler meals based on the ultrafresh California produce delivered daily to the area's farmers' markets (of which there are at least 20 and counting, according to the Center for Urban Education About Sustainable Agriculture).

Berkeley resident Michael Pollan's urging to eat "food your great-great-grandmother would have recognized as food" may seem like a call for old-fashioned, traditional American comfort food. But in San Francisco, where more than one out of three residents were born overseas, your great-great-grandmother may have been from Sichuan, Bangalore, or La Paz, and comfort food may mean anything from pho to goat meat tacos to gnocchi.

Here, global flavors have been woven into the local diet for generations. "During this recession, we're all getting back to our culinary roots, and in San Francisco, that means soul food from Mexico, Asia, and Europe—all those cuisines have been in San Francisco since the Gold Rush 160 years ago," explains Sarah Sung of the popular local trend-spotting blog UrbanDaddy.com. "We've grown up with tacos and kimchi for generations now, so that's our comfort food as much as pizza or mac 'n cheese."

And this just may be the key to San Francisco's edge: the combination of global influences in a temperate, gardenlike place.

So as the rest of America catches on to the locavore wave, San Francisco keeps on cooking. Today, its food scene seems more grounded than ever, serving responsible, good food at reasonable prices, impressing a demanding crowd of foodies—and their worldly grandmas.

VEGETABLES HAVE MOVED TO THE CENTER OF THE PLATE FOR MANY BAY AREA CHEFS.

Breakfast

Spinach, Green Onion, and Smoked Gouda Quiche

Born in Vietnam and raised in San Francisco's Chinatown, 2010 James Beard Outstanding Chef nominee Charles Phan combines California produce, classical technique, and Asian menu favorites at his fusion flagship Slanted Door (slanteddoor.com) and downtown dim sum phenomenon Heaven's Dog (heavensdog.com). Now Phan is taking on breakfast, serving hearty dishes like stuffed steamed buns and the spinach-packed quiche that inspired our recipe at Out the Door (outthedoors.com), his industrial Zen storefront eatery on the border of Pacific Heights and Japantown. We like the creamy, custardy consistency of this quiche when it's baked for 35 minutes. If you prefer a firmer texture, bake an additional 5 minutes.

Crust:
6 tablespoons butter, softened
2 tablespoons 1% low-fat milk
¼ teaspoon salt
1 large egg yolk
5.6 ounces all-purpose flour (about 1¼ cups)

Filling:
1 tablespoon extra-virgin olive oil
½ cup thinly sliced green onions
3 cups fresh baby spinach leaves
1 cup 1% low-fat milk
¾ cup (3 ounces) grated smoked Gouda cheese
¾ teaspoon salt
Dash of grated nutmeg
3 large eggs

1. To prepare crust, place butter in a large bowl; beat with a mixer at medium speed until light and fluffy. Combine milk, salt, and egg yolk in a small bowl; stir well with a whisk. Add milk mixture to butter, 1 tablespoon at a time, beating well after each addition. Add flour; beat just until combined. Press mixture into a 4-inch circle on plastic wrap; cover. Chill 1 hour.
2. Preheat oven to 350°.
3. Unwrap and place chilled dough on a lightly floured surface. Roll dough into a 10-inch circle. Fit dough into a 9-inch pie plate. Freeze 15 minutes.

Bake at 350° for 25 minutes or until lightly browned. Cool.

4. To prepare filling, heat oil in a large skillet over medium-high heat. Add onions; sauté 5 minutes or until tender. Add spinach; sauté 2 minutes.

5. Combine 1 cup milk and remaining ingredients in a bowl; stir well with a whisk. Stir in spinach mixture. Pour filling into crust. Bake at 350° for 35 minutes. Cut into 10 wedges. Yield: 10 servings (serving size: 1 wedge).

CALORIES 205; FAT 12.9g (sat 6.8g, mono 4.3g, poly 0.8g); PROTEIN 7.3g; CARB 15.4g; FIBER 1.1g; CHOL 113mg; IRON 1.5mg; SODIUM 405mg; CALC 120mg

Lunch

Open-Faced Roast Beef Sandwiches with Braised Cabbage Slaw and Russian Dressing

Chef Dennis Leary is bringing back the long-lost lunch break with The Sentinel (thesentinelsf.com), a converted cigar shop with ceviche specials and sandwiches made with pasture-raised roast beef and housemade Russian dressing. To keep flavors authentic and the line moving, sandwiches are served with condiments already on them. Not that you'd want any substitutions, anyway: The lamb meatball sandwich comes hot from the oven and slathered in thick, minty tomato sauce. Low-sodium roast beef keeps sodium levels in check for this hearty sandwich.

1 tablespoon olive oil
1 cup thinly sliced onion
1½ cups thinly sliced peeled Fuji apple
5 cups thinly sliced green cabbage
¼ cup water
2 teaspoons white wine vinegar
¼ teaspoon caraway seeds, crushed
¼ teaspoon salt
2 tablespoons chopped fresh parsley
2 tablespoons plain 2% reduced-fat Greek yogurt
1½ tablespoons canola mayonnaise
1 tablespoon prepared horseradish
1 tablespoon ketchup
1 teaspoon stone-ground mustard
½ teaspoon freshly ground black pepper
½ teaspoon fresh lemon juice

½ teaspoon Worcestershire sauce
¼ teaspoon salt
¼ teaspoon sweet paprika
Dash of ground red pepper
1 pound thinly sliced low-sodium deli roast beef
6 (1-ounce) slices rye bread, lightly toasted

1. Heat oil in a large skillet over medium heat. Add onion to pan; cook 10 minutes or until golden, stirring occasionally. Add apple; cook 1 minute. Add cabbage and next 3 ingredients; cover and cook 10 minutes or until cabbage is crisp-tender, stirring occasionally. Uncover and add ¼ teaspoon salt; cook 6 minutes or until liquid evaporates. Remove from heat; stir in parsley.

2. Combine yogurt and next 10 ingredients in a small bowl; stir well with a whisk.

3. Divide roast beef evenly among rye toasts; top each serving with ⅔ cup slaw. Drizzle about 1 tablespoon dressing over cabbage. Yield: 6 servings (serving size: 1 open-faced sandwich).

CALORIES 286; FAT 8.6g (sat 1.7g, mono 2.3g, poly 0.7g); PROTEIN 23.8g; CARB 27.8g; FIBER 4g; CHOL 41mg; IRON 3.3mg; SODIUM 639mg; CALC 95mg

Dinner

Grilled Lamb Chops with Roasted Summer Squash and Chimichurri

The sunny flavors at Frances (www.frances-sf.com) are clearly California-grown, but the precise balance of complementary tastes and textures reveals Chef Melissa Perello's classical training: Velvety gnocchi made from local Bellwether Farms ricotta are topped with perfectly crisp rounds of Broccolini and chunky breadcrumbs tossed in warm olive oil until golden and crunchy. Being tucked away on a quiet, tree-lined neighborhood street not far from Wine Country has obvious advantages: an unusually good selection of Sonoma wines by the glass, and a citrusy house white produced especially for Frances, served from a tap, much like beer. A quick blanching in boiling water mellows the garlic slightly.

2 cups water
2 garlic cloves, peeled
½ cup fresh flat-leaf parsley leaves
3 tablespoons extra-virgin olive oil, divided
1½ tablespoons coarsely chopped shallots
1 teaspoon fresh oregano leaves
1½ teaspoons sherry vinegar
1½ teaspoons fresh lemon juice
Dash of crushed red pepper
1 teaspoon salt, divided
1 teaspoon freshly ground black pepper, divided
3 medium yellow squash, cut lengthwise into ¼-inch-thick slices (about ¾ pound)
3 medium zucchini, cut crosswise into ¼-inch-thick slices (about ¾ pound)
6 (5-ounce) lamb loin chops, trimmed (about 1 inch thick)
Cooking spray

1. Bring 2 cups water to a boil in a small saucepan. Add garlic to pan; reduce heat, and simmer 3 minutes. Remove garlic from water; cool. Coarsely chop garlic.

2. Place garlic, parsley, 2 tablespoons oil, shallots, and next 4 ingredients in a food processor; process 1 minute or until almost smooth. Add ¼ teaspoon salt and ¼ teaspoon black pepper, and pulse 2 times.

3. Preheat oven to 450°.

4. Preheat grill to medium-high heat.

5. Combine squash, zucchini, and remaining 1 tablespoon oil in a bowl; toss well. Arrange squash and zucchini in a single layer on a baking sheet. Sprinkle with ¼ teaspoon salt and ¼ teaspoon black pepper. Bake at 450° for 16 minutes or until tender, turning after 8 minutes.

6. Lightly coat lamb with cooking spray. Sprinkle with remaining ½ teaspoon salt and remaining ½ teaspoon black pepper. Place lamb on grill rack coated with cooking spray; grill 5 minutes on each side or until desired degree of doneness. Divide squash and zucchini evenly among 6 plates. Top each serving with 1 lamb chop and 1½ teaspoons parsley puree. Yield: 6 servings.

CALORIES 288; FAT 15.5g (sat 4.4g, mono 8.4g, poly 1.5g); PROTEIN 30.9g; CARB 5.8g; FIBER 2.1g; CHOL 90mg; IRON 3.5mg; SODIUM 466mg; CALC 47mg

THE GREAT 1-COOLER, 1-WEEKEND GETAWAY

Five fun meals for four people. Easy to pack, easy to cook.

Here's the thing about cooking on vacation: You're on vacation. Yes, cooking is a pleasure, but so is a nice nap on a deck chair. The perfect getaway allows you to fit both in.

We combined a little bit of make-ahead planning with some double-duty ingredients to build a menu of easy, straightforward meals that feed four deliciously and healthfully—from Friday night cocktails and dinner to Sunday brunch—without ever resorting to boring standbys like cereal, cold-cut sandwiches, and chips.

How do you get all this food to wherever you're going? That's the easy part: All the cold items you'll need fit into a single large cooler. (Yes, we measured it.) Everything else fits in a grocery tote or two. And for the most part, you'll use every ingredient you bring. That Sunday afternoon needs to stretch as long as it possibly can; there's no need to waste a single minute of it repacking a bunch of leftovers.

MAKE AHEAD

Make Ahead • Freezable • Kid Friendly
Citrus Shortcake

Bake this lightly sweetened, sturdy cake-style shortcake in a square pan to use for both weekend desserts. You'll only need seven of the squares, so freeze the remaining two for another use (or go ahead and pack them; consider them secret snacks for the cook).

3/4 cup sugar
1/4 cup butter, softened
2 large eggs
1 tablespoon grated orange rind
1 tablespoon fresh orange juice
4.5 ounces all-purpose flour (about 1 cup)
2 tablespoons yellow cornmeal
3/4 teaspoon baking powder
1/2 teaspoon baking soda
1/4 teaspoon salt
2/3 cup low-fat buttermilk
Cooking spray

1. Preheat oven to 350°.
2. Place sugar and butter in a large bowl; beat with a mixer at medium speed until well blended (about 5 minutes). Add eggs, 1 at a time, beating well after each addition. Add rind and juice; beat well. Weigh or lightly spoon flour into a dry measuring cup; level with a knife. Combine flour and next 4 ingredients, stirring well with a whisk. Add flour mixture and buttermilk alternately to butter mixture, beginning and ending with flour mixture; mix after each addition.
3. Spoon batter into a 9-inch square metal baking pan coated with cooking spray. Bake at 350° for 25 minutes or until a wooden pick inserted in center comes out clean. Cool cake in pan 10 minutes on a wire rack; remove from pan. Cool completely on wire rack.
4. Cut cake into 9 squares. Reserve 4 squares for Brandied Peach Shortcakes and 3 squares for Mixed Berry Trifles; freeze remaining 2 squares for another use. Yield: 9 servings (serving size: 1 square).

CALORIES 195; **FAT** 6.5g (sat 3.7g, mono 1.7g, poly 0.4g); **PROTEIN** 3.8g; **CARB** 30.8g; **FIBER** 0.5g; **CHOL** 61mg; **IRON** 1mg; **SODIUM** 248mg; **CALC** 52mg

Make Ahead
Sweet Chipotle Snack Mix

Have this addictive mix on hand for nibbling all weekend (we also use some in a salad on Saturday). Ground chipotle pepper and chili spices combine with sugar to coat this three-part combo of pepitas (pumpkinseeds), almonds, and cashews. Make it ahead of time, and bring with you.

1/4 cup sugar
1 teaspoon salt
1 teaspoon ground chipotle chile pepper
1/2 teaspoon ground cumin
1/2 teaspoon dried oregano
1/2 teaspoon chili powder
1 large egg white
1 cup slivered almonds
1 cup unsalted cashews
1 cup unsalted pumpkinseed kernels

1. Preheat oven to 325°.
2. Combine first 6 ingredients in a small bowl; stir with a whisk.
3. Place egg white in a large bowl; stir with a whisk until foamy. Add almonds, cashews, and pumpkinseeds; toss well to coat. Sprinkle with spice mixture; toss well to coat. Spread nuts in an even layer on a baking sheet lined with parchment paper. Bake at 325° for 15 minutes, stirring once. Turn oven off. Remove pan from oven; stir snack mix. Immediately return pan to oven for an additional 15 minutes (leave oven off). Remove pan from oven and place on a wire rack; cool completely. Store snack mix in an airtight container for up to 2 weeks. Yield: about 3½ cups (serving size: 3 tablespoons).

CALORIES 130; **FAT** 9.7g (sat 1.4g, mono 5.8g, poly 2g); **PROTEIN** 4.5g; **CARB** 7.3g; **FIBER** 1.1g; **CHOL** 0mg; **IRON** 1.1mg; **SODIUM** 175mg; **CALC** 23mg

WEEKEND GETAWAY GUIDE

WEEKEND MENU

Cocktails & Dinner

(Friday night)
Daiquiri, barbecue chicken sliders with corn and slaw, and shortcakes
Recipes on pages 216 and 217

Quick & Easy Breakfast

(Saturday morning)
Orange french toast and berry smoothie
Recipes on page 217

Hearty, Healthy Lunch

(Saturday afternoon)
Grilled vegetable and goat cheese salad
Recipe on page 217

Steak & Potato Supper

(Saturday night)
Flat-iron steak with salad and potatoes and a berry trifle
Recipes on page 218

Steak & Eggs Brunch

(Sunday morning)
Steak hash and eggs with fruit salad and an iced latte
Recipes on page 219

PACK THESE IN A LARGE COOLER

PRODUCE

- 1 bunch parsley
- 1 (12-ounce) bag broccoli slaw
- 1 (5-ounce) package baby arugula
- 1 (5-ounce) package baby spinach
- 1 (16-ounce) container strawberries
- 2 (5-ounce) containers blackberries
- 1 lime
- 1 lemon
- 4 peaches
- 3 large oranges
- 4 ears of corn
- 1 large red bell pepper
- 2 pints grape tomatoes

CONDIMENTS

- Dijon mustard* (1/3 cup)
- Orange marmalade* (1/2 cup)

DAIRY & EGGS

- 1 stick butter*
- 1 quart plain fat-free Greek yogurt
- 1 quart 2% reduced-fat milk (3 1/2 cups used in recipes—use other 1/2 cup for coffee)
- 1 (4-ounce) log goat cheese
- 6 large eggs

MEAT

- 1 1/2 pounds skinless, boneless chicken thighs
- 2 (12-ounce) flat-iron steaks

BAG THE REST

PRODUCE

- 1 honeydew melon
- 5 kiwifruit
- 1 banana
- 1 large red onion
- 1 (1-pound) eggplant
- 2 1/2 pounds fingerling potatoes

GROCERIES

- Sugar* (1/2 cup; more if desired for coffee)
- Salt*
- Black pepper*
- Sherry vinegar* (1/2 cup)
- Honey* (1/3 cup)
- Cooking spray
- Coffee*
- Extra-virgin olive oil* (6 tablespoons)
- Ground red pepper* (optional)
- Ground cinnamon* (1/2 teaspoon; more if desired for sprinkling on coffee)
- 2 cinnamon sticks*
- Espresso powder*
- Garlic salt*
- Ground cumin*
- Dried oregano*
- Chili powder*

BAKERY

- 1 (12-ounce) ciabatta loaf
- 8 pull-apart dinner rolls

ALCOHOL

- 1 bottle red wine
- 1 (50-milliliter) bottle brandy
- 1 (50-milliliter) bottle Grand Marnier
- 1 half-pint light rum

*To save space, pack the amount specified rather than the whole jar, box, or bag.

6 SECRETS OF A WELL-PACKED COOLER

Cool the cooler: If yours is stored in a hot garage or attic, bring it inside overnight so it can cool off before you start packing it.

Fill it all the way up: A half-empty cooler is half full of room-temperature air, which means the ice inside it will melt faster.

Use solid ice: Solid ice melts slower than cubed or crushed. If you can't find solid blocks, use reusable gel-filled ice packs. Line the bottom of the cooler, then pack food on top, adding cubed or crushed ice (in bags) to fill gaps.

Pack foods in order: Raw meats, fish, and poultry belong on the bottom to avoid contamination. Seal them in plastic bags.

Keep it shut: Use a separate cooler to pack drinks and snacks for the trip.

Insulate it: Stow the cooler in the trunk, away from light, and put a blanket or sleeping bag around it for extra insulation.

FRIDAY DINNER

Make Ahead
Honeydew-Kiwi Daiquiris

A pitcher of slushy daiquiris is a great way to start the weekend. You'll use about half of the melon for this recipe and the rest in Sunday's fruit salad. If you don't think your rental place will have a blender, whir these up before you leave town, and freeze overnight in a zip-top plastic freezer bag. Thaw for a few minutes before serving (knead the bag to break up big pieces). If you brought extra orange liqueur, add a splash to the mix for more flavor.

3 cups chopped honeydew melon
4 kiwifruit, peeled and coarsely chopped
2 cups crushed ice
1/2 cup light rum
2 tablespoons sugar
1 teaspoon grated lime rind
2 tablespoons fresh lime juice

1. Arrange melon in a single layer on a baking sheet; freeze at least 30 minutes or until firm.
2. Place frozen melon and remaining ingredients in a blender; process mixture until smooth. Yield: 4 servings (serving size: about 1¼ cups).

CALORIES 183; FAT 0.6g (sat 0.1g, mono 0g, poly 0.3g); PROTEIN 1.6g; CARB 29.7g; FIBER 3.4g; CHOL 0mg; IRON 0.5mg; SODIUM 26mg; CALC 35mg

KICK THINGS OFF WITH BBQ SLIDERS, GRILLED CORN, AND PEACH SHORTCAKES. PERFECT.

Kid Friendly
Barbecue Chicken Sliders with Pickled Onions

Chicken thighs are dipped in Carolina-style barbecue sauce, a delicious vinegar-based mix.

1/4 cup thinly sliced red onion
3 tablespoons sherry vinegar, divided
1½ tablespoons honey, divided
2 tablespoons water
3 tablespoons Dijon mustard
3/4 teaspoon freshly ground black pepper, divided
1 tablespoon butter
1½ pounds skinless, boneless chicken thighs, trimmed
1/8 teaspoon salt
Cooking spray
8 (1.5-ounce) pull-apart dinner rolls (such as Sara Lee)

1. Preheat grill to medium-high heat.
2. Combine onion, 1 tablespoon vinegar, and 1½ teaspoons honey in a small bowl; toss well. Cover and refrigerate onion mixture at least 30 minutes.
3. Combine remaining 2 tablespoons vinegar, remaining 1 tablespoon honey, 2 tablespoons water, mustard, and 1/4 teaspoon pepper in a small saucepan over medium-low heat. Bring to a simmer (do not boil). Simmer 5 minutes; stir in butter. Remove from heat; keep warm.
4. Sprinkle chicken with remaining ½ teaspoon pepper and salt. Place on a grill rack coated with cooking spray; grill 4 minutes on each side or until done. Remove chicken from grill; cool slightly. Shred chicken into bite-sized pieces. Add chicken to saucepan with mustard mixture, and toss gently to coat.
5. Cut rolls in half crosswise. Place rolls, cut sides down, on grill; grill 1 minute or until toasted. Spoon about 1/3 cup chicken mixture over bottom half of each roll. Top each roll with about 1 teaspoon drained onion slices and top half of roll. Serve immediately. Yield: 4 servings (serving size: 2 sliders).

CALORIES 429; FAT 18.4g (sat 6g, mono 7.2g, poly 3.4g); PROTEIN 32.1g; CARB 31.9g; FIBER 1.8g; CHOL 108mg; IRON 3.2mg; SODIUM 569mg; CALC 82mg

Quick & Easy • Kid Friendly
Grilled Corn with Honey Butter

4 ears shucked corn
Cooking spray
1½ tablespoons butter, melted
1 tablespoon honey
1/8 teaspoon salt
1/8 teaspoon freshly ground black pepper
1/8 teaspoon ground red pepper (optional)

1. Preheat grill to medium-high heat.
2. Place corn on a grill rack coated with cooking spray; grill 8 minutes, turning frequently. Combine butter, honey, salt, black pepper, and red pepper, if desired; brush over corn. Yield: 4 servings (serving size: 1 ear).

CALORIES 131; FAT 5.3g (sat 2.9g, mono 1.4g, poly 0.7g); PROTEIN 3g; CARB 21.6g; FIBER 2.5g; CHOL 11mg; IRON 0.5mg; SODIUM 118mg; CALC 4mg

Brandied Peach Shortcakes

One small "airline bottle" of brandy is enough for this spirited dessert.

1/4 cup plain fat-free Greek yogurt
1 teaspoon sugar
1 (50-milliliter) bottle brandy, divided
1 tablespoon butter, melted
1 tablespoon honey
4 firm ripe peaches, halved and pitted
Cooking spray
4 Citrus Shortcake squares (page 214)

1. Preheat grill to medium-high heat.
2. Combine yogurt, sugar, and 1 teaspoon brandy. Cover and chill.
3. Combine remaining brandy, butter, and honey.
4. Place peach halves, cut sides down, on grill rack coated with cooking spray, and grill 2 minutes on each side or until grill marks appear. Remove peaches from grill; thinly slice and place in a bowl. Stir in honey mixture.
5. Split each Citrus Shortcake square in half, and spoon about 1¼ cups peach mixture over bottom half of each shortcake. Top with top half of

shortcake and 1 tablespoon yogurt mixture. Yield: 4 servings (serving size: 1 filled shortcake).

CALORIES 299; **FAT** 9.6g (sat 5.5g, mono 2.6g, poly 0.6g); **PROTEIN** 5.9g; **CARB** 46.1g; **FIBER** 2g; **CHOL** 69mg; **IRON** 1.2mg; **SODIUM** 273mg; **CALC** 69mg

Quick & Easy
Broccoli Slaw

¼ cup plain fat-free Greek yogurt
1 tablespoon fresh lemon juice
1 tablespoon extra-virgin olive oil
½ teaspoon sugar
½ teaspoon Dijon mustard
¼ teaspoon salt
¼ teaspoon freshly ground black pepper
¼ cup chopped fresh parsley
1 (12-ounce) package broccoli slaw

1. Combine first 7 ingredients in a large bowl; stir with a whisk. Add parsley and broccoli slaw; toss to coat. Yield: 4 servings (serving size: about 1 cup).

CALORIES 73; **FAT** 3.4g (sat 0.5g, mono 2.5g, poly 0.4g); **PROTEIN** 3.7g; **CARB** 6.4g; **FIBER** 2.6g; **CHOL** 0mg; **IRON** 0.8mg; **SODIUM** 188mg; **CALC** 30mg

SATURDAY BREAKFAST

Quick & Easy • Kid Friendly
Berry and Banana Smoothies

1 frozen sliced banana
½ cup fresh orange juice (about 1 large orange)
1 cup hulled strawberries
1 cup blackberries
1¾ cups plain fat-free Greek yogurt
1 tablespoon honey

1. Place all ingredients in a blender; process until smooth. Yield: 4 servings (serving size: about 1 cup).

CALORIES 138; **FAT** 0.4g (sat 0g, mono 0g, poly 0.2g); **PROTEIN** 9.8g; **CARB** 25.3g; **FIBER** 3.4g; **CHOL** 0mg; **IRON** 0.6mg; **SODIUM** 38mg; **CALC** 86mg

Quick & Easy • Kid Friendly
Ciabatta French Toast with Marmalade Drizzle

⅓ cup fresh orange juice
½ cup orange marmalade
½ cup 2% reduced-fat milk
½ teaspoon ground cinnamon
2 large eggs
8 (1-ounce) slices ciabatta bread
2 tablespoons butter

1. Place orange juice and marmalade in a small saucepan over medium heat; bring to a simmer. Remove from heat; keep warm.
2. Combine milk, cinnamon, and eggs in a shallow dish; stir with a whisk. Dip bread slices in egg mixture; let slices stand in egg mixture 20 seconds on each side.
3. Melt 1 tablespoon butter in a large nonstick skillet over medium-high heat. Place 4 bread slices in pan; cook 2 minutes on each side or until lightly browned. Remove from pan. Repeat procedure with remaining 1 tablespoon butter and 4 bread slices. Drizzle with marmalade syrup. Yield: 4 servings (serving size: 2 bread slices and about 3 tablespoons syrup).

CALORIES 360; **FAT** 11.3g (sat 5g, mono 4.5g, poly 0.8g); **PROTEIN** 9.4g; **CARB** 56.9g; **FIBER** 1.2g; **CHOL** 123mg; **IRON** 2.4mg; **SODIUM** 479mg; **CALC** 58mg

STURDY CIABATTA BREAD MAKES FOR GREAT FRENCH TOAST; YOU'LL USE THE REMAINING BREAD FOR LUNCH.

SATURDAY LUNCH

Grilled Vegetable and Goat Cheese Salad

1 (1-pound) eggplant, cut into ½-inch-thick slices
1 large red bell pepper, cut into 6 wedges
Cooking spray
½ teaspoon freshly ground black pepper, divided
4 (1-ounce) slices ciabatta bread
2 tablespoons sherry vinegar
1 tablespoon extra-virgin olive oil
½ teaspoon Dijon mustard
¼ teaspoon salt
2 cups arugula
1½ cups grape tomatoes, halved
1 (5-ounce) package fresh baby spinach
4 ounces goat cheese, cut into 4 slices
¼ cup Sweet Chipotle Snack Mix (page 214)

1. Preheat grill to medium-high heat.
2. Place eggplant and bell pepper on a grill rack coated with cooking spray; grill 4 minutes on each side or until tender. Place bell pepper wedges in a zip-top plastic bag; seal. Let stand 15 minutes. Peel bell pepper wedges. (Reserve 2 bell pepper wedges and 2 eggplant slices for Sunday's brunch.) Coarsely chop remaining bell pepper and remaining eggplant. Sprinkle with ¼ teaspoon black pepper.
3. Place bread slices on grill rack, and grill 2 minutes on each side or until golden brown.
4. Place remaining ¼ teaspoon black pepper, vinegar, and next 3 ingredients in a large bowl; stir well with a whisk. Add eggplant, bell pepper, arugula, tomatoes, and spinach; toss gently to combine. Arrange about 2½ cups salad on each of 4 plates; top each serving with 1 goat cheese slice and 1 tablespoon Sweet Chipotle Snack Mix. Serve each salad with 1 toast slice. Yield: 4 servings.

CALORIES 292; **FAT** 14.2g (sat 5.3g, mono 6.2g, poly 1.2g); **PROTEIN** 12.1g; **CARB** 32.5g; **FIBER** 7.6g; **CHOL** 13mg; **IRON** 3.5mg; **SODIUM** 584mg; **CALC** 110mg

SATURDAY DINNER

Chili-Espresso Rubbed Steaks with Warm Tomato Sauce

Because there is only one flat-iron steak per steer, it's a good idea to call ahead and order two steaks. Flank or tri-tip steaks make fine substitutes. You'll serve roughly two-thirds of the steak for dinner Saturday night and use the rest for Sunday brunch. If you don't have a mini chopper or blender, just dice the tomatoes and parsley by hand for a chunkier sauce.

2 teaspoons espresso powder
1 teaspoon garlic salt
1 teaspoon ground cumin
1 teaspoon dried oregano
1 teaspoon chili powder
1 teaspoon freshly ground black pepper
2 (12-ounce) flat-iron steaks
Cooking spray
1 cup grape tomatoes
2 tablespoons chopped fresh parsley
1 teaspoon extra-virgin olive oil
1 teaspoon sherry vinegar

1. Combine first 6 ingredients; stir well. Rub spice mixture evenly over both sides of steaks; cover and let stand at room temperature 30 minutes.
2. Preheat grill to medium-high heat.
3. Place steaks on a grill rack coated with cooking spray; grill 3 minutes on each side or until desired degree of doneness. Remove from grill; let stand 10 minutes.
4. Place tomatoes and remaining ingredients in a mini chopper or blender; process until coarsely chopped. Spoon tomato mixture into a microwave-safe bowl; microwave at HIGH 1 minute. Cut steaks diagonally across grain into thin slices. Place 3 ounces steak on each of 4 plates (roughly ⅔ of cooked meat). (Reserve remaining steak for Sunday brunch.) Top each serving with 2 tablespoons sauce. Yield: 4 servings.

CALORIES 216; **FAT** 12.3g (sat 4.5g, mono 5.4g, poly 0.6g); **PROTEIN** 21.9g; **CARB** 3.1g; **FIBER** 1.1g; **CHOL** 71mg; **IRON** 3.1mg; **SODIUM** 260mg; **CALC** 27mg

WINE NOTE: Coffee flavor in food can be a fabulous pairing point for some red wines. Cabernet sauvignon and syrah often have dark espresso flavors lurking around the edges. For Saturday's supper, though, you need a red with a little more bright acidity and juicy fruit than those two varieties bring on their own. Go for a blend of syrah and its common partner grenache: Bonny Doon Vineyard's Châteauneuf-du-Pape-styled 2006 Le Cigare Volant (California, $32), with spicy, toasty, earthy notes on one side and bright red fruit on the other.

Quick & Easy • Kid Friendly

Roasted Fingerling Potatoes with Dijon

Save half of the potatoes for Sunday's steak hash.

2½ pounds fingerling potatoes, cut in half lengthwise
2 tablespoons extra-virgin olive oil, divided
½ teaspoon salt
½ teaspoon freshly ground black pepper, divided
½ teaspoon Dijon mustard
3 tablespoons chopped fresh parsley

1. Preheat oven to 425°.
2. Place potatoes on a baking sheet. Drizzle potatoes with 1 tablespoon oil; sprinkle with salt and ¼ teaspoon pepper. Toss to coat. Bake at 425° for 30 minutes or until golden brown. Cool potatoes slightly.
3. Place remaining 1 tablespoon oil, remaining ¼ teaspoon pepper, and mustard in a large bowl; stir well with a whisk. Add half of roasted potatoes and parsley; toss gently to coat. (Reserve remaining potatoes for Sunday brunch.) Serve at room temperature. Yield: 4 servings (serving size: about 1 cup).

CALORIES 172; **FAT** 5.2g (sat 0.7g, mono 3.7g, poly 0.6g); **PROTEIN** 2.8g; **CARB** 29.4g; **FIBER** 2.9g; **CHOL** 0mg; **IRON** 1.8mg; **SODIUM** 173mg; **CALC** 16mg

Quick & Easy

Arugula Salad

1 tablespoon extra-virgin olive oil
1 tablespoon sherry vinegar
¼ teaspoon freshly ground black pepper
¼ teaspoon Dijon mustard
⅛ teaspoon salt
4 cups baby arugula
⅓ cup vertically sliced red onion

1. Combine first 5 ingredients in a large bowl; stir with a whisk. Add arugula and onion; toss well. Yield: 4 servings (serving size: about 1½ cups).

CALORIES 40; **FAT** 3.5g (sat 0.5g, mono 2.5g, poly 0.4g); **PROTEIN** 0.6g; **CARB** 1.7g; **FIBER** 0.5g; **CHOL** 0mg; **IRON** 0.4mg; **SODIUM** 82mg; **CALC** 35mg

Make Ahead • Kid Friendly

Mixed Berry Trifles

Any summer berries will work, and you can substitute other fruit liqueurs for the Grand Marnier. Reserve remaining liqueur for Sunday morning lattes.

3 Citrus Shortcake squares (page 214), each cut into 8 cubes
1¾ cups plain fat-free Greek yogurt
3 tablespoons sugar, divided
2 tablespoons Grand Marnier (orange liqueur), divided
½ teaspoon grated orange rind
1 cup strawberries, quartered
1 cup blackberries, halved

1. Preheat oven to 375°.
2. Place Citrus Shortcake cubes on a baking sheet lined with parchment paper. Bake at 375° for 10 minutes or until toasted, turning after 5 minutes. Cool completely on pan on a wire rack.
3. Combine yogurt, 2 tablespoons sugar, 1 tablespoon liqueur, and rind.
4. Combine strawberries, remaining 1 tablespoon sugar, and remaining 1 tablespoon liqueur in a medium bowl. Gently stir in blackberries.
5. Place 3 shortcake cubes in each of 4 (8-ounce) glasses or dessert bowls. Top each serving with about 1 tablespoon fruit mixture; top fruit mixture

with 1½ tablespoons yogurt mixture. Repeat layers, ending with yogurt. Serve immediately, or cover and refrigerate up to 1 hour. Yield: 4 servings (serving size: 1 trifle).

CALORIES 291; FAT 5.2g (sat 2.8g, mono 1.3g, poly 0.5g); PROTEIN 12.2g; CARB 45.5g; FIBER 3.1g; CHOL 46mg; IRON 1.1mg; SODIUM 223mg; CALC 123mg

SUNDAY BRUNCH

Make Ahead
Iced Mexican Latte

For this recipe, use the liqueur left over after making the trifles.

3 cups hot strong brewed coffee
2 (3-inch) cinnamon sticks
3 cups 2% reduced-fat milk
4⅛ teaspoons Grand Marnier (orange liqueur)

1. Combine coffee and cinnamon sticks; cover and steep 15 minutes. Discard cinnamon sticks. Stir in milk and liqueur; cover and refrigerate 1 hour or until thoroughly chilled. Serve over ice. Yield: 4 servings (serving size: 1½ cups).

CALORIES 111; FAT 3.6g (sat 2.2g, mono 1g, poly 0.1g); PROTEIN 6.3g; CARB 10.4g; FIBER 0g; CHOL 14mg; IRON 0.1mg; SODIUM 95mg; CALC 226mg

Steak Hash with Poached Eggs

Since the idea is to use up leftover steak and all the little bits of vegetables from your weekend getaway, don't worry if amounts don't match precisely.

1½ teaspoons extra-virgin olive oil
1 cup finely chopped red onion
1½ cups grape tomatoes, chopped
¼ cup chopped grilled eggplant (page 217)
¼ cup chopped roasted red bell pepper (page 217)
1¼ pounds Roasted Fingerling Potatoes (page 218), coarsely chopped
6 ounces grilled Chili-Espresso Rubbed Steak (page 218), chopped
⅜ teaspoon salt
½ teaspoon freshly ground black pepper, divided
1 tablespoon sherry vinegar
4 large eggs
3 tablespoons chopped fresh parsley

1. Heat oil in a large nonstick skillet over medium heat. Add onion; cook 6 minutes or until tender, stirring occasionally. Add tomatoes; cook 1 minute, stirring occasionally. Add eggplant and next 3 ingredients; cook 3 minutes or until heated. Stir in salt and ¼ teaspoon pepper. Keep steak mixture warm.
2. Add water to a large skillet, filling two-thirds full. Bring to a boil; reduce heat, and simmer. Add vinegar. Break eggs into pan; cook 3 minutes or until

desired degree of doneness. Carefully remove eggs from pan using a slotted spoon. Spoon about 1½ cups hash onto each of 4 plates; top each serving with 1 egg. Sprinkle evenly with remaining ¼ teaspoon pepper and parsley. Yield: 4 servings.

CALORIES 359; FAT 14.2g (sat 4.3g, mono 6.7g, poly 1.4g); PROTEIN 20.9g; CARB 37.7g; FIBER 5.3g; CHOL 247mg; IRON 4.4mg; SODIUM 583mg; CALC 73mg

Quick & Easy • Kid Friendly
Fresh Fruit Salad

Don't worry about exact measurements; you're using all of the remaining fruit for this salad.

2 tablespoons sugar
1 teaspoon grated orange rind
2 tablespoons fresh orange juice
3 cups cubed honeydew melon
1 cup strawberries, sliced
1 sliced peeled kiwifruit

1. Place first 3 ingredients in a large bowl; stir until sugar dissolves. Add honeydew, strawberries, and kiwifruit; toss gently to combine. Yield: 4 servings (serving size: about 1¼ cups).

CALORIES 99; FAT 0.4g (sat 0.1g, mono 0g, poly 0.2g); PROTEIN 1.2g; CARB 24.7g; FIBER 2.5g; CHOL 0mg; IRON 0.5mg; SODIUM 24mg; CALC 22mg

POACHED EGGS OVER LAST NIGHT'S ROASTED POTATOES ARE THE PERFECT SUNDAY WAKE-UP CALL. JUST ADD LATTES—ICED AND REFRESHING, WITH A LITTLE SPIKE.

FEARLESS FISH GRILLING

Enjoy restaurant-quality fish in the comfort of your backyard when you follow pointers from the pros.

There's a lot of buzz about the health benefits of eating fish: The American Heart Association recommends eating at least two servings a week. So it's more important than ever to expand your fish horizons, sampling a variety of sustainable species and cooking them in interesting ways. During the summer, the grill is a great tool to turn to. But let's face it: Grilling fish makes a lot of folks nervous since delicate fillets can stick and fall apart. Or worse, the fish can overcook, becoming dry and tough. In the following pages we share a few tips that will help you grill fish to perfection every time.

Kid Friendly

Striped Bass with Peach Salsa

2 cups water
1 tablespoon fine sea salt
2 teaspoons sugar
4 (6-ounce) striped bass fillets
Cooking spray
1 1/2 cups finely chopped peaches (about 2 medium)
2 tablespoons thinly sliced shallots
1 1/2 tablespoons fresh lemon juice
1 tablespoon extra-virgin olive oil
3/8 teaspoon table salt, divided
1/4 teaspoon black pepper
1 1/2 tablespoons torn small fresh mint leaves

1. Combine first 3 ingredients in a shallow dish, stirring until sea salt and sugar dissolve; add fish. Let stand 20 minutes. Drain; pat fish dry.
2. Prepare charcoal fire in a chimney starter; let coals burn 15 to 20 minutes or until flames die down. Carefully pour hot coals out of starter, and pile them onto one side of the grill. Coat grill grate with cooking spray; put grate in place over coals.
3. Combine peaches and next 3 ingredients in a medium bowl; stir in 1/8 teaspoon table salt. Sprinkle remaining

1/4 teaspoon table salt and pepper evenly over fish. Lightly coat fish with cooking spray. Place fish, skin sides down, over direct heat on grill rack coated with cooking spray; grill 2 minutes. Turn fish over and move over indirect heat; grill 12 minutes or until desired degree of doneness. Stir mint into peach mixture. Serve with fish. Yield: 4 servings (serving size: 1 fillet and about 1/3 cup salsa).

CALORIES 231; **FAT** 7.7g (sat 1.4g, mono 3.7g, poly 1.9g); **PROTEIN** 31.9g; **CARB** 8.1g; **FIBER** 0.8g; **CHOL** 140mg; **IRON** 1.8mg; **SODIUM** 514mg; **CALC** 31mg

Grilled Trout

2 cups water
1 tablespoon fine sea salt
2 teaspoons sugar
4 (7-ounce) dressed rainbow trout
Cooking spray
1/2 teaspoon table salt
1/4 teaspoon black pepper
2 (1-ounce) bunches fresh dill sprigs
2 medium limes, each thinly sliced

1. Combine first 3 ingredients in a shallow dish; add fish. Let stand 20 minutes. Drain.
2. Prepare charcoal fire in a chimney starter; let coals burn until flames die down. Pour hot coals out of starter;

pile on one side of grill. Coat grill grate with cooking spray; put grate in place over coals.
3. Sprinkle 1/2 teaspoon salt and pepper over fish flesh. Divide dill and lime slices evenly among fish cavities. Coat outside of fish with cooking spray. Place fish over direct heat, and grill 4 minutes. Turn over, and move to indirect heat. Grill 12 minutes or until done. Yield: 4 servings (serving size: 1 fish).

CALORIES 230; **FAT** 8.9g (sat 2.5g, mono 2.7g, poly 2.8g); **PROTEIN** 35g; **CARB** 0.3g; **FIBER** 0g; **CHOL** 105mg; **IRON** 0.6mg; **SODIUM** 553mg; **CALC** 132mg

Grilled Fresh Sardines

The average weight of a fresh sardine is 3 to 6 ounces, but they can grow up to about a pound. The number of servings and serving size will vary depending on the size of the fish you find.

1 teaspoon fennel seeds
1 teaspoon ground coriander
1 shallot, peeled and chopped
1 tablespoon olive oil
1/4 teaspoon kosher salt
12 (3-ounce) whole dressed sardines
Cooking spray

1. Place first 3 ingredients in a mini food processor; process until pureed. Add oil and salt to shallot mixture; pulse to combine. Place sardines in a shallow dish; rub inside and outside of fish evenly with shallot mixture. Cover and chill 3 hours.
2. Prepare charcoal fire in a chimney starter; let coals burn until flames die down. Pour hot coals out of starter, and pile on one side of grill. Coat grate with cooking spray; put grate in place.
3. Place sardines over direct heat, and grill 2 minutes on each side. Move fish over indirect heat, and grill 5 minutes or until desired degree of doneness. Yield: 4 servings (serving size: 3 fish).

CALORIES 143; **FAT** 7.6g (sat 1g, mono 3.9g, poly 2.3g); **PROTEIN** 12.7g; **CARB** 2.8g; **FIBER** 0.2g; **CHOL** 69mg; **IRON** 0.3mg; **SODIUM** 368mg; **CALC** 6mg

4 STEPS TO GRILLING FISH

1 PREPARE THE GRILL FOR INDIRECT GRILLING AND PREHEAT. To prepare a charcoal grill for indirect grilling, light the coals and let them burn until the flames die down. Then pile the hot coals off to one side of the grill. If you have a gas grill, preheat the entire grill to your desired temperature, and then shut off the heat on one side.

2 BRINE MOST FISH. Brining briefly before cooking helps fish stay moist on the grill, even if overcooked slightly. The brine is a mixture of water, sea salt, and a bit of sugar. There are a few exceptions. You don't need to brine fish like tuna that are usually not cooked beyond medium-rare. And oily fish, like sardines, are not as prone to drying out.

3 SEASON THE FISH. Great fish should have a fresh and bold flavor, so marinades are not really necessary. Stick to basic seasoning like salt, pepper, oil, and herbs. You can always add a little citrus and garlic, too, but be sure to let the fish shine.

4 GRILL IT. Make sure the grate is clean and dry; oil it and the fish lightly to prevent sticking. The fish should release easily when it's time to turn it over or remove it from the grill. If it's sticking, simply cook a bit longer, and the fish should release easily.

BEFORE YOU BUILD YOUR FIRE, MAKE SURE THE GRATE IS THOROUGHLY CLEAN.

Mahimahi with Bacon-Tomato Butter

Look for American mahimahi that were caught using the pole/troll method as this fishing practice has the least negative impact on the waters where they're caught, and it yields the freshest fish.

2 cups water
1 tablespoon fine sea salt
2 teaspoons sugar
4 (6-ounce) mahimahi fillets
Cooking spray
¼ teaspoon table salt, divided
1 slice center-cut bacon, finely chopped
1 garlic clove, thinly sliced
¼ teaspoon hot smoked paprika
2 plum tomatoes, seeded and diced
2 tablespoons butter

1. Combine first 3 ingredients in a shallow dish, stirring until sea salt and sugar dissolve; add fish. Let stand 20 minutes. Drain; pat dry.
2. Prepare charcoal fire in a chimney starter; let coals burn 15 to 20 minutes or until flames die down. Carefully pour hot coals out of starter, and pile them onto one side of the grill. Coat grill grate with cooking spray; put grate in place over coals.
3. Sprinkle ⅛ teaspoon table salt evenly over fish. Lightly coat fish with cooking spray. Place fish, skin sides down, over direct heat on grill rack coated with cooking spray; grill 2 minutes or until well marked. Turn fish over and move to indirect heat; grill 12 minutes or until desired degree of doneness.
4. Heat a small skillet over medium heat; add bacon to pan. Cook 5 minutes or until bacon is almost crisp, stirring occasionally. Add garlic; cook 2 minutes, stirring frequently. Add paprika, and cook 20 seconds, stirring constantly. Add tomatoes, and cook 3 minutes. Stir in butter. Remove from heat; stir in remaining ⅛ teaspoon table salt. Place 1 fillet on each of 4 plates; top each serving with about 2 tablespoons tomato mixture. Yield: 4 servings.

CALORIES 211; FAT 8g (sat 4.4g, mono 1.7g, poly 0.5g); PROTEIN 31.5g; CARB 1.9g; FIBER 0.4g; CHOL 137mg; IRON 2mg; SODIUM 561mg; CALC 31mg

GRILLED VEGGIES

Vegetables like asparagus and zucchini, cooked over an open flame, develop an intensity that seems to transform them.

Quick & Easy

Grilled Asparagus with Caper Vinaigrette

This side dish would pair well with a tomato and fresh mozzarella sandwich on grilled sourdough bread.

1½ pounds asparagus spears, trimmed
3 tablespoons extra-virgin olive oil, divided
½ teaspoon kosher salt, divided
Cooking spray
1 tablespoon red wine vinegar
½ teaspoon Dijon mustard
¼ teaspoon freshly ground black pepper
1 garlic clove, minced
2 teaspoons capers, coarsely chopped
¼ cup small fresh basil leaves

1. Preheat grill to medium-high heat.
2. Place asparagus in a shallow dish. Add 1 tablespoon oil and ¼ teaspoon salt, tossing well to coat. Place asparagus on grill rack coated with cooking spray; grill 4 minutes or until crisp-tender, turning after 2 minutes.
3. Combine remaining ¼ teaspoon salt, vinegar, and next 3 ingredients; stir with a whisk. Slowly pour remaining 2 tablespoons oil into vinegar mixture, stirring constantly with a whisk. Stir in capers. Arrange asparagus on a serving platter; drizzle with vinaigrette, and sprinkle with basil. Yield: 6 servings (serving size: about 4 asparagus spears and about 2 teaspoons vinaigrette).

CALORIES 91; **FAT** 7.2g (sat 1.1g, mono 5g, poly 1.1g); **PROTEIN** 2.6g; **CARB** 4.8g; **FIBER** 2.5g; **CHOL** 0mg; **IRON** 2.5mg; **SODIUM** 198mg; **CALC** 32mg

Grilled Peppers and Lentil Salad

(pictured on page 260)

You can substitute 1¼ teaspoons ground fennel seeds if fennel pollen is unavailable.

1 red bell pepper, quartered and seeded
1 green bell pepper, quartered and seeded
1 yellow bell pepper, quartered and seeded
Cooking spray
1⅛ teaspoons salt, divided
½ teaspoon freshly ground black pepper, divided
1½ cups dried lentils (about ¾ pound)
1 small onion, peeled and halved
1 bay leaf
⅔ cup chopped plum tomato
½ cup chopped green onions
⅓ cup fresh cilantro leaves
⅓ cup fresh lime juice
¼ cup chopped pitted kalamata olives
3 tablespoons extra-virgin olive oil
1 teaspoon fennel pollen

1. Preheat grill to high heat.
2. Lightly coat bell pepper pieces with cooking spray. Place bell pepper pieces, skin sides down, on grill rack, and grill 12 minutes or until skins are blackened. Place bell pepper pieces in a zip-top plastic bag; seal. Let stand 15 minutes; peel and chop bell peppers. Discard skins. Sprinkle with ½ teaspoon salt and ¼ teaspoon black pepper. Place bell peppers in a large bowl.
3. Rinse and drain lentils; place in a large saucepan. Cover with water to 3 inches above lentils; add onion and bay leaf to pan. Bring to a boil. Cover, reduce heat, and simmer 20 minutes or until lentils are just tender. Drain lentils. Discard onion halves and bay leaf. Add lentils to bell peppers. Add remaining ⅝ teaspoon salt, remaining ¼ teaspoon black pepper, tomato, and remaining ingredients to lentil mixture; stir well. Yield: 6 servings (serving size: 1⅓ cups).

CALORIES 287; **FAT** 8.8g (sat 1.1g, mono 5g, poly 1.1g); **PROTEIN** 15.7g; **CARB** 41g; **FIBER** 8.4g; **CHOL** 0mg; **IRON** 5mg; **SODIUM** 596mg; **CALC** 22mg

Grilled Eggplant Pita Sandwiches with Yogurt-Garlic Spread

This sandwich is also delicious cold the next day for lunch—to prevent the pita from getting soggy, don't assemble until you're ready to eat. We like thick, tangy Greek yogurt in this dish. Serve with tabbouleh salad.

1 (1-pound) eggplant, cut crosswise into ½-inch-thick slices
3¼ teaspoons kosher salt, divided
¼ cup plain 2% reduced-fat Greek yogurt
1 tablespoon fresh lemon juice
1 teaspoon chopped fresh oregano leaves
Dash of black pepper
1 small garlic clove, minced
½ small red onion, cut into ½-inch-thick slices
1 tablespoon extra-virgin olive oil
Cooking spray
2 (6-inch) pitas, cut in half
1 cup arugula

1. Place eggplant slices in a colander; sprinkle with 1 tablespoon salt. Toss well. Drain 30 minutes. Rinse thoroughly; pat dry with paper towels.
2. Combine remaining ¼ teaspoon salt, yogurt, and next 4 ingredients in a small bowl.
3. Preheat grill to medium-high heat.
4. Brush eggplant and onion slices with oil. Place eggplant and onion slices on grill rack coated with cooking spray; grill 5 minutes on each side or until vegetables are tender and lightly browned.
5. Fill each pita half with 1½ tablespoons yogurt mixture, one quarter of eggplant slices, one quarter of onion slices, and ¼ cup arugula. Yield: 2 servings (serving size: 2 pita halves).

CALORIES 311; **FAT** 8.2g (sat 1.6g, mono 5g, poly 1.2g); **PROTEIN** 12.7g; **CARB** 50.6g; **FIBER** 9.2g; **CHOL** 1.7mg; **IRON** 3.5mg; **SODIUM** 697mg; **CALC** 117mg

Plank-Grilled Zucchini with Couscous, Spinach, and Feta Stuffing

Cedar planks lend this dish a pleasant smoki-ness. If you don't have planks, cook the zucchini halves directly on the grill. Use zucchini with some heft; if it's too thin, it may get too soft.

2 (15 x 6½ x ⅜-inch) cedar grilling planks
2¼ cups organic vegetable broth
½ cup chopped shallots (about 1 large)
1 (10-ounce) package frozen chopped
   spinach, thawed and drained
¾ cup uncooked couscous
½ cup (2 ounces) diced feta cheese
¼ cup chopped fresh mint
2 teaspoons grated lemon rind
3 tablespoons fresh lemon juice
1 tablespoon extra-virgin olive oil
¼ teaspoon freshly ground black pepper
6 medium zucchini (about 2 pounds)
½ teaspoon kosher salt

1. Soak planks in water 1 hour; drain.
2. Preheat grill to medium-high heat.
3. Place broth in a large skillet over medium-high heat; bring to a boil. Add shallots and spinach; cook 5 minutes. Stir in couscous. Remove from heat; cover and let stand 5 minutes. Stir in cheese and next 5 ingredients.
4. Cut each zucchini in half lengthwise; scoop out pulp, leaving a ¼-inch-thick shell. Sprinkle salt evenly over zucchini. Spoon about ⅔ cup stuffing into each zucchini half.
5. Place planks on grill rack; grill 3 min-utes or until lightly charred. Turn planks over; place zucchini on charred sides of planks. Cover; grill 12 minutes or until tender. Yield: 6 servings (serving size: 2 stuffed zucchini halves).

CALORIES 192; **FAT** 5.8g (sat 2.4g, mono 2.3g, poly 0.7g); **PROTEIN** 8.7g; **CARB** 28.7g; **FIBER** 4.5g; **CHOL** 11mg; **IRON** 2mg; **SODIUM** 564mg; **CALC** 172mg

READER RECIPES
FROM YOUR KITCHEN TO OURS

After a year of marriage, Mary Ellen Smith tired of preparing the same basic dishes every night. Five years later, after poring through recipes, Smith discovered quinoa. "It was new to me, so I chose ingredients from one of my favorite cuisines, Italian." With endless options, Smith turned to the mellow nuttiness of roasted garlic to balance the tart flavor of tomato.

Preparing healthy meals wasn't always second nature for Nancee Melin, who learned about cooking and baking from her mother. "My family is Swed-ish and Norwegian, so we used a lot of butter and cream," she says. After retiring, she knew she had to make changes to lead a healthier lifestyle. In her recipe, whole-wheat pasta adds fiber, and edamame is a high-protein, nutritious substitute for peas.

For Amy Sokol, cooking for friends and family is a way to show that she cares. "Cooking for someone is giving out a lot of love; it's mushy, but true," she says. Inspired by a popular lettuce wrap appetizer at an Asian bistro chain, Sokol whipped up her own main dish rendition of this family favorite. Her version is lower in fat and sodium but just as flavorful. "It is much healthier and cheaper to make your own sauces, and the whole family loves the dish, which isn't always the case!" she says.

Although kids can be the pickiest eat-ers, Carma Van Allen coaxes her 2- and 5-year-olds to develop their palates by trying different flavors and textures. To encourage them to eat baked instead of fried fish, Van Allen used fresh orange and lime juice and a caramelized crust with mild-tasting tilapia. "I wanted to create a meal my husband and I could enjoy, too," she says. "I don't tend to abide by the idea of cooking separate meals for kids."

Quinoa with Roasted Garlic, Tomatoes, and Spinach

"Quinoa contains more protein than any other grain. The tiny, beige-colored seeds have a nice crunch. It's cooked and eaten like rice and other grains. Be sure to give it a good rinse before cooking, or it may have a bitter taste."
—Mary Ellen Smith, Doylestown, Pennsylvania

1 whole garlic head
1 tablespoon olive oil
1 tablespoon finely chopped shallots
¼ teaspoon crushed red pepper
½ cup uncooked quinoa, rinsed and drained
1 tablespoon dry white wine
1 cup fat-free, lower-sodium chicken broth
½ cup fresh baby spinach leaves
⅓ cup chopped seeded tomato (1 small)
1 tablespoon shaved fresh Parmesan cheese
¼ teaspoon salt

1. Preheat oven to 350°.
2. Remove papery skin from garlic head. Cut garlic head in half crosswise, breaking apart to separate whole cloves. Wrap half of head in foil; reserve remaining garlic for another use. Bake at 350° for 1 hour; cool 10 minutes. Separate cloves; squeeze to extract garlic pulp. Discard skins.
3. Heat oil in a saucepan over medium heat. Add shallots and red pepper to pan, and cook 1 minute. Add quinoa to pan; cook 2 minutes, stirring con-stantly. Add wine; cook until liquid is absorbed, stirring constantly. Add broth; bring to a boil. Cover, reduce heat, and simmer 15 minutes or until liquid is absorbed. Remove from heat; stir in garlic pulp, spinach, and remain-ing ingredients. Serve immediately. Yield: 4 servings (serving size: ½ cup).

CALORIES 130; **FAT** 5g (sat 0.7g, mono 3.1g, poly 1g); **PROTEIN** 4.1g; **CARB** 16.6g; **FIBER** 1.8g; **CHOL** 1mg; **IRON** 1.7mg; **SODIUM** 305mg; **CALC** 49mg

Whole-Wheat Pasta with Edamame, Arugula, and Herbs

"In my family, we have a motto for healthy food—eat the colors of the rainbow—which this one-dish meal exemplifies."
—Nancee Melin, Tucson, Arizona

8 ounces uncooked whole-wheat penne (tube-shaped pasta)
2 tablespoons olive oil
1 tablespoon butter
2 cups frozen shelled edamame (green soybeans), thawed
2 cups loosely packed baby arugula
1 cup grape tomatoes, halved
1/4 cup chopped fresh flat-leaf parsley
1/4 cup fresh lemon juice
3 tablespoons chopped fresh basil
1 tablespoon chopped fresh thyme
1/2 teaspoon kosher salt
2 ounces fresh Parmigiano-Reggiano cheese, shaved

1. Cook pasta according to package directions, omitting salt and fat. Drain.
2. Heat oil and butter in a large skillet over medium heat. Add edamame to pan; cook 2 minutes or until edamame are thoroughly heated, stirring occasionally. Combine pasta and edamame in a large bowl. Stir in arugula and next 6 ingredients, tossing well. Sprinkle each serving with cheese. Yield: 4 servings (serving size: about 1¾ cups pasta mixture and ½ ounce cheese).

CALORIES 477; **FAT** 21.6g (sat 5.4g, mono 7.8g, poly 6.1g); **PROTEIN** 25.6g; **CARB** 56.6g; **FIBER** 13.1g; **CHOL** 18mg; **IRON** 2.8mg; **SODIUM** 521mg; **CALC** 264mg

Quick & Easy • Kid Friendly

Sweet and Spicy Citrus Tilapia

"This is a very versatile marinade. It's great with chicken breasts, but I would recommend using the grill instead. Add green beans tossed with cilantro and lime."
—Carma Van Allen, South Orange, New Jersey

4 (6-ounce) tilapia fillets
Cooking spray
1/2 cup fresh orange juice (about 1 orange)
3 tablespoons fresh lime juice
1 tablespoon brown sugar
1 tablespoon extra-virgin olive oil
2 teaspoons lower-sodium soy sauce
1/2 teaspoon salt
1/2 teaspoon ground cumin
1/4 teaspoon black pepper
1/4 teaspoon ground red pepper
2 garlic cloves, crushed
1/2 teaspoon paprika

1. Arrange fish in a single layer in a shallow roasting pan coated with cooking spray. Combine orange juice and next 9 ingredients; pour over fish. Let stand 15 minutes.
2. Preheat broiler.
3. Sprinkle fish with paprika; broil 15 minutes or until desired degree of doneness. Drizzle sauce over fish. Yield: 4 servings (serving size: 1 fillet and about 2 teaspoons sauce).

CALORIES 225; **FAT** 6.6g (sat 1.5g, mono 3.4g, poly 1.2g); **PROTEIN** 34.8g; **CARB** 7.5g; **FIBER** 0.4g; **CHOL** 85mg; **IRON** 1.3mg; **SODIUM** 486mg; **CALC** 30mg

Quick & Easy

Asian Lettuce Cups

"This dish is cool and hot, sweet and spicy, fun and messy—not a date night meal!"
—Amy Sokol, San Antonio, Texas

1½ tablespoons canola oil, divided
3 cups coarsely chopped shiitake mushroom caps (about 1/2 pound)
1¼ pounds ground turkey
1/2 teaspoon minced garlic
1/2 teaspoon minced peeled fresh ginger
1 cup thinly sliced green onions (about 4)
1 (8-ounce) can sliced water chestnuts, drained and coarsely chopped
12 Boston lettuce leaves
3 tablespoons hoisin sauce
2 tablespoons lower-sodium soy sauce
1 tablespoon rice vinegar
2 teaspoons Sriracha (hot chile sauce, such as Huy Fong)
1/4 teaspoon salt

1. Heat 1 tablespoon oil in a large nonstick skillet over medium heat. Add mushrooms; sauté 5 minutes or until tender, stirring occasionally. Place mushrooms in a large bowl. Heat remaining 1½ teaspoons oil in pan over medium-high heat. Add turkey, garlic, and ginger to pan; cook 6 minutes or until turkey is browned, stirring to crumble. Add turkey mixture, onions, and water chestnuts to mushrooms in bowl; stir well.
2. Spoon ½ cup turkey mixture into each lettuce leaf. Combine hoisin, and remaining ingredients in a small bowl, stirring with a whisk. Serve sauce with lettuce cups. Yield: 6 servings (serving size: 2 filled lettuce cups and about 1 tablespoon hoisin sauce mixture).

CALORIES 247; **FAT** 13.1g (sat 2.6g, mono 5g, poly 3g); **PROTEIN** 18.8g; **CARB** 12.5g; **FIBER** 3.1g; **CHOL** 75mg; **IRON** 2.6mg; **SODIUM** 506mg; **CALC** 37mg

LESS MEAT, MORE FLAVOR
NEW SUPER HEROES
By Mark Bittman

Classic sandwiches—ham and cheese, smoked salmon and cream cheese—take on new nutritional powers in these tasty versions.

Here in America, sandwiches are sacred. The formula is etched into our daily diet, and it doesn't change much. We tinker with the ingredients to make fancier versions, and nowadays we may crisp, smash, or roll them. But only hippies and heretics fill sandwiches with vegetables.

Make that hippies, heretics, and me. Lately I've been changing sandwiches in much the same way as I have other recipes: flipping the animal protein-to-plant ratio by increasing the amount of vegetables and minimizing the meat, and favoring whole grains over refined, and enjoying these portable meals more than ever. If this concept is still a bit tough to swallow, then these two examples will convert you. The trick is to start with familiar combinations so the adjustments aren't so dramatic. And, pay close attention to the seasonings.

Take the classic bagel and smoked salmon model, the Sunday morning staple of my childhood and one we ate entirely vegetable-less (unless my mother cut up a tomato, a rare event). But since cucumbers have an affinity with fish, they seem a natural addition, and if we turn them into gingery relish that eats like a salad, we can get rid of the rich cream cheese (the salmon is fatty enough, don't you think?). Now we have a slightly acidic dressing that helps bridge the gap between bread and filling and brightens (rather than fattens) the fish. Spinach leaves act as a more nutritious form of lettuce, but romaine is good here, too. A slice of tomato doesn't hurt.

Or, to put a new spin on the traditional grilled cheese and meat (you might even call this a nuevo Cubano), I lean once again on companion ingredients. In this case a bit of mashed spicy black beans and some sliced fresh fruit keep the bread moist during cooking—without butter or tons of cheese. Choose tomato, which softens into an impromptu salsa for a saucier approach, or maintain the Caribbean spirit with sliced mango—unripe for a pleasing crunch or ripe for a juicy texture and tropical flavor. Either way, now the cheese and meat almost slip into the background, adding just enough richness to satisfy.

Any basic sandwich can be treated this way. Chicken or turkey salad? Load it up with chopped apples, celery, radishes, and a handful of chopped cashews; combine a little mayo and mustard with a lot of yogurt for a quick dressing. Ribbons of spinach or another tender green (raw, or cooked and squeezed dry, as you like) turn egg salad into a true salad so good you might not even want the bread. And since it takes shockingly little cheese to melt and glue bread together, why not slip some of last night's leftover veggies into today's grilled cheese sandwiches, too? Chop them up a bit, and away you go.

In fact, leftovers are among the best go-to fillings for healthier sandwiches, and obviously a vast improvement over bologna. Amounts of meat, fish, chicken, or cheese too small for any other use are ideal for this approach; combine them with cooked or raw vegetables or even sliced soft or crisp fruit. Slaws and salads are also excellent fillings, especially when seasoned with a little smoked meat (drain slaws and salads well before using). And instead of the usual smears of cream cheese, try mashing chickpeas, edamame, or white beans with a squeeze of lemon or some garlic, herbs, or spices; vegetable purees work well, too. Or simply brush a little vinegar on one side of the sandwich and olive oil on the other, and sprinkle with lots of black pepper.

As for the bread: Heroes, hoagies, and submarines depend on huge white torpedo rolls—all utterly flavorless and needlessly filling. Fortunately, most supermarkets today carry alternatives that contain at least some proportion of whole-wheat flour, and if you live near a good bakery, you can take advantage of its whole-grain rolls.

In almost all cases, the crust is the best part, so I pull out some of the soft interior and save it to make breadcrumbs. (This has the added benefit of leaving more room for the filling; it's an old New Orleans trick.) If you can't find good rolls, buy a whole loaf, cut it crosswise into a chunk 3 or 4 inches wide, and pull out the insides as described. Toasting the bread a bit in the oven helps stabilize the fillings, but it's not necessary.

One word of advice about traveling with vegetable-driven sandwiches: They tend to be more moist and will sog out the bread faster than their deli-meat counterparts. So if you're going on a picnic or bringing lunch to the office, consider packing the filling separately from the rolls and assembling them right before eating. They're still undeniably convenient and far better than anything you'll get from takeout.

Quick & Easy

Smoked Salmon Sandwiches with Ginger Relish

2 (7-ounce) cucumbers, peeled, seeded, and cut into chunks
1 (8-ounce) daikon radish, peeled and cut into chunks
4 green onions, cut into 2-inch pieces
1 (1-inch) piece fresh ginger, peeled and coarsely chopped
¼ cup rice vinegar
1 teaspoon sugar
1 teaspoon lower-sodium soy sauce
1 (16-ounce) whole-wheat baguette, cut in half lengthwise
12 large fresh spinach leaves
¼ pound thinly sliced cold-smoked salmon

1. Place cucumbers in a food processor; pulse 15 times or until finely chopped. Place in a large bowl. Add radish to food processor; pulse 15 times or until finely chopped. Add radish to bowl. Add green onions and ginger to food processor; process until minced. Add to bowl.
2. Combine vinegar, sugar, and soy sauce; stir until sugar dissolves. Pour over cucumber mixture; let stand at least 15 minutes. Drain in a fine mesh sieve, pressing to squeeze out excess moisture.
3. Preheat broiler.
4. Hollow out top and bottom halves of bread, leaving a ½-inch-thick shell; reserve torn bread for another use. Place bread on a baking sheet, cut sides up; broil 3 minutes or until toasted. Layer spinach, salmon, and relish on bottom half of bread; cover with top half of bread. Cut into 4 equal pieces. Yield: 4 servings (serving size: 1 sandwich).

CALORIES 267; **FAT** 2.2g (sat 0.3g, mono 1.1g, poly 0.4g); **PROTEIN** 14g; **CARB** 45.6g; **FIBER** 4g; **CHOL** 7mg; **IRON** 3.5mg; **SODIUM** 702mg; **CALC** 62mg

Nuevo Cubano

Quick & Easy • Kid Friendly

4 (3-ounce) whole-wheat sub rolls, cut in half lengthwise
1/4 cup chopped fresh cilantro
1 1/2 tablespoons fresh lime juice
1/4 teaspoon chili powder
2 garlic cloves, minced
1 (15-ounce) can no-salt-added black beans, rinsed and drained
1/4 pound thinly sliced reduced-sodium deli ham
1 peeled mango or 2 large tomatoes, thinly sliced
1/4 pound thinly sliced provolone cheese
2 tablespoons olive oil, divided

1. Hollow out top and bottom halves of bread, leaving a 1/2-inch-thick shell; reserve torn bread for another use.
2. Place cilantro and next 4 ingredients in a food processor; process until almost smooth and spreadable, adding a few drops of water, if necessary. Spread bean mixture evenly on bottom halves of prepared rolls. Layer rolls evenly with ham, mango, and cheese; replace top halves of rolls.
3. Heat 1 tablespoon olive oil in a large skillet over medium heat 5 minutes. Add 2 sandwiches to pan; place a cast-iron or other heavy skillet on top of sandwiches; press gently. Cook 2 to 3 minutes on each side or until sandwiches are golden brown (leave cast-iron skillet on sandwiches while they cook). Remove sandwiches from pan; repeat procedure with remaining 1 tablespoon oil and 2 sandwiches. Yield: 4 servings (serving size: 1 sandwich).

CALORIES 436; FAT 19.9g (sat 6.7g, mono 7.9g, poly 3g); PROTEIN 24.3g; CARB 44.6g; FIBER 7.2g; CHOL 32mg; IRON 3.5mg; SODIUM 792mg; CALC 328mg

BUDGET COOKING
FEED 4 FOR LESS THAN $10

Simple, summery recipes that will get you in and out of the kitchen in a flash.

Quick & Easy • Kid Friendly

Edamame Succotash

$2.47 per serving, $9.89 total
Edamame makes a hearty addition to this summer staple. If you can't find frozen, shelled edamame (green soybeans), substitute the more traditional lima beans. Serve with a baguette and Neufchâtel cheese.

1 slice center-cut bacon
1 tablespoon butter
2 cups chopped sweet onion
2 cups fresh corn kernels (about 3 ears)
1 (16-ounce) bag frozen, shelled edamame, thawed
2 tablespoons red wine vinegar
1/2 teaspoon salt
1/2 teaspoon freshly ground black pepper
1/2 teaspoon sugar
3 plum tomatoes, coarsely chopped
1 red bell pepper, seeded and coarsely chopped
3 tablespoons torn fresh basil

1. Cook bacon in a nonstick skillet over medium heat until crisp. Remove bacon from pan, reserving 2 teaspoons drippings in pan; coarsely chop bacon.
2. Increase heat to medium-high. Melt butter in drippings in pan. Add onion; sauté 3 minutes, stirring occasionally. Add corn; sauté 3 minutes or until lightly charred. Add edamame, and sauté 3 minutes, stirring occasionally. Stir in vinegar and next 5 ingredients; cook 30 seconds, stirring occasionally. Sprinkle with bacon and basil. Yield: 4 servings (serving size: 1 1/4 cups).

CALORIES 300; FAT 12.1g (sat 3.3g, mono 3.3g, poly 3.6g); PROTEIN 17.9g; CARB 37.2g; FIBER 10g; CHOL 10mg; IRON 0.9mg; SODIUM 386mg; CALC 28mg

Spicy Corn and Crab Chowder

Quick & Easy

$2.41 per serving, $9.63 total
Claw meat tends to be slightly darker than pristine lump crab, but it lends a robust flavor. Serve with corn muffins. Purchase a boxed corn muffin mix for maximum efficiency.

1 medium poblano chile
1 tablespoon butter
1 cup finely chopped onion
1/2 teaspoon salt
1/2 teaspoon sugar
1/4 teaspoon ground red pepper
1 (16-ounce) package frozen corn kernels, thawed
1 cup half-and-half, divided
1 (8-ounce) russet potato, peeled and chopped
2 cups water
2 tablespoons all-purpose flour
1 cup 2% reduced-fat milk
1 (8-ounce) container crab claw meat, shell pieces removed

1. Preheat broiler.
2. Place poblano on a foil-lined baking sheet. Broil 8 minutes on each side or until blackened. Place pepper in a small zip-top plastic bag; seal. Let stand 10 minutes. Peel and chop.
3. Melt butter in a Dutch oven over medium-high heat. Add onion and next 3 ingredients to pan; sauté 4 minutes, stirring occasionally. Add corn; sauté 2 minutes. Remove 3/4 cup corn mixture from pan. Place 3/4 cup corn mixture and 3/4 cup half-and-half in a blender; process until smooth. Add potato to pan; sauté 1 minute. Stir in 2 cups water; bring to a boil. Cook 4 minutes or until potato is almost tender. Reduce heat to medium.
4. Combine remaining 1/4 cup half-and-half and flour in a small bowl, stirring until smooth. Add flour mixture to pan. Cook 1 minute, stirring constantly. Return corn puree to pan. Stir in poblano, milk, and crab; bring to a simmer. Cook 3 minutes, stirring frequently. Yield: 4 servings (serving size: about 1 3/4 cups).

CALORIES 375; FAT 11.8g (sat 6.7g, mono 3.4g, poly 0.6g); PROTEIN 22.2g; CARB 47.6g; FIBER 4.4g; CHOL 82mg; IRON 1.7mg; SODIUM 597mg; CALC 233mg

Fettuccine with Mussels

$2.46 per serving, $9.85 total
Look for the small airline-sized bottles of wine that are packaged in 4-packs—they're the most economical way to buy wine when you just need a small amount for cooking.

8 ounces uncooked fettuccine
2 tablespoons butter
½ cup finely chopped onion
6 garlic cloves, coarsely chopped
½ cup dry white wine
3 plum tomatoes, chopped
⅓ cup bottled clam juice
1½ pounds mussels, scrubbed and debearded
¼ cup chopped fresh flat-leaf parsley

1. Cook pasta in boiling water until almost al dente; drain through a sieve over a large bowl. Reserve ⅓ cup pasta cooking water.
2. Melt butter in a large skillet over medium heat. Add onion to pan; cook 4 minutes, stirring occasionally. Add garlic; cook 1 minute, stirring constantly. Add wine; cook 3 minutes or until liquid evaporates, stirring occasionally. Add tomatoes; cook 2 minutes, stirring occasionally. Stir in reserved ⅓ cup pasta cooking water and clam juice; bring to a boil. Add mussels; cover and cook 4 minutes or until mussels open. Discard any unopened shells. Add cooked pasta to tomato mixture; cook 1 minute or until thoroughly heated, tossing well to combine. Sprinkle with parsley. Serve immediately. Yield: 4 servings (serving size: about 2 cups).

CALORIES 415; **FAT** 10.1g (sat 4.5g, mono 2.3g, poly 1.2g); **PROTEIN** 27g; **CARB** 54g; **FIBER** 2.9g; **CHOL** 58mg; **IRON** 8.6mg; **SODIUM** 530mg; **CALC** 76mg

WINE NOTE: With this fresh and affordable summer meal, look for a white wine with similar characteristics. Banrock Station Chardonnay 2009 ($7) is an Australian bargain that leaps easily from kitchen to table: The fresh fruit and lack of oak flavor allow it to work well in the recipe, while the wine's lighter body and crisp, citrusy flavors pair nicely with shellfish.

Chicken and Rice Casserole

$2.16 per serving, $8.65 total

Cooking spray
1 cup chopped onion
1 (8-ounce) bone-in chicken breast half, skinned
½ teaspoon black pepper, divided
1 (14-ounce) can fat-free, lower-sodium chicken broth
1 tablespoon butter
1 (8-ounce) zucchini, halved lengthwise and thinly sliced
1 (8-ounce) yellow squash, halved lengthwise and thinly sliced
2 cups cooked long-grain white rice
1 teaspoon minced fresh rosemary
1½ tablespoons all-purpose flour
1½ cups 2% reduced-fat milk
½ cup (2 ounces) grated fresh pecorino Romano cheese, divided
¼ teaspoon salt

1. Preheat oven to 350°.
2. Heat a large saucepan over medium-high heat. Lightly coat pan with cooking spray. Add onion to pan; sauté 5 minutes, stirring occasionally. Sprinkle chicken with ¼ teaspoon pepper, and add chicken, meaty side down, to pan. Cook 6 minutes or until browned; turn chicken over. Add broth to pan. Reduce heat, cover, and simmer 15 minutes or until chicken is done. Remove chicken from pan, reserving broth in pan. Let chicken stand 10 minutes. Remove chicken from bones; shred. Discard bones. Place chicken in a large bowl.
3. Bring broth to a boil; cook, uncovered, until reduced to ½ cup (about 10 minutes). Add broth mixture to chicken. Melt butter in pan over medium-high heat. Add zucchini and squash to pan; sauté 3 minutes or until lightly browned, stirring frequently. Add squash mixture, rice, and rosemary to chicken mixture, and toss gently to combine.
4. Place flour in a medium saucepan over medium heat. Gradually add milk, stirring until smooth; bring to a boil. Cook 1 minute or until thick, stirring constantly with a whisk. Remove from heat; let stand 30 seconds. Add ¼ cup cheese; stir with a whisk until smooth. Add remaining ¼ teaspoon pepper, milk mixture, and salt to chicken mixture; stir to combine. Spoon chicken mixture into a broiler-safe 8-inch ceramic baking dish coated with cooking spray. Sprinkle remaining ¼ cup cheese over rice mixture; bake at 350° for 20 minutes or until thoroughly heated. Remove casserole from oven.
5. Preheat broiler.
6. Broil 5 minutes or until golden. Yield: 4 servings (serving size: 1¼ cups).

CALORIES 337; **FAT** 9.7g (sat 5.7g, mono 2.7g, poly 0.6g); **PROTEIN** 23.9g; **CARB** 38.2g; **FIBER** 2.8g; **CHOL** 56mg; **IRON** 2.3mg; **SODIUM** 592mg; **CALC** 331mg

Easy Grilled Chicken Salad

$2.28 per serving, $9.10 total

4 (6-ounce) skinless, boneless chicken breast halves
1 tablespoon olive oil
½ teaspoon salt
½ teaspoon freshly ground black pepper
Cooking spray
⅓ cup finely chopped celery
⅓ cup sweetened dried cranberries
¼ cup chopped pecans, toasted
3 green onions, thinly sliced
3 tablespoons light sour cream
3 tablespoons canola mayonnaise
2 teaspoons fresh lemon juice

1. Preheat grill to medium-high heat.
2. Brush both sides of chicken evenly with oil; sprinkle with salt and pepper. Place chicken on a grill rack coated with cooking spray; grill 6 minutes on each side or until done. Let stand 10 minutes; shred. Place chicken in a large bowl. Add celery and next 3 ingredients; toss.
3. Combine sour cream, mayonnaise and lemon juice. Add sour cream mixture to chicken mixture; toss to coat. Yield: 4 servings (serving size: 1¼ cups).

CALORIES 391; **FAT** 22g (sat 3.4g, mono 11.4g, poly 5.1g); **PROTEIN** 36.1g; **CARB** 11.5g; **FIBER** 1.8g; **CHOL** 101mg; **IRON** 1.6mg; **SODIUM** 469mg; **CALC** 59mg

5-INGREDIENT COOKING

Quick & Easy

Herb and Lemon Roasted Striped Bass

Fresh herbs give mild-tasting bass vibrant flavor.

4 (6-ounce) striped bass fillets
1 lemon
1 tablespoon extra-virgin olive oil
1 teaspoon chopped fresh thyme
1 teaspoon chopped fresh oregano

Preheat oven to 425°. Coat a baking sheet with cooking spray. Place fish on pan. Grate lemon rind to measure 1 teaspoon; juice lemon to measure 1 tablespoon. Combine rind, juice, oil, thyme, oregano, ½ teaspoon salt, and ¼ teaspoon freshly ground black pepper; drizzle mixture over fish. Bake at 425° for 13 minutes or until desired degree of doneness. Yield: 4 servings (serving size: 1 fillet).

CALORIES 197; FAT 7.5g (sat 1.4g, mono 3.6g, poly 1.8g); PROTEIN 30.2g; CARB 0.6g; FIBER 0.1g; CHOL 136mg; IRON 1.5mg; SODIUM 412mg; CALC 29mg

THE FIVE INGREDIENTS

4 (6-ounce) striped bass fillets

1 lemon

1 tablespoon extra-virgin olive oil

1 teaspoon chopped fresh thyme

1 teaspoon chopped fresh oregano

Quick & Easy

Linguine with Peppery Shrimp

A generous amount of black pepper brings some welcome heat to this pasta dish.

2 pounds large shrimp, peeled and deveined
1 lemon
1 tablespoon chopped fresh thyme, divided
3 tablespoons butter
8 ounces uncooked linguine

Combine ½ teaspoon kosher salt, 1½ teaspoons freshly ground black pepper, and shrimp, tossing to coat shrimp. Heat a large nonstick skillet over medium-high heat. Coat pan with cooking spray. Add shrimp; sauté 4 minutes or until shrimp are done. Grate lemon rind to measure ½ teaspoon; juice lemon to measure 3 tablespoons. Combine rind and juice in a small saucepan over medium heat; add 2 teaspoons thyme. Bring to a boil; add butter, stirring constantly with a whisk until butter melts. Bring 6 quarts water to a boil; stir in 1 tablespoon kosher salt. Add pasta; cook 10 minutes or until al dente. Drain, reserving 2 tablespoons pasta water. Add shrimp, butter mixture, reserved pasta water, and ½ teaspoon kosher salt to pasta, tossing to coat. Sprinkle with remaining 1 teaspoon thyme. Yield: 6 servings (serving size: about 1⅓ cups).

CALORIES 352; FAT 8.9g (sat 4.3g, mono 1.9g, poly 1.2g); PROTEIN 36g; CARB 30.7g; FIBER 1.4g; CHOL 245mg; IRON 4.9mg; SODIUM 674mg; CALC 94mg

THE FIVE INGREDIENTS

2 pounds large shrimp,
peeled and deveined

1 lemon

1 tablespoon chopped
fresh thyme, divided

3 tablespoons butter

8 ounces uncooked linguine

SUPERFAST

A bit of heat and a lot of flavor in not much time: Banish the humdrum weeknight routine with these speedy 20-minute versions of Tex-Mex favorites.

Quick & Easy
Ancho Pork Medallions

Serve the sweet-spicy pork with a side salad of baby spinach, cilantro leaves, and sliced radish and red onion.

1 (1-pound) pork tenderloin, trimmed
3/4 teaspoon ancho chile powder
1/2 teaspoon salt
1/4 teaspoon sugar
1/4 teaspoon ground cumin
1/8 teaspoon ground allspice
2 tablespoons jalapeño pepper jelly
1 teaspoon fresh lime juice
2 teaspoons olive oil

1. Cut pork crosswise into 8 equal pieces. Combine chile powder and next 4 ingredients in a small bowl; rub evenly over both sides of pork. Combine jelly and lime juice; set aside.
2. Heat oil in a large heavy skillet over medium-high heat. Add pork to pan; cook 1 minute on each side. Brush pork with half of jelly mixture; turn and brush with remaining jelly mixture. Cook 1 minute on each side or until desired degree of doneness. Remove pork from pan; let stand 5 minutes before serving. Yield: 4 servings (serving size: 2 medallions).

CALORIES 168; **FAT** 6.1g (sat 1.6g, mono 3.2g, poly 0.6g); **PROTEIN** 22.5g; **CARB** 4.6g; **FIBER** 0.1g; **CHOL** 63mg; **IRON** 1.2mg; **SODIUM** 363mg; **CALC** 7mg

Quick & Easy
Superfast Chicken Posole

Look for canned tomatillos in the Mexican foods section of your supermarket.

1 tablespoon olive oil
1 teaspoon dried oregano
3/4 teaspoon ground cumin
1/2 teaspoon chili powder
2 garlic cloves, minced
1 (8-ounce) package prechopped onion and celery mix
4 canned tomatillos, drained and coarsely chopped
2 (14-ounce) cans fat-free, lower-sodium chicken broth
1 (15-ounce) can white hominy, rinsed and drained
2 cups chopped skinless, boneless rotisserie chicken breast
1 tablespoon fresh lime juice
1/4 teaspoon salt
1/4 teaspoon black pepper
1/2 ripe peeled avocado, diced
4 radishes, thinly sliced
Cilantro leaves (optional)

1. Heat oil in a large saucepan over medium-high heat. Add oregano and next 4 ingredients; sauté 2 minutes. Stir in tomatillos; cook 1 minute. Add broth and hominy; cover and bring to a boil. Uncover and cook 8 minutes. Stir in chicken; cook 1 minute or until heated. Remove from heat; stir in lime juice, salt, and pepper. Divide evenly among 4 bowls. Top with avocado and radish. Garnish with cilantro, if desired. Yield: 4 servings (serving size: 1½ cups soup, 2 tablespoons avocado, and 1 radish).

CALORIES 290; **FAT** 11.2g (sat 2.2g, mono 5.9g, poly 2g); **PROTEIN** 28.2g; **CARB** 20.2g; **FIBER** 4.5g; **CHOL** 60mg; **IRON** 2.4mg; **SODIUM** 452mg; **CALC** 62mg

INGREDIENTS FOR SOUTH-OF-THE-BORDER FLAIR

TORTILLAS
Try corn for soft tacos, flour for crispy salad shells.

SPICES
Chipotle adds smoke and heat; cumin offers earthiness.

FRUITS
Fresh zip from lime and creamy richness from avocado.

HERBS
Dried oregano adds depth. Fresh cilantro lends pungency.

Quick & Easy

Seared Pork Tortas

Torta is Spanish for "sandwich"—and is usually a hefty stack of meat, beans, and veggies.

2 teaspoons olive oil
1 teaspoon ground cumin
¼ teaspoon salt
6 (2-ounce) boneless center-cut pork loin chops (¼ inch thick)
1 (12-ounce) baguette, cut in half horizontally
½ cup canned pinto beans, rinsed and drained
2 tablespoons refrigerated fresh salsa
½ cup (2 ounces) shredded Monterey Jack cheese
¼ cup thinly sliced onion
1 large tomato, cut into 8 (¼-inch-thick) slices
1 jalapeño pepper, seeded and thinly sliced
½ ripe peeled avocado, cut into ⅛-inch-thick slices

1. Preheat broiler.
2. Heat oil in a large nonstick skillet over medium-high heat. Combine cumin and salt; sprinkle evenly over pork. Add pork to pan; cook 2 minutes on each side or until done. Let stand 5 minutes; cut into thin slices.
3. Hollow out top and bottom halves of bread, leaving a ¾-inch-thick shell; reserve torn bread for another use. Place bread halves, cut sides up, on a baking sheet. Broil 2 minutes or until golden brown.
4. Place beans and salsa in a small bowl; mash with a fork until almost smooth. Spoon bean mixture into bottom half of baguette. Top with pork, cheese, onion, tomato, jalapeño, avocado, and top half of baguette. Cut into 4 pieces. Yield: 4 servings (serving size: 1 sandwich).

CALORIES 441; FAT 15.2g (sat 5.2g, mono 7.3g, poly 1.5g); PROTEIN 30g; CARB 46.9g; FIBER 4.2g; CHOL 66mg; IRON 3.7mg; SODIUM 806mg; CALC 147mg

---

Quick & Easy

Pan-Grilled Salmon with Red Pepper Salsa

Salmon:
2 teaspoons chili powder
1 teaspoon ground cumin
½ teaspoon salt
½ teaspoon ground coriander
¼ teaspoon ground chipotle chile powder
4 (6-ounce) skinless salmon fillets
Cooking spray
Salsa:
1 cup prechopped red bell pepper
¼ cup chopped tomato
2 tablespoons prechopped red onion
1 tablespoon chopped fresh cilantro
1½ teaspoons fresh lime juice
⅛ teaspoon salt

1. To prepare salmon, heat a grill pan over medium-high heat. Combine first 5 ingredients; rub evenly over fillets. Coat pan with cooking spray. Add fillets to pan; cook 4 minutes on each side or until desired degree of doneness.
2. While fish cooks, prepare salsa. Combine bell pepper and remaining ingredients. Serve salsa with fillets. Yield: 4 servings (serving size: 1 fillet and about ⅓ cup salsa).

CALORIES 244; FAT 10.8g (sat 2.5g, mono 4.6g, poly 2.6g); PROTEIN 31.6g; CARB 3.6g; FIBER 1.2g; CHOL 80mg; IRON 0.9mg; SODIUM 484mg; CALC 25mg

---

Quick & Easy • Kid Friendly

Southwest Salsa Burgers

¼ cup finely chopped shallots
⅜ teaspoon salt
¼ teaspoon ground chipotle chile pepper
⅛ teaspoon black pepper
1 pound lean ground round
¼ cup refrigerated fresh salsa, divided
Cooking spray
4 (1-ounce) slices Monterey Jack cheese
4 Boston lettuce leaves
4 (1½-ounce) hamburger buns, toasted
8 (⅛-inch-thick) slices tomato

1. Combine first 5 ingredients and 2 tablespoons salsa. Divide mixture into 4 equal portions, shaping each into a ½-inch-thick patty.

2. Heat a large skillet or grill pan over medium-high heat. Coat pan with cooking spray. Add patties to pan; cook 5 minutes on each side or until desired degree of doneness. Top each patty with 1 cheese slice; cook 1 minute or until cheese melts.

3. Place 1 lettuce leaf on bottom half of each bun; top with 2 tomato slices, 1 patty, 1½ teaspoons salsa, and 1 bun top. Yield: 4 servings (serving size: 1 burger).

CALORIES 385; **FAT** 15.7g (sat 8.4g, mono 4.5g, poly 0.5g); **PROTEIN** 36.7g; **CARB** 24.3g; **FIBER** 1.3g; **CHOL** 86mg; **IRON** 4mg; **SODIUM** 720mg; **CALC** 282mg

Quick & Easy

Wild Mushroom, Flank Steak, and Poblano Tacos

1 tablespoon olive oil, divided
1 (8-ounce) flank steak, trimmed
½ teaspoon salt, divided
¼ teaspoon black pepper, divided
2 cups thinly sliced white onion
1 teaspoon dried oregano
2 teaspoons bottled minced garlic
½ teaspoon ground coriander
2 (4-ounce) packages presliced exotic mushroom blend
1 poblano pepper, seeded and thinly sliced
8 (6-inch) corn tortillas
½ cup (2 ounces) shredded reduced-fat Mexican blend cheese
½ cup refrigerated fresh salsa

1. Heat 1 teaspoon oil in a large skillet over medium-high heat. Sprinkle steak with ¼ teaspoon salt and ⅛ teaspoon black pepper. Add steak to pan; cook 4 minutes on each side or until desired degree of doneness. Remove steak from pan. Add remaining 2 teaspoons oil to pan. Add onion and next 5 ingredients; sauté 5 minutes or until vegetables soften. Cut steak across grain into thin slices. Add steak, remaining ¼ teaspoon salt, and remaining ⅛ teaspoon black pepper to pan; cook 1 minute. Place about ⅓ cup steak mixture in each

tortilla. Top each taco with 1 tablespoon cheese and 1 tablespoon salsa. Yield: 4 servings (serving size: 2 tacos).

CALORIES 332; **FAT** 12.1g (sat 4.4g, mono 4.3g, poly 1.5g); **PROTEIN** 21.8g; **CARB** 36.1g; **FIBER** 5.4g; **CHOL** 28mg; **IRON** 2.7mg; **SODIUM** 642mg; **CALC** 240mg

Quick & Easy

Chipotle-Rubbed Shrimp Taco Salad

(pictured on page 261)

3 tablespoons chopped fresh cilantro
3 tablespoons minced shallots
3 tablespoons fresh lime juice
2 teaspoons honey
⅛ teaspoon salt
2 tablespoons olive oil
1 refrigerated (8-inch) flour tortilla taco salad shell kit (such as Azteca)
1 pound peeled and deveined jumbo shrimp
½ teaspoon chili powder
¼ teaspoon ground chipotle chile powder
⅛ teaspoon salt
Cooking spray
6 cups packaged prechopped romaine hearts
1½ cups chopped peeled ripe mango (about 1 large)
½ cup cherry tomatoes, halved
4 radishes, quartered

1. Preheat oven to 350°.
2. Combine first 5 ingredients in a small bowl, stirring with a whisk. Gradually add oil, stirring constantly with a whisk.
3. Bake tortilla shells at 350° according to package directions.
4. While shells bake, heat a grill pan over medium-high heat. Combine shrimp and next 3 ingredients in a large bowl; toss well to coat. Coat pan with cooking spray. Add shrimp to pan; cook 2 minutes on each side or until done.
5. Combine lettuce and next 3 ingredients. Drizzle vinaigrette over salad; toss to coat. Place about 1½ cups salad in each tortilla shell; divide shrimp evenly among salads. Yield: 4 servings (serving size: 1 salad).

CALORIES 405; **FAT** 12.5g (sat 1.8g, mono 6.8g, poly 2.4g); **PROTEIN** 29.2g; **CARB** 45.9g; **FIBER** 3.4g; **CHOL** 172mg; **IRON** 4.9mg; **SODIUM** 598mg; **CALC** 200mg

DINNER TONIGHT

Fast weeknight menus from the *Cooking Light* Test Kitchens.

40 minutes

SHOPPING LIST

Summer Squash and Corn Chowder
green onions
celery
1 pound yellow summer squash
fresh thyme
1 quart 1% low-fat milk
extra-sharp cheddar cheese
applewood-smoked bacon
1 pound frozen white and yellow baby corn kernels

Tomato Bruschetta
garlic
1 large tomato
fresh basil
baguette
extra-virgin olive oil
balsamic vinegar

GAME PLAN

While oven preheats:
- Cook bacon.
- Prepare bruschetta topping.

While vegetables sauté:
- Puree corn mixture.
- Toast bread.

While soup cooks:
- Shred cheese.

continued

Quick & Easy • Kid Friendly

Summer Squash and Corn Chowder

with Tomato Bruschetta

(pictured on page 260)

Vegetarian Swap: Omit bacon and add 2 teaspoons olive oil in place of drippings.
Buy the Best: Choose small squash, 7 to 8 inches in length; they're sweeter and less stringy.
Simple Sub: Use any herb you like for the bruschetta—tarragon would be lovely.

2 slices applewood-smoked bacon
¾ cup sliced green onions, divided
¼ cup chopped celery
1 pound yellow summer squash, chopped
1 pound frozen white and yellow baby corn
   kernels, thawed and divided
2¼ cups 1% low-fat milk, divided
1 teaspoon chopped fresh thyme
½ teaspoon salt
¼ teaspoon freshly ground black pepper
⅛ teaspoon salt
¼ cup (1 ounce) shredded extra-sharp
   cheddar cheese

1. Cook bacon in a large Dutch oven over medium-high heat until crisp. Remove bacon from pan, reserving 2 teaspoons drippings in pan. Crumble bacon, and set aside. Add ½ cup onions, celery, and squash to drippings in pan; sauté 8 minutes or until vegetables are tender.
2. Reserve 1 cup corn; set aside. Place remaining corn and 1 cup milk in a blender; process until smooth. Add remaining 1¼ cups milk, thyme, ½ teaspoon salt, and pepper to blender; process just until combined. Add pureed mixture and reserved 1 cup corn to pan. Reduce heat to medium; cook 5 minutes or until thoroughly heated, stirring constantly. Stir in ⅛ teaspoon salt. Ladle about 1½ cups soup into each of 4 bowls; top each serving with about 1 tablespoon bacon, 1 tablespoon remaining onions, and 1 tablespoon cheese. Yield: 4 servings.

CALORIES 285; FAT 9.4g (sat 3.9g, mono 3.4g, poly 1.2g); PROTEIN 13.3g; CARB 37.8g; FIBER 5.4g; CHOL 20mg; IRON 1.3mg; SODIUM 605mg; CALC 260mg

---

For the Tomato Bruschetta:
Preheat oven to 425°. Arrange 12 thin baguette slices on a baking sheet; bake at 425° for 6 minutes or until toasted. Rub toasts with cut sides of a halved garlic clove. Combine ½ cup finely chopped tomato, 2 teaspoons chopped fresh basil, 1½ teaspoons extra-virgin olive oil, 1 teaspoon balsamic vinegar, and ⅛ teaspoon salt; top toasts evenly with tomato mixture.

40 minutes

SHOPPING LIST

Pepper Jack, Chicken, and Peach Quesadillas
1 lime
2 firm ripe peaches
fresh cilantro
rotisserie chicken
honey
8-inch flour tortillas
reduced-fat sour cream
3 ounces Monterey Jack cheese with
   jalapeño peppers

Spinach Salad with Cumin Vinaigrette
1 lime
5-ounce package fresh baby spinach
1 small red onion
extra-virgin olive oil
ground cumin

GAME PLAN

Prepare sauce; chill.
Prepare vinaigrette; set aside.
While quesadillas cook:
  ■ Slice onion.
  ■ Toss salad.

Quick & Easy

Pepper Jack, Chicken, and Peach Quesadillas

with Spinach Salad with Cumin Vinaigrette

Kid-Pleaser: Swap Monterey Jack or fontina cheese for the spicy pepper Jack.
Simple Sub: Try other seasonal fruits in place of peaches, like plums or nectarines.
Prep Pointer: Weighing down quesadillas with a skillet helps them cook faster and more evenly.

1 teaspoon honey
½ teaspoon fresh lime juice
½ cup reduced-fat sour cream
4 (8-inch) flour tortillas
¾ cup (3 ounces) shredded Monterey Jack
   cheese with jalapeño peppers
1 cup chopped skinless, boneless rotisserie
   chicken breast
1 cup thinly sliced peeled firm ripe peaches
4 teaspoons chopped fresh cilantro
Cooking spray

1. Combine honey and lime juice in a small bowl, stirring well with a whisk. Stir sour cream into honey mixture; cover and chill until ready to serve.
2. Place tortillas flat on a work surface. Sprinkle 3 tablespoons cheese over half of each tortilla; top each tortilla with ¼ cup chicken, ¼ cup peaches, and 1 teaspoon cilantro. Fold tortillas in half.
3. Heat a large nonstick skillet over medium-high heat. Coat pan with cooking spray. Place 2 quesadillas in pan, and top quesadillas with a cast-iron or other heavy skillet. Cook 1½ minutes on each side or until tortillas are crisp and lightly browned (leave cast-iron skillet on quesadillas as they cook). Remove quesadillas from pan; set aside, and keep warm. Repeat procedure with remaining quesadillas. Cut each quesadilla into wedges. Serve with sauce. Yield: 4 servings (serving size: 1 quesadilla and 2 tablespoons sauce).

CALORIES 364; FAT 15.8g (sat 7.4g, mono 5.8g, poly 1.4g); PROTEIN 21.3g; CARB 33.5g; FIBER 2.2g; CHOL 68mg; IRON 2.1mg; SODIUM 485mg; CALC 235mg

232 AUGUST

For the Spinach Salad with Cumin Vinaigrette:
Combine 1 tablespoon fresh lime juice, 1 tablespoon extra-virgin olive oil, ⅛ teaspoon salt, ⅛ teaspoon freshly ground black pepper, and ⅛ teaspoon ground cumin in a large bowl. Top with 1 (5-ounce) package fresh baby spinach and ½ cup thinly sliced red onion; toss gently to coat.

SHOPPING LIST

Flank Steak Salad with Plums and Blue Cheese

1 large lemon
4 ounces baby arugula
3 plums
olive oil
honey
1-pound flank steak
1 ounce blue cheese

Crunchy Cornmeal Breadsticks

yellow cornmeal
sugar
11-ounce can refrigerated breadstick dough
large egg

GAME PLAN

While oven preheats:
- Prepare seasoning rub.
- Prepare breadstick dough.
- Begin cooking steak.
While breadsticks bake:
- Finish cooking and rest steak.
- Prepare salad.

Quick & Easy

Flank Steak Salad with Plums and Blue Cheese

with Crunchy Cornmeal Breadsticks

You'll have leftover breadsticks; store them at room temperature in an airtight container, and reheat at 250° for 5 minutes or until warm.
Simple Sub: Use halved seedless red grapes in place of plums.
Prep Pointer: Be sure to slice the meat against the grain for tender bites.
Flavor Hit: Blue cheese is sharp, tangy, and creamy, the perfect foil to sweet fruit and rich beef.

½ teaspoon freshly ground black pepper
¼ teaspoon salt
1½ tablespoons olive oil, divided
4 teaspoons fresh lemon juice, divided
1 (1-pound) flank steak, trimmed
Cooking spray
1 teaspoon honey
⅛ teaspoon salt
8 cups loosely packed baby arugula
3 plums, thinly sliced
¼ cup (1 ounce) crumbled blue cheese

1. Combine pepper, ¼ teaspoon salt, 1½ teaspoons olive oil, and 1 teaspoon lemon juice in a small bowl; rub over both sides of steak.
2. Heat a large skillet over medium-high heat. Coat pan with cooking spray. Add steak to pan; cook 5 minutes on each side or until desired degree of doneness. Remove steak from pan; let rest 5 minutes. Cut steak diagonally across grain into thin slices.
3. Combine remaining 1 tablespoon olive oil, remaining 1 tablespoon lemon juice, honey, and ⅛ teaspoon salt in a large bowl; stir well with a whisk. Add arugula; toss gently to coat. Arrange about 1½ cups arugula mixture onto each of 4 plates; top each serving with 3 ounces steak, about ½ cup plums, and 1 tablespoon cheese. Yield: 4 servings.

CALORIES 290; FAT 15.8g (sat 5.4g, mono 7.7g, poly 1.3g); PROTEIN 26.1g; CARB 11.3g; FIBER 1.5g; CHOL 48mg; IRON 2.1mg; SODIUM 373mg; CALC 102mg

For the Crunchy Cornmeal Breadsticks:
Unroll 1 (11-ounce) can refrigerated breadstick dough. Brush with 1 lightly beaten large egg white. Combine 2 tablespoons yellow cornmeal, ½ teaspoon sugar, and a dash of salt in a shallow dish. Working with 1 breadstick at a time, press egg white–brushed side into cornmeal mixture; twist and place on an ungreased baking sheet. Repeat procedure with remaining breadsticks. Bake at 375° for 15 minutes or until golden brown.

SHOPPING LIST

Cobb Salad Pizza

cherry tomatoes
1 small red onion
2 ounces mixed baby greens
1 avocado
extra-virgin olive oil
white wine vinegar
Dijon mustard
11-ounce can refrigerated thin-crust pizza dough
1 ounce blue cheese
applewood-smoked bacon
8 ounces skinless, boneless chicken breast cutlets

Fresh Orange Spritzers

4 large oranges
fresh mint (optional)
sparkling water
sauvignon blanc (optional)

GAME PLAN

While oven preheats:
- Prepare vinaigrette.
- Cook bacon and chicken.
While crust bakes:
- Prep tomatoes, onion, and avocado.
- Squeeze orange juice.

continued

Quick & Easy

Cobb Salad Pizza
with Fresh Orange Spritzers

Simple Sub: Swap any salad greens you like (arugula, spinach, romaine) for mixed greens.
Buy The Best: Choose blemish-free avocados that are firm yet yield to gentle pressure.
Time-Saver: Pick up fresh orange juice from the refrigerated part of the produce section.

1 (11-ounce) can refrigerated thin-crust pizza dough
Cooking spray
¼ cup (1 ounce) crumbled blue cheese, divided
1 tablespoon extra-virgin olive oil
1 tablespoon white wine vinegar
½ teaspoon Dijon mustard
¼ teaspoon black pepper, divided
2 slices applewood-smoked bacon
8 ounces skinless, boneless chicken breast cutlets
½ cup quartered cherry tomatoes
2 tablespoons chopped red onion
2 cups lightly packed mixed baby greens
½ cup diced peeled avocado

1. Preheat oven to 425°.
2. Unroll dough on a baking sheet coated with cooking spray; pat dough into a 14 x 12–inch rectangle. Lightly coat dough with cooking spray. Bake at 425° for 8 minutes or until golden. Remove from oven; sprinkle evenly with 2 tablespoons cheese. Set aside.
3. Combine oil, vinegar, mustard, and ⅛ teaspoon pepper in a large bowl; stir with a whisk.
4. Cook bacon in a large nonstick skillet over medium heat until crisp. Remove bacon from pan; crumble bacon into oil mixture. Wipe pan clean with paper towels. Heat pan over medium-high heat. Coat pan with cooking spray. Sprinkle chicken with remaining ⅛ teaspoon pepper. Add chicken to pan; cook 4 minutes on each side or until done. Remove chicken from pan; chop into ½-inch pieces.
5. Add chicken, tomatoes, and onion to oil mixture; toss gently to combine. Add greens; toss gently. Top crust evenly with chicken mixture, avocado,

and remaining 2 tablespoons cheese. Cut into 8 pieces. Yield: 4 servings (serving size: 2 pieces).

CALORIES 377; **FAT** 13.9g (sat 3.1g, mono 7.1g, poly 2.4g); **PROTEIN** 21.8g; **CARB** 40.3g; **FIBER** 2.6g; **CHOL** 40mg; **IRON** 2.9mg; **SODIUM** 731mg; **CALC** 57mg

For the Fresh Orange Spritzers:
Combine 3 cups chilled sparkling water and 1 cup fresh, chilled orange juice in a pitcher. Pour into ice-filled glasses; garnish with fresh mint sprigs, if desired. For an adult twist, add a splash of sauvignon blanc.

40 minutes

SHOPPING LIST

Chunky Gazpacho with Sautéed Shrimp
1½ pounds red tomatoes
12 ounces yellow tomatoes
garlic
1 English cucumber
1 red bell pepper
fresh basil
1 lemon
low-sodium vegetable juice
ground red pepper
1 pound peeled and deveined large shrimp
plain fat-free Greek yogurt

Crispy Pita Chips
whole-wheat pitas
olive oil

GAME PLAN

While oven preheats:
■ Prepare soup; chill until ready to serve.
While pita chips cook:
■ Sauté shrimp.

Quick & Easy • Make Ahead

Chunky Gazpacho with Sautéed Shrimp
with Crispy Pita Chips

Flavor Hit: A touch of ground red pepper adds complexity and a hint of spice.
Simple Sub: Use any combination of colorful, flavorful tomatoes from your farmers' market.
Vegetarian Swap: Omit the shrimp and serve the soup with cheese toasts.

1½ cups chilled low-sodium vegetable juice
½ teaspoon salt
⅛ teaspoon ground red pepper
1½ pounds red tomatoes, cored, chopped, and divided
1 garlic clove, peeled
1 cup chopped English cucumber, divided
¾ cup chopped red bell pepper, divided
3 tablespoons chopped fresh basil, divided
1½ tablespoons fresh lemon juice
12 ounces yellow tomatoes, seeded and chopped
Cooking spray
1 pound peeled and deveined large shrimp
½ cup plain fat-free Greek yogurt

1. Place vegetable juice, salt, ground red pepper, half of red tomatoes, and garlic in a blender; process until smooth. Pour pureed tomato mixture into a large bowl. Place remaining red tomatoes, ⅔ cup cucumber, ½ cup bell pepper, 1 tablespoon basil, and lemon juice in blender; process until smooth. Add to pureed tomato mixture in bowl. Stir in remaining ⅓ cup cucumber, ¼ cup bell pepper, and yellow tomatoes. Cover and chill.
2. Heat a large grill pan over medium-high heat. Coat pan with cooking spray. Add shrimp to pan; grill 2 minutes on each side or until done. Remove from heat.
3. Ladle about 1¾ cups soup into each of 4 bowls; top each serving with 4 ounces shrimp, 2 tablespoons yogurt, and remaining 1½ teaspoons basil. Yield: 4 servings.

CALORIES 178; **FAT** 1.7g (sat 0.4g, mono 0.3g, poly 0.7g); **PROTEIN** 23.8g; **CARB** 17.7g; **FIBER** 4.3g; **CHOL** 168mg; **IRON** 4.1mg; **SODIUM** 581mg; **CALC** 105mg

For the Crispy Pita Chips:
Preheat oven to 375°. Split 2 whole-wheat pitas in half horizontally. Brush rough sides of pita halves with 1½ tablespoons olive oil; sprinkle with ¾ teaspoon cracked black pepper and ¼ teaspoon kosher salt. Cut each pita half into 8 wedges. Arrange in a single layer on baking sheet; bake at 375° for 14 minutes or until browned at edges and crisp.

RECIPE MAKEOVER
PASTA SALAD, PERFECTED

We ditch mayo and heavy seasonings for a lighter, summery noodle entrée.

The word "salad" in the title of a recipe doesn't always signal a healthy choice. Pasta salad proves that point, often dished out in huge portions, slathered with caloric dressings, and spiked with high-sodium ingredients. Our light, fresh twist returns this staple to your summer go-to list.

Before you reach for the usual rigatoni, consider an alternative noodle. We like protein- and fiber-filled legume-based pastas, partly because they don't taste healthy, though they give a nutrition boost. Instead of a high-calorie mayo-based dressing, we keep the dish light with a vinaigrette. Then we add some fresh melon and peppery arugula for zing. A little prosciutto and Parmigiano–Reggiano stand in for loads of salty seasonings. Presto! Instead of an overdressed, overportioned salad, our version offers brighter, lighter flavors in a truly healthy dish.

OLD WAY	OUR WAY
783 calories per serving	357 calories per serving
5.6 grams saturated fat	2.9 grams saturated fat
1,609 milligrams sodium	518 milligrams sodium
Gobs of mayo	Olive oil
Salt, seasoned salt, and seasoning mix	Judicious seasoning
Semolina pasta	Legume-based pasta

Quick & Easy
Prosciutto and Melon Pasta Salad

You can substitute whole-wheat pasta, if you like.

8 ounces uncooked legume-based farfalle pasta (such as Barilla Plus)
1½ tablespoons fresh lemon juice
1½ tablespoons white wine vinegar
¼ teaspoon Dijon mustard
¼ teaspoon salt
¼ teaspoon black pepper
⅛ teaspoon ground red pepper
1 garlic clove, coarsely chopped
2½ tablespoons extra-virgin olive oil
1 cup baby arugula
¾ cup diced cantaloupe
¼ cup thinly vertically sliced shallots
2 tablespoons torn fresh mint leaves
2 ounces thinly sliced prosciutto, cut into 2-inch-long strips
1 ounce shaved Parmigiano-Reggiano cheese

1. Cook pasta according to package directions, omitting salt and fat. Drain; cool to room temperature.
2. Place lemon juice and next 6 ingredients in a food processor; process until blended. With processor on, slowly pour olive oil through food chute; process 15 seconds or until blended.
3. Combine cooled pasta, arugula, and next 4 ingredients in a large bowl. Drizzle dressing over salad just before serving, and toss gently to coat. Top salad with cheese. Yield: 4 servings (serving size: 1¼ cups).

CALORIES 357; FAT 12.8g (sat 2.9g, mono 7.5g, poly 1.6g); PROTEIN 16.8g; CARB 44.3g; FIBER 4.7g; CHOL 13mg; IRON 2.5mg; SODIUM 518mg; CALC 134mg

GREAT NOODLES

A blend of chickpeas, multigrain flour, and legume flour, legume-based pasta yields a mild-flavored, al dente–textured noodle. The nutrition bonus: This type of pasta is higher in protein and fiber than regular semolina pasta.

PASTA SALADS AREN'T ALWAYS LIGHT, BUT OUR LIGHT FRESH TWIST RETURNS THIS STAPLE TO YOUR GO-TO LIST.

PRESTO!

For the healthy cook in a real hurry: 67 tips, 10 quick side dishes, 11 superfast entrées, and more...

HOW LONG DOES IT TAKE?

CHICKEN COOKING TIMES

Cooking chicken with the bone in may impart more flavor to the meat, but boneless cuts cook much faster. (See Spicy Honey-Brushed Chicken Thighs, page 237.)

BAKED AT 425°

Whole chicken	1 hour
Butterflied chicken (backbone and keel bone removed)	50 minutes
Whole chicken cut up into legs, thighs, breasts, and wings	35 minutes
Skinless, bone-in chicken thighs	35 minutes
Skin-on, bone-in chicken breasts	25 minutes

COOKED ON THE STOVETOP OVER MEDIUM-HIGH HEAT

Skinless, boneless chicken thigh	10 minutes
Skinless, boneless chicken breast	8 minutes
Chicken breast tenders	5 minutes
Chicken cutlets (¼ inch thick)	3 minutes

Quick & Easy
Favorite 20-Minute Recipe #1

Lemon-Splashed Shrimp Salad

You can purchase peeled and deveined shrimp to save prep time. Chop, measure, and prepare the remaining ingredients while the pasta water comes to a boil.

8 cups water
⅔ cup uncooked rotini (corkscrew pasta)
1½ pounds peeled and deveined large shrimp
1 cup halved cherry tomatoes
¾ cup sliced celery
½ cup chopped avocado
½ cup chopped seeded poblano pepper
2 tablespoons chopped fresh cilantro
2 teaspoons grated lemon rind
3 tablespoons fresh lemon juice
2 teaspoons extra-virgin olive oil
¾ teaspoon kosher salt

1. Bring 8 cups water to a boil in a large saucepan. Add pasta to pan; cook 5 minutes or until almost tender. Add shrimp; cook 3 minutes or until done. Drain. Rinse with cold water; drain well. Combine pasta mixture, tomatoes, and remaining ingredients; toss well. Yield: 4 servings (serving size: about 1¾ cups).

CALORIES 250; **FAT** 6.9g (sat 1.2g, mono 3.8g, poly 1.2g); **PROTEIN** 30.3g; **CARB** 17g; **FIBER** 2.6g; **CHOL** 252mg; **IRON** 5.1mg; **SODIUM** 667mg; **CALC** 74mg

---

Quick Side 1
Sautéed Spinach with Garlic and Red Pepper:
Heat 1 tablespoon olive oil and 2 teaspoons butter in a Dutch oven over medium-low heat. Add ¼ teaspoon crushed red pepper and 5 thinly sliced garlic cloves; cook 5 minutes, stirring occasionally. Increase heat to medium-high. Gradually add 2 (9-ounce) packages fresh spinach, tossing constantly until spinach wilts (about 2 minutes). Stir in ¼ teaspoon kosher salt. Yield: 4 servings (serving size: about ¾ cup).

CALORIES 82; **FAT** 5.8g (sat 1.8g); **SODIUM** 233mg

TIPS #1-4

SMART SHOPPING STRATEGIES WILL SAVE YOU TIME

1 Probably the biggest time-saver is the weekly menu plan and grocery list: a small Sunday chore but a real time-saver later, when weekday checkout lines can be long. Energetic? Do your grocery shopping on Sunday afternoon.

2 By now you probably know the layout of your favorite supermarket like the back of your hand. Use that navigation skill to your advantage: Organize the weekly grocery list by area, which will help keep you from backtracking.

3 Get supermarket staff to work for you—ask the butcher to divvy a family pack of chicken breasts into smaller packages or trim fat from roasts. Have the good folks at the seafood counter peel and devein your shrimp.

4 If you're really in a rush, call ahead to place orders with the butcher, bakery, deli, and seafood counters so that your ingredients will be ready for pickup—like the 1½ pounds of peeled and deveined shrimp you'll need for Lemon-Splashed Shrimp Salad, at left.

TIPS #5–8

GO-TO QUICK INGREDIENTS WITH BIG FLAVOR

5 Smoked paprika contributes smoky flavor to a dish without the hassle—and the messy grease spatters—of frying bacon.

6 Any nut that is sold shelled and roasted is a valuable time-saver that helps you work faster (faster than Tip #61, page 275, even).

7 The same idea applies in the case of pre-toasted sesame seeds, which can be found on the spice aisle of most grocery stores these days. Toasting brings out marvelous nutty flavor in sesame seeds, but doing it at home is tricky as they burn very easily.

8 Capers deliver bright briny flavor in a flash. Toss a tablespoon into pasta dishes, put on pizza, and use in sauces for chicken and fish.

Quick Side 2
Pan-Grilled Corn with Chipotle-Lime Butter:

Heat grill pan over medium-high heat. Coat pan with cooking spray. Add 4 ears shucked corn to pan; cook 8 minutes, turning frequently. Place 1 tablespoon butter in a microwave-safe dish. Microwave at HIGH 30 seconds or until butter melts. Stir in ½ teaspoon chipotle chile powder, ½ teaspoon grated lime rind, ¼ teaspoon salt, and ¼ teaspoon freshly ground black pepper. Brush butter mixture over corn. Yield: 4 servings (serving size: 1 ear).

CALORIES 103; FAT 3.9g (sat 2g); SODIUM 189mg

Quick & Easy
Favorite 20-Minute Recipe #2

Thai Beef Salad

Make this semi-involved recipe much faster by using the food processor's shredder attachment to shred the cabbage.

1 cup fresh cilantro leaves
¼ cup fresh lime juice (about 2 limes)
1 tablespoon lower-sodium soy sauce
1 tablespoon Thai fish sauce
1 tablespoon honey
2 teaspoons grated orange rind
2 garlic cloves, peeled
½ small serrano chile
2 teaspoons olive oil
4 (4-ounce) beef tenderloin steaks, trimmed
¼ teaspoon black pepper
⅛ teaspoon salt
2 cups shredded Napa cabbage
½ English cucumber, halved lengthwise and thinly sliced
⅓ cup thinly sliced green onions
3 tablespoons chopped fresh basil
1 (12-ounce) package broccoli coleslaw
1 (11-ounce) can mandarin oranges in light syrup, drained

1. Place first 8 ingredients in a food processor, and process until smooth.
2. Heat oil in a large nonstick skillet over medium-high heat. Sprinkle steaks evenly on both sides with pepper and salt. Add steaks to pan; cook 4 minutes on each side or until desired degree of doneness. Remove steaks from pan; let stand 5 minutes. Thinly slice steaks.
3. Combine cabbage and remaining ingredients in a large bowl. Drizzle slaw mixture with cilantro mixture; toss. Arrange 2 cups slaw mixture on each of 4 plates; top each serving with 3 ounces beef. Yield: 4 servings.

CALORIES 313; FAT 11.8g (sat 4g, mono 5.5g, poly 0.6g); PROTEIN 28.2g; CARB 22.6g; FIBER 5g; CHOL 71mg; IRON 2.8mg; SODIUM 612mg; CALC 105mg

---

Quick & Easy
Favorite 20-Minute Recipe #3

Spicy Honey-Brushed Chicken Thighs

Boneless chicken thighs cook in less than a third of the time it takes for bone-in thighs. Serve with Quinoa Salad with Peaches.

2 teaspoons garlic powder
2 teaspoons chili powder
1 teaspoon salt
1 teaspoon ground cumin
1 teaspoon paprika
½ teaspoon ground red pepper
8 skinless, boneless chicken thighs
Cooking spray
6 tablespoons honey
2 teaspoons cider vinegar

1. Preheat broiler.
2. Combine first 6 ingredients in a large bowl. Add chicken to bowl; toss to coat. Place chicken on a broiler pan coated with cooking spray. Broil chicken 5 minutes on each side.
3. Combine honey and vinegar in a small bowl, stirring well. Remove chicken from oven; brush ¼ cup honey mixture on chicken. Broil 1 minute. Remove chicken from oven and turn over. Brush chicken with remaining honey mixture. Broil 1 additional minute or until chicken is done. Yield: 4 servings (serving size: 2 chicken thighs).

CALORIES 321; FAT 11g (sat 3g, mono 4.1g, poly 2.5g); PROTEIN 28g; CARB 27.9g; FIBER 0.6g; CHOL 99mg; IRON 2.1mg; SODIUM 676mg; CALC 21mg

Quick Side 3
Quinoa Salad with Peaches:
Bring 1½ cups water to a boil in a medium saucepan; add ¾ cup uncooked quinoa. Cover, reduce heat, and simmer 20 minutes. Cool quinoa slightly. Stir in ¼ cup minced red bell pepper, ¼ cup chopped green onions, 3 tablespoons fresh lemon juice, 1½ tablespoons olive oil, ½ teaspoon kosher salt, 1½ teaspoons honey, ¼ teaspoon black pepper, and 1 sliced ripe peach. Yield: 4 servings (serving size: about 1 cup).

CALORIES 196; FAT 7.1g (sat 0.9g); SODIUM 245mg

THESE GADGETS REALLY DO SAVE YOU TIME

9 Toaster oven: It heats up quickly because it has less than 1 cubic foot of space, versus 5 for the average oven. It's ideal for small households—you can roast and toast portions for two in a fraction of the time it would take in the larger oven.

10 Food processor: Use its shredding blade attachment to make slaw in seconds. (See Thai Beef Salad recipe, page 237.)

11 Immersion blender: Stick it into a pot of soup, and you'll have a smooth puree in seconds. And you don't have to transfer hot soup from the pot to the conventional blender and back again. Easy to clean.

12 Egg slicer: Yes, your grandmother had one, but you should know it multitasks—use it for fresh hulled strawberries or small, firm mushrooms like button or cremini.

13 Kitchen scissors: Cut up canned whole tomatoes right in the can, snip away at a slice of bacon, and trim chives straight over dishes. (Just wash the scissors in between.)

Quick Side 4
Roasted Curried Cauliflower:
Preheat oven to 475°. Combine 6 cups cauliflower florets (about 1 medium head), 1½ tablespoons olive oil, ½ teaspoon kosher salt, and ½ teaspoon Madras curry powder on a baking sheet; toss to coat. Bake at 475° for 18 minutes or until browned and crisp-tender, stirring occasionally. Yield: 4 servings (serving size: about 1¼ cups).

CALORIES 82; FAT 5.2g (sat 0.7g); SODIUM 279mg

Quick & Easy • Kid Friendly
Favorite 20-Minute Recipe #4

Turkey and Bean Chili

To save time, chop off the top of a washed cilantro bunch rather than picking individual leaves (Tip #18, page 239). Serve this one-pot dish with corn bread for a warming weeknight supper.

1 cup prechopped red onion
⅓ cup chopped seeded poblano pepper (about 1)
1 teaspoon bottled minced garlic
1¼ pounds ground turkey
1 tablespoon chili powder
2 tablespoons tomato paste
2 teaspoons dried oregano
1 teaspoon ground cumin
¼ teaspoon salt
¼ teaspoon black pepper
1 (19-ounce) can cannellini beans, rinsed and drained
1 (14.5-ounce) can diced tomatoes, undrained
1 (14-ounce) can fat-free, lower-sodium chicken broth
½ cup chopped fresh cilantro
6 lime wedges

1. Heat a large saucepan over medium heat. Add first 4 ingredients; cook 6 minutes or until turkey is done, stirring frequently to crumble. Stir in chili powder and next 8 ingredients; bring to a boil. Reduce heat, and simmer 10 minutes. Stir in cilantro. Serve with lime wedges. Yield: 6 servings (serving size: about 1 cup chili and 1 lime wedge).

CALORIES 211; FAT 6.5g (sat 1.7g, mono 1.9g, poly 1.6g); PROTEIN 22.5g; CARB 16.4g; FIBER 4.7g; CHOL 54mg; IRON 3.4mg; SODIUM 474mg; CALC 52mg

---

Quick & Easy
Favorite 20-Minute Recipe #5

Maple-Glazed Salmon

(pictured on page 264)

Put together a big batch of the spice rub, and keep it in an airtight container; use it to add flavor to meat and fish on weeknights. Serve with Tomato-Dill Couscous.

1 teaspoon paprika
½ teaspoon chili powder
½ teaspoon ground ancho chile powder
¼ teaspoon ground cumin
¼ teaspoon brown sugar
1 teaspoon kosher salt
4 (6-ounce) Alaskan salmon fillets
Cooking spray
2 tablespoons maple syrup

1. Preheat broiler.
2. Combine first 6 ingredients; rub spice mixture evenly over flesh side of fillets. Place fish on a broiler pan coated with cooking spray; broil 6 minutes or until desired degree of doneness. Brush fillets evenly with syrup; broil 1 minute. Yield: 4 servings (serving size: 1 fillet).

CALORIES 352; FAT 20g (sat 3.2g, mono 7g, poly 2.7g); PROTEIN 34.6g; CARB 8.6g; FIBER 0.2g; CHOL 104mg; IRON 1.6mg; SODIUM 574mg; CALC 80mg

---

Quick Side 5
Tomato-Dill Couscous:
Heat a small saucepan over medium-high heat. Add 1 tablespoon olive oil to pan. Stir in 1 cup uncooked couscous; sauté 1 minute. Add 1 cup plus 2 tablespoons fat-free, lower-sodium chicken broth and ⅛ teaspoon salt; bring to a boil. Cover, remove from heat, and let stand 5 minutes. Fluff with a fork. Stir in ½ cup quartered cherry tomatoes, ¼ cup finely chopped red onion, and 2 tablespoons chopped fresh dill. Yield: 4 servings (serving size: ¾ cup).

CALORIES 201; FAT 3.7g (sat 0.5g); SODIUM 149mg

Favorite 20-Minute Recipe #6

Apricot Lamb Chops

(pictured on page 266)

Fruit preserves make a fast, simple glaze for roasted and grilled meats and poultry. Serve with Roasted Carrots with Fennel Seeds.

½ cup apricot preserves
2 teaspoons Dijon mustard
1 teaspoon bottled minced garlic
1 teaspoon lower-sodium soy sauce
½ teaspoon Worcestershire sauce
¼ teaspoon salt
⅛ teaspoon ground cinnamon
⅛ teaspoon black pepper
8 (4-ounce) lamb loin chops, trimmed
Cooking spray

1. Combine first 5 ingredients in a small bowl; set aside. Combine salt, cinnamon, and pepper, and sprinkle over both sides of lamb. Heat a large nonstick skillet over medium-high heat. Coat pan with cooking spray. Add lamb to pan; cook 5 minutes on each side or until desired degree of doneness. Remove skillet from heat; add apricot mixture, turning lamb to coat. Place 2 chops on each of 4 plates; spoon about 2 tablespoons remaining apricot mixture over each chop. Yield: 4 servings (serving size: 2 lamb chops and about 2 tablespoons sauce).

CALORIES 287; **FAT** 8.6g (sat 3g, mono 3.8g, poly 0.6g); **PROTEIN** 26.1g; **CARB** 26.7g; **FIBER** 0.3g; **CHOL** 81mg; **IRON** 2.1mg; **SODIUM** 350mg; **CALC** 32mg

Quick Side 6
Roasted Carrots with Fennel Seeds:
Preheat oven to 425°. Toss 2 cups (2-inch) diagonally cut carrot with 2 teaspoons olive oil, ½ teaspoon crushed fennel seeds, ¼ teaspoon salt, and ¼ teaspoon black pepper. Arrange carrots on a baking sheet. Roast at 425° for 15 minutes or until tender. Stir in ¼ cup chopped parsley. Yield: 4 servings (serving size: ½ cup).

CALORIES 46; **FAT** 2.4g (sat 0.3g); **SODIUM** 188mg

TIPS #14–16

COOKING SPRAY: THE QUICK COOK'S BEST KITCHEN FRIEND

14 When measuring syrupy items like honey, agave nectar, molasses, or, yes, syrup, coat the measuring spoon or cup with cooking spray. The ingredient will slip out easily—no need to scrape it out with a spatula to get the last bit.

15 Use cooking spray to coat your hands when you're forming meatballs or other sticky matter: You won't have to stop and wash nearly as often, if at all. (If you're a little squeamish about handling raw meat, use a cookie scoop to portion and form them instead. Lightly coat the inside of the scoop occasionally with cooking spray so the mixture doesn't stick.)

16 Lightly coat your knife blade to keep dried fruit and garlic from sticking to it as you chop.

TIPS #17–26

10 WAYS TO MAKE COMMON KITCHEN TASKS QUICKER AND EASIER

17 Boil water: Put a lid on it—4 quarts of water comes to a boil 1 minute faster in a covered pot. (OK, just 1 minute. But if you're in a rush, every second counts—think what you can do with 60.)

18 Chop herbs: To chop parsley or cilantro quickly, don't tediously pick leaves from the bunch; wash and dry the bunch while it's still bound together. Then make a diagonal cut (to avoid the thicker stems in the center) from the top of the bunch to chop off roughly the amount you'll need. (See Turkey and Bean Chili, page 238.)

19 Peel peaches: Place the peach in boiling water for about 30 seconds, remove it with a slotted spoon, and plunge it into an ice bath for a few seconds more. The peel will slip off easily.

20 Or just use nectarines: They're close enough to peaches for most recipes, and you won't have to bother with peeling at all.

21 If it's flat, stack it, and slice several at once—perfect for items like shiitake mushroom caps, bacon, and bread.

22 Peel garlic: Unless you need the garlic clove whole, just smash it with the flat side of your knife. The peel breaks apart so it's easy to remove. Mince away.

23 If you do need the whole peeled cloves, try this: Drop whole cloves into a lidded bowl, cover, and shake vigorously. The peels often fall right off. (This only works about half the time, but it's so cool when it does that we had to pass it on.)

24 Make a pasta toss: If you're including vegetables like broccoli rabe or peas, throw them into your pot of boiling pasta for the last minute of cooking. Drain everything together, toss, and add the remaining ingredients; one less dirty pot. If your recipe calls for wilted greens such as spinach or arugula, just drain the pasta over the leaves, and they'll wilt on the spot.

25 Make a spice rub: While you have the spices out, make an extra batch to use on meat, shrimp, or poultry on another night—it'll keep for months so there's no rush to use it. (See Maple-Glazed Salmon, page 238.) Or try this tasty rub on chicken, pork, or steak: Combine 2 tablespoons brown sugar, 2 tablespoons paprika, 4 teaspoons ground cumin, 2 teaspoons kosher salt, and 1 teaspoon ground red pepper; store in a dry, airtight container. Yield: about 6 tablespoons (serving size: 1 teaspoon).

26 Cook multiple toasted sandwiches or quesadillas: Use your broiler to cook several at once rather than using a skillet to cook batch after batch after (sigh) batch.

Quick Side 7
Greek Orzo Salad:

Cook ¾ cup uncooked orzo pasta according to package directions, omitting salt and fat. Drain and rinse under cold water; drain well. Stir in ⅓ cup sliced feta cheese, 3 tablespoons chopped kalamata olives, 1 tablespoon extra-virgin olive oil, 1 tablespoon fresh lemon juice, 1½ teaspoons chopped fresh oregano, ½ teaspoon freshly ground black pepper, and ¼ teaspoon kosher salt. Yield: 4 servings (serving size: about ¾ cup).

CALORIES 202; **FAT** 8.1g (sat 2.3g); **SODIUM** 412mg

TIPS #27–31

WORK FASTER WITH MEAT

27 If your recipe calls for superthin slices of meat—say, for Korean barbecue—chill the meat in the freezer for 10 to 15 minutes before slicing. It'll be much firmer, making it easier (and faster) to slice.

28 Just use your hands to shred cooked chicken, pork, or beef. The two-fork method can take forever.

29 To remove sausage from its casing, slice the link in half crosswise, then squeeze the meat out of the casing, bottom to top, toothpaste-style.

30 Fruit preserves make a quick, simple glaze for roasted and grilled meats, and the tasty results make you look like a chef. (Smucker's won't tell if you don't.) Just wait to brush it on until the final few minutes of cooking so it won't scorch. (See Apricot Lamb Chops, page 239.)

31 Use lower-sodium deli meats to quickly add protein to salads and turn them into a main course. (See Turkey and Romaine Salad, page 275.) In addition to meats that are labeled "low-sodium," roast beef often has less sodium than other deli meats. Low-sodium varieties of roast beef have about 80mg per 2-ounce serving.

Quick & Easy

Favorite 20-Minute Recipe #7

Gnocchi with Shrimp, Asparagus, and Pesto

Gnocchi—small Italian potato dumplings—are a hearty alternative to pasta. While making gnocchi from scratch could take more than an hour, premade vacuum-packed dumplings cook in a few minutes.

2 quarts plus 1 tablespoon water, divided
1 (16-ounce) package vacuum-packed gnocchi (such as Vigo)
4 cups (1-inch) slices asparagus (about 1 pound)
1 pound peeled and deveined large shrimp, coarsely chopped
1 cup fresh basil leaves
2 tablespoons pine nuts, toasted
2 tablespoons preshredded Parmesan cheese
2 teaspoons fresh lemon juice
2 teaspoons bottled minced garlic
4 teaspoons extra-virgin olive oil

1. Bring 2 quarts water to a boil in a Dutch oven. Add gnocchi to pan; cook 4 minutes or until done (gnocchi will rise to surface). Remove with a slotted spoon; place in a large bowl. Add asparagus and shrimp to pan; cook 5 minutes or until shrimp are done. Drain. Add shrimp mixture to gnocchi.
2. Place remaining 1 tablespoon water, basil, and next 4 ingredients in a food processor; process until smooth, scraping sides. Drizzle oil through food chute with food processor on; process until well blended. Add basil mixture to shrimp mixture; toss to coat. Serve immediately. Yield: 4 servings (serving size: 2 cups).

CALORIES 355; **FAT** 9.3g (sat 1.6g, mono 4.5g, poly 2.5g); **PROTEIN** 26.5g; **CARB** 42.7g; **FIBER** 3g; **CHOL** 170mg; **IRON** 5.7mg; **SODIUM** 747mg; **CALC** 108mg

---

Quick & Easy • Kid Friendly

Favorite 20-Minute Recipe #8

Quick Chicken and Dumplings

In this recipe, flour tortillas stand in for the traditional biscuit dough, while rotisserie chicken breast completes the dish in a jiffy.

1 tablespoon butter
½ cup prechopped onion
2 cups chopped roasted skinless, boneless chicken breast
1 (10-ounce) box frozen mixed vegetables, thawed
1½ cups water
1 tablespoon all-purpose flour
1 (14-ounce) can fat-free, lower-sodium chicken broth
¼ teaspoon salt
¼ teaspoon black pepper
1 bay leaf
8 (6-inch) flour tortillas, cut into ½-inch-wide strips
1 tablespoon chopped fresh parsley

1. Melt butter in a large saucepan over medium-high heat. Add onion, and sauté 5 minutes or until tender. Stir in chicken and vegetables; cook 3 minutes or until thoroughly heated, stirring constantly.
2. While chicken mixture cooks, combine 1½ cups water, flour, and broth. Gradually stir broth mixture into chicken mixture. Stir in salt, pepper, and bay leaf; bring to a boil. Reduce heat, and simmer 3 minutes. Stir in tortilla strips, and cook 2 minutes or until tortilla strips soften. Remove from heat; stir in parsley. Discard bay leaf. Serve immediately. Yield: 4 servings (serving size: about 1½ cups).

CALORIES 366; **FAT** 9.3g (sat 3.1g, mono 3.9g, poly 1.4g); **PROTEIN** 29.8g; **CARB** 40.3g; **FIBER** 5.3g; **CHOL** 67mg; **IRON** 3.4mg; **SODIUM** 652mg; **CALC** 104mg

continued on page 273

Upside-Down Fudge-Almond Tart, page 35

Beef and Pinto Bean Chili,
page 22

242

Chipotle Bean Burritos, page 49

Roast Chicken with Balsamic
Bell Peppers, page 46

Coconut Shrimp with
Fiery Mango Sauce, page 21

Chocolate-Cherry Heart Smart Cookies,
page 40

Quick Chicken Noodle
Soup, page 49

Apricot-Ginger Bellinis,
page 67

Maple-Mustard Pork Chops with
Winter Squash Puree, page 60

Pistachio Pavlovas with
Lemon Curd and Berries, page 79

Blue Cheese–Stuffed Chicken
with Buffalo Sauce, page 56

Bacon, Ranch, and Chicken
Mac and Cheese, page 54

Pasta with Mussels, Pine Nuts, and Orange, page 97

Black Bean Burgers with Mango Salsa, page 99

Lamb Chops with Pistachio Gremolata, page 109

No-Knead Overnight Parmesan
and Thyme Rolls, page 83

Salted Caramel
Ice Cream, page 128

Asparagus and Smoked Trout Frittata,
page 136

Crab Cakes with Spicy
Rémoulade, page 142

Spicy Asian Marinated Flank
Steak, page 161

Indian-Spiced Salmon
with Basmati Rice,
page 161

Grilled Chicken and Spinach Salad with
Spicy Pineapple Dressing, page 197

(Top) Salmon Burgers, page 175
(Bottom) Turkey Burgers with
Roasted Eggplant, page 173

Lattice-Topped Blackberry
Cobbler, page 178

Chicken and Guacamole
Tostadas, page 207

Summer Squash and Corn
Chowder, page 232

Grilled Peppers
and Lentil Salad,
page 222

Chipotle-Rubbed Shrimp Taco
Salad, page 231

261

Coconut Noodles with Scallops
and Pea Tendrils, page 209

Black Forest Cherry Cake,
page 283

263

Maple-Glazed Salmon, page 238

Mozzarella, Ham, and
Basil Panini, page 273

Oatmeal Pancakes, page 298

Apricot Lamb Chops, page 239

Peanut Butter Banana
Bread, page 312

Chicken with Lemon-Leek
Linguine, page 326

Roasted Red Pepper Hummus,
page 319

Mexican Turkey Stew, page 346

Halibut with Leeks, page 374

Christmas Stollen,
page 344

Peanut Butter,
Banana, and
Flax Smoothies,
page 372

Apple and Cranberry Turkey
Roulade, page 334

Curried Chicken Sauté,
page 375

OUR 10 BEST PREPARED-FOOD SHORTCUTS

Prepared foods can pack so much sodium and saturated fat that they're not worth the time they save in the kitchen. But Nutrition Editor Kathy Kitchens Downie, RD, has given these staff favorites a healthy thumbs-up.

32 Frozen stir-fry veggie bags by Birds Eye spare you lots of chopping time, and they don't come sauced, so you can control the sodium level.

33 Add cooked chicken or shrimp to refrigerated Cedar's Lentil Mediterranean Salad or Aegean Edamame Salad, and a high-fiber dinner is on the table in less than 10 minutes.

34 We love Amy's brand microwavable 6-ounce beans and rice burrito or black bean burrito for a light meal when there's a time crunch.

35 Mix steamed veggies and cooked chicken, shrimp, or tofu into authentically seasoned (but low in sodium) Seeds of Change Indian Simmer Sauces, and serve it over brown rice for a quick, tasty entrée.

36 Using Sunshine Southwest Organic Burgers or Morningstar Farms Spicy Black Bean Burgers, you can put a meatless meal together in a hurry. What's more, they're low enough in sodium to leave room for whole-grain buns and a little good cheese on top.

37 RiceSelect Royal Blend Texmati with Red Rice and Beans cooks up quickly and has a mix of white, brown, and red rices, so it has some whole grains in it. Pair with a quick-cooking protein to round out a fast but healthy meal.

38 Get sushi to go from Whole Foods, and try it with the multigrain rice.

39 Keep bags of Innovasian Cuisine chicken potstickers in your freezer. Build a fast dinner around them with steamed broccoli and rice noodles. They come with a sauce, but you can make your own lower-sodium dipping sauce.

40 Refrigerated fresh pastas by Buitoni and Vigo brand ready-made gnocchi cook in just a few minutes. (See Gnocchi with Shrimp, Asparagus, and Pesto, page 240.)

41 And then there are nights when only pizza will do. Frozen pizza is actually a viable option: Whole Foods 365 Chicken Caesar Pizza has less sodium and saturated fat than many other varieties.

10 THINGS TO DO WITH ROTISSERIE CHICKEN

42 Tuck breast meat slices into sandwiches for an easy, lower-sodium alternative to cold cuts.

43 Mix chopped chicken into a potato hash in place of corned beef or pork.

44 Add shredded chicken to any number of casseroles, from green bean to stratas. Use the dark meat—it can stand up to the extra cooking time without drying out.

45 Turn a variety of salads—whole grain, green, potato—into main dishes by using chicken as the protein.

46 Make fried rice a full meal by adding shredded breast and thigh meat.

47 Use whenever a recipe calls for cooked chicken, and save all that cooking time.

48 Toss chicken chunks with jarred salsa verde and preshredded Mexican blend cheese for a quick and easy filling for enchiladas, quesadillas, or tacos.

49 Combine shredded chicken with a mix of bottled barbecue sauce and light ranch dressing, and top a baked potato.

50 Make a simple chicken salad by adding canola mayonnaise, prechopped celery and onion, chopped walnuts, and halved red grapes.

51 Stir chopped or shredded breast meat into chilis, stews, and soups. (See Quick Chicken and Dumplings, page 240.)

Quick Side 8
Green Apple Slaw:
Combine 2 tablespoons cider vinegar, 1 tablespoon extra-virgin olive oil, 1½ teaspoons sugar, ¼ teaspoon kosher salt, and ¼ teaspoon freshly ground black pepper in a medium bowl; stir until sugar dissolves. Add 3 cups thinly sliced fennel bulb (about 1 large), 2 cups thinly sliced Granny Smith apple (1 large), ¼ cup fresh flat-leaf parsley leaves, and ¼ cup slivered red onion; toss to coat. Yield: 4 servings (serving size: about 1 cup).

CALORIES 91; FAT 3.6g (sat 0.5g); SODIUM 155mg

Quick & Easy • Kid Friendly
Favorite 20-Minute Recipe #9

Mozzarella, Ham, and Basil Panini

(pictured on page 264)
Fresh ciabatta bread and imported Dijon mustard make this quick sandwich seem like a treat.

1 (16-ounce) loaf ciabatta, cut in half horizontally
4 teaspoons Dijon mustard
4 teaspoons balsamic vinegar
1⅓ cups (8 ounces) thinly sliced fresh mozzarella cheese
12 basil leaves
8 ounces sliced 33%-less-sodium cooked deli ham (such as Boar's Head)
2 sweetened hot cherry peppers, sliced
1 large plum tomato, thinly sliced
Cooking spray

1. Brush cut side of bottom bread half with mustard; brush cut side of top half with vinegar. Top bottom half with mozzarella, basil, ham, peppers, and tomato. Top with remaining bread half. **2.** Heat a large nonstick skillet over medium heat. Coat pan with cooking spray. Add sandwich to pan; top with another heavy skillet. Cook 3 minutes on each side or until golden. Cut sandwich into 6 wedges. Yield: 6 servings (serving size: 1 wedge).

CALORIES 371; FAT 12.5g (sat 6.1g, mono 5g, poly 0.6g); PROTEIN 20.2g; CARB 44.9g; FIBER 1.8g; CHOL 46mg; IRON 3mg; SODIUM 976mg; CALC 220mg

5 WAYS TO PUT DINNER ON THE TABLE FASTER

52 Make sure you have everything you need—prepped ingredients, equipment—ready to roll before you start cooking. Chefs call it *mise en place* (literally, "putting in place"). Cooks who don't heed this can waste a lot of time backtracking in the middle of a recipe to prep ingredients they forgot.

53 Did we mention the importance of mise en place? Seriously: It bears repeating. Preparation is one of the big time-savers.

54 Cook simultaneously on as many burners as you can. Professional cooks can work six or more; you can handle at least two or three.

55 Rachael Ray didn't invent the practice of keeping a refuse bowl on the countertop, but she helped popularize it for good reason: Avoiding extra trips to the garbage will save you time.

56 Embrace sandwich night. Just make your sandwich good, and use a few premium ingredients like bakery-fresh bread or top-quality condiments like Maille Dijon mustard. (See Mozzarella, Ham, and Basil Panini, page 273.)

Quick Side 9
Green Beans with Browned Butter and Lemon:
Cook 1 pound trimmed green beans in boiling water 5 minutes or until crisp-tender. Drain and plunge beans into ice water; drain well. Melt 1½ tablespoons butter in a large skillet over medium-high heat; cook 2 minutes or until browned. Add beans to pan; cook 1 minute or until heated, stirring frequently. Stir in ½ teaspoon grated lemon rind, 1 teaspoon fresh lemon juice, ¼ teaspoon kosher salt, and ¼ teaspoon freshly ground black pepper. Yield: 4 servings (serving size: about 1 cup).

CALORIES 74; **FAT** 4.4g (sat 2.7g); **SODIUM** 155mg

USE SMALL FOOD FOR QUICKER COOKING

57 Baby vegetables cook in a flash because they're tiny and more tender than their full-grown counterparts.

58 Slice pork tenderloin crosswise into ½-inch-thick pieces. They'll cook about five times faster than a whole tenderloin.

59 Angel hair pasta is among the fastest-cooking dried pastas; it cooks in less than five minutes. Need pasta even more pronto? Then use refrigerated fresh pasta instead of dried; it cooks in less than four minutes. (See Chicken Puttanesca with Fettuccine, at right.)

Quick & Easy
Favorite 20-Minute Recipe #10

Chicken Puttanesca with Fettuccine

Refrigerated fresh fettuccine helps bring this dish together fast. We add olives, capers, crushed red pepper, and optional fresh basil to bottled pasta sauce for a quick variation on the classic recipe. Although we use chicken, you can also try this with shrimp.

8 ounces uncooked refrigerated fresh fettuccine
2 teaspoons olive oil
4 (6-ounce) skinless, boneless chicken breast halves
2 cups tomato-basil pasta sauce (such as Muir Glen Organic)
¼ cup pitted and coarsely chopped kalamata olives
2 teaspoons capers
¼ teaspoon crushed red pepper
¼ cup (1 ounce) shaved fresh Parmesan cheese
Chopped fresh basil or basil sprigs (optional)

1. Cook pasta according to package directions, omitting salt and fat. Drain and keep warm.
2. Heat oil in a large nonstick skillet over medium-high heat. Cut chicken into 1-inch pieces. Add chicken to pan. Cook chicken 5 minutes or until lightly browned, stirring occasionally. Stir in pasta sauce and next 3 ingredients; bring to a simmer. Cook 5 minutes or until chicken is done, stirring frequently. Arrange 1 cup pasta on each of 4 plates; top with 1½ cups chicken mixture. Sprinkle each serving with 1 tablespoon cheese. Garnish with basil, if desired. Yield: 4 servings.

CALORIES 462; **FAT** 9.9g (sat 2.2g, mono 4.2g, poly 1.5g); **PROTEIN** 49.7g; **CARB** 44g; **FIBER** 2.4g; **CHOL** 144mg; **IRON** 4.4mg; **SODIUM** 738mg; **CALC** 133mg

MAKE YOUR MICROWAVE WORK HARDER

60 To dissolve sugar in liquid, cook the mixture in the microwave for a minute or so until it comes to a boil. This beats stirring the mixture constantly until the tiny granules disappear.

61 Toast nuts quickly by microwaving on HIGH for one to two minutes. Automatic shutoff ensures you won't forget them in the oven and burn them to cinders.

62 Pouring cold or even room temperature broth into a pot for soup instantly slows down your cooking process. Bring the broth to a simmer in the microwave by heating it on HIGH for one or two minutes while you sauté your veggies; then pour it into your pot.

63 Jump-start baked potatoes by microwaving them on HIGH for about four minutes; then pop them into the oven to finish baking—you'll save half an hour or more, and still get that irresistible crunchy skin.

Quick Side 10
Roasted Potatoes with Thyme and Garlic:
Preheat broiler. Combine 1 (20-ounce) package refrigerated potato wedges (such as Simply Potatoes), 2 tablespoons olive oil, ½ teaspoon kosher salt, and ¼ teaspoon freshly ground black pepper on a baking sheet. Broil 12 minutes, stirring after 6 minutes. Stir in 1 tablespoon minced garlic; broil 2 minutes or until potatoes are tender. Remove from oven; sprinkle with 2 teaspoons chopped fresh thyme. Yield: 4 servings (serving size: about ¾ cup).

CALORIES 151; **FAT** 6.8g (sat 0.9g); **SODIUM** 385mg

Quick & Easy
Favorite 20-Minute Recipe #11

Turkey and Romaine Salad

Deli meats help turn a salad into a main dish with minimal effort.

¼ cup low-fat buttermilk
1 tablespoon light mayonnaise
1 tablespoon fresh lime juice
½ teaspoon salt
⅛ teaspoon ground red pepper
1 garlic clove, peeled
½ ripe peeled avocado, seeded and coarsely mashed
8 (½-ounce) slices diagonally cut French bread baguette (about ½ inch thick)
¼ cup (1 ounce) preshredded Parmesan cheese
4 cups bagged chopped romaine lettuce
2 cups diced deli, lower-salt turkey breast (about 8 ounces)
½ cup thinly sliced green onions
2 tablespoons chopped fresh cilantro

1. Place first 7 ingredients in a blender, and process until smooth, scraping sides. Set aside.
2. Preheat broiler.
3. Arrange bread slices in a single layer on a baking sheet. Sprinkle 1½ teaspoons cheese on each bread slice. Broil bread slices 2 minutes or until lightly browned.
4. Combine lettuce and remaining ingredients in a large bowl. Drizzle buttermilk mixture over lettuce mixture; toss gently to coat. Serve with cheese toasts. Yield: 4 servings (serving size: about 1½ cups salad and 2 cheese toasts).

CALORIES 260; **FAT** 8g (sat 2.4g, mono 3.5g, poly 1g); **PROTEIN** 24.2g; **CARB** 22.8g; **FIBER** 4g; **CHOL** 53mg; **IRON** 2.6mg; **SODIUM** 694mg; **CALC** 171mg

---

QUICK CLEANUP

64 Pour water into dirty pots and pans while they're still hot to prevent debris from sticking stubbornly (think of it as deglazing the dregs). Less scrubbing later.

65 Line your baking pans with foil. Do it thoroughly, and you might not even need to wash the pan. (It'll be our little secret.)

66 Use that same principle to build a dish with minimal cleanup—fish and veggies steamed in parchment, for instance.

67 Clean as you go: Wipe counters, rinse or wash dishes. Pro chefs do this religiously, and the kitchen can be 90 percent clean when you serve. Then institute a new house rule: "She who cooks does not clean." You're good. You're fast. You deserve it!

EDITORS' FAST FAVES

"A mandoline makes quick work of slicing—it yields perfectly uniform, thin pieces and spares you the hassle of dragging out your food processor."
—Test Kitchens Director Vanessa Pruett

"When you're making a puree, like gazpacho or butternut squash soup, don't bother with tedious cubing and just coarsely chop the ingredients—they get pulverized anyway so nobody could appreciate your ninja knife skills."
—Test Kitchens Staffer Robin Bashinsky

"Pull meat out of the fridge to take the chill off before you prep other ingredients. Meat will cook faster and more evenly when it's closer to room temperature."
—Associate Food Editor Tim Cebula

"If you have hardened caramel stuck to the inside of a pot, don't bother scrubbing it. Fill the pot halfway with water, and bring it to a boil, covered. The caramel will melt into the water, making it much easier to clean."
—Associate Food Editor Julianna Grimes

TOP 20 INGREDIENTS FOR THE QUICK COOK

Keep these essentials on hand and in mind. You can combine them in creative ways to yield deliciously quick and healthy weeknight meals.

Fast, fresh, and healthy: These three words represent the Holy Grail of the busy weeknight cook who wants to get a delicious meal on the table without sacrificing good nutrition (let alone good flavor) to the gods of the crazy-busy modern lives we all live. It's easy enough to open a box of fat-laden this and a package of supersalty that and turn out a 20-minute meal that doesn't quite meet the fast, fresh, and healthy goal. But this is not enough—not when a bit of planning, creativity, and smarts can have you quickly serving up dishes like Quick Crisp Ravioli with Roasted Tomato Sauce (at right), Quick Greek Couscous with Shrimp (page 279), or a spectacular, family-pleasing Quick Tex-Mex Confetti Pizza (page 277).

It all comes down to stocking up on healthy, easy-to-use, high-flavor ingredients and buying a few fast, fresh additions on your way home. We've identified 20 ingredients that get our creative juices flowing, from fresh, superconvenient products like bagged baby spinach, to go-to pantry standards like organic canned black beans, to high-flavor spice-rack heroes like smoked paprika, which gives a bacon-y savor to foods while adding zero calories and zero saturated fat.

With this list of 20 gold-standard quick-cooking ingredients in hand, we turned our Test Kitchens energies to some recipes. Each one uses just six ingredients (not including salt, pepper, water, oil, or cooking spray), with four coming from our list. We hope these inspire you to stock your own pantry and experiment further. Fast, fresh, and healthy can be something else, too—fun.

HEALTHY QUICK COOKING ALL COMES DOWN TO STOCKING UP ON HEALTHY, EASY-TO-USE, HIGH-FLAVOR INGREDIENTS AND BUYING A FEW FAST, FRESH ADDITIONS ON YOUR WAY HOME.

FRESH RAVIOLI, PANKO CRUMBS, AND TOMATOES

We're suckers for a bit of pan-fried crunchy goodness, and panko plus ravioli delivers *Quick Crisp Ravioli with Roasted Tomato Sauce.* Use your favorite ravioli—we like cheese or spinach filling. Serve with garlicky broccoli rabe or wilted greens, such as chard or kale.

Hands-on time: 25 minutes
Total time: 27 minutes

Quick & Easy • Kid Friendly

Quick Crisp Ravioli with Roasted Tomato Sauce

2 tablespoons water
1 large egg, lightly beaten
1 cup panko (Japanese breadcrumbs)
1/4 cup (1 ounce) grated fresh Parmigiano-Reggiano cheese
1 (9-ounce) package fresh ravioli
3 tablespoons olive oil, divided
4 cups grape tomatoes (about 2 pints), halved
1/2 teaspoon salt
1/4 teaspoon freshly ground black pepper
3 garlic cloves, coarsely chopped

1. Combine 2 tablespoons water and egg in a shallow dish, stirring well. Combine panko and cheese in a shallow dish, stirring well with a fork. Dip each ravioli in egg mixture; dredge in panko mixture.
2. Heat a large skillet over medium-high heat. Add 1½ tablespoons oil to pan; swirl to coat. Add half of ravioli to pan in a single layer; sauté 1 minute on each side or until golden. Remove ravioli from pan using a slotted spoon; drain on paper towels. Keep warm. Repeat procedure with remaining 1½ tablespoons oil and ravioli. Wipe skillet with paper towels.
3. Add tomatoes, salt, and pepper to pan; sauté 2 minutes, stirring frequently. Add garlic to pan; sauté 30 seconds, stirring constantly. Divide ravioli evenly among 4 plates; top each serving with ½ cup tomato sauce. Yield: 4 servings.

CALORIES 399; FAT 19.2g (sat 6.1g, mono 9.9g, poly 1.6g); PROTEIN 14.6g; CARB 42.4g; FIBER 4.1g; CHOL 93mg; IRON 1.9mg; SODIUM 747mg; CALC 159mg

POTATO WEDGES, EGGS,
BABY SPINACH, AND
MUSHROOMS

The simplest supermarket ingredients make a *Quick Garden Omelet* that works for breakfast, lunch, or dinner. Even faster: Buy presliced mushrooms.

Hands-on time: 32 minutes
Total time: 42 minutes

Quick & Easy
Quick Garden Omelet

Cooking spray
1/2 (20-ounce) package refrigerated red potato wedges (such as Simply Potatoes), coarsely chopped
6 ounces presliced cremini mushrooms
3/4 teaspoon salt, divided
4 teaspoons butter, divided
8 large eggs
1/2 teaspoon freshly ground black pepper
1 cup bagged fresh baby spinach leaves, coarsely chopped and divided
1/2 cup (2 ounces) crumbled goat cheese, divided

1. Heat a 12-inch nonstick skillet over medium-high heat. Coat pan with cooking spray. Add potatoes to pan; sauté 10 minutes, stirring occasionally. Stir in mushrooms and 1/4 teaspoon salt; sauté 8 minutes or until potatoes are tender, stirring occasionally. Remove from pan; set aside.
2. Wipe pan clean with paper towels. Melt 2 teaspoons butter in pan over medium-high heat. Combine eggs, remaining 1/2 teaspoon salt, and pepper in a bowl, stirring with a whisk until eggs are frothy. Pour half of egg mixture into pan, and stir briskly with a heatproof spatula about 10 seconds or until egg starts to thicken. Carefully loosen set edges of omelet with spatula, tipping pan to pour uncooked egg to sides. Continue this procedure for about 10 to 15 seconds or until almost no runny egg remains.
3. Remove pan from heat; arrange half of potato mixture, 1/2 cup spinach, and 1/4 cup cheese over omelet in pan. Run spatula around edges and under omelet to loosen it from pan. Fold omelet in half. Slide omelet from pan onto a platter. Cut in half crosswise. Repeat procedure with remaining butter, egg mixture, potato mixture, spinach, and cheese. Yield: 4 servings (serving size: 1 omelet half).

CALORIES 277; FAT 14.9g (sat 6.8g, mono 5.5g, poly 1.7g); PROTEIN 18.3g; CARB 13.7g; FIBER 2.2g; CHOL 377mg; IRON 2.8mg; SODIUM 744mg; CALC 89mg

SOY SAUCE, CANOLA MAYO,
AND CHILE PASTE

The tang of soy and spice of chile combine to yield tasty *Quick Pan-Fried Chicken Breast*. The creamy mayo helps panko crumbs cling to the chicken while you pan-fry it to a crispy finish.

Hands-on time: 22 minutes
Total time: 43 minutes

Quick & Easy
Quick Pan-Fried Chicken Breasts

4 (6-ounce) skinless, boneless chicken breast halves
3 tablespoons canola mayonnaise
2 tablespoons lower-sodium soy sauce
2 tablespoons fresh lemon juice
1 tablespoon chile paste (such as sambal oelek)
2 tablespoons olive oil, divided
1 1/2 cups panko (Japanese breadcrumbs)

1. Place each chicken breast half between 2 sheets of heavy-duty plastic wrap; pound to an even thickness (about 1/2-inch), using a meat mallet or small heavy skillet. Combine mayonnaise and next 3 ingredients in a large zip-top plastic bag. Add chicken to bag; seal and marinate in refrigerator 15 minutes. Remove chicken from bag; discard marinade.
2. Heat a large nonstick skillet over medium-high heat. Add 1 tablespoon oil to pan; swirl to coat. Place panko in a shallow dish. Dredge chicken evenly in panko. Add half of chicken to pan; sauté 4 minutes on each side or until chicken is done. Wipe pan clean with paper towels. Repeat procedure with remaining oil and chicken. Yield: 4 servings (serving size: 1 chicken breast half).

CALORIES 403; FAT 18g (sat 1.9g, mono 11.2g, poly 3.7g); PROTEIN 42.2g; CARB 14.6g; FIBER 0.7g; CHOL 102mg; IRON 1.4mg; SODIUM 498mg; CALC 21mg

FROZEN CORN AND
SMOKED PAPRIKA

Is there anything more prosaic than frozen corn? But when it's given a zing from the paprika, combined with other toppings like grape tomatoes and black beans, and all laid onto supermarket pizza dough: voilà, *Quick Tex-Mex Confetti Pizza*, a crowd-pleaser.

Hands-on time: 10 minutes
Total time: 30 minutes

Quick & Easy
Quick Tex-Mex Confetti Pizza

1 cup frozen corn kernels, thawed
1 tablespoon olive oil
1 teaspoon hot smoked paprika
1/8 teaspoon salt
1 pint grape tomatoes, halved
1 (15-ounce) can organic black beans, rinsed and drained
1 (16-ounce) package commercial pizza dough
3/4 cup (3 ounces) crumbled queso fresco cheese

1. Place a baking sheet in oven. Preheat oven to 450°.
2. Combine first 6 ingredients; toss. Roll dough out to a 13-inch circle; crimp edges to form a 1/2-inch border. Remove baking sheet from oven. Transfer dough onto preheated baking sheet. Spread bean mixture evenly over dough, leaving a 1/2-inch border, and top with cheese. Bake on bottom rack of oven at 450° for 20 minutes or until browned. Cut into 10 wedges. Yield: 5 servings (serving size: 2 wedges).

CALORIES 353; FAT 9.7g (sat 2.3g, mono 4.4g, poly 0.8g); PROTEIN 12.3g; CARB 56.7g; FIBER 3.9g; CHOL 6mg; IRON 3.3mg; SODIUM 721mg; CALC 73mg

20 ALL-STAR INGREDIENTS

PANTRY STAPLES

Boil-in-bag brown rice is one of the quickest ways to get more whole grains in your diet.
Use for: rice pilaf, rice salad, soups, and stews

Canned organic black beans offer options for main dishes and sides, and going with organic ensures there's minimal added salt.
Use for: black bean cakes, filling for tacos or burritos, salsa

Canned no-salt-added diced tomatoes save you the time and effort of seeding, chopping, and peeling fresh tomatoes.
Use for: marinara sauce, bruschetta, salsa

Canola mayonnaise has far less saturated fat than conventional store-bought mayo.
Use for: marinades, flavored sandwich spreads, dips

Couscous is one of the easiest and most versatile starches you can find.
Use for: salads, stuffing roasted veggies, serving with Moroccan tagines and other stews

Fat-free, lower-sodium chicken broth is indispensable for fast cooking.
Use for: poaching liquid, sauces, braising and stewing liquid

Pitted kalamata olives add a rich, meaty, and unique flavor to any dish they grace.
Use for: tapenade, pasta dishes, roast with chicken or vegetables

Smoked paprika packs a huge punch of flavor—and you don't need to fire up a grill.
Use for: replacing the smoky flavor of bacon, dry rubs on oven-roasted meats, stews, and chili

FROM THE FRIDGE AND FREEZER

Frozen corn kernels allow you to skip corn shucking and cutting the kernels from the cob.
Use for: cream-style corn, salsa, corn bread

Fresh pasta cooks in half the time it takes to cook dried. Here we focused on fresh ravioli.
Use for: soups, baked casseroles, appetizers

Frozen shelled edamame (soybeans) are a superconvenient way to add color, texture, and protein to most any dish.
Use for: salads, (pureed) dip or spread, whole-grain salads

Large eggs: There's simply no quicker protein, and they're just so versatile.
Use for: binder in patties and meatballs, salad topper, thickening and enriching sauces and salad dressings, or bulking up fried rice

Plain 2% reduced-fat Greek yogurt is luscious, smooth, and rich, not chalky like traditional plain yogurt.
Use for: dips, sauces, marinades

Refrigerated red potato wedges are ready to cook straight out of the bag.
Use for: potato salad, roasted potato sides, soup

PRODUCE

Bagged baby spinach saves you the time and trouble of removing the stems.
Use for: pizza topping, pasta dishes, wilted for a green side dish or salad

Grape tomatoes add a quick splash of color and flavor.
Use for: pasta tosses, salads, garnish

Presliced fresh cremini mushrooms allow you to simply dump and stir.
Use for: sauces, casseroles, stuffings, or fillings

ETHNIC

Panko (Japanese breadcrumbs) is every bit as convenient but tastes better than bland dry breadcrumbs. Panko also gives foods a supercrisp crust.
Use for: filler for meatballs, crab cakes, and the like; breading for oven-fried shrimp or fish fillets; casserole toppings

Lower-sodium soy sauce adds depth and flavor to a wide range of dishes, not just Asian foods.
Use for: fajita and other marinades, roasting veggies, dipping sauces

Chile paste (sambal oelek) is an all-purpose hot sauce.
Use for: marinades, vinaigrettes for steamed vegetables, scrambled or poached eggs

---

CANNED TOMATOES, BROWN RICE, EDAMAME, AND SMOKED PAPRIKA

Yes, it's possible to riff on the flavors of Spain's most famous dish and make a delicious *Quick Paella!* Boil-in-bag brown rice makes a fast, nutty, and nutritious foundation.

Hands-on time: 15 minutes
Total time: 29 minutes

Quick & Easy
Quick Paella

1 tablespoon olive oil
6 ounces Spanish chorizo, thinly sliced
2 (3.5-ounce) packages boil-in-bag brown rice (such as Uncle Ben's)
½ teaspoon salt
½ teaspoon hot smoked paprika
¼ teaspoon freshly ground black pepper
1½ cups water
1 (14.5-ounce) can no-salt-added diced tomatoes, undrained
1½ cups frozen shelled edamame
2 dozen mussels, scrubbed and debearded

1. Heat a Dutch oven over medium-high heat. Add oil to pan; swirl to coat. Add chorizo to pan; sauté 1 minute or until lightly browned, stirring occasionally. Remove rice from bags. Add rice to pan; sauté 1 minute, stirring frequently. Stir in salt, paprika, and pepper; sauté 30 seconds. Add 1½ cups water and tomatoes; bring to a boil. Cover, reduce heat to medium, and simmer 10 minutes or until rice is tender and liquid is almost absorbed.
2. Stir in edamame. Nestle mussels into rice mixture. Cover and cook 4 minutes or until mussels open and liquid is absorbed. Remove from heat. Discard any unopened mussels. Yield: 4 servings (serving size: 2 cups).

CALORIES 542; FAT 21g (sat 5.1g, mono 9g, poly 4.2g); PROTEIN 33.8g; CARB 55.6g; FIBER 8.1g; CHOL 27mg; IRON 4.9mg; SODIUM 636mg; CALC 42mg

Quick Black Bean and Corn Soup

Hands-on time: 12 minutes
Total time: 27 minutes

Cooking spray
1 cup frozen corn kernels
3 (15-ounce) cans organic black beans, rinsed, drained, and divided
1½ cups fat-free, lower-sodium chicken broth
1 (14.5-ounce) can no-salt-added diced tomatoes, undrained
1 tablespoon chile paste (such as sambal oelek)
³⁄₈ teaspoon salt
¼ cup plain 2% reduced-fat Greek yogurt

1. Heat a Dutch oven over medium-high heat. Coat pan with cooking spray. Add corn to pan, and sauté 4 minutes or until lightly browned, stirring occasionally.
2. Place 2 cans of beans and broth in a blender; process until smooth. Add bean mixture, remaining can of beans, tomatoes, chile paste, and salt to corn, stirring to combine; bring to a boil. Cover, reduce heat to medium, and simmer 15 minutes, stirring occasionally. Serve with yogurt. Yield: 4 servings (serving size: about 1¼ cups soup and 1 tablespoon yogurt).

CALORIES 295; FAT 1.6g (sat 0.3g, mono 0.4g, poly 0.6g); PROTEIN 17.8g; CARB 54.8g; FIBER 12.5g; CHOL 0.8mg; IRON 3.4mg; SODIUM 650mg; CALC 97mg

QUICK-COOKING PROTEINS

Combine ingredients from our list of essentials with meat or fish for a variety of quick and tasty dishes.
- Fish fillets
- Skinless, boneless chicken breast halves
- Boneless center-cut pork chops
- Peeled, deveined shrimp
- Shellfish: mussels, clams, and scallops
- Ground meats (beef, chicken, pork, or lamb)
- Lamb chops
- Beef tenderloin steaks
- Smoked or cured sausages, such as Spanish chorizo, andouille, chicken and apple sausage, etc.
- Smoked ham

GREEK YOGURT, KALAMATA OLIVES, COUSCOUS, AND GRAPE TOMATOES

These wonderful Mediterranean ingredients combine with quick seafood to produce *Quick Greek Couscous with Shrimp.* Yogurt adds a velvety texture.

Hands-on time: 18 minutes
Total time: 25 minutes

Quick & Easy • Kid Friendly

Quick Greek Couscous with Shrimp

1½ cups water
1⅓ cups uncooked couscous
½ teaspoon salt, divided
½ teaspoon freshly ground black pepper
3 tablespoons olive oil, divided
1½ pounds peeled and deveined medium shrimp
1 cup grape tomatoes, halved
½ cup thinly sliced green onions
⅓ cup pitted kalamata olives, halved
¼ cup plain 2% reduced-fat Greek yogurt (such as Fage)

1. Bring 1½ cups water to a boil in a large saucepan over medium-high heat. Add couscous, ¼ teaspoon salt, and pepper to pan. Cover, remove from heat, and let stand 5 minutes. Fluff with a fork.
2. Heat a large skillet over medium-high heat. Add 1 tablespoon olive oil to pan; swirl to coat. Sprinkle shrimp with remaining ¼ teaspoon salt. Add shrimp to pan, and sauté 3 minutes or until done. Add shrimp to couscous mixture.
3. Combine remaining 2 tablespoons oil, tomatoes, onions, and olives in a large bowl; toss. Add tomato mixture to couscous mixture; toss to combine. Serve with yogurt. Yield: 4 servings (serving size: 2 cups couscous mixture and 1 tablespoon yogurt).

CALORIES 487; FAT 15.3g (sat 2.4g, mono 9.5g, poly 2.3g); PROTEIN 35.3g; CARB 49.8g; FIBER 3.8g; CHOL 195mg; IRON 4mg; SODIUM 638mg; CALC 114mg

LESS MEAT, MORE FLAVOR
STIR-FRY SALADS

By Mark Bittman

A quick turn in a hot pan yields deliciously seared meat, crispy-crunchy vegetables, and intense flavors.

Fast is good, but frantic is not. So I sometimes take the urgency out of stir-fries by serving them at room temperature. This strategy works especially well when the sauce contains a splash of vinegar or citrus juice. The result is—in the very nicest way—a slightly soggy salad.

As the summer winds down, I'm also starting to get salad fatigue, so flash-cooking some or all the ingredients is a nice antidote to what sometimes seems like an overabundance of raw produce. A quick blast of heat intensifies the flavors of both vegetables and dressing, creates a variety of textures, and makes a salad feel more like dinner—all in a matter of minutes.

But first, a little debunking: Much has been written (some by me) about the importance of shuffling stir-fry ingredients in and out of the pan as they cook, the better to make sure they all brown, as they would in a superhot wok. I don't fuss about this as much as I used to; there's little reason to bother with several layers of cooking when you're turning the dish into a wilted salad anyway.

What is important is that whatever meat or seafood you use browns a bit, and that the vegetables soften somewhat but retain a little bite. You don't need a wok to accomplish this—in fact, unless your stove is set up with a well that allows flames to engulf the bottom third of the pan, a large, broad skillet with a lot of surface area is the best bet. Just be sure to turn the heat up fairly high and stir every once in a while—not constantly, which won't allow the meat and vegetables any time
continued

to sear. Leave the theatrics to Chinese restaurants.

A word about preparing the ingredients: You want the pieces to be small enough to cook quickly, but large enough that they don't turn to mush. And don't worry if they're not perfectly dry when you put them in the pan; the little bit of steam created during stir-frying helps cook the insides of the vegetables. I sometimes add a little water (especially with rugged foods like cabbage or root vegetables) for that reason. As an added benefit, a small amount of water adds volume to the sauce and helps distribute its flavors throughout the dish.

Don't be shy about seasoning here. Since cooking mitigates even the sharpest flavors, you can use more than you ever would in a raw tossed salad. I like to start the dressing with aromatics—ginger, onions, garlic, shallots—and build in deep flavors with soy or fish sauce. Chiles are almost always an option, as are spice blends like curry, five-spice, or chili powders. But it's the acidity that distinguishes these salads from most stir-fries. You want enough to brighten the other ingredients without overpowering them; again, a little water can come in handy here to dilute the strength of vinegar or citrus juice, if necessary.

The two salads here demonstrate the range of stir-fry approaches. In one, you start with a traditional bowl of lettuce and salad vegetables and toss it with piping hot stir-fried meat, tofu, and dressing. In the other recipe, the greens are added to the pan at the last minute to lightly cook them in the dressing. Feel free to improvise with seasonal produce and small amounts of seafood, poultry, meat, or soy protein in the form of tofu or tempeh. Whatever you do, undercook the vegetables just a tad so that, as the salad cools, they retain some crispness.

Quick & Easy
Spicy Beef and Tofu Salad

8 ounces firm tofu, cubed
6 cups torn or chopped romaine lettuce
½ cup torn fresh mint leaves
½ cup torn fresh basil leaves
1 large cucumber, peeled, halved lengthwise, seeded, and thinly sliced
1 small red onion, thinly sliced
¼ cup fresh lime juice
1 tablespoon Thai fish sauce
2 teaspoons dark sesame oil
½ teaspoon sugar
1 serrano pepper, minced
1 tablespoon peanut oil
4 ounces skirt steak, trimmed, cut into 3 equal pieces, and cut across grain into thin strips
¼ teaspoon salt
¼ teaspoon freshly ground black pepper

1. Arrange tofu on several layers of paper towels; cover with additional paper towels. Let stand 30 minutes, pressing down occasionally.
2. Combine lettuce and next 4 ingredients in a large bowl. Combine juice and next 4 ingredients in a small bowl, stirring with a whisk. Drizzle half of dressing over lettuce mixture; toss to coat.
3. Heat a large skillet over medium-high heat. Add peanut oil to pan; swirl to coat. Add tofu and beef; sprinkle with salt and black pepper. Cook 3 minutes or until tofu and meat are lightly browned, stirring once or twice. Remove pan from heat. Add remaining dressing to pan, scraping pan to loosen browned bits. Add tofu mixture to lettuce mixture; toss to combine. Yield: 4 servings (serving size: about 2¾ cups).

CALORIES 214; FAT 13.1g (sat 3g, mono 5.1g, poly 4.5g); PROTEIN 15g; CARB 10.8g; FIBER 3.2g; CHOL 17mg; IRON 2.9mg; SODIUM 527mg; CALC 105mg

Quick & Easy • Kid Friendly
Teriyaki Mushroom, Spinach, and Chicken Salad

2 tablespoons peanut oil, divided
8 ounces skinless, boneless chicken breast, cut into small pieces
½ teaspoon black pepper, divided
¼ teaspoon salt, divided
10 cups sliced shiitake mushroom caps (about 1 pound)
2 tablespoons minced peeled fresh ginger
1 tablespoon minced garlic
3 tablespoons lower-sodium soy sauce
3 tablespoons mirin (sweet rice wine) or 2 tablespoons water plus 1 tablespoon honey
1 teaspoon rice vinegar
8 cups fresh baby spinach (about 6 ounces)
1¾ cups chopped green onions

1. Heat a large skillet over high heat. Add 1 tablespoon oil to pan; swirl to coat. Add chicken; sprinkle with ¼ teaspoon pepper and ⅛ teaspoon salt. Cook 3 minutes or until chicken is just done, stirring occasionally. Remove chicken from pan.
2. Add mushrooms, remaining ¼ teaspoon pepper, and remaining ⅛ teaspoon salt to pan; stir-fry 6 minutes or until mushrooms brown and most of liquid evaporates. Add remaining 1 tablespoon oil, ginger, and garlic; cook 30 seconds, stirring constantly. Return chicken to pan; add soy sauce, mirin, and vinegar. Cook 2 minutes, scraping pan to loosen browned bits. Remove pan from heat; stir in spinach and onions. Yield: 4 servings (serving size: 1½ cups).

CALORIES 205; FAT 8.4g (sat 1.5g, mono 3.6g, poly 2.8g); PROTEIN 19.3g; CARB 13.4g; FIBER 3.1g; CHOL 33mg; IRON 2.9mg; SODIUM 629mg; CALC 82mg

FROM BOSTON TO THE BLACK FOREST

In a flight of fancy, we nabbed five classic desserts from famous places and made them deliciously light.

Cooking can be a more energetic variation of armchair travel, with this benefit: You end up with an evocative taste of the dreamed-of destination. Not long ago, we noticed the affinity of certain classic desserts to certain famous places. Cheesecake was not invented in New York, but New York has exerted unquestioned influence on the whole idea of cheesecake. It seems doubtful that the Black Forest Cake sprang whole out of a Black Forest cook's kitchen, but in its chocolate layers and cherry flavors is a lovely, dark symbol of a fabled place in Germany.

More fanciful ideas than this have sent our sweet tooths scurrying into the Test Kitchens. Our goal was to find the true nature of five destination desserts while rendering them lighter and brighter for the healthy appetite.

Make Ahead • Kid Friendly

Boston Cream Pie

In 1855, a French chef at Boston's Parker House Hotel cooked up this variant on an older pudding-cake dish, in which sponge cake is cut into two layers and filled with vanilla pudding or pastry cream, then glazed with chocolate. A New Yorker could get shirty about a cake that's called a pie, but is cheesecake really cake? Whatever: This is the state dessert of Massachusetts. Our version boozes up the chocolate glaze with a bit of Cointreau (orange-flavored liqueur), but feel free to omit it.

Cake:
Cooking spray
2 teaspoons cake flour
5 ounces sifted cake flour (about 1¼ cups)
1½ teaspoons baking powder
¼ teaspoon salt
½ cup granulated sugar
¼ cup butter, softened
1 teaspoon vanilla extract
1 large egg
¾ cup 1% low-fat milk
2 large egg whites
3 tablespoons granulated sugar

Filling:
½ cup granulated sugar
3 tablespoons cornstarch
⅛ teaspoon salt
1 cup plus 2 tablespoons 1% low-fat milk
⅓ cup egg substitute
1 tablespoon butter
½ teaspoon vanilla extract

Glaze:
2 ounces dark chocolate
2 tablespoons 1% low-fat milk
⅓ cup powdered sugar
2 teaspoons Cointreau (orange-flavored liqueur)

1. Preheat oven to 350°.
2. To prepare cake, coat bottom of a 9-inch round cake pan with cooking spray. Dust with 2 teaspoons cake flour; set aside.
3. Weigh or lightly spoon 5 ounces (about 1¼ cups) flour into dry measuring cups; level with a knife. Combine flour, baking powder, and ¼ teaspoon salt in a small bowl, stirring with a whisk. Place ½ cup granulated sugar and ¼ cup butter in a large bowl, and beat with a mixer at medium speed until light and fluffy (about 5 minutes).

Add 1 teaspoon vanilla and egg, beating until well blended. Add flour mixture and ¾ cup milk alternately to sugar mixture, beginning and ending with flour mixture.
4. Place egg whites in a medium bowl; beat with a mixer at high speed until foamy using clean, dry beaters. Gradually add 3 tablespoons granulated sugar, beating until stiff peaks form. Gently fold egg white mixture into batter; pour into prepared pan. Bake at 350° for 35 minutes or until a wooden pick inserted in center comes out clean. Cool in pan 10 minutes; run a knife around outside edge. Remove from pan, and cool completely on a wire rack.
5. To prepare filling, combine ½ cup granulated sugar, cornstarch, and ⅛ teaspoon salt in a medium saucepan. Gradually add 1 cup plus 2 tablespoons milk and egg substitute to pan, stirring with a whisk until well blended. Bring to a boil over medium heat, stirring constantly with a whisk until thick. Remove from heat; stir in 1 tablespoon butter and ½ teaspoon vanilla. Place pan in a large ice-filled bowl until custard cools to room temperature (about 15 minutes), stirring occasionally.
6. To prepare glaze, place chocolate and 2 tablespoons milk in a microwave-safe bowl. Microwave at HIGH 20 seconds or until chocolate melts. Add powdered sugar and liqueur, stirring with a whisk until smooth.
7. Split cake in half horizontally using a serrated knife; place bottom layer, cut side up, on a serving plate. Spread cooled filling evenly over bottom layer; top with remaining cake layer, cut side down. Spread glaze evenly over top cake layer. Yield: 10 servings.

CALORIES 281; **FAT** 8.7g (sat 5.2g, mono 1.9g, poly 0.4g); **PROTEIN** 5.1g; **CARB** 46.4g; **FIBER** 0.5g; **CHOL** 39mg; **IRON** 1.5mg; **SODIUM** 262mg; **CALC** 110mg

New York Cheesecake

More than one silly Web site claims this: "Ever since the dawn of time, mankind has striven to create the perfect cheesecake." Somehow, we doubt that (first, mankind had to invent fire, for example), but we don't doubt that the ancient Greeks produced a cheese-based sweet. Still, when cheesecake is dreamt of in the current millennium, it's not Athens but, say, Brooklyn that comes to mind—and that trademark rich, dense, creamy texture. This cake has a dense texture and rich cream cheese flavor. For a denser, creamier texture, cool the cake in the oven one hour with the oven door ajar instead of closed. Make a day ahead since the cooled cake needs to chill overnight.

Crust:

1 cup graham cracker crumbs (about 7 cookie sheets)

3 tablespoons sugar

1 large egg white

Cooking spray

Filling:

1 ounce all-purpose flour (about 1/4 cup)

1/2 cup 1% low-fat cottage cheese

3 (8-ounce) blocks fat-free cream cheese, softened, divided

2 (8-ounce) blocks 1/3-less-fat cream cheese, softened

1 3/4 cups sugar

1 1/2 teaspoons finely grated lemon rind

2 tablespoons fresh lemon juice

1/2 teaspoon vanilla extract

3 large eggs

3 large egg whites

1. Preheat oven to 350°.

2. To prepare crust, combine crumbs, 3 tablespoons sugar, and 1 egg white in a bowl; toss with a fork until well blended. Lightly coat hands with cooking spray. Press crumb mixture into bottom of a 9-inch springform pan coated with cooking spray. Bake at 350° for 8 minutes; cool on a wire rack. Reduce oven temperature to 325°.

3. To prepare filling, weigh or lightly spoon flour into a dry measuring cup; level with a knife. Place flour, cottage cheese and 8 ounces fat-free cream cheese in a food processor, and process until smooth. Add remaining 16 ounces fat-free cream cheese, 1/3-less-fat cream cheese, and next 4 ingredients; process until smooth. Add 3 eggs and 3 egg whites; process until blended. Pour cheese mixture into prepared pan. Bake at 325° for 65 minutes or until almost set (center will not be firm but will set as it chills). Turn oven off; cool cheesecake in closed oven 1 hour. Remove from oven; cool on a wire rack. Cover and chill 8 hours. Yield: 16 servings (serving size: 1 wedge).

CALORIES 259; **FAT** 8g (sat 4.8g, mono 2.5g, poly 0.4g); **PROTEIN** 12.7g; **CARB** 33.9g; **FIBER** 0.2g; **CHOL** 58mg; **IRON** 0.6mg; **SODIUM** 446mg; **CALC** 111mg

Mississippi Mud Pie

It's not the prettiest image, but many folks speculate this cross between a chocolate-bottomed pie and a chocolate cake was so named for its textural similarity to the rich, gooey mud found all along America's greatest river. Don't be tempted to use Dutch process cocoa powder in the crust or the pastry will be tough. However, it has a mild chocolate flavor and dark brown color perfect for the filling.

Crust:

4.5 ounces all-purpose flour (about 1 cup)

2 tablespoons sugar

2 tablespoons unsweetened cocoa

1/4 teaspoon salt

2 1/2 tablespoons vegetable shortening

2 tablespoons chilled butter, cut into small pieces

1/4 cup ice water

Cooking spray

Filling:

3 tablespoons butter

1 ounce semisweet chocolate chips

1 teaspoon vanilla extract

4 large egg whites

1 cup sugar

3.4 ounces all-purpose flour (about 3/4 cup)

1/3 cup Dutch process cocoa

1/2 teaspoon baking powder

Dash of salt

1. To prepare crust, weigh or lightly spoon 4.5 ounces (about 1 cup) flour into a dry measuring cup, and level with a knife. Place 4.5 ounces flour, 2 tablespoons sugar, 2 tablespoons unsweetened cocoa, and 1/4 teaspoon salt in a food processor; pulse 2 times or until blended. Add shortening and chilled butter; pulse 6 times or until mixture resembles coarse meal. With processor on, slowly pour 1/4 cup ice water through food chute, processing just until blended (do not allow dough to form a ball); remove from bowl. Gently press mixture into a 4-inch circle; wrap in plastic wrap. Chill 30 minutes.

2. Preheat oven to 350°.

3. Unwrap and place chilled dough on plastic wrap. Lightly sprinkle dough with flour; roll to a 10-inch circle. Fit dough, plastic wrap side up, into a 9-inch pie plate coated with cooking spray. Remove remaining plastic wrap. Fold edges under, and flute.

4. To prepare filling, place 3 tablespoons butter and chocolate in a microwave-safe bowl. Microwave at HIGH 30 seconds or until butter and chocolate melt, stirring well to combine. Place vanilla and egg whites in a bowl; beat with a mixer at medium speed until foamy. Gradually add 1 cup sugar; beat until soft peaks form (about 2 minutes). Gently fold melted chocolate mixture into egg white mixture.

5. Weigh or lightly spoon 3.4 ounces flour and 1/3 cup Dutch process cocoa into dry measuring cups; level with a knife. Combine flour, cocoa, baking powder, and dash of salt in a small bowl, stirring with a whisk. Fold flour mixture into egg white mixture. Pour mixture into prepared crust. Bake at 350° for 40 minutes or until a wooden pick inserted in center comes out clean. Cool on a wire rack. Yield: 10 servings (serving size: 1 slice).

CALORIES 277; **FAT** 10.2g (sat 5.5g, mono 2.5g, poly 1.2g); **PROTEIN** 4.7g; **CARB** 43.5g; **FIBER** 1.8g; **CHOL** 15mg; **IRON** 1.7mg; **SODIUM** 162mg; **CALC** 24mg

Kid Friendly

Key Lime Pie

The origin of the Key Lime Pie is obscure and disputed, but not the likely reason it came to be: Little refrigeration in the hot, remote Florida Keys meant a pie made from canned, sweetened condensed milk (invented in the middle of the 19th century) was a sensible thing. Add the juice of tart little local limes to balance the ferocious sweetness of the milk, and you have a wonderful pie. Even in its namesake area, there is no single recipe for Key Lime Pie. In Key West restaurants and homes, different crusts, meringues, and filling techniques abound. This dessert is best enjoyed the day it's made.

1½ cups graham cracker crumbs (about 10 cookie sheets)
2 tablespoons butter, melted
4 large egg whites, divided
1 tablespoon water
Cooking spray
2 large eggs
2 large egg yolks
½ cup fresh Key lime juice or fresh lime juice (about 6 Key limes)
1 (14-ounce) can fat-free sweetened condensed milk
1 teaspoon grated Key lime or lime rind
½ cup sugar
2½ tablespoons water

1. Preheat oven to 350°.
2. Combine crumbs and melted butter in a bowl. Place 1 egg white in a small bowl; stir well with a whisk until foamy. Add 2 tablespoons egg white to graham cracker mixture, tossing well with a fork to combine. Discard remaining beaten egg white. Add 1 tablespoon water to graham cracker mixture; toss gently to coat. Press into bottom and up sides of a 9-inch pie plate coated with cooking spray. (Moisten fingers, if needed, to bring mixture together.) Bake at 350° for 8 minutes. Cool completely on a wire rack.
3. Place 2 eggs and 2 egg yolks in a bowl; beat with a mixer at medium speed until well blended. Add juice and condensed milk, beating until thick; stir in rind. Spoon mixture into prepared crust. Bake at 350° for 20 minutes or until edges are set (center will not be firm but will set as it chills). Cool completely on a wire rack. Cover loosely, and chill at least 2 hours.
4. Place remaining 3 egg whites in a bowl; beat with a mixer at medium speed until foamy using clean beaters.
5. Combine sugar and 2½ tablespoons water in a small saucepan; bring to a boil. Cook, without stirring, until a candy thermometer registers 250°. Pour hot sugar syrup in a thin stream over egg whites, beating at high speed 2 minutes or until stiff peaks form. Spread meringue over chilled pie (completely cover pie with meringue).
6. Preheat broiler.
7. Broil pie 1 minute or until meringue is lightly browned. Yield: 8 servings (serving size: 1 slice).

CALORIES 320; FAT 6.8g (sat 2.8g, mono 2.3g, poly 1.1g); PROTEIN 9g; CARB 55.5g; FIBER 0.5g; CHOL 118mg; IRON 1mg; SODIUM 214mg; CALC 146mg

Make Ahead

Black Forest Cherry Cake

(pictured on page 263)

Filling:
⅔ cup sugar
⅔ cup cranberry juice cocktail
¼ cup water
3 tablespoons cornstarch
2 (14.5-ounce) cans pitted tart cherries in water, drained

Cake:
7.75 ounces all-purpose flour (about 1¾ cups)
2 cups sugar
¾ cup unsweetened cocoa
2 teaspoons baking soda
1 teaspoon baking powder
¼ teaspoon salt
1 cup nonfat buttermilk
1 cup fat-free milk
¼ cup canola oil
1 teaspoon vanilla extract
2 large eggs
Cooking spray
2 cups frozen reduced-fat whipped topping, thawed
1 tablespoon kirsch (cherry brandy)
½ ounce dark chocolate curls

1. To prepare filling, combine first 4 ingredients in a large saucepan; stir until cornstarch dissolves. Heat pan over medium-high heat; bring to a boil, stirring constantly. Cook 1 minute or until sugar mixture is very thick, stirring constantly. Remove sugar mixture from heat. Stir in cherries. Cool completely; cover and set aside.
2. To prepare cake, preheat oven to 350°.
3. Weigh or lightly spoon flour into dry measuring cups; level with a knife. Combine flour and next 5 ingredients in a large bowl; stir with a whisk. Combine buttermilk and next 4 ingredients in a bowl; stir with a whisk. Add buttermilk mixture to sugar mixture; beat with a mixer at medium speed just until well blended (batter will be thin).
4. Pour batter into 2 (9-inch) round cake pans coated with cooking spray. Bake at 350° for 40 minutes or until a wooden pick inserted in center comes out clean. Cool in pans 10 minutes; remove from pans. Cool completely on a wire rack.
5. Place 1 cake layer on a plate, and spoon half of cherry mixture (about 1½ cups) evenly over top, leaving a ¼-inch border around edges. Combine whipped topping and kirsch in a small bowl. Spoon 1 cup whipped topping mixture evenly over cherry mixture. Top with remaining cake layer. Spoon remaining 1½ cups cherry mixture onto cake layer, leaving a ½-inch border around edges. Spoon remaining 1 cup whipped topping mixture onto cherry mixture, leaving a 2-inch border from edge of cake layer. Garnish with chocolate curls. Cover loosely, and chill until ready to serve. Yield: 16 servings.

CALORIES 295; FAT 6.4g (sat 2.3g, mono 2.5g, poly 1.2g); PROTEIN 4.4g; CARB 58.2g; FIBER 2.1g; CHOL 27mg; IRON 1.9mg; SODIUM 259mg; CALC 70mg

EASY GRAIN SALADS

These light, meatless mains feature hearty whole grains, seasonal produce, and zesty dressings.

Golden Corn Salad with Fresh Basil

Corn is a starchy-sweet grain that makes a tasty base for a late-summer salad.

8 ounces small yellow Finnish potatoes or
    small red potatoes
3 cups fresh corn kernels (about 4 ears)
2 cups assorted tear-drop cherry tomatoes
    (pear-shaped), halved
1½ cups chopped red bell pepper
¼ cup minced shallots
3 tablespoons white balsamic vinegar
1 tablespoon Dijon mustard
½ teaspoon kosher salt
¼ teaspoon black pepper
3 tablespoons extra-virgin olive oil
6 cups arugula, trimmed
½ cup torn fresh basil leaves
2 ounces goat cheese, sliced

1. Place potatoes in a small saucepan; cover with water. Bring to a boil; cook 11 minutes or until tender. Drain and chill. Cut potatoes in half lengthwise. Combine potatoes, corn, tomatoes, and bell pepper in a large bowl.
2. Combine shallots and next 4 ingredients in a small bowl, stirring with a whisk. Slowly pour oil into shallot mixture, stirring constantly with a whisk. Drizzle over corn mixture; toss well. Add arugula; toss. Sprinkle with basil; top evenly with goat cheese. Yield: 4 servings (serving size: 2¼ cups).

CALORIES 337; **FAT** 16.5g (sat 4.7g, mono 8.9g, poly 2.4g); **PROTEIN** 10g; **CARB** 43.2g; **FIBER** 6.8g; **CHOL** 11mg; **IRON** 2.2mg; **SODIUM** 376mg; **CALC** 131mg

Farro Salad with Roasted Beets, Watercress, and Poppy Seed Dressing

Farro is an ancient grain from Tuscany available at Mediterranean and specialty foods stores. You can substitute wheat berries or spelt, but cook them a little longer than the farro.

2 bunches small beets, trimmed
⅔ cup uncooked farro
3 cups water
¾ teaspoon kosher salt, divided
3 cups trimmed watercress
½ cup thinly sliced red onion
½ cup (2 ounces) crumbled goat cheese
2 tablespoons cider vinegar
2 tablespoons toasted walnut oil
2 tablespoons reduced-fat sour cream
1½ teaspoons poppy seeds
2 teaspoons honey
½ teaspoon black pepper
2 garlic cloves, crushed

1. Preheat oven to 375°.
2. Wrap beets in foil. Bake at 375° for 1½ hours or until tender. Cool; peel and thinly slice.
3. Place farro and 3 cups water in a medium saucepan; bring to a boil. Reduce heat, and simmer 25 minutes or until farro is tender. Drain and cool. Stir in ½ teaspoon salt.
4. Arrange 1½ cups watercress on a serving platter; top with half of farro, ¼ cup onion, and half of sliced beets. Repeat layers with remaining 1½ cups watercress, remaining farro, remaining ¼ cup onion, and remaining beets. Sprinkle top with cheese.
5. Combine remaining ¼ teaspoon salt, vinegar, and remaining ingredients; stir well with a whisk. Drizzle vinegar mixture over salad. Yield: 4 servings (serving size: about 1¾ cups salad and about 3 tablespoons dressing).

CALORIES 351; **FAT** 13.8g (sat 4.2g, mono 2.9g, poly 4.8g); **PROTEIN** 11.7g; **CARB** 50.3g; **FIBER** 5.1g; **CHOL** 14mg; **IRON** 3.8mg; **SODIUM** 604mg; **CALC** 140mg

Curried Quinoa Salad with Cucumber-Mint Raita

This Indian-inspired dish features quinoa, a high-protein grain that cooks relatively quickly.

1 teaspoon olive oil
2 teaspoons Madras curry powder
1 garlic clove, crushed
1 cup uncooked quinoa
2 cups water
¾ teaspoon kosher salt
1 diced peeled ripe mango
½ cup diced celery
¼ cup thinly sliced green onions
3 tablespoons chopped fresh cilantro
3 tablespoons currants
¼ cup finely diced peeled English cucumber
2 teaspoons chopped fresh mint
1 (6-ounce) carton plain low-fat yogurt
1 (5-ounce) package fresh baby spinach

1. Heat oil in a medium saucepan over medium-high heat. Add curry and garlic to pan; cook 1 minute, stirring constantly. Add quinoa and 2 cups water; bring to a boil. Cover, reduce heat, and simmer 16 minutes or until tender. Remove from heat; stir in salt. Cool completely.
2. Add mango and next 4 ingredients to cooled quinoa; toss gently.
3. Combine cucumber, mint, and yogurt in a small bowl, and stir well. Divide spinach evenly among 6 plates, and top each serving with about ¾ cup quinoa mixture and about 2 tablespoons raita. Yield: 6 servings.

CALORIES 268; **FAT** 4.5g (sat 0.9g, mono 1.9g, poly 1.3g); **PROTEIN** 10.7g; **CARB** 46.8g; **FIBER** 6g; **CHOL** 2mg; **IRON** 4.4mg; **SODIUM** 418mg; **CALC** 122mg

Toasted Barley, Green Bean, and Shiitake Salad with Tofu

Toasting the barley before it boils brings out nutty flavor. Pressing and draining tofu helps it take on flavors more readily and improves its cooked texture (see information at right).

Tofu:
1 (12-ounce) package extra-firm tofu, drained and cut into 5 (1-inch-thick) slices
1 tablespoon brown sugar
2 tablespoons lower-sodium soy sauce
1 teaspoon grated peeled fresh ginger
1 teaspoon dark sesame oil
1 garlic clove, grated
Cooking spray

Salad:
2 tablespoons dark sesame oil, divided
1 cup uncooked pearl barley
5 cups water
3/4 teaspoon salt, divided
1 pound green beans, trimmed and cut into 2-inch pieces
10 ounces large shiitake mushrooms, stems removed
1 1/2 cups thinly sliced green onions
1/4 cup rice wine vinegar
2 tablespoons lower-sodium soy sauce
2 tablespoons agave nectar or honey
2 teaspoons finely grated peeled fresh ginger
1 garlic clove, minced

1. To prepare tofu, place tofu slices on several layers of paper towels; cover with additional paper towels. Top with a cutting board; place a heavy skillet on top of cutting board. Let stand 45 minutes, pressing down occasionally. Cut each tofu slice into 10 cubes; arrange in a single layer in a shallow dish.
2. Preheat oven to 375°.
3. Combine brown sugar and next 4 ingredients in a small bowl. Pour sugar mixture over tofu in dish, and turn to coat. Let stand 25 minutes. Arrange tofu in a single layer on a baking sheet coated with cooking spray. Bake at 375° for 35 minutes, turning after 15 minutes. Cool completely.
4. To prepare salad, heat 1 teaspoon sesame oil in a heavy saucepan over medium-high heat. Add barley to pan; cook 3 minutes or until lightly toasted, stirring frequently. Add 5 cups water and 1/2 teaspoon salt; bring to a boil. Reduce heat, and simmer 45 minutes or until barley is tender. Drain; cool completely. Place barley in a large bowl.
5. Cook green beans in boiling water 4 minutes or until crisp-tender. Drain and plunge green beans into ice water. Drain well; pat dry. Add beans to barley.
6. Heat a grill pan over medium-high heat. Brush tops of mushrooms with 2 teaspoons oil. Add mushrooms to pan, oiled side down. Cook 5 minutes or until browned. Sprinkle evenly with remaining 1/4 teaspoon salt. Cool slightly; slice mushrooms thinly. Add tofu, mushrooms, and green onions to barley mixture.
7. Combine remaining 1 tablespoon oil, rice wine vinegar, 2 tablespoons soy sauce, agave nectar or honey, grated ginger, and minced garlic in a small bowl, stirring with a whisk. Drizzle over barley mixture in bowl; stir well to combine. Serve at room temperature or chilled. Yield: 6 servings (serving size: about 1 1/2 cups).

CALORIES 304; FAT 9.7g (sat 1.5g, mono 3.2g, poly 4.7g); PROTEIN 13.1g; CARB 44.4g; FIBER 9.6g; CHOL 0mg; IRON 4.1mg; SODIUM 628mg; CALC 123mg

HOW TO PRESS TOFU

We used pressed tofu in Toasted Barley, Green Bean, and Shiitake Salad with Tofu because it absorbs the marinade better and cooks up firmer.

1 CUT the block of tofu into slices.

2 WEIGH DOWN THE SLICES to extract the liquid.

3 MARINATE. Cut the tofu slices into cubes and marinate.

4 BAKE. Arrange the tofu in a single layer on a baking sheet coated with cooking spray, and bake.

SAUTÉ SECRETS

Employ this technique for sides and entrées that are irresistibly browned and cook in a flash.

Sautéing is a cooking method that's made for the busy cook. It's fast, easy, and best of all, it yields deliciously healthy results. Start by heating a heavy skillet. Make sure the pan is good and hot before swirling just a bit of fat around in it. The hot pan and oil or butter will give foods a tasty golden exterior. And when you add your ingredients, be sure you don't overcrowd the pan, as that causes food to steam instead of sauté. This method works best for smallish, lean cuts of meat like boneless chicken breasts and beef fillets or small chunks of fruits and vegetables. (If ingredients are too large and require long cooking times, they'll burn on the outside before they fully cook.) So simplify your weeknight cooking by mastering the art of sautéing.

Quick & Easy

Sautéed Striped Bass with Lemon-Caper Sauce

Wild striped bass is plentiful along the East Coast, but if you live inland it might be hard to find and expensive. Look for farmed striped bass, which is actually a hybrid of striped bass and white bass.

1 tablespoon olive oil
4 (6-ounce) striped bass fillets
½ teaspoon salt
¼ teaspoon freshly ground black pepper
2 teaspoons drained capers, chopped
½ cup clam juice
1 tablespoon fresh lemon juice
2 tablespoons unsalted butter
1 tablespoon chopped fresh parsley

1. Heat a large stainless steel skillet over medium-high heat. Add oil to pan; swirl to coat. Sprinkle fillets with salt and pepper. Add fillets to pan, skin sides up; sauté 4 minutes or until lightly browned. Turn fillets over; sauté 4 minutes or until desired degree of doneness. Remove from pan; keep warm.
2. Add capers to pan; cook 15 seconds, stirring frequently. Add clam juice and lemon juice; bring to a boil, scraping pan to loosen browned bits. Cook until reduced to ¼ cup (about 3 minutes). Remove pan from heat. Add butter; stir with a whisk until butter melts. Stir in parsley. Serve sauce with fish. Yield: 4 servings (serving size: 1 fillet and about 1 tablespoon sauce).

CALORIES 248; **FAT** 13.2g (sat 5g, mono 5.1g, poly 2.1g); **PROTEIN** 30.4g; **CARB** 0.6g; **FIBER** 0.1g; **CHOL** 152mg; **IRON** 1.6mg; **SODIUM** 520mg; **CALC** 34mg

Quick & Easy

Sautéed Brussels Sprouts and Shallots

Slicing Brussels sprouts lengthwise helps them cook more quickly. They'll retain just a hint of crunch but develop a lovely flavor from the browned bits created in the hot skillet.

2 tablespoons olive oil
1 cup thinly sliced shallots
2 garlic cloves, minced
1 teaspoon sugar
¾ pound Brussels sprouts, trimmed and thinly sliced lengthwise
¼ teaspoon salt
⅛ teaspoon freshly ground black pepper

1. Heat a large stainless steel skillet over medium-high heat. Add oil to pan; swirl to coat. Add shallots; sauté 3 minutes or until almost tender, stirring occasionally. Add garlic; sauté 30 seconds, stirring constantly. Add sugar and Brussels sprouts; sauté 5 minutes or until brown, stirring occasionally. Sprinkle with salt and pepper; toss. Yield: 4 servings (serving size: about ¾ cup).

CALORIES 135; **FAT** 7.3g (sat 1g, mono 5.4g, poly 0.8g); **PROTEIN** 4g; **CARB** 15.9g; **FIBER** 3.6g; **CHOL** 0mg; **IRON** 1.7mg; **SODIUM** 174mg; **CALC** 53mg

Quick & Easy • Kid Friendly

Herbed Potatoes

This recipe is so versatile you can serve it at any—and every—meal throughout the day. Pair it with eggs for breakfast or brunch or alongside any roast meat and salad for lunch or dinner.

1½ pounds Yukon gold potatoes, peeled and cut into ½-inch chunks
2 tablespoons olive oil, divided
1 teaspoon butter
2 garlic cloves, minced
½ teaspoon salt
¼ teaspoon freshly ground black pepper
2 tablespoons small fresh basil leaves
2 tablespoons coarsely chopped fresh flat-leaf parsley

1. Place potatoes in a saucepan; cover with cold water. Bring to a boil. Remove from heat, and let stand 5 minutes; drain and pat dry with paper towels.
2. Heat a large cast-iron or stainless steel skillet over medium-high heat. Add 1 tablespoon oil to pan; swirl to coat. Add half of potatoes; sauté 8 minutes or until lightly browned, stirring occasionally. Remove from pan. Repeat procedure with remaining 1 tablespoon oil and potatoes. Add butter and garlic to pan. Stir in reserved potato mixture, salt, and pepper; sauté 1 minute or until mixture is thoroughly heated and golden brown, stirring occasionally. Remove from heat; sprinkle with herbs. Yield 6 servings (serving size: about ⅔ cup).

CALORIES 132; **FAT** 5.4g (sat 1.1g, mono 3.5g, poly 0.7g); **PROTEIN** 2g; **CARB** 20g; **FIBER** 1.9g; **CHOL** 2mg; **IRON** 0.4mg; **SODIUM** 202mg; **CALC** 10mg

Chicken and Mushrooms with Marsala Wine Sauce

Serve with mashed potatoes or egg noodles to soak up the tasty sauce.

½ cup dried porcini mushrooms (about ½ ounce)
4 (6-ounce) skinless, boneless chicken breast halves
4 teaspoons all-purpose flour, divided
¾ teaspoon salt, divided
¼ teaspoon freshly ground black pepper
2 tablespoons olive oil, divided
½ cup chopped onion
¼ teaspoon crushed red pepper
5 garlic cloves, thinly sliced
1½ cups thinly sliced shiitake mushroom caps (about 4 ounces)
1½ cups thinly sliced button mushrooms (about 4 ounces)
1 teaspoon dried oregano
½ cup dry Marsala wine
⅔ cup fat-free, lower-sodium chicken broth
1 cup halved cherry tomatoes
¼ cup small fresh basil leaves

1. Place porcini mushrooms in a small bowl; cover with boiling water. Cover and let stand 30 minutes or until tender. Drain and rinse; drain well. Thinly slice.

2. Place each chicken breast half between 2 sheets of heavy-duty plastic wrap; pound chicken to ½-inch thickness using a meat mallet or small heavy skillet. Combine 3 teaspoons flour, ¼ teaspoon salt, and black pepper in a shallow dish. Dredge chicken in flour mixture.

3. Heat a large stainless steel skillet over medium-high heat. Add 1 tablespoon oil to pan; swirl to coat. Add chicken; cook 3 minutes on each side or until done. Remove from pan; cover and keep warm.

4. Heat remaining 1 tablespoon oil in pan over medium-high heat. Add onion, red pepper, and garlic; sauté 2 minutes or until onion is lightly browned. Add remaining ½ teaspoon salt, porcini, shiitake, button mushrooms, and oregano; sauté 6 minutes or until mushrooms release moisture and darken. Sprinkle with remaining 1 teaspoon flour; cook 1 minute, stirring constantly. Stir in wine; cook 1 minute. Add broth; bring to a boil. Reduce heat, and simmer 1 minute. Add chicken and tomatoes; cook 2 minutes or until thoroughly heated, turning chicken once. Sprinkle with basil. Yield: 4 servings (serving size: 1 chicken breast half and about ½ cup sauce).

CALORIES 384; **FAT** 10g (sat 1.6g, mono 5.9g, poly 1.6g); **PROTEIN** 48.2g; **CARB** 20.3g; **FIBER** 4.8g; **CHOL** 99mg; **IRON** 6.1mg; **SODIUM** 644mg; **CALC** 50mg

3 STEPS TO SAUTÉ SUCCESS

PICK YOUR PAN
Be sure to choose a good-quality, heavy skillet (also known as a sauté pan). Thin pans don't conduct heat as evenly, creating hot spots where foods can burn. And although there are subtle differences in performance between the straight-sided sauté and slope-sided pans (also called a skillet), either will work just fine for this technique. For the best browning, use a regular stainless steel or cast-iron pan—you just can't get nonstick pans as hot, and they don't brown food as well.

1 HEAT IT UP: Place the dry pan over medium-high heat until it's thoroughly heated.

2 ADD THE FAT: Swirl enough fat in the preheated pan just to coat the surface—this ensures the food will take on a nice golden color and helps prevent it from sticking. Oils like olive or canola, with a reasonably high smoke point, are ideal for this application, but you can also use a mixture of oil and butter to add more flavor.

3 SAUTÉ AWAY: Add the ingredients to the pan, but be sure you don't overcrowd it; you can work in batches, if necessary. Foods brown and cook quickly, but don't stir them too often. You want to allow all surfaces of the food to remain in contact with the pan until they brown nicely.

NUTRITION NOTE

Butter adds flavor, but every tablespoon has 7.3 grams of saturated fat; fortunately, just a bit goes a long way.

PSSSSSST... THE AMAZING, TIME-SAVING PRESSURE COOKER, DEMYSTIFIED

Once the tool of military cooks and fearless grandmas, the new, improved pressure cooker is a safe, quick worker of wonders.

There's no denying the appeal of the pressure cooker: slow cooking done faster. Water and steam under high pressure can reduce cooking times by up to 70 percent, which means, at least theoretically, that you could cook a whole chicken in 20 minutes or a potato in eight minutes (theoretically, because some of the setup can add time to the process).

The science is pretty straightforward: Pressure increases the boiling temperature of water. In your unpressurized Dutch oven, water can only heat to 212°F. In a pressure cooker, water, sealed inside a strong pot, can heat up to 250°F before boiling. Imagine climbing to the top of Mount Everest and discovering that water, at such low atmospheric pressure, boils at a measly 160°F or so; should you decide to boil some coffee up there, it would not be piping hot.

There's nothing new about the pressure-cooker concept—it dates at least to the 17th century. Indeed, it carries the whiff of an old-fashioned, fusty method used long ago by addled cooks who caused occasional minor explosions. The old cookers had pretty simple safety valves on them and a reputation for potential disaster.

"Here's the thing," says James Beard award-winning chef Michael Schlow. "It might be time to retire grandma's pressure cooker and invest in a modern one. The modern ones have gaskets on the outside, locking handles, and pressure release valves, so they won't explode on you. As long as you carefully follow the directions, you really don't have to be afraid of it."

What's more, he finds its uses are myriad. "While I'm a big fan of low and slow cooking, there are times when you need to get something done in a hurry, and that's when a pressure cooker really comes in handy," he says. "Speed is its main calling card, but it's also that one-pot, no-mess idea. A pressure cooker is a great way to put out cool-weather dishes like braised lamb and osso bucco without having something on the stove for five or six hours."

Schlow says when you're dealing with any sort of braise, normally you wouldn't want the ingredients to boil away fiercely, as it could result in tough, dry meats. "But somehow the pressure cooker throws that ideology out the window, creating instead a moist, delicious stew."

Quick & Easy

Prosecco and Parmesan Risotto

Time saved: 20 minutes

The pressure cooker creates creamy risotto in a hands-free way. We tried this with Carnaroli and Arborio; we liked the forgiving nature of Carnaroli, which remained al dente, while Arborio rice produced a softer grain in the cooker. Don't worry if the rice is a tad runny after cooking—it thickens as it stands before serving.

1½ tablespoons butter
⅔ cup finely chopped shallots
3 garlic cloves, minced
1⅓ cups uncooked Carnaroli or other medium-grain rice
1 cup prosecco or other sparkling white wine, divided
3 cups fat-free, lower-sodium chicken broth
2 ounces fresh Parmigiano-Reggiano cheese, divided
1 teaspoon fresh thyme leaves
½ teaspoon grated lemon rind
¼ teaspoon freshly ground black pepper

1. Heat a 6-quart pressure cooker over medium-high heat. Add butter to cooker; swirl until butter melts. Add shallots; sauté 2 minutes. Add garlic; sauté 30 seconds, stirring constantly. Add rice; cook 1 minute, stirring constantly. Add ½ cup prosecco; cook 1 minute or until liquid is absorbed, stirring constantly. Stir in remaining ½ cup prosecco and broth. Close lid securely; bring to high pressure over high heat. Adjust heat to medium or level needed to maintain high pressure; cook 8 minutes. Remove from heat; release pressure through steam vent, or place cooker under cold running water to release pressure. Remove lid. Grate 1¾ ounces cheese; stir in grated cheese and remaining ingredients. Let stand 4 minutes to thicken. Shave remaining ¼ ounce cheese; top risotto with shavings. Yield: 6 servings (serving size: ¾ cup).

CALORIES 239; FAT 5.9g (sat 3.4g, mono 1.5g, poly 0.2g); PROTEIN 8.8g; CARB 38.7g; FIBER 2.5g; CHOL 14mg; IRON 0.9mg; SODIUM 371mg; CALC 134mg

1-Hour Spanish Chickpea Soup

Time saved: 1 hour of cooking, 8 hours of soaking

Dried chickpeas are typically soaked overnight and then simmered for up to two and a half hours to become tender. These, though, go into the pressure cooker dry and come out tender in just one hour! Use high-quality, cured Spanish chorizo (and not the fresh or raw Mexican version) for the best flavor and texture in this earthy, satisfying soup.

1 tablespoon olive oil
1½ cups chopped onion
5 garlic cloves, minced
4 ounces Spanish chorizo, diced
2½ cups water
2½ cups fat-free, lower-sodium chicken broth
1½ cups dried chickpeas (garbanzo beans)
2 bay leaves
6 cups chopped escarole
1 tablespoon sherry vinegar
½ teaspoon kosher salt
½ teaspoon freshly ground black pepper
¼ teaspoon crushed red pepper

1. Heat a 6-quart pressure cooker over medium-high heat. Add oil to pan; swirl to coat. Add onion; sauté 3 minutes. Add garlic and chorizo; sauté 2 minutes. Stir in 2½ cups water and next 3 ingredients. Close lid securely; bring to high pressure over high heat. Adjust heat to medium or level needed to maintain high pressure; cook 1 hour. Remove from heat; release pressure through steam vent, or place cooker under cold running water to release pressure. Remove lid. Discard bay leaves. Add escarole and remaining ingredients, stirring just until escarole wilts. Serve immediately. Yield: 6 servings (serving size: about 1¼ cups).

CALORIES 318; **FAT** 12.8g (sat 3.4g, mono 6g, poly 2.6g); **PROTEIN** 15.8g; **CARB** 36.3g; **FIBER** 10.6g; **CHOL** 16mg; **IRON** 4mg; **SODIUM** 571mg; **CALC** 108mg

Quick & Easy
Beets with Dill and Walnuts

Time saved: 35 minutes

Beets are ready when they can be pierced with a fork without too much resistance. If they're not quite tender enough, put them back under pressure for a minute or two. Prep the dressing while the beets cook.

2 pounds beets (about 6)
2½ cups water
1 tablespoon cider vinegar
1 tablespoon fresh lemon juice
2 teaspoons sugar
1½ teaspoons Dijon mustard
¾ teaspoon kosher salt
½ teaspoon freshly ground black pepper
3 tablespoons extra-virgin olive oil
2 tablespoons chopped fresh dill
2 tablespoons finely chopped walnuts

1. Leave root and 1-inch stem on beets, and scrub with a brush. Place in a 6-quart pressure cooker; add 2½ cups water. Close lid securely; bring to high pressure over high heat. Reduce heat to medium or level needed to maintain high pressure; cook 10 minutes. Remove from heat; let stand 6 minutes. Release pressure through steam vent, or place cooker under cold running water to release pressure. Remove lid. Drain and rinse beets with cold water. Drain; cool. Trim off beet roots; rub off skins. Cut beets in half vertically; cut each half into 4 wedges. Place in a medium bowl.
2. Combine vinegar and next 5 ingredients in a small bowl; stir with a whisk. Slowly drizzle in oil, stirring constantly with a whisk until well combined. Toss oil mixture with beets; let stand 15 minutes, tossing gently occasionally. Stir in dill. Top with walnuts just before serving. Yield: 6 servings (serving size: ⅔ cup).

CALORIES 148; **FAT** 8.5g (sat 1.1g, mono 5.3g, poly 1.8g); **PROTEIN** 3.1g; **CARB** 16.5g; **FIBER** 4.4g; **CHOL** 0mg; **IRON** 1.4mg; **SODIUM** 370mg; **CALC** 27mg

OUR TOP PRESSURE COOKER PICKS

We tested five stovetop models and two electric ones, covering several price points. These scored high for cooking results, instruction manuals, ease of cleaning, and overall performance.

KUHN RIKON 7-QUART DUROMATIC
This stovetop model handles like a Rolls-Royce version of pressure cookers. This sleek, heavyweight cooker works on all cooking surfaces, even induction. Two pressure settings, an easy-to-seal lid that stays locked while the pot is under pressure, and stay-cool handles mean that there is no pressure-cooking anxiety. We also liked the informative recipe and instruction books that are included.
Price: about $219
Buy at: Sur La Table (surlatable.com), amazon.com, or cooking.com

PRESTO STOVE-TOP 6-QUART STAINLESS STEEL PRESSURE COOKER
This is the no-frills pressure cooker, but it does the job on all stovetop cooking surfaces and is easy to clean. This model has one high-pressure setting, and the handle also has an auto-lock device that is activated when at pressure. The instruction book has many diagrams, and the recipe section is full of culinary inspiration and cook-time charts. The downside: some assembly required, since you must screw handles onto the pot and lid (screws included).
Price: about $75
Buy at: large retailers and amazon.com

CUISINART ELECTRIC PRESSURE COOKER CPC-600 SERIES
For the slow-cooker fan, the electric pressure cooker may be the way to go. This very heavy, sturdy cooker is quiet while it works. Safety is covered, too, with a locked-in-place lid while under pressure. The LED display is nice and serves as a timer. This machine does all the work for you, achieving and attaining high or low pressure, so there's no need to fidget with temperatures to maintain high pressure like with stove-top models. Bonus: Download recipes and instruction book at cuisinart.com.
Price: about $100
Buy at: Williams-Sonoma, Macy's, Bed Bath & Beyond, or at amazon.com

Kid Friendly

Chicken Fricassee

Time saved: 28 minutes

Don't limit your pressure cooker to stewing tough cuts of beef, pork, or lamb: You can prepare elegant entrées, too, like this chicken with a rich sauce and vegetables. For the best textured vegetables in this dish, allow the carrots, onions, and mushrooms to come to pressure, and then immediately take them off the heat and release the pressure.

1 pound baby carrots with green tops
1 tablespoon butter
1 tablespoon olive oil
4 chicken leg quarters, skinned
½ teaspoon kosher salt
½ teaspoon freshly ground black pepper
4.5 ounces all-purpose flour (about 1 cup)
1 pound cremini mushrooms, quartered
¾ cup dry white wine
3 fresh thyme sprigs
2 fresh sage sprigs
2 cups fat-free, lower-sodium chicken broth
10 ounces fresh pearl onions, peeled
1 tablespoon chopped fresh thyme
1 tablespoon chopped fresh sage

1. Trim tops of carrots to 1-inch; peel. Set aside.
2. Melt butter in an 8-quart pressure cooker over medium-high heat. Add oil to cooker; swirl to coat. Sprinkle chicken evenly with salt and pepper. Place flour in a shallow dish. Dredge chicken in flour. Place 2 chicken leg quarters, flesh sides down, in cooker; sauté 5 minutes or until browned. Set aside. Repeat procedure with remaining 2 chicken leg quarters. Place mushrooms in cooker; sauté 4 minutes or until liquid evaporates. Remove mushrooms from cooker using a slotted spoon; set aside.
3. Stir in wine, scraping cooker to loosen browned bits. Bring to a boil; cook 30 seconds. Tie thyme and sage sprigs together with twine. Add chicken, herb sprigs, and broth to cooker. Close lid securely; bring to high pressure over high heat. Reduce heat to medium or level needed to maintain high pressure; cook 6 minutes. Remove from heat; release pressure through steam vent, or

place cooker under cold running water to release pressure. Remove lid.
4. Add carrots, mushrooms, and onions to cooker; close lid securely. Return cooker to high pressure and immediately remove from heat; release pressure through steam vent, or place cooker under cold running water to release pressure. Remove lid. Transfer chicken to a platter. Remove vegetables from cooker using a slotted spoon; arrange on platter with chicken. Cover and keep warm. Strain cooking liquid through a cheesecloth-lined sieve into a large bowl; discard solids. Transfer liquid to a large, wide skillet over medium-high heat; bring to a boil. Cook until reduced to 1 cup (about 12 minutes). Stir chopped thyme and sage into sauce. Serve with chicken and vegetables. Yield: 4 servings (serving size: 1 chicken leg quarter, 1¼ cups vegetable mixture, and about ¼ cup sauce).

CALORIES 398; FAT 12g (sat 3.7g, mono 4.9g, poly 2.1g); PROTEIN 34g; CARB 37.6g; FIBER 6.4g; CHOL 112mg; IRON 4.3mg; SODIUM 659mg; CALC 108mg

Kid Friendly

Beef Pot Roast and Gravy

Time saved: 45 minutes

2 teaspoons olive oil
1 (3-pound) boneless chuck roast, trimmed
1 teaspoon kosher salt
¼ teaspoon freshly ground black pepper
3 cups Fast, Rich Pressure-Cooker Beef
  Stock (page 291)
½ cup dry red wine
4 fresh thyme sprigs, tied securely together
  with twine
3 garlic cloves, chopped
3 large parsnips, peeled and diagonally cut
  into 2-inch pieces
3 large carrots, peeled and diagonally cut
  into 2-inch pieces
1 pound turnips, each cut into 8 wedges
1 pound Yukon gold potatoes, peeled and cut
  into 2-inch pieces
1 large onion, cut into 8 wedges
2 tablespoons all-purpose flour
Thyme sprigs (optional)

1. Heat a 6- or 8-quart pressure cooker over medium-high heat. Add oil to cooker; swirl to coat. Sprinkle roast evenly with salt and pepper. Add roast to cooker; sauté 5 minutes, browning on all sides. Stir in 3 cups Fast, Rich Pressure-Cooker Beef Stock and wine. Close lid securely; bring to high pressure over high heat. Reduce heat to medium or level needed to maintain high pressure; cook 35 minutes. Remove from heat; release pressure through steam vent, or place cooker under cold running water to release pressure. Remove lid; add thyme sprigs and next 6 ingredients. Close lid securely. Return to high pressure; cook 1 minute. Remove from heat; release pressure through steam vent, or place cooker under cold running water to release pressure. Remove lid; let stand 5 minutes. Remove roast; slice roast thinly, and place on a platter. Remove vegetables from cooker using a slotted spoon, and place on platter with roast. Cover and keep warm.
2. Strain cooking liquid through a cheesecloth-lined sieve into a large bowl; discard solids. Bring cooking liquid to a boil over medium-high heat in a large, wide skillet; cook until reduced to 1½ cups (about 15 minutes). Remove ¼ cup cooking liquid from pan; add flour, stirring with a whisk. Return flour mixture to pan; cook 2 minutes or until slightly thick, stirring with a whisk. Serve with roast and vegetables. Garnish each serving with fresh thyme sprigs, if desired. Yield: 12 servings (serving size: 3 ounces beef, ⅔ cup vegetables, and 2 tablespoons sauce).

CALORIES 264; FAT 11.2g (sat 3.5g, mono 4.9g, poly 0.7g); PROTEIN 23.1g; CARB 15.4g; FIBER 2.6g; CHOL 70mg; IRON 3.3mg; SODIUM 254mg; CALC 41mg

Make Ahead • Freezable

Fast, Rich Pressure-Cooker Beef Stock

Time saved: 5 hours, 40 minutes

This beef broth delivers all the savory flavor of the slow-simmered recipe in about one-tenth of the cook time. Chilling the stock is an easy way to remove excess fat, but you can also cool the strained liquid slightly and spoon off the excess fat for immediate use.

2 tablespoons tomato paste
3 pounds meaty beef marrow bones
2½ pounds (1-inch-thick) beef shanks
2 celery stalks, diagonally cut into 2-inch
   pieces
1 large carrot, peeled and diagonally cut into
   2-inch pieces
1 large onion, peeled and cut into 8 wedges
Cooking spray
1 tablespoon black peppercorns
2 bay leaves
½ bunch fresh flat-leaf parsley
8 cups cold water

1. Preheat oven to 500°.
2. Brush tomato paste evenly over bones and shanks; place in a large roasting pan. Add celery, carrot, and onion to pan; lightly coat with cooking spray. Bake at 500° for 30 minutes.
3. Transfer bone mixture to a 6- or 8-quart pressure cooker; add peppercorns, bay leaves, and parsley. Pour 8 cups water over mixture. Close lid securely, and bring to high pressure over high heat. Reduce heat to medium or level needed to maintain high pressure; cook 35 minutes. Remove from heat; release pressure through steam vent, or place cooker under cold running water to release pressure. Remove lid, and let stand 20 minutes. Strain stock through a cheesecloth-lined sieve into a large bowl, pressing solids to release excess moisture. Discard solids. Cover and chill overnight. Skim solidified fat from surface; discard. Yield: 9 cups (serving size: 1 cup).
Note: Refrigerate stock for up to 1 week or freeze for up to 3 months.

CALORIES 4; FAT 0.1g (sat 0g, mono 0.1g, poly 0g);
PROTEIN 0.3g; CARB 0.3g; FIBER 0.1g; CHOL 1mg;
IRON 0.1mg; SODIUM 5mg; CALC 2mg

GREAT FOR BEANS & GRAINS

A pressure cooker makes quick work of whole grains and beans, heart-healthy ingredients that often require lots of soaking and cooking. Check your pressure cooker's manual for any specific guidelines about handling beans and grains in your model.

DRIED NAVY BEANS: Place 6 cups water, 1 cup dried navy beans, 1 teaspoon olive oil, and 1 bay leaf in pressure cooker. Close lid securely; bring to high pressure over high heat. Adjust heat to medium or level needed to maintain high pressure; cook 40 minutes. Remove from heat; release pressure through steam vent, or place cooker under cold running water to release pressure. Remove lid; drain beans. Discard bay leaf.

BROWN RICE: Place 1¼ cups water and 1 cup uncooked long-grain brown rice in the pressure cooker. Close lid securely; bring to high pressure over high heat. Adjust heat to medium or level needed to maintain high pressure; cook 17 minutes. Remove from heat; release pressure through steam vent, or place cooker under cold running water to release pressure. Remove lid.

WILD RICE: Place 2⅓ cups water and 1¼ cups uncooked wild rice (1 [8-ounce] package) in pressure cooker. Close lid securely; bring to high pressure over high heat. Adjust heat to medium or level needed to maintain pressure; cook 30 minutes. Remove from heat; release pressure through steam vent, or place cooker under cold running water to release pressure. Remove lid; drain any excess liquid.

KAMUT: Place 3 cups water, 1½ teaspoons canola oil, and 1 cup uncooked kamut in pressure cooker. Close lid securely; bring to high pressure over high heat. Adjust heat to medium or level needed to maintain pressure; cook 10 minutes. Remove from heat; allow pressure to release naturally through steam vent. Remove lid; drain kamut.

PEARL BARLEY: Place 4½ cups water, 1 cup uncooked pearl barley, and 1 tablespoon canola oil in pressure cooker. Close lid securely; bring to high pressure over high heat. Adjust heat to medium or level needed to maintain pressure; cook 18 minutes. Remove from heat; allow pressure to release naturally through steam vent. Remove lid; drain barley.

RECIPE HALL OF FAME
OUR DESSERT FAVORITE

Quick & Easy

Rum-Spiked Grilled Pineapple with Toasted Coconut

Six ingredients make one delicious dessert in less than 10 minutes.

¼ cup packed brown sugar
¼ cup dark spiced rum (such as Captain
   Morgan's)
1 pineapple (about 1½ pounds), peeled,
   cored, halved lengthwise, and sliced
   lengthwise into 12 wedges
1 tablespoon butter
2 tablespoons sweetened flaked coconut,
   toasted
3 cups low-fat vanilla ice cream

1. Combine sugar and rum in a microwave-safe bowl. Microwave at HIGH 1½ minutes or until sugar dissolves. Brush rum mixture evenly over pineapple wedges.
2. Melt butter in a grill pan over medium-high heat. Add pineapple to pan; grill 3 minutes on each side or until grill marks form and pineapple is thoroughly heated. Sprinkle with coconut. Serve with ice cream. Yield: 6 servings (serving size: 2 pineapple wedges, 1 teaspoon coconut, and ½ cup ice cream).

CALORIES 226; FAT 4g (sat 2.6g, mono 0.5g, poly 0.1g);
PROTEIN 3.7g; CARB 43.1g; FIBER 4.7g; CHOL 10mg;
IRON 0.5mg; SODIUM 78mg; CALC 123mg

BREAKFAST, LUNCH, AND DINNER IN... LONDON

It's been 20 years since the London restaurant boom banished the notion that eating out in the U.K. capital was something to be endured rather than enjoyed. And yet while nineties and naughties London served as the showcase for every major cooking trend to emerge from the global kitchen, the one cuisine typically bypassed by British culinary fashion was British food itself.

Not anymore: Recent years have seen an explosion of interest in Britain's native ingredients and its classic dishes, timed perfectly with the more general rise of the seasonal, organic, and local food movement. In February, Yorkshire rhubarb joined the ranks of Parma ham and Roquefort cheese as one of the regional specialties to be given "Protected Designation of Origin" status by the European Union. And the nationwide supermarket chain Waitrose will soon offer six types of heritage apples grown on its Hampshire farm. What's more, Waitrose made a multimillion-pound investment in Duchy Originals, the U.K.'s most famous organic food brand, founded by Prince Charles, with plans to increase the range to 500 organic British-produced products. (Not that U.K. shoppers are restricted to buying organic only from the heir to the throne: High-street supermarkets sell an impressively wide range of organic foodstuffs.)

London dining isn't all about hyper-local food, though. Centuries of immigration combined with Londoners' seemingly insatiable hunger for culinary experimentation means that, from Afghan to Australian, the city is a melting pot of global cooking.

Breakfast

Corn Fritters with Roasted Tomatoes and Lime Aioli

Over the last two years, a new breed of "cool caff" has appeared in London. Leading the way is Lantana (lantanacafe.co.uk), opened by Shelagh Ryan after she moved to London and couldn't find the sort of laid-back, quality café of her native Australia. Dishes like sourdough toast with roasted tomatoes, basil, and shaved Parmesan or corn fritters stacked with crispy bacon, arugula, corn salsa, and lime aioli— which inspired our lightened version—give Londoners a taste of why Sydney is the brunch capital of the world. For convenience, you can make the tomatoes and fritters in advance, then reheat them to serve. Reheating the fritters in an oven or toaster oven will keep them from being soggy.

4 ripe tomatoes, halved (about 1 pound)
2 teaspoons olive oil, divided
½ teaspoon black pepper, divided
2.25 ounces all-purpose flour (about ½ cup)
1 teaspoon baking powder
⅓ cup fat-free milk
1 large egg, beaten
1½ cups fresh corn kernels (3 ears)
⅓ cup finely chopped green onions
¼ teaspoon salt
3 tablespoons reduced-fat mayonnaise
2 tablespoons fresh lime juice
½ garlic clove, minced
1 teaspoon cold water
4 cups loosely packed arugula
4 (¼-ounce) slices prosciutto

1. Preheat oven to 375°.
2. Arrange tomato halves, cut sides up, on a baking sheet. Drizzle tomatoes with 1 teaspoon oil; sprinkle with ¼ teaspoon pepper. Bake at 375° for 1 hour and 30 minutes or until tomatoes are soft and have lost a lot of their moisture.
3. Weigh or lightly spoon flour into a dry measuring cup; level with a knife. Combine flour and baking powder in a medium bowl. Add milk and egg; stir until smooth. Stir in remaining ¼ teaspoon pepper, corn, green onions, and salt.
4. Heat ½ teaspoon oil in a large non-stick skillet over medium heat. Drop batter by level tablespoonfuls into pan to make 6 fritters; cook 2 minutes or until tops are covered with bubbles and edges are golden. Carefully turn fritters over; cook 2 minutes or until golden. Repeat procedure with remaining ½ teaspoon oil and remaining batter.
5. Combine mayonnaise and next 3 ingredients. Place 1 fritter on each of 4 plates. Top each with 1 tomato half and ½ cup arugula. Repeat layers with remaining fritters, tomato halves, and arugula, ending with fritters. Top each serving with 1 prosciutto slice; drizzle with 4 teaspoons aioli. Yield: 4 servings.

CALORIES 284; FAT 7.8g (sat 1.2g, mono 2.6g, poly 2.3g); PROTEIN 12.6g; CARB 48.4g; FIBER 7.4g; CHOL 49mg; IRON 2.9mg; SODIUM 526mg; CALC 185mg

BREAKFAST IN LONDON USED TO MEAN PARTING WITH BIG BUCKS IN A HOTEL DINING ROOM OR HAVING YOUR CLOTHES ABSORB THE SMELL OF COOKING FAT OVER A "FULL ENGLISH." NO MORE.

Lunch

Skillet-Cooked Shrimp with Romesco Sauce

Maybe it's the sort of attention-deficit disorder that comes from living in a city with 7 million inhabitants, but Londoners can't get enough of tapas-sized plates—especially from a cuisine not usually served in mini portions. Polpo (polpo.co.uk) is modeled on a Venetian wine bar. At Terroirs (terroirswinebar.com), the French bistro furnishings are the background for tapas-sized plates of charcuterie and seafood, like the recipe below. If you're unable to find jumbo shrimp, large will work just fine. We like the flavor and texture of shrimp cooked in its shell, but take the shells off before cooking, if you prefer. To make the sauce even faster, use a bottled roasted red pepper.

1 large red bell pepper
2 tablespoons chopped fresh flat-leaf parsley
2 tablespoons olive oil, divided
1 tablespoon fresh lemon juice
⅛ teaspoon crushed red pepper
16 unpeeled jumbo shrimp (about 1⅓ pounds)
1½ tablespoons blanched slivered almonds
¼ ounce white bread, torn into pieces
1 garlic clove, sliced
1¾ cups chopped tomato
1 tablespoon sherry vinegar or red wine vinegar
½ teaspoon salt

1. Preheat broiler.
2. Cut bell pepper in half lengthwise; discard seeds and membranes. Place pepper halves, skin sides up, on a foil-lined baking sheet; flatten with hand. Broil 8 minutes or until blackened. Place in a zip-top plastic bag; seal. Let stand 10 minutes. Peel and coarsely chop.
3. Combine parsley, 1 tablespoon oil, juice, crushed red pepper, and shrimp in a bowl; let stand 15 minutes.
4. Heat remaining 1 tablespoon oil in a large skillet over medium-high heat. Add almonds and bread to pan; sauté 2 minutes or until nuts are golden. Add garlic; sauté 1 minute. Add tomato and roasted bell pepper; sauté 4 minutes or until tomato begins to break down.

Place tomato mixture in a blender or food processor; process until smooth. Add vinegar and salt to tomato mixture; pulse until combined. Cool to room temperature.
5. Heat a nonstick skillet over medium-high heat. Add half of shrimp mixture to pan; cook 2 minutes on each side or until shrimp are done. Remove from pan. Repeat procedure with remaining shrimp mixture. Serve with sauce. Yield: 4 servings (serving size: 4 shrimp and about ⅓ cup sauce).

CALORIES 273; FAT 11.7g (sat 1.7g, mono 6.5g, poly 2.6g); PROTEIN 32.7g; CARB 9.2g; FIBER 2.3g; CHOL 229mg; IRON 4.4mg; SODIUM 534mg; CALC 104mg

Dinner
Kid Friendly

Chunky Fish Fingers with Pea and Mint Puree

Mark Hix has three restaurants to his name in London, but it's Hix (www.hixsoho.co.uk) that's grabbing attention now—not only for the fact that Hix's artist chums such as Damien Hirst have provided pieces for the decor, but also for its simply served, utterly indulgent dishes made from rigorously sourced native ingredients. Cornish fish soup with Julian Temperley's cider brandy might be followed by Ayrshire veal stew with Mendip snails and January king cabbage. Traditional British comfort is found in Hix's upscale take on fish, chips, and mushy peas. This kid-friendly entrée pairs flaky fish sticks with sweet, herby mashed peas.

2 (1-ounce) slices white bread
1 pound skinless Pacific cod or other firm-fleshed white fish fillet
½ teaspoon salt, divided
½ teaspoon freshly ground black pepper, divided
2 tablespoons all-purpose flour
1 large egg, beaten
Cooking spray
¼ cup fat-free, lower-sodium chicken broth
2 cups frozen green peas
1 tablespoon butter
8 fresh mint leaves
Lemon wedges (optional)

1. Preheat oven to 425°.
2. Place bread in a food processor; pulse 10 times or until coarse crumbs measure 1¼ cups. Arrange breadcrumbs on a baking sheet. Bake at 425° for 5 minutes or until light golden. Cool; place in a shallow dish.
3. Cut fish into 16 (3 x 1-inch) pieces; pat dry with paper towels. Sprinkle fish evenly with ¼ teaspoon salt and ¼ teaspoon pepper. Place flour and egg in separate shallow dishes. Dredge 1 fish finger in flour, shaking off any excess. Dip fish in egg; dredge in breadcrumbs. Repeat procedure with remaining fish, flour, egg, and breadcrumbs. Arrange coated fish on a wire rack on a baking sheet; lightly coat fish with cooking spray. Bake at 425° for 8 minutes or until desired degree of doneness.
4. Bring chicken broth to a simmer in a saucepan over medium heat. Stir in peas; cover and cook 2 minutes. Remove from heat; stir in butter, mint, remaining ¼ teaspoon salt, and remaining ¼ teaspoon pepper. Place pea mixture in a food processor; process until smooth. Place about ⅓ cup pea puree in middle of each of 4 plates. Stack 4 fish fingers on puree. Serve with lemon wedges, if desired. Yield: 4 servings.

CALORIES 242; FAT 5.1g (sat 2.4g, mono 1.4g, poly 0.8g); PROTEIN 26.4g; CARB 19.6g; FIBER 3.5g; CHOL 101mg; IRON 2.2mg; SODIUM 514mg; CALC 49mg

FEED 4 FOR LESS THAN $10

These economical recipes bridge summer and fall with vibrant flavors.

Quick & Easy

Warm Pasta Salad with Shrimp

$2.07 per serving, $8.28 total

Toss warm pasta with the tangy dressing so it will absorb more flavor. If you prefer to serve this salad chilled, make it up to a day ahead, toss, and refrigerate until you're ready to serve.

3 cups uncooked farfalle (bow tie pasta)
1/4 cup fresh lemon juice
1 1/2 tablespoons Dijon mustard
1 teaspoon minced fresh garlic
1/4 cup olive oil
1/2 teaspoon kosher salt
1/2 teaspoon freshly ground black pepper
Cooking spray
12 ounces medium shrimp, peeled and deveined
1 1/2 cups chopped fresh spinach
1 cup canned cannellini beans, rinsed and drained
1/4 cup minced red onion
2 tablespoons chopped capers

1. Cook pasta according to package directions, omitting salt and fat; drain.
2. Combine juice, mustard, and garlic in a small bowl, stirring well with a whisk. Gradually add oil, stirring constantly with a whisk. Stir in salt and pepper.
3. Heat a large nonstick skillet over medium-high heat. Coat pan with cooking spray. Add shrimp to pan; cook 2 minutes or until done. Stir in spinach and next 3 ingredients; toss to combine. Add pasta and juice mixture to shrimp mixture; toss. Yield: 4 servings (serving size: about 2 cups).

CALORIES 487; **FAT** 16.4g (sat 2.4g, mono 10.1g, poly 2g); **PROTEIN** 28.9g; **CARB** 56.2g; **FIBER** 4.9g; **CHOL** 129mg; **IRON** 5.6mg; **SODIUM** 664mg; **CALC** 103mg

Gingery Pork Meatballs with Noodles

$2.06 per serving, $8.23 total

Wide rice noodles are available on the ethnic-foods aisle at most major supermarkets and at Asian grocers. If you can't find them, any rice noodle or even spaghetti will work in this dish. You can also use ground sirloin, if you can't find pork.

Meatballs:
1/2 cup chopped fresh cilantro
1/4 cup dry breadcrumbs
1/4 cup finely chopped red onion
2 tablespoons lower-sodium soy sauce
2 teaspoons grated peeled fresh ginger
3 garlic cloves, minced
1 pound lean ground pork
1 large egg, lightly beaten

Noodles:
8 ounces uncooked wide rice noodles
1 tablespoon dark sesame oil
1 cup red bell pepper strips
1 cup julienne-cut snow peas
1/2 teaspoon salt
1/2 teaspoon crushed red pepper
1/2 cup thinly sliced green onions

1. Place a foil-lined jelly-roll pan in oven. Preheat oven to 450°.
2. To prepare meatballs, combine first 8 ingredients in a large bowl; stir gently just until blended. Cover and chill 30 minutes. Divide pork mixture into 20 equal portions; shape each portion into a meatball. Arrange meatballs in a single layer on preheated pan. Bake at 450° for 20 minutes or until done.
3. To prepare noodles, cook noodles according to package directions, omitting salt and fat; drain. Rinse noodles under cool water; drain. Heat oil in a large nonstick skillet over medium-high heat. Add bell pepper and next 3 ingredients; cook 5 minutes, stirring occasionally. Add noodles; toss. Place 1 3/4 cups noodle mixture on each of 4 plates; top each serving with 5 meatballs. Sprinkle each serving with 2 tablespoons green onions. Yield: 4 servings.

CALORIES 506; **FAT** 15.4g (sat 5.1g, mono 6.2g, poly 3.3g); **PROTEIN** 30.6g; **CARB** 58.8g; **FIBER** 3.7g; **CHOL** 138mg; **IRON** 3.4mg; **SODIUM** 700mg; **CALC** 81mg

Quick & Easy • Make Ahead

Minty Tomato Soup

$2.42 per serving, $9.68 total

Look for large tomatoes as they're easier to work with. If you make the soup ahead, the flavors will meld with time, but give the soup a quick stir before serving. Cheesy toasts add a bit of extra protein to this end-of-summer soup.

4 1/2 pounds plum tomatoes
2 tablespoons finely chopped fresh mint
5/8 teaspoon kosher salt, divided
1 teaspoon red wine vinegar
2 garlic cloves, crushed
1/2 cup packed fresh mint leaves
2 1/2 tablespoons olive oil
4 ounces French bread baguette
1 (3-ounce) package 1/3-less-fat cream cheese, softened

1. Preheat broiler.
2. Core tomatoes, and halve crosswise. Working with 1 tomato at a time, squeeze tomato halves over a sieve over a bowl; press sieve gently with back of a wooden spoon to extract remaining juice, reserving tomato halves and juice. Discard seeds.
3. Press tomato halves through large holes of a box grater into a large bowl; discard skins. Add reserved tomato juice to bowl. Stir in 2 tablespoons chopped mint, 1/2 teaspoon salt, and vinegar.
4. Place garlic in a food processor; process until chopped. Add 1/2 cup mint leaves and remaining 1/8 teaspoon salt; process until pureed. With motor running, gradually pour oil through food chute, processing until oil is fully incorporated, scraping sides as necessary.
5. Slice bread crosswise into 8 slices. Spread cream cheese evenly over 1 side of bread slices. Place bread, cheese sides up, in a single layer on a baking sheet. Broil 2 minutes or until golden. Ladle about 1 cup soup into each of 4 bowls; divide pesto evenly among bowls. Serve each with 2 toasts. Yield: 4 servings.

CALORIES 328; **FAT** 15.7g (sat 4.7g, mono 8g, poly 2g); **PROTEIN** 10.4g; **CARB** 42g; **FIBER** 7.3g; **CHOL** 16mg; **IRON** 5.2mg; **SODIUM** 614mg; **CALC** 85mg

Roasted Lemon–Garlic Chicken with Potatoes

$2.33 per serving, $9.33 total

This classic meal is economical and easy to prepare. Although we call for thyme, you can use any fresh herbs you have on hand—tarragon, chives, rosemary, or a mix of any of them will work in the potatoes.

2 lemons
1 teaspoon kosher salt, divided
1 teaspoon black pepper
4 garlic cloves, minced and divided
1 (3½-pound) whole chicken
6 garlic cloves, crushed
1½ pounds red potatoes, quartered
2 tablespoons butter, softened
1 tablespoon minced fresh thyme leaves

1. Grate rind from lemons to measure 2 tablespoons. Reserve lemons. Combine 5 teaspoons rind, ¾ teaspoon salt, pepper, and 2 minced garlic cloves in a small bowl.
2. Remove and discard chicken giblets and neck. Loosen skin from breast and drumsticks by inserting fingers and gently pushing between skin and meat. Rub rind mixture under loosened skin over flesh. Tuck wing tips under chicken. Place chicken in a shallow dish; refrigerate, uncovered, 4 hours or overnight.
3. Preheat oven to 425°.
4. Quarter reserved lemons. Place lemon quarters and 6 crushed garlic cloves into chicken cavity; tie ends of legs together with cord. Place chicken, breast side up, in a roasting pan. Bake at 425° for 25 minutes. Reduce oven temperature to 375° (do not remove chicken from oven). Bake 40 minutes or until a thermometer inserted into meaty portion of thigh registers 165°. Remove from oven; let stand 15 minutes.
5. Place potatoes in a saucepan; cover with cold water. Bring to a boil. Cook 10 minutes or until tender; drain. Combine potatoes, remaining 1 teaspoon rind, remaining ¼ teaspoon salt, remaining 2 minced garlic cloves, butter, and thyme. Discard chicken skin; carve. Yield: 4 servings (serving size: 1 chicken breast half or 1 thigh and 1 drumstick, and ½ cup potatoes).

CALORIES 379; **FAT** 12.7g (sat 5.5g, mono 4.1g, poly 1.8g); **PROTEIN** 30.9g; **CARB** 33.3g; **FIBER** 2.7g; **CHOL** 94mg; **IRON** 3.1mg; **SODIUM** 601mg; **CALC** 35mg

WINE NOTE: With all the bright lemon woven through this comfort dish, you need a wine with a great squeeze of citrus at its core. Look no further than Columbia Crest's 2009 Two Vine Pinot Grigio (Washington, $8). Lemon expands to pink grapefruit and peach, with a refreshing, zesty finish—all of which make the citrus and thyme on the chicken and potatoes pop.

Southwest Turkey Burgers

$2.44 per serving, $9.74 total

Serve these budget-friendly burgers with Grilled Corn.

2 poblano chiles (about ½ pound)
1 ounce French bread baguette
¼ cup 1% low-fat milk
½ teaspoon chili powder, divided
1 teaspoon ground cumin
½ teaspoon salt
¼ teaspoon black pepper
¼ teaspoon ground red pepper
1 pound ground turkey breast
Cooking spray
2 tablespoons canola mayonnaise
4 (1½-ounce) hamburger buns, toasted
4 (½-inch-thick) slices tomato
4 green leaf lettuce leaves

1. Preheat grill to medium-high heat.
2. Cut poblanos in half lengthwise; discard seeds and membranes. Place poblanos, skin sides down, on grill rack; grill 10 minutes or until blackened. Place poblanos in a small zip-top plastic bag; seal. Let stand 15 minutes. Peel and dice.
3. Place bread in a food processor; pulse 5 times or until coarse crumbs measure ½ cup. Combine breadcrumbs and milk in a large bowl; let stand 5 minutes. Add poblano chiles, ¼ teaspoon chili powder, cumin, and next 4 ingredients; gently mix just until combined. Divide turkey mixture into 4 equal portions; shape each portion into a ½-inch-thick patty. Place patties on grill rack coated with cooking spray; grill 3 minutes on each side or until done.
4. Combine remaining ¼ teaspoon chili powder and mayonnaise. Top bottom half of each bun with 1 tomato slice, 1 lettuce leaf, 1 patty, about 1½ teaspoons mayonnaise mixture, and 1 bun top. Yield: 4 servings (serving size: 1 burger).

CALORIES 321; **FAT** 8.5g (sat 1.1g, mono 4.2g, poly 2.9g); **PROTEIN** 27.8g; **CARB** 32.5g; **FIBER** 2.6g; **CHOL** 56mg; **IRON** 3.5mg; **SODIUM** 658mg; **CALC** 108mg

Grilled Corn:

Combine 1½ tablespoons melted butter, ½ teaspoon grated lime rind, ¼ teaspoon salt, and ¼ teaspoon chili powder in a bowl. Coat 4 shucked corn ears with cooking spray. Place corn on a grill rack coated with cooking spray, and grill 10 minutes or until charred, turning every 2 minutes. Cut corn from ears, and toss with butter mixture. Yield: 4 servings.

CALORIES 115; **FAT** 5.3g (sat 2.9g); **SODIUM** 196mg

DARK GREEN POBLANO CHILES HAVE MILD TO MODERATE HEAT. THE DARKER THE CHILE, THE MORE FIERY IT WILL BE.

NEW USES FOR LIGHT COCONUT MILK

With 70 percent less saturated fat, lower-fat coconut milk adds a sweet, nutty richness to all kinds of foods.

1. MAKE FLUFFY PANCAKES

Combine 4.5 ounces (about 1 cup) all-purpose flour, 1 tablespoon sugar, 2 teaspoons baking powder, and ¼ teaspoon salt. Whisk together 1 cup light coconut milk, 1½ tablespoons canola oil, and 1 egg; combine with dry ingredients. Cook as usual for pancakes. Yield: 4 servings (or double the recipe for a taller stack).

CALORIES 228; **FAT** 9.8g (sat 3.7g); **SODIUM** 425mg

2. BLEND UP A SMOOTHIE

Place ½ cup frozen mango cubes, ⅓ cup light coconut milk, ¼ cup nonfat coconut-flavored yogurt, 1 tablespoon fresh lime juice, and 1½ teaspoons sugar in a blender; process until smooth. Yield: 1 serving.

CALORIES 157; **FAT** 4.3g (sat 3.8g); **SODIUM** 56mg

3. MAKE COCONUT ICE

Freeze coconut milk in ice-cube trays. Use the coconut cubes for margaritas on the rocks, rum and colas, or in place of regular ice for daiquiris or other slushy blended drinks.

4. MAKE A COCO-FIZZ

Try this refreshing fizzy drink. Combine ¼ cup light coconut milk, 1½ tablespoons agave nectar or simple syrup, and 1 teaspoon fresh lime juice; add ½ cup sparkling water. Serve over ice. (There will be some coconut solids in the drink—not to worry.) Yield: 1 serving.

CALORIES 125; **FAT** 3g (sat 2.8g); **SODIUM** 20mg

5. JAZZ UP YOUR MORNING CEREAL

Use a combination of coconut milk and dairy or soy milk to enliven your everyday breakfast bowl. Try a ratio of roughly 2 parts dairy or soy milk to 1 part light coconut milk for a hint of sweetness and a surprisingly nice hit of nutty essence.

5-INGREDIENT COOKING

Quick & Easy

Seared Scallops with Farmers' Market Salad

Look for dry-packed scallops, which will brown best.

2 cups chopped tomato (about 1 pound)
1 cup chopped fresh basil
1 tablespoon canola oil
1½ pounds sea scallops
2 cups fresh corn kernels (about 3 ears)

Combine tomato, basil, ¼ teaspoon kosher salt, and ⅛ teaspoon freshly ground black pepper; toss gently. Heat a large cast-iron or heavy skillet over high heat. Add oil to pan, swirling to coat. Pat scallops dry with paper towels; sprinkle with ½ teaspoon kosher salt and ⅛ teaspoon freshly ground black pepper. Add scallops to pan; cook 2 minutes or until browned. Turn scallops; cook 2 minutes or until done. Remove scallops from pan; keep warm. Coat pan with cooking spray. Add corn to pan; sauté 2 minutes or until lightly browned. Add to tomato mixture; toss gently. Serve salad with scallops. Yield: 4 servings (serving size: about 1 cup salad and about 3 scallops).

CALORIES 251; **FAT** 5.7g (sat 0.5g, mono 2.4g, poly 1.9g); **PROTEIN** 31.6g; **CARB** 19.4g; **FIBER** 3.3g; **CHOL** 56mg; **IRON** 1.4mg; **SODIUM** 641mg; **CALC** 70mg

THE FIVE INGREDIENTS

2 cups chopped tomato (about 1 pound)

+

1 cup chopped fresh basil

+

1 tablespoon canola oil

+

1½ pounds sea scallops

+

2 cups fresh corn kernels (about 3 ears)

Quick & Easy

Gemelli with Broccoli Rabe, Bacon, and Chickpeas

Penne works well in this dish if gemelli isn't available.

1 pound broccoli rabe, trimmed and coarsely
   chopped
8 ounces uncooked gemelli pasta
6 slices center-cut bacon
3 garlic cloves, thinly sliced
1 (15-ounce) can no-salt-added chickpeas
   (garbanzo beans), rinsed and drained

Bring 4 quarts water to a boil in a large Dutch oven. Add broccoli rabe to pan; cook 2 minutes. Remove with a slotted spoon; drain well. Coarsely chop. Return water to a boil. Add pasta to pan; cook according to package directions, omitting salt and fat. Drain in a colander over a bowl; reserve ¾ cup pasta water. Cook bacon in a large skillet over medium heat until crisp. Remove bacon from pan, reserving 1 tablespoon drippings in pan; crumble bacon. Increase heat to medium-high. Add garlic and chickpeas to drippings in pan; sauté 2 minutes or until garlic is golden. Stir in broccoli rabe, ½ teaspoon salt, and ¼ teaspoon freshly ground black pepper; cook 3 minutes or until broccoli rabe is heated. Stir in pasta, ¾ cup pasta water, and bacon; toss well. Yield: 4 servings (serving size: 1¾ cups).

CALORIES 357; **FAT** 7g (sat 2.2g, mono 2.6g, poly 1.1g); **PROTEIN** 179g; **CARB** 57.4g; **FIBER** 4.4g; **CHOL** 11mg; **IRON** 3.7mg; **SODIUM** 537mg; **CALC** 88mg

THE FIVE INGREDIENTS

1 pound broccoli rabe,
trimmed and coarsely chopped

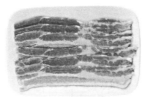

8 ounces uncooked
gemelli pasta

6 slices center-cut bacon

3 garlic cloves,
thinly sliced

1 (15-ounce) can no-salt-added chickpeas
(garbanzo beans), rinsed and drained

READER RECIPES

FROM YOUR KITCHEN TO OURS

Raised in an Italian-American home, Nicolette Manescalchi began cooking with her parents at an early age. "My mom would bake, and my dad would cook every night," she says. "We would never buy anything packaged." Now a professional chef, Manescalchi spends her time whipping up Southern Italian cuisine for patrons at A16 restaurant in San Francisco. She pairs her pasta with a simple chicory salad with lemon-olive oil dressing.

When it was Linda Stoneking's turn to host her supper club, she decided to incorporate in-season corn as a theme to challenge her guests. Her salad creation was the favorite that night. Yogurt in the marinade tempers the heat from the Sriracha and keeps this dish family-friendly.

After falling in love with some oatmeal pancakes she had at a bed-and-breakfast, Kathy Brown set out to replicate their light and fluffy texture. "The original recipe called for regular oats to be soaked overnight in buttermilk, but I discovered that using quick oats and not soaking them turned out a better and lighter product," she says.

Although many cooks consider sauce a condiment or an afterthought, Lisa Richardson developed this recipe around her homemade sauce based on store-bought tahini. Richardson enjoys creating recipes and encourages her 8-year-old daughter to get involved in cooking. "She has her own recipe cards on which she jots down her new dishes," she says.

continued

Spiced-Up Linguine with Clams

"I wanted to use spice to add bold flavors with-out adding calories. Soak and clean the clams well to avoid sand in your dish."

—Nicolette Manescalchi, San Francisco, California

12 ounces uncooked linguine
3 tablespoons extra-virgin olive oil
1 teaspoon dried thyme
1 teaspoon crushed red pepper
6 canned anchovy fillets, chopped
4 garlic cloves, minced
⅓ cup dry white wine
¼ cup clam juice
30 littleneck clams
2 tablespoons butter
½ cup chopped fresh parsley
¼ teaspoon kosher salt
¼ teaspoon freshly ground black pepper

1. Cook pasta according to package directions, omitting salt and fat. Drain.
2. Heat oil in a large saucepan over medium heat. Add thyme and next 3 ingredients; cook 2 minutes. Stir in wine and clam juice. Add clams; cover and cook 4 minutes or until shells open. Remove from heat; discard any unopened clam shells. Add cooked pasta, butter, and remaining ingredients to pan; toss well. Yield: 6 servings (serving size: 1⅓ cups pasta mixture and 5 clams).

CALORIES 388; **FAT** 13.1g (sat 3.9g, mono 6.2g, poly 1.5g); **PROTEIN** 21.5g; **CARB** 46.6g; **FIBER** 2.4g; **CHOL** 46mg; **IRON** 15.9mg; **SODIUM** 336mg; **CALC** 90mg

Chicken Dinner Salad

"You can arrange the salad on a platter for a supper club. It's a colorful main dish and great family meal."

—Linda Stoneking, Broadview Heights, Ohio

6 medium beets
4 (6-ounce) skinless, boneless chicken breast halves
½ cup plain 2% reduced-fat Greek yogurt
¼ cup Sriracha (hot chile sauce, such as Huy Fong)
3 tablespoons olive oil, divided
1 teaspoon freshly ground black pepper, divided
½ teaspoon kosher salt, divided
¼ cup white wine vinegar
1 tablespoon honey
1 shallot, minced
6 ears shucked corn
6 cups packed fresh spinach
4 ounces goat cheese, cut into 6 slices
6 tablespoons chopped toasted pecans

1. Leave root and 1-inch stem on beets; scrub with a brush. Place beets in a saucepan; cover with water. Bring to a boil. Reduce heat; simmer 1 hour or until tender. Drain. Cool beets slightly. Trim off beet roots and stems; rub off skins. Chop beets.
2. While beets cook, place each chicken breast half between 2 sheets of heavy-duty plastic wrap; pound to ½-inch thickness using a small heavy skillet. Combine yogurt and Sriracha in a heavy-duty zip-top plastic bag. Add chicken to bag; seal. Marinate in refrigerator 30 minutes, turning occasionally. Remove chicken from bag; discard marinade.
3. Preheat grill to medium-high heat.
4. Combine 2 tablespoons oil, ½ teaspoon pepper, ¼ teaspoon salt, and next 3 ingredients in a small bowl; stir with a whisk.
5. Place chicken on grill rack; grill 6 minutes on each side or until done. Cut chicken into 1-inch strips.
6. Brush remaining 1 tablespoon oil over corn; sprinkle with remaining ½ teaspoon pepper and remaining ¼ teaspoon salt. Grill 10 minutes or until lightly charred, turning corn occasionally. Cool. Cut kernels from ears of corn.
7. Place 1 cup spinach on each of 6 plates; top each serving with 3 ounces chicken, ⅓ cup beets, ⅓ cup corn, 1 cheese slice, and 1 tablespoon pecans. Drizzle 1 tablespoon dressing over each salad. Yield: 6 servings.

CALORIES 456; **FAT** 21.9g (sat 6.5g, mono 10.5g, poly 3.6g); **PROTEIN** 35.1g; **CARB** 33.5g; **FIBER** 7.4g; **CHOL** 78mg; **IRON** 4.9mg; **SODIUM** 614mg; **CALC** 175mg

Oatmeal Pancakes

(pictured on page 265)

"I like to serve the pancakes with fresh fruit, such as peaches and blueberries. You can also add fresh berries to the batter for an interesting twist."

—Kathy Brown, Tomball, Texas

1.1 ounces all-purpose flour (about ¼ cup)
1 cup quick-cooking oats
1 tablespoon sugar
½ teaspoon baking powder
½ teaspoon baking soda
¼ teaspoon ground cinnamon
⅛ teaspoon salt
1 cup nonfat buttermilk
2 tablespoons butter, melted
1 large egg
Cooking spray

1. Weigh or lightly spoon flour into a dry measuring cup; level with a knife. Combine flour and next 6 ingredients in a medium bowl, stirring with a whisk.
2. Combine buttermilk, butter, and egg in a small bowl. Add to flour mixture, stirring just until moist.
3. Heat a nonstick griddle over medium heat. Coat pan with cooking spray. Spoon about 2½ tablespoons batter per pancake onto griddle. Turn pancakes over when tops are covered with bubbles; cook until bottoms are lightly browned. Yield: 3 servings (serving size: 4 pancakes).

CALORIES 273; **FAT** 11.2g (sat 5.7g, mono 3.3g, poly 1.3g); **PROTEIN** 10g; **CARB** 34.7g; **FIBER** 2.8g; **CHOL** 91mg; **IRON** 2.1mg; **SODIUM** 526mg; **CALC** 184mg

Quick & Easy

Turkey Burger Pitas with Tahini Sauce

"My husband and I also enjoy the tahini sauce on other types of sandwiches—the Greek yogurt is so thick, you'd think it was full-fat."
—Lisa Richardson, Glendale, California

½ cup plain 2% reduced-fat Greek yogurt
1 tablespoon tahini (sesame seed paste)
1 teaspoon fresh lemon juice
1 garlic clove, minced
Dash of salt
¼ cup chopped green onions
3 tablespoons finely chopped fresh parsley
½ teaspoon salt
¼ teaspoon onion powder
1 pound ground turkey
Cooking spray
2 (6-inch) whole-wheat pitas, cut in half
4 green leaf lettuce leaves
4 (¼-inch) slices tomato

1. Combine first 5 ingredients in a small bowl.
2. Combine onions and next 4 ingredients in a large bowl. Divide mixture into 4 equal portions, shaping each into a ½-inch-thick patty.
3. Heat a large nonstick skillet over medium-high heat. Coat pan with cooking spray. Add patties to pan, and cook 4 minutes on each side or until done.
4. Line each pita half with 1 lettuce leaf; add 1 patty, 1 tomato slice, and 2 tablespoons tahini sauce to each pita half. Yield: 4 servings (serving size: 1 filled pita half).

CALORIES 302; FAT 11.9g (sat 3.5g, mono 3.9g, poly 3.3g); PROTEIN 30.6g; CARB 21.1g; FIBER 2.8g; CHOL 73mg; IRON 2.7mg; SODIUM 599mg; CALC 93mg

SUPERFAST

Enjoy late-summer bounty with light, fresh entreés that are chock-full of produce and ready in 20 minutes.

Quick & Easy

Prosciutto, Fresh Fig, and Manchego Sandwiches

Prosciutto and fresh figs are a classic Italian combination. Here, along with the cheese and jam, they create a sweet-savory sandwich that's simple yet memorable. Great ingredients make all the difference here, so look for a fine loaf of artisan bread and quality prosciutto. Use a sharp vegetable peeler to shave the Manchego, a Spanish cheese similar to pecorino Romano (which you can substitute).

4 teaspoons Dijon mustard
8 (¾-ounce) slices Italian bread, toasted
1 cup baby arugula
2 ounces very thin slices prosciutto
2 ounces Manchego cheese, shaved
8 fresh figs, cut into thin slices
2 tablespoons fig jam

1. Spread 1 teaspoon mustard over 4 bread slices. Arrange ¼ cup arugula over each bread slice. Divide prosciutto evenly over arugula; top evenly with cheese and fig slices. Spread 1½ teaspoons jam over remaining 4 bread slices. Top each serving with 1 bread slice, jam sides down. Yield: 4 servings (serving size: 1 sandwich).

CALORIES 295; FAT 5.3g (sat 2.6g, mono 2.1g, poly 0.6g); PROTEIN 11.5g; CARB 52.3g; FIBER 4.2g; CHOL 18mg; IRON 1.8mg; SODIUM 805mg; CALC 114mg

Quick & Easy

Grilled Yellowfin Tuna with Romaine and Tropical Fruit

4 cups packaged chopped romaine lettuce
2 cups chopped fresh pineapple
1 cup refrigerated presliced mango, chopped
⅓ cup chopped red onion
2 tablespoons chopped fresh cilantro
2 tablespoons fresh lime juice
2 tablespoons fresh orange juice
1 tablespoon olive oil, divided
½ teaspoon salt, divided
⅜ teaspoon freshly ground black pepper, divided
8 (3-ounce) Yellowfin tuna steaks
Cooking spray
4 lime wedges (optional)

1. Combine first 7 ingredients in a large bowl; add 1 teaspoon oil, ¼ teaspoon salt, and ⅛ teaspoon pepper, tossing to combine.
2. Heat a large heavy grill pan over medium-high heat. Rub remaining 2 teaspoons olive oil over tuna; sprinkle tuna evenly with remaining ¼ teaspoon salt and ¼ teaspoon pepper. Coat pan with cooking spray. Add tuna to pan; cook 3 minutes on each side or until desired degree of doneness. Arrange 1½ cups salad on each of 4 plates; top each serving with 2 tuna steaks. Serve with lime wedges, if desired. Yield: 4 servings.

CALORIES 292; FAT 5.4g (sat 0.9g, mono 2.8g, poly 1g); PROTEIN 39.8g; CARB 21.5g; FIBER 3.3g; CHOL 74mg; IRON 2.1mg; SODIUM 362mg; CALC 66mg

Pasta with Fresh Tomato-Basil Sauce

Though we paired this chunky sauce with fettuccine, it would also be nice with short pasta shapes, like penne, gemelli, or farfalle.

1 (9-ounce) package refrigerated fresh
    fettuccine
2 tablespoons olive oil
3 garlic cloves, minced
4 cups cherry tomatoes, halved
½ teaspoon salt
1 cup fresh basil leaves, torn
¼ teaspoon freshly ground black pepper
2 ounces Parmigiano-Reggiano cheese,
    shaved (about ½ cup)

1. Cook pasta according to package directions, omitting salt and fat. Drain; place pasta in a large bowl.
2. While pasta cooks, heat oil in a medium saucepan over medium heat. Add garlic to pan; cook 1 minute, stirring frequently. Add tomatoes and salt; cover and cook 4 minutes. Remove from heat; stir in basil and pepper. Add tomato mixture to pasta; toss well to combine. Top with cheese. Yield: 4 servings (serving size: about 1½ cups pasta and about 2 tablespoons cheese).

CALORIES 343; **FAT** 13.3g (sat 4.2g, mono 6.2g, poly 1.1g); **PROTEIN** 14.8g; **CARB** 43.4g; **FIBER** 3.7g; **CHOL** 51mg; **IRON** 2.6mg; **SODIUM** 541mg; **CALC** 201mg

LATE-SEASON PRODUCE FOR QUICK MEALS

TOMATOES
Colorful, juicy, sweet, and tangy—great in most any entrée

FIGS
Heavenly fruit for elegant salads and sandwiches

BELL PEPPERS
Sweeter and less expensive in summer

FRESH HERBS
Fresh, vibrant, and abundantly available

Chicken Kebabs with Creamy Pesto

2 teaspoons grated lemon rind
4 teaspoons fresh lemon juice, divided
2 teaspoons bottled minced garlic
2 teaspoons olive oil
½ teaspoon salt
¼ teaspoon black pepper
8 (1-inch) pieces yellow bell pepper
8 cherry tomatoes
1 pound skinless, boneless chicken breasts,
    cut into 1-inch pieces
1 small red onion, cut into 8 wedges
Cooking spray
2 tablespoons plain low-fat yogurt
2 tablespoons reduced-fat sour cream
1 tablespoon commercial pesto

1. Preheat broiler.
2. Combine rind, 1 tablespoon juice, garlic, and next 3 ingredients. Toss with bell pepper and next 3 ingredients. Thread vegetables and chicken onto 4 (12-inch) skewers. Place skewers on a broiler pan coated with cooking spray. Broil 12 minutes or until chicken is done, turning occasionally.
3. Combine remaining 1 teaspoon juice, yogurt, sour cream, and pesto. Serve sauce with kebabs. Yield: 4 servings (serving size: 1 kebab and 1 tablespoon sauce).

CALORIES 211; **FAT** 7.3g (sat 2.1g, mono 3g, poly 0.7g); **PROTEIN** 279g; **CARB** 7g; **FIBER** 1.2g; **CHOL** 70mg; **IRON** 1.4mg; **SODIUM** 441mg; **CALC** 48mg

Grilled Chicken and Tomato Salad

4 (6-ounce) skinless, boneless chicken breast
    halves
¼ teaspoon salt
¼ teaspoon black pepper
Cooking spray
5 cups arugula
1 cup halved multicolored cherry tomatoes
¼ cup thinly sliced red onion
¼ cup olive oil and vinegar salad dressing,
    divided
10 pitted kalamata olives, chopped
½ cup crumbled goat cheese

1. Heat a large grill pan over medium-high heat. Sprinkle chicken with salt and pepper. Coat pan with cooking spray. Place chicken in pan; cook 6 minutes on each side or until done.
2. While chicken cooks, combine arugula, tomatoes, onion, 3 tablespoons dressing, and olives; toss gently. Arrange about 1 cup salad on each of 4 plates; top each with 2 tablespoons cheese. Brush chicken with remaining 1 tablespoon dressing. Cut chicken into slices. Arrange 1 sliced chicken breast half on each salad. Yield: 4 servings (serving size: 1 salad).

CALORIES 305; **FAT** 15.9g (sat 4.6g, mono 7.1g, poly 1.4g); **PROTEIN** 33.6g; **CARB** 5.2g; **FIBER** 1g; **CHOL** 85mg; **IRON** 1.7mg; **SODIUM** 581mg; **CALC** 102mg

RECIPE MAKEOVER
TAMING A CLASSIC CASSEROLE

Say *arrivederci* to heavy, greasy Eggplant Parmesan.

Talk about a dish that could stand to lose a few: The Italian-American favorite of eggplant, tomato sauce, and cheese—spelled variously "Parmesan," "parmigian," or "parmigiana"—knows no nutritional boundaries. Fried-eggplant goodness is buried under piles of gooey cheese, with the tangy counterpoint of the tomato. It's delicious, but a serving has enough saturated fat and almost enough sodium for a whole day.

To walk this recipe back, we dredge eggplant slices in crispy, whole-wheat panko, then bake them to crunchy, meaty perfection. Leaner part-skim ricotta is jazzed up with garlic, crushed red pepper, basil, and cheese. Some thinly sliced mozzarella stretches our cheese budget, while gourmet jarred pasta sauce streamlines the method. This tasty casserole loses the heaviness, not to mention the grease, of the old standard. You'll have room for dessert.

Eggplant Parmesan

Use whole-wheat panko in this recipe; we found the regular type becomes soggy.

Eggplant:

2 large eggs, lightly beaten

1 tablespoon water

2 cups whole-wheat panko (Japanese breadcrumbs)

¼ cup (1 ounce) grated fresh Parmigiano-Reggiano cheese

2 (1-pound) eggplants, peeled and cut crosswise into ½-inch-thick slices

Cooking spray

Filling:

½ cup torn fresh basil

¼ cup (1 ounce) grated fresh Parmigiano-Reggiano cheese

½ teaspoon crushed red pepper

1½ teaspoons minced garlic

¼ teaspoon salt

1 (16-ounce) container part-skim ricotta cheese

1 large egg, lightly beaten

Remaining Ingredients:

1 (24-ounce) jar premium pasta sauce

¼ teaspoon salt

8 ounces thinly sliced mozzarella cheese

¾ cup (3 ounces) finely grated fontina cheese

1. Preheat oven to 375°.

2. To prepare eggplant, combine 2 eggs and 1 tablespoon water in a shallow dish. Combine panko and ¼ cup Parmigiano-Reggiano in a second shallow dish. Dip eggplant in egg mixture; dredge in panko mixture, pressing gently to adhere and shaking off excess. Place eggplant 1 inch apart on baking sheets coated with cooking spray. Bake at 375° for 30 minutes or until golden, turning once and rotating baking sheets after 15 minutes.

3. To prepare filling, combine basil and next 6 ingredients.

4. To assemble, spoon ½ cup pasta sauce in bottom of a 13 x 9–inch glass baking dish coated with cooking spray. Layer half of eggplant slices over pasta sauce. Sprinkle eggplant with ⅛ teaspoon salt. Top with about ¾ cup pasta sauce; spread half of ricotta mixture over sauce, and top with a third of mozzarella and ¼ cup fontina. Repeat layers once, ending with about 1 cup pasta sauce. Cover tightly with aluminum foil coated with cooking spray. Bake at 375° for 35 minutes. Remove foil; top with remaining third of mozzarella and ¼ cup fontina. Bake at 375° for 10 minutes or until sauce is bubbly and cheese melts; cool 10 minutes. Yield: 10 servings (serving size: 1 slice).

CALORIES 318; **FAT** 15.1g (sat 8.2g, mono 2.7g, poly 0.6g); **PROTEIN** 19.3g; **CARB** 26.8g; **FIBER** 4.8g; **CHOL** 99mg; **IRON** 1.6mg; **SODIUM** 655mg; **CALC** 365mg

OLD WAY	OUR WAY
1,053 calories per serving	318 calories per serving
30.4 grams saturated fat	8.2 grams saturated fat
1,965 milligrams sodium	655 milligrams sodium
Deep-fried eggplant	Baked breaded eggplant
Breadcrumbs	Whole-wheat panko
4+ pounds cheese	1¾ pounds cheese

PANKO BREADING TECHNIQUE

A too-heavy or too-thin coating of these Japanese breadcrumbs will prevent you from getting the coveted crispy "oven-fried" effect that is the crux of this dish. Here's how to get the crumb count just right.

1 Give the eggplant slices a quick dip in egg wash; let excess drip off.

2 Gently press the panko onto the slice to help it adhere.

3 The whole-wheat panko barely browns, but it will create a perfectly crisp coating.

DINNER TONIGHT

Here are a handful of fast weeknight menus from the *Cooking Light* Test Kitchens.

SHOPPING LIST

Grilled Steak with Fresh Mango Salsa

1 mango
1 cucumber
fresh cilantro
1 lime
fresh ginger
garam masala
brown sugar
1-pound flat-iron or flank steak

Garlic Flatbread

garlic
olive oil
naan or other flatbread

GAME PLAN

While grill preheats:
- Rub steak with spice rub.
- Prepare and chill salsa.

Grill steak.

While steak rests:
- Grill flatbread.

Quick & Easy

Grilled Steak with Fresh Mango Salsa

with Garlic Flatbread

Make-Ahead Tip: Refrigerate the salsa up to a day ahead.

1 teaspoon garam masala
1 teaspoon brown sugar
½ teaspoon salt
½ teaspoon freshly ground black pepper
1 (1-pound) flat-iron or flank steak
1 cup diced peeled fresh mango (about 1)
¼ cup diced seeded cucumber
1 tablespoon chopped fresh cilantro
1 tablespoon fresh lime juice
¼ teaspoon minced peeled fresh ginger
Dash of salt
Cooking spray

1. Preheat grill to medium-high heat.
2. Combine first 4 ingredients; rub evenly over both sides of steak. Let steak stand at room temperature 10 minutes.
3. Combine mango and next 5 ingredients; cover and chill.
4. Lightly coat both sides of steak with cooking spray. Place steak on grill rack; grill 5 minutes on each side or until desired degree of doneness. Remove steak from grill; let stand 5 minutes. Cut steak diagonally across grain into thin slices. Serve with salsa. Yield: 4 servings (serving size: about 3 ounces steak and about ¼ cup salsa).

CALORIES 223; FAT 11.1g (sat 4.4g, mono 4.6g, poly 0.5g); PROTEIN 21.5g; CARB 8.6g; FIBER 1.2g; CHOL 71mg; IRON 2.8mg; SODIUM 399mg; CALC 19mg

For the Garlic Flatbread:
Preheat grill to medium-high heat. Combine 1 tablespoon olive oil, 1 minced garlic clove, and dash of salt in a microwave-safe bowl; cover and microwave at HIGH 8 seconds or until warm. Let stand 5 minutes. Brush both sides of 2 (3.25-ounce) naan flatbreads or other flatbreads with oil mixture. Place bread on grill rack; grill 1 minute on each side or until browned. Yield: 4 servings.

CALORIES 160; FAT 6g (sat 1.1g); SODIUM 251mg

SHOPPING LIST

Arctic Char with Cilantro-Yogurt Sauce

1 cucumber
fresh cilantro
1 lime
olive oil
plain 2% reduced-fat Greek yogurt
4 (6-ounce) arctic char or salmon fillets

Red Pepper–Coconut Rice

small red bell pepper
jasmine rice
crushed red pepper
1 (14-ounce) can light coconut milk

GAME PLAN

While rice cooks:
- Prepare sauce; chill.
- Rub fish with seasonings.

While fish cooks:
- Stir bell pepper into rice and let stand.

Quick & Easy

Arctic Char with Cilantro-Yogurt Sauce

with Red Pepper-Coconut Rice

Kid Pleaser: Strike the crushed red pepper from the rice; serve raita with pita chips.
Simple Sub: Replace cilantro with fresh mint or basil.
Flavor Hit: Jasmine rice has a nutty aroma and flavor; you can also use basmati rice.

½ cup plain 2% reduced-fat Greek yogurt
¼ cup finely chopped peeled cucumber
2 tablespoons chopped fresh cilantro
½ teaspoon fresh lime juice
⅛ teaspoon salt
2 teaspoons olive oil
4 (6-ounce) arctic char or salmon fillets, skinned
½ teaspoon salt
¼ teaspoon freshly ground black pepper
Lime wedges (optional)

1. Combine first 5 ingredients; chill.
2. Heat oil in a large nonstick skillet over medium-high heat. Sprinkle fillets with ½ teaspoon salt and pepper. Add to pan; cook 3 minutes on each side or until desired degree of doneness. Serve fillets with sauce and lime wedges, if desired. Yield: 4 servings (serving size: 1 fillet and about 3 tablespoons sauce).

CALORIES 271; FAT 13.5g (sat 3.3g, mono 6.4g, poly 2.7g); PROTEIN 33.9g; CARB 1.7g; FIBER 0.1g; CHOL 82mg; IRON 0.5mg; SODIUM 446mg; CALC 47mg

For the Red Pepper–Coconut Rice:
Bring 1 cup jasmine rice, ¼ teaspoon salt, ¼ teaspoon crushed red pepper, and 1 (14-ounce) can light coconut milk to a boil. Cover, reduce heat, and simmer 20 minutes. Remove from heat. Stir in ½ cup diced red bell pepper; cover and let stand 5 minutes. Yield: 4 servings.

CALORIES 138; FAT 4.7g (sat 4.4g); SODIUM 172mg

SHOPPING LIST

Crab and Grilled Corn Salad
6 ears corn
celery
fresh cilantro
green onions
2 limes
Boston lettuce
1 bottle roasted red bell peppers
canola mayonnaise
ground red pepper
12 ounces lump crabmeat

Manchego–Black Pepper Breadsticks
11-ounce can refrigerated breadstick dough
Manchego cheese

GAME PLAN

While oven preheats:
- Grill corn.
- Pick out shell pieces from crabmeat.
- Prepare breadstick dough.
While breadsticks bake:
- Toss salad.

Quick & Easy

Crab and Grilled Corn Salad

with Manchego-Black Pepper Breadsticks

Simple Sub: Use Asiago or Parmigiano-Reggiano in place of the Manchego cheese.
Prep Pointer: Rinse and drain the bell peppers to freshen their flavor.
Flavor Hit: Charring the corn adds toasty, nutty depth.

6 ears shucked corn
1 cup finely chopped celery
1 cup chopped bottled roasted red bell pepper, rinsed and drained
½ cup chopped fresh cilantro
⅓ cup thinly sliced green onions
12 ounces lump crabmeat, shell pieces removed
¼ cup fresh lime juice
3 tablespoons canola mayonnaise
½ teaspoon freshly ground black pepper
⅜ teaspoon salt
⅛ teaspoon ground red pepper
12 Boston lettuce leaves

1. Heat a large grill pan over medium-high heat. Place corn in pan; cook 8 minutes or until slightly charred, turning frequently. Cool slightly. Cut kernels from ears of corn; place in a large bowl. Add celery and next 4 ingredients to corn; toss gently to combine.
2. Combine lime juice and next 4 ingredients in a small bowl, stirring well with a whisk. Pour dressing over crab mixture; toss gently to coat. Serve salad over lettuce leaves. Yield: 6 servings (serving size: 1⅓ cups salad and 2 lettuce leaves).

CALORIES 249; FAT 8.3g (sat 0.6g, mono 2.4g, poly 4.7g); PROTEIN 16.8g; CARB 31g; FIBER 4.9g; CHOL 59mg; IRON 1.9mg; SODIUM 475mg; CALC 90mg

For the Manchego–Black Pepper Breadsticks:
Preheat oven to 375°. Separate 1 (11-ounce) can refrigerated breadstick dough to form 12 dough pieces. Twist each dough piece, and place on an ungreased baking sheet pressing ends down. Combine ½ cup shredded

---

Manchego cheese and 1 teaspoon cracked black pepper. Gently press cheese mixture onto tops of breadsticks. Bake at 375° for 13 minutes or until breadsticks are browned. Yield: 12 servings.

CALORIES 94; FAT 3g (sat 1.2g); SODIUM 222mg

SHOPPING LIST

Chicken Stuffed with Spinach, Feta, and Pine Nuts
5 ounces fresh spinach
fresh thyme
1 lemon
garlic
pine nuts
olive oil
fat-free, lower-sodium chicken broth
2 ounces crumbled feta cheese
4 (6-ounce) skinless, boneless chicken breast halves

Currant Couscous
fresh parsley
olive oil
Israeli couscous
dried currants

GAME PLAN

While oven preheats:
- Toast nuts.
- Cook spinach.
- Stuff chicken.
- Sauté couscous.
While chicken bakes:
- Prepare couscous.

continued

Chicken Stuffed with Spinach, Feta, and Pine Nuts

with Currant Couscous

Kid Pleaser: For milder flavor, use shredded mozzarella or provolone cheese.
Simple Sub: Try raisins or dried apricots in place of currants.
Prep Pointer: Use a sharp paring knife or utility knife to cut a pocket in the chicken.

5 ounces fresh spinach, chopped
1/2 cup (2 ounces) crumbled feta cheese
2 tablespoons pine nuts, toasted
1 teaspoon fresh thyme, minced
2 teaspoons fresh lemon juice
2 garlic cloves, minced
4 (6-ounce) skinless, boneless chicken breast halves
1/4 teaspoon salt
1/4 teaspoon freshly ground black pepper
1 tablespoon olive oil
1/2 cup fat-free, lower-sodium chicken broth

1. Preheat oven to 350°.
2. Heat a large nonstick ovenproof skillet over medium-high heat. Add spinach to pan, and cook 1 minute or until spinach wilts, tossing constantly. Place spinach in a colander; press until barely moist. Wipe pan clean.
3. Combine spinach, cheese, and next 4 ingredients. Cut a horizontal slit through the thickest portion of each chicken breast half to form a pocket. Stuff 3 tablespoons filling into each pocket. Seal with wooden picks. Sprinkle chicken with salt and pepper.
4. Heat oil in pan over medium-high heat. Add chicken; cook 3 minutes on each side or until brown. Add broth, and cover pan. Place pan in oven. Bake at 350° for 15 minutes or until done. Yield: 4 servings (serving size: 1 stuffed chicken breast half).

CALORIES 297; **FAT** 11.6g (sat 3.4g, mono 4.4g, poly 2.4g); **PROTEIN** 43.3g; **CARB** 3.4g; **FIBER** 1.2g; **CHOL** 111mg; **IRON** 2.7mg; **SODIUM** 493mg; **CALC** 131mg

For the Currant Couscous:
Heat 2 teaspoons olive oil in a saucepan over medium-high heat. Add 1 cup uncooked Israeli couscous; sauté 2 minutes. Add 2 cups water and 1/4 cup dried currants; bring to a boil. Cover, reduce heat, and simmer 12 minutes. Remove from heat; stir in 1/4 cup chopped fresh parsley and 1/4 teaspoon salt. Yield: 4 servings.

CALORIES 236; **FAT** 2.8g (sat 0.3g); **SODIUM** 148mg

30 minutes

SHOPPING LIST

Lamb and Turkey Pita Burgers
1 lemon
prechopped onion
green leaf lettuce
whole-wheat pitas
ground cumin
ground red pepper
ground cinnamon
ground ginger
canola mayonnaise
tomato paste
8 ounces lean ground lamb
8 ounces ground turkey breast

Tomato-Cucumber Salad
1 English cucumber
2 large tomatoes
fresh flat-leaf parsley
1 lemon
kalamata olives
extra-virgin olive oil

GAME PLAN

While cucumbers drain:
■ Prepare sauce; chill.
■ Prepare patties.
While patties cook:
■ Cut pitas.
■ Prepare lettuce.
■ Make salad.

Lamb and Turkey Pita Burgers

with Tomato-Cucumber Salad

Sauce:
1/4 cup canola mayonnaise
2 teaspoons fresh lemon juice
1/4 teaspoon ground cumin
1/8 teaspoon ground red pepper
Burgers:
1/4 cup prechopped onion
1 tablespoon tomato paste
1/4 teaspoon salt
1/8 teaspoon ground cinnamon
1/8 teaspoon ground ginger
8 ounces lean ground lamb
8 ounces ground turkey breast
Cooking spray
8 small green leaf lettuce leaves
4 (6-inch) whole-wheat pitas, halved

1. To prepare sauce, combine first 4 ingredients; cover and chill.
2. To prepare burgers, combine onion and next 6 ingredients in a large bowl. Divide mixture into 8 equal portions, shaping each into a 1/3-inch-thick oval patty.
3. Heat a large grill pan over medium-high heat. Coat pan with cooking spray. Add patties to pan; cook 5 minutes on each side or until well-marked and done. Arrange 1 lettuce leaf, 1 patty, and about 1½ teaspoons sauce in each pita half. Yield: 4 servings (serving size: 2 stuffed pita halves).

CALORIES 423; **FAT** 18.8g (sat 3.2g, mono 6.2g, poly 8.2g); **PROTEIN** 27.3g; **CARB** 37.6g; **FIBER** 5.3g; **CHOL** 70mg; **IRON** 3.4mg; **SODIUM** 658mg; **CALC** 29mg

For the Tomato-Cucumber Salad:
Combine 2 cups thinly sliced English cucumber and 1/4 teaspoon salt in a colander; let stand 10 minutes. Squeeze out excess moisture. Combine cucumber, 2 cups thin tomato wedges, 2 tablespoons chopped fresh flat-leaf parsley, 2 tablespoons chopped pitted kalamata olives, 1 tablespoon fresh lemon juice, and 2 teaspoons extra-virgin olive oil. Yield: 4 servings.

CALORIES 53; **FAT** 3.3g (sat 0.4g); **SODIUM** 158mg

WHY DID THE CHICKEN CROSS THE GLOBE?

To escape all those busy weeknight cooks, of course. Here, supersimple recipes jazz up the bird.

For so many cooks on so many nights, the basic chicken breast is the go-to protein for a healthy meal in a hurry. It can be a snoozer after awhile, until you start importing flavors and ingredients from around the world. Chicken is favored just about everywhere for its versatility—from Vietnam and Korea to Greece and Mexico. The recipes here use five ingredients or fewer (not including salt, pepper, water, oil, and cooking spray, which are freebies), but those ingredients are chosen for maximum impact: lemongrass, soy, fresh herbs, Gorgonzola, Dijon.

Quick & Easy • Kid Friendly
Korean Meatballs

Serve with store-bought kimchi and Quick Pickled Cucumbers to add heat and tang to the meal.

2 tablespoons brown sugar
2 tablespoons canola oil
8 garlic cloves
3 tablespoons lower-sodium soy sauce
¼ teaspoon salt
1 pound skinless, boneless chicken breasts, cut into 1-inch pieces
Cooking spray

1. Preheat oven to 400°.
2. Place first 3 ingredients in a food processor; process until finely ground. Add soy sauce, salt, and chicken; process until finely ground. Divide chicken mixture into 20 equal portions. With moist hands, shape each portion into a meatball.
3. Heat a large cast-iron skillet over medium-high heat. Add 10 meatballs to pan; sauté 4 minutes, turning to brown meatballs on all sides. Arrange browned meatballs on a jelly-roll pan coated with cooking spray. Repeat procedure with remaining meatballs. Bake at 400° for 5 minutes or until done. Yield: 4 servings (serving size: 5 meatballs).

CALORIES 225; FAT 9.7g (sat 1.3g, mono 5g, poly 2.7g); PROTEIN 23.9g; CARB 9.7g; FIBER 0.2g; CHOL 63mg; IRON 1.2mg; SODIUM 606mg; CALC 30mg

Quick Pickled Cucumbers:
Slice 1 English cucumber crosswise into thin rounds. Combine cucumber and 2 crushed garlic cloves in a medium bowl. Combine 1 cup rice vinegar, ¾ cup water, 2 tablespoons sugar, and ½ teaspoon salt; microwave at HIGH 2 minutes or until boiling. Pour hot vinegar mixture over cucumber mixture; stir in 1 tablespoon sambal oelek (such as Huy Fong). Cover and chill at least 4 hours. Serve with a slotted spoon, or drain before serving. Garnish with sliced green onions, if desired. Yield: 4 servings.

CALORIES 12; FAT 0.1g (sat 0.1g); SODIUM 31mg

Quick & Easy
Vietnamese Stir-Fry

Serve with wide rice noodles tossed with sliced green onions and fresh cilantro leaves.

1 tablespoon canola oil
⅓ cup finely chopped peeled fresh lemongrass
1 pound skinless, boneless chicken breasts, cut into bite-sized pieces
¼ teaspoon kosher salt
1½ tablespoons sambal oelek (such as Huy Fong)
¼ cup lower-sodium soy sauce

1. Heat a large skillet over medium-high heat. Add oil to pan; swirl to coat. Add lemongrass; sauté 1 minute, stirring frequently. Add chicken to pan, and sprinkle with salt. Sauté 3 minutes or until lightly browned, stirring occasionally. Stir in sambal; sauté 30 seconds. Add soy sauce; bring to a boil. Reduce heat, and simmer 5 minutes or until chicken is done. Yield: 4 servings (serving size: about ⅔ cup).

CALORIES 177; FAT 6.2g (sat 1g, mono 3g, poly 1.6g); PROTEIN 24.4g; CARB 4.7g; FIBER 0g; CHOL 63mg; IRON 1.3mg; SODIUM 678mg; CALC 18mg

3 MORE WAYS TO USE LEMONGRASS

• Add lemon essence to vichyssoise or other soup.

• Infuse poaching liquid or stew.

• Puree with chiles, ginger, garlic, shallots, cilantro, and lime juice to make a curry paste or sauce.

Greek-Style Skewers

Serve with orzo tossed with crumbled feta cheese and pitted kalamata olives.

1 pound skinless, boneless chicken breasts, cut into 32 cubes
24 cherry tomatoes (optional)
3/4 teaspoon salt, divided
1/4 teaspoon freshly ground black pepper
Cooking spray
1 lemon
2 garlic cloves
1/4 cup fresh oregano leaves
3 tablespoons extra-virgin olive oil

1. Preheat grill to medium-high heat.
2. Thread 4 chicken cubes alternately with 3 tomatoes, if desired, onto each of 8 (12-inch) skewers. Sprinkle skewers with 1/2 teaspoon salt and pepper; coat with cooking spray. Place skewers on a grill rack coated with cooking spray; grill 3 minutes. Turn skewers over; grill 2 minutes or until chicken is done.
3. Grate 1 1/2 teaspoons rind from 1 end of lemon; cut lemon in half, crosswise. Cut ungrated lemon half into quarters; reserve remaining lemon half for another use. Place remaining 1/4 teaspoon salt, lemon rind, garlic, and oregano in a food processor; process until finely ground, scraping sides. With motor running, slowly drizzle oil through food chute; process until well blended. Brush oregano mixture over skewers; serve with lemon wedges. Yield: 4 servings (serving size: 2 skewers and 1 lemon wedge).

CALORIES 221; FAT 13.3g (sat 2.3g, mono 8.4g, poly 2.1g); PROTEIN 23.2g; CARB 1.9g; FIBER 0.3g; CHOL 63mg; IRON 0.9mg; SODIUM 498mg; CALC 36mg

3 MORE WAYS TO USE GUANCIALE

- Sauté with aromatic ingredients as a base for soups and stews.

- Simmer with dried beans for meaty richness.

- Flavor pasta sauces, such as carbonara.

Pork and Gorgonzola–Stuffed Chicken Breasts

Serve with creamy polenta and garlicky broccoli rabe sautéed in olive oil. Guanciale is a lean, full-flavored Italian pork product. Although it contains less fat than either, it's similar to pancetta or cured bacon—which you can substitute if you can't find guanciale. And Gorgonzola is Italy's most famous blue cheese, but any blue cheese will work in this dish.

2 ounces guanciale, finely chopped
1/2 cup (2 ounces) crumbled Gorgonzola cheese
1/3 cup finely chopped seeded tomato
1/2 teaspoon salt, divided
4 (6-ounce) skinless, boneless chicken breast halves
1/4 teaspoon freshly ground black pepper
1 1/2 teaspoons olive oil

1. Preheat oven to 400°.
2. Cook guanciale in a large ovenproof skillet over medium heat 10 minutes or until crisp, stirring frequently; remove from pan using a slotted spoon. Combine guanciale, 1 tablespoon drippings, cheese, tomato, and 1/4 teaspoon salt in a small bowl, stirring well.
3. Cut a horizontal slit through thickest portion of each chicken breast half to form a pocket. Stuff 2 tablespoons cheese mixture into each pocket; secure with a wooden pick. Sprinkle both sides of chicken evenly with remaining 1/4 teaspoon salt and pepper.
4. Wipe pan clean with paper towels. Return pan to medium-high heat. Add oil to pan; swirl to coat. Add chicken; sauté 4 minutes. Turn chicken over. Place pan in oven; bake at 400° for 8 minutes or until chicken is done. Let stand 5 minutes. Discard wooden picks. Cut chicken diagonally into 1/2-inch-thick slices, if desired. Serve with pan juices. Yield: 4 servings (serving size: 1 chicken breast half and 1 tablespoon pan juice).

CALORIES 330; FAT 18.3g (sat 7.1g, mono 6.7g, poly 2.1g); PROTEIN 38.3g; CARB 1.6g; FIBER 0.5g; CHOL 118mg; IRON 1.3mg; SODIUM 558mg; CALC 86mg

Chicken Breasts with Classic French Pan Sauce

Serve this simple, rich dish with steamed haricots verts or fresh green beans and silky mashed potatoes. Adding a pinch of flour is an easy way to thicken the sauce quickly. If you prefer, you can omit the flour and simply allow the sauce to simmer longer, just until it thickens naturally.

1 tablespoon olive oil
4 bone-in chicken breast halves
5/8 teaspoon salt, divided
1/4 teaspoon freshly ground black pepper
1/4 cup dry white wine
2 teaspoons Dijon mustard
1/4 cup heavy whipping cream
1/2 teaspoon all-purpose flour

1. Preheat oven to 350°.
2. Heat a large ovenproof skillet over medium-high heat. Add oil to pan; swirl to coat. Sprinkle chicken evenly with 1/2 teaspoon salt and pepper. Add chicken to pan, skin sides down; sauté 4 minutes or until browned. Turn chicken over. Place pan in oven; bake at 350° for 40 minutes or until a thermometer inserted in thickest portion registers 160°. Remove chicken from pan, and let stand 10 minutes.
3. Return skillet to medium-high heat. Add wine to pan; bring to a boil. Cook 1 minute or until reduced to 2 tablespoons, scraping pan to loosen browned bits. Stir in mustard. Combine cream and flour, stirring until smooth. Add cream mixture to pan; bring to a boil. Cook until slightly thick, stirring constantly with a whisk. Stir in remaining 1/8 teaspoon salt. Serve with chicken. Yield: 4 servings (serving size: 1 chicken breast half and about 1 1/2 tablespoons sauce).

CALORIES 239; FAT 12.1g (sat 4.8g, mono 5.2g, poly 1.4g); PROTEIN 27g; CARB 1.6g; FIBER 0g; CHOL 93mg; IRON 0.9mg; SODIUM 498mg; CALC 23mg

Sautéed Chicken Breasts with Pico de Gallo

Although Mexican cuisine usually involves a variety of complex flavors, you'll find three base ingredients in most dishes: tomatoes, white onions, and chiles. Here we use jalapeño peppers, which give a nice kick, but you can substitute the hotter serrano chile if you're a fan of spicy foods. Serve the chicken with Cilantro Rice.

1 cup chopped, seeded tomato
⅓ cup chopped white onion
1 jalapeño pepper, finely chopped
2½ tablespoons canola oil, divided
¾ teaspoon salt, divided
4 (6-ounce) skinless, boneless chicken breast halves
¼ teaspoon freshly ground black pepper

1. Combine first 3 ingredients, 2 tablespoons oil, and ¼ teaspoon salt.
2. Heat a large skillet over medium-high heat. Add remaining 1½ teaspoons oil to pan; swirl to coat. Sprinkle both sides of chicken with remaining ½ teaspoon salt and pepper. Add chicken to pan; sauté 6 minutes on each side or until done. Serve with pico de gallo. Yield: 4 servings (serving size: 1 chicken breast half and about ⅓ cup pico de gallo).

CALORIES 275; FAT 12.8g (sat 1.8g, mono 6.5g, poly 3.5g); PROTEIN 34.9g; CARB 3.3g; FIBER 0.9g; CHOL 94mg; IRON 1.3mg; SODIUM 527mg; CALC 25mg

Cilantro Rice:
Combine 2 cups hot cooked long-grain white rice with ¼ cup chopped fresh cilantro, 1 teaspoon grated lime rind, ½ teaspoon ground cumin, and ¼ teaspoon salt.

CALORIES 104; FAT 0.3g (sat 0.1g); SODIUM 149mg

IT'S CRUNCH TIME

And tart time. And sauce time. A bunch of apples a day keeps the healthy cook at play.

As the weather gets crisp and the crispness of apples signals the sweet, fleeting passage of fall, it's time to get cooking. You may find eight varieties of apples for sale in a good grocery store these days, and a dozen or more in a big farmers' market. There are more than 2,500 kinds of apples grown in the United States alone, with rare, old heirloom varieties on a welcome rebound. All this means you have a bumper crop of fruit to cook with—and apples are a great cooking fruit. We matched some favorite varieties to recipes designed to unlock the unique charm of each fruit.

Make Ahead
Apple-Parsnip Soup

Pink Lady apples are wonderful for applesauce and so work very well in this pureed appetizer soup. Sweet Fuji or all-purpose Spartan apples would also lend themselves nicely to the dish.

2 tablespoons olive oil
1 cup chopped onion
2½ cups chopped peeled Pink Lady apple (about 1 pound)
1 tablespoon curry powder
1½ teaspoons grated peeled fresh ginger
1 teaspoon ground cardamom
1 garlic clove, chopped
3½ cups chopped peeled parsnip (about 1½ pounds)
4 cups fat-free, lower-sodium chicken broth
1 cup apple cider
½ teaspoon salt
⅛ teaspoon freshly ground black pepper
8 teaspoons crème fraîche

1. Heat oil in a Dutch oven over medium heat. Add onion; cook 5 minutes or until tender, stirring frequently. Add apple and next 4 ingredients; cook 1 minute, stirring constantly. Add parsnip, broth, and cider; bring to a boil. Cover, reduce heat, and simmer 30 minutes or until parsnip is tender.

2. Place half of parsnip mixture in a blender. Remove center piece of blender lid (to allow steam to escape); secure blender lid on blender. Place a clean towel over opening in blender lid (to avoid splatters). Blend until smooth. Pour into a large bowl. Repeat procedure with remaining parsnip mixture. Stir in salt and pepper. Ladle about ¾ cup soup into each of 8 bowls; top each serving with 1 teaspoon crème fraîche. Yield: 8 servings.

CALORIES 136; FAT 5.6g (sat 1.6g, mono 2.6g, poly 0.6g); PROTEIN 1.8g; CARB 21.2g; FIBER 4.2g; CHOL 5mg; IRON 0.7mg; SODIUM 381mg; CALC 30mg

APPLES PERFORM VERY DIFFERENTLY WHEN COOKED. MATCHMAKING IS AN ART. ONE APPLE FOR A SWEET SANGRIA, ANOTHER FOR A SILKY SOUP.

Squash-Apple Turnovers

Jonagold apples bring some tartness to the lightly sweet squash-based filling. You can also use other good baking apples like Honeycrisp or Rome. Serve as a side dish or appetizer.

2 teaspoons olive oil
1/2 cup minced onion
2 cups (1/4-inch) diced peeled butternut
    squash
1 cup (1/4-inch) diced peeled Jonagold apple
    (about 1/2 pound)
1/2 teaspoon kosher salt
1/4 teaspoon freshly ground black pepper
1/4 cup (1 ounce) crumbled goat cheese
2 teaspoons chopped fresh thyme
1 (11.3-ounce) can refrigerated dinner roll
    dough
1 tablespoon honey mustard
2 teaspoons water
2 tablespoons 1% low-fat milk
Cooking spray

1. Preheat oven to 375°.
2. Heat oil in a large skillet over medium-high heat. Add onion; sauté 3 minutes. Add squash; sauté 5 minutes. Add apple; cook 6 minutes or until squash and apple are tender. Stir in salt and pepper. Remove from heat, and cool to room temperature. Gently stir in cheese and thyme.
3. Separate dough into 8 pieces. Roll each portion into a 5-inch circle on a lightly floured surface. Combine mustard and 2 teaspoons water in a small bowl. Lightly brush top sides of dough circles with mustard mixture. Spoon about 2 tablespoons squash mixture onto half of each circle, leaving a 1/4-inch border. Fold dough over filling; press edges together with a fork to seal. Brush milk over dough. Place turnovers 1 inch apart on a baking sheet lightly coated with cooking spray. Bake at 375° for 19 minutes or until golden brown. Serve warm. Yield: 8 servings (serving size: 1 turnover).

CALORIES 177; **FAT** 4.5g (sat 1g, mono 2.3g, poly 0.8g); **PROTEIN** 5.7g; **CARB** 29g; **FIBER** 2.1g; **CHOL** 3mg; **IRON** 1.6mg; **SODIUM** 427mg; **CALC** 51mg

---

Make Ahead
Apple Sangria

Sugary-sweet Honeycrisp apples balance the spiced wine in this festive drink. Pink Lady or Ambrosia apples—which are slow to oxidize—would make good substitutes.

3 1/2 cups chopped Honeycrisp apple
    (about 2 pounds)
1/2 cup apple schnapps
1/4 cup honey
4 whole cloves
2 (3-inch) cinnamon sticks
2 (1/4-inch) slices peeled fresh ginger
1 large navel orange, quartered
1 (750-milliliter) bottle fruity red wine
    (such as Beaujolais)
1/4 cup club soda, chilled, divided
4 thin horizontal slices cored Honeycrisp
    apple

1. Combine first 8 ingredients in a large bowl; stir well. Refrigerate 4 hours or until thoroughly chilled.
2. Strain wine mixture through a sieve into a bowl; discard solids. Pour about 2/3 cup sangria over ice in each of 4 glasses; top each serving with 1 tablespoon club soda and 1 apple slice. Yield: 4 servings.

CALORIES 209; **FAT** 0g; **PROTEIN** 0.3g; **CARB** 23.7g; **FIBER** 0.5g; **CHOL** 0mg; **IRON** 1mg; **SODIUM** 4mg; **CALC** 4mg

---

EAT YOUR HEIRLOOMS

There has been a resurgence of heirloom varieties, which were dropped by many growers during the rush to supermarket efficiencies. The Golden Russet variety is one of thousands of varieties, many of which boast quirky names like Sheep's Nose, Esopus Spitzenburg, Winter Banana, and Sine Qua Non. These apples can run the gamut from still-life gorgeous to mirror-cracking homely and often have vibrant flavors that will challenge your perceptions of how an apple should taste. Try buying a mixed bag and do an heirloom tasting at home as a fun family activity.

Make Ahead
Apple Upside-Down Cake

Mild Rome apples are great for baking. You can also use Pink Lady, Honeycrisp, or Jonagold apples. Dollop the cake with a bit of whipped cream, if desired.

Topping:
Cooking spray
3/4 cup sugar
1/4 cup water
3 cups (1/4-inch-thick) slices peeled Rome
    apple (about 2 large)
1/4 cup chopped walnuts
Cake:
5.3 ounces cake flour (about 1 1/3 cups)
1 1/2 teaspoons baking powder
1/4 teaspoon salt
2/3 cup sugar
3 tablespoons butter, softened
2 large egg yolks
1 teaspoon vanilla extract
1/2 cup 1% low-fat milk
3 large egg whites

1. Preheat oven to 350°. Coat a 9-inch round cake pan with cooking spray.
2. To prepare topping, combine 3/4 cup sugar and 1/4 cup water in a small heavy saucepan over medium-high heat; cook until sugar dissolves, stirring gently as needed to dissolve sugar evenly (about 3 minutes). Continue cooking for 4 minutes or until golden (do not stir). Immediately pour into prepared cake pan, tipping quickly to coat bottom of pan. Arrange apple slices in concentric circles in pan over warm caramel. Sprinkle with nuts; set aside.
3. To prepare cake, weigh or lightly spoon flour into dry measuring cups; level with a knife. Combine flour, baking powder, and salt; stir with a whisk.
4. Combine 2/3 cup sugar and butter in a large bowl; beat with a mixer at medium speed until light and fluffy. Add egg yolks and vanilla to sugar mixture; beat until combined. Add flour mixture and milk alternately to sugar mixture, beginning and ending with flour mixture; mix after each addition.
5. Place egg whites in a large, clean bowl. Beat egg whites with mixer at

high speed until stiff peaks form using clean, dry beaters. Gently fold egg whites into batter. Spread batter over apples. Bake at 350° for 35 minutes or until a wooden pick inserted in center comes out clean. Cool on a wire rack in pan 5 minutes. Loosen edges of cake with a knife; invert cake onto a serving plate. Serve warm or at room temperature. Yield: 10 servings (serving size: 1 slice).

CALORIES 253; FAT 6.6g (sat 2.8g, mono 1.6g, poly 1.7g); PROTEIN 3.9g; CARB 45.8g; FIBER 0.9g; CHOL 52mg; IRON 1.5mg; SODIUM 163mg; CALC 79mg

WHICH APPLE TO EAT AND COOK?

PINK LADY: Crisp and tangy-sweet, the Pink Lady is very good for eating raw or baking.

JONAGOLD: A cross between a Jonathan and a Golden Delicious apple, this variety is crisp and sweet yet balanced with acidity. Jonagolds are good for both raw and cooked applications.

LIBERTY: Balanced sweet-tart flavor makes this a good apple for eating raw.

AMBROSIA: Slightly crisp, sweet, and low in acid, this variety is slow to oxidize, so the flesh will stay white longer in raw applications.

ROME: This mild-tasting variety is best for baking because the raw flesh can sometimes be soft or mealy.

HONEYCRISP: Every bit as sweet and firm as the name suggests, this juicy apple is great for raw uses but also holds its shape very well and develops complex flavor when baked.

SPARTAN: This sweet, juicy hybrid variety is descended from McIntosh apples. It's a good all-purpose apple, suitable for baking, sauces, or eating raw.

FUJI: The candy-sweet, crisp Fuji is best for raw uses.

Kid Friendly

French Toast with Maple-Apple Compote

Sweet Pink Lady apples hold up well to being sautéed for the compote. Liberty, Fuji, or Jonagold apples would also work. Substitute Hawaiian bread if challah isn't available.

Compote:
Cooking spray
1 tablespoon butter
3 cups sliced peeled Pink Lady apples (about 1½ pounds)
¼ cup maple syrup
½ teaspoon ground cinnamon
French Toast:
2 tablespoons granulated sugar
1 teaspoon ground cinnamon
1 cup 2% reduced-fat milk
2 teaspoons vanilla extract
⅛ teaspoon salt
4 large eggs, lightly beaten
12 (1-ounce) slices challah bread
4 teaspoons butter
Powdered sugar (optional)

1. Preheat oven to 250°. Place wire rack on a baking sheet and place in oven.
2. To prepare compote, heat a large nonstick skillet over medium-high heat. Coat pan with cooking spray; melt 1 tablespoon butter in pan. Add apples to pan; sauté 8 minutes or until tender. Stir in maple syrup and ½ teaspoon cinnamon. Keep warm.
3. To prepare French toast, combine granulated sugar and 1 teaspoon cinnamon in a medium bowl, stirring with a whisk. Add milk and next 3 ingredients; whisk until well blended. Working with 1 bread slice at a time, place bread slice into milk mixture, turning gently to coat both sides.
4. Heat a large nonstick skillet over medium-high heat. Coat pan with cooking spray; melt 1 teaspoon butter in pan. Add 3 coated bread slices, and cook 2 minutes on each side or until lightly browned. Place on rack in oven to keep warm. Repeat procedure three times with cooking spray, remaining 3 teaspoons butter, and remaining

9 coated bread slices. Serve French toast with compote. Sprinkle with powdered sugar, if desired. Yield: 6 servings (serving size: 2 pieces toast and about ⅓ cup compote).

CALORIES 370; FAT 12.1g (sat 5.3g, mono 4g, poly 1.3g); PROTEIN 11.3g; CARB 55.3g; FIBER 2.9g; CHOL 185mg; IRON 2.7mg; SODIUM 427mg; CALC 146mg

Quick & Easy

Brie, Apple, and Arugula Quesadillas

Fuji apples offer a crisp counterpoint to the rich, creamy cheese. Substitute Honeycrisp or Ambrosia apples, if you prefer.

1 tablespoon Dijon mustard
2 teaspoons apple cider
3 (10-inch) flour tortillas
6 ounces Brie cheese, rind removed and cut into ¼-inch-thick slices, divided
1 Fuji apple, cored and cut into ¼-inch-thick slices (about ½ pound), divided
3 cups arugula, divided
¾ teaspoon freshly ground black pepper, divided

1. Combine mustard and cider in a small bowl; stir well.
2. Heat a large nonstick skillet over medium heat. Spread each tortilla with about 1½ teaspoons mustard mixture. Place 1 tortilla, mustard side up, in pan. Arrange one-third of cheese slices over half of tortilla; cook 1 minute or until cheese begins to melt. Arrange one-third of apple slices over cheese; top with 1 cup arugula. Sprinkle with ¼ teaspoon pepper. Fold tortilla in half; press gently with a spatula. Cook 2 minutes on each side or until golden brown. Remove from pan. Repeat procedure twice with remaining 2 tortillas, cheese, apple slices, 2 cups arugula, and ½ teaspoon pepper. Cut each quesadilla into 4 wedges. Yield: 6 servings (serving size: 2 wedges).

CALORIES 182; FAT 7.4g (sat 4.4g, mono 1.9g, poly 0.2g); PROTEIN 8.2g; CARB 20.6g; FIBER 3.2g; CHOL 24mg; IRON 0.8mg; SODIUM 397mg; CALC 111mg

Fresh Apple Salsa

This sweet-tart condiment features crisp, slightly acidic Spartan apples, though Fuji, Jonagold, and Liberty apples would also work nicely. Serve with pork or roast chicken.

2 cups diced peeled Spartan apple (about ³/₄ pound)
½ cup diced red bell pepper
⅓ cup fresh lime juice
¼ cup diced red onion
¼ cup minced fresh cilantro
1 tablespoon honey
¼ teaspoon salt
¼ teaspoon freshly ground black pepper
1 jalapeño pepper, seeded and minced

1. Combine all ingredients, stirring well. Yield: 12 servings (serving size: ¼ cup).

CALORIES 21; **FAT** 0.1g; **PROTEIN** 0.2g; **CARB** 5.7g; **FIBER** 0.8g; **CHOL** 0mg; **IRON** 0.1mg; **SODIUM** 50mg; **CALC** 4mg

SOME BAKE BETTER THAN OTHERS

If you're baking a whole apple, choose carefully. We baked nine varieties for 1 hour at 350° and found that the firm Granny Smith apple collapsed and turned to complete mush. The Honeycrisp, however, retained its shape and had a pleasing, slightly firm texture and full apple flavor, faring the best of the nine varieties. Other varieties that kept their shape: Rome, Jonagold, and Spartan.

COOKING CLASS

GOING BANANAS, BETTER

America's favorite quick bread gets a nutritional makeover with a classic version and three yummy-gooey variations.

We're not kidding when we say the peanut butter–glazed banana bread is one of the tastier treats to come out of our kitchen, and the grown-up Bananas Foster treatment on page 312 is a kick. And despite the rich flavor, our recipes don't use a cup of oil or butter, as many others do; we use less than half that without sacrificing the moist texture that makes banana bread a treat. Baking consistently good loaves—especially lightened versions—does require some attention. Follow our steps for perfect results. Banana bread freezes well, but for a glazed version, slather on the gooey goodness after you've thawed the loaf.

Make Ahead • Freezable • Kid Friendly
Basic Banana Bread

Ground flaxseed adds heart-healthy omega-3 fatty acids and nutty flavor. Look for whole ground flaxseed (sometimes labeled "flaxseed meal") on the baking aisle.

1½ cups mashed ripe banana
⅓ cup plain fat-free yogurt
5 tablespoons butter, melted
2 large eggs
½ cup granulated sugar
½ cup packed brown sugar
6.75 ounces all-purpose flour (about 1½ cups)
¼ cup ground flaxseed
¾ teaspoon baking soda
½ teaspoon salt
½ teaspoon ground cinnamon
⅛ teaspoon ground allspice
Cooking spray
⅓ cup powdered sugar
1½ teaspoons 1% low-fat milk

1. Preheat oven to 350°.
2. Combine first 4 ingredients in a large bowl, and beat with a mixer at medium speed. Add granulated and brown sugars; beat until combined.
3. Weigh or lightly spoon flour into dry measuring cups; level with a knife. Combine flour and next 5 ingredients. Add flour mixture to banana mixture, and beat just until blended. Pour batter into a 9 x 5–inch loaf pan coated with cooking spray. Bake at 350° for 55 minutes or until a wooden pick inserted in center comes out clean. Remove from oven, and cool 10 minutes in pan on a wire rack. Remove bread from pan, and cool completely. Combine powdered sugar and milk, stirring until smooth; drizzle over bread. Yield: 16 servings (serving size: 1 slice).

CALORIES 167; **FAT** 5.1g (sat 2.5g, mono 1.3g, poly 0.9g); **PROTEIN** 2.9g; **CARB** 28.3g; **FIBER** 1.5g; **CHOL** 32mg; **IRON** 1mg; **SODIUM** 173mg; **CALC** 24mg

Make Ahead • Kid Friendly

Banana-Chocolate-Walnut Bread

Mini chocolate chips disperse well and melt nicely for the glaze.

1½ cups mashed ripe banana
⅓ cup plain fat-free yogurt
5 tablespoons butter, melted
2 large eggs
⅓ cup granulated sugar
⅓ cup packed light brown sugar
6.75 ounces all-purpose flour (about 1½ cups)
¼ cup ground flaxseed
¾ teaspoon baking soda
½ teaspoon salt
½ teaspoon ground cinnamon
⅛ teaspoon ground allspice
⅔ cup semisweet chocolate minichips, divided
⅓ cup chopped walnuts, toasted
Cooking spray
2 tablespoons fat-free milk

1. Preheat oven to 350°.
2. Combine first 4 ingredients in a large bowl; beat with a mixer at medium speed until blended. Add granulated and brown sugars; beat until blended.
3. Weigh or lightly spoon flour into dry measuring cups; level with a knife. Combine flour and next 5 ingredients in a small bowl; stir well with a whisk. Add flour mixture to banana mixture; beat just until blended.
4. Fold ⅓ cup minichips and nuts into batter; pour batter into a 9 x 5–inch loaf pan coated with cooking spray. Bake at 350° for 55 minutes or until a wooden pick inserted in center comes out clean. Remove from oven; cool 10 minutes in pan on a wire rack. Remove bread from pan; cool completely on wire rack. Combine remaining ⅓ cup minichips and milk in a microwave-safe bowl; microwave at HIGH 30 seconds, stirring until smooth. Drizzle over bread. Yield: 16 servings (serving size: 1 slice).

CALORIES 195; **FAT** 8.9g (sat 4g, mono 2.3g, poly 2.1g); **PROTEIN** 3.6g; **CARB** 27.3g; **FIBER** 2.1g; **CHOL** 32mg; **IRON** 1.2mg; **SODIUM** 174mg; **CALC** 29mg

4 STEPS TO THE BEST BANANA BREAD

1 COMBINE THE WET INGREDIENTS. This is a hybrid between a muffin method (combining wet and dry ingredients separately by hand) and a cake method (whipping butter and sugar with a mixer).

2 ADD THE SUGAR. Next, add the sugars and beat to incorporate air into the batter. The recipes use a mix of granulated and brown sugars to add straight sweetness and caramel notes.

3 ADD THE DRY INGREDIENTS. Weighing flour is the most accurate way to measure. If you don't have a scale, lightly spoon flour into dry measuring cups and level with a knife. Then add the remaining dry ingredients; stir into the sugar mixture.

4 STIR IN YOUR FLAVORING ADDITIONS. Besides the requisite bananas, you can add lots of tasty ingredients to the batter—chopped nuts, chocolate chips, spices, dried fruit, and alcohol, to name a few.

Bananas Foster Bread

This adult interpretation switches all the sugar to brown sugar and cooks the mashed bananas with butter and cognac or dark rum, which adds depth to the flavor of this variation. And it's topped with a slightly boozy glaze.

1½ cups mashed ripe banana
1 cup packed brown sugar, divided
6 tablespoons butter, melted and divided
¼ cup cognac or dark rum, divided
⅓ cup plain fat-free yogurt
2 large eggs
6.75 ounces all-purpose flour (about 1½ cups)
¼ cup ground flaxseed
¾ teaspoon baking soda
½ teaspoon salt
½ teaspoon ground cinnamon
⅛ teaspoon ground allspice
Cooking spray
⅓ cup powdered sugar

1. Preheat oven to 350°.
2. Combine banana, ½ cup brown sugar, 5 tablespoons butter, and 3 tablespoons cognac in a nonstick skillet. Cook over medium heat until mixture begins to bubble. Remove from heat; cool. Place banana mixture in a large bowl. Add yogurt, remaining ½ cup brown sugar, and eggs. Beat with a mixer at medium speed.
3. Weigh or lightly spoon flour into dry measuring cups; level with a knife. Combine flour and next 5 ingredients in a small bowl. Add flour mixture to banana mixture; beat just until blended. Pour batter into a 9 x 5–inch loaf pan coated with cooking spray. Bake at 350° for 1 hour or until a wooden pick inserted in center comes out clean. Remove from oven; cool 10 minutes in pan on a wire rack. Remove bread from pan; place on wire rack.
4. Combine remaining 1 tablespoon melted butter, remaining 1 tablespoon cognac, and powdered sugar; stir until well blended. Drizzle over warm bread. Yield: 16 servings (serving size: 1 slice).

CALORIES 194; FAT 5.8g (sat 3g, mono 1.5g, poly 0.9g); PROTEIN 2.9g; CARB 31.1g; FIBER 1.5g; CHOL 34mg; IRON 1.1mg; SODIUM 181mg; CALC 32mg

Peanut Butter Banana Bread

(pictured on page 267)

A small amount of chopped roasted peanuts offers delightfully surprising crunch.

Bread:
1½ cups mashed ripe banana
⅓ cup plain fat-free yogurt
⅓ cup creamy peanut butter
3 tablespoons butter, melted
2 large eggs
½ cup granulated sugar
½ cup packed brown sugar
6.75 ounces all-purpose flour (about 1½ cups)
¼ cup ground flaxseed
¾ teaspoon baking soda
½ teaspoon salt
½ teaspoon ground cinnamon
⅛ teaspoon ground allspice
2 tablespoons chopped dry-roasted peanuts
Cooking spray
Glaze:
⅓ cup powdered sugar
1 tablespoon 1% low-fat milk
1 tablespoon creamy peanut butter

1. Preheat oven to 350°.
2. To prepare bread, combine first 5 ingredients in a large bowl; beat with a mixer at medium speed. Add granulated and brown sugars; beat until blended.
3. Weigh or lightly spoon flour into dry measuring cups; level with a knife. Combine flour and next 5 ingredients in a small bowl. Add flour mixture to banana mixture; beat just until blended. Stir in nuts. Pour batter into a 9 x 5–inch loaf pan coated with cooking spray. Bake at 350° for 1 hour and 5 minutes or until a wooden pick inserted in center comes out clean. Remove from oven; cool 10 minutes in pan on a wire rack. Remove bread from pan; cool.
4. To prepare glaze, combine powdered sugar, milk, and 1 tablespoon peanut butter in a small bowl, stirring with a whisk. Drizzle glaze over bread. Yield: 16 servings (serving size: 1 slice).

CALORIES 198; FAT 7.4g (sat 2.3g, mono 2.7g, poly 1.8g); PROTEIN 4.7g; CARB 29.7g; FIBER 1.9g; CHOL 28mg; IRON 1.1mg; SODIUM 200mg; CALC 27mg

LESS MEAT, MORE FLAVOR
BETTER BOLOGNESE

By Mark Bittman

The classic sauce, rethought: Hearty vegetables and smart techniques yield robust, complex, meaty flavors.

Back in the days when I ate half-pound bowls of pasta, if I wanted meat sauce (which was frequently), I usually made a rich, slow-simmered Bolognese loaded with ground pork and beef and finished with a cup of milk and maybe a splash of cream. Marinara—the lighter, faster, all-tomato sauce—was almost a snack.

Now I eat more sauce and less pasta in my bowl, with tons of vegetables, and I'm often satisfied with a simple tomato sauce. But to retool Bolognese, I wanted to do more than just add meat to a basic marinara. The goal was to duplicate the luxury of the classic meat sauce—the texture, the flavor, the creaminess, all of it—without the hours of cooking. So I turned to the two meatiest vegetables on the planet: eggplant and mushrooms.

What gives traditional Bolognese that sublime texture is the way the ingredients coalesce as they cook. It goes beyond a sum of parts: The meat, tomatoes, token vegetables, and dairy work together to create a sauce that's hearty and silky, without turning lumpy or gritty. To duplicate that effect, the eggplant and mushrooms must be chopped fairly small and cooked until browned, just like the meat. And, like the meat, both of these vegetables will break down during cooking and enrich and thicken the tomatoes in the sauce by partially melting into them.

Trust me: A little patience at the beginning of the process pays off later. It's important—though counterintuitive—to encourage stuff to stick to the bottom of the pot. Do so and you will be rewarded. Just keep an eye on the heat so that everything browns nicely without burning. Once you add liquid to the pot (a technique known as deglazing), those little darkened crispy bits will go a long way to flavor the sauce.

Browning the vegetables and meat creates the foundation for the sauce, but the flavor can't stop there. For acidity, we've got the tomatoes, and a little tomato paste is a nice shortcut here when you're trying to reduce cooking time, especially when used in combination with canned tomatoes. Because the eggplant sauce is a little quicker and brighter tasting, red wine helps add some depth. In the mushroom version, the liquid from soaking the dried porcini intensifies the mushroom flavor, so a splash of white wine works the opposite way to keep things light. Both sauces benefit from a final sprinkle of fresh herbs.

A final word about the pasta: Whole-wheat noodles are my first choice with a sauce this hearty, but eat whatever type you like. What's more important is the ratio of sauce to pasta—ultimately, you want to be eating sauce with a bit of pasta rather than the other way around.

Staff Favorite • Quick & Easy
Make Ahead • Kid Friendly
Mushroom Bolognese

½ ounce dried porcini mushrooms
1 cup boiling water
1 tablespoon olive oil
2½ cups chopped onion
¾ teaspoon kosher salt, divided
½ teaspoon freshly ground black
  pepper, divided
½ pound ground pork
8 cups finely chopped cremini mushrooms
  (about 1½ pounds)
1 tablespoon minced garlic
2 tablespoons tomato paste
½ cup white wine
1 (14-ounce) can whole peeled
  tomatoes, undrained
¼ cup whole milk
10 ounces uncooked whole-wheat spaghetti
1 tablespoon kosher salt
1½ ounces Parmigiano-Reggiano
  cheese, grated
¼ cup chopped fresh parsley

1. Combine porcini and boiling water in a bowl; cover and let stand 20 minutes or until soft. Drain porcini in a colander lined with a paper towel over a bowl, reserving liquid. Rinse and chop porcini.
2. Heat olive oil in a Dutch oven over medium-high heat. Add onion, ½ teaspoon salt, ¼ teaspoon pepper, and pork; cook 10 minutes or until pork is browned, stirring to crumble pork. Add cremini mushrooms, garlic, remaining ¼ teaspoon salt, and remaining ¼ teaspoon pepper; cook 15 minutes or until liquid almost evaporates, stirring occasionally. Add porcini; cook 1 minute. Add tomato paste; cook 2 minutes, stirring constantly. Add reserved porcini liquid and wine; cook 1 minute, scraping pan to loosen browned bits. Add tomatoes; bring to a boil. Reduce heat; simmer 30 minutes, stirring occasionally and breaking up tomatoes as necessary. Stir in milk; cook 2 minutes.
3. Cook pasta according to package directions, adding 1 tablespoon salt to cooking water. Drain. Toss pasta with sauce; top with cheese and parsley. Yield: 6 servings (serving size: ¾ cup sauce, about ¾ cup pasta, about 1 tablespoon cheese, and 2 teaspoons parsley).

CALORIES 344; **FAT** 8.6g (sat 2.9g, mono 3.8g, poly 1.1g); **PROTEIN** 22.1g; **CARB** 49.6g; **FIBER** 9.6g; **CHOL** 34mg; **IRON** 3.5mg; **SODIUM** 544mg; **CALC** 130mg

THE GOAL WAS TO DUPLICATE THE LUXURY OF THE CLASSIC MEAT SAUCE WITHOUT THE HOURS OF COOKING.

Quick & Easy • Make Ahead
Eggplant Bolognese

2 tablespoons olive oil
2¼ cups chopped onion
¾ teaspoon kosher salt, divided
½ teaspoon freshly ground black
  pepper, divided
½ pound ground sirloin
8 cups chopped eggplant (about 1½ pounds)
1 tablespoon minced garlic
1 tablespoon tomato paste
½ cup red wine
1 (28-ounce) can whole tomatoes, undrained
1 tablespoon red wine vinegar
10 ounces uncooked whole-wheat fettuccine
1 tablespoon kosher salt
¼ cup small fresh basil leaves

1. Heat olive oil in a Dutch oven over medium-high heat. Add onion, ¼ teaspoon salt, ¼ teaspoon pepper, and beef; cook 10 minutes or until beef is browned, stirring to crumble beef. Add eggplant, garlic, ¼ teaspoon salt, and remaining ¼ teaspoon pepper; cook 20 minutes or until eggplant is very tender, stirring occasionally. Add tomato paste; cook 2 minutes, stirring constantly. Add wine; cook 1 minute, scraping pan to loosen browned bits. Add tomatoes; bring to a boil. Reduce heat; simmer 10 minutes, stirring occasionally and breaking up tomatoes as necessary. Add remaining ¼ teaspoon salt and vinegar.
2. Cook pasta according to package directions, adding 1 tablespoon kosher salt to cooking water. Drain. Toss pasta with sauce; sprinkle with basil leaves. Yield: 6 servings (serving size: 1 cup sauce, about ¾ cup pasta, and 2 teaspoons basil).

CALORIES 323; **FAT** 7.3g (sat 1.5g, mono 4.1g, poly 1.1g); **PROTEIN** 17.3g; **CARB** 53.1g; **FIBER** 12.3g; **CHOL** 20mg; **IRON** 3.9mg; **SODIUM** 553mg; **CALC** 92mg

DINNER IN PARADISE

Beautiful weather, locally sourced food, wine made on site: a meal at a Sonoma estate is nothing short of stunning.

Sandra Simile checks on the chicken and fingerling potatoes roasting in the oven, then kicks a step stool into place, allowing her to climb up and stir a tall pot on the cooktop in the kitchen at Lynmar Estate. At 4-foot-10, Simile needs help with her reach but certainly not with her deft, confident cooking.

She crumbles fresh goat cheese over a citrus-dressed salad and gently stirs a creamy butternut squash risotto, pleased with the meal's progress. This is local food as California's bounty can provide it on a sweet, sunny fall day: All of the ingredients she is using for this harvest dinner for Lynmar Estate proprietors Lynn and Anisya Fritz and friends were plucked that day from the garden outside her door or purchased from artisanal producers not too far afield.

Simile is one of those lucky cooks whose ranks have been growing in California as the food-wine equation has matured: the winery chef. It's her job to match delicious, locally sourced meals to the top-notch chardonnays and pinot noirs produced at the Russian River Valley winery Lynmar Estate.

Simile and the Fritzes enjoy exquisite weather from April through November when warm, sunny days and cool nights favor both grapes and growers. Local gardens and farms yield an embarrassment of fresh, locally grown and raised foods. Seafood arrives from the nearby Pacific Ocean. Few who love Sonoma believe there is a better place in America to share food and wine with neighbors and lucky customers.

The story begins, of course, with the grapes. "Wines are made in the vineyard," Lynmar winemaker Bibiana González Rave says, "and my role as winemaker is to preserve what Mother Nature has given to us. When I came to the Russian River Valley, I knew that it could produce world-class pinot noir and chardonnay, wines that are especially elegant and aromatically complex." González Rave, a native of Colombia, acquired her enological chops at universities and wineries in France. She then worked 14 harvests in California before discovering Lynmar in early 2009.

In the summer and fall, the grapes reach maturity and harvest begins, typically in early September for white grapes and ending in October with red. Even in October, days are hot, but a nightly blanket of cooling fog from the Pacific Ocean drops the temperature 35 to 40 degrees. This famous chill-down helps the grapes retain their natural acidity—the zip that makes wine so refreshing—and develop balanced flavors over a slow, steady period.

Over time, Lynn and Anisya expanded the vineyards and winemaking facilities, built an airy, inviting visitor center that includes Chef Simile's spacious kitchen, and planted the two-acre organic garden that keeps gardener Michael Presley busy and Chef Simile smiling.

"My menus show what we can do in our organic garden and with our wine," she says. "I think about recipes that are healthy, and I don't use a lot of fat, yet I don't set out to make low-calorie dishes. The cooking comes naturally, letting the fresh flavors from the garden dictate the preparation."

This harvest menu, created for *Cooking Light*, is a sort of upscale stone soup party. The estate garden contributed most of the ingredients, the "soup" finished by additions such as Trumpet Royale mushrooms from Sebastopol's Gourmet Mushrooms to the green bean dish, Petaluma Poultry's Rosie organic chicken to the entrée, and Laura Chenel Sonoma goat cheese to the salad.

FALL HARVEST MENU

(serves 8)

First course
Mixed Lettuce, Pear, and Goat Cheese Salad with Citrus Dressing
(page 315)

Wine: Lynmar Russian River Valley Chardonnay

Second course
Roasted Butternut Squash Risotto with Sugared Walnuts
(page 315)

Wine: Lynmar Russian River Valley Pinot Noir

Third course
Roasted Breast of Chicken with Pinot Noir Sauce
(page 316)

Rosemary Roasted Fingerling Potatoes
(page 316)

Buttered Green Beans and Mushrooms
(page 316)

Wine: Lynmar Hawk Hill Vineyard Pinot Noir

Fourth course
Honey-Baked Black Mission Figs with Orange and Ginger
(page 317)

FEW WHO LOVE SONOMA BELIEVE THERE IS A BETTER PLACE IN AMERICA TO SHARE FOOD AND WINE WITH FRIENDS.

Mixed Lettuce, Pear, and Goat Cheese Salad with Citrus Dressing

If you can't find Meyer lemons, use regular lemon juice and add a pinch of sugar to approximate the flavor.

Dressing:
1 tablespoon finely chopped shallots
1 teaspoon Dijon mustard
1/4 cup fresh orange juice
4 teaspoons fresh Meyer lemon juice
1/4 teaspoon kosher salt
1/8 teaspoon freshly ground black pepper
4 teaspoons extra-virgin olive oil

Salad:
2 tablespoons fresh orange juice
2 firm ripe Bosc pears, cored and thinly sliced
6 cups mixed baby lettuces
1 head Boston or butter lettuce, torn (about 2 cups)
3/4 cup (3 ounces) crumbled goat cheese

1. To prepare dressing, combine shallots and mustard in a medium bowl, stirring with a whisk. Stir in 1/4 cup orange juice and next 3 ingredients. Gradually add oil, stirring constantly with a whisk.
2. To prepare salad, combine 2 tablespoons orange juice and pears, tossing to coat. Combine lettuces in a large bowl. Drizzle with dressing; toss gently to coat. Arrange about 1 cup lettuce mixture on each of 8 salad plates. Top each serving with about 1/4 cup pear and 1 1/2 tablespoons cheese. Yield: 8 servings.

CALORIES 100; FAT 5.6g (sat 2.5g, mono 2.4g, poly 0.4g); PROTEIN 3.5g; CARB 10.2g; FIBER 2.5g; CHOL 8mg; IRON 1.1mg; SODIUM 141mg; CALC 67mg

"WINES ARE MADE IN THE VINEYARD, AND MY ROLE AS WINEMAKER IS TO PRESERVE WHAT MOTHER NATURE HAS GIVEN TO US."

—*Bibiana González Rave, Lynmar winemaker*

Roasted Butternut Squash Risotto with Sugared Walnuts

1/2 cup coarsely chopped walnuts
1 tablespoon butter, melted
1 teaspoon brown sugar
1/8 teaspoon freshly ground black pepper
2 cups (1/2-inch) cubed peeled butternut squash
1 tablespoon olive oil
2 teaspoons minced fresh garlic
4 cups fat-free, lower-sodium chicken broth
1/2 cup water
1 ounce pancetta, finely chopped (about 1/4 cup)
1 cup finely chopped onion
1 1/4 cups uncooked Arborio rice
1/2 cup chardonnay
2 tablespoons finely chopped fresh lemon thyme or 1 1/2 tablespoons thyme plus 1/2 teaspoon grated lemon rind
1/4 teaspoon salt
1/4 teaspoon freshly ground black pepper
1/4 cup (1 ounce) shaved Parmigiano-Reggiano cheese

1. Preheat oven to 400°.
2. Arrange nuts in a single layer on a jelly-roll pan. Bake at 400° for 5 minutes or until toasted, stirring twice. Place nuts in a bowl. Drizzle butter over warm nuts; sprinkle with sugar and 1/8 teaspoon pepper. Toss well to coat.
3. Combine squash and 1 tablespoon oil, tossing to coat. Arrange squash in a single layer on jelly-roll pan. Bake at 400° for 15 minutes or until squash is just tender. Remove from pan; stir in garlic. Set aside.
4. Bring broth and 1/2 cup water to a simmer in a saucepan (do not boil). Keep warm over low heat.
5. Heat a large saucepan over medium heat. Add pancetta to saucepan; cook 5 minutes or until browned, stirring frequently. Add onion; cook 3 minutes or until tender, stirring occasionally. Add rice; cook 2 minutes, stirring constantly. Add wine; cook 1 minute or until liquid is nearly absorbed, stirring constantly. Add broth mixture, 1/2 cup at a time, stirring constantly until each portion of broth is absorbed before adding the next (about 20 minutes total). Stir in squash, thyme, salt, and 1/4 teaspoon pepper. Top with cheese and nuts. Yield: 8 servings (serving size: about 2/3 cup risotto, 1 1/2 teaspoons cheese, and 1 tablespoon nuts).

CALORIES 259; FAT 10.7g (sat 2.7g, mono 2.6g, poly 3.8g); PROTEIN 7.5g; CARB 35.5g; FIBER 3.9g; CHOL 9mg; IRON 1.3mg; SODIUM 397mg; CALC 95mg

LYNMAR AT WORK

From organic farming to untampered aging, Lynmar treats its wines as gently as possible. The result: Nature's wine, from vine to bottle.

1 HARVEST
Handpicked grapes grown in nutrient-rich soil arrive at the winery still cool from the early morning chill. The cold harvest temperature ensures grapes will not oxidize before fermentation. Handpicking and hand sorting allow for quality control throughout.

2 FERMENTATION
Once the grapes are crushed, they're placed in fermentation tanks that are carefully monitored as the grapes convert their sugars into alcohol. No outside yeasts are introduced. When ready, the tanks are drained and solids are pressed. Once settled, the wine will drain into barrels.

3 AGING
The wine is aged in French oak barrels up to 15 months. Aside from weekly quality checks, the barrels are never disturbed. This allows natural settling to occur, eliminating the need to filter the wine, which could damage its complexity.

Roasted Breast of Chicken with Pinot Noir Sauce

For this gathering, the chicken is organic, from Sonoma's Petaluma Poultry. Seek out the best organic chicken in your area for this dish. Chef Simile's tips: Resting the chicken after roasting and then slicing against the grain will give you juicy, tender bites. To slice against the grain, position the chicken breast on a cutting board so the part that was attached to the wing is at the top of the board; slice from this point on a diagonal down the length of the breast.

2 teaspoons chopped fresh thyme
1/2 teaspoon salt, divided
1/2 teaspoon freshly ground black pepper, divided
1/2 teaspoon chopped fresh rosemary
8 (6-ounce) skinless, boneless chicken breast halves
1/4 cup all-purpose flour
1 tablespoon olive oil, divided
Cooking spray
3 tablespoons finely chopped shallots
2 cups pinot noir
1 1/2 cups fat-free, lower-sodium chicken broth
3/4 teaspoon sugar
3 tablespoons chilled butter, cut into small pieces

1. Preheat oven to 425°.
2. Sprinkle thyme, 1/4 teaspoon salt, 1/4 teaspoon pepper, and rosemary evenly over chicken. Dredge chicken in flour; shake off excess flour. Heat 1 1/2 teaspoons oil in a large skillet over medium-high heat. Add 4 chicken breast halves to pan; cook 2 minutes or until browned. Turn chicken over; cook 1 minute. Remove chicken from pan. Repeat procedure with remaining 1 1/2 teaspoons oil and remaining chicken. Arrange chicken in a single layer on rack of a roasting pan coated with cooking spray; place rack in pan. Bake at 425° for 12 minutes or until a thermometer inserted into thickest part of chicken registers 160°. Remove from oven. Cover and let stand 10 minutes.
3. Heat a medium saucepan over medium-high heat. Coat pan with cooking spray. Add shallots to saucepan; sauté 30 seconds, stirring frequently. Stir in wine, scraping pan to loosen browned bits. Increase heat to high; bring to a boil. Cook 10 minutes or until wine is reduced to 1 cup. Add broth; cook 16 minutes or until broth mixture is reduced to 1/3 cup. Remove from heat; stir in remaining 1/4 teaspoon salt, remaining 1/4 teaspoon pepper, and sugar. Gradually add butter, stirring constantly with a whisk until smooth. Serve sauce with chicken. Yield: 8 servings (serving size: 1 breast half and about 1 tablespoon sauce).

CALORIES 258; **FAT** 10g (sat 4.1g, mono 3.7g, poly 1.2g); **PROTEIN** 35.2g; **CARB** 5g; **FIBER** 0.2g; **CHOL** 105mg; **IRON** 1.7mg; **SODIUM** 349mg; **CALC** 26mg

Freezable

Rosemary Roasted Fingerling Potatoes

The simplicity of this dish is part of what makes it so special.

2 1/2 pounds fingerling potatoes, halved
2 tablespoons olive oil
3/4 teaspoon kosher salt
1 teaspoon finely chopped fresh rosemary
1/2 teaspoon freshly ground black pepper

1. Preheat oven to 375°.
2. Place potatoes on a jelly-roll pan. Drizzle potatoes with oil; sprinkle with salt, rosemary, and pepper. Toss to combine; spread into a single layer on pan. Bake at 375° for 30 minutes or until lightly browned and tender. Yield: 8 servings (serving size: about 2/3 cup).

CALORIES 147; **FAT** 3.4g (sat 0.5g, mono 2.5g, poly 0.4g); **PROTEIN** 3.4g; **CARB** 25.1g; **FIBER** 1.7g; **CHOL** 0mg; **IRON** 1.3mg; **SODIUM** 185mg; **CALC** 1mg

Quick & Easy • Kid Friendly

Buttered Green Beans and Mushrooms

The beans were plucked from Lynmar's garden; the mushrooms were supplied by nearby Sebastopol's Gourmet Mushrooms.

3/4 pound green beans, trimmed
2 tablespoons butter
6 ounces cremini mushrooms, thinly sliced
4 ounces shiitake mushroom caps, thinly sliced
3/4 teaspoon kosher salt, divided
1/2 teaspoon coarsely ground black pepper, divided
1 teaspoon minced fresh garlic

1. Steam green beans, covered, 4 minutes or until crisp-tender. Plunge beans into ice water; drain. Pat dry with a towel; set aside.
2. Melt butter in a large nonstick skillet over medium-high heat. Add mushrooms, 1/2 teaspoon salt, and 1/4 teaspoon pepper; sauté 8 minutes or until mushroom liquid evaporates. Stir in garlic; sauté 1 minute, stirring constantly. Add remaining 1/4 teaspoon salt, remaining 1/4 teaspoon pepper, and green beans; cook 3 minutes or until thoroughly heated, tossing to combine. Yield: 8 servings (serving size: 1/2 cup).

CALORIES 44; **FAT** 3g (sat 1.8g, mono 0.7g, poly 0.2g); **PROTEIN** 1.7g; **CARB** 3.9g; **FIBER** 1.9g; **CHOL** 8mg; **IRON** 0.4mg; **SODIUM** 198mg; **CALC** 23mg

Honey-Baked Black Mission Figs with Orange and Ginger

The Lynmar property indeed offers its bounty, supplying these Black Mission figs as well as the honey that's the base for the saucy drizzle. If you cannot find fresh figs, try the dessert with dried figs: Place 24 small stemmed, halved dried figs in a large saucepan with ¾ cup fresh orange juice, 2 tablespoons honey, ¼ teaspoon ginger, and ¼ teaspoon vanilla; bring to a simmer. Simmer 3 minutes; cover, remove from heat, and let stand 15 minutes.

12 ripe Black Mission figs, stemmed and
   halved lengthwise
Cooking spray
3 tablespoons orange blossom honey
3 tablespoons fresh orange juice
¼ teaspoon grated peeled fresh ginger
¼ teaspoon vanilla extract
4 large navel oranges, peeled and sectioned
½ cup heavy whipping cream
1½ tablespoons superfine sugar
1 tablespoon Grand Marnier (orange-
   flavored liqueur)
Mint leaves (optional)

1. Preheat oven to 350°.
2. Arrange fig halves, cut sides down, in a single layer in an 8-inch square baking dish coated with cooking spray. Combine honey and next 3 ingredients, stirring with a whisk. Drizzle honey mixture over figs. Bake at 350° for 10 minutes; turn figs over. Bake an additional 2 minutes. Remove from oven; cool to room temperature. Combine orange sections and fig mixture, tossing gently.
3. Place cream in a medium bowl; beat with a mixer at high speed until soft peaks form. Add sugar and liqueur; beat at high speed until stiff peaks form. Divide fig mixture evenly among 8 bowls; top each serving with about 2 tablespoons whipped cream. Garnish with mint leaves, if desired. Yield: 8 servings.

CALORIES 177; **FAT** 5.9g (sat 3.5g, mono 1.7g, poly 0.3g); **PROTEIN** 1.7g; **CARB** 32.1g; **FIBER** 3.8g; **CHOL** 20mg; **IRON** 0.5mg; **SODIUM** 8mg; **CALC** 70mg

EVERYDAY VEGETARIAN
ROOT VEGETABLES

Sweet, earthy, creamy, and starchy—sweet potatoes, turnips, beets, parsnips, and more create meatless meals brimming with hearty flavors.

Pasta with Black Kale, Caramelized Onions, and Parsnips

Black kale—sometimes called cavolo nero— *is dark green and becomes very tender when cooked. If black kale is unavailable, use regular kale.*

2 tablespoons extra-virgin olive oil, divided
3 cups (⅓-inch) diagonally cut parsnip
   (about 1 pound)
2½ cups sliced onion (about 1 large)
1 tablespoon chopped fresh thyme
4 garlic cloves, chopped
½ cup dry white wine
8 cups trimmed chopped black kale (about
   3 bunches)
½ cup organic vegetable broth
8 ounces uncooked penne pasta
½ cup (2 ounces) shaved Parmigiano-
   Reggiano cheese, divided
½ teaspoon salt
½ teaspoon freshly ground black pepper

1. Heat 1 tablespoon oil in a large nonstick skillet over medium heat. Add parsnip to pan; cook 12 minutes or until tender and browned, stirring occasionally. Place in a large bowl; keep warm.

2. Heat remaining 1 tablespoon oil in pan over medium-low heat. Add onion to pan; cook 20 minutes or until tender and golden brown, stirring occasionally. Stir in thyme and garlic; cook 2 minutes, stirring occasionally. Add wine; cook 3 minutes or until liquid almost evaporates. Stir in kale and broth; cook, covered, 5 minutes or until kale is tender. Uncover; cook 4 minutes or until kale is very tender, stirring occasionally.
3. Cook pasta according to package directions, omitting salt and fat. Drain pasta in a sieve over a bowl, reserving ¾ cup cooking liquid. Add drained pasta to kale mixture. Stir in parsnip, ½ cup reserved cooking liquid, ¼ cup cheese, salt, and pepper; cook 1 minute or until thoroughly heated. Add remaining ¼ cup cooking liquid if needed to moisten. Top with remaining ¼ cup cheese. Yield: 6 servings (servings size: 1⅔ cups).

CALORIES 324; **FAT** 8g (sat 2.1g, mono 4g, poly 1.1g); **PROTEIN** 12g; **CARB** 54.7g; **FIBER** 7.3g; **CHOL** 6mg; **IRON** 3.5mg; **SODIUM** 428mg; **CALC** 242mg

LIGHTLY BROWNING THE PARSNIP HELPS ITS NATURAL SUGARS EMERGE, LENDING RICH, CARAMELIZED FLAVOR TO THE DISH.

Make Ahead

Creamy Root Vegetable Stew with Gruyère Crostini

Pair this rustic stew with a green salad.

1 tablespoon olive oil
1 cup chopped onion
3 tablespoons chopped garlic
1 tablespoon chopped fresh rosemary, divided
2½ cups (¾-inch) diced peeled Yukon gold potato (about 1 pound)
2¼ cups (¾-inch) diced peeled rutabaga (about ¾ pound)
2 cups (¾-inch) diced peeled turnip
1¼ cups (¾-inch) diced peeled parsnip (about ½ pound)
2 cups organic vegetable broth
2 cups water
2 tablespoons heavy whipping cream
½ teaspoon freshly ground black pepper
¼ teaspoon salt
8 (⅛-inch) slices diagonally cut French bread baguette
½ cup (2 ounces) shredded Gruyère cheese

1. Heat oil in a Dutch oven over medium heat. Add onion to pan; cook 5 minutes or until tender, stirring occasionally. Add garlic and 2 teaspoons rosemary; cook 1 minute, stirring occasionally. Stir in potato and next 5 ingredients. Bring to a simmer; cook, covered, 20 minutes or until vegetables are tender.
2. Place 3 cups vegetable mixture in a blender. Remove center piece of blender lid (to allow steam to escape); secure blender lid on blender. Place a clean towel over opening in blender lid (to avoid splatters). Blend until smooth. Return to pan. Stir in cream, pepper, and salt.
3. Preheat broiler.
4. Arrange bread slices on a baking sheet. Sprinkle each bread slice with 1 tablespoon cheese; top evenly with remaining 1 teaspoon rosemary. Broil 1 minute or until cheese melts. Yield: 4 servings (serving size: 2 cups stew and 2 crostini).

CALORIES 383; FAT 12.8g (sat 5.2g, mono 5.2g, poly 1.7g); PROTEIN 11g; CARB 57.7g; FIBER 7.5g; CHOL 26mg; IRON 2.5mg; SODIUM 639mg; CALC 246mg

Staff Favorite

Two Potato and Beet Hash with Poached Eggs and Greens

2 tablespoons extra-virgin olive oil, divided
1 cup finely chopped onion
2 cups cubed peeled Yukon gold potato (about ¾ pound)
2 cups cubed peeled sweet potato (about ¾ pound)
1 tablespoon chopped fresh sage, divided
3 garlic cloves, minced
1 cup cubed peeled cooked beets (about ½ pound)
½ teaspoon salt, divided
½ teaspoon black pepper, divided
5 teaspoons red wine vinegar, divided
4 large eggs
½ teaspoon Dijon mustard
6 cups torn frisée or curly endive

1. Heat 1 tablespoon oil in a large nonstick skillet over medium-high heat. Add onion to pan; sauté 5 minutes or until tender and golden brown. Add potatoes, 2 teaspoons sage, and garlic; cook 25 minutes or until potatoes are tender, stirring occasionally. Stir in beets, ¼ teaspoon salt, and ¼ teaspoon pepper; cook 10 minutes, stirring occasionally.
2. Add water to a large skillet, filling two-thirds full. Bring to a boil; reduce heat, and simmer. Add 1 tablespoon vinegar. Break each egg into a custard cup, and pour gently into pan. Cook 3 minutes or until desired degree of doneness. Remove eggs from pan using a slotted spoon. Sprinkle ½ teaspoon sage evenly over eggs.
3. Combine remaining 1 tablespoon oil, remaining 2 teaspoons vinegar, remaining ¼ teaspoon salt, remaining ¼ teaspoon pepper, remaining ½ teaspoon sage, and mustard in a large bowl, stirring with a whisk. Add frisée; toss to coat. Serve with hash and eggs. Yield: 4 servings (serving size: about 1 cup hash, 1 poached egg, and about 1½ cups frisée).

CALORIES 329; FAT 11.5g (sat 2.3g, mono 6.9g, poly 1.9g); PROTEIN 11.7g; CARB 45.5g; FIBER 8.1g; CHOL 180mg; IRON 3.6mg; SODIUM 472mg; CALC 124mg

WINE NOTE: Sweet, earthy beets and the tangy combo of greens and mustard are balanced by The Velvet Devil Merlot (Columbia Valley, Washington State, 2008; $12). The wine's opulent cooked cherry and chocolate aromatic profile give new life to this sadly scorned grape variety.

READER RECIPES
FROM YOUR KITCHEN TO OURS

For Peg Palmasano, food is a reminder of family. "I think I acquired my love for cooking from my grandmother," she says. "She cooked with such ease, and everything was to perfection." Spending time in the kitchen as a child whetted her appetite for Italian cuisine. "The flavors and aromas are so welcoming," she says. Her Tuscan chicken recipe reminds her not only of a recent trip to Italy but also of warmth, heritage, and home.

A seasoned baker, Barbara Estabrook often looks for ways to improve the nutritional profile of traditional recipes by eliminating saturated fats. She frequently adds applesauce to her baked products for flavor and moisture. "I love dried figs and almonds, which along with the canola oil boost this quick bread's unsaturated fats," she says.

Mary Pellum grew up watching her father create meals for her family. "He always let me help out in the kitchen when I was growing up," she says. When her father whipped up a Mediterranean-inspired meal six years ago, Pellum fell in love with the menu, which included hummus. Pellum has passed her passion for food on to her daughter, who requested this for her third birthday.

Tuscan Baked Chicken and Beans

"While the chicken roasts in the oven, you can prepare a fresh green salad and still have time to relax with your family and friends before dinner."

—Peg Palmasano,
St. Michaels, Maryland

1 (3½-pound) roasting chicken
¼ teaspoon kosher salt
¼ teaspoon freshly ground black pepper
3 center-cut bacon slices
1 cup chopped onion
⅛ teaspoon kosher salt
2 cups packed torn spinach
½ teaspoon chopped fresh rosemary
2 (16-ounce) cans cannellini or other white beans, rinsed and drained
1 (14.5-ounce) can diced tomatoes, undrained

1. Preheat oven to 350°.
2. Remove and discard giblets and neck from chicken. Trim excess fat. Cut chicken into 2 breast halves, 2 drumsticks, and 2 thighs. Season with ¼ teaspoon salt and pepper. Cook bacon in a 12-inch ovenproof skillet over medium-high heat until crisp. Remove bacon from pan; chop and set aside, reserving drippings in pan. Add chicken pieces to reserved drippings in pan; cook 2 minutes on each side or until browned. Remove chicken from pan; set aside.
3. Add onion and ⅛ teaspoon salt to pan; reduce heat to medium, and cook 5 minutes or until onion begins to brown. Stir in bacon, spinach, and remaining ingredients; remove from heat. Arrange chicken pieces on top; bake, uncovered, at 350° for 40 minutes. Discard skin before serving. Yield: 4 servings (serving size: 1 breast half or 1 leg and 1 thigh and about 1¼ cups bean mixture).

CALORIES 307; FAT 4.9g (sat 1.2g, mono 1.5g, poly 1.4g); PROTEIN 36g; CARB 30g; FIBER 9.5g; CHOL 91mg; IRON 5mg; SODIUM 759mg; CALC 238mg

Fig, Applesauce, and Almond Breakfast Loaf

"Since retirement, watching my calories is a daily ritual. I enjoy a slice for breakfast with a light smear of cream cheese and jam."

—Barbara Estabrook, Rhinelander, Wisconsin

Streusel:
2½ tablespoons brown sugar
2 tablespoons all-purpose flour
1½ tablespoons coarsely chopped almonds
1 tablespoon chilled butter, cut into small pieces
⅛ teaspoon ground cinnamon
Bread:
1 cup dried figs
½ cup boiling water
Cooking spray
1 tablespoon all-purpose flour
2 large egg whites
1 large egg
¾ cup applesauce
⅓ cup plain fat-free yogurt
¼ cup canola oil
½ teaspoon almond extract
¾ cup granulated sugar
6.75 ounces all-purpose flour (about 1½ cups)
2.5 ounces whole-wheat flour (about ½ cup)
⅓ cup chopped almonds, toasted
1 teaspoon baking powder
1 teaspoon ground cinnamon
½ teaspoon salt
½ teaspoon baking soda

1. Preheat oven to 350°.
2. To prepare streusel, combine first 5 ingredients in a small bowl, stirring with a fork until crumbly; set aside.
3. To prepare bread, combine figs and ½ cup boiling water in a small bowl; let stand 30 minutes. Coat 2 (8-inch) loaf pans with cooking spray; dust with 1 tablespoon flour.
4. Place egg whites and egg in a medium bowl; stir well with a whisk. Add applesauce and next 3 ingredients; stir well. Add granulated sugar; stir well.
5. Weigh or lightly spoon 6.75 ounces all-purpose flour and 2.5 ounces whole-wheat flour into dry measuring cups; level with a knife. Combine flours and next 5 ingredients in a large bowl, stirring with a whisk. Drain figs, and coarsely chop. Add figs and applesauce mixture to flour mixture, stirring until just combined. Divide batter between prepared pans. Sprinkle streusel over batter. Bake at 350° for 55 minutes or until a wooden pick inserted in center comes out clean. Cool in pans 15 minutes on a wire rack; remove from pans. Cool completely on wire rack. Yield: 2 loaves, 9 servings per loaf (serving size: 1 slice).

CALORIES 185; FAT 5.9g (sat 0.9g, mono 3.1g, poly 1.5g); PROTEIN 3.8g; CARB 30.9g; FIBER 2.5g; CHOL 14mg; IRON 1.2mg; SODIUM 140mg; CALC 58mg

Roasted Red Pepper Hummus
(pictured on page 268)

"I have tried many variations of hummus, but this one is especially flavorful and unique. Serve with pita chips or vegetable crudités."

—Mary Pellum,
Louisville, Kentucky

⅓ cup tahini (sesame seed paste)
¼ cup water
¼ cup chopped bottled roasted red bell peppers, rinsed and drained
2 tablespoons fresh lemon juice
¼ teaspoon salt
1 garlic clove, minced
1 (15½-ounce) can chickpeas, rinsed and drained

1. Place all ingredients in a food processor; process until smooth. Yield: 2 cups (serving size: ¼ cup).

CALORIES 102; FAT 5.7g (sat 0.8g, mono 2.1g, poly 2.5g); PROTEIN 3.5g; CARB 10.5g; FIBER 2g; CHOL 0mg; IRON 1mg; SODIUM 199mg; CALC 26mg

EATING IN RALEIGH-DURHAM-CHAPEL HILL, NORTH CAROLINA

The Piedmont, the rolling terrain in the middle of North Carolina, has long been known as Tobacco Road for its most famous farming export. Lately, however, the region has turned its attention to a more healthful harvest. Not that the area has forgotten its agricultural roots—you can still drive half an hour in just about any direction from the capitol building in Raleigh and find yourself surrounded by farmland. But instead of tobacco rows, you're now more apt to see fields of sustainably grown heirloom tomatoes or pastures of grazing dairy goats.

What prompts that kind of change? Eating from the land is woven into the culture here. The diverse topography of North Carolina (only 500 miles separate western mountains from eastern coast) means chefs can source everything from oysters to apples, both likely harvested within the same day. Public health policy has certainly helped, too; with smoking rates dwindling, North Carolina farmers have turned to other crops just in time for the rising local-food movement.

But the main driver is an increasingly cosmopolitan population drawn to the region by the three major universities (Duke, UNC Chapel Hill, NC State) and scores of international technology firms that now make their homes in Raleigh, Durham, and Chapel Hill—the three cities in the eastern Piedmont that are collectively known as The Research Triangle.

While the recession hasn't cast as dark a cloud over the region as it has over other parts of the country (thanks in large measure to the strong presence of nearby electronics and pharmaceutical manufacturers and researchers), its shadow can still be seen in a dramatic increase in fine dining establishments now offering bargain meals. The quality of ingredients isn't sacrificed, but portion size is often reduced—a silver lining for those seeking to eat healthy.

One thing you won't find at these spots (or any other bar in the area) is a haze of cigarette smoke. In January of this year, North Carolina—whose name has been synonymous with tobacco since the days of Sir Walter Raleigh—passed a statewide ban on smoking in restaurants and bars.

Nowadays, if there's any smoking going on in a restaurant on Tobacco Road, it's probably something tasty being cooked up.

FISH WITH SWEET POTATO CUSTARD. TUSCAN GREENS, PORK, AND RED-EYE GRAVY. THIS IS THE NEW SOUTHERN COOKING.

Fall Salad with Apples, Walnuts, and Stilton

After more than a decade of supplying some of the area's best restaurants and sandwich shops, local artisanal bakeries are now offering their own dine-in options. At La Farm Bakery (lafarmbakery.com) in the nearby town of Cary, master baker Lionel Vatinet fills his Parisian baguettes with charcuterie and Gruyère, and transforms his rustic farm bread into croques monsieurs. When the weather is fair, the landscaped patio at Guglhupf (guglhupf.com) fills quickly with customers hungry for light salads of shrimp salad with radicchio, local tomatoes, and green goddess dressing or sandwiches ranging from roasted beef with arugula and blue cheese spread to house-roasted turkey with watercress. Use crumbled goat cheese in place of Stilton, if you prefer a milder flavored cheese.

1 tablespoon minced shallot
1½ tablespoons champagne or white wine vinegar
1 tablespoon fresh lemon juice
1 tablespoon honey
1 teaspoon Dijon mustard
1 dried apricot, finely chopped
3 tablespoons extra-virgin olive oil
¼ teaspoon salt
⅛ teaspoon freshly ground black pepper
2 cups torn green leaf lettuce leaves
2 cups thinly sliced Belgian endive (about 2 heads)
¼ cup (1 ounce) Stilton cheese, thinly sliced
¼ cup walnuts, coarsely chopped
1 (5-ounce) package baby arugula
1 ounce very thin slices prosciutto, torn
1 Granny Smith apple, cored and thinly sliced

1. Place first 6 ingredients in a blender. With blender on, slowly add oil; process until well combined. Stir in salt and pepper.
2. Combine lettuce and remaining ingredients in a large bowl; add apricot mixture, tossing gently to coat. Yield: 4 servings (serving size: 2 cups).

CALORIES 294; FAT 18.4g (sat 3.6g, mono 8.9g, poly 5g); PROTEIN 9.2g; CARB 28g; FIBER 10.8g; CHOL 9.5mg; IRON 3.7mg; SODIUM 429mg; CALC 254mg

Dinner

Coconut Red Curry Hot Pot with Braised Chicken and Mushrooms

For the menu at bu•ku (bukuraleigh.com), Chef William D'Auvray draws inspiration from the pushcarts and markets of the world. Diners can embark on a gastronomic tour that might include Colombian arepas, Polish beer–braised chicken pierogis, and Thai-style barbecued pike. Look for Kaffir lime leaves and galangal—also known as Thai ginger—at ethnic markets and gourmet grocers. If you can't find them, use an extra ¼ cup chopped peeled fresh lemongrass to flavor the broth. You can use regular ginger in place of galangal.

2 cups fat-free, lower-sodium chicken broth
¾ cup chopped peeled fresh lemongrass
6 Kaffir lime leaves, torn
5 (¼-inch) slices fresh galangal
1½ tablespoons red curry paste
1 (4-ounce) package presliced exotic
  mushroom blend (such as shiitake, cremini,
  and oyster)
8 ounces skinless, boneless chicken breast,
  cut into bite-sized pieces
1 (13.5-ounce) can light coconut milk
1 tablespoon Thai fish sauce
2 teaspoons brown sugar
⅓ cup thinly diagonally cut green onions
2 tablespoons fresh lime juice
6 tablespoons coarsely chopped fresh
  cilantro, divided
3 ounces uncooked wide rice noodles

1. Bring broth to a boil in a medium saucepan over medium-high heat; stir in lemongrass, lime leaves, and galangal. Reduce heat, and simmer 5 minutes. Remove from heat; let stand 30 minutes. Strain through a sieve over a bowl; discard solids. Return broth to pan; add curry paste, stirring with a whisk. Bring to a simmer over medium-high heat. Add mushrooms; cook 2 minutes or until tender. Stir in chicken; cook 3 minutes or until chicken is done. Add coconut milk, stirring well to combine. Stir in fish sauce and sugar, stirring until sugar dissolves. Remove from heat; stir in onions, juice, and ¼ cup cilantro.

2. Cook noodles according to package directions, omitting salt and fat; drain. Add noodles to coconut milk mixture. Ladle 1 cup soup into each of 6 bowls; sprinkle evenly with remaining 2 tablespoons cilantro. Yield: 6 servings.

CALORIES 221; FAT 5.4g (sat 4.4g, mono 0.2g, poly 0.2g); PROTEIN 17.2g; CARB 27.3g; FIBER 1g; CHOL 33mg; IRON 1.8mg; SODIUM 681mg; CALC 20mg

FROM OUR NEW COOKBOOK

This is just the thing if you're hungry and in a hurry: Cooking Light Complete Meals in Minutes, which contains all our best quick recipes.

Quick & Easy • Kid Friendly

Wild Rice and Mushroom Soup with Chicken

20 Minutes
Make it a meal: Add sliced whole-wheat French bread and a mixed greens salad.

4 cups fat-free, lower-sodium chicken broth,
  divided
1 (2.75-ounce) package quick-cooking wild
  rice (such as Gourmet House)
1 tablespoon olive oil
½ cup prechopped onion
½ cup chopped red bell pepper
⅓ cup matchstick-cut carrots
1 teaspoon bottled minced garlic
½ teaspoon dried thyme
1 teaspoon butter
2 (4-ounce) packages presliced exotic
  mushroom blend (such as shiitake, cremini,
  and oyster)
2 cups shredded rotisserie chicken breast
⅛ teaspoon salt
⅛ teaspoon black pepper

1. Bring 1⅓ cups broth to a boil in a medium saucepan; add rice to pan. Cover,

reduce heat, and simmer 5 minutes or until liquid is absorbed. Set aside.

2. Heat oil in a Dutch oven over medium-high heat. Add onion and next 4 ingredients to pan; sauté 3 minutes, stirring occasionally. Stir in butter and mushrooms; sauté 3 minutes or until lightly browned. Add remaining 2⅔ cups broth, rice, chicken, salt, and pepper to pan; cook 3 minutes or until thoroughly heated, stirring occasionally. Yield: 4 servings (serving size: 1½ cups).

CALORIES 281; FAT 7.5g (sat 1.9g, mono 3.8g, poly 1.3g); PROTEIN 28.9g; CARB 23g; FIBER 4g; CHOL 62mg; IRON 2.8mg; SODIUM 541mg; CALC 42mg

Quick & Easy

Spicy Filet Mignon with Grilled Sweet Onion

15 Minutes
Serve with a tossed salad.

Cooking spray
2 cups vertically sliced Vidalia or other
  sweet onion
⅛ teaspoon salt
⅛ teaspoon black pepper
1 teaspoon garlic powder
½ teaspoon ground cumin
½ teaspoon dried oregano
¼ teaspoon salt
¼ teaspoon ground red pepper
¼ teaspoon black pepper
4 (4-ounce) filets mignons

1. Heat a grill pan over medium-high heat. Coat pan with cooking spray. Add onion; sprinkle with ⅛ teaspoon salt and ⅛ teaspoon black pepper. Cook 8 minutes or until browned, stirring occasionally. Remove from pan; keep warm.

2. Combine garlic powder and next 5 ingredients in a small bowl; sprinkle over both sides of beef. Add beef to pan. Grill 5 minutes on each side or until desired degree of doneness. Serve with onion mixture. Yield: 4 servings (serving size: 1 filet and ¼ cup onion mixture).

CALORIES 313; FAT 22g (sat 8.7g, mono 9.2g, poly 0.9g); PROTEIN 21g; CARB 6.7g; FIBER 1.1g; CHOL 74mg; IRON 3mg; SODIUM 269mg; CALC 27mg

5-INGREDIENT COOKING

Quick & Easy

Tomato-Citrus Salmon

Tangy tomatoes, sweet oranges, and briny olives bring lively color and bold flavor to this simple dish.

3 large navel oranges, divided
4 (6-ounce) skinless salmon fillets
1 cup thinly sliced red onion
1½ cups diced plum tomato
¼ cup chopped pimiento-stuffed green olives

Grate ½ teaspoon orange rind; squeeze ¼ cup juice from 1 orange into a sieve over a bowl. Section remaining 2 oranges to equal 1 cup sections. Sprinkle ½ teaspoon salt and ¼ teaspoon freshly ground black pepper over fish. Heat a large nonstick skillet over medium-high heat. Coat pan with cooking spray. Add fish, top sides down, to pan; cook 5 minutes. Remove fish from pan. Add onion to pan; sauté 3 minutes or until tender and lightly browned. Add tomato, olives, orange juice, and orange rind to pan; cook 3 minutes, stirring occasionally. Stir in ¼ teaspoon salt and ¼ teaspoon freshly ground black pepper. Arrange fish, browned sides up, over tomato mixture in pan. Cover, reduce heat, and simmer 3 minutes. Add orange sections; cook 1 minute or until desired degree of doneness. Yield: 4 servings (serving size: 1 fillet and ⅓ cup tomato mixture).

CALORIES 380; **FAT** 19.8g (sat 3.8g, mono 7.1g, poly 7.3g); **PROTEIN** 35.5g; **CARB** 13.7g; **FIBER** 2.7g; **CHOL** 100mg; **IRON** 1mg; **SODIUM** 663mg; **CALC** 57mg

THE FIVE INGREDIENTS

3 large navel oranges, divided

4 (6-ounce) skinless salmon fillets

1 cup thinly sliced red onion

1½ cups diced plum tomato

¼ cup chopped pimiento-stuffed green olives

Quick & Easy

Buffalo Chicken Panini

This toasted sandwich delivers classic bar-food taste in a healthier package.

¼ cup hot pepper sauce, divided
1 pound chicken breast tenders
½ cup (2 ounces) crumbled blue cheese
6 tablespoons canola mayonnaise
8 (1-ounce) slices white or sourdough bread

Preheat broiler; coat broiler pan with cooking spray. Combine 2 tablespoons sauce and chicken in a medium bowl, tossing to coat. Arrange chicken in a single layer on broiler pan; broil 4 minutes on each side or until done. Place chicken in a bowl; toss with remaining 2 tablespoons sauce. Combine cheese and mayonnaise. Spread 3 tablespoons cheese mixture on each of 4 bread slices; top each with one-fourth of cooked chicken and 1 bread slice. Heat a grill pan over medium-high heat. Coat pan with cooking spray. Arrange 2 sandwiches in pan. Place a cast-iron or heavy skillet on top of sandwiches; press gently. Cook 3 minutes on each side or until bread is toasted (leave skillet on sandwiches while they cook). Repeat procedure with remaining 2 sandwiches. Yield: 4 servings (serving size: 1 sandwich).

CALORIES 402; **FAT** 16.2g (sat 4.9g, mono 6g, poly 3.5g); **PROTEIN** 32.4g; **CARB** 29.1g; **FIBER** 3g; **CHOL** 75mg; **IRON** 0.8mg; **SODIUM** 724mg; **CALC** 100mg

THE FIVE INGREDIENTS

¼ cup hot pepper sauce, divided

+

1 pound chicken breast tenders

+

½ cup (2 ounces) crumbled blue cheese

+

6 tablespoons canola mayonnaise

+

8 (1-ounce) slices white or sourdough bread

WHAT TO EAT RIGHT NOW
PEARS

Perfectly ripe pears have no peers: sensuous with a quenching, dripping juiciness and perfumed, honey-buttery sweetness—like the last hurrah of summer's sunshine. Their texture, mealy in the best way, offers a slight give followed by a mouthwatering giving-in. This year's U.S. crop—grown mostly in Washington and Oregon—comes into full glory now. If rotund, short-necked Comice is the Cadillac of the pear world, Anjou is the workhorse. Forelle and Seckel are petite, fleeting beauties. Grab them while you can!

Fresh Pear Cocktail

The philosophy at Rouge Tomate, a health-mindful restaurant with locations in New York and Brussels, is guided by seasonal ingredients and bright flavors. Beverage Director Pascaline Lepeltier shares this delicious cocktail.

Shred 1 medium Bosc pear; place pulp on several layers of cheesecloth. Gather edges of cheesecloth together; squeeze over a glass measuring cup to yield ⅓ cup juice. Discard solids. Combine pear juice, 2 tablespoons citrus-infused vodka, 1 tablespoon pomegranate juice, 1 tablespoon fresh lime juice, and 1 tablespoon agave syrup (or sugar syrup) in a martini shaker with ice; shake. Strain about 3 tablespoons vodka mixture into each of 2 martini glasses. Top each serving with 1½ tablespoons hard apple cider or *cidre doux*. Garnish with pear slices. Yield: 2 servings.

CALORIES 156; **FAT** 0.2g (sat 0g); **SODIUM** 5mg

Pear Relish

Serve this over chicken, fish, or quesadillas, or just spoon into fresh endive spears.

Combine 2 cups chopped red Anjou pear, ⅓ cup sliced kumquat, 2 tablespoons fresh lemon juice, and 1 tablespoon honey; let stand 10 minutes. Add ⅓ cup sliced green olives, 3 tablespoons thinly sliced shallots, 1½ tablespoons extra-virgin olive oil, 1½ tablespoons chopped fresh chives, 1½ teaspoons chopped fresh flat-leaf parsley, ¼ teaspoon salt, and ⅛ teaspoon ground red pepper; toss. Yield: 12 servings (serving size: ¼ cup).

CALORIES 47; **FAT** 2.4g (sat 0.3g); **SODIUM** 105mg

PEAR PAIRINGS

Ripe pears are the ideal match for many sweet and savory ingredients. Try using them in places you would use apples:
- The next time you cook pork, make homemade pear sauce just as you would fresh applesauce; just substitute pears for apples.
- Pears love blue cheese (or brie and other pungent cheeses), and their honey sweetness is a nice foil for supertart cranberries.
- Put in pies, tarts, crisps, and crumbles.
- Or play their sweetness against bitter endive or radicchio, tangy citrus such as kumquats or oranges, earthy nuts (especially walnuts), and woodsy herbs like fresh thyme or sage. Pear has a mysterious ability to show its true, pure flavor in alcohol better than many fruits.

DID YOU KNOW?

Each pear is harvested by hand and ripened off the tree so the fragile fruit is not bruised.

DINNER TONIGHT

Fast weeknight menus from the *Cooking Light* Test Kitchens.

Quick & Easy

Spicy Shrimp Noodle Bowl

with Cucumber Salad

Simple Sub: Try shredded rotisserie chicken breast instead of shrimp.

1 pound tail-on peeled and deveined medium shrimp
1½ cups water
1 cup fat-free, lower-sodium chicken broth
1 (8-ounce) bottle clam juice
2 (¼-inch-thick) slices peeled fresh ginger
1 teaspoon olive oil
¾ cup thinly sliced red bell pepper
¼ cup thinly sliced yellow onion
1 garlic clove, minced
½ cup sugar snap peas
2 teaspoons chili garlic sauce or ½ teaspoon crushed red pepper
¼ teaspoon salt
3 ounces uncooked rice sticks
2 tablespoons fresh cilantro leaves
Lime wedges

1. Remove shrimp tails; set aside. Combine shrimp tails, 1½ cups water, and next 3 ingredients in a saucepan, and bring to a boil. Reduce heat, and simmer, uncovered, 10 minutes. Strain broth mixture through a sieve into a bowl; discard solids.
2. Heat oil in a medium saucepan over medium-high heat. Add bell pepper, onion, and garlic; sauté 3 minutes. Add reserved broth; bring to a simmer. Add shrimp, peas, and next 3 ingredients; cook 5 minutes or until noodles are done. Ladle 1¼ cups soup into each of 4 bowls; top each serving with 1½ teaspoons cilantro. Serve with lime wedges. Yield: 4 servings.

CALORIES 236; **FAT** 3.6g (sat 0.7g, mono 1.3g, poly 1g); **PROTEIN** 26.5g; **CARB** 25.4g; **FIBER** 1.9g; **CHOL** 174mg; **IRON** 3.7mg; **SODIUM** 506mg; **CALC** 84mg

---

For the Cucumber Salad:
Combine 4 teaspoons rice vinegar, 2 teaspoons dark sesame oil, ¼ teaspoon black pepper, and ⅛ teaspoon salt in a medium bowl. Add 2 cups thinly sliced cucumber, ½ cup thinly sliced radishes, and 3 tablespoons thinly sliced green onions; toss well to combine. Yield: 4 servings.

CALORIES 32; **FAT** 2.4g (sat 0.4g); **SODIUM** 83mg

SHOPPING LIST

Spicy Shrimp Noodle Bowl
fresh ginger
1 red bell pepper
1 small yellow onion
garlic
sugar snap peas
fresh cilantro
1 lime
olive oil
fat-free, lower-sodium chicken broth
8-ounce bottle clam juice
chili garlic sauce
3 ounces rice sticks
1 pound tail-on peeled, deveined medium shrimp

Cucumber Salad
1 large cucumber
radishes
green onions
rice vinegar
dark sesame oil

GAME PLAN

While broth mixture simmers:
- Slice bell pepper and onion.
- Mince garlic.
- Slice cucumber and radish.

While noodle mixture cooks:
- Prepare green onions.
- Toss salad.

Quick & Easy

Mushroom and Provolone Patty Melts

with Quick-Roasted Potato Wedges

Time-Saver: Presliced mushrooms are widely available and save a lot of prep work.
Flavor Hit: Porter beer has strong notes of malt and hops.
Kid Tweak: Use beef broth in place of beer, and try mild-tasting wheat bread.

1 pound ground sirloin
Cooking spray
1 tablespoon olive oil
¼ cup thinly sliced yellow onion
⅛ teaspoon salt
⅛ teaspoon black pepper
1 (8-ounce) package presliced cremini mushrooms
1½ teaspoons all-purpose flour
¼ cup dark beer (such as porter)
8 (1.1-ounce) slices rye bread
4 (¾-ounce) slices reduced-fat provolone cheese

1. Heat a large nonstick skillet over medium-high heat. Shape beef into 4 (4-inch) patties. Coat pan with cooking spray. Add patties; cook 4 minutes on each side or until done.
2. Heat oil in a medium skillet over medium-high heat. Add onion and next 3 ingredients; sauté 3 minutes. Sprinkle flour over mushroom mixture; cook 1 minute, stirring constantly. Stir in beer; cook 30 seconds or until thick. Remove from heat; keep warm.
3. When patties are done, remove from large skillet. Wipe pan clean; heat over medium-high heat. Coat 1 side of each bread slice with cooking spray. Place 4 bread slices, coated sides down, in pan. Top each with 1 patty, 1 cheese slice, and one-fourth of mushroom mixture. Top with remaining bread slices, and coat with cooking spray. Cook 2 minutes on each side or until browned. Yield: 4 servings (serving size: 1 sandwich).

CALORIES 416; **FAT** 17.1g (sat 6.2g, mono 7.7g, poly 1.4g); **PROTEIN** 30g; **CARB** 34.3g; **FIBER** 4.1g; **CHOL** 42mg; **IRON** 3.9mg; **SODIUM** 708mg; **CALC** 232mg

For the Quick-Roasted Potato Wedges:
Preheat oven to 425°. Cut 1 pound small red potatoes into wedges; toss with 1 tablespoon olive oil, ½ teaspoon black pepper, and ¼ teaspoon salt. Arrange on a baking sheet. Bake at 425° for 25 minutes or until tender, stirring once. Toss with 2 tablespoons chopped fresh parsley. Yield: 4 servings.

CALORIES 110; **FAT** 3.5g (sat 0.5g); **SODIUM** 154mg

40 minutes

SHOPPING LIST

Mushroom and Provolone Patty Melts

8-ounce package presliced cremini mushrooms
1 small yellow onion
all-purpose flour
olive oil
dark beer (porter)
rye bread
presliced reduced-fat provolone cheese
1 pound ground sirloin

Quick-Roasted Potato Wedges

1 pound red potatoes
fresh parsley
olive oil

GAME PLAN

While oven preheats:
  ■ Cut potatoes.
  ■ Cook burger patties.
While potatoes roast:
  ■ Cook mushroom mixture.
  ■ Assemble and cook sandwiches.

Quick & Easy • Make Ahead
Fall Vegetable Curry
with Cashew Basmati Rice

Simple Sub: No Madras? Try 1½ teaspoons regular curry and ½ teaspoon red pepper.
Flavor Hit: Tangy, creamy Greek yogurt mitigates the curry's heat.
Prep Pointer: Cutting the sweet potato into small pieces helps it cook more quickly.

1½ teaspoons olive oil
1 cup diced peeled sweet potato
1 cup small cauliflower florets
¼ cup thinly sliced yellow onion
2 teaspoons Madras curry powder
½ cup organic vegetable broth (such as Swanson)
¼ teaspoon salt
1 (15-ounce) can chickpeas (garbanzo beans), rinsed and drained
1 (14.5-ounce) can no-salt-added diced tomatoes, undrained
2 tablespoons chopped fresh cilantro
½ cup plain 2% reduced-fat Greek yogurt

1. Heat oil in a large nonstick skillet over medium-high heat. Add sweet potato to pan; sauté 3 minutes. Decrease heat to medium. Add cauliflower, onion, and curry powder; cook 1 minute, stirring mixture constantly. Add broth and next 3 ingredients; bring to a boil. Cover, reduce heat, and simmer 10 minutes or until vegetables are tender, stirring occasionally. Sprinkle with cilantro; serve with yogurt. Yield: 4 servings (serving size: 1 cup curry and 2 tablespoons yogurt).

CALORIES 231; **FAT** 3.9g (sat 0.9g, mono 1.6g, poly 0.9g); **PROTEIN** 10.4g; **CARB** 40.8g; **FIBER** 8.6g; **CHOL** 2mg; **IRON** 2.5mg; **SODIUM** 626mg; **CALC** 106mg

For the Cashew Basmati Rice:
Cook 1 cup basmati rice according to package directions, omitting salt and fat. Stir in ¼ cup unsalted cashew pieces and ¼ teaspoon salt. Yield: 4 servings.

CALORIES 129; **FAT** 4g (sat 0.8g); **SODIUM** 149mg

WINE NOTE: Tangent 2008 Paragon Vineyard Viognier (Edna Valley, CA; $17) is your must-try wine here, with notes of gardenia, peach, and apricot. It is full-bodied enough to meet the chickpeas halfway but crisp enough to hold up to the tangy tomatoes and yogurt.

30 minutes

SHOPPING LIST

Fall Vegetable Curry

1 large sweet potato
cauliflower
1 small yellow onion
fresh cilantro
olive oil
Madras curry powder
organic vegetable broth
(15-ounce) can chickpeas
(14.5-ounce) can no-salt-added diced tomatoes
plain 2% reduced-fat Greek yogurt

Cashew Basmati Rice

basmati rice
unsalted cashew pieces

GAME PLAN

While water for rice comes to a boil:
  ■ Prep sweet potato, cauliflower, and onion.
While rice cooks:
  ■ Cook curry.
  ■ Chop cilantro.

Chicken with Lemon-Leek Linguine
with Mixed Greens Salad
(pictured on page 267)

Prep Pointer: Leeks can be full of grit, so it's a good idea to rinse well after slicing.
Flavor Hit: Fresh lemon juice packs more of a punch than its bottled counterpart.
Vegetarian Swap: Omit chicken, use vegetable broth, and top with crumbled goat cheese.

6 ounces uncooked linguine
4 (6-ounce) skinless, boneless chicken
    breast halves
½ teaspoon salt, divided
¼ teaspoon black pepper
¼ cup all-purpose flour
3 tablespoons butter, divided
3 garlic cloves, thinly sliced
1 leek, trimmed, cut in half lengthwise, and
    thinly sliced (1½ cups)
½ cup fat-free, lower-sodium chicken broth
2 tablespoons fresh lemon juice
2 tablespoons chopped fresh flat-leaf parsley

1. Cook pasta according to package directions, omitting salt and fat. Drain; keep warm.
2. Place chicken between 2 sheets of heavy-duty plastic wrap; pound to an even thickness using a meat mallet or small heavy skillet. Sprinkle chicken with ¼ teaspoon salt and pepper. Place flour in a shallow dish; dredge chicken in flour, shaking to remove excess.
3. Heat 1 tablespoon butter in a large nonstick skillet over medium-high heat. Add chicken; cook 3 minutes on each side or until done. Remove chicken from pan; keep warm.
4. Melt 1 tablespoon butter in skillet over medium-high heat. Add garlic, leek, and remaining ¼ teaspoon salt; sauté 4 minutes. Add broth and juice; cook 2 minutes or until liquid is reduced by half. Remove from heat; stir in remaining 1 tablespoon butter. Add pasta to leek mixture; toss well to combine. Serve chicken over pasta

mixture; sprinkle with parsley. Yield: 4 servings (serving size: 1 chicken breast half and 1 cup pasta mixture).

CALORIES 474; **FAT** 11.5g (sat 6.2g, mono 2.7g, poly 0.9g); **PROTEIN** 46.8g; **CARB** 44g; **FIBER** 2.3g; **CHOL** 121mg; **IRON** 3.8mg; **SODIUM** 592mg; **CALC** 57mg

For the Mixed Greens Salad:
Combine 1 tablespoon olive oil, 2 teaspoons white wine vinegar, ½ teaspoon Dijon mustard, and a dash of salt in a large bowl. Add 4 cups mixed baby greens; toss. Yield: 4 servings.

CALORIES 40; **FAT** 3.5g (sat 0.5g); **SODIUM** 66mg

30 minutes

SHOPPING LIST

Chicken with Lemon-Leek Linguine
garlic
1 leek
1 lemon
fresh parsley
all-purpose flour
6 ounces linguine
fat-free, lower-sodium chicken broth
butter
4 (6-ounce) skinless, boneless chicken
    breasts

Mixed Greens Salad
4 cups mixed baby greens
olive oil
white wine vinegar
Dijon mustard

GAME PLAN

While water comes to a boil:
 ▪ Pound chicken.
 ▪ Dredge chicken in flour.
While pasta cooks:
 ▪ Cook chicken.
 ▪ Prepare leek sauce.
 ▪ Prepare salad.

White Wine–Marinated Steak
with Chive Smashed Potatoes and Lemon Green Beans

Simple Sub: Use thyme instead of chives for the potatoes.
Prep Pointer: If the potatoes are a little too thick, add more milk, 1 tablespoon at a time.

3 tablespoons white wine
1 tablespoon olive oil
1 teaspoon Dijon mustard
1 pound chuck eye steaks, trimmed
¼ teaspoon salt
¼ teaspoon black pepper
Cooking spray
1 large shallot, sliced
¼ cup fat-free, lower-sodium beef broth

1. Combine first 3 ingredients in a shallow dish. Add steaks, and let stand at room temperature 10 minutes. Remove steaks from marinade; reserve marinade. Sprinkle steaks evenly with salt and pepper.
2. Heat a large heavy skillet over medium-high heat. Coat pan with cooking spray. Add steaks to pan; cook 4 minutes on each side or until desired degree of doneness. Remove steaks from pan; keep warm. Add shallots to pan; sauté 1 minute. Add reserved marinade and broth, scraping pan to loosen browned bits; cook 2 minutes or until reduced by half. Spoon sauce over steaks. Yield: 4 servings (serving size: 3 ounces steak and 1 tablespoon sauce).

CALORIES 227; **FAT** 14.4g (sat 4.8g, mono 7g, poly 1g); **PROTEIN** 21.6g; **CARB** 1.4g; **FIBER** 0.1g; **CHOL** 71mg; **IRON** 2.6mg; **SODIUM** 273mg; **CALC** 10mg

For the Chive Smashed Potatoes:
Cut 1 pound Yukon gold potatoes into ¾-inch pieces. Steam potato 15 minutes or until tender. Combine potato, ⅓ cup plain 2% reduced-fat Greek yogurt, 2 tablespoons minced fresh chives, 2 tablespoons fat-free milk, and ¼ teaspoon salt. Mash to desired consistency. Yield: 4 servings.

CALORIES 111; **FAT** 0.5g (sat 0.3g); **SODIUM** 165mg

For the Lemon Green Beans:
Steam ¾ pound trimmed green beans
for 5 minutes or until crisp-tender. Toss
with 2 tablespoons lemon rind strips,
1 tablespoon olive oil, ¼ teaspoon salt,
and ¼ teaspoon black pepper. Yield:
4 servings.

CALORIES 57; **FAT** 3.5g (sat 0.5g); **SODIUM** 154mg

40 minutes

SHOPPING LIST

White Wine–Marinated Steak
1 large shallot
olive oil
Dijon mustard
fat-free, lower-sodium beef broth
white wine
1 pound chuck eye steaks

Chive Smashed Potatoes
1 pound Yukon gold potatoes
fresh chives
plain 2% reduced-fat Greek yogurt
fat-free milk

Lemon Green Beans
³/₄ pound green beans
1 lemon
olive oil

GAME PLAN

While steaks marinate:
- Steam potatoes.
- Slice shallot.
- Mince chives.
- Slice lemon rind.
While steaks cook:
- Finish potatoes.
- Steam green beans.

SUPERFAST

Don't let the speeded-up pace of fall keep
you from the rich, comforting tastes of the
season. Yes, you can have it all—even on
weeknights.

Quick & Easy

Beef Filets with Pomegranate-Pinot Sauce

*Pomegranate seeds make a pretty garnish
(look for convenient, ready-to-eat seeds in the
produce section). Serve with potato wedges.*

4 (4-ounce) beef tenderloin steaks, trimmed
½ teaspoon salt
½ teaspoon freshly ground black pepper,
   divided
Cooking spray
1 tablespoon minced shallots
⅓ cup pinot noir or burgundy wine
⅓ cup pomegranate juice
⅓ cup fat-free, lower-sodium beef broth
1 fresh thyme sprig
1½ tablespoons chilled butter, cut into small
   pieces

1. Heat a large heavy skillet over
medium-high heat. Sprinkle steaks
evenly with salt and ¼ teaspoon pepper. Coat pan with cooking spray. Add
steaks to pan; cook 3 minutes on each
side or until desired degree of doneness.
Remove steaks from pan; keep warm.
2. Add shallots to pan; sauté 30 seconds. Add remaining ¼ teaspoon pepper, wine, and next 3 ingredients; bring
to a boil. Cook 7 minutes or until reduced to about 3 tablespoons. Remove
from heat; discard thyme sprig. Add
butter to sauce, stirring until butter
melts. Serve sauce with steaks. Yield:
4 servings (serving size: 1 steak and
about 2 teaspoons sauce).

CALORIES 227; **FAT** 12.3g (sat 5.7g, mono 4.2g, poly 0.5g);
PROTEIN 24g; **CARB** 3.8g; **FIBER** 0.1g; **CHOL** 82mg;
IRON 3.4mg; **SODIUM** 428mg; **CALC** 15mg

Quick & Easy

Sandwich of the Month

Prosciutto, Pear, and Blue Cheese Sandwiches

8 slices 100% multigrain bread
1 tablespoon butter, softened
3 cups arugula
1 medium shallot, thinly sliced
1 tablespoon extra-virgin olive oil
2 teaspoons red wine vinegar
⅛ teaspoon freshly ground black pepper
2 ounces thinly sliced prosciutto
1 ripe pear, cored and thinly sliced
2 ounces blue cheese, sliced

1. Preheat broiler.
2. Arrange bread in a single layer on a
baking sheet; broil 3 minutes or until
toasted. Turn bread slices over; spread
butter evenly over bread slices. Broil an
additional 2 minutes or until toasted.
3. Combine arugula and shallots in a
medium bowl. Drizzle arugula mixture
with oil and vinegar; sprinkle with pepper. Toss well to coat. Divide arugula
mixture evenly among 4 bread slices,
buttered sides up; top evenly with prosciutto. Divide pear slices and cheese
evenly among sandwiches; top each
sandwich with 1 bread slice, buttered
sides down. Yield: 4 servings (serving
size: 1 sandwich).

CALORIES 324; **FAT** 13.8g (sat 5.4g, mono 5g, poly 0.8g);
PROTEIN 15g; **CARB** 36.4g; **FIBER** 9.7g; **CHOL** 26mg;
IRON 2.1mg; **SODIUM** 706mg; **CALC** 408mg

Herbed Couscous Pilaf

Start with the basic side dish, and try any of our flavorful riffs below.

1 tablespoon olive oil
¼ cup finely chopped shallots
1 cup uncooked couscous
1 cup plus 2 tablespoons fat-free, lower-
    sodium chicken broth
¼ teaspoon salt
1 tablespoon chopped fresh flat-leaf parsley
1 teaspoon chopped fresh thyme

1. Heat a small saucepan over medium-high heat. Add oil to pan, swirling to coat. Add shallots; sauté 2 minutes or until tender. Stir in couscous; sauté 1 minute. Add broth and salt; bring to a boil. Cover, remove from heat, and let stand 5 minutes. Fluff with a fork. Stir in parsley and thyme. Yield: 4 servings (serving size: ¾ cup).

CALORIES 205; **FAT** 3.7g (sat 0.5g, mono 2.5g, poly 0.5g); **PROTEIN** 6.5g; **CARB** 35.6g; **FIBER** 2.6g; **CHOL** 0mg; **IRON** 0.8mg; **SODIUM** 263mg; **CALC** 20mg

Tex-Mex Variation:
In place of broth, use ½ cup canned diced tomatoes with chiles, ¾ cup broth, and ½ cup frozen corn. Omit salt and herbs; stir in 1 tablespoon lime juice and 1 tablespoon cilantro. Yield: 4 servings.

CALORIES 227; **FAT** 3.9g (sat 0.6g); **SODIUM** 283mg

Curried Currant Variation:
Add ¼ teaspoon curry powder to shallots as they sauté. Increase broth to 1¼ cups. Add ¼ cup dried currants to pan with broth. Omit thyme. Yield: 4 servings.

CALORIES 231; **FAT** 3.8g (sat 0.6g); **SODIUM** 275mg

Tomato-Feta Variation:
Prepare Herbed Couscous Pilaf; decrease salt to ⅛ teaspoon. Stir in ¾ cup quartered grape tomatoes, ⅓ cup crumbled feta cheese, 1 tablespoon chopped fresh basil, and 1 tablespoon lemon juice. Yield: 4 servings.

CALORIES 244; **FAT** 6.5g (sat 2.4g); **SODIUM** 330mg

Easy Guacamole

The food processor makes quick work of this basic dip that's rich in heart-healthy monoun-saturated fats. We like the heat from leaving the seeds in the jalapeño, but you can seed the pepper for a milder guac. To test for ripeness without bruising, place your thumb on the bottom and your middle finger on top of the avocado. Squeeze gently, feeling for a slight give. If it feels mushy, keep looking. Serve with tortilla chips or crudités.

1½ tablespoons coarsely chopped red onion
1 tablespoon fresh lime juice
⅛ teaspoon salt
1 garlic clove
½ small jalapeño pepper
1 ripe peeled avocado
1 tablespoon fresh cilantro leaves

1. Place first 5 ingredients in a food processor; pulse 5 times or until finely chopped. Add avocado; process until smooth. Sprinkle with cilantro. Yield: 4 servings (serving size: about ¼ cup).

CALORIES 85; **FAT** 7.7g (sat 1.2g, mono 4.8g, poly 1g); **PROTEIN** 1.1g; **CARB** 4.8g; **FIBER** 2.7g; **CHOL** 0mg; **IRON** 0.6mg; **SODIUM** 77mg; **CALC** 9mg

Loaded Potato Soup

4 (6-ounce) red potatoes
2 teaspoons olive oil
½ cup prechopped onion
1¼ cups fat-free, lower-sodium chicken broth
3 tablespoons all-purpose flour
2 cups 1% low-fat milk, divided
¼ cup reduced-fat sour cream
½ teaspoon salt
¼ teaspoon freshly ground black pepper
3 bacon slices, halved
⅓ cup shredded cheddar cheese
4 teaspoons thinly sliced green onions

1. Pierce potatoes with a fork. Microwave at HIGH 13 minutes or until tender. Cut in half; cool slightly.
2. While potatoes cook, heat oil in a saucepan over medium-high heat. Add onion; sauté 3 minutes. Add broth. Combine flour and ½ cup milk; add to pan with 1½ cups milk. Bring to a boil; stir often. Cook 1 minute. Remove from heat; stir in sour cream, salt, and pepper.
3. Arrange bacon on a paper towel on a microwave-safe plate. Cover with a paper towel; microwave at HIGH 4 minutes. Crumble bacon.
4. Discard potato skins. Coarsely mash potatoes into soup. Top with cheese, green onions, and bacon. Yield: 4 servings (serving size: about 1¼ cups).

CALORIES 325; **FAT** 11.1g (sat 5.2g, mono 4.5g, poly 0.8g); **PROTEIN** 13.2g; **CARB** 43.8g; **FIBER** 3g; **CHOL** 27mg; **IRON** 1.3mg; **SODIUM** 670mg; **CALC** 261mg

Quick & Easy • Kid Friendly
Cider-Glazed Chicken with Browned Butter–Pecan Rice

1 (3.5-ounce) bag boil-in-bag brown rice (such as Uncle Ben's)
2 tablespoons butter, divided
1 pound chicken breast cutlets (about 4 cutlets)
3/4 teaspoon salt, divided
1/4 teaspoon freshly ground black pepper
1/2 cup refrigerated apple cider
1 teaspoon Dijon mustard
1/4 cup chopped pecans
2 tablespoons chopped fresh flat-leaf parsley

1. Cook rice according to package directions in a small saucepan, omitting salt and fat; drain.
2. While rice cooks, melt 1 teaspoon butter in a large heavy skillet over medium-high heat. Sprinkle chicken with 1/4 teaspoon salt and pepper. Add chicken to pan; cook 3 minutes on each side or until done. Remove from pan. Add cider and mustard to pan, scraping pan to loosen browned bits; cook 2 to 3 minutes or until syrupy. Add chicken to pan, turning to coat. Remove from heat; set aside.
3. Melt remaining 5 teaspoons butter in saucepan over medium-high heat; cook 2 minutes or until browned and fragrant. Lower heat to medium; add pecans, and cook 1 minute or until toasted, stirring frequently. Add rice and remaining 1/2 teaspoon salt; toss well to coat. Serve rice with chicken. Sprinkle with parsley. Yield: 4 servings (serving size: 1 cutlet and about 1/2 cup rice).

CALORIES 333; FAT 13g (sat 4.4g, mono 4.9g, poly 2.2g); PROTEIN 29.1g; CARB 24.2g; FIBER 1.9g; CHOL 81mg; IRON 1.5mg; SODIUM 601mg; CALC 23mg

Quick & Easy • Kid Friendly
Spiced Pork Tenderloin with Sautéed Apples

Sweet spices coat the tenderloin, while apples get a savory treatment. Serve with a spinach salad.

1/2 teaspoon salt
1/4 teaspoon ground coriander
1/4 teaspoon freshly ground black pepper
1/8 teaspoon ground cinnamon
1/8 teaspoon ground nutmeg
1 pound pork tenderloin, trimmed and cut crosswise into 12 pieces
Cooking spray
2 tablespoons butter
2 cups thinly sliced unpeeled Braeburn or Gala apple
1/3 cup thinly sliced shallots
1/8 teaspoon salt
1/4 cup apple cider
1 teaspoon fresh thyme leaves

1. Heat a large cast-iron skillet over medium-high heat. Combine first 5 ingredients; sprinkle spice mixture evenly over pork. Coat pan with cooking spray. Add pork to pan; cook 3 minutes on each side or until desired degree of doneness. Remove pork from pan, and keep warm.
2. Melt butter in pan; swirl to coat. Add apple, shallots, and 1/8 teaspoon salt; sauté 4 minutes or until apple starts to brown. Add apple cider to pan, and cook 2 minutes or until apple is crisp-tender. Stir in thyme. Serve apple mixture with pork. Yield: 4 servings (serving size: 3 pork medallions and about 1/2 cup apple mixture).

CALORIES 234; FAT 9.7g (sat 5g, mono 3.2g, poly 0.7g); PROTEIN 24.4g; CARB 12.3g; FIBER 1.5g; CHOL 89mg; IRON 1.7mg; SODIUM 468mg; CALC 18mg

BUDGET COOKING
FEED 4 FOR LESS THAN $10

Spend very little for some of the big flavors of fall.

Make Ahead
Lamb Tagine

$2.45 per serving, $9.79 total
Serve this Moroccan-style lamb stew with 2 cups hot cooked couscous.

Cooking spray
1 (1-pound) boneless leg of lamb roast, trimmed and cut into 1/2-inch cubes
3/4 teaspoon kosher salt, divided
1 1/2 cups chopped onion
1 teaspoon ground cumin
1/2 teaspoon ground cinnamon
1/2 teaspoon ground red pepper
6 garlic cloves, coarsely chopped
2 tablespoons honey
1 tablespoon tomato paste
1/2 cup dried apricots, quartered
1 (14-ounce) can fat-free, lower-sodium beef broth

1. Heat a Dutch oven over medium-high heat. Coat pan with cooking spray. Sprinkle lamb evenly with 1/2 teaspoon salt. Add lamb to pan; sauté 4 minutes, turning to brown on all sides. Remove from pan. Add onion; sauté 4 minutes, stirring frequently. Add remaining 1/4 teaspoon salt, cumin, and next 3 ingredients; sauté 1 minute, stirring constantly. Stir in honey and tomato paste; cook 30 seconds, stirring frequently. Return lamb to pan. Add apricots and broth; bring to a boil. Cover, reduce heat, and simmer 1 hour or until lamb is tender, stirring occasionally. Yield: 4 servings (serving size: 1 cup).

CALORIES 395; FAT 17.8g (sat 8.3g, mono 7g, poly 0.8g); PROTEIN 28.3g; CARB 30g; FIBER 3.2g; CHOL 90mg; IRON 3.7mg; SODIUM 617mg; CALC 71mg

Roasted Cauliflower Pasta

$1.84 per serving, $7.37 total

Fruity, briny olives add meaty flavor to this meatless one-dish meal.

2 tablespoons butter
2 tablespoons olive oil
2 medium shallots, peeled and cut into wedges
1 (1½-pound) head cauliflower, trimmed and cut into florets
⅓ cup sliced Spanish olives
½ teaspoon salt
½ teaspoon crushed red pepper
5 garlic cloves, crushed
12 ounces uncooked penne (tube-shaped pasta)
3 tablespoons coarsely chopped fresh parsley
1 ounce fresh pecorino Romano cheese, shaved

1. Place a small heavy roasting pan in oven. Preheat oven to 450°.
2. Remove preheated pan from oven. Add butter and oil to pan; swirl to coat. Add shallots and cauliflower to pan; toss to coat. Bake at 450° for 10 minutes. Add olives and next 3 ingredients to pan; toss to combine. Bake an additional 7 minutes or until cauliflower is tender and browned.
3. Cook pasta in boiling water 7 minutes or until almost tender. Drain pasta through a sieve over a bowl, reserving ½ cup pasta cooking liquid. Return pasta to pan over medium-high heat. Add reserved cooking liquid and cauliflower mixture; toss. Cook 2 minutes or until pasta is al dente, stirring occasionally. Remove from heat; sprinkle with parsley, and garnish with cheese. Yield: 4 servings (serving size: 2 cups).

CALORIES 531; **FAT** 18g (sat 6.4g, mono 8.6g, poly 1.3g); **PROTEIN** 18.3g; **CARB** 77.4g; **FIBER** 8g; **CHOL** 22mg; **IRON** 4.1mg; **SODIUM** 701mg; **CALC** 156mg

Mushroom and Sausage Ragù with Polenta

$2.49 per serving, $9.95 total

Cook the polenta while the ragù simmers so everything will be ready and hot at the same time. Use mild sausage, if you prefer.

1½ tablespoons olive oil, divided
8 ounces hot turkey Italian sausage
½ cup chopped onion
1 pound cremini mushrooms, sliced
2 large garlic cloves, minced
¼ teaspoon kosher salt, divided
1 (14.5-ounce) can no-salt-added diced tomatoes, undrained
2½ cups fat-free, lower-sodium chicken broth
1½ cups water
1 cup uncooked polenta
4 ounces ⅓-less-fat cream cheese
1 tablespoon butter

1. Heat a skillet over medium-high heat. Add 1½ teaspoons oil to pan; swirl to coat. Remove sausage from casings. Add sausage to pan; sauté 3 minutes or until browned, stirring to crumble. Remove sausage from pan.
2. Add remaining 1 tablespoon oil to pan; swirl to coat. Add onion; sauté 3 minutes, stirring occasionally. Add mushrooms; sauté 4 minutes, stirring occasionally. Add garlic; sauté 1 minute, stirring constantly. Stir in sausage, ⅛ teaspoon salt, and tomatoes; bring to a simmer. Reduce heat to medium; simmer gently 15 minutes.
3. Bring broth and 1½ cups water to a boil in a medium saucepan. Add polenta, stirring well. Reduce heat to medium, and simmer 20 minutes or until thick, stirring occasionally. Stir in remaining ⅛ teaspoon salt, cheese, and butter. Serve with sausage mixture. Yield: 4 servings (serving size: 1 cup polenta and 1 cup ragù).

CALORIES 428; **FAT** 18.7g (sat 8.4g, mono 8.5g, poly 1.4g); **PROTEIN** 18.2g; **CARB** 46g; **FIBER** 4.6g; **CHOL** 53mg; **IRON** 3.3mg; **SODIUM** 821mg; **CALC** 74mg

WINE NOTE: At $3.99, who wouldn't jump for joy about the La Granja 360 Tempranillo (Carinena, Spain, 2008). Although a tad tight upon opening, this wine mellows to unveil a touch of licorice, tart cherry, and a dry spice rack concoction that echoes the mushrooms' depth, stands up to the spice of the sausage, and complements the creamy polenta.

Chicken and Rice

$2.41 per serving, $9.63 total

1 tablespoon olive oil
8 bone-in chicken thighs, skinned
¾ teaspoon salt
¼ teaspoon ground black pepper
2 cups chopped onion
1 carrot, thinly sliced
8 ounces cremini mushrooms, sliced
4 garlic cloves, minced
1 cup long-grain white rice
Cooking spray
1 cup fat-free, lower-sodium chicken broth
¼ cup water
3 tablespoons heavy whipping cream
⅓ cup (1½ ounces) grated fresh pecorino Romano cheese

1. Preheat oven to 350°.
2. Heat oil in a skillet over medium-high heat. Sprinkle chicken with salt and pepper. Add 4 chicken thighs to pan; sauté 3 minutes on each side or until browned. Remove chicken from pan. Repeat with remaining chicken.
3. Add onion and carrot to pan; sauté 4 minutes. Add mushrooms; sauté 5 minutes. Add garlic; sauté 1 minute, stirring constantly. Add rice; sauté 1 minute. Spoon rice mixture into a 13 x 9–inch baking dish coated with cooking spray; stir in broth, ¼ cup water, and cream. Arrange chicken over rice mixture; sprinkle with cheese. Bake at 350° for 45 minutes or until chicken is done. Yield: 4 servings (serving size: 2 chicken thighs and ½ cup rice mixture).

CALORIES 519; **FAT** 16.3g (sat 6.4g, mono 6.3g, poly 2.1g); **PROTEIN** 37.3g; **CARB** 53.5g; **FIBER** 2.9g; **CHOL** 141mg; **IRON** 3.8mg; **SODIUM** 717mg; **CALC** 188mg

KITCHEN HOW-TO

Make Ahead • Kid Friendly

Caramel Apples

Gooey homemade caramel may take a little time, but it's totally worth the effort.

16 wooden sticks
16 small apples, chilled
2 cups granulated sugar
½ cup light-colored corn syrup
½ cup water
2 cups half-and-half
2 teaspoons vanilla extract
¼ teaspoon salt

1. Push wooden sticks into top of chilled apples. Return apples to refrigerator until caramel is ready for dipping.
2. Place sugar, corn syrup, and ½ cup water in a large saucepan; boil, stirring until dissolved. Boil, without stirring, 9 minutes or until light golden.
3. Combine half-and-half, vanilla, and salt; slowly stir into pan. Boil until candy thermometer reaches 235° (45 minutes), stirring frequently.
4. Pour caramel into a bowl sitting in a hot water bath. Swirl apples in caramel, and place on baking sheet lined with wax paper. Yield: 16 apples (serving size: 1 apple).

CALORIES 221; FAT 3.7g (sat 2.2g, mono 1g, poly 0.2g); PROTEIN 1.2g; CARB 48.9g; FIBER 2.5g; CHOL 11mg; IRON 0.2mg; SODIUM 57mg; CALC 40mg

KIDS LOVE THIS SWEET-TART, BUTTERY TREAT.

RECIPE MAKEOVER
BAKING BETTER BROWNIES

How much do you love those fudgy squares? Now picture them lighter, but just as scrumptious.

Brownies are a piece of cake to make, but as rich-tasting as any buttery bar cookie—and in the portions that are served at some bakeries and coffee-houses, they could sugar-daze an entire family. Our goal was to retain the deep chocolate yum in a much slimmer profile.

We tinkered with all kinds of leaven-ers, egg whites, and even, in a fit of mad creativity, mayonnaise. Then we back-tracked to traditional ingredients and found, as sometimes happens, the best results. Unsweetened cocoa provides a hit of pure chocolate flavor with less saturated fat and fewer calories. A little butter, one egg, and two egg yolks serve to keep our brownies rich, while a bit of low-fat milk enhances moisture. The result? A treat that delivers the fudge-bar goods in a package that cuts out three-quarters of the fat and slims the calories by more than half.

OLD WAY	OUR WAY
366 calories per serving	147 calories per serving
23.8 grams total fat	6.1 grams total fat
14.1 grams saturated fat	3.6 grams saturated fat
Plenty of dark chocolate	Dark chocolate plus cocoa powder
Tons of butter and sugar	Enough butter and sugar for richness
Gargantuan portion	Just-right portion

Make Ahead • Kid Friendly

Fudgy Brownies

4.5 ounces all-purpose flour (about 1 cup)
½ cup unsweetened cocoa
¼ teaspoon salt
⅓ cup butter
2 ounces dark chocolate, chopped
1 cup granulated sugar
¼ cup 1% low-fat milk
1 teaspoon vanilla extract
2 large egg yolks
1 large egg
Cooking spray

1. Preheat oven to 350°.
2. Weigh or lightly spoon flour into a dry measuring cup; level with a knife. Combine flour, cocoa, and salt in a medium bowl; stir with a whisk.
3. Place butter and chocolate in a medium microwave-safe bowl, and microwave at HIGH 45 seconds, stirring every 15 seconds. Stir until smooth, and set aside. Cool slightly. Add sugar and next 4 ingredients; stir with a whisk to combine. Add butter mixture to flour mixture, stirring just until combined. Pour batter into an 8-inch square metal baking pan coated with cooking spray. Bake at 350° for 20 minutes or until a wooden pick inserted in center comes out almost clean. Yield: 16 squares (serving size: 1 square).

CALORIES 147; FAT 6.1g (sat 3.6g, mono 1.5g, poly 0.3g); PROTEIN 2.3g; CARB 22.4g; FIBER 1.3g; CHOL 47mg; IRON 1mg; SODIUM 73mg; CALC 15mg

HOLIDAY COOKBOOK

This year we took classic holiday and entertaining recipes and made them healthier, of course, but also quicker or more contemporary—and sometimes all three. And we've added international recipes to liven the mix. Tradition, renewed: Enjoy the blessings of family, food, and friends.

STARTERS & DRINKS

In starters and drinks there's a quick pâté, rich with cherries and a hint of bacon. There's, yes, an update of the classic holiday cheese ball, and for a sweet drink, light eggnog.

Quick & Easy
Pomegranate Gin Sling

A classic gin sling is dressed for festive parties when made with seasonal pomegranate juice and decorated with crimson pomegranate fruit. Both simple syrup and agave syrup are widely available at liquor stores. To make your own simple syrup, boil 2 parts sugar to 1 part water, stirring just until sugar dissolves; reduce until thickened. Cool before using.

1/4 cup gin
1/4 cup pomegranate juice, chilled
1 tablespoon agave syrup or simple syrup
1 teaspoon fresh lime juice
8 pomegranate seeds
2 lime slices

1. Combine first 4 ingredients; divide evenly between 2 chilled glasses; divide seeds between glasses. Garnish with lime slices. Yield: 2 servings.

CALORIES 115; FAT 0g; PROTEIN 0.2g; CARB 13.5g; FIBER 0.1g; CHOL 0mg; IRON 0.1mg; SODIUM 4mg; CALC 7mg

Make Ahead • Vegetarian
Date, Walnut, and Blue Cheese Ball

1 cup (4 ounces) crumbled blue cheese
1 tablespoon nonfat buttermilk
5 ounces fat-free cream cheese, softened
3 ounces 1/3-less-fat cream cheese, softened
3 tablespoons minced pitted Medjool dates (2 to 3 dates)
1 tablespoon minced shallots
1/2 teaspoon grated lemon rind
1/4 teaspoon kosher salt
1/4 teaspoon black pepper
1/4 cup minced fresh flat-leaf parsley
2 1/2 tablespoons finely chopped walnuts, toasted

1. Place first 4 ingredients in a large bowl; beat with a mixer at medium speed 2 minutes or until smooth and creamy. Add dates and next 4 ingredients; beat at medium speed until well blended, scraping sides of bowl as necessary.
2. Spoon cheese mixture onto a large sheet of plastic wrap. Form into a ball, using a rubber spatula. Wrap cheese ball in plastic wrap; chill overnight.
3. Combine parsley and walnuts in a shallow dish. Unwrap cheese ball; gently roll in nut mixture, coating well. Place on a serving plate. Serve immediately, or cover and refrigerate until ready to serve. Yield: 14 servings (serving size: 2 tablespoons).

CALORIES 78; FAT 4.8g (sat 2.6g, mono 1.2g, poly 0.7g); PROTEIN 4.2g; CARB 5.3g; FIBER 0.5g; CHOL 12mg; IRON 0.2mg; SODIUM 229mg; CALC 74mg

Make Ahead
Eggnog

No need to forgo one of the holidays' favorite indulgences—creamy, rich eggnog. This version gives you all the satisfaction of the full-fat version without the guilt, and it can be made up to a week in advance.

3 1/2 cups 1% low-fat milk
1/2 cup fat-free sweetened condensed milk
1 tablespoon all-purpose flour
1/4 teaspoon grated whole nutmeg
1/8 teaspoon salt
2 large egg yolks
1/4 cup bourbon
2 tablespoons brandy
1 teaspoon vanilla extract
Additional grated whole nutmeg (optional)

1. Combine first 5 ingredients in a medium saucepan. Bring to a boil over medium heat, stirring constantly with a whisk. Place egg yolks in a medium bowl. Gradually whisk one-third of hot milk mixture into egg yolks. Add yolk mixture to remaining hot milk mixture, stirring with a whisk. Cook over medium heat 1 minute or until slightly thickened. Pour into a pitcher; stir in bourbon, brandy, and vanilla.
2. Cover surface of eggnog with wax paper; refrigerate at least 4 hours or overnight. Garnish with additional nutmeg, if desired. Yield: 8 servings (serving size: 1/2 cup).

CALORIES 147; FAT 2.3g (sat 1.1g, mono 0.8g, poly 0.2g); PROTEIN 5.8g; CARB 18.1g; FIBER 0g; CHOL 58mg; IRON 0.2mg; SODIUM 113mg; CALC 187mg

Orange Salad with Arugula and Oil-Cured Olives

This minty salad makes a refreshing first course for a holiday feast. Every component of the salad can be prepared and ready to serve well in advance. Make the dressing several hours or even a day ahead; just bring to room temperature before tossing with arugula. Buy washed and ready-to-use arugula. It takes time to peel and slice the oranges, so do that ahead, arranging the oranges on a plate and covering with plastic wrap. If you can find fresh blood oranges, they make a stunning presentation.

Dressing:
1/3 cup thinly sliced shallots
1/4 cup fresh lemon juice
2 tablespoons finely chopped fresh mint leaves
1 teaspoon sugar
2 teaspoons Dijon mustard
1/4 teaspoon kosher salt
1/8 teaspoon freshly ground black pepper
1/4 cup extra-virgin olive oil
Salad:
1 (5-ounce) package arugula
5 oranges, peeled and thinly sliced crosswise
30 oil-cured black olives
1/2 teaspoon kosher salt
Freshly ground black pepper (optional)

1. To prepare dressing, combine first 7 ingredients in a medium bowl, stirring with a whisk. Gradually add oil, stirring constantly with a whisk.
2. To prepare salad, combine arugula and three-fourths of dressing in a large bowl; toss gently to coat. Arrange about 1/2 cup arugula mixture on each of 10 salad plates; arrange orange slices evenly over salads. Drizzle remaining one-fourth of dressing evenly over salads; top each salad with 3 olives. Sprinkle evenly with 1/2 teaspoon salt and additional black pepper, if desired. Serve immediately. Yield: 10 servings.

CALORIES 132; FAT 9.5g (sat 1.6g, mono 6.6g, poly 1.3g); PROTEIN 1g; CARB 16.7g; FIBER 5.3g; CHOL 0mg; IRON 0.5mg; SODIUM 404mg; CALC 56mg

Quick Liver Pâté

This pared-down pâté is based on liverwurst. Use Usinger's or Schaller & Weber brand liverwurst for best results.

1/4 cup dried tart cherries
2 slices thick-cut bacon
2 tablespoons finely chopped shallots
1 teaspoon finely chopped fresh thyme
1/4 teaspoon salt
1/8 teaspoon black pepper
1 garlic clove, finely chopped
1 bay leaf
2 tablespoons cognac
1/4 cup whipped cream cheese
8 ounces liverwurst
2 tablespoons chopped unsalted dry-roasted pistachios (optional)

1. Place cherries in a small saucepan with just enough water to cover; bring to a simmer over medium heat. Cook 3 minutes or until soft. Drain cherries; cool slightly, and finely chop.
2. Cook bacon in a small skillet over medium heat until crisp; remove bacon from pan, reserving 1 tablespoon drippings in pan. Finely chop bacon.
3. Add shallots and next 5 ingredients to drippings in pan; cook 2 minutes or until softened, stirring occasionally. Remove pan from heat. Add cognac, scraping pan to loosen browned bits.
4. Remove and reserve bay leaf. Place shallot mixture, cream cheese, and liverwurst in a food processor; process until smooth. Place in a small bowl; stir in bacon and cherries. Place bay leaf on top of pâté. Cover surface of pâté with plastic wrap; chill at least 8 hours. Sprinkle with pistachios before serving, if desired. Yield: 12 servings (serving size: about 2½ tablespoons).

CALORIES 110; FAT 8.3g (sat 3.5g, mono 3.3g, poly 0.7g); PROTEIN 3.4g; CARB 3.5g; FIBER 0.4g; CHOL 36mg; IRON 1.4mg; SODIUM 266mg; CALC 12mg

Roasted Chestnut Soup with Thyme Cream

Roasting bottled chestnuts brings back fresh-toasted flavor.

3 cups whole roasted bottled chestnuts
2 cups chopped yellow onion
3/4 cup thinly sliced carrot
1 tablespoon olive oil
6 cups fat-free, lower-sodium chicken broth
5/8 teaspoon kosher salt, divided
1/4 teaspoon freshly ground black pepper
1/3 cup heavy whipping cream
1½ teaspoons chopped fresh thyme leaves

1. Preheat oven to 400°.
2. Place chestnuts on a jelly-roll pan. Bake at 400° for 15 minutes. Place chestnuts in a large bowl; cool to room temperature.
3. Combine onion, carrot, and oil on pan; toss to coat vegetables. Bake at 400° for 1 hour or until tender, stirring occasionally. Add to chestnuts; stir in broth. Pour half of broth mixture into a blender; blend until smooth. Pour pureed mixture into a Dutch oven. Repeat procedure with remaining broth mixture. Stir in ½ teaspoon salt and pepper. Place pan over medium-high heat; bring to a simmer. Reduce heat, and simmer 20 minutes.
4. Place cream in a medium bowl; beat with a mixer at high speed until soft peaks form. Add remaining ⅛ teaspoon salt; beat at high speed until stiff peaks form (do not overbeat). Ladle about ¾ cup soup into each of 10 bowls; top each serving with about 1 tablespoon cream. Sprinkle with thyme. Serve immediately. Yield: 10 servings.

CALORIES 172; FAT 5.5g (sat 2.3g, mono 2.3g, poly 0.7g); PROTEIN 3.5g; CARB 27.5g; FIBER 3.6g; CHOL 11mg; IRON 0.8mg; SODIUM 364mg; CALC 38mg

CRUNCHY CELERY, SWEET-CHEWY RAISINS, AND GRASSY PARSLEY CREATE A FRESH, WHIMSICAL SALAD COURSE.

Make Ahead • Vegetarian

Celery and Parsley Salad with Golden Raisins

What a light, crunchy, and refreshing palate cleanser to accompany a holiday meal!

2/3 cup golden raisins
1/2 cup white balsamic vinegar
7 cups thinly diagonally sliced celery (including leaves)
4 cups loosely packed fresh flat-leaf parsley leaves
3/4 teaspoon kosher salt
1/2 teaspoon black pepper
1/4 cup extra-virgin olive oil

1. Combine raisins and vinegar in a small microwave-safe bowl; microwave at HIGH 1 minute and 15 seconds or until raisins are plump. Drain raisins in a sieve over a medium bowl, reserving 3 tablespoons vinegar; discard remaining vinegar.
2. Combine raisins, celery, and parsley in a large bowl.
3. Add salt and pepper to reserved vinegar, stirring with a whisk. Gradually add oil, stirring constantly with a whisk. Drizzle dressing over salad; toss gently to coat. Cover and refrigerate at least 2 hours. Yield: 12 servings (serving size: about 2/3 cup).

CALORIES 87; **FAT** 5g (sat 0.7g, mono 3.4g, poly 0.8g); **PROTEIN** 1.4g; **CARB** 11g; **FIBER** 2g; **CHOL** 0mg; **IRON** 1.5mg; **SODIUM** 191mg; **CALC** 60mg

Oyster Bisque

Thickened with vegetables and finished with a touch of half-and-half, this silky soup makes an elegant first course. Small oysters, such as Kumamoto or Prince Edward Island, are preferable, but you can use your favorite fresh raw oysters.

2 dozen small oysters
1 quart seafood stock (such as Kitchen Basics)
1 3/4 cups diced peeled red potato
1 cup diced peeled parsnip
1 cup chopped leek, white part only
1/4 teaspoon salt
1/8 teaspoon freshly ground black pepper
1/4 cup half-and-half
2 tablespoons coarsely chopped fresh chives

1. Shuck oysters, reserving oyster liquid. Strain oyster liquid through a sieve over a large saucepan. Pick over oysters to remove any bits of shell. Chill oysters.
2. Add stock and next 5 ingredients to oyster liquid; bring to a simmer. Cover and simmer 20 minutes or until vegetables are tender. Place half of stock mixture in a blender. Remove center piece of blender lid (to allow steam to escape); secure blender lid on blender. Place a clean towel over opening in blender lid (to avoid splatters). Blend until smooth. Pour into a large bowl. Repeat procedure with remaining stock mixture.
3. Return pureed soup to saucepan; bring to a simmer. Stir in half-and-half and oysters; simmer 2 minutes or until oyster edges curl; stir in chives. Yield: 8 servings (serving size: about 3/4 cup).

CALORIES 82; **FAT** 2.2g (sat 1.1g, mono 0.5g, poly 0.3g); **PROTEIN** 4.5g; **CARB** 11.7g; **FIBER** 1.6g; **CHOL** 18mg; **IRON** 2.2mg; **SODIUM** 320mg; **CALC** 34mg

MAIN DISHES

Kid Friendly

Apple and Cranberry Turkey Roulade
(pictured on page 271)

Prepare the filling, stuff the tenderloins, roll, and tie them a day ahead. Let them stand at room temperature for 20 minutes before cooking. You won't need any cranberry sauce, as the sweet and savory stuffing does double duty. If you can't find turkey tenderloins, use skinless, boneless turkey breast halves.

2 slices center-cut bacon, chopped
1 cup chopped onion
1 teaspoon chopped fresh rosemary
1 teaspoon salt, divided
3/4 teaspoon freshly ground black pepper, divided
1 1/2 cups fat-free, lower-sodium chicken broth, divided
3 cups chopped peeled Granny Smith apple (about 2 medium)
1/2 cup dried cranberries
3 (12-ounce) turkey tenderloins
2 teaspoons canola oil
3 fresh rosemary sprigs
1 tablespoon all-purpose flour

1. Preheat oven to 325°.
2. Cook bacon in a large skillet over medium heat 7 minutes or until bacon begins to brown, stirring occasionally. Stir in onion, chopped rosemary, 1/4 teaspoon salt, and 1/4 teaspoon pepper; cook 8 minutes or until onion begins to brown, stirring occasionally. Stir in 1 cup broth, apples, and cranberries. Bring to a boil. Reduce heat, and simmer until liquid evaporates and apples are almost tender (about 15 minutes), stirring occasionally. Remove from heat, and cool slightly. Set aside 1 cup apple mixture.
3. Slice turkey tenderloins lengthwise, cutting to, but not through, the other side. Open halves, laying tenderloins flat. Place each tenderloin between 2 sheets of heavy-duty plastic wrap; pound to 1/2-inch thickness using a meat mallet or small heavy skillet. Discard plastic wrap.

4. Sprinkle remaining ¾ teaspoon salt and remaining ½ teaspoon black pepper evenly over both sides of tenderloins. Spread ⅓ cup apple mixture over each tenderloin; roll up jelly-roll fashion, starting with long sides. Secure at 2-inch intervals with twine.

5. Heat oil in a large Dutch oven over medium-high heat. Add tenderloins; cook 6 minutes, turning to brown on all sides. Add remaining ½ cup broth and rosemary sprigs; bring to a boil. Cover and bake at 325° for 25 minutes or until a thermometer inserted in thickest portion registers 165°. Remove tenderloins from pan; let stand 10 minutes. Slice crosswise into ½-inch-thick slices.

6. Strain cooking liquid through a fine mesh sieve over a bowl; discard solids. Combine flour and ¼ cup cooking liquid, stirring with a whisk until smooth. Return flour mixture and remaining cooking liquid to pan. Stir in reserved 1 cup apple mixture; bring to a boil. Cook 1 minute or until thickened, stirring constantly. Serve with turkey. Yield: 8 servings (serving size: about 2 turkey slices and ¼ cup sauce).

CALORIES 220; FAT 3.3g (sat 0.8g, mono 0.6g, poly 0.9g); PROTEIN 33.2g; CARB 12.8g; FIBER 1.4g; CHOL 82mg; IRON 1.8mg; SODIUM 486mg; CALC 23mg

---

THANKSGIVING MENU

serves 12

Apple-Poblano Whole Roast Turkey
(recipe at right)

Framboise Cranberry Sauce
(page 345)

Sausage and Sourdough Bread Stuffing
(page 339)

Rosemary Mashed Sweet Potatoes with Shallots
(page 340)

Citrus Green Beans with Pine Nuts
(page 341)

(To serve 12, triple the green beans, double the sweet potatoes, and make 1.5 times the cranberry sauce.)

Apple-Poblano Whole Roast Turkey

Turkey Brine:
8 cups water
8 cups apple cider
½ cup packed brown sugar
⅓ cup kosher salt
2 tablespoons black peppercorns, crushed
1 jalapeño pepper, quartered lengthwise
Turkey:
1 (12-pound) organic fresh turkey
1 tablespoon brown sugar
1 teaspoon kosher salt
¾ teaspoon dried oregano
½ teaspoon ground cumin
½ teaspoon freshly ground black pepper
½ teaspoon ground red pepper
¼ teaspoon ground coriander
3 Gala apples, quartered and divided
2 poblano chiles, quartered, seeded, and divided
1 cup fresh cilantro leaves
Cooking spray
3 cups water
3 cups fat-free, lower-sodium chicken broth, divided
2 tablespoons butter
2 cups chopped onion
5 garlic cloves, crushed
1.13 ounces all-purpose flour (about ¼ cup)
1 cup apple cider
3 tablespoons chopped fresh cilantro
2 tablespoons fresh lime juice

1. To prepare brine, combine first 6 ingredients, stirring well.
2. To prepare turkey, remove giblets and neck from turkey; reserve neck and giblets. Trim excess fat. Place a turkey-sized oven bag inside a second bag to form a double thickness. Place bags in a large stockpot. Place turkey inside inner bag. Add brine. Secure bags with several twist ties. Refrigerate 12 to 24 hours.
3. Preheat oven to 500°.
4. Remove turkey from bags; discard brine. Pat turkey dry. Starting at neck cavity, loosen skin from breast and drumsticks by inserting fingers, gently pushing between skin and meat. Combine 1 tablespoon brown sugar and next 6 ingredients in a small bowl. Rub spice mixture under loosened skin over flesh.

Place 1 apple quarter and 1 poblano quarter in the neck cavity; close skin flap. Arrange 5 apple quarters, 1 poblano quarter, and 1 cup cilantro leaves in body cavity. Secure legs with kitchen twine. Arrange turkey, neck, and giblets on rack of a roasting pan coated with cooking spray. Arrange remaining 6 apple quarters and 6 poblano quarters in bottom of roasting pan coated with cooking spray. Place rack with turkey in pan. Roast at 500° for 30 minutes.
5. Reduce oven temperature to 350° (do not remove turkey from oven). Place a foil tent over turkey breast. Pour 3 cups water in bottom of pan.
6. Bake turkey at 350° for 40 minutes. Rotate turkey, and baste with ¾ cup broth. Roast 30 minutes; rotate turkey. Baste with ¾ cup broth. Roast 20 minutes or until a thermometer inserted in thickest part of thigh registers 165°. Remove from oven. Place turkey, breast side down, on a jelly-roll pan or cutting board. Let stand, covered, 30 minutes. Serve breast side up. Chop giblets. Discard neck.
7. Strain pan drippings through a sieve into a bowl; discard solids. Melt butter in a large saucepan over medium-high heat. Add onion; sauté 5 minutes or until translucent. Stir in reserved chopped giblets and garlic; sauté 2 minutes, stirring constantly. Weigh or lightly spoon flour into a dry measuring cup, and level with a knife. Sprinkle flour over onion mixture; sauté 2 minutes, stirring frequently. Add drippings, remaining 1½ cups broth, and 1 cup apple cider; bring to a boil. Reduce heat, and simmer until reduced to 3 cups (about 15 minutes). Strain through a sieve over a bowl, and discard solids. Stir in chopped cilantro and lime juice. Discard turkey skin; carve. Serve with gravy. Yield: 12 servings (serving size: 6 ounces turkey and about ¼ cup gravy).

CALORIES 302; FAT 3.4g (sat 1.7g, mono 0.5g, poly 0.8g); PROTEIN 55g; CARB 9.7g; FIBER 0.6g; CHOL 154mg; IRON 3.1mg; SODIUM 637mg; CALC 31mg

WHAT WINES GO WITH THESE HOLIDAY MEATS?

PORK

Lean pork tenderloin benefits from juicy fruit found in riesling and pinot gris. Pork chops or standing rib roasts have a little more fat, so they work with lighter red wines, like pinot noir from Burgundy, or one of Austria's food-friendly red wines from grapes like Blaufränkisch and St. Laurent.

HAM

A meat like salty, smoky ham craves wines that have a lot of fruit. German or American riesling is an ideal choice, as are many American rosé wines, with their berry fruit and light tannins. Sparkling wines are an elegant option, and you might consider a demi-sec style with a hint of sweetness—especially nice with good ham.

Feeling adventurous? If the answer is yes, seek out a soft, fruity, and fizzy red lambrusco from Italy's Emilia Romagna, which is a classic partner for the region's similarly salty prosciutto.

TURKEY

The best pairings with turkey are determined by the accompanying ingredients that flavor the bird. Unoaked whites, like riesling and pinot gris, and lighter-bodied reds, like pinot noir and Beaujolais, work well with fruity flavors, such as those found in Apple and Cranberry Turkey Roulade (page 334).

Savory notes and herbal accents, meanwhile, work better with a particularly versatile red: barbera. This affordable wine from Italy's Piedmont region is a good choice for the crisp acidity, berry fruit, and light tannins, which won't overpower the bird's lean white meat.

LAMB

Lamb pairs beautifully with any number of reds. Syrah, in an Australian shiraz or an earthy and spicy red from France's Rhône Valley, is a can't-miss choice. Lamb also works well with New Zealand pinot noir; fruity, young rioja joven from Spain; and softly fruity, occasionally smoky merlot and a cabernet sauvignon from Argentina.

BEEF

There are two ways to think about pairing wine with beef. The first is to mirror the flavor profile. An earthy dish will pair well with a smoky, earthy wine, like tempranillo from the Ribera del Duero, for example.

The other approach is to balance the fat in the dish with a red wine's tannin structure. A tannic wine, mouth-puckering on its own, cuts through and balances rich meat in a very pleasant way. With a fatty steak like rib-eye, seek out a tannic, young California cabernet. For a cut like filet mignon, look for a soft, silky merlot from Bordeaux.

Quick & Easy

Beef Filets with Mushroom Sauce and Parmesan Popovers

Popovers:

1 cup fat-free milk

2 large eggs

4.5 ounces all-purpose flour (about 1 cup)

½ teaspoon kosher salt

Cooking spray

2 tablespoons grated fresh Parmigiano-Reggiano cheese

Sauce:

½ ounce dried porcini mushrooms

2 cups boiling water

1½ teaspoons olive oil

⅓ cup thinly sliced shallots

4 ounces sliced fresh cremini mushroom caps (about 2 cups)

2 garlic cloves, minced

¼ teaspoon kosher salt

¼ teaspoon black pepper

½ cup pinot noir

2 tablespoons all-purpose flour

2 tablespoons chopped fresh sage

1 tablespoon chopped fresh thyme

Beef:

1 tablespoon olive oil

6 (4-ounce) beef tenderloin steaks

1 teaspoon kosher salt

½ teaspoon black pepper

1. Preheat oven to 400°.

2. To prepare popovers, combine milk and eggs in a bowl. Weigh or lightly spoon 4.5 ounces flour into a dry measuring cup; level with a knife. Add flour and ½ teaspoon salt to milk mixture, stirring well; let stand 30 minutes. Place a popover tin in oven for 5 minutes. Remove tin from oven; lightly coat popover cups with cooking spray. Spoon ¼ cup batter into each cup, and sprinkle with cheese. Bake at 400° for 35 minutes or until puffed and golden.

3. To prepare sauce, place porcini mushrooms in a bowl, and cover with 2 cups boiling water. Let stand 15 minutes. Drain through a sieve over a bowl, reserving mushrooms and soaking liquid. Heat a large saucepan over medium-high heat. Add 1½ teaspoons oil to pan; swirl to coat. Add shallots to pan; sauté 1 minute, stirring frequently. Add cremini mushrooms to pan; sauté 2 minutes or until almost tender. Add garlic; sauté 30 seconds, stirring constantly. Stir in porcini, ¼ teaspoon salt, and ¼ teaspoon pepper, and sauté 1 minute, stirring frequently. Add wine to pan; bring to a boil. Cook until liquid almost evaporates (about 3 minutes). Sprinkle 2 tablespoons flour over mushroom mixture; cook 1 minute, stirring frequently.

Gradually add reserved mushroom soaking liquid, stirring constantly; bring to a simmer. Cook 2 minutes or until slightly thick, stirring frequently. Stir in sage and thyme.

4. To prepare beef, heat a large skillet over medium-high heat. Add 1 tablespoon oil. Sprinkle beef with 1 teaspoon salt and ½ teaspoon pepper. Add beef to pan; sauté 4 minutes on each side or until desired degree of doneness. Remove from pan, and let stand 10 minutes. Yield: 6 servings (serving size: 1 steak, 1 popover, and ⅓ cup sauce).

CALORIES 405; **FAT** 19.9g (sat 6.9g, mono 9.1g, poly 1.2g); **PROTEIN** 29.7g; **CARB** 24.8g; **FIBER** 1.5g; **CHOL** 146mg; **IRON** 3.6mg; **SODIUM** 675mg; **CALC** 113mg

WINE NOTE: Beef Filets with Mushroom Sauce and Parmesan Popovers pairs well with 2007 Bodeaga Catena Zapata Malbec from Mendoza, Argentina ($20). It has a smooth tobacco aroma that opens into deep waves of vanilla and cassis—filled out by roasted plums and caramelized grapefruit.

Pork Tenderloin Agrodolce

¾ cup balsamic vinegar
½ cup green olives
½ cup dried sweet cherries
¼ cup fat-free, lower-sodium chicken broth
2 tablespoons sugar
6 garlic cloves
3 fresh thyme sprigs
1 pound cipollini onions, peeled
1 teaspoon kosher salt, divided
2 tablespoons olive oil
2 (1-pound) pork tenderloins, trimmed
½ teaspoon freshly ground black pepper

1. Preheat oven to 500°.
2. Combine first 8 ingredients in a medium saucepan; stir in ½ teaspoon salt. Bring to a boil. Cover, reduce heat to medium-low, and cook 45 minutes or until onions are almost tender, stirring occasionally. Uncover, increase heat to medium-high, and cook 7 minutes or until thick, stirring frequently.
3. Heat oil in a large cast-iron skillet over medium-high heat. Sprinkle pork evenly with remaining ½ teaspoon salt and pepper. Add pork to pan, and cook 1 minute. Turn pork over. Place pan in oven; bake at 500° for 12 minutes or until a thermometer registers 155° (slightly pink). Remove from oven; let stand 10 minutes. Slice pork crosswise into ½-inch-thick slices. Serve with sauce. Yield: 8 servings (serving size: 3 ounces pork and about ⅓ cup sauce).

CALORIES 238; **FAT** 7.7g (sat 1.7g, mono 4.5g, poly 1.1g); **PROTEIN** 18.9g; **CARB** 21.4g; **FIBER** 2.3g; **CHOL** 55mg; **IRON** 1.4mg; **SODIUM** 416mg; **CALC** 43mg

WINE NOTE: With subtle fragrance of black tea and charred embers of warm fire, Montepulciano d'Abruzzo, Cantina Zaccagnini, 2007, il vino "dal tralcetto" ($14), keeps up with both the sweet and sour notes in this dish.

Easy Coq au Vin

Serve with noodles, rice, or boiled potatoes.

4 slices applewood-smoked bacon, cut into
    1-inch pieces
4 chicken drumsticks, skinned
4 chicken thighs, skinned
¼ teaspoon kosher salt
½ teaspoon freshly ground black pepper,
    divided
1 cup finely chopped onion
½ cup finely chopped celery
½ cup finely chopped carrot
1 teaspoon finely chopped fresh thyme
4 garlic cloves, minced
2 bay leaves
1 tablespoon tomato paste
1 (750-milliliter) bottle red wine
2 cups fat-free, lower-sodium chicken broth
1 tablespoon extra-virgin olive oil
8 ounces button mushrooms, quartered
6 ounces frozen pearl onions
¼ cup chopped fresh flat-leaf parsley

1. Cook bacon in a large, deep skillet over medium heat until crisp. Remove bacon from pan. Reserve 2 tablespoons drippings in pan. Sprinkle chicken with salt and ¼ teaspoon pepper. Add chicken to drippings in pan; cook 5 minutes on each side or until browned. Remove chicken from pan.
2. Add onion and next 5 ingredients to pan; cook 5 minutes. Add tomato paste; cook 1 minute. Stir in wine; bring to a boil. Cook 10 minutes or until reduced by half, stirring occasionally. Return chicken to pan. Add broth; bring to a simmer. Cover and simmer 35 minutes or until chicken is done, turning after 20 minutes. Remove chicken from pan; cover.
3. Heat a large heavy skillet over medium heat. Add oil to pan, and swirl to coat. Add button mushrooms and pearl onions; sprinkle with remaining ¼ teaspoon pepper. Cook 10 minutes or until golden, stirring occasionally. Remove from heat.
4. Place chicken cooking liquid over medium-high heat; bring to a boil. Cook until reduced by half (about 10 minutes). Discard bay leaves. Stir in mushroom mixture. Return chicken to pan; simmer 5 minutes or until heated.

Sprinkle with parsley and bacon. Yield: 4 servings (serving size: 1 thigh, 1 drumstick, and about 1 cup sauce).

CALORIES 319; **FAT** 13.2g (sat 3.6g, mono 4.1g, poly 1.8g); **PROTEIN** 33.9g; **CARB** 16.1g; **FIBER** 2.7g; **CHOL** 115mg; **IRON** 3.2mg; **SODIUM** 727mg; **CALC** 78mg

Crab Eggs Benedict

This Benedict is served with a "mock" hollandaise sauce made from mayonnaise and buttermilk. Serve with steamed asparagus.

⅓ cup reduced-fat buttermilk
⅓ cup canola mayonnaise
½ teaspoon grated lemon rind
1 tablespoon fresh lemon juice
1½ teaspoons Dijon mustard
¼ teaspoon freshly ground black pepper
1½ teaspoons butter
1 tablespoon white wine vinegar
8 large eggs
4 English muffins, toasted
8 ounces fresh lump crabmeat, shell pieces
    removed
Cracked black pepper
2 tablespoons chopped fresh chives
    (optional)
1 tablespoon chopped fresh tarragon
    (optional)

1. Combine first 6 ingredients in a small saucepan over low heat, stirring well with a whisk. Add butter; stir until butter melts. Keep warm.
2. Add water to a large skillet, filling two-thirds full. Bring to a boil; reduce heat, and simmer. Add 1 tablespoon white wine vinegar. Break each egg into a custard cup; pour gently into pan. Cook 3 minutes or until desired degree of doneness. Place 1 muffin, cut sides up, on each of 4 plates; divide crab among muffins. Remove eggs from pan using a slotted spoon. Gently place 1 egg on each muffin half. Top each serving with about 3 tablespoons sauce. Sprinkle with cracked pepper. Garnish with chives and tarragon, if desired. Yield: 4 servings.

CALORIES 503; **FAT** 28.2g (sat 5.7g, mono 12.4g, poly 5.7g); **PROTEIN** 32.1g; **CARB** 29.5g; **FIBER** 1.9g; **CHOL** 478mg; **IRON** 4.8mg; **SODIUM** 711mg; **CALC** 127mg

Rabbit à la Moutard

Rabbit is becoming more popular and accessible. Look for it at specialty markets or sometimes frozen in supermarkets. You can also order online from dartagnan.com. Cook the egg noodles as the rabbit finishes simmering.

2 tablespoons canola oil, divided
1 cup coarsely chopped peeled turnip
1 cup chopped peeled carrot
1 (3-pound) rabbit, cut into 8 pieces
3/4 teaspoon kosher salt
1/2 teaspoon freshly ground black pepper
1/2 teaspoon whole black peppercorns
2 fresh thyme sprigs
2 whole cloves
1 bay leaf
1 tablespoon unsalted butter
2 cups chopped leek
1 cup finely chopped celery
1/2 cup finely chopped shallots
1 tablespoon minced garlic
1 cup dry white wine
2 cups fat-free, lower-sodium chicken broth
2 tablespoons stone-ground mustard
1 tablespoon Dijon mustard
1/4 cup heavy cream
1 tablespoon chopped fresh chives
1 tablespoon chopped fresh flat-leaf parsley
1 1/2 teaspoons chopped fresh tarragon
12 ounces fettuccine or egg noodles

1. Preheat oven to 350°.
2. Heat a Dutch oven over medium-high heat. Add 1 1/2 teaspoons oil to pan; swirl to coat. Stir in turnip and carrot; sauté 12 minutes or until vegetables begin to brown, stirring occasionally. Remove vegetables from pan; set aside.
3. Sprinkle both sides of rabbit evenly with salt and pepper. Add 2 1/4 teaspoons oil to pan; swirl to coat. Add half of rabbit; cook 3 minutes on each side or until browned. Remove rabbit from pan; keep warm. Repeat procedure with remaining 2 1/4 teaspoons oil and rabbit. Wipe pan clean with a paper towel.
4. Place peppercorns and next 3 ingredients on a double layer of cheesecloth. Gather edges of cheesecloth together; tie securely. Melt butter in pan over medium heat. Add leek and next 3 ingredients; sauté 8 minutes or until tender, stirring occasionally. Add wine and cheesecloth bag; bring to a boil. Stir in broth and stone-ground mustard; return rabbit to pan. Cover and bake at 350° for 40 minutes or until rabbit is done.
5. Remove rabbit from bones; shred with 2 forks. Discard bones. Strain cooking liquid through a fine mesh sieve over a bowl; discard solids. Return meat and cooking liquid to pan. Stir in reserved turnip mixture, Dijon mustard, and cream; bring to a boil. Cook 15 minutes or until vegetables are tender and liquid is slightly thick, stirring occasionally. Remove from heat; stir in chives, parsley, and tarragon. Discard cheesecloth bag.
6. Cook noodles according to package directions, omitting salt and fat; drain. Place about 1 cup hot cooked noodles in each of 6 shallow bowls, and divide rabbit mixture evenly among servings. Yield: 6 servings.

CALORIES 521; FAT 20.2g (sat 7.1g, mono 7.9g, poly 4.2g); PROTEIN 36g; CARB 47.7g; FIBER 3.9g; CHOL 159mg; IRON 4.6mg; SODIUM 577mg; CALC 80mg

Quick Cassoulet

2 tablespoons olive oil
4 (4-inch) pork sausages, sliced (about 8 ounces)
4 (4-inch) lamb sausages, sliced (about 6 1/2 ounces)
4 (4-inch) duck sausages, sliced (about 8 1/2 ounces)
Cooking spray
1 cup finely chopped onion
1/2 cup finely chopped carrot
1/2 cup finely chopped celery
2 tablespoons minced garlic
1/2 teaspoon freshly ground black pepper
1/4 teaspoon salt
1/2 cup dry white wine
1/4 cup cognac or brandy
5 fresh thyme sprigs
2 bay leaves
2 whole cloves
1 cup fat-free, lower-sodium chicken broth
3 (15-ounce) cans cannellini beans, rinsed and drained
1 (14.5-ounce) can no-salt-added diced tomatoes, drained
1 (4-ounce) piece French bread baguette
1 1/2 tablespoons unsalted butter

1. Preheat oven to 325°.
2. Heat a large Dutch oven over medium heat. Add oil to pan; swirl to coat. Add sausages; cook 6 minutes, stirring frequently. Remove sausages from pan using a slotted spoon; drain. Wipe pan with paper towels, leaving browned bits on bottom of pan. Coat pan with cooking spray. Add onion and next 5 ingredients; cook 8 minutes, stirring occasionally. Add wine and cognac; bring to a boil. Cook 10 minutes or until liquid almost evaporates, scraping pan to loosen browned bits.
3. Place thyme sprigs, bay leaves, and cloves on a double layer of cheesecloth. Gather edges of cheesecloth together; tie securely. Add cheesecloth bag, broth, beans, and tomatoes to vegetable mixture; stir to combine. Return sausages to pan; stir. Bring mixture to a boil, and remove from heat.
4. Place bread in a food processor; pulse 10 times or until fine crumbs measure 2 cups. Melt butter in a large skillet over medium-high heat. Add crumbs to pan; sauté 5 minutes or until golden, stirring frequently. Sprinkle crumbs evenly over bean mixture. Bake at 325° for 40 minutes. Discard cheesecloth bag before serving. Yield: 8 servings (serving size: about 1 cup).

CALORIES 423; FAT 26.8g (sat 9.7g, mono 10.8g, poly 2.8g); PROTEIN 14.7g; CARB 27g; FIBER 5.4g; CHOL 73mg; IRON 4.4mg; SODIUM 685mg; CALC 55mg

A MIXTURE OF MEAT ADDS DEPTH TO THIS CASSOULET, AND THE MEDLEY OF SAUSAGES SPEEDS UP THE COOK TIME WITHOUT SACRIFICING FLAVOR.

Spicy Moroccan Chickpeas

¼ cup extra-virgin olive oil
3 large garlic cloves, peeled
2 cups thinly sliced red onion
½ cup dried apricots, sliced
1 tablespoon ras el hanout (Moroccan spice blend) or garam masala
1 teaspoon salt
¾ teaspoon black pepper
¼ teaspoon crushed red pepper
1 (3-inch) cinnamon stick
½ cup water
1½ teaspoons grated lemon rind
1½ tablespoons fresh lemon juice
2 (15-ounce) cans chickpeas (garbanzo beans), rinsed and drained
1 (28-ounce) can no-salt-added whole tomatoes, undrained and chopped
6 cups escarole, torn into 1-inch pieces
1 cup fresh cilantro leaves
¼ cup fresh mint leaves
½ cup roasted whole almonds, coarsely chopped
4 cups hot cooked couscous

1. Heat a large skillet over medium-high heat. Add oil to pan; swirl to coat. Add garlic; cook 1 minute, stirring constantly. Remove garlic from pan using a slotted spoon; discard or reserve for another use. Add onion and next 6 ingredients to pan; sauté 7 minutes or until onion is lightly browned, stirring occasionally. Add ½ cup water and next 4 ingredients; bring to a boil. Reduce heat, and simmer 7 minutes, stirring occasionally.
2. Stir in escarole; simmer 1 minute or until escarole wilts. Remove from heat. Sprinkle with cilantro and mint; top with almonds. Serve over couscous. Yield: 8 servings (serving size: ¾ cup chickpea mixture, 2 tablespoons cilantro, 1½ teaspoons mint, 1 tablespoon almonds, and ½ cup couscous).

CALORIES 406; **FAT** 12.7g (sat 1.5g, mono 8.1g, poly 2.4g); **PROTEIN** 12.6g; **CARB** 62.8g; **FIBER** 9.6g; **CHOL** 0mg; **IRON** 3.8mg; **SODIUM** 512mg; **CALC** 127mg

SIDE DISHES

Sausage and Sourdough Bread Stuffing

10 cups (½-inch) cubed sourdough bread (about 1 pound)
3 tablespoons unsalted butter
2 cups finely chopped onion
1 cup finely chopped celery
15 ounces hot turkey Italian sausage, casings removed
3 tablespoons chopped fresh thyme
3 tablespoons chopped fresh sage
3 tablespoons chopped fresh flat-leaf parsley
½ teaspoon black pepper
2 cups fat-free, lower-sodium chicken broth
1 cup water
1 large egg, lightly beaten
Cooking spray

1. Preheat oven to 350°.
2. Arrange bread in single layers on 2 jelly-roll pans. Bake at 350° for 20 minutes or until golden, rotating pans after 10 minutes. Turn oven off; leave pans in oven for 30 minutes or until bread is crisp.
3. Melt butter in a large skillet over medium heat. Add onion and celery; cook 11 minutes or until tender, stirring occasionally. Transfer vegetables to a large bowl. Add sausage to pan. Increase heat; sauté 8 minutes or until browned, stirring to crumble. Remove sausage from pan using a slotted spoon; add sausage to vegetable mixture. Stir in bread, thyme, and next 3 ingredients; toss. Combine broth, 1 cup water, and egg, stirring well. Drizzle broth mixture over bread mixture; toss. Spoon mixture into a 13 x 9–inch glass or ceramic baking dish coated with cooking spray; cover with foil. Bake at 350° for 25 minutes. Uncover and cook 20 minutes or until browned. Yield: 14 servings (serving size: about ¾ cup).

CALORIES 149; **FAT** 6.3g (sat 1.8g, mono 1g, poly 0.5g); **PROTEIN** 7.2g; **CARB** 15.9g; **FIBER** 1.3g; **CHOL** 34mg; **IRON** 1.6mg; **SODIUM** 396mg; **CALC** 61mg

HOW TO MAKE SAUSAGE AND SOURDOUGH BREAD STUFFING

1 Spread bread cubes on two jelly-roll pans in a single layer. Bake for 20 minutes or until golden brown. Rotate the pans halfway through cooking so the cubes brown evenly. Turn the heat off, and leave bread in oven for 30 minutes.

2 Place toasted bread in a large bowl. Add sautéed onion and celery, browned sausage, herbs and spices, broth, water, and egg, tossing well to combine. Spoon into a broiler-safe 13 x 9-inch baking dish coated with cooking spray.

3 Cover baking dish with aluminum foil, and bake at 350° for 25 minutes. Uncover and cook 20 minutes or until browned. For extra crispness, broil for 1 to 2 minutes. Watch closely; stuffing can burn quickly.

Rosemary Mashed Sweet Potatoes with Shallots

You don't need butter and cream to make wonderfully creamy mashed sweet potatoes. Heart-healthy olive oil adds flavor and silkiness without saturated fat.

2 tablespoons plus 2 teaspoons extra-virgin olive oil, divided
3/4 cup thinly sliced shallots (about 2 large)
2 teaspoons brown sugar
2 pounds sweet potatoes, peeled and diced
1 tablespoon finely chopped fresh rosemary
1/2 teaspoon coarse sea salt
1/4 teaspoon black pepper

1. Heat 2 tablespoons oil in a medium skillet over low heat. Add shallots to pan, and cook 5 minutes, stirring occasionally. Sprinkle with sugar; cook 20 minutes or until shallots are golden, stirring occasionally.
2. Place potato in a medium saucepan; cover with water. Bring to a boil; cook 8 minutes or until tender. Drain. Place potato in a large bowl; beat with a mixer at medium speed until smooth. Add rosemary, salt, and pepper; beat until blended. Spoon into a bowl; top with shallots, and drizzle with remaining 2 teaspoons oil. Yield: 6 servings (serving size: about ½ cup).

CALORIES 202; **FAT** 6.3g (sat 0.9g, mono 4.5g, poly 0.9g); **PROTEIN** 2.9g; **CARB** 34.9g; **FIBER** 4.8g; **CHOL** 0mg; **IRON** 1.2mg; **SODIUM** 278mg; **CALC** 55mg

A BIT OF BACON ADDS A RICH NOTE TO BITTER BRUSSELS SPROUTS.

Brussels Sprouts Gratin

Braise the Brussels sprouts and toast the bread-crumbs up to a day ahead. Then assemble and reheat before serving.

2 slices hickory-smoked bacon
4 large shallots, thinly sliced
2 pounds Brussels sprouts, trimmed and halved
1 cup water
1/2 teaspoon kosher salt, divided
1/4 teaspoon freshly ground black pepper
Cooking spray
1 (2-ounce) slice French bread baguette
3 tablespoons butter

1. Preheat broiler.
2. Cook bacon in a large skillet over medium heat until crisp. Remove bacon from pan, reserving drippings; crumble. Increase heat to medium-high. Add shallots to drippings in pan; sauté 2 minutes or until tender, stirring occasionally. Add Brussels sprouts and 1 cup water; bring to a boil. Cover pan loosely with aluminum foil; cook 6 minutes or until Brussels sprouts are almost tender. Uncover and remove from heat. Sprinkle with ¼ teaspoon salt and pepper; toss to combine. Spoon Brussels sprouts mixture into a 2-quart broiler-safe glass or ceramic baking dish coated with cooking spray.
3. Place bread in a food processor, and process until finely ground. Melt butter in skillet over medium-high heat. Add breadcrumbs and remaining ¼ teaspoon salt to pan; sauté 2 minutes or until toasted, stirring frequently. Sprinkle breadcrumb mixture over Brussels sprouts mixture. Broil 3 minutes or until golden and thoroughly heated. Yield: 6 servings (serving size: about ¾ cup).

CALORIES 133; **FAT** 5.8g (sat 3.2g, mono 1.1g, poly 0.3g); **PROTEIN** 5.9g; **CARB** 17.9g; **FIBER** 4.6g; **CHOL** 14mg; **IRON** 2.1mg; **SODIUM** 280mg; **CALC** 57mg

Wild Rice Dressing with Roasted Chestnuts and Cranberries

2 cups uncooked wild rice
2 cups fat-free, lower-sodium chicken broth
2 cups water
1/2 teaspoon kosher salt, divided
1½ cups whole roasted bottled chestnuts
1 cup sweetened dried cranberries
1½ tablespoons unsalted butter
1½ cups halved lengthwise and thinly sliced carrot
1½ cups chopped yellow onion
1¼ cups thinly sliced celery
1/2 cup minced fresh flat-leaf parsley
2 tablespoons minced fresh sage
1 tablespoon fresh thyme leaves
1/4 teaspoon black pepper
Cooking spray

1. Preheat oven to 400°.
2. Combine rice, broth, 2 cups water, and ¼ teaspoon salt in a saucepan; bring to a boil. Partially cover, reduce heat, and simmer 40 minutes or until rice is tender, stirring occasionally. (Do not drain.) Place rice in a large bowl; cover.
3. Arrange chestnuts on a baking sheet. Bake at 400° for 15 minutes. Cool slightly; cut chestnuts into quarters.
4. Place cranberries in a small bowl; cover with hot water. Let stand 20 minutes or until soft. Drain and add to rice.
5. Melt butter in a large nonstick skillet over medium heat. Add carrot, onion, and celery; cook 15 minutes or until vegetables are tender, stirring occasionally. Stir in parsley, sage, and thyme; remove from heat. Add to rice mixture. Stir in remaining ¼ teaspoon salt, chestnuts, and pepper.
6. Spoon rice mixture into a 13 x 9–inch glass or ceramic baking dish coated with cooking spray. Cover and bake at 400° for 10 minutes or until thoroughly heated. Yield: 12 servings (serving size: about ¾ cup).

CALORIES 213; **FAT** 2.4g (sat 1.1g, mono 0.6g, poly 0.5g); **PROTEIN** 5.5g; **CARB** 44.4g; **FIBER** 4.5g; **CHOL** 4mg; **IRON** 1.2mg; **SODIUM** 182mg; **CALC** 31mg

Quick & Easy • Vegetarian

Garlic-Roasted Kale

Roasting kale is amazing—the leaves turn from a dusty dark green to dark emerald with brown-tinged curly edges that crunch. This vegetable side is delicious served hot from the oven; the leaves lose their crisp texture as the dish stands.

3 tablespoons extra-virgin olive oil
½ teaspoon kosher salt
3 garlic cloves, thinly sliced
1½ pounds kale, stems removed and
   chopped
2 teaspoons sherry vinegar

1. Arrange oven racks in center and lower third of oven. Preheat oven to 425°. Place 2 large jelly-roll pans in oven for 5 minutes.
2. Combine first 4 ingredients in a large bowl; toss to coat. Divide kale mixture evenly between hot pans, spreading with a silicone spatula to separate leaves. Bake at 425° for 7 minutes. Stir kale, and rotate pans. Bake an additional 5 minutes or until edges of leaves are crisp and kale is tender.
3. Place kale in a large bowl. Drizzle with vinegar; toss to combine. Serve immediately. Yield: 10 servings (serving size: about ⅔ cup).

CALORIES 72; **FAT** 4.7g (sat 0.7g, mono 3g, poly 0.8g); **PROTEIN** 2.3g; **CARB** 7.1g; **FIBER** 1.4g; **CHOL** 0mg; **IRON** 1.2mg; **SODIUM** 125mg; **CALC** 93mg

Quick & Easy • Kid Friendly
Vegetarian

Citrus Green Beans with Pine Nuts

1 pound green beans, trimmed
2 teaspoons extra-virgin olive oil
¾ cup sliced shallots (about 2 large)
1 teaspoon grated orange rind
1 tablespoon fresh orange juice
¼ teaspoon black pepper
⅛ teaspoon coarse sea salt
1 tablespoon pine nuts, toasted

1. Cook green beans in boiling water 2 minutes. Drain and rinse under cold running water. Drain well.

2. Heat a large nonstick skillet over medium-high heat. Add oil to pan; swirl to coat. Add shallots; sauté 2 minutes or until tender. Add green beans; stir well. Add rind and next 3 ingredients; sauté 2 minutes. Spoon onto a platter; sprinkle with nuts. Yield: 4 servings (serving size: 1 cup).

CALORIES 86; **FAT** 3.8g (sat 0.4g, mono 2.1g, poly 1.1g); **PROTEIN** 2.5g; **CARB** 12.8g; **FIBER** 4.5g; **CHOL** 0mg; **IRON** 1mg; **SODIUM** 76mg; **CALC** 68mg

Make Ahead • Kid Friendly
Vegetarian

Winter Jeweled Fruit Salad

In Mexico, copas de frutas (fruit cups) are popular street food. They typically consist of fresh fruit sprinkled with lime juice and chili powder and are the inspiration for this jewel-colored fruit salad. Jicama (pronounced HEE-kah-mah), also known as a Mexican potato or turnip, tastes like a cross between an apple and a potato and adds crunch to the salad.

½ cup pomegranate seeds (about
   1 pomegranate)
½ cup julienne-cut peeled jicama
⅓ cup sliced seeded kumquats (about
   6 medium)
2 medium ripe mangoes, peeled and cut
   into thin slices
2 tangerines or clementines, peeled and
   sectioned
2 blood oranges, peeled and sectioned
1 pear, thinly sliced
2 tablespoons fresh lime juice
2 tablespoons honey
¼ teaspoon ground red pepper
⅛ teaspoon coarse sea salt

1. Combine first 7 ingredients in a large bowl; toss gently. Combine juice and remaining ingredients in a small bowl, stirring well with a whisk. Pour over fruit; toss gently to coat. Serve at room temperature. Yield: 8 servings (serving size: 1 cup).

CALORIES 118; **FAT** 0.4g (sat 0.1g, mono 0.1g, poly 0.1g); **PROTEIN** 1.3g; **CARB** 30g; **FIBER** 4.2g; **CHOL** 0mg; **IRON** 0.4mg; **SODIUM** 37mg; **CALC** 39mg

DESSERTS

Make Ahead • Kid Friendly

Apple Kuchen

3 Fuji apples, peeled, cored, and sliced
2 tablespoons fresh lemon juice
1 cup granulated sugar, divided
½ teaspoon ground cinnamon
½ teaspoon salt, divided
6.75 ounces all-purpose flour (about 1½ cups)
1 teaspoon baking powder
½ cup butter, softened and divided
3 ounces cream cheese, softened
2 large eggs
1 teaspoon vanilla extract
⅔ cup nonfat buttermilk
½ cup chopped walnuts, toasted
Cooking spray
¼ cup apricot preserves
2 teaspoons apple juice

1. Preheat oven to 350°.
2. Combine apples and juice; toss. Add ¼ cup sugar, cinnamon, and ¼ teaspoon salt; toss to combine.
3. Weigh or lightly spoon flour into dry measuring cups; level with a knife. Combine flour, remaining ¼ teaspoon salt, and baking powder in a bowl, stirring well. Place remaining ¾ cup sugar, 6 tablespoons butter, and cheese in a bowl; beat with a mixer at medium speed until light and fluffy. Add eggs, beating well. Stir in vanilla. Add flour mixture and buttermilk alternately to butter mixture, beginning and ending with flour mixture, beating just until combined. Stir in walnuts.
4. Scrape batter into a 13 x 9–inch metal baking pan coated with cooking spray. Arrange apples over batter. Melt remaining 2 tablespoons butter; brush over apples. Bake at 350° for 45 minutes or until set.
5. Combine preserves and juice, and microwave at HIGH 30 seconds or until melted, stirring once. Brush apricot mixture over apples; cool. Cut into 15 squares. Yield: 15 servings (serving size: 1 square).

CALORIES 251; **FAT** 11.4g (sat 5.6g, mono 2.8g, poly 2.3g); **PROTEIN** 3.9g; **CARB** 35.1g; **FIBER** 1.7g; **CHOL** 51mg; **IRON** 1mg; **SODIUM** 185mg; **CALC** 58mg

Make Ahead • Kid Friendly

Crema Catalana

2 cups whole milk
3 (3 x 1–inch) strips fresh lemon rind
1 (2-inch) cinnamon stick
7 tablespoons sugar, divided
2 tablespoons cornstarch
⅛ teaspoon salt
3 large egg yolks

1. Heat milk over medium-high heat in a small heavy saucepan to 180° or until tiny bubbles form around edge (do not boil). Remove from heat. Add rind and cinnamon; cover and let stand 30 minutes. Discard rind and cinnamon.
2. Combine ¼ cup sugar, cornstarch, and salt in a small bowl, stirring well with a whisk. Add ¼ cup milk to sugar mixture, stirring until smooth. Return milk mixture to pan; cook over medium-low heat 7 minutes or until almost thick, stirring constantly with a whisk. Place egg yolks in a small bowl. Gradually pour one-third of hot milk mixture into yolks, stirring constantly with a whisk. Carefully return yolk mixture to pan. Cook over low heat 4 minutes or until a thermometer registers 180°, stirring constantly with a whisk. Divide custard evenly among 6 (4-ounce) custard cups; press plastic wrap against surface of custard. Chill at least 4 hours.
3. Remove plastic; discard. Sprinkle remaining 3 tablespoons sugar evenly over custards. Holding a kitchen blowtorch about 2 inches from top of each custard, heat sugar, moving torch back and forth, until sugar is completely melted and caramelized (about 1 minute). Serve immediately or within 1 hour. Yield: 6 servings.

CALORIES 142; FAT 4.9g (sat 2.3g, mono 1.6g, poly 0.5g); PROTEIN 3.9g; CARB 21g; FIBER 0g; CHOL 111mg; IRON 0.3mg; SODIUM 86mg; CALC 103mg

Make Ahead • Kid Friendly

Pumpkin Pie Pudding

½ cup sugar, divided
2 tablespoons cornstarch
1¾ cups 1% low-fat milk
1 large egg
½ cup canned unsweetened pumpkin
1 teaspoon vanilla extract
½ teaspoon ground cinnamon
⅛ teaspoon salt
⅛ teaspoon ground nutmeg
Cooking spray
¼ cup chopped walnuts
Dash of salt
¼ cup heavy whipping cream

1. Combine 6 tablespoons sugar and 2 tablespoons cornstarch in a medium saucepan over medium heat. Combine milk and egg, stirring well with a whisk. Gradually add milk mixture to sugar mixture, stirring constantly, and bring to a boil. Cook 1 minute, stirring constantly. Remove from heat.
2. Combine pumpkin and next 4 ingredients in a bowl, stirring well. Slowly add pumpkin mixture to milk mixture, whisking constantly. Place pan over low heat, and cook 3 minutes or until thoroughly heated, stirring constantly (do not boil). Divide pudding evenly among 4 dessert bowls, and cover surface of pudding with plastic wrap. Chill.
3. Line a baking sheet with foil, and coat foil with cooking spray. Place remaining 2 tablespoons sugar, walnuts, and a dash of salt in a small nonstick skillet; cook over low heat until sugar dissolves and is golden (about 3 minutes), stirring frequently to coat nuts. Transfer mixture to prepared baking sheet, and cool completely. Coarsely chop nuts.
4. Place cream in a bowl. Beat with a mixer at high speed until stiff peaks form. Top each serving with 2 tablespoons whipped cream and about 1 tablespoon nuts. Yield: 4 servings.

CALORIES 288; FAT 12.8g (sat 5g, mono 3.1g, poly 3.9g); PROTEIN 6.9g; CARB 38g; FIBER 1.6g; CHOL 78mg; IRON 1mg; SODIUM 190mg; CALC 167mg

Make Ahead • Kid Friendly

Chocolate Walnut Tart

A riff on the classic pecan pie, this dessert is rich, chocolaty, and a little fancier with its free-standing fluted sides. Of course, you can use a 9-inch pie plate if you don't have a tart pan with a removable bottom.

⅓ cup packed brown sugar
2 tablespoons all-purpose flour
¼ teaspoon salt
½ cup light-colored corn syrup
2 tablespoons butter (at room temperature)
4 ounces bittersweet chocolate, finely chopped
1 cup walnut halves
½ teaspoon vanilla extract
3 large eggs, lightly beaten
½ (15-ounce) package refrigerated pie dough (such as Pillsbury)
Cooking spray

1. Arrange 1 rack in lower third of oven. Preheat oven to 350°.
2. Combine first 3 ingredients in a medium heavy saucepan over medium heat, stirring well with a whisk. Stir in corn syrup, and bring mixture to a boil. Cook 1 minute, stirring occasionally until sugar dissolves. Remove from heat. Add butter and chocolate; stir with a whisk until smooth. Cool to room temperature; stir in walnuts, vanilla, and eggs.
3. Fit pie dough into a 9-inch round removable-bottom tart pan coated with cooking spray, pressing dough into bottom and up sides of pan.
4. Spoon walnut mixture into prepared crust. Bake on bottom oven rack at 350° for 33 minutes or until set. Cool 20 minutes in pan on a wire rack. Remove sides of tart pan; slide tart onto a serving platter. Cut into wedges. Yield: 12 servings (serving size: 1 wedge).

CALORIES 292; FAT 18.3g (sat 5.9g, mono 5.1g, poly 6.2g); PROTEIN 4.2g; CARB 32.3g; FIBER 1.4g; CHOL 60mg; IRON 0.9mg; SODIUM 165mg; CALC 24mg

Ricotta Semifreddo

Semifreddo is an Italian term that refers to any number of frozen or chilled desserts. Here we offer a frozen orange-scented mousse made with ricotta cheese. It's worth the effort to search out the best ricotta you can find.

½ cup sugar
¼ cup fat-free milk
¼ cup honey
2 teaspoons grated orange rind
1½ teaspoons vanilla extract
⅛ teaspoon salt
3 ounces fat-free cream cheese, softened
1 (16-ounce) container part-skim ricotta cheese (such as Calabro)
½ cup chilled heavy cream
Fresh orange sections (optional)
Fresh currants (optional)

1. Line a 9 x 5–inch loaf pan with plastic wrap. Place first 8 ingredients in a blender; process until smooth. Pour mixture into a large bowl. Pour cream into a medium bowl, and beat with a mixer at high speed until stiff peaks form. Fold ¼ cup whipped cream into ricotta mixture. Fold in remaining cream.
2. Spoon mixture into prepared loaf pan. Cover with plastic wrap, and freeze at least 8 hours or until set. Remove from freezer, and let stand 20 minutes. Discard top piece of plastic wrap. Invert loaf pan onto a serving platter, and tap to remove semifreddo. Discard remaining plastic wrap, and slice semifreddo crosswise. Serve with orange sections and currants, if desired. Yield: 8 servings (serving size: 1 slice).

CALORIES 226; FAT 10.1g (sat 6.3g, mono 2.9g, poly 0.4g); PROTEIN 8.6g; CARB 25.8g; FIBER 0.1g; CHOL 39mg; IRON 0.3mg; SODIUM 176mg; CALC 193mg

Pear Tarte Tatin

2 tablespoons butter, divided
½ cup sugar, divided
4 peeled ripe Anjou pears, cored and halved lengthwise
1 tablespoon canola oil
5 (14 x 9–inch) sheets frozen phyllo dough, thawed
3 tablespoons crème fraîche

1. Preheat oven to 400°.
2. Coat a 10-inch cast-iron skillet with 1½ tablespoons butter. Sprinkle 6 tablespoons sugar into pan. Arrange 7 pear halves, cut sides up, in a circle in pan; place remaining pear half in center. Cover skillet, and place over medium-low heat. Cook, without stirring, 15 minutes or until sugar mixture is bubbly and caramelized. Place pan in oven. Bake at 400° for 5 minutes.
3. Place 1½ teaspoons butter and oil in a bowl. Microwave at HIGH 30 seconds or until butter melts. Lay 1 phyllo sheet horizontally on a flat work surface; brush lightly with butter mixture. Sprinkle 2 teaspoons sugar evenly over phyllo. Place next phyllo sheet vertically on top of first. Repeat procedure twice with remaining butter mixture, sugar, and phyllo, ending with phyllo. Fold edges to form a 9-inch circle.
4. Place phyllo circle in pan over pears, pressing gently. Bake at 400° for 16 minutes or until filling is bubbly and crust is browned. Remove from oven, and let stand 5 minutes. Place a plate upside-down on top of pan; invert tart onto plate. Cut tart into 6 wedges. Top each wedge with 1½ teaspoons crème fraîche. Yield: 6 servings.

CALORIES 258; FAT 10.3g (sat 4.4g, mono 2.9g, poly 1g); PROTEIN 2g; CARB 41.7g; FIBER 3g; CHOL 17mg; IRON 0.5mg; SODIUM 79mg; CALC 70mg

WINE NOTE: Match this tart with Muscat de Beaumes de Venise, 2006, from Domaine Durban ($26). Filled with the unctuous fragrance of pears and sweet citrus, the wine's balanced and bright acidity is a palate-cleansing drop of gold.

EXTRAS

Orange-Buttermilk Dinner Rolls

1¼ cups warm buttermilk (100° to 110°)
2 tablespoons sugar
1 tablespoon honey
1 package dry yeast
3 tablespoons butter, melted and divided
4 teaspoons grated orange rind
1 teaspoon kosher salt
14 ounces all-purpose flour (about 3 cups)
Cooking spray

1. Combine first 3 ingredients in bowl of an electric mixer. Sprinkle yeast over milk mixture; let stand 5 minutes or until bubbly. Stir in 2 tablespoons butter, rind, and salt. Weigh or lightly spoon flour into dry measuring cups; level with a knife. Add flour to yeast mixture; mix on low speed with a dough hook until a soft, elastic dough forms (about 5 minutes). Dough will be sticky. Place dough in a large bowl coated with cooking spray, turning to coat top. Cover and let rise in a warm place (85°) for 1 hour or until doubled in size.
2. Punch dough down; turn out onto a lightly floured surface. Cut dough into 13 equal pieces. Working with 1 piece at a time, roll dough into a ball by cupping your hand and pushing against dough and surface while rolling. Arrange dough balls 2 inches apart on a baking sheet coated with cooking spray. Brush lightly with remaining 1 tablespoon butter. Cover; let rise 1 hour or until doubled in size.
3. Preheat oven to 375°.
4. Bake at 375° for 20 minutes or until rolls are golden. Remove rolls from pan; cool slightly on a wire rack. Yield: 13 rolls (serving size: 1 roll).

CALORIES 163; FAT 3.7g (sat 2.2g, mono 0.7g, poly 0.2g); PROTEIN 4.2g; CARB 28.1g; FIBER 1g; CHOL 10mg; IRON 1.5mg; SODIUM 192mg; CALC 7mg

WRAP THIS FRUITED BREAD IN A TEA TOWEL AND TIE WITH A PRETTY RIBBON FOR A LOVELY HOMEMADE GIFT.

Make Ahead • Freezable • Kid Friendly
Vegetarian

Christmas Stollen
(pictured on page 270)

Order candied citron from amazon.com, or omit it and add extra dried apricots and increase lemon rind to 1 tablespoon.

16.9 ounces all-purpose flour (about 3³/₄ cups), divided
½ teaspoon salt
½ teaspoon freshly grated nutmeg
¼ cup fresh orange juice
2 tablespoons brandy
½ cup dried cherries
⅓ cup golden raisins
⅓ cup chopped dried apricots
½ cup warm 2% reduced-fat milk (100° to 110°)
¼ cup granulated sugar
1 package dry yeast
6 tablespoons butter, melted
2 large eggs, lightly beaten
½ cup diced candied citron
½ cup sliced almonds, toasted
1½ teaspoons grated lemon rind
Cooking spray
2 tablespoons 2% reduced-fat milk, divided
1 large egg
½ cup powdered sugar

1. Weigh or lightly spoon flour into dry measuring cups, and level with a knife. Combine 15.75 ounces (about 3½ cups) flour, salt, and nutmeg. Combine orange juice and brandy; microwave at HIGH 45 seconds. Add cherries, raisins, and apricots; let stand 20 minutes.

2. Combine warm milk, granulated sugar, and yeast; let stand 5 minutes. Stir butter and 2 eggs into yeast mixture. Stir in juice mixture, ½ cup citron, almonds, and rind. Add flour mixture to yeast mixture, stirring until a soft dough forms. Turn dough out onto a lightly floured surface. Knead 5 minutes or until dough is smooth and elastic, adding remaining ¼ cup flour, 1 tablespoon at a time, to prevent dough from sticking to hands (dough will feel sticky).

3. Place dough in a large bowl coated with cooking spray, turning to coat top. Cover and let rise in a warm place (85°) 1 hour or until doubled in size. Punch dough down. Divide dough into 2 equal portions; roll each into an 11 x 8–inch oval. Fold 1 short end toward center; fold other short end toward center until it overlaps first end. Place loaves, seam sides down, on a baking sheet lined with parchment paper. Cover and let rise 1 hour or until doubled in size.

4. Preheat oven to 350°.

5. Combine 1 tablespoon milk and 1 egg. Uncover dough, and brush gently with milk mixture. Bake at 350° for 32 minutes or until golden. Cool on wire racks. Combine 1 tablespoon milk and powdered sugar, stirring until smooth; drizzle over loaves. Yield: 24 servings (serving size: 1 slice).

CALORIES 168; FAT 4.8g (sat 2.2g, mono 1.7g, poly 0.5g); PROTEIN 3.8g; CARB 26.5g; FIBER 1.4g; CHOL 34mg; IRON 1.4mg; SODIUM 83mg; CALC 26mg

Make Ahead • Freezable • Vegetarian

Cheese and Chive Challah

The traditional yeasted egg bread is enriched even more by adding cheese to the dough. We love the flavor of fontina, but Gruyère or another Swiss cheese would also work.

1 cup warm 2% reduced-fat milk (100° to 110°)
1 teaspoon sugar
1 package dry yeast (about 2¼ teaspoons)
3 tablespoons butter, melted
1½ teaspoons salt
5 large egg yolks
3 large eggs
³/₄ cup (3 ounces) shredded aged fontina cheese
½ cup finely chopped fresh chives
10.7 ounces bread flour (about 2¼ cups)
13.5 ounces all-purpose flour (about 3 cups), divided
Cooking spray
1 large egg
2 tablespoons water
2 tablespoons grated fresh Parmigiano-Reggiano cheese

1. Combine first 3 ingredients in a large bowl; let stand 5 minutes or until bubbly. Stir in butter and next 3 ingredients. Stir in fontina and chives. Weigh or lightly spoon flours into dry measuring cups; level with a knife. Add 10.7 ounces bread flour (about 2¼ cups) and 12.4 ounces (about 2¾ cups) all-purpose flour to yeast mixture, stirring until a soft dough forms (dough will be sticky).

2. Turn dough out onto a lightly floured surface. Knead until smooth and elastic, adding remaining ¼ cup all-purpose flour, 1 tablespoon at a time, to prevent dough from sticking to hands. Place dough in a large bowl coated with cooking spray, turning to coat top. Cover with plastic wrap, and let rise in a warm place (85°), free from drafts, 45 minutes or until doubled in size. Punch down dough; cover and let rise 50 minutes or until doubled in size. (Gently press two fingers into dough. If indentation remains, dough has risen enough.)

3. Divide dough into 6 equal portions. Roll each portion into a ball. Roll each ball into a rope about 15 inches long. Place 3 ropes parallel to one another; braid ropes. Pinch ends together, and tuck under loaf. Repeat procedure with remaining 3 ropes. Place loaves on a baking sheet lined with parchment paper; coat with cooking spray. Cover and let rise 30 minutes or until doubled in size.

4. Preheat oven to 375°.

5. Combine 1 egg and 2 tablespoons water, stirring well with a whisk. Brush loaves gently with egg mixture. Sprinkle loaves evenly with Parmigiano-Reggiano. Bake at 375° for 25 minutes or until golden. Remove from baking sheet; cool on a wire rack. Yield: 24 servings (serving size: 1 slice).

CALORIES 160; **FAT** 4.7g (sat 2.3g, mono 1.5g, poly 0.5g); **PROTEIN** 6.2g; **CARB** 22.5g; **FIBER** 0.8g; **CHOL** 78mg; **IRON** 1.6mg; **SODIUM** 210mg; **CALC** 51mg

---

Quick & Easy • Make Ahead
Vegetarian

Framboise Cranberry Sauce

Belgian Framboise Lambic beer—a frothy, berry-colored beverage—adds an underlying sweetness that complements the cranberries.

1 (12-ounce) bottle Framboise Lambic beer
    (such as Lindemans)
½ cup sugar
1½ teaspoons grated orange rind
1 (12-ounce) package fresh cranberries

1. Bring beer to a boil in a medium saucepan over medium heat. Add sugar, rind, and cranberries; bring to a simmer. Cook 18 minutes or until slightly thick, stirring occasionally. Remove from heat; cool to room temperature. Spoon into a bowl; cover and chill. (Sauce will thicken as it chills.) Yield: 9 servings (serving size: ¼ cup).

CALORIES 81; **FAT** 0.1g (sat 0g, mono 0g, poly 0.1g); **PROTEIN** 0.2g; **CARB** 19.6g; **FIBER** 1.8g; **CHOL** 0mg; **IRON** 0.1mg; **SODIUM** 1mg; **CALC** 4mg

---

Make Ahead • Freezable • Kid Friendly
Vegetarian

Spiced Persimmon and Pecan Muffins

¾ cup chopped pecans, divided
5.6 ounces all-purpose flour (about
    1¼ cups)
4.75 ounces whole-wheat flour (about
    1 cup)
½ cup packed dark brown sugar
1½ teaspoons baking soda
1 teaspoon salt
1 teaspoon ground cinnamon
½ teaspoon ground nutmeg
⅛ teaspoon ground cloves
1 cup plain fat-free yogurt
⅓ cup ripe mashed Hachiya persimmon
⅓ cup honey
¼ cup canola oil
2 teaspoons grated peeled fresh ginger
1 teaspoon vanilla extract
2 large eggs, lightly beaten
½ cup diced peeled Fuyu persimmon
½ cup dried cranberries
Cooking spray

1. Preheat oven to 375°.

2. Place ½ cup pecans in a single layer on a baking sheet. Bake at 375° for 8 minutes or until pecans are fragrant and toasted. Cool.

3. Weigh or lightly spoon flours into dry measuring cups, and level with a knife. Combine flours and next 6 ingredients in a bowl, stirring well with a whisk. Combine yogurt and next 6 ingredients in a bowl, stirring well with a whisk. Add egg mixture to flour mixture, and stir just until combined. Fold in Fuyu persimmon, cranberries, and toasted pecans. Spoon batter into 18 muffin cups coated with cooking spray. Sprinkle tops with remaining ¼ cup pecans.

4. Bake muffins at 375° for 18 minutes or until a wooden pick inserted in center comes out clean. Cool in pans 5 minutes on a wire rack, and remove from pans. Yield: 18 servings (serving size: 1 muffin).

CALORIES 202; **FAT** 7.4g (sat 0.7g, mono 4.1g, poly 2.2g); **PROTEIN** 3.7g; **CARB** 31.8g; **FIBER** 2.4g; **CHOL** 20mg; **IRON** 1.2mg; **SODIUM** 255mg; **CALC** 36mg

---

TRADITIONAL SPICED MUFFINS SUDDENLY SEEM STYLISH WHEN MADE WITH SEASONAL PERSIMMONS. THERE ARE TWO DISTINCT TYPES: CREAMY-FLESHED HACHIYA IS MASHED TO KEEP THE MUFFINS MOIST, WHILE FIRMER FUYU IS DICED FOR FRUITY BITS WITH SOME BITE.

GLOBAL TWISTS ON THE SAME OLD LEFTOVERS

There's nothing finer than a turkey-and-stuffing sandwich. But when that's been munched, turn to turkey with hominy and Mexican spice, or cranberry and Champagne.

Thanksgiving dinner is nearly as treasured for its leftovers as for the feast itself. In fact, wise cooks cook with the goal of having lots of leftovers left over. The first round of dishes are DIY treats that kids or visitors can fish out of the fridge themselves. But then the cook recovers her or his energy and, staring at a bowl of cold spuds, remembers a wonderful British pub dish called Cottage Pie, based on humble mash. Or recalls the shredded turkey in a spicy Mexican posole from a vacation long ago. Thanksgiving leftovers, being in the best way rather basic foods, lend themselves to internationally inspired twists. Here we dish up more than a half-dozen delicious, playful uses for those precious Turkey Day leftovers.

Make Ahead
Mexican
Mexican Turkey Stew
(pictured on page 269)

3 large Anaheim chiles, seeded and halved lengthwise
2 teaspoons canola oil
Cooking spray
1½ cups chopped onion
4 garlic cloves, minced
2 tablespoons ground guajillo chile powder
1½ teaspoons dried oregano
4 cups water
3 cups fat-free, lower-sodium chicken broth
1 (15-ounce) can golden or white hominy, drained
4 cups leftover shredded cooked turkey breast
⅓ cup chopped fresh cilantro
¼ teaspoon salt
½ cup roasted unsalted pumpkinseed kernels
½ cup thinly sliced radishes
½ cup thinly sliced green onions
½ cup (2 ounces) crumbled queso fresco cheese
Lime wedges (optional)

1. Preheat broiler.
2. Place chile halves, skin sides up, on a foil-lined baking sheet. Broil 6 minutes or until blackened. Place in a paper bag, and fold to close tightly. Let stand 15 minutes. Peel and chop; set aside.
3. Heat oil in a large Dutch oven coated with cooking spray over medium heat. Add onion to pan; cook 6 minutes, stirring occasionally. Add garlic; cook 1 minute, stirring occasionally. Add chile powder and oregano; cook 1 minute, stirring constantly. Stir in 4 cups water, broth, and hominy; bring to a boil. Reduce heat, and simmer, uncovered, 10 minutes. Stir in Anaheim chiles and turkey; cook 2 minutes. Stir in cilantro and salt; cook 3 minutes. Ladle about 1⅓ cups soup into each of 8 bowls. Top each with 1 tablespoon pumpkinseeds, 1 tablespoon radishes, 1 tablespoon green onions, and 1 tablespoon cheese. Serve with lime wedges, if desired. Yield: 8 servings.

CALORIES 213; **FAT** 6.8g (sat 2.3g, mono 1.9g, poly 1.6g); **PROTEIN** 25.4g; **CARB** 13.5g; **FIBER** 3.2g; **CHOL** 56mg; **IRON** 1.7mg; **SODIUM** 483mg; **CALC** 88mg

BEER NOTE: With Anaheim and guajillo chiles lending their subtle heat, reach for a flavorful chilled beer, like a Scottish-style ale. Oskar Blues Old Chub Scotch Ale ($8.99/six-pack), from Colorado, has a rich, malty sweetness, hinting of caramel, that works to balance the peppery posole, while the beer's dark chocolate, toasted nut, and smoky notes complement the roasted pumpkinseeds in this richly layered soup.

Make Ahead
French
Cranberry Kir Royale

Leftover cranberry sauce helps concoct a lightly sweet homemade cranberry liqueur in this twist on a classic French cocktail. Allow four days to steep the liqueur. Garnish with cranberries, if you like.

¼ cup water
3 tablespoons sugar
½ cup leftover whole-berry cranberry sauce
¾ cup vodka
4 cups dry prosecco or sparkling wine, chilled

1. Combine ¼ cup water and sugar in a small saucepan over medium heat. Cook 5 minutes or until sugar melts. Remove from heat; stir in cranberry sauce. Let cool. Stir in vodka; pour mixture into a bowl. Cover and refrigerate 4 days.
2. Strain mixture through a cheesecloth-lined sieve into a small jar; discard solids. Cover jar with an airtight lid; chill until ready to use.
3. To make cocktails, spoon 2 tablespoons cranberry liqueur into each of 8 champagne flutes. Top each with ½ cup wine. Serve immediately. Yield: 8 servings.

CALORIES 188; **FAT** 0g; **PROTEIN** 0g; **CARB** 13.1g; **FIBER** 0.3g; **CHOL** 0mg; **IRON** 0mg; **SODIUM** 4mg; **CALC** 0.1mg

Kid Friendly
Colombian
Turkey Arepas

Arepas are corn cakes popular in Latin American countries. Look for arepa flour in the international food section of large supermarkets or in an ethnic market. Don't substitute masa harina or cornmeal for the arepa flour, which is precooked. Store the flour in an airtight container in your freezer to extend its shelf life.

7.5 ounces yellow arepa flour (about 1½ cups; such as P.A.N. or masarepa)
1 teaspoon salt, divided
2 cups hot water
2 tablespoons canola oil, divided
1 cup finely chopped onion
1 cup finely chopped green bell pepper
2 teaspoons minced seeded jalapeño pepper
½ teaspoon cumin seeds
2 garlic cloves, minced
2 cups chopped leftover cooked turkey breast
¼ cup chopped fresh cilantro
½ teaspoon freshly ground black pepper
⅓ cup (3 ounces) shredded reduced-fat sharp white cheddar cheese

1. Preheat oven to 400°.
2. Weigh or lightly spoon flour into dry measuring cups; level with a knife. Combine flour and ½ teaspoon salt; stir well. Add 2 cups hot water; stir until well combined and smooth. Let stand 10 minutes. Divide dough into 12 equal portions, shaping each into a ball. (Dough should be moist.) Working with 1 portion at a time, roll each portion into a 3-inch circle (about ½ inch thick).
3. Heat 1½ teaspoons oil in a large nonstick skillet over medium-high heat. Add 6 arepas to pan; cook 2 minutes on each side or until browned and crisp. Place on a baking sheet. Repeat procedure with 1½ teaspoons oil and remaining arepas. Bake at 400° for 20 minutes or until arepas sound hollow when lightly tapped.
4. Heat remaining 1 tablespoon oil in a large nonstick skillet over medium heat. Add onion and bell pepper; cook 5 minutes, stirring occasionally. Add jalapeño, cumin seeds, and garlic; cook 2 minutes, stirring occasionally. Stir in remaining ½ teaspoon salt, turkey, cilantro, and black pepper; cook 1 minute. Remove from heat; stir in cheese.
5. Remove arepas from oven; let stand 2 minutes. Cut a 3-inch pocket in side of each arepa; spoon turkey mixture into arepas. Yield: 6 servings (serving size: 2 filled arepas).

CALORIES 282; FAT 10.4g (sat 3g, mono 3.3g, poly 2.3g); PROTEIN 20.8g; CARB 26.5g; FIBER 4.8g; CHOL 42mg; IRON 3mg; SODIUM 547mg; CALC 162mg

Make Ahead • Freezable • Vegetarian
Indian
Vegetable Samosas with Mint Chutney

This dish uses leftover mashed potatoes in a big batch of Indian-inspired snacks, which are good for parties.

Chutney:
1 cup fresh mint leaves
1 cup fresh cilantro leaves
1 tablespoon fresh lime juice
1 tablespoon water
1 teaspoon finely chopped seeded jalapeño pepper
1 teaspoon chopped garlic
½ teaspoon minced peeled fresh ginger
⅛ teaspoon salt
Samosas:
2 tablespoons olive oil, divided
¼ cup finely chopped onion
⅔ cup shredded carrot
⅔ cup frozen green peas, thawed
2 teaspoons mustard seeds
1½ teaspoons garam masala
½ teaspoon salt
1 cup leftover mashed potato
8 (14 x 9–inch) sheets frozen phyllo dough, thawed
Cooking spray

1. Preheat oven to 350°.
2. To prepare chutney, place first 8 ingredients in a food processor; process 1 minute or until smooth. Spoon mixture into a bowl; cover and refrigerate.
3. To prepare samosas, heat 1 tablespoon oil in a large nonstick skillet over medium heat. Add onion to pan, and cook 2 minutes, stirring occasionally. Add carrot, and cook 2 minutes, stirring occasionally. Add peas and next 3 ingredients; cover and cook 2 minutes. Stir in potato; remove from heat.
4. Working with 1 phyllo sheet at a time, cut each sheet lengthwise into 3 (3 x 14–inch) strips, and coat with cooking spray. (Cover remaining phyllo dough to keep from drying.) Spoon 1 tablespoon potato mixture onto 1 end of each strip. Fold 1 corner of phyllo dough over mixture, forming a triangle; keep folding back and forth into a triangle to end of strip. Place triangles, seam sides down, on a baking sheet. Brush triangles with remaining 1 tablespoon oil. Bake at 350° for 23 minutes or until lightly browned. Serve warm or at room temperature with chutney. Yield: 12 servings (serving size: 2 samosas and 1½ teaspoons chutney).

CALORIES 89; FAT 3.6g (sat 0.7g, mono 2.3g, poly 0.5g); PROTEIN 2.2g; CARB 13g; FIBER 1.6g; CHOL 1mg; IRON 0.9mg; SODIUM 217mg; CALC 21mg

3 MORE WAYS TO USE GARAM MASALA

1 Stir it into cooked lentils.
2 Add to curry dishes.
3 Sprinkle onto roasted or sautéed butternut squash for an exotic, fragrant flourish.

Make Ahead • Kid Friendly
Spanish

Sweet Potato Buttered Rum Flan

This flan—a Spanish baked custard—is best when made with leftover sweet potatoes that have been simply prepared and minimally seasoned. Use ground nutmeg in place of grated whole nutmeg, if you prefer.

1/2 teaspoon canola oil
1/2 cup granulated sugar
1 tablespoon water
1 cup leftover mashed sweet potato
1/2 cup packed brown sugar
2 tablespoons white rum
2 tablespoons butter, melted
1/4 teaspoon ground cinnamon
1/8 teaspoon salt
1/8 teaspoon grated whole nutmeg
3 large eggs
1 1/2 cups 1% low-fat milk

1. Preheat oven to 325°.
2. Coat an 8-inch metal cake pan with high sides with oil, tipping to fully coat.
3. Combine granulated sugar and 1 tablespoon water in a small heavy saucepan over medium-high heat; cook 5 minutes or until golden. Immediately pour into prepared pan, tipping quickly until caramelized sugar coats bottom of pan.
4. Place sweet potato and next 7 ingredients in a blender; process until smooth. Add milk; process just until blended. Pour mixture over caramel in pan. Place pan in a 13 x 9–inch glass or ceramic baking dish; add hot water to dish to a depth of 1 inch.
5. Bake at 325° for 1 hour or until a knife inserted in center comes out clean. Remove pan from water. Cool completely on a wire rack. Cover and chill 8 hours or overnight. Invert flan onto a platter, and cut into 8 wedges. Drizzle any remaining caramel syrup over flan. Yield: 8 servings (serving size: 1 wedge).

CALORIES 230; FAT 6.6g (sat 3.5g, mono 2.1g, poly 0.6g); PROTEIN 4.6g; CARB 36.1g; FIBER 0.6g; CHOL 81mg; IRON 1.1mg; SODIUM 219mg; CALC 90mg

---

3 MORE WAYS TO USE GRATED WHOLE NUTMEG

1 Add a dash or two to sautéed spinach to build complex flavor.
2 Mix 1/4 teaspoon into spice rubs for meats.
3 Use it to top chai tea, cappuccinos, or eggnog.

Kid Friendly
English

English Cottage Pie

Leftover mashed potatoes are mixed with white cheddar cheese to form the top crust for this British pub-food staple. Ground beef is traditionally used, but lean ground turkey will work, as well. Brown the crust under the broiler for a minute or two, if you like.

1 tablespoon all-purpose flour
1 tablespoon butter, softened
Cooking spray
1 1/2 cups chopped onion
1/2 cup chopped carrot
1 (8-ounce) package cremini or button mushrooms, thinly sliced
1 pound extra-lean ground beef
2 tablespoons no-salt-added tomato paste
1 cup fat-free, lower-sodium beef broth
1/4 teaspoon freshly ground black pepper
1/4 cup chopped fresh parsley
1 tablespoon fresh thyme leaves
1/2 teaspoon salt
3 cups leftover mashed potato
3/4 cup (3 ounces) shredded reduced-fat sharp white cheddar cheese, divided
Paprika (optional)

1. Preheat oven to 350°.
2. Combine flour and butter; stir well. Heat a large nonstick skillet over medium-high heat. Coat pan with cooking spray. Add onion and carrot; sauté 5 minutes. Add mushrooms; sauté 5 minutes or until lightly browned. Remove vegetables from skillet. Add beef to pan; cook 5 minutes or until browned, stirring to crumble. Stir in tomato paste, and cook 3 minutes. Stir in broth and pepper. Return vegetables to pan, and bring to a simmer. Stir in parsley, thyme, and salt. Add flour mixture, and cook 1 minute or until thick, stirring constantly.
3. Spoon meat mixture into an 8-inch square glass or ceramic baking dish coated with cooking spray. Combine potatoes and half of cheese; spread potato mixture evenly over meat mixture. Top with remaining cheese. Sprinkle with paprika, if desired. Bake at 350° for 20 minutes or until bubbly. Yield: 6 servings (serving size: 2/3 cup).

CALORIES 288; FAT 10g (sat 5.6g, mono 2.3g, poly 0.5g); PROTEIN 24.1g; CARB 29.9g; FIBER 4g; CHOL 60mg; IRON 2.8mg; SODIUM 626mg; CALC 164mg

---

Make Ahead • Vegetarian
Greek

Green Bean, Feta, and Black Olive Salad

Serve this Mediterranean-flavored side dish with roasted, simply seasoned chicken, pork, beef, or fish.

1 1/4 cups uncooked bulgur
1 1/4 cups boiling water
2 cups leftover cooked green beans, cut into 1-inch pieces
3/4 cup (3 ounces) crumbled reduced-fat feta cheese
1/4 cup chopped fresh parsley
1/4 cup chopped fresh mint
1/4 cup thinly sliced red onion
1/2 teaspoon grated lemon rind
1/4 cup fresh lemon juice
2 1/2 tablespoons extra-virgin olive oil
1/2 teaspoon salt
1/4 teaspoon freshly ground black pepper
4 kalamata olives, pitted and finely chopped

1. Combine bulgur and 1 1/4 cups boiling water in a large bowl. Let stand 30 minutes or until water is absorbed. Add green beans and remaining ingredients to bulgur; toss gently. Serve at room temperature. Yield: 6 servings (serving size: 1 cup).

CALORIES 208; FAT 8.9g (sat 2.3g, mono 4.7g, poly 1.1g); PROTEIN 7.8g; CARB 28g; FIBER 7.3g; CHOL 4.2mg; IRON 1.2mg; SODIUM 441mg; CALC 72mg

RECIPE MAKEOVER
CHICKEN FINGERS, ALL GROWN UP

Leaving the deep fryer in the ditch, we create a crunchy new version of a fast-food staple that adults (and kids) will love.

Battered and deep-fried strips of poultry populate most family-restaurant and drive-through menus in America because their crunchy, salty blandness is a nice foil for a dipping sauce, and finger foods please the kids. But check out the left side of the nutrition panel on this page: a full gram of salt and 703 calories per serving! You shouldn't cross the road for those chicken fingers.

Can this marriage of batter and tenders be saved? Certainly: Our Test Kitchens found the perfect coating in a nutty, fiber-filled whole-grain cereal. No need to deep-fry these fingers for crunch now—there's plenty of that in the coating already. For sauce, we keep it simple but zingy, using lime juice, soy sauce, and Sriracha to boost the mayo base, creating the perfect complement to a new version of America's family favorite.

EASY AS 1, 2, 3, 4

Sure, too much saucing can lead to a world of sugar, salt, and calories, but don't walk away from the saucy verities: tang, savor, sweet heat, and body. This delivers all those.

TANG
From the heady juice of fragrant limes

SAVOR
Salty richness from lower-sodium soy sauce

SWEET HEAT
Via the chile kick of our go-to Thai sauce, Sriracha

BODY
Mayo base clings, while canola delivers heart-healthy fats.

OLD WAY	OUR WAY
703 calories per serving	414 calories per serving
1,000 milligrams sodium	495 milligrams sodium
10.7 grams saturated fat	1.5 grams saturated fat
Deep-fried in lard	Pan-seared in canola oil
Drowning in sauce	Just enough spicy mayo sauce
Greasy, heavy coating	Light, crispy, crunchy

Kid Friendly
Pan-Fried Chicken Fingers with Spicy Dipping Sauce

Use less hot chile sauce (or none at all) if serving to children.

Sauce:
¼ cup canola mayonnaise
2 teaspoons Sriracha (hot chile sauce, such as Huy Fong)
1 teaspoon fresh lime juice
½ teaspoon lower-sodium soy sauce
Chicken:
¼ cup all-purpose flour
1½ teaspoons freshly ground black pepper
1½ teaspoons paprika
2 large eggs, lightly beaten
1 tablespoon water
3 cups whole-grain flake cereal (such as Kashi 7-Grain Flakes), finely crushed (about 2½ cups)
1 pound chicken breast tenders
¼ teaspoon salt
1½ tablespoons canola oil

1. To prepare sauce, combine first 4 ingredients in a small bowl, stirring with a whisk. Cover and chill.
2. To prepare chicken, combine flour, black pepper, and paprika. Place flour mixture in a shallow dish. Combine eggs and 1 tablespoon water, and place in another shallow dish. Place crushed cereal in another shallow dish.
3. Sprinkle chicken evenly with salt. Working with 1 piece at a time, dredge chicken in flour mixture. Dip in egg mixture; dredge in cereal.
4. Heat a large skillet over medium-high heat. Add oil to pan, swirling to coat. Add chicken pieces to pan, and cook 2 minutes on each side or until done. Serve immediately with sauce. Yield: 4 servings (serving size: about 3 ounces chicken fingers and 1 tablespoon sauce).

CALORIES 414; FAT 14g (sat 1.5g, mono 7g, poly 4.2g); PROTEIN 34.3g; CARB 37.6g; FIBER 4.5g; CHOL 156mg; IRON 2.8mg; SODIUM 495mg; CALC 38mg

INSTEAD OF BATTER-COATED, DEEP-FRIED CHICKEN DROWNING IN FATTY SAUCE, OUR CHICKEN GETS A CRUNCHY EXTERIOR FROM CEREAL AND IS SERVED WITH JUST ENOUGH SPICY MAYO FOR DIPPING.

THE PLEASURES OF LEARNING TO COOK IN FRANCE

If you have never skinned a skate, filleted a turbot, or even shucked an oyster, a cooking class with Susan Herrmann Loomis is a rewarding way to plunge into those salty waters.

Y ou don't have to be long in France or speak any French to see that many people share this quasi-religious view about the glory of the raw ingredient, much as they do about the blessed avocations of the cheesemaker and the winemaker and the baker. At the end of a very long and intricate French food chain are the alchemical skills of the cook—not only the Michelin chef but also the competent home cook. There is grace in finding, handling, cooking, and eating well. There is something divine in what the Italians (and now a lot of other people) call slow food, which is simply food that has not suffered from factory farming and factory-sized supermarket selling.

In 2001 Susan Herrmann Loomis published *On Rue Tatin,* her account of moving from America, buying, and then laboriously restoring a 17th-century house in the small city of Louviers, northwest of Paris, with her then-husband, who did most of the construction work. It's beautifully written, and we see exactly why Loomis loves France, but it is full of travail, mingled with early poverty that was anything but charming. The couple worked so damned long and hard to fix their decrepit old house that you conclude Loomis earned every bit of the joys she takes in the place, the people, and the food, and along the way discovered a lot to teach.

Still, when she opened a cooking school in the renovated home in 2001, students arrived expecting a simple taste of *la vie en France.*

"People came and didn't care about cooking," Loomis said. "They just wanted to be in my life because they had read my book. And I was kind of discouraged because I wanted to cook: I'm a serious cook. But now I find people are really interested in every aspect of cooking. Every word that comes out of my mouth they're writing down notes, asking questions." This she attributes to the explosion of interest in food and cooking back home, in America, and word of mouth.

What does healthy eating learn from a cooking lesson in France? Much about how precise technique and direct approaches bring bright flavors forward in service of precious ingredients. Loomis puts vegetables in the middle of her plate, and many of her seafood recipes are naturally light, broth-based, and herb-infused. She has been a preacher of the organic, the sustainable, the local from the beginning. But she would no more avoid cream or butter than a songwriter would avoid C or G.

Welcome, again, to the French paradox. Cream, butter, cheese, meat, duck fat, sausage…all remain central to the idea of good eating, not just as "flavor agents" but things to be appreciated straightforwardly and with appetite. The prevailing theory is that a culture of mindfulness about food, about the integration of food into sociability and happiness (rather than food as a sort of distinct category of chest-beating construction and consumption) explains all this.

Basil-Steamed Halibut with Lemon-Crème Sauce

A simple, quick fish stock is used for steaming the fish and for the sauce. Ask your fishmonger for white fish bones; the flavor from darker-fleshed fish might be too strong. It's important to thoroughly rinse fish bones and remove any blood before preparing the stock.

1½ pounds white fish bones
2 medium carrots, peeled and coarsely
  chopped
1 medium onion, peeled and coarsely
  chopped
1 garlic clove, minced
4 cups water
¼ cup crème fraîche
2¼ teaspoons fresh lemon juice
1 large egg yolk
1½ tablespoons unsalted butter
½ teaspoon fine sea salt, divided
¼ teaspoon freshly ground black pepper
1 bunch fresh basil leaves (about 1 ounce)
4 (6-ounce) halibut fillets, skinned
Torn fresh basil leaves (optional)

1. Combine first 4 ingredients in a large Dutch oven; add 4 cups water. Bring to a boil; reduce heat, and simmer 20 minutes. Strain mixture through a sieve into a bowl, reserving stock. Discard solids.
2. Pour ¼ cup stock into a small saucepan (set remaining stock aside); bring to a boil over high heat. Boil 2 minutes or until stock is reduced to 2 tablespoons. Reduce heat to low. Combine crème fraîche, juice, and egg yolk in a small bowl, stirring with a whisk. Slowly pour egg mixture into reduced stock, stirring constantly with a whisk. Remove from heat; stir in butter, ¼ teaspoon salt, and pepper. Set aside.
3. Pour remaining stock into a large skillet; bring to a simmer over medium-high heat.
4. Line a vegetable steamer with 1 bunch basil leaves; arrange fillets in a single layer over basil. Place steamer in skillet; cover and steam fillets 15 minutes or until fish flakes easily when tested with a fork. Carefully remove steamer from skillet. Sprinkle fillets

with remaining ¼ teaspoon salt; let stand 5 minutes. Serve with sauce. Garnish with basil leaves, if desired. Yield: 4 servings (serving size: 1 fillet and 2 tablespoons sauce).

CALORIES 290; FAT 14.4g (sat 6.9g, mono 4.2g, poly 1.8g); PROTEIN 36.6g; CARB 0.5g; FIBER 0.1g; CHOL 131mg; IRON 1.6mg; SODIUM 387mg; CALC 88mg

Quick & Easy • Vegetarian

Roasted Eggplants with Herbs

This simple preparation yields irresistible results. Use very firm, small eggplants; if young and fresh enough, they won't be bitter.

6 small eggplants (about 1¼ pounds)
¼ cup extra-virgin olive oil, divided
½ teaspoon fine sea salt
¼ teaspoon freshly ground black pepper
½ cup chopped fresh basil
1 tablespoon chopped fresh sage
1 tablespoon chopped fresh rosemary

1. Preheat oven to 450°.
2. Cut each eggplant into ¼-inch slices, cutting to, but not through, stem end. Fan eggplants, and place on a baking sheet lined with parchment paper. Brush 2 tablespoons oil evenly over eggplant slices. Bake at 450° for 15 minutes; remove from oven. Press eggplants gently to fan slices. Brush eggplants with 1½ tablespoons oil; sprinkle evenly with salt and pepper. Bake an additional 10 minutes or until flesh is tender and edges are browned and slightly crisp.
3. Drizzle remaining 1½ teaspoons oil evenly over eggplants; sprinkle with basil, sage, and rosemary. Yield: 6 servings (serving size: 1 eggplant).

CALORIES 104; FAT 9.2g (sat 1.3g, mono 6.6g, poly 1g); PROTEIN 1.1g; CARB 5.7g; FIBER 3.4g; CHOL 0mg; IRON 0.4mg; SODIUM 194mg; CALC 18mg

—Adapted with permission from *Nuts in the Kitchen*

Quick & Easy

Nutty Mussels

The beard, or byssus, on a mussel is like a string the mussel uses to attach itself to something solid. It must be removed right before the mussel is cooked, but not in advance or the mussel might spoil. Hazelnuts are key to the flavor of this dish, so be sure to scoop some into every serving.

3 tablespoons extra-virgin olive oil
2 garlic cloves
2 tablespoons fresh lemon juice
3 pounds mussels, scrubbed and debearded
⅓ cup chopped hazelnuts, toasted
1 tablespoon minced fresh rosemary
¼ teaspoon salt
¼ teaspoon freshly ground black pepper

1. Heat a wok or large Dutch oven over medium-high heat. Add oil to pan; swirl to coat. Add garlic; stir-fry 2 minutes or until just golden. Carefully add lemon juice and mussels to pan; cook 4 minutes or until shells open, stirring constantly. Remove mussels from pan using a slotted spoon; keep warm. Discard any unopened shells. Cook pan juices 3 minutes or until reduced to 1 tablespoon; stir in nuts. Return mussels to pan; cook 2 minutes or until thoroughly heated, stirring to combine. Remove from heat; sprinkle with rosemary, salt, and pepper, tossing gently to combine. Divide mussel mixture evenly among 4 bowls; serve immediately. Yield: 4 servings.

CALORIES 284; FAT 19.4g (sat 2.5g, mono 12.5g, poly 2.7g); PROTEIN 19.4g; CARB 8.5g; FIBER 1.1g; CHOL 42mg; IRON 6.5mg; SODIUM 577mg; CALC 56mg

—Adapted with permission from *Nuts in the Kitchen*

Quick & Easy • Vegetarian

Green Salad with Hazelnut Vinaigrette

1 tablespoon red wine vinegar
½ teaspoon Dijon mustard
¼ teaspoon fine sea salt
¼ teaspoon freshly ground black pepper
3 tablespoons toasted hazelnut oil
8 cups packaged herb salad blend (such as Fresh Express)
1 shallot, thinly sliced

1. Combine first 4 ingredients in a large bowl, stirring with a whisk. Gradually add oil to vinegar mixture, stirring constantly with a whisk. Add salad blend and shallot, tossing to coat. Serve immediately. Yield: 8 servings (serving size: about 1 cup).

CALORIES 59; FAT 5.2g (sat 0.4g, mono 4g, poly 0.6g); PROTEIN 1g; CARB 2.6g; FIBER 1.2g; CHOL 0mg; IRON 0.8mg; SODIUM 94mg; CALC 32mg

SO SIMPLE, SO LOVELY—THIS SALAD IS THE PERFECT EXAMPLE OF HOW A FEW WELL-CHOSEN, HIGH-QUALITY INGREDIENTS COME TOGETHER FOR A TRULY MEMORABLE DISH.

Mackerel Gravlax with Roasted Red Pepper Puree

Serve this unique gravlax with seedy whole-grain crackers.

2 (10-ounce) mackerel fillets
3 tablespoons fine sea salt
3 tablespoons sugar
1 bunch fresh cilantro sprigs
1/2 cup thinly sliced shallots
2 medium red bell peppers
2 tablespoons fresh cilantro leaves
1 teaspoon balsamic vinegar

1. Run fingers along flesh side of fillets, and remove any pin bones with a pair of kitchen tweezers. Turn fillets over, and score skin by making 4 (1-inch) crosswise cuts in each fillet with a sharp knife.
2. Combine salt and sugar in a small bowl. Sprinkle 1 tablespoon salt mixture over skin side of each fillet; let stand 10 minutes.
3. Arrange half of cilantro sprigs in a 13 x 9–inch glass or ceramic baking dish. Arrange fillets in a single layer, skin sides down, on top of cilantro. Spread remaining salt mixture over flesh side of fillets; top evenly with shallots and remaining cilantro sprigs. Cover loosely with plastic wrap. Place a cast-iron skillet or other heavy object on top of fillets to weigh them down; refrigerate 24 hours.
4. Remove skillet; set aside. Uncover fillets; drain any accumulated liquid. Carefully turn fillets over; cover loosely with plastic wrap. Place skillet or heavy object on top of fillets; refrigerate 24 hours.
5. Preheat broiler. Cut bell peppers in half lengthwise; discard seeds and membranes. Place pepper halves, skin sides up, on a foil-lined baking sheet; flatten with hand. Broil 12 minutes or until blackened. Place in a paper bag; fold to close tightly. Let stand 10 minutes. Peel. Place bell peppers, cilantro leaves, and vinegar in a food processor; process until smooth.
6. Remove skillet from fillets, and discard plastic wrap. Scrape off and discard cilantro and salt mixture, and discard liquid. Using a sharp knife, remove skin from fillets. Cut fillets into 1/16-inch slices. Serve with bell pepper puree. Yield: 8 servings (serving size: about 2 ounces fish and 1½ tablespoons sauce).

CALORIES 95; **FAT** 1.7g (sat 0.3g, mono 0.6g, poly 0.4g); **PROTEIN** 16.3g; **CARB** 3.1g; **FIBER** 0.9g; **CHOL** 41mg; **IRON** 1.6mg; **SODIUM** 385mg; **CALC** 28mg

—Adapted with permission from *The Great American Seafood Cookbook*

Scallops with Green Tea Cream

This dish makes a uniquely delicious first course. Look for matcha, a Japanese green tea powder with a vibrant color and deep, somewhat bitter flavor, in Asian grocery stores or gourmet markets. If you can't find it, pulverize regular green tea in a spice grinder.

1/3 cup crème fraîche
1¼ teaspoons matcha (Japanese green tea powder), divided
1/2 teaspoon fresh lemon juice
1/8 teaspoon fine sea salt
1/8 teaspoon Hungarian hot paprika
1/2 teaspoon ground ginger
18 large sea scallops (about 1¾ pounds)
1 tablespoon extra-virgin olive oil, divided
1/4 teaspoon fleur de sel or other sea salt
2 tablespoons fresh chervil (optional)

1. Place crème fraîche in a medium bowl; beat with a mixer at high speed until stiff peaks form. Add ½ teaspoon matcha, lemon juice, 1/8 teaspoon salt, and paprika, stirring with a whisk.
2. Combine remaining ¾ teaspoon matcha and ginger in a fine mesh sieve over a bowl; press ginger mixture through sieve. Sprinkle ginger mixture evenly over scallops.
3. Heat a large heavy skillet over high heat. Add 1½ teaspoons oil to pan; swirl to coat. Arrange half of scallops in a single layer in pan; cook 2 minutes on each side or until browned and desired degree of doneness. Remove scallops from pan. Repeat procedure with remaining 1½ teaspoons oil and scallops. Arrange 3 scallops and about 1 tablespoon crème fraîche mixture on each of 6 plates. Sprinkle evenly with fleur de sel and chervil, if desired. Yield: 6 servings.

CALORIES 155; **FAT** 7.6g (sat 3.3g, mono 2.9g, poly 0.7g); **PROTEIN** 17.3g; **CARB** 2.7g; **FIBER** 0.1g; **CHOL** 46mg; **IRON** 0.3mg; **SODIUM** 310mg; **CALC** 25mg

5 OTHER USES FOR MATCHA

Until you are accustomed to the powerful flavor of matcha, start with a small amount (1/4 to 1/2 teaspoon per serving), and then increase as you prefer.

1 Stir into a smoothie—this is particularly great with banana-yogurt smoothies, like the one on page 372.

2 Dust a tiny amount over a chocolate-glazed cake for a green tinge and big flavor.

3 Stir some into your favorite vanilla-flavored cupcake batter or standard buttercream frosting for a unique twist.

4 Make shortbread cookies with a delicious can't-quite-identify-the-secret-ingredient quality by adding some matcha.

5 Make green tea ice cream—it's incredibly easy. Stir some matcha into softened vanilla ice cream.

FIVE SAUCES TO MASTER

Ignore the intimidation factor. Sauces are not hard, and they're oh so worth it.

A healthy cook can't afford to ignore the power of a good sauce. Sauces add richness to lean meats and fish, coat pastas, add zing to pizzas, and generally turn tasty meals into memorable ones.

Yet sauce making has a reputation for being difficult, a culinary-school skill that separates the home cook from the pro, and not worth the time at home.

Here is the good news: Most sauces are just not that hard. Follow a few simple steps—we'll walk you through them on the next few pages—and success will be yours. With these five fundamental sauces in your repertoire (and a few variations and short-cuts for when you really don't have time), new horizons open up.

Quick & Easy • Kid Friendly
Vegetarian

Béchamel Sauce

Béchamel, one of the "mother" sauces in classic French cuisine, is versatile: It's used in dishes such as lasagna, macaroni and cheese, and moussaka, and it can also serve as the base for soufflés, soups, and savory pie fillings. What's more, add a little Swiss cheese, and voilà— you've got Mornay Sauce (see recipe at right). We call for white pepper so it isn't visible in the sauce. If it's unavailable, you can omit it.

1¾ cups 2% reduced-fat milk
½ cup thinly sliced onion
Dash of freshly grated whole nutmeg
1 bay leaf
2 tablespoons butter
1½ tablespoons all-purpose flour
¼ teaspoon salt
Dash of ground white pepper

1. Combine first 4 ingredients in a small saucepan over medium-high heat; bring to a simmer. Remove from heat; cover and let stand 15 minutes. Strain milk mixture through a sieve over a bowl; discard solids.
2. Wipe pan clean with paper towels. Melt butter in pan over medium heat. Add flour to pan; cook 1 minute, stirring constantly. Gradually add strained milk, stirring with a whisk until blended. Bring to a boil; cook 9 minutes or until thickened, stirring constantly. Remove from heat; stir in salt and pepper. Yield: 8 servings (serving size: about 2½ tablespoons).

CALORIES 57; FAT 3.9g (sat 2.4g, mono 1g, poly 0.2g); PROTEIN 2g; CARB 3.8g; FIBER 0.1g; CHOL 12mg; IRON 0.1mg; SODIUM 121mg; CALC 66mg

For Mornay Sauce:
Stir ½ cup (2 ounces) shredded Gruyère cheese into thickened Béchamel Sauce, stirring over medium-low heat until smooth. Yield: 8 servings (serving size: about 2½ tablespoons).

CALORIES 87; FAT 6.2g (sat 3.8g, mono 1.8g, poly 0.3g); SODIUM 144mg

BÉCHAMEL BRINGS RICH CREAMINESS TO A DISH WITHOUT RESORTING TO SATURATED FAT-LADEN CREAM.

STEP-BY-STEP BÉCHAMEL

1 Combine milk, onion, grated nutmeg, and bay leaf in a saucepan; bring to a simmer.

2 After milk mixture stands for 15 minutes, strain through a fine sieve over a bowl.

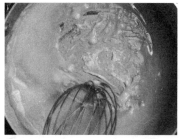

3 Cook flour and butter to form a roux that will thicken the sauce.

4 Gradually add milk mixture to pan. Cook until thickened, stirring constantly.

FLAVOR BOOST
Onion lends the sauce a faintly sweet note. For even more aroma, add a crushed garlic clove to the steeping milk.

STEP-BY-STEP MARINARA

1 Roast seasoned tomato halves, cut sides up, at 250° for 7 hours.

2 Pass roasted tomatoes through a food mill, or puree the sauce in a blender or food processor and strain through a sieve.

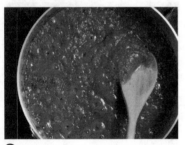

3 Simmer tomato mixture along with wine and sautéed aromatics.

QUICK TIP
Instead of slow roasting, you can blast the tomatoes at 450° for 20 minutes or until they begin to brown. The sauce will be slightly thinner but still vibrantly flavored.

Make Ahead • Freezable • Kid Friendly
Vegetarian

Slow-Roasted Tomato Marinara

Slow roasting concentrates the flavor in the tomatoes, making for a much heartier and somewhat thicker sauce. You can freeze the sauce in pint containers for up to six months. If you don't have a food mill, puree the sauce in a blender or food processor and strain through a sieve.

1 tablespoon sugar
1 tablespoon extra-virgin olive oil
3/4 teaspoon dried basil
1/2 teaspoon dried oregano
4 pounds plum tomatoes, halved lengthwise
Cooking spray
1/3 cup water
4 teaspoons extra-virgin olive oil
3/4 cup chopped onion
1 teaspoon dried basil
1/2 teaspoon dried oregano
3 garlic cloves, minced
1/3 cup dry red wine
2/3 cup water
1/2 teaspoon salt
1/4 teaspoon freshly ground black pepper

1. Preheat oven to 250°.
2. Combine first 5 ingredients in a large bowl, tossing gently to coat. Arrange tomato halves, cut sides up, on a jelly-roll pan coated with cooking spray. Bake tomatoes at 250° for 7 hours. Remove pan from oven. Add 1/3 cup water to pan, scraping pan to loosen browned bits. Place a food mill over a large bowl; spoon tomato mixture into food mill. Press mixture through food mill; keep warm.
3. Heat oil in a saucepan over medium-high heat. Add onion and next 3 ingredients; sauté 5 minutes or until tender. Add wine; cook 3 minutes or until liquid nearly evaporates. Stir in tomato mixture and 2/3 cup water; bring to a boil. Cover, reduce heat, and simmer 15 minutes, stirring occasionally. Remove from heat; stir in salt and pepper. Yield: 8 servings (serving size: about 1/2 cup).

CALORIES 99; FAT 4.9g (sat 0.7g, mono 3g, poly 0.9g);
PROTEIN 2.3g; CARB 14.4g; FIBER 3g; CHOL 0mg;
IRON 1.4mg; SODIUM 167mg; CALC 27mg

Quick & Easy • Make Ahead
Vegetarian

Rémoulade

Start with a base of Mayonnaise (see recipe below). Add 2 teaspoons capers for a more briny flavor. You can substitute dill pickle for cornichons (tiny gherkin pickles). If you're short on time, use store-bought canola mayonnaise in this recipe and the Tartar Sauce recipe (page 355).

3/4 cup Mayonnaise (below)
2 teaspoons finely chopped onion
2 teaspoons chopped cornichons
1 teaspoon chopped fresh flat-leaf parsley
1 teaspoon chopped fresh chives

1. Combine all ingredients in a medium bowl, and stir well. Yield: 12 servings (serving size: about 1 tablespoon).

CALORIES 128; FAT 14.4g (sat 1.5g, mono 9g, poly 3.5g);
PROTEIN 0.2g; CARB 0.3g; FIBER 0g; CHOL 17mg;
IRON 0.1mg; SODIUM 60mg; CALC 2mg

Quick & Easy • Make Ahead
Kid Friendly • Vegetarian

Mayonnaise

The key to creamy homemade mayo is to add just a few drops of oil at a time to the egg mixture, then pour in a slow, thin drizzle—whisking constantly—to ensure the mayonnaise emulsifies (blends smoothly).

2 teaspoons fresh lemon juice
1 teaspoon Dijon mustard
1 large pasteurized egg yolk
1/2 cup canola oil
1/4 cup olive oil
1/4 teaspoon salt
1/8 teaspoon freshly ground black pepper

1. Combine first 3 ingredients in a medium bowl; stir well with a whisk. Combine oils; slowly drizzle oil mixture into egg mixture, stirring constantly with a whisk until mixture is thick and smooth. Stir in salt and pepper. Yield: 12 servings (serving size: 1 tablespoon).

CALORIES 127; FAT 14.4g (sat 1.5g, mono 9g, poly 3.5g);
PROTEIN 0.2g; CARB 0.2g; FIBER 0g; CHOL 17mg;
IRON 0mg; SODIUM 53mg; CALC 2mg

STEP-BY-STEP RÉMOULADE

1 Combine lemon juice, Dijon mustard, and pasteurized egg yolk in a medium bowl; stir well with a whisk.

2 Add oils to egg yolk mixture, drop by drop at first, then in a thin drizzle, stirring constantly with a whisk.

3 Stir in onion, pickle, and fresh herbs.

For Tartar Sauce:
½ cup Mayonnaise (page 354)
2 tablespoons sweet pickle relish
2 teaspoons chopped fresh parsley
2 teaspoons minced onion
½ teaspoon fresh lemon juice
½ teaspoon Dijon mustard

1. Combine all ingredients in a small bowl; stir well. Yield: 10 servings (serving size: 1 tablespoon).

CALORIES 106; **FAT** 11.5g (sat 1.2g, mono 7.2g, poly 2.8g); **PROTEIN** 0.2g; **CARB** 1.3g; **FIBER** 0.1g; **CHOL** 14mg; **IRON** 0.1mg; **SODIUM** 70mg; **CALC** 2mg

---

Kid Friendly
Mushroom Gravy

Sage gives this gravy a more traditional Thanksgiving flavor, but to change it up, try some chopped rosemary, tarragon, thyme, or parsley. This is slightly thinner than some gravies because we found the consistency to be more pleasing to the palate. Add 1 tablespoon flour to the slurry for a thicker gravy. You can substitute fat-free, lower-sodium chicken broth for the Roasted Chicken Stock—but if you do, decrease the salt to ⅛ teaspoon or add none at all.

1 tablespoon olive oil
½ cup chopped onion
1½ tablespoons chopped fresh sage
¼ teaspoon salt
1 (8-ounce) package presliced mushrooms
¼ cup Madeira wine or dry sherry
3 cups Roasted Chicken Stock (page 356)
1½ tablespoons all-purpose flour
2 tablespoons water
2 tablespoons butter
⅛ teaspoon freshly ground black pepper

1. Heat oil in a nonstick skillet over medium-high heat. Add onion to pan; sauté 1 minute. Add sage, salt, and mushrooms; sauté 11 minutes or until mushrooms are browned. Add wine; cook 30 seconds or until liquid almost evaporates. Stir in Roasted Chicken Stock. Boil; cook until reduced to 2 cups (about 14 minutes).
2. Combine flour and 2 tablespoons water in a bowl, stirring until smooth. Add flour mixture to pan; return to a boil. Reduce heat; simmer 2 minutes or until slightly thickened, stirring occasionally. Remove from heat. Stir in butter, 1 tablespoon at a time, stirring until butter melts. Stir in pepper. Yield: 8 servings (serving size: about ¼ cup).

CALORIES 71; **FAT** 5.5g (sat 2.2g, mono 2.4g, poly 0.6g); **PROTEIN** 2.8g; **CARB** 3.4g; **FIBER** 0.6g; **CHOL** 14mg; **IRON** 0.4mg; **SODIUM** 104mg; **CALC** 9mg

---

STEP-BY-STEP MUSHROOM GRAVY

1 Sauté onion, mushrooms, and sage until mushrooms are browned.

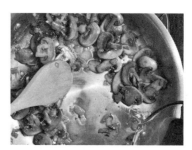

2 Add wine, and cook until liquid almost evaporates; add stock, and reduce to 2 cups.

3 Whisk flour slurry into mushroom mixture; cook until slightly thickened.

4 Remove from heat, then whisk in butter.

Make Ahead • Freezable
Roasted Chicken Stock

Roasting the chicken and vegetables browns the chicken and caramelizes the vegetables, lending a deeper, richer flavor—and color—to the stock and your sauces. Freeze extra stock for up to six months.

7 pounds chicken wings
Cooking spray
3 cups coarsely chopped onion
2½ cups coarsely chopped celery
2¼ cups coarsely chopped carrot
1 tablespoon olive oil
1 cup water
5 quarts water
15 fresh parsley sprigs
15 black peppercorns
8 fresh thyme sprigs
3 bay leaves

1. Preheat oven to 450°.
2. Arrange chicken in a single layer on a jelly-roll pan coated with cooking spray. Combine onion and next 3 ingredients in a bowl; toss well to coat vegetables. Arrange vegetable mixture in a single layer on another jelly-roll pan coated with cooking spray. Roast chicken and vegetables at 450° for 1 hour and 20 minutes or until browned, turning occasionally.
3. Place wings and vegetables in a stockpot. Pour ½ cup water into each baking sheet, scraping to loosen browned bits. Pour water mixture into pot. Add 5 quarts water and remaining ingredients to pot. Place pot over medium-high heat. Bring to a boil. Reduce heat to low, and simmer 4 hours, skimming off and discarding foam as needed. Strain stock through a fine sieve into a large bowl; discard solids. Cool stock to room temperature. Cover and refrigerate 5 hours or overnight. Skim solidified fat from surface; discard fat. Yield: 24 servings (serving size: ½ cup).

CALORIES 25; **FAT** 1.4g (sat 0.3g, mono 0.7g, poly 0.3g); **PROTEIN** 2.6g; **CARB** 0.3g; **FIBER** 0.1g; **CHOL** 11mg; **IRON** 0.2mg; **SODIUM** 13mg; **CALC** 4mg

Red Wine Reduction

You can turn this into a pan sauce for steak by removing the cooked steak from the pan, adding the stock to the pan and scraping to loosen browned bits, then proceeding with the recipe as follows. The deglazed bits add wonderful depth of flavor to the sauce.

2 cups Roasted Chicken Stock (at left)
1 cup zinfandel or other fruity dry red wine
⅓ cup finely chopped shallots
1 tablespoon tomato paste
1 fresh thyme sprig
5 teaspoons butter
⅛ teaspoon salt
⅛ teaspoon freshly ground black pepper

1. Place Roasted Chicken Stock in a small saucepan over medium-high heat; bring to a boil. Cook until reduced to ½ cup (about 20 minutes). Place stock in a bowl; keep warm.
2. Combine wine and next 3 ingredients in pan over medium-high heat; bring to a boil. Cook until reduced to ⅓ cup (about 8 minutes). Stir in reserved stock; return mixture to a boil. Cook until reduced to ⅔ cup (about 7 minutes). Strain mixture through a sieve over a bowl; discard solids. Stir in butter, 1 teaspoon at a time, stirring until butter melts. Stir in salt and pepper. Yield: 4 servings (serving size: 2 tablespoons).

CALORIES 79; **FAT** 5.8g (sat 3.3g, mono 1.7g, poly 0.4g); **PROTEIN** 2.8g; **CARB** 4.3g; **FIBER** 0.5g; **CHOL** 21mg; **IRON** 0.7mg; **SODIUM** 156mg; **CALC** 20mg

STEP-BY-STEP RED WINE SAUCE

1 Reduce stock to ½ cup in a small saucepan.

2 Combine wine, shallots, tomato paste, and thyme; cook until reduced to ⅓ cup. Stir in reduced stock.

3 Strain wine-stock mixture through a sieve over a bowl.

4 Whisk butter into sauce to enrich and slightly thicken it.

QUICK TIP
In a pinch, you can substitute purchased fat-free, lower-sodium chicken broth for the Roasted Chicken Stock, and omit salt.

LIGHTER LAYER CAKES

You can have your cake, eat it, and eat the crumbs, too.

There are several reasons to take the time to make a homemade cake. First, flavor, texture, and pride. Second, a majestic layer cake puts the exclamation point on a holiday table and doubles as a stunning centerpiece for your dessert buffet. Third, this impressive production actually has big make-ahead potential: You can bake layers up to a month ahead and freeze them, and most fillings and frostings can be made in advance, too. All you need to do is thaw and assemble the day before. Finally, our light cakes really do save on calories and fat. There are, naturally, a few tricks to coaxing great taste and texture from a cake that leans less heavily on butter and sugar. Here, the secrets are revealed.

Staff Favorite • Make Ahead
Kid Friendly

Vanilla Cake with Italian Meringue Frosting

Cake:
Cooking spray
2 teaspoons cake flour
11 ounces cake flour (about 2¾ cups)
½ teaspoon baking powder
½ teaspoon baking soda
½ teaspoon salt
1 cup nonfat buttermilk
¼ cup 1% low-fat milk
1 cup plus 2 tablespoons sugar, divided
5 tablespoons butter, softened
2 tablespoons canola oil
3 large egg yolks
1 teaspoon vanilla extract
3 large egg whites
Frosting:
²/₃ cup plus 2 tablespoons sugar, divided
¼ cup water
Dash of salt
¼ teaspoon cream of tartar
3 large egg whites
½ teaspoon vanilla extract
Filling:
½ cup bottled lemon curd

1. Preheat oven to 350°.
2. To prepare cake, lightly coat 2 (8-inch) round metal cake pans with cooking spray; line bottoms of pans with wax paper. Coat wax paper with cooking spray; dust each pan with 1 teaspoon flour.
3. Weigh or lightly spoon 11 ounces (about 2¾ cups) flour into dry measuring cups; level with a knife. Combine 11 ounces flour, baking powder, baking soda, and ½ teaspoon salt in a medium bowl, stirring well with a whisk. Combine buttermilk and low-fat milk. Combine 1 cup sugar and butter in a large bowl; beat with mixer at medium speed until well blended. Add canola oil and egg yolks, 1 at a time, beating well after each addition. Beat in 1 teaspoon vanilla. Add flour mixture and milk mixture alternately to butter mixture, beginning and ending with flour mixture and beating just until combined.
4. Place 3 egg whites in a medium bowl; beat with a mixer at high speed until foamy, using clean, dry beaters. Gradually add remaining 2 tablespoons sugar, beating until stiff peaks form. Gently fold egg white mixture into batter. Divide batter evenly between prepared pans. Bake at 350° for 28

minutes or until a wooden pick inserted into center comes out clean. Cool in pans 10 minutes on wire racks. Loosen edges with a knife, and invert cakes onto racks. Cool completely; discard wax paper.
5. To prepare frosting, combine ²/₃ cup sugar, ¼ cup water, and dash of salt in a small saucepan over medium-high heat; bring to a boil, stirring just until sugar dissolves. Cook, without stirring, until a candy thermometer registers 240° (about 4 minutes). Combine cream of tartar and 3 egg whites in a large bowl; beat with a mixer at high speed until foamy. Gradually add remaining 2 tablespoons sugar, beating at high speed until medium peaks form. Gradually pour hot sugar syrup into egg white mixture, beating first at medium speed and then at high speed until stiff peaks form. Beat in ½ teaspoon vanilla.
6. To prepare filling, place lemon curd in a medium bowl. Gently fold ⅓ cup meringue into curd. Fold an additional ²/₃ cup meringue into curd mixture.
7. Place 1 cake layer on a plate; spread filling over top of cake, leaving a ¼-inch border. Top with remaining cake layer. Spread remaining frosting over sides and top of cake. Yield: 16 servings (serving size: 1 wedge).

CALORIES 274; **FAT** 7.5g (sat 3.3g, mono 2.4g, poly 0.8g); **PROTEIN** 4.2g; **CARB** 48.4g; **FIBER** 1.3g; **CHOL** 59mg; **IRON** 1.7mg; **SODIUM** 214mg; **CALC** 23mg

4 STEPS TO LUSCIOUS LAYERS

1 PREPARE PANS. Prevent cake layers from sticking to the pan and crumbling when you try to remove them by spraying the pan with cooking spray, lining it with wax paper, spraying again, and dusting with flour.

2 CAREFULLY MEASURE INGREDIENTS. Precision is important when baking, especially light baking, where there's less margin for error. For absolute accuracy, weigh the flour instead of scooping and measuring with a cup.

3 INCORPORATE AIR. Fluffy batter will result in a moist cake with a fine crumb. The first step of the mixing process—creaming butter with sugar—whips air into the batter. More air is added as you incorporate eggs into the batter by beating it.

4 GENTLY STIR IN FLOUR. Slow the mixer speed before adding flour and milk. Start with flour, then alternate with liquid (often milk). Finish with flour, as well. Beat only until combined. If overbeaten at this stage, the cake will become tough.

Make Ahead • Kid Friendly

Pecan Spice Cake with Maple Frosting

Work quickly to spread the warm frosting over the first layer, stack the second on top, and then spread the remaining frosting over the top and sides before it sets.

Cake:
Cooking spray
2 teaspoons all-purpose flour
9 ounces all-purpose flour (about 2 cups)
½ teaspoon baking soda
½ teaspoon salt
½ teaspoon ground cinnamon
¼ teaspoon ground nutmeg
Dash of ground cloves
1 cup packed brown sugar
½ cup butter, softened
3 large eggs
1 teaspoon vanilla extract
1 cup buttermilk
⅓ cup chopped pecans, toasted

Frosting:
½ cup packed brown sugar
¼ cup heavy whipping cream
¼ cup maple syrup
1 tablespoon butter
Dash of salt
2 cups powdered sugar
½ teaspoon vanilla extract
2 tablespoons chopped pecans, toasted

1. Preheat oven to 350°.
2. To prepare cake, coat 2 (8-inch) round metal cake pans with cooking spray. Line bottoms of pans with wax paper; coat with cooking spray. Dust each pan with 1 teaspoon flour. Weigh or lightly spoon 9 ounces flour (about 2 cups) into dry measuring cups; level with a knife. Combine 9 ounces flour, baking soda, and next 4 ingredients, stirring well with a whisk.
3. Place 1 cup brown sugar and ½ cup butter in a large mixing bowl; beat with a mixer at medium-high speed until light and fluffy (about 3 minutes). Add eggs, 1 at a time, beating well after each addition. Beat in 1 teaspoon vanilla. Add flour mixture and buttermilk alternately to butter mixture, beginning and ending with flour mixture and beating just until combined. Fold in ⅓ cup

pecans. Divide batter evenly between prepared pans.

4. Bake at 350° for 24 minutes or until a wooden pick inserted in center comes out clean. Cool in pans 5 minutes on wire racks. Invert cake layers onto racks; cool completely. Discard wax paper.

5. To prepare frosting, place ½ cup brown sugar and next 4 ingredients in a heavy saucepan over medium-high heat; bring to a boil, stirring just until sugar dissolves. Cook 3 minutes, without stirring. Scrape brown sugar mixture into a bowl. Add powdered sugar; beat with a mixer at high speed 2 minutes or until slightly cooled and thick. Beat in ½ teaspoon vanilla. Place 1 cake layer on a plate. Spread about ¾ cup frosting evenly over 1 layer, and top with second layer. Spread remaining frosting over sides and top of cake, and sprinkle with 2 tablespoons pecans. Let cake stand until frosting sets. Yield: 16 servings (serving size: 1 wedge).

CALORIES 325; FAT 11.8g (sat 5.7g, mono 3.8g, poly 1.2g); PROTEIN 3.8g; CARB 52.1g; FIBER 0.8g; CHOL 64mg; IRON 1.5mg; SODIUM 209mg; CALC 36mg

IF YOU PREFER, YOU CAN SUBSTITUTE WALNUTS FOR THE PECANS IN THIS LUSCIOUS PECAN SPICE CAKE.

Make Ahead • Kid Friendly

Chocolate-Orange Layer Cake

Cake:
1 cup boiling water
⅔ cup unsweetened cocoa
2 ounces bittersweet chocolate, finely chopped
Cooking spray
2 teaspoons all-purpose flour
1¾ cups sugar
6 tablespoons butter, softened
1 teaspoon vanilla extract
3 large egg whites
½ cup fat-free sour cream
7.4 ounces cake flour (about 1⅔ cups)
1 teaspoon baking powder
¾ teaspoon baking soda
½ teaspoon salt

Filling:
⅓ cup orange juice
3 tablespoons sugar
1½ teaspoons cornstarch
2½ teaspoons unsweetened cocoa
¾ teaspoon all-purpose flour
Dash of salt
¼ ounce bittersweet chocolate, finely chopped
¾ cup frozen fat-free whipped topping, thawed

Glaze:
2 tablespoons evaporated low-fat milk
1 tablespoon butter
4 ounces bittersweet chocolate, finely chopped

1. Preheat oven to 350°.
2. To prepare cake, combine 1 cup boiling water and ⅔ cup cocoa in a bowl, stirring until smooth. Add 2 ounces bittersweet chocolate; stir until smooth. Cool to room temperature. Coat 2 (8-inch) round metal cake pans with cooking spray; line bottoms of pans with wax paper. Coat wax paper with cooking spray; dust each pan with 1 teaspoon flour.

3. Place 1¾ cups sugar, 6 tablespoons butter, and 1 teaspoon vanilla in a large bowl; beat with a mixer at medium speed 1 minute. Add egg whites, 1 at a time, beating well after each addition. Add sour cream; beat at medium speed 2 minutes. Weigh or lightly spoon 7.4 ounces flour (about 1⅔ cups) into dry measuring cups; level with a knife. Combine 7.4 ounces flour, baking powder, baking soda, and ½ teaspoon salt in a bowl, stirring well. Add flour mixture and cocoa mixture alternately to sugar mixture, beginning and ending with flour mixture and beating just until combined.

4. Divide batter evenly between prepared pans. Bake at 350° for 30 minutes or until a wooden pick inserted into center comes out clean. Cool in pans 10 minutes on wire racks. Invert cake layers onto racks; cool completely. Discard wax paper.

5. To prepare filling, combine juice and next 6 ingredients in a small saucepan over low heat; bring mixture to a boil, stirring frequently. Cook 1 minute, stirring constantly. Pour into a bowl. Cover and chill. Uncover; fold in whipped topping.

6. To prepare glaze, combine milk, 1 tablespoon butter, and 4 ounces bittersweet chocolate in a medium microwave-safe bowl; microwave at HIGH 1 minute, stirring every 15 seconds until smooth.

7. Place 1 cake layer on a plate. Spread filling over top, leaving a ¼-inch border. Top with remaining cake layer. Spoon warm glaze over top of cake, allowing it to drip over edges of cake. Yield: 16 servings (serving size: 1 wedge).

CALORIES 280; FAT 10.4g (sat 5.7g, mono 1.3g, poly 0.3g); PROTEIN 4.2g; CARB 46g; FIBER 1.9g; CHOL 14mg; IRON 1.5mg; SODIUM 229mg; CALC 38mg

FROM YOUR KITCHEN TO OURS

After retiring from her job as a registered nurse, Christine Vaught found she had more time to prepare healthy meals for her family.

"We're getting away from the heavy meals of meat and potatoes," she says. Inspired by a coleslaw recipe in her local newspaper, Vaught, who often plays with Asian flavors, created a lighter version but packed more punch in the soy-honey dressing with ginger and crushed red pepper.

Inspired by her Greek heritage, Marina Delio began to include more Greek recipes in her family's weekly menus but also wanted to incorporate more fish into their diets. "I like tilapia because it is mild flavored and raised in an environmentally friendly way," she says. The thin white fish fillets became the perfect filling for her gyros, which are kept simple with fresh tomatoes, avocado, and yogurt sauce.

Growing up, Judith McIntire never experienced good home cooking. "My mother detested cooking, hated to go into the kitchen," she says. Now a grandmother, McIntire discovered a multitude of fresh fruits and vegetables when she started cooking and makes sure she puts a healthy spin on favorite recipes. Her Banana Snacking Cake is always gone before it is time for dessert.

Despite having cooked for more than 45 years, retired nurse Gale Moody only recently began preparing healthier meals, gravitating toward a Mediterranean diet of fish and vegetables.

Quick & Easy • Make Ahead
Vegetarian

Broccoli Slaw with Oranges and Crunchy Noodles

"Good food usually has a variety of colors, textures, and flavors. I often use these criteria when creating new recipes."
—Christine Vaught, Salem, Oregon

Slaw:
6 cups thinly sliced napa cabbage
1 cup diagonally sliced celery
1 cup finely chopped broccoli florets
½ cup grated carrot (1 medium)
¼ cup thinly sliced green onions
¼ cup unsalted sunflower seed kernels
1 (5-ounce) can whole water chestnuts, drained and chopped

Dressing:
¼ cup lower-sodium soy sauce
3 tablespoons rice vinegar
1 tablespoon fresh lime juice
1 tablespoon honey
1 teaspoon crushed red pepper
⅛ teaspoon ground ginger
1 garlic clove, crushed
⅓ cup canola oil

Remaining Ingredients:
1 cup fresh orange sections
¼ cup sliced almonds, toasted
1 (3-ounce) package ramen noodles, crumbled and toasted (discard seasoning packet)

1. To prepare slaw, combine first 7 ingredients in a large bowl; toss well to combine.
2. To prepare dressing, combine soy sauce and next 6 ingredients in a small bowl, stirring with a whisk. Gradually add oil to soy sauce mixture, stirring constantly with a whisk. Drizzle dressing over slaw, tossing gently to coat. Top slaw with oranges, almonds, and noodles. Yield: 12 servings (serving size: ½ cup).

CALORIES 162; FAT 10.7g (sat 1.3g, mono 5.4g, poly 3.4g); PROTEIN 3.7g; CARB 15.2g; FIBER 3.6g; CHOL 0mg; IRON 1.2mg; SODIUM 308mg; CALC 51mg

Quick & Easy

Broiled Tilapia Gyros

"I love the fresh flavors of the tzatziki with the fish. The gyros are lighter and brighter than traditional ones."
—Marina Delio, Santa Barbara, California

Fish:
1½ pounds tilapia fillets
1½ tablespoons olive oil
½ teaspoon freshly ground black pepper
¼ teaspoon salt
Cooking spray

Tzatziki:
¾ cup plain 2% reduced-fat Greek yogurt
2 teaspoons chopped fresh dill
1½ teaspoons fresh lemon juice
½ teaspoon freshly ground black pepper
¼ teaspoon salt
2 garlic cloves, minced

Remaining Ingredients:
4 (2.75-ounce) Mediterranean-style wheat flatbreads (such as Toufayan)
½ cup vertically sliced red onion (about ½ small onion)
1 ripe avocado, peeled and cut into 12 thin slices
1 medium tomato, thinly sliced
½ small English cucumber, thinly sliced (about ½ cup)

1. Preheat broiler.
2. To prepare fish, brush fish with oil; sprinkle with ½ teaspoon pepper and ¼ teaspoon salt. Place fish on a broiler pan coated with cooking spray. Broil 6 minutes or until fish flakes easily when tested with a fork or desired degree of doneness.
3. To prepare tzatziki, place yogurt and next 5 ingredients in a food processor or blender; pulse until smooth.
4. Spread 2 tablespoons tzatziki in center of each flatbread. Divide fish evenly among flatbreads. Top each serving with 2 tablespoons onion, 3 avocado slices, 2 tomato slices, and about 6 cucumber slices; fold in half. Yield: 4 servings (serving size: 1 filled gyro).

CALORIES 479; FAT 16.8g (sat 3.7g, mono 9.4g, poly 2.2g); PROTEIN 46.1g; CARB 39.7g; FIBER 9.4g; CHOL 88mg; IRON 3.5mg; SODIUM 538mg; CALC 120mg

Banana Snacking Cake

"This cake is fun, quick, and easy to throw together. It also freezes well and is a great portable dessert."

—Judith McIntire, Sarasota, Florida

6.75 ounces all-purpose flour (about 1½ cups)
⅓ cup sugar
1 teaspoon baking powder
1 teaspoon baking soda
1 teaspoon ground cinnamon
¼ teaspoon salt
1 cup plain low-fat yogurt
¾ cup mashed ripe banana (about 1 medium)
¼ cup canola oil
1 teaspoon vanilla extract
1 large egg, lightly beaten
Cooking spray
½ cup frozen fat-free whipped topping, thawed

1. Preheat oven to 375°.
2. Weigh or lightly spoon flour into dry measuring cups; level with a knife. Combine flour and next 5 ingredients in a large bowl; stir with a whisk. Make a well in center of flour mixture.
3. Combine yogurt and next 4 ingredients in a small bowl; stir until well blended. Add yogurt mixture to flour mixture in large bowl, stirring just until moist.
4. Pour batter into a 9-inch square metal baking pan coated with cooking spray. Bake at 375° for 20 minutes or until a wooden pick inserted in center comes out clean. Cool cake in pan 10 minutes on a wire rack; remove from pan. Cool completely on wire rack. Serve with whipped topping. Yield: 8 servings (serving size: 1 cake piece and 1 tablespoon topping).

CALORIES 235; **FAT** 8.3g (sat 1g, mono 4.4g, poly 2.3g); **PROTEIN** 4.8g; **CARB** 35g; **FIBER** 1.3g; **CHOL** 26mg; **IRON** 1.6mg; **SODIUM** 304mg; **CALC** 104mg

Roasted Red Pepper and Herb Pasta with Shrimp

2 red bell peppers
8 ounces uncooked fettuccine
2 tablespoons extra-virgin olive oil
1 tablespoon unsalted butter
1 cup finely chopped onion
1 tablespoon minced garlic
½ pound peeled and deveined large shrimp
¼ cup fresh lemon juice (about 2 lemons)
2 tablespoons chopped fresh flat-leaf parsley
1 teaspoon chopped fresh thyme
½ teaspoon chopped fresh sage
¾ teaspoon salt
½ teaspoon freshly ground black pepper
½ teaspoon crushed red pepper
1 teaspoon extra-virgin olive oil
2 tablespoons shaved fresh Parmesan cheese

1. Preheat broiler.
2. Cut bell peppers in half lengthwise; discard seeds and membranes. Place pepper halves, skin sides up, on a foil-lined baking sheet; flatten with hand. Broil 15 minutes or until blackened. Place in a paper bag; fold to close tightly. Let stand 20 minutes. Peel and chop; set aside.
3. Cook fettuccine according to package directions, omitting salt and fat; drain well. Set aside; keep warm.
4. Heat 2 tablespoons oil and butter in a large skillet over medium-high heat. Add onion and garlic to pan, and cook 4 minutes or until onion is tender, stirring frequently. Add shrimp to pan, and cook 2 minutes. Add bell peppers and lemon juice to pan, and cook 4 minutes or until shrimp are done and half of the liquid has evaporated. Add parsley and next 5 ingredients to shrimp mixture. Remove pan from heat.
5. Combine fettuccine and 1 teaspoon oil in a large bowl; toss well. Add shrimp mixture, tossing gently to coat. Top each serving with cheese. Yield: 4 servings (serving size: 1½ cups shrimp and pasta mixture and 1½ teaspoons cheese).

CALORIES 378; **FAT** 10.5g (sat 3.3g, mono 4.6g, poly 1.7g); **PROTEIN** 20.7g; **CARB** 51g; **FIBER** 4.9g; **CHOL** 96mg; **IRON** 4mg; **SODIUM** 573mg; **CALC** 91mg

"TO SAVE TIME, YOU CAN SIMPLY PURCHASE THE ROASTED RED PEPPERS IN A JAR."

—Gale Moody, Woodstock, Georgia

BREAKFAST, LUNCH, AND DINNER IN... SEATTLE

Seattle is a city on the verge of so many things. Unlike the more staid, settled food destinations whose stories and signature dishes are already so well known (there's not a Seattle equivalent of Boston clam chowder or Chicago deep dish), the Emerald City's culinary scene is still building to its boom. It's a place of constant revolution, of paradigm shifts that come like the changing of the seasons, where notions of corporate versus local and historic versus cutting-edge are debated in every dining room of note and on every menu worth tasting. It's where a young, hungry chef can still make his mark, can still change the course of things from behind the pass of a small, fiercely independent restaurant, and establish himself as elemental and indispensable, all, it sometimes seems, in a matter of months.

Those looking for a simple description of Seattle will be disappointed. It is not a "steak town" or a "fine-dining destination." Rather than having a single cuisine that identifies it, the city has a food culture that makes good use of all the disparate influences spread through its neighborhoods. It's difficult to navigate but (contrary to reputation) surprisingly welcoming to all those who approach it with willing appetites. This was not always the case.

For most of its history, Seattle has been a blue-collar town with blue-collar tastes—a boom-and-bust city where dining was fine when everyone was flush, but sometimes seemed the last thing on anyone's mind. Before Boeing, Starbucks, or Microsoft (and before the floods of money and notoriety that came with them), it was a place where a fat steak, a baked potato, a fried fish, or a plate of clams was the height of cuisine.

These days, there's a kind of punk rock, do-it-yourself ethos at play here, borne out in the profusion of pop-up and walk-up restaurants, as well as food trucks.

SEATTLE TAKES ITS SUSHI SERIOUSLY—FROM THE 100-YEAR-OLD MANEKI RESTAURANT TO 100 PERCENT SUSTAINABLE OPTIONS AT MASHIKO.

Vegetarian
Breakfast
Egg White and Sun-Dried Tomato Frittata

Volterra (volterrarestaurant.com) hosts a weekend brunch that those in the Ballard neighborhood can't seem to get enough of. And with good reason. Chef Don Curtiss (who named Volterra after the small town in Tuscany where he married his wife and partner, Michelle Quisenberry) makes chestnut flour pancakes with sautéed apples that are justifiably famous. Francesco's Eggs—a mix of Italian sausage, spinach, pecorino Romano, and mushrooms— make a good start to any morning. Inspired by Curtiss's dish, this ethereally fluffy frittata tastes rich, thanks in part to the cheese wedges. Substitute feta if ricotta salata is unavailable. A green or fruit salad would make this dish into a nice brunch.

1/8 teaspoon kosher salt
8 large egg whites
1/2 teaspoon cream of tartar
1/8 teaspoon freshly ground black pepper
1/3 cup chopped drained oil-packed sun-dried tomatoes
1/4 cup chopped green onions
1 1/2 teaspoons olive oil
4 ounces ricotta salata, cut into 6 thin wedges
1 tablespoon sun-dried tomato oil
Chopped fresh parsley (optional)

1. Preheat oven to 400°.
2. Place salt and egg whites in a large bowl; beat with a mixer at high speed until foamy. Add cream of tartar and pepper; beat until soft peaks form. Gently fold in tomatoes and onions.
3. Heat olive oil in a 10-inch ovenproof nonstick skillet over medium-high heat. Spread egg white mixture evenly in pan; arrange ricotta wedges on top. Drizzle with tomato oil. Bake at 400° for 16 minutes or until puffed and golden. Loosen with a spatula, and slide onto a platter. Serve immediately. Garnish with parsley, if desired. Yield: 6 servings (serving size: 1 wedge).

CALORIES 132; FAT 7.5g (sat 3.3g, mono 3.3g, poly 0.5g); PROTEIN 9g; CARB 7g; FIBER 1.5g; CHOL 17mg; IRON 1mg; SODIUM 335mg; CALC 100mg

Toasted Guajillo and Pork Posole

Posole is infinitely customizable. Though the recipe is fairly standardized, there are as many variations as there are cooks who make it. At Seattle's La Carta de Oaxaca (lacartadeoaxaca.com) in the Ballard neighborhood, lunch crowds descend for the kitchen's pulled pork version with homemade tortillas. Serve with lime wedges, chopped onion, cilantro leaves, and sliced radish and cabbage, if desired.

3 dried guajillo chiles
1½ pounds pork shoulder, trimmed and cut into 2-inch pieces
½ teaspoon kosher salt
¼ teaspoon freshly ground black pepper
1 tablespoon canola oil
3 cups fat-free, lower-sodium chicken broth
3 cups water
2 teaspoons ground cumin
¼ teaspoon ground cloves
3 garlic cloves, crushed
1 medium onion, cut into 4 wedges
1 (7-ounce) can chipotle chiles in adobo sauce
1 (29-ounce) can hominy, rinsed and drained

1. Preheat oven to 400°.
2. Place chiles on a baking sheet; bake at 400° for 4 minutes or until dark. Cool; remove stems and seeds.
3. Sprinkle pork with salt and pepper. Heat oil in a large Dutch oven over medium-high heat. Add pork to pan; cook 5 minutes or until browned. Remove pork from pan. Wipe drippings from pan; return pork to pan. Add broth and next 5 ingredients, scraping pan to loosen browned bits. Add guajillo chiles and 1 tablespoon adobo sauce; reserve remaining chipotle chiles and sauce for another use. Bring to a boil; cover, reduce heat, and simmer 2 hours or until pork is tender.
4. Remove chiles, onion, garlic, and 1 cup cooking liquid; place in a blender. Remove center piece of blender lid (to allow steam to escape); secure blender lid on blender. Place a clean towel over opening in blender lid

(to avoid splatters). Blend until smooth; return to pan. Stir in hominy; cook 10 minutes. Yield: 6 servings (serving size: 1¼ cups).

CALORIES 273; FAT 10.4g (sat 2.7g, mono 4.8g, poly 1.8g); PROTEIN 25.1g; CARB 17.7g; FIBER 3.2g; CHOL 74mg; IRON 2.5mg; SODIUM 704mg; CALC 33mg

Dinner

Chicken with Smoked Chanterelles and Potatoes

At Chef Jason Wilson's Crush (chefjasonwilson.com), the menu is borderless, shifting effortlessly between Japanese, Mediterranean, and American regional. Too cold to grill? Sauté the mushrooms and chicken instead.

2 cups 1% low-fat milk
1 teaspoon chopped fresh thyme
½ teaspoon chopped fresh rosemary
¼ teaspoon kosher salt
3 garlic cloves, thinly sliced
1 shallot, peeled and sliced
1 bay leaf
1 pound Yukon gold potatoes, peeled and cut into (⅛-inch-thick) slices
½ teaspoon all-purpose flour
¼ teaspoon freshly ground black pepper
Cooking spray
¾ cup (3 ounces) shredded white cheddar cheese, divided
2 cups cedar wood chips
6 fresh thyme sprigs
3 fresh rosemary sprigs
1 pound chanterelle mushrooms, sliced lengthwise
1 slice center-cut bacon, thinly sliced
1 tablespoon butter
2 cups chopped kale
¼ cup fat-free, lower-sodium chicken broth
¼ teaspoon kosher salt
⅛ teaspoon freshly ground black pepper
4 (6-ounce) skinless, boneless chicken breast halves
¼ teaspoon kosher salt
⅛ teaspoon freshly ground black pepper

1. Preheat oven to 350°.
2. Place first 7 ingredients in a medium saucepan; bring to a boil. Reduce heat, and simmer 10 minutes. Add potatoes

to pan; simmer 5 minutes. Remove potatoes with a slotted spoon. Strain milk mixture through a fine mesh sieve over a bowl, reserving liquid; discard solids. Return liquid to pan. Add flour and ¼ teaspoon pepper to pan; cook 4 minutes or until slightly thickened, stirring constantly with a whisk. Remove from heat. Arrange half of potatoes in a 9 x 5–inch metal loaf pan coated with cooking spray. Sprinkle half of cheese over potatoes. Arrange remaining potatoes over cheese. Pour milk mixture over potatoes. Cover; bake at 350° for 1 hour. Remove from oven.
3. Preheat broiler.
4. Sprinkle remaining half of cheese over potatoes. Broil 5 minutes or until browned.
5. Prepare grill for indirect grilling, heating one side to high and leaving one side with no heat. Pierce bottom of a disposable aluminum foil pan several times. Place pan on heated side of grill; add wood chips, thyme sprigs, and rosemary sprigs to pan. When chips are smoking, place another foil pan (do not pierce) on unheated side of grill; add mushrooms. Cover and smoke 20 minutes.
6. Cook bacon in a large nonstick skillet over medium heat until crisp. Remove bacon from pan. Increase heat to medium-high. Add butter to drippings in pan. Add mushrooms to pan; sauté 3 minutes or until tender. Add kale and next 3 ingredients; cook until kale is tender and liquid almost evaporates, stirring occasionally. Sprinkle with bacon.
7. Preheat grill to high heat for direct grilling.
8. Sprinkle chicken with ¼ teaspoon salt and ⅛ teaspoon pepper. Place chicken on a grill rack coated with cooking spray; grill 5 minutes on each side or until done. Serve with potatoes and mushroom mixture. Yield: 4 servings (serving size: 1 chicken breast half, 1 cup potatoes, and ¾ cup mushroom mixture).

CALORIES 521; FAT 15.5g (sat 8.4g, mono 3.6g, poly 1g); PROTEIN 58.2g; CARB 34.7g; FIBER 2.7g; CHOL 140mg; IRON 3.5mg; SODIUM 856mg; CALC 390mg

HYBRID HORS D'OEUVRES

By Mark Bittman

Yes, you can have it all—festive finger foods that are make-ahead, healthy, slightly decadent, and delicious.

The whole point of a celebration is to have fun, so I have little patience when anyone tells me not to over-indulge at a party—until regrets set in the next day.

The risk of overeating makes it tough to enjoy back-to-back holiday events, so for purely practical reasons it makes sense to find a way to stay spry throughout the seasonal marathon. The key is more vegetables, but no one's idea of fun is to stand eternally over a platter of raw produce and yogurt dip. The real solution is *hybrid hors d'oeuvres*: fresh-tasting finger foods that aren't quite cheese fondue but remind you that you are, after all, at a holiday party.

Convenience is another factor, so I want dishes that can be mostly prepared in advance, especially for impromptu gatherings and potlucks. The following recipes deliver on all counts: They're satisfying, just slightly decadent, and easy to prepare and store. And they happen to work well together, so you can cherry-pick one or two for your own menu or lift the entire lineup and throw a party tomorrow.

Let's start with one of my all-time favorites, the roasted cauliflower: Oven cooking reduces the cabbage-y flavor and leaves the florets crumbly, slightly chewy, and uniquely appealing. With a light dressing and a little mashing, the bits of vegetable come together nicely into a loose spread that tastes even better at room temperature. One added tip: The smaller you chop the cauliflower, the less time it takes to crisp up and brown. (If you're feeling really energetic, serve the cauliflower in hollowed-out halves of boiled new potatoes.)

Crab is standard festive fare, but I find it counterproductive to bury the slightly sweet, rich meat in a load of sour cream or gooey cheese. Far better to use just enough mayo for tang and delicate binding, then play on crab's affinity for celery with a spin on classic rémoulade. This bright salad comes together in a flash; grate the celery root in a food processor, and you can use the work bowl to make the dressing. A sprinkle of Old Bay seasoning on top is a nice touch.

The best way to eat crudités is with *bagna cauda*, little more than warmed olive oil and anchovies. It's almost pure fat by design, but tempering the key ingredients with a ton of roasted red peppers is more than a decent compromise. Roasting your own peppers is beneficial, but not crucial: Cook the peppers directly on a gas flame or under the broiler until they are charred all over. Put them in a covered pot or paper bag to cool, then rub off the skin, and remove the stem and seeds. If you don't want the hassle, you can use peppers from the jar; just be sure to rinse them off a bit first.

As a bonus, these dishes easily make the transition from the holidays into your weekday repertoire: The cauliflower makes a terrific side dish or base for a frittata; the crab and celery root combo is a perfect sandwich filling; and the peppers make an excellent sauce for braising chicken or tossing with pasta. That's one way to keep the party going.

Quick & Easy • Make Ahead

Crab and Celery Root Rémoulade

2 cups shredded peeled celery root
  (about 1 pound)
½ cup finely chopped red onion
8 ounces lump crabmeat, drained and
  shell pieces removed
3 tablespoons mayonnaise
1 tablespoon Dijon mustard
1 tablespoon fresh lemon juice
1 teaspoon finely chopped tarragon
¼ teaspoon kosher salt
¼ teaspoon freshly ground black pepper
⅛ teaspoon ground red pepper
2 tablespoons olive oil
24 baby Boston lettuce leaves

1. Combine first 3 ingredients in a medium bowl.
2. Combine mayonnaise and next 6 ingredients in a small bowl, stirring with a whisk. Gradually add oil, stirring well with a whisk. Drizzle dressing over crab mixture, tossing well to combine. Spoon about 1½ tablespoons crab mixture in center of each lettuce leaf. Yield: 12 servings (serving size: 2 filled leaves).

CALORIES 70; FAT 4g (sat 0.6g, mono 2.1g, poly 1.2g); PROTEIN 4.5g; CARB 4.4g; FIBER 0.7g; CHOL 20mg; IRON 0.5mg; SODIUM 155mg; CALC 38mg

Make Ahead

Cauliflower "Caviar" with Frizzled Prosciutto

4 cups coarsely chopped cauliflower florets
  (about 2 pounds)
5 teaspoons olive oil, divided
¾ teaspoon freshly ground black pepper
¼ teaspoon kosher salt
4 ounces prosciutto, chopped
1 tablespoon minced garlic
1 tablespoon sherry vinegar
¼ cup chopped fresh parsley
24 belgian endive leaves (about 2 small
  heads)

1. Preheat oven to 400°.
2. Arrange cauliflower florets in a single layer in a 13 x 9–inch metal baking pan. Drizzle with 1 tablespoon oil; sprinkle with pepper and salt, tossing to combine. Bake at 400° for 40 minutes or until cauliflower is lightly browned.
3. Heat remaining 2 teaspoons oil in a small skillet over medium heat. Add prosciutto; sauté 10 minutes or until crisp, stirring occasionally. Add garlic; sauté 1 minute. Drain on paper towels.
4. Combine cauliflower mixture, prosciutto mixture, and vinegar in a large bowl; coarsely mash with a fork. Stir in parsley. Spoon 2 tablespoons cauliflower mixture into each endive leaf. Serve warm or at room temperature. Yield: 12 servings (serving size: 2 filled leaves).

CALORIES 59; FAT 3g (sat 0.6g, mono 1.8g, poly 0.5g); PROTEIN 3.8g; CARB 4.8g; FIBER 2.2g; CHOL 6mg; IRON 0.6mg; SODIUM 205mg; CALC 21mg

Make Ahead

Roasted Red Pepper Bagna Cauda

Serve with fennel bulb slices, blanched broccoli florets, steamed new potatoes, and carrots.

1 whole garlic head
6 red bell peppers
¼ cup olive oil
8 small canned anchovy fillets, drained
2 tablespoons fresh lemon juice
½ teaspoon crushed red pepper
¼ teaspoon kosher salt
¼ teaspoon freshly ground black pepper
1½ tablespoons chopped fresh parsley

1. Preheat oven to 350°.
2. Remove white papery skin from garlic head (do not peel or separate cloves). Wrap in foil. Bake at 350° for 1 hour; cool 10 minutes. Separate cloves; squeeze to extract garlic pulp. Discard skins. Set aside 1 tablespoon garlic pulp; reserve remaining pulp for another use.
3. Preheat broiler.
4. Cut bell peppers in half lengthwise, and discard seeds and membranes. Place pepper halves, skin sides up, on a foil-lined baking sheet; flatten with hand. Broil 15 minutes or until blackened. Place in a paper bag; fold to close tightly. Let stand for 20 minutes; peel.
5. Place bell peppers, reserved garlic, oil, and next 5 ingredients in a food processor; process until smooth. Sprinkle with parsley. Yield: 12 servings (serving size: about 2½ tablespoons).

CALORIES 66; FAT 5.3g (sat 0.8g, mono 3.4g, poly 0.8g); PROTEIN 1.4g; CARB 4.2g; FIBER 1.3g; CHOL 2mg; IRON 0.4mg; SODIUM 140mg; CALC 11mg

EVERYDAY VEGETARIAN

SOUPS AND STEWS

Whether brothy-slurpy or thick and filling, these bowls will warm you up.

Vegetarian

Mushroom Stew with Spaetzle

Spaetzle—small German noodles or dumplings—are paired with a thick mushroom gravy. For more broth, soak porcini in 1 cup water, and use all the liquid.

4.5 ounces all-purpose flour (about 1 cup)
¼ teaspoon salt
3 tablespoons 1% low-fat milk
2 large eggs
2 quarts water
⅓ cup dried porcini mushrooms (about ⅜ ounce)
½ cup boiling water
1 tablespoon canola oil
1½ cups chopped onion
2 garlic cloves, minced
7 cups (½-inch) sliced cremini mushrooms (about 14 ounces)
10 ounces button mushrooms, halved
2 tablespoons all-purpose flour
1 tablespoon paprika
¼ cup red wine
1½ cups organic vegetable broth
½ cup chopped fresh flat-leaf parsley, divided
2 teaspoons balsamic vinegar
¼ teaspoon salt
¼ teaspoon freshly ground black pepper

1. Weigh or lightly spoon 4.5 ounces flour into a dry measuring cup, and level with a knife. Sift together flour and ¼ teaspoon salt. Combine milk and eggs in a medium bowl; stir with a whisk. Add flour mixture to egg mixture, stirring until well combined. Let stand 10 minutes.
2. Bring 2 quarts water to a boil in a large saucepan. Hold a colander with large holes (about ¼ inch in diameter) over boiling water; spoon about ½ cup dough into colander. Press dough through holes with a rubber spatula (droplets will form spaetzle); set colander aside. Cook 3 minutes or until done (spaetzle will rise to surface). Remove with a slotted spoon; drain in a strainer (spaetzle will stick to a paper towel). Repeat procedure with remaining dough.
3. Combine porcini mushrooms and ½ cup boiling water in a small bowl; cover and let stand 30 minutes. Drain mushroom mixture in a colander over a bowl, reserving ¼ cup liquid. Rinse and chop mushrooms.
4. Heat oil in a Dutch oven over medium-high heat. Add onion and garlic to pan; sauté 2 minutes. Add reserved porcini mushrooms, cremini mushrooms, and button mushrooms to pan; sauté 15 minutes or until moisture almost evaporates. Stir in 2 table-spoons flour and paprika. Add wine to pan; cook 1 minute or until liquid is absorbed. Stir in reserved mush-room liquid and broth; bring to a boil. Reduce heat, and simmer 15 minutes, stirring occasionally. Add ¼ cup parsley, vinegar, ¼ teaspoon salt, and pepper to pan; cook 1 minute. Add spaetzle to pan; cook 2 minutes or until thoroughly heated. Garnish with remaining ¼ cup parsley. Yield: 4 servings (serving size: about 1½ cups stew and 1 tablespoon parsley).

CALORIES 300; FAT 7g (sat 1.2g, mono 3.3g, poly 1.5g); PROTEIN 12.8g; CARB 45.7g; FIBER 5.1g; CHOL 106mg; IRON 4.3mg; SODIUM 571mg; CALC 76mg

Vegetarian

Ribollita (Italian Bread Soup)

3 cups (1-inch) cubed hearty Italian
  country bread (about 6 ounces)
Cooking spray
3 tablespoons extra-virgin olive oil,
  divided
1 cup chopped onion
¼ cup chopped celery
1 tablespoon minced garlic
6 cups water, divided
6 cups (1-inch) chopped kale
6 cups chopped Savoy cabbage
4 cups chopped broccoli rabe
2 cups (1-inch) cubed peeled Yukon gold
  or red potato
1 cup thinly sliced carrot
1 (14.5-ounce) can whole plum tomatoes,
  undrained and chopped
2 (15-ounce) cans cannellini beans or
  other white beans, rinsed, drained,
  and divided
¾ teaspoon salt
½ teaspoon dried thyme
½ teaspoon dried oregano
¼ teaspoon crushed red pepper
½ cup (2 ounces) shaved or grated
  Parmigiano-Reggiano cheese

1. Preheat oven to 375°.
2. Place 3 cups bread on a baking sheet,
and lightly coat with cooking spray.
Bake at 375° for 15 minutes or until
toasted, stirring occasionally. Remove
from oven; cool.
3. Heat 1 tablespoon oil in a large
stockpot or Dutch oven over medium-
high heat. Add onion and celery to pan;
sauté 5 minutes. Add garlic, and sauté
1 minute. Add 5 cups water and next
6 ingredients. Cover, reduce heat, and
simmer 20 minutes or until greens are
wilted, stirring occasionally. Mash
1 can of beans. Add mashed beans and
remaining 1 cup water to pan; bring
to a boil. Reduce heat, and simmer
35 minutes or until potato and carrot
are tender.
4. Stir in bread, remaining can of beans,
salt, and next 3 ingredients; bring to a
boil. Reduce heat, and simmer 10 minutes. Remove from heat; cover and let

stand 10 minutes. Ladle about 1½ cups
soup into each of 8 bowls. Sprinkle
each serving with 1 tablespoon cheese,
and drizzle with ¾ teaspoon oil. Yield:
8 servings.

CALORIES 305; FAT 8.7g (sat 2.8g, mono 4.3g, poly 1g);
PROTEIN 11.7g; CARB 45.6g; FIBER 10.7g; CHOL 4.4mg;
IRON 4.1mg; SODIUM 693mg; CALC 161mg

Vegetarian

Lentil-Barley Soup

2 teaspoons canola oil
1 cup sliced leek
3 cups organic vegetable broth
1 cup water
¾ cup beer
1 cup chopped carrot
1 cup chopped celery
½ cup chopped parsnip
¼ cup chopped celery leaves
¼ cup chopped fresh dill
¼ cup uncooked pearl barley
½ teaspoon freshly ground black
  pepper
¼ teaspoon dried thyme
2 bay leaves
½ cup dried lentils
¼ teaspoon salt

1. Heat oil in a Dutch oven over
medium-high heat. Add leek to pan;
sauté 2 minutes. Add broth, 1 cup water,
and beer; bring to a boil. Add carrot and
next 8 ingredients; return to a boil. Cover,
reduce heat, and simmer 15 minutes. Stir
in lentils; cover and cook 30 minutes.
Discard bay leaves.
2. Place 1½ cups broth mixture in a
blender. Remove center piece of blender
lid (to allow steam to escape); secure
blender lid on blender. Place a clean
towel over opening in blender lid (to
avoid splatters). Blend until smooth.
Return pureed mixture to pan, and stir
in salt. Return mixture to a boil; cover,
reduce heat, and simmer 10 minutes or
until thoroughly heated, stirring occasionally. Yield: 4 servings (serving size:
about 1⅓ cups).

CALORIES 300; FAT 4.7g (sat 2.2g, mono 1.5g, poly 0.8g);
PROTEIN 11.8g; CARB 53.6g; FIBER 15.7g; CHOL 0mg;
IRON 6.6mg; SODIUM 667mg; CALC 63mg

Vegetarian

Black Bean Soup

*A topping of chopped hard-cooked eggs adds
interesting texture and lends a cooling effect to
this spicy Southwestern soup. Chopped cilantro supplies bright, fresh flavor and a welcome
hit of color.*

1 cup dried black beans (about 6 ounces)
1 teaspoon olive oil
¼ cup chopped onion
1 garlic clove, minced
2½ cups water
½ teaspoon dried oregano
¼ to ½ teaspoon ground red pepper
¼ teaspoon ground cumin
1 (14-ounce) can organic vegetable broth
1 (4-ounce) can chopped green chiles,
  drained
¼ cup tomato paste
⅜ teaspoon salt
3 hard-cooked large eggs, coarsely chopped
Chopped fresh cilantro (optional)

1. Sort and wash beans; place in a large
Dutch oven. Cover with water to 2
inches above beans; bring to a boil.
Cook 2 minutes; remove from heat.
Cover and let stand 1 hour. Drain beans.
2. Heat oil in pan over medium-high
heat. Add onion and garlic to pan; sauté
3 minutes or until tender. Add beans,
2½ cups water, and next 5 ingredients;
bring to a boil. Cover, reduce heat, and
simmer 1½ hours or until beans are
tender.
3. Place half of bean mixture in a
blender. Remove center piece of blender
lid (to allow steam to escape); secure
blender lid on blender. Place a clean
towel over opening in blender lid (to
avoid splatters). Blend until smooth.
Pour pureed soup into a bowl. Repeat
procedure with remaining soup. Return
to pan. Stir in tomato paste and salt;
cook 3 minutes or until thoroughly
heated. Ladle 1¼ cups soup into each
of 4 bowls; top each serving with about
⅓ cup chopped eggs. Sprinkle each
serving with cilantro, if desired. Yield:
4 servings.

CALORIES 235; FAT 4.2g (sat 1g, mono 2.3g, poly 0.7g);
PROTEIN 13.7g; CARB 33.2g; FIBER 5.3g; CHOL 135mg;
IRON 3.1mg; SODIUM 631mg; CALC 50mg

BUDGET COOKING
FEED 4 FOR LESS THAN $10

Bold flavors bring warmth and comfort to your table without breaking the bank.

Quick & Easy • Kid Friendly

Balsamic-Glazed Pork Chops and Polenta

$2.34 per serving, $9.34 total

Reduce the vinegar while the polenta simmers so the entire meal is ready and hot at the same time.

2 cups whole milk
1 cup fat-free, lower-sodium chicken broth
3/4 cup uncooked polenta
3 ounces 1/3-less-fat cream cheese, softened
6 tablespoons balsamic vinegar
1 1/2 teaspoons chopped fresh rosemary
1/4 teaspoon kosher salt
1/2 teaspoon freshly ground black pepper
2 large garlic cloves, minced
4 (4-ounce) boneless center-cut pork chops, trimmed

1. Bring milk and broth to a simmer in a medium saucepan over medium heat. Gradually add polenta. Cook 20 minutes or until thick and bubbly, stirring frequently with a whisk; remove from heat. Stir in cream cheese. Keep warm.
2. Place vinegar in a small saucepan over medium-high heat. Bring to a boil, and cook until reduced by half (about 5 minutes).
3. Place a grill pan over medium-high heat. Combine rosemary and next 3 ingredients; rub mixture over pork. Place pork in pan; cook 5 minutes on each side or until desired degree of doneness, basting with vinegar. Let stand 5 minutes before slicing. Serve with polenta. Yield: 4 servings (serving size: 3 ounces pork and about 1/2 cup polenta).

CALORIES 408; FAT 16.1g (sat 7.7g, mono 4.6g, poly 1.2g); PROTEIN 29.7g; CARB 34.2g; FIBER 2.4g; CHOL 84mg; IRON 3.2mg; SODIUM 685mg; CALC 218mg

Quick & Easy

Sesame-Soy Meatballs

$2.50 per serving, $9.98 total

Serve these garlicky, spicy meatballs with steamed sugar snap peas and two cups cooked rice tossed with 1 tablespoon chile paste—you'll find it on the ethnic aisle of most supermarkets or at Asian grocers.

1/3 cup minced green onions
2 tablespoons brown sugar
3 tablespoons lower-sodium soy sauce
2 tablespoons dark sesame oil
1 tablespoon chile paste (such as sambal oelek)
1/4 teaspoon salt
6 garlic cloves, finely minced
1 pound ground sirloin
Cooking spray

1. Preheat oven to 400°.
2. Combine first 7 ingredients in a large bowl. Add beef; mix gently to combine. With moist hands, shape beef mixture into 20 (1 1/2-inch) meatballs.
3. Heat a large cast-iron skillet over medium-high heat. Add half of meatballs to pan; cook 4 minutes, turning to brown meatballs on all sides. Arrange browned meatballs in a single layer on a jelly-roll pan coated with cooking spray. Repeat procedure with remaining meatballs. Bake meatballs at 400° for 7 minutes or until done. Yield: 4 servings (serving size: 5 meatballs).

CALORIES 241; FAT 11.3g (sat 2.7g, mono 4.8g, poly 3g); PROTEIN 23.5g; CARB 10.3g; FIBER 0.3g; CHOL 42mg; IRON 1.9mg; SODIUM 491mg; CALC 36mg

3 MORE WAYS TO USE CHILE PASTE

1 Add to marinades for beef, pork, chicken, or seafood.

2 Spice up salads by stirring some into dressings.

3 Toss with hot cooked rice or potatoes.

Quick & Easy • Kid Friendly
Vegetarian

Rotini and Cheese

$1.01 per serving, $4.05 total

This hearty one-dish meal combines smoky bacon with tangy cheddar for a family-friendly midweek meal that comes together in a flash. Use cavatappi, fusilli, or your favorite short pasta if you can't find rotini.

2 bacon slices
1 tablespoon butter
1 tablespoon olive oil
1 cup finely chopped onion
2 garlic cloves, minced
1 1/2 teaspoons all-purpose flour
2 teaspoons Dijon mustard
1 cup 1% low-fat milk
3/4 cup (3 ounces) shredded sharp cheddar cheese
1/2 teaspoon kosher salt
1/4 teaspoon freshly ground black pepper
5 cups hot cooked rotini (about 8 ounces uncooked pasta)
3/4 cups frozen green peas, thawed

1. Cook bacon in a large nonstick skillet over medium heat until crisp. Remove bacon from pan; crumble. Increase heat to medium-high. Add butter and oil to drippings in pan; swirl to coat. Add onion; sauté 5 minutes, stirring occasionally. Add garlic; sauté 30 seconds, stirring constantly. Add flour, and sauté 1 minute, stirring frequently. Stir in mustard. Gradually add milk, stirring constantly with a whisk, and bring to a boil. Cook 3 minutes or until slightly thickened. Remove from heat. Let stand 5 minutes. Add cheese, salt, and pepper, stirring with a whisk until smooth.
2. Place pan over low heat. Stir in bacon, pasta, and peas; cook 1 minute or until thoroughly heated, tossing to coat. Yield: 4 servings (serving size: about 1 1/2 cups).

CALORIES 470; FAT 19.9g (sat 9.1g, mono 7.7g, poly 1.3g); PROTEIN 18.4g; CARB 54.8g; FIBER 3.7g; CHOL 40mg; IRON 2.7mg; SODIUM 667mg; CALC 258mg

Make Ahead • Freezable • Kid Friendly

Pork and Herbed White Beans

$2.37 per serving, $9.48 total

Although this dish takes a while to cook, the majority is hands off. You can easily prepare it over the weekend and reheat during the week. Garnish with small sage leaves, if desired.

1 cup dried white beans
6 cups boiling water
1½ tablespoons olive oil, divided
1 (1-pound) boneless pork picnic roast, cut into ½-inch pieces
½ teaspoon salt, divided
½ teaspoon black pepper
2 cups fat-free, lower-sodium chicken broth
½ cup water
2 fresh thyme sprigs
1 fresh sage sprig
2 cups coarsely chopped onion
½ cup coarsely chopped carrot
6 garlic cloves, coarsely chopped

1. Place beans in a Dutch oven; cover with 6 cups boiling water. Let stand 1 hour; drain.
2. Preheat oven to 325°.
3. Heat a Dutch oven over medium-high heat. Add 1 tablespoon olive oil to pan, and swirl to coat. Sprinkle pork evenly with ¼ teaspoon salt and pepper. Add pork to pan; sauté 6 minutes, turning to brown on all sides. Stir in beans, remaining ¼ teaspoon salt, broth, and next 3 ingredients; bring to a boil. Cover and bake at 325° for 1 hour.
4. Heat a skillet over medium-high heat. Add remaining 1½ teaspoons oil to pan; swirl to coat. Add onion and carrot; sauté 4 minutes, stirring occasionally. Add garlic, and sauté 1 minute, stirring constantly. Stir onion mixture into bean mixture; bake at 325° an additional 1½ hours or until beans are tender. Drain solids through a sieve over a bowl, reserving solids and cooking liquid. Skim fat from top of liquid; discard fat. Stir cooking liquid back into pork mixture. Yield: 4 servings (serving size: 1¼ cups).

CALORIES 559; **FAT** 19.6g (sat 5.6g, mono 10.4g, poly 2.1g); **PROTEIN** 51.7g; **CARB** 43.5g; **FIBER** 10.6g; **CHOL** 129mg; **IRON** 7.6mg; **SODIUM** 631mg; **CALC** 164mg

Make Ahead

Curried Potatoes and Squash

$2.42 per serving, $9.66 total

Substitute vegetable broth for chicken, if you prefer a meatless dish. Serve with warm flatbread to soak up the flavorful juices.

2 tablespoons butter
1 cup chopped onion
1½ tablespoons grated peeled fresh ginger
4 garlic cloves, minced
3 cups (½-inch) cubed peeled baking potato (about 1½ pounds)
3 cups (½-inch) cubed peeled butternut squash (about 1¼ pounds)
½ teaspoon salt
½ teaspoon ground cumin
½ teaspoon ground red pepper
1 (14.5-ounce) can whole tomatoes, undrained and chopped
1 (14-ounce) can fat-free, lower-sodium chicken broth
¾ cup light coconut milk
1 cup frozen green peas, thawed
½ cup thinly diagonally sliced green onions (about 4 medium)

1. Melt butter in a large skillet over medium-high heat. Add onion to pan, and sauté 4 minutes, stirring occasionally. Add ginger and garlic; sauté 1 minute, stirring constantly. Add potato and next 4 ingredients; sauté 1 minute, stirring constantly. Stir in tomatoes and broth; bring to a boil. Cover and cook 5 minutes.
2. Stir in coconut milk and peas; bring to a simmer. Cook, uncovered, 12 minutes or until squash is tender, stirring occasionally. Sprinkle with green onions. Yield: 4 servings (serving size: 1¾ cups).

CALORIES 356; **FAT** 8.8g (sat 5.9g, mono 1.6g, poly 0.5g); **PROTEIN** 10.5g; **CARB** 66g; **FIBER** 9.3g; **CHOL** 15mg; **IRON** 4.9mg; **SODIUM** 668mg; **CALC** 166mg

DINNER TONIGHT

Here are a handful of fast weeknight menus from the *Cooking Light* Test Kitchens.

Quick & Easy

Sautéed Chicken and Zucchini with Parsley-Chervil Pan Sauce

with Golden Mashed Potatoes

Simple Sub: Instead of dried chervil, you can use 1 teaspoon chopped fresh tarragon.
Prep Pointer: Finishing the sauce with cold butter enriches it and adds body.
Flavor Hit: A hint of acidity from lemon juice balances the taste of the sauce.

4 (6-ounce) skinless, boneless chicken breast halves
½ teaspoon salt, divided
½ teaspoon freshly ground black pepper
6½ teaspoons chilled butter, divided
2 teaspoons olive oil
3 cups (¾-inch-thick) slices zucchini (about 2 medium)
½ cup fat-free, lower-sodium chicken broth
½ teaspoon dried chervil
1 teaspoon fresh lemon juice
1 tablespoon chopped fresh parsley

1. Sprinkle chicken with ¼ teaspoon salt and black pepper. Heat 1 teaspoon butter and oil in a large skillet over medium-high heat. Add chicken, and cook 4 minutes on each side or until done. Remove from pan; keep warm.
2. Add zucchini and remaining ¼ teaspoon salt to pan; cook 2 minutes on each side or until crisp-tender. Remove from pan; keep warm.
3. Melt 1 teaspoon butter in pan, scraping pan to loosen browned bits. Add broth and chervil; bring to a boil. Cook 3 minutes or until reduced to ¼ cup. Remove from heat; stir in remaining 1½ tablespoons butter, lemon juice, and parsley. Serve chicken with sauce

and zucchini. Yield: 4 servings (serving size: 1 chicken breast half, 1½ tablespoons sauce, and ½ cup zucchini).

CALORIES 276; FAT 12.6g (sat 5.4g, mono 4.6g, poly 1.4g); PROTEIN 35.9g; CARB 3.8g; FIBER 1.3g; CHOL 110mg; IRON 1.7mg; SODIUM 479mg; CALC 39mg

For the Golden Mashed Potatoes:

Place 3 cups cubed Yukon gold potatoes (about 1 pound) in a large saucepan; cover with water. Bring to a boil. Cover, reduce heat, and simmer 10 minutes or until tender; drain. Place potatoes in a large bowl. Add ⅓ cup 2% reduced-fat milk, 1 teaspoon butter, ⅜ teaspoon salt, and ¼ teaspoon freshly ground black pepper; mash to desired consistency. Yield: 4 servings.

CALORIES 124; FAT 1.3g (sat 0.8g); SODIUM 246mg

SHOPPING LIST

Sautéed Chicken and Zucchini with Parsley-Chervil Pan Sauce
2 medium zucchini
1 lemon
fresh parsley
olive oil
fat-free, lower-sodium chicken broth
dried chervil
butter
4 (6-ounce) skinless, boneless chicken breast halves

Golden Mashed Potatoes
1 pound Yukon gold potatoes
2% reduced-fat milk
butter

GAME PLAN

While potatoes and water come to a boil:
- Cook chicken.
- Slice zucchini.
While potatoes cook:
- Sauté zucchini.
- Finish sauce.

Quick & Easy • Make Ahead
Chicken and Parsnip Soup
with Herb-Scented Drop Biscuits

Vegetarian Swap: Use mushroom broth, omit chicken, and use two cans of chickpeas.
Buy The Best: Choose firm, small to medium-sized parsnips.
Simple Sub: Try sliced cremini or button mushrooms in place of the gourmet blend.

1½ teaspoons olive oil
¾ cup thinly diagonally sliced parsnip (2 parsnips)
¾ cup thinly sliced shallots (2 shallots)
1 (4-ounce) package gourmet mushroom blend
1 garlic clove, minced
2½ cups fat-free, lower-sodium chicken broth
1 cup water
1 cup chickpeas (garbanzo beans), rinsed and drained
1 cup shredded skinless, boneless rotisserie chicken breast
½ teaspoon freshly ground black pepper
¼ teaspoon salt
⅛ teaspoon hot sauce
1 fresh thyme sprig
2 tablespoons chopped fresh parsley

1. Heat olive oil in a medium saucepan over medium-high heat. Add parsnip and next 3 ingredients; sauté 3 minutes. Add broth and next 7 ingredients; bring to a simmer, and cook 10 minutes or until parsnips are tender. Remove from heat; stir in parsley. Yield: 4 servings (serving size: 1⅓ cups).

CALORIES 204; FAT 4.1g (sat 0.8g, mono 1.9g, poly 0.9g); PROTEIN 17.4g; CARB 25.3g; FIBER 5.1g; CHOL 30mg; IRON 2.3mg; SODIUM 607mg; CALC 62mg

---

For the Herb-Scented Drop Biscuits:

Preheat oven to 450°. Combine 4.5 ounces (about 1 cup) all-purpose flour, ¾ teaspoon baking powder, and ¼ teaspoon salt; cut in 1 tablespoon cold unsalted butter until mixture resembles coarse meal. Make a well in center of mixture; add ⅓ cup 1% low-fat milk, 2 tablespoons plain fat-free Greek yogurt, and 1½ teaspoons fresh thyme leaves, stirring just until combined. Drop by heaping tablespoonfuls onto a baking sheet coated with cooking spray to form 8 biscuits; coat tops with cooking spray. Bake at 450° for 15 minutes or until golden brown. Yield: 4 servings.

CALORIES 156; FAT 3.5g (sat 2.1g); SODIUM 256mg

SHOPPING LIST

Chicken and Parsnip Soup
2 parsnips
2 shallots
4 ounces gourmet mushroom blend
garlic
fresh thyme
fresh parsley
olive oil
hot sauce
2 cans fat-free, lower-sodium chicken broth
1 can chickpeas
rotisserie chicken

Herb-Scented Drop Biscuits
fresh thyme
all-purpose flour
baking powder
unsalted butter
1% low-fat milk
plain fat-free Greek yogurt

GAME PLAN

While oven preheats:
- Prep vegetables for soup.
- Sauté vegetables for soup.
- Make biscuit dough.
While biscuits bake:
- Simmer soup.

Rosemary Lamb Chops

with Maple-Hazelnut Sweet Potatoes
and Fall Apple Salad

*Simple Sub: In place of hazelnuts, try walnuts
or pecans.*
*Flavor Hit: Maple syrup intensifies the sweet-
ness of the potatoes and adds caramel notes.*
*Time-Saver: You can forgo the "custom blend"
of lettuces and pick up a boxed mix.*

1½ teaspoons chopped fresh rosemary
½ teaspoon salt
¼ teaspoon freshly ground black pepper
1 garlic clove, minced
8 (3-ounce) lamb rib chops, trimmed
2 teaspoons olive oil

1. Combine first 4 ingredients in a small
bowl. Sprinkle herb mixture evenly over
lamb; gently rub over lamb.
2. Heat a large skillet over medium-
high heat. Add oil to pan; swirl to coat.
Add lamb; cook 3 minutes on each side
or until desired degree of doneness.
Remove lamb from pan; let stand
5 minutes. Yield: 4 servings (serving
size: 2 lamb chops).

CALORIES 157; **FAT** 9.7g (sat 3g, mono 4.6g, poly 0.9g);
PROTEIN 16g; **CARB** 0.4g; **FIBER** 0.1g; **CHOL** 52mg;
IRON 1.4mg; **SODIUM** 344mg; **CALC** 12mg

For the Maple-Hazelnut Sweet Potatoes:
Pierce 2 (8-ounce) sweet potatoes a few
times with a fork; place potatoes on
a layer of paper towels in microwave.
Microwave at HIGH 10 minutes or
until tender; let stand 5 minutes. Peel
potatoes; discard skins. Place potatoes
in a medium bowl; mash with a potato
masher to desired consistency. Add
¼ cup 1% low-fat milk, 2 tablespoons
butter, 1 tablespoon maple syrup, and
¼ teaspoon salt; stir until well combined. Top with 2 tablespoons chopped
blanched hazelnuts. Yield: 4 servings.

CALORIES 159; **FAT** 8.2g (sat 3.9g); **SODIUM** 220mg

For the Fall Apple Salad:
Combine 1 tablespoon red wine vinegar, 1½ teaspoons honey, 1 teaspoon
Dijon mustard, ¼ teaspoon cracked
black pepper, ⅛ teaspoon salt, and
1 minced garlic clove in a large bowl;
gradually whisk in 2 tablespoons extra-
virgin olive oil. Add 2 cups torn butter
lettuce, 1 cup sliced endive, 1 cup torn
radicchio, and 1 cup thinly sliced apple
(about 1 small apple); toss gently to
coat. Yield: 4 servings.

CALORIES 91; **FAT** 6.9g (sat 1g); **SODIUM** 110mg

30 minutes

SHOPPING LIST

Rosemary Lamb Chops
fresh rosemary
garlic
olive oil
8 (3-ounce) lamb rib chops

Maple-Hazelnut Sweet Potatoes
2 (8-ounce) sweet potatoes
maple syrup
blanched hazelnuts
1% low-fat milk
butter

Fall Apple Salad
garlic
butter lettuce
2 endive heads
radicchio
1 small apple
red wine vinegar
honey
Dijon mustard
extra-virgin olive oil

GAME PLAN

While potatoes microwave:
- Rub lamb chops with seasonings.
- Prepare vinaigrette.
While potatoes stand:
- Cook lamb.
- Prepare salad.

Halibut à la Provençal over Mixed Greens

with Toasted Garlic Bread

*Prep Pointer: For the best browning, make sure
the skillet is very hot before adding the fish.*
*Simple Sub: The flavors of herbes de Provence
would also work well with chicken.*
*Time-Saver: Be sure to purchase pitted
kalamata olives.*

1 teaspoon dried herbes de Provence
2 tablespoons fresh lemon juice, divided
½ teaspoon salt, divided
4 (6-ounce) halibut fillets
3 tablespoons olive oil, divided
½ teaspoon chopped fresh parsley
½ teaspoon chopped fresh thyme
¼ cup minced shallots
½ teaspoon Dijon mustard
1 teaspoon honey
¼ teaspoon freshly ground black pepper
2 tablespoons finely chopped pitted kalamata
   olives
1 (6-ounce) package gourmet salad greens

1. Combine herbes de Provence, 2 teaspoons juice, and ¼ teaspoon salt. Rub
over tops of fillets. Heat 2 teaspoons
oil in a large skillet over medium-high
heat. Add fish to pan; cook 3 minutes
on each side or until desired degree
of doneness. Remove fish from pan;
sprinkle with parsley and thyme.
2. Heat remaining 7 teaspoons oil in
skillet over medium-high heat. Add
shallots; sauté 2 minutes or until tender.
Remove from heat; stir in remaining
4 teaspoons lemon juice, remaining
¼ teaspoon salt, mustard, honey, and
pepper. Gently stir in olives.
3. Combine greens and olive mixture
in a large bowl, tossing well to coat.
Arrange 1½ cups salad on each of 4 plates;
top each serving with 1 fillet. Yield: 4
servings.

CALORIES 308; **FAT** 15.6g (sat 2.2g, mono 9.8g, poly 2.5g);
PROTEIN 35.2g; **CARB** 6.2g; **FIBER** 1.4g; **CHOL** 52mg;
IRON 2.4mg; **SODIUM** 502mg; **CALC** 115mg

For the Toasted Garlic Bread:
Preheat broiler. Arrange 8 (½-ounce) slices French bread baguette in a single layer on a baking sheet. Lightly coat tops with olive oil cooking spray. Broil bread slices 1 minute or until lightly browned. Turn slices over; lightly coat with olive oil cooking spray. Broil 30 seconds or until lightly browned. Rub toasts with cut side of a halved garlic clove. Yield: 4 servings.

CALORIES 84; **FAT** 1g (sat 0g); **SODIUM** 184mg

SHOPPING LIST

Halibut à la Provençal over Mixed Greens
1 lemon
1 shallot
fresh thyme
fresh parsley
6-ounce package gourmet salad greens
dried herbes de Provence
olive oil
Dijon mustard
honey
pitted kalamata olives
4 (6-ounce) halibut fillets

Toasted Garlic Bread
baguette
garlic
olive oil cooking spray

GAME PLAN

While broiler heats:
- Slice bread.
- Season fish.
While fish cooks:
- Toast bread.
- Prepare salad.

Quick & Easy
Deviled Chicken
with Broccoli with Shallots and Herbed Rice

Flavor Hit: This dish gets its name from the spicy kick of ground red pepper.
Kid Tweak: Omit the red pepper and use an equal amount of mild chili powder.
Simple Sub: The vegetable side would be good with cauliflower or Brussels sprouts, too.

4 (8-ounce) skinless, bone-in chicken breast halves
½ teaspoon freshly ground black pepper
¼ teaspoon salt
Cooking spray
2 tablespoons prepared mustard
½ teaspoon ground red pepper
2 (1-ounce) slices French bread baguette

1. Preheat oven to 475°.
2. Sprinkle chicken with black pepper and salt; lightly coat with cooking spray.
3. Place chicken on rack of a broiler or roasting pan coated with cooking spray. Bake at 475° for 15 minutes; remove pan from oven.
4. Combine mustard and red pepper in a small bowl; brush over chicken. Place bread in food processor; pulse 10 times or until crumbs measure 1 cup. Sprinkle breadcrumbs evenly over mustard mixture on chicken, pressing lightly to adhere. Lightly coat breadcrumbs with cooking spray. Return pan to oven. Bake at 475° for 10 minutes or until breadcrumbs are browned and a thermometer registers 165°. Yield: 4 servings (serving size: 1 chicken breast half).

CALORIES 214; **FAT** 3.8g (sat 1.1g, mono 1.3g, poly 0.8g); **PROTEIN** 34.2g; **CARB** 8.8g; **FIBER** 0.4g; **CHOL** 90mg; **IRON** 1.6mg; **SODIUM** 408mg; **CALC** 17mg

---

For the Broccoli with Shallots:
Cook 12 ounces fresh broccoli florets in boiling water 2 minutes; drain. Heat 1 teaspoon butter and 1 teaspoon olive oil in a skillet over medium-high heat. Add 3 tablespoons minced shallots; sauté 2 minutes. Add broccoli, ¼ teaspoon salt, and ¼ teaspoon black pepper; sauté 2 minutes. Yield: 4 servings.

CALORIES 48; **FAT** 2.4g (sat 0.8g); **SODIUM** 178mg

For the Herbed Rice:
Cook 1 cup basmati rice according to package directions. Stir in 1 tablespoon chopped fresh thyme, 1 teaspoon chopped fresh oregano, ½ teaspoon cracked black pepper, and ⅜ teaspoon salt. Yield: 4 servings.

CALORIES 182; **FAT** 0g; **SODIUM** 221mg

SHOPPING LIST

Deviled Chicken
baguette
prepared mustard
ground red pepper
4 (8-ounce) skinless, bone-in chicken breast halves

Broccoli with Shallots
12-ounce package fresh broccoli florets
1 shallot
olive oil
butter

Herbed Rice
fresh thyme
fresh oregano
basmati rice

GAME PLAN

While oven preheats:
- Bring water to a boil for rice.
- Make breadcrumbs.
While chicken bakes:
- Cook rice.
- Prepare broccoli.

SUPERFAST

Fresh flourishes and seasonal ingredients cook up quickly for lively weeknight meals.

Quick & Easy • Vegetarian
Side Dish of the Month
Romaine Salad with Balsamic Vinaigrette

Customize this basic salad by using other fruit, such as dried cranberries, apricots, or raisins, or different cheeses, like blue or goat.

3 tablespoons balsamic vinegar
2 tablespoons olive oil
1 tablespoon minced shallots
1 tablespoon chopped fresh parsley
1 teaspoon Dijon mustard
¼ teaspoon salt
¼ teaspoon freshly ground black pepper
1 garlic clove, crushed
6 cups chopped romaine lettuce
¼ cup dried cherries, chopped
¼ cup (1 ounce) crumbled feta cheese

1. Combine first 8 ingredients in a large bowl; stir well with a whisk. Add lettuce, dried cherries, and cheese; toss gently to coat. Yield: 4 servings (serving size: 1½ cups).

CALORIES 144; **FAT** 9g (sat 2.4g, mono 5.4g, poly 0.9g); **PROTEIN** 3.1g; **CARB** 12.8g; **FIBER** 2.6g; **CHOL** 8mg; **IRON** 1.2mg; **SODIUM** 294mg; **CALC** 86mg

Lemony Sugar Snap Variation: Omit vinegar and garlic; add 3 tablespoons lemon juice. Use 6 cups torn butter lettuce. Omit cherries and feta; add 1 cup sliced sugar snap peas and 3 tablespoons toasted sliced almonds. Yield: 4 servings.

CALORIES 116; **FAT** 9.2g (sat 1.1); **SODIUM** 152mg

Cilantro-Lime Variation: Omit vinegar; add 3 tablespoons lime juice. Use 1 tablespoon cilantro in place of parsley. Omit cherries and feta. Add ½ cup diced yellow bell pepper and ¼ cup sliced green onions. Yield: 4 servings.

CALORIES 86; **FAT** 7.1g (sat 1g); **SODIUM** 159mg

Honey-Balsamic-Arugula Variation: Decrease vinegar to 2 tablespoons. Add 1 teaspoon honey. Use 6 cups arugula. Omit cherries and feta; add ¼ cup sliced red onion, ¼ cup shaved Parmesan, and 2 tablespoons chopped walnuts. Yield: 4 servings.

CALORIES 136; **FAT** 11.2g (sat 2.4g); **SODIUM** 272mg

Quick & Easy
Chicken Piccata with Orzo

Lemon rind gives the orzo floral, muted citrus notes, a nice companion to the zingy sauce.

1 cup uncooked orzo
2 teaspoons grated lemon rind
4 (4-ounce) chicken cutlets
¼ teaspoon kosher salt
¼ teaspoon freshly ground black pepper
1 tablespoon olive oil
¼ cup white wine
½ cup fat-free, lower-sodium chicken broth
1 tablespoon fresh lemon juice
1 tablespoon chilled butter, cut into small pieces
2 tablespoons chopped fresh parsley
1 tablespoon capers

1. Cook orzo according to package directions. Drain. Stir in rind.
2. While orzo cooks, heat a large skillet over medium-high heat. Sprinkle chicken with salt and pepper. Add oil to pan; swirl to coat. Add chicken; cook 3 minutes on each side or until done. Remove from pan; keep warm. Add wine; cook 1 minute or until liquid almost evaporates, scraping pan to loosen browned bits. Add broth and lemon juice; bring to a boil. Cook 2 minutes or until reduced to ½ cup. Remove from heat; add butter, stirring until butter melts. Stir in parsley and capers. Serve over orzo. Yield: 4 servings (serving size: about ½ cup orzo, 1 cutlet, and 2 tablespoons sauce).

CALORIES 345; **FAT** 8.5g (sat 2.7g, mono 3.6g, poly 0.8g); **PROTEIN** 32g; **CARB** 33g; **FIBER** 1.9g; **CHOL** 73mg; **IRON** 1.1mg; **SODIUM** 328mg; **CALC** 22mg

Quick & Easy • Kid Friendly
Snack of the Month
Peanut Butter, Banana, and Flax Smoothies
(pictured on page 270)

If the smoothies seem too thick, add another tablespoon or two of milk.

½ cup 1% low-fat milk
½ cup vanilla fat-free yogurt
2 tablespoons ground golden flaxseed
1 tablespoon creamy peanut butter
1 teaspoon honey
¼ teaspoon vanilla extract
1 ripe banana, sliced

1. Place all ingredients in a blender; process until smooth. Yield: 2 servings (serving size: about ¾ cup).

CALORIES 229; **FAT** 8.4g (sat 1.7g, mono 2.8g, poly 3.5g); **PROTEIN** 9.2g; **CARB** 32g; **FIBER** 4g; **CHOL** 3mg; **IRON** 0.8mg; **SODIUM** 113mg; **CALC** 211mg

Quick & Easy
Soup of the Month
White Bean Soup with Kale and Chorizo

Be sure to use smoked Spanish chorizo, not raw Mexican chorizo.

2 ounces Spanish chorizo sausage, finely chopped
1 cup prechopped onion
3 garlic cloves, minced
3 cups fat-free, lower-sodium chicken broth
2 (15-ounce) cans organic cannellini beans, rinsed and drained
4 cups prechopped kale
½ teaspoon freshly ground black pepper
Cracked black pepper (optional)

1. Heat a large saucepan over medium-high heat. Add chorizo to pan; sauté 1 minute. Add onion and garlic to pan; sauté 5 minutes or until tender.
2. While onions cook, pour broth into a microwave-safe bowl; microwave at HIGH 3 minutes. Add hot broth and beans to pan; bring to a boil. Partially

mash beans with potato masher. Stir in kale and ½ teaspoon pepper; cook over medium heat 6 minutes. Sprinkle with cracked pepper, if desired. Yield: 4 servings (serving size: about 1¼ cups).

CALORIES 235; FAT 7.3g (sat 2.1g, mono 3.4g, poly 1.2g); PROTEIN 13.4g; CARB 30.7g; FIBER 7.6g; CHOL 12mg; IRON 3.5mg; SODIUM 586mg; CALC 157mg

Quick & Easy

Maple-Glazed Chicken with Apple–Brussels Sprouts Slaw

Chicken cutlets can range in size from about 2 ounces each to close to 5 or 6 ounces each. For this dish, we chose the smaller ones.

8 (2-ounce) chicken cutlets
½ teaspoon kosher salt, divided
½ teaspoon freshly ground black pepper, divided
2 tablespoons olive oil, divided
3 tablespoons red wine vinegar, divided
2 tablespoons maple syrup
8 ounces Brussels sprouts
¼ cup dried currants
1 medium Fuji or Gala apple, cut into ⅛-inch-thick slices

1. Heat a large skillet over medium-high heat. Sprinkle chicken with ¼ teaspoon salt and ¼ teaspoon pepper. Add 1 tablespoon oil to pan; swirl to coat. Add chicken to pan; cook 3 minutes on each side or until done. Remove from pan; keep warm. Add 2 tablespoons vinegar and syrup to pan; bring to a boil. Cook 1 minute or until reduced to 3 tablespoons. Return chicken to pan; turn to coat with glaze.
2. Cut Brussels sprouts in half lengthwise; thinly slice crosswise. Place remaining 1 tablespoon oil, 1 tablespoon vinegar, ¼ teaspoon salt, and ¼ teaspoon pepper in a large bowl; stir well with a whisk. Add Brussels sprouts, currants, and apple; toss to combine. Serve slaw with chicken. Yield: 4 servings (serving size: 2 cutlets and about ¾ cup slaw).

CALORIES 282; FAT 8.7g (sat 1.4g, mono 5.4g, poly 1.5g); PROTEIN 28.6g; CARB 23.4g; FIBER 3.7g; CHOL 66mg; IRON 2.1mg; SODIUM 331mg; CALC 54mg

Quick & Easy • Kid Friendly

Ginger-Soy Chicken Thighs with Scallion Rice

If you can't find ginger preserves, you can substitute ½ cup apricot preserves plus 2 teaspoons grated peeled fresh ginger.

1 (3½-ounce) bag boil-in-bag long-grain rice
2 tablespoons thinly sliced green onions
1 tablespoon olive oil
8 (2-ounce) skinless, boneless chicken thighs
½ cup ginger preserves
2 tablespoons lower-sodium soy sauce
2 garlic cloves, minced

1. Prepare rice according to package directions. Drain; fluff rice with a fork. Gently stir in green onions.
2. While rice cooks, heat a large skillet over medium-high heat. Add oil to pan; swirl to coat. Add chicken; cook 5 minutes on each side or until done. Remove from pan; keep warm. Add preserves, soy sauce, and garlic to pan; bring to a boil. Cook sauce 2 minutes or until reduced to ⅓ cup, stirring occasionally. Return chicken to pan; turn to coat with sauce. Yield: 4 servings (serving size: 2 thighs, about ½ cup rice, and about 1½ tablespoons sauce).

CALORIES 355; FAT 7.8g (sat 1.6g, mono 3.8g, poly 1.5g); PROTEIN 24.5g; CARB 47.3g; FIBER 0.2g; CHOL 94mg; IRON 2.2mg; SODIUM 366mg; CALC 18mg

FROM OUR NEW COOKBOOK

Following the success of *Way to Cook* comes *Way to Cook Vegetarian*—tips, techniques, and recipes for meatless meals.

Vegetarian

Pan-Crisped Tofu with Greens and Peanut Dressing

⅓ cup white miso (soybean paste)
⅓ cup mirin (sweet rice wine)
⅓ cup rice vinegar
1 tablespoon finely grated peeled fresh ginger
½ cup chopped dry-roasted peanuts, divided
5 tablespoons canola oil, divided
2 (14-ounce) packages water-packed firm tofu, drained
8 cups gourmet salad greens
Minced fresh chives (optional)

1. Combine first 4 ingredients, ¼ cup peanuts, and 3 tablespoons oil in a small bowl; stir with a whisk.
2. Cut each tofu block crosswise into 8 (½-inch-thick) slices. Arrange tofu on several layers of paper towels. Top with several more layers of paper towels; top with a cast-iron skillet or other heavy pan. Let stand 30 minutes. Remove tofu from paper towels.
3. Heat 1 tablespoon oil in a large nonstick skillet over medium-high heat. Add 8 tofu slices to pan; sauté 4 minutes on each side or until crisp and golden. Remove from pan, and drain tofu on paper towels. Repeat procedure with remaining 1 tablespoon oil and remaining 8 tofu slices. Place 1 cup greens on each of 8 plates. Top each serving with 2 tofu slices, 3 tablespoons miso mixture, and 1½ teaspoons chopped peanuts. Garnish each serving with chives, if desired. Yield: 8 servings.

CALORIES 266; FAT 18g (sat 1.8g, mono 8.3g, poly 6.8g); PROTEIN 13.9g; CARB 13g; FIBER 4.1g; CHOL 0mg; IRON 3mg; SODIUM 375mg; CALC 227mg

POMS AWAY

Is there a more gorgeous fruit than the crimson pomegranate, brimming with ruby gems? Open one up and receive a spritz of juice and oils, a whiff of tannins. Tucked into its complex web of pith are a thousand jewels called arils (the only edible parts). Healthy antioxidants have made it a vogue fruit, and you can buy all sorts of juices and teas and even sodas, some of which are delicious. But start by taking the time to enjoy one fresh—it's a bit of work, and don't wear your Sunday best.

Kid Friendly

Moroccan Roasted Pomegranate Chicken

1 (3-pound) whole chicken
1 teaspoon kosher salt, divided
Cooking spray
1 pomegranate, quartered
3 tablespoons dry white wine
2 teaspoons sugar
¼ teaspoon ground cinnamon
¼ teaspoon black pepper
1 garlic clove, minced
2 teaspoons fresh lemon juice

1. Preheat oven to 450°.
2. Remove and discard giblets and neck from chicken. Lift wing tips up and over back; tuck under chicken. Sprinkle ¾ teaspoon salt over chicken. Place chicken, breast side up, on rack of a roasting pan coated with cooking spray. Place rack in pan. Bake at 450° for 45 minutes or until a thermometer inserted in meaty part of thigh registers 165°. Remove chicken and rack from pan; let stand 10 minutes. Remove skin from dark meat; discard.
3. Remove seeds from pomegranate; set 1 tablespoon seeds aside. Place remaining seeds in a blender; pulse to crush. Strain mixture through a sieve over a bowl to yield ¼ cup juice; discard solids.

4. Place roasting pan over medium heat. Add wine to drippings in pan, scraping pan to loosen browned bits. Pour mixture into a medium saucepan; stir in pomegranate juice, sugar, and next 3 ingredients. Bring to a boil. Cook 16 minutes or until reduced to ⅓ cup. Remove from heat; stir in lemon juice and remaining ¼ teaspoon salt. Serve sauce with chicken. Sprinkle with reserved 1 tablespoon seeds. Yield: 4 servings (serving size: about 5 ounces chicken, about 1½ tablespoons sauce, and ¾ teaspoon seeds).

CALORIES 327; FAT 12.6g (sat 3.4g, mono 4.6g, poly 2.7g); PROTEIN 41.6g; CARB 10.1g; FIBER 1.7g; CHOL 124mg; IRON 1.9mg; SODIUM 595mg; CALC 29mg

Pomegranate-Orange Salsa

Serve with shrimp, flaky white fish, chicken, or tortilla chips.

Combine 1 cup chopped orange sections, ⅔ cup pomegranate seeds (about 2 pomegranates), ⅓ cup fresh pomegranate juice, ¼ cup minced shallots, 2 tablespoons minced jalapeño pepper, 1 tablespoon chopped fresh cilantro, 1 tablespoon fresh lime juice, ¼ teaspoon kosher salt, and ¼ teaspoon freshly ground black pepper. Yield: 6 servings (serving size: ¼ cup).

CALORIES 46; FAT 0.1g (sat 0g); SODIUM 81mg

Pomegranate and Pear Jam

Combine 2 cups sugar, 2 cups chopped peeled Seckel (or other) pear, ⅔ cup strained fresh pomegranate juice (about 2 pomegranates), and ¼ cup rosé wine in a large saucepan over medium heat; stir until sugar melts. Bring to a simmer; simmer 25 minutes or until pear is tender. Remove from heat; mash with a potato masher. Add ¼ cup pomegranate seeds and ½ teaspoon butter; bring to a boil. Stir in 2 tablespoons fruit pectin for less- or no-sugar recipes (such as

Sure-Jell in pink box). Return mixture to a boil; cook 1 minute, stirring constantly. Remove from heat; stir in 1 tablespoon grated lemon rind and 1 teaspoon minced fresh rosemary. Cool to room temperature. Cover and chill overnight. Yield: 2 cups (serving size: 4 teaspoons).

CALORIES 90; FAT 0.3g (sat 0.1g); SODIUM 1mg

5-INGREDIENT COOKING

Quick & Easy

Halibut with Leeks
(pictured on page 269)

Raisins and vinegar lend sweet-tart appeal to a dish inspired by a classic Italian approach.

3 tablespoons extra-virgin olive oil
6 cups ½-inch-thick sliced leeks (about 4 medium)
¾ cup golden raisins
2½ tablespoons tarragon vinegar
4 (6-ounce) halibut fillets

Heat a large saucepan over medium heat. Add olive oil to pan, swirling to coat. Add leeks and ½ teaspoon kosher salt to pan; cover and cook 6 minutes, stirring occasionally. Add ¾ cup water to pan; bring to a boil. Cover, reduce heat, and simmer 6 minutes or until leeks are tender. Remove from heat. Stir in raisins, vinegar, and ¼ teaspoon freshly ground black pepper; keep warm. Heat a large nonstick skillet over medium-high heat. Coat pan with cooking spray. Sprinkle fish evenly with ½ teaspoon kosher salt and ½ teaspoon freshly ground black pepper. Add fish to pan; cook 4 minutes on each side or until desired degree of doneness. Serve fish with leek mixture. Yield: 4 servings (serving size: 1 halibut fillet and about ⅔ cup leek mixture).

CALORIES 453; FAT 14.6g (sat 2.1g, mono 8.7g, poly 2.6g); PROTEIN 38.5g; CARB 43.8g; FIBER 3.7g; CHOL 54mg; IRON 4.9mg; SODIUM 603mg; CALC 177mg

THE FIVE INGREDIENTS

3 tablespoons extra-virgin olive oil

6 cups ½-inch-thick sliced leeks (about 4 medium)

¾ cup golden raisins

2½ tablespoons tarragon vinegar

4 (6-ounce) halibut fillets

Quick & Easy

Curried Chicken Sauté

(pictured on page 272)

This simple dish delivers bold, complex flavors. Serve with steamed rice.

1½ teaspoons curry powder, divided
1 pound skinless, boneless chicken breasts
1 (8-ounce) package presliced mixed bell peppers
1 cup light coconut milk
1 lime

Heat a nonstick skillet over medium-high heat. Sprinkle 1 teaspoon curry powder, ½ teaspoon salt, and ½ teaspoon black pepper over chicken. Coat pan with cooking spray. Add chicken to pan; cook 5 minutes on each side or until done. Remove chicken from pan; keep warm. Add bell peppers and remaining ½ teaspoon curry powder to pan; sauté 1 minute. Add coconut milk, and bring to a boil; reduce heat, and simmer 4 minutes or until mixture is slightly thickened. Cut lime in half. Squeeze 1 tablespoon juice from 1 lime half; slice other half into 4 wedges. Stir juice and ¼ teaspoon salt into bell pepper mixture. Cut chicken across grain into thin slices. Serve chicken with bell pepper mixture and lime wedges. Yield: 4 servings (serving size: 3 ounces chicken, ½ cup pepper mixture, and 1 lime wedge).

CALORIES 175; **FAT** 5.9g (sat 3.6g, mono 1g, poly 0.7g); **PROTEIN** 24.4g; **CARB** 7.1g; **FIBER** 1.7g; **CHOL** 63mg; **IRON** 1.6mg; **SODIUM** 515mg; **CALC** 20mg

---

THE FIVE INGREDIENTS

1½ teaspoons curry powder, divided

1 pound skinless, boneless chicken breasts

1 (8-ounce) package presliced mixed bell peppers

1 cup light coconut milk

1 lime

THE 12 DISHES OF CHRISTMAS...AND HANUKKAH AND NEW YEAR'S...

Presenting a dozen versatile recipes, rich with the flavors of winter cheer, perfect for your holiday repertoire. We cooked up 5 menus, but there are so many possibilities.

GLOBAL FLAVORS DINNER MENU

serves 8

Fennel and Spinach Soup with Roasted Pepper Yogurt

Roast Chicken with Five-Spice Sauce

Quinoa with Dried Cherries and Pistachios

Broccolini with Anchovy Gremolata

Braised Kale

Rustic Apple Tart

Make Ahead • Kid Friendly

Rustic Apple Tart

We like the flavor combo of sweet Golden Delicious and tart Granny Smith apples, but you can use any apple you like. If you'd like to keep strictly kosher when making this dessert, use walnut oil in place of butter, and look for pie dough made with shortening (and containing no lard).

2 tablespoons unsalted butter
1/4 cup packed brown sugar
2 tablespoons granulated sugar
4 1/2 cups sliced peeled Golden Delicious apple (about 1 1/2 pounds)
4 1/2 cups sliced peeled Granny Smith apple (about 1 1/2 pounds)
2 teaspoons fresh lemon juice
1 teaspoon ground cinnamon
1/4 teaspoon ground nutmeg
1/2 (15-ounce) package refrigerated pie dough (such as Pillsbury)
1 teaspoon ice water
1 teaspoon granulated sugar
1 tablespoon apricot preserves
1 teaspoon water

1. Melt butter in a large skillet over medium-high heat. Add brown sugar and 2 tablespoons granulated sugar; cook 2 minutes or until sugars dissolve. Stir in apples and next 3 ingredients. Cover, reduce heat, and cook 20 minutes or until apples are tender, stirring occasionally. Remove from heat; cool to room temperature.
2. Preheat oven to 400°. Set oven rack to lowest third of oven.
3. Place dough on a piece of parchment paper. Roll dough into a 14-inch circle. Place dough and parchment paper on a baking sheet. Arrange cooled apples in center of dough, leaving a 2-inch border. Fold edges of dough toward center, pressing gently to seal (dough will only partially cover apple mixture). Brush dough with 1 teaspoon ice water; sprinkle dough evenly with 1 teaspoon granulated sugar. Bake at 400° for 45 minutes or until golden brown.
4. Place preserves and 1 teaspoon water in a small microwave-safe bowl. Microwave at HIGH 30 seconds or until bubbly. Brush mixture over warm tart. Cut into wedges; serve warm or at room temperature. Yield: 8 servings (serving size: 1 wedge).

CALORIES 241; FAT 10g (sat 4.8g, mono 2.7g, poly 0.8g); PROTEIN 1.4g; CARB 40.1g; FIBER 1.8g; CHOL 11mg; IRON 0.2mg; SODIUM 140mg; CALC 16mg

Make Ahead

Fennel and Spinach Soup with Roasted Pepper Yogurt

You can serve this light, bright-tasting soup hot or at room temperature—or if you want to get a head start, make it ahead and serve it chilled. If the soup seems a little too thick after pureeing, add a few tablespoons of water to thin it out.

2 red bell peppers
2 large fennel bulbs with stalks
2 tablespoons extra-virgin olive oil
2 cups chopped leek (about 2 medium)
1 cup chopped shallots (about 2 large)
1 tablespoon chopped fresh thyme
3/8 teaspoon salt
2 cups fat-free, lower-sodium chicken broth
1 cup water
1 bay leaf
4 ounces fresh spinach
1/4 teaspoon freshly ground black pepper
1/2 cup fat-free Greek yogurt
1 teaspoon grated lemon rind
1 teaspoon fresh lemon juice
Dash of ground red pepper

1. Preheat broiler.
2. Cut bell peppers in half lengthwise; discard seeds and membranes. Place pepper halves, skin sides up, on a foil-lined baking sheet; flatten with hand. Broil 15 minutes or until blackened.

Place in a paper bag; fold to close tightly. Let stand 10 minutes. Peel and chop; set aside.

3. Trim tough outer leaves from fennel; mince feathery fronds to measure 2 tablespoons. Remove and discard stalks. Cut bulbs in half lengthwise; discard core. Chop bulbs to measure 4 cups.

4. Heat oil in a large Dutch oven over medium heat. Add fennel bulb, leek, and next 3 ingredients; cover and cook 10 minutes, stirring occasionally. Add broth, 1 cup water, and bay leaf; bring to a boil. Cover, reduce heat, and simmer 12 minutes. Discard bay leaf. Stir in spinach and black pepper. Remove from heat; cover and let stand 5 minutes at room temperature.

5. Pour half of fennel mixture into a blender. Remove center piece of blender lid (to allow steam to escape); secure blender lid on blender. Place a clean towel over opening in blender lid (to avoid splatters). Blend until smooth. Pour into a large bowl. Repeat procedure with remaining fennel mixture. Return pureed soup to pan; heat over medium heat 2 minutes or until heated.

6. Place roasted bell pepper, yogurt, and next 3 ingredients in a food processor; process until smooth.

7. Ladle about ¾ cup soup into each of 8 bowls; top each serving with 2 tablespoons yogurt mixture. Garnish with fennel fronds. Yield: 8 servings.

CALORIES 96; **FAT** 3.8g (sat 0.5g, mono 2.5g, poly 0.5g); **PROTEIN** 4g; **CARB** 13g; **FIBER** 3g; **CHOL** 0mg; **IRON** 1.8mg; **SODIUM** 255mg; **CALC** 73mg

---

SOUTHERN-STYLE FEAST MENU

serves 8

Beer-Braised Brisket with Honey-Lime Glaze

Hoppin' John's Cousin

Braised Kale

Roasted Winter Vegetables

Gingery Banana Pudding with Bourbon Cream

Beer-Braised Brisket with Honey-Lime Glaze

You can partially prepare this delicious, fork-tender roast a day ahead: Cook for four hours, cool to room temperature, and chill. Remove from refrigerator and let stand at room temperature for 30 minutes to an hour (to take the chill off), and proceed with step 3. You'll have leftovers that are great for saucy open-faced sandwiches or beef-and-potatoes hash.

2 teaspoons canola oil
1 (5-pound) flat-cut beef brisket, trimmed
1 teaspoon kosher salt, divided
1 teaspoon freshly ground black pepper
4 cups water
3 cups dark beer (such as a Belgian Chimay)
2 cups chopped carrot
1 cup vertically sliced onion
¼ cup chopped peeled fresh ginger
¼ cup no-salt-added ketchup
1 teaspoon lower-sodium soy sauce
¼ teaspoon crushed red pepper
20 fresh cilantro sprigs
10 fresh thyme sprigs
6 orange rind strips
6 lemon rind strips
2 bay leaves
1 apple, cored and cut into 6 wedges
1 (3-inch) cinnamon stick
¼ cup honey
3 tablespoons fresh lime juice
¼ cup chopped fresh cilantro

1. Preheat oven to 325°.

2. Heat oil in a heavy roasting pan over medium-high heat. Sprinkle beef with ¾ teaspoon salt and black pepper. Add beef to pan; cook 15 minutes, browning on both sides. Drain oil from pan. Add 4 cups water and next 14 ingredients to pan. Bring to a boil; cover with foil and bake at 325° for 4 hours. Remove beef from pan, reserving cooking liquid. Strain cooking liquid through a sieve into a bowl; skim fat from surface. Return liquid and beef to pan.

3. Cook beef, uncovered, at 325° for 1½ to 2 hours or until meat is fork-tender, basting occasionally with cooking liquid. Remove beef from pan, reserving cooking liquid; cover and keep warm.

4. Place a large zip-top plastic bag inside a bowl. Pour cooking liquid into bag. Carefully snip off 1 bottom corner of bag; drain liquid into a medium saucepan, stopping before fat layer reaches opening. Discard fat. Cook liquid over medium-high heat until reduced to about 1 cup. Add remaining ¼ teaspoon salt, honey, and lime juice; stir with a whisk. Cut beef diagonally across grain into thin slices; serve with sauce. Sprinkle evenly with chopped cilantro. Yield: 16 servings (serving size: about 3 ounces beef and 1½ tablespoons sauce).

CALORIES 224; **FAT** 7.5g (sat 2.7g, mono 3.3g, poly 0.4g); **PROTEIN** 28.3g; **CARB** 9.8g; **FIBER** 0.7g; **CHOL** 68mg; **IRON** 2.6mg; **SODIUM** 191mg; **CALC** 23mg

---

Braised Kale

For easy prep, look for bags of prewashed, prechopped kale in the produce section.

1 tablespoon olive oil
1½ cups thinly sliced onion
⅓ cup thinly sliced garlic (about 9 cloves)
10 cups loosely packed chopped kale (about 2 pounds)
1 cup fat-free, lower-sodium chicken broth
1 cup water
¾ teaspoon crushed red pepper
2 teaspoons red wine vinegar
¼ teaspoon salt
¼ teaspoon freshly ground black pepper

1. Heat oil in a large Dutch oven over medium heat. Add onion and garlic; cook 10 minutes or until golden, stirring frequently. Add kale and next 3 ingredients; cover and bring to a boil. Reduce heat and simmer 20 minutes, stirring occasionally. Stir in vinegar, salt, and black pepper. Yield: 8 servings (serving size: ¾ cup).

CALORIES 88; **FAT** 2.6g (sat 0.4g, mono 1.3g, poly 0.6g); **PROTEIN** 4.5g; **CARB** 14.8g; **FIBER** 2.9g; **CHOL** 0mg; **IRON** 2.1mg; **SODIUM** 173mg; **CALC** 167mg

VEGETARIAN SUPPER MENU

serves 8

Granny Smith, Radish, and Radicchio Salad with Orange-Walnut Vinaigrette

Truffled Wild Mushroom Lasagna

Broccolini with Anchovy Gremolata

(omit anchovies for a vegetarian side)

Rustic Apple Tart

CHRISTMAS DINNER MENU

serves 8

Granny Smith, Radish, and Radicchio Salad with Orange-Walnut Vinaigrette

Roast Chicken with Five-Spice Sauce

Broccolini with Anchovy Gremolata

Braised Kale

Roasted Winter Vegetables

Gingery Banana Pudding with Bourbon Cream

Make Ahead • Vegetarian

Granny Smith, Radish, and Radicchio Salad with Orange-Walnut Vinaigrette

We love the look of this salad when the ingredients are cut into julienne or matchstick pieces—but you can also chop or slice them.

3 tablespoons fresh orange juice

3 tablespoons walnut oil

1 tablespoon red wine vinegar

2 teaspoons Dijon mustard

¼ teaspoon freshly ground black pepper

⅛ teaspoon salt

4 cups thinly sliced radicchio (1 [12-ounce] head)

1 cup thinly sliced radishes (about 6)

2 Granny Smith apples, quartered and cut into julienne strips (about 1 pound)

¼ cup coarsely chopped walnuts, toasted

1. Combine first 6 ingredients in a large bowl, stirring with a whisk. Add radicchio, radish, and apple to bowl; toss gently to coat. Place about ¾ cup salad on each of 8 plates; sprinkle each serving with 1½ teaspoons nuts. Yield: 8 servings.

CALORIES 101; **FAT** 7.7g (sat 0.7g, mono 5g, poly 1.5g); **PROTEIN** 1.3g; **CARB** 8.2g; **FIBER** 1.6g; **CHOL** 0mg; **IRON** 0.5mg; **SODIUM** 82mg; **CALC** 16mg

Roast Chicken with Five-Spice Sauce

A big, fat roasting hen is an excellent choice for an eight-person gathering—just as impressive as a roast turkey but downsized so you don't end up with lots of leftovers. Though the recipe doesn't include Chinese five-spice powder, it does capture the flavors of the classic blend with fennel, cinnamon, cloves, star anise, and pepper.

1 (6-pound) whole roasting chicken

1 medium fennel bulb with stalks

12 fresh thyme sprigs, divided

8 garlic cloves, crushed and divided

4 lemon wedges

1 (3-inch) cinnamon stick, broken in half and divided

1 whole clove

1 tablespoon olive oil

1 teaspoon freshly ground black pepper, divided

¾ teaspoon salt, divided

1 onion, vertically sliced

2 cups red wine

1 cup lower-sodium chicken broth

2 orange rind strips

1 star anise

½ cup chopped dried apricots

1 tablespoon butter

1. Preheat oven to 450°.

2. Remove and discard giblets and neck from chicken. Trim tough outer leaves from fennel; mince feathery fronds to measure 2 tablespoons.

Remove and discard stalks. Cut bulb into quarters. Place 1 fennel quarter, 6 thyme sprigs, 4 garlic cloves, lemon wedges, ½ cinnamon stick, and whole clove in body cavity. Combine fennel fronds, oil, ¾ teaspoon pepper, and ½ teaspoon salt. Starting at neck cavity, loosen skin from breast and drumsticks by inserting fingers, gently pushing between skin and meat. Rub salt mixture under skin. Lift wing tips up and over back; tuck under chicken. Tie legs together with twine. Place chicken, breast side up, on rack of a roasting pan. Arrange remaining 4 garlic cloves, remaining fennel quarters, and onion in bottom of roasting pan; place rack with chicken in pan. Bake at 450° for 20 minutes.

3. Reduce oven temperature to 375°.

4. Add remaining 6 thyme sprigs, remaining cinnamon stick half, wine, and next 3 ingredients to bottom of pan; baste chicken. Bake at 375° for 40 minutes; baste chicken. Bake an additional 10 minutes or until a thermometer inserted in meaty part of thigh registers 165°. Remove from oven; let stand 20 minutes.

5. Place a zip-top plastic bag inside a 2-cup glass measure. Pour drippings into bag; let stand 5 minutes (fat will rise to top). Seal bag; carefully snip off 1 bottom corner of bag. Drain drippings back into roasting pan, stopping before fat layer reaches opening; discard fat. Cook over medium heat, scraping pan to loosen browned bits, until reduced to 1¼ cups (about 15 minutes). Remove from heat; stir in remaining ¼ teaspoon salt, remaining ¼ teaspoon pepper, apricots, and butter.

6. Remove skin from chicken; discard skin. Carve chicken; arrange on a platter. Serve with sauce. Yield: 8 servings (serving size: about 3½ ounces chicken and 3 tablespoons sauce).

CALORIES 275; **FAT** 11.1g (sat 3.3g, mono 4.5g, poly 2.1g); **PROTEIN** 36g; **CARB** 6.2g; **FIBER** 0.8g; **CHOL** 119mg; **IRON** 2.4mg; **SODIUM** 415mg; **CALC** 29mg

Make Ahead

Hoppin' John's Cousin

Traditionally, Hoppin' John is served in the South at New Year's because the black-eyed peas represent coins—they're meant to herald prosperity in the coming year. Our version, with all its veggies, is a fresher, healthier update.

1 cup dried black-eyed peas
2 teaspoons olive oil
1 cup chopped onion
½ cup finely chopped red bell pepper
½ cup finely chopped green bell pepper
3 garlic cloves, minced
1 jalapeño pepper, seeded and minced
½ teaspoon paprika
½ teaspoon ground cumin
2 cups water, divided
1½ cups fat-free, lower-sodium chicken broth
1½ teaspoons chopped fresh thyme
½ teaspoon freshly ground black pepper
¼ teaspoon salt
¼ teaspoon hot pepper sauce (such as Tabasco)
3 ounces andouille sausage, cut into ¼-inch cubes
1 (14.5-ounce) can diced tomatoes, drained
1 bay leaf
½ cup uncooked long-grain rice
¼ cup thinly sliced green onions (optional)

1. Sort and wash peas; place in a large bowl. Cover with water to 2 inches above peas; soak 8 hours or overnight. Drain.
2. Heat oil in a Dutch oven over medium-high heat. Add onion and next 4 ingredients; sauté 7 minutes or until vegetables are tender. Stir in paprika and cumin; sauté 1 minute. Add peas, 1 cup water, and next 8 ingredients, stirring to combine. Bring to a boil; cover, reduce heat, and simmer 50 minutes or until peas are tender. Discard bay leaf.
3. Combine remaining 1 cup water and rice in a small saucepan; bring to a boil. Cover, reduce heat, and simmer 12 minutes or until rice is tender and water is absorbed. Fluff rice with a fork; stir into pea mixture. Top with green onions, if desired. Yield: 8 servings (serving size: about ¾ cup).

CALORIES 112; FAT 2.6g (sat 0.6g, mono 0.9g, poly 0.2g); PROTEIN 4.2g; CARB 18.1g; FIBER 2.7g; CHOL 11mg; IRON 1.4mg; SODIUM 294mg; CALC 45mg

Vegetarian

Truffled Wild Mushroom Lasagna

The secret to the intense mushroom character delivered in this dish is the layering of flavor achieved by sautéing fresh mushrooms and incorporating truffle oil into the mixture.

1 tablespoon olive oil
2 cups thinly sliced leek
8 garlic cloves, thinly sliced
⅜ teaspoon salt, divided
7 cups sliced cremini mushrooms (about 1½ pounds), divided
4 cups sliced shiitake mushroom caps (about 1 pound)
⅔ cup Côtes du Rhône or other fruity red wine
1 tablespoon chopped fresh thyme
1 tablespoon chopped fresh oregano
1 tablespoon chopped fresh sage
3 tablespoons white truffle oil
1 teaspoon freshly ground black pepper, divided
2½ cups 1% low-fat milk
1 bay leaf
2 tablespoons butter
3½ tablespoons all-purpose flour
⅛ teaspoon ground nutmeg
2 cups fat-free ricotta cheese
¼ cup chopped fresh flat-leaf parsley
1 tablespoon grated lemon rind
Cooking spray
1 (8-ounce) package precooked lasagna noodles
1 cup (4 ounces) shredded part-skim mozzarella cheese
1 cup (4 ounces) grated fresh Parmesan cheese

1. Heat olive oil in a large Dutch oven over medium-high heat. Add leek, garlic, and ¼ teaspoon salt; sauté 2 minutes. Add 4 cups cremini mushrooms and shiitake mushrooms; sauté 10 minutes or until mushrooms release moisture and begin to brown. Stir in wine; cook 3 minutes or until liquid almost evaporates, stirring frequently. Remove from heat; stir in thyme, oregano, sage, truffle oil, and ½ teaspoon pepper.
2. Combine milk and bay leaf in a heavy saucepan; cook over medium-high heat to 180° or until tiny bubbles form around edge (do not boil). Remove from heat; cover and let stand 10 minutes. Strain mixture through a sieve into a bowl; discard bay leaf. Set aside.
3. Melt butter in saucepan over medium heat. Add remaining 3 cups cremini mushrooms; sauté 4 minutes or until tender. Add flour, stirring with a whisk until blended. Cook 1 minute, stirring constantly; gradually add milk. Bring to a boil; reduce heat, and simmer 8 minutes or until thick. Stir in remaining ⅛ teaspoon salt, ¼ teaspoon pepper, and nutmeg.
4. Preheat oven to 350°.
5. Combine ricotta, parsley, lemon rind, and remaining ¼ teaspoon black pepper in a bowl. Spread ½ cup sauce in bottom of an 11 x 7–inch glass or ceramic baking dish coated with cooking spray. Arrange 3 noodles over sauce; top with 2 cups mushroom mixture. Sprinkle with ¼ cup mozzarella and ¼ cup Parmesan. Arrange 3 noodles over cheese. Top with 1 cup ricotta mixture. Repeat layers once with 3 noodles, 2 cups mushroom mixture, ¼ cup mozzarella, ¼ cup Parmesan, 3 noodles, and 1 cup ricotta (dish will be very full); spread remaining sauce over top. Cover with foil; place baking dish on a baking sheet. Bake at 350° for 30 minutes. Remove from oven; increase oven to 450°. Uncover lasagna and sprinkle with remaining ½ cup mozzarella and remaining ½ cup Parmesan; bake at 450° an additional 10 minutes or until golden brown. Yield: 8 servings (serving size: 1 piece).

CALORIES 424; FAT 17.7g (sat 6.4g, mono 2.2g, poly 8.1g); PROTEIN 23.7g; CARB 41.3g; FIBER 2.8g; CHOL 31mg; IRON 2.6mg; SODIUM 455mg; CALC 393mg

Vegetarian
Roasted Winter Vegetables

Use any combination of vegetables you like for this riotously colorful side dish. To ensure all the vegetables are done at the same time, place the second pan in the oven after the first pan has been in for 20 minutes.

16 fresh thyme sprigs, divided
4 medium beets, peeled and quartered
4 carrots, peeled and cut in half lengthwise
2 medium turnips, peeled and quartered
2 tablespoons extra-virgin olive oil, divided
1/2 teaspoon salt, divided
1/2 teaspoon freshly ground black pepper, divided
8 unpeeled garlic cloves
2 medium red onions, peeled and cut lengthwise into quarters
2 fennel bulbs, cored and cut lengthwise into quarters
1 teaspoon chopped fresh thyme

1. Preheat oven to 425°.
2. Place 8 thyme springs, beets, carrots, and turnips in a large bowl. Drizzle with 1 tablespoon oil; sprinkle with 1/4 teaspoon salt and 1/4 teaspoon pepper. Toss to coat. Arrange vegetables in a single layer in a jelly-roll pan. Bake at 425° for 45 minutes or until vegetables are tender and begin to brown, stirring occasionally.
3. Place remaining 8 thyme sprigs, garlic, onions, and fennel in a bowl. Drizzle with remaining 1 tablespoon oil; sprinkle with remaining 1/4 teaspoon salt and remaining 1/4 teaspoon pepper. Arrange vegetables in a single layer in a jelly-roll pan. Bake at 425° for 25 minutes or until vegetables are tender and begin to brown, stirring occasionally. Combine beet mixture and onion mixture; sprinkle with chopped thyme. Yield: 8 servings (serving size: 1 cup).

CALORIES 103; **FAT** 3.7g (sat 0.5g, mono 2.5g, poly 0.5g); **PROTEIN** 2.5g; **CARB** 16.7g; **FIBER** 4.9g; **CHOL** 0mg; **IRON** 1.1mg; **SODIUM** 253mg; **CALC** 67mg

---

HEALTHY HANUKKAH MENU

serves 8

Fennel and Spinach Soup with Roasted Pepper Yogurt

Beer-Braised Brisket with Honey-Lime Glaze

Quinoa with Dried Cherries and Pistachios

Braised Kale

Roasted Winter Vegetables

Rustic Apple Tart

Vegetarian
Quinoa with Dried Cherries and Pistachios

1 3/4 cups uncooked quinoa
2 tablespoons plus 2 teaspoons extra-virgin olive oil, divided
3 tablespoons finely chopped shallots
2 cups water
1/3 cup dry white wine
1/2 teaspoon salt
3 tablespoons fresh lemon juice
1/4 teaspoon freshly ground black pepper
1/2 cup dried sweet cherries, chopped
1/2 cup dry-roasted pistachios, chopped
1/4 cup chopped fresh mint
1/4 cup chopped fresh parsley

1. Rinse and drain quinoa. Heat 2 teaspoons oil in a large saucepan over medium-high heat. Add shallots; sauté 2 minutes or until tender. Add 2 cups water, wine, and salt to pan; bring to a boil. Add quinoa; cover, reduce heat, and simmer 15 minutes or until liquid is absorbed and quinoa is tender. Remove from heat; set aside and cool slightly.
2. Combine remaining 2 tablespoons oil, lemon juice, and pepper in a large bowl; stir with a whisk. Add quinoa, cherries, and remaining ingredients; toss gently to combine. Yield: 8 servings (serving size: 3/4 cup).

CALORIES 256; **FAT** 10.3g (sat 1.3g, mono 5.8g, poly 2.8g); **PROTEIN** 7.6g; **CARB** 34g; **FIBER** 4.3g; **CHOL** 0mg; **IRON** 2.4mg; **SODIUM** 184mg; **CALC** 38mg

---

Gingery Banana Pudding with Bourbon Cream

Leave the booze out of the kids' desserts—more for you.

1/2 cup sugar
5 tablespoons cornstarch
1/8 teaspoon salt
4 cups 1% low-fat milk, divided
2 large egg yolks
2 teaspoons vanilla extract
4 ripe bananas
12 gingersnaps, coarsely crumbled and divided
1/2 cup heavy whipping cream
1 teaspoon sugar
1 tablespoon bourbon (optional)
1/4 cup chopped pecans, toasted
2 tablespoons finely chopped crystallized ginger

1. Combine first 3 ingredients in a medium saucepan. Gradually add 3 cups milk, stirring with a whisk until blended. Heat mixture to 180° or until tiny bubbles form around edge (do not boil).
2. Combine remaining 1 cup milk and egg yolks in a bowl; stir with a whisk. Gradually add 1 cup hot milk mixture to egg yolk mixture, stirring constantly with a whisk. Add egg yolk mixture to pan. Bring to a boil; cook 2 minutes or until thick, stirring constantly. Remove from heat; stir in vanilla. Place pan in a large ice-filled bowl 20 minutes or until mixture cools to room temperature, stirring occasionally. Cover surface of pudding with plastic wrap. Refrigerate 2 hours or until thoroughly chilled. Mash 2 bananas; cut remaining 2 bananas into 1/4-inch-thick slices. Stir mashed and sliced bananas and half of gingersnaps into pudding; chill 30 minutes.
3. Combine cream and 1 teaspoon sugar in a medium bowl. Beat with a mixer at high speed until stiff peaks form; stir in bourbon, if desired.
4. Spoon 2/3 cup pudding into each of 8 dessert glasses; divide remaining gingersnaps among servings. Top each serving with about 2 tablespoons whipped

cream, 1½ teaspoons pecans, and ¾ teaspoon ginger. Yield: 8 servings.

CALORIES 311; FAT 10.5g (sat 5g, mono 3.9g, poly 1g); PROTEIN 6.3g; CARB 48.9g; FIBER 2g; CHOL 76mg; IRON 1.2mg; SODIUM 176mg; CALC 177mg

Broccolini with Anchovy Gremolata

A gremolata is a quickly made condiment used to finish savory dishes with bright citrus-herb flavors. Usually a combination of minced parsley, lemon zest, and garlic, ours also includes anchovy, but don't be scared—it doesn't come across as fishy. All you'll taste is a hit of salty goodness. If including this dish in a vegetarian meal, simply omit the anchovies.

⅓ cup chopped fresh flat-leaf parsley
1½ tablespoons grated lemon rind
4 canned anchovy fillets, rinsed, drained, and finely chopped
4 garlic cloves, minced
5 quarts water
1½ pounds Broccolini
2 tablespoons fresh lemon juice
1 tablespoon olive oil
¼ teaspoon salt
¼ teaspoon freshly ground black pepper

1. Combine first 4 ingredients in a small bowl.
2. Bring 5 quarts water to a boil. Add half of Broccolini to boiling water; cook 4 minutes or until crisp-tender. Remove Broccolini from pan with a slotted spoon. Repeat procedure with remaining Broccolini. Place Broccolini in a large bowl. Add lemon juice and next 3 ingredients; toss to combine. Divide Broccolini mixture evenly among 8 plates; top each serving with about 1 tablespoon gremolata. Yield: 8 servings.

CALORIES 59; FAT 1.9g (sat 0.3g, mono 1.3g, poly 0.2g); PROTEIN 3.8g; CARB 7.2g; FIBER 1.3g; CHOL 1.7mg; IRON 1mg; SODIUM 174mg; CALC 73mg

THE ANNOTATED GUIDE TO HAPPY, HEALTHY HOLIDAY BAKING

This year, before you step into the kitchen to wield your holiday whisk, consider brushing up on a few kitchen science fundamentals. Not that tasty treats require a PhD, but what Grandma knew about baking was as much about chemistry as tradition or art. In fact, successful baking can be summed up with one simple formula: You have to strike a balance between structure and moisture. Everything else is frosting on the cake.

The main ingredients responsible for providing structure are flour and eggs, while sugar and fat contribute and hold moisture. Too much flour in your cookie dough is what results in those sad little hockey pucks. But too little structure— which is to say too much moisture—can make your cake too dense or, worse, a wet, gooey mess. And that's before you tackle light baking, which by definition alters and adjusts this delicate balance.

Here, we offer a collection of healthful recipes developed by a couple of pastry chefs and put through the paces in our Test Kitchens. We've added annotations that explain the basic kitchen science that yields best results. Pick a treat, and step up to your stove with new confidence as you gear up for the sweetest season.

Make Ahead
Bourbon-Caramel Truffles

Truffles typically have the added richness of cream and butter. These ingredients help stabilize chocolate, which tends to scorch, separate, or become grainy if not heated slowly and carefully. We add corn syrup and evaporated milk for smooth, creamy confections.
Recipe Notes:
• Evaporated whole milk won't curdle when heated with sugar.
• Chopped chocolate bits melt smoothly and quickly.

3 tablespoons brown sugar
2 tablespoons evaporated whole milk
1 tablespoon golden cane syrup (such as Lyle's Golden Syrup)
Dash of salt
1 tablespoon bourbon
½ teaspoon vanilla extract
3.5 ounces bittersweet chocolate, finely chopped
1.75 ounces milk chocolate, finely chopped
2 tablespoons unsweetened cocoa

1. Combine first 4 ingredients in a small saucepan over medium-high heat; bring to a boil. Cook 1 minute or until sugar dissolves. Remove from heat. Stir in bourbon and vanilla. Add chocolates; let stand 1 minute. Stir until smooth. Pour mixture into a shallow dish; cover and refrigerate 4 hours or until firm.
2. Heat a tablespoon measure with hot water; pat dry. Scoop chocolate mixture with spoon; dip in cocoa. Quickly roll chocolate into balls. Cover and refrigerate until ready to serve. Yield: 19 truffles (serving size: 1 truffle).

CALORIES 60; FAT 2.7g (sat 1.6g, mono 0.5g, poly 0g); PROTEIN 0.8g; CARB 8g; FIBER 0.7g; CHOL 1mg; IRON 0.2mg; SODIUM 14mg; CALC 12mg

COPING WITH COOKIE CONUNDRUMS

Cookies may seem like one of the simplest things to bake, but they offer so many examples of what can go wrong. Lighter cookies can be even trickier because less fat means less moisture. Light cookies require precise measuring of flour—weighing is most accurate. Just a smidge too much turns a perfect cookie into a doorstop! Almond paste is an ingenious way to flavor, tenderize, and sweeten our Pine Nut Cookies because it won't cause spreading like excess sugar or warm butter will. And be sure to pull light cookies from the oven a bit sooner than you would full-fat ones—they tend to go from perfectly toasty to overbrowned quickly.

Make Ahead

Pine Nut Cookies

Recipe Notes:
- *Stacking two baking sheets is a smart trick to prevent overbrowning.*
- *Small amounts of butter yield a rich flavor payoff.*
- *Ground nuts act like flour but don't dry out the cookies.*

1/3 cup almond paste
3/4 cup sugar
6 tablespoons butter, softened
1/4 teaspoon salt
1 large egg white
1/2 cup pine nuts, divided
4.5 ounces all-purpose flour (about 1 cup)
1 teaspoon baking powder

1. Preheat oven to 375°.
2. Grate almond paste on large holes of a box grater. Combine paste and next 4 ingredients in a large bowl; beat with a mixer at medium speed until light and fluffy (about 5 minutes).
3. Place 1/4 cup pine nuts in a mini food processor; pulse until finely ground. Weigh or lightly spoon flour into a dry measuring cup; level with a knife. Combine ground nuts, flour, and baking powder, stirring with a whisk. Add flour mixture to butter mixture; beat on low speed just until combined.

4. Stack two baking sheets one on top of the other; line top sheet with parchment paper. Shape dough into 48 equal-sized balls (about 1 tablespoon each). Press 3 to 5 of remaining pine nuts in a sunburst shape on top of each ball. Place 12 balls 2 inches apart on top baking sheet (keep sheets stacked). Bake 14 minutes or until edges of cookies are lightly browned. Cool 5 minutes on pan. Cool completely on a wire rack. Repeat procedure 4 times. Yield: 24 servings (serving size: 2 cookies).

CALORIES 103; FAT 5.7g (sat 2g, mono 1.8g, poly 1.3g); PROTEIN 1.4g; CARB 12.2g; FIBER 0.4g; CHOL 8mg; IRON 0.5mg; SODIUM 43mg; CALC 22mg

Make Ahead

Walnut Cupcakes with Maple Frosting

Recipes Notes:
- *Cake flour is low in gluten that yields a tender cake.*
- *You can tell if you've overbaked cupcakes if the edges are too dark and dry.*

Cupcakes:
1/2 cup granulated sugar
1/2 cup packed brown sugar
6 tablespoons butter, softened
3 large eggs
1 teaspoon vanilla extract
8 ounces cake flour (about 2 cups)
1/2 teaspoon baking soda
1/4 teaspoon salt
1/4 teaspoon ground cinnamon
1/2 cup buttermilk
1/3 cup plus 2 tablespoons walnuts, toasted, chopped, and divided
Frosting:
1/2 teaspoon cream of tartar
3 large egg whites
3/4 cup maple sugar or granulated sugar
1/4 cup water
Dash of salt

1. Preheat oven to 350°.
2. To prepare cupcakes, combine first 3 ingredients in a medium bowl; beat with a mixer at medium speed until light and fluffy. Add eggs, 1 at a time, beating well after each addition. Stir in vanilla. Increase speed to high; beat for 1 minute.
3. Weigh or lightly spoon flour into dry measuring cups; level with a knife. Combine flour and next 3 ingredients in a bowl, stirring well with a whisk. Add flour mixture and buttermilk alternately to sugar mixture, beginning and ending with flour mixture, beating until just combined. Stir in 1/3 cup walnuts.
4. Place 12 paper muffin cup liners in muffin cups; divide batter evenly among cups. Bake at 350° for 19 minutes or until a wooden pick inserted in center comes out with moist crumbs clinging. (Cupcakes will look slightly pale.) Cool in pan 5 minutes. Remove from pan; cool on a wire rack.
5. To prepare frosting, place cream of tartar and egg whites in a large bowl; beat with a mixer at high speed until soft peaks form. Combine maple sugar, 1/4 cup water, and dash of salt in a small saucepan; bring to a boil. Cook, without stirring, until candy thermometer registers 238°. Gradually pour hot sugar syrup into egg white mixture, beating until stiff peaks form. Spread about 3 rounded tablespoonfuls frosting over each cupcake. Sprinkle with remaining 2 tablespoons nuts. Yield: 12 servings (serving size: 1 cupcake).

CALORIES 291; FAT 10.4g (sat 4.5g, mono 2.4g, poly 2.6g); PROTEIN 5.4g; CARB 44.7g; FIBER 0.7g; CHOL 69mg; IRON 2.4mg; SODIUM 203mg; CALC 33mg

AVOIDING CAKE CATASTROPHES

Unlike their full-fat cousins, which get their softness from oil and butter, light cakes rely less on fat and more on sugar and liquids. More sugar minimizes the development of gluten proteins (the primary source of toughness in cakes), but it can also cause excess browning, especially if dairy products are present. Pull the cake from the oven when a wooden pick inserted in the center comes out with moist crumbs still clinging to it.

PERFECTING PIECRUST

Making perfect pastry depends mostly on how well you coat flour proteins with fat—more difficult in a low-fat recipe. You want to leave small clumps of fat in the dough (here, from vegetable shortening) so they'll melt during cooking and give off steam, creating luscious layers. Meanwhile, we melted the butter so it would coat more than it would in solid form.

Meringue-Topped Cranberry Curd Tart

Recipe Notes:
• *Vegetable shortening creates flaky layers in the crust.*
• *Overworking the dough will make it tough.*
• *Plastic wrap prevents dough from sticking and falling apart.*

Crust:
5 ounces all-purpose flour (about 1¼ cups)
1 tablespoon sugar
¼ teaspoon salt
¼ teaspoon baking powder
¼ cup vegetable shortening
¼ cup boiling water
4 teaspoons butter, melted
Cooking spray
Filling:
1 (12-ounce) package fresh cranberries
1 cup sugar, divided
¾ cup water, divided
⅛ teaspoon salt
¼ cup cornstarch
2 large egg yolks
2 tablespoon butter, softened
Meringue:
3 large egg whites
⅛ teaspoon salt
½ cup sugar
¼ cup water

1. To prepare crust, weigh or lightly spoon flour into dry measuring cups; level with a knife. Combine flour and next 3 ingredients in a bowl; cut in shortening with a pastry blender or two knives until mixture resembles coarse meal. Make a well in center of flour mixture. Combine ¼ cup boiling water and 4 teaspoons melted butter in a bowl. Pour butter mixture into center of flour mixture. Gently draw flour mixture into butter mixture until moist clumps form. Press dough gently into a 4-inch circle on plastic wrap; cover. Chill 30 minutes.
2. Preheat oven to 400°.
3. Unwrap dough; place between 2 sheets of plastic wrap. Roll dough into an 11-inch circle. Remove top sheet of plastic wrap. Fit dough, plastic wrap side up, into a 9-inch round tart pan coated with cooking spray. Remove plastic wrap. Press dough into bottom and up sides of pan; fold excess crust back in, and press to reinforce sides. Pierce bottom and sides of dough lightly with a fork; freeze 10 minutes. Line bottom of dough with a piece of foil; arrange pie weights or dried beans on foil. Bake at 400° for 18 minutes. Remove foil and pie weights. Bake 15 minutes or until lightly browned. Cool on a wire rack.
4. To prepare filling, combine cranberries, ½ cup sugar, ¼ cup water, and ⅛ teaspoon salt in a medium saucepan. Cook over medium-high heat 10 minutes or until cranberries burst, stirring occasionally. Combine remaining ½ cup sugar, remaining ½ cup water, cornstarch, and egg yolks in a small bowl; stir with a whisk until smooth. Gradually add 1 cup hot cranberry mixture to egg mixture, stirring constantly. Return egg mixture to pan. Cook 2 minutes or until a thermometer registers 160°, stirring constantly.

5. Place a food mill or fine sieve over a large bowl. Pour cranberry mixture into food mill, and press through. Discard solids. Add 2 tablespoons softened butter; stir until smooth. Spoon into baked crust. Cover and chill.
6. Preheat broiler.
7. To prepare meringue, place egg whites and ⅛ teaspoon salt in a large bowl; beat with a mixer at high speed until soft peaks form. Combine ½ cup sugar and ¼ cup water in a small saucepan; bring to a boil. Cook, without stirring, until candy thermometer registers 238°. Pour hot sugar syrup in a thin stream over egg white mixture, beating at high speed until stiff peaks form. Spread meringue over cranberry curd.
8. Broil meringue 30 seconds or until lightly browned. Yield: 12 servings (serving size: 1 wedge).

CALORIES 245; **FAT** 8.1g (sat 3.8g, mono 2.3g, poly 1.5g); **PROTEIN** 2.7g; **CARB** 41.1g; **FIBER** 1.7g; **CHOL** 43mg; **IRON** 0.7mg; **SODIUM** 147mg; **CALC** 15mg

KEEPING CUSTARDS CREAMY

Heating a creamy custard over an intense flame can scramble the eggs, and light custards made with milk are even more fragile because milk is less stable than cream. If you add sugar or any acidic ingredients to milk as it heats, it's almost sure to curdle. To keep things smooth and silky, combine sugar, egg yolks, and any flavorings separately, and gradually add hot milk to the mixture so eggs can slowly come up to the proper temperature (also called tempering), stirring the mixture constantly with a whisk.

continued

Kid Friendly
Butterscotch Pots de Crème

Recipe Notes:
- *Eggs are the key to creaminess but only if heated carefully.*
- *A water bath cooks gently for smooth results.*

¾ cup whole milk
¾ cup 2% reduced-fat milk
7 tablespoon brown sugar
2 tablespoons water
1 tablespoon dark molasses
½ teaspoon salt
2 large eggs
2 large egg yolks
1½ teaspoons butter
½ teaspoon vanilla extract
¼ cup heavy whipping cream
1 tablespoon powdered sugar

1. Preheat oven to 325°.
2. Heat milks over medium-high heat in a small, heavy saucepan to 180° or until tiny bubbles form around edge (do not boil). Combine brown sugar and next 5 ingredients in a medium bowl, stirring well with a whisk. Gradually pour ½ cup hot milk mixture into egg mixture, stirring constantly with a whisk. Return egg mixture to pan, stirring constantly until sugar dissolves. Strain mixture through a fine sieve into a bowl. Stir in butter and vanilla. Cover and chill 1 hour.
3. Divide mixture evenly among 6 (8-ounce) custard cups. Place cups in a 13 x 9–inch metal baking pan; add enough hot water to come halfway up sides of cups. Bake at 325° for 24 minutes or until center barely moves when cup is touched. Remove cups from pan; cool 20 minutes on a wire rack. Cover and chill at least 1 hour.
4. To prepare whipped cream, place cream and powdered sugar in a small bowl; beat with a mixer at high speed until stiff peaks form. Top custards with whipped cream. Yield: 6 servings (serving size: 1 custard and about 1 tablespoon cream).

CALORIES 195; FAT 9.3g (sat 4.9g, mono 3g, poly 0.7g); PROTEIN 5.4g; CARB 23g; FIBER 0g; CHOL 160mg; IRON 1.3mg; SODIUM 271mg; CALC 132mg

COCKTAILS & NIBBLES

Spritzers, mimosas, cheese straws, and crab cups: simple, fun recipes for an easy cocktail party.

Quick & Easy • Make Ahead
Salty Chihuahua

Red grapefruit juice and Cointreau combine for a margarita-style drink. As the name implies, a dash of salt is put in the cocktail or on the rim. Make the juice mixture up to one day ahead, and chill.

8 cups fresh red grapefruit juice (about 12 grapefruits)
1½ cups silver tequila
¾ cup Cointreau (orange-flavored liqueur)
1½ teaspoons kosher salt
Ice cubes
Lime slices (optional)

1. Combine first 3 ingredients; stir well. Coat rim of each of 12 glasses with ⅛ teaspoon salt. Fill each glass with ice; pour 1 cup juice mixture into each glass. Garnish each glass with a lime slice, if desired. Yield: 12 servings (serving size: 1 cup).

CALORIES 187; FAT 0.2g (sat 0g, mono 0.1g, poly 0.1g); PROTEIN 0.8g; CARB 20g; FIBER 0g; CHOL 0mg; IRON 0.3mg; SODIUM 242mg; CALC 15mg

Quick & Easy
Prosciutto-Wrapped Stuffed Dates

Assemble up to one day ahead and refrigerate, then let come to room temperature and bake as directed when ready to serve.

¾ cup (6 ounces) goat cheese
1 tablespoon minced shallots
1 tablespoon chopped fresh thyme
¼ teaspoon freshly ground black pepper
24 whole pitted dates
6 thin slices prosciutto

1. Preheat oven to 350°.
2. Combine first 4 ingredients in a small bowl, stirring with a fork. Slice dates lengthwise, cutting to, but not through, other side. Open dates; place 1 rounded teaspoon cheese mixture into each date. Cut 1 prosciutto slice in half lengthwise and then crosswise to make 4 equal pieces. Repeat procedure with remaining prosciutto to form 24 pieces. Wrap each date with 1 prosciutto piece; place dates on a baking sheet lined with parchment paper. Bake at 350° for 8 minutes or until filling is thoroughly heated. Serve immediately. Yield: 12 servings (serving size: 2 stuffed dates).

CALORIES 91; FAT 3.7g (sat 2.3g, mono 1g, poly 0.2g); PROTEIN 4.6g; CARB 10.8g; FIBER 1.2g; CHOL 11mg; IRON 0.5mg; SODIUM 159mg; CALC 27mg

Quick & Easy
Campari Mimosa

A bitter Italian liqueur, Campari takes the sweet edge off a traditional mimosa while tinting the drink a beautiful red-orange color.

¾ cup Campari
3 cups fresh orange juice, chilled
3 (750-milliliter) bottles chilled prosecco, brut Champagne, or sparkling wine
Orange rind strips (optional)

1. Fill each of 12 Champagne flutes with 1 tablespoon Campari and ¼ cup juice; stir. Tilt each glass slightly and add about ¾ cup prosecco. Garnish each glass with an orange rind strip, if desired. Serve immediately. Yield: 12 servings (serving size: about ¾ cup).

CALORIES 179; FAT 0.1g (sat 0g, mono 0g, poly 0.1g); PROTEIN 0.4g; CARB 9.6g; FIBER 0.1g; CHOL 0mg; IRON 0.1mg; SODIUM 2mg; CALC 7mg

White Cranberry Spritzer

White cranberry juice is made with young cranberries before they develop their tart flavor and red color—it's milder and sweeter than regular cranberry juice.

2¾ cups white cranberry juice drink (such as Ocean Spray)
2 tablespoons sugar
1 teaspoon chopped fresh rosemary
12 fresh mint leaves
¼ cup fresh lime juice
3 cups club soda, chilled
1½ cups white rum
Crushed ice

1. Combine first 4 ingredients in a small saucepan; bring to a boil. Remove from heat; cool to room temperature. Strain juice mixture through a sieve into a bowl; discard solids. Stir in lime juice; cover and refrigerate.
2. Combine juice mixture, club soda, and rum in a large pitcher; stir well to combine. Serve over crushed ice. Yield: 12 servings (serving size: about ⅔ cup).

CALORIES 101; **FAT** 0g; **PROTEIN** 0g; **CARB** 9.7g; **FIBER** 0g; **CHOL** 0mg; **IRON** 0mg; **SODIUM** 21mg; **CALC** 4mg

Blue Cheese and Chive Straws

Make up to two days ahead, and store in an airtight container at room temperature.

6.75 ounces all-purpose flour (about 1½ cups)
¼ cup chilled butter, cut into small pieces
1 cup (4 ounces) crumbled blue cheese
⅓ cup finely chopped chives
¼ teaspoon salt
¼ teaspoon freshly ground black pepper
1 to 2 tablespoons cold water

1. Weigh or lightly spoon flour into dry measuring cups; level with a knife. Place flour and butter in a food processor; pulse to blend. Add cheese and next 3 ingredients; pulse until mixture resembles coarse meal. Drizzle 1 to 2 tablespoons water into flour mixture until dough forms a ball. Roll dough into a 16 x 8–inch rectangle. Wrap dough in plastic wrap, and refrigerate 4 hours or until firm.
2. Preheat oven to 350°.
3. Cut dough crosswise into 64 (¼-inch-wide) slices. Place ½ inch apart on a baking sheet lined with parchment paper. Bake at 350° for 10 minutes or until edges are lightly browned. Cool completely on wire racks. Yield: 32 servings (serving size: 2 straws).

CALORIES 47; **FAT** 2.5g (sat 1.6g, mono 0.7g, poly 0.1g); **PROTEIN** 1.4g; **CARB** 4.7g; **FIBER** 0.2g; **CHOL** 6mg; **IRON** 0.3mg; **SODIUM** 78mg; **CALC** 21mg

Mini Crab Cups

Make the crab filling up to one day ahead, and keep chilled.

1 tablespoon water
1 tablespoon honey
2 teaspoons canola oil
30 gyoza skins
½ cup finely chopped celery
½ cup chopped seeded tomato
½ cup light mayonnaise
¼ cup chopped fresh chives
3 tablespoons finely chopped fresh cilantro
1 teaspoon minced seeded jalapeño pepper
1 teaspoon grated lime rind
3 tablespoons fresh lime juice
1 tablespoon Worcestershire sauce
¼ teaspoon freshly ground black pepper
1 pound lump crabmeat, shell pieces removed
Cilantro leaves (optional)

1. Preheat oven to 375°.
2. Combine first 3 ingredients, stirring with a whisk; brush mixture evenly over both sides of each gyoza. Fit 1 gyoza into each of 30 miniature muffin cups, pressing gyoza firmly into base of cups. Bake at 375° for 12 minutes or until lightly browned; cool in pans on wire racks. Carefully remove cups from pans.
3. Combine celery and next 10 ingredients in a large bowl; toss gently. Spoon 1½ tablespoons crab mixture into each gyoza cup. Garnish each cup with a cilantro leaf, if desired. Yield: 15 servings (serving size: 2 cups).

CALORIES 108; **FAT** 4.1g (sat 0.6g, mono 1.9g, poly 1.3g); **PROTEIN** 6.1g; **CARB** 12g; **FIBER** 0.5g; **CHOL** 31mg; **IRON** 0.9mg; **SODIUM** 332mg; **CALC** 24mg

Vanilla-Spice Nuts

Bring a little heat to this popular party snack by adding ¼ teaspoon ground red pepper to the spice mix. Returning the spice-coated nuts to the oven after it's been turned off ensures they won't overtoast. Prepare up to one week ahead, and store in an airtight container at room temperature.

1 tablespoon vanilla extract
1 large egg white
1 cup sliced almonds
1 cup pecan halves
1 cup macadamia nuts
¼ cup sugar
1 teaspoon kosher salt
¾ teaspoon ground cinnamon
¾ teaspoon ground allspice
¼ teaspoon ground cardamom

1. Preheat oven to 325°.
2. Combine vanilla and egg white in a large bowl, stirring with a whisk until foamy. Stir in nuts. Combine sugar and remaining ingredients in a small bowl; sprinkle sugar mixture over nuts, tossing to coat. Place nut mixture on a baking sheet lined with parchment paper. Bake at 325° for 15 minutes. Remove pan from oven. Turn off oven. Toss nuts, and break large pieces apart. Return pan to oven; leave pan in oven 10 minutes. Cool to room temperature; store in an airtight container. Yield: 24 servings (serving size: 2 tablespoons).

CALORIES 108; **FAT** 9.6g (sat 1.1g, mono 4.4g, poly 0.6g); **PROTEIN** 1.9g; **CARB** 4.5g; **FIBER** 1.3g; **CHOL** 0mg; **IRON** 0.3mg; **SODIUM** 83mg; **CALC** 16mg

HOLIDAY BREAKFASTS

By Mark Bittman

Start your day with food that breaks from the excesses of the season—lighter, fresher, flavor-packed meals.

I've never understood why the predominant flavors in most breakfasts are sugar and fat, especially during the holidays—precisely the time of year our stomachs could use a break. I prefer to start the day with something a little more interesting or, at the very least, something that has the true taste of the main ingredients.

And since my usual routine is to eat a vegan meal in the morning—no animal products, not even dairy—I usually emphasize fresh fruits and vegetables. Eggs and butter have become so rare at breakfast that even small amounts feel like a huge treat.

Here are one savory and one sweet recipe to illustrate these points: an egg-and-sauce dish that's a far cry from the classic Benedict, yet not completely unrelated, and an apple-and-nut phyllo pastry. Neither could be considered austere. In fact, they're quite satisfying precisely because you can actually taste what you're eating.

Curry might seem a tad strident for the morning, but in aromatic tomato sauce, spiked with light coconut milk, any assertive flavors are tempered by acidity and richness. Toast the spices in oil first, which takes their edge off while building more complexity. And let the sauce simmer and mellow a bit.

The dish is inspired by an Indian recipe that calls for braising hard-boiled eggs in a spicy sauce, but I prefer gently poaching eggs in the flavorful liquid; just make sure before you add the eggs that the sauce is wet enough so it doesn't stick to the bottom of the pan when you stir it. (If it does, add enough water so it bubbles evenly and steadily, rather than occasional, eruptive "plops.") It's also important that the lid fit fairly tightly so the eggs steam a bit and stay tender. You'll be surprised how fast they cook, so keep an eye on them.

A whole-wheat English muffin is a nice vehicle for the sauce and egg, but so is brown basmati rice, or a whole-grain paratha or other chewy flatbread.

For a little something sweet, try the strudels. It's almost a miracle how flaky and crisp the results are with so little fat. The secret is a light dusting of ground nuts between the layers. I won't say the texture is akin to that of a Danish, but they are certainly more luxurious than toast and jam. They're prepared without too much work, and once they're in the oven, there's no fuss at all, freeing you to prepare the remainder of your brunch spread or simply to relax with another cup of coffee.

A couple of technical notes: If juice collects in the bottom of the bowl with the apples, leave it behind as you fill the strudels; they'll get plenty juicy as they cook. And consider the apples a mere suggestion, nodding to the season. Pears or bananas are other obvious options. In the summer, try peaches, plums, or nectarines (but not berries, which bleed too much liquid). And tropical fruits like mangoes, papayas, or pineapple instantly steer the pastries toward the exotic.

BREAKFASTS DON'T HAVE TO BE LADEN WITH SUGAR AND FAT, AND THESE TWO RECIPES—ONE SAVORY AND ONE SWEET—ILLUSTRATE THESE POINTS.

Eggs Poached in Curried Tomato Sauce

Make the sauce up to three days ahead; prepare through step 1, cool, cover, and refrigerate. Bring back to a gentle simmer before proceeding.

2 tablespoons peanut oil
1½ cups chopped onion
1 tablespoon minced garlic
1 tablespoon minced peeled fresh ginger
1 jalapeño pepper, minced
2 teaspoons curry powder
3/8 teaspoon kosher salt
1/4 teaspoon freshly ground black pepper
Dash of sugar
1 (28-ounce) can diced tomatoes, undrained
1/2 cup light coconut milk
1/2 cup chopped fresh cilantro
4 large eggs
4 whole-wheat English muffins, split and toasted
1/4 cup chopped green onions
Cilantro leaves (optional)

1. Heat oil in a large skillet over medium-high heat. Add onion and next 3 ingredients; sauté 5 minutes or until vegetables are tender, stirring occasionally. Add curry powder and next 3 ingredients; cook 2 minutes, stirring constantly. Drain tomatoes in a colander over a bowl; reserve liquid. Add tomatoes to pan; cook 5 minutes, stirring frequently. Add half of reserved tomato liquid; bring to a boil. Add coconut milk and chopped cilantro; return to a boil. Cover, reduce heat, and simmer 10 minutes. If sauce is too thick, add remaining reserved tomato liquid; maintain heat so that sauce bubbles gently.
2. Break each egg into a custard cup; pour gently into pan over sauce. Cover and cook 5 minutes, just until whites are set and yolks have filmed over but are still runny. Arrange 1 muffin, cut sides up, on each of 4 plates. Carefully scoop 1 egg and about ½ cup sauce onto each serving. Sprinkle each serving with 1 tablespoon green onions; garnish with cilantro leaves, if desired. Yield: 4 servings.

CALORIES 335; **FAT** 14.6g (sat 4.3g, mono 5.3g, poly 3.4g); **PROTEIN** 13.7g; **CARB** 40.9g; **FIBER** 6.4g; **CHOL** 212mg; **IRON** 3.7mg; **SODIUM** 637mg; **CALC** 175mg

Make Ahead • Kid Friendly

Individual Apple Strudels

You can make these several hours ahead; tent loosely with foil and leave at room temperature. Put in a 400° oven for a few minutes to warm and crisp just before serving.

½ cup shelled dry-roasted pistachios
4 cups diced peeled apple (about 1½ pounds)
¼ cup turbinado sugar
1 tablespoon cornstarch
½ teaspoon ground cardamom
32 (14 x 9–inch) sheets frozen whole-wheat phyllo dough, thawed
3 tablespoons unsalted butter, melted and divided
2 tablespoons powdered sugar

1. Preheat oven to 375°.
2. Place pistachios in a food processor; process until finely ground.
3. Combine apple and next 3 ingredients in a large bowl; toss well.
4. Stack 2 phyllo sheets on a large cutting board or work surface (cover remaining dough to keep from drying). Lightly brush phyllo stack with butter; sprinkle with about 1 tablespoon ground pistachios. Top with 2 more phyllo sheets. Spoon about ½ cup apple mixture along 1 short edge of phyllo stack, leaving a 2-inch border on all sides. Fold over long edges of phyllo to cover about 1½ inches of apple mixture on each end. Starting at short edge with 2-inch border, roll up jelly-roll fashion. (Do not roll tightly, or strudel may split.) Place strudel, seam side down, on a baking sheet lined with parchment paper. Repeat procedure with remaining phyllo sheets, butter, pistachios, and apple mixture to form 8 strudels total.
5. Pierce each strudel 2 times with a fork. Brush tops of strudels with remaining butter. Bake at 375° for 35 minutes or until crisp and golden brown. Sprinkle evenly with powdered sugar. Serve warm or at room temperature. Yield: 8 servings (serving size: 1 strudel).

CALORIES 278; **FAT** 10.8g (sat 3.9g, mono 4.5g, poly 1.7g); **PROTEIN** 5.3g; **CARB** 41.8g; **FIBER** 2.7g; **CHOL** 11.5mg; **IRON** 1.9mg; **SODIUM** 261mg; **CALC** 19mg

COOKING CLASS

LATKES

Commemorate the ancient miracle of the oil with crisp, golden, delicious potato pancakes.

These delectable potato pancakes are, for Jews and anyone lucky enough to be at a Jewish table when there's a latke expert in the house, the tastiest tradition of Hanukkah. But as with all frying, latke making requires a deft hand and a good eye. Once you have the knack for crispy-tender success—easily gained in these pages—it's easy to vary the effect by adding fruit or by using interesting vegetable combinations (like the butternut squash version, page 388). As with many traditional Hanukkah foods, latkes are always fried in oil, usually olive oil, a reminder of the miracle story at the heart of this happy holiday.

Classic Potato Latkes

3½ cups shredded peeled baking potato (about 1½ pounds)
1¼ cups grated onion
6 tablespoons all-purpose flour
1 teaspoon chopped fresh thyme
½ teaspoon kosher salt
¼ teaspoon freshly ground black pepper
1 large egg
¼ cup olive oil, divided
¾ cup unsweetened applesauce
Dash of ground cinnamon

1. Combine potato and onion in a colander. Drain 30 minutes, pressing occasionally with the back of a spoon until barely moist. Combine potato mixture, flour, and next 4 ingredients in a large bowl; toss well.

2. Heat a large skillet over medium-high heat. Add 2 tablespoons oil to pan; swirl to coat. Spoon ¼ cup potato mixture loosely into a dry measuring cup. Pour mixture into pan, and flatten slightly. Repeat procedure 5 times to form 6 latkes. Sauté 3½ minutes on each side or until golden brown. Remove latkes from pan; keep warm. Repeat procedure with remaining 2 tablespoons oil and potato mixture to yield 12 latkes total. Combine applesauce and cinnamon in a bowl. Serve applesauce with latkes. Yield: 6 servings (serving size: 2 latkes and 2 tablespoons applesauce).

CALORIES 215; **FAT** 8.7g (sat 1.3g, mono 6.1g, poly 1g); **PROTEIN** 4.4g; **CARB** 31.6g; **FIBER** 2.6g; **CHOL** 30mg; **IRON** 1.6mg; **SODIUM** 173mg; **CALC** 30mg

YOU'LL NEED TO COOK LATKES IN BATCHES. PLACE THE COOKED ONES IN A SINGLE LAYER ON A BAKING SHEET LINED WITH PAPER TOWELS, AND KEEP THEM WARM IN A LOW OVEN AS YOU FRY THE NEXT BATCH.

3 STEPS TO CRISP, LIGHT LATKES

TO GET STARTED, shred potatoes and other main ingredients. Although potatoes are the staple, you can also add flavor and texture by adding shredded onions or squash. If you want to add a touch of sweetness, try sweet potatoes, root vegetables like carrots or parsnips, or even apples.

1 DRAIN MOISTURE. Shredding the ingredients causes them to release more moisture than they would if chopped. Moisture is the enemy of starch, which helps hold the cakes together until they're cooked. (Moisture released in the pan will also prevent a crisp crust from forming.) So be sure to drain as much of the moisture off the mixture as possible.

2 MIX INGREDIENTS. Next, combine your shredded mixture with egg, a bit of flour, and any flavoring options you want to add, and toss.

3 FRY THEM. Finally, you'll portion and form the pancakes in one swoop of the measuring cup. Flatten the top slightly, and pan-fry until golden brown.

Curried Butternut and Potato Latkes with Apple Salsa

Serrano chiles are more fiery than jalapeños. To tame the heat, substitute a jalapeño.

1½ cups finely chopped peeled Gala apple
1 tablespoon fresh lime juice
¼ cup thin vertically sliced red onion
1 finely chopped seeded serrano chile
5 tablespoons chopped fresh cilantro, divided
⅝ teaspoon kosher salt, divided
3 cups shredded peeled butternut squash (about ¾ pound)
3 cups shredded peeled baking potato (about ¾ pound)
1 cup grated onion
6 tablespoons all-purpose flour
1 teaspoon curry powder
½ teaspoon ground coriander
¼ teaspoon freshly ground black pepper
⅛ teaspoon ground cinnamon
1 large egg
¼ cup olive oil, divided

1. Combine apple and lime juice in a bowl; toss. Add onion, chile, 1 tablespoon cilantro, and ⅛ teaspoon salt; toss. Cover and chill.
2. Combine squash, potato, and onion in a colander; drain 30 minutes, pressing occasionally with the back of a spoon until barely moist. Combine potato mixture, remaining 4 tablespoons cilantro, remaining ½ teaspoon salt, flour, and next 5 ingredients in a large bowl; toss well.
3. Heat a large skillet over medium-high heat. Add 4 teaspoons oil to pan; swirl to coat. Spoon ¼ cup potato mixture loosely into a dry measuring cup. Pour mixture into pan; flatten slightly. Repeat procedure 4 times to form 5 latkes. Sauté 3½ minutes on each side or until golden brown and thoroughly cooked. Remove latkes from pan; keep warm. Repeat procedure twice with remaining oil and potato mixture to yield 14 latkes total. Serve with salsa. Yield: 7 servings (serving size: 2 latkes and about ¼ cup salsa).

CALORIES 218; FAT 10.1g (sat 1.6g, mono 6.9g, poly 1.2g); PROTEIN 4g; CARB 30.2g; FIBER 3.6g; CHOL 35mg; IRON 1.7mg; SODIUM 265mg; CALC 53mg

Cilantro-Jalapeño Latkes with Chipotle Sour Cream

6 tablespoons light sour cream
1 tablespoon chopped chipotle chile, canned in adobo sauce
¾ teaspoon grated lime rind
1 teaspoon fresh lime juice
6 cups shredded peeled baking potato (about 1½ pounds)
1 cup grated fresh onion
6 tablespoons all-purpose flour
½ cup chopped fresh cilantro
2 tablespoons finely chopped, seeded jalapeño pepper
1 large egg
1 teaspoon ground cumin
½ teaspoon salt
¼ cup olive oil, divided

1. Combine first 4 ingredients in a small bowl, stirring well. Cover and chill until ready to serve.
2. Combine potato and onion in a colander. Drain 30 minutes, pressing occasionally with the back of a spoon until barely moist. Combine potato mixture, flour, and next 5 ingredients in a large bowl; toss well.
3. Heat a large skillet over medium-high heat. Add 2 tablespoons oil to pan; swirl to coat. Spoon ¼ cup potato mixture loosely into a dry measuring cup. Pour mixture into pan; flatten slightly. Repeat procedure 5 times to form 6 latkes. Sauté 3½ minutes on each side or until golden brown and thoroughly cooked. Remove latkes from pan; keep warm. Repeat procedure with remaining 2 tablespoons oil and potato mixture to yield 12 latkes total. Serve with sour cream mixture. Yield: 6 servings (serving size: 2 latkes and about 1½ tablespoons sour cream mixture).

CALORIES 260; FAT 11g (sat 2.2g, mono 6.9g, poly 1.2g); PROTEIN 5.6g; CARB 35.3g; FIBER 3.8g; CHOL 35mg; IRON 2.1mg; SODIUM 268mg; CALC 36mg

DAZZLING HOLIDAY DESSERTS

Cranberries' brilliant crimson hue, sparkling diamond-like sugar, rich dark chocolate—these showstopper sweets capture the indulgent spirit of the season.

Make Ahead
Cranberry Swirl Cheesecake

If the cranberry mixture gets too thick, add a tablespoon of water, and whirl it around in the food processor. You can also make this in an 8-inch springform pan; it'll be very full, so you should cook over a foil-lined baking sheet. Cook time will be the same.

Crust:
4 ounces chocolate graham crackers
3 tablespoons canola oil
Cooking spray
Swirl:
1½ cups fresh cranberries
½ cup sugar
¼ cup Chambord (raspberry-flavored liqueur)
3 tablespoons water
Filling:
1 cup sugar
2 (8-ounce) packages block-style ⅓-less-fat cream cheese, softened
½ cup (4 ounces) block-style fat-free cream cheese, softened
1 cup plain fat-free Greek yogurt
2 teaspoons vanilla extract
⅛ teaspoon salt
3 large eggs
2 large egg whites

1. Preheat oven to 375°.
2. Wrap outside and bottom of a 9-inch springform pan tightly with a double layer of heavy-duty foil; set pan aside.
3. To prepare crust, place crackers in a food processor; process until finely ground. Drizzle with oil; pulse until combined. Using bottom of a dry measuring cup, press mixture into bottom and ½-inch up sides of prepared pan coated with cooking spray. Bake at 375° for 8 minutes. Cool on a wire rack.
4. Reduce oven temperature to 325°.
5. To prepare swirl, place cranberries and next 3 ingredients in a small saucepan; bring to a boil over medium-high heat. Cook 8 minutes or until cranberries pop and mixture is slightly syrupy. Cool 20 minutes. Place mixture in a food processor; process 1 minute or until smooth. (Mixture will thicken while sitting. Pulse again just before spooning onto cheesecake.)
6. To prepare filling, combine 1 cup sugar and cheeses in a large bowl; beat with a mixer at medium speed until smooth. Add yogurt, vanilla, and salt; beat until blended. Add whole eggs, 1 at a time, beating well after each addition.
7. Place 2 egg whites in a medium bowl; beat with a mixer at high speed until soft peaks form using clean, dry beaters. Fold beaten egg whites into cream cheese mixture. Pour filling over prepared crust. Spoon cranberry mixture over filling; swirl mixtures together using the tip of a knife. Place springform pan in a 13 x 9–inch metal baking pan. Add hot water to pan to a depth of 2 inches. Bake at 325° for 50 minutes or until center of cheesecake barely moves when pan is touched.
8. Turn oven off. Cool cheesecake in closed oven 30 minutes. Remove cheesecake from oven. Run a knife around outside edge. Cool to room temperature on a wire rack. Cover and chill 8 hours. Yield: 12 servings (serving size: 1 wedge).

CALORIES 321; FAT 14.1g (sat 6.1g, mono 5g, poly 1.5g); PROTEIN 10g; CARB 37.8g; FIBER 0.9g; CHOL 81mg; IRON 0.5mg; SODIUM 333mg; CALC 81mg

Chocolate-Cranberry Parfaits

1⅓ cups granulated sugar, divided
1 cup water
1 cup fresh cranberries
½ cup sparkling white sugar or turbinado sugar
3 tablespoons cornstarch
¼ teaspoon salt
2½ cups fat-free milk, divided
2 large egg yolks
1 teaspoon vanilla extract
4 ounces semisweet chocolate, chopped
1 cup frozen fat-free whipped topping, thawed
¼ cup mascarpone cheese

1. Combine 1 cup granulated sugar and 1 cup water in a small heavy saucepan over medium-high heat, stirring until sugar dissolves. Bring to a simmer; remove from heat. Combine sugar syrup and cranberries in a small bowl. Cover and chill 4 hours.
2. Drain cranberries in a colander over a bowl, reserving liquid for another use, if desired. Place sparkling sugar in a shallow dish. Add cranberries, rolling to coat. Spread sugared cranberries in a single layer on a baking sheet; let stand at room temperature 1 hour or until dry.
3. Combine remaining ⅓ cup granulated sugar, cornstarch, and salt in a large bowl, stirring well. Combine ½ cup milk and egg yolks in a small bowl, stirring with a whisk. Heat remaining 2 cups milk in a medium heavy saucepan to 180° or until tiny bubbles form around edge (do not boil). Stir egg yolk mixture into cornstarch mixture. Gradually add half of hot milk to sugar mixture, stirring constantly with a whisk. Add egg yolk mixture to pan; bring to a boil. Cook 1 minute, stirring constantly with a whisk. Remove from heat. Add vanilla and chocolate, stirring until chocolate melts. Spoon pudding into a bowl; place bowl in a large ice-filled bowl 15 minutes or until pudding cools, stirring occasionally. Cover surface of pudding with plastic wrap; chill 20 minutes.
4. Combine whipped topping and mascarpone in a bowl, stirring until well blended. Spoon about ⅓ cup pudding into each of 8 bowls or footed glasses; top each serving with about 3 tablespoons mascarpone mixture and about 2 tablespoons cranberries. Yield: 8 servings.

CALORIES 286; FAT 11.7g (sat 6.5g, mono 3.5g, poly 0.7g); PROTEIN 5.3g; CARB 41.9g; FIBER 0.5g; CHOL 71mg; IRON 0.5mg; SODIUM 121mg; CALC 121mg

EVERYDAY VEGETARIAN

SMALL-PLATE SPECIALS

Great flavors in little tapas-style packages are perfect for holiday entertaining.

Chickpeas and Spinach with Smoky Paprika

Look for smoked paprika in the spice section of your supermarket, or substitute 1 teaspoon sweet paprika and ¼ teaspoon ground red pepper. Serve on grilled or toasted bread.

1 tablespoon olive oil
4 cups thinly sliced onion
5 garlic cloves, thinly sliced
1 teaspoon Spanish smoked paprika
½ cup dry white wine
¼ cup organic vegetable broth
1 (14.5-ounce) can fire-roasted diced tomatoes, undrained
1 (15-ounce) can chickpeas (garbanzo beans), rinsed and drained
1 (9-ounce) package fresh spinach (about 10 cups)
2 tablespoons chopped fresh flat-leaf parsley
2 teaspoons sherry vinegar

1. Heat oil in a large Dutch oven over medium heat. Add onion and garlic to pan; cover and cook 8 minutes or until tender, stirring occasionally. Stir in paprika; cook 1 minute. Add wine, broth, and tomatoes; bring to a boil. Add chickpeas; reduce heat, and simmer until sauce thickens slightly (about 15 minutes), stirring occasionally. Add spinach; cover and cook 2 minutes or until spinach wilts. Stir in parsley and vinegar. Yield: 10 servings (serving size: ⅔ cup).

CALORIES 86; FAT 1.9g (sat 0.2g, mono 1g, poly 0.2g); PROTEIN 3.1g; CARB 14.6g; FIBER 3.5g; CHOL 0mg; IRON 1.8mg; SODIUM 168mg; CALC 64mg

Polenta Squares with Gorgonzola and Pine Nuts

These are also tasty with chopped dried figs or cranberries in place of the currants.

4 cups water
1 cup quick-cooking polenta
1 teaspoon kosher salt
1 tablespoon butter
Cooking spray
¼ cup boiling water
3 tablespoons currants
⅓ cup (about 1½ ounces) crumbled Gorgonzola cheese
3 tablespoons pine nuts, toasted
1 teaspoon grated orange rind
⅔ cup balsamic vinegar
2 tablespoons chopped fresh flat-leaf parsley

1. Bring 4 cups water to a boil in a medium saucepan. Gradually add polenta and salt, stirring constantly with a whisk. Reduce heat to low; cook 4 minutes or until thick, stirring frequently. Stir in butter. Spoon polenta into a 9-inch square baking pan coated with cooking spray, spreading evenly. Press plastic wrap onto surface of polenta; chill 1 hour or until very firm. Cut into 30 squares.
2. Combine ¼ cup boiling water and currants in a small bowl. Let stand 10 minutes or until currants are plump; drain. Combine currants, cheese, pine nuts, and orange rind in a small bowl.
3. Heat vinegar in a small saucepan; cook over medium-low heat until reduced to 2 tablespoons (about 10 minutes). Cool slightly.
4. Heat a large nonstick skillet over medium-high heat. Coat pan with cooking spray. Add half of polenta

squares to pan; cook 6 minutes on each side or until golden. Remove from pan; keep warm. Repeat procedure with remaining polenta. Top each square with rounded ½ teaspoon of cheese mixture, and drizzle with about ¼ teaspoon balsamic. Garnish with parsley. Yield: 10 servings (serving size: 3 topped polenta squares).

CALORIES 130; FAT 4.2g (sat 1.7g, mono 1.1g, poly 1g); PROTEIN 3.1g; CARB 19.8g; FIBER 1.9g; CHOL 6mg; IRON 0.7mg; SODIUM 268mg; CALC 33mg

Tortilla Español with Romesco Sauce

In Spain, a tortilla is an omelet with potatoes. Spanish Manchego cheese and a robust romesco—red pepper sauce—add flair to the tapas favorite. Make the sauce up to three days in advance.

Romesco:
3 red bell peppers
2 tablespoons blanched almonds, toasted
1 tablespoon extra-virgin olive oil
2 teaspoons sherry vinegar
¼ teaspoon kosher salt
⅛ teaspoon ground red pepper
1 garlic clove, peeled

Tortillas:
3 cups (½-inch) diced peeled Yukon gold potato
1 tablespoon extra-virgin olive oil
¼ cup finely chopped shallots
2 garlic cloves, minced
Cooking spray
½ cup (about 2 ounces) grated aged Manchego cheese
2 teaspoons dried oregano
10 large eggs
½ teaspoon kosher salt
½ teaspoon freshly ground black pepper
Chopped fresh parsley (optional)

1. Preheat broiler.
2. To prepare romesco, cut bell peppers in half lengthwise; discard seeds and membranes. Place bell pepper halves, skin sides up, on a foil-lined baking sheet; flatten with hand. Broil 6 minutes or until blackened. Place in a paper bag; fold to close tightly. Let stand 20 minutes. Peel and chop. Place chopped bell pepper in a food processor. Add almonds and next 5 ingredients; process until smooth.
3. Preheat oven to 325°.
4. To prepare tortillas, place potato in a medium saucepan; cover with water. Bring to a boil over medium-high heat. Cook 6 minutes or just until tender. Drain and cool completely.
5. Heat 1 tablespoon oil in a large nonstick skillet over medium heat. Add shallots and minced garlic; cook 1 minute, stirring occasionally. Add potatoes; increase heat to medium-high. Cook 4 minutes or until potatoes are golden brown, stirring occasionally. Cool completely.
6. Coat 10 (4-ounce) ramekins with cooking spray; place in a roasting pan. Add cheese and oregano to potato mixture; toss well to combine. Divide potato mixture evenly among prepared ramekins. Combine eggs, ½ teaspoon salt, and black pepper, stirring with a whisk until well blended. Pour egg mixture over potato mixture in each ramekin. Add enough hot water to roasting pan to come halfway up sides of ramekins. Bake at 325° for 25 minutes or until set. Run a knife around outside edges of tortillas. Serve with romesco sauce. Sprinkle with parsley, if desired. Yield: 10 servings (serving size: 1 tortilla and 2 tablespoons sauce).

CALORIES 187; FAT 9.8g (sat 3.1g, mono 4.5g, poly 1.4g); PROTEIN 9.4g; CARB 13.9g; FIBER 1.8g; CHOL 186mg; IRON 1.4mg; SODIUM 252mg; CALC 114mg

Sweet Potato and Black Bean Empanadas

These savory pies are great served hot at a party, and the leftovers also make a tasty room-temperature snack.

Dough:
9 ounces all-purpose flour (about 2 cups)
¾ teaspoon kosher salt
⅓ cup canola oil
¼ cup cold water
1 tablespoon cider vinegar
1 large egg, lightly beaten

Filling:
1 poblano chile
1 tablespoon cumin seeds
1 cup mashed cooked sweet potatoes
1 cup canned black beans, rinsed and drained
⅓ cup chopped green onions
2 tablespoons chopped fresh cilantro
1 teaspoon ancho chile powder
½ teaspoon kosher salt
1 large egg white, lightly beaten
Cooking spray

1. To prepare dough, weigh or lightly spoon flour into dry measuring cups; level with a knife. Combine flour and ¾ teaspoon salt in a large bowl, stirring with a whisk. Combine oil and next 3 ingredients. Gradually add oil mixture to flour mixture, stirring just until moist. Knead lightly until smooth. Shape into a ball; wrap in plastic wrap. Chill 1 hour.
2. Preheat broiler.
3. To prepare filling, place poblano on a foil-lined baking sheet; broil 8 minutes or until blackened, turning after 6 minutes. Place in a paper bag; fold to close tightly. Let stand 15 minutes. Peel chile; cut in half lengthwise. Discard seeds and membranes. Finely chop.
4. Preheat oven to 400°.
5. Cook cumin seeds in a large saucepan over medium heat 1 minute or until toasted, stirring constantly. Place cumin in a clean spice or coffee grinder; process until ground. Combine cumin, poblano, sweet potatoes, and next 5 ingredients; mash with a fork until almost smooth.
6. Divide dough into 10 equal portions, shaping each into a ball. Roll each portion into a 5-inch circle on a lightly floured surface. Working with 1 portion at a time (cover remaining dough to keep from drying), spoon 3 level tablespoons poblano mixture into center of each circle. Moisten edges of dough with egg white; fold dough over filling. Press edges together with a fork to seal. Place on a large baking sheet coated with cooking spray. Cut 3 diagonal slits across top of each. Bake at 400° for 16 minutes or until lightly browned. Yield: 10 servings (serving size: 1 empanada).

CALORIES 209; FAT 8.4g (sat 0.7g, mono 5g, poly 2.3g); PROTEIN 5.1g; CARB 29g; FIBER 2.9g; CHOL 18mg; IRON 2.3mg; SODIUM 359mg; CALC 32mg

WHAT TO EAT RIGHT NOW
MANDARIN ORANGES

As winter settles in, tangerines, satsumas, and clementines begin to sing their siren songs. These sun-colored squatty orbs—all members of the Mandarin orange family—stand out amid the other seasonal offerings. Loose (and generally thin) skin is a snap to peel, and these gems of the citrus world have less weblike pith than regular oranges encasing their delicate juicy segments. Just one taste of the refreshing sweet-tart flavor will stave off the winter doldrums.

Holiday Vodka-Tini

Place 1 cup fresh cranberries, 1 cup vodka, ½ cup sugar, and 4 whole satsumas in a food processor; process until pureed. Refrigerate 8 hours or overnight. Strain mixture through a cheesecloth-lined sieve over a bowl, pressing to extract juice. Discard solids. Stir in ¾ cup Grand Marnier and ¼ cup fresh lime juice. Place 1 cup satsuma mixture in a martini shaker with ½ cup crushed ice; shake. Strain mixture into 2 martini glasses. Repeat procedure four times. Yield: 10 servings.

CALORIES 187; **FAT** 0.2g (sat 0g); **SODIUM** 2mg

Clementine Glaze

Combine 3 cups fresh clementine juice, 1 chopped shallot, and 1 fresh thyme sprig in a heavy saucepan; bring to a boil. Cook until syrupy and reduced to ⅓ cup. Strain mixture; discard solids. Stir in 2 tablespoons butter and ¼ tea-spoon salt. Brush on pork, chicken, or beef while roasting. Yield: 6 servings (serving size: about 1 tablespoon).

CALORIES 90; **FAT** 4.1g (sat 2.5g); **SODIUM** 127mg

10 THINGS ABOUT COFFEE

1. MUCH DEPENDS ON THE SOIL—BUT NOT EVERYTHING.
Coffee talk is all about the *terroir,* the taste derived from the soil. And flavor profiles follow continental patterns. But processing and freshness tend to have a bigger effect on taste than they do in the case of wine, because beans, after roasting, are volatile. Time between roasting and packing is important, as is the quality of the package, and time between opening the package and brewing the beans.
African: Aromatic with strong fruity or floral notes.
Asia/Indo-Pacific: Full-bodied and earthy; also less acidic and bright.
Latin American: Notes of nuts and cocoa; not as aromatic as African varieties.

2. SO, WHEN WERE THESE BEANS ROASTED?
That's when the clock starts ticking, and you've got about two weeks before flavor starts to fade. There are no guidelines for coffee labeling; some vendors list the roasting date, and some don't. Open bins of beans are not promising; nor are bags without valves (see #3). Some vendors, like Peet's Coffee & Tea (www.peets.com), roast to order.

3. IS THE BAG GOOD?
Freshly roasted beans off-gas carbon dioxide. Valve-sealed bags let the gas escape in transit. Cans or vaccuum-sealed bags contain beans that have been aired out. And note what air does to beans in point #4.

4. STORE WELL; GRIND AS YOU GO.
Store beans in an airtight canister away from light, then grind just before brewing. Once ground, more of the bean's surface area is exposed to air, causing the oils (and the flavor) to evaporate faster. Ground coffee lasts just a day or two; whole beans, up to two weeks.

5. THE BLADE VS BURR DEBATE:
Blade grinders chop beans into bits, yielding grounds of varying sizes, leading to an inconsistent brew. Burr grinders, little millstones, grind beans to a uniform size between two plates. And you can adjust grind size according to your own brewing method. Coffee aficionados like the more costly burrs for that reason.

6. THE WATER MATTERS.
If your tap water tastes weird, it's doing your brew no favors. Filter it. Then, pay attention to temperature. The water needs to reach from 195° to 205°, and many automatic-drip coffeemakers don't reach that mark. The best way to control temperature is to use a brewing method that requires you to heat the water yourself. Two words: French press. Extra work, but worth it.

7. TRY THE COFFEEHOUSE RATIO.
Using better machines and higher-quality beans makes for richer, more intensive flavor. But good coffeehouses use more coffee when brewing, too: 2 tablespoons of coffee per 6 ounces of water.

8. CHECK YOUR POT'S MATH.
A standard cup measure is 8 ounces, but it's obvious to the eye that many 8- and 10-cup coffeemakers use a different measure. Some use a 6-ounce standard, some even less. Check the manual or test your pot. Important because you want to use the right coffee-water ratio. See #7.

PROCESSING AND FRESHNESS GREATLY AFFECT TASTE, BECAUSE UNLIKE WINE, COFFEE DOES NOT AGE GRACEFULLY.

9. KNOW YOUR GRINDS.
Dry raw beans can keep a long time, ship well to distant roasters.
Roasting, light to dark, moves beans from terroir notes to deep-roasted notes.
Coarse grind is best for a French press.
Medium grind is best for auto-drip machines.
Fine grind is best for espresso or cone filters.

10. WHO GETS FAIR-TRADE DOLLARS?
Fair-trade coffee is certified to come from small farmer cooperatives that are paid a premium of 10 cents per pound (20 cents for organic). You absorb that cost—plus another 5 to 10 cents for the certifying agency.

4 TIPS FOR A BETTER AUTOMATIC DRIP EXPERIENCE

So you refuse to part with the convenience of automatic drip? We understand. Here's how to get a better brew.

1 AVOID HEAT PLATES. What you see as a coffee warmer is also a coffee cooker. It keeps heating the oil that's been extracted from the ground beans, making the brew bitter. Look for a coffeemaker with a thermal carafe instead.

2 ADD FRESH WATER. Don't let it sit in the machine overnight—stagnant water in a warm, moist environment...no thanks!

3 START BREWING as soon as you finish grinding.

4 CLEAN YOUR EQUIPMENT (even your grinder) after each use. Residue builds up and can taint the taste of your coffee.

DINNER TONIGHT

Here are a batch of fast weeknight menus from the *Cooking Light* Test Kitchens.

Quick & Easy • Make Ahead
Mexican Chicken-Hominy Soup
with Cumin-Lime Tortilla Chips

Simple Sub: Use 1 cup frozen thawed corn in place of hominy.
Make-Ahead Tip: Refrigerate cooked, cooled soup up to two days.
Flavor Hit: A spritz of lime in the soup and on the chips adds bright notes.
This is a mild, brothy, comforting soup. For more kick, leave the seeds in part or all of the jalapeño.

1 tablespoon olive oil
1¾ cups chopped onion
3 garlic cloves, minced
1 jalapeño pepper, seeded and minced
2 cups shredded skinless, boneless rotisserie chicken breast
¼ teaspoon freshly ground black pepper
2 (14-ounce) cans fat-free, lower-sodium chicken broth
1 (15.5-ounce) can hominy, rinsed and drained
½ cup thinly sliced radishes
2 tablespoons fresh cilantro leaves
4 lime wedges

1. Heat oil in a large saucepan over medium-high heat. Add onion to pan; sauté 2 minutes. Stir in garlic and jalapeño; sauté 1 minute. Add chicken, black pepper, and broth; bring to a boil. Reduce heat, and simmer 5 minutes. Stir in hominy; bring to a boil. Cook 5 minutes. Ladle about 1½ cups soup into each of 4 bowls; top each serving with 2 tablespoons radishes and 1½ teaspoons cilantro. Serve with lime wedges. Yield: 4 servings.

CALORIES 235; FAT 6.6g (sat 1.3g, mono 3.5g, poly 1.2g); PROTEIN 24.8g; CARB 18g; FIBER 3.3g; CHOL 60mg; IRON 1.5mg; SODIUM 641mg; CALC 43mg

For the Cumin-Lime Tortilla Chips:
Preheat oven to 350°. Cut each of 4 (6-inch) yellow corn tortillas into 8 wedges. Arrange wedges in a single layer on a baking sheet. Brush wedges evenly with 1½ tablespoons canola oil. Combine ⅜ teaspoon ground cumin and ⅛ teaspoon salt; sprinkle evenly over wedges. Bake at 350° for 15 minutes or until crisp and golden. Cool slightly; drizzle with 2 tablespoons fresh lime juice. Yield: 4 servings.

CALORIES 119; FAT 6.3g (sat 0.4g); SODIUM 109mg

30 minutes

SHOPPING LIST

Mexican Chicken-Hominy Soup
1 large onion
garlic
1 jalapeño pepper
radishes
fresh cilantro
1 lime
olive oil
2 (14-ounce) cans fat-free, lower-sodium chicken broth
15.5-ounce can hominy
rotisserie chicken

Cumin-Lime Tortilla Chips
yellow corn tortillas
canola oil
ground cumin
1 lime

GAME PLAN

While oven preheats:
 ■ Prep tortillas.
 ■ Sauté aromatics for soup.
While tortilla chips bake:
 ■ Finish cooking soup.

Quick & Easy
Chicken and Black Bean Stuffed Burritos
with Citrus and Radish Salad

Shopping Tip: Refrigerated salsa tastes vibrant.
Simple Sub: You can also use preshredded Mexican blend cheese.
Vegetarian Swap: Omit the chicken, and use the whole can of beans.

¼ cup water
2 tablespoons fresh lime juice
½ teaspoon chili powder
¼ teaspoon ground cumin
¼ teaspoon black pepper
⅛ teaspoon ground red pepper
2 cups shredded skinless, boneless rotisserie chicken breast
¼ cup thinly sliced green onions
¾ cup canned black beans, rinsed and drained
½ cup refrigerated fresh salsa or pico de gallo
4 (8-inch) flour tortillas
½ cup (2 ounces) shredded Monterey Jack cheese
Cooking spray

1. Combine first 6 ingredients in a small saucepan; bring to a boil. Stir in chicken and green onions; cook 2 minutes or until thoroughly heated.
2. Combine beans and salsa. Working with 1 tortilla at a time, spoon ¼ cup bean mixture and ½ cup chicken mixture down center of tortilla. Sprinkle evenly with 2 tablespoons cheese; roll up. Repeat procedure with remaining tortillas, bean mixture, chicken mixture, and cheese.
3. Heat a large skillet over medium-high heat. Coat pan with cooking spray. Add 2 burritos to pan. Place a cast-iron or other heavy skillet on top of burritos; cook 3 minutes on each side or until browned (leave skillet on burritos while they cook). Remove from pan; repeat procedure with remaining 2 burritos. Yield: 4 servings (serving size: 1 burrito).

CALORIES 353; **FAT** 9.8g (sat 4.1g, mono 3.6g, poly 1.3g); **PROTEIN** 30.9g; **CARB** 33.1g; **FIBER** 2.4g; **CHOL** 72mg; **IRON** 1.6mg; **SODIUM** 595mg; **CALC** 137mg

For the Citrus and Radish Salad:
Combine 2 tablespoons fresh orange juice, 2 tablespoons olive oil, and ⅛ teaspoon ground red pepper, stirring with a whisk. Toss with 4 cups prechopped romaine lettuce, ½ cup thinly sliced radishes, 2 tablespoons fresh cilantro leaves, and 1 ripe peeled sliced avocado. Yield: 4 servings.

CALORIES 154; **FAT** 14.3g (sat 2g); **SODIUM** 13mg

40 minutes

SHOPPING LIST

Chicken and Black Bean Stuffed Burritos
1 lime
green onions
refrigerated fresh salsa
chili powder
ground cumin
ground red pepper
1 can black beans
8-inch flour tortillas
Monterey Jack cheese
rotisserie chicken

Citrus and Radish Salad:
1 orange
prechopped romaine lettuce
radishes
fresh cilantro
1 avocado
olive oil
ground red pepper

GAME PLAN

While water mixture heats:
- Shred chicken.
- Slice green onions.
- Rinse and drain black beans.

While burritos cook:
- Prepare salad.

Quick & Easy
Salisbury Steak with Mushroom Gravy
with Herbed Smashed Potatoes and Buttered Peas with Shallots

Flavor Hit: A hint of vinegar rounds out the sauce.
Kid Tweak: Omit the red wine and use all broth instead.

⅓ cup grated onion, divided
½ teaspoon black pepper
¼ teaspoon salt
2 garlic cloves, minced
1 pound ground sirloin
Cooking spray
1 tablespoon butter
1 (8-ounce) package cremini mushrooms, quartered
⅓ cup dry red wine
1¼ cups fat-free, lower-sodium beef broth
1 tablespoon all-purpose flour
1 teaspoon red wine vinegar

1. Combine ¼ cup onion, pepper, and next 3 ingredients in a bowl. Divide mixture into 4 equal portions; shape each into a ½-inch-thick patty. Heat a large nonstick skillet over medium-high heat. Coat pan with cooking spray. Add patties to pan; cook 3 minutes on each side or until browned. Remove from pan; keep warm.
2. Melt butter in pan, swirling to coat. Add mushrooms; sauté 4 minutes or until liquid evaporates. Stir in wine and remaining onion; cook 2 minutes or until liquid is absorbed. Combine broth and flour, stirring with a whisk; add to pan and bring to a boil. Cook 5 minutes or until thickened. Add patties and vinegar to pan; cook 2 minutes or until desired degree of doneness. Yield: 4 servings (serving size: 1 steak and about ¼ cup gravy).

CALORIES 192; **FAT** 7.9g (sat 3.8g, mono 2.7g, poly 0.7g); **PROTEIN** 24.9g; **CARB** 6g; **FIBER** 0.7g; **CHOL** 68mg; **IRON** 2.3mg; **SODIUM** 380mg; **CALC** 20mg

For the Herbed Smashed Potatoes:
Place 1 pound small red potatoes in a medium saucepan; cover with water and bring to a boil. Cook 10 minutes or until tender; drain. Mash slightly with a potato masher. Add ⅓ cup half-and-half, 1 tablespoon butter, 1 tablespoon mixed fresh herbs, ⅜ teaspoon salt, and ⅛ teaspoon black pepper, stirring to combine. Yield: 4 servings.

CALORIES 132; **FAT** 5.4g (sat 3.3g); **SODIUM** 257mg

For the Buttered Peas with Shallots:
Cook 2 cups frozen green peas according to package directions. While peas cook, heat 1 tablespoon butter and 2 teaspoons olive oil in a skillet over medium-high heat. Add 1 thinly sliced large shallot; sauté 3 minutes or until browned. Add peas, ¼ teaspoon salt, and ¼ teaspoon black pepper; toss to coat. Yield: 4 servings.

CALORIES 118; **FAT** 5.4g (sat 2.1g); **SODIUM** 226mg

GRATING THE ONION ALLOWS IT TO COOK QUICKLY IN THE PATTIES AND DOESN'T LEAVE ANY CRUNCHY BITS BEHIND.

40 minutes

SHOPPING LIST

Salisbury Steak with Mushroom Gravy
1 small onion
garlic
8-ounce package cremini mushrooms
1 can fat-free, lower-sodium beef broth
all-purpose flour
red wine vinegar
1 pound ground sirloin
butter
dry red wine

Herbed Smashed Potatoes
1 pound small red potatoes
mixed fresh herb blend
half-and-half
butter

Buttered Peas with Shallots
1 large shallot
olive oil
butter
frozen green peas

GAME PLAN

While patties cook:
- Cook peas.
- Cook potatoes.

While gravy cooks:
- Mash potatoes.
- Finish peas.

HOW TO MAKE SMASHED POTATOES

When making smashed potatoes with larger potatoes, such as baking potatoes, you'll need to cut the potato into uniform pieces—about 1-inch pieces—to ensure even cooking. But smaller potatoes, such as red potatoes, can be left whole.

1 Cook the potatoes in boiling water until tender. Drain and return them to the pan over low heat.

2 Mash slightly with a potato masher.

3 Add butter, cream, and any herbs and seasonings you like, and mash them until they reach the desired consistency.

4 If you like, add cheese and stir to combine.

40 minutes

SHOPPING LIST

Kung Pao Chicken
1 small onion
garlic
bottled minced ginger
1 large red bell pepper
1 cup snow peas
dark sesame oil
lower-sodium soy sauce
cornstarch
brown sugar
crushed red pepper
unsalted, dry-roasted peanuts
1 pound skinless, boneless chicken thighs

Coconut Jasmine Rice
fresh cilantro
jasmine rice
light coconut milk

GAME PLAN

While rice mixture comes to a boil:
- Chop onion and garlic.
- Prep chicken.
- Slice bell pepper.
While rice simmers:
- Cook entrée.

Quick & Easy
Kung Pao Chicken
with Coconut Jasmine Rice

Vegetarian Swap: Omit chicken, and sauté cubed tofu in its place.
Flavor Hit: Dark sesame oil lends deep toasty essence.

2 tablespoons dark sesame oil
1 cup chopped onion
2 garlic cloves, minced
1 pound skinless, boneless chicken thighs,
  cut into 1-inch pieces
¾ cup water
3 tablespoons lower-sodium soy sauce
2 teaspoons cornstarch
1 teaspoon brown sugar
½ teaspoon bottled minced ginger
1 to 1½ teaspoons crushed red pepper
1 cup thinly sliced red bell pepper (about
  1 large pepper)
1 cup snow peas, trimmed
2 tablespoons chopped unsalted, dry-roasted
  peanuts

1. Heat oil in a large skillet over medium-high heat. Add onion to pan; sauté 3 minutes or until softened. Add garlic; sauté 30 seconds, stirring constantly. Add chicken; sauté 3 minutes or until chicken begins to brown.
2. Combine ¾ cup water and next 5 ingredients, stirring until sugar dissolves. Add water mixture to pan; bring to a boil. Add bell pepper and snow peas to pan; cook 2 minutes or until vegetables are crisp-tender. Sprinkle with nuts. Yield: 4 servings (serving size: 1 cup).

CALORIES 275; FAT 13.8g (sat 2.6g, mono 5.3g, poly 4.8g); PROTEIN 25.3g; CARB 11.9g; FIBER 2.2g; CHOL 94mg; IRON 2mg; SODIUM 502mg; CALC 41mg

For the Coconut Jasmine Rice:
Combine 1 cup uncooked jasmine rice, 1¼ cups water, ½ cup light coconut milk, and ¼ teaspoon salt in a medium saucepan; bring to a boil. Cover and reduce heat to a simmer; cook 15 minutes or until liquid is absorbed and rice is tender. Remove from heat; fluff rice with a fork. Stir in ¼ cup chopped fresh cilantro. Yield: 4 servings.

CALORIES 97; FAT 1.5g (sat 1.4g); SODIUM 155mg

BUDGET COOKING
FEED 4 FOR LESS THAN $10

Crab gumbo, roast lamb: expensive tastes on a penny-wise leash.

Crab and Vegetable Gumbo

$2.49 per serving, $9.97 total

3 tablespoons butter
1 cup chopped onion
⅓ cup chopped carrot
½ teaspoon kosher salt
½ teaspoon ground cumin
½ teaspoon ground red pepper
½ teaspoon freshly ground black pepper
¼ teaspoon garlic powder
1 celery stalk, chopped
2 cups fat-free, lower-sodium chicken broth
1 (16-ounce) package frozen gumbo-blend
  vegetables
1 cup water
2 tablespoons all-purpose flour
1 (8-ounce) container crab claw meat, shell
  pieces removed
2 cups hot cooked long-grain white rice

1. Melt butter in a large Dutch oven over medium heat; cook 2 minutes or until lightly browned. Add onion and next 7 ingredients to pan; cook 4 minutes, stirring occasionally.
2. Increase heat to medium-high. Add broth and vegetable blend. Combine 1 cup water and flour, stirring well; stir into broth mixture. Bring to a boil. Reduce heat to medium; simmer 18 minutes. Add crab; simmer 2 minutes. Serve over rice. Yield: 4 servings (serving size: 1½ cups gumbo and ½ cup rice).

CALORIES 323; FAT 10.3g (sat 5.8g, mono 2.6g, poly 0.9g); PROTEIN 17.2g; CARB 41.3g; FIBER 5.2g; CHOL 67mg; IRON 3.1mg; SODIUM 702mg; CALC 151mg

Roast Lamb with Pomegranate Sauce

$2.44 per serving, $9.75 total

2 teaspoons olive oil
1 (1-pound) boneless leg of lamb, trimmed
³/₄ teaspoon kosher salt, divided
½ teaspoon freshly ground black pepper
³/₄ cup coarsely chopped onion
2 garlic cloves, crushed
¹/₃ cup red wine
1½ cups fat-free, lower-sodium chicken broth, divided
¼ cup pomegranate juice
2 teaspoons sugar
2 teaspoons all-purpose flour

1. Preheat oven to 375°.
2. Heat a large ovenproof skillet over medium-high heat. Add oil to pan; swirl to coat. Sprinkle lamb evenly with ½ teaspoon salt and pepper; add lamb to pan. Sauté 10 minutes, turning to brown on all sides. Place pan in oven; bake at 375° for 15 minutes or until a thermometer inserted in thickest portion registers 130°. Remove lamb from pan; let stand 10 minutes.
3. Place pan over medium-high heat. Add onion and garlic to pan; sauté 3 minutes, stirring occasionally. Add wine to pan; bring to a boil. Cook until liquid almost evaporates, scraping pan to loosen browned bits. Stir in remaining ¼ teaspoon salt, 1 cup broth, juice, and sugar; bring to a boil. Cook until reduced to ½ cup (about 10 minutes), stirring occasionally. Combine remaining ½ cup broth and flour, stirring until smooth. Add flour mixture to juice mixture; bring to a boil. Cook 1 minute, stirring occasionally. Strain mixture through a fine-mesh sieve; discard solids. Serve with lamb. Yield: 4 servings (serving size: 3 ounces lamb and about 3 tablespoons sauce).

CALORIES 317; FAT 18.8g (sat 7.4g, mono 8.4g, poly 1.6g); PROTEIN 22.5g; CARB 9.6g; FIBER 1g; CHOL 77mg; IRON 2.4mg; SODIUM 574mg; CALC 29mg

Mushroom and Barley Risotto

$2.27 per serving, $9.08 total

2 cups boiling water
½ ounce dried porcini mushrooms
2 tablespoons olive oil
1½ cups chopped onion
1 (8-ounce) package cremini mushrooms, sliced
5 garlic cloves, minced
2 cups uncooked pearl barley
3 tablespoons brandy
1³/₄ cups water
1 cup fat-free, lower-sodium chicken broth
2 ounces fresh pecorino Romano cheese, divided
½ teaspoon kosher salt
¼ cup chopped fresh flat-leaf parsley

1. Combine 2 cups boiling water and porcini mushrooms; let stand 20 minutes. Drain mushrooms through a sieve over a bowl, reserving liquid. Finely chop mushrooms.
2. Heat a large Dutch oven over medium-high heat. Add oil to pan; swirl to coat. Add onion; cook 4 minutes, stirring occasionally. Add cremini mushrooms; cook 5 minutes, stirring occasionally. Add reserved porcini mushrooms and garlic; cook 1 minute, stirring constantly. Add barley; cook 30 seconds, stirring occasionally. Add brandy; bring to a boil. Cook until liquid almost evaporates (about 1 minute), stirring occasionally.
3. Stir in reserved mushroom liquid, 1³/₄ cups water, and broth; bring to a boil. Cover; reduce heat, and simmer 55 minutes or until liquid evaporates and barley is tender, stirring occasionally. Remove from heat. Grate 1 ounce cheese; stir grated cheese and salt into barley mixture. Sprinkle with parsley. Shave remaining 1 ounce cheese over top. Yield: 4 servings (serving size: 1²/₃ cups).

CALORIES 487; FAT 8.1g (sat 1.2g, mono 5.1g, poly 1.3g); PROTEIN 14.2g; CARB 88.4g; FIBER 18.6g; CHOL 0mg; IRON 4.1mg; SODIUM 654mg; CALC 61mg

Pork and Sweet Potato Hash

$2.16 per serving, $8.64 total

1 pound boneless pork shoulder (Boston butt), trimmed
½ teaspoon kosher salt
½ teaspoon freshly ground black pepper
Cooking spray
3½ cups fat-free, lower-sodium chicken broth
6 garlic cloves, crushed
1 tablespoon olive oil
4 cups (½-inch) cubed peeled sweet potato (about 1 pound)
1 cup chopped onion
¼ teaspoon ground red pepper
1 (8-ounce) package cremini mushrooms, thinly sliced
3 tablespoons sliced green onions

1. Heat a 12-inch cast-iron skillet over medium-high heat. Sprinkle pork evenly with salt and black pepper. Coat pan with cooking spray. Add pork to pan; sauté 8 minutes, turning to brown on all sides. Add broth and garlic to pan; bring to a boil. Cover, reduce heat to low, and simmer 45 minutes or until pork is fork-tender. Remove pork from pan, reserving cooking liquid and garlic. Place cooking liquid in a bowl. Cool pork slightly; shred with two forks.
2. Heat a large skillet over medium-high heat. Add oil to pan; swirl to coat. Add potato and onion; sauté 6 minutes or until lightly browned, stirring occasionally. Add red pepper and mushrooms; cook 3 minutes. Add cooking liquid and garlic; bring to a boil. Reduce heat to medium, and cook, uncovered, 20 minutes or until liquid nearly evaporates, stirring occasionally. Stir in pork; cook 1 minute or until thoroughly heated. Sprinkle with green onions. Yield: 4 servings (serving size: 1¼ cups).

CALORIES 340; FAT 11.8g (sat 3.4g, mono 6.2g, poly 1.3g); PROTEIN 28.3g; CARB 29g; FIBER 5.7g; CHOL 76mg; IRON 2.9mg; SODIUM 732mg; CALC 78mg

Bacon Pierogi Bake

$1.84 per serving, $7.34 total

Pierogies are yummy potato-filled dumplings you can purchase from the freezer section of most major supermarkets. Using this convenience item to jump-start dinner is not just economical, but it'll save you lots of time in the kitchen, as well. Serve with a green salad.

1 (16-ounce) package frozen potato and onion pierogies (such as Mrs. T's)
Cooking spray
2 center-cut bacon slices, chopped
2 garlic cloves, minced
⅓ cup (3 ounces) ⅓-less-fat cream cheese
½ cup fat-free, lower-sodium chicken broth
½ cup (2 ounces) shredded sharp cheddar cheese
¼ cup thinly diagonally sliced green onions
¼ cup chopped seeded plum tomato
½ teaspoon freshly ground black pepper

1. Preheat oven to 400°.
2. Arrange pierogies in an 11 x 7–inch glass or ceramic baking dish coated with cooking spray. Cook bacon in a saucepan over medium heat until crisp; remove from pan. Set aside.
3. Add garlic to drippings in pan; cook 30 seconds, stirring constantly. Add ⅓ cup cream cheese to pan; cook 1 minute or until cream cheese begins to melt, stirring frequently. Gradually add broth to pan, stirring with a whisk until smooth. Pour cream cheese mixture evenly over pierogies. Top evenly with ½ cup cheddar cheese. Bake at 400° for 20 minutes or until bubbly and thoroughly heated. Remove from oven; sprinkle with bacon, green onions, tomato, and pepper. Yield: 4 servings (serving size: 3 pierogies and 2 tablespoons sauce).

CALORIES 303; **FAT** 12.8g (sat 6g, mono 4.3g, poly 0.4g); **PROTEIN** 12.1g; **CARB** 36.4g; **FIBER** 2.2g; **CHOL** 38mg; **IRON** 0.4mg; **SODIUM** 646mg; **CALC** 141mg

READER RECIPES
FROM YOUR KITCHEN TO OURS

After a recent trip to Israel, Pam Riesenberg was inspired to include more quinoa and fresh salads in her family's meals. "It's a very healthy cuisine, and quinoa figures into the Israeli diet a lot." Now she's spreading the word through cooking classes.

Gloria Piantek grew up in an Italian neighborhood and has been baking rosemary focaccia for years. But this time she kicked the flavors up by adding toasty almonds and a sweet honey glaze. There's a wee bit of red pepper, too, for a little extra bite.

While in Delaware on a business trip, Janet Cabibi ordered the famous local crab cakes. Tasty, she thought, but why so much fat? Back home, she wanted to match the crabby flavor in a lighter version—and succeeded. "This recipe works because the combination of ingredients complement but don't overwhelm the flavor of fresh crab," she says. "My version has been a big hit with all of the guests I have served it to." For a satisfying main meal, try two crab cakes, some slices of whole-wheat baguette, and tomatoes with a balsamic drizzle. Or serve these quick and easy crab cakes as an appetizer for eight.

Bunny Pryor always admired her mother-in-law's kitchen expertise, but she also wanted to devise healthier versions of her husband's favorite dishes. "I tried to create foods even my steak-loving father-in-law could enjoy without feeling cheated," she says. This soup makes a perfect one-pot meal. You can layer on other flavors: Avocado makes a cool, creamy topping, and you can add hot sauce for some zing.

Quinoa and Parsley Salad

"If you don't have quinoa, Israeli couscous would also work well in this salad."
—Pam Riesenberg, Millburn, New Jersey

1 cup water
½ cup uncooked quinoa
¾ cup fresh parsley leaves
½ cup thinly sliced celery
½ cup thinly sliced green onions
½ cup finely chopped dried apricots
3 tablespoons fresh lemon juice
1 tablespoon olive oil
1 tablespoon honey
¼ teaspoon salt
¼ teaspoon black pepper
¼ cup unsalted pumpkinseed kernels, toasted

1. Bring water and quinoa to a boil in a medium saucepan. Cover, reduce heat, and simmer 20 minutes or until liquid is absorbed. Spoon into a bowl; fluff with a fork. Add parsley, celery, onions, and apricots.
2. Whisk lemon juice, olive oil, honey, salt, and black pepper. Add to quinoa mixture, and toss well. Top with pumpkinseed kernels. Yield: 4 servings (serving size: about ⅔ cup).

CALORIES 238; **FAT** 8.6g (sat 1.3g, mono 4.3g, poly 2.8g); **PROTEIN** 5.9g; **CARB** 35.1g; **FIBER** 3.6g; **CHOL** 0mg; **IRON** 4.6mg; **SODIUM** 172mg; **CALC** 47mg

Honey-Almond Focaccia with Rosemary

"This bread is not only attractive but also has a wonderful, rich flavor."
—Gloria Piantek, West Lafayette, Indiana

½ cup sliced almonds
½ cup olive oil
1 tablespoon chopped fresh rosemary
⅛ teaspoon salt
⅛ teaspoon crushed red pepper
1 cup warm 1% low-fat milk (100° to 110°)
1½ teaspoons granulated sugar
1 package dry yeast (about 2¼ teaspoons)
14.7 ounces all-purpose flour (about 3¼ cups), divided
1 teaspoon salt
1 large egg yolk
2 tablespoons olive oil, divided
3 tablespoons powdered sugar
1½ teaspoons honey
1 large egg white

1. Combine first 3 ingredients in a small saucepan; bring to a boil over medium-high heat. Cook 1 minute or until golden. Drain nut mixture through a fine sieve into a bowl, reserving oil. Toss nuts with ⅛ teaspoon salt and red pepper in a bowl.
2. Combine milk, granulated sugar, and yeast in a large bowl; let stand 5 minutes or until bubbly. Weigh or lightly spoon flour into dry measuring cups; level with a knife. Add reserved oil, 6.75 ounces flour (about 1¼ cups), 1 teaspoon salt, and egg yolk to yeast mixture; beat with a mixer at low speed until combined. Gradually add remaining 9 ounces flour (about 2 cups) to oil mixture; beat at low speed until a soft, elastic dough forms (about 3 minutes). Press dough into a jelly-roll pan coated with 1½ tablespoons oil. Cover with plastic wrap; let rise in a warm place (85°) for 40 minutes or until almost doubled in size.
3. Preheat oven to 350°.
4. Press dough gently with fingertips. Combine remaining 1½ teaspoons oil, powdered sugar, honey, and egg white; stir with a whisk until smooth. Gently brush dough with half of egg white mixture. Bake at 350° for 20 minutes. Remove pan from oven. Brush top of bread with remaining egg white mixture; sprinkle with almonds. Bake an additional 10 minutes or until golden brown. Remove from pan; cool 10 minutes on a wire rack. Yield: 24 servings (serving size: 1 [2½-inch square] piece).

CALORIES 137; FAT 7.1g (sat 1g, mono 4.9g, poly 0.9g); PROTEIN 2.9g; CARB 15.5g; FIBER 0.8g; CHOL 8mg; IRON 1mg; SODIUM 119mg; CALC 21mg

Crab Cakes

"Shape the uncooked crab cakes, and refrigerate them in advance to save preparation time."
—Janet Cabibi, Clermont, Florida

3 (1-ounce) slices white bread
¼ cup chopped green onions
2 tablespoons reduced-fat mayonnaise
1½ tablespoons fresh lemon juice
1½ teaspoons Dijon mustard
1½ teaspoons Worcestershire sauce
½ teaspoon black pepper
¼ teaspoon hot pepper sauce
2 large egg whites, lightly beaten
1 pound lump crabmeat, drained and shell pieces removed
1 teaspoon olive oil
4 lemon wedges

1. Place bread in a food processor; pulse 10 times or until coarse crumbs measure 1½ cups. Combine breadcrumbs and next 9 ingredients in a large bowl. Divide mixture into 8 equal portions, shaping each into a ½-inch-thick patty.
2. Heat oil in a large nonstick skillet. Add patties; cook 4 minutes on each side or until golden brown. Serve with lemon wedges. Yield: 4 servings (serving size: 2 crab cakes).

CALORIES 203; FAT 5.3g (sat 0.8g, mono 1.7g, poly 2.1g); PROTEIN 23.4g; CARB 14.2g; FIBER 0.8g; CHOL 69mg; IRON 1.5mg; SODIUM 624mg; CALC 94mg

Make Ahead

Pork and Wild Rice Soup

"Prepare the soup ahead of time, if you like, so the flavors can marry. The soup always tastes better the next day!"
—Bunny Pryor, Hollyglen, California

1 tablespoon extra-virgin olive oil, divided
1 pound pork tenderloin, trimmed and cut into ½-inch pieces
⅓ cup brown and wild rice blend (such as Lundberg)
¼ cup finely chopped onion
3 garlic cloves, minced
2 serrano chiles, seeded and minced (about 2½ tablespoons)
1 cup water
1 teaspoon chopped fresh oregano
1 (32-ounce) carton fat-free, lower-sodium chicken broth
1 (15-ounce) can black beans, rinsed and drained
¼ cup chopped fresh cilantro
2½ tablespoons fresh lime juice
¼ teaspoon kosher salt
¼ teaspoon freshly ground black pepper
3 tablespoons crumbled queso fresco
1 sliced peeled avocado
24 baked tortilla chips

1. Heat 1½ teaspoons oil in a Dutch oven over medium-high heat. Brown pork on all sides. Remove pork from pan.
2. Heat remaining 1½ teaspoons oil in pan, scraping pan to loosen browned bits. Add rice and next 3 ingredients; sauté 3 minutes or until onion is tender. Add pork, 1 cup water, and next 3 ingredients; bring to a boil over high heat. Cover, reduce heat, and simmer 15 minutes or until rice is tender. Stir in cilantro and next 3 ingredients; simmer 2 minutes or until thoroughly heated. Top each serving with cheese, avocado, and chips. Yield: 6 servings (serving size: about 1⅓ cups soup, 1½ teaspoons cheese, 2 avocado slices, and 4 chips).

CALORIES 282; FAT 12.1g (sat 2.7g, mono 6.7g, poly 1.7g); PROTEIN 21.6g; CARB 24.6g; FIBER 5.1g; CHOL 52mg; IRON 2.3mg; SODIUM 638mg; CALC 61mg

RECIPE MAKEOVER
BRING ON THE BRIOCHE

Toasty, buttery French brioche gets a makeover in time for the holidays.

Fluffy, flaky morsels of butter-laden brioche exemplify the art of the French baker, and this rich bread is deliciously adaptable in holiday dishes. Brioche dough makes a splendid base for bread pudding or sticky buns, and the baked bread makes delicious croutons and breadcrumbs. It's also wonderful alone, traditionally slathered with a bit more butter. But the Nutrition Grinch will point out that you can eat 27 grams of fat in just one fluffy roll—and he has a point.

How to keep this chubby carb from weighing down the holiday table? Our approach does not banish the trinity of butter, eggs, and sugar— it just slims it down. A stand mixer streamlines prep, and muffin tins keep portions in check. An overnight rise in the fridge builds flavor and develops texture. The result? Flaky rolls, buttery essence, and a top Test Kitchens rating. Brioche is back, better than ever.

Make Ahead • Freezable
Brioche Rolls

We streamline the kneading process by incorporating the butter with a stand mixer. No brioche pans needed—use a muffin tin to corral the rolls while they bake. Start this a day ahead as the overnight dough rise is essential to coax out bakery-like flavor.

1 package dry yeast (about 2¼ teaspoons)
⅓ cup warm 1% low-fat milk (100° to 110°)
15.75 ounces all-purpose flour (about 3½ cups)
⅓ cup sugar
½ teaspoon salt
4 large eggs, lightly beaten
8½ tablespoons unsalted butter, softened and divided
Cooking spray
1 tablespoon water
1 large egg white

1. Dissolve yeast in warm milk in bowl of a stand mixer fitted with paddle attachment; let stand 5 minutes. Weigh or lightly spoon flour into dry measuring cups; level with a knife. Add flour and next 3 ingredients to milk mixture; beat with a stand mixer at low speed until smooth, scraping down sides of bowl with spatula as needed. Remove paddle attachment; insert dough hook. Mix dough at low speed 5 minutes or until soft and elastic and dough just begins to pull away from sides of bowl. Cut 6½ tablespoons butter into large cubes; add half of cubed butter to dough, mixing at medium speed to blend. Add remaining half of butter to dough; mix at medium speed until incorporated. Mix dough on medium speed 4 minutes or until smooth and elastic. Place dough in a large bowl coated with cooking spray, turning to coat top. Cover and let rise in a warm place (85°), free from drafts, 1 hour or until doubled in size. (Gently press two fingers into dough. If indentation remains, dough has risen enough.) Punch dough down; form into a ball. Return dough to bowl; cover with plastic wrap, and refrigerate 8 hours or overnight.

2. Uncover dough; let stand 90 minutes or until dough comes to room temperature. Divide dough into 4 equal pieces. Working with 1 portion at a time (cover remaining dough to prevent

OLD WAY	OUR WAY
524 calories per serving	128 calories per serving
27.1 grams total fat	4.9 grams total fat
15.7 grams saturated fat	2.8 grams saturated fat
511 milligrams sodium	94 milligrams sodium
Loads of butter	Loads of flavor and rich, tender crumb with just the right amount of butter
Rich flavor from butter and sugar	Overnight rise to develop complex flavors
Over-the-top portion	Sensible, satisfying portion

drying), cut dough into 6 equal pieces. Roll each piece into a 1½-inch ball. Repeat procedure with remaining 3 dough portions to make 24 rolls total. Place rolls in muffin cups coated with cooking spray. Cover and let rise 45 minutes or until almost doubled in size.

3. Preheat oven to 350°.

4. Combine 1 tablespoon water and egg white, stirring with a whisk. Gently brush rolls with egg mixture. Bake at 350° for 14 minutes or until golden. Place pans on wire racks. Place remaining 2 tablespoons butter in a small microwave-safe bowl; microwave at HIGH 20 seconds or until butter melts. Brush butter evenly onto rolls. Yield: 24 rolls (serving size: 1 roll).

Note: Freeze baked, cooled brioche for up to 4 weeks. Reheat rolls by placing in a warm preheated oven for a few minutes.

CALORIES 128; **FAT** 4.9g (sat 2.8g, mono 1.4g, poly 0.4g); **PROTEIN** 3.4g; **CARB** 17.2g; **FIBER** 0.6g; **CHOL** 41mg; **IRON** 1.1mg; **SODIUM** 94mg; **CALC** 13mg

BETTER BRIOCHE

Enhance your bread-baking adventure with these visual cues:

1 The butter is sufficiently incorporated when the dough forms a rough mass and rides with the dough hook, pulling away from the sides of the bowl.

2 Once risen, the dough should be satiny and smooth. Gently press two fingers into dough; if indentation remains, dough is ready to go.

3 Roll the dough pieces into 1½-inch balls, and place in muffin cups coated with cooking spray.

4 Gently brush dough with the egg wash to create a golden, flaky crust. Once the brioche is baked, a final brush of butter ensures rich flavor in each roll.

5-INGREDIENT COOKING

Quick & Easy

Seared Scallops with Fennel and Grapefruit Salad

Licorice and citrus notes highlight the sweetness of the scallops.

2 large red grapefruit
3 cups thinly sliced fennel bulb (about 1 medium)
¾ cup fresh flat-leaf parsley leaves
1 tablespoon extra-virgin olive oil, divided
1½ pounds large sea scallops

Peel and section grapefruit to measure 1½ cups sections over a bowl; squeeze membranes to extract ½ cup juice. Set juice aside. Combine grapefruit sections, fennel, and parsley in a medium bowl. Add 2 teaspoons oil and ¼ teaspoon kosher salt; toss gently to combine. Heat remaining 1 teaspoon oil in a large nonstick skillet over medium-high heat. Sprinkle scallops with ¼ teaspoon kosher salt and ¼ teaspoon freshly ground black pepper. Add scallops to pan; cook 2 minutes on each side or until desired degree of doneness. Remove scallops from pan; keep warm. Add reserved ½ cup juice to pan; cook until reduced to ¼ cup (about 2 minutes). Remove from heat. Place 1 cup fennel mixture on each of 4 plates. Divide scallops evenly among plates; top each serving with 1 tablespoon reduced juice. Yield: 4 servings.

CALORIES 292; **FAT** 5g (sat 0.6g, mono 2.6g, poly 0.8g); **PROTEIN** 27g; **CARB** 37.4g; **FIBER** 5.7g; **CHOL** 47mg; **IRON** 2mg; **SODIUM** 507mg; **CALC** 122mg

THE FIVE INGREDIENTS

2 large red grapefruit

+

3 cups thinly sliced fennel bulb (about 1 medium)

+

¾ cup fresh flat-leaf parsley leaves

+

1 tablespoon extra-virgin olive oil, divided

+

1½ pounds large sea scallops

Tex-Mex Pork

Quick & Easy

Fresh salsa simmers to create a surprisingly complex and zesty sauce in this quick entrée.

1 pound pork tenderloin, trimmed and cut into ³/₄-inch cubes
1½ cups refrigerated fresh salsa
2 cups hot cooked long-grain rice
¼ cup light sour cream
³/₄ cup cubed avocado

Heat a large nonstick skillet over medium-high heat. Coat pan with cooking spray. Add pork to pan; sprinkle with ¾ teaspoon kosher salt and ¾ teaspoon freshly ground black pepper. Sauté 8 minutes or until lightly browned. Add salsa and ¼ cup water to pan; bring to a boil, reduce heat, and simmer 5 minutes or until slightly thickened. Serve pork mixture over rice; top with sour cream and avocado. Yield: 4 servings (serving size: ¾ cup pork mixture, ½ cup rice, 1 tablespoon sour cream, and 3 tablespoons avocado).

CALORIES 322; **FAT** 8.3g (sat 2.4g, mono 4.2g, poly 1g); **PROTEIN** 27g; **CARB** 28.9g; **FIBER** 2.3g; **CHOL** 79mg; **IRON** 2.3mg; **SODIUM** 658mg; **CALC** 38mg

THE FIVE INGREDIENTS

1 pound pork tenderloin, trimmed and cut into ³/₄-inch cubes

+

1½ cups refrigerated fresh salsa

+

2 cups hot cooked long-grain rice

+

¼ cup light sour cream

+

³/₄ cup cubed avocado

SUPERFAST

Big tastes from bold ingredients boost bowls of Italian comfort.

Quick & Easy

Sausage, Tomato, and Arugula Fettuccine

1 (9-ounce) package refrigerated fettuccine
1 tablespoon olive oil
6 ounces Italian turkey sausage
2 teaspoons minced garlic
1 pint cherry tomatoes
¼ teaspoon salt
¼ teaspoon freshly ground black pepper
3 cups baby arugula leaves
2 ounces pecorino Romano cheese, shaved

1. Cook pasta according to package directions, omitting salt and fat. Drain in a colander over a bowl, reserving ⅔ cup cooking liquid.
2. While pasta cooks, heat oil in a large skillet over medium-high heat. Remove casings from sausage. Break sausage into bite-sized pieces and add to pan; cook 3 minutes or until browned, stirring frequently to crumble. Add garlic; cook 30 seconds, stirring constantly. Add tomatoes, salt, and pepper; cover and cook 2 minutes. Mash tomatoes with back of a wooden spoon to break them up. Cover pan; reduce heat to low, and cook 3 minutes. Remove pan from heat. Add pasta, reserved ⅔ cup cooking liquid, and arugula; toss well. Sprinkle with cheese. Yield: 4 servings (serving size: 1⅓ cups pasta and about 2 tablespoons cheese).

CALORIES 356; **FAT** 13g (sat 4.2g, mono 4.2g, poly 2.4g); **PROTEIN** 19.8g; **CARB** 39.3g; **FIBER** 3.9g; **CHOL** 92mg; **IRON** 3mg; **SODIUM** 706mg; **CALC** 168mg

402   DECEMBER

Vegetarian Dish of the Month

Fontal Polenta with Mushroom Sauté

This comforting one-dish meal hits many high notes—creamy, cheese polenta is crowned with a meaty, herby mushroom sauté. Fontal is a soft, mild cow's milk cheese that creates buttery taste and texture in the polenta; if you can't find it, substitute fontina.

2 tablespoons olive oil
2 (4-ounce) packages exotic mushroom blend, chopped
1 (8-ounce) package presliced cremini mushrooms
1 teaspoon minced fresh thyme
½ teaspoon minced fresh oregano
3 garlic cloves, chopped
⅓ cup organic vegetable broth
2 teaspoons fresh lemon juice
⅛ teaspoon salt
⅛ teaspoon freshly ground black pepper
2 cups 2% reduced-fat milk
1½ cups organic vegetable broth
¾ cup instant polenta
1 cup (4 ounces) shredded fontal or fontina cheese
¼ teaspoon salt

1. Preheat broiler.
2. Heat oil in a large skillet over high heat. Add mushrooms to pan; sauté 4 minutes or until softened. Add thyme, oregano, and garlic; sauté 1 minute. Stir in ⅓ cup broth and next 3 ingredients; cook 1 minute. Keep warm.
3. Bring milk and 1½ cups broth to a boil in a large saucepan. Gradually add polenta, stirring with a whisk; cook 4 minutes or until thick, stirring constantly. Stir in ½ cup cheese and ¼ teaspoon salt. Divide polenta among 4 gratin dishes; top evenly with ½ cup cheese. Broil 5 minutes. Top each serving with ½ cup mushrooms. Yield: 4 servings (serving size: 1 gratin).

CALORIES 377; **FAT** 18.2g (sat 7.9g, mono 8.1g, poly 1.3g); **PROTEIN** 16.9g; **CARB** 30.5g; **FIBER** 4.6g; **CHOL** 42mg; **IRON** 1.2mg; **SODIUM** 784mg; **CALC** 322mg

Orecchiette with Kale, Bacon, and Sun-Dried Tomatoes

Orecchiette (little ears pasta) is a classic shape that's ideal for this chunky sauce. You can also use short pasta shapes like penne or rigatoni.

8 ounces uncooked orecchiette pasta
5 cups bagged prewashed kale
2 center-cut bacon slices
¼ cup oil-packed sun-dried tomatoes, drained and roughly chopped
½ teaspoon crushed red pepper
3 large garlic cloves, chopped
½ teaspoon freshly ground black pepper
⅜ teaspoon salt
¼ cup (1 ounce) grated Parmigiano-Reggiano cheese
2 tablespoons fresh lemon juice

1. Cook pasta in boiling water 8 minutes or until almost tender, omitting salt and fat. Add kale; cook 2 minutes. Drain in a colander over a bowl, reserving ½ cup cooking liquid.
2. While pasta cooks, cook bacon in a large skillet over medium-high heat 4 minutes or until crisp. Remove bacon from pan with a slotted spoon; crumble and set aside. Reduce heat to medium-low. Add tomatoes, red pepper, and garlic to drippings in pan; cook 1 minute, stirring frequently. Add pasta mixture, reserved ½ cup cooking liquid, black pepper, and salt to pan; toss to combine. Top evenly with bacon and cheese; drizzle evenly with lemon juice. Yield: 4 servings (serving size: about 1¼ cups pasta).

CALORIES 350; **FAT** 9.2g (sat 3.1g, mono 3.4g, poly 1.3g); **PROTEIN** 14.7g; **CARB** 53.7g; **FIBER** 4.1g; **CHOL** 12mg; **IRON** 3.7mg; **SODIUM** 486mg; **CALC** 218mg

Snack of the Month

Spicy Maple-Cashew Popcorn

For a more kid-friendly version, omit the ground red pepper. Store in an airtight container for up to two days.

1 tablespoon canola oil
¼ cup unpopped popcorn kernels (about 6 cups popped)
¼ cup dry-roasted cashews
⅓ cup sugar
⅓ cup maple syrup
1 tablespoon butter
½ teaspoon salt
¼ teaspoon ground red pepper

1. Heat oil in a medium, heavy saucepan over medium-high heat. While pan heats, line a jelly-roll pan with parchment paper; set aside. Add popcorn to pan; cover and cook 2 minutes or until kernels begin to pop, shaking pan frequently. Continue cooking 2 minutes, shaking pan constantly. When popping slows down, remove pan from heat. Let stand 1 minute or until all popping stops. Stir in cashews.
2. Combine sugar and next 4 ingredients in a small saucepan, and bring to a boil. Cook 1 minute, stirring constantly. Remove from heat; cool 1 minute.
3. Pour hot syrup mixture over popcorn mixture; toss well to coat. Immediately spread popcorn mixture out onto prepared jelly-roll pan. Cool 3 minutes. Yield: 6 servings (serving size: 1 cup).

CALORIES 188; **FAT** 7.3g (sat 1.9g, mono 3.4g, poly 1.2g); **PROTEIN** 1.7g; **CARB** 30.5g; **FIBER** 1.4g; **CHOL** 5mg; **IRON** 0.7mg; **SODIUM** 248mg; **CALC** 15mg

HOW TO COOK PERFECT PASTA

Most pasta packages give directions for how to prepare them, but here are some additional tips. Use a Dutch oven or stockpot to allow room for the pasta to move freely in the boiling water and cook evenly. You'll want to use as much water as possible. For 8 ounces of dried pasta, use 4 quarts of water.

1 Fill the pot with water, cover, and bring the water to a full rolling boil over high heat before adding the pasta. It isn't necessary to add salt (for flavor) or oil (to prevent) the pasta from sticking) to the water, so omit them to avoid adding sodium and fat.

2 Add the pasta and start timing the cooking when the water returns to a rolling boil. If you use fresh pasta, remember that it cooks more quickly than dried. After adding pasta to boiling water, put the lid on the pot, but prop it open slightly with a wooden spoon so the water doesn't boil over.

3 Start testing the pasta for doneness a few minutes before the end of the indicated cooking time. Pasta that offers resistance to the bite but has no trace of brittleness is al dente, and that's how you want it. If an undercooked piece of pasta is cut in half, a white dot or line is clearly visible in the center. Al dente pasta has only a speck of white remaining, meaning the pasta has absorbed just enough water to hydrate it. Drain the cooked pasta in a colander, and shake it well to remove the excess water.

4 If you plan on using the pasta in a salad or filling it, such as in stuffed manicotti shells, rinse the pasta with cold running water. This removes the light coating of starch that covers cooked pasta.

Quick & Easy

Pasta with Anchovy-Walnut Sauce

8 ounces uncooked spaghetti
1 tablespoon olive oil
3 cups prechopped onion
½ cup sliced red bell pepper
6 canned anchovy fillets in oil, drained
4 large garlic cloves, chopped
½ cup fat-free, lower-sodium chicken broth
½ teaspoon crushed red pepper
½ cup fresh flat-leaf parsley leaves
½ cup chopped walnuts, toasted
½ teaspoon salt
½ teaspoon freshly ground black pepper

1. Cook pasta according to package directions, omitting salt and fat. Drain in a colander over a bowl, reserving ½ cup cooking liquid.
2. While pasta cooks, heat oil in a large skillet over medium-high heat. Add onion; sauté 5 minutes or until lightly browned. Add bell pepper, anchovies, and garlic; cook 1 minute, stirring frequently to break anchovies into small pieces. Add broth and red pepper; cook 3 minutes or until most of liquid evaporates. Add pasta, reserved ½ cup cooking liquid, parsley, and remaining ingredients to pan; toss to combine. Yield 4 servings (serving size: 2 cups).

CALORIES 376; **FAT** 14.7g (sat 1.7g, mono 4.2g, poly 7.9g); **PROTEIN** 12.6g; **CARB** 49.8g; **FIBER** 4.1g; **CHOL** 5mg; **IRON** 3.3mg; **SODIUM** 574mg; **CALC** 67mg

---

Quick & Easy

Sandwich of the Month

Turkey Meatball Reuben Subs

This sandwich combines two deli favorites—the hearty meatball sub and zesty Reuben sandwich.

2 teaspoons paprika, divided
1½ teaspoons ground coriander
1 teaspoon bottled minced garlic
¾ teaspoon freshly ground black pepper
½ teaspoon sugar
¼ teaspoon salt
¼ teaspoon ground red pepper
1 pound ground turkey
Cooking spray
4 (3-ounce) wheat submarine rolls (such as Cobblestone Mill)
1⅓ cups packaged coleslaw
¼ cup reduced-fat Thousand Island dressing
4 (1-ounce) slices Swiss cheese

1. Preheat broiler.
2. Combine 1½ teaspoons paprika, coriander, and next 6 ingredients in a bowl. Shape into 16 meatballs (about 1 heaping tablespoon each). Place meatballs on a broiler pan coated with cooking spray; broil 8 minutes or until done, turning once.
3. While meatballs cook, hollow out bread, leaving a ½-inch-thick shell; reserve torn bread for another use. Combine coleslaw, dressing, and remaining ½ teaspoon paprika. Arrange 4 meatballs and 1 cheese slice inside each roll. Place sandwiches on broiler pan; broil 1 minute or until cheese melts. Divide slaw among sandwiches. Yield: 4 servings (serving size: 1 sandwich).

CALORIES 428; **FAT** 16.8g (sat 7g, mono 5.5g, poly 1.1g); **PROTEIN** 31.5g; **CARB** 40g; **FIBER** 4.1g; **CHOL** 76mg; **IRON** 3.7mg; **SODIUM** 723mg; **CALC** 308mg

THE *COOKING LIGHT* BUYING GUIDE

HOW TO BUY THE BEST FISH

With the enormous variety of fresh fish available at supermarkets today, there's a fish to suit anyone's palate—from assertive salmon to subtle tilapia, from buttery, delicate halibut to meaty tuna and swordfish and beyond. Here, you'll learn the essentials so you can choose the tastiest, healthiest, and most sustainable fish at the market and enjoy it at your table.

Fish Facts

Top chefs often feature "day-boat" fish caught locally on restaurant menus, but unless you live near water, it can be challenging to find the freshest fish. Often the fresh fish you buy to prepare at home has been frozen. Fish sold as fresh can be anywhere from one day to two weeks out of the water. Large fishing vessels may stay at sea for two weeks, keeping their catch on ice to sell fresh. Even locally caught fish may take days traveling from boat to truck to wholesaler to retailer to your kitchen.

For top quality, look for "Frozen-at-Sea" (FAS)—fish that has been flash-frozen at extremely low temperatures in as little as three seconds onboard the ship. When thawed, sea-frozen fish are almost indistinguishable from fresh fish, according to the United Nations Food and Agriculture Organization.

Fish Nutrition

Fish contain 17 to 25 percent protein and are generally a good source of B vitamins. Fatty fish are good sources of vitamins A and D. The small, soft, edible bones of fresh sardines and smelts and canned bone-in fish like salmon are valuable sources of calcium.

Some fish also contain heart-healthy omega-3s. Dark-fleshed fish that swim in

continued

cold, open waters, such as tuna, herring, and mackerel, store fat in their flesh and are high in omega-3s. Fresh water fish from cold waters, such as lake herring, lake trout, salmon, and whitefish, are also high in omega-3s. In general, white-fleshed fish, such as cod, tilapia, or flounder, are low in all types of fat, including omega-3s. That's because they store fat in their livers (as in cod-liver oil).

Dietary recommendations: Although the Dietary Guidelines for Americans do not make specific recommendations regarding seafood, other public health organizations, like the American Heart Association and American Dietetic Association, recommend two servings weekly because seafood is a quality protein source that is high in "good" fats.

weakfish; Gulf amberjack and black drum in the South; Great Lakes Coho salmon and smelts in the Midwest; and Pacific sardines and albacore tuna on the West Coast.

• **Try whole fish.** Whole fish shrink less than fillets when cooking, giving you more value for your per-pound price. Whiting, croaker, porgy, and Pacific rockfish can be great values. Also, consider summer flounder (sometimes called fluke), red snapper, farmed striped bass, and Arctic char.

• **Consider canned.** Canned fish is an excellent budget-friendly option. It can also be a nutritious one, particularly varieties like canned tuna and salmon that are low in sodium and rich in omega-3s. Keep them— along with flavorful sardines and ancho-vies—on hand for fish cakes and salads.

Fish Glossary

Amberjack: Full flavor and firm flesh make amberjack, which stands up to more asser-tive flavors, ideal to grill, pan-fry, or broil. Amberjack is available in fillets and steaks year-round.

Arctic char (farmed freshwater): Arctic char, most often sold in fillets, has a distinc-tive pink flesh with a rich flavor similar to salmon and steelhead trout. Substitute arctic char for salmon in almost any recipe, and vice versa.

Catfish (farmed freshwater): Farmed cat-fish is available fresh year-round. Its sweet flavor and firm texture make it ideal for grilling, roasting, pan-frying, and braising. It can also substitute for other firm-flesh fish, such as pompano.

At the Market

• **Choose a quality fish market.** Choose a fish market with knowledgeable salespeople. Fish should be displayed attractively and surrounded by plenty of clean, crushed ice.

• **Be flexible.** The best approach to buying and eating fish is to aim for variety. You'll consume fish of varying omega-3 levels and from a variety of sources without over-dependence on one. Let freshness be your guide. It's easy to substitute one fish for another (at right and page 407), so if the mahimahi looks and smells fresher than the pompano, buy it instead.

• **Handle properly.** When shopping, ask for your fish to be packed with a separate bag of crushed ice to keep it cold. Refriger-ate whole fish up to two days; fillets and steaks one to two days. Place the fish in a plastic bag, then top with a zip-top plastic bag filled with ice. Thaw frozen fish in the refrigerator. To defrost safely and quickly in one to two hours, place the fish in a sealed plastic bag in a bowl of cold water, changing the water often.

Ways to Save

• **Know your local fish.** Buying local fish when they're abundant often means you'll get a higher quality fish for a lower cost. In the East, try Atlantic black sea bass and

Cod: Cod is a delicate, flaky white fish with mild, sweet flavor—so mild, in fact, those who are wary of seafood tend to gravitate to it. Cod is often used to make fish cakes and fish sticks and frequently appears in chowders and stews.

Halibut: Popular because of its mild flavor, this flaky white fish should be prepared with subtle flavors that won't overwhelm its delicacy. Fresh halibut is plentiful and available fresh from March to November. It's sold frozen the rest of the year.

Mahimahi: Popular because of its versatility, mahimahi pairs well with fruits and spicy sauces. It grills, broils, pan-fries, and braises beautifully.

Pompano: Pompano has a delicate, sweet flavor. Catfish makes a suitable substitute when pompano is scarce. Grill, broil, or pan-fry it.

Red snapper: The most prized member of the large snapper family is the American red snapper, which has a pronounced sweet flavor, similar to shrimp. Many varieties of snapper are available year-round, and though they may not be quite as sweet as American red snapper, they're excellent substitutions.

Salmon: Most of what you'll find at the grocery store is farmed Atlantic salmon. While wild Atlantic salmon is virtually extinct, wild Pacific salmon is still available. The high fat content of salmon keeps it moist when cooked by almost any method—you can pan-fry, grill, roast, steam, poach, or smoke it.

Sole/Flounder: Although sole are actually members of the flounder family, the words sole and flounder are often used interchangeably. (You're likely to see flounder at the fish market and sole on restaurant menus.) For this fish, you can substitute turbot, plaice, or fluke (sometimes called summer flounder).

Swordfish: Popular for its mild flavor and meaty texture, swordfish appears in markets year-round, usually as steak, and is best pan-fried or grilled.

Tilapia (farmed freshwater): Tilapia has a slightly firm, flaky texture and mild flavor that makes it an ideal canvas on which to paint layers of flavor. Like cod, this is a great fish for people who say they don't like fish. Readily available year-round, tilapia can be pan-fried, broiled, baked, or braised.

Trout (farmed freshwater): The flavor of trout ranges from subtle and mild to sweet. Most of the trout sold at markets is rainbow trout, although you'll also see other varieties such as brook trout. At its best, trout is subtle; prepare it simply to avoid masking its flavor.

Tuna: The many species of tuna vary in flavor and texture. Sashimi-grade tuna has a clean, subtle flavor and a delicate texture, and it's higher in fat. The tuna found in most grocery stores is meatier, with a more assertive flavor. Tuna is ideal for grilling or searing, which caramelizes the outside and leaves the interior moist. It is less forgiving than other fish, and when overcooked it can be dry and tough. Tuna is sold fresh and frozen year-round.

continued

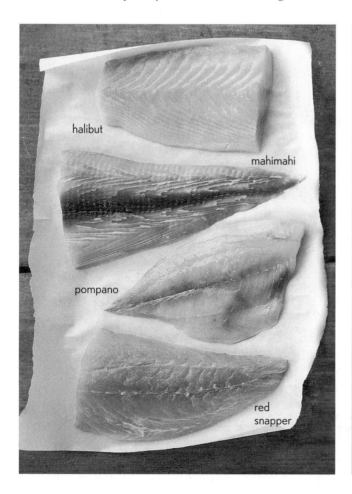

BUYING THE BEST FISH: WHAT TO LOOK FOR

Whole fresh fish ▼
• Look for shiny skin; tightly adhering scales; bright, clear eyes; firm, taut flesh that springs back when pressed; and a moist, flat tail.
• Gills should be cherry-red, not brownish.
• Saltwater fish should smell briny; freshwater fish should smell like a clean pond.

Fresh fillets, steaks ▶
• When buying white-fleshed fish, choose translucent-looking fillets with a pinkish tint.
• When buying any color fish, the flesh should appear dense without any gaps between layers.
• If the fish is wrapped in plastic, the package should contain little to no liquid.
• Ask the fishmonger to remove any pin bones, which run crosswise to the backbone.

Frozen fish ▲
• Look for shiny, rock-hard frozen fish with no white freezer-burn spots, frost, or ice crystals.
• Choose well-sealed packages from the bottom of the freezer case that are at most three months old.

TYPES OF FISH

Fish can be categorized many ways. For simplicity's sake, we have identified five categories.
Generally, you can substitute any fish within one category for another, although you'll notice differences in taste.

White, firm, and oil-rich
• Albacore tuna
• Atlantic shad
• California white sea bass
• Chilean sea bass
• Cobia
• Lake trout
• Lake whitefish
• Pacific escolar
• Pacific sablefish
• White sturgeon

White, lean, and flaky
• Atlantic croaker
• Black sea bass
• Flounder
• Pacific cod
• Rainbow smelt
• Rainbow trout

• Red snapper
• Tilapia
• Weakfish (sea trout)
• Whiting

Dark and oil-rich
• Anchovies
• Atlantic or Boston mackerel
• Bluefin tuna
• Farmed salmon
• Grey mullet
• Herring
• King mackerel
• King (Chinook) salmon
• Sardines
• Skipjack tuna

Medium color and oil-rich
• Amberjack
• Arctic char

• Coho salmon
• Hawaiian kampachi
• Mahimahi
• Paddlefish
• Pompano
• Sockeye salmon
• Wahoo
• Yellowfin tuna

White, lean, and firm
• Alaska pollock
• Catfish
• Grouper
• Haddock
• Pacific halibut
• Pacific rockfish
• Pacific sand dab and sole
• Striped bass (wild and hybrid)
• Swordfish

HOW TO BUY THE BEST BEEF

Did you know that there are about 97 million cattle in the United States? That's one cow for every three people in the country—no wonder Americans love beef. We eat nearly 63 pounds per person each year. Here, you'll learn the basics about beef so you can choose the type that's best for you.

Beef Background

Humans began domesticating cattle about 8,500 years ago. Columbus first brought cattle to the New World, and by 1690, descendants of Columbus's cattle ranging in Mexico were driven north and became known as Texas Longhorns. Others arrived later with the colonists. America's top five cattle breeds are Angus from Scotland, Hereford from England, Limousin from France, Simmenthal from Switzerland, and Charolais from France.

More than 90 percent of the beef we buy originates in America, while most of the rest is Canadian bred. The beef we eat comes mostly from 18- to 24-month-old steers, averaging about 1,000 pounds and yielding about 450 pounds of meat. Each is divided for wholesale into eight primals (major portions): the chuck (shoulder and upper ribs), the rib, the loin, the sirloin (hip), the round (upper leg), the brisket (breast), the plate (belly), and the small flank. Organs like liver and kidneys are called variety meats.

• **Grain-finished:** Nearly 75 percent of U.S. beef comes from cattle fattened on grain (usually corn) for three to six months in feedlots. Since corn is not a natural part of a cow's diet, cattle fed on it may experience stress and other ailments, so they are routinely treated with antibiotics. They also receive growth hormones to increase their size (and value, as beef is sold by weight). Until recently, inexpensive corn has helped keep down the price of beef.

continued

• **Grass-finished:** Grass- or pasture-finished beef comes from cattle that forage on grasses and legumes. Their meat is lower in saturated fat, cholesterol, and calories than grain-finished. (Because it is quite lean, cook rare to medium-rare for juiciness.) Grass-fed beef has a distinct flavor, often described as bold, complex, and gamy. Many people believe that grass-fed cattle are a more sustainable choice. However, raising grass-fed cattle is time-consuming and requires large open spaces, variables that raise its price. Most is imported from Canada, followed by Australia, New Zealand, Argentina, and Brazil.

• **Aging:** Dry-aging is the traditional process preferred by many steak lovers. The concentrated, intense flavor of dry-aged beef develops as it hangs in special temperature- and humidity-controlled rooms from 10 days to six weeks. The longer the aging, the better the flavor and tenderness, but also the more the shrinkage as water evaporates and a dark crust develops, which must be cut away. About 90 percent of American beef is sold as large vacuum-packed cuts. During the average seven-day period the beef spends "in the bag," it ages in a process called "wet-aging."

• **Processing and packaging:** Until the 1960s, butcher shops bought beef as half- or quarter-carcasses. Packers then began selling vacuum-packed beef, the same large cuts sold at warehouse club stores. Retailers refrigerated the boxes until needed, then opened the package and cut the meat into portions for sale. Next came case-ready meat, which precluded the need for skilled butchers on-site in markets. Leak-proof and easily stackable, case-ready packages are produced in USDA-inspected plants and have a longer shelf life. Packages covered with a sealed layer of clear plastic are modified-atmosphere packages, which have a gas-filled space inside to help preserve freshness and color.

BUYING THE BEST BEEF: WHAT TO LOOK FOR

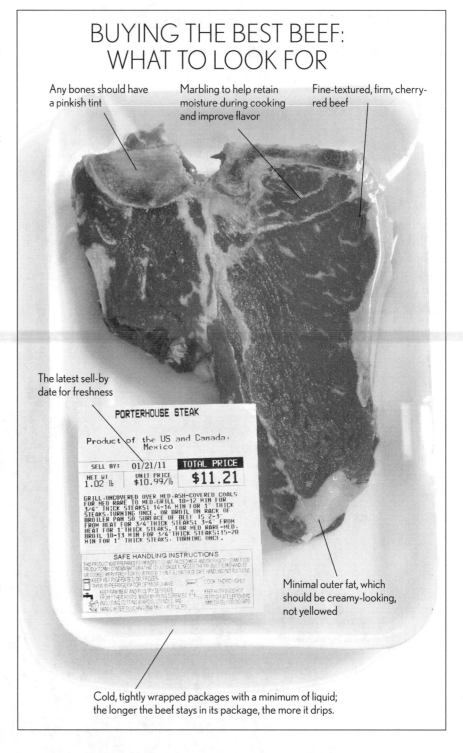

Any bones should have a pinkish tint

Marbling to help retain moisture during cooking and improve flavor

Fine-textured, firm, cherry-red beef

The latest sell-by date for freshness

PORTERHOUSE STEAK

Product of the US and Canada, Mexico

| SELL BY: | 01/21/11 | **TOTAL PRICE** |
| NET WT 1.02 lb | UNIT PRICE $10.99/lb | **$11.21** |

GRILL UNCOVERED OVER MED.ASH-COVERED COALS FOR MED RARE TO MED.GRILL 10-12 MIN FOR 3/4" THICK STEAKS; 14-16 MIN FOR 1" THICK STEAKS.TURNING ONCE. OR BROIL ON RACK OF BROILER PAN SO SURFACE OF BEEF IS 2-3" FROM HEAT FOR 3/4" THICK STEAKS; 3-4" FROM HEAT FOR 1" THICK STEAKS. FOR MED RARE-MED, BROIL 10-13 MIN FOR 3/4" THICK STEAKS; 15-20 MIN FOR 1" THICK STEAKS. TURNING ONCE.

SAFE HANDLING INSTRUCTIONS
THIS PRODUCT WAS PREPARED FROM INSPECTED AND PASSED MEAT AND/OR POULTRY. SOME FOOD PRODUCTS MAY CONTAIN BACTERIA THAT COULD CAUSE ILLNESS IF THE PRODUCT IS MISHANDLED OR COOKED IMPROPERLY FOR YOUR PROTECTION, FOLLOW THESE SAFE HANDLING INSTRUCTIONS.
KEEP REFRIGERATED OR FROZEN. THAW IN REFRIGERATOR OR MICROWAVE.   COOK THOROUGHLY.
KEEP RAW MEAT AND POULTRY SEPARATE FROM OTHER FOODS. WASH WORKING SURFACES   KEEP HOT FOODS HOT REFRIGERATE LEFTOVERS
(INCLUDING CUTTING BOARDS), UTENSILS, AND   IMMEDIATELY OR DISCARD.
HANDS AFTER TOUCHING RAW MEAT OR POULTRY.

Minimal outer fat, which should be creamy-looking, not yellowed

Cold, tightly wrapped packages with a minimum of liquid; the longer the beef stays in its package, the more it drips.

IDENTIFY A PROPER PORTION: A SINGLE SERVING OF COOKED BEEF IS ABOUT THE SIZE OF A DECK OF CARDS.

GROUND-BEEF SPECIFICS

To accurately gauge the amount of fat in ground beef, look to the percentages. If the package is labeled "80% lean," that means it's 20% fat. In addition to ground chuck (20% fat), round (15% fat), and sirloin (10% fat), you may also find ground beef simply labeled "lean ground beef." At 7% fat, it's the leanest ground beef available.

Fresh ground beef goes through a number of natural color changes. The beef may look bright red on the surface, where it has been exposed to oxygen, while the inside remains purplish-red.

Beef Nutrition

• **Fat content:** The USDA defines "lean beef" as having less than 10 grams (g) of total fat, 4.5g or less of saturated fat, and less than 95 milligrams of cholesterol per 3½-ounce serving (100g) of cooked beef. Half of the fat is saturated and half is heart-healthy monounsaturated. There are 29 naturally lean cuts of beef, including many familiar to *Cooking Light* readers, such as tenderloin, flank steak, and sirloin. Others, such as ribeye or chuck roast, naturally contain more fat, although it is similarly divided between saturated and monounsaturated. Because lean beef contains less fat, it's best cooked to medium-rare (145°) or medium (160°) to optimize tenderness. If using fattier cuts, slice away the outer rim of fat and cut or pull out any pockets of fat before cooking. For larger cuts, allow the fat to baste the meat while cooking, then trim it away before eating, or skim it from the surface of braised dishes or stews.

• **Other nutrients:** A 3½-ounce serving provides 27g to 30g of protein—more than half of the 50g recommended daily in a 2,000-calorie-per-day diet. All beef is an excellent source of iron, zinc, and phosphorus. In general, the redder the meat, the more iron it contains (beef liver has the most). Beef also contains thiamin, riboflavin, and niacin and is a rich source of B12, found naturally only in animal foods.

At the Market

• **Inspection and grading:** USDA inspectors examine all live animals and beef shipped out of state, which encompasses most of today's supermarket beef. Grading is voluntary and done by the same inspectors. The more marbling—the small white flecks of fat within the muscles—the higher the grade.

Three grades of beef are sold to consumers. Only 3 percent is highly marbled Prime, sought after by top steak houses and butcher shops. About 57 percent is moderately marbled Choice, the most common supermarket grade. The remaining 40 percent is lean Select.

• **Private labels:** Supermarket chains and large food distributors also have developed private brands with their own specifications. The first such program began in 1978 with Certified Angus Beef, which must come from Angus cattle. Niman Ranch Natural Beef and Certified Hereford Beef are two others.

• **Natural and organic:** Beef labeled "natural" must not contain any artificial ingredients and cannot be more than minimally processed, such as ground beef. "Organic" beef must come from cattle raised and certified according to the USDA's National Organic Program. Organic cattle must be fed 100-percent organically and without antibiotics or hormones. Both natural and organic beef can be either grass- or grain-finished.

Ways to Save

• **Buy lean cuts.** Often, leaner cuts are cheaper than fatty ones. And when the fat cooks away, lean cuts provide more meat for your dollar.

• **Buy in bulk.** Large or family-sized packages cost less per pound than smaller packages. Divide into portions, and freeze the surplus.

• **Be your own butcher.** Beef that has been presliced into steaks or made into patties costs more than less processed meat. Buy bigger cuts, and do some of the preparation work yourself.

• **But don't go overboard.** Advice to buy a side or quarter of beef may seem sensible, but you'll likely have more meat than you can store. Such a purchase may yield what one buyer describes as "cheap steak and expensive hamburger."

SINCE BEEF IS SOLD BY WEIGHT, LEAN CUTS ARE OFTEN SMART, ECONOMICAL BUYS—YOU PAY FOR MORE MEAT AND LESS FAT.

HOW TO BUY THE BEST DAIRY

Buy 2 percent milk or fat-free milk? Salted butter or unsalted butter? Cheddar or Gorgonzola? From milk to butter to cheese, the dairy department in your grocery store is stocked with hundreds of options for you to choose from. Here, you'll find information that will help you make the right decisions.

MILK

Today's supermarket shelves are stocked with conventional, organic, hormone-free, enriched, and sometimes even raw (that is, unpasteurized) milk. Each type is available with varying levels of fat—whole, 2 percent (reduced-fat), 1 percent (low-fat), fat-free (skim), along with half-and-half and cream, both heavy and light.

Milk Basics

• **Processing:** About 95 percent of milk is pasteurized—quickly heated to 162° and then cooled to destroy bacteria and microorganisms. (The remaining 5 percent is unpasteurized and known as "raw" milk.) UHT (Ultra-High Temperature) milk is flash-sterilized at temperatures up to 300 degrees, then packed in shelf-stable aseptic cartons. Most milk is also homogenized to prevent fat molecules from separating, keeping it smooth and creamy.

• **Hormones:** All cows generate natural bST, a hormone that helps them produce milk. Some dairy farmers supplement with synthetic rbST (recombinant bovine somatotropin), boosting production by as much as one gallon a day per cow. According to the FDA and World Health Organization, among others, milk from these cows is safe, but the use of rbST is illegal in many countries, and critics question its safety.

Milk Nutrition

Which type of milk is right for your family? Here's what you need to know to help you choose.

• **Varied fat content:** In its unadulterated state, milk is about 87 percent water, 5 percent sugar or carbohydrate, 3.5 percent protein, and less than 4 percent fat. In times gone by, to make reduced-fat milk, dairy farmers would simply skim off the high-fat cream layer that naturally rose to the top. Today, dairies use centrifuges to spin off the fat, resulting in milk of varying fat levels.

Most major health authorities, including the USDA Dietary Guidelines for Americans, recommend you choose low-fat or fat-free milk and other dairy foods to meet the recommended three daily servings. All forms of dairy find a place in our recipes, depending on the need.

• **Organic:** About 3 percent of America's milk is organic, and the market is growing. New USDA rules require that organic cows be kept on pasture at least half the year so they can obtain plenty of fresh grass. Organic cows must not be treated with synthetic hormones to boost milk production.

Nutritional differences are currently under study. Two studies compared organic to conventional milk and found organic contains slightly more antioxidants and vitamins, and higher levels of omega-3 fatty acids and conjugated linoleic acid.

LESS FAT, MORE CALCIUM

Because calcium is contained in the nonfat part of milk, reduced-fat dairy foods contain slightly more of the mineral than full-fat varieties. Here's the amount of calcium, in milligrams, contained in an 8-ounce serving of each type of milk:

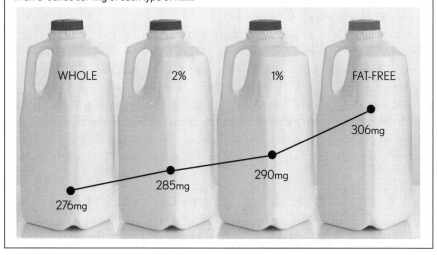

WHOLE — 276mg
2% — 285mg
1% — 290mg
FAT-FREE — 306mg

WHAT ONE SERVING LOOKS LIKE

Current Dietary Guidelines for Americans recommend that adults consume 3 servings of milk or other dairy products daily, with an emphasis on low-fat or fat-free types. Children ages 2 to 8 should consume 2 servings per day. Choose from some of the following options to meeting your daily requirement:

| 8 oz. low-fat or fat-free milk (plain or chocolate) | ½ cup cottage cheese | 1 cup low-fat or fat-free yogurt |

| 1½ oz. natural cheese | 2 oz. processed cheese | ⅓ cup shredded cheese |

| 1 cup low-fat pudding | 1 cup frozen yogurt | ½ cup low-fat ice cream |

At the Market

• **Examine the packaging.** Look for milk in opaque containers; milk in clear containers can lose significant amounts of vitamin A and riboflavin through exposure to light.

• **Buy the freshest.** Choose the container with the latest sell-by date from the coldest part of the refrigerator case. (You may have to reach to the back of the case.)

• **Keep it that way.** Keep milk cold on the way home, preferably in an insulated bag. For each 18-degree increase in temperature, the spoilage rate of milk doubles. If it takes 45 minutes to get milk from the dairy case to your home, milk may already have risen from its preferred temperature of 33 to 40 degrees to nearly 60 degrees on a warm day. If stored properly, milk will keep up to five days beyond the sell-by date.

• **But don't freeze it.** Freezing is not recommended as it causes separation and graininess.

Ways to Save

• **Compare store brands and national brands.** Store-brand (or private-label) dairy products are often made by the same dairies that sell the products for a higher price under their own brand name.

• **Flavor your own.** To save money, add your own chocolate syrup or sweetened cocoa powder to plain milk. If needed, package individual servings in a reusable container. (Do the math and you'll see that a cute little 8-ounce container of organic chocolate milk can cost more than $5 per quart.)

• **Buy fresh.** Contrary to what you might expect, using reconstituted powdered milk won't save much money. You'll need about one dollar's worth or 3.2 ounces (about 1⅓ cups) of powdered milk to make one quart of milk, about the same cost as a quart of fresh milk if you buy it by the half or full gallon.

• **Consider signing up for home delivery.** Look into home delivery. The extra cost is usually low (about $3.75 per week), and you'll be assured of fresh milk (often delivered in reusable glass bottles) from a local dairy that may also deliver other products, such as cheese and eggs.

Milk Glossary

Whole milk: With none of its inherent fat removed, whole milk is thick and rich. Each 8-ounce glass has 146 calories, 7.9 grams of fat, and 276 milligrams of calcium. Whole milk is recommended for children under the age of two, but in most cases it is considered too high in fat for adults and older children to drink regularly. It can, however, play an important role in cooking. It adds silky texture to sauces and soups, contributes flavor and texture to baked goods, and lends golden gloss to doughs and crusts.

Two percent milk: An 8-ounce glass of 2 percent (reduced-fat) milk contains 121 calories, 4.7 grams of fat, and 297 milligrams of calcium. The higher fat content makes it creamier than 1 percent milk or fat-free milk, which can be beneficial in cooking.

One percent milk: An 8-ounce glass of 1 percent, or low-fat, milk has 102 calories, 2.6 grams of fat, and 300 milligrams of calcium. Some dishes rely on other ingredients or techniques for texture and are dependent on milk mostly for flavor and liquidity. So a lower-fat milk works fine in these cases.

Fat-free milk: Fat-free milk is many people's milk beverage of choice. Also called skim milk, it contains no fat, only 83 calories, and 306 milligrams of calcium per 8-ounce glass.

continued

BUTTER

Although made up completely of fat, butter has a place in a healthful diet. This is partly because fat is satisfying, but mostly because when it comes to flavor, there's simply no substitute.

The key to cooking with butter in light recipes is to use techniques that stretch it so you enjoy its benefits. Small amounts add richness to sauces, keep baked goods tender, and enhance the flavor of other ingredients. So go ahead and dab some on—just do so sparingly. Your cooking, like butter itself, will be golden.

Storage Savvy

Air and bright light break down fat molecules and eventually turn butter rancid, which is why butter is best stored in cool, dark places—like refrigerators. Since refrigerator door temperatures vary considerably, skip the butter compartment and store butter near the back. In a cold refrigerator, a stick of salted butter in its original wrapping will keep for about two months (the salt acts as a preservative); unsalted butter will keep for one and a half months. Butter freezes well for up to six months.

Salted vs. Unsalted

The difference between salted and unsalted butter is simple: about 80 milligrams of sodium per tablespoon. Salt acts as a preservative and prolongs the shelf life of butter. Most people use salted butter, and most of our recipes were tested with that variety. Some cooks prefer unsalted butter because it allows them to control the amount of salt in a dish and preserves the mellow sweetness of butter. If you want unsalted butter, look for the phrase "sweet butter" or "unsalted." The term "sweet cream butter" is used for both salted and unsalted butter.

Lower-fat milks have more calcium per cup than whole milk because in whole milk some of the volume is displaced by milk fat, which has no calcium. Use fat-free milk on cereal, in coffee, as a drink—and to make certain dishes, such as puddings and cheese sauces, where the milk provides background flavor, and other ingredients, such as flour or cornstarch, lend texture.

Whipping cream: Whipping cream (or heavy whipping cream) has 51 calories and 5.6 grams of fat per tablespoon. When beaten, whipping cream doubles in volume to create a classic dessert topping. (Neither light whipping cream nor light cream contains enough fat to hold its shape when whipped.) Whipping cream is the only type of milk that is heat stable—it won't curdle when brought to a boil. Use it to enrich sauces and soups, adding just a bit at a time—as little as a tablespoon can add the right amount of body and rich taste.

Half-and-half: A mixture of equal parts milk and cream, half-and-half weighs in with only 20 calories and 1.7 grams of fat per tablespoon. Use it to finish sauces and soups, but add it off the stove or over lower heat to prevent it from curdling.

Buttermilk: Traditionally, buttermilk was the liquid that remained after butter was churned from cream. Today, buttermilk is made by adding bacteria cultures to fat-free, low-fat, or whole milk. Buttermilk has a thick consistency and tart flavor. It's often used for cakes, biscuits, pancakes, and quick breads.

Acidophilus milk: Acidophilus milk is whole, reduced-fat, or fat-free milk with friendly *Lactobacillus acidophilus* bacteria added to it. The bacteria is believed to benefit the digestive tract, much the same way yogurt does.

Butter Glossary

Cultured cream butter: Cultured cream butter is made by adding lactic acid to butter. Before the advent of large-scale commercial butter production, farmers made butter from cream collected over several days of milking. During this time, the cream soured from the natural formation of lactic acid and made a pleasingly tart butter. Some people prefer its sharper taste.

Organic butter: Organic butter is made from organic milk. By law, the cream used to produce it must be free of antibiotics, synthetic growth hormones, and pesticides.

Whipped butter: Whipped butter is standard butter pumped with air or nitrogen gas to create a light, fluffy texture. (Oxygen hastens rancidity.) This is a good choice to serve at the table because it has a spreadable texture even when cold.

European-style butter: European-style butter contains more milk fat than the standard 80 percent for American butters, and as a result, it has a creamier taste and a smoother texture. Because of its lower water content, this type of butter makes rich sauces, pastries, and frostings. You can use it in any application for which you would use regular butter.

Stick butter: Stick butter, the most widely available form, comes salted or unsalted. Light butter, made by combining butter with fat-free milk, has half the fat and calories of regular butter. It's fine as a spread, but its lower fat content makes it a poor choice for baking or frying.

CHEESE

No matter how tasty a dish may be, it's almost always better with cheese. Because cheese is naturally high in fat (particularly saturated fat), it's important to use it wisely.

Cheese Glossary

There are hundreds of specific cheese varieties, ranging in flavor from sweet and nutty to bitter and acidic, so we focus here on the ones we use most often.

Saint André: This French cheese is made from cow's milk and is surrounded in a soft white rind. Inside the rind, the creamy center is about 75 percent buttermilk fat. Saint André has a buttery texture and rich flavor similar to Brie.

Feta: Feta is a fresh Greek cheese that is tangy and salty as a result of the brine in which it's cured. It's traditionally made from sheep's milk, but it can also be made from goat's or cow's milk. Its crumbly yet creamy texture lends it to a variety of culinary applications. A choice addition to salads, feta is also good for fillings, sauces, and pasta dishes.

Brie: Brie's soft texture oozes at peak ripeness. Creamy, buttery, rich, and slightly sweet, it is spreadable and completed by its edible white rind. The soft-ripened French cheese is best enjoyed as an appetizer or dessert at room temperature, or it can be baked with an array of savory or sweet toppings.

Goat cheese: Goat cheese—or chèvre, French for "goat"—is a fresh, unripened goat's milk cheese that has a fruity flavor early on but develops a sharper and slightly tart quality as it ages. Crumble it over salads, or serve it with herbs as a spread on crusty bread. You can also use it as a topping for pizzas, quesadillas, or open-faced sandwiches.

Mascarpone: This Italian cheese has a silky texture and a rich, creamy flavor. It's a very spreadable cheese, but, depending on how it's processed, the texture can range from very soft to more stiff, like butter. It's a traditional dessert cheese that's used in classic Italian desserts such as tiramisu and zabaglione.

Saint André

feta

Brie

mascarpone

goat cheese

chèvre (goat cheese)

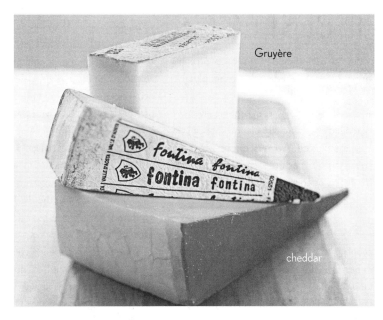

Gruyère

fontina

cheddar

Parmigiano-Reggiano

blue cheeses

Gruyère: Produced in Switzerland, Gruyère has a smooth yet pliable texture with a mild nutty or toasty flavor. This semifirm cheese also has fruity or sweet hints and should have a pale yellow interior and slightly browned edges. Flavorful and moist, it's a popular dessert cheese and also melts well for sauces or fondues. Gruyère is traditional in veal dishes and chicken cordon bleu and is excellent for gratins and soufflés.

Fontina: Semisoft but dense with small holes, fontina is encased by a dark gold, crusty rind. With a fruity overtone, its buttery qualities make it a natural for dessert. Fontina is a good melting cheese, often used in sauces and on pizzas or casseroles.

Cheddar: The salty tang of cheddar cheese can range from mild to sharp, making it versatile for both cooking and snacking. It can be white or dyed orange; both deliver a robust quality that can stand alone or incorporate well into soups, casseroles, and sandwiches.

Parmesan: Parmesan cheese is perhaps the most widely used hard cheese. Parmigiano-Reggiano is considered the finest of Parmesan. It has an appealing grainy texture and a rich and strong nutty flavor. This grade of Parmesan must be aged at least 12 months and is specific to the Italian province bearing its name—Parma. Its piquant quality makes it a versatile cheese that can be grated and incorporated into soups, salads, and pasta dishes.

Gorgonzola: Among blues, Gorgonzola is moist, creamy, savory, earthy, and slightly spicier than its relatives. A pleasing addition to salads, it's excellent paired with apples, pears, figs, and peaches, and it works well with pastas, sauces, and meat and poultry dishes.

HOW TO BUY THE BEST EGGS

Eggs are an adaptable, quick-cooking food that offers an abundance of nutrients—protein, vitamins, minerals, and antioxidants—all in one handily self-contained package. Simply open, and use.

Inexpensive white eggs sell for just over $1 per dozen, while eggs from organically pastured chickens may sell for $6 a dozen, so price differences are significant, especially if you buy eggs in quantity. But buying eggs isn't just about price. We must choose among eggs that are local, organic, humanely-raised, vegetarian-fed, pastured, cage-free, special diet, pasteurized, or liquid mixes. Here, we feature all you need to know so you can purchase the kind that best suits your needs.

Nutrition and Health

Eggs are an excellent source of protein, with more than 6 grams in a single large egg, and about 70 calories. They are a good source of vitamin B12, and they provide lutein, which helps prevent age-related macular degeneration and cataracts.

• **Cholesterol:** A large Harvard School of Public Health study found no association between eating up to one egg a day and heart disease, except in people with diabetes. Dietary cholesterol, found in eggs, raises blood cholesterol in only about one-third of people, and eggs don't appear to contribute to heart disease in most people. It's the foods high in saturated fat (like bacon, sausage, and cheese) often served with eggs that seem to be the culprits.

The American Heart Association recommends that most people limit cholesterol consumption to 300 milligrams a day. That number decreases to 200 milligrams for people with heart disease, high cholesterol, or other coronary risk factors. For reference, one large egg has 212 milligrams of cholesterol.

• **Omega-3 eggs:** These specialty eggs result from hens fed special diets, which affects the nutrients their eggs contain. When considering omega-3 eggs, check the packaging to ensure they contain the two types of omega-3 fatty acid with the strongest links to heart health: DHA and EPA. Even if they do, know that omega-3 eggs contain no more than the amount in less than two teaspoons of salmon, according to the Center for Science in the Public Interest.

• **Salmonella:** It's rare, but salmonella bacteria can exist inside eggs, and if the eggs are eaten raw or undercooked, serious illness can result. To kill salmonella, cook eggs fully (until the yolk and white are both firm), cook egg custards until they thicken visibly (at a temperature of 160°), and bake meringue-topped pies at 350° for 15 minutes. If you prefer eggs runny, use pasteurized eggs. Eggs are pasteurized by keeping them in a water bath for about an hour at a controlled temperature to destroy bacteria without cooking the eggs.

continued

SIZING UP EGGS

Egg sizes cause the nutrition profile to vary slightly. *Cooking Light* usually calls for large eggs in most recipes.

	SMALL	MEDIUM	LARGE	EXTRA LARGE	JUMBO
Calories	54	63	72	80	90
Fat	3.78g	4.37g	4.97g	5.57g	6.26g
Saturated fat	1.18g	1.36g	1.55g	1.74g	1.95g

Where the Nutrients Are

White: Accounts for two-thirds of an egg's weight, water, more than half of its protein, and minerals such as iron, selenium, and trace amounts of calcium.

Yolk: Accounts for one-third of the egg's weight and all of the fat and any fatty acids, such as omega-3s, about half the protein, most of the vitamins such as A, B12, E, and all of the antioxidants, such as lutein. Because it contains all of the fat, and fat is higher in calories per gram than protein or carbohydrate, the yolk also has most of the calories—76 percent.

At the Market

• **Look them over.** Open the carton and check eggs for cracks. While they are perfectly fine to eat, eggs with oddly-shaped or thin shells often come from older hens. Extremes in humidity and overcrowding are the main causes of mottled shells, which are more common in brown eggs.

• **Keep them cool.** Get eggs home quickly and (if possible) keep them cool on the way in an insulated bag. An egg stored for one hour at room temperature ages more than a refrigerated egg ages in one week.

Ways to Save

• **Choose the store brand.** Store brand eggs have the same quality as name brands, but they're almost always less expensive.

• **Buy in bulk.** Eggs stay fresh a lot longer than you might expect, says Patricia Curtis, PhD, director of the Poultry Product Safety and Quality program at Auburn University in Auburn, Alabama. In fact, many people mistakenly think the "sell-by" date on the carton (intended to tell grocers the last day they can sell the eggs) is the date eggs go bad. Eggs will stay fresh in your refrigerator for about a month after purchase, even if the sell-by date expires during that length of time.

• **Use them before you lose them.** Use older eggs for hard cooking. A hard-cooked egg will keep for up to one week, extending your eggs' shelf life.

EGG LABELS: WHAT THEY MEAN

Organic: Meets the standards of the USDA's National Organic Program: Birds must be cage free with outdoor access, cannot be given antibiotics, and their food must be organic and vegetarian.

Certified humane raised and handled: A program audited by the USDA and endorsed by many animal welfare organizations with humane requirements for raising and handling chickens and their eggs.

Cage free: The chickens are out of cages with continuous access to food and water, but may not necessarily have access to the outdoors.

Animal welfare approved: A new label by the Animal Welfare Institute is given to independent family farmers with flocks of up to 500 birds, where chickens are free to spend as much time as they desire outside on pesticide-free pasture, cannot have their beaks trimmed (a practice often done in crowded egg farms), or fed animal by-products. Because this label applies to smaller egg producers, you may only encounter it at farmers' markets or specialty grocers.

United Egg Producers Certified: "Eighty percent of industrial egg producers are certified this way," says New York University professor Marion Nestle, PhD, in her book *What to Eat.* "This certification merely attests that a company gives food and water to its caged hens." Natural, naturally raised, no hormones, no antibiotics.

Storage Savvy

Buy the freshest eggs available (check the sell-by date). At home, refrigerate immediately in the original carton, which prevents moisture loss and absorption of odors from other foods in the refrigerator. Store on an inside shelf—not in the egg "cups" on the door where the temperature is not as cold—for three to five weeks from the day they're purchased.

HOW TO BUY THE BEST OILS

Many of our recipes call for cooking and salad oils, but selecting the best kind for various uses can confuse even seasoned cooks. Read on as we explain how to choose the best oils, keeping in mind flavor, health benefits, shelf life, and value for price.

About Oils

Oils are mostly liquid at room temperature. They come from plants such as seeds like sunflowers, fruits like olives, nuts like walnuts, and legumes like soybeans. In the kitchen, oils carry flavors and aromas of spices and herbs and lend their smooth mouthfeel to sauces, dressings, stews, marinades, and soups; they also impart smooth texture and rich body to baked goods.

Nutrition and Health

Oils are 100 percent fat, so they contain 9 calories per gram (that's 120 calories per tablespoon). Their fat is made up of various proportions of three fatty acids: polyunsaturated, monounsaturated, and saturated. An ideal all-purpose oil is low in saturated fat and high in mono- or polyunsaturated fats. Our favorites at *Cooking Light:* olive and canola oils. Other good options are walnut oil or peanut oil, respectively.

Dietitians often call mono- and polyunsaturated fats "good" fats because they can help improve blood cholesterol profiles, ease arterial inflammation, and stabilize heart rhythms, resulting in a healthier cardiovascular system. Saturated fats are known as "bad" fats because they elevate harmful LDL cholesterol (however, like most dietary fats, they also elevate protective HDL).

Oils have other benefits, too. Some types, like sunflower and canola, are among the richest food sources of vitamin E. And adding a little oil to cooked vegetables helps us absorb their fat-soluble vitamins (A, E, and K) and antioxidant carotenoids (beta-carotene, lycopene, and lutein).

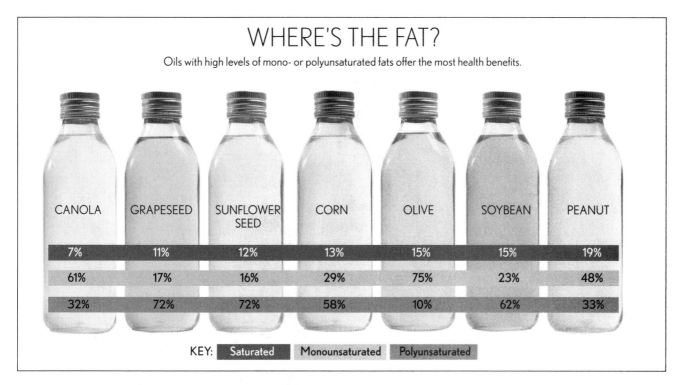

WHERE'S THE FAT?

Oils with high levels of mono- or polyunsaturated fats offer the most health benefits.

	CANOLA	GRAPESEED	SUNFLOWER SEED	CORN	OLIVE	SOYBEAN	PEANUT
Saturated	7%	11%	12%	13%	15%	15%	19%
Monounsaturated	61%	17%	16%	29%	75%	23%	48%
Polyunsaturated	32%	72%	72%	58%	10%	62%	33%

KEY: Saturated Monounsaturated Polyunsaturated

Trans Fats

Manufacturers create trans fats by altering the chemical structure of oil to be solid at room temperature. This is done by infusing oil with hydrogen, thus the term "partially hydrogenated oils." Using these oils increases the shelf life of processed foods. If you see partially hydrogenated oils in a food's ingredient list, the food contains trans fats. Trans fats are now listed on food labels, though servings containing less than a half gram can be noted as zero. Trans fats decrease HDL cholesterol, raise LDL, and have been linked to disease.

Dietary Recommendations

MyPyramid.gov suggests daily allowances for oils since they can be such a rich source of healthful fats. For adults, these vary from five to seven teaspoons daily, based on age, gender, and activity level. Remember, though, that foods such as nuts and fish contain oils naturally and count toward the allowance.

At the Market

Two oils will suffice for most of your every-day cooking needs:

• **Extra-virgin olive oil:** There is no substitute for its bitter-fruity flavor. Extra-virgin olive oil is costly but also high in antioxidants, especially if harvested and dated from the most recent season. Less than 10 percent of olive oils are extra-virgin, which by European Union regulations can contain no more than 0.08 percent oleic acid, a type of monounsaturated fatty acid.

• **Canola oil:** Canola oil has the least amount of saturated fat of any cooking oil. Its mellow, adaptable flavor and high smoke point make it well suited for a wide range of uses.

Prevent Spoilage

Clear glass bottles expose oils to harmful ultraviolet rays. While this isn't as much of a concern for vegetable oils, which are more stable because they have been refined, exposure to light is a potential threat to unrefined olive and nut oils. Look for unrefined oils sold in metal tins or dark green or black glass bottles. This ensures that the oil has been protected from light from the time it was bottled until you bring it home. Some brands' labels feature a helpful freshness date. To reduce your chances of buying spoiled oil, buy from a store that has a high turnover rate. At home, store your oils in a cool, dark place, such as your pantry or cupboard.

Ways to Save

• **Think small.** Vegetable oils like corn, canola, and soybean can last for more than a year once you've opened them, so it makes sense to buy them in large containers, which are often less expensive. But just the opposite is true for more fragile nut, peanut, sesame, and olive oils. Buying only the amount you'll use within three to six months ensures that they'll always taste fresh. Plus, you won't waste money by throwing out oil that's past its peak.

• **Spend where it counts.** A moderately priced olive or canola oil may work perfectly well for cooking onions or sautéing meat, chicken, or fish. But dishes where the oil's flavor shines—salads, pesto, bruschetta, or vegetables—are where you may want to spring for quality.

continued

Oil Glossary

Extra-virgin olive oil: Extra-virgin olive oil has a rich range of flavors, from pungent and bold to smooth and buttery. Because the flavor of extra-virgin olive oil can diminish with heat, it's often used to finish a dish, drizzled over pasta, or whisked into a vinaigrette (though many chefs cook with it, too).

Regular olive oil: Also called "pure" or "light" olive oil, which are simply marketing tags and not an indication of nutritional qualities, this olive oil is a blend of refined olive oil and extra-virgin olive oil. It costs less and has a mild flavor. Use it when you want to preserve the flavors of the food rather than impart the character of the oil to it. We often use it for sautés or stir-fries.

Canola oil: Derived from a strain of rapeseed in Canada in the 1970s that yields oil with lower acidity than traditional rapeseed, this oil's name is an amalgam of the words "Canada" and "oil." A major export crop for its namesake country, canola oil is high in mono- and polyunsaturated fats and very low in saturated fat. Its neutral flavor makes it a good choice when you don't want to detract from the flavors of the food.

Sesame oil: This oil is pressed from crushed sesame seeds. The lighter-colored oil comes from raw seeds and has a mild, neutral taste. Dark sesame oil, also called toasted sesame oil, has been pressed from toasted sesame seeds and has an intense, nutty flavor and aroma. Both are considered a seasoning.

Walnut oil: Unrefined walnut oil tastes just like the nut from which it comes. It's rich and flavorful (especially if made from toasted walnuts) and perfect as a finishing drizzle on salads, rice, pasta, or even desserts like tarte tatin or rice pudding.

HOW TO STOCK UP ON SEASONINGS AND SPICES

Need a flavor boost for your next meal? Take a detour to the often-forgotten seasoning aisle. With hundreds of salts, spices, and sauces to choose from, the possibilities are practically endless.

SALT

From a culinary perspective, salt is indispensable. It enhances and rounds out the flavors of almost every other ingredient it touches, even sweets. Salt brightens flavors, balances the bitterness of certain foods, acts as a preservative, and tenderizes. In essence, salt makes food taste more like itself.

Due to a proven link between eating too much salt and high blood pressure, many people have to watch their sodium intake. We've found that it doesn't take a lot of salt to achieve its many culinary benefits. Using a small amount of salt in a strategic way helps flavors bloom without overloading on sodium. Learn how thoughtful use of this ingredient can enhance many of your favorite foods.

How Your Daily Sodium Intake Measures Up

• Daily sodium needed for basic physiological functions: scant $1/8$ tsp salt = 250mg sodium
• Daily sodium limit for seniors: $1/2$ tsp salt = 1,200mg sodium
• Daily sodium limit for adults: scant 1 tsp salt = 2,300mg sodium
• Daily sodium the average American consumes: heaping $1^{1}/_{2}$ tsp salt = 4,000mg sodium

Low-Sodium Alternatives

For cooks who seek to minimize sodium in their recipes, there are ways to play up flavors without extra salt. Highlight a dish's savory notes with a finishing spritz of lemon or lime juice or a flavored vinegar. Fresh herbs or homemade blends of dried spices also enhance taste.

Salt Storage

Salt doesn't spoil, but if it comes into contact with humidity, it can cake. Add toothpicks or roasted grains of rice to table salt in salt shakers to help absorb the humidity. Open salt cellars (great for kosher salt, which cooks pinch into often) left out near the stovetop benefit from the drying effects of any residual heat. In the pantry, large quantities of salt of any sort are best kept in airtight containers, such as glass jars with rubber-lined lids, to lock out humidity. If, however, moisture causes your salt to cake, it can simply be dried out in a cool oven and easily repulverized with a mortar and pestle.

continued

Salt Glossary

Kosher salt: For chefs and many home cooks, this cousin of table salt has become the standard. Kosher salt, named as such because it's used by Jewish butchers, is chemically identical to table salt. But it has fewer additives and comes in coarser particles, which make it easy to pinch and sprinkle.

Fleur de sel: The crystalline "flower of salt," skimmed from the tops of marshes in northwestern France, may be the most special and sought-after sea salt. It's considered a comparably pure sea salt, free of most trace elements that define many other varieties. Its clean, well-balanced bite makes it nice for finishing simple dishes, such as grilled vegetables or pasta tossed in olive oil and garlic.

Sea salt: These salts come from all over the world in a variety of textures and colors. Sea salt doesn't contain additives, but it does contain more minerals than table salt. Because their taste nuances become almost untraceable once absorbed in food and they tend to be pricier, sea salts are often used as finishing touches.

Rock salt: In culinary terms, rock salt generally refers to the large-crystal salt sprinkled on the ice used in the making of ice cream. (Salt lowers the freezing point of water, making ice cold enough to freeze sugared cream.) Also, since salt is a potent and quick conductor of heat, rock salt can be packed around foods such as fish or shrimp for fast baking.

Table salt: This fine-grain salt has been a staple of American pantries for more than 100 years. In 1924, iodine was added to address what was then an epidemic of thyroid disorders. World health organizations continue to implore table salt producers to add it. But the supplement's presence—and that of anticaking agents—slightly alters the salt's flavor, so table salt has fallen out of favor with many food-lovers.

SUGAR

Sugar is essential to cooking. At the simplest level, it imparts sweetness. But it often performs more than one role in a recipe, and it can be key in dishes other than desserts because it balances bitter and sour tastes.

Sugar Glossary

Granulated sugar: Granulated sugar, chemically designated "sucrose," is bright white, dry, and free-flowing. All-purpose granulated sugar is the most commonly used sugar—for everything from sweetening coffee to being mixed into cake and cookie batters. Its flavor is pure sweetness, with no other taste.

Superfine granulated sugar: Called caster sugar in Britain, superfine granulated sugar is more finely ground granulated sugar, often used in applications where it's important for the sugar to dissolve quickly (such as in meringues, angel food cakes, and iced tea).

Brown sugar: Brown sugar is either partially refined sugar with traces of molasses remaining or refined white sugar to which molasses has been added. Molasses gives these varieties their unique flavors and textures. Light brown sugar (often called just "brown sugar") possesses a subtle caramel taste, while dark brown sugar has more molasses and thus a fuller, more robust molasses flavor. Light and dark brown sugar can be used interchangeably in recipes, but the final product will taste more subtle or more assertive depending on which you use. Brown sugar is often used for cookies and savory applications (such as barbecue sauce or rubs) where a richer taste is desired.

Powdered sugar: Also known as confectioners' sugar, powdered sugar is granulated sugar ground to a fine powder with an anticaking agent such as cornstarch added. The "X" designation on powdered sugar products denotes how finely the sugar has been ground—the more Xs, the finer (10X is the finest); they can be used interchangeably in recipes. Because it dissolves quickly, it's often used for uncooked cake frostings. It's also a pretty decoration when dusted over cookies or cakes.

Turbinado sugar: Turbinado sugar is a dry, pourable sugar (as opposed to many brown-colored sugars, which are moist) that has been only partially refined and steam cleaned. Blond in color and made up of large, coarse crystals, it has subtler molasses flavor than brown sugar. It derives its name from the part of the sugar-making process where raw cane is spun in a turbine. It's often sprinkled atop cakes, cookies, and other baked goods to add crunch.

continued

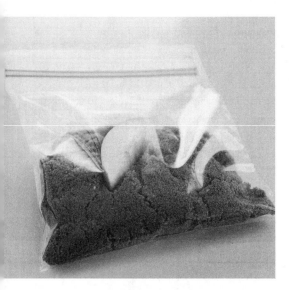

Storage Savvy

To help granulated sugar stay dry and pourable, keep it in an airtight container or moisture-proof heavy-duty plastic bag. Properly stored, it keeps indefinitely. If humidity causes it to clump, place it in a heavy-duty zip-top plastic bag, and give it a few whacks with a mallet or the flat side of a meat cleaver. You can also whirl it in a food processor or blender or use a mortar and pestle or a spice grinder.

Powdered sugar is harder to salvage if humidity strikes. If it becomes lumpy, try sifting it.

Brown sugar, which needs to retain its moisture, should also be stored in an airtight container. There are a number of tricks to bring dried-out brown sugar back to life. Let it stand overnight in a zip-top plastic bag with a damp paper towel or an apple slice from which the sugar can absorb moisture (see photo above). Or warm it for a few minutes in a 250° oven or in the microwave for about 1 minute per cup, but be careful—the sugar will be hot, and it should be measured and mixed quickly before it rehardens.

SPICES

Spices are derived from the bark, pods, fruit, roots, seeds, or stems of plants and trees. They appeal to our senses, and they're key in healthy cooking. You often don't need fat to enhance the flavor of a dish because spices alone can add intrigue, zest, and depth to food without increasing calories.

Spice Glossary

Allspice: As the name suggests, the flavor and aroma of allspice are a mixture of cinnamon, nutmeg, and a touch of clove. It's a delicious spice that adds deep, warm flavor to dishes. Buy whole rather than ground allspice. Whole allspice stores almost indefinitely in an airtight jar and will grind in a pepper mill.

Anise: Two spices give us anise flavor. The first is sweet anise; warm it gently before use to release its aroma. The second and more familiar spice is star anise. Buy star anise whole. One or two "stars" usually impart sufficient flavor to infuse an entire dish. To substitute star anise for aniseed in a recipe, reduce the quantity to half or a third of the recipe's recommendation.

Black peppercorns: The strongest in flavor and bite, black peppercorns are the world's most popular spice. They're picked when slightly underripe and then air-dried, which results in their dark color.

Caraway: Caraway has a pungent aroma and a slightly lemony, anise flavor. The caraway seed is soft and easy to grind, but it loses its scent quickly once it's ground. Buy it whole, and warm or lightly toast the seeds to bring out the flavor before using them.

Cardamom: The best pods will be pale sage green and have sticky black seeds inside. They're intensely aromatic and have an orangy flavor. Since cardamom's essential oils are volatile, the flavor of ground cardamom dissipates quickly. Bruise whole pods before using them to allow the flavor to escape. If the seeds are dry and light brown, they're old and have lost their flavor and aroma.

Cloves: Cloves have an intensely sharp, slightly bitter taste. Use sparingly because they can overpower other flavors. Use whole or ground, but if you use whole cloves to flavor a dish, remove them before serving. Cloves don't need toasting before use.

Cinnamon: Although cinnamon may be more familiar in sweet dishes, its distinctive notes blend with meats and fish and perk up grains and vegetables in a surprising way. Buy it as sticks (or quills) or ground. Cinnamon sticks have a sweeter, subtler flavor and a longer shelf life than ground. Whole cinnamon is best ground in a clean coffee mill.

Cumin seeds: These small seeds have a nutty, peppery flavor and are an essential component of curry powders and chile powders. They add a punch of flavor to dishes, particularly when toasted. Keep them in a tightly sealed glass container in a cool, dark, dry place. Whole seeds will stay fresh for about a year.

Five-spice powder: Chinese five-spice powder is a fragrant blend of cinnamon, cloves, fennel seed, star anise, and Szechuan peppercorns. The licorice-like anise and fennel melded with the sweet, pungent cloves and cinnamon contrast the woodsy flavor of peppercorn.

Ground cumin: Cumin has a pungent, nutty flavor. It's common in Mediterranean cuisines and is also featured in Indian curries and garam masala, Mexican chile powders and salsas, and Thai marinades. Cumin is typically found ground, but you can also purchase whole seeds.

Nutmeg: Each kernel of nutmeg comes wrapped in a lacy covering that we use separately as the spice mace. They both share a warm, sweet, musky flavor suited to desserts, cookies, and cakes. Use nutmeg freshly grated or milled. Except in cakes, add nutmeg toward the end of cooking to retain its evanescent aroma and warm, spicy flavor.

Paprika: Paprika is made from grinding sweet red bell peppers into a fine powder. Most paprikas are mild and slightly sweet, but you'll also find hot paprikas that are made from more intense peppers. Paprika

can be used to add flavor and color to a variety of dishes, but it only releases its flavor when heated. Sprinkling some on a dish may help improve its color, but it won't do much for the flavor.

Saffron: It's the world's most expensive spice, but you need only a few dried stigmas to color a dish golden yellow and impart a warm, aromatic, and slightly bitter quality. For most dishes, saffron is best soaked in a few tablespoons of warm liquid to allow the color and flavor to develop fully before adding it to the rest of the ingredients.

Tumeric: Turmeric gives food a golden color and a peppery, slightly pungent flavor. It's best known as one of the ingredients used to make curry, and it gives ballpark mustard its signature bright yellow color.

Buying and Storing Spices

Purchase small quantities, particularly those that you won't use often, from a store that has frequent turnover. You don't want to buy spices that have been sitting on the shelf for a long time. Ground spices tend to lose their flavor after a year. The best way to tell if your spices are past their prime is to smell them—they should still be vibrant when you use them and have a strong, aromatic scent.

Light, heat, and humidity all can diminish the color and potency of spices. The best place to store spices is in airtight containers in a cool, dry, dark place, such as a drawer or pantry. If stored properly, they'll last up to 18 months, but for maximum flavor, it's best to use them within six months to a year. If you don't think you'll use certain spices in that time frame, store them in the freezer to keep them fresher longer.

SAUCES

Sauces help make life in the kitchen a little easier. They are a quick and convenient way to add a punch of flavor to any dish.

Chipotles in adobo sauce: Chipotle chile peppers in adobo sauce are smoked jalapeños canned in a sauce of tomatoes, onions, garlic, spices, and vinegar. Taking a cue from Mexican cooks, we often reach for these to add complex, smoky flavor to a dish. If these fiery chiles are new to you, start easy—a little goes a long way. Chipotles are a natural in barbecue recipes, braised and stewed meats and poultry, and chili. Add minced chipotles to turkey burgers, bean dips, soups, salsas, and even scrambled eggs.

Coconut milk: The "cream" of the tropics is produced by blending freshly grated coconut with hot water. A "lite" coconut milk is also available—it's great to use in healthy Caribbean cooking.

Fish sauce: Widely used in southeast Asia as a condiment and flavoring for various dishes, fish sauce is a salty, light-brown liquid made from fermented fish, water, and salt. It's best used sparingly—just a spoonful makes a world of difference in many dishes. Combine fish sauce with sugar and lime juice to make a dipping sauce for vegetables and spring rolls, or use it as a base to add pungent flavor.

Hoisin sauce: This sauce is made with soybeans, sugar, vinegar, and spices. Sweet and fairly thick, it's often used in marinades for barbecuing and roasting and in dipping sauces.

Oyster sauce: This Cantonese staple, usually sold in bottles, is made from oysters, salt, and seasonings. It's often used in sauces for seafood, meat, and vegetable dishes. You can substitute an equal amount of soy sauce.

Sambal oelek (chile paste with garlic): This Chinese condiment is often added to stews as a flavoring. It's essentially pureed fresh chiles, but some varieties have bean paste or garlic added. We prefer the basic variety. This somewhat thin sauce has intense heat. Stir it into sauces and marinades.

Soy sauce: Made from fermented soybeans and wheat, the flavor of soy sauce varies by manufacturer and aging process. Regular soy sauce contains approximately 900 milligrams of sodium per tablespoon; light or low-sodium versions have 500 to 600 milligrams.

CONTRIBUTORS

Kwaku Alston

Sang An

Mary Drennen Ankar

Charlotte Autry

John Autry

Melanie Barnard

Lindsey Ellis Beatty

Lisa Bell

Alison Bing

Mark Bittman

François Blais

SaBrina Bone

David Bonom

Elisa Bosley

Philippa Brathwaite

Barbara Seelig Brown

Maureen Callahan, M.S., R.D.

Megan Caponetto

Julie Chai

Jamie Chung

Melanie J. Clarke

Martha Condra

Kathryn Conrad

Lorrie Hulston Corvin

Ruth Cousineau

Greg Cox

Tara Donne

Laura Dotolo

Thom Driver

Karen Evans

Kathy Farrell-Kingsley

Kim Ficaro

Sidney Fry, M.S., R.D.

Lynsey Fryers

Jan Gautro

Amit Gawajani

Carol Gelles

Bobby Ghosh

Victoria Granof

Paul Grimes

Dina Guillen

Cynthia Hacinli

Tamar Haspel

Anissa Helou

Brian Henn

Nick Higgins

Jason Horn

Jill Hough

Lia Huber

Nancy Hughes

Beverly Hyde

Raghavan Iyer

Sally James

Bill Jamison

Cheryl Jamison

Liza Jernow

Margaret M. Johnson

Telia Johnson

Kathleen Kanen

Elizabeth Karmel

Jeanne Kelley

John Kernick

Jamie Kimm

Todd Kliman

Hannah Klinger

Manfred Koh

Jean Kressy

Ellie Krieger

Corby Kummer

Jee Levin

Karen Levin

Mindi Shapiro Levine

Jeffery Lindenmuth

Judy Lockhart

Susan Herrmann Loomis

J. Kenji Lopez-Alt

Becky Luigart-Stayner

Karen MacNeil

Ivy Manning

Domenica Marchetti

Jennifer Martinkus

Charles Masters

Ben McCormack

Nancie McDermott

Angus McRitchie

Alma Melendez

William Meppem

Douglas Merriam

Jackie Mills, M.S., R.D.

Katie Morford, M.S., R.D.

Diane Morgan

Pam Morris

Megan Morton

Mary Catherine Muir

Linda Murphy

Elizabeth Nelson

Jackie Newgent, R.D.

Marcus Nilsson

Chris Nuttall-Smith

Michael O'Neill

Jamie Oliver

Violet Oon

Susan Ottaviano

Laraine Perri

Marge Perry

James Peterson

Plamen Petkov

José Picayo

Laura E. Pitts

Michele Powers

Janine Ratcliffe

Nicole Rees

Maria Ricapito

Victoria Abbott Riccardi

Amy Rosen

Anthony Rosenfeld

Maggie Ruggiero

Susan Russo

Amelia Saltsman

Ariana Salvato

Mark Scarbrough

Sara Schneider

Liza Schoenfein

Melissa Scott

Barton Seaver

Mary Britton Senseney

Jason Sheehan

Sandra Simile

Marie Simmons

Marcia Smart

Darren Soh

Sue Spitler

Hagen Stegall

Jane Strode

Jeremy Strode

Billy Strynkowski

Susan Sugarman

Kim Sunée

Adeena Sussman

Elizabeth Taliaferro

Jess Thomson

Corinne Trang

Julie Upton, M.S., R.D.

Jonny Valiant

Gary Vaynerchuk

Sara Vigneri

Coral Von Zumwalt

Robb Walsh

Carole Walter

Phillip Ward

Kate Washington

Mary-Ellen Weinrib

Bruce Weinstein

Joanne Weir

Ann Willan

Deborah Williams

Caroline Wright

Phoebe Wu

Romulo Yanes

Laura Zapalowski

SEASONAL PRODUCE GUIDE

When you use fresh fruits, vegetables, and herbs, you don't have to do much to make them taste great. Although many fruits, vegetables, and herbs are available year-round, you'll get better flavor and prices when you buy what's in season. The Seasonal Produce Guide below helps you choose the best produce so you can create sensational meals all year long.

SPRING

Fruits

Bananas
Blood oranges
Coconuts
Grapefruit
Kiwifruit
Lemons
Limes
Mangoes
Navel oranges
Papayas
Passionfruit
Pineapples
Strawberries
Tangerines
Valencia oranges

Vegetables

Artichokes
Arugula
Asparagus
Avocados
Baby leeks
Beets
Belgian endive
Broccoli
Cauliflower
Dandelion greens
Fava beans
Green onions
Green peas
Kale
Lettuce
Mushrooms
Radishes
Red potatoes
Rhubarb
Snap beans
Snow peas
Spinach
Sugar snap peas
Sweet onions
Swiss chard

Herbs

Chives
Dill
Garlic chives
Lemongrass
Mint
Parsley
Thyme

SUMMER

Fruits

Blackberries
Blueberries
Boysenberries
Cantaloupes
Casaba melons
Cherries
Crenshaw melons
Grapes
Guava
Honeydew melons
Mangoes
Nectarines
Papayas
Peaches
Plums
Raspberries
Strawberries
Watermelons

Vegetables

Avocados
Beets
Bell peppers
Cabbage
Carrots
Celery
Chili peppers
Collards
Corn
Cucumbers
Eggplant
Green beans
Jicama
Lima beans
Okra
Pattypan squash
Peas
Radicchio
Radishes
Summer squash
Tomatoes

Herbs

Basil
Bay leaves
Borage
Chives
Cilantro
Dill
Lavender
Lemon balm
Marjoram
Mint
Oregano
Rosemary
Sage
Summer savory
Tarragon
Thyme

AUTUMN

Fruits

Apples
Cranberries
Figs
Grapes
Pears
Persimmons
Pomegranates
Quinces

Vegetables

Belgian endive
Bell peppers
Broccoli
Brussels sprouts
Cabbage
Cauliflower
Eggplant
Escarole
Fennel
Frisée
Leeks
Mushrooms
Parsnips
Pumpkins
Red potatoes
Rutabagas
Shallots
Sweet potatoes
Winter squash
Yukon gold potatoes

Herbs

Basil
Bay leaves
Parsley
Rosemary
Sage
Tarragon
Thyme

WINTER

Fruits

Apples
Blood oranges
Cranberries
Grapefruit
Kiwifruit
Kumquats
Lemons
Limes
Mandarin oranges
Navel oranges
Pears
Persimmons
Pomegranates
Pomelos
Tangelos
Tangerines
Quinces

Vegetables

Baby turnips
Beets
Belgian endive
Brussels sprouts
Celery root
Chili peppers
Dried beans
Escarole
Fennel
Frisée
Jerusalem artichokes
Kale
Leeks
Mushrooms
Parsnips
Potatoes
Rutabagas
Sweet potatoes
Turnips
Watercress
Winter squash

Herbs

Bay leaves
Chives
Parsley
Rosemary
Sage
Thyme

NUTRITIONAL ANALYSIS

How to Use It and Why

Glance at the end of any *Cooking Light* recipe, and you'll see how committed we are to helping you make the best of today's light cooking. With chefs, registered dietitians, home economists, and a computer system that analyzes every ingredient we use, *Cooking Light* gives you authoritative dietary detail like no other magazine. We go to such lengths so you can see how our recipes fit into your healthful eating plan. If you're trying to lose weight, the calorie and fat figures will probably help most. But if you're keeping a close eye on the sodium, cholesterol, and saturated fat in your diet, we provide those numbers, too. And because many women don't get enough iron or calcium, we can help there, as well. Finally, there's a fiber analysis for those of us who don't get enough roughage.

Here's a helpful guide to put our nutritional analysis numbers into perspective. Remember, one size doesn't fit all, so take your lifestyle, age, and circumstances into consideration when determining your nutrition needs. For example, pregnant or breast-feeding women need more protein, calories, and calcium. And women older than 50 need 1,200mg of calcium daily, 200mg more than the amount recommended for younger women.

IN OUR NUTRITIONAL ANALYSIS, WE USE THESE ABBREVIATIONS

sat	saturated fat	**CHOL**	cholesterol
mono	monounsaturated fat	**CALC**	calcium
poly	polyunsaturated fat	**g**	gram
CARB	carbohydrates	**mg**	milligram

Daily Nutrition Guide

	Women Ages 25 to 50	Women over 50	Men over 24
Calories	2,000	2,000 or less	2,700
Protein	50g	50g or less	63g
Fat	65g or less	65g or less	88g or less
Saturated Fat	20g or less	20g or less	27g or less
Carbohydrates	304g	304g	410g
Fiber	25g to 35g	25g to 35g	25g to 35g
Cholesterol	300mg or less	300mg or less	300mg or less
Iron	18mg	8mg	8mg
Sodium	2,300mg or less	1,500mg or less	2,300mg or less
Calcium	1,000mg	1,200mg	1,000mg

The nutritional values used in our calculations either come from The Food Processor, Version 8.9 (ESHA Research), or are provided by food manufacturers.

METRIC EQUIVALENTS

The information in the following charts is provided to help cooks outside the United States successfully use the recipes in this book. All equivalents are approximate.

Cooking/Oven Temperatures

	Fahrenheit	Celsius	Gas Mark
Freeze Water	32° F	0° C	
Room Temp.	68° F	20° C	
Boil Water	212° F	100° C	
Bake	325° F	160° C	3
	350° F	180° C	4
	375° F	190° C	5
	400° F	200° C	6
	425° F	220° C	7
	450° F	230° C	8
Broil			Grill

Liquid Ingredients by Volume

¼ tsp	=					1 ml		
½ tsp	=					2 ml		
1 tsp	=					5 ml		
3 tsp	=	1 tbl	=	½ fl oz	=	15 ml		
2 tbls	=	⅛ cup	=	1 fl oz	=	30 ml		
4 tbls	=	¼ cup	=	2 fl oz	=	60 ml		
5⅓ tbls	=	⅓ cup	=	3 fl oz	=	80 ml		
8 tbls	=	½ cup	=	4 fl oz	=	120 ml		
10⅔ tbls	=	⅔ cup	=	5 fl oz	=	160 ml		
12 tbls	=	¾ cup	=	6 fl oz	=	180 ml		
16 tbls	=	1 cup	=	8 fl oz	=	240 ml		
1 pt	=	2 cups	=	16 fl oz	=	480 ml		
1 qt	=	4 cups	=	32 fl oz	=	960 ml		
				33 fl oz	=	1000 ml	=	1 l

Dry Ingredients by Weight

(To convert ounces to grams, multiply the number of ounces by 30.)

1 oz	=	¹⁄₁₆ lb	=	30 g
4 oz	=	¼ lb	=	120 g
8 oz	=	½ lb	=	240 g
12 oz	=	¾ lb	=	360 g
16 oz	=	1 lb	=	480 g

Length

(To convert inches to centimeters, multiply the number of inches by 2.5.)

1 in	=				2.5 cm		
6 in	=	½ ft		=	15 cm		
12 in	=	1 ft		=	30 cm		
36 in	=	3 ft	=	1 yd	90 cm		
40 in	=				100 cm	=	1 m

Equivalents for Different Types of Ingredients

Standard Cup	Fine Powder (ex. flour)	Grain (ex. rice)	Granular (ex. sugar)	Liquid Solids (ex. butter)	Liquid (ex. milk)
1	140 g	150 g	190 g	200 g	240 ml
¾	105 g	113 g	143 g	150 g	180 ml
⅔	93 g	100 g	125 g	133 g	160 ml
½	70 g	75 g	95 g	100 g	120 ml
⅓	47 g	50 g	63 g	67 g	80 ml
¼	35 g	38 g	48 g	50 g	60 ml
⅛	18 g	19 g	24 g	25 g	30 ml

MENU INDEX

A topical guide to all the menus that appeared in *Cooking Light Annual Recipes 2011*. See page 448 for the General Recipe Index.

Christmas Dinner Menu (page 378)

serves 8

Granny Smith, Radish, and Radicchio Salad with Orange-Walnut Vinaigrette

Roast Chicken with Five-Spice Sauce

Broccolini with Anchovy Gremolata

Braised Kale

Roasted Winter Vegetables

Gingery Banana Pudding with Bourbon Cream

Healthy Hanukkah Menu

(page 380)

serves 8

Fennel and Spinach Soup with Roasted Pepper Yogurt

Beer-Braised Brisket with Honey-Lime Glaze

Quinoa with Dried Cherries and Pistachios

Braised Kale

Roasted Winter Vegetables

Rustic Apple Tart

CASUAL ENTERTAINING

An Al Fresco Dinner Menu (page 143)

serves 6

Sparkling Rosemary-Peach Cocktails

Muhammara with Crudités

Grilled Chicken with Cucumber-Melon Salsa

Green salad

Apricot-Thyme Galette

Farmers' Market Veggie Plate Menu

(page 148)

serves 6

Cranberry Beans with Parsley Pesto

Roasted Summer Squashes with Caper Gremolata

Summer Peach and Tomato Salad

Corn bread

Sydney Beach Menu

(page 180)

serves 6

Tiger Prawn, Noodle, and Herb Salad

Whole Baby Snapper and Green Sauce

Ocean Trout with Coleslaw and Crispy Smoked Bacon —or—

Marinated Chicken Thighs with Sweet Potato

Heirloom Tomato, Baby Basil, and Sourdough Salad

Sheep's-Milk Yogurt Cheesecakes with Grilled Figs and Pistachios

Weekend Getaway Menu (page 215)

serves 4

Cocktails & Dinner (Friday night)
Daiquiri, barbecue chicken sliders with corn and slaw, and shortcakes
Quick & Easy Breakfast (Saturday morning)
Orange french toast and berry smoothie
Hearty, Healthy Lunch (Saturday afternoon)
Grilled vegetable and goat cheese salad
Steak & Potato Supper (Saturday night)
Flat-iron steak with salad and potatoes and a berry trifle
Steak & Eggs Brunch (Sunday morning)
Steak hash and eggs with fruit salad and an iced latte

Quick Summer Meal for a Pasta Fix Menu

(page 147)

serves 6

Quick-Roasted Cherry Tomato Sauce with Spaghetti

Romano Bean Salad

Garlic bread

Global Flavors Dinner Menu (page 376)

serves 8

Fennel and Spinach Soup with Roasted Pepper Yogurt

Roast Chicken with Five-Spice Sauce

Quinoa with Dried Cherries and Pistachios

Broccolini with Anchovy Gremolata

Braised Kale

Rustic Apple Tart

Southern-Style Feast Menu (page 377)

serves 8

Beer-Braised Brisket with Honey-Lime Glaze

Hoppin' John's Cousin

Braised Kale

Roasted Winter Vegetables

Gingery Banana Pudding with Bourbon Cream

Vegetarian Supper Menu

(page 378)

serves 8

Granny Smith, Radish, and Radicchio Salad with Orange-Walnut Vinaigrette

Truffled Wild Mushroom Lasagna

Broccolini with Anchovy Gremolata
(omit anchovies for a vegetarian side)

Rustic Apple Tart

RECIPE TITLE INDEX

An alphabetical listing of every recipe title that appeared in the magazine in 2010. See page 448 for the General Recipe Index.

MONTH-BY-MONTH INDEX

A month-by-month listing of every food story with recipe titles that appeared in the magazine in 2010. See page 448 for the General Recipe Index.

May

The Cooking Light® Summer Cookbook

July

The Cooking Light® Holiday Cookbook

December

GENERAL RECIPE INDEX

A listing by major ingredient and food category for every recipe that appeared in the magazine in 2010.

Fish *(continued)*

Sauces *(continued)*

Marsala Wine Sauce, Chicken and Mushrooms with, 287
Morel and Tarragon Cream Sauce, Scrambled Eggs with, 156
Mornay Sauce, 353
Mornay Sauce, Savory Buckwheat Crepes with Ham and, 133
Mushroom and Sausage Ragù with Polenta, 330
Mushroom Bolognese, 313
Mushroom Sauce and Parmesan Popovers, Beef Filets with, 336
Mustard-Parsley Sauce, Broiled Tilapia with Frisée-Apple Salad and, 98
Mustard Sauce, Irish Bacon and Cabbage with, 64
Orange Basil Sauce, Swordfish Kebabs with, 170
Parsley-Chervil Pan Sauce, Sautéed Chicken and Zucchini with, 368
Peanut Dipping Sauce, 188
Pinot Noir Sauce, Roasted Breast of Chicken with, 316
Poblano Mole, Bison Steak with, 43
Pomegranate-Pinot Sauce, Beef Filets with, 327
Pomegranate Sauce, Roast Lamb with, 397
Red Wine Reduction, 356
Rémoulade, 354
Rémoulade, Crab Cakes with Spicy, 142
Romesco Sauce, Tortilla Español with, 391
Soy-Citrus Sauce, Gyoza with, 84
Spicy Dipping Sauce, Pan-Fried Chicken Fingers with, 349
Tahini Sauce, Turkey Burger Pitas with, 299
Tartar Sauce, 355
Tartar Sauce, Fried Catfish with Hush Puppies and, 92
Ti-Malice, Griot with Sauce, 120
Tomato
Curried Tomato Sauce, Eggs Poached in, 386
Fresh Tomato-Basil Sauce, Pasta with, 300
Marinara, Slow-Roasted Tomato, 354
Pizza Sauce, Basic, 116
Quick-Roasted Cherry Tomato Sauce with Spaghetti, 147
Roasted Tomato Sauce, Quick Crisp Ravioli with, 276
Romesco Sauce, Skillet-Cooked Shrimp with, 293
Simple Tomato Sauce, Spaghetti with Sausage and, 105
Warm Tomato Sauce, Chili-Espresso Rubbed Steaks with, 218
Tonnato Sauce, Sautéed Chicken with, 44
Yogurt-Mint Sauce, Lamb Burgers with Indian Spices and, 174
Yogurt-Tahini Sauce, Grilled Vegetables with, 183
Zucchini Pistou, Penne with, 184
Sausage
Braid, Jalapeño, Sausage, Jack, and Egg Breakfast, 39
Cassoulet, Quick, 338

Chorizo and Fingerlings, Grilled Salmon with, 160
Chorizo Pizza, Manchego and, 61
Fettuccine, Sausage, Tomato, and Arugula, 402
Hoppin' John's Cousin, 379
Paella, Quick, 278
Pan Roast, Smoky Spanish-Style, 153
Pepperoni Deep-Dish Pizza, 116
Ploughman's Lunch Platter, 64
Ragù with Polenta, Mushroom and Sausage, 330
Rice Balls with Sausage and Dried Shrimp, Sticky, 211
Soup with Cheese "Crackers," Vegetable and Spicy Sausage, 60
Soup with Kale and Chorizo, White Bean, 372
Spaghetti with Sausage and Simple Tomato Sauce, 105
Stuffing, Sausage and Sourdough Bread, 339
Subs, Sausage-Fennel, 141
Scallops
Green Tea Cream, Scallops with, 352
Noodles with Scallops and Pea Tendrils, Coconut, 209
Pan-Seared Scallops with Bacon and Spinach, 113
Seared Scallops with Farmers' Market Salad, 296
Seared Scallops with Fennel and Grapefruit Salad, 401
Seafood. See also specific types and Fish.
Paella, Quick, 278
Salad, Thai Seafood, 197
Sotong Bakar (Barbecue Squid), 187
Soup, Creamy Garlic-Seafood, 20
Tiger Prawn, Noodle, and Herb Salad, 180
Shrimp
Cilantro Shrimp, 209
Coconut Shrimp with Fiery Mango Sauce, 21
Couscous with Shrimp, Quick Greek, 279
Dried Shrimp, Sticky Rice Balls with Sausage and, 211
Egg Rolls, Pan-Fried, 158
Fra Diavolo, Shrimp, 46
Gnocchi with Shrimp, Asparagus, and Pesto, 240
Gumbo, Shrimp and Okra, 106
Kebabs, Mango Shrimp, 104
Lemongrass and Garlic Shrimp, 152
Noodle Bowl, Spicy Shrimp, 324
Pan Roast, Smoky Spanish-Style, 153
Pasta with Arugula and Shrimp, Peppery, 101
Pasta with Shrimp, Roasted Red Pepper and Herb, 361
Peppery Shrimp, Linguine with, 228
Risotto, Pan-Seared Shrimp and Arugula, 122
Salads
Chipotle-Rubbed Shrimp Taco Salad, 231
Chipotle Shrimp Salad, Spicy, 202
Lemon-Splashed Shrimp Salad, 236
Lime Shrimp Salad with Bean Sprouts and Thai Basil, 210
Pasta Salad with Shrimp, Warm, 294

Taco Salad, Southwestern-Style Shrimp, 130
Seviche, Golden Peach Soup with Shrimp and Crab, 145
Skillet-Cooked Shrimp with Romesco Sauce, 293
Spicy Shrimp and Grits, 78
Spicy Shrimp, Linguine with, 168
Stir-Fry, Garlic-Ginger Shrimp, 158
Stuffed Poblanos, Cheese and Shrimp-, 20
Thai Red Curry Shrimp, 163
Snacks
Mix, Sweet Chipotle Snack, 214
Samosas with Raita, Spicy Chickpea, 203
Soufflé, Parmesan and Eggplant, 156
Soups. *See also* **Chili, Chowder, Gumbo, Stews.**
Apple-Parsnip Soup, 307
Avocado-Buttermilk Soup with Crab Salad, 208
Beef-Noodle Soup with Asian Greens, Vietnamese, 107
Bean
Black Bean and Corn Soup, Quick, 279
Black Bean Soup, 366
Chickpea, Bread, and Leek Soup with Harissa and Yogurt, 102
Chickpea Soup, 1-Hour Spanish, 289
White Bean Soup with Kale and Chorizo, 372
Carrot Soup with Yogurt, 82
Chicken
Chili-Spiced Chicken Soup with Stoplight Peppers and Avocado Relish, 66
Hominy Soup, Mexican Chicken-, 393
Noodle Soup, Quick Chicken, 49
Parsnip Soup, Chicken and, 369
Superfast Chicken Posole, 229
Clams Fagioli, Steamed, 99
Coconut Red Curry Hot Pot with Braised Chicken and Mushrooms, 321
Fennel and Spinach Soup with Roasted Pepper Yogurt, 376
Garlic-Seafood Soup, Creamy, 20
Gazpacho with Sautéed Shrimp, Chunky, 234
Hot and Sour Soup with Tofu, 96
Leek and Potato Soup, 36
Lentil-Barley Soup, 366
Oyster Bisque, 334
Pea Soup, Habitant, 29
Peach Soup with Shrimp and Crab Seviche, Golden, 145
Pork and Wild Rice Soup, 399
Potato Soup, Loaded, 328
Ribollita (Italian Bread Soup), 366
Roasted Chestnut Soup with Thyme Cream, 333
Stocks
Beef Stock, Fast, Rich Pressure-Cooker, 291
Chicken Stock, Homemade, 122
Chicken Stock, Roasted, 356
Tomato Soup, Minty, 294
Vegetable and Spicy Sausage Soup with Cheese "Crackers," 60
Wild Rice and Mushroom Soup with Chicken, 321